For Reference

Not to be taken from this room

D1275494

CITIES OF THE WORLD

ISSN 0889-2741

SIXTH EDITION

CITIES OF THE WORLD

A Compilation of Current Information on Cultural, Geographic, and Political Conditions in the Countries and Cities of Six Continents, Based on the Department of State's "Post Reports"

In Four Volumes

Volume 2:
The Western Hemisphere
(exclusive of the United States)

Cumulative Index Volumes 1-4

GALE®

THOMSON
™
GALE

Detroit • New York • San Diego • San Francisco • Cleveland • New Haven, Conn. • Waterville, Maine • London • Munich

CITIES OF THE WORLD SIXTH EDITION
Karen Ellicott, Editor

Project Editor
Kathleen Droste

Permissions
Lori Hines

Imaging and Multimedia
Dean Dauphinais, Leitha Etheridge-Sims,
Dave Oblender, Robert Duncan, Lezlie Light

Manufacturing
Nekita McKee

set:	0787639125
vol.1	0787639133
vol.2	0787639141
vol.3	078763915X
vol.4	0787639168

Printed in the United States of America
10 9 8 7 6 5 4 3 2 1

CONTENTS

PREFACE

Cities of the World represents a compilation of government reports and original research on the social, cultural, political, and industrial aspects of the nations and cities of the world. Most of the country profiles included here are based on official personnel briefings issued as *Post Reports* by the U.S. Department of State. The *Post Reports* are designed to acquaint embassy personnel with life in the host country. Consequently, the reports concentrate on cities in which the U.S. government has embassies or consulates. To increase coverage of other important cities, the editors have added information on a large number of cities—31 of which are new to this editon—not reported on by the Department of State.

Since the fifth edition of *Cities of the World,* the Department of State has issued 62 new or revised *Post Reports,* all of which have been incorporated into this sixth edition. Selected data in *Post Reports* not revised by the Department of State since the last edition of *Cities of the World* have been updated by the editors with revised statistics acquired through independent research. In addition, articles have been written on thirty-three countries for which no *Post Report* exists.

Readers familiar with the fourth edition of this publication will notice that with the fifth edition the page size was enlarged to accommodate more information. This sixth edition includes new photographs selected by the Gale editors. The photographs depict scenes found in a city and countryside and, in many cases, reveal the cultural flavor of the area as well. As in the prior edition, many chapters feature a map of that country's capital or major city, with a superimposed locator map indicating the nation's geographic location in relation to its regional neighbors.

Volumes in This Series
This series includes four volumes:
- Volume 1: Africa;
- Volume 2: The Western Hemisphere (exclusive of the United States);
- Volume 3: Europe and the Mediterranean Middle East;
- Volume 4: Asia, the Pacific, and the Asiatic Middle East.

In all, this set provides coverage of over 2,000 cities in 193 countries.

Format and Arrangement of Entries
Cities of the World is arranged alphabetically by country name. Its chapters are divided into two basic sections, Major Cities and Country Profile, each of these with several subdivisions. A Major City listing might comprise information on Education, Recreation, and Entertainment. Other Cities, smaller cities and towns which are designated as other than major, are discussed in brief paragraphs at the end of the Major City section. Country Profile sections are subdivided into: Geography and Climate; Population; Government; Arts, Science, Education; Commerce and Industry; Transportation; Communications; Health; Clothing and Services; Local Holidays; Recommended Reading; and Notes for Travelers. Thus, *Cities of the World* presents not only basic information, but also comprehensive data on local customs, political conditions, community services, and educational and commercial facilities.

Contents and Index
The Contents and Index in each volume provide easy access to these reports. Listed under each country in the Contents are the cities that appear in its Major Cities section, as well as listings for the Other Cities and Country Profile sections. A Cumulative Index, combining the four individual volumes is found at the end of each volume. The Index is arranged alphabetically by city name, including listings for both major and minor cities that are mentioned in each volume; as well as by country name with names of cities indented below.

Acknowledgments
The editors would like to thank the U.S. Department of State for providing copies of *Post Reports* to aid in the compilation of these volumes. The editors would also like to thank Adam A. Gall and Marlon C. Tussel for their editorial assistance.

Suggestions Welcome
The editors invite comments and suggestions concerning *Cities of the World.* Please write to: Editors, *Cities of the World,* The Gale Group, Inc., 27500 Drake Road, Farmington Hills, MI 48331-3535; fax (248) 699-8074; or call toll-free (800) 877-4253.

CITIES OF THE WORLD

Volume 2:
The Western Hemisphere
(exclusive of the United States)

ANTIGUA AND BARBUDA

Major City:
St. John's

INTRODUCTION

ANTIGUA (pronounced An-tee-ga) is a three-island nation located about 1,200 miles southeast of Miami. The country consists of the islands of Antigua, Barbuda, and the uninhabited island of Redonda. Each of these islands is unique. Antigua's topography is varied. In the north and west, the gently undulating terrain consists of limestone, marls, and sandstone. In the south and east, the land is of volcanic origin, with high ridges and forests common to many other Caribbean islands. Thirty-two miles to the north, Barbuda is a 62-square mile flat island composed of limestone, ancient coral reefs, and sand. It has a 14-mile long beach. Twenty miles west lies Redonda, a solitary volcanic cone jutting directly out of the sea to a height of over 1,000 feet. Steep cliffs surround the area of less than one-half square mile.

Among Antigua's attractions are 365 beautiful white sand beaches. Tourists arrive by cruise ship, yachts, and airliners to relax in the sea, sun, and surf, or enjoy all kinds of water sports. In the off-season, it is possible to find many uninhabited beaches. History buffs will find Antigua rich in human events, agriculture, and strategic importance.

MAJOR CITY

St. John's

St. John's, with a population of 24,000 (2000 estimate) is the capital of Antigua and Barbuda. It is situated on Deep Water Harbor, where as many as five Caribbean cruise ships dock for the day, adding hundreds of tourists to the daily activity. From this protected location nearly all commerce occurs; from the quaint fish market to the modern mini-mall, people come to trade and transact business. In daytime, people scurry about in the narrow streets, taking time to greet friends along the way. On cool evenings, people stroll leisurely in the refreshing sea breeze.

Clothing

Antiguans dress in moderation and are conditioned to tropical living. As a result, it is common for men to work in blue jeans and long sleeve shirts, and women in synthetic fabric dresses. It is acceptable for tourists to wear shorts. However, American women living in Antigua find dresses or slacks more appropriate. North Americans who are not accustomed to living in tropical climates should bring lightweight clothing. Cotton or cotton-blend garments are the most comfortable. Antigua has a few fine-quality clothing stores, but clothing is expensive. Expatriates should bring an ample supply of shoes as local varieties are not well made and sizes are different from U.S. standards. In the heat and humidity, shoes one-half size larger are more comfortable.

Clothing and accessories suitable for men include wash-and-wear business suits, sport jackets, shirts worn with or without ties, sport shirts, and slacks. Shirt jacs or a *guayabera*, and slacks are popular. Working attire for women is usually a modest suit, a cotton dress, or a blouse and skirt. Stockings are not normally worn. Hats are not normally worn except occasionally to church or at a sunny beach. Antiguan women are fashion conscious and like to dress for cocktail and dinner parties. Nights are occasionally cool, so a lightweight cotton sweater or shawl is useful. For children, normal U.S. summer wear is suitable, with lightweight jackets or cardigans for cool evenings. All schools, including preschool, require uniforms. Girls wear simple one-piece dresses, or skirts and blouses. Boys wear slacks and shirts. In secondary schools, a tie completes the dress code. Uniforms are made and sold locally.

Supplies & Services

In general, it is possible to buy most anything in Antigua. However, prices are often highly inflated. Stocks are often small and selections are poor compared to the U.S. American expatriates often order most items via catalogs. St. John's offers an interesting variety of stores and boutiques. Specialties include straw goods, pottery, batik and silk-screened fabrics and jewelry incorporating semiprecious Antiguan stones. China, crystal, watches and perfumes are obtainable at duty-free prices. Heritage Quay and Redcliffe Quay are the two main shopping areas in St. John's. Many expatriates also making shopping trips to St. Martin's or Puerto Rico.

The number of establishments offering basic services is limited. Dry-cleaning services are poor. Many people restrict the need for dry-cleaning because of the expense, and availability of cotton and synthetic substitutes. Shoe and leather repair service is good, and some crafters do custom work. Barbershops are adequate and charge reasonable prices. A wide range of hair care services are available, including permanents, tints, and stylings. Many hairdressers are expatriates. Dressmakers vary in skill, but some can take a length of fabric and fashion anything from sundresses to formal wear. Some repair work is good, but the standard of most is uneven, particularly if unsupervised. Progress is often slow and further

Street in St. John's, Antigua

© Dave G. Houser/Corbis. Reproduced by permission.

hampered by periodic unavailability of materials and electrical failures. Repair work on cars, electronic equipment, and household appliances varies in quality, because of the lack of expertise and unfamiliarity with certain electronic devices.

Food

St. John's has four supermarkets, several well-stocked minimarkets, and numerous small stores. Many canned and packaged goods are U.S. name brands, the rest are from Europe or nearby islands. Imported dairy products are safe; local products are not. Most eggs are imported. Cattle, hogs, and chickens are raised and processed locally. All are safe to eat if cooked properly. Cuts vary widely from those in U.S. meat markets. Beware of frozen packaged meats in smaller stores; power failures are frequent and meat lockers may not have generator backup. Local bakeries make fresh breads and pastries. Packaged cereals may not be fresh, and grain products are subject to bug infestations.

Fresh seafood is always available at the Saturday morning market; for other times, it is wise to establish contact with a local fisherman. Fresh vegetables and fruits are also sold at the Saturday market and stores. Most are imported, since the economy does not have an agricultural base. Most stores sell wines, hard liquor, and brand name soft drinks. Diet foods and products are rarely available.

A local cuisine specialty is *roti*. It is an unleavened bread shell folded in half and filled with a curry gravy, vegetables, and a meat. *Roti* made from conch meat is considered a delicacy. Barbudan lobsters are excellent. Cockles are an island favorite, especially around Whit's Day. Numerous downtown restaurants cater to the professional community. Antigua has a U.S.-based fast-food chicken restaurant.

For dining out, it is possible to choose from a variety of hotel restaurants, offering everything from smorgasbords to full course meals. Most specialties are "the catch of the day" seafoods. Also, ethnic restaurants featuring Italian, French, Chinese, British, and American cuisine exist. Dress is casual at restaurants, but hotels are slightly more formal. Hotels that cater to tourists may inflate some prices.

Domestic Help

Domestics are available for laundry and household chores. Some families with large gardens may also hire a part-time gardener. Reliable employees can usually be found through friends. However, it is best to hire on a temporary basis at first and set out the terms of employment.

Wages are governed by law; minimum wage is generally EC $20 a day from 9 a.m. to 1 p.m., five days a week. Workers have one paid holiday a month. Domestic help is entitled to all local holidays, and a Christmas bonus is suggested. All workers over 18 years of age must register. Employers pay social security and medical insurance that is accumulated by a deduction of 5.5% from employee wages and an employer contribution of 7.5%. Employers provide either transportation or bus fares.

Education

The children of American expatriates attend local schools. Schooling is adequate through high school. However, American history and geography are not taught. Many parents select private schools as they are perceived to have a higher quality of education. Schools in St. John's follow the British educational system and are in session from September until the last week in June. Instruction is in English. Teachers and teaching assistants may be hired locally or recruited from neighboring islands or the expatriate community. All schools have open play areas and all-purpose playing fields; however, they do not have closed auditoriums. Some extracurricular activities are available such as scouting, cricket, basketball, volleyball, and soccer.

Schools in Antigua cannot support special educational requirements. Children with learning disabilities, or physical, behavioral, or emotional handicaps should be placed in U.S. schools.

Recreation

As in most Caribbean countries, cricket is Antigua's national sport. Soccer (locally called football) and basketball are played in the off-season. A local board game, called *warri*, is played on a board with hollowed pockets. Two opponents move warri beans about, seeking to capture the opponents' beans. Warri is popular with cabbies and bus drivers awaiting fares.

Antigua has two golf courses open for year-round play. Cedar Valley Golf Club has an 18-hole championship course. This challenging course has narrow fairways, deep roughs, and hilly terrain. Clubs and accessories are available at the recreation building. Half Moon Bay Hotel, located on the opposite side of the island, has a 9-hole course more hospitable to casual players. Equipment can be rented.

All water sport activities abound. It is possible to rent sailboats, both large and small. Powerboating is used mainly for fishing, but in some places, powerboats are used for parasailing, water skiing, and sightseeing. Small craft and inexperienced pilots should not operate in the open Atlantic. Coral reefs and shoals encircle Antigua, and novices must learn to identify and navigate these hazards. Antigua's clear waters offer abundant marine flora and fauna.

St. John's offers many sight-seeing opportunities. St. John's has an old fort that can be readily explored. Fort James, built in 1703, guarded the entrance to St. John's Harbor. Many of the original buildings no longer exist, but some buildings that remain date back to 1749. The fort still has ten cannons. Each weigh about two and one half tons and can propel a cannonball one and one half miles. Another tourist attraction is St. John's Cathedral. Built in 1722, the cathedral's interior is encased in wood to protect it from hurricane and earthquake damage.

In addition to sights in St. John's, there are points of interest throughout the island. Nelson's Dockyard, built in 1784 as the headquarters of Admiral Horatio Nelson, is situated in one of the safest landlocked harbors in the world. Today, the Dockyard has been restored to its original state and houses a museum that is very popular among visitors. Indian Town, one of Antigua's national parks, features Devil's Bridge, carved out by the forces of the Atlantic Ocean. Clarence House, the Governor's residence, is open to the public when the Governor is absent. The house was once the home of the "Sailor King," William IV, when he was Duke of Clarence.

Many old sugarcane mills are familiar landmarks throughout the island. Betty's Hope is one of the oldest plantation sites in Antigua, dating back to 1655. It was Antigua's foremost sugar plantations for large-scale sugar cultivation and innovative processing methods. The Sugar Factory had twin stone windmill towers, a laborers' village, and an extensive water catchment system. Most buildings are in ruins, but restoration plans are underway.

Antigua hosts several international events. In late July, Antigua hosts a ten-day Carnival. Visitors come from all over the world. It is a time when people celebrate the people's emancipation and freedom from subjugation. During "J'Ouvert," a Carnival highlight, everyone comes together jumping and jamming to the pulsing, rhythmic sounds of steel pan and brass bands. Carnival Monday is a riot of color. The elaborate costumes are combinations of sequins, feathers, beads, and glitter, often towering ten to fifteen feet in the air. Each represents countless hours of painstaking work to design and create.

Antiguan Sailing Week has evolved into one of the world's top sailing regattas. It attracts many spectators to watch the excitement of the races and to join in the parties that follow. Sailing Week, which begins the last week in April and continues during the first week in May, is a blend of international, regional, and local yachts. Many colorful sails catch the wind as yachts jostle to pass each other on the sea. Races are organized into different categories.

Entertainment

St. John's has limited forms of entertainment. One popular discotheque occasionally offers performances by regionally well-known groups. Apart from this, nightlife is confining. The one movie theater, in the shopping district, offers a mix of martial arts movies, "B" movies, and an occasional recently released film. Video clubs are coming to Antigua, but prices are high.

Many hotels offer live entertainment on particular nights. Steel drums and reggae bands, along with other musical groups, are featured. Casino gambling is popular; however, odds heavily favor the house.

Among expatriates, cocktail parties, small suppers, or dining out are common ways to entertain. Community fund-raising events are held throughout the year. The American Women's Club coordinates philanthropic and community activities. Most people find the life-style on Antigua limiting and feel a periodic need to leave the island. Many expatriates also enjoy golf, bridge, and special hobbies.

COUNTRY PROFILE

Geography and Climate

Antigua is roughly oval in shape, 10 miles by 12 miles, with a land area of 108 square miles. Although Antigua is volcanic in origin, it also has extensive limestone geology. Various coral reefs surround the island. Antigua's shores are washed by the Atlantic Ocean on the east and the Caribbean Sea on the west. This makes Antigua unique and diverse in both terrestrial and marine flora and fauna. Boggy Peak, at 1,330 feet, is the highest prominent landmark. Barbuda, which is not commercialized or overly developed, promises a nearly unspoiled fishing,

snorkeling, and scuba-diving paradise. Most of the 1,500 Barbudans live in the town of Codrington.

Antigua's climate is heavily influenced by the easterly trade winds and sea currents that are present all year. Drier than most other Caribbean islands, Antigua and Barbuda's climate is tropical, with low humidity and an average rainfall of 42 inches. Most homes in Antigua have cisterns, and the island has numerous ponds, reservoirs, and catchment systems to store rain water, which until recently was the only natural fresh-water source on the island. During the cool season, December-February, night temperatures range from 60°F to 65°F. Average daytime temperatures are 76°F, December-April, and 85°F in August and September.

Although the official hurricane season begins June 1 and ends November 30, August and September are the two most active months. At this time, tropical storms form in the eastern Atlantic Ocean and spend days building their wind velocities as they approach the Caribbean. On September 16, 1989, Hurricane Hugo passed within 40 miles south of Antigua, causing extensive damage to the entire island. Historically speaking, the threat of a major hurricane hitting Antigua is small; the last direct strike was in 1952.

Population

The people of Antigua and Barbuda are almost exclusively of black African origin. Antiguans and Barbudans are largely descendants of African slaves who were transported from West Africa in the seventeenth and eighteenth centuries. Several minorities are also represented. These persons are the descendants of Lebanese and Syrian traders, British colonial settlers, and Portuguese laborers. Statistically, life expectancy is 68 years for males and 73 years for females (2001 estimates). The educational requirement is a compulsory 9 years, and the literacy rate is roughly 90%. Antigua and Barbuda

has an estimated population of 64,500; 98% live on Antigua. Redonda is uninhabited.

History

The earliest known human-made artifacts have been carbon dated at least to 1775 B.C. These people have been named the "Siboney," the Stone People. Their society was that of nomadic food gatherers having no agriculture or permanent settlements.

About the time of Christ, an agricultural society made its way up the chain of islands from South America. They brought with them new plants such as peanut, pineapple, cotton, and tobacco plants.

Later, A.D. 1200–1300, two Amerindian societies with opposing lifestyles coexisted; the peaceful and pottery-making Arawaks, and the fierce and warlike Caribs. Arawaks came here for clay, a resource in short supply elsewhere and essential for making pottery. The Caribs are thought to have exploited another earth resource, flint, a hard mineral necessary in the making of arrowheads and spear points.

The first Western explorer believed to have discovered Antigua was Christopher Columbus. In his second voyage in 1493, Columbus was sailing from the south when he spotted Antigua on the horizon. It was at this time that he named Antigua after a sainted miracle worker, Santa Maria de Antigua, from Seville Cathedral, Spain. Columbus did not stop or set foot on Antigua, he continued northbound to Hispaniola, convinced that gold and spices existed there.

For the next 200–300 years, there was great imperial rivalry for control and possession of the Caribbean islands. The Spanish Armada, the Dutch and French fleets, and British Navy all had a military presence.

The English successfully colonized Antigua in 1632. Although the island was held briefly by the French in 1666, Antigua remained thereafter under British control.

Sir Christopher Codrington established the first large sugar estate in Antigua in 1674 and leased Barbuda to raise provisions for the plantation. Barbuda's only settlement is named for him. Sir Codrington and others brought slaves from Africa's west coast to work the plantation. To exploit the land for sugar cane production, plantation owners cleared the forest and woods. Today, many Antiguans attribute frequent droughts to the island's early deforestation. Antigua's profitable sugar plantations were soon the envy of other European powers. To defend the island's growing wealth, the British built several large forts. The ruins of these forts are notable tourist attractions.

Antiguan slaves were emancipated in 1834, but they remained bound to their plantation owners. A lack of surplus farming land, no access to credit, and an economy built on agriculture rather than manufacturing limited economic opportunities for the freed men. Poor labor conditions continued until 1939, when a member of a Royal Commission urged the formation of a trade union movement. The Antigua Trades and Labor Union, formed shortly afterward, became the political vehicle for Vere Cornwall Bird, who became the union's president in 1943. The Antigua Labor Party (ALP), formed by Bird and other trade unionists, first ran candidates in the 1946 elections, thus beginning a long history of electoral victories. In 1971, general elections swept the Progressive Labor Movement into power, but Bird and the ALP returned to office in 1976. Prime Minister Bird's ALP government has led the country since, winning a renewed mandate in the 1989 general election.

Government

Antigua and Barbuda is a member of the British Commonwealth. As head of the Commonwealth, Queen Elizabeth II is represented in Antigua and Barbuda by a Governor General, who acts on the advice of the Prime Minister and the Cabinet. The Prime Minister is the leader of the majority party of the House, and the Cabinet conducts affairs of state. Antigua and Barbuda has a bicameral legislature: a 17-member popularly elected Upper House or Senate appointed by the Governor General (mainly on the advice of the Prime Minister and the leader of the opposition) and a 17-member popularly elected House of Representatives. The Prime Minister and Cabinet are responsible to the Parliament, which has a normal term of five years.

Constitutional safeguards include freedoms of speech, press, worship, movement, and association. Like its English-speaking neighbors, Antigua and Barbuda has an outstanding human rights record. Its judicial system is modeled on British practice and procedure, and its jurisprudence on English Common Law.

The flag of Antigua and Barbuda is red with an inverted isosceles triangle based on the top edge of the flag; the triangle contains three horizontal bands of black (top), light blue, and white with a yellow sun rising in the black band.

Arts, Science, Education

The longest established gallery is The Art Center at English Harbor. It only displays local art, but it has influenced the development of art in the Caribbean. The island's newest addition is the Seahorse Studio's Art Gallery. This studio was established in 1985 to provide graphics and layout services for local businesses. In addition to Caribbean art displays are unique gold and bronze marine crafts made in Antigua by "The Goldsmitty." The Island Arts Foundation has four galleries in Antigua, and six associate galleries throughout the islands. Island Arts offers the widest variety of Caribbean art anywhere in the region. It is a nonprofit company devoted to economic support of Caribbean-based artists. Coates College and The Art Gallery both feature local artists' exhibits year round. Harmony Hall of Jamaica has a branch studio on Antigua at Brown's Bay. Exhibitions change every three to four weeks, November to March. Aiton Place has art pieces at numerous fine hotels.

The Antigua Arts Society, a group of local and regional artists, actively provides direction and promotes growth in all art forms. The Society sponsors regional art fairs and showings.

Antigua has four museums. The Museum of Antigua and Barbuda has tours, book libraries, and computer libraries open to visitors and residents. It is also a research area for foreign students. The museum has direct links with several universities, such as Tulane, Brown, Northern Illinois, and Cambridge. Students can research in areas from geology and archeology to sociology and communications. A second museum, the Museum of Marine and Living Art, offers a stunning collection of seashells and relics salvaged from old shipwrecks.

The oldest museum in Antigua was established in 1953 at English Harbor. The Dockyard Museum is near the waterfront and deals with naval history. Antigua was Britain's major Caribbean naval base for much of the colonial period. The museum has large ship models on loan from the British National Maritime Museum.

The newest museum is on the road to Shirley Heights. This once was the largest fort, and its main function was to reinforce Antigua's defenses. It now houses the Military and Infantry Museum.

In Antigua, public education is free and compulsory for children ages five-16. The education system is modeled after British schools. Parents provide books and uniforms for the three local coeducational elementary schools. One is secular, a second is Roman Catholic, and a third is Lutheran. Tuition varies according to the school's funding.

Antigua has two Roman Catholic high schools, one for girls and one for boys. Both schools are highly regarded. Uniforms are required, and a demerit system governs discipline and conduct. Classes in history, geography, and literature are regional in nature.

The University of the West Indies (UWI) has campuses in Barbados, Trinidad, and Jamaica, and maintains extramural departments in several other islands including Antigua. Antiguans interested in higher education enroll at UWI campuses, or schools in Britain, the United States, Europe, and Canada.

The Venezuelan Institute for Culture and Cooperation offers many interesting programs, free to the public. Spanish lessons are provided for adults at all conversational and grammatical levels. Sewing lessons are offered throughout the year. Occasionally, cooking, music, and art classes are also given.

Commerce and Industry

Sugar cultivation, long dominating Antigua and Barbuda's economy, was a major export until 1960, when prices fell dramatically and crippled the industry. By 1972, the industry was largely dismantled. The agricultural pattern in Antigua has shifted to a multiple cropping system. Though fruit and vegetable production predominates, the Antiguan government has encouraged investment in livestock, cotton, and export-oriented food crops.

Currently, the economy is based on services rather than manufacturing. Tourism is the economic backbone and main source of foreign exchange. Over 150,000 cruise ship visitors and 250,000 overnight visitors arrive each year.

In the private sector, domestic and foreign investments are encouraged. Private businesses benefit from a stable political environment, good transportation to and from the island, and a pleasant climate. Government policies also provide liberal tax holidays, duty-free import of equipment and materials, and subsidies for training local personnel. The country's reasonably sound infrastructure is an added incentive.

Nontraditional exports have grown in recent years. Foreign investors, lured by Antigua's good transportation connections to North America and Europe, have set up light manufacturing industries on the island, primarily in the finished textile and electronic component assembly sectors. Some of the newer industries produce durable household appliances, paints, furniture, mattresses, metal and iron products, and masonry products for the local market as well as for export.

Barbuda supports a tremendous diversity of unexploited native habitats, including a bird sanctuary. It is hoped that development will focus on preserving these natural attributes.

Redonda's economic importance lies in the past. In 1860, Redonda was worked for its valuable bird guano, and later for aluminum phosphate. At the outbreak of World War I, mining operations ceased. After the war, technological advances made during the war made further mining uneconomical. Today, the island's only inhabitants are the birds. Redonda's quarry works stand alone, mute testimony to a bygone day.

Transportation

Americans need private cars. Most Americans buy cars here, as right-hand drive vehicles are more appropriate for local driving. Japanese cars predominate locally; other Asian Pacific Rim cars make up the difference. There is a 100% duty

rate for locally purchased or imported cars. U.S. Government employees are exempt from this tax. Landrovers are popular, especially for exploring the island or towing a boat. Many people consider air- conditioning indispensable, particularly in the rainy, hot season. Fuel-injected or sport cars are not recommended due to the inferior quality and low octane of imported gasoline.

Auto mechanics and repair shops service locally sold cars satisfactorily, but parts are generally unavailable for other imports. Expatriates should bring an ample supply of spare parts with them, including a dry-charged battery, fanbelts and hoses, a tune-up kit, fuel and water pumps, windshield wiper blades, oil, gasoline and air filters, headlights, indicator lamps, and an extra set of tires.

An Antiguan drivers license is required for all drivers. To obtain a license, present a valid U.S. drivers license to the local constabulary. A three-month temporary permit is issued and should be used until the permanent license is received. The U.S. drivers license is also returned.

Antiguan roads are not well maintained. Potholes are numerous, and roads are narrow and steep in hilly areas. Newcomers should exercise extreme care when driving in Antigua. The accident rate is very high because of poor road conditions, excessive speeding and passing by some residents, and because Americans are unfamiliar with driving on the left. Speed limit signs are infrequent and poorly observed or enforced. Taxis and buses frequently stop in the middle of the road for passengers. Road markings, such as center lines, are absent. In the city of St. John's, only a few streets are identified with signs. Rural roads do not have signs. Caution should be observed when driving in rural areas because livestock often wander aimlessly into traffic.

For those who do not have their own cars, taxis and rental cars are the main source of transportation. It is important to negotiate fares before getting into a cab because the cabs are not metered. Some comfortable, newer buses and minivans commute between St. John's and outlying communities. However, they are often overcrowded and driven recklessly. Several car rental firms offer mostly small Japanese models for rent by the day, week, or month. Rates are expensive.

Vere Cornwall Bird International Airport handles all international flights. Nonstop connections to Antigua from London, New York, Miami, Puerto Rico, Toronto, Frankfurt, Guadeloupe, Baltimore, and St. Maarten are available. Connections from several U.S. cities are routed through San Juan, Puerto Rico. Regularly scheduled air service is provided by British Airways, American Airlines, British West Indies Airways, Air Canada, and Continental Airlines. The regional airline, Leeward Island Air Transport (LIAT) provides service from Antigua and Barbuda to many locations within the Caribbean.

Communications

Antigua Public Utilities Authority (APUA) suffered extensive damage from Hurricane Hugo and is slowly repairing and upgrading its telephone equipment. Phones often stop working, and service is slow and unreliable. Long-distance, direct-dialing is available to most of the world.

The government-operated Antigua and Barbuda Broadcasting Service (ABBS) has one radio station and a television station. A privately owned radio station, Radio ZDK, broadcasts from St. John's. The format of Radio ZDK consists primarily of local news and features and sometimes includes prerecorded programs from U.S. satellite services. Antigua's one Christian broadcast radio station, Caribbean Radio Lighthouse, is affiliated with the Baptist Church. Many Americans enjoy listening to GEM-94, which broadcasts from the island of Montserrat. This satellite syndicated station features contemporary and oldies music.

Because it experiences little electromagnetic interference, Antigua is an ideal location for shortwave reception. Stations from around the world, including BBC Caribbean and Radio Deutsche Welle, can be received. The Voice of America also has a relay station on Antigua that broadcasts daily. Programming is mainly regional and world news, with some special music features and world reports aired on the weekends.

Antigua has three weekly publications that publish local and regional events but do not cover social and international events. Freedom of the press is guaranteed by law. *The Nation* and *The Worker's Voice* are government owned and abridged. *The Outlet* is privately owned and unabridged.

U.S. paperbacks and magazines are readily found. *The Miami Herald* and *USA Today* are available one day late. Bookshops, although small, sell a wide range of paperback novels, some reference books, and hardcovers at about twice U.S. prices. The small public library in St. John's has a good reference section. Library fees are reasonable.

Health

Antigua has some qualified doctors who were trained in the U.S. or Britain. However, specialists in pediatrics, surgery, ear, nose, and throat, cardiology, oncology, dermatology, neurology, orthopedics, and more advanced internal medicine are limited. Emergency obstetrical care is not immediately available. Holberton Hospital is old and inadequate. Nursing care is limited.

Current community health requirements fall below U.S. standards. In St. John's, open gutters carry untreated waste. Sewage treatment is inadequate, and the limited public restroom facilities are unclean. The weekly garbage pickup is deposited into open dump sites.

In St. John's, water is treated and has been safe to drink. However, the distribution system is old, and broken water mains can lead to contamination. If this occurs, unpotable water must be boiled and filtered before use. Homes have cisterns as an alternative source.

Infectious hepatitis, gastroenteritis, and intestinal parasites are common. Tropical weather and high humidity are conducive to skin and fungal infections.

Frequent power outages can result in food spoilage. Therefore, exercise caution when purchasing frozen foods. Meats purchased in Antiguan markets should be thoroughly cooked. Some large predatory fish that feed from the reef environment food chains contain a neurotoxin, which can produce diarrhea, vomiting, muscle aches, numbness, tingling of the mouth and extremities, itching, and severe headaches. Neurological symptoms can last a few days or longer.

Although none of the following inoculations is required for entry, they are highly recommended. Visitors and expatriates should be inoculated against typhoid, polio, tetanus, and hepatitis. Children should be have measles, mumps, rubella, and DPT (diphtheria, pertussis, and tetanus) shots, and an oral polio vaccine (OPV).

Although no special preparation of fruits and vegetables is required, visitors and expatriates should be aware of some toxic plants. The manchineel is a tropical American tree that has a poisonous fruit and a poisonous milky sap that causes skin blisters on contact. Three other common ornamental plants with a similar alkaline sap are the candelabra cactus, the frangipani bush, and the poinsettia. They too can cause skin redness and irritation.

Antigua and Barbuda do not have poisonous snakes since the introduction of the mongoose. However, there are scorpions, centipedes, and tarantulas. Their sting or bite is toxic and painful, and immediate care should be sought. The islands also have rodents and flying and crawling insects. Certain types of coral formations (the fire coral) can cause severe skin irritation, and spiny sea urchins can cause major foot infections if stepped on and left untreated. Visitors should also be aware that the stings of Portuguese man-of-war and the scorpion fish can be very painful and possibly deadly. Broken glass and sharp metal objects are often found at old ruins and abandoned sites. Caution should be exercised when exploring these areas.

Gradual exposure to the tropical sun's rays is the best protection against painful sunburn. Gradually increasing the length of exposure time each day will build up a protective tan. A hat should be worn between 11 am and 2 pm as the sun is most intense during this period. A sunscreen with an SPF of 15 or better should be worn.

LOCAL HOLIDAYS

Jan. 1 . . . . New Year's Day

Feb. 14 . . . . Valentine's Day

Mar/Apr. . . . . Good Friday*

Mar/Apr. . . . . Easter*

Mar/Apr. . . . . Easter Monday*

May . . . . Labor Day*

May . . . . Queen's Official Birthday

June . . . . Whitsunday*

June . . . . Whitmonday*

Aug. . . . . Carnival*

Nov. 1 . . . . State Day

Dec. 25 . . . . Christmas Day

Dec. 26 . . . . Boxing Day

*variable

NOTES FOR TRAVELERS

Passage, Customs & Duties

A valid passport or certified birth certificate and picture identification, such as a driver's license, are required of U.S. citizens entering Antigua and Barbuda. A return ticket is sometimes requested. Immigration officials are strict about getting exact information about where visitors are staying. There is no fee for entering the country, but there is a departure tax. U.S. citizens entering with documents other than U.S. passports should take special care in securing those documents while traveling. It can be time-consuming and difficult to acquire new proof of citizenship to facilitate return travel.

The possession, use, or sale of non-prescription controlled substances such as cocaine, heroin, marijuana, etc., is expressly forbidden. Bring prescriptions in their original containers with prescription labels attached.

Americans living in or visiting Antigua and Barbuda are encouraged to register at the Consular Section of the U.S. Embassy in Bridgetown, Barbados. Travelers may contact the Embassy to obtain updated information on travel and security within Antigua and Barbuda. The Embassy is located in the Canadian Imperial Band and Commerce (CIBC) Building on Broad Street, telephone (246) 436-4950, web site http://www.usembassy.state.gov/posts/bb1/wwwhemb1.html. The Consular Section is located in the American Life Insurance Company (ALICO) Building, Cheapside, telephone (246)431-0225 or fax (246)431-0179, web site http://www.usembassy.state.gov/posts/bb1/wwwhcons.html. Hours of operation are 8:00 a.m. to 4:00 p.m., Monday - Friday, except local and U.S. holidays.

U.S. citizens may also register with the U.S. Consular Agent in Antigua, whose address is Bluff House, Pigeon Point, English Harbour, telephone (268)463-6531, fax (268)460-1569, or e-mail ryderj@candw.ag. The Consular Agent's hours of operations are 9:00 a.m. to 4:00 p.m., Monday-Friday, except local and U.S. holidays (please call for an appointment).

Pets

Only pets currently residing in Britain may be imported, accompanied by appropriate veterinary certificates, into Antigua and Barbuda. This rule offers no waivers or relaxations. Pets from the U.S. can be sent to Britain for six months' quarantine. This is, however, extremely costly. Mongrel dogs and cats abound in Antigua, and many strays need homes. Antigua has an American veterinarian. The most common endemic parasites treated are tapeworm, hookworm, and heartworm. Rabies is not present on the island.

Firearms & Ammunition

Prior approval by the Chargé d'Affaires is required to import weapons and ammunition. In addition to obtaining the prior approval of the Chargé, all authorized weapons must be registered and licensed by the Police Commissioner. Separate applications must be made for the licensing of each gun including air rifles and pellet guns. Licenses are issued for a twelve-month period.

Currency, Banking and Weights and Measures

The official currency of Antigua is the Eastern Caribbean (XCD) dollar. All currency is graced with the likeness of Queen Elizabeth II. Paper bill denominations are in the amounts of 5, 10, 20, and 100 dollar notes. Coins are minted in 1-, 2-, 5-, 10-, and 25-cent denominations and a EC$1 coin. The official exchange rate in May 2002 was 2.70XCD to $1 U.S.

Travelers checks and major credit cards are honored at many hotels, restaurants, and most businesses.

Personal checks drawn on U.S. accounts are not generally accepted.

Antigua has no personal income taxes or general sales taxes. However, hotel and restaurant bills include a 7% government tax, and many restaurants also add a 10% gratuity.

The U.S. standards of measurement are the most widely observed in daily commerce. However, since virtually everything is imported, metric units are often used in food stores and appliance centers.

Disaster Preparedness

Like all Caribbean countries, Antigua can be affected by hurricanes. The hurricane season normally runs from June to the end of November, but there have been hurricanes in December in recent years. General information about natural disaster preparedness is available via the Internet from the U.S. Federal Emergency Management Agency (FEMA) at http://www.fema.gov/.

RECOMMENDED READING

The following titles are provided as a general indication of the material published on this country:

Ali, Arif. *A Little Bit of Paradise, Antigua and Barbuda.* London: Hansib Publications, 1988.

Antigua & Barbuda. New York: Chelsea House, 1988.

Crewe, Quentin. *Touch the Happy Isles.* Terra Alta, WV: Headline Book Publishers, 1988.

Dyde, Brian. *Antigua and Barbuda: The Heart of the Caribbean.* London: MacMillan Caribbean, 1990.

Kincaid, Jamaica. *A Small Place.* New York: New American Library, 1989.

Michener, James A. *The Caribbean.* New York: Random House, 1989.

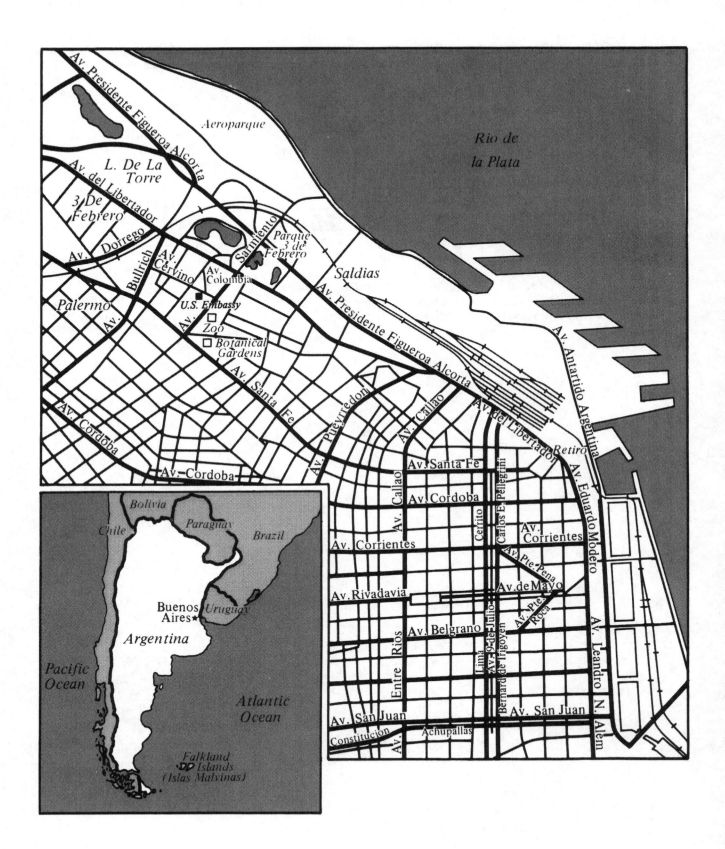

Buenos Aires, Argentina

ARGENTINA

Major Cities:
Buenos Aires, Córdoba, Rosario, La Plata, Mendoza, San Miguel de Tucumán, Mar del Plata, Salta

Other Cities:
Avellaneda, Bahía Blanca, Catamarca, Comodoro, Rivadavia, Concordia, Corrientes, Godoy Cruz, Paraná, Posadas, Resistencia, Río Cuarto, San Juan, Santa Fe

◦ EDITOR'S NOTE

This chapter was adapted from the Department of State Post Report dated February 1997. Supplemental material has been added to increase coverage of minor cities, facts have been updated, and some material has been condensed. Readers are encouraged to visit the Department of State's web site at http://travel.state.gov/ for the most recent information available on travel to this country.

INTRODUCTION

ARGENTINA is different from most Latin American countries in that 97% of its population is Caucasian, with Spanish and Italian strains predominating. There were few Indians in the area when the first permanent Spanish colony was established in 1536 on the site of what is now Buenos Aires. As a result, the Indian genealogical influence is slight. In the early years of this century, large-scale European immigration stimulated the modernization of the country, giving it economic and cultural status in the Western Hemisphere. Argentina is the second largest country in South America (after Brazil).

MAJOR CITIES

Buenos Aires

Buenos Aires is the capital of Argentina and its largest city. Situated on the Rio de la Plata 100 miles from the Atlantic Ocean, it is the country's major port and the center of virtually all activity.

Greater Buenos Aires has approximately 12,431,000 people; it is the world's fifth largest metropolitan area.

The general atmosphere of Buenos Aires is cosmopolitan and its people are quite sophisticated. The change from leisurely 19th century European living to present-day patterns is striking in the residential areas of Barrio Norte, Palermo, and Belgrano. Here, Paris-inspired mansions with wrought iron grillwork and carved doors pass from private hands to become Ambassadorial residences, government agencies, museums, or make way for tall apartment buildings boasting penthouses and swimming pools. In the high rise apartments and in the comfortable houses of the northern suburbs of Olivos, Martinez, and San Isidro, it is possible to reproduce U.S. patterns of living while enjoying much of the Argentine way of life.

The streets and avenues of Buenos Aires tell the story of the city, from afternoon tea at a sidewalk restaurant on Avenida Callao to late night on Avenida Corrientes, the "Broadway" of Buenos Aires. There is, for instance, Avenida 9 de Julio, claimed to be the world's widest avenue, and Calle Florida, an exclusively pedestrian mall where tourists shop year round. Avenida Santa Fe could be called the Fifth Avenue of Buenos Aires, while on Avenida Alvear, the small, elegant shops remind you of Paris and Vienna. The Costanera, the wide riverside boulevard, boasts dozens of open-air cafes.

There is a modern system of transportation with bus, train, and subway complexes contrasted with horse-drawn vehicles, whose drivers offer carriage rides through Palermo Park. Buenos Aires has some supermarkets and department stores. However, small businesses abound, from open and covered marketplaces to arcades lined with small boutiques and cafe bars.

Entertainment is plentiful and varied in Buenos Aires. The Colon Theater, one of the world's great opera houses, each year plays host to ballet troupes, opera stars, and symphony orchestras from Europe and the U.S. Folkloric music can be heard at various restaurants around the city. In small out-of-the-way places, the Tango is still danced to the music of small combos; and the colorful water front area of La Boca offers noisy nightlife. With over 60 legitimate theaters in the city, Buenos Aires is popular with traveling theatrical groups as well as outstanding local professional companies.

The city is very sports minded, too. Golf, tennis, riding, fishing, horse racing, polo, soccer, rugby, and boating are all popular sports. "Pato," considered the Argentine national game, is played on horseback with a leather ball (about soccer size) with six leather handles. More than a dozen private golf courses and a municipal course in Palermo Park are near the city center. In recent years bowling has become popular, with automatic alleys in both the city and northern suburbs.

The foreign community is extensive. The passport-holding Italian community is the largest (488,000), followed by the Spanish (374,000), the Polish (57,000), and the German (24,000). The British number about 22,000; North, Central, and other South Americans number about 800,000.

Food
Food is plentiful in Argentina. Supermarkets are well stocked, and carry some U.S. brands.

Clothing
Most clothing items are more expensive in Argentina, but are plentiful and fashionable although for women, smaller sizes only. When planning and packing, remember that when it is summer in the U.S., it is winter in Argentina.

Men: Men wear medium-weight woolen suits during cool months (mid-April to mid-November) and tropical worsted and wash-and-wear suits during the warm months. Many wear vests or sweaters under suit coats for extra warmth in July and August. The same type wardrobe worn in Washington, D.C. is needed here except that heavy overcoats are seldom needed. Due to the high cost of dry cleaning, wash-and-wear suits are a wise investment.

Good woolen cloth is manufactured in Argentina, and good tailors are available. Nice, reasonably-priced winter suits can be bought locally, but few wash-and-wear suits are sold. Raincoats with zip-out linings are useful. Good leather coats and jackets are made here with prices similar to the U.S., as are woolen sweaters and socks.

Women: Woolen suits, dresses, pants, blouses, and sweaters are basics for Argentine winter wardrobes. Ready-made woolen and knit clothing can be found locally in sophisticated styles but more expensive than comparable qualities in the U.S. Raincoats and coats are necessary although winter weather is less severe than in Washington, D.C. Lightweight summer clothing is recommended for the warm, humid months. Local cotton fabrics are available but drip-dry fabrics are seldom found. Tall and large sizes are virtually nonexistent.

Some opera evenings are very formal, but most performances can be attended in afternoon attire. Shorts can be worn on the streets and golf courses, but are more commonly used for beach wear, tennis, and casual outdoor parties.

Argentine shoes are of excellent quality leather, but the lasts are different and sometimes uncomfortable for Americans. Broad feet are more easily fitted than narrow and large sizes (9 and up) are very difficult to find. Gloves, belts, purses and other leather items can be purchased locally in a wide variety of styles, colors and prices. Hats, except for rain, are seldom used in Buenos Aires. Woolen sweaters of excellent quality are available at fairly reasonable prices.

Children: Beautiful knit clothes for babies are sold locally, however, most children's and babies' clothing is of lower quality than in the U.S. and is very expensive. Rubber pants and disposable diapers are often of inferior quality. U.S. diapers are better for keeping babies dry at night.

Shoes are of fairly good quality although narrow and small shoes are hard to find. Woolen sweaters and coats are generally of good quality. Snowsuits are often used for infants as winters are damp and cold. Winter pajamas with feet are popular with children and blanket-type sleeping bags are often used for babies. Warm socks, sweaters, trousers, and coats are standard wear.

Supplies and Services
Common household supplies are available in Buenos Aires on the local market, and nearby pharmacies dispense first aid supplies, pills, and other drugstore needs. Special prescriptions should be brought in quantity. Many well-known cosmetic firms have branches in Argentina, although their products may be slightly different, and the prices higher. Bring along a good first aid kit.

All books are expensive in Buenos Aires.

Tailoring and dressmaking as well as mending services for hosiery and shoes, are available. Beauty shops are plentiful Radio and TV repairs are generally good if parts are available. Occasional problems are experienced with stereo repairs.

Religious Activities
Argentina is predominantly Roman Catholic. Other denominations include Anglican, Baptist, Methodist, Latter-Day Saints, Lutheran, Seventh-day Adventist, Presbyterian, Jewish, Russian, Greek Orthodox and Christian Scientist. English services are conducted at some of the churches.

Education
Most American children in Argentina attend the Asociacion Escuelas Lincoln, generally known as the American Community School. It is a tuition-supported school which also receives periodic grants from the U.S. It is accredited by the Southern Association of Colleges and Schools.

It is essential that you begin the enrollment process at least 60 days prior to your arrival. Screening tests are given to all new students in grades K-8. Lincoln School has established English proficiency standards based on testing for full admission as well as for conditional admission.

Students admitted without knowledge of Spanish are provided with special Spanish classes until they can integrate with their regular classes. Students are screened for placement in the Special Spanish program.

Lincoln maintains an Elementary Resource Room which is setup to attend to the needs of students with minimal learning difficulties on a part-time pull out basis, grades 1-8. Due to the nature of the school and curriculum, it is not possible to provide a special program for every student as is the norm in most U.S. school districts. It is ESSENTIAL for parents of students with a history of learning problems to contact the school WELL IN ADVANCE so that it can be determined if Lincoln is a suitable educational environment and, if so, to obtain the necessary testing data. There is no special education program in the high school.

Diagnostic Testing—In grades K-6, based on teacher and parent referral, the Guidance Counselor and Resource Room Teacher administer specific diagnostic tests to students who exhibit learning problems. These tests are used to diagnose learning styles and achievement levels so that individual educational programs can be developed to meet each student's needs. The American School maintains a preschool, kindergarten, and grades 1-12. It is located in the Buenos Aires suburb of La Lucila along the shores overlooking the Rio de la Plata. Enrollment is about 800 students.

Approximately 35% of the student body is American but also includes Argentines and children from about 40 other countries. The property of the school includes a playground, athletic field, auditorium/gymnasium, cafeteria, and large swimming pool. The school has well-stocked libraries and suitable laboratory facilities.

© Pablo Corral Vega/Corbis. Reproduced by permission.
Aerial view with La Plata River, Buenos Aires, Argentina

The curricula of both private and public schools in Argentina must conform with that stipulated by the National Council of Education. By Argentine law, all students through the first semester of the 8th grade must pursue the Argentine course with instruction in Spanish.

Approximately one third of each day must be devoted to these studies. Newcomers are placed in language classes commensurate with their knowledge or abilities. New students should not be too concerned, as a "grace period" of one semester is allowed before testing in Spanish proficiency is attempted. New students are not expected to be proficient in the language upon arrival. All high school courses are taught in English, except for foreign language courses.

School terms run from early August to late December, and from mid-February to late June. The summer holiday of about five weeks starts in July. The American Community School's academic year corresponds as closely as possible to the school year in the U.S.; i.e., the second term of the academic year begins after the long summer vacation.

Bus service and hot lunches are available to children attending the American School. The school has no boarding facilities. School hours are 8:00 a.m. - 3:15 p.m.

In addition to academic education, extracurricular opportunities abound for adults and children within Greater Buenos Aires, including lessons in guitar, piano, riding, dancing, yoga, art, and ceramics. Children may join scout groups or participate in Little League, soccer, basketball, and other sports.

Sports

Recreational opportunities abound in Argentina. There are excellent private golf clubs and one public course, the Municipal Course in Palermo Park. Good tennis clubs and facilities for yachting, fishing, rowing, swimming, horseback riding, bowling, skiing, and hunting are available. There are also tennis courts which can be rented by the hour, with or without lessons. Jogging, biking and roller blading in the parks are popular exercises. Indoor facilities include several gymnasiums, one of which—the YMCA—is equipped for handball, fencing, boxing, wrestling, and many other sports. Most clubs specialize in only one or two activities, making the cost of participating in a variety of interests, quite high.

Avenida 9 de julio, Buenos Aires, Argentina

Ocean swimming is available in Uruguay or south of Buenos Aires in Mar del Plata, Pinamar, Miramar and other beach resorts. The nearest ski areas are in Bariloche and Neuquen in the Argentine Patagonia (4 hours, depending on type of aircraft; 2 days by train or car), or in Chile.

Hunting licenses are easily obtained. Most hunting is done on private lands and is by invitation or arrangement. Hunters find an abundance of game birds, including the "perdiz" (similar to partridge), copetona (resembling guinea hen), "colorado" (a pheasant-like bird having all white meat) and duck. You can also hunt deer, rheas (the Argentine ostrich), wild boar, hare, and fox. Guanaco and mountain goats are found in the high mountains, and pumas are found in many parts of the country. U.S. hunting equipment is highly prized here. Guns can only be imported with a customs declaration and special

permit. Satisfactory shotguns and 22 caliber ammunition are available locally. High quality ammunition should be brought with you.

Fishing catches include dorado, a large, gold-colored fish found only in the rivers of Argentina, Uruguay, Paraguay, and Brazil. Deep sea tackle is used for these game fish. The country abounds in trout and landlocked salmon, which grow to fantastic sizes. Trout fishing with a fly rod is very popular. Bring a fairly heavy casting rod to do double-duty casting and trolling. Spinning reels are recommended. Equipment for most sports can be bought in Buenos Aires, but quality is inferior to U.S. equipment and prices are higher.

Spectator sports include the immensely popular football (soccer), played year round at every level from sandlot to professional (at many stadiums in the city); the aristocratic polo; tennis; horseracing (tracks in Palermo, suburban San

Isidro, and nearby La Plata); pato, the rough gaucho-on-horseback spectacle; rugby; car racing; and boxing and wrestling at the Luna Park Stadium.

Polo was first played in Argentina by a group of Britons on August 30, 1875. They called it the game "of the mad Englishmen", but it was taken up with enthusiasm by the Argentines. The game spread with the founding of the Buenos Aires Polo Club in 1882 and was made popular among Argentines with the emergence of great players.

In 1920 Argentine polo made its presence felt internationally and soon became known as the best in the world, a label it has never lost. Argentina is known to have the best polo ponies, which are much sought after by the rest of the polo-playing world. While the early matches were played on farm horses, the breeding of polo ponies soon became a fine art. Today's polo ponies are fast, strong, agile, docile, and intelligent, and often crossbred with racehorses.

In Argentina the horse has always been associated with the country dweller's work and play. Pato is a game played on horseback, and forms part of the native tradition. It is played by two teams of four players each. A stuffed leather ball similar in size to a soccer ball, but with six leather handles attached, is held by one of the players. The name of the game derives from the original ball—a live duck tied up in a sack. The object is to throw the ball through a vertical ring defended by the opposing team. The game requires both skill and strength and puts the horses' speed and endurance to the test. The match is divided into four or six tiempos (sets) of 8 minutes each, with 5-minute intervals between them. The pato season in Buenos Aires runs from the end of April to November.

Touring and Outdoor Activities

While expensive and generally far from Buenos Aires, Argentina has numerous beautiful and interesting tourist areas. One of the most popular recreation spots for the Argentines and an exception to the previous sentence is Tigre, 28 miles from Buenos Aires on the Parana River delta, reached by train, bus, or car. Facilities are available for sailing, fishing, rowing, and cruising among the main islands and channels at the mouth of the river.

Mar del Plata, about 250 miles southeast of Buenos Aires, is the principal seaside resort in Argentina and is 30 minutes by plane, 5½ hours by train, 5 hours by car, or 6½ hours by bus. Mar del Plata is an important city and seaport. It has magnificent residences, parks, wide beaches, hotels, restaurants, shops of all kinds, and a huge, luxurious casino. A smaller casino is attached to the famous Hotel Provincial, one of the city's best. Mar del Plata is one of Argentina's most popular vacation spots, and the atmosphere is similar to Atlantic City. Several smaller seaside resorts near Mar

del Plata include: Pinamar, more expensive and exclusive, with more private homes than hotels; and Miramar, called the "City of Children," which attracts many American visitors. Attractive beaches in the River Plate area are found at Punta del Este near Montevideo, a ferry trip from Buenos Aires or 35 minutes by air.

In northeastern Argentina at the junction of the Argentine, Paraguayan, and Brazilian borders lies the spectacular 237-foot-high Iguazu Falls (Niagara is 167 feet high). It may be reached by a two-day car ride or by plane. Excellent hotels are available on both the Brazilian and Argentine sides of the falls. There are 14 large falls, most of them of great height and beauty. The river areas below the Falls provide excellent fishing. Because of cooler temperatures and more abundant rainfall, the best months to visit Iguazu are from May to September.

Bariloche, in the lake district of Nahuel Huapi in the Patagonian Andes and about 950 miles southwest of Buenos Aires, is another popular tourist resort. It is very pleasant in summer and an excellent place to escape from the city heat. Winter skiing can be done over well-developed trails. Bariloche may be reached by plane, train, or car. Often called the "Argentine Switzerland", it boasts beautiful scenery, with snowcapped mountains, noble forests, mirrorlike lakes, and numerous trout streams.

The city of Mendoza, at the foot of the Andes, is the center of the wine-growing district. The Transandine Railway connects Mendoza with Santiago, Chile, and passes the tallest mountain in the western hemisphere, Aconcagua—almost 23,000 feet high. The Chilean beach resort of Vina del Mar is three hours by car from Santiago.

For the traveler who is looking for something extra, it is possible to visit the Antarctic though a very expensive trip. Other attractions within a few hours by air of Buenos Aires include Asuncion, Paraguay,

which also can be reached by river boat or bus from Iguazu; Ushuaia in Tierra del Fuego, the southernmost city in the world; and such Brazilian cities as Sao Paulo and Rio de Janeiro.

Camping is very popular and campsites are numerous. Some have water, electricity, bathrooms with hot water, and general stores, while others are open land where you must set up a tent. Many beautiful National Parks have camping sites next to lakes or high in the mountains. Caution: Do not bring a tall tent. Argentine camping requires mountain tents, even in the flat lands, due to occasional high winds. For those who are interested in camping, it is advisable to purchase equipment in the U.S.

Entertainment

If you have a good knowledge of Spanish, the scope of entertainment in Buenos Aires is unlimited. Local theater is active, with good professional companies and amateur groups. Modern and classic plays by Spanish and Argentine authors, as well as translations of Broadway and European hits, are presented year-round. In summer, open-air performances are given in the Teatro Caminito, located in a section of Buenos Aires called "La Boca," one of the older parts of the city with tenements gaily painted in corals, greens, and blues. In this period (December to March), several outdoor theaters present classical plays, while operas, concerts, and ballets are held in San Martin Theater and Palermo Park, and the grounds of the National Library. Many of these summer performances are free.

Teatro Colon, the huge opera house, is typical of Old World magnificence. According to Arturo Toscanini, it has the best acoustics in the world; it was inaugurated on May 25, 1908. It covers an area of 7,050 square meters, is 117.5 meters long, 60 meters wide, and is 43 meters tall at its highest point.

The regular opera and symphonic season lasts from April to November with a full program each year of operas, concerts, soloists, and ballets. As the season in Buenos Aires falls during summer in the Northern Hemisphere, many of the great opera stars from Europe and the U.S. have been able to appear at the Colon. Argentina's symphony orchestras give many performances throughout the year. Ballets are also presented by local companies.

Movies are numerous, imported from the U.S. and Europe, and represent a good cross section of the world's cinematography. Most foreign films, including American, are subtitled and are heard in the original language.

The city has several good museums and many art galleries. There are many guided tours of the city with English-speaking guides available. Local newspapers publish schedules of cultural events in the entertainment section.

Small nightclubs, called "boites," are common in the city, and larger places have open-air dancing in the suburbs along the river. The music, orchestral and recorded, alternates between Latin and North American dance beats. Argentine folk music, while little known outside the country, is becoming increasingly popular with Americans here. "Penas Folkloricas" (public folk music clubs) offer the whole range of native music, from the lively carnavalitos of the far northwest to the slower samba and the familiar tango of Buenos Aires.

Social Activities

The American Club of Buenos Aires, at Viamonte 1133 on the top three floors of a 10-story building, is principally a lunching club, open Monday through Friday. The dining room accommodates members and guests for lunch only. Private dining rooms for parties up to 120 people are available on the 8th floor, and the 9th floor dining room is used for private functions of up to 500 people for cocktails or 350 for lunch or dinner.

The American Women's Club meets twice a month week. All female citizens of Western Hemisphere nations may join. In addition to biweekly teas and monthly meetings, activities are planned around the members' interests, and are in English. In the recent past, classes have been held in art, bridge, Spanish, cooking, music, and Argentine literature and poetry. The American Women's Club holds a charity benefit each year.

The American Society of the River Plate is the social and welfare organization of the American community in Argentina. Citizens of the U.S. and sons and daughters of U.S. citizens may join. The society has no clubrooms but meets in the American Club. The society promotes and maintains friendly relations between the U.S. and Argentina, encourages friendly relations between U.S. and Argentine citizens and promotes their respective interests, assumes responsibility for the celebration of days of national remembrance and Thanksgiving, and gives aid to institutions and/or individuals in need of assistance.

The American Chamber of Commerce in Argentina represents over 500 U.S. business firms. It publishes trade statistics, a weekly newsletter, a monthly magazine, and an annual business directory.

The Chamber holds monthly membership luncheons with guest speakers from government (both Argentine and U.S.) who are prominent in international business. Various committees are active. For example, the Export Committee (AGEX) gives seminars in Argentina and other countries on the technicalities of exporting, and a communications committee arranges—among other things—a lecture program designed to convince students in 15 Argentine universities of the advantages of the free enterprise system. Also active are a legal committee, an industrial relations committee, involved in salary studies among other things, and other committees.

Americans have many opportunities to meet and work with Argentines and representatives of other nations.

The University Women's Club meets monthly for luncheons featuring guest speakers. The club offers orientation courses, tours, and study groups. Programs are generally in English. Any woman, regardless of nationality, who has attended an accredited university or college for 2 years is eligible for membership.

Special Information

By the terms of Law 12.665, the Argentine National Commission of Museums, Monuments, and Historic Places is empowered to register, control the transfer of, and expropriate private property which it considers to be "of historic-artistic interest." Objects of this nature may not be removed from Argentina. When ownership of such antiquities is transferred, the former owner is obliged to report the transaction, together with the name and address of the new owner, to the Commission within 10 days. Failure to do so automatically raises a presumption of concealment. Anyone guilty of such concealment, or of illegally transferring or exporting such articles, is subject to fine. The law specifically includes historical documents in the category of national treasures and lists such things as old maps, autographed letters and memoranda, and public documents.

Córdoba

Córdoba, a cultural and intellectual center on the Primero River about 400 miles northwest of Buenos Aires, is Argentina's second largest city. It is the capital of Córdoba Province and one of the earliest cities in the country. Founded in 1573, it predates the first permanent settlement at Buenos Aires. Córdoba prospered during colonial times as a link on the commercial route between Buenos Aires and Chile. The advent of the railroad in the 19th century also increased its prosperity. In 2000, it had a population of 1,407,000.

Córdoba is the seat of the country's oldest university, which was founded in 1613 by priests of the Jesuit order as the College of Monserrat. The original building still stands. The college became a university in 1622 and is now, as Paraná, part of the national educational system. A new Catholic university was founded in the city in 1956.

Córdoba is noted for its excellent astronomy observatory; the beautiful and well-preserved colonial architecture; its museums and theaters; its numerous new, large buildings which have transformed the skyline; and its physical beauty, which is emphasized by its location on the slopes of the Sierra de Córdoba.

Near the city, on the Primero, is one of South America's most important dams. (Dique San Roque) Formerly used for cattle ranches, the surrounding land has been enriched by irrigation and transformed into orchards, vineyards, and grain fields. Wheat, cattle, lumber, and minerals are exported from Córdoba.

In recent decades, many industries have developed (textiles, leather, food processing, chemicals, glass), and the city is now one of Argentina's principal commercial and transportation centers. The city is serviced by a modern airport, Pajas Blancas, as well as excellent highways and railways. Also, the tourist industry in and around Córdoba continues to grow.

Education

There are two schools in Córdoba which are recommended to English-speaking students, although Spanish is used as an integral part of their curricula. Academia Arguello is located in the city on Avenida Rafael Nunez, and Reydon School for Girls is at 5178 Cruz Chica, Provincia de Córdoba, Argentina.

Rosario

Rosario is the principal city of Santa Fe Province in the north-central part of the country. It is a major rail terminal and the nation's largest inland port. Rosario lies on the Paraná River, 190 miles northwest of Buenos Aires, and is a commercial city and export center for the neighboring agricultural provinces. Its population of over 1,228,000 includes a large British expatriate community. Nearby Fisherton Airport serves the city.

Rosario was settled in 1689, and founded as a city under its present name in 1725. After the Argentine war of independence, the nation's first flag was raised here in 1816 and, each summer, commemorative ceremonies are held at the site.

Rosario began developing into a major center late in the 19th century, and is now an important industrial city known for sugar refining, flour milling, automobile production, steel milling, and meat processing. It has a national university, founded in 1968.

The city has several museums, among them the Municipal Decorative Arts Museum, the Municipal Fine Arts Museum, and the Museum of Provincial History. Tourists also enjoy viewing Rosario's Renaissance-Style Cathedral, Municipal Palace, and the Monument of the Flag which commemorates the raising of the first Argentine Flag.

La Plata

La Plata, 35 miles southeast of the capital, was built as a new city after Buenos Aires became a federal district in 1880. For a brief period, from 1952 to 1955, La Plata's name was changed to Eva Perón, in honor of the wife of Juan Perón, who was president at that time. The city's name was returned to the original when Perón fell from power.

La Plata, the capital of Buenos Aires Province, has a population of 676,000. Its commercial enterprises include meat packaging, textiles, oil refineries, and sawmills. Among its cultural institutions are a national university, a museum with a world-famous collection of anthropological artifacts, a national library, and fine zoological gardens.

Mendoza

Mendoza, situated in an oasis in western Argentina called the "Garden of the Andes," is a major metropolis and the center of a fruit- and wine-producing region which was settled mostly by Italian immigrants. Its vast fields are irrigated by the Mendoza River. Each March, the city celebrates the grape harvest with the Fiesta de la Vendimia, and *bodegas* (wine cellars) in the surrounding area are open to the public for the sampling of the new wine.

Mendoza was founded in 1516. It belonged to Chile until 1776, when it came under the viceroyalty of Río de la Plata. José de San Martín began his final preparation here in 1817 for the liberation of Chile. The city was destroyed by an earthquake and fire in 1861, but rebuilding was well underway within two years.

Mendoza is the eastern terminus of the 75-year-old Transandine Railway, which traverses the Andes at Uspallata Pass, connecting the city with Santiago, Chile. It passes the tallest mountain in the Western Hemisphere, Aconcagua, at a height of 22,834 feet. In Mendoza, from the summit of Cerro de la Gloria, which is crowned with a statue of San Martín, there are spectacular views of the Andean peaks to the west.

Mendoza, with a greater area population of 943,000 is noted for its museums and parks, and for its numerous restaurants which offer fine food at moderate prices. The city has several theaters, the National University of Cuyo and two other private universities. The population of the city proper, considerably smaller, is somewhat over 120,000.

San Miguel de Tucumán

San Miguel de Tucumán is a city of about 642,000 inhabitants in northern Argentina, and is the center of the country's sugar industry. Its more than one million acres of sugarcane are irrigated by tributary waters of the Dolce River at the foot of the Sierra de Aconquija, in the eastern range of the Andes. Large maize-producing plantations are also in operation in the area. A mild, pleasant climate and rich flora has earned the city a reputation as "the garden of the republic." The surrounding district is also known as a lumbering center, and the entire area is rich in mineral deposits.

It was at Tucumán on July 9, 1816, in the first congress of the republic, that the United Provinces of La Plata (the River Plate) proclaimed their independence from Spain after a bitter war against the royalists.

The city had been founded originally in 1565 on the Río del Tejar, south of the present site, in a place now known as the Pueblo Viejo, but was moved to its present location in 1685 in the aftermath of a disastrous flood. Many colonial buildings of the 18th century remain.

The National University of Tucumán was founded here in 1914. The city also boasts a shrine to Our Lady of Mercy, which is visited annually by throngs of tourists. Tourists also visit the city's museums, colonial cathedral, and the Casa de Gobierno (Government House).

Mar del Plata

Mar del Plata, about 250 miles southeast of Buenos Aires, is the principal seaside resort in Argentina and is six hours from the capital by train, car, or bus. It is an important city and seaport, with an atmosphere similar to that of Atlantic City. It has magnificent residences, parks, wide beaches, luxury hotels, restaurants, and shops of all kinds. Each year, during Easter and the November "spring" holidays (Southern Hemisphere seasons are the reverse of those in the U.S.), the population figure of about 533,000 is swelled to more than a million by the influx of tourists. All activities during these weeks seem to revolve around the huge casino which is one

of the largest in the world. A smaller casino is attached to the Hotel Provincial, one of the city's best.

Several smaller seaside resorts near Mar del Plata include: Pinamar, expensive and exclusive, where there are more private homes than hotels; and Miramar, called the "City of Children," which attracts many American visitors. Lovely beaches in the Río de la Plata area are found near Montevideo (Uruguay), just an overnight boat trip from Buenos Aires, or 45 minutes by air. Costs are higher there than in Mar del Plata.

Mar del Plata is home to the Stella Maris University, and the National University of Mar del Plata, as well as several museums. The city is linked by modern highways, railways, and air transport with other major Argentine cities.

Salta

Salta, capital of the northwestern Argentine province whose name it bears, has a population over 350,00. It is situated in the Lerma Valley, close to the foothills of the Andes, and is considered one of the country's prettiest cities. It is the commercial center of the region, exporting sugar, farm products, minerals, tobacco, wine grapes, and livestock. Its access to the Pacific came with the completion of a railroad extending to the north Chilean port of Antofagasta in 1848.

Founded in 1582, Salta is one of the oldest cities in the country. Here, in 1813, Argentine patriots under Manuel Belgrano defeated Spanish royalists in a battle leading to national independence. The city has experienced severe earthquakes throughout the centuries. However, many of Salta's colonial buildings remain intact. Of particular interest are the Church of San Francisco, which is reported to have the tallest tower of any South American house of worship, and the city's well-known cathedral. One of the best Argentine museums, the Cabildo Histórico, is located here. Other tourist attractions include the ther-

mal springs located near the city and the Miracle Fiesta, a festival held every September to celebrate Salta's survival after a severe earthquake in 1692. During the Miracle Fiesta (Fiesta del Milagro), religious icons are paraded through the city streets. The tourist office is at Avenida Buenos Aires 93.

OTHER CITIES

AVELLANEDA (formerly called Barracas al Sud), on the estuary of the Río de la Plata in east central Argentina, was named in honor of Argentine President Nicolás Avellaneda in 1904. Avellaneda is situated just south of Buenos Aires. The city is a major seaport and an industrial center. Wool and hides are shipped, and industries include meat-packing, textile production, and oil refineries. The population is approximately 350,000.

BAHÍA BLANCA ("white bay") is an Atlantic port approximately 370,000 in southwestern Buenos Aires Province. It is situated at the head of a deep, sheltered bay, and is the chief shipping port of the country's southern region. Bahía Blanca is also an industrial center and rail terminus. It originated as a trading post in 1828, but development came in the early 20th century with the increased production of the south *Pampa* area. The city conducts a huge import-export business; oil, grains, wool, and hides are the major exports. Bahía Blanca has a university, founded in 1956.

CATAMARCA (also called San Fernando del Valle de Catamarca) is located in the foothills of the Andes in northwestern Argentina, 210 miles northwest of Córdoba. Situated in a fertile valley, the city's economy depends on the agricultural products of the region; These include the production and processing of cotton, grapes, cereals, meats, and hides. Catamarca is known for its hand-woven woolen ponchos. Tourists enjoy the city's pleasant winter climate, hot springs, excellent scenery, and historical buildings dating to 1694. Catamarca also has a museum of art and an art gallery. The city also has many fine examples of colonial architecture such as the Church of the Virgin of the Valley. Its population is about 100,000.

The city of **COMODORO RIVADAVIA** is a seaport in southern Argentina on the Golfo San Jorge, about 1,000 miles south of Buenos Aires. It is significant to Argentina's economy because of nearby oil production. A 1,100-mile-long pipeline supplies natural gas to Buenos Aires, and tankers from the city's port deliver oil to refineries in northern Argentina. Comodoro Rivadavia has a population of approximately 126,000. The city's university was founded in 1961. Comodoro Rivadavia is linked by a national highway and air transport with Buenos Aires and La Plata. The city is the site of a major base of the Argentine Air Force.

A trading hub in northeastern Argentina, **CONCORDIA** is 225 miles north of Buenos Aires. It is situated on the Uruguay River, opposite Salto, Uruguay. As one of the largest cities in the region, Concordia enjoys a flourishing shipping market and trades with Uruguay and Brazil. Its main industry is food processing. Other industries include sawmills, flour mills, rice mills, and tanneries. The modern city was founded in 1832 and has a race track, a theater, a golf course, and parks. Salmon and dorado fishing in the Uruguay River is an added tourist attraction. Its population is about 120,000.

CORRIENTES is the center of a rich agricultural region, and the capital of Corrientes Province in the northeastern part of the country, close to the border with Paraguay. This commercial city of nearly 270,000 is an important port on the Paraná River, exporting cotton, *quebracho* (a sumac-like wood), cabinet woods, grains, rice, tobacco, citrus fruits, and livestock. Founded by the Spanish in 1588, Corrientes was the scene of a dramatic uprising in 1762 against the colonial governor, an

event which foreshadowed the wars of independence. The city and province were also among the first to rebel against the tyrant Juan Manuel de Rosas in 1844. Corrientes boasts a museum, founded in 1854, and a university, founded in 1957. The city is noted for its colonial architecture and served as the setting for the novel *The Honorary Consul* by Graham Greene.

GODOY CRUZ is located in western Argentina, less than 20 miles south of Mendoza. The city is a major manufacturing center with flour mills, canneries, breweries, sawmills, and meat-packing plants among its industries. It is also known for its wine-making. A highway and railroad link the city with Mendoza. A hydroelectric power plant is located near the city. Its population is about 180,000.

PARANÁ, a port city on the river of the same name, is the capital of Entre Ríos Province in northeastern Argentina, 80 miles north of Rosario. The city, with an approximate population of 207,000, was founded in the late 16th century by settlers from Santa Fe. It is the center of the grain and cattle district, and the home of an agricultural school. Paraná was the capital of the Argentine Confederation from 1853 to 1861. Paraná is the site of several notable buildings and monuments, among them are the Bishop's Palace, the Cathedral of Parana, the Museum of Entre Rios, the Senate of the Argentine Confederation building, and the home of Argentina's first president, General Justo Jose de Urquiza.

Located in eastern Argentina near the border with Paraguay, **POSADAS** is the capital of the Misiones Province. Situated on the Paraná River opposite the Paraguayan city of Encarnación, Posadas was established as a Paraguayan trading post and port. In 1879, the city was named in honor of Gervasio Antonio Posadas, a national hero. Most of its 140,000 residents work in public service. The city is an administrative center, and also manufactures iron and

wood products. A ferry between Posadas and Encarnación links Argentina and Paraguayan railways.

RESISTENCIA, the capital of Chaco Province in northern Argentina, lies opposite Corrientes on the banks of the Paraná. A city of 230,000, it is a center for the shipping of cattle, hides, lead, and *quebracho* wood. Resistencia is connected by a bridge with the city of Corrientes.

RÍO CUARTO is located in north-central Argentina, 350 miles northwest of Buenos Aires and 125 miles south of Córdoba. It was established in 1794. The city's economy is basically agricultural, but there has been some light industrial development. Fruit, meat-packing, and flour milling are important activities. Historical landmarks include the Museo Municipal de Bellas Artes and a cathedral built in 1794. The city is also the site of a military base and an arsenal. Río Cuarto's population is about 150,000.

SAN JUAN, capital of the eponymous province in western Argentina, is also a center for wine-growing; its vineyards add to the charm of the surrounding landscape. The province also produces fruit, raises cattle, and is rich in minerals. Situated 100 miles north of Mendoza, San Juan was founded in 1562 and moved to its present location after 1593. This city of about 120,000 residents figured prominently in the civil wars of the 19th century. Domingo Faustino Sarmiento, the romantic writer and president of the republic from 1868-74 was born in San Juan. In 1944, a disastrous earthquake almost leveled the city.

SANTA FE, a city with an approximate population near 350,000, is the capital of Santa Fe Province in east-central Argentina, 90 miles north of Rosario. It is a port connected to the nearby Paraná River by canal; the port was opened to ocean going vessels in 1911. Santa Fe's modern port is the most inland seaport in the world and accommodates ocean going vessels. It also is a shipping point for grain, meat, and *quebracho* (a sumac-like wood), from the country's northwest. Several industries are located in Santa Fe, among them are dairy plants, flour mills, mineral smelters, and automobile manufacturers. Santa Fe has several notable churches and is the seat of the National University of the Littoral, founded in 1889. A Catholic university also opened here in 1960. The Argentine constitution was promulgated in Santa Fe in 1853.

COUNTRY PROFILE

Geography And Climate

Argentina is South America's second-largest country, after Brazil, in size and population. It occupies most of the continent's southern region between the Andes Mountains and the Atlantic Ocean. Argentina stretches from 22 to 55 south latitude—a distance of about 2,300 miles—and is shaped roughly like an inverted triangle that tapers southward from a base about 1,000 miles wide. It borders on five South American countries: Chile to the west, Bolivia and Paraguay to the north, and Brazil and Uruguay to the Northeast.

In climate, size, and topography Argentina can be compared with the portion of the U.S. between the Mississippi River and the Rocky Mountains, although the North American region has colder winters. The humid lowlands of eastern Argentina, especially along the rivers of the Rio de la Plata system, resemble the Mississippi Valley. In northern Argentina, the savannas and swamps of the Chaco region find a parallel in coastal Louisiana. Westward, the humid Pampa (plain) gives way to rangeland and finally to desert that is broken only by irrigated oases, just as the Great Plains of the U.S. become drier toward the west. The Andes present a far more imposing barrier than the Rockies, but both mountain systems mark the western end of the plains.

Argentina's area of 1,072,067 square miles is about one-third that of the U.S. Although Argentina is narrower than the U.S., it extends much farther from north to south. Thus, Argentina has a range of climates that supports a broad diversity of vegetation, tropical as well as temperate. But the extreme temperatures that characterize comparable latitudes in North America are mitigated in Argentina by the oceanic influences that affect much of the country.

Except for its northernmost fringe, which lies in the Tropics, all of Argentina is in the Southern Hemisphere's Temperate Zone, which includes the world's most economically advanced regions south of the Equator. Climates in the Temperate Zone range from subtropical in the extreme north to sub-Antarctic in southern Patagonia. About 22% of Argentina's land area consists of accessible forests; another 3% is inaccessible forests. The variety of vegetation in Argentina is striking. The Patagonian-Fuegian Steppe in the south is characterized by a cold, windy, and very dry climate. Trees are scarce, and vegetation is dominated by low plants bearing a cluster of leaves that grow in a dense, cushion-like tuft. North and northeast are desert and scrub regions of the interior parts of central and northern Argentina. This desert/scrub area, known as the monte, has a climate as dry as that of the Patagonian-Fuegian Steppe, but somewhat warmer and essentially without a winter season. Its vegetation is highly drought-resistant and consists partly of low trees. In the Chaco region of northern Argentina the vegetation is a mixture of forests and savannas. The trees often grow in salt-impregnated soils, marshes, or swampy areas. The southern Andes region has high intermountain valleys with dry grasslands and often sub-desert shrubs and trees.

In sharp contrast with such areas of limited economic efficiency is the vast Pampa region. It is the most extensive level grassland in South America, and covers roughly one-

quarter of the nation. A great nation has been fashioned from its economic potential. It fans out for almost 500 miles from Buenos Aires. Containing some of the richest topsoil in the world, the Pampa is extensively cultivated in wheat and corn and provides year-round pasturage for most of Argentina's 50 million head of cattle. Average annual rainfall ranges from 20 inches in the west to 40 inches in the east.

The Andean region extends from the dry north to the heavily glaciated and ice-covered mountains of Patagonia, and includes the dry mountain and desert west of Cordoba and south of Tucuman, embracing the irrigated valleys on the eastern slopes and foothills of the Andes. Annual precipitation ranges from 4 inches to 24 inches in the arid regions and 20 inches to 120 inches in the heaviest rainfall areas.

Patagonia is a region of arid, wind-swept plateaus, covering about 300,000 square miles. Except for some irrigated valleys, this is poor, scattered pasture land. Far south, the weather is continuously cold and stormy; the region has no summer, and winters can be severe.

The alluvial plain of the Chaco in the north has a subtropical climate with dry winters and humid summers. Rainfall decreases from 60 inches to 20 inches and temperatures reach 120°F.

The Argentine Mesopotamia, which consists of the provinces between the Uruguay and Parana rivers, is made up of flood plains and gently rolling plains. The highest precipitation falls in the extreme north of Misiones Province, where it amounts to about 80 inches yearly.

Buenos Aires, is located on the right margin of the Rio de la Plata, and is part of the vast Pampa. The terrain within the city varies from low flatland only inches above the high tide line to slightly rolling country with a maximum elevation of 129 feet. The city's climate is similar to that of Washington, D.C., except that winters are less severe and it never snows.

Average rainfall in Buenos Aires is 39 inches (Washington—41.4 inches), distributed evenly throughout the year. Humidity is high year-round (yearly mean is 76%). High humidity makes winters seem colder and summers hotter. Abrupt temperature changes are experienced throughout the year, bringing relief to summer's heat and winter's cold.

Population

Argentina's population is approximately 37,215,000 (2000 est.). Ninety-seven percent of the people are Caucasian, mostly of European origin, with Italian and Spanish strains predominating. The population also includes many Germans and Central Europeans, and about 700,000 of Arab descent, most of them Lebanese Christians. Practically no Indians or mestizos reside in Buenos Aires; however, some 650,000 are concentrated in the northern and western border provinces.

Since most of the land is habitable, space is available for an increase in population. The Pampa's 15th century settlers were the offspring of Indian mothers and Spanish fathers. For more than 200 years they and their descendants populated the Pampa. The gaucho, or cowboy, was the typical country dweller who herded cattle, was an expert in breaking horses, and was said to be quick with his knife. Gauchos were the rank and file of the revolutionary army that won independence from Spain in the early 19th century.

During the 19th century the population grew rapidly. From then on the Spanish element lost its numerical dominance, blacks practically disappeared as a visible group, Indians were reduced to a few thousand living on reservations, and the mestizo population decreased. Much of the present population stems from a European immigration that was concentrated in the years 1880-1930, with a spurt after World War

II. The proportion of foreign born reached a peak of 30% in 1944. Of the total European migration between 1859 and 1937, Argentina received 11%. Birth rates were much higher than death rates during this period of population increase.

Since 1910 the Argentine nation has been more urban than rural. Over half its people reside in places of more than 2,000 population. Much of urban Argentina is concentrated in one area, Greater Buenos Aires, where more than a third of the Argentine population lives. Argentina is by tradition a rural, agricultural country, and the transition since 1910 to an urban society and an industrial economy has created strains in the social structure.

Industry developed and business flourished. Urban society was much like that of European countries, with a growing middle class of business and professional men and women. By the end of World War II many rural workers migrated to the cities in search of a better living. The pace of this migration has since increased. At the same time industry and commerce have grown substantially, requiring more workers.

Most Argentines are city dwellers, and most of them live in apartment buildings. Family life is close and affectionate. Women frequently work outside the home, if they do not have young children.

Argentine people eat well, and their per capita consumption of meat is one of the world's highest. Salads are popular; vegetables and fruits are abundant and available year-round. Many Argentines dress well and keep up with international fashion trends.

In sports, the Argentines favor football (soccer), horseracing, boxing, and tennis. Their polo teams are said to be the best in the world. "Pato" is a gaucho equestrian sport.

Argentines read widely. A tradition of public libraries goes back to 1870, when then-President Sarmiento established 100 free libraries. Some

of the best known Latin American book publishers can be found in Argentina and Buenos Aires is the home of thousands of book shops; the annual book fair is a major public event.

Public Institutions

Argentina is a republic of 23 provinces and a federal capital district (the city of Buenos Aires). The Argentine Constitution, modeled on the United States Constitution, provides for an executive branch with ministries, a bicameral legislature, and a Supreme Court.

Roman Law forms the basis of Argentine jurisprudence. Although provincial and federal courts, and ultimately Supreme Court-appointed judges traditionally administer justice behind closed doors, public, oral trials for criminal cases are increasingly common.

In 1983, free elections were held after 7 years of military government, and the country returned to constitutional rule. Full liberties were restored following years of a state of siege and the suspension of many civil and political rights originally aimed at combating leftist-inspired political violence. National, provincial and local elections have been held regularly since then; the most recent were presidential elections in May 1995. The national congress and provincial legislatures function normally again, alongside elected governors, mayors, and other municipal authorities.

The Argentine military is under the civilian control of the President, who is Commander-in-Chief, and the Ministry of Defense. While there have been three minor military uprisings since 1983 (the last in 1991), the armed forces as a whole have pledged their respect for democratic institutions and civilian government.

Argentina is a member of the UN, the OAS, the World Health Organization (WHO), the Inter-American Development Bank, the World Trade Organization (WTO), the World

Bank, the Red Cross, and many other international organizations.

Arts, Science, and Education

Buenos Aires is the cultural capital of Latin America and is one of the world's largest book publishing centers. It has more than 60 theaters where internationally known groups (such as the Comedie Francaise or well-known English theater groups) and artists (such as the New York Philharmonic Orchestra or American Ballet Theater) perform during the cultural season (April to October). Along with these international attractions, local performers compete with experimental avant-garde groups in this lively city. The Colon Theater, one of the world's most beautiful, is the leading opera house in Latin America; it features famous artists, both foreign and Argentine.

The National Library holds 1,700,000 volumes. Every day public lecturers present talks in Buenos Aires on diverse cultural and artistic subjects. More than 100 art galleries exhibit the works of important foreign and local artists. Other cities, such as Rosario, Cordoba, and Mendoza, also take great pride in their extensive cultural life.

Argentina has 75 officially accredited universities with a total of 740,545 students. The largest, the University of Buenos Aires, has 173,345 students.

The country has a high literacy rate, estimated at 96%. The educational system provides free primary and secondary schooling. Primary (or elementary) education is compulsory up to grade 9 - the pupils' ages range from 6 to 14 years.

Private, foreign, and religious schools are permitted but must conform to a nationally prescribed pattern of teaching in the Spanish language. The Lincoln (American Community) School offers classes in Spanish and English in conformity with government regulations.

Commerce and Industry

Argentina has the second largest economy in South America with a gross domestic product of $476 billion (2000 est.) and a per capita income of about $7,600, the highest in Latin America. The strength of the economy is largely related to economic restructuring in the 1990s, which included major new investments in services and industry. As a result, Argentine exports have more than doubled in eight years – from about $12 billion in 1992 to about $26.4 billion in 2000. Imports also grew rapidly during the same period, rising from $15 billion to about $25.2 billion.

Argentina is traditionally a leading exporter of agricultural products, including sunflower seeds, lemons, soybeans, grapes, corn, tobacco, peanuts, teas, wheat and edible oils. Other exports include fuels and energy, and motor vehicles.

One major boost to trade came from MERCOSUR—the customs union of Argentina, Brazil, Paraguay and Uruguay, which entered into force in January 1995. Chile signed a free trade agreement with MERCOSUR which became effective in October 1996 and Bolivia is expected to join soon.

Foreign trade now equals approximately 18% of GDP and plays an increasingly important role in Argentina's economic development. Still, exports represent only 10% of Argentine GDP.

Foreign capital has been a key component in Argentina's recent economic growth. U.S. direct investment in Argentina is concentrated in telecommunications, petroleum and gas, electric energy, financial services, chemicals, food processing and vehicle manufacturing. The stock of U.S. direct investment in Argentina approached $18 billion at the end of 2000.

Transportation

Local

Buenos Aires has an extensive transportation system. Five separate privately-owned subway lines serve many parts of the city. At certain stops you can transfer from one subway line to another without paying an additional token.

The most extensive above-ground transportation is by "colectivos" (privately owned buses holding about 40 passengers). Bright colors indicate the line and route traveled. The average fare is about 50 cents and there are no transfers.

Fares for Buenos Aires metered taxis are quite reasonable. Small tips are appreciated, though not always expected. Taxi meters show units based on distance and time.

The "remise", a kind of taxi-limousine service, is telephone dispatched, but you can hail them in front of major hotels. Charges are lower than U.S. cab fares. Always establish the fare before riding.

Traffic moves on the right. Buenos Aires has many wide streets and highways (such as Avenida del Libertador, Santa Fe, and the Costanera), but few modern superhighways such as the Ricchieri Autopista from Ezeiza Airport into the city limits, the General Paz which follows the city limits along three sides of Buenos Aires, 25 de Mayo which runs east to west, and the Pan American Highway.

Driving in Buenos Aires has been described as being at least as hectic as Rio, Tokyo, or Mexico City, as your first ride in a taxi or "colectivo" will reveal.

Regional

Travel outside Buenos Aires can be by train, air, bus, or auto. But since the general points of interest in Argentina are so far apart, a great deal of time is lost if you do not go by air. Some overnight train service is available to main cities with sleeping cars and service (room and food). Two main airports are accessible to the city. One is Aeroparque Jorge Newbery, near the downtown section and the River Plate. This airport handles propeller aircraft and smaller jets such as the Fokker-28 and Boeing 727 and 737. All domestic flights, and several regional flights to Asuncion, Montevideo, Santiago, Rio de Janeiro, Sao Paulo, and Santa Cruz, use the Aeroparque. The International Airport of Ezeiza is about a 45-minute drive from the city center. It handles all large jets and most international flights.

Communications

Telephone and Telegraph
The telephone company (former ENTEL), which was a government entity, has been privatized. Presently, former ENTEL has split up into private companies (Telefonica and Telecom), which are responsible for different sectors and TELINTAR, which is mainly responsible for international service. Phone service in Buenos Aires is generally very dependable.

A telephone is essential in Buenos Aires.

Long distance calls can be made from your home. Many people use a call-back service which is less expensive than using a calling card, or direct dialing.

Users of ATT, Sprint, and MCI credit cards receive a substantial discount on overseas calls.

The government owns and runs a telegraph and telex system.

Radio and TV
Buenos Aires has a wide range of radio programming on both AM and FM, featuring talk, music, news and sports (particularly soccer). Radio Mitre, Radio Del Plata, Radio Continental and Radio America, plus the government-owned Radio Nacional, are the most popular stations in Buenos Aires. VOA broadcasts are available by shortwave and Radio Nacional will begin using at least one hour daily of VOA programming late in 1996 after the installation of a VOA-donated antenna.

Television viewing in Buenos Aires changed dramatically over the past several years. From having five "air" channels available, one of them government-owned, television viewers in the federal capital now have the option of 65 channels from one of the big three cable TV systems: Cablevision-TCI; VCC; or Multicanal. Local programming is competing with a wide range of foreign programs, especially from the U.S. American channels, such as HBO, Fox, Warner Brothers, Cinemax, Sony, ESPN, CNN, TNT and others are heavily represented on the Cablevision-TCI (51% American-owned) cable system and, to a lesser degree on the others. Certain U.S. channels are broadcast with two audio tracks, Spanish and English, which can be accessed using a stereo television, or only in English with Spanish subtitles. USIA's Worldnet television network is also available on all Buenos Aires' cable systems.

Newspapers, Magazines, and Technical Journals
Buenos Aires is an important Spanish-language publishing capital. There are 10 daily newspapers, varying in importance and size from "La Nacion" and "Clarin" to small circulation money-losers. The "Buenos Aires Herald" is the only English-language daily. Newspapers are very expensive in Buenos Aires, costing an average of $1.25 per copy. Economic hard-times have forced many people to reduce the number of newspapers they buy daily from two or three to one, further pressuring the highly-competitive newspaper market place.

A wide variety of magazines are available locally, from picture and news magazines such as *Noticias*, and *Gente* to trade, technical, and professional journals. *Time, Newsweek* and many other American magazines are available on local news stands, but some are very costly. For example, an issue of "Vanity Fair" costs over $7.00 on the local market.

Bookstores are numerous in Buenos Aires and books in major languages, from publishing centers around the world, are available here. Stores such as ABC and Rodriguez have large stocks of English-language books but all imported hardbacks and paperbacks are expensive.

Health and Medicine

Medical Facilities
Buenos Aires has many good hospitals which in the private sector are called either "clinicas" or "sanatorios." U.S. trained physicians practice in all specialties. Medical costs are higher than in the U.S.

Community Health
Sanitary conditions in public facilities, such as restaurant kitchens are usually good. Health and sanitary controls are enforced and immunizations for school children are checked by the Health Ministry.

Hepatitis does occur, and all susceptible travellers should be immunized with the newer Hepatitis A vaccine. The Hepatitis B carrier state has been estimated at 1.1%. Vaccination against hepatitis B is recommended. Yellow fever is present in the northeastern portion of Argentina, and vaccination may be required when entering into another country. Carrying your yellow "International Health Certificate" with you is advisable. Malaria does occur below 4000 feet elevation in Jujuy and Salta provinces, and has on occasion been found in the Missiones and Corrientes provinces. Risk is higher in the summer months (December through May).

Water supplies are considered to be potable in Buenos Aires; higher risk of water-borne illness occurs countrywide outside of Buenos Aires.

The humid climate, vegetation, and diesel fuel can aggravate sinus conditions. Colds sore throats and mild forms of flu are common.

Traffic is generally heavy, and the risk of accidents is high. Seat belts and child restraint systems should always be used.

Keep these immunizations current: diphtheria, tetanus, typhoid, yellow fever, measles, mumps and rubella. Hand-carry your "yellow" International Immunization card. You do need special malaria prevention for in-country travel.

Flies and mosquitoes are common in summer. Most houses and apartments are not equipped with screens.

LOCAL HOLIDAYS

Jan. 1 . . . . New Year's Day
Jan. 6 . . . . Epiphany
Mar/Apr. . . . . Holy Thursday*
Mar/Apr. . . . . Good Friday*
Mar/Apr. . . . . Easter*
May 1 . . . . Labor Day
May 25 . . . . Revolution Day
June 10. . . . . Sovereignty Day
June
(Mon nearest
June 20) . . . . Flag Day*
July 9 . . . . Independence
                       Day
Aug. 20 . . . . Death of San
                       Martin
Sept. 21. . . . . Students' Day
Oct. 12 . . . . Columbus Day
Dec. 8 . . . . Immaculate
                       Conception
Dec. 25 . . . . Christmas Day
*variable

NOTES FOR TRAVELERS

Passage, Customs & Duties
American and United Airlines have regular flights between the U.S. and Argentina. The flights take approximately eight hours from Miami.

The most rapid and direct transport from Ezeiza International Airport is by remise (rental car with driver) which will charge a flat rate from point to point (maximum three passengers per car). Bus service is also available in front of the terminal and will drive to major hotels and/or a bus terminal in central Buenos Aires where taxis are available.

Buses are convenient for one passenger. For more than one passenger, the cost of the bus is almost the same as the cost of a remise.

A passport is required. U.S. citizens do not need a visa for visits up to 90 days for tourism and business.

The age of majority in Argentina is 21 years. Minors who are permanent or temporary residents of Argentina who are traveling alone, with one parent, or in someone else's custody, are required to present at departure from Argentina a notarized document which certifies both parents' permission for the child's travel. A parent with sole custody should carry a copy of the judicial custody decree. Although Argentine regulations do not require that minors who enter Argentina as tourists carry certified parental permission, immigration officials infrequently do request such a certification upon arrival in Argentina. Either document should be notarized before an Argentine consular officer or, if in Argentina, a local notary (escribano). For current information concerning entry and customs requirements for Argentina, travelers can contact the Argentine Embassy at 1600 New Hampshire Ave., N.W., Washington, D.C. 20009, tel. (202) 939-6400. Internet: http://athea.ar/cwash/homepage. Travelers may also contact the nearest Argentine consulate in Los Angeles, Miami, Atlanta, Chicago, New York, or Houston.

Americans living in or visiting Argentina are encouraged to register at the Consular Section of the U.S. Embassy in Buenos Aires and obtain updated information on travel and security within Argentina. The U.S. Embassy is located at 4300 Avenida Colombia, 1425 Buenos Aires, Argentina. The main Embassy switchboard telephone is (011)(54)(11) 5777-4533. Recorded consular information, including instructions on whom to contact in case of an American citizen emergency, is available at telephone (54)(11) 4514-1830. The main embassy fax is (54)(11) 5777-4240. The Consular Section fax is

(011)(54)(11) 5777-4205. Additional information is available through the Embassy's web site at http://us-embassy.state.gov/baires embassy, which has a link to the Consular Section's email inquiry Address: BuenosAiresConsulate@state.gov.

Pets
For the importation of pets into Argentina, you will need veterinary certificates of good health and rabies vaccination, each accompanied by a photograph of the animal. The signature and license of your veterinarian must be authenticated by a federal veterinary officer in the country in which you are living. In addition, the certificates must be validated by an Argentine Consul.

If such certificates are not presented at the Argentine port of entry and/or if the animal shows symptoms of sickness, it will be quarantined for 40 days at the owner's expense.

Limited boarding facilities exist for pets in Buenos Aires. You should investigate them carefully in advance for cleanliness and quality of service. Some residential hotels will accept pets.

Currency, Banking and Weights and Measures
The unit of currency in Argentina is the Argentine peso (ARS) It is issued in both bills and coins, with the bills in the same denominations as US currency. The value of coins are of 5, 10, 25, 50 centavos and 1 peso.

The value of the peso is pegged to the US dollar at a fixed rate. 1ARS=US$1.

Argentina uses the metric system of weights and measures.

RECOMMENDED READING

These titles are provided as a general indication of the material published in this country. The

Department of State does not endorse unofficial publications.

American University *Area Handbook for Argentina* U.S. Government Printing Office, Washington, D.C., 1969

Argentina. Insight Guides Series. Englewood Cliffs, NJ: Prentice Hall, 1992.

Brusca, Maria Cristina. *One the Pampas.* New York: H. Holt, 1991.

Caistor, Nick. *Argentina.* Austin, TX: Steck-Vaughan Library, 1991.

Fox, Geoffrey. *The Land and People of Argentina.* New York: Lippincott, 1990.

Jacobsen, Karen. *Argentina.* Chicago: Children's Press, 1990.

Mares, Michael A., Ricardo A. Ojeda, and Ruben M. Barquez. *Guide to the Mammals of Salta Province, Argentina.* Norman, OK: University of Oklahoma Press, 1989.

Morrison, Marion. *Argentina.* Englewood Cliffs, NJ: Silver Burdett Press, 1989.

Wynia, Gary W. *Argentina: Illusions & Realities.* 2d rev. ed. New York: Holmes & Meier, 1991.

History

Andersen, Martin. *Dossier Secreto: Argentina's Desaparecidos & the Myth of the "Dirty War."* Westview Press. 1993

Avni, Haim. *Argentina and the Jews: a History of Jewish Immigration.* Translated by Gila Brand. Tuscaloosa, AL: University of Alabama Press, 1991.

Brown, Jonathan C. *Rearrangement of Power in Argentina, 1776-1860.* Unv. Nebraska Press, 1994

Burns, J. *The Land that Lost Its Heroes: The Falklands, the Postwar and Alfonsin.* North Pomfret, VT: David & Charles, 1989.

Ivereigh, Austen. *Catholicism & Politics in Argentina, 1810-1960.* Saint Martin's Press, Inc. 1995

Moyano, Maria J. *Argentina's Lost Patrol: Armed Struggle, 1969-1979.* Yale University Press. 1995

Shumway, Nicolas. *The Invention of Argentina.* Berkeley, CA: University of California Press, 1991.

Politics and Government

Brysk, Alison. *The Politics of Human Rights in Argentina: Protest, Change, & Democratization.* Stanford Univ. Press, 1994

Calvert, Susan. *Argentina: Political Culture and Instability.* Pittsburgh, PA: University of Pittsburgh Press, 1989.

Gibson, Edward L. *Class & Conservative Parties: Argentina in Comparative Perspective.* Johns Hopkins Univ. Press, 1996

Gough, Barry *The Falkland Islands - Malvinas: The Contest for Empire in the South Atlantic.* Humanities Press International, Inc. 1992

Hodges, Donald Clark. *Argentina's "Dirty War": an Intellectual Biography.* Austin, TX: University of Texas Press, 1991.

Norden, Deborah L. *Military Rebellion in Argentina: Between Coups and Consolidation.* Univ. of Nebraska Press, 1996

Snow, Peter G. *Political Forces in Argentina.* Westport, Ct., Praeger, 1993

Tulchin, Joseph S. *Argentina & the United States: A Conflicted Relationship.* Macmillan Publishing Co., 1990

Economics and Sociology

Argentina: From Insolvency to Growth. World Bank. 1993

De La Blaze, Felipe. *Remaking the Argentine Economy.* Council of Foreign Relations. 1995

Hudson, William Henry *Far Away and Long Ago The Purple Land Tales of the Pampas*

Lewis, Paul H. *The Crisis of Argentina Capitalism.* Chapel Hill, NC: University of North Carolina Press, 1990.

Nolan, James L. et al., *Argentina Business.* San Rafael, CA. World Trade Press, 1996

Rojas, Ricardo *San Martin: Knight of the Andes* Cooper Square, 1966

Sarmiento, Domingo F. *Life in the Argentine Republic in the Days of the Tyrants: Civilization and Barbarism* Translation by Mrs. Horace Mann, Gordon Press Publishers, 1976

The Political Economy of Argentina, 1946-83. Di Tella, Guida and Dornbush, Rudiger. ed. Univ. of Pittsburgh Press, 1988

Wynia, Gary W. *Argentina: Illusions & Realities.* 2nd Ed. Holmes & Meier Publishers, Inc., 1992

Works in Spanish

Borges, Jorge Luis and *El Lenguaje de Buenos Aires* Jose E. Clemente Buenos Aires, 1965

Di Tella, T.S., *Argentina, Sociedad de Masas* Gino Germani, and Buenos Aires, 1962 Jose Graciarena

Escardo, Florencio *Geografia de Buenos Aires* Buenos Aires 1966

Imaz, Jose Luis de *Los que Mandan* Buenos Aires, 1964

Martinez Estrada, Ezequiel *Radiografia de la Pampa* Buenos Aires 1961

Travel

Ball, Deidre. *Insight Guide to Argentina*, 3rd Ed. Houghton Miffin Co., 1995

Benmayor, Lily. *This is Buenos Aires.* Buenos Aires: Ediciones Arte y Turismo, 1989.

Greenburg, Arnold. *Buenos Aires Alive & the Best of Argentina.* Hunter Publishing, Inc. 1995

Quesada, Maria S. *Estancias: Las Grandes Haciendas de Argentina.* Abbeville Press, Inc. 1992

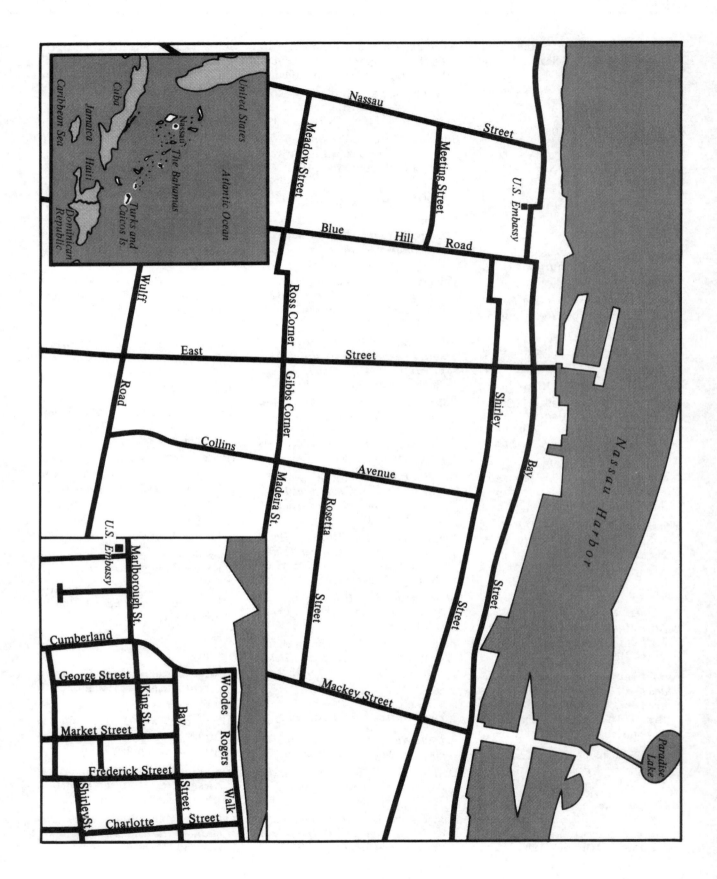

Nassau, Bahamas

THE BAHAMAS

Commonwealth of the Bahamas

Major Cities:
Nassau, Freeport

EDITOR'S NOTE

This chapter was adapted from the Department of State Post Report dated September 1994. Supplemental material has been added to increase coverage of minor cities, facts have been updated, and some material has been condensed. Readers are encouraged to visit the Department of State's web site at http://travel.state.gov/ for the most recent information available on travel to this country.

INTRODUCTION

The Commonwealth of the **BAHAMAS** is a chain of islands, cays, and reefs that sweep in a broad arc from 50 miles off the Florida coast, southward to the northern limits of the Caribbean. Blue skies and sparkling waters have lured generations of winter visitors to this subtropical archipelago, which was British colonial territory as recently as 14 years ago. The islands now comprise a fully independent state within the community of the British Commonwealth, having achieved autonomy in July 1973.

Close historical, social, cultural, and economic ties with the United States have left their imprint here. American investments and tourism in this island nation continue to make the Bahamas substantially more important to the U.S. than its small size and population would indicate. However, it retains its own distinctive character, and the society and institutions which lie behind its facade defy easy classification. Bahamian culture is a blend of the islands' African, English, and American origins, combined with the influence of the sun, the sea, and the tourists.

MAJOR CITIES

Nassau

Nassau, capital of the Bahamas and its major port and city, is nearly 300 years old. Time and the elements—hurricanes, decay, fires, and termites—have destroyed many of the old buildings. The downtown area has a distinctive architecture accented by columns, verandas, jalousies, and pastel colors. More Victorian than anything else, Nassau's narrow walks, streets, and prolific flowering bougainvillea and hibiscus have helped preserve its charm.

Nassau's population in 2000 was estimated at 195,000.

Nassau is located on the island of New Providence—21 miles long and 7 miles wide—one of the smallest and most central of the Bahamas chain. Nassau and its suburbs, which range east and west along and behind Bay Street, occupy mostly the northern half of the island. Miami is 210 miles to the northwest and New York is 1,080 miles almost due north.

History

Proprietary governors of Carolina and other North American colonies administered the Bahamas as trading markets with little pretense of civil administration. By 1700, the islands were well established as pirate camps for such immortals as Blackbeard and Calico Jack. In 1718, the First Governor, Captain Woodes Rodgers (an ex-privateer), gave the Bahamian pirates the choice of either confronting the small army he brought with him, or accepting a Royal Amnesty. Most took the latter, but eventually drifted off to other islands to resume their profession.

During the American Revolution, the Bahamas served as a supply point. Afterwards, the islands saw

Government building in Nassau, Bahamas

Susan Rock. Reproduced by permission.

their biggest change, as some 8,000 British loyalists and their slaves fled the U.S. These settlers brought the plantation system to some of the smaller islands, but poor soil, over-cultivation, and the boll weevil exhausted the chances of large-scale cotton crops in less than 10 years.

With the agricultural exhaustion of lands, poverty became more serious. However, the American Civil War brought prosperity as Nassau became the center for Confederate blockade running and the Royal Victoria Hotel (a once grand, now largely demolished) old building in the center of downtown Nassau became the haunt for both spies and gunrunners. In 1866, depression returned and for the next 50 years a succession of attempts to create wealth from conch (pronounced "conk") shells, tobacco, fruits, vegetables, sponges, and shipbuilding

failed. The Florida land boom from the early 1900s and again in 1920 drew many Bahamian immigrants to the U.S.

With the Prohibition Act of 1920, the Bahamas reemerged as a major base for blockade running, this time for bootleggers. World War II and the establishment of U.S. bases and facilities in the Bahamas brought back the prosperity of the 1920s.

Food

The selection and quality of food found in Bahamian food stores in Nassau is comparable to those of an average American supermarket with some exceptions. Certain popular brands may not be available, and specialty items such as delicatessen and ethnic food selections are usually meager. Produce is not comparable to an American supermarket,

but a broad selection does exist and fresh vegetables can be found through careful shopping. Prepared food items often cost twice as much as the same products in southern Florida.

Clothing

Local tastes and standards are similar to those of southern Florida. Summer clothing is worn year round, but with somewhat heavier material during the Bahamian "winter." Fabrics comfortable for the season range from lightweight washables to heavier fabrics and knits. Winter can be quite cool and clothes tend to be more formal. Wardrobes should include sweaters and possibly lightweight woolens. Heavy clothing is not necessary unless winter trips abroad are contemplated. Sportswear is available locally at reasonable prices.

Bahamian women often dress elegantly when attending church services and other special occasions.

Children's clothing is dictated by the time of year. All schools require uniforms which are available locally, so children probably need little more than play clothes. Children's clothing is available, but expensive. Parents may wish to purchase additional children's clothing before arrival.

All students wear uniforms for school and casual clothes at other times. Attractive casual clothes, including a sport jacket or suit for boys and appropriate dresses for girls are necessary, as young people are often included in social functions. Clothing for girls is readily available, but student sizes for boys are difficult to find.

Supplies and Services

Nassau drugstores, supermarkets, and speciality shops stock a variety of brand name toiletries, cosmetics, feminine personal supplies, home medicines, and common household needs. Prices are higher than in the U.S., and stores do not always maintain adequate supplies.

There are at least five custom tailor shops and six dressmakers in Nassau, and 23 custom drapery shops. The quality of the tailoring and dressmaking shops is spotty; only a few are recommended. Custom-made drapes and reupholstery in Nassau are expensive and believed to be on a par with the more expensive shops in large U.S. cities.

Dry-cleaning and laundry outlets are conveniently located. The quality of dry-cleaning service is poor. Some individuals have experienced difficulty with delicate fabrics and specialty cleaning, such as removing difficult stains from linens or silks.

Most skilled appliance and automotive service personnel are employed by major appliance stores and auto-

mobile dealers. Preference is given to customers who have purchased the appliance or automobile from the dealer. Warranties on items imported from the U.S. are not valid. Several independent automotive and appliance repair shops exist. Service varies greatly. Some independent repair shops take on projects for which they lack proper tools, equipment, training, or knowledge and can create more service/repair-related problems than they solve.

All the major hotels have qualified beauticians and barbers who meet U.S. standards of sanitation, styling, and beauty care services.

Shoe repair is limited but heels and soles can be repaired while you wait. Only two watch repair shops are located in Nassau but the quality of service is good. Some small, independent jewelers also do limited watch repairs and produce high quality custom-made jewelry. U.S. companies, such as IBM, Xerox, and Wang, provide reliable service on electric typewriters and personal computers.

Religious Activities

Full freedom of religion exists in the Bahamas, which has no favored or official State religion. The Bahamas is a predominately Christian country, and over ninety churches on New Providence represent Protestant, Roman Catholic, and interdenominational religions. Most of these churches are members of the Bahamas Christian Council, a national association which coordinates church activities and represents church services. Church services are conducted in English, but one church conducts services in Creole for Haitian residents. New Providence has no Jewish synagogues or Islamic Mosques.

Education

The Bahamian school system, including most private schools, offers curricula based on the British system. All the Catholic schools are

based on the American system. However, parents should be prepared to supplement their children's education with studies of American history and literature, especially for students in grade 7 and above. Overall, the resource centers, libraries, and curricula are inadequate by comparison. On the other hand, most private schools in Nassau have smaller class sizes and less disciplinary problems than many public schools in the U.S. No American International School exists in Nassau. The school systems follow the British in terms of grade levels.

A major concern is that teachers in many schools are not required to fit their study programs into a planned, step by step overall program, resulting in some gaps in subject coverage. Elementary Schools in Nassau range from thoroughly inadequate (Bahamian public schools) to very good. The upper grades (9-11), however, offer neither breadth nor depth in their study programs. Many college-bound high school students go to boarding schools in the U.S., Canada, or Britain. However, there are some good high schools in the Bahamas.

People with school-age children should complete and forward school applications to the CLO upon learning of their assignment to the Bahamas. Many schools have waiting lists.

A short description of the highest rated schools follows:
Lyford Cay School, located on the extreme western end of New Providence, occupies a six-acre wooded site within the boundaries of Lyford Cay. The school is able to take advantage of a 24-hour private security system. The children have access to two superb beaches and a 20-meter swimming pool at the Lyford Cay Club.

The school receives children from all over the island and accommodates up to 175 children ages 3-11. The pupils come from many different backgrounds and nationalities.

The school curriculum is based on the British system and is geared to the resources of the Bahamian environment. The children are tested annually by the Bahamian government and the Educational Research Bureau. Tuition for the 1993-94 school year ranged from $3105 to $3500.

St. Andrew's School is interdenominational, and coeducational. The children come from families in the middle and upper income brackets. Approximately 75% are Bahamian and the teaching staff is mostly British, with 3-year teaching certificates. The campus is large, the buildings are in good condition, and the student-teacher ratio is approximately 20 to 1. The school offers many extracurricular activities and has excellent sports facilities, including an outdoor swimming pool.

Structured on the British system, the school offers programs for approximately 750 students as young as 3 in a preschool program, and ranging to the late teens for children in the 12th grade. Tuition for the 1993-94 school year ranged from $4,755 to $5,790 per year depending on grade level. Even though the school is structured on the British system of eleven grades, the twelfth year was added to help students compete with other 18 year olds in the U.S. system.

St. Augustine's College (high school, grades 7-12) St. Augustine's is Roman Catholic, and coeducational. The students are 90% Bahamian, from middle and upper socioeconomic bracket families. All the teaching staff is Bahamian, most with teaching certificates.

The buildings are well kept, on a large and beautiful campus. Religious education and regular church attendance are mandatory. The school has excellent sports facilities, including an outdoor swimming pool.

The curriculum is equivalent to British Comprehensive schools, incorporating elements of American junior and senior prep school along with computer science. In addition, the S.A.T. is taken in the final year for admission to American colleges and universities. The library is inadequate and most books date from 1967 or before. The physical education program is good, and a few extracurricular programs are offered. Tuition for the 1993-94 school year was $2,040.

Tambearly School is an independent, recently established school with a curriculum for children age 4 (Reception) through eighth grade. It has a well planned study program using a combination of textbooks and workbooks (rare for Bahamian schools), combined with frequent field trips. Its goal is to prepare students for integration into schools abroad. All students utilize the computer and take French and Spanish.

Tambearly has a student enrollment of approximately 130, and is located at Sandyport, West Bay Street. The school accommodates up to 15 students per class, and has a staff of 12 full-time teachers and four part-time. Tuition for the 1993-94 school year was $4,050.

Special Educational Opportunities

The College of The Bahamas offers programs leading to the Bachelors Degree, the Associate Degree, Advanced Level G.C.E. (London), College Diplomas, and Certificates in Business Administration, Education, Humanities, Natural Sciences, Nursing and Health Sciences, Social Sciences, and Technology. The College's first Bachelor's Degree program, a B.B.A. in Banking and Finance, was introduced in September 1991. The College operates on a semester system—two semesters, and one summer session. Tuition fees are about $25 per credit hour per semester for Bahamians and $50 for non-Bahamians.

The Bahamas Hotel Training College and the University of the West Indies (degree program) offer courses in tourism and hotel management.

The University of Miami, Barry University, and Nova University, conduct a 2-year program in Nassau leading to an MBA. Courses are held on weekends and are designed for business executives and managers. American family members who have enrolled have found it challenging and worthwhile. Additional information on the University of Miami program is available by telephoning the University at (305) 284-2510, or contacting the CLO or USIS Education Advisor.

Several business schools offer courses in secretarial skills, business, word processing, and computer programming. The Industrial Training Center offers one-year courses in the technical/vocational curricula.

Sports

The emerald and turquoise waters of the Bahamas set the backdrop for sports in the country. Swimming, fishing, boating, sailing, scuba diving, snorkeling, and water skiing are excellent year round. Instruction is available for all sports, but may entail club memberships.

Golf and tennis are also popular. Nassau has four 18-hole golf courses, but green fees are expensive. Paradise Island's seaside course offers a view as well as a challenge. Divi Beach Golf Course is the newest course. Like Paradise Island, it can be crowded and expensive. Electric carts are required at all courses. The course at Lyford Cay has a limited membership and is very expensive. Many hotels have tennis courts. Several private tennis clubs are available, as well as athletic clubs, gyms, and spas. The world-class "Gold's Gym" opened in October 1993.

New Providence Island has in-season pigeon and duck shooting. The

Family Islands also have seasonal pigeon, duck, and wild boar shooting. Horseback riding is offered by stables in the Coral Harbour area as well as on Paradise Island and Nassau East.

Spectator sports include boxing, baseball, cricket, softball, soccer, rugby, basketball, American football, and volleyball. Some events are free; others charge a small admission fee.

Touring and Outdoor Activities

Literally all of New Providence can be explored in less than a week's time. The Family Islands, including Eleuthera, the Exumas, Bimini, and Abaco, are most popular with Americans. The terrain is flat as in New Providence. The islands can be reached by air, charter boat, or mailboat. Tours can be taken by taxi, bicycle, and surrey, or by glass-bottomed boat trips, sailing cruises or even an air-conditioned submarine which dives 80 feet below the surface.

Entertainment

The major importance of the tourist industry to the Bahamian economy has determined to a large extent the type of entertainment facilities here, which mirror those of a popular American resort city.

Luxury hotels on Paradise Island and on the north shore of New Providence offer a wide variety of specialty restaurants, cocktail lounges, cabarets, and discos. Two large casinos exist in Nassau, one on Paradise Island at the Brittania Towers Hotel and the other at the Crystal Palace Casino. Both the Crystal Palace Hotel and the Brittania Towers Hotel produce a Las Vegas-style extravaganza or floor show. Several other night clubs located in hotels and separate from hotels offer Bahamian and American-style shows and dancing.

Apart from the luxury-class restaurants, many good restaurants featuring Bahamian, American, Italian, and Greek food are patronized by nontourists.

Many choirs exist in Nassau and the Dundas Centre for the Performing Arts produces numerous well-known musicals and plays throughout the year. In addition, it also produces folk ballets and dramas written by Bahamians. Several of the larger hotels offer aerobic and other dance classes.

Two movie theaters operate in Nassau. They features popular American films.

Social Activities

An American Men's Club and an American Women's Club, the latter affiliated with the Federation of Women's Clubs of America, coordinate philanthropic and community activities among resident Americans. Outstanding among these are the annual Fourth of July picnic and the annual Christmas season wine and cheese tasting and dinner dance

An Hispanic Women's Club, including many U.S. members, is also active in the community.

Some organized activities exist for children, ages 7 to 15 years, including Boy and Girl Scouts, and extracurricular school events. Two swimming clubs for children offer competitive swimming. A riding school exists for those interested in horses. Some children also participate in operetta society productions, gymnastics, tennis, and Little League baseball.

You may contribute your time and skills through churches, the American Women's Club, the Hispanic Women's Club, the Bahamas National Trust, the Yellowbirds (Princess Margaret Hospital volunteers), the Bahamas Humane Society, Animals Require Kindness, the Red Cross Society, Ranfurly Home, the Women's Crisis Center, and assorted clinics. The Historical Society and the National Trust offer lectures on the Bahamas.

Special Information

The primary hazard facing anyone living in or visiting Nassau comes from residential and street crime, primarily burglary, robbery, and larceny. Residents and visitors should exercise caution and common sense. Doors and windows should be kept locked at all times, and deserted beaches, back streets, and poorly lighted areas should be avoided.

As the Bahamas remains a transit area for drugs designated for the United States, narcotics are easily obtainable. Parents should take extra precaution to educate their children on the dangers of illegal drug use. Parents should also become involved in their children's outside activities and closely monitor the company they keep. Drug offenses are dealt with very seriously in the Bahamas.

Temporary duty visitors to The Bahamas and newcomers should exercise extreme care while driving. The accident rate in Nassau is high due to the driving habits of Bahamians, poor enforcement of speed limits, and adverse road conditions. Accident rates among visitors who rent motorbikes and motorscooters are particularly high.

Freeport, Grand Bahama Island

Freeport is a modern community located on the southwestern shore of Grand Bahama Island, 120 miles northwest of Nassau. In 2000, Freeport's population was approximately 41,000. The island is 530 square miles in area, and the highest point of elevation is 68 feet. Although cooler than Nassau and with a higher rainfall, effects of the climate are similar to those in Nassau.

Freeport boasts a 450-seat Regency Theater in which the Freeport Players Guild presents several plays throughout the year. In addition, the Grand Bahama Players also present plays by Bahamian playwrights. The Freeport Friends of the Arts are active in bringing music and dance performers to Freeport. In the past, the group has brought in the Billy Taylor Jazz trio, the Alvin Ailey Dance Repertoire Ensemble, the English Chamber Orchestra, Russian concert pianist Boris Block, and singer Harry Belafonte.

Tourism is an important factor on Grand Bahama Island, and more than 5,000 resort hotel rooms are available for tourists. Planned less than 30 years ago, Freeport is still hopeful of attracting more investors. Major industries in Freeport include an oil transshipment company, several pharmaceutical plants, a perfume factory, a liquor blending company, three shipping companies, and a cancer immunology research center.

Taxis are readily available. No public transportation system exists, but jitneys are sometimes available. Roads are excellent and better designed than in Nassau. Most major highways are divided expressways.

Communications

Telephone service in Freeport is reliable, but callers to the U.S. find that the circuits are often busy. Direct dialing to long distance numbers is possible. Listings for Freeport and Grand Bahama are contained in the Commonwealth of The Bahamas Telephone Directory published by the BATELCO.

The Broadcasting Corporation of the Bahamas operates radio station ZNS-3 out of Freeport to service Grand Bahama, Abaco, and Bimini with local as well as national programming originating in Nassau. AM reception of Florida stations is fair to good depending on atmospheric conditions, but FM reception from Miami requires special antennae. A Miami-based company operates a CATV positive cable system which provides good reception to seven television stations from southern Florida. In addition, viewers can tune into Bahamian Channel 13, ZNS. Satellite dishes are popular, but expensive.

Three Bahamian newspapers, the *Guardian*, the *Tribune*, and the *Freeport News*, are available as are the Miami Herald and the New York Times.

Health

Medical facilities in Freeport are adequate for routine medical care, but are more limited than those in Nassau. The government-owned Rand Memorial Hospital has 50 beds and includes departments of surgery, general medicine, obstetrics and gynecology, radiography, and an emergency room. The Antoni Clinic is privately owned, and in addition to the services provided at Rand Memorial, this clinic includes plastic surgery, dentistry, and orthodontics, as well as oral and maxillo-facial surgery. The Lucayan Medical Center is limited to family medicine, internal medicine, and obstetrics.

Community health conditions in Freeport are comparable to those in Nassau, but Freeport does not have a large Haitian expatriate population.

Education

The same concerns that affect choice of education in Nassau hold true for Freeport. Numerous private schools, mostly church affiliated, offer programs for preschool age (3-5) children through high school. School years are divided into three terms. Brief descriptions of major schools follow.

Freeport Nursery School and Play Group—Calvary Academy This kindergarten offers three terms during the period September-June for children ages 3-5. Classes are from 9 am to 2:30 pm. In addition, the day care center operates from 8 am to 5:30 pm for children between the ages of 3 months and 5 years. Tuition varies from about $300 per term.

Sunland Lutheran School Sponsored by Our Savior Lutheran Church, this coeducational school accepts children ranging from nursery school through grade 10. Fees range from $508 per term for nursery school children, and are graduated for older children up to $650 per term. Enrollment is approximately 500, with 35 faculty members.

Mary, Star of the Sea School This Roman Catholic school offers coeducational training from nursery school through 8th grade, and is staffed by two Franciscan sisters and about 40 lay teachers. Enrollment is approximately 850, and at times applicants are put on a waiting list. Term fees range to about $440.

St. Paul's Methodist College This coeducational school accepts children ages 3-16 and is administered by the same Board of Trustees as Queens College in Nassau. Term fees range from $435 to $554. The faculty consists of 40 teachers and maximum enrollment is 800.

Freeport High School This coeducational high school (grades 7-12) is administered by the Anglican Diocese of the Bahamas. Normal term fees are $550. A special college preparatory program is also available for an additional fee. Enrollment is about 400, with 25 teachers.

Grand Bahama Catholic High School This coeducational high school schedules its instruction in two semesters and offers a 4-year program to prepare students to take the American College Board examinations based on the British System. Tuition is approximately $1680 per year. Enrollment is 340 and the faculty consists of 18 lay teachers.

Recreation and Social Life

Grand Bahama offers an unusual activity for underwater explorers that is unavailable in Nassau. Due to the unique "sponge-like" structure of the Grand Bahama land mass, many ocean holes or small underground lakes connect to the sea. These underground, water-filled caverns are popular with scuba divers who enjoy exploring. One of the larger underground caverns, the Lucayan Cavern, contains over 33,000 feet of exploration line. Due to abuse by some souvenir hunters, the Bahamas National Trust closed this cavern to the public for an indefinite period.

COUNTRY PROFILE

Geography and Climate

The Bahama Islands lie between 20 and 27 °N. latitude and 72 and 79 °W. longitude. Separated from the North American Continent by the Florida Channel and cooled in the summer by the northeast trade winds, the Bahamas enjoys a moderate climate. During the summer, temperatures rarely rise above 90°F, while the lowest winter temperatures vary between 40° and 50°F Rainfall ranges 40-60 inches a year.

The Bahamas extends over 100,000 square miles of sea, with slightly less than half lying in the Tropics. The Tropic of Cancer crosses the lower part of Long Island.

The Bahamas covers a distance of some 760 miles from northwest to southeast and include 29 inhabited islands, 661 cays, and about 2,387 exposed reefs. The total land area is approximately 5,380 square miles, about the size of Wales or two-thirds the size of Massachusetts. The largest island is Andros, with an area of 2,300 square miles, and the smallest is Spanish Wells, with an area of one-half mile. Some of the most

beautiful beaches and lagoons in the world are located in the Bahamas.

Over 50 varieties of trees can be found here, including such exotic species as the African tulip, the casuarina (hardy Australian pine), the cork tree, several varieties of palm trees, and about 40 varieties of fruit trees. In addition, large varieties of shrubs, climbers, vines, vegetables, and herbs are found here.

Significant seasonal changes requiring winter clothing or central heating do not occur here. The rainy season is from May to October, and the hurricane season extends from May to November. In the winter, temperatures rarely fall below 60°F, and usually reach 77°F by midafternoon. During the summer, temperatures fluctuate between 90°F in the daytime and 75°F or less in the evening.

Although humidity can reach above 80% (relative humidity for September is 82%), prevailing easterly winds lessen personal discomfort. Temperatures vary from a low of 76.7°F in January to a high of 89.1°F in August. Humidity causes mildew on leather and textile products, but homes equipped with central air-conditioning or dehumidifiers neutralize the harmful effects.

Rainfall often occurs in the form of fairly intense showers, frequently accompanied by strong, gusty winds. These storms are usually short and are followed by clear skies. Weather conditions can change rapidly. Statistically, a hurricane can be expected to occur in some part of the Bahamas every nine years. The last hurricane (Andrew) struck in August 1992.

Population

In 2000, the approximate total resident population of the Bahamas was 287,550. The statistics show that New Providence (where Nassau is located), has 171,542 persons accounting for 67.35% of the population, representing a 2.7% increase compared to the 1980 census. Grand Bahama, with the second largest population, has 41,035 persons representing 16.11% of the population, an increase of 31% over 1980. Abaco follows with a population of 10,061 or 3.95% of the population, Andros with 8,155, and Eleuthera with 8,017 accounting for 3.20% and 3.15%, respectively. Exuma had 3,539 persons and 1.39% of the total population, while Long Island with 3,107 persons had 1.22% of the population.

The Lucayan Indians, a branch of the Arawaks, discovered the islands in the ninth century. Some 600 years later, on October 12, 1492, Christopher Columbus made his first landfall in the New World on San Salvador Island. Some studies by historians have disputed the San Salvador theory, however, and suggest that the landfall may have occurred at Samana Cay instead. Spanish adventurers followed Columbus to the Bahamas and soon shipped the remaining Lucayan population as slaves to mines in Cuba and Santo Domingo, where the race was extinguished.

The islands were the setting for several attempts at establishing colonies of religious refugees, including the Eleutherian Adventurers. Although they all ultimately failed, many family names in the Bahamas derive from seventeenth century English settlers.

Most Bahamians are of mixed African and European descent. Of the European portion of the population, 90% are descendants of early British and American settlers, most notably loyalists from New York, Virginia, and the Carolinas. The Bahamas also has a considerable Greek community. Most are second and third generation Bahamians, whose descendants came to the islands as sponge fishermen.

English is universally spoken as is Bahamian, a variant of Caribbean English. A wide variety of religious denominations and interfaith and evangelical churches are found in the Bahamas.

Public Institutions

The Bahamas is a constitutional, parliamentary democracy. As a fully independent member of the British Commonwealth of Nations, the nominal Head of State is Queen Elizabeth II, represented in the Bahamas by an appointed Governor General. The Head of Government is the Prime Minister. The 1973 Bahamian Constitution was enacted by a Parliament composed of the Senate and the House of Assembly.

The House of Assembly consists of 49 members, elected by constituency every 5 years on the basis of universal adult suffrage. The Senate consists of 16 members appointed by the Prime Minister and the Leader of the Opposition. The Parliament performs all major legislative functions. The leader of the majority party serves as Prime Minister. The Cabinet, which answers to the House of Assembly, consists of the Prime Minister, a Deputy Prime Minister, an Attorney General, and other Ministers of executive departments.

The judiciary consists of a Supreme Court, a Court of Appeals, and various Magistrates' Courts, with the right to appeal to Her Majesty's Privy Council in the United Kingdom. The Chief Justice of the Supreme Court is appointed by the Governor General on the advice of the Prime Minister and the Leader of the Opposition.

In January 1993, the government instituted a form of local government for the Family Islands (Bahamian islands beyond New Providence) by appointing individuals to local licensing boards. Commissioners, who formerly served as administrators for the Family Islands, now serve as secretaries to these boards in addition to their duties as local magistrates.

Arts, Science, and Education

The historic Bahamian cultural experience is essentially British (English), but American cultural values have had an increasingly important impact on Bahamian society due to modern media, the large number of Bahamians who visit Florida, and the increased number of American tourists who visit the Bahamas

Education is free and compulsory between ages 5 and 14. The Ministry of Education has responsibility for all Bahamian educational institutions. Ninety-six primary schools, 29 secondary schools, and 46 all-age schools receive government funding. In addition, 6 special schools, and 45 independent schools operate in the Bahamas.

Courses lead to the Bahamas Junior Certificate (B.J.C.) taken in grade 9. In 1993, a new Bahamian National Examination (administered in grade 12 as an exit examination), the Bahamas General Certificate of Secondary Education (BGCSE), was instituted in both private and government schools.

The College of The Bahamas (COB) is the only tertiary level institution in the country. Founded in 1974, it currently enrolls some 2,500 full and part-time students. Essentially a 2-year institution offering Associate of Arts degrees in liberal arts and sciences, the COB recently instituted a Bachelors Degree program in banking and is working on plans to add additional 4-year degree programs. It also administers a School of Nursing. In conjunction with the University of the West Indies (UWI), it offers a Bachelors Degree in Education. UWI operates a Center for Hotel and Tourism Management, also a degree program, which draws students from throughout the Caribbean.

Success Training College offers certificates, diplomas, some associate degrees in business, computer science, and electrical technology. Several U.S. universities (St. Benedict's/St. John's, Nova University, Barry University, and the University of Miami) offer in-country programs to be followed by courses on the parent campus which lead to Bachelors or Masters degrees.

A large number of Bahamians complete university studies in the United States; fewer further their education at schools in Great Britain, Canada, and at UWI.

The Dundas Center For the Performing Arts, located in Nassau, presents two repertoire seasons each year including performing artists in drama, dance, and song. The Bahamas National Dance Theatre and the National Youth Choir were founded in 1992 as part of the country's activities in commemoration of the Quincentennial Celebrations of Christopher Columbus's discovery of the islands and the New World. Other active cultural groups include the Nassau Music Society, The Renaissance Singers, The Nassau Players, and the Freeport Player's Guild, located in Freeport, Grand Bahama.

Two of the most spectacular folk cultural events in the Bahamas each year are the Junkanoo Parades held on December 26 (Boxing Day) and New Year's Day. The parades begin at 2:00 am and continue until 9:00 am. Participants prepare costumes, rehearse months in advance, and compete for various individual and group prizes. The Junkanoo is an integral part of the traditional culture of the Bahamas, dating back to the days of slavery when slaves were given three days off during the Christmas holidays.

Music is provided by goatskin drums, cowbells, whistles, conch shells, and bicycle horns. Junkanoo music can also be heard whenever Bahamians feel in a festive mood or wish to celebrate.

Commerce and Industry

Since World War II, the Bahamas has become a tourist and financial center. These two industries remain the mainstays of the Bahamian economy.

The Bahamas was a vacation destination for over 4.2 million visitors in 2000. Realizing the importance of tourism for the economy, more than more than $1.5 billion has been spent on hotel construction and refurbishment in The Bahamas over the past five years. Tourism and related services now account for up to 60% of GDP and employ nearly two-thirds of the labor force.

About 80% of the tourists who come each year are from the U.S. The luxury hotels and casinos are clustered in Nassau, Paradise Island, and Freeport. New directions in tourism include a growing interest in the smaller, sometimes very luxurious, resort hotels of the Family Islands. About half the tourists visiting The Bahamas arrive by cruise ship, and port facilities in Nassau and the Family Islands have been upgraded to accommodate this growing market. In October 1995, The Casino Taxation Act was amended to allow for the establishment of small-scale casinos and the Lotteries and Gaming Acts allowed for sports betting.

Financial services, the second major sector of the Bahamian economy, consists primarily of banking, trust administration, insurance and mutual funds. The 400 banks and trust companies engage primarily in the business of managing assets of wealthy individuals. Strict banking secrecy laws are enforced. The Bahamas are widely known as a tax haven for non-Bahamians seeking to avoid income tax payments. As a result of new anti-money laundering laws passed in response to an initiative with the G-7's Financial Action Task Force (FATF), government revenues from International Business Companies (IBCs) declined from $2.5 million in the first four months of 2000 to $908,701 for the corresponding period in 2001.

The Bahamian Government recognizes the need for diversification, new industry development, exploration, and exploitation of agriculture and fisheries resources. The Bahamas imports over $250 million in agricultural goods per year, representing about 80% of its food consumption.

The agriculture and fisheries sectors together only account for about 5% of GDP and employ about 5% percent of the work force full time. A larger portion of the workforce is employed on a temporary basis during the opening weeks of lobster (crawfish) season. In an attempt to meet more of its own food needs, the government is working with local farmers to introduce new varieties of crops. However, foreign investment will be needed for this project.

The U.S. is the Bahamas' most important trading partner. Principal Bahamian exports to the U.S. are pharmaceuticals, lobster, salt, and hormones. Most food and other consumer goods are imported from the U.S. Brand name products are readily available, although transport and considerable import duties add some 50% or more to comparable U.S. consumer prices.

Freeport, the industrial center of the country, is a planned community built by foreign investors. A subsidiary of a major U.S. pharmaceutical manufacturing company has a sizeable facility there and there are several smaller export-oriented pharmaceutical and chemical plants. Solar salt and aragonite, two of the Bahamas' otherwise scanty natural resources, are exported from other points in the island chain.

The Bahamas have several labor unions, the largest and strongest of which is the Hotel Workers' Union.

Transportation

Local

Most areas of New Providence are serviced by small mini buses called jitneys. The jitneys operate from 6:30 a.m. to 7:30 p.m., although service to some residential areas is infrequent and hours of operation more limited than in the downtown area. The fare is about 75¢. No inexpensive limousine or bus connections serve Nassau International Airport. Taxis are metered and rates are controlled by the government. Cabs can also be hired for about $25 -$30 per hour. Limousines cost $50 per hour.

Several automobile rental agencies are in Nassau and Freeport, including subsidiaries of some well-known American agencies. Rental fees vary with the size and type of vehicle and the duration of the rental period, but are much higher than in the U.S. Several agencies also rent motorbikes, but they should be avoided because of the vehicles' very high accident rates.

Regional

Traffic moves on the left side of the road in the Bahamas. Road conditions vary greatly from four-lane highways to narrow streets with sharp curves. Some road surfaces are very poor with potholes and badly eroded shoulders that could damage a vehicle. Surface drainage is poor and large areas of standing water can be found on the roads after a heavy rainstorm. Posted highway speeds vary from 25 to 45 miles per hour. Cars, taxis, and buses often stop unexpectedly in the middle of the road to pick up or discharge passengers.

Regional travel throughout the Bahamas is principally by commercial, charter, and private aircraft. Fares on car ferries serving Eleuthera, Andros, and Abaco from Nassau are $200 for a car and two passengers, or $59 for foot passengers. Some travelers use the services of interisland mailboats. More than 20 mailboats depart Nassau for the Family Islands each week; one way fares range from $20 to $45.

Several direct flights connect Nassau with major American airports daily. American Eagle provides hourly service to Miami. Bahamasair, Delta, U.S. Air, Carnival Airlines, Paradise Island Airlines, and others provide direct service to Atlanta, Charlotte, Raleigh-Durham, Fort Lauderdale, Miami, New York, Orlando, and West Palm Beach. Air Canada has flights to Toronto on Thursday, Saturday, and Sunday only. Schedules change frequently.

Communications

Telephone and Telegraph

New Providence (Nassau) has a 24-hour telephone and telegraph service provided by the Bahamas Telecommunications Corporation (BATELCO). BATELCO has in the past few years completed systems upgrades, modernization, and increased features for its customers. For instance, direct dialing service is now available to 120 countries around the world, including the U.S., except Alaska. Direct dial calls are considerably less than for operator-assisted calls. For example, a 3 minute night call to Virginia costs $1.05, whereas the same operator assisted call costs $6. In some overseas areas the savings are more dramatic; a 3 minute call to Switzerland is $4 if dialed directly, whereas an operator assisted call costs $15. New digital exchanges have enabled BATELCO to offer several new features in addition to the standard services. Two speed calling services are now available. The eight most frequently called numbers can be reached by dialing only one digit. The other allows calls to 30 most frequently dialed numbers by dialing just two digits. Both services include long distance direct dial numbers. Other services available include call-forwarding and three-person conference calls. These new features and services are not yet available to all subscribers, although some 90 to 95% of the population is currently covered.

While BATELCO has made dramatic strides in modernizing its equipment and in expanding its range of services, it is still plagued by chronic problems associated with growth and older equipment. In some areas of Nassau, customers have waited months and even years for a telephone line. In other areas, frequent malfunctions occur and telephones can be out of order for weeks. The quality of calls to the U.S. is excellent. BATELCO maintains an over-the-horizon link with Florida City and a submarine cable links Nassau, Grand Bahama Island, and West Palm Beach, Florida. The quality of calls to other overseas locations is comparable to calls placed from U.S. telephones.

The monthly rental charge for one basic telephone instrument is $9.50, with additional costs for added features and extensions.

Telegrams may be telephoned to the telegraph office and charged on the regular telephone bill. Full rate telegrams to the U.S. cost $.24 per word and night letters cost $.12 per word (minimum 22 words).

Health and Medicine

Medical Facilities

While at times strained by the volume of cases, adequate medical facilities and sufficiently trained physicians in Nassau provide reliable medical care for most routine needs. The principal hospital is the government-operated Princess Margaret Hospital offering 24-hour emergency medical service and has 484 beds. Doctors Hospital is privately owned and operated, and has 72 beds and offers 24-hour emergency medical services. Rooms are considerably more expensive than those in Princess Margaret. Both are located in downtown Nassau. On the western end of New Providence in Lyford Cay, the Western Medical Clinic has a 14-bed care facility with a four-bed intensive care unit. It specializes in plastic and reconstructive surgery. The hospital houses the cardiac diagnostic center providing such services as doppler echocardiography, 24-hour electrocardiograms, exercise electrocardiograms, and facilities for pacemaker implantations and evaluations. The Sandilands Rehabilitation Center, with 344 beds, is a psychiatric hospital and a 133-bed geriatrics facility, including a maximum security unit, a child and family guidance center, and a combined substance abuse facility for drug and alcoholic patients.

Nassau has over 111 physicians including specialists in pediatrics, obstetrics and gynecology, dermatology, cardiology, gastroenterology, nephrology, neurosurgery, ophthalmology, orthopedics, anesthetics, pathology, radiology, and internal medicine. Among the 42 dentists in Nassau, two are oral surgeons.

Most doctors and dentists attended medical or dental schools either in the U.S., Canada, or the United Kingdom. The ophthalmological service at Princess Margaret Hospital is partially staffed by Yale Medical School ophthalmology residents who rotate every three months.

Community Health

Nassau has no major medical hazards. The water, however, tends to be brackish, and at times is not potable. Some visitors have experienced gastroenteritis, vomiting, and diarrhea after drinking tap water. These symptoms usually run 24-72 hours and subside without medication. Tuberculosis, hepatitis, and malaria have been reported among Haitian refugees living in close quarters, but no major outbreaks have occurred.

Newcomers should be aware that at certain times of the year, some large predatory fish which feed from reef environment food chains contain a neurotoxin (ciguatera) that can produce diarrhea, vomiting, muscle aches, dysesthesia (abnormal sensations), paresthesia (numbness and tingling) of the mouth and extremities, itching, and severe headaches. Neurological symptoms can last a few days, several months, or years. No known specific treatment for ciguatera exists. Barracuda and certain species of jack and grouper have been known to cause ciguatera. Deep ocean fish such as shark, marlin, salmon, and tuna do not feed on the reef and therefore are usually safe. Lobster, shrimp, and other shellfish are not affected. Occasionally, food poisoning associated with raw or "scorched" conch occurs, usually from improper handling by street vendors.

Preventive Measures

No serious, prevalent, endemic diseases exist in Nassau. Sanitary standards for food handlers, barbers, and beauticians are high. Food is imported from the U.S., Europe, and New Zealand and subject to inspection by the country of origin. Locally produced dairy foods meet U.S. health and sanitary standards. No special preparation of fruit and vegetables is required. Sewage is adequate but, in some low areas where drainage is poor, septic tanks and drainage pits require frequent waste water removal.

Although New Providence has no poisonous snakes, it does have poisonous insects, such as black widow spiders and scorpions. Certain types of coral formations can cause severe skin irritation and spiny sea urchins can cause severe foot infections if stepped on. No known cases of rabid animals have been reported on New Providence Island.

NOTES FOR TRAVELERS

Passage, Customs and Duties

Ample flights are available on American air carriers and should be used. Bahamasair, which flies the Miami-Nassau route, is a Bahamian carrier.

For the traveler who may have forgotten that airplanes were once powered only by propellers, Paradise Island Airlines, an American carrier, offers flights from downtown Miami and Fort Lauderdale International Airport in an amphibious, propeller-driven aircraft. The flights land in Nassau Harbor.

U.S. citizens must present original proof of U.S. citizenship (a valid or expired passport, a certified U.S. birth certificate or a Certificate of Naturalization), photo identification, and an onward/return ticket for entry into The Bahamas. Voter registration cards, driver's licenses, affidavits and other similar documents are not acceptable as proof of U.S. citizenship. Visas are not required for U.S. citizens for stays up to eight months. There is an airport departure tax of $15 for travelers age six years and older. For further information, U.S. citizens may contact the Embassy of the Commonwealth of The Bahamas, 2220 Massachusetts Avenue, N.W., Washington, D.C. 20008, telephone (202) 319-2660, or the Bahamian consulates in Miami or New York. Additional information is available on The Bahamas Tourist Board web site at http://www.bahamas.com or telephone 1-800-422-4262, and on the official web site of the Government of the Bahamas at http://www.bahamas.gov.bs/.

The Bahamas Dangerous Drug Act makes it an offense for an unauthorized person to import, export, or be in possession of marijuana, morphine, opium, or lysergic acid (LSD) in the Bahamas. The provisions of this Act are strictly enforced.

Firearms & Ammunition

It is illegal to import firearms or ammunition into The Bahamas or to possess a firearm in the country without appropriate permission. Tourists who arrive by private boat are required to declare firearms to Bahamian Customs and leave firearms on the boat while in The Bahamas. Penalties for illegal possession of a firearm or ammunition are strict and can involve heavy fines, lengthy prison terms, or both. For further information on firearms in The Bahamas, please contact the Embassy of the Commonwealth of The Bahamas in Washington, D.C., or the Bahamian consulates in Miami or New York

Americans living in or visiting The Bahamas are encouraged to register at the Consular Section of the U.S. Embassy in Nassau and obtain updated information on travel and security within The Bahamas. The U.S. Embassy is located next to McDonald's restaurant on Queen Street in downtown Nassau; telephone (242) 322-1181, after hours: (242) 328-2206. The Consular Section hours are 8:00 a.m. - 12 noon, Monday - Friday, except local and U.S. holidays. The U.S. Embassy is also responsible for consular services in the Turks and Caicos Islands, an overseas territory of the United Kingdom. The Consular Information Sheet for the British West Indies provides additional information on the Turks and Caicos Islands.

Laws

Boaters should be aware that long-line fishing in Bahamian waters is illegal. All long-line fishing gear must be stowed below deck while transiting through Bahamian waters. Fishermen should note that stiff penalties are imposed for catching crawfish (lobster) or other marine life out of season or in protected areas.

U.S. citizens should exercise caution when considering time-share investments and be aware of the aggressive tactics used by some time-share sales representatives. Bahamian law allows time-share purchasers five days to cancel the contract for full reimbursement. Disputes that arise after that period can be very time-consuming and expensive to resolve through the local legal system.

Pets

There are no known cases of rabid animals in the Bahamas. No pit bulls and no dogs under six months of age are permitted to enter the Bahamas.

An Import Permit is required from the Bahamian Ministry of Agriculture and Fisheries for all animals brought to the Bahamas. Applications for such permits should be made several weeks in advance to the Ministry of Agriculture and Fisheries, P.O. Box N-3028, Nassau, Bahamas. The telephone number is (809) 322-1277.

Dogs and cats over the age of 6 months, imported from the U.S. or Canada, must be accompanied by a Veterinary Health Certificate issued within 24 hours of embarkation and a certificate of Rabies Vaccination issued not less than 10 days or more than 9 months before.

Pets under 6 months do not require a Rabies Vaccination Certificate, but must have a Veterinary Health Certificate. Dogs under six months are not permitted to enter.

Dogs and cats traveling to the U.S. from the Bahamas need a Health Certificate issued within 24 hours of departure. If you intend to ship pets to the U.S., check with the U.S. Department of Agriculture Animal and Plant Inspector at Nassau International Airport well in advance of planned travel to confirm this policy.

Disaster Preparedness

The Bahamas, like all countries in the Caribbean basin, is subject to the threat of hurricanes. Hurricane season officially runs from June 1 to November 30, although hurricanes have been known to occur outside that time period. Visitors to The Bahamas during hurricane season are advised to monitor weather reports in order to be prepared for any potential threats. General information about disaster preparedness is available via the Internet from the U.S. Federal Emergency Management Agency (FEMA) at http://www.fema.gov.

Currency, Banking, and Weights and Measures

Virtually all stores, restaurants, hotels, and other commercial facilities accept American currency, which is on par with the Bahamian dollar. Major credit cards and travelers checks are also widely accepted. No restriction is placed on the amount of currency brought into or taken out of the Bahamas.

American currency, usually exchanged on a one-to-one basis with Bahamian dollars, can be used throughout the Bahamas. Most major stores, hotels, and restaurants will accept major credit cards and travelers checks, but will not accept a personal check without a check cashing card (Chekard).

Standard U.S. weights and measures are used in the Bahamas.

LOCAL HOLIDAYS

Jan. 1	New Year's Day
Mar/Apr.	Good Friday*
Mar/Apr.	Easter Monday*
Mar/Apr.	Easter Monday*
May/June	Whitsunday*
May/June	Whitmonday*
June (first Friday)	Labour Day
July 10	Independence Day
Aug. 3	Emancipation Day
Oct. 12	Discovery Day
Dec. 25	Christmas Day
Dec. 26	Boxing Day

*variable

RECOMMENDED READING

These titles are provided as a general indication of the material published on this country.

The Department of State does not endorse unofficial publications.

Ajlouny, Joe. *The Bahamas: A Colorful & Concise History.* Oak Park, MI: JSA Publications, 1989.

Blount, S. *Diving and Snorkeling Guide to the Bahamas.* Houston, TX: Pisces Books, 1991.

Christmas, R.J. *Fielding's Bermuda and the Bahamas.* New York: Fielding Travel Books, 1990.

Collinwood, Dean W. *The Bahamas Between Worlds.* Decatur, IL: White Sound Press, 1989.

Dalleo, Peter T. *The New Bahamian History: Africa's Image Revisited.* Decatur, IL: White Sound Press, 1988.

Dupuch, Jr., Etienne, Bahamas *Handbook and Businessman's Annual.* Nassau.

Fodor's Bahamas 1992. New York: McKay, 1992.

Fox, L. *Romantic Island Getaways.* New York: John Wiley & Sons, 1991.

Greenfield, Eloise. *Under the Sunday Tree.* New York: Harper Collins Children's Books, 1988.

Johnson, Dr. Doris, *The Quiet Revolution.* Nassau.

Lloyd, H. *Isles of Eden.* Akron, OH: Benjamin Publishing, 1991.

McCulla, Patricia E. *Bahamas.* New York: Chelsea House, 1988.

Marshall, Dawn I., *The Haitian Problem, Illegal Migration to the Bahamas.* Kingston, Jamaica.

Saunders, Dr. Gail, *Islanders In The Stream.* University of Georgia, 1992.

Stone, William T., and Anne M. Hays. *A Cruising Guide to the Caribbean: Including the North Coast of South America, Central, & Yucatan.* New York: Putnam Publishing Group, 1991.

White, Virginia. *The Outermost Island: An Oral History of San Salvador, the Bahamas.* Port Charlotte, FL: Bahamian Field Station, 1987.

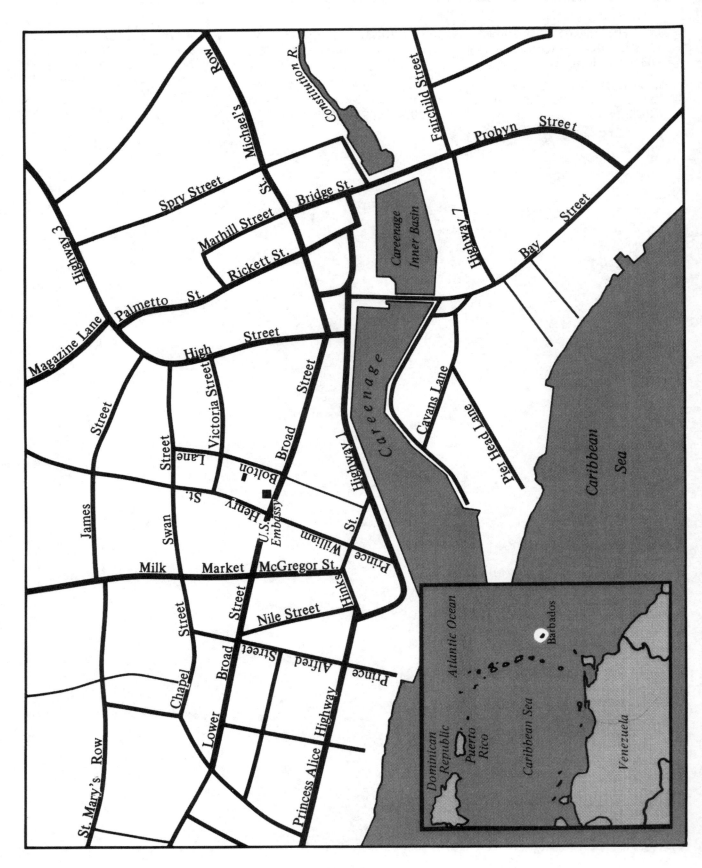

Bridgetown, Barbados

BARBADOS

Major Cities:
Bridgetown

EDITOR'S NOTE

This chapter was adapted from the Department of State Post Report dated November 1995. Supplemental material has been added to increase coverage of minor cities, facts have been updated, and some material has been condensed. Readers are encouraged to visit the Department of State's web site at http://travel.state.gov/ for the most recent information available on travel to this country.

INTRODUCTION

The British influence remains alive and strong in **BARBADOS**. Although this small Caribbean nation has been independent for more than two decades, the mark of the Crown survives in its language, in its passion for cricket, in conservative dress, and in the carefully nurtured observance of afternoon teatime. A renowned tourist mecca, Barbados is, in many ways, the most advanced of the smaller Caribbean islands, and it enjoys its position as a stable, independent state within the British Commonwealth.

The island is geographically isolated and offers few sophisticated cultural amenities, but the sun shines nearly every day, and the sea beckons to visitors throughout the year. From quiet coves to sprawling, luxurious resorts, Barbados is well-equipped for tourism.

The island was settled by the English, but it is thought that perhaps it had been named earlier by Portuguese explorers—*Los Barbados*—for the bearded fig trees they found in such profusion.

MAJOR CITY

Bridgetown

Bridgetown, founded in 1629, is Barbados' capital and largest city. It has about 123,000 inhabitants. The Careenage, a small inlet of the Atlantic Ocean, divides the city. Some tourist charter boats and fishing boats are docked there. Two of the old warehouses lining the Careenage have been partly renovated and provide space for some cafes and shops.

Broad Street is the principal tourist shopping and banking street. A small statue of Lord Nelson stands in the square, commissioned by the Bridgetown merchants in gratitude for Nelson's saving the West Indies by defeating the French at Trafalgar.

A deep-water harbor was constructed in 1961, and interisland shipping has since been moved from the Careenage to a shallow draft harbor. The government has built Bridgetown Fishing Harbour, which provides piers and moorings for the fishing fleet and a fish market.

The Garrison Savannah, once the training ground for the British West Indies Regiment, is now a park. Horse-racing is held at the track there on most Saturdays in season and on some holidays. Surrounding the Savannah are private buildings that once housed the British forces. One of these is the Barbados Museum.

Many of the older buildings in Bridgetown have been destroyed to make way for modern, utilitarian structures. In recent years, the Barbados National Trust has become interested in preserving Barbados' architectural heritage. As a result, a few of the charming old buildings have been repainted and renovated.

Food

Most meat sold locally, except for chicken, is imported. American beef is available, but quite expensive. Local pork, chicken, and lamb are available, fresh and frozen. Fresh fish is sold every afternoon at fish markets around the island. Kingfish, dorado (referred to locally as

Boats in Bridgetown Harbor, Barbados

Susan Rock. Reproduced by permission.

dolphin), and flying fish are staples; red snapper is available during the summer months. Tuna, shark, and marlin are also available. Shrimp and lobster are available, but at high prices.

Pasteurized milk, cream, yogurt, cottage cheese, and sour cream are available from the local dairy and are safe for consumption. They are also expensive by U.S. standards and tend to spoil rapidly. Ice cream and frozen yogurt are also produced locally, but are very expensive.

The variety and quality of fruits and vegetables available are disappointing. Prices are high by U.S. standards, whether the produce is locally grown or imported. Most fruit sold in the supermarkets is imported. Local lettuce is available, as are cucumbers, green beans, carrots, bell peppers, and cabbage, but with frequent shortages of these items, especially during the tourist season (mid-December to mid-April). Tomatoes, avocados, melon, squash, broccoli, mangoes, and papayas are seasonally available. Quality varies and you may have to search through the local vendors stalls to find good ones. All bananas sold in Barbados are grown locally. Oranges, grapefruit, and pineapple are imported from the other CARI-COM countries. The market at

Cheapside, open mornings, Monday through Saturday, is where many local small farmers sell their produce. Although the variety is limited, the prices are much lower than in supermarkets, and some families find this a better source than the supermarkets.

Clothing

Dress in Barbados is more traditional and conservative than elsewhere in the Caribbean. This translates to more suits and ties and dresses than may be expected from perusal of tourist brochures of cruises and vacations in the Caribbean.

Lightweight, informal clothing is worn by both men and women. The selection available locally is limited and expensive.

Keep in mind that clothing will be laundered more frequently here; it fades and wears out quickly. Elastic loses its stretch; metal pieces rust. When purchasing new items for Barbados try to avoid metal buckles, zippers, snaps, or buttons. Leather belts and shoes tend to mildew.

Clothes not worn frequently that are left in closets on metal hangers may be damaged by rusting of the hangers, sometimes even rusting

through the fabric at the shoulders. Leave most woolen clothing or other items that require dry-cleaning in storage. The humidity increases the amount of mildew forming on clothing kept in closets, resulting in the need to wash or dry-clean clothing that has not been worn.

Men: A suit is worn to the office and most social functions. The locally available "shirt jac" (something like the guya-bera in Latin America or safari suit in Africa) is acceptable on some occasions. When selecting your wardrobe for Barbados, keep in mind the heat, the humidity, the island's limited professional cleaning facilities, and the fact that clothing fades and wears out quickly here.

Women: Short-sleeved cotton dresses or skirts and blouses are suitable for work. Short-sleeved or sleeveless cotton dresses, sundresses, blouses, and skirts or shorts are suitable for home or running errands, although residents do not generally wear shorts downtown—only the tourists do. Slacks are also worn in the evening or when the weather is cooler. Bring 100% cotton clothing and lingerie. Synthetics are fine for the office or evening. Hats (except on the beach), gloves, and hose are rarely worn. Sweaters are rarely needed, except at the office.

Children: School-age children wear uniforms. Each school has their own color uniform. Some pieces (i.e., white shirts, brown or black shoes) may be purchased in the U.S. at a lower cost. Some specific items must be purchased locally. Children will live in swimsuits, shorts, and T-shirts. Children's clothing is more expensive and of poorer quality than that available in the U.S.

Supplies and Services

Tailors and dressmakers are hard to find, and the quality of workmanship varies. Dry-cleaning is much more expensive than in the U.S., and the quality is not always the best. Several good beauty shops operate with prices that are similar to those in the U.S.

Religious Activities

More than 140 different religious denominations and sects are represented in Barbados. The Anglican Church predominates and Anglican churches abound. The island has six Catholic churches. Protestant denominations include Methodist, Seventh-day Adventist, Moravian, Pilgrim Holiness, New Testament Church of God, Church of the Nazarene, Assembly of God, Baptist, and the United Christian Brethren. Christian Science, Mormon, and Jehovah's Witnesses are also here. More Caribbean in character and African in outlook are the Sons of God Apostolic Church or "Spiritual Baptists" and Rastafarians. Barbados has two Greek Orthodox churches, a synagogue, and a mosque. Baha'is and Hindus are also here.

Education

The education system in Barbados is modeled on the British system and is in many ways not comparable to education in the U.S. In addition to the stress of coping with a different education system, the educational environment lacks amenities taken for granted in the U.S. The schools have no science labs or theaters; the libraries and gyms are inadequate or nonexistent; very little computer training is available. The buildings generally appear rundown; the walls are bare. Children coming from an American education system have found the adjustment especially difficult at the secondary level.

Many parents are satisfied with local preschools and primary schools. The local schools are not obliged to accept U.S. children, however, and it is difficult to find places after June 30.

Primary school children usually attend St. Gabriel's, St. Angela's, or St. Winifred's. All schools require uniforms. Some schools have Brownie and Cub Scout troops.

Secondary education begins at age 11 upon completion of the 11 plus examination.

The differences in the educational system are most apparent at the secondary level, where emphasis is on memorization of material in preparation for taking public examinations. The curriculum is inflexible, and course offerings are limited by the form (grade) in which a child is placed. For example, if your child is ready to begin the second year of Spanish and the form is in the third year of French, the child will have to do third-year French or no foreign language at all. Creativity is not rewarded and often discouraged. No credit is given for having completed course work; scores on the year end public examination determine success or failure. Extracurricular activities such as sports, drama, music, journalism, or other special interests are not normally available. Pressure is placed on children to compete with their classmates to be "first in form."

Special Educational Opportunities

Children can take lessons in ballet, modern dance, swimming, tennis, riding, piano, Spanish, French, chess, table tennis, drawing, karate, judo, gymnastics, and recorder. The Barbados Yachting Association offers sailing lessons in the summer for children 8 and older.

The Barbados Community College also offers courses to adults in foreign languages, computers, and other continuing education. The Alliance Francais offers French-language courses at various levels.

The University of the West Indies will allow a college-age dependent to enroll as an "occasional student" and audit courses on a noncredit basis. Expenses are equal to a non-resident student at a U.S. university. Computer courses are held at a local institute.

The Office of Overseas Schools advises against bringing handicapped children to Barbados.

Sports

Cricket is the national sport, and most Barbadians take an avid interest in it. The quality of cricket played locally is high, especially the test matches, and the West Indian team is one of the world's top test match teams.

Soccer, rugby, golf, field hockey, running, cycling, and tennis are popular, and basketball is becoming increasingly so. Individuals have access to three courses: the 18-hole Sandy Lane Hotel Course, the 18-hole course at the new Royal Westmoreland Golf Course, and the 9-hole course at Rockley. Tennis courts are available, although few are public, and most require club membership. At least five squash clubs are available and several gyms and fitness centers offer exercise classes as well as Nautilus equipment. Bodybuilding is a very popular sport in Barbados. The country has produced a number of world-class bodybuilders, including a former Mr. Universe and a former Mr. World.

All beaches in Barbados are public. A certain amount of harassment by panhandlers and itinerant vendors is a problem with some selling drugs. Women who are alone can expect to be approached by several persistent young men who make a living that way. Swimming, water skiing, sailing, windsurfing, scuba diving, snorkeling, and fishing are popular sports. The water is warm year round. Some of the hotels offer use of their pools gratis or for a small fee. Most swimming areas do not have lifeguards, and swimming on the east coast can be very dangerous.

Sailing conditions are good, but possible local destinations are very limited. No marinas or docks are available to pleasure boat owners in Barbados. Those that exist are only for commercial fishing boats. Boats may be moored along the coast; most are moored in Carlisle Bay adjacent to the Yacht Club. No charge is made for your mooring. The Yacht Club has modest fees to join for both boating and tennis and sponsors serious sailing races for racing, cruising, and dinghy classes.

Thoroughbreds on the island are limited in number, although the Barbados Turf Club holds periodic races during the year. Horses are occasionally brought in from Trinidad or Martinique. Polo matches are held during winter.

Barbados offers opportunities for water polo, horseback riding, rifle shooting, Ping-pong, and netball. For runners, two or three 10K races and a marathon are held each year. The Barbados Hash House Harriers meet every Saturday afternoon at various spots on the island for a run or walk through the countryside. The National Trust sponsors walks each Sunday morning and afternoon that offer great views as well as good exercise.

Touring and Outdoor Activities

All touring on Barbados is done by car. Distances are not great, but travel can sometimes be time consuming due to narrow, congested, and unevenly maintained roads.

Barbados has several old plantation "Great Houses" open to the public. Sam Lord's Castle, Villa Nova, and St. Nicholas Abbey are the best known, but Sunbury and Francia are also interesting to visit. Farley Hill, a great house now in ruins, is a National Park with beautiful views of both coasts, a picnic area, and playground. The Flower Forest, Welchman Hall Gully, and Andromeda Gardens are botanical parks. The Wildlife Reserve has monkeys, caiman, peacocks, tortoises, and other small animals and is a favorite with children. Harrison's Cave is a large limestone cavern also very popular with the younger set.

St. Vincent and the Grenadines offer some of the most beautiful sailing waters in the world. It is a short flight from Barbados to Grenada, Union Island, or St. Vincent. Chartering a sailboat and sailing among the Grenadine islands is a memorable experience for those who are able to take advantage of the opportunity to explore the unique character and attractions of each of the islands.

Entertainment

Entertainment possibilities in Barbados, beyond the tourist-oriented shows, are limited and hard to find. Those who seek them out, begin by asking long-term residents and Barbadians. The island's drive-in movie theater is a great treat on balmy evenings with a cooler of drinks and a vat of popcorn.

Most Americans in Barbados have VCRs (VHS predominant) and get current copies of releases from the many video clubs located around the island. Many of these copies are of indifferent quality and do not appear authorized. Amateur and semiprofessional theater, music, and dance groups perform occasionally. In addition, most larger hotels provide calypso and steelband music of varying quality year round. The island also has some nightclubs and discos.

Barbados has many restaurants that, in general, offer standard tourist fare at tourist prices. A few noteworthy restaurants offer excellent cuisine at prices comparable to those of similar quality in Washington, D.C. Some of the hotels offer buffet specials, which can be more reasonably priced.

The Barbados National Trust holds an open house each week from January to April at some of the finer homes on the island. The plantation houses are varied, with luxury winter homes. These tours are popular with residents and tourists alike. The Barbados Museum supports an amateur archeological group that has been digging with great success at a pre-Columbian Indian site.

Amateur photographers and artists will find both scenic beauty and human interest shots. Art materials are limited. Film can be purchased locally, but is expensive.

Several active bridge clubs hold regular sessions. The Barbados Bridge League offers duplicate bridge four times a week. A chess club and a ham radio club accept members.

Social Activities

The American Women's Club is a large local organization that meets monthly. Membership is open to both Americans and others. The club sponsors several activities, including a book group, a cooking group, bridge, a literary group, and an occasional charity ball.

Opportunities exist to meet Barbadians officially and in community activities. These contacts can later broaden into more personal relationships, but may require more effort to overcome the reserved distance characteristic of Barbadian culture. Nationals of other countries, particularly the U.K. and Canada, are easy to meet and share many interests with Americans. The Multi-National Women's Committee sponsors an annual fundraising fair to benefit a variety of children's charities each February, thereby offering opportunities to get involved in Barbadian society and meet people from many countries.

International organizations represented in Barbados include, among others, UNDP, PAHO, EEC, IDB, UNICEF, and the OAS.

COUNTRY PROFILE

Geography and Climate

Barbados lies about 270 miles northeast of Venezuela and 1,612 miles southeast of Miami. It is 21 miles long and 14 miles wide with an area of 166 square miles. Constant westward tradewinds temper the tropical climate much of the year.

Situated 100 miles to the east of the Caribbean Windward Island chain, Barbados is distinct from those islands in many ways. It is a coral island, rather than volcanic, and relatively flat.

Mt. Hillaby, the highest point, is only 1,104 feet above sea level. Bridgetown, the capital, is located on the southwest corner of the island. The west and south coasts leading out of the city are densely populated, with hotels, residential, and commercial areas intermingling. The rugged, windswept east coast boasts the scenic Scotland district. The currents on the east coast are very dangerous, and swimming is forbidden in many areas. The interior of the island rises gently and sugarcane fields are interspersed with villages, farms, and the occasional plantation Great House.

Actual temperatures in Barbados vary little during the year, averaging about 77°F (25°C) and rarely rising above 89°F (32°C) or falling below 65°F (18°C). The intensity of the sun this near the Equator makes it seem much hotter, but the effects of the changes in humidity are even stronger. During the summer months, which make up the rainy season and coincide with the hurricane season, high humidity levels greatly intensify the discomfort of the higher temperatures. During the winter, which is the "dry" tourist season, it can feel almost cold in the evenings. Even during those months a significant amount of rain falls.

Population

Approximately 260,000 people live in Barbados, with about 123,000 of them residing in the capital of Bridgetown.

Arawak Indians are thought to have lived here once, only to be destroyed by the fierce Carib Indians who then abandoned the island. Barbados was uninhabited when British sailors landed at what is now Holetown, in 1625. As the sugar industry developed into the main commercial interest, Barbados was divided into huge estates. Slaves were brought from Africa to work the plantations until slavery was abolished throughout the British Empire in 1834.

Barbados is much more densely populated than its Eastern Caribbean island neighbors. The people of Barbados came from Africa, England, South America, North America, other Caribbean nations, and, more recently, from Asian countries. Over 90% of the population is directly descended from African slaves, and they dominate the island's politics. Over the last 15 years, a growing interest in exploring their African cultural heritage has occurred. Approximately 20% of the population are of mixed black and white blood, with shades of skin color playing an important role in defining how Barbadians view one another. This can be seen in the variety of terms used to describe the variations between black and white—brown skin, light skin, fair skin, high brown, red, and mulatto among them. About 7% of the population is white, and still control much of the economic activity on the island. Since the mid-1980s, a willingness on the part of educated blacks and others to discuss racial problems and concepts has often led to heated debates. Racially motivated violence, however, is rare to nonexistent.

Barbadians consider themselves as friendly, relaxed, and informal, and many visitors to Barbados who stay for only a few days or weeks leave with that same impression. Outsiders who live here, however, perceive Barbadians as more reserved, formal, and less spontaneous and outgoing than any other people in the West Indies. They are not nearly so quick as Americans to deal with others on a first- name basis, resorting more often to titles and formal forms of address. A proud people, Barbadians may take offense easily to any perceived slight, and sometimes seem to be looking for signs of disrespect or condescension.

English is the official language, but dialects vary from country to country in the region, as well as from parish to parish on each island. Most Americans need some time to adapt to the heavy Barbadian dialect, which can become absolutely impenetrable at will. A French patois is spoken widely in St. Lucia, Dominica, and in certain areas of St. Vincent as these islands were all under French control at one time or another.

Public Institutions

From the arrival of the first British settlers in 1627 until independence in 1966, Barbados was under British control. Its House of Assembly, which began meeting in 1639, is the third oldest legislative body in the Western Hemisphere, preceded only by Bermuda's legislature and the Virginia House of Burgesses.

Local politics at that time were dominated by a small group of British plantation owners and tradesmen. It was not until the 1930s that a movement for political rights was begun by educated descendants of the emancipated slaves. One of the leaders, Sir Grantley Adams, founded the Barbados Labor Party in 1938.

Progress toward a more democratic government was made in 1950 when universal suffrage was introduced. This was followed by steps toward increased self-government until full internal autonomy was achieved in 1961.

From 1958 to 1962, Barbados was one of 10 members in the West Indies Federation. When the Federation was terminated, Barbados reverted to its former status as a self-governing colony. Following several attempts to form another federation composed of Barbados and the Leeward and Windward Islands, Barbados negotiated its own independence at a constitutional conference with the U.K. in June 1966. After years of peaceful, democratic, and evolutionary progress toward self-rule, Barbados attained independence on November 30, 1966.

Barbados is now an independent and sovereign state within the Commonwealth. Under the current constitution, Barbados is a Westminster-style parliamentary democracy. The Queen of England,

Barbados titular head of state, appoints a Governor General as her representative in Barbados. The bicameral Parliament, consisting of an appointed Senate and an elected House of Assembly, is supreme. The Prime Minister (normally the leader of the House majority party) and other Cabinet members are appointed from among the House members. The Senate consists of 21 members; the House, 28. The Governor General appoints all Senators: 7 without advice to represent religious, economic, social, or other interests; 12 on the advice of the Prime Minister; and 2 on the advice of the opposition leader. The country's two major political parties, the Barbados Labor Party and the Democratic Labor Party (which arose out of the labor movement in the West Indies) have precipitated much of the country's political change.

The judiciary comprises the Supreme Court of Barbados and numerous courts of summary jurisdiction. The Supreme Court includes a Court of Appeal and a High Court.

The island is divided into 11 parishes and the city of Bridgetown. No local government exists, and all these divisions are administered by the central government.

The territories are linked in various ways, but little popular support exists to merge the islands into a common Caribbean or other regional political grouping. There have been unsuccessful attempts to form a single political union.

Arts, Science, and Education

The educational system, traditionally geared to prepare administrative and clerical personnel as well as some university entrants, has changed recently. Certain branches of technical training, especially manufacturing, engineering service, hotel management, and management training, have progressed greatly.

The government operates primary and secondary schools, and through grants, aids some private schools, all of which offer regular academic subjects—English, math, languages, science, history, and geography. The educational system is patterned after the British model. The Cave Hill Campus of the University of the West Indies (UWI) has faculties of law, arts, and general studies, natural and social sciences, and a school of education. Other UWI facilities are located at the Jamaica and Trinidad campuses. The Barbados Community College offers junior college-level courses in commercial, engineering subjects and liberal arts and recently introduced the associate degree program modeled after the U.S. system. The Samuel Jackman Prescod Polytechnic Institute concentrates on vocational and technical education. Erdiston College conducts a 2-year teacher training course. Codrington College, an Anglican seminary dating back to the early 1700s, now is also affiliated with UWI.

Each year the National Cultural Foundation (NCF) sponsors a guitar festival in February, and the National Independence Festival of Creative Arts (NIFCA) in November. The Caribbean and Latin American Music Society (CLAMS) sponsors a series of classical chamber music concerts in January, and the Barbados Dance Theater sponsors a "season of dance" in March. All of these activities involve a limited number of amateur performances (usually fewer than six) over the space of a few days. The NCF also sponsors the island's largest festival, Crop-Over, from June to August. This is similar to the Carnival celebrated on other islands in the Caribbean. It includes calypso competitions and other festivities, culminating in "Kadooment," a street parade of costumes and general merrymaking.

Throughout the year, performances by calypso artists, amateur theatrical productions, the Barbados Symphonia (a local orchestral ensemble), and a variety of talent competitions and concerts by local groups and church choirs are offered. Several local art shows are also here.

Commerce and Industry

Historically, sugar production was Barbados' largest industry since its introduction in the 17th century. But in recent years, tourism and light industry have surpassed sugar both as foreign exchange earners and employers.

Tourism is a major industry in Barbados and continues to increase each year, with an 8% growth in 2000. The majority of visitors are from the United Kingdom, but U.S. visitors have increased in the past few years. To encourage tourism and industrial development, the government is expanding the recently completed major highway program that links the airport, deep-water harbor, several industrial parks.

Sugar production continues and even rose by about 10% in 2000 to its highest yield since 1997. Most of the sugar produced is sold to the European Community at a guaranteed price. Non-sugar agricultural production, vegetables and cotton, grew by about 6%%. However, agriculture only accounts for about 4% of the GDP, and imports are still needed to provide Barbados with much of what it needs to survive, not only in foods, but in energy and other consumer products. In 2000, Barbados import expense was about $800 million. Major trading partners are the U.K. and the U.S.

Barbados is a member of CARICOM, a regional trade alliance.

Unions play an important role in the nation's political and economic development. Some 40% of the work force is unionized, and the labor movement, particularly the Barbados Workers Union, has traditionally been a significant factor in the political process in Barbados.

Transportation

Local

Barbados has an extensive road network—900 miles of paved roads—but the roads are narrow, poorly developed, and many are indifferently maintained. Blind corners and dangerous intersections are encountered throughout the island. The tropical climate includes frequent brief rains that leave the roadway extremely slippery. The lack of sidewalks means pedestrians are often encountered in the road. Traffic tends to be congested in Bridgetown during daytime hours.

Inexpensive public bus service covers nearly all the island. Buses are not air-conditioned and are overcrowded during rush hours and on Saturdays when people go to market. Independently owned minivans operate at low cost and breakneck speed, with a minimum of regulation and according to no published schedule. Taxis are available in population centers and at most hotels, but fares are too high for regular use.

Regional

Daily flights are available to Miami, New York, and through San Juan to other cities. Travel from the U.S. to the other islands of the Caribbean can be expensive, particularly in the high season—mid-December to mid-April. Travel within the Caribbean islands costs the same year round. Several local travel agents offer moderately priced packages over holiday weekends and during the low season to the other Caribbean islands, Puerto Rico, and Caracas. Martinique, St. Vincent and the Grenadines, St. Lucia, and Grenada are close.

Communications

Telephone and Telegraph

The telephone system in Barbados is good, with direct-dial service via satellite to the U.S. Repairs can take a very long time. The area code for Barbados and most of the Caribbean is 809. Direct calls are expensive, but cheaper when charged to a U.S. telephone credit card (currently, AT&T and cable and wireless have an agreement to permit use of AT&T cards in Barbados). Telegraph service is also good.

Radio and TV

Two local AM radio stations, four local FM radio stations, and one wired service are available only to subscribers. The AM stations favor West Indian sounds, with lively discussions on local issues and extensive local news coverage. The FM stations present American pop, easy listening, and religious formats. One of the FM stations also presents a classical program on the weekends. The wire service, Redifusion, carries classical music, drama, and literature. The BBC's *World News* is broadcast on both AM and FM daily. In addition to the Barbados stations, several regionally based radio stations can be picked up on the AM band, including Radio Francaise Outre-Mer and stations in Grenada, St. Vincent, Puerto Rico, Trinidad, and Venezuela. VOA is carried 7 hours a day over Radio Antilles (930 AM).

The Caribbean Broadcasting Corporation's (CBC) TV station carries 12 hours of programming daily, including about 4 hours of CNN *Headline News* weekday mornings. Evening programming is a mix of older American and British serials, locally produced news, and information and entertainment shows. *Sesame Street* is telecast weekday afternoons. CBC broadcasts in NTSC and U.S. sets operate without adjustment. They have recently made available four subscriber channels, ESPN, CNN, TNT South, and Lifetime, at a fee comparable to U.S. cable services that have many more channels.

Newspapers, Magazines, and Technical Journals

Barbados has two daily newspapers, *The Nation* and *The Advocate*, both published in Bridgetown and available throughout the island. These concentrate on local and regional news. Their coverage of international news not directly affecting Barbados is limited. Home delivery is available. A local distributor offers same day or 1-day-later provision of The *Wall Street Journal,* *USA Today*, The *Herald Tribune* and The *New York Times*.

Popular U.S. magazines may be purchased at the three or four local bookstores and newsstands, but they are expensive. International editions of U.S. news magazines are available locally.

Barbados has a public library system, and the small central library has a fair collection. Several local bookstores carry a very limited selection of paperbacks and hardbound books at very high prices.

Health and Medicine

Medical Facilities

Barbados has good medical facilities, and most medical specialties have practitioners here. Some areas of medical practice are lacking, however, and certain ailments and injuries cannot be adequately treated locally.

Medical facilities on the other islands are barely adequate, and most lack the facilities to treat major medical problems. Each island has at least one hospital, but complicated cases are usually transferred to Barbados.

Two main hospitals, the government-supported Queen Elizabeth Hospital and the private Bayview Hospital are available, along with local polyclinics. The selection of a personal or family physician is the responsibility of the individual and should be done as soon as possible. The physician with whom you register will determine at which hospital you will receive treatment. In case of emergency, your private physician will meet you at the hospital, which will greatly speed the care given.

Individual or family counseling is available through recommended community resources.

Therapy services, including physical, occupational, and speech, are available both privately and through government services. Most therapists are trained abroad in the U.S., U.K., or Canada and provide good-quality care by U.S. standards.

General dental and orthodontic services are available. When possible, crowns, root canals, dental surgery, etc., should be done in the U.S.

Not all local pharmacists will fill U.S. physician prescriptions. In general, pharmacists will supply a medicine to someone who has run out of a supply while visiting, if the vial and some form of identification are produced. Drug agencies in Barbados order from all over the world, including the U.S., with many of the brand names supplied in the U.S. available here, sometimes at a lower price.

Community Health

The Government of Barbados is continuing its efforts to improve sanitation. Most residences in Bridgetown are connected to sewers. Free garbage pickup is provided once or twice a week in many areas. Sanitation inspectors periodically check homes, hotels, restaurants, and factories to control flies and mosquitoes.

Barbados has pure water, filtered through 600 feet of coral. Tap-water is potable. The water is not fluoridated. The water's lime and calcium content are high. Do not assume the tap-water is potable on the other islands. Drink bottled water, soft drinks, etc.

Preventive Measures

The intense sunlight is a serious hazard. Use sunscreen daily before leaving home. Children particularly need to be protected from overexposure. Sunscreen is available locally. The climate can cause heat exhaustion, sunburn, and fatigue. Drink plenty of fluids to offset increased perspiration.

Local milk and milk products are safe. Fruits and vegetables need only washing.

Skin problems such as acne and fungal infections may be aggravated by the humid climate, and extra measures of hygiene are necessary. Photosensitivity reactions from taking certain medications may occur. Pollen from cane, cashews, and other flora may cause allergic reactions. Some people suffer gastrointestinal disturbances after arrival, but the effects are generally slight and mainly due to the change in eating habits, climate, and water. External ear infections are common. Hookworms, roundworms, and pinworms are common, but normally do not present a problem to resident Americans.

Dengue fever occurs periodically. No protection is available other than the avoidance of mosquito bites. Use coils and repellants. A few cases of bilharzia (schistosomiasis) continue to be reported annually on St. Lucia as well as the French islands of Martinique and Guadeloupe. To avoid the disease, do not expose any part of the body to any freshwater streams, lakes, or pools. Tuberculosis is a recurrent problem in Dominica, and, to a lesser extent, in St. Lucia. Skin tests for tuberculosis are available in the Medical Unit.

LOCAL HOLIDAYS

The exact dates of some religious holidays are based on the lunar calendar and change each year.

Jan. 1	New Year's Day
Jan. 21	Errol Barrow's Birthday
Mar/Apr.	Good Friday*
Mar/Apr.	Easter Sunday*
May 1	Labor Day
May/June	Whitsunday*
May/June	Whitmonday*
Aug. 1	Emancipation Day
August (first Monday)	Kadooment Day
October (first Monday)	United Nations Day
Nov. 30	Independence Day
Dec. 25	Christmas Day
Dec. 26	Boxing Day

*variable

NOTES FOR TRAVELERS

Passage, Customs & Duties

You can reach Bridgetown from Washington, D.C., by air via New York or Miami. American Airlines has daily flights from JFK and Miami with a stopover in San Juan. No regularly scheduled U.S. passenger liner service is available between the U.S. and Barbados.

U.S. citizens may enter Barbados for up to 28 days without a valid passport, but must carry original documentation proving U.S. citizenship (i.e. valid or expired U.S. passport, certified U.S. birth certificate, Consular Report of Birth Abroad, Certificate of Naturalization, or Certificate of Citizenship), state-issued photo identification and an onward or return ticket. U.S. citizen visitors who enter Barbados without these items, even if admitted by immigration authorities, may encounter difficulties in boarding flights for return to the United States. U.S. citizens entering with documents other than U.S. passports should take special care to secure those documents while travelling. It can be time-consuming and difficult to acquire new proof of citizenship to facilitate return travel. The Barbados government requires payment of a service tax upon departure from the island.

Barbados customs authorities may enforce strict regulations concerning temporary importation into or export from Barbados of items such as firearms and agricultural products. It is advisable to contact the Embassy of Barbados in Washington, D.C. or one of Barbados's consulates in the United States for specific information regarding customs requirements.

Americans living in or visiting Barbados are encouraged to register at the Consular Section of the U.S. Embassy in Barbados and obtain updated information on travel and security within Barbados. The U.S. Embassy is located in Bridgetown at the Canadian Imperial Bank of Commerce (CIBC) Building on Broad Street, telephone (246) 436-4950, web site http://usembassy.state.gov/posts/bb1/wwwhemb1.html. The Consular Section is located in the American Life Insurance Company (ALICO) Building, Cheapside, telephone (246) 431-0225 or fax (246) 431-0179, web site http://www.usembassy.state.gov/posts/bb1/wwwhcons.html. Hours of operation are 8:00 a.m. to 4:00 p.m. Monday through Friday, except local and U.S. holidays.

Pets

Barbados is rabies free, and the authorities are determined to keep it so. Most families purchase animals locally. Some purebred animals are sold locally, but they are expensive. Dogs and cats can generally be imported into Barbados only from the U.K. If you want to import a dog or cat, strict quarantine regulations require that the animal be quarantined for 6 months in the U.K. You must then apply for an import permit from the Barbados Ministry of Agriculture at least 30 days in advance of pet's arrival date. Importation from another rabies-free country is not always permitted, but the cost savings make it worth taking the steps to apply for an import permit from the Ministry of Agriculture well in advance of your arrival. The U.K. Ministry of Agriculture will supply a list of recommended kennels for quarantine upon request. If you want to import other animals, you must obtain an import permit from the Barbados Ministry of Agriculture before shipping the animal. Excellent veterinarians are located on the island who offer boarding facilities as well.

Currency, Banking, and Weights and Measures

The monetary unit is the Barbados dollar (BDS$), comprising 100¢. US$1= BDS$2 (fixed rate). Most hotels and restaurants on the island accept U.S. currency. The East Caribbean dollar (EC$), comprising 100¢, is also accepted. US$1=EC$2.70. Rates seldom fluctuate.

The Central Bank of Barbados issues Barbados currency in denominations of $100, $50, $20, $10, $5, and $2 in notes. Coins are issued in $1, 25¢, 10¢, 5¢, and 1¢ denominations. The Caribbean Currency Authority issues East Caribbean notes in denominations of $100, $20, $10, $5, and $1. Coins are minted in 50¢, 25¢, 10¢, 5¢, 2¢, and 1¢ denominations.

Barbados and the other islands of the Eastern Caribbean use the metric system.

Disaster Preparedness

All Caribbean countries can be affected by hurricanes. The hurricane season normally runs from June to the end of November, but there have been hurricanes in December in recent years. General information about natural disaster preparedness is available via the Internet from the U.S. Federal Emergency Management Agency (FEMA) at http://www.fema.gov.

RECOMMENDED READING

The following titles are provided as a general indication of the material published on this country. The Department of State does not endorse unofficial publications.

Several books are available in Barbados regarding West Indian life, history, and culture. Most are not widely available outside of the Caribbean. Rather than include a long list of these books here, members of the Embassy staff recommend newcomers read the following books, which are available in the U.S. as an introduction to Barbados.

A-Z of Barbadian Heritage. Kingston, Jamaica: Heinemann Publications, 1990.

Alleyne, W. *The Barbados Garrison and Its Buildings*. Hampshire, England: Macmillan Caribbean, 1990.

Beckles, Hilary. *A History of Barbados*. Cambridge: Cambridge University Press, 1990.

Broberg, Merle. *Barbados*. New York: Chelsea House, 1988.

Hoefer, Hans. *Barbados: Insight Guides*. APA Publications: Singapore, 1985.

Hoyos, F.A. *Barbados: A History from Amerindians to Independence*. Macmillan Publishers.

Michener, James. *Caribbean*. New York: Random House, 1989.

Pariser, H. *Adventure Guide to Barbados*. New York: Hunter Publishing, 1990.

Potter, Robert B., and Graham M.S. Dann, comps. *Barbados*. Santa Barbara, CA: ABC-Clio, 1987.

Wouk, Herman. *Don't Stop the Carnival*. Garden City, NY: Doubleday, 1965.

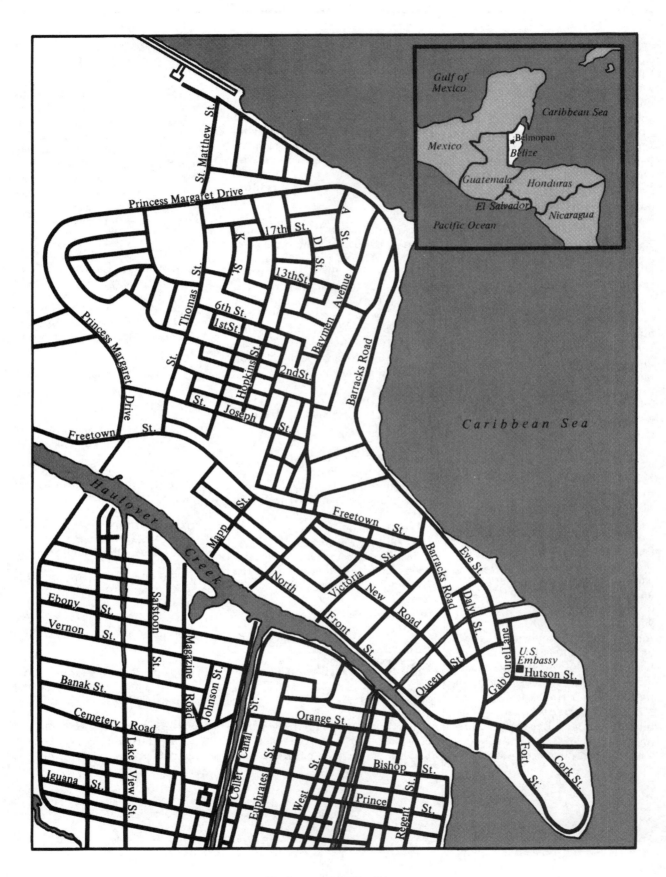

Belmopan, Belize

BELIZE

Major Cities:
Belmopan, Belize City

Other Cities:
Dangriga, Orange Walk, Punta Gorda, San Ignacio

EDITOR'S NOTE

This chapter was adapted from the Department of State Post Report 1999 for Belize. Supplemental material has been added to increase coverage of minor cities, facts have been updated, and some material has been condensed. Readers are encouraged to visit the Department of State's web site at http://travel.state.gov/ for the most recent information available on travel to this country.

INTRODUCTION

The tiny country once known as British Honduras, lies on the Caribbean coast of Central America, tucked in between Mexico on the north and Guatemala on the west and south. Its first European settlement was made in 1638 by shipwrecked British sailors but, subjected to repeated attacks by neighboring Spanish colonies, it endured a troubled 150-year period until the British established control just before the turn of the 19th century. Full status as a crown colony was formally declared in 1862. Belize has been independent since 1981. Although Britain had sovereignty, Guatemala had long disputed Britain's claim to the territory, maintaining its own territorial claim allegedly inherited from Spain. Guatemala finally recognized Belize's independence in 1991. The Guatemalan claim, however, remains unresolved.

Belize is a land of natural wonders and broad ecological diversity. It is noted for its virgin rain forests and pine savannas; the richness of its marine and wildlife; and, especially, for its 176-mile-long barrier reef, second only in size to the Great Barrier Reef of Australia. Estuaries, caves, and cascading waterfalls add further wealth to the tropical environment.

Archaeological sites at Xunantunich and Altun Ha reveal the extensive Mayan civilization that flourished here approximately 1,500 years ago. With almost every new excavation, spectacular discoveries are made, and the country becomes ever more notable for its pre-Columbian culture.

MAJOR CITIES

Belmopan

Belmopan is situated some 50 miles inland in the foothills of the Maya Mountains, at the country's geographic center. When the capital was moved here in 1970 from Belize City, the principal municipality, the area first had to be cleared of its dense jungle growth. The city was built after the devastation wrought in 1961 upon Belize City by Hurricane Hattie. Although Belmopan is also vulnerable to hurricane winds, its mean altitude of 182.5 feet above sea level is greater than Belize City's, and this protects it against the waters which have inundated the latter in previous times, causing widespread damage and loss of life.

Belmopan is easily accessible by one of the country's two good highways, although heavy rains can cause severe flooding on the sections of road close to Belize City.

The capital's main point of interest is the National Assembly building, patterned on an ancient Mayan motif, and flanked by government ministries around a spacious esplanade.

The official residences of the governor-general and the prime minister also are here, as are some foreign consulates. The city is administered by an agency of the national government rather than by an elected municipal authority.

Belmopan lacks the amenities found in Belize City. It has a handful of shops and stores, a market, one movie theater, a hotel, two commercial banks, one service station, and a small hospital for minor health problems. On weekends, many people travel the short distance to Belize City for shopping and entertainment.

Current plans for Belmopan's future include expansion to accommodate several times its present population of about 6,000 with the addition of residential, governmental, commercial, industrial, educational, and medical facilities. A 20-room hotel has convention facilities. Also, the broad, fertile valley of the Belize River, stretching several miles to the north and west of Belmopan, provides an excellent area for agricultural development.

Belize City

Belize City is a mixture of modern concrete buildings, Victorian-style wood houses, and old buildings dating back to the 1800s. A branch of the Belize River, known as Haulover Creek, divides the city into "northside" and "southside". Three bridges join the two halves. Downtown (alternately described as dumpy and charming) and the poorer sections of town are southside. The Fort George area and the Southern Foreshore, facing each other at the mouth of the Creek, are the older residential areas. Kings Park, Caribbean Shores and Bell Vista, where most Mission personnel live, are newer developments on the nourished, upriver toward the airport.

The city is built on reclaimed mangrove swamp and expansion can occur only by further reclamation, an expensive process. The two roads leaving the city pass through several miles of wetland before reaching slightly higher ground.

Seaward, the view is interesting. Four or five scenic cayes with good fishing, swimming, and skin-diving, lie within a 30-minute boat ride. The island villages of San Pedro and Caye Caulker are the favorite jumping-off spots where skin-diving and scuba equipment can be rented.

Close in to Belize City, the sea is shallow, muddy, and polluted. Freighters dock at a cargo pier outside the city, while cruise ships often anchor offshore in winter. Though locals can often be seen swimming along the city shoreline, there are no beaches. You should swim only at the cayes, along the reef, up rivers or at designated beach areas. The nearest white-sand beaches are 30 minutes east by boat or a one-hour drive south.

Food

Most packaged, canned and bottled items needed in the average household can be bought in Belize. Four supermarkets and several small groceries carry a good supply of imported U.S. and British food and housekeeping supplies. Most baby foods, formulas and disposable diapers are available. Prices on all items are high. The supermarkets have imported fresh butter, margarine, various cheeses and a modest assortment of frozen products, including fruits, vegetables, bakery goods, and processed meats. Frozen whole chickens, chicken parts, beef and pork from local producers are stocked as well. Fresh meat is sold in various meat markets and, with the exception of lamb which is increasing in popularity, is in generous supply. Beef is not as tender here as in the U.S., but is lean and of quite acceptable quality. Local chickens are good, as are local dairy products in general.

Fish, conch, shrimp and lobster are caught and frozen locally. The supply of fresh fish varies according to the weather and prices are cheaper than in the U.S.

Mexico offers less expensive shopping: Chetumal is just over the border (two-hour drive), while Cancun and Merida (six-hour drives) boast fully stocked Wal-Marts and Sam's Clubs.

Clothing

The most important thing to keep in mind when buying clothing to wear in Belize is that the fabric must be suitable for the hot and humid climate. No garment will be wearable if the fabric is heavy or retains heat. Synthetics and double knits are too hot. Pure cotton is ideal, but always think lightweight and permanent press. There is one dry-cleaner in Belize City. Another consideration is the type of recreational activity most popular here. Casual clothing is acceptable for swimming, fishing, boating and travel to out-of-the-way archeological ruins. It also is a good idea to have a hat for protection from the sun. Ladies straw hats and men's summer caps can be purchased in Belize, but beachwear is best brought to post. Remember that clothes wear out quickly, as there is no change of season. Therefore, bring more, rather than less; little is available on the local market. Lightweight hiking boots and outdoor clothing or jungle fatigues are a good idea for hiking in the rainforest.

Men: Dress is cool and casual. Guayaberas (embroidered Mexican shirts with evenly hemmed tails worn outside the pants) are appropriate on most occasions and are worn in the office and for evening social events. Any open-necked short- or long-sleeved shirts are acceptable for business and most informal social occasions. Lightweight suits are worn for a few special events, especially official functions. Black-tie is almost never worn, but when it is, both black and white jackets are acceptable. Poor drainage in the city, which is one foot below sea level, floods streets and hides ditches during the rainy season, so getting wet is a part of life here. Sweaters are needed for winter evenings.

Women: Dressing is casual, although less so in the office where air-conditioning is efficient. Dresses or slacks are worn. Lightweight slacks and tops, and sleeveless dresses are worn for shopping and marketing. Sun-dresses are also popular for everyday wear. Stockings are never worn except occasionally in the evening and in the office. Hats are rarely required. Short cocktail dresses and patio-type clothes are worn at evening parties. Formal parties are rare, so the need for long evening dresses is minimal. In December and January, dresses with sleeves are comfortable. A light stole is useful to have in the evening during the cooler months. Bring a sweater and heavier clothing for traveling to mountain areas.

Completely closed leather or synthetic shoes are a bit warm for Belize. So canvas espadrilles and sandals are common daytime wear. Women's casual shoes are sold here, but styles and fit are limited. Narrow sizes are not available.

Children: Infants and children wear simple clothing. Cotton T-shirts, light pants, shorts, and simple dresses are worn. Sneakers are the usual footwear, so bring a supply. Children tend to dress up for birthday parties and religious services.

All schools mandate that uniforms be worn. Children's shoes are available, but don't count on the local selection. Some British and American toys and baby supplies are sold, but prices are high.

Supplies and Services

Most all necessities can be bought at one of the several department, hardware, and drugstores, but shortages occur. Hobby, recreational, beauty and medicinal/medical items can be another story. If they are available, they're expensive. Make sure you bring along books, art supplies, CDs and special needs like cosmetics, medicines and toiletries. A good rule of thumb is: If it's not in every store in the U.S., don't assume it's to be found anywhere in Belize (though sometimes Belize can surprise you).

There is one dry cleaner in Belize City and three or four commercial laundromats. Electricians, plumbers, carpenters, auto mechanics, etc., are easy to find, but service is generally slow, and replacement parts not always on hand. Barbers and hairdressers are competent, as are upholsterers, drapery makers, dressmakers and jewelers.

Domestic Help

Most American households have a maid, though experienced and trained servants are difficult to find. Domestic workers typically do not live in, and work 6-8 hours per day. The legal minimum wage for domestics is Bz$2.25 per hour. Overtime is paid for extra hours. Employers pay Social Security tax for all domestics who work over 23 hours per week. Maids do routine cleaning, laundry and child care, and may speak Spanish and/or English. Night baby-sitting and help at parties requires overtime pay. Hours and fringe benefits should be agreed upon at time of employment.

Religious Activities

Belize is roughly 60% Roman Catholic and 38% Protestant. Although church attendance is relatively low, the country is very religious; prayers accompany virtually every public ceremony. Denominations represented in Belize include Anglican, Assemblies of God, Baptist, Hindu, Jehovah's Witnesses, Mennonite, Methodist, Mormon, Muslim, Nazarene, Pentecostal, Presbyterian, Roman Catholic and Seventh Day Adventist. All conduct services in English.

Education

Local schools provide good education through the junior high school level. The basics are taught, but creative art, music and laboratory science are lacking. The school year usually begins the first Monday after September 10, and ends in mid-June. There is a three-week vacation at Christmas and a two-week vacation at Easter.

Some schools have U.S. priests and nuns on their staff, but most of the schools are staffed by Belizeans. The educational system is basically British (although the textbooks in some schools come from the U.S.), and some of the curriculum and the approach to learning differs from that in the U.S. Most students re-entering schools in the U.S. have no difficulty at their expected grade level.

To enter first grade, a child must be five years old by January 1, following the beginning of the school year. Infant I (kindergarten) enrolls children from ages three to five, and there are morning and afternoon sessions.

Most foreign grade-school children attend the British Toucan School, located at the Belize Defense Forces Airport Camp. Some others attend the new and privately operated Belize Elementary School.

At the high school level, girls can attend St. Catherine Academy or Palloti, both of which are run by Roman Catholic nuns. St. John's College, run by Jesuit priests, is the premier school for boys. The Anglican Cathedral College is a coeducational high school. Belmopan Christian Academy in Belmopan offers an American curriculum and several American teachers. These schools are regarded as the best in Belize.

Special Educational Opportunities

St. John's Sixth Form is a coeducational junior college with U.S. accreditation. St John's College Extension and the Extramural Department of the University of the West Indies offer a few evening courses for adults. Several people have learned Spanish through these courses as well as the Mexican Cultural Institute. These night classes are attended by working people who are studying to pass the high school equivalency test or who are upgrading then office skills by taking commercial courses

The University College of Belize provides higher education. Degrees are offered in Business Administration, Math English, Chemistry, Biology, Environmental Health, Education and Social Work Elective courses are in English, Literature Economics, History and Mathematics

Sports

Adequate exercise and outdoor recreation are essential to morale and physical wellbeing in Belize. Opportunities for outdoor recreation are limitless, while those who don't like the outdoors are likely to find life here frustrating. Jogging and bicycling are popular. Close proximity to some of the world's most beautiful boating and swimming makes this an ideal post for water sports. Sailing, canoeing (on rivers), sea kayaking, motor-boating, SCUBA, snorkeling, fishing, and exploring the barrier reef and the cayes are popular activities. From Belize City, water taxis take you out to the cayes. There are plenty of boats for hire, or bring your own. Outboard motors are in ample supply and cheaper than in the U.S. Races for various classes of local and imported sailboats are held two or three times a year. Fishing tournaments, too, are held several times a year. Manatee can be seen upriver; and it is possible to canoe from the Guatemalan border into Belize City in 3 or 4 days (experienced outfitters can arrange the trip). The Belize Pickwick Club, the main tennis and social club, is in decline and membership is expensive. There are a few free or less expensive courts to be found around town, and partners are easy to find.

There is one private golf course. The Caye Chapel course is on an island ten miles east, and is being upgraded whilst the entire island is remade into an exclusive resort. It charges Bz$50/round. (Bring your own set of clubs, rentals don't exist here.) Golf is also possible in Cancun.

The cost of recreational and hobby equipment is high. It's a good idea to bring your own supplies and equipment. A fully equipped gymnasium is available northside at reasonable monthly fees.

Bird watching and hiking are popular activities. Belize is a world famous bird watching destination with over 560 species. An enthusiastic and professional Belize Audubon Society is active throughout the country. Belize has several caves to explore. Some can even be floated through on rivers in inner tubes.

The Radisson Fort George Hotel and Marina, and the Fiesta Inn open

their main pools to non-hotel guests, who have come for a meal. Also, a public pool has just been completed.

The Belize Fishing Association benefits sports fishermen and promotes fishing-related tourism. The association explores all kinds of sport fishing, organizes fishing tournaments, and advances marine conservation by maintaining records of fish caught in Belizean waters, such as grouper, snapper, tuna, marlin and swordfish.

Popular sports include karate, softball, basketball, horse racing, body building, soccer and cross-country bicycle racing.

The government reciprocally issues amateur radio licenses upon presentation of a U.S. license. The Belize Amateur Radio Society offers code and technical courses. In addition to high frequency operations, there is wide-spread two-meter activity across the country, with the assistance of active repeaters.

Touring and Outdoor Activities

Possibilities for weekend excursions are limitless. Roads, hotels, food and restaurants are generally good, the language is English, distances are short, and the variety of scenery great. A wide variety of ethnic groups can be found, and rural people are friendly. Particularly welcoming are the resident Americans, who are scattered all across the country, and are preeminent in the tourism industry.

A number of Mayan ruins in Belize have been excavated and partially restored. The two well-excavated ruins are Xunantunich, 70 miles west of Belize City, and Altun Ha, 30 miles north. The latest ruin, Caracol, rivaled (and in fact once defeated) Tikal, and requires an adventurous 4-wheel trek into Belize's tropical rainforest. Many sites are still under excavation and archeologists sometimes welcome visitors.

The Belize Zoo and Tropical Education Center, 30 miles west of the city, is a trend-setting world-class

facility, started and run by an American. It offers not only an interesting selection of Belizean wildlife in their natural settings, but also has educational programs on the flora and fauna of the region. A Baboon Sanctuary (actually black howler monkeys), butterfly farms across the country, bird sanctuaries (featuring the Western Hemisphere's largest bird, the jabiru) near Belize City and several national parks nationwide have established trails and guides. The world's only jaguar reserve is in the south.

The Mountain Pine Ridge, about three hours from Belize City off the Western Highway, provides a change of climate with cool nights. A number of resorts in the 3,000-foot high Pine Ridge offer horseback riding through Mayan ruins, inner tubing through ancient river caves, and ecological camping trips. Caves, waterfalls, natural pools and scenic views abound. The Mexican town of Chetumal (a two-hour drive), with freshwater, crystal clear lagoons for swimming close by, makes a good weekend excursion. The modern resorts of Cancun, Cozumel, Playa del Carmen and Isla Mujeres are six hours by car and are popular vacation sites. Cancun boasts every American chain restaurant and a Wet n Wild water park. Merida, the capital city of the Yucatan is also a six hour drive. It has excellent shopping and sightseeing facilities, and can be used as a base for visits to the famous ruins of Uxmal and Chichen-Itza.

Guatemala City and the colonial town of Antigua are an inexpensive and easy flight away. The quaint, sinking Guatemalan island village of Flores and the nearby Mayan ruins of Tikal are three hours by car.

Closer to home is Ambergris Caye, a large sandy island, only 15 minutes by plane or 1-1/2 hours by boat from Belize City. A fishing village turned tourist hub, San Pedro, is the premier jumping off spot for the best fishing, diving and boating. Many other lovely cayes are minutes from Belize City by boat, a couple with cabana guest rooms. Placencia, a rustic, mainland fishing village about 30 minutes by air or three hours by car, is one of several popular beach-front village vacation spots in the south.

Entertainment

The Calypso Bar and Grill, part of the Fiesta Inn, has a live band and dancing every Thursday through Saturday nights, and attracts an older crowd. Lindbergh's Landing is a popular hangout, and the happy hour at Mangos restaurant is well-attended. The Bellevue Hotel is favored by older young people. Karaoke is popular. There are several nightclubs, but no movie theaters.

There are a number of festivals year round. September 10, the anniversary of the Battle of St. George's Caye, and September 21, Independence Day, both feature parades, beauty contests, street dances and special events. Pan American Day and Garifuna Settlement Day (the anniversary of their arrival in Belize) are also celebrated.

Social Activities

The 3,000-strong American community consists mainly of business people who have enterprises, hotels or farms on the cayes or in the interior. Several American clergy and religious orders live in Belize City and in the districts. An American Chamber of Commerce formed in 1998.

Your social life can be active or quiet depending on inclination. Belizeans are friendly and easy to get to know, and a wide circle of acquaintances can easily develop. Most social activity takes place in the home, out on the cayes, and through scheduled events of the various clubs. Both Rotary and Lions have active branches in Belize.

OTHER CITIES

DANGRIGA (formerly called Stann Creek) is located in east-central Belize on the Caribbean Sea. The town was founded by black refugees from Honduras in 1823. It soon became a trading center and port for timber, fish, coconuts, and bananas. Dangriga has facilities for canning and freezing orange juice. The town's population is about 7,000.

Situated on the New River in northeastern Belize, **ORANGE WALK** is about 50 miles north of the capital. During the late 19th and early 20th century, Orange Walk enjoyed prosperous mahogany trading. Today, the economy is based on sugarcane and rum distilling. The area's inhabitants are a mixture of Maya Indians, Creoles, and a small number of Mennonites. The city's population is about 10,400.

PUNTA GORDA, in southern Belize, lies on a coastal plain about 75 miles south of Belmopan. Livestock are raised locally. Punta Gorda is linked to Belmopan by the Southern and Hummingbird highways via Dangriga. Its exports include coconuts, sugarcane, and bananas. Most of the 2,600 residents are Caribs.

SAN IGNACIO (formerly called El Cayo or Cayo) is the administrative center of the Cayo district in west-central Belize. The town lies on the Belize River, near the border with Guatemala. Rice, beans, cattle, and corn are traded in San Ignacio. The town's inhabitants are mostly Maya Indians, *mestizos*, and a substantial number of Mennonites. The population is about 8,000.

COUNTRY PROFILE

Geography and Climate

Belize is located along Central Americas eastern coast, bordered to the north by Mexico, to the west and south by Guatemala and to the east by the Caribbean Sea. It measures 175 miles north to south and 69 miles across at its widest point. Total land area is about the same as New Jersey.

The savannas of northern Belize are flat and dry compared to the rest of the country (receiving only 50 inches of rain a year). The primary source of income for the predominantly Mestizo population there is sugarcane. South and westward, the hilly inland terrain is more forested, including some remaining stands of mahogany. Next is the Mountain Pine Ridge range, with pine-covered peaks of over 3,000 feet that enjoy cool nights year round. To the south are citrus plantations, fishing, and rainforests where the annual rainfall increases to 120 inches. The Mayan Indian and Garifuna inhabitants subsist primarily upon small-scale farm - subsist and fishing.

Much of the coastline consists of either dense growths of mangrove habitats or broken, low-lying and narrow sandy shoreline. Belize City itself rests upon filled mangrove forest, with an elevation that is actually a foot below sea level.

The central Belize District is the most populated of six and is predominantly Creole. Economic activity centers around commerce and some light manufacturing Belize's barrier reef is the second largest in the world, running some 150 miles nearly the entire length of the coast, featuring three of the Caribbean's four atolls Small islands or cayes (pronounced keys; abound in the crystal-clear waters of the reefs.

Belize's subtropical climate is hot and humid most of the year. In Belize City the average daily temperature is 85°F, but the daytime high is often in the 90s between May and October, with uncomfortably high humidity. Dry season runs from January through April. Heavy rains begin in June and can continue through December. Mosquito outbreaks are a perennial result. From March to November, a fairly steady breeze makes the heat in Belize City less intolerable. The coolest period is December to February, when the average daily temperature is only 75°E During this period, night temperatures can drop into the upper 50s.

Tropical storms and hurricanes can occur from June through November.

In 1931 and 1961, hurricanes devastated Belize City; Hattie in 1961 put 15 feet of water in the chancery. Hurricane Greta (1978) was much less intense, but still covered the first floor of the chancery with 18 inches of water.

The country's capital is Belmopan, at the country's geographic center in the foothills of the Maya Mountains. It was conceived and constructed as the capital after hurricane Hattie's devastation. Though Belmopan is still vulnerable to hurricane winds, its distance inland (50 miles) and 180-foot elevation protect it from the waters that inundate Belize City. Belmopan is an easy hour away by paved highway.

Belmopan's modest main point of interest is its government buildings, styled after ancient Mayan architecture, arranged around a wide plaza. While it lacks the amenities of Belize City, it does have a handful of shops and produce stalls, a supermarket, banks, three hotels and a hospital. Plans to increase the city's 7,000+ population have stalled in recent years, and Belize City remains the principal shopping, business and entertainment center.

Population

Belize's three major ethnic groups are the Mestizo (Spanish/Indian descent), the Creole (African/European descent) and the indigenous Maya Indians. Garifuna (African/Arawak Indian descent), East Indian, Lebanese, European, Mennonite and Chinese people make up the rest of the population, which is estimated at 230,000. Average annual growth rate is 2.6%, due to a high birth rate coupled with a higher immigration than emigration rate.

The Creole and Garifuna together comprise roughly 36% of the population. Descended from African slaves, the two groups are distinguished by lineage and culture. The Creole, who predominate in Belize City, intermarried with Europeans, and their local English dialect is

AP/Wide World Photos, Inc. Reproduced by permission.

Street in Belize City, Belize

also known as Creole. Their culture is a blend of West Indian, British and American. The Garifuna are slaves intermarried with Carib Indians, who were deported by the British from the French West Indies around 1800. Garifuna communities are in the south. They maintain distinctly African cultural traits, while their first language combines an African dialect with Maya and Spanish words.

About 45% of Belizeans are of Latin and/or Indian lineage. Some are direct descendants of the regional Mayan tribes, who have become part of the money economy, learned Spanish, and married Latin descendants; this group is often referred to as the Mestizo. In remote areas, such as in the south, some Mayans still maintain some ethnic purity in custom and language.

In recent years, the influx of Hispanic refugees has had a significant impact on the population of Belize. The refugees came mostly from El Salvador, Guatemala, and Honduras during the wars of the 1980s. A reduced number still come, primarily for economic reasons. Official estimates place their numbers at 40,000. Some are being assimilated into Belizean society, working as laborers or in service industries in the larger towns. Many live as squatters, practicing slash-and-burn agriculture on interior lands.

Mennonites of European stock are often seen in black clothing and horse and buggy. They inhabit the northwest, and produce lovely furniture and much of the country's poultry and vegetables. The few remaining British subjects, the Lebanese, East Indian and Chinese business communities are predominantly in Belize City. English is the official language and mother tongue of over half of the population, with Spanish, Mayan dialects and Garifuna spoken as the first language of the rest of the population. Literacy is liberally estimated at 90%.

Public Institutions

After more than 200 years of British colonization, independence was granted on September 21, 1981. But Belize has enjoyed internal self-government since 1964, boasting the most stable democracy in the region, with a British-style parliamentary government, headed by a Prime Minister and 10 or more Cabinet ministers who all serve in the House of Representatives or Senate. Upon independence, Belize joined the Commonwealth, making Queen Elizabeth the head of state. The monarch is represented by a Governor General, whose appointment is recommended by the Prime Minister.

In 1993, British Forces withdrew all but a small training detachment of its former garrison. Today, defense is the responsibility of the small but dedicated Belize Defence Force (BDF). Policemen, like the British bobby, are unarmed on the beat.

There are two principal political parties-the People's United Party (PUP), and the United Democratic Party (UDP). The two have exchanged control of the government in every election since independence.

Arts, Science, and Education

Most exponents of Belizean art are the Garifuna, Creole, Maya and East Indian peoples. The work of wood and slate carvers, black coral jewelers, and local musicians and vocalists are readily available in stores where tourists shop, although much of the handicrafts are imported from Guatemala. There are many talented and popular painters, some of whom are exhibited fairly regularly in Belize City, especially at the National Handicraft Center and the Mexican Cultural Center.

Various choral societies practice and perform regularly. There are five national dance companies under the auspices of the National Arts Council, a couple of which have toured overseas on occasion.

The Belize National Theater Company and the Arts Council put on three to four shows a year, favoring works by local and Caribbean writers.

Scientific activity centers around the excavation of some of the 900 pre-Mayan/Mayan ruins throughout the country. A historical society, run by an American expatriate, is active.

The government and private citizens have set aside tens of thousands of acres of wildlife and ecological habitats where researchers study everything from herbal medicines to the coral reefs, manatees, mangrove trees and the spiny lobster. Reportedly, Belize has a higher percentage of its land (40%)

held as nature reserves or parks than any other country; and ecotourism is popular.

The University College of Belize (UCB), the only 4-year junior college with U.S. accreditation; the Belize Agricultural College; the University of the West Indies (UWI) Belize campus; and the Belize Teachers College are the premier institutions of higher learning. Check with the individual institutions, however, for their accreditation and academic levels of proficiency, as relevance and carryover to American programs may differ greatly.

There are relatively few cultural traces of two centuries of British colonialism; widespread cable television in particular, has increasingly Americanized the country.

Commerce and Industry

Sugar, citrus, rice, bananas, fishing, cattle ranching, and tourism have long since surpassed logging as the country's major economic activities. Still, only a small percentage of the cultivable land is in use, and tourism is now the largest industry (160,000 tourists, 65% of them Americans, visited in 1997).

Historically, Belize has exported agricultural products such as sugar and bananas, and has imported everything else. Through the efforts of Mennonite and Central American immigrants, it has achieved a modicum of self-sufficiency in basic foodstuffs like rice, corn, and red kidney beans. There are only a handful of small industries - cigarettes, beer, soft drinks, floor milling, concrete blocks, dairy products and agricultural processing.

Since Belize's modest market imports almost everything from the U.S., the UK or the English-speaking Caribbean, the cost of living remains high. Many Belizeans do their shopping in Mexico or Guatemala, where goods are cheaper.

Transportation

Automobiles

Private cars are a necessity and air-conditioned, heavy-duty vehicles are popular. High clearance vehicles are needed for traveling out of town. Parts and service are most easily obtained for Fords and Toyotas, which have full dealerships here. Jeep, Chrysler, Land Rover, Mitsubishi and Suzuki have agencies, with a limited supply of parts. The Ford Explorer and Suzuki Vitara or Sidekick are among the most popular models. Flood damage and poor maintenance make urban streets so full of potholes that tires and shock absorbers often need replacement (some would say high clearance is needed in town as well).

Driving licenses and registration certificates are issued with minimum formality and free of charge. Third-party liability insurance is compulsory and can be obtained locally at reasonable rates. Regular, high-octane, leaded and unleaded, and diesel fuels are readily available.

Local

Tropic Air and Maya Island Airways are the two local airlines, using single- and twin-engine planes to serve the district towns, resort cayes and Tikal, Guatemala.

Paved roads link Belize City north to the Mexican and west to the Guatemalan borders. A dry-weather road (now being paved) connects to Punta Gorda in the far south. Roads on to Tikal, Guatemala and Cancun and Merida, Mexico are paved and in good shape.

Regular, inter-city bus service (on modern as well as aging buses) operates on the all-weather roads. In-town bus service is infrequent. Traffic moves on the right, American-style. Taxis are reasonably priced (Bz$5 per person within the city during the day), and are usually available.

Regional

From Houston and Miami, Belize is a 2 hour flight. TACA makes daily flights from these cities, San Salvador (with connections to all Central

America), and Roatan and San Pedro Sula, Honduras. Continental Airlines flies twice daily from Houston, while American Airlines flies daily from Miami. Commuter airlines link Belize City to Tikal, Guatemala, and Chetumal and Cancun, Mexico.

Commercial cargo flights arrive in Belize weekly. Freighters make port calls from Miami two or three times a week, taking three days to make the journey. It is also possible to sail on cruise ships that call at Belize City in the winter.

Communications

Telephone and Internet

Belize enjoys excellent but expensive telephone service. All districts and major population centers are now linked by dial service. Direct-dial capability to the U.S. and many other countries is available through the local phone company. It is possible to use USA Direct for both AT&T and MCI from Belize if you have a calling card.

The country is Internet-friendly, with a well developed net, lots of web sites and home e-mail service readily available.

Mail

International airmail service between Belize and the U.S. is reliable. Postage for a one-half ounce letter to the U.S. is 75¢ (US3 80 equivalent). International air parcel post from the U.S. is expensive, but fast and reliable. Airmail packages sent from Belize to the U.S. are slightly less expensive and service is equally reliable. International mail from Belize can be registered and insured.

Personal mail between the U.S. and Belize can take from four days to a week (first class or priority mail). The same is true of parcel post. Fourth class mail generally arrives within a month; and mail is received on a daily basis.

Radio and TV

There are few facilities for entertainment and recreation, so two local TV stations and 60-plus cable channels make a TV and VCR a necessity.

There has also been a rapid increase in the number of radio stations across the country. For the most part, programming consists of contemporary and Caribbean music. Live programming takes the form of newscasts, talk shows, government and public service announcements and political propagandizing. Though the country is English-speaking, Spanish stations and programs are on the rise.

British Forces Belize broadcast on FM in Belize City, and IBB/VOA can be heard on AM. Short-wave reception is good.

Newspapers, Magazines, and Technical Journals

There are five weekly newspapers in circulation in Belize. All are in English and each represents a different point of view. Four are published in Belize City, and one in San Pedro on Ambergris Caye.

A variety of U.S. magazines, including the Latin American editions of Time and Newsweek are sold locally. Several poorly stocked bookstores carry detective, Western, gothic romance and comic books. Belize City has a new public lending library with novels, text and reference books, but few are new.

Health and Medicine

Medical Facilities

Some local doctors are well-trained and competent to thwart common ailments. Diagnosis and treatment of complicated illnesses are difficult due to lack of equipment and facilities. Trained laboratory technicians are available, but equipment and supplies in the government hospitals are limited. For these reasons, serious conditions and cases involving special care are treated in Miami. Many Belizeans travel to Mexico or Guatemala for medical attention. Local ophthalmologists provide high quality care, and glasses, contact lenses, and exams are comparatively priced to the U.S. Emergency dental work should be evacuated to the U.S.

Several pharmacies carry a wide variety of basic medicines. However, bring to post a supply of prescription drugs, medicines and first aid supplies, since these items are imported and scarcities occur.

Community Health

Although Belize City now has a modern water treatment plant, and sanitation has improved greatly in recent years, things are still well below U.S. standards. About 90% of urban households are connected to the citywide sewage system, but sewage still runs in some open canals which empty into the sea. Although there is regular removal of city garbage, it is common to see it strewn about.

Houseflies, horseflies, sandflies, mosquitoes, roaches, land crabs, rats, and mice are widespread, and mildew, rot rust, and salt air corrosion are a continuous problem. For pets, ticks and fleas are a constant annoyance. Bring plenty of tick/flea shampoo, spray, collars, powder or whatever you normally use to control the problem (what is available here is expensive).

The constant mildew and dust in the city can aggravate allergies and sinus conditions, and colds are common. The high heat and humidity make this a debilitating climate, and extra exertion can quickly bring on heat exhaustion and dehydration.

Preventive Measures

No specific immunizations are recommended for Belize.

Bring an ample supply of insect repellent (Belizean mosquitoes are immune to Skin So Soft) and sunscreen to avoid the damaging effects of overexposure to the sun's rays. The latter is particularly important when traveling to the cayes by boat where the sun's intensity is amplified by the reflection from the sea.

NOTES FOR TRAVELERS

Passage, Customs & Duties

From the Texas border, it is a 1,650 mile drive across Mexico to Belize City, most of it on 4-lane toll expressways. Good hotels, restaurants, spectacular scenery and mild mountain temperatures mark the route. Or, one can drive to Miami and take a plane from there to Belize City.

Plane connections to Belize are through Miami and Houston.

U.S. citizens need a passport valid for duration of stay. U.S. citizens do not need visas for tourist visits up to thirty days, but they must have onward or return air tickets and proof of sufficient funds. Visitors for other purposes must obtain a visa. Additional information on entry and customs requirements may be obtained from the Embassy of Belize at 2535 Massachusetts Ave., N.W., Washington, DC 20008, telephone (202) 332-9636. Information is also available at the Belizean Consulate in Miami or at the Belizean Mission to the UN in New York.

U.S. citizens living in or visiting Belize are encouraged to register at the Consular Section of the U.S. Embassy in Belize City and obtain updated information on travel and security in Belize. The U.S. Embassy is located at the intersection of Gabourel Lane and Hutson Street in Belize City; telephone 011 (501) 2-77161/62/63. The Embassy is open from 8:00 a.m. to 5:00 p.m., Monday through Friday, except for the 12:00 noon to 1:00 p.m. lunch hour.

Pets

Although no restrictions exist for bringing pets, and no quarantine is imposed, a current rabies shot and a health certificate (valid for no more than six months prior to arrival in country) are required. Also, a pet importation permit is required from the Vet Clinic in Belize, and a copy of it is required by the international carrier before personnel can board with their pet(s). A fee of BA 10 per pet is levied, and the permit is valid for 60 days. A veterinarian's health certificate must show an examination conducted not more than 10 days before arrival in country.

Heartworm is a deadly illness in Belize, therefore all dogs must receive constant preventative medication. Daily and monthly worming medicines are available, but you may want to bring your own supply to guard against shortages. Belize has a good clinic with several veterinarians, usually trained in the U.S. or Britain.

Firearms and Ammunition

Weapons must be registered with local authorities upon arrival. Only the following non-automatic firearms and ammunition may be brought to Belize.

Item Quantity: Pistols 1, Rifles 1, Shotgun 1. Ammunition: Rifle/pistols 100 rounds, Shotgun 50 rounds.

Currency, Banking, and Weights and Measures

The Belize dollar (BA) rate of exchange has remained steady for over 20 years at Bz$2 - US$1. U.S. dollars are accepted everywhere. It is not possible to access U.S. bank accounts through automated teller machines (ATMs) in Belize. Travelers, however, can obtain cash advances from local banks, Monday through Friday, using major international credit cards.

Distances are measured in miles and weights in pounds.

Disaster Preparedness

Belize is a hurricane-prone country. The coastal islands of Belize, which are low-lying and lack high ground, are particularly vulnerable to direct hits by hurricanes and tropical storms. The islands have been cut off from communications and assistance during previous hurricanes. Extensive flooding as a result of storm activity is common both on the islands and in areas of the country not directly affected by hurricanes. General information about natural disaster preparedness is available via the Internet from the U.S. Federal Emergency Management Agency (FEMA) at http://www.fema.gov/

LOCAL HOLIDAYS

Jan. 1	New Year's Day
Mar. 9	Baron Bliss Day
Mar/Apr.	Good Friday*
Mar/Apr.	Holy Saturday*
Mar/Apr.	Easter Monday*
May 1	Labor Day
May	Commonwealth Day*
May 28	Memorial Day
Sept. 10	National Day
Sept. 21	Independence Day
Oct. 12	Pan American Day
Nov. 19	Garifuna Day
Dec. 25	Christmas Day
Dec. 26	Boxing Day

*variable

RECOMMENDED READING

The following titles are provided as a general indication of the material published on this country:

Conroy, Richard (vice-consul here 196062). *Our Man in Belize*. St. Martins Press, 1998.

Fernandez, Julio. Belize: *A Case Study for Democracy in Central America*. Avebury, 1989.

National Geographic. "Belize, the Awakening Land." January 1972. *National Geographic*. "La Rita Maya." October 1989.

Rabinowitz, Alan. Jaguar. S*truggle and Triumph in the Jungle of Belize*. Arbor House: New York, 1986.

Smithsonian Magazine. "Illuminating the Maya's Path in Belize." December 1989.

Sutherland, Anne. *The Making of Belize: Globalization in the Margins*. Bergen & Garvey, 1998..

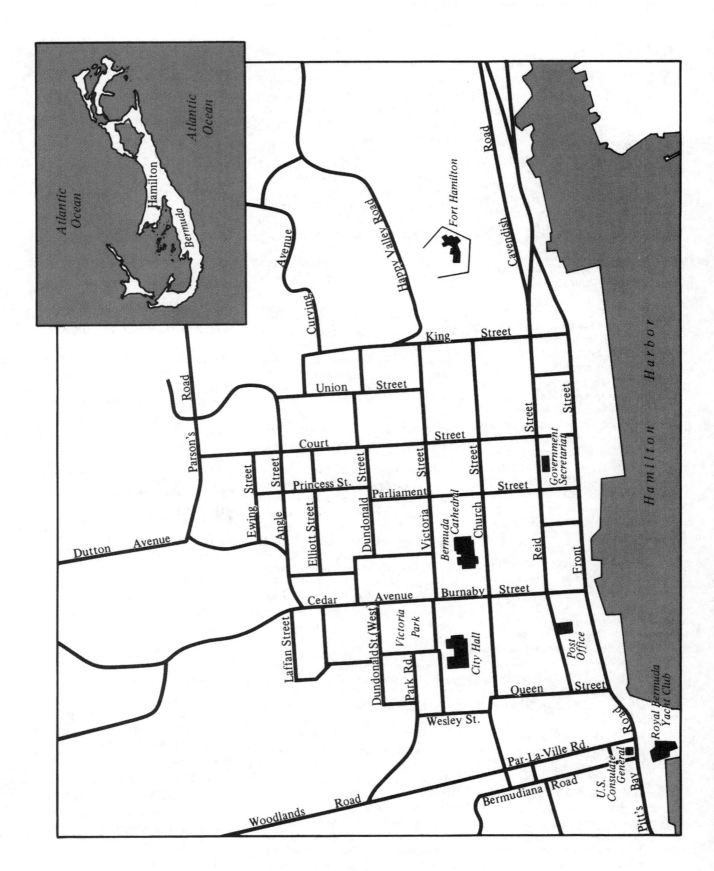

Hamilton, Bermuda

BERMUDA

Major City:
Hamilton

Other City:
St. George

INTRODUCTION

Bermuda is the most northerly group of coral islands in the world, lying just beyond the Gulf Stream some 650 miles off the coast of the Carolinas. Although very small and isolated in its part of the ocean, it offers a wide variety of places to see, people to meet, and things to do. With an economy based on tourism and international business, Bermudians enjoy a high standard of living with almost no unemployment, no national debt, and no income tax. They do face, however, a high cost of living and an increasing share of the stress associated with maintaining the lifestyle of an economically developed western society.

Places to see vary from Hamilton, the capital, with its smart shops and busy harbor, to St. George, the only other municipality, with its Old World lanes and fortresses. You can sightsee from the North Shore, with its bizarre rock formations, to the South Shore with its pink and white beaches. From end to end Bermuda is picturesque. Nature has endowed it with an abundance of verdant trees and colorful flowers. The landscape is dotted with pastel-hued, white-roofed houses and stately, tasteful hotels. No factories, billboards, or neon signs blot the quaint scenery.

In addition to the pleasant and hospitable Bermudians, the people include large numbers of more recent arrivals from around the world, some official representatives of the UK and their families, hundreds of Americans and Canadians who live on the island all or part of the year, a constant stream of tourists from the U.S. and Canada, a small but long-settled Portuguese community, and many residents and workers from the West Indies.

Bermuda offers many things to do. For recreation, Bermuda offers a host of outdoor sports including golf, tennis, fishing, sailing, diving, and swimming, and an adequate number of pursuits such as movies, occasional theatrical productions, and musical concerts.

Life in Bermuda is confined, yet varied. The island can be restful, yet interesting, busy, but not hectic

MAJOR CITY

Hamilton

Only 2,000 people reside within Corporation limits, but as the island's business center Hamilton's daytime population swells to about 14,000. The city's main attractions are its restaurants and its smart shops and department stores along Front Street, which faces the busy quay side of Hamilton's harbor. The city's low traditional buildings are rapidly giving way on many streets to international-style low-rise business buildings with a few Bermudian architectural grace notes, but the town still retains a basically

British-colonial appearance. From across the harbor, its central skyline is dominated by the towers of City Hall, the Bermuda Cathedral, and the Sessions House or parliament building. The last contains the chambers of the House of Assembly and Supreme Court. Nearby on Front Street is the Cabinet Building, which houses the Senate chamber and the offices of the Premier and his staff. On a hill just north of the city stands Government House, the official residence and office of the Governor, overlooking the city and the harbor to the south, the Dockyard across the water to the west, and the ocean to the north. Hamilton's other attractions include Albouy's Point, site of the Royal Bermuda Yacht Club and a park overlooking the harbor, the Bermuda Library, which houses the Museum of Bermuda History, and the adjacent Par-La-Ville Gardens. The remains of Fort Hamilton are on the east side of the city, also pro-

View of the harbor, Hamilton, Bermuda

Susan Rock. Reproduced by permission.

months. A piano becomes "tinny" after a year or two of exposure to the subtropical climate. The wooden structure of a violin or guitar may warp. A brass instrument may corrode, unless frequently polished.

Domestic Help

Good, reliable domestic help is hard to find and is expensive because the demand greatly exceeds the supply. For general housekeeping, count on paying about $15 per hour. Very few live-in domestics or nannies are available. Importing one from elsewhere may be useful. Baby-sitters are available but are also expensive. The going rate for an average teenage babysitter is approximately $7 per hour. Gardeners are provided where needed at leased housing.

Education

Bermuda is in the process of reorganizing its public education system to provide middle schools and reduce the number of existing secondary schools. Professionally, the Ministry of Education seems to rely heavily on advice from educationists in the Province of Ontario and has followed many of their approaches to educational policy.

The Bermuda College, established in 1974, provides post-secondary education on a level with American junior or community colleges. Courses offered include "academic studies" (designed for preuniversity work), "commerce and technology" (designed to prepare students for various trades and business skills), and "hotel technology." In 1980, the government opened Stonington Beach Hotel, which is operated by the College and staffed by students training for careers in the hotel industry. The College offers some courses from Queens University in Canada.

Bermuda has a number of private schools. In addition to denominational (Roman Catholic and Seventh-Day Adventist) schools, there is one girls' school and two co-educational English style grammar schools, one of which offers a postgraduate year designed to prepare qualified graduates of any Bermuda

viding harbor and city views from its ramparts

Utilities

Electricity in Bermuda is U.S. standard, 110/60 cycle. All American electric or electronic equipment can be used here. The electrical supply is fairly reliable, with the occasional weather-associated or equipment-failure outages to be expected by residents of islands.

Food

Almost all of the island's food supply is imported. With transportation costs and import duties, all consumer good prices are much higher than in the US. A few foods-some vegetables, bakery goods, fresh milk and eggs, meats and several species of fish-are produced locally but are expensive. U.S.-style supermarkets abound.

Clothing

Clothing which would be suitable for wear during summer in Washington, D.C., may be worn in Bermuda from April through November. Moderately heavy clothing is useful during Bermuda's frost-free but chilly winters. Sweaters are essential but are something of a bargain at times in local stores.

Fashionable clothing of all sorts is available in local stores, usually but not always at prices somewhat above those of Washington. Wash-and-wear clothing is a great boon in Bermuda's climate, especially since dry cleaning is very expensive.

Office wear is more casual than in Washington, and Bermudians often wear Bermuda shorts with long socks, blazers, and ties. In general, dress in Bermuda is informal and colorful, but not to the extent associated with the tropical tourist islands to the south. Most social occasions and visits to all the better restaurants and hotels require at least jackets and ties, if not suits, for men and comparable outfits for women. Formal wear can be rented locally.

Supplies and Services

Virtually everything is available in Bermuda at a price or can be obtained quickly by mail order from the United States.

Numerous satisfactory beauty salons and barber shops are available in Hamilton and elsewhere. Nearly all appliance repairs are available somewhere in Bermuda but can be difficult if the right parts are not in stock. As with everything else, this can be expensive.

Musical instruments suffer in the climate and need tuning every few secondary school for attendance at American and Canadian universities. Another private school on the university level is Webster University which operates associate, bachelor's, and master's degree programs.

The reorganization of the public school system has created distrust among the public in the system as a whole. This in turn has nurtured a growing rush by parents to place their children in private schools, so waiting lists may apply.

The island's proximity to the U.S. east coast opens a wide choice of specialized schools for those who wish it.

Sports

Much of the island's life centers around outdoor activity. The island boasts of having more golf courses per square mile than any other country in the world. Of nine courses on the island, three are public, four are associated with hotels, and two are private with long waiting lists for membership. Greens fees are more expensive than at comparable courses in the U.S.

Tennis is also popular and almost all hotels have courts. The National Tennis Stadium has five courts available at moderate charges, and five tennis clubs throughout the island may be joined easily.

Sailing is the outdoor sport supreme; racing in the various classes takes place throughout the year, but the sport is expensive. Sailing classes for children are held three mornings a week at the Royal Bermuda Yacht Club and the Royal Hamilton Amateur Dinghy Club during the summer. The Bermuda Yachting Association also offers a subsidized sailing program in the summer.

Excellent light tackle fishing is available and more than 200 species of fish are found in the waters off Bermuda. Charter boats equipped with outriggers and all modern equipment are available at reasonable prices.

Bermuda's beaches are the main recreational areas. Along the South Shore stretch superb white and pink sand beaches which are ideal for swimming and sunbathing. Throughout the year hardy individuals can bathe in the sea, although the popular swimming season is from late May to early October. A Bermudian would not think of taking a dip in the sea between October and May, but visitors and foreign residents do. Water skiing can be enjoyed in the protected waters of the harbors and sounds. Skin-diving with mask and snorkel or with aqualungs is popular, and even inexperienced swimmers can soon learn how to explore reefs close off Bermuda's shore.

Most sporting equipment can be bought from local shops. Every make of camera and film can be found in Hamilton's shops.

Entertainment

Hamilton has two modern movie theaters. Other movie theaters are located at Dockyard and St. George's. Visiting concert musicians and ballet troupes sometimes perform in the small theater at Hamilton's City Hall. In recent years several excellent plays have also been presented by overseas theatrical groups.

As a tourist mecca, Bermuda has a varied program of spectator events. The Queen's Birthday in June and other national holidays are celebrated with military parades on Front Street. The opening of Parliament each autumn is also marked by impressive ceremonies. The International Yacht Race between Newport, Rhode Island, and Bermuda, held every other year in June, brings well over 100 entries from North America, South America, and Europe to Hamilton Harbor where they form as large a fleet of ocean-going sailing vessels as may be seen anywhere in the world. Another popular sports event is the two-day cricket Cup Match each August. Both days of the match are national holidays. 1997 also saw the third annual "ShootOut" professional golf tournament, and the

inaugural offerings of a celebrity golf tournament and a Bermuda Film Festival.

There is an active International American Women's Club and Junior Service League for women.

Good restaurants are available throughout the island, and most hotels have first-class dining rooms. However virtually all dining establishments are priced for the tourist trade and are expensive. "Continental" and Italian cuisine predominate. Ethnic restaurants-Chinese, Indian, and Mexican-exist, but are far from authentic. Many hotels and clubs offer dancing nightly. Prices are scaled to the tourist traffic.

OTHER CITY

The only other municipality in Bermuda is **ST. GEORGE,** on the extreme east, about 12 miles from Hamilton. It is much larger than Hamilton, with an area of 400 acres, but has a population of less than 1,700. St. George is probably the oldest English-speaking community in the Western Hemisphere, and it preserves the atmosphere and appearance of a 17th-century settlement. A series of high-walled, cannon-bedecked fortresses dating from the early 1600s line its eastern seacoast. The most imposing is Fort St. Catherine, and in one of its chambers an illuminated diorama illustrates scenes from the colony's history. Nearby is Gunpowder Cavern, a brick-lined cluster of chambers and walkways deep within a man-made hill—formerly an ammunition magazine, but today a charming restaurant.

In King's Square, the former marketplace, stands a replica of an ancient stock and pillory. Around the square are most of the city's main attractions: St. Peter's Church, probably the oldest Anglican church site in the New World, in use, although often restored, since 1612; the Old State House, the colony's first stone building, constructed in 1619; Tucker House, a high-ceilinged mansion built in 1711, and the St. George Town Hall, in use since 1782. The square is lined on the south by the busy docks on the harbor.

Across St. George's harbor, to the south, lies St. David's Island, most of which is occupied by the U.S. Naval Air Station. The base's runways are shared with the Bermuda Civil Air Terminal, the colony's only civilian airport. The southernmost tip is the site of the Bermuda National Aeronautics and Space Administration (NASA) installation, which has played an important role in manned space programs.

Separating St. David's and St. George's Islands from the 15-mile-long central island—sometimes called Main Island—is Castle Harbor, a six-square-mile body of seawater. Much of the eastern portion of Main Island is occupied by Harrington Sound, a three square-mile incursion of the sea that almost forms a lake.

Along the narrow strip of land between Castle Harbor and Harrington Sound are several caves where visitors may view impressive formations of stalactites and stalagmites. On the neck of land between Harrington Sound and the sea lies the village of Flatts, the most populous settlement between St. George and Hamilton. Nearby is the aquarium, where a fascinating collection of more than 200 varieties of fish and other marine life found in Bermuda's waters may be seen. Adjoining is the Natural History Museum, which displays shells, fossils, and marine antiques, and the Zoological Garden, featuring an array of tropical birds and animals.

At the southernmost point of Harrington Sound is Devil's Hole, a natural saltwater pool stocked with large fish and tortoises. Here visitors can drop baited, but hookless, lines to lure the creatures part way out of the water.

The western portion of Bermuda has its attractions, too. The large village of Somerset occupies much of Somerset Island, which lies just off the western terminus of Main Island, about 12 miles from Hamilton. Like St. George, Somerset retains much of the atmosphere and appearance of a 17th-century settlement. This island is connected with Main Island by Somerset Bridge, reputed to be the smallest functioning drawbridge in the world. It has a 22-inch-wide plank across its center which is raised by hand to allow clearance of sailboat masts.

Near Somerset, on a peninsula off Main Island, lies the U.S. Naval Air Station Annex, occupying about 268 acres. North of the base are the waters of Great Sound and, to the south, lies Little Sound. On Main Island, directly south of the base across Little Sound, stands Gibbs Hill Lighthouse, one of the most powerful lighthouses in the world. Completed in 1846, it stands on a 245-foot hill and is, itself, 117 feet high. Its rotating beam of a half-million candle power is visible as far away as 40 miles. Visitors may mount the spiral stairway to the top during the daytime.

COUNTRY PROFILE

Area and Geography

Bermuda is an archipelago of seven main islands and some 150 other islands and islets. The main islands, joined by bridges or causeways, stretch from northeast to southwest in a long, narrow formation that hooks northward at the western end. On the map the shape is much like that of a fishhook. The main islands are in close proximity, and since being joined the Bermuda Islands (or Somers Isles, their other name) are generally called the island of Bermuda.

Total land area is about 20 square miles-some 22 miles in length and an average of less than a mile in width. This is slightly smaller than the area of Manhattan. During World War 11, the U.S. military created 1.25 square miles of the present area by uniting and enlarging some of the islands with material dredged from the sea bottom.

The archipelago is the summit of a submerged volcanic mountain range, 14,000 -15,000 feet high, which has been extinct since before the first ice age. Over the volcanic foundation and just under the inches-thin layer of soil capping it lies a 200-foot thick layer of limestone formed by deposits of mollusks, coral polyps, and other sea creatures. The coral content in the limestone substructure justify Bermuda's classification as a "coral island," though it is more accurately a mixed superstructure of aeolian petrified sand hills and limestone upon an eroded volcanic base. Only the surrounding reefs are true coral growths, and Bermuda is the most northerly point on the globe where reef-building coral exists.

Bermuda lies at latitude 32' 18" N and longitude 65'46" W Geographically, it is remote and does not lie within or near the West Indies or Caribbean, with which it is often erroneously identified. The nearest land is Cape Hatteras, North Carolina, 570 nautical miles away. New-York City is 733 nautical miles to the northwest.

The terrain is hilly. Some hills exceed 200 feet in height; the highest, Gibbs Hill, is 260 feet above sea level. A fertile valley extends along the length of the main island. On the rocky northern shore wind-carved cliffs cascade into the sea. Similar rock formations form a dramatic backdrop for the long beaches and small coves of the sandy south shore. The enclosing reef, a few yards offshore on the south coast and up to several miles offshore on the north, emerges from the sea each day at low tide, framing the islands and completing the topographical picture.

Except for a few small ponds, no rivers, streams, lakes, or other freshwater surface formations exist on the islands. For most of its history, Bermuda was thought to have no ground water, but in the 1920s and 30s, freshwater lens formations lying above underground salt water were discovered and exploited to supplement the island's main source of drinking water; rainwater collected on roofs and paved catchments.

Though far north from tropical latitudes, Bermuda has a mild, humid, frostfree climate. The annual mean temperature is 70.2 F. Highs in summer rarely top 90 E, lows in winter rarely are below the upper 50s. The lowest temperature ever officially recorded was 44 E The Gulf Stream, running west and north of the island, is the main reason for the good climate. Average annual rainfall is 57.6 inches, spread evenly across the 12 months. The year-round high humidity, averaging more than 75%, makes some days uncomfortably sticky in summer and damp in winter.

January through March tends to be overcast and squally, though when the sun shines it can be just breezy and spring-like. April and May are very pleasant. June through August are like summer in Washington, D.C., except that Bermuda nights are comfortable in houses positioned to catch southerly breezes. September is the stormy season; the hurricane season extends from June through November. Barring hurricanes, October through December are calm, usually sunny, mild months, considered by many the most pleasant part of the year. The climate plus the well-distributed rainfall and heavy dew make for a luxuriant growth of vegetation of every description, despite the dearth of soil.

Palms, Australian and Norfolk Island pines, mangrove, poinciana, casuarina, and ficus trees, along with citrus and some tropical fruits, grow well in Bermuda. Oleander and hibiscus are common. The famous Bermuda cedar trees which for centuries dominated the landscape and were the islands' pride were afflicted by a blight in the early 1940s and by 1944 more than 90% of them were dead. They are now protected but few are as robust as formerly. Some cedar reforestation, with blight-resistant stock, is being undertaken.

History

Bermuda is named for the Spanish seafarer Juan de Bermudez, who discovered the island in 1503. There is evidence of occasional visits by Spanish or Portuguese seamen, and at least one fruitless Spanish plan to settle the island, but generally the local reefs and raucous native birds gave Bermuda a bad name among Spanish sailors, who avoided a place they thought inhabited by devils. In 1609, Admiral Sir George Somers' ship Sea Venture, carrying a new lieutenant governor to Virginia, ran aground on Bermuda's eastern reef. The crew was stranded until they built a new ship from local timber to continue their voyage. Descriptions of Bermuda attracted great interest, and in 1612 about 60 colonists (including some of Somers' crew) sailed for what were then called the Somers Isles. Shortly after landing, they founded the town of St. George at the eastern end of the island. In 1790, the more centrally located town of Hamilton was incorporated. In 1815 the seat of government was transferred from St. George to Hamilton, which had a larger harbor and was more central to a greatly-expanded British program of fortification building that saw the creation of the massive Royal Dockyard at the West End, and Fort Prospect (the principal land garrison) and other forts in the parishes near Hamilton.

During the first three centuries of the Colony's existence, except for its function as a military bastion of the Empire and periods of prosperity generated by the American Revolutionary War and Civil War, Bermuda itself remained quite isolated from developments abroad. The industrial revolution virtually passed it by. By the turn of the 20th century, wealthy Americans, Canadians, and Britons, seeking refuge from the pressures of modern life, were renting or buying homes and estates for seasonal occupancy in Bermuda. Soon shops and restaurants sprang up to cater to this carriage trade. As the economic benefits of tourism became apparent, the colony sought to cultivate and broaden it. During the 1920s several impressive luxury hotels were built. In the early 1930s large passenger steamships were put into liner service between New York and Bermuda. In 1937, passenger seaplane service between New York and Bermuda was inaugurated. The tourist industry continued to develop until the outbreak of World War II.

The war gave new significance to the Colony as a strategic outpost for the AngloAmerican forces. In 1941, the UK granted the U.S. a 99-year rent-free lease for construction and maintenance of two bases in Bermuda. The bases, the U.S. Naval Air Station, Bermuda, on St. David's Island, and the U.S. Naval Air Station Annex in Southampton, were for fifty years an integral and important part of the Bermudian scene and economy. The U.S. bases closed, however, in September of 1995. The airfield built by U. S. forces as part of the base during World War II now also serves as Bermuda's international airport.

Population

Bermuda's population is 58,460 (1991 census). This includes about 15,800 foreign-born residents without Bermuda status (the nearest thing to citizenship this British Dependent Territory has). The racial composition of the native Bermudian population is about 76% black and 24% white; of the total population the proportion is nearer 60% - 40%.

Several thousand Americans and Canadians live on the island either all or part of the year. About half the 6,000 or so Portuguese (Azoreans) on the island are now Bermudians, with the other half contract workers expected to return to their homeland. Several hundred Europeans-

British, Italians, Yugoslavs, Irish, Austrians, Swiss, and French-are employed in Bermuda's hotels, restaurants, guest houses, and other service areas, as are an equal number of Filipinos, other Asians, and West Indians. Some 600,000 tourists visit the island every year, most of them Americans.

Slavery was abolished in the British Empire in 1834, but racial segregation was practiced in Bermuda's schools, restaurants, hotels, and other public places until the 1960s. Racial discrimination in any form is not tolerated in today's multiracial Bermudian society.

English is the official and vernacular language of Bermuda. The traditional Bermudian dialect is characterized by broad vowels and a frequent transposition of "v" and "w" sounds. Educated Bermudians have accents ranging from standard British to standard American, with the "typical" accent sounding to the American ear like a cross between New England and Maritime Canadian. British visitors often find the local accent American, while many American visitors think it is vaguely British-sounding. Some Azorean Portuguese is also heard in Bermuda.

Bermuda has a strong religious tradition, rooted in its rural past. Many Christian denominations are represented on the island, distributed among the Church of England (28%), Roman Catholic Church (15%), African Methodist Episcopal (12%), Methodist (5%), and Seventh Day Adventist (6%), along with many other smaller Protestant followings. Baha'i, Moslem, and other groups are also present. Jewish services are held informally; there is no synagogue on the island.

Public Institutions

Bermuda is the oldest self-governing colony in the British Commonwealth. Representative government was first introduced to the Colony in 1620. Since 1684, the Governor of the Island has been appointed by the Crown and the colony's laws

enacted by a local legislature. Though Bermuda is a British Dependent Territory, it has a separate written Constitution, giving its elected Cabinet government almost complete self-determination in conducting local affairs. The Bermuda Parliament is the third-oldest in the world, following Iceland's and Britain's.

The Queen appoints the Governor, who is responsible for external affairs, defense, and internal security. In other matters the Governor acts on the advice of the Cabinet. The Deputy Governor is appointed by the Foreign & Commonwealth Office, and is normally a British Foreign Service Officer. These two officials are the only representatives of the United Kingdom on the island.

The Legislature consists of the Senate and the House of Assembly. Members of the Senate are appointed by the Governor, five on the advice of the Premier, three on the advice of the Leader of the Opposition, and three by the Governor at his own discretion. The Senate elects its own president and vice president. The House of Assembly, consisting of 40 popularly elected members from 20 constituencies, elects a Speaker and a Deputy Speaker. Universal suffrage on the one-person, one vote principle has existed since 1968. In 1989, the voting age was lowered from 21 to 18.

The Cabinet consists of the Premier and at least six other members of the Assembly or the Senate. The Governor appoints the majority leader in the House of Assembly as Premier, who in turn nominates the other Cabinet Ministers. They are responsible for government departments and related business. The Opposition Leader, which in British parliamentary practice is a formally designated position, is the leader of the largest minority party in the House of Assembly.

The judiciary consists of the Court of Appeal, the Supreme Court, and the Magistracy. The Chief Justice presides over the Supreme Court

and is consulted by the Governor in the appointment of judges, magistrates, and court officers.

Hamilton, the capital, was made a city by an act of legislature in 1897 and is governed by a Corporation. The town of St. George, one of the oldest English settlements in the New World, was founded in 1612 and remained the capital until 1815. Charges for water and dock facilities and municipal taxes are the main sources of revenue for both.

Aside from the two municipalities, Bermuda is divided into nine districts, called parishes. From east to west, these are St. George's, Hamilton (not to be confused with the city of Hamilton), Smith's, Devonshire, Pembroke, Paget, Warwick, Southampton, and Sandys.

Politics

The United Bermuda Party (UBP) is the ruling party and has not lost an election since its founding in 1968. It is a multiracial party, and has combined moderately progressive social policy with conservative fiscal policy. The UBP saw significant erosion in its parliamentary majority in the 1989 elections, falling from 31 to 22 of the 40 seats in the House, largely because of internal party dissension arising from disputes over independence for Bermuda. In the 1993 elections, the UBP's majority slipped even further, and the party now maintains only 21 seats in the House, as well as five Senate positions. New elections must be held every five years, and thus the next scheduled vote must take place by the Fall of 1998.

The opposition Progressive Labor Party (PLP) holds 18 seats in the House and three in the Senate. The PLP is largely identified with the black population, closely allied to organized labor, and favors independence for Bermuda.

In August of 1995, former Premier Sir John Swan, the head of government for 13 years, bucked UBP supporters and staked his political career on an independence referendum, which was defeated at the polls by a three to one margin. The new Premier and UBP leader, Pamela Gordon, has held her position since March 1997. She previously served as Minister for the Environment & Minister for Youth, Sports & Recreation.

Arts, Science, and Education

Bermuda hosts a variety of cultural events featuring both local talent and groups touring from abroad. The Bermuda Festival is held in January-February, attracting additional tourists during the winter and providing cultural entertainment for local residents. The Festival features performances by international-class artists, which have included The Dance Theater of Harlem, the Flying Karamazov Brothers, the Vienna Choir Boys, Wynton Marsalis, and The Empire Brass Quintet.

Local amateur arts groups include the Bermuda Musical and Dramatic Society (performing arts), Bermuda Society for the Arts (exhibitions, art gallery), and the Gilbert and Sullivan Society (light opera). Memberships and participation are open to all.

The Bermuda Biological Station, on Ferry Reach at the island's eastern end, was founded by a group of North American universities to further the study of marine sciences, and receives both Government of Bermuda and U.S. National Science Foundation support. It hosts researchers from the U.S. and elsewhere, conducting research at sea with its own ocean-going research vessels.

Conservation/preservation groups include the Bermuda National Trust, Audubon Society, the Bermuda Maritime Museum, and the Bermuda Zoological Society (responsible for the popular Aquarium, Zoo, and Natural History Museum). The Bermuda Botanical Garden (also site of the Premier's official residence, Camden) and an Arboretum are publicly maintained.

Commerce and Industry

Bermuda's GDP is over $9 billion, or about $27,500 per capita-one of the highest per capita income rates in the world. Most Bermudians owe their livelihood, directly or indirectly, to tourism, which provides 55% of GDP.

Bermuda's other source of national income is foreign companies operating out of offices in Bermuda. These offshore "exempt" and "nonresident" companies, almost all of them reinsurance or captive insurance companies, for the most part conduct international operations unrelated to Bermuda. The fees, charges, and taxes they pay, and their local expenditures, contribute about 40% of GDP, a share that is growing relative to tourism. Some 8,700 foreign firms are registered in Bermuda, though only a few actually maintain a physical presence here.

Total exports for 1996 were estimated at $67.7 million. Roughly 98% of total exports fell under the tariff #99.7000 - "Other Miscellaneous Manufactured Items". The re-export of pharmaceutical goods accounts for roughly 99% of this tariff number. Trading countries for pharmaceutical items include: Holland (50%), Brazil (13%), Canada (6%), Caribbean (5%), and all other countries (26%). The remaining export items are traded to the following partner countries: USA (91%), Canada (1%), Caribbean (1%), and UK (7%).

Fishing and agriculture (vegetables, fruits, eggs, and some milk) produce only a fraction of Bermuda's needs. Almost all manufactures and foodstuffs are imported, nearly two-thirds of them from the United States.

The largest single source of government revenue is customs duties, supplemented by a land tax, employment taxes, hotel occupancy taxes, departure taxes, and a hospital levy. There is no local income tax. Government spending in the FY 95 budget totaled $406 million on current account, including $34.5 million on capital projects. Bermuda traditionally does not borrow for current expenditure, and public borrowing for the capital account is limited to 10% of GDP.

Bermuda has tight immigration and property ownership and management regulations. The Immigration Board will grant permission for a non-Bermudian to work only if no qualified Bermudian, or person with Bermudian status, is available for the position. Applications for work permits are scrutinized carefully, and the procedure is complicated and time-consuming. Foreigners may purchase only those houses or condominiums listed as available for sale to nonBermudians. The list is short and the properties are expensive. Such properties may not pass by inheritance beyond the children of the original purchasers.

Transportation
Automobiles
Cars have been a part of the Bermuda scene only since 1946. The law limits a car's size and horsepower, forbids the use of private cars by all but residents, and provides for only one car per household (and only members of that household may drive it). Because of the latter restriction, most families own one (or more) motorbike, motor scooter, or motorcycle in addition to a car. Rental cars are not available.

Bermuda's laws restrict passenger vehicles to a maximum of 169 inches in overall length and 67 inches in overall width, with a maximum engine capacity of 2,000 cc (2.0 liters). There are technical restrictions that might bar other vehicles, such as sports cars or unusual models. Most cars in Bermuda are of Japanese manufacture (Mitsubishi, Nissan, Honda, Toyota, and Mazda, etc.). Volkswagen, British Ford, Hyundai, Peugeot, BMW,

Fishermen cleaning their catch in Hamilton, Bermuda

and various other makes are also sold here. Bermudians drive on the left, so almost all cars are right-hand drive. Right-hand drive cars are not compulsory, however. Because most roads are narrow and winding, Bermuda's speed limit is 35 km/h (21.7 mph).

Bermuda's laws virtually forbid the import of used cars. A vehicle may be imported only if it was purchased new within 6 months of importation. The local used car market is small and prices tend to be high, as they reflect the 75% duty that new car buyers pay. New cars may be purchased through local dealers.

Cars brought to Bermuda should be undercoated to protect the chassis against the corrosive effects of the climate and seasprayed roads. Bermuda has adequate repair shops for most popular makes of small cars; spare parts are usually in stock. Labor and materials are expensive.

All drivers must, without exception, pass a driving test. The Transport Control Department (TCD) does not recognize any foreign licenses for use by Bermuda residents. A driver's license issued in Bermuda is normally valid only for the licensee's car.

All motorized vehicles must be registered with and inspected by TCD. Motorized vehicles with engines of 50cc or less may be driven with a local learner's permit or a foreign license (this permits tourists to rent 50cc mopeds or scooters on temporary visits to Bermuda). TCD vehicle inspection requirements are similar to examinations in the U.S. Third-party liability insurance is also compulsory on all vehicles. Most Bermuda insurance firms grant no-claim discounts; travelers with a record of accident-free driving should bring letters from their previous insurance firms attesting to this.

Used motorbikes or scooters are readily available. As with cars, duty must be paid on a new vehicle bought from a local dealer's existing stocks.

Gasoline sold at local service stations costs about $4.60 a gallon. Safety helmets must be worn when driving any two-wheeled vehicle.

Local

More than 600 taxis are available. Some 300 Bermudian taxi drivers have attained "Qualified Tour Guide" status by successfully completing special government exams. Taxi fares are high; the fare from the airport to Hamilton is about $25.

Local bus service is extensive and reasonable in price and is heavily used by both Bermudians and tourists. The government ferry service connects Hamilton with points in Paget and Warwick (across the harbor from Hamilton) running at frequent intervals. Less frequent service on larger ferries goes to three points in Somerset, including the Dockyard. The ferries are heavily used by tourists and are a convenient form of commuting for those living near the landing points. The ferries are canceled, however, whenever sea conditions are unfavorable.

Regional

Flights are available daily between Bermuda and New York. Good non-stop services also connect Bermuda with Baltimore, Boston, Atlanta, London, and Toronto. Baltimore-Washington International Airport is about 2 hours away by plane. British Air and Air Canada are the only non-American carriers serving Bermuda. Passengers on the many U.S. carrier flights to the U.S. are pre-cleared by U.S. Immigration and U.S. Customs at Bermuda's airport, arriving at domestic terminals on the mainland. Bermuda is on Atlantic Time, one hour ahead of the East Coast throughout the year.

Cruise ships service Bermuda from New York and Boston from May to October, with occasional voyages from other ports during this period.

Communications

Telephone and Telegraph

Telephone and fax service extends throughout the island. Long distance service is rapid and efficient, with direct dialing to the U.S. and most of the world.

Rental rates and local service costs are comparable to those in the U.S. A 3-minute direct-dialed station-to-station call to the East Coast averages $3.75. Calls to Bermuda from the U.S. are cheaper than the other way around. The Bermuda Telephone Company, Ltd. uses Canadian-built equipment and many international brands of telephone and fax sets are available for home and business use.

International telegraph service is operated by Cable & Wireless Ltd.

Round the clock service is available by calling 297-7000. Communications in Bermuda are state-of-the-art, with multiple satellite, ocean cable, and fiber-optic cable facilities in place.

TV and Radio

The three local TV stations can be received on any standard American TV set without alteration. One is a CBS affiliate, another carries NBC programs, and the other carries some ABC programs. A fourth station offers some CNN and BBC programming. Cable service is also available, similar to that in most American cities.

Newspapers, Magazines, and Technical Journals

Bermuda has one daily newspaper, the morning Royal Gazette. The Mid-Ocean News and Bermuda Sun appear weekly on Fridays. While all newspapers concern themselves mainly with local events, they have wire-service coverage of leading US. and other foreign news stories. The New York Times and Washington Post are received by local vendors daily and usually arrive by air the same day of publication, or the following morning. Several other leading American and British newspapers are available on local stands.

American newspaper and magazine subscriptions should be sent via pouch. Magazines are normally sent by surface mail, arriving at least two weeks after publication. Current books, including paperbacks, are available in Hamilton bookstores, but are quite expensive. Subscription to book-buying services or clubs in the U.S. is advisable.

Health and Medicine

Medical Facilities

All physicians in the yellow pages of the Bermuda telephone directory are licensed by the Bermuda Government and are considered acceptable.

The only hospital in Bermuda is the King Edward VII Memorial Hospital just east of Hamilton. It is a well-equipped and modern general medical and surgical hospital with about 300 beds. All customary services are available at King Edward, including an emergency and outpatient department. The hospital is accredited under a Canadian system. Local dentists are competent, most trained in the U.S. or Canada.

Community Health

Immunization and preventive care in Bermuda are undertaken vigorously and the general health of the community is good. Immunization programs exist for diphtheria, whooping cough, tetanus, poliomyelitis, and measles. Vaccination against smallpox is compulsory. No unusual communicable disease or severe epidemics have been recorded in the past few years. A successful diabetic program and the family limitation and birth control programs are being continued. The decrease in the number of births has continued annually since 1963.

As in any subtropical region, Bermuda is afflicted with a variety of insect pests. Most households, no matter how clean or how fumigated, may have ants and/or cockroaches and termites. These are kept under control by regular spraying under commercial contracts. Few mosquitoes are found on the island, due to the scarcity of standing fresh water, and mosquito-borne diseases have been eliminated. Small and harmless lizards, mostly chameleons, may enter houses but are often welcomed as scavengers of insects. Bermuda has no snakes and few household rodents.

The Department of Health monitors food operations of all hotels, restaurants, shops, food manufacturers, pasteurizing plants, dairy farms, and slaughterhouses. A close watch is kept on the quality of imported foods. The health standards of housing and sanitary engineering are supervised by the Bermuda Government. Garbage is collected once a week as are recyclables. Recycling at present is limited to aluminum cans and glass. Virtually all homes have septic tanks for sewage disposal, utilizing either brackish or fresh water. In the latter case, the supply is dependent on rainfall and may run short during droughts.

Preventive Measures

Few health hazards exist in Bermuda. Because the source of home water supply is rainwater stored in cisterns, the possibility of contamination always exists. Simple precautions and periodic testing of each water supply has made this problem minimal.

Foodstuffs available on the island present no health hazard. Milk from local dairies is safe. No unusual dangerous insects or animals are present, and the island is rabies free.

You can be severely sunburned during the summer, and standard precautions should be taken. The Portuguese man of-war abounds in the waters off Bermuda; its presence near shore depends on prevailing currents. Its sting produces serious but not fatal illness among swimmers. If you are stung, get immediate medical care.

No special treatment of raw fruits and vegetables is required. All milk is pasteurized. Some people add chlorine to the water in underground storage tanks.

The Bermuda Department of Health recommends that those coming to Bermuda be vaccinated against smallpox, diphtheria, tetanus, and whooping cough, but merely as a precautionary measure. Tuberculosis exists in Bermuda, but its incidence is decreasing and cases are rigidly controlled.

Those with respiratory ailments may suffer from the humid climate, which also seems to activate potential arthritis in those susceptible. Asthma and hay fever sufferers, however, will find some relief here. You need not bring any special medicines or drugs; any medication can be bought locally. It would be economical to stock up on any regular medications needed, however, as local pharmacy prices are high. Fluoride supplements are provided for all children over 6 months old at government expense, as part of a 25-year study.

NOTES FOR TRAVELERS

Passage, Customs & Duties

U.S. citizens entering Bermuda must present a U.S. passport or a certified U.S. birth certificate, and photo identification. The Consulate strongly recommends that visitors travel with a valid passport at all times. A U.S. driver's license or a voter registration card is not sufficient for entry into Bermuda. For additional information on entry requirements, travelers may contact the British Embassy at 3100 Massachusetts Avenue, N.W, Washington, D.C. 20008, telephone (202) 462-1340, or the British consulate in Atlanta, Boston, Chicago, Dallas, Los Angeles, New York or San Francisco; Internet: http://www.britain-info.org or the Bermuda Department of Immigration;http://www.immigration.bdagov.bm.

U.S. citizens who are taking prescription medication must inform Bermuda customs officials at the point of entry. Medicines must be in labeled containers. Travelers should carry a copy of the written prescription and a letter from the physician or pharmacist confirming the reason the medicine is prescribed.

Bermuda customs authorities may enforce strict regulations concerning temporary importation into or export from Bermuda of items such as animals, arms, ammunition and explosives, building sand, crushed rock, gravel, peat and synthetic potting media, foodstuffs (animal origin), fumigating substances, gaming machines, historic articles (relating to Bermuda), lottery advertisements and material, motorcycles, motor vehicles, obscene publications, organotin anti-fouling paint, plants, plant material, fruits and vegetables (living or dead, including seeds), pesticides, prescription drugs, prohibited publications, seditious publications, soil, VHF radios, radar and citizens band (CB) radios. For additional information on temporary admission, export and customs regulations and tariffs, please contact Bermuda Customs at telephone 1-441-295-4816, or email customs@bdagov.bm, or visit the Bermuda Customs web site at http://www.customs.gov.bm.U.S. citizens may register with the Consular Section of the U.S. Consulate General located at Crown Hill, 16 Middle Road, Devonshire DV03, telephone 1-441-295-1342, where they may also obtain updated information on travel and security in Bermuda. Office hours for American Citizens Services are 8:30 a.m.-11:30 a.m., Monday through Thursday, except Bermudian and U.S. holidays. American citizens in need of after-hours emergency assistance may call the duty officer at telephone 1-441-235-3828.

Pets

Bermuda has no quarantine restriction, for pets arriving on the island, but an animal entry permit from the Bermuda Department of Agriculture is required. Failure to satisfy all requirements for this permit can result in the animal being refused entry, and there are no facilities at the airport or elsewhere for storing animals while the permit is straightened out. Veterinarians are available in Bermuda, as is pet grooming. Fleas abound.

Firearms and Ammunition

Bermuda laws are extremely strict with regard to firearms and ammunition. No private firearms may be brought into Bermuda. There are no exceptions to this regulation.

Currency, Banking, and Weights and Measures

Bermuda's currency is on the decimal system; notes come in $100, $50, $20, $10, $5, $2 denominations, and metal coinage in $1, .25, .10, .05, and .01 issues. U.S. money, while not legal tender in Bermuda, is freely accepted by all trading establishments on a one-for-one basis, although the official exchange rate makes the Bermuda dollar worth slightly more than the U.S. dollar.

Most local concerns accept U.S. credit cards and many vendors take checks drawn on U.S. banks. No restrictions are placed on the importation of U.S. dollars, other currency, or travelers checks-the export of Bermudian currency requires a foreign exchange permit (usually granted) from the Bermuda Monetary Authority.

British Imperial standard weights and measures are in general used in Bermuda and many Bermudians habitually use American terms of measurement-but the Bermuda Government has adopted a policy of gradual shift to the metric system. Road signs and local gas pumps are metric.

LOCAL HOLIDAYS

Jan. 1	New Year's Day
Mar/Apr.	Good Friday*
Mar/Apr.	Easter*
May 24	Bermuda Day
June	Queen's Birthday*
Aug.2	Emancipation Day
Aug.	Somers Day*
Sept.3	Labor Day
Nov. 12	Remembrance Day
Dec. 25	Christmas Day
Dec. 26	Boxing Day

*Variable

RECOMMENDED READING

The following titles are provided as a general indication of the material published on this country:

Bermuda Travel Guide. New York: Macmillan, 1989.

Cancelino, Jesse, and Michael Strohofer. *Diving Bermuda*. Locust Valley, CA: Aqua Quest Publications, 1990.

Christmas, Rachel J., and Walter Christmas. *Fielding's Bermuda & the Bahamas Nineteen Ninety-Two*. New York: Fielding Travel Books, 1991.

Fodor, Eugene. *Fodor's Bermuda, 1991*. New York: McKay, 1991.

Fox, Larry, and Barbara Radin-Fox. *Romantic Island Getaways: The Caribbean, Bermuda & the Bahamas*. New York: Wiley, 1991.

LaBrucherie, Roger A. *Images of Bermuda*. Rev. ed. Pine Valley, CA: Imagenes Press, 1989.

Raine. *The Islands of Bermuda*. Edison, NJ: Hunter Publishing, 1990.

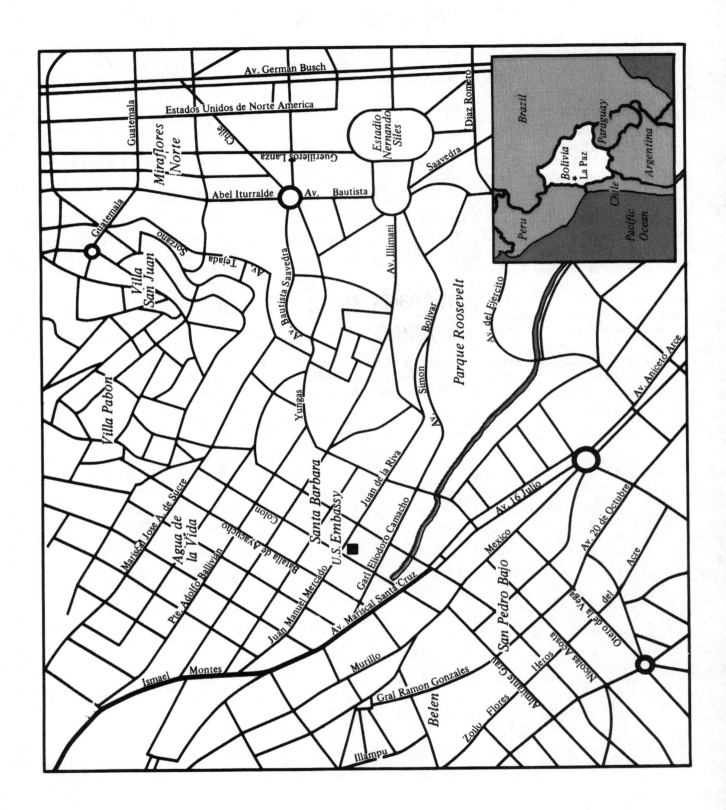

La Paz, Bolivia

BOLIVIA

Republic of Bolivia

Major Cities:
La Paz, Santa Cruz, Cochabamba, Sucre, Potosí

Minor Cities:
Oruro, Tarija, Trinidad

EDITOR'S NOTE

This chapter was adapted from the Department of State Post Report dated June 1996. Supplemental material has been added to increase coverage of minor cities, facts have been updated, and some material has been condensed. Readers are encouraged to visit the Department of State's web site at http://travel.state.gov/ for the most recent information available on travel to this country.

INTRODUCTION

BOLIVIA can be described as a land of contrasts. There are spectacular geographic contrasts—its natural beauty varying from the dramatically barren *altiplano*, to the snowcapped Andean mountains, to the lush jungles of the Amazon lowlands. Its chief cities, which lie in the *altiplano*, are some of the highest in the world, and Lake Titicaca, also situated on this two-and-a-half-mile-high plateau, is the largest freshwater lake in all of South America.

Furthermore, Bolivia is endowed with some of the richest mineral resources in the world. An international leader in tin production, it also mines copper, silver, tungsten, bismuth, antimony, and zinc. But despite these mineral riches, Bolivia is one of the poorest countries in Latin America; most Bolivians live by subsistence farming, raising sugarcane, potatoes, corn, wheat, and rice.

The people of Bolivia are predominantly Indian. They descend from the Aymara, who produced a highly advanced culture between the seventh and the 10th centuries, and from the Quechua-speaking Incas, one of the world's greatest imperial dynasties. The Spaniards arrived from Peru in 1535 to conquer Bolivia, and during most of the colonial period kept it as a dependency of the viceroyalty of Lima. Independence was established in 1825.

MAJOR CITIES

La Paz

La Paz, the de facto capital of Bolivia, is in the west-central part of the country, in a deep canyon about 60 miles south of Lake Titicaca. At about 12,500 feet, it is the highest capital city in the world and has a metropolitan population of about 1.5 million.

La Paz was founded in 1548 by the Spanish conquistadors, who chose the site as a halfway station for the llama pack trains bearing silver ore from Potosí to Lima. After Bolivia achieved independence, La Paz grew to be the commercial and financial center of the country. Although Sucre remains the constitutional capital, all government offices except the Supreme Court are in La Paz.

The city's architecture is a mixture of colonial and modern styles. The older sections, with their narrow cobblestone streets, contain some fine colonial buildings from the 16th century. Many high-rise office and apartment buildings have been completed or are under construction in the center of the city. Most business is conducted in small shops or in local markets run by colorfully clad Indian women.

Business activity within the city is mainly light industry, such as clothing and food manufacture, and commercial and financial enterprises, which support the country's mining economy.

One of the few level areas in La Paz is directly adjacent to Avenida 16 de Julio (El Prado) in the center of the city. Virtually all major streets radiate from the Prado, and some are so steep that they are difficult to negotiate.

Deeply eroded water courses cut through the city at a number of points, contributing to the irregular street pattern. The slopes of the canyon are rocky and bleak, except where eucalyptus trees have been planted. Although the *altiplano* countryside is barren, the magnificent snowcapped mountain peaks (particularly Mount Illimani) that overlook the canyon and the multicolored eroded hillsides provide a most spectacular setting for the city.

La Paz Airport, above the city on the *altiplano*, is the highest international airport in the world, at 13,300 feet above sea level. The descent from the *altiplano* provides a beautiful panorama of the entire canyon and city. Most of the year, particularly during "winter," the air is crystal clear and the sky is a magnificent blue.

Clothing

Temperatures in La Paz are not extremely hot or cold. Spring and fall clothing may be worn all year. Temperatures vary considerably in the sun or in the shade. Although lightweight clothing may be comfortable in sunshine, temperature drops are sudden in the shade.

During winter—May through August—a light winter coat is worn in the morning and evening. With the sun, daytime temperatures become quite warm, especially at midday. During rainy weather a raincoat (preferably with a zip-in lining), boots, and umbrella are needed. Warm bathrobes or sweatsuits and slippers are comfortable at home during mornings and evenings.

Except for fur and wool items, clothing in La Paz is expensive, hard to find, and usually behind U.S. styles. Shoes in La Paz (except for Italian imports) are poorly made, wide, and expensive. Due to steep and very slippery sidewalks, low-heeled, rubber-soled shoes are needed.

Some good seamstresses and tailors in La Paz copy fashions from photographs. Fabrics (including British wool imports) are available but at

© Stephanie Colasanti/Corbis. Reproduced by permission.

Aerial view of La Paz, Bolivia

higher prices, making it cheaper to buy material in the U.S.

Men wear medium-weight suits all year. Some men wear vests or sweaters with their jackets on cooler days. A good supply of shirts, shoes, underwear, socks, and accessories should be brought from the U.S. as well as lightweight clothing and sportswear.

Clothing worn in the U.S. in early spring and fall is worn by women year round in La Paz. Skirts and sweaters, as well as basic medium-weight suits and dresses that can be dressed up or down are best. Three-piece suits and dresses with jackets are practical, since they can be varied to suit temperatures. It is advisable to bring shoes, undergarments, purses, and sportswear from the U.S. These items are expensive and hard to find. Sweaters are essential and available locally. Pantsuits, slacks, and jeans are seen everywhere and are worn for casual wear to provide warmth

in unheated buildings. Some summer clothes, including a bathing suit, are needed for trips to warmer climates.

In general, children's clothing in La Paz resembles what is worn in Washington, DC in the fall. Emphasis should be on layered clothing that can be added or subtracted according to temperature changes, rather than on extra heavy clothing. All types of clothing for babies and some children's clothing are available in La Paz. Locally made clothing is inexpensive. Imports are limited and expensive. Dress for school-age children is informal. Girls wear jeans, slacks, skirts, sweaters, and dresses to school. Boys wear jeans, slacks, and shirts without ties. Both need windbreakers or jackets, sweaters, raincoats, and sturdy shoes. Children use lightweight jackets, sweaters, or sweatshirts almost daily. Locally made blouses and shirts and velour sweatshirts are well-made and can be bought at reasonable prices.

Food

Availability of most foodstuffs is good, through there are occasional shortages of basic and specialty items in the marketplace. Processed food in La Paz costs much more than in the U.S. since many goods are imported. Stocks are less varied and almost no frozen foods exist. Major food sources in La Paz are local shops, open-air markets, and a supermarket in Obrajes. Markets sell fresh produce, meats (beef, pork, lamb, and poultry), fresh fish (especially trout from Lake Titicaca and tropical fish from Cochabamba), and dairy products. The wide variety of fruits and vegetables is of good quality and reasonably priced. Meat is not cut U.S. style, varies in quality, and supply is sometimes limited. In addition to open-air markets, small shops and several supermarkets stock expensive canned and packaged items and specialty shops carry good quality, expensive cheeses and other imports. Although called "supermarkets," these stores only slightly resemble U.S. chains.

Reconstituted pasteurized milk, butter, and limited cheeses are available. Locally canned fruits and vegetables are expensive and of lower-than-average quality.

Meats and vegetables require longer cooking in La Paz due to altitude. Pressure cookers save time and energy and tenderize tougher meat cuts. Cakes and other pastries require adjustments in ingredients and baking time. Although local cooks are familiar with high-altitude cooking, Americans find the *Andean Cookbook*, written in Spanish and English, very useful.

The wine industry in Bolivia is just being developed, but a couple of local wineries are marketing some good wines.

Supplies & Services

La Paz has several adequate dry cleaners and prices are reasonable, but to rid clothes of strong cleaning fluid odors, they must be aired. A few laundries are available, but most laundry is done at home by maids or laundresses.

Men's tailoring costs about the same as in the U.S. but quality is somewhat lower. Good quality women's tailoring is available. Fair shoe repair and leather service is available and costs compare with those in the U.S.

La Paz has good barbers and beauticians who offer all standard services at moderate prices.

Electrical and mechanical repairs vary in quality. Prices depend on parts availability. Labor costs are reasonable; quality work is rare. It is advisable to check and repair electrical and mechanical items before coming to La Paz. Automobile body service is very satisfactory.

Film developing is available but of poor quality, high cost, and not all films can be processed. Camera and watch repairs can be made here.

Religious Activities

Most churches in Bolivia are Roman Catholic. Services are usually conducted in Spanish. An English mass is said every Saturday at the Santa Rosa Church in La Florida, and La Paz Community Church, a nondenominational Protestant church, has services in English every Sunday. Most major Protestant denominations have at least one Spanish-speaking church in La Paz. The Church of Jesus Christ of Latter-Day Saints (Mormon) has several Spanish-speaking branches in the capital and other Bolivian cities. The headquarters of the Andes South Mission is in La Paz. The Jewish community in La Paz holds religious services at two synagogues, and also maintains a school.

Domestic Help

Virtually all foreigners find domestics necessary due to marketing difficulties and the extra time needed to prepare and cook food at the high altitude. A combination maid/cook is generally sufficient for a couple with one or two children in a small house. Many Americans with more than two children employ a cook and a general maid or houseboy.

Everyone with gardens needs a part-time gardener.

The salaries for domestics are reasonable. The employer provides meals, uniforms, medical care, and lodging for live-in servants. Local law requires an extra month's pay as a Christmas bonus and a patriotic bonus paid in July. Domestics are entitled to 10 days of paid vacation per year. If mutually acceptable, extra pay may be given in lieu of vacation.

Domestics vary in efficiency and dependability, but all need training. During a three-month probationary period, an employee may be terminated without notice or compensation. After this period, 15 days' discharge notice or 15 days' pay are required. When employees are discharged after 12 months' service they can receive a longevity bonus equal to 15 days' pay for each year of employment.

The prospective employer pays for medical checkups (which include a chest X-ray) before hiring domestics. All employees sign a work contract.

Education

Most American children living in La Paz attend the American Cooperative School in the residential suburb of Calacoto. The school also sponsors a kindergarten and pre-kindergarten at the same location. In 1994, the school had 500–600 students, 25% American, 55% Bolivian, and 20% third country nationals. The school had 60 full-time teachers, 80% of these teachers were American. The student-teacher ratio was less than 25 students per teacher. An American director supervises American high-school and elementary school principals, and the teaching staff. Instruction is in English, secondary-level courses compare to college preparatory courses in U.S. schools. Spanish is taught as a foreign language.

The American Cooperative School has maintained a good rating and is accredited by the Southern Association of Colleges and Schools. School runs from mid-August to late May,

Skyscraper in Cochabamba, Bolivia

Cory Langley. Reproduced by permission.

with the usual holidays and vacations. The school also runs a six-week summer school offering a variety of courses, including remedial math and English classes, Spanish, sports, and others. Special education resources are also available at the school.

In addition to the regular curriculum, several extracurricular activities are offered. Among these are student government, a school newspaper, intramural and interscholastic sports program, drama, forensics, Knowledge Bowl, astronomy, photography, the Cultural Convention, and a jazz band. Various Boy and Girl Scout troops sponsored by the American community also use school facilities.

School facilities include modern buildings, housing science laboratories, auditorium with stage, cafeteria, library, audiovisual center, gymnasium, all-purpose room, sports field, volleyball and basketball courts, and shower and dressing rooms.

There are several other schools available in La Paz, all opening in February or March and running to late October or early November. The American Institute is a coeducational school operated by Methodist missionaries. It has regular primary

and secondary grades and also offers a three-year commercial course. Classes are held in Spanish, and English is taught as a foreign language.

St. Andrew's is a Catholic-administered, nonsectarian school with a U.S.-trained Bolivian headmaster. Classes are taught in Spanish.

Franco Boliviano is a French coed school, supported partly by the French Embassy. Classes are conducted in French with Spanish and English taught as foreign languages.

San Calixto and La Salle are Catholic coed schools; classes are taught in Spanish with English as a foreign language.

School of the Sacred Heart is a coed school directed by a French mother superior. Classes are in Spanish, with French and English taught as foreign languages.

The German community in La Paz directs and supports nonsectarian Mariscal Braun. Classes are in both Spanish and German.

Kindergartens are maintained by the English Catholic College, the Mariscal Braun School. Several private kindergartens, not connected with schools or institutions, are also available. Little English, if any, is taught in private kindergartens. A Spanish-speaking Montessori school is available for preschool children.

Private instruction in photography, art, music, folk dancing, and ballet is available. The American Cooperative School provides the community with a program of after school and evening sports and educational activities for both students and adults. Depending on demand and availability of teachers, these include photography, ballet, exercise, square dancing, handicrafts, business courses, language, and culture.

The German, American, and French binational centers periodically offer courses and lectures in various fields. Once each semester, a graduate-level course for credit is offered at the American Cooperative School through the University of Arkansas. For those with a working knowledge of Spanish, other special educational opportunities exist. The municipal government sponsors a cultural foundation (Casa Juvenil de la Cultura "Juancito Pinto") which offers music, folk dancing, and puppetry to children, free of charge.

Recreation

Bolivia's varied climate is ideal for outdoor sports. The elevation at La Paz adds a sense of novelty to participation in sports such as skiing, golf, and tennis. Tennis balls are depressurized especially for the high altitude, and 300-yard drives on the golf course at La Paz are occasionally enjoyed by the competent player. Soccer is the national sport, but basketball and volleyball are sufficiently important to support national federations. The American Cooperative School's evening programs include a men's basketball league.

La Paz boasts the Mallasilla Golf Club, an 18-hole course with magnificent vistas, about 25 minutes from the city. There are tennis clubs, a rod and gun club, a bowling alley, and a glider club. The climate in the capital discourages swimming, but in warmer areas of the country swimming can be enjoyed.

Many Americans enjoy trout fishing in the areas surrounding La Paz. The trout of Lake Titicaca and nearby glacier lakes are of the salmon family. Catches in Lake Titicaca have been reported as weighing up to 28 pounds; however, fishing here has been poor in recent years due to netting, trapping, and dynamiting by commercial fishermen. The small glacier lakes, about three hours from La Paz, produce rainbow trout weighing up to four pounds. Fly fishing is found two-to-three hours from La Paz in the streams of the lowland valleys of the Yungas. Stream fishing is as effective as lake fishing, but is more difficult due to the rugged terrain

and fast waters. Better fishing may be found farther from La Paz, but reaching the least-fished waters requires four-wheel-drive vehicles or transportation by air. Other tropical varieties of fish are found in the warmer waters of the Beni and Sata Cruz.

Opportunities for partridge, duck, and wild fowl shooting are available year round on the eastern shore of Lake Titicaca, and at certain other high-altitude lakes. The Beni area in the lowlands offers big-game hunting possibilities, including wild hog, puma, ocelot, anteater, deer, and alligator. Hunting and fishing licenses are required in Bolivia. Bolivia has a long list of protected animals and birds with which one should be familiar. No special clothing nor dogs are required for hunting. Hunters or fishing enthusiasts should bring their own gear.

Sailing on Lake Titicaca, the world's highest navigable lake, is rewarding. Actually it is two lakes, separated by a narrow strait. The lower lake—Huinamarca—is much smaller and shallower than Upper Chucuito, a veritable inland sea, with water horizons and persistent swells. Visibility is generally almost unlimited. The most consistent winds and sunniest weather occur on winter afternoons. Summer, though generally warmer, is characterized by light, variable winds, and frequent rain showers.

Chacaltaya, site of the highest ski run in the world at 17,400 feet, offers a spectacular course for expert skiers on a glacier during the October through April season. When snow cover is heavy enough to fill gullies in upper headwalls, experts will find very challenging skiing. The primitive, 5,000-foot cable tow operates on Saturdays, Sundays, and holidays when there is skiing. The slopes adjacent to deep precipices are wide and steep, with varying and unpredictable snow conditions. Chacaltaya is about a 90-minute drive from La Paz; the Andino Club provides transportation from La Paz. A four-wheel-drive vehicle is recom-

mended for driving the steep dirt road, although normal cars can manage under good conditions. A day lodge serves soft drinks and some snacks.

Bolivia offers excellent opportunities for mountain climbing and hiking. Two major cordilleras, the Cordillera Real and Cordillera de las Tres Cruces, are accessible by mining roads. The third significant cordillera, Apolobamba, is harder to reach. Bolivia's highest peak is Nevada Ancohuma (21,489 feet) near the Peruvian border. Other mountains over 20,000 feet include Illampu, Sajama, Illimani, Huayna Potosí, and Chachacomani. Hundreds of peaks in the 17,500- to 18,500-foot class are excellent for experienced climbers. Although most summits have been reached, many new routes are possible, and climbing is still very challenging. Backpacking is another popular pastime, and Bolivia offers superb opportunities. Mountain hiking is aided by a network of Indian paths and ancient trails on the dry western slopes, and a less extensive network on the wet and steep eastern side. It is on these eastern slopes, however, that hikers in good condition find excellent opportunities for walks of from two days to a week through magnificent scenery, often over trails originally engineered by the Incas. Stretches of these well-designed ancient roads remain in use today.

Good one-day rock and ice climbs can be found in the Khala Cruz-Charquini-Sora Patilla group south of Huayna Potosí and on nearby 18,700-foot Cerro Milluni and its rocky satellites. Climbers and walkers should bring their own equipment to Bolivia.

La Paz has a glider club. Some hang gliding has been done, but thin air makes this sport difficult and dangerous. Andean air currents offer some of the world's most challenging and highest gliding for experienced pilots, but this area is not considered suitable for novices. An equestrian club offers boarding facilities for privately owned horses and classes in horsemanship. Another club offers rentals and lessons. Periodically, public horse races are held.

By far, the most popular spectator sport in Bolivia is football, or soccer. Several Bolivian teams are often in international competition. Other spectator sports include wrestling, basketball, and an occasional bullfight.

Bolivia has many interesting tour sites. A popular place is Copacabana, a resort town 88 miles from La Paz on Lake Titicaca. It is noted especially for the Shrine of the Virgin of Copacabana, to which many Bolivians make a pilgrimage. Copacabana can be reached by car from La Paz in about four hours. It also is possible to take a hydrofoil from Huatajata (a town on Lake Titicaca) to Copacabana. Day trips by motorboat to the Isles of the Sun and Moon, famous in Incan mythology, can be made from Copacabana.

En route to the western shore of Lake Titicaca, 60 miles from La Paz, are the ruins of the advanced Aymara culture of Tiwanaku, which can be reached by car from La Paz in about two-and-a-half hours.

Situated 95 miles from La Paz at 8,700 feet, Sorata provides relief from the high altitude of the capital and the *altiplano*. Sorata is in a valley at the foot of Illampu, one of the highest mountains in Bolivia. There are some interesting caves that can be explored nearby. The trip takes roughly four hours, one way, by car. In the vicinity of Sorata, along the east shore of Lake Titicaca, is a tremendous slough that provides some of the best duck and goose shooting in Bolivia.

The Yungas are a series of deep valleys sloping from the cordillera into the eastern jungle region. They can be reached by car in three-to-four hours. Landslides may block roads during rainy months. The road from La Paz to the Yungas crosses the eastern cordillera through a 15,000-foot pass, then drops down rapidly into lush, semitropical valleys in less than 50 miles, one of the most spectacular sights in the country. Hotel accommodations are available at Coroico, Chulumani, and a few other points.

North of Lake Titicaca in Peru is Cuzco, center of the ancient Inca civilization and famed site of the Incas' last stand. Cuzco and nearby Machu Picchu, the "lost city of the Incas," are sight-seeing attractions for tourists from all over the world. The trip from La Paz to Cuzco by air takes 50 minutes.

Arica, a Chilean seaport 20 minutes away by air or 12 hours by train, is a good change of scene for those who enjoy the seashore.

The tropical lowlands facing Brazil provide another interesting change from La Paz. These areas are interlaced with large rivers, are heavily forested, and abound in many varieties of wild game. Driving trips to some parts of the area are possible but require elaborate preparation and four-wheel-drive vehicles.

The region around Santa Cruz is the fastest developing area in Bolivia. Santa Cruz can be reached by road and by air. Northwest of Santa Cruz is the department of Beni, a sparsely populated region with great potential for agricultural development and increased cattle production. The region is traversed by the major rivers in Bolivia and offers excellent fishing. These tropical lowlands facing Brazil provide a pleasant change from La Paz. They are interlaced with large rivers, and are heavily forested, with a large variety of game. Road trips during dry months to some areas are possible but require elaborate arrangements and four-wheel-drive cars.

Entertainment

Adequate entertainment is available in most of the large cities. La Paz has a few nightclubs, and the most popular among these are the discotheques. Others have dance bands, and most feature additional entertainment on weekends. Americans as well as Bolivians enjoy the *peñas* or clubs which specialize in authentic folk singing, dancing, and art. These clubs have shows on Fri-

day and Saturday nights, and serve drinks and meals. A visit to one of these *peñas* is a good way to be introduced to Bolivian folklore.

Some unique folklore festivals highlight the year in La Paz. In January, a week-long fair, "Alacitas," centers around Ekeko, the Aymaran talisman of prosperity and good fortune. Miniatures, from clothes to buses, are bought (and given) with the hope that what they represent will be obtained soon. Carnival is celebrated with parades (a very charming one features children in costumes) and dancing in La Paz. "Jesús, el Gran Poder" is honored in June in La Paz with a parade of dancers and musicians. Year round, small pueblos in the outskirts of La Paz stage interesting festivals.

Several restaurants have good quality food, service, and atmosphere that Americans normally associate with dining out.

Movie theaters in La Paz are inexpensive and show many American films as well as films from Argentina, Brazil, Italy, and France. All films are in the original soundtrack with Spanish subtitles. Films make their debut in La Paz a year or more after their release.

Video clubs recently have become very popular. The variety is not the best, but tapes can be rented for very reasonable prices. Local clubs carry Beta and VHS tapes.

Santa Cruz

Santa Cruz, the seat of early Spanish culture, was founded in the mid-16th century, and reestablished in 1595 by settlers from Paraguay. With a population of 1,110,000 (2000 est.), it is the second largest city in Bolivia. Its economy is based on exports of oil and agricultural products.

The people of Santa Cruz call themselves Crucenos or Cambas. They are staunchly proud of their land and of their heritage. The Crucenos are innately polite and hospitable, slow to anger, generous, and proud. Typical of the people of tropical climates in Latin America, Crucenos maintain a very active social calendar, and are extremely warm, friendly, and outgoing.

Education

The Santa Cruz Cooperative School is a coeducational, day, school for pre-kindergarten through grade 12. The school was originally established to serve the children of the Gulf Oil Company personnel. When Gulf Oil was nationalized, many Americans left Bolivia. The school continued as a cooperative, and over the years, the percentage of host country students has increased to a large majority. Currently about 10% of the students at SCCS are American, 65% are Bolivian, and 25% are from other various nations. Facilities include two science laboratories, a computer lab, a new library/media center, and a comprehensive sports/fine arts complex. Classes follow a U.S. school year and a U.S. curriculum, granting both American and Bolivian secondary diplomas.

Cochabamba

Cochabamba is Bolivia's third largest city. Its population is approximately 377,260 (2000 est.). This valley city is 8,430 feet above sea level. Cochabamba was founded in 1574 and was originally called Villa de Oropeza. The city has many historical buildings and is an important alpaca handicraft center and vacation spot.

Education

Cochabamba Cooperative School is a coeducational school for pre-kindergarten through grade 12. A U.S. curriculum is used for its 100 students.

The American International School of Bolivia offers the International Baccalaureate(IB) as well as U.S. and Bolivian degrees. It receives a State Department grant and has about 100 students in kindergarten through grade 12.

The Carachipampa Christian School is run by the Andes Evangelical Mission and has about 100 students kindergarten through grade 12.

Sucre

Sucre is the judicial center and constitutional capital of Bolivia. Its population is 152,000 (2000 est.). The city lies in a mountain valley on the eastern slope of the Andes, 9,320 feet above sea level. A learning center for centuries and the city where Bolivia proclaimed independence, Sucre is now a university town. It offers large monasteries, fine churches, exquisite colonial architecture, colonial paintings, and Old World art collections.

Potosí

Potosí, at 4,000 meters (over 14,000 feet), is the highest city in the world. Today it is a mining town producing some silver and substantial amounts of tin, lead, and zinc, but in 1553 it was decreed an Imperial City by Charles V, Holy Roman Emperor and King of Spain, due to the discovery of silver here by the Spanish conquistadors in 1545. During the late 1500s, it was one of the largest cities in the world (population 160,000), and the name Potosí became synonymous with the idea of untold riches. It is estimated that over a billion dollars' worth of silver was extracted from the Cerro Rico Mountain overlooking Potosí. By the 18th century the silver mines were depleted and the city was in decline. In 2000, Potosí had a population of 114,092.

However, the aura of its fabulous past still lingers and can be seen in some of the colonial architecture, much of which is baroque in design. The colonial Art Museum in Sucre contains detailed color drawings of Potosí in its prime. One of the chief attractions and places of renown in Potosí is the Casa de la Moneda, or mint, established to control the minting of colonial wealth. The restored building has been called the most important monument of civilian building in all of South America. It houses an important collection of colonial paintings, sculptures, and archaeological and minting materials.

OTHER CITIES

ORURO, with a population of 125,240 (2000 est.), is 120 miles southeast of La Paz, situated at an altitude of 12,160 feet. Capital of Oruro Department, the city is also the country's railroad center. Founded early in the 17th century to exploit the nearby silver deposits, Oruro nearly became a ghost town in the 19th century when silver production declined. However, other mineral resources, primarily wolfram, copper, and tin are now mined and are the basis of the city's economy. Due to the altitude, agriculture is almost nonexistent. A technical university was founded in Oruro in 1892. A major tin refinery is located here. An outstanding celebration takes place here; day-long parades feature the world-famous *diabladas* (devil dancers), bears, and *morenadas*, creating an outstanding display of folkloric costumes and *altiplano* music. Oruro is a major hub for Bolivia's railway system.

TARIJA, at an altitude of 6,398 feet, is located in a fertile Andean valley, about 160 miles southeast of Potosí. The area has rich soil and a moderate climate, making the region famous for its vineyards and orchards. Vegetables, wheat, potatoes, corn, and other crops are grown near Tarija. However, due to the city's remote location, they are consumed by the local population. Founded in 1574, the city's commercial growth lagged due to a lack of communications. With a population of nearly 403,000 (2000), Tarija is known for its *Vendimia*, or grape harvest festival, held each February. Residents of the city are noted for their outdoor religious processions. A university, founded in 1966, is also located in Tarija.

TRINIDAD, capital city of the Beni Department, is located in northeastern Bolivia, about 250 miles north of La Paz. The city has a sugar refinery and also trades in sugarcane, rice, beef, and cotton. A busy commercial center, Trinidad has an airport and several roads leading to other cities. The city is the seat of the "Mariscal Jose Ballivian" Bolivian University.

COUNTRY PROFILE

Geography and Climate

Landlocked Bolivia shares borders on the north and east with Brazil, on the south with Argentina and Paraguay, on the southwest with Chile, and on the northwest with Peru. With an area of 420,000 square miles, Bolivia is about the size of Texas and California combined. The country has three well-defined geographic zones—the high plateau (*altiplano*); the temperate and semitropical valleys of the eastern mountain slopes (*yungas*); and the tropical lowlands (*llanos*) of the Amazon River Basin. Each of these regions differs from the others in a significant way.

Lying between the main eastern and western ridges of the Andean Mountains, the *altiplano* is 500 miles long and 80 miles wide, at altitudes varying between 12,000 and 14,000 feet. It is one of the world's highest inhabited regions. Lake Titicaca is situated in the *altiplano* and straddles Bolivia's border with Peru in the north. It has an area of 3,500 square miles with depths of up to 700 feet, and maintains a constant temperature of 55°F. The land surrounding the lake is the most agriculturally productive and heavily populated section of the *altiplano*, with a population density of more than 125 per square mile in some localities. Most of the region's inhabitants are Aymara and Quechua Indians, who maintain a primitive subsistence agricultural and grazing economy. Principal animals are sheep, alpacas, llamas, and the fast-disappearing vicunas. The rich mineral deposits that form the backbone of the Bolivian economy are found on

Cory Langley. Reproduced by permission.

Going to the market in Bolivia

the *altiplano* and in nearby mountainous areas. Several cities (La Paz, the capital; Oruro; and Potosí) and industries are located here.

To the east and northeast of the *altiplano* lie the *yungas*, the temperate and semitropical valleys. Cochabamba, Sucre, and Tarija are major cities in the more arid mountain valleys to the southeast of the capital. These areas vary in altitude from 1,600 feet to 9,000 feet above sea level and have a moderately warm and humid climate. This region is mainly agricultural—chief crops are corn, barley, coffee, cacao, citrus fruits, and sugarcane.

The *llanos* cover more than two-thirds of the country. Through the *llanos* flow the major tributaries of the Amazon: the Mamoré, Beni,

Ichilo, Itenes, and Madre de Dios rivers. With the exception of the Santa Cruz area, the lowlands are sparsely populated and are only now being developed. This fertile region offers excellent possibilities for agriculture and stock-raising. Santa Cruz (Bolivia's second largest city), Trinidad, Riberalta, and Cobija are the principal cities in the lowlands.

Bolivia lies entirely within the tropics, but the extreme differences in elevation—as low as 300 feet along the Brazilian border and more than 21,000 feet on the highest mountain peaks—produce a great variety of climatic conditions. These, coupled with a wide diversity in soils, result in vegetation ranging from the sparse cover of scrub in the semiarid highlands to lush rain forests in the abundantly watered plains of the east.

La Paz has only two seasons: rainy and dry. The rainy season begins in December and continues through March; some rain falls almost daily during this period. Even in the rainy season, the humidity is very low. Average annual rainfall is 20 inches. The climate is cool, but the warm sunshine raises the temperature during the daytime, making outdoor parties and activities at midday very pleasant.

Population

Reliable demographic data is difficult to obtain in Bolivia. Bolivia's estimated population is about 8.1 million (2000), with an estimated 1.5 million people inhabiting the capital city of La Paz. Population density, the lowest in Latin America, is approximately 7 per square mile, but varies greatly by area.

An estimated 55% of the people are Aymara- and Quechua-speaking, descended from peoples of pre-Inca cultures. Virtually all Indians live in rural areas or villages. The hard daily life of the Indian population is occasionally brightened by colorful fiestas which often last for days. Bolivians of mixed Indian and European ancestry (*mestizos*) comprise 30% of the population and work mostly in small businesses, factories, and government offices. *Mestizos* generally speak Spanish as a first language, but often know at least one native language.

The rest of the population is of European descent and fill most professional and management positions in Bolivian society. The most recent large-scale immigration of Europeans to Bolivia took place before and during World War II. More recently, there have been smaller immigrations of Taiwanese, Japanese, Koreans, and Mennonites to the underpopulated tropical lowlands of Santa Cruz.

Although Roman Catholicism is the recognized religion of Bolivia and 95% of the population is Catholic, other religions are freely practiced.

History

Between A.D. 600 and 900, Aymara Indians living at the southern end of Lake Titicaca produced an advanced native civilization known as Tiahuanaco. In about 1200, the Quechua-speaking Incas invaded the area and incorporated much of what is now Bolivia under their control, until the Spaniards arrived from Peru and conquered Bolivia in 1535.

The area became a dependency of the viceroyalty of Lima, and the principal cities were Chuquisaca (now Sucre), the seat of the Audlencia de Charcas, La Paz, and Potosí, for many years the largest city in the Western Hemisphere. The Bolivian silver mines were a major source of the wealth of the Spanish Empire. As Spanish royal authority weakened during the Napoleonic Wars, Bolivia swarmed with secret patriotic societies. Although independence was proclaimed in 1809, 16 years of struggle followed before the Republic (named for the patriot and liberator, Simón Bolívar) was established on August 6, 1825.

The 19th century saw one military leader after another succeed to power, frequently by force. This political disorder and instability impeded social and economic progress. A disastrous war with Chile (1879–84) caused Bolivia to lose its seacoast and the rich nitrate fields and copper mines of the region around Antofagasta, Chile. A major aim of Bolivian foreign policy since then has been to recover a port on the Pacific coast.

Government

Political stability improved during the early 20th century, although the Chaco War with Paraguay (1932-35) exhausted Bolivia economically and discredited its traditional ruling classes. A protracted period of political unrest ended in the revolution of April 9, 1952, which put in power the Nationalist Revolutionary Movement (MNR). The MNR introduced universal suffrage, agrarian and educational reform, and nationalized the three largest private tin enterprises under the state mining corporation, COMIBOL.

Divisions within the MNR and growing opposition to its rule led to its overthrow in November 1964 by a military junta. The Ovando-Barrientos junta retained the MNR's major reforms. In August 1966, the junta leader was elected president. On September 26, 1969, the military overthrew the president and formed a civilian-military government.

From 1969 to 1982, Bolivia experienced several coups and rapid changes of government. The first two years of the UDP (Popular Democratic Unity, 1982-85) were marked by national disasters, a deteriorating economy, and lack of political consensus. The fragile government was teetering by 1984, threatened by political extremists and undercut by its lack of coherency. The president, responding to an initiative of the Catholic Church, began talks with the opposition, and, as a result, curtailed his term, calling for elections in 1985.

Since then, despite continual changes in players, elections have been held peacefully and on schedule.

The 1967 constitution, revised in 1994, provides for balanced executive, legislative, and judicial powers. The traditionally strong executive, however, tends to overshadow the Congress, whose role is generally limited to debating and approving legislation initiated by the executive. The judiciary, consisting of the Supreme Court and departmental and lower courts, has long been riddled with corruption and inefficiency. Through revisions to the constitution in 1994, and subsequent laws, the government has initiated potentially far-reaching reforms in the judicial system and processes.

Bolivia's nine departments received greater autonomy under the Administrative Decentralization law of 1995, although principal departmental officials are still appointed by the central government. Bolivian cities and towns are governed by elected mayors and councils. The Popular Participation Law of April 1994, which distributes a significant portion of national revenues to municipalities for discretionary use, has enabled previously neglected communities to make striking improvements in their facilities and services.

The Bolivian flag consists of three horizontal bands in red, yellow, and green.

Arts, Science, Education

Education, from primary to postsecondary, is currently the subject of much debate in Bolivia, focusing on how to provide educational opportunities for all and still maintain quality.

Bolivia has nine state universities and eight private universities. In addition to their usual curriculum, the universities serve as centers of scientific activities with programs in space sciences, geology, mineralogy, genetics, and other sciences. The University of San Andrés Observatory at Chacaltaya (near La Paz) is world famous for its work on cosmic rays.

The National Symphony Orchestra and the Coral Nova choir, based in La Paz, give several concerts a year. A national ballet company performs occasionally and visiting music and dance performers are sponsored by the Casa de la Cultura, the Centro Boliviano Americano, and other cultural institutions. There are also a Chamber Orchestra and a Youth Orchestra in La Paz. Folk music can be enjoyed at the various folklore nightclubs called *peñas* on weekends and some week nights at programs of the Centro Boliviano Americano. The Municipal Theater offers various programs, including visiting artists, jazz groups, and other entertainers. These performances vary in quality, from very good to mediocre.

Art exhibits are held in the National Museum of Art, the Casa de la Cultura, the University of San Andrés, the Centro Boliviano Americano, the lobby of the newspaper *El Diario*, and in a number of private galleries, and commercial art galleries in the major cities. La Paz has several museums. The National Museum of Archaeology and the Diez de Medina Museum both house good collections of Inca and pre-Inca artifacts. The National Folklore Museum and the Fine Arts Museum are located in beautifully restored colonial palaces. The latter contains interesting examples of colonial art, but the finest collections are in Sucre and Potosí.

A wealth of handicraft art is found in colorful Indian markets or urban boutiques in Bolivia, ranging from the crude and primitive to the refined. Gold and silver jewelry is a good buy; Bolivian goldsmiths can make jewelry in any design at a cost below that in the U.S. A great deal of work is done with pewter and in a metal similar to silver, and the products are handsome. Good quality sweaters, coats, scarves, and rugs of sheepskin, llama, and alpaca are reasonably priced.

Commerce and Industry

Since 1985, the Government of Bolivia has been implementing a far-reaching program of macroeconomic stabilization and structural reform aimed at restoring price stability, creating conditions for sustained growth, and alleviating poverty. Important components of these structural reform measures include the capitalization of state enterprises and strengthening of the country's financial system.

The most important recent structural changes in the Bolivian economy have involved the capitalization of numerous public sector enterprises. (Capitalization in the Bolivian context is a form of privatization where investors acquire a 50% stake and management control of public enterprises in return for a commitment to undertake capital expenditures equivalent to the enterprise's net worth). Parallel legislative reforms have locked into place market-oriented policies, especially in the hydrocarbon and mining sectors, that have encouraged private investment. Foreign investors are accorded national treatment, and foreign ownership of companies enjoys virtually no restrictions in Bolivia. The privatization program has generated commitments of $1.7 billion in foreign direct investment over the period 1996-2002.

In 1996, three units of the Bolivian state oil corporation (YPFB) involved in hydrocarbon exploration, production, and transportation were capitalized. The capitalization of YPFB allowed agreement to be reached on the construction of a gas pipeline to Brazil. A priority in the development strategy for the sector is the expansion of export markets for natural gas. The Brazil pipeline contract projects natural gas exports of 9 million metric cubic meters per day (mmcmd) by the end of 2000, increasing to over 30 mmcmd by 2004. The government plans to position Bolivia as a regional hub for exporting hydrocarbons.

By May 1996, three of the four Bolivian banks that had experienced difficulties in 1995 were recapitalized and restructured under new ownership with support from the Bolivian Government's Special Fund for Strengthening the Financial System (FONDESIF), which helped restore confidence in the banking system. In November 1996, the Bolivian Congress approved a comprehensive pension reform that replaces the old pay-as-you-go system by a system of privately managed, individually funded retirement accounts, and the new system began operations in May 1997.

Bolivia's trade with neighboring countries is growing, in part because of several regional preferential trade agreements it has negotiated. Bolivia is a member of the Andean Community and has free trade with other member countries--Peru, Ecuador, Colombia, and Venezuela. Bolivia began to implement an association agreement with MERCOSUR (Southern Cone Common Market) in March 1997. The agreement provides for the gradual creation of a free trade area covering at least 80% of the trade between the parties over a 10-year period. The U.S. Andean Trade Preference Act (ATPA) allows numerous Bolivian products to enter the United States free of duty on a unilateral basis. Tariffs have to be paid on clothing and leather products only.

The U.S. remains Bolivia's largest trading partner. In 1998, the U.S. exported $626 million of merchandise to Bolivia and imported $149 million, according to the World Trade Atlas of the Global Trade Information Service. Bolivia's major exports to the U.S. are tin, gold, jewelry, and wood products. Its major imports from the United States are computers, vehicles, wheat, and machinery.

Agriculture accounts for roughly 15% of Bolivia's GDP. The amount of land cultivated by modern farming techniques is increasing rapidly in the Santa Cruz area, where weather allows for two crops a year and soybeans are the major cash crop. The extraction of minerals and hydrocarbons accounts for another 10% of GDP. Bolivia exports natural gas to Brazil. Manufacturing represents less than 17% of GDP.

The Government of Bolivia remains heavily dependent on foreign assistance to finance development projects. Most payments to other governments have been rescheduled on several occasions since 1987 through the Paris Club mechanism. External creditors have been willing to do this because the Bolivian Government has generally achieved the monetary and fiscal targets set by IMF programs since 1987. Some countries have forgiven substantial amounts of Bolivia's bilateral debt.

Transportation

Jet service to and from the U.S. is available daily. Flights to Guayaquil (Ecuador), Cali (Colombia), and Asunción (Paraguay) are also possible. LAN Chile, and LAB (Lloyd Aéreo Boliviano) also fly to and from Santiago (Chile). Lufthansa Airlines has two flights a week to and from Lima (Peru). LAB, the national airline, has frequent flights to other major cities in Bolivia as well as international flights to Arica (Chile), Asunción, Cuzco (Peru), Caracas (Venezuela), Panama, Santiago, Rio de Janeiro (Brazil), Buenos Aires (Argentina), São Paulo (Brazil), Lima, and Miami. Argentine, Brazilian, and Paraguayan Airlines have flights to several Bolivian cities.

Train service is generally limited and slow. Trains run from La Paz to Antofagasta and Arica (Chile); and from La Paz to some interior cities and to Argentina. An interesting train trip is one between La Paz and Cochabamba. Many points in Bolivia can be reached only by car, truck, or bus over inferior roads, and many interesting and important areas are frequently inaccessible except by four-wheel-drive vehicles.

Cars move on the right in Bolivia. La Paz has few stop signs, and automatic and hand-operated traffic lights are erratic. Uphill traffic has the right-of-way; car horns are sounded to signal right-of-way at intersections. Most Bolivian drivers use no lights or only parking lights for night driving. Defensive driving means adjusting to hazardous conditions. Streets in La Paz are steep, narrow, and often slippery, particularly during the rainy season. Outside the city, most roads are unpaved, can be dangerous, and are sometimes impassable during the rainy season.

Bus and taxi service is erratic at best. Small buses, or *micros*, operate to the suburbs. They seat about 21 persons, and carry as many standees as possible. The large *littoral* buses are cheaper, but seldom used by Americans because they are slow

and overcrowded. Taxis must be hailed on the street (no call service) and can be identified by their orange license plates with a "T" prefix. *Trufi* taxis, following several set routes, operate from the suburbs to the city. These taxis are identified by flags on their bumpers. All taxis are collectives, so one usually must share a cab with others going in the same direction.

Communications

Telephone service within Bolivia is steadily improving, and direct-dialing between most major cities and between the U.S. and some major cities is possible. Empresa Nacional de Telecomunicaciónes (ENTEL) provides long-distance service to the U.S. A microwave system links La Paz, Oruro, Sucre, Potosí, Trinidad, Tarija, Cochabamba, and Santa Cruz, with calls made through an operator, but service is good. Calls to other parts of the country are reached through the long-distance operator. Telegraphic service is available to all foreign points. International airmail between Bolivia and the United States takes between five and eight days, and surface mail six to eight weeks.

La Paz has 18 AM and nine FM radio stations which broadcast in Spanish and in two Indian languages. Music programs include Bolivian and Latin music, American popular music, and some classical selections. Some stations specialize in covering sports events; others emphasize news or cultural programs. All stations currently tie into the government news broadcasts. A shortwave radio is essential for receiving American or English stations. The quality of shortwave and FM reception varies with location and ionospheric conditions, but is generally adequate. Several Americans operate ham radios in La Paz with satisfactory results.

Eleven television stations currently broadcast in La Paz; seven are privately owned and the one is owned by the government. The other three broadcast in the UHF band. All programming is in Spanish. A private cable company also offers English-language programming for an installation fee and a monthly charge.

Six daily newspapers are printed in Spanish in La Paz. The better papers contain fair coverage of international news along with extensive local coverage. No English-language newspapers are published in La Paz but U.S. newspapers can occasionally be found. Except for the Latin American editions of *Time* and *Newsweek*, American magazines are outdated and expensive in La Paz.

Several bookstores carry English-language books and paperbacks at prices about double those in the U.S. Records are also available here, but prices are high. La Paz has a municipal public library, used only for research. The library at the Centro Boliviano Americano lends books and magazines including works in English. The La Paz Book Club maintains a lending library also.

Health

The newcomer to Bolivia is sometimes apprehensive, often because of stories about serious altitude effects. Most of these stories are exaggerated. Altitude sickness symptoms are grouped under the term *soroche* and may include headaches, sleeplessness or sudden awakening, shortness of breath, loss of appetite, abdominal cramps, nausea or vomiting, chest pains, and dizziness. For most people these symptoms, if present at all, gradually decrease or disappear after the first few days. Many of the symptoms are due to dehydration; therefore, sufficient fluids should be taken. Humidifiers and vaporizers are also helpful. Newcomers are advised to rest for three days after arrival, eat only light meals, and not drink alcoholic beverages or smoke cigarettes for the first week.

You should make sure you consult with you doctor before making the trip to Bolivia, particularly if you have one of the following illnesses or conditions: sickle cell anemia or sickle cell trait, heart disease, lung disease, elevated cholesterol or blood pressure, diabetes, or asthma.

Respiratory infections such as colds, sinusitis, and bronchitis are relatively common. Colds are treated with rest, aspirin, and occasionally antihistamines. The most common complaint is nasal stuffiness and dryness, usually caused by the extreme dryness of the altitude rather than by allergies. Fungal skin infections are rare in dry climates. Severe sunburn and excessive skin dryness are the most troublesome skin disorders. Ultraviolet radiation is high; light-skinned persons should have no more than 15 minutes of direct or reflected exposure at one time. Some people report difficulty with contact lenses due to diminished atmospheric pressure and dry air; plenty of lubricating solution should be brought along.

Several good physicians and dentists—many trained in the U.S.—practice in La Paz. Hospitals and inpatient clinics, for the most part, are inadequate by U.S. standards. Travellers should carry a sufficient supply of medications, prescription and over-the-counter, along with first aid supplies.

Bolivia's sanitation procedures are poor, and sewage disposal is inefficient and inadequate. Purification of city water is not reliable, and few official inspection systems for water and food products exist. These conditions increase the incidence of intestinal disorders, especially during the December, January, and February rainy season. Flies transmit bacteria and amoebic cysts. Water for drinking, making ice cubes, brushing teeth, and rinsing vegetables must be filtered and then boiled for at least 20 minutes. For out-of-town trips, water should be treated with Globaline tablets.

Rabies exist here because many wild or loose dogs roam freely through the cities and countryside. Routing pre-exposure rabies vaccine is recommended. All animal bites and scratches should be reported immediately to a physician. Pets should be vaccinated against rabies, distemper, and parvo virus. Snakes and venomous insects are rare except in tropical areas.

NOTES FOR TRAVELERS

Passage, Customs & Duties

Commercial travel from U.S. to La Paz is by air. Service to Bolivia is available from Washington, New York, Miami, Houston, and New Orleans. Direct flights to La Paz via Panama take 10 to 15 hours, depending on point of departure. Surface travel to other places in Latin America and then overland to landlocked Bolivia is possible, but complicated and time consuming.

A valid U.S. passport is required to enter and depart Bolivia. U.S. citizens do not need a visa for a stay of one month or less (that period can be extended upon application to 90 days). Visitors for other purposes must obtain a visa in advance. U.S. citizens whose passports are lost or stolen in Bolivia must obtain a new passport and present it, together with a police report of the loss or theft, to the Bolivian government immigration office in La Paz, Cochabamba, or Santa Cruz to obtain permission to depart. An exit tax must be paid at the airport when departing Bolivia. Travelers who have Bolivian citizenship or residency must pay an additional fee upon departure. For further information regarding entry, exit, and customs requirements, travelers should contact the Consular Section of the Bolivian Embassy at 1819 H Street, N.W, Suite 240, Washington, DC 20006; telephone (202) 232-4827/4828; or the Bolivian consulate in Houston, Los Angeles, Miami, New Orleans, New York, San Francisco, or Seattle.

The Bolivian government has very strict laws concerning attempted theft or removal from Bolivia of any item that it considers to be a national treasure. The Bolivian and

U.S. governments are currently completing renewal of a cultural property protection agreement. In addition to the traditional examples of pre-Colombian artifacts, certain historical paintings, items of Spanish colonial architecture and history, and some native textiles, the Bolivian government also considers certain flora, fauna, and fossils as national treasures. It is illegal to remove any such items from Bolivia without prior written permission from the appropriate Bolivian authority. Any type of fossil excavation, even picking up a fossil, without prior written authorization from the appropriate Bolivian authority, is also illegal. Violation of the law can result in lengthy jail sentences and fines. Please contact the Embassy of Bolivia in Washington, D.C. or one of Bolivia's consulates in the United States for specific information regarding customs requirements.

U.S. citizens living in or visiting Bolivia are encouraged to register at the Consular Section of the U.S. Embassy in La Paz and obtain updated information on travel and security in Bolivia. The Consular Section is open for U.S. citizen services, including registration, from 8:30 a.m. to 12:30 p.m. weekdays, excluding U.S. and Bolivian holidays. The U.S. Embassy is located at 2780 Avenida Arce in La Paz; tel. (591-2) 2433-812 during business hours 8:30 a.m.-5:30 p.m., or (591-2) 2430-251 for after-hours emergencies; fax (591-2) 2433-854; Internet: http://www.megalink.com/usembla-paz. There are also U.S. consular agencies in Santa Cruz and Cochabamba, which are open weekday mornings from 9:00 a.m.-12:00 noon, excluding U.S. and Bolivian holidays. The Consular Agency in Santa Cruz is located at Calle Guemes 6, Barrio Equipetrol; tel. (591-3) 3363-842 or 3330-725; fax (591-3) 3325-544. The Consular Agency in Cochabamba is located at Avenida Oquendo 654, Torres Sofer, Room 601; tel. (591-4) 4256-714; fax (591-4) 4257-714.

Pets

Pets may be imported by presenting a valid certificate of vaccination against rabies certified by a Bolivian consul or other official. No quarantine is imposed. Pets obtained in Bolivia should be inoculated against distemper and rabies. Veterinarians will make house calls to provide these shots. Other medication for pets is difficult to obtain.

Firearms & Ammunition

The only firearms which may be imported are pistols, rifles, and shotguns (one each), and a total of 500 rounds of ammunition. All firearms must be registered with the police immediately.

Currency, Banking and Weights and Measures

The time in Bolivia is Greenwich Mean Time (GMT) minus four.

The unit of currency is the *peso* Boliviano ($b). Banking facilities are readily available in La Paz, where there are several branches of U.S. banks. Dollars in cash or travelers checks are widely acceptable and can be exchanged at favorable rates at most banks or *cambio* (exchange houses). They are accepted at hotels, restaurants, and stores at very favorable rates. American Express and Visa cards are accepted on a limited basis.

The metric system is used in local weights and measures, except in the markets, where pounds and kilos are both used.

LOCAL HOLIDAYS

Jan. 1	New Year's Day
Feb/Mar (Mon. & Tues. before Ash Wed. . .	Carnival*
Mar/Apr.	Good Friday*
Mar/Apr.	Easter*
May 1	Bolivian Labor Day
June	Corpus Christi*
July 16	La Paz Day (in La Paz only)
Aug. 6	Bolivian Independence Day
Nov. 2	All Saints Day
Dec. 25	Christmas Day

*Variable

RECOMMENDED READING

These titles are provided as a general indication of the material published on this country:

Blair, David Nelson. *The Land and People of Bolivia*. New York: J.B. Lippincott, 1990.

Griffiths, John. *Let's Visit Bolivia*. Bridgeport CT: Burke Publishing, 1988.

Jacobsen, Karen. *Bolivia*. Chicago: Childrens Press, 1991.

Klein, Herbert S. *Bolivia: The Evolution of a Multi-Ethnic Society*. 2nd ed. New York: Oxford University Press, 1992.

Lawlor, Eric. *In Bolivia*. New York: Vintage Books, 1989.

Morales, Waltraud Q. *Bolivia: Land of Struggle*. Boulder, CO: Westview Press, 1992.

Morrison, Marion. *Bolivia*. Chicago: Childrens Press, 1988.

Odijk, Pamela. *The Incas*. Englewood Cliffs, NJ: Silver Burdett Press, 1990.

Rasnake, Roger Neil. *Domination and Cultural Resistance: Authority and Power among an Andean People*. Durham, NC: Duke University Press, 1988.

Sachs, Jeffrey, and Juan A. Morales. *Bolivia: Nineteen Fifty-Two to Nineteen Eighty-Six*. San Francisco, CA: ICS Press, 1988.

Schimmel, Karen. *Bolivia*. New York: Chelsea House, 1990.

Swaney, Deanna. *Bolivia: A Travel Survival Kit*. Oakland, CA: Lonely Planet, 1988.

Yeager, Gertrude M., comp. *Bolivia*. Santa Barbara, CA: ABC-Clio, 1988.

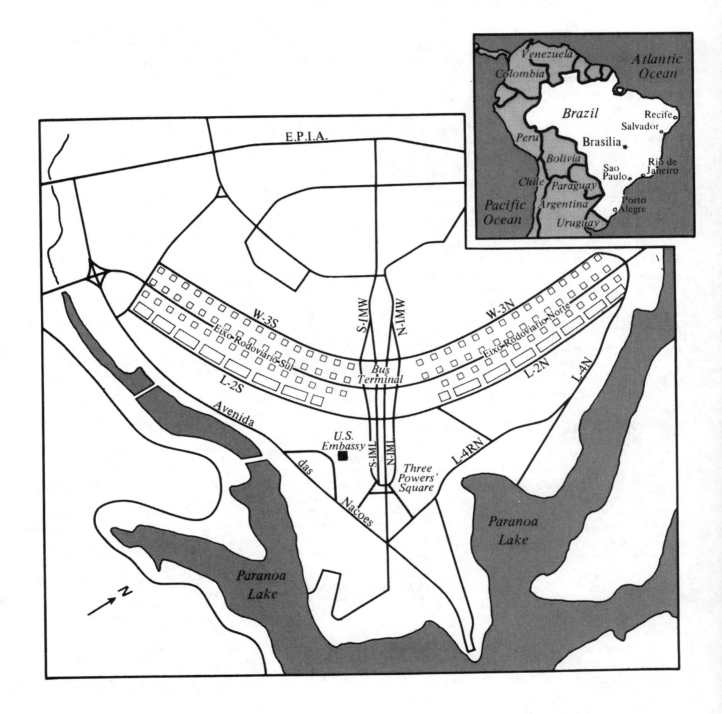

Brasilia, Brazil

BRAZIL

Federative Republic of Brazil

Major Cities:

Brasilia, Rio de Janeiro, São Paulo, Recife, Pôrto Alegre, Salvador da Bahia, Belo Horizonte, Belém, Manaus, Fortaleza, Curitiba, Goiânia

Other Cities:

Anápolis, Aracaju, Campina Grande, Campinas, Campo Grande, Caxias do Sul, Corumbá, Florianópolis, João Pessoa, Juiz de Fora, Maceió, Natal, Olinda, Ouro Prêto, Ribeirão Prêto, Santos

EDITOR'S NOTE

This chapter was adapted from the Department of State Post Report 1999 for Brazil. Supplemental material has been added to increase coverage of minor cities, facts have been updated, and some material has been condensed. Readers are encouraged to visit the Department of State's web site at http://travel.state.gov/ for the most recent information available on travel to this country.

INTRODUCTION

The Federative Republic of **BRAZIL,** occupying almost half of continental South America, is the fifth largest country in the world. With a 1996 population of roughly 160 million people, it sprawls across 3.3 million square miles of forest and plain, and shares boundaries with every South American state except Chile and Ecuador. In spite of profound economic problems, Brazil is an intriguing country. Its daring venture, nearly three decades ago, of carving a new capital city out of almost inaccessible territory, captured the interest of the world. Its bustling cities offer a broad contrast to the beauty of the countryside, and the widespread intermixtures among Caucasians, Negroes, and native Indians have resulted in a land of varied cultures and fascinating people.

MAJOR CITIES

Brasilia

The city of Brasilia, one of the wonders of the modern world. Modern buildings, is a futuristic city design and road system, rolling landscape, and a lake are features of the city. Brasíia, 600 air miles northwest of Rio de Janeiro in the central plateau of Brazil, is similar in topography and vegetation to western Texas. The Federal District, home of Brasíia and its satellite cities, lies within the State of Goids and comprises some 2,200 square miles. The District lies at the junction of the headwaters of three major Brazilian river systems, with an elevation of about 3,700 feet.

Brasíia is growing steadily but retains many U.S. small-town characteristics, such as an emphasis on family life. People are friendly and lifestyles tend to be informal. Construction of Brasíia began in 1957. In 1960, the city formally became the capital of Brazil. Over the next decade, the President, Congress, Federal Supreme Court, Foreign Ministry, and most other government agencies moved to Brasíia from the former capital, Rio de Janeiro. All official acts are signed in Brasíia, and all embassies are here.

Brasíia's demographics and economy make it a unique city. Brasíia's standard of living (the highest in Brazil) is stable due to regular employment in the government. Indeed, most of the population depends either directly or indirectly on government employment. Locals consider Brasíia as being on the Plano Piloto, while other cities in the Federal District are satellite cities. Satellite cities, originally created to house construction workers early in Brasíia's history and intended to disappear after construction was completed, have remained to be Brasíia's suburbs. Although construction workers originally populated them, skilled and semi-skilled workers and government bureaucrats now mostly populate satellite cities.

The city's population comes from all parts of Brazil and is heterogeneous. The native population is small. The appearance, thinking, and idiosyncrasies common to each area within Brazil are present in Brasíia. People consider themselves state citizens and form close associations with state groups.

Brazilians rely heavily on the family unit, spend their free time together, and depend on one another for assistance. The big Sunday family dinner is far more common here than in the U.S. Although some Brasilienses speak English, Portuguese is important for dealing with any stratum of Brazilian society. Limited recreational facilities and cultural activities, close living, and isolation can be problems, unless you develop hobbies or other leisure-time activities. Most who have served here have found life in Brasíia pleasant.

Outside the official U.S. Embassy community, most Americans living in Brasíia are missionaries, farmers who only work part of the year within the Federal District, and teachers employed by the American School.

Brasíia's moderate temperatures make the climate pleasant. Winter temperatures drop as low as 55°F at night and reach about 80°F during the day. Summer temperatures average from 65°F to 85°F. Average relative humidity varies from 50% to 70% during the summer's rainy season. Rainfall averages 60 inches annually, falling mostly between October and April. During this period, mildew is sometimes a problem. During the rainy season, flash storms bring several inches of rain in a short time. It rains in the morning or afternoon, followed by clear skies. Brasíia has spectacular sunrises; the sunsets are equally breathtaking.

The dry season, from April to September, has little or no rainfall, with humidity as low as 10%. Days are warm, but nights are cool.

Although pests do not plague Brasíia, ants, roaches, mosquitoes, flies, lizards and spiders are sometimes plentiful. Snakes are not generally found in populated areas.

Food

Brasíia has several well-stocked, large supermarkets. Vegetables and fruits are in good supply. They can also be purchased in small shops, Japanese markets, or from large, open, suburban markets where fruits and vegetables are fresher, cheaper, and found in greater quantity and variety. Frozen meats and prepared foods are available.

Almost all American-type fresh fruits and vegetables are available. Tropical fruits such as papaya, pineapple, mango, tamarind, passion fruit, sweetsop, Chinese gooseberry, and even more exotic fruits are available seasonally. Other fruits such as strawberries, apples, grapes, pears, peaches and nectarines are imported. Standard U.S. beef cuts are not widely available, but Brazilian cuts are acceptable. Beef filet, chicken, and fresh pork are excellent. Lamb is also available. Fresh and frozen fish are abundant, but shellfish is expensive. Local fresh, pasteurized, powdered, and long-life milk are available. Dairy products, such as butter, cream, yogurt, and cheese, are available in grocery stores, cheese stores, health food stores, delicatessens, and bakeries.

Brasíia has many good restaurants. Chinese, French and Mexican cuisine is available, as well as outstanding, traditional Brazilian barbecued meat (churrasco), and other national and international dishes. The American fast-food chains McDonald's and Arby's have representation here, too.

Clothing

Men: Summer and spring suits are worn year round. Bring primarily lightweight suits and one or two medium weight suits for the cool season. Generally, the quality of dry-cleaners is good, but expensive. Slacks and sports shirts (short or long sleeved) are suitable for off-duty hours. Bring a variety of clothes for a warm climate, from casual to semi-formal. Sport jackets, sweaters, light jackets, and wind breakers are comfortable during the cool season. Local clothing prices vary from city to city and U.S. sizes are not always available. Styles are more European than American.

Women: Fashion-conscious Brazilian women follow all the latest trends abroad, and have some of their own. Although entertaining is informal, elegant sports clothes are often worn. You can buy chic well-made clothing, but prices are high. Cotton suits and lightweight knit dresses can be worn during the cool and rainy seasons and evenings. Some warmer clothing is occasionally necessary. Except for the rainy period, days are often hot, so bring cotton and synthetic blends. If you are planning to travel to Bolivia, Chile, Argentina, or south of Brasíia during winter, you will need winter clothes. Generally, informality prevails in Brasíia. However, evening wear is often considered "elegant casual." Bring sweaters or lightweight jackets for occasional cooler days and nights of the rainy season and the evenings of the dry season. A raincoat may be too warm, but an umbrella is essential. Wool slacks and long-sleeved blouses or dresses for cool, rainy days and a warm robe are welcome.

Bring plenty of sportswear, including washable slacks and shorts. Local prices for underwear and beach ensembles are high. Women's and girl's swimwear is available in all sizes, but run small. Brazilian swimwear, even one-piece suits, exposes more than U.S. styles. Sun hats are advisable.

Bring shoes or leave shoe size with a U.S. store and order as needed. All types of shoes, sandals, and tennis shoes are found in Brasíia, but it is difficult to find good fits, particularly for half and narrow sizes. Brazil manufactures many kinds of footwear available at a variety of prices, though for the most part the quality is inferior to shoes found in the U.S.

Children: Bring washable children's clothing, swimwear, and shoes. Include sweaters and lightweight jackets for cool nights and mornings. Blue jeans are a must for outside play. Light-colored play clothes stain easily from Brasíia's red clay. Dress at the American School is informal; both boys and girls may wear jeans. Elementary school-aged children wear shorts with short-sleeved shirts or T-shirts most of the year.

Supplies & Services

Toiletries and patent medicines of Brazilian manufacture may be bought locally. Many are U.S. brands manufactured under license and are expensive. Bring or order specialty items from the U.S. Bring all essential store items with you such as Tylenol, children's cough syrup, toothpaste, suntan lotion, contact lens solution, etc. If you have a baby or are expecting, bring all items with you. These items are imported to Brasíia and the costs are about double that in the U.S. Baby food and diapers can be ordered through the commissary or the internet Netgrocer shopping service.

Litter boxes are not available in Brasíia. Pet supply stores sell leashes, brushes, flea collars, and a few toys. Pet treats and rawhide chew sticks are available. Fleas are prevalent year round. Consult your veterinarian regarding flea repellents and flea collars. Anti-flea sprays and lotions, shampoos, etc. are roughly twice the price here than they are in the States. Program is also sold here, although it is more expensive than in the States.

Laundry and dry-cleaning services are available throughout Brasíia.

Beauty shops and barbershops do acceptable work and some are reasonably priced. Specialty services such as hair coloring/frosting and perms are generally more expensive than in the U.S. Massages, manicures, and pedicures are available at varying prices.

Domestic Help

Part-time servants usually suffice, although full-time and live-in help are desired by some. Wages vary from USD 150-200 (at an exchange rate of R$2 to USD 1) a month for live-in maids, plus the cost of various benefits guaranteed them under Brazil's Constitution.

In addition to wages, the employer of a live-in servant provides bed linens, towels, food, and, if desired, uniforms. Live in maids are sometimes scarce, as many prefer to work during the day only. Housekeeping and laundry services are fair, but you must train the maids to use modern appliances.

Day cleaning personnel currently charge USD 15-20 per day (again, with an exchange rate of R$2 to USD 1). They are generally available for 1 or 2 days a week per family, with services divided among two or three employers. The 1988 Constitution guarantees various rights to domestic workers.

Religious Activities

Brasíia has many Catholic churches. An English-language mass is conducted each Saturday at one of the churches. Several Protestant churches and a Greek Orthodox church have congregations in Brasíia. English-language worship services and religious instruction are held Sunday mornings by an interdenominational Protestant group and a Baptist church. A small Jewish cultural association welcomes members from the official and diplomatic communities. Services are conducted weekly and on all holidays at the local synagogue.

Education

The American School of Brasíia (EAB) was founded in 1964 and offers preschool through grade 12 based on a U.S. public school curriculum. Instruction is in English, but English-speaking students are required to study Portuguese. The school has about 600 students from about 40 countries. Facilities include a soccer/softball field, a library with 10,000 volumes, a science lab, a computer classroom, a gym, and a canteen. Enrollment is close to school capacity.

The Southern Association of Colleges and Secondary Schools of the U.S. accredits the school. The lower school is recognized by the Secretary of Education in the Federal District. The educational allowance currently covers all school expenses

for grades K-12. Preschool is not covered by the educational allowance. The school year runs from early August to early June, with a one-week vacation at Carnaval and a four-week vacation during the Christmas season.

Some supervised extracurricular sports, as well as other after-school activities including band, are available, though they are quite limited, especially for the lower grades. Bring music materials, as they are expensive in Brasíia.

EAB participates in sports and some academic competitions along with other American schools in Brazil and the region, giving students the opportunity to travel and take part in these events while meeting a variety of South American and international students.

Another school that is used by some in the American community in Brasíia is the School of Nations, a B'hai school. Instruction is bilingual, one-half in English and one-half in Portuguese. The school is not accredited. The School of Nations offers instruction from pre-kindergarten through 11th grade and offers a US-based curriculum with a strong emphasis on diversity and values.

Preschool aged children may attend the Affinity Arts pre-school. There is a strong emphasis on music in the program along with other activities such as language, science, theater, swimming, cooking and playground.

Other schools in the Federal District include public, private, and parochial institutions. Instruction is given from nursery school through grade 12, but not in English. Children with a good background in Portuguese may attend these schools. Note: the Brazilian school year has summer vacation during December, January, and February, with a midterm break in July.

Sports

Sociedade Hipica de Brasíia (Horse Riding Club): This is the most complete and centrally located

Atlantic coast development, Rio de Janeiro, Brazil

horse-riding club in Brasíia. Horses are rented. Nonmembers can ride on weekends at scheduled times.

Other facilities include a social clubhouse with bar and restaurant, two swimming pools, tennis court, basketball, volleyball, soccer, and a large riding pavilion. Riding lessons are available.

The following clubs are available for membership, but memberships are extremely expensive: the Yacht Club of Brasíia (late Clube), the Club of Nations (Clube das Naçðes and the Brasíia Country Club, Cota Mil Yacht Club, and the Academia de Tenis (Tennis Academy). There are numerous commercial health clubs (called academias) whose fees are similar to health-club fees in the U.S.

Touring and Outdoor Activities

Brasíia's Lake Paranoá is beautiful. However, floating debris and raw sewage make all water-related activities in the lake unsafe. Swimming in pools is a popular pastime. Bring diving masks, goggles, and flippers if desired.

Brazil's national sport is soccer. Numerous games are played in Brasíia between various amateur teams, and a small professional league. Brasíia has a team in the national league.

Hunting for birds and small game is prohibited in all states except Rio Grande do Sul. Fishing for any but the smallest kinds of fish requires a 3- to 4-hour drive to the Verde River or an 8-hour drive to the Araguaia River in Goiás State. Excellent fishing is found on the Island of Ban--nal, accessible only by 1-1/2 hours' flight by small plane.

Brasíia offers limited sightseeing with few museums and galleries. A well-laid out zoo houses several species of Brazilian wildlife and is con-

tinually expanding. You can view various types of vegetation and plant life can be seen at the botanical reserve.

Brasíia's TV tower is the fourth tallest in the world at 715 feet. Oscar Niemeyer, the famous architect who designed much of Brasíia, designed it. The top of the tower is 4,403 feet above sea level, and a lookout platform provides a panoramic view of the city and surrounding countryside. A "hippie" fair, featuring handicrafts, clothes, shoes, and wood and leather items, is held at the foot of the tower on Saturdays, Sundays, and holidays. There is a lovely gem museum located on the Center level of the TV tower. At Christmas, the tower is strung with lights to resemble an enormous Christmas tree.

An outstanding landmark in Brasíia is the national flag flown on Three Powers Square. The enormous 286-square meter flag flies from a 100-meter high flagpole that consists of 22 joined staffs representing the states of Brazil. A different Brazilian state donates a new flag on the first Sunday of every third month. The new flag is raised amidst a colorful ceremony with music and traditional folk dancing.

In late June, Brasíia hosts the "Feira dos Estados," a charity state fair including state displays, local products, regional cuisine for sale, folk dancing performances, and a midway. Representatives of foreign countries also participate.

In May, one of the liveliest and most colorful festivals is the Cavalhadas in Pirenópolis about 2 hours from Brasíia. During this brilliant pageant, richly caparisoned horses and riders simulate ancient Iberian Peninsula tournaments. Both fine horsemanship and wild stunt riding by masked riders are displayed in this fascinating folk festival.

Driving outside Brasíia can be a pleasant pastime. The town of Cristalina, a gem seeker's paradise, is about 2 hours south of Brasíia. The shops located around the town-square offer Brazilian precious and semiprecious stones and other gifts or souvenirs. You can visit some working pit mines a short drive out of town. A quaint country restaurant serving local fare is located in Luziania, mid-way between Brasíia and Cristalina, and is a popular place to stop for lunch when returning from a shopping expedition.

Goiánia, about 2-3 hours southwest of Brasíia, is the capital of Goiás and its largest city. The city, founded in 1933, is a planned city like Brasíia. With an altitude much lower than Brasíia's, it is warmer and more humid. Goiánia is a pretty town with tree-lined streets, interesting 1930s architecture, a centralized shopping center, good hotels, tall apartment buildings, and some excellent restaurants. On weekends, a "hippie fair" offers a variety of goods and crafts.

The beautiful Itiquira waterfalls, amid a rugged terrain, are located 2 hours north of Brasíia over newly paved roads. For those interested in a health spa, a first-class resort hotel and several warm, natural pools are located near Caldas Novas, about 5 hours from Brasíia in Goiás. Visit this resort for a relaxing 3-day weekend.

Travel to São Paulo - Brazil's largest city, or to Rio de Janeiro - world famous for its natural beauty - for a real change of pace and scenery. By highway, Rio is 753 miles and 15-20 hours away; São Paulo is 627 miles from Brasíia with driving time of 14-17 hours. Frequent air connections to both cities are available. Air travel time is about 1-1/2 hours.

If you want to leave the main road, secondary roads are often unpaved and difficult. Four-wheel-drive vehicles are useful, especially for camping.

There are two softball seasons, and several coed teams, with participants from the American and international community. Bowling is available at Park Shopping.

The Parque da Cidade (City Park), located in Asa Sul, offers opportunities for outdoor activities such as bicycle riding, jogging, walking, paddleboats, children's amusement park, barbecue sites, etc. Additionally, one of the main highways is closed on Sundays and made available to bicyclists and joggers.

Entertainment
Dinner parties, cookouts and casual buffets are a popular form of home entertainment. The American Women's Club International (AWCI) organizes monthly meetings with speakers on various topics. Weekly and monthly AWCI activity groups meet to enjoy such things as tennis, bridge, playgroup, Portuguese conversation and social services work, to name just a few. The AWCI book clubs buy a wide selection of current bestsellers with membership fees. The American School sponsors a Christmas Bazaar, Fun Run, International

Fair, Flea Market, and two stage productions which are attended by the Brasíia community at large. The Casa Thomas Jefferson, which is actually three Brazilian-American binational centers, sponsors art exhibits and musical events that feature both American and Brazilian artists and performers.

Brasíia has many movie theaters. Admission costs are comparable to the U.S. English-language films are popular. Most films are American originals with Portuguese subtitles. Children's films tend to be dubbed. Some French and Italian films are also shown in the respective embassies as well as in Brazilian theaters.

The National Theater presents concerts and occasionally has ballet or other dance performances. The circus comes to town once a year, as do various foreign performers. The University of Brasíia holds interesting performances by staff members in its music school. Military and police groups hold parades and other activities on various national holidays. Americans are welcome at all cultural and national celebrations.

Brasíia has some nightclubs; most have dancing, some have floor shows. Several popular discotheques attract various age groups. Outdoor cafes featuring drinks and snacks are popular evening meeting places.

Shopping malls have movie theaters, a variety of shops and eateries. Park Shopping, adjacent to one of the largest supermarkets in the area, has eleven movie theaters, a 24 lane bowling alley built by Brunswick, a McDonald's, an international food court, and approximately 175 shops. Many other new malls have been built recently, including Brasíia Shopping and Patio Brasil, each with stores, eateries and move theaters. There is an arcade with small amusement rides and video games, and an in-door skating rink during the Christmas holidays.

Rio De Janeiro

Rio de Janeiro, the center of a metropolitan area of about 11 million people, offers one of the world's most beautiful physical settings. Set adjacent to an ocean bay off the Atlantic Ocean and facing south, Rio is surrounded by mountains with spectacular formations and tropical greenery, and is truly what its residents, the Cariocas, call the Cidade Maravilhosa (marvelous city). Its landmarks are the striking Sugar Loaf Mountain Pão de Açucar and Corcovado Mountain with its famous Christ Statue overlooking the city. Brazil's seasons are the reverse of those in the U.S., with summer from December to March. Rio's normal temperatures range from 75 to 95°F. Extremes vary from 40°F during winter to 105°F in the hot, humid summer. Intense rainfall also occurs throughout the year and may occasionally cause severe flooding within the city itself. Infrequent landslides affect housing on mountain slopes in densely populated slum areas known as favelas.

The city was Brazil's capital until 1960, and many government offices are located here. Rio is a focus of transportation, communications, military, cultural and journalistic activity. However, its history is as a seashore resort famous for its beaches, Carnaval, and its outgoing people But the continued population increase within Rio has created other problems common to a megalopolis: traffic congestion, air and noise pollution, and a high crime rate. Pollution and crime have, it fact, jeopardized the traditional tourist industry. The Department of State has designated the crime threat rating level for Rio as critical.

While Rio is cosmopolitan, Portuguese is necessary for everyday use (shopping, newspapers, and social events). Its beaches are often a focal point for recreational activities but they can be overcrowded and polluted.

Cariocas commonly refer to Rio being divided into three residential areas: Zona Sul (South Zone) and Zona Norte (North Zone) and Barra da Tijuca. There is a mountain range, which forms a spectacular, scenic separation between the zones. The Zona Sul area is significantly smaller. less than 1 million people and is also the area where virtually all official Americans reside. The sparsely populated area known as Centro, separates the relatively more affluent south zone from poorer neighborhoods in the north zone.

Another fast-growing and relatively new part of Rio de Janeiro is the southern suburb of Barra da Tijuca. This area which was once considered out of town is the fastest growing district in the city. Barra da Tijuca features several large shopping centers as well as large megamarkets, which include everything from groceries to clothes to hardware to car supplies (i.e., similar to Super Wal-Marts in the States). In addition to the shopping, dozens of new condominiums have sprung up. American fast food outlets are common. Office parks are also being built, not to mention major amusement parks. Barra da Tijuca is also home to the cleanest beaches in the city of Rio de Janeiro.

The American community in Rio is fairly large, with about 6,000 registered at the Consulate General. Only a relatively small number participate in activities that bring the expatriate community together. Rio's American Society organization is active. The American business community in Rio is strongly represented with Fortune 500 firms. The American Chamber of Commerce meets regularly and maintains full-time offices. However, significant reductions in the presence of American businessmen have had a marked affect on community life, including reduced enrollment by American students at the American School of Rio.

Food

Rio has many large supermarkets. Selection is generally good. Many employees purchase fresh produce from weekly markets (feiras) that rotate through residential areas; costs can be higher but the quality is better. Each neighborhood has its own smaller grocery store, butcher, bakery, and other specialty shops which results in decentralized frequent shopping (Brazilians often shop on a daily basis). Local beef is not aged and lacks tenderness but is reasonably priced; lamb is generally not available. Fish and seafood are plentiful, but expensive. The COBAL in Leblon is another market similar to the feiras, but is covered. It is open Tuesday through Sunday. Fresh fruits, vegetables, fresh cut flowers, meat, seafood and poultry are available. The prices vary from stand to stand, but the quality is similar to those at the feiras or (better).

Recognized international and U.S. food companies manufacture many of their products in Brazil but retail prices are higher than in the U.S. Employees are supplied bottled drinking water. One and a half liter plastic bottles are now available at the supermarket; larger size containers can be home-delivered.

Clothing

General: Bring lightweight, washable, comfortable clothing. Dry-cleaning is available but is expensive and not always reliable. Small clothing stores line shopping malls and shopping areas with reasonable selections and often focus on designer clothing. During summer days, beachwear is frequently the norm in shopping areas and restaurants. Shoes available here may not conform to U.S. sizes or durability. Good sandals and casual shoes are available locally. Shoe repair workmanship is good and reasonably priced.

Women: Although temperature differences between summer and winter are not wide, seasonal differences in dress are noticed. In summer, bright, gay colors, and patterns in lightweight materials predominate; in winter, lightweight woolens and knits in darker tones appear. A light jacket is occasionally needed, and during damp, rainy weather, a sweater or sweatshirt would be comfortable. Slacks and jogging suits are worn year round. Hose is rarely worn, except on dressier occasions or in office settings. Locally produced panty hose is of variable quality, so bring a supply from the U.S. A good selection of casual wear is a must for both seasons.

Bikinis dominate beach wear (Cariocas actually prefer the even briefer tanga), but all styles are worn. Frequent swimmers or sunbathers should have several changes of beachwear to avoid drying problems. All styles of swimsuits and beach cover-ups are available locally, but larger sizes (above a US size 10) may be difficult to find. Evening social events require dressier clothing. Brazilian women favor long or very short dresses of silk and other fine materials. Dressy cottons and synthetics are practical.

Many seamstresses are available, but finding the right one is difficult. Some prefer to work in their own homes; others will work in a customer's home and must be provided a sewing machine. U.S. patterns are not available locally; some seamstresses make their own patterns, use those in Brazilian fashion magazines, or copy from ready made clothing or pictures. If you sew, bring a supply of U.S. patterns. A wide variety of Brazilian textiles, some in wash-and-wear materials, is available. Many fabrics are not preshrunk. Quality materials cost more than U.S. goods.

Stylish belts, costume jewelry, purses and other accessories are available in Rio. Brazilian gems and jewelry designs are world renown. The quality of Brazilian ready-made clothing is adequate, but expensive. Women's sizes are not comparable to those in the U.S., particularly undergarments. Bring an ample supply of hot weather clothes, as during the long summer, repeated laundering and intense sun cause fabrics to fade and lose body.

Men: Heavy wool suits are never necessary. Suits of lightweight wool, linen, or other natural fiber are comfortable and practical. Dark

suits are useful for evening events. The need for formal clothing is negligible in Rio.

Raincoats or overcoats are rarely seen on men except during a cool winter's rain. Ready-made suits in various materials are available locally, but cuts differ from the U.S. Tailors are expensive but offer quality continental-style tailoring.

Sports clothing is necessary. Long sleeved sports shirts in conservative colors and sports jackets are commonly worn to social functions and restaurants. A wide variety of good-quality sports clothes, including jeans, is available locally at prices roughly comparable to those in the U.S. Bring cheap, generic baseball caps for use on the beach. Cotton sweaters and light jackets are useful on cooler days.

Children: Children's shoes and clothes are more expensive and sometimes less durable. Most families order clothes from U.S. catalog companies.

Supplies and Services

Rio has several large shopping areas and malls where one can find both local and imported products. The variety is impressive. More specialized malls include the São Conrado Fashion Mall, emphasizing clothing, and the Rio Design Center in Leblon, with beautiful furniture and decorative accent pieces for the home. Many international pharmaceutical and cosmetic companies manufacture locally under license. Suntan lotion is an expensive item in Brazil. Appliances, household tools, electrical supplies, plastic ware, and a wide range of consumer goods are manufactured locally. Inmost instances, prices are higher than comparable U.S. items.

Beauty shops and barbershops abound. Prices are generally higher than U.S. levels, depending on location and reputation of the shop. Quality is good if language is no barrier. Some hairdressers for both men and women have trained in either the U.S. or Europe. Repair costs for electrical equipment and

appliances, such as radios and TVs, are higher than U.S. prices. Reliable service is a problem.

Print film can be developed locally and 1-hour processing is available. Several good automobile repair shops exist. General bodywork is adequate but more sophisticated electronic repairs are difficult to obtain. Costs are sometimes high, especially for spare parts, and estimates should be requested before repairs are authorized. Spare parts for U.S. cars must be imported; tires are available locally for U.S. cars. Repair services for Brazilian made cars (Chevrolet, Ford, Fiat and VW) are good.

Domestic Help

The quality of domestic help varies and turnover is high. Domestics who have worked for other Americans are helpful, but few understand English, and you need at least a rudimentary knowledge of Portuguese. Most apartments have domestic quarters that are located off of the kitchen area. Employers furnish room and board, uniforms, and linens. A cook or housekeeper currently receives about $200-$400 monthly, plus the Brazilian Social Security contribution, currently 12% of salary. Day workers are paid from $20 to $40 per day plus lunch. Occasionally transportation cost will be assessed.

Religious Activities

Brazil is the most populous Roman Catholic nation in the world. Many Catholic churches are found in Rio. The Chapel of Our Lady of Mercy has services in English.

Protestant churches with English language services include the Union Church, a Protestant nondenominational church; the Christ Church (American Episcopal Church of England), which has an international membership; the International Baptist Church; the Christian Science; and the English Lutheran.

Jewish services are held at the Sinagoga Copacabana (Orthodox), the Associação Religiosa Israelita

(Conservative), and the Centro Israelita Brasileiro (highly Conservative, Sephardic). All services are in Hebrew.

Education

The American School, Escola Americana of Rio de Janeiro (EARJ), is a coeducational school offering a U.S. curriculum from preschool through grade 12, including the International Baccalaureate degree. Accredited by the Southern Association of Colleges and Secondary Schools of the U.S., it is a member of the National Association of Independent Schools. Its enrollment is about 1,000, and U.S. colleges readily accept its graduates. The faculty numbers 118 (37 Americans). Students with American citizenship make up about 10% of the student body with about 85% being Brazilian students.

The first semester begins in early August and runs to mid-December; the second term runs from early February to mid-June. Extracurricular activities are at an extra expense. Classes are 5 days weekly, from 8:00 a.m. to 2:30 p.m., in a modern, hillside complex of 9 interconnected buildings. Full cafeteria facilities are available; extracurricular activities are similar to those in U.S. schools. School buses serve most residential areas.

Arrangements for enrollment can be made directly with the Escola Americana, Estrada da Gavea, 132, Gavea Rio de Janeiro, RJ 22451-260 Brazil.

Our Lady of Mercy School, a coeducational Catholic school, follows an American curriculum for grades 1 through 12. The U.S. Southern Association of Colleges and Secondary Schools accredits the school. The school is sponsored by the Society of Our Lady of Mercy and provides a chapel for English-speaking Catholics. Graduates have been readily accepted in U.S. colleges. Our Lady of Mercy also offers a prenursery school program for children age 2 and up.

The school term is similar to the American School. Hot lunches are available. Extracurricular activities are similar to those in U.S. Schools. Make enrollment arrangements directly with the Headmaster, Rua Visconde de Caravelas 48, Botafogo, Rio de Janeiro RJ 22271-030, Brazil.

The British School is coeducational and offers instruction from prenursery through age 13. Following a British curriculum, it qualifies students for the British common entrance examinations. School terms are from February to July and August to December. Lunch is provided for all, except pre-nursery and kindergarten children who go home at noon. Large playground and playing fields are available for sports. School bus transportation is available. Average class size is 24. Enrollment is arranged through the Headmaster, The British School, Rua da Matriz, 76, Botafogo Rio de Janeiro, RJ 22260-100 Brazil.

Several pre-schools accept children as young as 1 year old. One such institution, St. Patrick's, teaches in English. All are more expensive than comparable U.S. facilities. Bus service is available for many. Arrangements for these schools may be made after you arrive at post. Generally, St. Patrick's accepts children age 2 and up. Classes are taught in English through the 4th grade.

Special Education Opportunities

Working knowledge of Portuguese greatly enhances any trip to Rio. Portuguese language training is available through various institutions. The Brazilian-U.S. Institute offers frequent Portuguese language courses. Tutors for private lessons are available. Portuguese courses are also available at any of several local universities. There are no programs of higher learning in the English language in Rio.

Sports

The main recreational activities relate to the beach. The popular beach promenades have all been illuminated and are now enjoyed by many both day and night. Games of soccer, volleyball and that incredible combination of the two, fute volley, seem to be going on 24 hours of the day. There are no public recreational facilities with swimming pools or golf courses. Club memberships within Rio range in price from the nicely affordable (Clube Flamengo) to the extravagantly expensive (Country Clube). While a few apartment buildings have facilities reserved for tenants, most buildings do not. The city does have a bicycle path that follows along certain beach areas. On Sundays and holidays, half of the primary beach avenue is closed to normal traffic to the great enjoyment of walkers, joggers, cyclists, and rollerbladers.

Soccer is the national sport. Brazil won the 1994 World Cup; the popularity of the sport is reflected by the size of Rio's Maracaña Stadium. It is one of the world's largest, originally configured to seat 200,000 people. The nearby smaller Maracañazinho Stadium is used for special events, such as ice shows and basketball games. Neighborhood soccer and volleyball games are also played frequently, as are weekend games on nearly every beach.

Rio's extensive beaches are popular for swimming, boogy boarding, and surfing but one must be alert to publicized, regular health warnings and avoid dangerous levels of water pollution. The advisability of beach swimming is published daily in the local newspapers. Strong undertow is also a common hazard. Many people with their own transportation travel to cleaner, less heavily populated beaches south of the city.

Sports equipment is manufactured locally and imported, but prices are generally higher than U.S. prices. Be sure to bring your bicycles and rollerblades.

Touring and Outdoor Activities

As a transportation and communications center, Rio offers excellent opportunities for touring all parts of Brazil. The cost of domestic air transportation is high. If possible, try to purchase the special Brazil Air Pass from the Brazilian carrier Varig prior to your arrival (not all travel agents can/ will sell these since one purchase requirement may be the possession of a round trip ticket to Brazil from the U.S.).

For overland travel, many highways are good but sometimes crowded. Brazilian drivers are impatient in heavy traffic. Highway fatality rates are among the highest in the world. Night highway driving is exceptionally dangerous and is not recommended. Bus service, including the sleeper bus, is frequent, and not overly expensive. The bus conditions are varied but can be cramped.

An automobile trip of about an hour and a half will lead you to cooler mountain are. Quaint colonial cities, lovely seaside communities, and modern industrial centers are all within a 3-6 hour drive. Few roadside motel accommodations are available; lodgings at major destinations are satisfactory.

Camping, hang-gliding, surfing, surf fishing, mountain climbing, and water skiing are other activities available within Rio's vicinity. Deep-sea fishing is fair but expensive; freshwater fishing is available in the mountains. Hunting is prohibited in Brazil, except in Rio Grande do Sul.

Entertainment

The greatest single annual entertainment event in Rio is its famed Carnaval. During the 4 nights and 3 days preceding Ash Wednesday, commercial and official activities come to a complete standstill. Then samba schools, street parades, and night-long parties dominate Rio's scene. Carnaval also attracts many foreign visitors. Tickets for Carnaval balls and main parade seating are relatively expensive but the events, especially the parades, are exceptional and should not be missed.

From June to September, outstanding Brazilian and foreign artists offer varied programs of music,

opera, and dance at several theaters. The Brazilian theater season is year round; both original Brazilian works and foreign plays are presented in Portuguese, and in an informal off-Broadway style. Children's plays are offered regularly in Portuguese. An English-language small theater group offers productions and performance opportunities on an irregular basis.

Nightclubs and small boate offer shows of varying quality; many feature jazz, samba music, and dancers. Well known foreign entertainers and groups appear occasionally at some larger theaters and nightclubs.

Movie theaters are numerous and good. First-run American and European films are shown with original dialogue and Portuguese subtitles at prices comparable to the U.S. Late-night network TV sometimes features programs in English. Rio has several good TV stations, which can help improve Portuguese language abilities. Many neighborhoods offer cable TV for a monthly fee with programs such as CNN, ESPN, and MTV Excellent FM radio broadcasting is also available.

Restaurants offer varied national and international cuisine at comparable U.S. prices. A churrascaria (specializing in barbecued meat) is a popular type of Rio restaurant.

Many art and historical museums are available. Rio also has interesting and photogenic churches, a large botanical garden, a major tropical forest park (Tijuca National Park), and a zoological park. Art galleries abound, and although prices of established Brazilian artists are high by U.S. standards, new painters always await discovery. Art courses in Portuguese are available at the Parque Lage, the Museum of Modern Art, and the Catholic University.

Rio has no English-language newspapers. Local newsstands regularly offer the Miami Herald and the International Herald Tribune; individual subscriptions can be

arranged at reduced cost, but are still expensive. English language editions of some leading U.S. news magazines are also available.

Social Activities

The American Society and the International Newcomers Club help integrate the social activities of the American community. Another organization, "The Players," has periodic English language performances that provide opportunities related to the theater.

São Paulo

São Paulo is the largest and one of the fastest growing cities in South America. It is a thriving metropolis of contrasts, with skyscrapers built alongside small, residential houses; narrow cobblestone streets feed wide avenues; street vendors hawk their wares near five star hotels. A dynamic city rich in historic and modern culture, it boasts three symphony orchestras, many fine art galleries, and an international selection of museums. Thousands of avid spectators follow everything from soccer matches to horse races. São Paulo is the industrial and financial heart of Brazil, and the bustling city sets a pace that resembles New York City. [It is also home to fine restaurants, theaters, nightclubs, first-run movie theatres, and performances by major international stars.] With something of appeal from every point of view, these inviting contrasts make living and working in São Paulo exciting, interesting and challenging.

Utilities

The water supply is plentiful in São Paulo. Water pressure is reasonable in all areas of the city. All parts of the city now have fluoridated water, although levels of fluoridation are below recommended U.S. levels. Tap water is not consistently potable anywhere in Brazil. Electric current is 110v 60 cycle, AC; 220v, 3-phase, AC, is available for ranges, high-voltage heaters, and dryers. Power interruptions are uncommon, though voltage regulators are recommended for occasional current

Aerial view of Sao Paulo, Brazil

© Stephanie Maze/Corbis. Reproduced by permission.

tral heating is nonexistent. Electric blankets and space heaters are recommended. Blankets and comforters are more expensive in São Paulo, so bring a sufficient supply. As a side note, pollution tends to be heavier in the winter months. Occasionally, this affects individuals with allergies or respiratory problems. You may want to bring air purifiers.

Food

Most foods are available locally. Pasteurized fresh milk, butter, cheeses, and other products are plentiful. Almost all fresh fruits and vegetables are available year round in supermarkets, as well as open-air fruit and vegetable markets. Oranges, tangerines, bananas, pineapples, papayas, melons, mangoes, and other fruits are always in season. Locally grown apples, pears, peaches, plums, strawberries, and grapes are available seasonally, and imported varieties, year round. Ample supplies of meat and fish exist. American-type supermarkets and European-style hypermarkets carry locally made goods that compare with U.S. brands. Some of these supermarkets also offer U.S. cuts of beef (Brazilian cuts differ markedly from U.S. cuts). Local wines and spirits are of good quality.

Clothing

Although São Paulo's climate is milder than that of the northeastern U.S., bring clothes for cool and rainy weather, including sweaters, fall suits, raincoats, and umbrellas. Rain is common in São Paulo and during the summer there can be heavy rainstorms each afternoon. Every family member needs at least one good umbrella. Temperatures vary, so layered dressing is important. Fall and winter (June - October) can be chilly. Bring light and warm clothing that can be worn indoors due to of lack of central heating. An all-weather coat with removable lining should meet your outdoor needs. Those accustomed to living in very warm climates may need a pair of gloves, a scarf, and a knit hat.

fluctuations. Electrical outlets vary even within households and you will need several different types of adapters. They are available locally for a reasonable price, but you may want to bring an assortment.

In the past, U. S.-made appliances were preferred for quality and price to local products. However, appliances are now increasingly comparable to U.S. products in price, quality and availability.

Like any large U.S. city, São Paulo has a wide variety of local radio stations, including several FM stations with continuous (mostly American and Brazilian popular) music, classical music and talk radio. Radio

short-wave bands receive VOA and BBC in the evening.

Local TV is on the PAL-M system, so U.S.-purchased sets (NTSC or European PAL sets) will only receive in black and white, unless modified-a process that is commonly performed for around 150 Reals. Videocassette recorders are popular and video clubs like Blockbuster are plentiful. However, U.S. VCRs are not compatible with PAL-M-only TVs and must be converted, the cost of which is about 100 Reals. Cable is available at costs comparable to U.S. prices.

São Paulo winters can be cold and damp. The temperature rarely drops below 32 Fahrenheit, and cen-

Local shoes vary in quality though shoes are stylish and easily found although narrow widths are not readily available. Walking shoes are a must and, due to uneven, cobblestone sidewalks, occasional heel repair is necessary. Leather is of good quality. São Paulo is a high fashion city; every new fashion can be seen and is acceptable, from conservative to trendy. All types of sports goods and clothing are sold in São Paulo, at prices similar to those found in the U.S.

Dress for social functions is often business attire, depending on the nature of the event. Tuxedo or formal dress rental places are abundant throughout the city. Long dresses are seldom worn to formal dinners. For women, local lingerie, hose, and other nylon clothing are of lesser quality than U.S. made products, but are readily available.

Supplies and Services

It is important to note that the Brazilian economy is drastically changing and therefore it is difficult to state with certainty that Brazilian-made products are higher or lower in cost relative to the U.S., although imported items are generally higher-priced (e.g., some clothing, luxury items). The cost of living is comparable to that in Washington, D.C. Dining out, food purchases, and entertainment (theater, movies, etc.) cost the same or less.

Cathedral Brasilia, Brasilia, Brazil

Miscellaneous toiletries, cosmetics, household needs, cigarettes, tobacco, and liquor products are sold on the Brazilian market. However, not every brand is consistently available. American-style supermarkets and superstores like Wal-Mart and Sam's Club sell all types of household cleaning equipment. Prescription and nonprescription drugs, many made by subsidiaries of U.S. or European companies, are available at reasonable prices. Imported cosmetics are more expensive, but some U.S. brand names (Revlon, Helena Rubinstein, etc.) are manufactured locally. Travellers with infants or small children may want to bring disposable diapers, a supply of baby food, any special

baby formula, and a bottle warmer in accompanied airfreight. Disposable diapers are available locally, but are expensive.

Dry-cleaning and laundry services are common and equal to U.S. prices. Shoe repair is inexpensive, workmanship is good, and rubber and leather are used for heels and heel tips. Nylon is not generally available. Hair salons are less expensive than in the U.S.; work is good and reasonably priced. Consider bringing your favorite hair shampoos, rinses, and sprays, as these are not consistently available. Repair work on watches, radios, stereos, televisions, and other electrical appliances is good.

The quality of auto maintenance and repair facilities is inconsistent. Repair work is good, but most services take more time than in the U.S. GM, Ford, Fiat, and VW produce cars locally at favorable prices.

Domestic Help

Domestic help is readily available, but trained servants are hard to find and few speak English. Salaries depend on class of servant, i.e., trained cooks earn R$100 to R$150 a week; live-in housekeeper, R$100 and up. Staff with newborns often hire a live-in nurse who has had about 6 months of formal education in pediatric nursing. The live-in nurse earns around R$125 a week. Families with older children often employ a live-in nanny. Salaries may change as the economy settles.

Brazilian houses and apartments are designed with a maid's room and private bath, located near the laundry and kitchen area. Employers can provide uniforms, and live-ins normally receive bedding, towels, and furniture. Servants get one day off weekly, plus major national and religious holidays. Under the Brazilian Constitution, employers must give servants a 13th-month bonus equal to one month's salary or prorated to the length-of-employment during the year. Also, the employer must contribute to the local Brazilian retirement system for the domestic employee.

Medical Care

São Paulo has very competent doctors and dentists. Many speak English and were trained in the U.S. Quality orthodontic services are available as well. In general, the costs for an office visit are equal to fees in the U.S. Maternity and other in-hospital care is good, despite a lack of thorough training for support personnel.

Religious Activities

São Paulo has many churches and synagogues. Many Protestant churches, including the Fellowship Community Church, inter-denominational; St. Paul's (Anglican); Calvary International Church; First Church of Christ Scientist; and the Church of Jesus Christ of Latter Day Saints, hold English-language services. The American priests of the Order of the Oblate Fathers conduct services in English at the Chapel School. A Greek Orthodox Cathedral also exists. The city has several synagogues. The largest, Congregacão Israelita Paulista, follows the conservative traditions and has an American rabbi.

Religious-oriented summer camps are available for children.

Education

Three schools in São Paulo follow the U.S. public school curriculum: the São Paulo Graded School, the Chapel School (School of Mary Immaculate), and the Pan American Christian Academy. The Southern Association of Colleges and Schools accredits all three schools.

The local Chamber of Commerce established the São Paulo Graded School, in 1929. The faculty, though predominantly American, employs teachers of several nationalities. Instruction is from kindergarten through grade 12. There is also a large preschool for 3-year-olds and older. The preschool and lower grades are taught on a modified Montessori program. The school follows curriculum standards of New York State. Enrollment is about 1,168; 38% are U.S. citizens. Facilities include a gym, auditorium, science labs, computer center, satellite TV, libraries, and a cafeteria serving hot lunches. Buses serve all residential areas. Most sports played in the U.S., except American football, are offered; teams compete within the school and with other American schools in Brazil. Additional extracurricular activities include theater, yearbook, and scouting. A program for students with special learning problems is available.

Felician Sisters and lay teachers staff Escola Maria Imaculada (The Chapel School) under the direction of the Oblate Fathers of Mary Immaculate. Instruction is from nursery school through grade 12. Advanced placement and the International Baccalaureate are integral parts of its quality academic program. Most graduates are accepted into universities and colleges of their first choice. The students represent over 30 countries; 40% of the students are non-Catholics and enrollment is 700; 25% are U.S. citizens. Facilities include: two libraries, a gym, a large playing field, a cafeteria, an auditorium, science labs, a computer center, an audiovisual room, an infirmary staffed by a nurse, and a student union. Organized sports include soccer, basketball, gymnastics, softball, tennis, handball, and volleyball both varsity and junior varsity teams. The school is a member of the São Paulo High School League. Twice a year, sports meets are held with American schools in São Paulo, Brasilia, and Rio de Janeiro at alternating locations. Additional extracurricular activities include judo, cooking, ballet, debating, choral groups, and band.

The Pan-American Christian Academy is operated by evangelical missionaries and is located some distance outside the city. Instruction from kindergarten through grade 12 is conducted in English. The level of instruction and discipline is reportedly high. Enrollment is approximately 317; 40% are U.S. citizens.

Each school begins in early August and runs through early June, with a 6-week midyear vacation in December and January. Requirements for enrollment are similar to those in the U.S. Schools adequately prepare students for entrance into U.S. colleges and universities.

Two preschool programs often used by American families are: Playpen, a Montessori school that has classes in English, and Portuguese and Tiny Tots, a preschool operated by a British-Brazilian family, with instruction in both English and Portuguese. Both often offer instruction during periods when the major schools (Graded, Chapel, etc.) are not in session. There are numerous other preschool programs in Portuguese throughout the city.

Tuition costs vary according to school and grade, with higher costs for middle school and senior high school.

A French-language school and a British school, St. Paul's, are also available. Also, many Brazilian nursery schools and kindergartens offer excellent, inexpensive programs. The required Portuguese language programs at the American schools are good, but some families send younger children to a public or private Brazilian school to learn Portuguese. Most Brazilian schools do not have facilities for children with speech or learning problems. Differences exist in preparation for American and Brazilian universities; therefore it is not recommended that you use Brazilian schools beyond the primary level.

Special Educational Opportunities

Although São Paulo has several fine universities, among which are the University of São Paulo, Mackenzie University, and Fundacao Getulio Vargas (FGV), you must be fluent in Portuguese in order to take advantage of their study programs. The Alumni Association and Uniao Cultural, two U.S. Brazil binational centers in the city, offer Portuguese language courses that can be used to supplement the post's language training program. However, there are certain opportunities for educational advancement available in English.

Through the Graded School, graduate level education courses are periodically offered for teachers, parents, and community members, with priority for enrollment in that order. These courses are taught by visiting professors from U.S. universities. The Graded School also offers courses in computers for teachers, parents, and members of the community. Other computer courses, in English and Portuguese, are available at private institutes throughout the city. Many schools of dance, adult exercise classes, and tutors in music, ballet, and painting are available.

Sports

Like other metropolis areas, São Paulo has various spectator sports. The most popular sport is soccer. Horse, auto and motorcycle racing, basketball games, tennis and golf tournaments, sailing regattas, polo, boxing, and wrestling matches complete the picture. São Paulo has no public golf courses or tennis courts, but many private tennis, squash, and racquetball courts are widely available on a pay-as-you-go basis. Private clubs include facilities for golf, tennis, swimming, horseback riding, boating, and basketball. Membership is expensive.

Most sporting equipment sold locally is comparable to price and quality of products in the U.S.

Touring and Outdoor Activities

The area around São Paulo is ideal for weekend excursions. Many beach and mountain resorts are within 100 miles of São Paulo and connected by good roads. Hotel quality and prices vary greatly, though most are very reasonable. Weekend houses are sometimes available for rent. The northern coast has various little towns and pristine beaches where hotel rooms are as little as $15 a night and rental boats will take you to secluded natural pools.

Iguaçu Falls (2 hours by air) offers one of Latin America's unique tourist sights. You may want to take an extra day to visit the falls from the Argentine side. The huge Itaipu hydroelectric project is nearby. Other popular outings for weekends or vacations include Rio de Janeiro; Ouro Preto, a mining town in Minas Gerais, with colonial baroque churches and other old towns nearby; Campos do Jordão; and Brasilia, a stunning example of city planning and modern architecture. Local travel agencies can be helpful in obtaining tour packages throughout Brazil and to other South American locations. Sdo Paulo and Mato Grosso offer excellent fishing and camping along the coast.

Weekly artist fairs are held on Sundays at the Praça da Republica, in the Asian neighborhood of Liberdade, and in Embu, on the outskirts of Sdo Paulo. These fairs offer local artwork, handicrafts, and geological specimens. The city also has many shopping facilities reminiscent of those in American cities.

Entertainment

Sdo Paulo offers excellent, professional theater in Portuguese. During winter, several symphonies often offer concerts, some with guest soloists. Operas are presented and local and touring concert groups and ballet companies also perform. Most movie theaters feature first-run American or foreign movies, as well as many Brazilian films. Foreign movies are usually shown with Portuguese subtitles. The city has many world-class art museums and galleries. Every 2 years, São Paulo hosts the Biennial, an internationally important modern art exposition, with extensive multinational representation.

With about 25,000 restaurants, cafes, and bars, São Paulo is one of the world's greatest cities for dining out. The city is especially rich in Italian, Japanese, and continental restaurants, and almost all ethnic communities are well represented. Brazilian churrascarias abound, serving a wide variety of richly seasoned, grilled meats accompanied by generous salad bars and side dishes. Fast food branches of American chains or local imitations are increasingly available.

Social Activities

There is a wide range of both business and social events, while home entertaining is also common. Much of the entertaining in the American community consists of luncheons and dinners.

The Newcomers Club, an English speaking club composed of all nationalities, is open to individuals for their first 2 years in Brazil. The club helps newcomers get acquainted and settled, and provides an opportunity for members to exchange information. Social activities include coffees and teas, museum outings, luncheons, dinners, book exchanges, and trips.

The American Society is a social and philanthropic organization for Americans in São Paulo. It organizes an annual field day for American Society members on the Fourth of July, an eggnog party at Christmas, and sponsors other social activities during the year. The American Society also issues an annual directory of members, a handy classified shopper's guide in English, and publishes a monthly newspaper with news of the English-speaking community. The American Society has a welfare program that provides financial, medical, and educational assistance to U.S. citizens in distress and also sponsors little league baseball, soccer, and flag football.

The São Paulo Women's Club, an international English-speaking club, provides social, cultural, and charitable activities. These include two book clubs, a free circulating library, a chorus, small theater group, current events group, and classes in bookbinding, painting, languages, and gems.

Masons, Rotary, and Lions clubs meet regularly in São Paulo. Illinois and São Paulo participate in a program called Joint Partners of the Americas. Finally, the PTAs of the three American schools sponsor many children's activities, such as sports teams and competitions, scouting, drama, dances, and school trips.

Special Information

If you are traveling between June and October, include cool weather clothing in ac companied baggage; other times brim warm weather clothing.

The winter is brief but can be chilly. An all-weather coat with zip out lining should meet your needs. Those accustomed to living in warm climates may need a pair of gloves, a scarf, and a knit hat. Children need a warm jacket. For the rest of the year, cardigan and pullover sweaters and sweatshirts in assorted weights will suffice.

It rains nearly every afternoon in summer (December to February). Therefore, each family member needs at least one good umbrella. Plastic rainwear is uncomfortable, and a lightweight cloth raincoat would be preferable. Footwear for wet weather is also useful.

Travelers with infants or small children should include disposable diapers, a supply of baby food, any special baby formula, and a bottle warmer in accompanied airfreight.

Disposable diapers are available locally, but are expensive and of poor quality.

São Paulo has competent doctors and dentists. Many speak English and were trained in the U.S. Their fees for an office visit are higher than fees in the U.S. Adequate orthodontic services are available at prices higher than those in the U.S.

Maternity and other hospital care is good, despite the absence of thorough training for support personnel. Admission to private institutions, even for an emergency, requires a substantial cash deposit if you do not belong to a local health plan.

São Paulo is a major metropolitan area with all the noise, pollution, and congestion found in large cities. Pollution levels are high, which affects those with allergies or respiratory problems. Heavy traffic and noise are common problems.

Recife

Recife, a city of startling contrasts, stretches 30 miles along Brazil's east coast. Miles of attractive beaches front the modern, luxury suburbs of Boa Viagem and Piedade at the city's southern tip. The central city, situated on two islands and the delta formed by the Capibaribe and Beberibe Rivers, is laced with numerous old and new bridges. It is a bustling, dynamic area, with thousands of taxis and small passenger vans clogging the narrow streets. The total absence of a grid system, the rivers winding through the city, and maze of one-way streets (at times unmarked) make finding one's way a challenge.

Recife's many small parks and plazas are well maintained. The thriving open market, Mercado de São Jose, is a principal tourist attraction, as are feiras (smaller markets) scattered throughout the city. Colonial Portuguese churches abound, the railroad station is a well-restored Victorian marvel, and an adjacent former prison has been converted into the Casa da Cultura, where hundreds of stalls feature

local handicrafts. Neighboring Olinda is considered one of Brazil's greatest colonial treasures and offers a fascinating glimpse into 17th century architecture.

Recife is the capital of Pernambuco and is the principal port city of Brazil's developing northeast. It is the commercial, cultural, and political center of the consular district, which has about 40 million people. The city has 2 million inhabitants; the greater metropolitan area has 3.5-4 million inhabitants. The city skyline is an impressive jumble of modern skyscrapers and sturdy old church towers. Residential areas along the Boa Viagem, Piedade and Candeias beaches feature kilometers of 2030 story apartment buildings.

Developing industrialization includes sugar refining, alcohol distillation, truck assembly, aluminum fabrication, and the manufacture of textiles, rum, vegetable oils, leather, glass, ceramics, canned goods, pharmaceuticals, paint, electronic equipment, and synthetic rubber. Tourism is an expanding industry with a growing influx of tourists traveling from southern Brazil during winter and summer and from Europe in winter. Agriculture remains the base of the Pernambuco economy; sugar has been the principal crop for over 300 years. Cotton raised in the interior, sisal, livestock, and fruits, vegetables, and grain crops are also economically important. Over the past few years, Brazil's largest center for the production of irrigated tropical fruit has developed in Petrolina, about 700 km west of Recife.

The countryside surrounding Recife is tropical, hilly, and fertile; it reaches inland some 20-30 miles. The undulating foothills and low mountains of the drier agreste region offer some relief from the tropical monotony of the coast. The agreste gives way to the semiarid sertão which stretches far into the central regions of the Northeast. It is dry and desolate most of the year; its cowboy folklore reminds one of the American southwest. Its location on the eastern extremity of Brazil places Recife about 1,500 miles across the south Atlantic from Dakar, Senegal, and about 1,300 miles north of São Paulo. Recife's geographic location makes it an important refueling point for transatlantic flights from South America to Europe. There are currently several non-stop flights a week to Miami as well as to destinations in Europe. Local connections to other Brazilian cities are also widely available and deregulation in recent years has led to a drop in domestic airfares. While few American tourists visit Recife, increasing numbers are visiting other beach cities in the consular district, most notably Natal and Fortaleza. Fernando de Noronha, an archipelago approximately 400 miles northeast of Recife which belongs to Pernambuco state, is rapidly gaining international notoriety as a destination for ecotourism.

Recife is located on the eastern edge of Brazil's time zone; sun time is over an hour ahead of clock time. Throughout the year it is dark soon after the Consulate closes at 5 pm, and there are never daylight hours for outdoor activities in the evening. Many Brazilians rise with the sun at 4:30 or 5:30 am and exercise on Boa Viagem beach or use the 8-kilometer walkway that stretches the length of the beach. For the late starter, for whom vigorous early morning exercise has little appeal, there are other options, including golf, equestrian sports and sports facilities at local clubs.

Recife has year-round rainfall, but the winter rainy season (May-September) has heavy daily rains that account for most of the annual 77 inches along the Pernambuco coast. Summer (October-April) is drier, with many clear, beautiful days. During the winter rainy season humidity is high and temperature variations are slight; the thermometer rises from 80°F to almost 90 degrees F, distinguishing winter from summer. The Northeast averages 250 days of sun per year, and the sun shines at least part of the day even during the rainy season.

The climate is not unbearably tropical, due to prevailing trade winds. Nevertheless, many expatriates experience problems with upper respiratory allergies during the rainy season, and post has obtained dehumidifiers to alleviate problems with some success.

Brazilians are a mixture of many ethnic groups: Portuguese, African, and Brazilian Indian backgrounds predominate in the Northeast. The largest foreign community is Portuguese, but small French, German, Israeli, Italian, Japanese, and Middle East groups exist. There are over 2,000 Americans registered in the Consular district and approximately 25% live in Recife. Many of those registered are dual nationals, although there is an important American missionary community.

Food

Recife's modern, air-conditioned supermarkets are well stocked and provide all the essentials to meet food and other household requirements of the average American family. In addition, the city is host to several specialty stores that provide oriental and other ethnic foods. Some types of meat, veal for example, are hard to obtain, but aside from this, you can maintain a perfectly adequate nutritional regimen with the food products available locally. Exceptional local tropical fruits and vegetables are available year round. Temperate climate fruits are brought in from southern Brazil and Argentina.

Clothing

Men: Summer clothes may be worn year round as temperatures seldom fall below 70 degree F. Most businessmen are casual in their dress, although some, such as bankers, still prefer suits to sport shirts.

Wash-and-wear items are most practical. Local custom-made linen, tropical worsteds, and Brazilian-made wash-and-wear suits range from $200 to $300, but are of lower quality. Bring at least one or two dark, lightweight suits for business calls and evening social functions.

You do not need hats (although caps for use in outdoor activities are highly recommended), but bring shirts, underwear, socks, and shoes. You can buy good-quality imported shirts in Recife, but they are expensive. Summer-weight washable slacks and shorts are useful, as is beach attire. Dry cleaning is available, but of questionable quality and expensive. Formal attire, such as a tuxedo or smoking jacket, is rarely required (only for the Carnaval ball). Tuxedos can be purchased or rented locally.

Women: Clothing stores are plentiful and varied, although Brazilian styles are considerably tighter fitting than U.S. clothing. Bring plenty of comfortable summer clothing: skirts, shorts, shirts, and bathing suits. A good basic evening wardrobe might consist of washable cocktail separates (pants, skirts, blouses, etc.) and a few washable evening dresses. Cotton dresses and separates are preferable for afternoon functions.

Dressmakers range from expensive designers to tailors who take in mending; in between are competent, reasonable dressmakers who can adequately copy the simple lines of current fashions. Fabrics are available locally. Hats are seldom worn (except for informal hats and caps for outdoor activities). Carnaval calls for costumes of fancy dress or shorts and a T-shirt.

Children: Bring children's clothing from the U.S. Given the weather, do not purchase winter clothes. Spring and summer weight clothing can be used year-round. Children rarely require long pants. Local seamstresses can be hired to mend and alter clothing and to make play clothing for children, although inexpensive locally manufactured play clothing is available and of acceptable quality.

Supplies and Services

Brazilian cosmetics and toiletries, many manufactured under agreements with U.S. firms, resemble U.S. products and are plentiful but more expensive than their U.S.

Teatro do Amaznas, Manaus, Brazil

counterparts. Internet buying services offer an excellent option for the purchase of U.S. goods.

Dry-cleaning service is available in Recife, but the quality is not up to U.S. standards. Full- or part-time launderers work in homes. Good beauty shops are available. Men's haircuts average $10. Women's cuts and styling range from $20-$40.

Repair work on radios, TVs, and other electrical appliances is not always satisfactory, but authorized service centers are available for most major brands. Parts are available, but expensive. Recife has the second most developed medical infrastructure in Brazil, and as a result medical and dental care is excellent, but more expensive than in the U.S. Note: Check your health insurance before arrival to see if overseas claims are based on an U.S. fee schedule or on a straight percentage of charges.

Domestic Help

Servants are necessary in Recife for the American or Brazilian running a household. The system benefits the family in that necessary household help is supplied, and employment and security is provided for semiliterate and untrained persons. Nannies are also common and readily available. Current monthly wages (including all benefits are estimated as follows: cook/housekeeper, $200; nanny $200; cook, $150; housekeeper, $150. Fringe benefits include quarters for the live-in cook and housekeeper (all housing, including smallest apartments, provides separate servants quarters and bath), food, uniforms, and social security/health insurance (for those that do not live in, a transportation allowance is also provided). Live-in employees are more common and less expensive. Part-time domestic employees charge on average $200 a month. A note of caution, finding suitable servants can be difficult and challenging.

Religious Activities

Recife has churches of almost every denomination including a synagogue, but few English-speaking services. English-language Baptist church services and a children's Sunday school are held every Sunday. Many beautiful and historical Catholic churches are located in Recife and in the adjoining town of Olinda. Mass is conducted in Portuguese. Many Catholic churches hold special Masses for adults, family, and youth. The youth mass is particularly interesting for young people who bring their guitars for group singing.

Education

The American School of Recife, founded in 1957, is a private, nonsectarian coeducational school that offers an instructional program from pre-kindergarten through grade 12 for students of all nationalities. The school is governed by a seven-member Board of Directors elected for a 2-year term by the Association, composed of the parents of children enrolled in the School. The Principal Officer is a non-voting member of the school board.

The curriculum is mainly that of U.S. general academic, preparatory, public schools. The Southern Association of Colleges accredits the school. There are 32 full-time and 6 part-time faculty members, of which 13 are U.S. citizens, 20 Brazilians, and 5 of other nationalities. Enrollment is approximately 350 students of which 40 are U.S. citizens, 250 host-country nationals, and 60 third-country nationals.

The school occupies an 8.5-acre site in a beautiful residential area of Recife. The pre-K/Kindergarten, elementary and high schools are in separate buildings. General facilities include classrooms, a science laboratory, two audio/visual rooms, a computer laboratory, a library with 12,000 volumes and a small theater. The school also has an adequate snack bar and lunch area as well as spacious sports and playground facilities.

Special Educational Opportunities

An art academy and a music conservatory are located in Recife. The Federal University of Pernambuco School of Fine Arts offers courses in theory, instrumentation, and ensemble playing. Private instruction is available on musical instruments. Private art instruction and group ballet lessons are also available.

Spouses need a basic command of Portuguese before coming to Recife; all practical day-to-day communications is in Portuguese. Additional language instruction for adult dependents is available.

Sports

Many health clubs and fitness centers in the city offer aerobics, gymnastics, dance, and exercise equipment. They are similar to those in the U.S., with trained instructors and such amenities as saunas, steam baths, and optional massages. Membership fees are low

by U.S. standards and are paid monthly.

Other social clubs offer recreational facilities in the city. There is also a golf and equestrian club.

Touring and Outdoor Activities

The Northeast offers some of the best beaches in Brazil, and many are less than a day's drive from Recife. Beaches range from established resorts to isolated stretches and most are easily accessible by vehicle, although a four-wheel drive vehicle would be preferable. Other one-day sightseeing trips afford visits to sugarcane plantations and mills, forts from the Dutch era in the 17th century, and quaint fishing villages on the coast and inlets. Most major routes are paved, and the remote, adventuresome routes are passable, except during the rainy season.

Several small towns, from 2-3 hours away offer a cooler, drier climate than the coastal region. Satisfactory overnight accommodations are available. Other cities in the consular district, such as Fortaleza, Natal and João Pessoa offer considerable tourist attractions. Salvador, the colorful, historic first capital of Brazil is approximately an hour's flight south. Rio de Janeiro and São Paulo are a 2-1/2-hour flight south.

Entertainment

Recife has several modern multiplex theaters offering first-run U.S. and Brazilian movies. Several comfortable movie theaters also show other foreign films. Foreign films are in their original language with Portuguese subtitles, although children's films are dubbed. Recife has many restaurants ranging from simple, beachfront seafood houses in Olinda, to luxurious and expensive restaurants in Boa Viagem. Downtown restaurants are patronized mainly at lunchtime. Open-air restaurants along the beach in Boa Viagem are popular for evenings and weekends. Cuisines include Chinese, Italian, and seafood restaurants; churrascarias for grilled meats are also available. Prices

vary, but dinner for two with wines is less than in the U.S.

The renovated old city, Recife Antigo, offers an excellent option for nightlife. Open-air bars and sidewalk cafes, along with cultural events sponsored by the city, make Recife Antigo the center of nightlife in the city. There are several large discos and nightclubs (including Brazil's largest) which are very popular.

Recife also has several large modern shopping centers with many services, including bowling alleys and arcades. One, Shopping Recife, is the largest shopping center in South America.

Several radio stations and five color TV stations broadcast in Recife. An American black-and-white TV operates with a transformer and a voltage regulator. U.S. color sets need a PAL-M to NTSC converter, which can be purchased in the U.S. Local TVs are readily available, although more expensive than U.S. TVs.

Local TV offers numerous variety shows, popular Brazilian novelas (soap operas), daily national news programs, public interest features, Brazilian soccer and, occasionally, world sports events. Direct TV is available as are affordable satellite TV services offering US premium cable channels.

No English-language newspapers are published in Recife; foreign news is sparsely covered in the local press. The Latin American editions of Time and Newsweek are available weekly. However, internet service is readily available and inexpensive (approximately $20 per month for unlimited access).

Recife's Carnaval is world famous. It is considered the largest street carnival in the world. Two events during Carnaval, the Bloco de Parceria on the Sunday before Carnaval and the Galo de Madrugada the Saturday of Carnaval vie for the title of largest concentration of people in the Guinness Book of World Records (each brings an estimated 2 million people together). Tourists from around the world flock to Olinda and Recife Antigo for more traditional carnivals. Other important celebrations include the São Joao festival in June, which offers typical northeastern music and dancing and special Brazilian dishes, and Recifolia, one of the largest out-of-season carnivals in Brazil. Several libraries are located in Recife for those who can read Portuguese, although books cannot be loaned out. A small library of American books and current periodicals is located at the binational center.

Social Activities

This region of Brazil is known for its hospitality and receptivity to foreigners. Most of the social activity in Recife revolves around the extended family, which often includes close family friends. Dinners are also common. Most entertaining, both in a family or more formal setting, is done at home. Entertaining is also more informal in nature, reflecting this family orientation.

The social life in Recife is active and Americans are readily welcomed into the community. Adults, adolescents and children quickly develop their own social life and meet frequently for parties and various activities.

Pôrto Alegre

Pôrto Alegre, capital of the State of Rio Grande do Sul, is the center of one of the most prosperous areas of Brazil. The city, with an estimated population of 2.9 million, lies at sea level at the mouth of the Guaíba River, the head of the sea's freshwater outlet, Lagoa dos Patos. The State of Rio Grande do Sul covers 108,951 square miles, and is slightly larger than Colorado. It is bordered on the north by the State of Santa Catarina, on the west by Argentina, and on the south by Uruguay.

Traditionally an agricultural state, it grows and processes rice, corn, wheat, soybeans, livestock, and a variety of other products. Extensive industrial expansion, including the refining of petroleum and its by-products, and the production of steel, ships, footwear and leather products, wine, wood, paper and cellulose, textiles, and electrical products has occurred in recent years.

Although Pôrto Alegre's basic cultural pattern is dominated by its Luso-Brazilian heritage, this has been modified by Texas-like gaucho traditions, and (more recently) by heavy German and Italian immigration.

Pôrto Alegre's architecture reflects its historical development: early colonial buildings, baroque structures derived from Italy and France, and Brazilian modern design. Pôrto Alegre is built on hills, some of them quite steep. Narrow cobblestone streets, buses, and taxis, and many office buildings in the downtown district contribute to traffic congestion that is out of proportion to the city's size.

The Americans in Pôrto Alegre include those on assignment with agencies of the U.S. Government, a small number of business firms, and several religious organizations. The British community is somewhat larger. Periodically, American business representatives visit the city. Membership in the American Chamber of Commerce is almost entirely Brazilian.

Schools for Foreigners

Rio Grande do Sul, and Pôrto Alegre in particular, has one of the best school systems in Brazil, but all instruction is in Portuguese. Fluency in that language is more or less mandatory for admission and for satisfactory performance in Brazilian schools.

The only English-language school in Pôrto Alegre is the Pan-American School, which offers kindergarten through eighth grade, and can provide correspondence-school supervision for grades nine through 12. The school was organized in 1966, and had a 1991 enrollment of about 87 students. There were nine full-time and seven part-time teachers at the school in 1991. The Pan-American School is a coeducational institution with a U.S.-style curriculum. The school has 12 classrooms, a 5,000-volume library, playing field, computer lab, and science lab. Extracurricular activities include soccer, field trips, and school newspaper. Information is available from the school at Rua João Paetzel 440, 90.000 Pôrto Alegre, Rio Grande do Sul, Brazil.

Four private American missionary schools exist but, as the founders have died or been replaced by Brazilian teachers, the schools have lost their U.S. character. The schools are Colegio Americano (Methodist for girls), Instituto Pôrto Alegre (Methodist for boys), Colegio Batista (Baptist, coeducational), and Ginasio Menino Deus (Catholic, coeducational in the primary grades, operated by the Bernardine Sisters from the U.S., but taught mostly by Brazilian nuns). All offer first grade through high school. Children, especially girls, must wear uniforms.

Several good Portuguese-language schools are in Pôrto Alegre—the Colegio Anchieta (Jesuit, coeducational), Colegio Farroupilha (coeducational), Colegio de Aplicacão (junior high and high school, coeducational), Colegio Rosario (Marist Brothers for boys), and Colegio Sevigne (Sisters of St. Joseph for girls). Pôrto Alegre's Jewish community runs the Ginasio Israelita Brasileiro. Schools are in session about four hours a day, morning or afternoon, six days a week. Children too young to travel alone are taken to and from school by parents. A few private institutions have buses.

Principal universities in Pôrto Alegre, among the first in Brazil, are Catholic University and Federal University. Courses are taught in Portuguese. Private Portuguese-language instruction on a reasonable hourly basis may be arranged.

Recreation

Many sports are available in the Pôrto Alegre area, among them tennis, golf, yachting, fishing, swimming, riding, and trap, skeet, and target shooting. A number of clubs maintain good tennis courts, and several clubs also have swimming pools. Ocean swimming is available at beach resorts such as Torres, Capão da Canoa, Tramandaí, and Cassino, two to six hours by car from the city. There is a fine harbor at Veleiros do Sul, one of the two major yacht clubs. The other club, Jangadeiros, caters to day sailors and holds frequent regattas for small centerboard sloops. Motorboating is also popular.

Spectator sports are soccer and horse racing.

Those interested in touring will find Caxias do Sul an interesting spot. About 75 miles north of Pôrto Alegre in the center of the mountainous wine-growing region, it is a clean and attractive city well worth visiting. The Italian community holds an annual wine festival there. Slightly closer than Caxias do Sul is the mountain resort town of Gramado. Many people living temporarily in Pôrto Alegre also make trips to Florianópolis, the capital of Santa Catarina, to enjoy the fine beaches. Iguaçú Falls are accessible by scheduled airlines in a three-hour flight or a one-day drive over good roads. Bordered by Brazil, Argentina, and Paraguay, the falls are world renowned for their volume and beauty.

Entertainment

Pôrto Alegre has several air-conditioned movie theaters. U.S films (six months to one year old) predominate, supplemented by French, Italian, German, British, and Brazilian productions.

The Pôrto Alegre Symphony Orchestra plays at least once a month in season, and another concert series brings international guest artists to the city. Professional Brazilian theater companies perform occasionally. The city offers many good restaurants, some featuring German, Italian, or Chinese cuisine, as well as the traditional *churrasco* (barbecue). Several nightclubs exist.

Celebration of *Carnaval* season is fairly moderate and is best represented by social events organized by clubs and neighborhood groups.

Many members of the English-speaking community join the British Club. Facilities include tennis courts, swimming and wading pools, and playground equipment. Although the club serves as a gathering place for English speakers, membership is not confined to persons familiar with the language. The International Women's Association also offers opportunities for social activities.

One of the attractive features of visiting or living in Pôrto Alegre is the chance to meet and know Brazilians, and the only limit to the newcomer's international contacts is language. Pôrto Alegre has several active Rotary and Lions clubs and Masonic lodges. The ability to speak Portuguese fluently will greatly enhance opportunities for social contact.

Special Information

Santa Catarina, in the U.S. consular district of Pôrto Alegre, is in the south temperate zone of Brazil. Its climate is similar to that of Rio Grande do Sul. The state is divided into three distinct geographical zones: the coastal plain, the central highlands, and the western highlands. The state borders Argentina to the west, Paraná to the north, and Rio Grande do Sul to the south. The capital is Florianópolis.

Blessed with abundant rainfall and numerous lakes, the state is one of Brazil's most beautiful. The coastal area includes superb beaches and coves, and attracts visitors from many parts of Brazil, Uruguay, and Argentina.

The State of Santa Catarina's population of four million includes 30 percent German, 30 percent Italian, 15 percent Portuguese, 10 percent Polish, five percent Russian, five percent Negro, and five percent of mixed origin. Santa Catarina is the most European of Brazil's states. Entire communities of German-speaking peoples abound, especially in the Blumenau-Joinville-Brusque area. The architecture, language, music, and cultural traditions all give the state the air of a central European country.

Santa Catarina has elementary and secondary schools in all municipalities of 2,000 inhabitants or more. In the western highlands, few secondary and preparatory schools exist.

The only accredited university in the state, the Federal University of Santa Catarina, is in Florianópolis. Present enrollment is about 6,000 full-time students. Separate faculties also exist in Joinville (economics and public administration) and in Lages (chemistry and industrial engineering). Blumenau has a municipal university.

Santa Catarina's many lakes and ocean-front beaches make it a fisherman's heaven. For hunters, all sorts of wild game abound, including rabbit, squirrel, bobcat, puma, bear, raccoon, wild boar, and over 25 species of game birds. The western portion is ideal for overnight camping.

Salvador Da Bahia

Salvador Da Bahia, formerly Salvador, is Brazil's oldest city, located in one of the most historic parts of the country. The Portuguese first landed in Brazil at Pôrto Seguro in the southern part of the State of Bahia, and when they colonized the country, they built the city which is now Salvador da Bahia. It was Brazil's capital from 1549 to 1763.

Situated on a hilly peninsula at the entrance to All Saints' Bay (Bahia de Todos os Santos), it is a picturesque city famed for its many baroque churches, distinctive food, colorful costumes, and religious ceremonies. Although strong African influences are found in Bahia, the main cultural tradition is Western, influenced at first by Portugal, and more recently by France and the U.S.

Salvador da Bahia is one of Brazil's largest modern ports. Cocoa, tobacco, sugar, sisal, diamonds, iron ore, aluminum, hides, and petroleum are exported through Salvador da Bahia's port. The city has many important industries, among them textiles, ceramics, food and tobacco processing, automobiles, chemicals, and shipbuilding.

The metropolitan area has an estimated population of 2.4 million and is growing rapidly. Although this growth is accompanied by modern urban problems, the city retains much of its charm because of its privileged location by the bay and ocean, its varied topography, and its rich collection of historic buildings, many of which are registered and cannot be torn down.

Salvador da Bahia is divided into two parts—the "lower city" at sea level with the old port and commercial district; and the "upper city," reached by stone steps, and the site of government buildings, residential areas, museums, and churches. Some of the old and historically significant churches have been made into museums.

Schools for Foreigners

The Pan-American School of Bahia, with a student body of about 470, representing many nationalities, is partially sponsored by the U.S. Government. It offers an English-language curriculum from kindergarten through 12th grade. In 1991, the school had 50 full-time teachers, 25 of whom were Americans. Located 15 minutes from downtown Salvador da Bahia, the school consists of two buildings, 25 classrooms, a 35,000-volume library, two playing fields, two science labs, and a computer lab. In December 1977, Pan-American was accredited by the Southern Association of Colleges and Schools. Its program follows the U.S. educational system, and students have transferred easily into American schools and universities. Extracurricular activities include field trips, computers, year-

book, basketball, volleyball, and soccer. The school address is: Caixa Postal 231, Salvador da Bahia 4000, Brazil.

Two universities in Bahia offer interesting courses, seminars, and lectures for those with a firm command of Portuguese. Many Americans study that language with private tutors or at the Binational Center.

Recreation

Golf, tennis, sailing, swimming, and volleyball are the sports which normally attract members of the foreign community in Bahia. Skin diving, rock fishing, and deep-sea fishing are also available. Game in the area is scarce, but duck hunting is possible.

Many Americans join clubs which, in addition to offering sports facilities, provide a place to dine and relax on weekends. The Yacht Club, with a large freshwater pool, a boathouse, and restaurant/bar in attractive surroundings, makes available a temporary (four-month) membership. The Associação Atletica also offers a temporary (six-month) membership. Both the Bahia Tennis Club and the Cajazeira Golf Club provide either transferable or temporary memberships. The British Club, strictly a social organization, is the gathering place for the English-speaking community, and an English-language library is maintained there.

Salvador da Bahia and many nearby historic towns are good for sight-seeing. In the city itself, there is the excellent Museum of Sacred Art, considered the most beautiful in all of Brazil; it contains many works of Brazil's renowned baroque sculptor, Aleijadinho (Antônio Francisco Lisboa), known as "the little cripple." The visitor will also find numerous churches, forts, a small zoo, and many buildings of historical and architectural interest.

It is possible, by prior arrangement, to attend a *condomble* (voodoo religious ceremony). Photographs may

not be taken at such ceremonies without specific permission.

Entertainment

Movies in English, with Portuguese subtitles, are shown in many theaters. A cultural society presents a series of musical recitals and concerts during the May-to-December season.

The few nightclubs, generally discotheques without live entertainment, compare in price to those in large cities of the U.S. Salvador da Bahia has many fine restaurants.

Local radio programs are good, and shortwave is usually satisfactory, but sets should be tropicalized and powerful because of the distances involved. Most people on extended assignments have stereo equipment for home entertainment, and they find that the humidity makes it necessary to use cartridges of variable inductance rather than the ceramic type. There are three television stations in the city. No adjustments are needed for reception on black-and-white American sets.

The closely knit international community in Salvador da Bahia consists mainly of Americans (executives from the private industrial sector and petrochemical complex, and petroleum industry workers), Scandinavians, Swedes, English, Germans, and Argentines. Most speak English and send their children to the Pan-American School. In several book clubs, English-speaking members collectively purchase and share publications. The International Women's Club is one of the city's active social and charitable organizations.

Foreigners participate actively in the city's normal social life. Bahians are friendly and welcome contact with foreigners, especially Americans. English-speaking business representatives meet each Wednesday for lunch at the Clube do Comércio.

Because of the interesting scenery and relaxed life in Salvador da Bahia, many prominent artists

Transporting soda pop in Brazil

make their homes in the area, and are easily accessible to foreigners.

Belo Horizonte

Belo Horizonte (Beautiful Horizon), capital of Minas Gerais, is Brazil's third largest city, with a population of over 4 million. Minas Gerais is Brazil's second most important state economically, after São Paulo. It is a major center of mining, steel production, automobile (Fiat), electronics, heavy machinery, and agriculture.

Minas Gerais maintains a higher economic growth rate than the nation as a whole. The state's utilities are generally well run providing better than average services, for Brazil. However, investment in basic infrastructure, especially roads, has not kept pace with the state's economic growth. The effects of rapid economic growth of the past decades are evident in the prolifera-

tion of common urban problems, such as air pollution (especially severe during the dry season), a crowded downtown area, and slums. Nevertheless, the city is less crowded and congested than Rio or São Paulo, and seems much smaller than a city of 4 million.

Accelerated economic growth in the past few years has also brought an explosion in the cost of living in Belo Horizonte. Consumer prices and rents are comparable to Rio de Janeiro and São Paulo. Officers stationed in Belo Horizonte do not receive tax-free gasoline privileges.

Belo Horizonte, founded in 1897, is spread out over a rolling terrain and many streets are steep. The crosswork of avenues, streets, and diagonals can be confusing to a newcomer. Belo Horizonte has few landmarks of historical significance. The most interesting features of the city include the Praça da Liberdade, the center for the state government;

the Municipal Park with tree-shaded paths, a small recreation area for children, small lake, and the Lagoa da Pampulha area with a larger lake; and the Oscar Niemeyer-designed São Francisco de Assis Church, with murals and frescoes by the internationally famed Brazilian painter, Portinari. Brazil's colonial past is illustrated by a series of beautifully preserved historical cities such as Ouro Preto and Sabará, within 2 hours' drive of the capital. The city has an active night life, with many bars, clubs, restaurants and music.

Belo Horizonte enjoys a warm and dry climate. Winters are mild and sunny, with few genuinely cold days. Summers (December-March) are warm with few spells of hot, muggy weather. Most precipitation occurs from November to February with intermittent rain, heavy at times, causing severe, dangerous flooding.

The city is a junction for highways, connecting Rio de Janeiro (4-4-1/2 hours by car), São Paulo (8 hours), and Brasilia (10 hours). Highways are paved and in good condition, although overcrowded with trucks carrying mineral and steel products and agricultural goods. The city's streets are well kept generally, although the quality of pavement is poor in many areas. Most of the city is paved and has a clean look, although pollution is becoming a problem. Modern shopping centers are located in and around the city, offering many stores, including many international chains.

Two airports, Confins (60 min. downtown) and Pampulha (20-30 min.), provide frequent connections to Brasilia, São Paulo Rin de Janeiro and other cities

Food

Food is available locally in adequate quantity and variety. Fresh meat is plentiful. Fruits and vegetables in season are plentiful. Canned goods, frozen foods, and a growing variety of packaged and convenience foods are available but expensive. The central market and neighborhood markets continue to be important sources of supply for fruit, vegetables, and meats. Large supermarkets carrying a wide variety of merchandise, in addition to food items, are available.

Clothing

All types of temperate climate clothing are useful, including a limited number of woolens for occasionally chilly winter mornings, evenings, or when traveling in southern Brazil during winter. Styles for men and women are informal, but some business and social occasions call for business suits or formal wear. Brazilian women are style conscious and women coming to post may wish to vary their wardrobe after arrival according to local fashions. Various pants, blouses, and pantsuits will suffice for most occasions, with long dresses used only for formal social events.

Supplies and Services

Basic supplies are available locally. Officers stationed in Belo Horizonte should make arrangements to buy items available at the commissary in Brasilia.

Local tailors and dressmakers are adequate. Shoe repair is good. Laundry and dry cleaning services are good, but prices are high.

Local physicians, surgeons, and dentists can treat all but the most serious medical problems. Many have studied or done residencies in the U.S. and speak some English. The cost of medical services in Belo Horizonte is high. An office call currently costs about $70. You can obtain advanced and highly specialized medical services in Rio de Janeiro and São Paulo. Pharmacies carry adequate stocks of Brazilian-produced prescription and nonprescription medicines.

Repair facilities for foreign automobiles, appliances, or electronic items are difficult to find. The reliability of repairs varies. Local carpenters and cabinetmakers are competent, but slow.

Good household help is difficult to find. Increased job opportunities for women in manufacturing industries and businesses have sharply reduced the number interested in domestic employment. Finding and keeping skilled and reliable help is a problem. Personal recommendations are the best way of finding help; employment agencies are not recommended.

Education

American and English-speaking children attend the American School. Classes are from kindergarten through grade 12.

The Federal University of Minas Gerais and the Catholic University of Minas Gerais provide programs in most subject areas. Foreign students are few. The binational center and the Federal University offer Portuguese courses.

Sports

Free public recreation facilities are limited and crowded. These include the Municipal Park downtown, a zoo in the Pampulha area, Mangabeiras Park, and Minas Gerais and Fernão Dias Parks.

Many local residents join sports and social clubs and memberships cost $2,000 and up. Clubs offer swimming and tennis facilities. Monthly fees cost $200 and up. Fishing and boating are available on the San Francisco River, some 200 miles from the city. Spectator sports include professional soccer, basketball, and volleyball.

Entertainment

Several colonial cities famous for their baroque architecture and colorful settings are located in Minas Gerais State and are popular tourist attractions. Movie theaters often feature international films with Portuguese subtitles. The Palacio das Artes is home of the Minas Gerais Symphony Orchestra and sponsors performances by local and international musical and theatrical groups. A growing number of art galleries exhibit the works of local artists. The city has an active night life, with many bars, restaurants, nightclubs, concerts, and dancing. The small American community offers limited opportunities for social contact and activities. It consists of temporary residents working for American firms with local branches, missionaries, and permanent residents, including Americans settling in Minas Gerais after marrying Brazilians. A monthly picnic is held at the American School for all members of the community. The city has a small diplomatic community with consulates from Portugal, Argentina, Italy, and Chile.

Mineiros, as natives of the state are known, are friendly but reserved. Host country and other officials meet through business, commercial, fraternal organizations, country clubs, and artistic and cultural events. Family life centers in the home in Minas Gerais. However, once new acquaintances are established, families welcome friendly relationships in their homes.

Belém

Belém, a port city, lies about 1°S. of the equator. The ninth largest city in Brazil, it is the capital of the State of Pará. Belém is the economic and political center of the Amazon region. Its narrow streets, tile-fronted homes, random Victorian architecture, modern high-rise office and apartment buildings, and wide streets lined with mango trees bear testimony to Belém's rich and varied history. The city was founded in 1616 by the Portuguese as a base to protect their territorial holdings in what now is northern Brazil. Throughout its history, as now, Belém has served as the port of entry to the vast Amazon Basin, and port of exit for regional products. Products exported via Belém include Brazil nuts, cassava, jute, black pepper, and aluminum.

Some of Brazil's most beautiful old churches are in Belém, among them the Santo Alexandre, the Basílica da Nossa Senhora de Nazaré, and the 17th-century Mercês Church. The city's Catedral (cathedral) dates from 1748. Noteworthy among the modern structures is Teatro da Paz, one of the country's largest theaters, the public library, and archives building.

The city is 90 miles inland from the Atlantic Ocean, at the junction of the Guamá River and Guajara Bay, which form part of the southern estuary of the Amazon River system. High temperatures and relative humidity make the climate debilitating and, at times, exhausting, but moderate easterly winds bring some relief. Insect and animal pests flourish.

About 25 percent of the city's estimated population of 1.5 million is of European descent, mostly Portuguese. The remainder is either of Indian or mixed racial origin. The foreign community includes some 25,000 Portuguese, 10,000 Japanese, and several hundred English, Dutch, French, German, Italian, Spanish, Lebanese, and Eastern Europeans. About 1,000 Americans live in and around Belém, and another 1,500 are scattered throughout the district.

A modern airport, which is one of Brazil's largest, is maintained in Belém.

Manaus

Manaus (formerly spelled Manáos) is the capital of Amazonas State and the major city of the Amazon Basin, standing near the confluence of the Amazon and the Río Negro. The rubber boom of the late 19th century effected temporary prosperity, but the decline in that industry left the city to shrink in influence until a renewed interest in the Amazon Basin brought economic growth. Approximately 615,000 people now live in Manaus. It is the major port of northwestern Brazil, and its floating docks can accommodate oceangoing vessels. Brazil nuts, rubber, rosewood oil, and several forest products constitute Manaus' primary exports. Several industries make their home in Manaus, including ship building, soap manufacturing, brewing, petroleum refining, and chemical production. An international airport has been built, and coexists with the British-built customs house, the Portuguese townhouses, and the lavish Opera House, where Sarah Bernhardt once sang.

Manaus features a cathedral, zoological and botanical gardens, and the Museu Indígena Salesiano, which is dedicated to the region's Indian cultures. The tourist office is at Praça 24 de Outubro, Rua Taruma 329, and there are information kiosks at the airport and at the floating docks. Most banks in the city will change foreign currency only in the morning, but money can be exchanged at *Selvatour* in the Hotel Amazónas. One- and two-day river trips up the Río Negro from Manaus are readily available, and considered worthwhile excursions; it is possible to stop along the river banks to explore the fringes of the forest or to canoe in the clear lakes of the interior.

Fortaleza

Fortaleza (Portuguese for fortress), a city with an estimated population of 2.8 million residents, is the capital of the State of Ceará in northeastern Brazil. The city (often referred to as Ceará, the state designation, by foreigners) served as a center for the sugar plantations in colonial times and, today, processes sugar and cotton, and ships exotic products such as carnauba wax and oiticica oil. Fortaleza is also known for traditional handicrafts, especially lace-making.

The Dutch occupied Fortaleza in the mid-17th century, and Nossa Senhora da Assuncão, a fort built by them, still stands. Excellent seafood is brought to the nearby beaches by the fishermen in their hand-crafted vessels each day at about sundown, and the lobsters here are considered particular delicacies. The 1,393-acre Ubajará National Park, featuring caves of the same name, is close by. Fortaleza's tourist office is located at Rua Senador Pompeu 250, and there is a branch in the old prison.

Curitiba

Curitiba, a rapidly growing city of more than 1.4 million residents, is a commercial and processing center, and also the capital, of the southeastern State of Paraná. It was founded in 1654, but developed slowly until the influx of German, Italian, and Slavic immigrants in the early part of the 20th century. The metropolitan area now accommodates well over one million residents.

During the past 30 years, Curitiba has seen swift expansion and modernization. New housing and public buildings have sprung up both in the central city and the burgeoning suburbs, yet the city has not succumbed to the clutter and confusion which often accompanies urban growth. Beautiful, wide avenues and vast expanses of park land remain, bestowing an aura of tranquility seldom found in a modern setting.

Curitiba is home to several industries which manufacture textiles, automobiles, furniture, matches, tobacco, soft drinks, lumber, and tea. Tourist attractions in the city include the Paranáense Museum and an Egyptian-style temple located near Lake Bacacheri.

Two institutes of higher learning are located here—Federal University of Paraná, dating from 1912, and Catholic University, which opened in 1959. Curitiba also is the site of the State Library. The International School of Curitiba, which follows a U.S. curriculum and employs six American teachers, is in a suburb overlooking the city.

Goiânia

Goiânia, capital of the State of Goiás and its largest city, is about two-and-a-half hours west of Brasilia. Like Brasilia, it is a planned city, and was built in 1933 to replace the old city of Goiás as the state capital. With an altitude much lower than Brasilia's, it is usually considerably warmer and more humid. Goiânia is an attractive city with tree-lined streets, attractive parks, interesting 1930s architecture, a shopping center, good hotels, and some excellent restaurants. It also has fine museums and art galleries, and a good urban transportation system. The Sunday fair is one of the best in the area.

Goiânia's population has grown to over 702,000. The city is a shipping and processing center for livestock, crops, and minerals. It is the seat of two schools of higher learning, Federal and Catholic universities, as well as several technical institutes. The city is accessible by air, road, and railway.

OTHER CITIES

The city of **ANÁPOLIS,** in the State of Goiás, is situated in central Brazil, 82 miles south of the capital. Lumber, rice, coffee, and livestock are processed in this industrial center. Anápolis distributes diamonds, gold, maize, and rubber by rail. A highway and an airport are located nearby. Its population is about 161,000.

ARACAJU is the capital city of Sergipe State in northeastern Brazil. It is near the mouth of the Sergipe River and has an excellent harbor. As the state's commercial hub, it ships cotton, sugar, hides, and rice. The city has several industries which process salt, cotton, sugar, beans, bananas, cashews, and leather. Several roads and airports link Aracaju to Recife, Maceió, and Salvador da Bahia. Aracaju's population is about 289,000.

CAMPINA GRANDE is situated in northeastern Brazil in the State of Paraíba. Since Campina Grande is located in a cotton-growing region, most of its industries are mainly based on that product. Other factories in the city manufacture metallurgical products, pharmaceuticals, and plastics. It also produces sugarcane, fruit, vegetables, and tobacco. The city is the home of an art museum and a regional university. Road, river, air, and rail transportation is available to Recife, João Pessoa and several other cities. The population of Campina Grande is about 222,000.

Located in the State of São Paulo, **CAMPINAS** is about 57 miles northwest of the city of São Paulo. At one time, Campinas was Brazil's top coffee producer. Today, its industries include the processing of cereals, cotton, and sugarcane as well as coffee. Cosmetics, soap, textiles, motorcycles and agricultural machinery are also produced. Campinas has a symphony orchestra, as well as theaters, museums, and art galleries. A tourist attraction near Campinas is the Salto d'Ita Falls, located five miles north of the city. There are two universities here. The city's population is approximately 567,000.

CAMPO GRANDE, in southwestern Brazil, is the fastest-growing city in the State of Mato Grosso. Industries include tanneries, meat-packing plants, and slaughterhouses. Coffee, corn, rice, and beans are grown in areas surrounding the city. The railroads and airways in Campo Grande are an essential means of transportation for the surrounding region. Campo Grande's population of 282,800 is the largest in Mato Grosso.

CAXIAS DO SUL (formerly called Caxias) is an Italian immigrant settlement in the State of Rio Grande do Sul in southern Brazil. Regional farming supports the city's industries which include cattle-raising, wine making, and hog slaughtering. The city's population is close to 199,000.

CORUMBÁ, a small southwestern port city of approximately 66,000 residents on the Río Paraguai, is the chief trade center for Mato Grosso State. Visitors often take boat trips north from here through the Pantanal, a vast wildlife preserve. Other attractions are the regional museum, and the arts and crafts center at the old jail. Corumbá, a junction on the railroad connecting Brazil and Bolivia, was a key strategic point in the War of the Triple Alliance (1865), and changed hands often. Factories in the city process xarque (dried beef) and animal hides.

FLORIANÓPOLIS is located on Santa Catarina Island, off the coast of southeastern Brazil, and is connected to the mainland by two spans, the oldest of which is the handsome and historical Hercílio Luz Bridge. The city has spilled over onto the Estreito strip of the mainland, and the total population is estimated at 154,000. The city produces a number of products including pharmaceuticals, communications equipment, perfume, and plastics. Now a bustling commercial center and the capital of Santa Catarina, Florianópolis' colonial houses still stand along the narrow streets of the city's older section. An anthropology museum at Federal University is worth visiting, and excellent beaches have made the area popular with tourists. The city, named for an early Brazilian president, Floriano Peixoto, was once known as Destêrro. It is linked by excellent roads with the coastal cities of Pôrto Alegre and Curitiba. Flights are available from Florianópolis to Rio de Janeiro, Pôrto Alegre, and São Paulo.

Located in northeastern Brazil, **JOÃO PESSOA** is the capital of Paraíba State. Founded in 1585, João Pessoa today supplies cement, clothing, beverages, and cigars locally. One of its better-known historical buildings is the 18th-century Church of São Francisco. The church still has its original wooden grilles, entrance, and decorative towers and domes. The city manufactures chemicals, metals, plastics, and electrical products. The city is the home of Paraíba University. João Pessoa's population is close to 290,250.

JUIZ DE FORA is 80 miles north of Rio de Janeiro in the southeastern State of Minas Gerais. The city, with an estimated population of 300,000, is an important manufacturer of knitwear. Many crops are grown near Juiz de Fora, among them bananas, sugarcane, coffee, and rice. Textiles and plastics are also manufactured here. A major tourist attraction is the Mariano Procopio museum. In 1960, the Federal University of Juiz de Fora was opened here.

Situated 125 miles southwest of Recife, in northeastern Brazil, **MACEIÓ** is the capital of Alagoas State. An industrial city, Maceió produces household items, cotton textiles, chemicals, cigarettes, sugar, and foods. Exports include tobacco, cotton, rum, and sugar. Reflecting its colonial background, the city's landmarks include a lighthouse in the center of the city the Church of Bom Jesus dos Mártires, the Metropolitan Cathedral, and the Government Palace. Maceió is linked with Recife and cities to the north by road and rail. The population here is about 375,700.

NATAL, with a population of close to 376,500, is situated in northeastern Brazil. It is the capital of Rio Grande do Norte State. A major port, it ships hides, salt, cotton, and sugar. Important industries include salt refining and cotton spinning and weaving. The city was founded on December 25, 1599; "natal" means "Christmas" in Portuguese. The coastline has nice beaches and a folk museum housed in a 16th-century fort. Railroads and highways extend from Natal to the interior and to coastal urban centers. Flights are available to the cities of Recife and Teresina.

Located on the Atlantic coast in Pernambuco State, **OLINDA** is about 60 miles south of Natal and about 50 miles north of Maceió. Less than four miles from Recife, Olinda is one of the major architectural centers of Brazil. The narrow, steep streets here are flanked by beautiful churches and centuries-old houses. A large colony of artists in the city produce wood carvings and pottery. The colorful Moorish fountains give an added dimension to this historic town of 267,000 residents.

OURO PRÊTO, located in the mountains of eastern Brazil, was founded during the gold rush at the turn of the 18th century, and became a prosperous mining town in the following decades. Since 1933, the city has been considered a national museum, and bears the designation, "world monument," an honor bestowed by United Nations Educational, Scientific, and Cultural Organization (UNESCO). The city's colonial-era houses, churches, and public buildings have been preserved and restored. On June 24 of each year, it becomes the capital of Minas Gerais State for one day (it was superseded by Belo Horizonte in 1897). The 18th-century atmosphere of twisting streets, and the old houses and churches of the town have been preserved. At the churches of Sáo Francisco and Carmo, one may view the baroque sculpture of Aleijadinho, the "little cripple." The museum of the Inconfidencia, housed in a large colonial penitentiary, is dedicated to the history of gold mining and culture in Minas Gerais. For those interested in mineralogy, a museum at the old colonial governor's palace contains a beautiful collection of minerals native to Brazil. The still-operating gold mines three miles north of town are of interest. The tourist office at Praça Tiradentes 41 features films about Ouro Prêto several times daily. Maps in English are available at the Luxor Hotel. The population here is about 27,900.

Once the coffee capital of Brazil, **RIBEIRÃO PRÊTO** is located in southeastern Brazil in São Paulo State. It was founded in 1856 and has over 300,000 residents. Several crops are grown near the city, among them corn, rice, cotton, sugar, and fruits. Cottonseed oil, beer, and textiles are manufactured in Ribeirão Prêto. The city is accessible by road, air, and rail from São Paulo.

SANTOS, a city of approximately 416,000 in São Paulo State, is the world's largest coffee-exporting port, and one of the principal ports of Brazil. Settled in 1543, it is situated on the island of São Vicente, near the town of the same name, which was the first permanent Portuguese settlement in the New World (1532). Several factories are located in the city. These factories produce soap, soft drinks, cement, and candy. Santos' energy needs are met by a large hydroelectric plant and the petroleum refinery at Cubatão. Santos' humid climate and marshy terrain once made living conditions difficult, but new housing, drainage canals, and updated sanitation facilities have dramatically improved the city. Santos, with its fine beaches and seaside facilities (particularly at suburban Guarujá), is a fashionable residential and resort area.

COUNTRY PROFILE

Geography and Climate

Brazil, with a land area of 3.3 million square miles, is larger than the continental U.S. It extends from the Amazonian equatorial plains at latitude 4°N. to cool uplands at 30°S., where frost often occurs. It borders all South American countries except Chile and Ecuador and, to the east, the coastline runs along the Atlantic Ocean for 4,600 miles.

The vast regions of the Amazon and La Plata River basins occupy about three-fifths of the total area. The huge plateau, rising from 1,000 to 3,000 feet above sea level in São Paulo and Rio Grande do Sul, is the country's main physical feature. This is crossed by two mountain ranges; the highest, at 9,823 feet, is near Rio de Janeiro. A second mountain system, in central Brazil, has an eastern range with a maximum altitude of 4,206 feet, and a western peak of 4,500 feet near the city of Goiânia. Because of its great plains and basins, 40 percent of the country has an average altitude of only 650 feet.

Although Brazil is immense in size and varies in topography from the sweeping sea-level Amazon basin south to the mountains of São Paulo and Pôrto Alegre, the temperature range is narrow. The seasons are the reverse of those in the U.S., with summer from December to February. The rainy season usually extends from October to March.

Population

Brazil's population of roughly 160 million is composed of four major groups: indigenous. Indians, the Portuguese, Africans brought to Brazil as slaves, and various. European and Asian immigrant groups. The Portuguese navigator Pedro Alvares Cabral discovered Brazil in 1500, and the country was subsequently colonized by the Portuguese. A strong African influence exists in the northeast, the legacy of slaves brought to Brazil. The population in the southern half of the country reflects various waves of immigration, with many Brazilians of German and Italian descent in Santa Catarina and Rio Grande do Sul. A large Japanese population is concentrated in the agricultural and

industrial area around São Paulo, and Brazil also has a significant population of Arab descent. Travelers to Brazil will note a distinct atmosphere and population in each region-the result of the wide diversity in Brazil's ethnic composition.

Brazilians are warm and friendly people eager to know foreigners and their habits and customs. In large cities, many Brazilians speak some English, but appreciate Americans who speak Portuguese. A knowledge of the language is necessary to understand and enjoy the people and their intriguing culture.

Some 90% of the population live in the central plateau and the narrow coastal plain along the Atlantic. The tropical Amazon River basin, comprising almost half of Brazil's total area, is sparsely settled. The Trans-Amazonian Highway Project, as well as several large development projects such as Carajas, are aimed at developing the local economy and encouraging migration into the less populated regions of northern Brazil.

Almost every religion is represented in Brazil, but Roman Catholics are predominant (89%). Animism is widespread and is practiced alongside Catholicism. Religious freedom and separation of church and state prevail.

Public Institutions

Brazil is a constitutional federal republic with broad powers granted to the federal government. The 1988 constitution establishes, at the national level, a presidential system with three branches - executive, legislative, and judicial. Brazilians reelected President Fernando Henrique Cardoso and his vice-president, Marco Maciel, to second four-year terms beginning January 1, 1999. This marked the fourth direct election for Congress, governorships and the President.

The bicameral national Congress consists of 81 senators (three from each state and the Federal District)

elected to eight-year terms, and 513 federal deputies elected at large in each state to four year terms, based on a complex proportional representation system, weighted in favor of less populous states. The apex of the judicial system is the Supreme Federal Tribunal, whose 11 justices are appointed by the president to serve until age 70.

Brazil is divided administratively into 27 states and a federal district, which includes the capital, Brasíia. The structure of state and local governments closely parallels that of the federal government. Governors are elected for four year terms. A federal revenue-sharing system, in place since the 1988 constitution, provides states with considerable resources.

Arts, Science, and Education

Brazil's tremendous ethnic and regional diversity makes for a vibrant and varied cultural scene. São Paulo and Rio audiences enjoy a constant menu of outstanding national music and art events, and a steady diet of top international fare as well. Brasíia and Recife are less tied into the international circuit, but local and national cultural options are regularly available.

Brazil's federal and state higher education institutions include some of the finest in Latin America, a product of heavy government investment in graduate-level programs and university research capacity since the 1960s. Of the 68 major universities in Brazil, 35 are federal, 20 are private or church-related, two are municipal and 11 are state supported. Every state but one (Tocantins) and the Federal District of Brasíia has one or more federal universities, all of which operate directly under the Ministry of Education. In many states there are also one or more state universities and one or more Catholic universities. In addition to the universities, there are approximately 800 other degree-granting colleges and institutions of higher education in such areas as engineering, medicine, agriculture, law, economics and business administration.While bloated payrolls and an innovation-stifling bureaucracy have come to pose a serious challenge to the health and quality of the system, a number of reforms stressing greater teacher and student performance based accountability and more streamlined budgetary processes promise to address many concerns.

The Cardoso Administration recognizes that to be competitive in today's more open and service-driven economy places greater demands on workforce education at all levels, and resources are being shifted to the long-neglected primary and secondary levels. Both access and quality are showing improvement. Although eight years of schooling have been legally compulsory since 1973, 1992 figures revealed that the average Brazilian worker had fewer than five years of formal education. That figure is expected to be closer to seven years in 1998 figures, and the sharply upward trend is likely to continue based on much better retention rates in primary schools over the past four years and surging enrollment rates in secondary schools.

During the 70s and 80s, the poor quality of public schools prompted almost all Brazilian middle- and upper-class families to send their children to private or church-affiliated schools. Those children were then better prepared to pass the difficult entry exams for the public universities, creating a paradox in which the less affluent Brazilians were the least able to benefit from the free public universities. Today that trend is showing some signs of softening as quality improvements and economic pressures lead an increasing number of middle-class families to opt again for public schools.

Commerce and Industry

Brazil's gross domestic product (GDP) of US$800 billion in 1998 makes it the world's ninth largest economy. Brazil's population of 160 million makes it the fourth most populous country, and its territory is the fifth largest. Rich resources make Brazil a country of tremendous potential. Per capita income averages US$5,000, with sharp disparities; in general, the south and southeast are more prosperous, while the northeast is much poorer.

Brazil's economy is highly diversified both agriculturally and industrially. Brazil is a major exporter of manufactured products (73 percent of total exports). It is the world's largest exporter of coffee and orange juice concentrate and a major exporter of soybeans, sugar, cocoa, meat and cotton. Mining is also important, particularly iron ore production.

After many years of high inflation, Brazil achieved its most sustained period of stability, beginning in July 1994 with the introduction of a new currency, the real (plural is reais; abbreviation is R$). This stabilization plan was developed when current President Fernando Henrique Cardoso was Finance Minister (May 1993 - April 1994). The inflation rate, which had reached 50 percent per month by June 1994, declined to less than two percent per month throughout 1995. Inflation came down as a result of a strongly valued currency bolstered by very high real interest rates.

In order to consolidate the stabilization program, attract more long-term investment, and put Brazil on the path to long-term sustainable growth, the government must implement wide-ranging structural reforms. Over the years, Brazil has built a cumbersome government-dominated economy that has benefited a few special interests at the expense of the overall society. Many of the necessary reforms require amendment of Brazil's 1988 Constitution. The Congress passed in 1995 five reforms opening the economy to greater investment by the private sector, including foreign investors. Since then some US$80 billion of mostly federally owned assets have been privatized with another US$20 billion of state and local enterprises set for the auction block in 1999.

The GOB has been engaged in a multifaceted program to stabilize its economy in the face of a global financial crisis which began in Asia in late 1997 and was further aggravated with Russia's default and the devaluation of its currency in September 1998. Brazil's vulnerability was its high fiscal deficit. To address this, the Brazilian government has cut spending modestly while simultaneously raising taxes. In early 1999, it abandoned its foreign exchange policy which had closely bound the real to the dollar in a "crawling peg," embracing, instead, a floating exchange.

There was strong consensus that the real has been overvalued for some time. The result was a nearly 50 percent devaluation against the dollar in its first month. To further address the fundamental causes of fiscal deficit, Brazil continues to make structural reforms, primarily in the area of social security and public sector retirement programs. Other reforms currently under consideration include an overhaul of its tax system, labor reform, and political reform to strengthen party organization and discipline.

Transportation

Automobiles

Parts for cars not produced in Brazil must be ordered from abroad. Few mechanics are trained for repair of imported vehicles. Brazil manufactures gasoline, alcohol, and some service-type, diesel-powered vehicles. Gasoline available is only a 72-octane gasohol mixture. Nearly all gasoline sold in Brazil contains up to 25% anhydrous alcohol. Non-Brazilian-manufactured vehicles run well on the local gasohol. But low-compression engines, either imported or produced locally, are recommended. The gasoline is non-leaded and therefore it is not necessary to remove the catalytic converter.

Ford, Chevrolet, Fiat and VW manufacture full lines of vehicles in Brazil. Most models are based on the companies' European models, but a few are similar to models sold in the U.S. Toyota, Honda and Renault manufacture a limited selection of models in Brazil. Brazilians overwhelmingly prefer vehicles with manual transmissions; automatic transmission is available on a few models, though not all. Used cars are readily available.

The number of imported cars in Brazil is increasing, and dealers are improving service and parts availability. However, it would still be prudent to bring a shop/repair manual and some make/model specific spare parts. There are several competent mechanics in town.

All POVs must carry mandatory and third-party insurance. The mandatory insurance covers personal medical expenses resulting from an accident and costs about R$60 a year. The third-party insurance may be obtained from a Brazilian or a U.S. firm. The minimum required coverage is $400,000 for property damage and $400,000 for personal injury or death. Insurance should include coverage for all persons who may, with permission, operate the vehicle.

The Brazilian Transit Department (DETRAN) issues Brazilian drivers licenses. Those without a valid U.S. or other foreign license are required to have an eye exam. Only eligible family members (EFMs) 18 years old or older are eligible to obtain a Brazilian license.

Brasíia: Taxis are available and offer adequate transportation, particularly for short runs. They are, however, expensive. Municipal governments set metered taxi rates, with higher rates being charged after 11 p.m. on weekends and holidays. All cabs have red license plates with white numbers. Tips are not required, but 10% of the metered fare is appropriate for excellent service.

Bus transportation passes through the center of the city, as well as on other major thoroughfares and is good. Bus service is also available to Brasíia's many satellite cities.

Rio de Janeiro: Many metered taxis are available at reasonable prices, depending on the distance to be traveled. Radio controlled taxis which can be requested by phone are also available. Drivers have a reputation for being reckless. The Security Office advises personnel to avoid riding public buses because of the high incidence of theft. The Metro is also another form of transportation from Copacabana to downtown. The Metro is reasonably priced at R$1.00 each way. Air conditioned buses are widely available and the price ranges from R$3.00 to R$5.00. The air-conditioned buses are generally safer than the public buses. Public bus price is R$.70 each way if you choose to take this route of transportation.

São Paulo: Metered taxis are available at reasonable prices.

Recife: Recife's extensive bus system is efficient and inexpensive. Taxis are abundant and inexpensive. Although we recommend against their use, inexpensive gypsy cab vans ply regular routes.

Belo Horizonte: The rapid growth of this city has overburdened the city's transportation system. Bus lines are extensive and inexpensive, but some knowledge of the city is required. The bus system is chaotic, with most lines ending in the downtown area requiring a change of bus for cross town trips. Although economical, city buses are overcrowded and offer only minimal comfort.

Taxis are plentiful and can be found at stands situated throughout the downtown and principal residential areas. Taxi fares are moderate. Trips to outlying areas require a fare supplement. Taxi companies provide radio-controlled service.

Crowded traffic conditions and a limited number of parking spaces in the downtown and adjacent commercial areas of the city make the use of private cars impractical at times. Trips to this area during business hours are best taken on foot or by taxi.

Regional

Direct international air service is available to and from the U.S., Africa, and Europe. Rio de Janeiro and São Paulo are the primary entry airports for U.S. flag carriers. However, some international flights terminate in Manaus, Belem, Recife, Brasíia, Belo Horizonte, and other Brazilian cities. Intracountry connections to Brazil's major cities by national airlines are excellent, but airfares are high. Air transportation to and from Belo Horizonte is excellent, as the city is served by all four Brazilian commercial air carriers and American and United Airlines. Air transportation to and from Porto Alegre is also excellent, although most destinations require an intervening stop in Rio or Sdo Paulo.

Bus transportation between cities is inexpensive and widely used. Some of the longer routes have air-conditioned buses with sleeper chairs (leito), coffee service, and toilets. Most intracity buses are not air conditioned and are crowded during rush hours, but run frequently and are inexpensive. Metro service operates in Rio de Janeiro and São Paulo.

The highway system in southeastern Brazil and as far north as Salvador is good. Brasíia is connected directly to Foz do Iguacu, Belem, Goidnia, and to Rio de Janeiro and São Paulo. Gas stations, restaurants, and hotel accommodations are scarce on some highways.

The Amazon and Plata Rivers with their tributaries provide 25,600 miles of navigable rivers. Regular water transportation is available from Rio de Janeiro south to Buenos Aires and up the Amazon to Iquitos on the Peruvian border. You can obtain information in Belem on ships traveling up the Amazon.

Communications

Telephone and Telegraph

Brazil's telephone service is good. Local rates are higher than in the U.S., however. Reception on incoming international calls is excellent; for outgoing calls reception varies considerably. Direct dialing is available internationally and throughout Brazil. A telephone calling card from a major carrier (AT&T, Sprint, MCI, etc.) is quite useful. Cellular phone service is Brazil is popular.

Mail

Registered mail service is available at Rio de Janeiro only.

Radio and TV

Brazil has some 3,000 radio stations and more than 400 television stations. For most Brazilians, TV and radio act as the principal source of news, sports and entertainment. TV Globo, with 107 stations, is known throughout the world for its telenovelas (soap operas), which bring Brazilian stories to TV fans throughout the Americas, Europe, Asia and Africa.

Unlike the U.S. standard NTSC system, Brazil television is broadcast with the PALM system. A U.S.-purchased NTSC set can receive the PAL-M signal, but only in black and white. NTSC-PAL-M converters that will allow you to use your NTSC set and receive the normal color transmission are available in large cities for prices that range between $60 and $100. Multisystem TVs are available in Brazil, as well; as of February 1999, a 29-inch SONY multisystem set was selling for about $600.

While Brazil's commercial and public networks provide an ample selection of Portuguese-language news, talk shows, soap operas, sports and variety programs, most expatriates also subscribe to one of the cable systems. Since the launch of cable service in 1993, it has grown rapidly, with projections to reach an estimated 6 million subscribers in the year 2000. The major companies are Globo's NET, TVA/Abril and Direct TV Monthly fees range from about $25 to $40, depending on the package selected. CNN, ESPN, HBO, Cartoon Network, Discovery Kids and similar cable fare are available via all three systems.

Video rental outlets, including U.S. giant Blockbuster, are common throughout Brazil. American-made films for children are generally dubbed into Portuguese; those for adults generally carry subtitles. Video rental prices range from $1 to $3 at February 1999 exchange rates.

Radio fare runs the gamut from MPB (Brazilian Popular Music) and Bossa Nova to Motown and classical music. U.S. music fans can easily identify several stations that focus on music from back home, and Portuguese-speaking news hounds will find a growing selection of all-news or mostly-news formats. The Brazilian Government continues to require all commercial broadcasters to air the government-run Radiobras news program from 7 to 8 p.m. During election time, the public airwaves are also dedicated to a couple of hours a day of free campaign spots for candidates.

Internet use has grown rapidly in Brazil. An estimated 3.5 million Brazilians will be surfing the net by the year 2000, and Brazilian web sites are proliferating daily. Those who would like to practice their Portuguese from the U.S. can start by accessing dozens of Brazilian newspapers via http:llwww.zaz.com.brl-noticias/ jornais.chtm or listen to Brazilian radio stations via the Internet at http://www. lancc. utexas.edu/ilas/brazctr/ radio. html

Internet providers are multiplying throughout the country, and prices have become more competitive over the past couple of years. You can expect to pay $20 to $35 for monthly service, depending on the amount of usage and your location. AOL is coming into Brazil shortly, so the U.S. standby will also be an option. Phone lines have historically been the limiting factor with Internet service, as 56k modems were wasted on bad lines. With the privatization of phone companies throughout Brazil, the future looks brighter (and faster).

Newspapers, Magazines, and Technical Journals

Brazilian newsstands are jammed with an array of newspaper and magazines, ranging from the serious to the frivolous. Major dailies such as *Folha de São Paulo*, *Jornal do Brasil*, *O Estado de São Paulo*, and *O Globo* are great sources for information about Brazilian politics, society and culture. They and many smaller, regional newspapers can be accessed on-line via http:llwww.zaz.com.brlnoticias/ J.ornais.chtm. *Veja*, the most widely circulated weekly magazine in Brazil, offers both newcomers and veterans an excellent overview of the country.

International newspapers such as the *International Herald Tribune*, *The Wall Street Journal*, *The Miami Herald* and *The New York Times* are available at major newsstands, but the news will be at least a day - and sometimes a week - old. Single editions sell for the equivalent of USD 2.50 to USD 4.00, and subscriptions are available.

Latin American editions of *Time* and *Newsweek*, which focus more on international events and issues, are available both at newsstands and via subscription. National bookstore chains such as Saraiva and Livraria Siciliano carry a selection of English-language paperbacks alongside their Brazilian titles, but prices tend to be significantly higher than what readers can find via amazon.com or other U.S. providers.

Internet Support: Computers and associated hardware are more expensive in Brazil than in the U.S. Parts for personal computers made by international vendors (Dell, Compaq, Hewlett-Packard, etc.) are usually available. Qualified repair personnel can be difficult to find. Be sure to bring power and telephone line protection for computer equipment.

Health and Medicine

Medical Facilities

Most of the pharmaceuticals used in the United States are available in the Brazilian post cities. In some cases the identical brand name medication is marketed locally. However, in some instances, the quality or availability of locally marketed medication is suboptimal.

The testing of blood products for transfusion purposes in Brazil has improved considerably over the past several years and blood supplies are considered safe.

Brasíia: There are several very adequate hospitals available and the level of competence and technical sophistication among the local health care providers is very good. Dental, orthodontic, and prosthodontic care is available and of good quality. Supplies of medications are good. There is an abundance of specialist consultant physicians available, many of whom are English speaking and have had training in the United States.

Rio de Janeiro: As in Brasíia, there are inspected and satisfactory hospitals, well trained specialist physicians, and other medical support services are readily available. Likewise, dental, orthodontic, and prosthodontic care is available and of good quality. Supplies of medications are good.

São Paulo: São Paulo is the largest city in Brazil and as such has a very sophisticated and excellent medical infrastructure.

Community Health

Bottled water, available on a post-reimbursable basis, is recommended for direct consumption, at all locations. Municipality supplied water is treated and considered acceptable for bathing, laundering, and cooking. Fluoride content is variable and not directly added to bottled water and so fluoride supplementation is advised, for children under the age of twelve.

Food inspection and cleanliness of marketed meats and produce is very variable. Fruits and vegetables that are eaten uncooked and or unpeeled should be thoroughly washed and soaked in a disinfecting solution prior to consumption. Meats should be cooked thoroughly. Adequate pasteurization of dairy products is much improved but still variable and "long life" milk is recommended. Likewise, restaurant inspection is less enforced than in the United States. It is advisable to keep this constantly in mind and use discretion in ordering choices, and particularly to be careful with buffet type presentations in regard to freshness and adequacy of food chilling.

Several insect borne diseases are a problem in different areas of Brazil. In the Amazon and Northern regions malaria and Chagas disease are endemic. Dengue fever, a mosquito-transmitted viral illness, is becoming more disseminated throughout the country. To date, Brasíia and São Paulo are still considered nonendemic cities. There is no vaccine available for dengue fever. The malaria in Brazil is considered chloroquine resistant. As important, is to make provision for avoidance of mosquito bites by means of protective clothing, bed netting, and insect repellents. Schistosomiasis, a tissue-invasive worm infestation, is present throughout the countryside. The parasite is transmitted by a microscopic water dwelling larval form, which can invade through the skin unnoticed. Bathing in lakes and river pools is inadvisable because of this organism.

Viral hepatitis, both A and B types, is a significant danger in Brazil and immunization for both is strongly recommended. Tuberculosis is a widespread illness in the country and biannual skin testing for the disease is appropriate. The incidence of HIV AIDS is rapidly increasing in Brazil. Appropriate protective measures and diligent awareness of the problem are essential. Education of potentially at-risk individuals is well advised.

Rabies is present in the country, but not in sufficient intensity to warrant universal immunization for individuals. Pets accompanying the employee should be current in rabies vaccination. Environmental hazards include heat prostration, air pollution in Rio de Janeiro and São Paulo, dehydration during the dry season (May-October) particularly in Brasíia, and sun exposure-related skin problems. Liberal use of sun screens lotions/creams while outdoors along with wearing protective clothing and headgear is a good habit to develop.

Preventive Measures

You should be immunized against yellow fever. Likewise, immunization against polio, typhoid fever, tetanus, diphtheria, and hepatitis A and B should be current for those coming to Brazil. Due to Brasíia's elevation and proximity to the equator, the sun's ultraviolet rays are more intense and hence more dangerous to skin exposed to the sun. It is important to protect against this hazard with clothing, hats, and sunscreen application.

Persons with ongoing health problems requiring medication or medical appliances and equipment should bring several months' supply of the prescribed drugs along with them. If you use corrective lenses, bring an extra pair of glasses as well as the lens prescription with you, the same applies to contact lenses. The local supply of these items is actually quite adequate, but some delay may be involved in the replacement process.

NOTES FOR TRAVELERS

Passage, Customs & Duties

Direct Delta, United, and American flights to Brazil are available from New York, Miami, San Francisco, and Los Angeles. Usual ports of entry are Rio de Janeiro and São Paulo.

A passport and visa are required for Americans traveling to Brazil for any purpose. Brazilian visas must be obtained in advance from the Brazilian Embassy or consulate nearest to the traveler's place of residence. There are no "airport visas," and immigration authorities will refuse entry to Brazil to anyone not possessing a valid visa. All Brazilian visas, regardless of validity, are considered invalid if not used within 90 days of the issuance date. Immigration authorities will not allow entry into Brazil without a valid visa. Minors (under 10) traveling alone, with one parent or with a third party, must present written authorization by the absent parent(s) or legal guardian, specifically granting permission to travel alone, with one parent or with a third party. This authorization must be notarized, authenticated by the Brazilian Embassy or Consulate, and translated into Portuguese. For current entry and customs requirements for Brazil, travelers may contact the Brazilian Embassy at 3009 Whitehaven St. N.W., Washington, D.C., 20008; telephone (202) 238-2818, e-mail consular@brasilemb.org.; Internet: http://www.brasilemb.org. Travelers may also contact the Brazilian consulates in Boston, Houston, Miami, New York, Chicago, Los Angeles, or San Francisco. Addresses, phone numbers, web and e-mail addresses, and jurisdictions of these consulates may be found at the Brazilian Embassy web site above.

Americans living in or visiting Brazil are encouraged to register at the Consular Section of the U.S. Embassy or Consulates in Brazil and obtain updated information on travel and security within Brazil. The U.S. Embassy is located in Brasilia at Avenida das Nacoes, Lote 3, telephone 011-55-61-321-7272, after-hours telephone 011-55-61-321-8230; web site at http//www.embaixada-americana.org.br. Consular Section public hours are 8:00 a.m.-12:00 noon and 1:30 p.m.-4:00 p.m., Monday through Friday except Brazilian and American holidays. There are consulates in the following cities:

Recife: Rua Goncalves Maia 163, telephone 011-55-81-3421-2441, after-hours telephone 011-55-3421-2641; web site at http://www.consulado-americano.org.br. Consular Section public hours are 8:00am-12noon and 1:00pm-4:00pm Monday through Friday except Brazilian and American holidays.

Rio de Janeiro: Avenida Presidente Wilson 147, telephone 011-55-21-2292-7117, after-hours 011-55-21-2220-0489; web site at http://www.consulado-americano-rio.org.br. Consular Section public hours are 8:30am-11:00am and 1:00pm-3:00pm, Monday through Friday except Brazilian and American holidays.

Sao Paulo: Rua Padre Joao Manoel 933, telephone 011-55-11-3081-6511, after-hours telephone 011-55-113064-6355; web site at http://www.consuladoamericanosp.org.br. Consular Section public hours are 8:30am-11:00am, Monday through Friday and 2:00pm-3:30pm Monday, Wednesday, and Friday except Brazilian and American holidays.

There are Consular Agencies in:

Belem: Rua Oswaldo Cruz 165; telephone 011-55-91-242-7815.

Manaus: Rua Recife 1010, Adrianopolis; telephone 011-55-92-633-4907.

Salvador da Bahia: Rua Pernambuco, 51, Pituba; telephone 011-55-71-345-1545 and 011-55-71-345-1548.

Forteleza: The Instituto Cultural Brasil-Estados Unidos (IBEU), Rua Nogueira Acioly 891, Aldeota; telephone 011-55-85-252-1539.

Porto Alegre: The Instituto Cultural Brasil-Norteamericano, Rua Riachuelo, 1257, Centro; telephone 011-55-512-225-2255.

Pets

Dogs and cats are required to have the following documentation before their arrival: (1) certificate of vaccination against rabies, and (2) a U.S. public health certificate issued within 30 days of departure and validated by the U.S. Department of Agriculture (USDA). Veterinarians are familiar with this procedure.

The same procedure is followed for pets coming from outside the U.S., i.e., a public health certificate from the country where the pet is located.

Firearms and Ammunition

The importation of personal firearms is to be for sporting purposes only. Those wishing to import a personal firearm into Brazil or purchase one locally should be aware of the following restrictions: There are restrictions on the number and caliber of weapons that can be imported or purchased locally. All personal firearms must be legally registered with the Brazilian Government. The focal point for all matters pertaining to personal firearms is the regional security office in Brasilia. All questions pertaining to personal firearms should be directed to that office. A written request which includes the make, model, serial number, and a copy of the original sales receipt must be forwarded to that office a minimum of 120 days prior to the intended date for shipping personal firearms.

Currency, Banking, and Weights and Measures

The currency of Brazil is the real. The rate of exchange is determined by market forces and varies from day to day. It is illegal to purchase currency from individuals or entities that are not authorized by the Central Bank of Brazil to perform exchange services.

In Recife and Belo Horizonte, authorized exchange dealers provide these services. A limited number of automated teller machines (ATMs) accept U.S. ATM cards. This service is expanding. As an added convenience, many personal bills for things like residential telephones and cable television services may be paid at banks.

Brazil has many banks, including Citibank and the Bank of Boston.

Most banks also offer ATM service for account holders.

International credit cards are beginning to enjoy widespread acceptance in Brazil. Major credit cards include Diner's Club, American Express, Master Charge, Visa, and Credicard. They may be used for a variety of purchases and for travel expenses. The rates of exchange offered on credit card purchases are competitive at this time.

The international metric system of weights and measures is standard for Brazil.

LOCAL HOLIDAYS

Jan. 1 . . . . New Year's Day
Feb/Mar.
(Mon & Tues
before Ash Wed.) . Carnival*
Feb/Mar . . . . Ash
 Wednesday*
Mar. 19 . . . . St. Joseph's Day
Mar/Apr. . . . . Good Friday*
Mar/Apr. . . . . Easter*
Apr. 21 . . . . Tiradentes Day
May 1 . . . . Labor Day
June . . . . Corpus Christi*
Sept. 7 . . . . Independence
 Day
Oct. 12 . . . . Our Lady of
 Aparecida
Nov. 1 . . . . All Saints' Day
Nov. 2 . . . . All Souls' Day
Nov. 15 . . . . Proclamation of
 the Republic
Dec. 25 . . . . Christmas Day
*variable

RECOMMENDED READING

The following titles are provided as a general indication of the material published on this country:

Amado, Jorge. Gabriela, Clove and Cinnamon. New York: Knopf. 1962. America's Watch. *The Struggle for Land in Brazil: Rural Violence in Brazil*. New York: Human Rights Watch, 1991.

Atkins, G., Editor. *South America into the 1990's: Evolving International Relationships*. Boulder, Co.: Westview, 1989.

Baer, Werner and Joseph S. Tulchin. *Brazil & the Challenge of Economic Reform*. Washington, D.C.: Woodrow Wilson Center Press, 1993.

Bastide, Roger. *The African Religions of Brazil: Toward a Sociology of the Interpenetrating of Civilizations*. Baltimore: Johns Hopkins University Press, 1978.

Bishop, Elizabeth. *Anthology of 20th Century Brazilian Poetry*. Wesleyan University Press, 1971.

Bradbury, Alex. *Backcountry Brazil: The Pantanal, Amazon, and the Northeast Coast*. Edison, N.J.: Hunter Publishing, 1990.

Bunker, Steven G. *Under Developing the Amazon: Extraction, Unequal Exchange, and the Failure of the Modern State*. Champaign, IL: University of Illinois Press, 1985.

Burns, E. Bradford. *History of Brazil*. New York: Columbia University Press, 1980.

Costa, Emilia Viotti da. *The Brazilian Empire: Myths and Histories*. Chicago: University of Chicago Press, 1985.

Costa, Gino R *Brazil's Foreign Policy: Toward Regional Dominance*. Boulder, Co.: Westview, 1989.

DaCunha, Euclides. *Rebellion in the Backlands*. Chicago: University of Chicago Press, 1957.

Damatta, Roberto. *Carnivals, Rogues, & Heroes: An Interpretation of the Brazilian Dilemma*. South Bend, Ind: University of Notre Dame Press, 1991.

Degler, Carl L. *Neither Black Nor White: Slavery and Race Relations in Brazil and the U.S.* New York: The Macmillan Company, 1971.

Dos Passos, John. *Brazil on the Move*. New York: Paragon, 1963.

Everson, Norma. *Two Brazilian Capitols: Architecture and Urbanism in Rio de Janeiro and Brasilia*. New Haven: Yale University Press, 1973.

Fontaine, Pierre-Michel. *Race, Class and Power in Brazil*. Los Angeles: University of California Press, 1985. Freyre, Gilberto. *The Masters and the Slaves: A Study in the Development of Brazilian Civilization*. New York: Knopf, 1964.

Guillermoprieto, Alma. *Samba*. New York: Alfred Knopf, 1990.

Guimarães Roberto. *Politics & Environment in Brazil: The Ecopolitics of Development in the Third World*. Lynne Rienner Publishers, Inc., 1995.

Hagopian, Frances. *Traditional Politics & Regime Change in Brazil*. New York: Cambridge University Press, 1996.

Jesus, Carolina Maria de. *Child of the Dark*. NAL, 1963.

Johnson, Randal and Robert Stam. *Brazilian Cinema*. East Brunswick, N.J.: Associated University Presses, 1982.

Kanitz, S. *Brazil: The Emerging Economic Boom, 1995-2005*. New York: McGraw-Hill Publishing, 1995.

Mainwaring, Scott. *The Catholic Church in Brazil, 1916-1985*. Palo Alto, Ca.: Stanford University Press, 1986.

McCann, Frank. *The Brazilian-American Alliance 1937-1945*. Princeton University Press: 1973.

Nyrop, Richard F., ed. *Brazil: A Country Study*. American University, Foreign Area Studies, 1982.

Page, Joseph A. *The Brazilians*. New York: Addison-Wesley Publishing Co. Inc., 1995.

Parker, Richard. *Bodies, Pleasure and Passions: Sexual Culture in*

Contemporary Brazil. Beacon Press, 1993.

Pang, Eul-Sol. *Bahia in the First Republic*. Gainesville: University of Florida, 1979.

Penglase, Ben. *Final Justice: Police and Death Squad Homicides of Adolescents in Brazil*. New York: Human Rights Watch, 1994.

Poppino, Rollie E. *Brazil the Land and the People*. New York: Oxford University Press, 1973.

Revkin, Andrew. *The Burning Season: The Murder of Chico Mendes and the Fight for the Amazon Rain Forest*. Boston: Houghton Mifflin Company, 1990.

Roett, Riordan. *Brazil, Politics in a Patrimonial Society*. New York: Praeger 1984.

Schmink, Marianne and Charles H. Wood (eds.). *Frontier Expansion in Amazonia*. Gainesville, FL: University Presses of Florida, 1985.

Shoumatoff, Alex. *The Capital ofHope: Brasilia and Its People*. New York: Random House, New York, 1980.

Skidmore, Thomas E. *Black into White: Race and Nationality in Brazilian Thought*. Durham, N.C.: Duke University Press, 1993.

Vianna Moog, Clodomiro. *Bandeirantes and Pioneers*. New York: George Braziller, 1964.

Updike, John. *Brazil*. 1991.

Wagley, Charles. *Introduction to Brazil*. New York: Columbia University Press, 1971.

Ottawa, Ontario, Canada

CANADA

Major Cities:

Ottawa, Toronto, Montreal, Quebec City, Vancouver, Calgary, Halifax, Winnipeg, Hamilton, Regina, Edmonton, London, St. John's, Victoria, Windsor

Other Cities:

Antigonish, Brampton, Brantford, Charlottetown, Dawson, Fredericton, Gander, Guelph, Kingston, Kitchener, Medicine Hat, Niagara Falls, Niagara-on-the-lake, North Bay, Oakville, Oshawa, Peterborough, Prince Albert, Prince George, Saint Catherines, Saint John, Saskatoon, Sault Sainte Marie, Stratford, Sudbury, Thetford Mines, Thompson, Thunder Bay, Trois Rivières, Whitehorse, Yellowknife

EDITOR'S NOTE

This chapter was adapted from the Department of State Post Report dated April 1996. Supplemental material has been added to increase coverage of minor cities, facts have been updated, and some material has been condensed. Readers are encouraged to visit the Department of State's web site at http://travel.state.gov/ for the most recent information available on travel to this country.

INTRODUCTION

The vast nation of **CANADA**, which borders on three oceans and spans seven time zones, abounds in contrasts. It boasts magical coasts, majestic mountains, wild rivers, untrod forests, and untouched lakes. It also boasts sky-scraping cities, sophisticated shopping, and culinary delights. From the Calgary Stampede to the Shakespearean Festival, from ethnic festivals to the changing of the guard in Ottawa, Canada is a fascinating blend of English and French, historic and modern, ceremonial and casual.

Canada has always had close ties with the United States, as evidenced by the fact that the two countries share the longest unguarded border in the world. In spite of its extensive geographical, cultural, financial, and economic ties with the U.S., however, Canada retains a unique distinction from its southern neighbors.

MAJOR CITIES

Ottawa

Ottawa (from an Indian word meaning "near the water") is a clean, attractive, modern city at the junction of the Ottawa, Rideau, and Gatineau Rivers, about 60 miles north of the New York State border and 120 miles west of Montreal. City residents total over 400,000, and the total metropolitan population is over one million. The climate is healthful and bracing, and the area abounds with opportunities for outdoor activities and family living.

Samuel de Champlain reached the site of what is now Ottawa in 1613; however, a permanent settlement did not develop until after the Rideau Canal was built in 1827. Originally named Bytown, Ottawa was incorporated as a city under its present name in 1854. It was selected as the national capital by Queen Victoria in 1888.

As Canada's capital, Ottawa's main business is government and, as in Washington, DC, little industry exists. Living conditions are similar to those in comparably sized U.S. cities, although social life is geared to demands of diplomatic and government circles.

Small Oriental, Lebanese, Portuguese, and Italian colonies exist in Ottawa, but the majority of residents are of British or French descent. Most francophones (35% of the population) are also fluent in English. Approximately 15,000 Americans live in the Ottawa district; they have merged into the population and do not constitute a discernible American colony. About 50 U.S. companies have subsidiaries or affiliates in the area, but only a few have American citizens on their local staffs.

During summer, there is a flow of U.S. tourists through the city, and all year government officials and business representatives visit Ottawa in their respective roles.

The diplomatic community is large and growing. Some 146 nations maintain relations with Canada, although only 100 have resident missions in Ottawa. Most are small, with two or three officers and a chief of mission. The only large missions are those of the U.S., U.K., Russia,

View of Ottawa

France, Germany, and the People's Republic of China.

Education

Ottawa's public school system offers instruction from kindergarten through grade 13. There are 55 elementary schools for kindergarten through grade eight, and 15 high schools with English instruction and five with French instruction, both covering grades 9 to 13. Tuition is free for Ottawa residents attending public schools. Children may enter kindergarten at age five, or four if the child will be five before December 31 of that year.

Courses meet the standards established by the Ontario Ministry of Education. The teacher-student ratio in elementary schools is about 1:16, and in secondary schools about 1:12, ratios which have remained constant for several years.

Parents may place their children in one of two language programs: the immersion program consisting of instruction totally in French in the first few years, and a gradual phasing in of English instruction until the program becomes bilingual; or the core program consisting of at least 20 minutes daily of French instruction from kindergarten through eighth grade and making it optional at some level after that. The core program is not a rigid one and may vary from school to school.

While some students coming from U.S. schools have found the Ottawa high schools somewhat less demanding than their own, most students and parents report few differences or problems. Instructional programs and course offerings vary from school to school within a particular area.

Students pursuing a commercial, technical, or vocational curriculum in high school can receive a diploma after grade 12. Those planning to continue their studies beyond high school, especially if applying for admission to colleges and universities in Ontario, have, until recently, been required to complete grade 13, but this proviso is currently being phased out.

The Roman Catholic Church maintains a "separate school" system in Ottawa composed of 42 primary schools (19 with French instruction, 23 with English); six intermediate schools (five with French instruction, one with English); and two junior high schools, all with English instruction. Tuition through grade 10 is free for Ottawa residents. The curriculum of the "separate schools" meets all the requirements of the Ontario Ministry of Education.

The schools located in the suburban areas of Ottawa come under either the Carleton Public or Carleton Roman Catholic School Boards. Tuition for schools in both systems is free for residents of the school district. The Carleton Public School Board has 60 elementary schools (including 28 offering French immersion). There are 16 high schools, grades nine through 13, including several with a French immersion program. In addition to the schools offering French immersion, many schools in the Carleton jurisdiction offer French instruction similar to the Ottawa Board's core program. As with the Ottawa Board, parents are advised to check with the school in their neighborhood for specific details regarding the French program.

The Carleton Roman Catholic School Board has 51 elementary schools (32 with English instruction, 19 with French), all of which provide kindergarten to grade eight, and five high schools, grades nine through 13. However, after grade 10, the schools are considered private and tuition must be paid by parents. Many English- instruction elementary schools have French programs similar to those offered in the public school system. For details, parents should check with the neighborhood school their children will attend. The Carleton Roman Catholic School Board has no high schools where the language of instruction is French.

As in the Ottawa public and separate school boards, the curriculum in both boards in Carleton meets all the requirements of the Ontario Ministry of Education.

While a few American families live in Quebec Province (across the Ottawa River in the greater Hull area), the U.S. Embassy strongly discourages families with school-age children from residing in Quebec. The volatile French-language issue and related educational controversies, plus frequent teachers' strikes, have created considerable turmoil in the schools. Children not already reasonably conversant in French will probably encounter problems, especially at the high school level, even if enrolled in an English-language school.

Quebec Province requires all high school students to take French throughout high school and to pass a standard provincial French-language examination before graduation.

Both public and separate school systems in Ottawa and the suburban areas offer extracurricular activities similar to those found in the U.S., including athletics, drama, music, and student government. The Ottawa school year, longer than that of the U.S., runs from Labor Day to the last week in June. Students have a week-long vacation at Christmas and a spring break of 10 days (usually in March). Grades are released quarterly.

Ottawa has a number of nursery schools which accept children from age three. In addition, there are a number of "play schools" for children 18 months to age four. These are usually two or three half days a week, and these require some type of parent participation.

There are two private preparatory schools in the Ottawa area: Elmwood School for girls (kindergarten through the fourth grade is coeducational; grades five through 13 are only for girls), and Ashbury College for boys (covering grades five through 13). Ashbury enrolls both day and boarding students.

Two universities, a technical institute, a teachers' college, and a variety of business and professional schools provide ample opportunity for education on a full- or part-time basis. These include Carleton University (English-language and private, founded in 1942); and University of Ottawa (bilingual and government-supported, founded in 1848). These universities offer a multitude of courses at the undergraduate and graduate levels leading to degrees in liberal arts, sciences, engineering, theology, business administration, education, medicine, nursing, law, and applied sciences. Evening courses at both universities provide many opportunities for both degree and nondegree study. Both universities have extensive evening programs for part-time students as well. Unlike most U.S. colleges, courses are generally conducted on a yearly rather than semester basis.

Algonquin College of Applied Arts and Technology, a community college with four campuses, offers a wide range of day and evening courses, one-year certificate programs, and two- and three-year diploma programs. In general, tuition and fees for colleges and universities in Ottawa are less than those of state colleges and universities in the U.S.

Ottawa has four schools for trainable, mentally handicapped children. They are École Jeanne-Lajoie, the Clifford Bowie School, McHugh School (affiliated with the Royal Ottawa Psychiatric Center), and the Crystal Bay School (Carleton Board of Education). One school, Centennial, is for the physically handicapped, and additionally, the Ottawa Crippled Children's Treatment Center has teaching facilities for physically handicapped and autistic children.

Other educational opportunities include tutoring or group study in languages, music, dance, art, and related activities. These are available for all ages at reasonable cost, usually through the various school systems, Algonquin College, the universities, and the YMCA. Often, however, waiting lists are encountered for those wishing to obtain the most competent instruction available. This is particularly true of French-language courses.

Recreation

Extensive opportunities for participation in many recreational sports activities exist in and around Ottawa. In winter, cross-country and downhill skiing are very popular. Trails and slopes abound within a 100-mile radius of the city, ranging from those for the beginner or casual skier to expert slopes for the advanced enthusiast.

Main roads are kept open and passable in winter, providing access to a number of ski trails and tows in developed ski complexes. Bus service is available. There is one ski area within the Ottawa city limits—Carlington Park. Within an hour's drive are the ski complexes of Camp Fortune and Edelweiss Valley. Camp Fortune, located in Quebec Province (in Gatineau Park) is one of the country's largest ski complexes, offering downhill and cross-country skiing at all levels of difficulty, day and night skiing, instruction, and rentals. It is a 20-minute drive from Ottawa.

Farther afield, the slopes at Mount St. Marie (Quebec) and Calabogie (Ontario) are 60 miles away. All have a variety of slopes and trails and offer instruction and rentals. Season passes for instruction, rentals, and tows are offered at most ski facilities. The elaborate winter sports resorts of Mount Tremblant, Quebec, can be reached from Ottawa in about three hours.

Ottawa also boasts what is billed as the world's largest outdoor skating rink. During the winter, a five-mile stretch of the Rideau Canal, built by the British after the War of 1812, between Dow's Lake and the National Arts Center is cleared and partially lighted for ice skating. Warming huts and snack bars are located at convenient intervals along the canal. It is not unusual to see business-people, with briefcases in tow, skate to work on the canal.

Ample facilities for all types of sports have been developed in and around Ottawa, including ice skating arenas, curling rinks, bowling alleys, indoor and outdoor swimming pools, and tennis and squash courts. One of the largest, and most unique, is the Nepean Sportsplex located in West Ottawa. Under one roof it contains an ice skating rink, hockey arena, curling rink, gymnasium, squash courts, indoor swimming pool, auditorium, sauna, pub, and restaurant. It offers instruction for all age groups in sports activities as well as physical fitness classes, ski fitness clinics, arts and crafts, ballroom dancing, and ballet and tap dancing. The sportsplex publishes an annual bulletin of activities; enrollment in some courses is limited, and first preference is given to Nepean Township residents.

In the summer, ample opportunity for all types of water sports exists on the Ottawa, Rideau, and Gatineau Rivers, and at nearby lakes. There are several yacht clubs with extensive sailing programs. Beaches within Ottawa city limits are limited to one or two spots along the Rideau River, and Britannia Beach on the Ottawa River; facilities at these places are often crowded. On some of the lakes in the area, both in Ontario and Quebec, there are developed-access roads, beaches, and docks for canoes and boats, while other lakes are more isolated and primitive.

Some private golf clubs keep their courses open from May to October; several operate their dining rooms all winter. Ottawa also has public courses.

Tennis and squash facilities are available at a number of private clubs, such as the Ottawa Athletic Club. Municipal tennis courts are scattered about the area as well, offering seasonal membership at reasonable cost, or free use on a space-available basis. Instruction is also provided at the private and public tennis facilities.

Bicycling and jogging are very popular during summer, and there are numerous cycling and jogging trails in Ottawa and across the Ottawa River in Quebec's Gatineau Park. Some roads are closed to auto traffic on Sundays for the exclusive use of hikers, joggers, and cyclists. Additional popular participant sports include archery, badminton, bowling, camping, cricket, flying, judo,

riding, rugby, rowing, soccer, snow-shoeing, and sailing.

For the spectator in winter, ice hockey, Canada's national sport, is virtually a mania. National Hockey League games are televised several times a week. In 1992 the Ottawa Senators, a new National Hockey League franchise, began play. The Ottawa Rough Riders represent Ottawa in the Canadian professional football league. The season begins in late July and ends in early December with the Grey Cup finals between the champions of the Eastern and Western Conferences.

Canadians are avid baseball fans, too, and root for the American major league teams as well as the Canadian entries in Toronto (Blue Jays) and Montreal (Expos). Tickets for Montreal Expo games are sold in Ottawa, and there are chartered buses from downtown Ottawa to the baseball stadium in Montreal for selected games. Stock car racing is held in Stittsville, about 20 miles from Ottawa, in the summer months.

In the greater Ottawa area, which includes suburban areas in and around Hull, Quebec, there are numerous parks operated by various municipal, provincial, and federal authorities. Much of the land adjacent to the Ottawa River on the Ontario side is part of the National Capital Commission and is maintained as park land, with hiking and bicycle trails which serve as cross-country skiing trails in winter. In nearby Quebec is the largest of the area parks, Gatineau Park, whose 75,000 acres are maintained by the National Capital Commission. It offers opportunities to painters, hikers, photographers, naturalists, skiers, and picnickers.

Ottawa citizens often form private fishing and hunting clubs, which acquire and stock private lakes within driving distance. Public or crown lands, other than in the protected areas of Gatineau Park, are generally open to hunters and fishermen. Ontario hunting licenses are issued for a nominal fee upon pre-

sentation of a valid hunting license from another province or from the U.S., or after passing a basic firearms handling test.

In Ottawa there are several museums of interest, including the National Gallery of Art; the Museum of Science and Industry, with unique viewer-participation exhibits especially recommended for school-age children; the Museum of Man; the Bytown Museum (natural history); and Laurier House (former residence of Canadian prime ministers).

Tours of the Parliament buildings are conducted daily throughout the year. During the summer there are sight-seeing tours and moonlight cruises on the Rideau Canal and the Ottawa River. Tours of the Royal Canadian Mounted Police headquarters, the Queen's Printer, the Royal Canadian Mint, and other government agencies can be arranged upon request. Within an easy drive of Ottawa are the St. Lawrence Seaway, the Thousand Islands area, and the restored pioneer settlement of Upper Canada Village.

Toronto and Montreal, Canada's two largest urban centers, are both close to Ottawa—Toronto is 275 miles to the west, and Montreal 120 miles to the east. Toronto, five hours away by road and rail and 55 minutes by air, is the business center of Canada. Here, visitors find a wide variety of reasonable hotel accommodations, extensive shopping facilities, museums, restaurants, and a lively theater district. Montreal is only two hours from Ottawa by road and rail, or 35 minutes by air, and offers a definite French-Canadian atmosphere, which can be enjoyed in a day's visit or for a longer period. There are attractive shopping areas, numerous restaurants, nightclubs, museums, and theaters.

Washington, DC (Dulles) and Baltimore, Maryland (BWI) airports are connected to Ottawa by direct air service. There are daily flights between Ottawa and BWI. Air travelers to other cities in the U.S. must make connections in either Montreal or Toronto. Washington, DC is about 600 miles by road from Ottawa, via excellent interstate highways. New York City can be reached in one day by car and is about 455 miles from Ottawa, also via interstate highways.

Entertainment

Ottawa offers a wide variety of entertainment. The National Arts Center is a cultural center of the first rank, where national and international stars, orchestras, and ballet and theatrical troupes perform regularly. Top-flight soloists and musical groups also are featured at Ottawa and Carleton Universities in programs which are open to the public. The Ottawa Little Theater, with a cast of amateur players, offers a full season of plays.

Ottawa now has some 20 movie houses, and an active National Film Theater whose thrice-weekly showings of classic and foreign films attract crowds of movie buffs to the auditorium in the Public Archives.

The National Gallery of Canada owns and displays a small but excellent collection of European and Canadian paintings, and a small group of contemporary American art. Special exhibits are scheduled throughout the year; the opening ceremonies and receptions are well-attended social events. The gallery also sponsors film shows and art lectures.

The number and quality of Ottawa's restaurants has been rising, and ethnic cuisine is available in a range of prices. Dancing is provided nightly in hotels, in the National Arts Center, and in several of the nightclubs in town and across the Ottawa River in Hull, Quebec. Another attraction in Hull is the abundance of excellent restaurants which may be found in that predominantly French-Canadian city.

Annual events of interest are the Winterlude Festival in February; the Tulip Festival in the latter half of May; and the Central Canada

Ontario Place, Toronto, Canada

David Johnson. Reproduced by permission.

Exhibition, a week-long country fair held each September.

Because of the absence of a language barrier and the openness of Canadian society, Americans blend easily into the local scene. Ottawa has a number of social clubs and public activities which provide opportunities for contact with Canadians. These include an International Women's Club; Boy and Girl Scout groups; and a number of civic organizations, such as Lions, Rotary, Kiwanis, and Optimists.

Toronto

Toronto, Canada's largest city, occupies the site of an old French trading post, Fort Rouillé founded in the 1790s. The city was founded as a British Army garrison town, Fort York, on the shores of Lake Ontario in 1793. It succeeded Niagara-on-the-Lake as capital of Upper Canada in 1797. Chartered as a city in 1834, its name was then changed to Toronto. Toronto served as the country's capital from 1849 to 1851, and from 1855 to 1859.

The Municipality of Metropolitan Toronto consists of the city of Toronto and five boroughs, with an estimated population of 4.7 million (2000), and covering an area of about 625 square miles. It is a beautiful city of parks and trees with a mixture of old and new buildings, connected by an excellent network of roads. Tall construction has been kept to a minimum, creating a feeling of spaciousness. The city is the capital of the Province of Ontario, the most populous and industrialized province in Canada. Toronto is the commercial, financial, and industrial center of Canada.

With the opening of the St. Lawrence Seaway, Toronto has become an important shipping center with modern harbor facilities. It is also one of Canada's principal aviation and railway focal points. Well over 1,000 U.S.-controlled companies have plants or representation within the U.S. consular district, and American investment in the area is enormous. This area is said to contain the largest concentration of American-owned or American-controlled plants in any consular district outside the U.S.

Toronto is the headquarters of the Canadian book and magazine publishing industry, three large daily newspapers, and English-language radio and TV broadcasting. It is the center of English-speaking culture in Canada.

An estimated 200,000 U.S. citizens live in the district; many are dual

Skyline of Toronto, Ontario

nationals. In addition, tens of thousands of Americans visit the city annually, many of them in connection with conventions, or while en route to and from recreation and vacation areas north of the city.

Education

English is the language of instruction in virtually all public schools and in the universities. For those families who may be interested, French has been offered recently as the language of instruction at certain selected public schools throughout the metropolitan area. French is also taught as a required subject in elementary schools.

Toronto's public school system, used by most expatriates, consists of kin-

dergarten, eight years of elementary school, and four or five years of secondary school, depending on the course selected. The fifth year of high school (grade 13), once necessary for admission to most universities in Ontario, is currently being phased out to put Ontario in step with the rest of Canada and the United States. Standards in Toronto secondary schools are comparable to those in the U.S. Course work may be on a yearly basis or semester system, depending on the school attended. Some students entering during the later high school years may have difficulty with subjects that are not taught as a matter of course in American schools. In Canadian schools, many subjects build on a foundation established

the year or two before. It does not seem to be an impossible problem, but young people should come prepared to study hard if they wish to enter a collegiate school. It also should be remembered that, in this bilingual country, French is required of all students. All college entrance examinations are offered in Toronto.

A separate school system is maintained for Roman Catholic children. Catholic schools receive financial support from the property taxes assessed on those homes occupied by Roman Catholic families. Education is free through grade 10, but tuition must be paid from grade 11. Uniforms are required beginning in ninth grade, and only a couple of Catholic schools are coeducational.

Several excellent private schools accept both boarding and day pupils. Tuition rates are about the same as in comparable schools in the northeastern U.S. These schools are usually not coeducational, and uniforms are worn.

Toronto offers extensive educational opportunities, ranging from the University of Toronto to night courses available at the local high schools.

The University of Toronto (founded in 1827), an institution of high academic standing, offers undergraduate and postgraduate courses in virtually all fields of endeavor, including the arts, sciences, commerce, medicine, applied sciences, and engineering. The Ontario College of Art and the Royal Conservatory of Music are affiliated with the university.

York University is Toronto's second university; founded in 1959, it is much newer, and has faculties of art, administrative studies, environmental studies, fine arts, science, and law.

Admission standards at both universities are high, and completion of grade 13 or an equivalent year is mandatory. Undergraduate courses are offered in the evening, and summer school is also available.

In addition to university-level education, the past few years have seen a rise in the number of community colleges. These schools offer post-secondary education in numerous fields, primarily in technical areas.

The Toronto area offers exceptional facilities for the education of the mentally retarded. Special full-time programs are available through the public schools; counseling, special classes, and parent relief activities by the Provincial Ministry of Community and Social Services' Surrey Place Center; and a very active association for the retarded with its own nursery and training programs and community activities (summer camp, meetings with specialists, etc.). These combine to provide families with retarded children greater opportunities for development. However, as possibilities may depend on the age of the child and the nature of the retardation, advanced contact with the Metropolitan Toronto Association for the Mentally Retarded and with Surrey Place Center is advised.

Recreation
Toronto and the nearby areas have much to offer the sports enthusiast, both as spectator and participant. For the spectator there are both professional and amateur hockey, football, soccer, lacrosse, tennis, wrestling, boxing, baseball, and horse racing.

Hockey is by far the most popular professional spectator sport, and is followed by all ages with such enthusiasm that it ranks as a national craze. The Toronto Maple Leafs, an entry in the National Hockey League, play to packed houses at Maple Leaf Gardens from October through April.

Close behind hockey in popularity is football. The Toronto Argonauts are members of the Canadian Football League. There are two horse racing tracks within the metropolitan area offering both thoroughbred and harness racing. Pari-mutuel betting is

permitted. The Toronto Blue Jays baseball team became a member of the American League in 1977, and has gained an enthusiastic following of fans of all ages; they won the Eastern Division pennant in 1985 and the World Series in 1992.

For the sports participant, there are swimming, tennis, roller and ice skating, curling, golf, bowling, skiing, fishing, and hunting. Swimming is a popular summer sport and there are many public pools, operated by the Toronto Parks Commission. Because these pools are usually overcrowded on weekends, and because the waters of Lake Ontario are generally considered too cold for anything other than wading, many Torontonians head north to the lake regions for swimming.

Tennis can be played on a number of public courts. Artificial ice skating rinks are located throughout the metropolitan area. Curling, a new game to most Americans, is another popular winter sport, played indoors on ice in arenas built expressly for this purpose.

Numerous golf courses are in the Toronto area or within a 30- or 40-mile drive. They range from crowded public courses to the exclusive, well-maintained, and expensive private clubs.

Because of Toronto's proximity to Lake Ontario and the lake regions to the north, boating is a popular summer pastime, and the city has several yacht clubs. Good fishing and hunting can be found by driving about 120 to 150 miles north of the city. Skiing in and around Toronto is possible, but the real skiing enthusiast will go north 60 to 100 miles to the Collingwood and Gravenhurst areas.

The Province of Ontario maintains an excellent system of toll-free expressways and paved secondary roads, making all but the most remote parts of the province accessible by car. However, traffic is heavy, particularly during the summer months. Distance by road (miles) to

the following points are: Buffalo, New York, 100; Windsor-Detroit, 235; Ottawa, 286; Montreal, 350; Quebec City, 480; New York City, 478; and Washington, DC, 520.

Toronto's fine park system offers a variety of activities, winter and summer. The pride of the system is Centre Island Park, located on a large island in Lake Ontario off the harbor area, and accessible only by ferry. Ontario Place is also located on a series of man-made islands in Lake Ontario, adjacent to the Canadian National Exhibition grounds, the largest annual exhibition in the world. The Canadian National Exhibition is a popular event. The exhibition features theatrical and musical events, animals, farm and horticultural displays, and an international air show.

Children's playgrounds are located throughout the city and, in summer, playground directors supervise children's activities. During winter, the Parks Department operates numerous ice skating and hockey rinks.

Entertainment
Toronto does not lack cultural or entertainment activities, and offers everything normally found in a cosmopolitan city of comparable size.

Many first-run and neighborhood movie theaters show American, British, and foreign films. Live theater is also very much in evidence in the Toronto area. The 3,200-seat O'Keefe Centre for the Performing Arts and the Royal Alexandra Theatre both present full seasons of opera, ballet, and musical and dramatic productions, featuring not only the top Canadian companies, but also the best American and British companies. Toronto's concert hall, Massey Hall, a venerable old building with near-perfect acoustics, housed the Toronto Symphony Orchestra until the Roy Thomson Hall was opened. Recitals are given here by touring internationally known artists.

In Stratford, Ontario, about 90 miles southwest of Toronto, the Stratford Shakespearean Festival features world famous actors. Niagara-on-the-Lake, about 80 miles south of Toronto, is the home of the Shaw Festival. Both have become very popular spots for the theater lover during the summer season.

Jazz, folk music, chamber music, and numerous smaller professional and amateur theatrical groups can be found throughout Toronto. The city is purported to be the third most important center for theater in the world, after New York and London. There are also many fine restaurants of every cuisine, cocktail lounges, coffee shops, and nightclubs to suit every taste.

The Royal Ontario Museum, the Ontario Art Gallery, the McLaughlin Planetarium, and the Ontario Science Centre provide many hours of interesting viewing.

Montreal

Montreal, with an estimated metropolitan population of 3.4 million, is the second largest city in Canada and the second-largest French speaking city in the world. When Jacques Cartier visited the area that is presently Montreal in 1535, he found the Indian village of Hochelaga. The island was visited in 1603 by Samuel de Champlain, but was not settled by the French until 1642, when Sieur de Maisonneuve founded the Ville Marie de Montreal. The city became the center of fur trade and a starting point of expeditions into the interior. Montreal was the last Canadian city held by the French; it surrendered to the British in 1760. From 1844 to 1849, Montreal was the seat of Canadian government.

Montreal is a cosmopolitan city of charm and variety, where skyscrapers share space with 200-year-old buildings. More than two-thirds of its people are French-speaking. Most of the rest are English-speaking, primarily of English, Irish, Scottish, and Welsh descent. Italians are the third largest ethnic group. About 60% of all the people in Montreal speak English fluently. Several million Americans visit the

© Paul Almasy/Corbis. Reproduced by permission.

Street in Montreal, Quebec

Province of Quebec every year, and nearly all visit Montreal.

The visitor soon discovers that Montreal has everything needed for a pleasant stay—an absorbing history, a rich and varied culture, outstanding cultural and recreational facilities, comfortable and attractive apartments and houses, a French cuisine which justifies the title of "Paris of America," and over 3,000 restaurants specializing in the foods of many other nationalities. The general standard of living is high. Montrealers, particularly well-to-do French-Canadians, are more fashion-conscious than most Americans and accept European style trends more readily.

Montreal is located in the southern part of the Province of Quebec, 120 miles east of Ottawa, and about 40 miles from the New York and Vermont borders. By car, it is 400 miles from New York City and 615 miles from Washington, DC. It is situated

on an island some 30 miles long, and seven to 10 miles wide, at the junction of the St. Lawrence and Ottawa Rivers. Mount Royal, for which it is named, rises almost in the center of the city to a height of about 765 feet above sea level (the city's average altitude is 63 feet). Most of Mount Royal is a natural park, providing areas for picnics in summer and skating and skiing in winter.

Education

Over the last several years, the school system in Quebec has been in a state of some turmoil because of strikes and linguistic and pedagogical issues. The current provincial language law severely restricts access to English education, although exceptions are granted to children expecting to live in Quebec Province for temporary periods only.

The public school system in Montreal consists of 11 grades (grades one through six is elementary school; grades seven through 11 is high school). Some public schools have kindergartens, but this is not the general rule. The public schools, which are free, are run by two separate school boards: Catholic and Protestant, each administering francophone and anglophone schools. For public school purposes, Protestant generally means non-Catholic. Basic instruction can be in French or English. Moreover, English schools provide French immersion courses in which students may elect to take a portion of their subjects in French.

Students entering the Quebec system in the elementary grades will generally find the education to be on a par with that in the U.S., with the bonus of being able to develop a sound knowledge of French. Students entering at the secondary level may, however, encounter problems as a result of French-language requirements and the 11-grade system.

Provincial regulations require that any student who has been in Quebec for more than two years pass a French equivalency test, given to all 11th-grade students, in order to receive a school leaving certificate, which is the equivalent of a high school diploma. Most students entering in the eighth or ninth grades will therefore require extra tutoring to enable them to attain required proficiency levels in French.

Grading procedures in Quebec are also different than in the U.S. For the upper grades, class marks, which are reflected in transcripts, are heavily based on standardized provincial examinations, given at the end of the year to all Quebec students.

The absence of a 12th grade presents other problems. For the Quebec student, the normal sequence is to graduate from high school at the end of the 11th year, enter the two-year CEGEP system (somewhat like a U.S. junior college), and subsequently go on to a university. Based on recent experience, education authorities will not authorize

entry to the CEGEP system for any American student who has not graduated from an American high school. The alternatives for an entering student who would normally enter the 12th grade in the U.S. are to repeat the 11th grade, which Quebec authorities insist is equivalent to the American 12th grade, or to go to school in the U.S.

American students finishing the 11th grade in Quebec have several alternatives. They may elect to go to a boarding school in the U.S. for the 12th grade, although a graduating student could elect to stay in Montreal, since one private boy's school offers a 12th-grade program. However, no 12th-grade programs for girls exist in Montreal. Alternatively, the student could elect to enter the CEGEP system or apply directly to an American college. Some Quebec students enter U.S. colleges after the 11th grade. The willingness of an American college to consider the application of an American student from Quebec would depend, however, on the success of the student in fulfilling course requirements by the end of the 11th grade.

Montreal has a number of private schools. Entrance to these schools is based on competitive examinations, and most of them have waiting lists for entry. The role of private schools in Quebec and the extent to which they should receive government support are under review by the provincial government. Most private schools in Quebec require uniforms.

Montreal has adequate facilities for any type of education from nursery school to the most advanced academic and scientific degrees; private tutoring in any subject; instruction in music, dancing, painting, and the other arts; and special training in crafts, hobbies, sports, gardening, use of power equipment, and other skills.

The Montreal school system has facilities at all grade levels for both physical (including the deaf and blind) and learning handicaps.

The school year runs from just after Labor Day until mid-June. The opening and closing dates for Catholic and Protestant schools differ by a few days, but time in school is the same. All schools have a five-day week. Schools have a two-week holiday at Christmas and a few days at Easter, usually Holy Thursday through Easter Monday.

While extracurricular activities are similar to those in the U.S., they tend to be less extensive, particularly in the area of sports.

Montreal's universities have many American students. The largest of the universities is the French-language Université de Montreal, founded in 1876. The Université du Quebec à Montreal (founded in 1969) is also a French-language institution. Most popular with Americans is the English-language McGill University, founded in 1821. The other large English-language institution is Concordia University, formed by the amalgamation of Sir George Williams University and Loyola College. Concordia has an extensive evening program where it is possible to earn degrees in a variety of fields. All of Montreal's universities offer evening extension programs, but not all lead to degrees.

Recreation

Canada's national sport is hockey. Canadian children learn to skate almost as soon as they learn to walk, and start playing hockey soon thereafter. In winter, free public skating and hockey rinks are found in every section of the city. During the season, Les Canadiens, Montreal's almost legendary National Hockey League team, play at the Forum. Announcements at Canadiens games are made in both French and English.

Montreal's professional baseball team, the Expos, is part of the National Baseball League. The Expos utilize the 1976 Olympic Stadium for their home games. Bowling and curling also are popular, and there are a number of clubs and leagues.

The city has many public tennis courts, and a number of tennis clubs, some with indoor courts. The Montreal area is dotted with private golf courses. A few public courses exist, but they are usually crowded. Excellent and extensive jogging paths are located on Mount Royal. Joggers also enjoy running along the seven-mile Lachine Canal. The Montreal International Marathon, run in late September, attracts over 10,000 participants annually.

Boating is popular. Several yacht clubs on Lake St. Louis (about a half-hour by car from the city) and on the Lake of Two Mountains offer keen inter-club competition and a limited cruising area. Most sailboats on Lake St. Louis are centerboard types because of the large shoal areas, but there are many larger boats, and the International Dragon Class is very active. Two- to three-week cruises to the Thousand Islands, Ottawa, and the Rideau or Lake Champlain are popular with local yachters.

Montreal has an excellent range of readily accessible year-round recreational opportunities in Quebec Province and in northern New York and New England. The Laurentian mountain area, which begins about 45 miles from the city and includes Mont Tremblant Park, is one of the most attractive winter and summer resort areas in Canada. Mont Tremblant, 100 miles from Montreal, and Stowe, Vermont, 120 miles away, provide the best skiing in eastern North America. There is limited skiing in Montreal itself on Mount Royal, but the nearest really good skiing areas begin about 50 miles away. Cross-country skiing is very popular both in and outside of Montreal.

The many lakes in the Laurentians and other nearby areas provide swimming, boating, and water-skiing. There are good camping facilities and accommodations, from luxury hotels to simple lodgings in all areas.

Fishing and hunting are good and are possible close to Montreal. The lakes, rivers, and streams of the province have a variety of fish; speckled trout are the most common. Partridge are found in most woods. The flyways over Lake St. Francis and Lake St. Peter, each about 75 miles from Montreal, offer some of the finest duck shooting in North America. About 150 miles down the St. Lawrence is the only place in the world for hunting the beautiful snow goose. Deer and bear are found within 100 miles of the city.

Montreal has 362 parks. The top of Mount Royal has been preserved as a 500-acre natural forest park. Both the Chalet, at the peak, and Beaver Lake, at the beginning of the park area, are popular in winter and summer. The Chalet has a remarkable view of the city. Beaver Lake, an artificial lagoon, is a favorite place for model-boat enthusiasts. In addition to skiing and tobogganing in winter, the Beaver Lake Pavilion has a large ice skating rink. Mount Royal also has bridle paths for horseback riders.

Another delightful park is located on St. Helen's and Notre Dame Islands in the middle of the St. Lawrence, between the harbor and the seaway. It has an amusement park (the site of Expo '67), swimming pools, picnic areas and playgrounds, and other attractions, including Montreal's Military and Maritime Museum. Its Helene-de-Champlain Restaurant, in a castle-like chalet, provides a picturesque setting and good food.

The Garden of Wonders, better known as the Children's Zoo, is a fascinating feature of Lafontaine Park, which also has two lagoons. Rowboats are for rent, and rides can be taken in a miniature paddle-wheeler "showboat" and in a miniature train.

The extensive greenhouses of Montreal's Botanical Gardens, conveniently located on a principal street, are open all year; its outdoor gardens are open from May or June to October. There are spectacular exhibitions in November and at Easter, and excellent shows at various other times.

Montreal has a number of fine museums. The best historical museum is the Chateau de Ramezay, built in 1705 as the residence for the governor of Montreal. It was the headquarters of the American Army of Occupation in 1775–76, and well-known Americans who stayed there included Benjamin Franklin, Charles Carroll of Carrollton, and Benedict Arnold. Redpath Museum has interesting geological and zoological exhibits and Indian relics. McGill University's McCord Museum, now associated with the Montreal Museum of Fine Arts, has a unique collection of Canadian historical and North American archaeological exhibits. The Wax Museum has more than 200 life-size figures, depicting scenes from Canada's earliest history to modern times. The Bell Telephone Company of Canada has an industrial science museum with original equipment, replicas, and pictures of communications from ancient sight and sound signals to Telstar. Many of these exhibits can be seen in operation.

The Montreal Museum of Fine Arts, entering its second century, is located in the city's center, and houses a formidable collection of paintings, decorative arts, and sculptures, as well as ancient glass and textile collections.

Several Catholic churches have museums with collections of paintings and religious and other exhibits. The museum of Notre Dame de Bon Secours Church, also known as the Sailor's Church, has model ships presented by sailors and an excellent collection of fine dolls. There is also the Museum of Contemporary Art, which opened prior to the 1976 World's Fair held in Montreal. A planetarium and an aquarium were established within the city during 1966–67.

In February 1990, the Montreal Insectarium opened to the public. Built to resemble a stylized insect, the building has a total area of

View of Quebec City, Quebec

approximately 7,000 square feet and includes exhibition areas, open-space laboratories, a multipurpose hall and a 40-seat theater.

Entertainment

Nowhere is Montreal's cosmopolitan nature better reflected than in its entertainment. Plays may be seen throughout the year in both English and French, with occasional productions in other languages. A mobile summer theater for children is operated by the Montreal Parks Department. The Montreal ballet company, Les Grands Ballets Canadiens, performs regularly, and there are other ballet performances as well.

Montreal's modern Place des Artes is the city's center for symphonies, ballets, stage productions, and visiting national and international performers. Place des Arts houses three theaters, the largest seating approximately 3,000 people. Throughout the year, there are many vocal and instrumental recit-

als. The International Music Competition, held in May or June of each year, is one of the most important artistic events held in Montreal. The Montreal International Jazz Festival, held in June or July, features concerts and shows by many of the world's great jazz musicians. The World Film Festival is held annually in August and September.

There are many movie houses, both downtown and in the neighborhoods. New American films are shown at the same time as in the U.S. Films are in English and French. A few theaters show films in their original languages, with English or French subtitles.

The midwinter Carnival festivities in Quebec City are attended by many people from Montreal, Quebec, New England, New York, and elsewhere. The Sherbrooke Festival des Cantons features Quebecois shows, horse-pulling, and gourmet cuisine.

Almost every social group contains a number of the Americans living in Montreal. An American Women's Club meets regularly for lunch and has annual bazaars, fashion shows, dances, and bridge tournaments for the benefit of Canadian charities. The Montreal Post of the American Legion is also active. No other American community organizations exist.

Quebec City

Quebec City is the provincial capital and the center of French Canada. The city takes its name from an Algonquin Indian word meaning where the river narrows, but its many residents, although North American, bear the clear imprint of their French ancestry and culture. The city is located on the site of the old Indian town of Stadacona and was visited by Jacques Cartier in 1535 and 1541. In 1608, Samuel de Champlain established a trading post here which became the first permanent settlement. The area was briefly controlled by the British and was the capital of New France from 1663 to 1763. It also served as capital of Canada from 1851 to 1855, and from 1859 to 1867.

Greater Quebec is a metropolitan area of about 646,000. Quebec, the largest municipality, is divided into two distinct areas. These are Lower Town (which winds around the base of the promontory, along the banks of the St. Lawrence into the St. Charles River Valley), and Upper Town (on heights 200 to 300 feet above the St. Lawrence). When viewed from the sister city of Levis (part of Greater Quebec), Upper Town has a distinctly Old World appearance, including the imposing roof and turrets of the Château Frontenac. Stone walls encircle part of the business and residential section of Upper Town and reach to the ramparts of the Citadelle. The area within the old city walls is recognized as a historic monument. Building restrictions and the tasteful restoration of old houses preserve the Old World flavor of the area. Most buildings in the city have painted tin roofs, dormer windows, colorful shutters, and wooden doors.

The city's population is about 96% French-speaking. Most of the remainder are English Canadians, and only a small minority is of other national and racial origins. In the surrounding countryside, the population is almost totally French-speaking, and is descended from French colonists led by Champlain, who established the first settlement in 1608. Although they are undeniably French in origin, their attitudes and viewpoints reflect the fact that development of their distinctive society has taken place in North America.

Quebec harbor is one of the most important in Canada. It has extensive passenger and freight-handling facilities, including large elevators for the transshipment of grain. Quebec is a regularly scheduled port of call for steamship lines during the ice-free months from April through November and, for several years, has enjoyed an increasing volume of winter freight traffic as well.

The Port City life has been reanimated at the Vieux-Port de Quebec. La Societé du Vieux-Port, commissioned by the Canadian Government, manages this facility which consists of a walkway, outdoor amphitheater, marina, market, and residential units.

In 1977, developers and artists pooled their resources to rescue North America's oldest neighborhood from an undeserved fate. Warmed with color and flowers, the Quartier Petit Champlain is once again a community and a real delight. Its beautifully restored houses shelter more than 50 businesses, outdoor cafes and restaurants ranging from classic French to European fast-food, art galleries, a theater, and charming boutiques. One can meet artists and crafts-people in their studios, or in the street, where pedestrians, musicians, clowns, and jugglers mingle.

Currently 2,000 Americans are registered with the U.S. Consulate and about 7,700 Americans live within the district, many of them French-Canadian descent.

Education

Quebec's public and private schools, from preschool through eighth grade, are generally comparable to American schools. High schools, however, are organized somewhat differently and, in general, are less demanding than their American counterparts.

The final year of high school is the 11th year of studies. Provincial regulations require that every student have two years of high school French and pass both oral and written examinations in French before graduation. The exception to that rule is only for dependents of diplomats, who are exempt from the language law, and who may attend either English- or French-language schools.

Public schools in the province are Catholic or Protestant, but the emphasis on religion has diminished considerably in recent years. Quebec now generally minimizes the importance of religious study much the same as in U.S. public schools.

Quebec has no French-language Protestant schools, public or private. Protestant parents are free to enroll their children in the French-language Catholic schools located throughout the city.

Excellent boarding schools are found throughout the neighboring New England states and in Montreal.

There are a number of specialized schools and organizations in the area for physically and mentally handicapped individuals. Children with learning disabilities attend special classes in the regular school system. For those more severely handicapped, special education, including vocational training, is available through grade nine. Interested individuals should contact the U.S. Consulate in Quebec for further information.

At Laval University (founded in 1852), many faculties, such as medicine and law, accept students only at the graduate level. Other faculties accept students at what would be considered the undergraduate level. Students wishing to enter Laval should discuss the matter with university authorities.

Laval offers evening courses during the academic year in a variety of subjects at the undergraduate level. Instruction in these courses is in French. Laval also offers an intensive summer French-language program which is well known in the U.S. and is attended by several thousand Americans each year. At other times, French-language instruction is offered in the evening at both beginning and advanced levels.

Recreation

Many opportunities exist for ice skating, skiing, and other winter sports in Quebec City. Good ski slopes are within 30 miles of town. Mount Ste. Anne—the highest—has a vertical drop of over 2,000 feet and is one of the best ski mountains in eastern North America. Cross-country skiing is enjoying a major boom, and cross-country trails are maintained in a great number of federal and provincial parks within easy driving distance. For those who prefer to break trail on their own, the open rolling countryside near the city offers virtually unlimited opportunities.

In winter, two or three professional ice hockey games are played each week by the National Hockey League's Quebec Nordiques. The Coliseum was recently renovated and enlarged. Announcements at Nordiques games are made only in French. Several other ice arenas in the municipal area provide instruction and organized competition in both hockey and figure skating.

Quebec City's premier cold-weather event is the annual 10-day Winter Carnival, held in February. There are ice sculpture contests, a majestic ice castle on Place du Palais, a canoe race on the St. Lawrence, and two parades through city streets.

Several indoor curling clubs admit both men and women to membership. There is great interest in this ancient sport here, and membership in one of these clubs affords an opportunity to meet a large number of business and professional persons.

There is good hunting and fishing close to Quebec. The provincial government runs camps in the Laurentides Park. Summertime can be very pleasant in Quebec, in spite of the overwhelming number of tourists who crowd into the city. Golf, tennis, sailing, and fishing are available near town, as well as swimming, hiking, and camping.

Quebec City is the gateway to the Laurentides Park, which begins about 30 miles north of the city and is easily accessible on one of the newest and most modern highways in the province. The areas north and east of Quebec City abound in wooded hills and mountains, with numerous small lakes perfect for flat-water canoeing and boating. These areas can be reached in a short time on good roads. Fishing and hunting are excellent. There are opportunities for day-hiking and backpacking in the park, particularly in the valley of the Jacques Cartier River. The valley also affords supervised rock-climbing, as well as white-water canoeing and kayaking.

A popular summer resort is located at Murray Bay (La Malbaie), on the north shore 100 miles down-river from Quebec. The principal hotel is the Manor Richelieu, operated by the Quebec Government. There is a fine swimming pool and golf course, both of which are open to the public. Another resort, Tadoussac, is 50 miles farther down-river at the mouth of the Saguenay River, but this resort is primarily popular with older people, and there is little excitement or activity to be found. Murray Bay can be reached by train, car, or the Saguenay excursion boats in half a day. Tadoussac can be reached by car, although the road is not well surfaced. The trip is best made by boat.

Baie St. Paul, on the north shore 89 miles down-river from Quebec, has an art center and several art galleries. This artists' haven is also a favorite among crafts-people.

Chicoutimi, a city of 60,000, located 130 miles north of Quebec City, is a tourist base for exploring the Saguenay area. The Saguenay River itself is a fjord with steep canyon walls which can be viewed from sight-seeing boats from June to September. The city is also surrounded by true "wilderness," offering excellent hunting and fishing as well as numerous other outdoor activities.

The south shore of the St. Lawrence and the Gaspé Peninsula has many small resorts of interest during the warmer months, and the trip around this spectacular peninsula can be made comfortably in four or five days by car. Lake St. Joseph and Lake Beauport, about 30 to 15 miles, respectively, from Quebec, are pleasant places to spend a day or weekend during summer.

An attraction only five miles from Quebec is the thunderous Montmorency Falls; just beyond that lies the Island of Orleans, accessible by bridge, which retains much of the charm of the early French-Canadian countryside. The island has several good restaurants and numerous artisan stores offering handwoven articles and ceramics. In summer, visitors can buy fresh fruit at farmers' stands, or pick their own in the fields.

A short distance farther along the north shore of the river is Cap Tourmente National Wildlife Refuge, where virtually the entire east coast population of snow geese congregate in a vast honking horde twice a year, in the spring and fall, on their way to breeding or wintering grounds.

Entertainment

Quebec has several good movie theaters showing American, French, French Canadian and, occasionally, English films. One or two theaters show English-language pictures, but most American films are shown with French soundtracks.

Many visiting companies and artists stop in Quebec. The Quebec Symphony Orchestra, the oldest in Canada, has a full season. There are several avant-garde stock theater groups of considerable talent. An opera company performs occasionally during the winter season, and gifted local folk singers offer concerts. The Grand Théâtre, dedicated in January 1971, has a large auditorium for music, plays, and opera, and a small auditorium for experimental theater. The Grand Théâtre is the home of the Quebec Symphony Orchestra. Several societies, such as the Institut Canadien, offer interesting series of lectures and concerts.

Canada Place, Vancouver, British Columbia

Susan Rock. Reproduced by permission.

The Quebec Winter Carnival is a major event in the area. For three weeks before the beginning of Lent, little else occupies the minds and time of the Quebecois. Among the principal events are the masquerade and regency balls, peewee hockey played by boys 12 and under, boat races over and around the ice floes on the St. Lawrence River, dog-sled races, huge parades, and street dancing. A three-story palace is constructed of enormous blocks of ice, and ice snow statues are carved and placed along many city streets.

During July, the city sponsors a 10-day music festival offering jazz, folk, rock, and classical music in several public parks in the old town. The city, in general, is particularly lively during summer as numerous Quebecois stroll through the historic area and frequent outdoor cafes.

The historic area of Quebec City is beautifully preserved and is completely surrounded by ramparts. The city's oldest hotel, the Chateau Frontenac, and the Citadel, a star-shaped military fortress, are two main historical attractions.

Quebec boasts some excellent restaurants offering French cuisine, among them the Continental, Marie Clarisse, Rabelais, and the Serge Broyere; and out of town, the Manoir St. Castin at Lac Beauport. The variety of nightclubs is limited.

The recently-opened Museum of Civilization is a popular attraction in Quebec City. This museum contains an entire hall dedicated to the history of games—board games, cards, gambling, toys, and other recreational activities.

There are few resident Americans in Quebec, and they are well integrated into the community. A group called the American Colony Club meets infrequently, but participates in community activities and organizes an annual Thanksgiving dinner, a children's Christmas party, a summer picnic, and receptions. Rotary Club also has a chapter in the city.

The city's tourism office, located at 60 rue d'Auteuil, has advice and free booklets for tourists.

Vancouver

Vancouver, the third largest city after Toronto and Montreal, is the largest, most cosmopolitan, and most exciting city in western Canada. Strategically located in the extreme southwest corner of mainland British Columbia, it is the gateway to Alaska, to the Pacific Ocean, to the American Northwest, and to the Orient. The provincial capital and seat of government is Victoria, on Vancouver Island.

The first settlement in the area was established by 1865 and called Granville. It was incorporated as a city in 1881 and named for Captain George Vancouver. Vancouver's development was aided by the completion of the trans-Canada railroad in 1887. Fire destroyed Vancouver in 1886, the year it was incorporated. Reconstruction began immediately and an area known as Gastown became the new city center. The Gastown area declined when the commercial district expanded away from the waterfront; in 1969 restoration of Gastown began and it was preserved as a vital link to the city's past.

As of 2000, Vancouver had an estimated population near 2 million. It is by far the largest city in the Province of British Columbia. Vancouver is located on the eastern shore of the Strait of Georgia, between the Fraser River on the south and Burrard Inlet on the north. The city has a beautiful, landlocked, ice-free harbor, with wooded mountains to the north rising to 4,000 feet and snow-capped much of the year. Its glittering skyscrapers are softened by a dazzling array of parks that bring British Columbia's great outdoors to the heart of the urban setting. At its doorstep are 10 beaches and miles of sheltered cruising waters, with the lighted ski runs on Grouse Mountain only a half-hour to the north.

Vancouver's year-round port handles more dry tonnage than all five U.S. West Coast ports combined. The port is a hub for most passenger ships and Alaskan cruises from May to October.

The climate is comparable to that of Seattle, with few extremes of heat or cold. The temperature rarely exceeds 80°F in summer, and winters have relatively few days when the temperature drops below the freezing point. The mean temperature is 63°F in summer and 36°F in winter. Rainfall averages 59 inches annually in Vancouver, but is considerably less in the outlying districts south of the city. There is also very little snowfall. Living conditions are comparable to those of many other large modern cities in North America, with the additional attraction of extensive and readily accessible outdoor recreational facilities.

The U.S. consular district covers both the Province of British Columbia and the Yukon Territory—a total of 573,331 square miles. It is an area greater than California, Oregon, Washington, Wyoming, and Montana combined. The population is relatively small in British Columbia (3,105,000 in 1989) and in the Yukon (29,000 in 1990), but British Columbia is Canada's second fastest growing province.

People from the prairie provinces, as well as immigrants to Canada, are moving into British Columbia in large numbers, attracted by the climate and economic opportunities. These include Australians, Indians, Iranians, Germans, Dutch, Italians, Scandinavians, French, Swiss, Filipinos, Chinese, and Japanese. Next to San Francisco and New York City, Vancouver has the third largest Chinatown in North America. As a result, many shops specializing in ethnic goods or foods are found in the city, in addition to a host of Chinese restaurants. Chinese laborers were instrumental in building the Canadian-Pacific Railway in this part of Canada.

Currently, about 60,500 American citizens reside in British Columbia and the Yukon. Tourism plays a major role in the economics of the province. About two million Americans visit "The Evergreen Playground" each year. Vancouver was the site of the world's fair—Expo '86—in 1986. It was opened on May 2 by the Prince and Princess of Wales, Charles and Diana.

Education
Public and private schools are on a par with those in the U.S. The Vancouver public school system consists of roughly 95 elementary schools and 18 secondary schools. Roman Catholic schools are run by the church and charge monthly tuition. One public elementary school offers a French immersion program through sixth grade. French is also offered as an optional subject, along with other foreign languages at the secondary level.

Vancouver has three provincial universities: the University of British Columbia (founded in 1890 at Point Gray), University of Victoria (founded in 1902, elevated to university status in 1963), and Simon Fraser University (founded in 1963 at Burnaby).

In addition to credit and non-credit programs and courses offered by technical institutes, vocational training centers, and community colleges, Vancouver and the surrounding municipalities offer adult education day and evening classes. Subjects range from strictly academic courses to instruction in sewing, golf, and ceramics. Fees are moderate.

Vancouver has about 30 educational facilities for the mentally retarded and physically handicapped. Treatment is available for most age groups in schools specializing in disabilities ranging from autistic and behavior disorders to the multi-handicapped. Schools specifically for the deaf and blind are also available. A complete listing of facilities may be obtained by writing directly to the U.S. Consulate General.

Recreation
Vancouver is a sportsman's paradise. There are a number of excellent golf courses, both public and private, where the visitor can play most of the year. The city also has many public tennis courts. Horseback riding is available, but expensive. The surrounding mountains offer skiing from December through April. Popular runs are found on Seymour and Grouse Mountains in North Vancouver; Garibaldi Park, 30 miles from Vancouver; Whistler Mountain, some 75 miles away; and Mount Baker, east of Bellingham, Washington, where skiing is possible most of the year. Also available are numerous cross-country trails, some close by on the North Shore. There are several public and private ice skating rinks.

Boating and water-skiing are very popular, and numerous small-boat launching sites and mooring facilities are found in the surrounding salt water. Many of the interior lakes also provide boating facilities. The boating season runs from late May through September. Bowling (both indoor and lawn variety) and curling are popular. The many mountain trails offer good hiking possibilities.

For the spectator-sports fan, Vancouver has three professional teams. The British Columbia Lions play in the Western Conference of the Canadian Football League; the Vancouver Canucks are in the National Hockey League; and the Vancouver Canadians, the top farm club of the Milwaukee Brewers, are members of the Pacific Coast League. Major U.S. sporting events are telecast in Vancouver as well.

British Columbia is famous for its fishing and hunting. Freshwater trout and salmon are the most popular catches of the sport fisherman. For big game, including bear, deer, moose, mountain goat, and wild fowl, the hunter usually has to travel some distance into the interior of the province.

Camping is a popular summer activity, but facilities are often rough in the interior regions.

Numerous points of scenic interest are within easy driving distance of Vancouver. Vancouver Island, the largest island on the west coast of North and South America, features the provincial capital of Victoria, unusual gardens, beaches, and mountain scenery. One of the most scenic attractions in the Province of British Columbia, Victoria is just an hour's drive along the highway overlooking Howe Sound. The spectacular Fraser River Canyon is several hours away via Hope and Cache Creek.

In the interior of the province, east of Quesnel, lies the historic ghost town of Barkerville, a booming gold town a century ago. The Rocky Mountain Resorts of Banff and Lake Louise, about 650 miles east, just across the British Columbia-Alberta border, can be reached by car, rail, or plane almost all year. Alaska can also be reached via weekly sailings from Vancouver.

Metropolitan Vancouver contains many attractive parks, the largest being world-famous Stanley Park on a 1,000-acre forested peninsula adjacent to the downtown area. Governor General Lord Stanley, in whose honor the NHL's championship cup was named, dedicated the peninsula as a park in 1889, a year after its official opening. Stanley's life-size statue graces the park's entrance. It is a prime tourist attraction, with a zoo, gardens, one of North America's finest aquariums, picnic areas, woodland trails, playgrounds, and scenic viewpoints overlooking the entrance to Vancouver harbor. The MacMillan-Bloedel Conservatory is in the park. Queen Elizabeth Park, south of the downtown section, is another picturesque area, noted for its flowers and views of the city and surrounding area.

Vancouver has a strong international flavor, with large Italian, Greek, and East Indian communities. The city has the second largest Chinatown in North America. Every possible kind of ethnic cuisine is served somewhere in the city.

Gastown is Vancouver's "heritage" area—a colorful redevelopment of the original settlement. Cobbled streets, a steam clock restored heritage buildings housing shops and restaurants, a town square and a statue of Vancouver pioneer Gassy Jack are all part of the ambience. Handicrafts and local artists flourish here.

Shopping in Vancouver tends to be mall oriented and, because it is a port city, many exotic goods can be found. The corner of Georgia and Grandville is the key to a major downtown shopping area. The city

has two underground malls, Pacific Centre and Vancouver Centre. A $100-million extension to the Pacific Centre complex has made it one of the largest retail-office complexes in Canada. It is linked to the rest of the shopping center by overhead walkway and a tunnel. The extension added 100 stores to the existing 127 retail outlets, and features a covered central atrium and a waterfall.

Numerous beaches exist in Vancouver proper and in north and west Vancouver, although the water is usually chilly, even in summer.

Vancouver also has a small but growing art gallery, an excellent maritime museum, and a new planetarium. The Anthropological Museum at the University of British Columbia is excellent.

Entertainment
Entertainment to suit all tastes is available at some time during the year. The excellent Vancouver Symphony Orchestra has a regular concert season extending from fall to spring. This and other orchestras, an opera company, soloists, and first-class theatrical companies, ballets, and choruses from many parts of the world perform at the modern Queen Elizabeth Theater, which has a capacity of 2,800.

Vancouver has a large pool of professional actors from which resident theater companies draw for stage productions of a high order. The Playhouse Theater Company, based in the Queen Elizabeth Theater, and the 450-seat Arts Club Theater, located on Granville Island, each offers seven or more major annual productions, ranging from Shakespeare to Tennessee Williams and modern Canadian playwrights.

The Waterfront Theater, Carousel Theater (for young people), and City Stage add to the variety of what is available on almost a year-round basis. A six-week Festival of Arts each summer features both local and visiting artists of distinction. A Jeunesses Musicales chapter fosters youthful musical activities in Van-

couver and throughout the province. The city has many first-run movie theaters and assorted nightclubs.

Many cultural events also take place from October to June at the University of British Columbia and Simon Fraser University.

The Pacific National Exhibition (PNE), held the last two weeks of August, draws exhibitors from across Canada, the U.S., and other countries. Many top entertainers perform here during the exhibition's run. The "midway" section of the PNE also is open during summer and on weekends during good weather. An Oktoberfest is also held in Vancouver.

The excellent main public library has branches in every neighborhood.

Vancouver social life is like that in any large U.S. city. Americans soon find opportunities to make acquaintances among Canadians. People in Vancouver are hospitable and extend numerous invitations to various social or public affairs.

Organized groups include, among many others, the Board of Trade, Rotary, the English-Speaking Union, and the Consular Corps—both a men's and women's group. Vancouver has three downtown men's luncheon clubs; the Vancouver Club, the Terminal City Club, and the University Club. All of these offer comfortable, convenient facilities, pleasant associations, and good food. American men and women are welcome to participate in the charitable organizations that exist in Vancouver.

Calgary
Calgary is located in the foothills of the Rocky Mountains, 3,440 feet above sea level. From the city, one can see jagged peaks of the Rockies rising to a height of 12,000 feet only 65 miles to the west. Calgary is 160 miles north of the U.S. border.

Calgary, with an estimated population of 888,000 (2000), is one of Canada's fastest growing cities. It is the center of Canada's oil industry (there are about 400 oil companies producing 90% of Canada's oil in the city) and the heart of an extensive ranching area. Calgary was founded in 1875 when the Royal Northwest Mounted Police established a fort at the junction of the Bow and Elbow Rivers. The Canadian-Pacific railroad reached Calgary in 1883; soon a bustling town had outgrown the fort to become the hub of cattle ranches and meat-packing plants. By 1891, the town had attracted 3,100 people. It was chartered as a city in 1893. By the 1950s, it had grown into a peaceful, prosperous provincial city of nearly 100,000.

A U.S. consular agency was established at Lethbridge in 1891, soon after railway connections were opened to Great Falls, Montana. This later was closed, and a consulate was established in Calgary in 1906, a year after Alberta became a province. In 1963, that Consulate was made a consulate general. The consular district includes the Provinces of Alberta, Saskatchewan, and Manitoba and the MacKenzie and Keewatin Districts of the Northwest Territories.

Calgary was the host of the XV Winter Olympic Games in 1988. To prepare for this event, downtown office complexes, hotels, and department stores were connected by climate-controlled elevated skyways.

Downtown Calgary, Alberta

© Brian A. Vikander/Corbis. Reproduced by permission.

Education

Calgary has a good public school system, which includes elementary, junior high, senior high, and combined junior and senior high schools. Tuition is free for all Calgary residents attending public schools. Instruction is in English, and in some schools, in French.

Physical education is compulsory through grade 10, after which it becomes an extra elective. Interschool athletic competitions are an integral part of school life. French is, in general, the only language offered through grade 12. Two years of a foreign language are among the requirements for a high school diploma. Music and art instruction is offered in all grades.

Several private nursery schools and kindergartens are available. Nursery schools generally accept children from the age of three.

The Catholic Church maintains a separate system of elementary, junior high, combined elementary and junior high, and high schools. French and Latin are the only languages offered through grade 12. Textbooks are supplied free through grade nine, and no tuition fees are charged for Calgary residents.

The University of Calgary gives complete courses in arts, commerce, education, engineering, music, physical education, and science, premed. The student body totals about 20,000.

The Southern Alberta Institute of Technology provides educational programs in technology, art, business, trades, correspondence, instruction, and adult education. The institute is operated by the Alberta Department of Education and is financed by the provincial and federal governments.

Mount Royal Junior College is a public institution offering several types of programs: vocational training; high school completion at accelerated rate; course make-up while studying at the University of Calgary; and a transfer program geared to enrollment at a degree-granting institution.

The Calgary School Board offers a wide range of evening courses and services, primarily in high schools. Academic subjects for adults as well as general interest courses are also offered at the University of Calgary and Southern Alberta Institute of Technology.

Calgary has programs to aid the mentally and physically handicapped and children with learning disabilities. Special educational services provide alternative educational programs for children unable to cope with or benefit adequately from the regular school programs. Emphasis is placed at the elementary level, but programs for some students are available through grade 12. Schooling for the handicapped is also available at the Children's Hospital.

Recreation

Football is the main spectator sport in Calgary, and the Stampeders play in the Western Conference of the Canadian Football League. Beginning with the 1980-81 season, Calgary also has a team in the National Hockey League. The Flames moved to the Canadian city from Atlanta, and play during the winter at the Saddledome, which was also used during the 1988 Winter Olympics.

Several good horse shows are held during the year, and pari-mutuel horse racing is held regularly. Good public and private golf clubs are nearby; both the Banff Springs Hotel and Jasper Park Lodge have excellent courses.

The city has several tennis clubs. During the winter many enjoy badminton, curling, and ice skating. Boating and canoeing are also popular. Within the city, many parks and playgrounds have community swimming pools. Bowling, both five-pin and 10-pin, is popular. Downhill and cross-country skiing are available just outside the city limits, as well

as on the slopes at Banff and Lake Louise. Several riding academies on nearby ranches offer lessons. Calgary also has an excellent planetarium and zoo.

A spectacular annual event is the Calgary Stampede, held during the first part of July. This event, which began in 1912, has since grown into a 10-day celebration. Rodeo and western enthusiasts are drawn from all over Canada and the U.S. during this time, when the city completely surrenders to the spirit of the Old West. Besides rodeo programs and chuck wagon races, street dancing, chuck wagons selling flapjacks and bacon, and marching bands are popular. More than half-a-million Americans pass through Calgary every year to see the stampede and to enjoy nearby scenic attractions.

Within a few hours of Calgary, in the Canadian Rockies, are some of the most scenic areas of North America: Banff (also known as a center for native arts and crafts), Lake Louise, and Jasper National Park. Banff, about 75 miles to the northwest, may be reached by car in about one-and-a-half hours; another half-hour will take the traveler to Lake Louise. The "Badlands" at Drumheller, and the dinosaur burying ground, some 85 miles north and east, are also of interest, as is the Cypress Hills area in the southeastern corner of the province.

To the south, straddling the Canadian-U.S. border at the junction of Alberta, British Columbia, and Montana, is Waterton-Glacier International Peace Park. This rustic recreation area comprises large park sites of both countries. The oil and natural gas fields in Turner Valley, just southwest of Calgary, are points of interest, as are the Pembina and Leduc oil fields to the north. The tourist may drive on the Alaska Highway to Dawson Creek and beyond. Excellent highways extend into British Columbia through beautiful scenery. The nearest U.S. border points from Calgary are the small Montana towns of Babb, 165 miles to the south, and Sweetgrass, 195 miles to the south-

east. Other road mileages from Calgary are: Helena, Montana, 395; Great Falls, Montana, 330; Seattle, Washington, 760; Boise, Idaho, 680; and Salt Lake City, Utah, 995.

Edmonton, Alberta's capital, is connected to Calgary by an excellent highway and frequent air service.

Big-game hunting is possible, and antelope, caribou (woodland), bear (black and grizzly), deer, elk, mountain goat, bighorn sheep, and moose are found within easy driving distance of Calgary. On the flyway for millions of migratory water fowl, Alberta offers excellent hunting for several varieties of duck and geese. Pheasant, grouse, partridge, and ptarmigan are hunted in many areas.

The larger northern Alberta lakes are inhabited by huge northern pike and lake trout; pike, perch, and pickerel can be found in most Alberta lakes. In the Rocky Mountain lakes and streams are found Dolly Varden trout, rainbow trout, and grayling. The Bow River, which flows through Calgary, is one of the best rainbow trout streams in North America.

Camping is popular in Alberta, and campsites are available in the three Rocky Mountain National Parks, as well as in 37 provincial parks. The national parks offer superb recreation throughout the year; entry permits, valid for a year, can be bought for a nominal fee.

Entertainment

Calgary has a philharmonic orchestra, a chamber music society, several choral groups, an amateur theater, an opera association, and a large number of movie houses. The permanent home of the Calgary Philharmonic Orchestra is the splendid new Calgary Centre for the Performing Arts. In addition, traveling orchestras, ballets, and musicals visit the city each year. The Glenbow Museum houses displays of Eskimo and Indian artifacts, as well as exhibits on ranching, railroads, farming, oil, and the mounted police.

Calgary's Chinatown is small compared to those in Vancouver, Toronto, and Montreal, but the restaurants on South Centre Street are lively late into the evening. There are very good Italian, Greek, Hungarian, Italian, Mexican, and Vietnamese restaurants, and first-class French cuisine.

Calgary has several public libraries. New works of fiction and nonfiction from Canadian, American, and British publishers are regularly added to the stacks. An almost complete array of U.S. magazines and pocketbooks can be found at most newsstands, department stores, and supermarkets.

Social contact between members of the American community is informal. The American Women's Club is a group of mainly longtime Calgary residents, many of whom are Canadian citizens.

Other gatherings include both Canadians and Americans. Many opportunities exist for contributing voluntary time, skill, and effort to Canadian charitable and other activities. Rotary, Kiwanis, and Lions Clubs are active in the city. Several ranking men's clubs are available downtown, including the Calgary Petroleum Club, the Ranchman's Club, and the 400 Club.

Halifax

Halifax is the center of economic, political, and military activity in the Atlantic provinces. The capital of the province of Nova Scotia and the largest, most important city in the Atlantic region, Halifax is located on the south coast of the Nova Scotia peninsula. The city itself is a tiny peninsula with one of the finest natural harbors in the world.

Halifax was founded in 1749 by Edward Cornwallis as a British stronghold, and became the capital of Nova Scotia in place of Annapolis Royal the following year. It was incorporated as a city in 1842 and has been an important Canadian naval base since 1910.

Beginning life as a fort, its situation was so ideal for trade that, during the early 19th century, Halifax was the wealthiest part of Canada. Today, Halifax is an interesting mix of old and new. Province House where the Nova Scotia legislature meets, is a fine example of Georgian architecture. The residence of the lieutenant governor is also a beautiful building with lovely period furniture. The Old Town Clock on Citadel Hill, ordered by the Duke of Kent, father of Queen Victoria, during his tenure as commander of the Halifax Garrison, has been the symbol of Halifax for many years, but is now challenged by the towers of encroaching high-rise office and apartment buildings.

The Halifax Container port, Halifax Shipyards Ltd., and HMC Dockyard (the largest naval base in Canada) are the most important waterfront industries. Although Halifax spent the first half of the 20th century tearing down its old buildings, it is spending the latter half restoring those which are left. A fine example of this change of heart is the Historic Properties waterfront development, which features warehouses, banks, and other buildings of historic value.

The population of metropolitan Halifax (including its twin city of Dartmouth and other contiguous communities) is estimated at 321,000 (2000). The decline in merchant shipping has adversely affected the local economy, as have the recent severe problems in the fishing industry, an important one in this area. Nova Scotia now bases its hopes for economic prosperity on the gas finds off Sable Island, just as Newfoundland has great expectations founded on offshore oil. Although the oil glut has dimmed these hopes for the moment, exploration is still going on. Dartmouth, until recently best known as the bedroom of Halifax, is doing better with related industry which supplies the drilling rigs. Unlike Halifax which, cramped into its small peninsula, literally has no place to go, Dartmouth is able to provide space for industry in its Burnside

Industrial Park. Halifax International Airport is located in Kelly Lake, about a 20-minute drive from Dartmouth.

Halifax is the Atlantic regional headquarters of the Canadian Broadcasting Corporation (CBC); the federal departments of Manpower and Immigration; Northern and Indian Affairs; Public Works; and Transport. It is also the principal military, rescue, and emergency planning headquarters of eastern Canada. The main office of the Atlantic Provinces Economic Council is in Halifax, as are the regional headquarters of many banks and corporations.

The U.S. consular district was originally established in 1827 as the first consular office in British North America. Now, it covers four of Canada's 10 provinces—New Brunswick, Nova Scotia, Prince Edward Island, and Newfoundland. The first three are known as the Maritime Provinces; along with Newfoundland, they are known as the Atlantic Provinces.

Education
Educational opportunities are excellent in Halifax, which is the center of the largest concentration of institutions of higher learning in Atlantic Canada, attracting students and teachers from many parts of the world. This contributes to the area's growing cosmopolitan atmosphere.

Within the corporate boundaries of the city are seven degree-granting institutions—Dalhousie University (founded in 1818), St. Mary's University (founded in 1841), King's College, Nova Scotia Technical College (founded in 1907), Mount St. Vincent University (founded in 1873), Atlantic School of Theology, and the Nova Scotia College of Art and Design. Also available is the Nova Scotia Institute of Technology.

School attendance is compulsory for all children ages six to 16. The language of instruction for most of Nova Scotia is English. The Halifax public schools are divided into elementary schools and junior and

Old Town Clock in Halifax, Nova Scotia

© Wolfgang Kaehler/Corbis. Reproduced by permission.

senior high schools. Vocational and technical training is offered by the provincially operated vocational school.

Tuition is free for Halifax residents. No school bus transportation is provided; students either walk or rely on public transportation. French instruction is available on a voluntary basis at all levels, and one school offers a French immersion program in elementary grades. It is anticipated that the program will expand gradually to include upper grades as well.

The Catholic Church operates one private school in Halifax—the Convent School of the Sacred Heart.

Tuition is charged. The school offers classes for girls through grade 12, and for boys in grades primary to six.

Another private school is the Armbrae Academy. It is coeducational and offers classes for grades primary through twelve.

Halifax has a number of nursery schools, one popular school being the Halifax Early Childhood School, on Inglis Street.

Special education opportunities in Halifax include facilities for the mentally handicapped and those with learning disabilities, grades primary through nine, and for the

physically handicapped, grades primary through 12. In addition, educational facilities are available for the emotionally disturbed and those with behavioral difficulties in grades one through nine. Transportation, if required, is available, and in very special cases, teaching in the home is possible.

A school for the blind (primary to 11th grade) is also located in Halifax. An effort is made to keep visually handicapped children within the regular school system, particularly at the high school level. A school for the deaf, serving New Brunswick, Prince Edward Island, and Nova Scotia, is located in Amherst, Nova Scotia, about 125 miles from Halifax.

Recreation

Several beaches are on both the south and east shores within two hours' drive of Halifax. Sea bathing is for the hardy only, since the water temperature is rarely over 65°F. Freshwater swimming is available at Grand Lake outside Halifax and in the Dartmouth Lakes. Indoor pools are located at the YMCA, the YWCA, and Centennial Pool. The Halifax Dalplex and the Dartmouth Sportsplex offer swimming, skating, and gym facilities, as well as exercise classes. Skating and curling clubs are popular. Outdoor skating on the various lakes is limited because of the changeable climate.

Most of the city's leading business and professional people belong to one of two yacht clubs, the Royal Nova Scotia Yacht Squadron or the Armdale Club, even if they do not own boats.

The area has four golf clubs: a public club, the Ashburn Golf and Country Club in Halifax (the largest); Brightwood in Dartmouth; and a private club, Oakfield Golf and Country Club, Ltd., outside the city.

A majority of the tennis courts are controlled by the tennis clubs and universities. Among the clubs with tennis courts are the South End Tennis Club, the Waegwoltic Club, St. Mary's Boat Club, and the

Northwest Arm Rowing Club. Indoor tennis is available at the Burnside Tennis Club in Dartmouth. Public tennis courts are located on the Halifax Common and at other parks throughout the city. Other court games available (at private clubs) are squash, handball, and badminton.

Persons who have some skill in football, basketball, or hockey can join amateur leagues or club teams. Health-building programs and gym facilities are available at the local YMCA, YWCA, and at various health clubs. Nova Scotians are also interested in skating and curling. Many people join skating clubs. The ancient Scottish game of curling is entirely a club activity, and membership in either of two curling organizations is an easy way to get to know the Haligonians.

Wentworth, about 90 miles north of Halifax, and Mount Martoc near Windsor have limited skiing.

Halifax is far from the larger Canadian and U.S. cities, but is well situated for excursions within the Maritimes. Its coastal scenery is beautiful, and the provinces contain many places of interest, with sailing, sunbathing, hunting, and fishing as the chief attractions. These points are not resort towns in the usual sense, so a car is useful. Bus transportation is available; railway travel is slow, except on the main line.

Two main highway routes connect most points of interest. One leads from Halifax to Yarmouth, on the southwestern end of the province, close to the famous tuna fishing grounds, then northeast along the Bay of Fundy through the apple-growing belt of the Annapolis Valley and Evangeline country. The Evangeline trail covers the country first colonized by the French. The oldest permanent settlement in North America was at Port Royal, and the French Habitation built there in 1605 has been reconstructed.

The other route leads northeast from Halifax, across the Strait of Canso and around the scenically magnificent Cabot Trail to Sydney, a city of about 35,000 and Cape Breton's steel center. Cape Breton Island, with its Cabot Trail, Louisbourg Fortress, and the Alexander Graham Bell Museum at Baddeck, is a very popular tourist attraction.

Hubbards, Chester, Mahone Bay, and Lunenburg, all with less than 5,000 population, lie along the Atlantic Coast, some 20 to 100 miles southwest of Halifax. These towns have comfortable accommodations for visitors in the tourist season, as do most Nova Scotian towns. Peggy's Cove and colorful fishing villages lie along the bays of the south coast.

Nova Scotia's 4,500 lakes, 50 rivers, and numerous streams offer fantastic fishing—shad, brook trout and, especially, Atlantic salmon. Some of the best smoked salmon can be found in the small Nova Scotian town of Tangier.

In New Brunswick, Fundy National Park, maintained by the federal government, features camping facilities, hiking, boating, horseback riding, nature trails, and many other worthwhile recreational activities. New Brunswick also has a number of festivals related to the area's fishing industry, including the Shediac Lobster Festival and the Campbellton Salmon Festival. Not far away is the former summer home of President Franklin D. Roosevelt at Campobello Island, now maintained jointly by the U.S. and Canada. The picturesque resort town of St. Andrews-by-the-Sea, with its white frame houses, reminds the visitor of the U.S. New England states.

Prince Edward Island (P.E.I.), the garden province, is alive with activity in the summertime, with its many museums, beaches, parks, and theaters. Music camps and the Atlantic Canada Institute Summer School are held in July at the University of P.E.I. Country Days and Old Home Week feature music, agri-

cultural displays, handicrafts, and parades. The Anne of Green Gables Festival, along with lobster, strawberry, and potato blossom festivals and craft fairs, are also part of its summer attractions. P.E.I. is a favorite vacation spot for young families.

Newfoundland offers many opportunities for camping, hunting, fishing, and sight-seeing. Its capital, St. John's, is a good base from which to explore the province's scenic and historic Avalon Peninsula.

Year-round ferry service to Port Aux Basques on Newfoundland's southwest coast is offered from North Sydney, Nova Scotia. Many summertime visitors to Newfoundland, however, prefer to take the ferry which operates during summer months from North Sydney to Argentia, Newfoundland, an Avalon Peninsula port (in Placentia Bay near the site where Roosevelt and Churchill drafted the Atlantic Charter), only 85 miles from St. John's. Newfoundland's annual regatta is one of the oldest sporting events in North America.

Air service is provided by Air Canada and Eastern Provincial Airways to numerous cities in the Atlantic Provinces. Two ferry services connect Nova Scotia with Prince Edward Island at two points: one, operating throughout the year, crosses from Cape Tormentine in New Brunswick to Port Borden, about 35 miles to the west of Charlottetown, Prince Edward Island; the other, which operates only when there is no ice, crosses from Pictou, Nova Scotia, to Woods Island, about 35 miles southeast of Charlottetown.

Entertainment
Halifax has a professional repertory theater, The Neptune, and is the home of Symphony Nova Scotia, a professional orchestra, recently formed under the musical direction of Boris Brott, a well-known and talented Canadian conductor. The orchestra performs chamber music as well as symphonic programs. Rebecca Cohn Auditorium, located

at Dalhousie University, is the locale for various kinds of entertainment, including concerts by such well-known Canadians as André Gagnon and Liona Boyd. An ensemble called Nova Music performs classical music by contemporary composers. Distinguished films are shown in the auditorium on Sunday nights.

Dalhousie University, St. Mary's University, and the Canadian Broadcasting Corporation (CBC) sponsor concert series throughout the season which feature international and national artists. Local amateur groups also present plays and operettas. Spectator sports include football, basketball, hockey, boxing, and wrestling. The various university and service teams compete in amateur football, basketball, and baseball.

Several movie theaters in Halifax and Dartmouth show current American and British films. Nova Scotia is also the home of the Annapolis Apple Blossom Festival and the Highland Games.

Two Canadian television stations have studios in Halifax, and there are several radio stations in the metro area, both AM and FM. Halifax Cablevision Limited provides a cable service which picks up the U.S. public broadcasting channel, NBC, and ABC from Maine transmitters. French-language broadcasts are presented on radio and TV.

The Halifax Memorial Library, established in 1951, offers free library service from its collection of about 130,000 volumes. It has a good selection of late and current fiction and nonfiction and an excellent reference section. A mobile service for the city and the county has been operating for several years. Books are available at local bookstores, but cost 20% more than in the U.S.

Art exhibits are held at the Art Gallery of Nova Scotia and at various universities.

Some excellent restaurants are located in Halifax, specializing in seafood delicacies and French cuisine.

Winnipeg

Metropolitan Winnipeg is the fifth largest city in Canada, ranking after Toronto, Montreal, Vancouver, and Calgary. It is known worldwide for its seemingly endless wheat fields, its blizzards, and its hockey team, the Jets.

A fur trading post was established on the site of modern-day Winnipeg in 1738, and later a colony was founded by the Scots. The village of Winnipeg was settled in the late 1860s, and incorporated as a city in 1873.

Winnipeg resembles cities of comparable size in the middle western plains in the U.S. Situated on the eastern edge of an 800-mile stretch of prairie-land, it is the home of the Canadian Wheat Board and the Board of Grain Commissioners. Winnipeg is also located almost midway between the two oceans, near the geographical center of North America. Its people are friendly and hospitable. Their interests, habits, and mode of life are similar to those of the American Westerner.

The capital of the Province of Manitoba, Winnipeg is situated at the junction of the Red and Assiniboine Rivers, about 70 miles north of the international boundary. It is 485 miles, by car, from Minneapolis, Minnesota. It is 760 feet above sea level, and the surrounding area within a 100-mile perimeter is flat, broken by occasional wooded areas and streams. The area has a healthy climate, comparable to that of Minneapolis, although colder. Winter temperatures drop to as low as 40°F or more below zero. Winters are fairly dry and summers are cool and pleasant.

Greater Winnipeg's population was about 652,400 in 2000. English is the principal language spoken in the city. However, in St. Boniface, a part of metropolitan Winnipeg, more than 40% of the present population is of French or Belgian ancestry, and most people speak French as well as English.

Although about 40% of Winnipeg's population is British in origin, with a strong Scottish strain, there are a number of other nationalities, including Ukrainians, Germans, French, Italians, Dutch, Philippines, Vietnamese, and Chinese. There is no American colony as such in Winnipeg. In fact, the social, economic, and cultural background of the city is practically the same as in the contiguous areas of the U.S. There is a constant shift of population in both directions across the border, and estimates place the number of persons in the district with claim to U.S. citizenship above 10,000. Upwards of one-and-a-half million American tourists have annually visited the Province of Manitoba.

Education

Winnipeg's good, free education for kindergarten through grade 12 is comparable to American standards. Two nondenominational private schools and two Roman Catholic schools are also of good reputation. The nondenominational school for girls, Balmoral High School, has classes from kindergarten through grade 12. The Roman Catholic school, St. Mary's Academy for Girls, provides facilities for grades seven through 12. St. John's Ravenscourt School for Boys (and girls from grades nine through 12) provides excellent education from grades one through 12. St. Paul's College (Roman Catholic) provides education for boys and young men (grades nine through 11 and through university). Tuition and annual fees at private schools are slightly lower than those in the U.S.

Special educational opportunities are available in each school division in Winnipeg for children who have learning disabilities or who are mentally or physically handicapped. Special educational institutions are also available for severely physically handicapped or mentally retarded children.

Winnipeg has two universities. The University of Manitoba, is the oldest university in Western Canada. Founded in 1877, it is a first-class provincially operated institution and offers a large number of undergraduate and graduate programs. The University of Winnipeg, located in the center of the city, is a relatively new institution (founded in 1967), with undergraduate courses in the liberal arts and pre-professional education.

Red River Community College specializes in practical courses for both degree and nondegree students. All three institutions have evening and summer sessions.

Various levels of instruction are offered at the Winnipeg School of Ballet. Students taking private lessons in music may take examinations leading to the certificate of Associate of the Toronto Conservatory of Music. The University of Manitoba gives a bachelor's degree (AMM) in music. The Winnipeg Art Gallery also offers art classes.

Recreation

Winnipeg offers numerous and varied year-round recreational facilities for adults as well as children. Nearly every residential neighborhood has school playgrounds and local community clubs where instruction is given to children in handicrafts, dancing, skating, hockey, football, tennis, and other sports. Four large and some small parks, the largest of which is Assiniboine Park (which has a fine zoo, formal gardens, and conservatory), provide pleasant surroundings for picnicking, sports, and walking. All parks are conveniently served by local transportation.

Golf, tennis, swimming, and boating are the most popular summer sports in Winnipeg. Golf may be played at several very good municipal courses or at a number of semiprivate clubs where reasonable greens fees are charged. Winnipeg has a number of neighborhood wading pools, one

large municipal outdoor pool, and several indoor pools. An Olympic-size indoor pool, one of the largest in the world and the site of the 1967 Pan American Games' swimming events, is located in the city.

Several local skiing clubs teach the fundamentals of skiing and jumping on the banks of the Red and Assiniboine Rivers, but it is necessary to travel some distance from the city for really good downhill skiing conditions. Cross-country skiing is popular in and around Winnipeg. Indoor sports such as badminton, squash, bowling, curling, and roller skating may also be enjoyed.

Excellent hunting abounds in Manitoba. Deer, moose, and even polar bear are found in the north. Duck, geese, prairie chicken, and grouse are found only a few hours' drive from Winnipeg in some of the best hunting regions in Canada. Good fishing can be found throughout the district, and both open water and ice fishing are very popular.

The Precambrian Shield, 50 miles east of the city, is an area of woods, rocks, and lakes. The nearest resort area is the district on the southern shores of Lake Winnipeg, about 35 miles to the north by road, where many people have small cottages. There are limited bathing facilities in several of the beach towns.

The western section of the very attractive Lake of the Woods area is about 120 miles east of Winnipeg and easily accessible by car, bus, or train. Among the pleasant resorts closest to Winnipeg are Kenora, Whiteshell Forest Reserve and, to the west, Riding Mountain National Park. Many attractive summer homes are found throughout the area. Hotel accommodations are good; motels are satisfactory. Most resort spots offer special camping facilities.

To the north, places such as Flin Flon, a copper-zinc-gold mining center, and Fort Churchill on Hudson Bay are interesting places to visit. There is a good paved road to Flin Flon (560 miles) and to Thompson (a

nickel mining town), but Fort Churchill is reached only by rail or air. Each year a few rail excursions of several days' duration are run to Churchill, with the tourists living on the train. The Selkirk Navigation Company operates a five-day cruise on Lake Winnipeg during June, July, August, and September. Accommodations on the modern *Lord Selkirk* are comfortable.

Northwest of Winnipeg, at the south end of Lake Dauphin, is the town of Dauphin (population 9,000). Known for barley, timber, and fisheries, Dauphin is also host to Canada's National Ukrainian Festival, held annually in August.

Entertainment

Winnipeg prides itself as being "The Convention City" and, as might be expected, it offers a wide variety of entertainment opportunities. These include the internationally renowned Royal Winnipeg Ballet, the Winnipeg Symphony Orchestra, the Manitoba Theater Center, the Contemporary Dancers, and the Opera. Performances are usually held in the Concert Hall and the Manitoba Theater Center, both located at the Centennial Center adjacent to City Hall. There is also an open-air theater—Rainbow Stage—where plays, musicals, and other attractions are held during the summer.

Also in the Centennial Center is the Museum of Man and Nature, which offers a wide variety of exhibits on the general theme of man in relation to the environment. There are several other museums in the city, the most impressive of which is the new and strikingly handsome Winnipeg Art Gallery.

The city's ethnic diversity is reflected in the variety of festivals held throughout the year, including Festival du Voyageur (a winter festival in St. Boniface), Ukrainian Week, and Folklorama, a major event each summer, during which pavilions representing various ethnic groups provide entertainment in the form of traditional songs, dancing, and food.

Probably the most popular attraction in the city is hockey, with its National Hockey League franchise, the Jets. The Winnipeg Arena is located on Maroons Road, named after a senior hockey team which brought honor to the city 20 years ago. When the Jets joined the NHL, the roof of Winnipeg Arena was raised and 5,400 additional seats were installed. This brought the arena up to NHL standards of at least 15,000 seats.

Other spectator sports include football and curling games, as well as thoroughbred racing at Assiniboine Downs.

There are about 15 motion picture theaters in the city. Several of these are first class and feature the latest American and, on occasion, European films. Winnipeg also has a 200,000-volume, Carnegie-endowed public library located in a new, attractive building.

Weather dictates the nature of much of the activity: concerts, theater, ballet, bridge, and winter sports when it is cold; and fishing, touring tennis, golf, cycling, and walking when the glorious spring and summer weather arrives.

Hamilton

Hamilton, on the western tip of Lake Ontario, is about 40 miles southwest of Toronto. Explored by Robert LaSalle in 1669 and first settled in 1813, it is Canada's most important steel-producing center, and also is a transportation hub with a harbor, an airport, and a rail terminus. Other industries include the manufacture of automobiles, tires, railroad equipment, clothing, chemicals, and farm implements. The metropolitan population is approximately 599,800 (2000 est.).

Hamilton has many attractions for the visitor. Its 1,900-acre Royal Botanical Gardens are among the most beautiful on the North American continent. There are also gardens in Gage Park, and formal gardens close to the Art Gallery of Hamilton. The city is home to Canada's largest open-air market, which teems with residents and visitors during the growing season. Hamilton Beach on Lake Ontario is a summer playground.

One of the major tourist sites in the city is the 72-room Dundurn Castle, which houses a museum and a children's theater. It was built by Sir Allan Napier MacNab from 1832 to 1835 and bought by the city in 1900. MacNab was prime minister of the United Province of Upper and Lower Canada from 1854–1856.

The Hamilton Visitors and Convention Bureau is located at 155 James Street South.

Regina

Regina is the capital city of Saskatchewan, Canada's fifth largest province. Founded in 1822, it was the capital of the Northwest Territories from its inception until 1905 and, that year, when Saskatchewan was designated as a separate province, it became the seat of provincial government. It is called by Canadians the "Queen City of the Plains."

Regina is a transportation and commercial center in the midst of a large farming region. It is the site of Campion College (founded in 1917), the Canadian Bible College (founded in 1941), the Regina branch of the University of Saskatchewan, and Luther College (founded in 1921). Among its points of interest are the Museum of Natural History, the Regina Plains Museum, the Telecommunications Historical Museum, the Saskatchewan Archives, and MacKenzie Art Gallery, with its extensive collection of Canadian and European art and antiquities from the ancient world. Sports enthusiasts can spend a day amidst memorabilia and artifacts at the Saskatchewan Sports Hall of Fame and Sport Museum. Its population is approximately 192,800.

Regina was named by Princess Louise of Great Britain in honor of her mother, Queen Victoria. It was the headquarters of the Royal Canadian Mounted Police until 1920. The Royal Canadian Mounted Police Centennial Museum contains buffalo coats, guns, saddles, uniforms, and photographs illustrating the legendary police force's intriguing past.

Regina hosts a number of major events each year: the Western Canada Farm Progress Show in June, Buffalo Days in July, the International Arabian Horse Show in August, and the Canadian Western Agribition each November.

The city has a rich cultural tradition as evidenced by its many theater, dance, music and ethnic performing groups and by the Saskatchewan Center of the Arts, one of the finest concert halls in North America. The Regina Symphony is the oldest continuously operating symphony orchestra in Canada.

The city operates a number of excellent parks and complexes, the Regina Sportplex, five outdoor swimming pools and several excellent golf courses. Wascana Centre, located in the heart of the city, has a man-made lake, bicycle paths, paddle-boat rentals, a waterfowl park, double-decker bus tours, and several historic points of interest.

Just north of Regina, in the small town of Craven, the largest outdoor country music extravaganza in Canada is held annually in July. The Big Valley Jamboree features many U.S. country music performers.

Saskatchewan's rich Indian heritage can be explored at the summer powwows held on most Indian reserves. Major ceremonies include the Poundmaker Powwow near Cutknife, and the Standing Buffalo Indian Powwow at Sioux Bridge near Fort Qu'Appelle.

Edmonton

Edmonton, Alberta's capital, is Canada's "Gateway to the North," known for its excellent quality of life. It boasts a population of 940,000 and is the oil capital of the country. In addition to oil, Edmonton's major industries include flour milling, meat-packing, plastics, tanning, dairying, lumbering, and petrochemical production. Established in 1795 as a Hudson's Bay trading post, it expanded and developed during the gold rush to the Klondike in 1898. The quiet town of 1,500 settlers became the supply center for miners drawn by the promise of gold. It is now a modern city with a new international airport. The city's numerous rail lines have contributed to Edmonton's reputation as the transportation hub of northwestern Canada.

Located 350 miles north of the U.S. border, Edmonton is the northernmost major city in Canada. Just 185 miles from the center of Alberta, Edmonton is surrounded by a rare natural setting. Verdant foothills banked with wood and the mighty North Saskatchewan River soften the effect of all the city's new concrete. Along the river runs an impressive 35 miles of greenbelt.

The University of Alberta (founded in 1906) is located in the city, as are St. Joseph's College (founded in 1927), the Christian Training Institute, and other specialized schools.

Football and curling are popular spectator and participant recreational activities, but of greatest interest is Edmonton's National Hockey League team, the two-time Stanley Cup champion (1984 and 1985) Oilers.

Attractions in Edmonton range from various types of theater, particularly at the Citadel, to galleries and the domed Provincial Legislature buildings. Several rodeos are held during the summer months. In July, when the sun hardly sets, Edmonton hosts Klondike Days. The city's frontier past and gold rush days are celebrated at that time with sourdough raft races, beard growing contests, and other events. In August, the city hosts a Folk Music Festival. This festival features traditional and bluegrass music, country, blues, and Celtic

music, arts and crafts displays, and a food fair.

Perhaps the biggest attraction in Edmonton is West Edmonton Mall, located seven miles from downtown. It is the world's largest shopping mall and the world's largest indoor amusement park—all under one roof. Covering 110 acres and housing 836 stores on two levels, the mall also includes a reproduction of the Versailles fountains; a recreation of New Orleans' Bourbon Street; a miniature golf course; an indoor amusement park called Canada Fantasyland; a water park that offers water-skiing and body surfing on artificial waves; an NHL regulation-size ice rink (the Oilers practice here often); and a hotel, with fantasy-style rooms.

Built in phases (the first was opened in 1980) by four Iranian-immigrant brothers at a cost of $750 million, the mall attracts 400,000 visitors a week, two-thirds of them from out of town.

London

London, a city of 381,500, is the chief municipality of southwestern Ontario. It is an industrial and railroad center, first settled in 1826, on the Thames River, about 20 miles north of Lake Erie. Much of its architecture and atmosphere is suggestive of the more famous city on another Thames, and visitors find that the Ontario London has many characteristics reminiscent of England's capital. London is surrounded by a rich agricultural area. Vegetables, fruits, grain, and dairy products are produced in this region. Several products are manufactured in London, including brass and steel products, textiles, diesel locomotives, food products, clothing, and electrical appliances.

London is well known for its art museum and for its Museum of Indian Archaeology and Pioneer Life, housed at the University of Western Ontario. Other popular tourist spots include the Storybook Gardens for children and the Royal Canadian Regiment Museum.

There is also a unique Guy Lombardo Museum.

The city offers theaters and cultural activities (many connected with the several private colleges and the university) and other opportunities for sports and entertainment.

St. John's

St. John's, the capital of Newfoundland, is the oldest city in North America north of Mexico. Located on the southeast coast of the province, on the Atlantic Ocean, St. John's is the commercial center and principal port of Newfoundland. With a metropolitan population of about 173,000 the city has an excellent natural harbor and is the terminus of the railroad which crosses the island.

The area was colonized by Sir Humphrey Gilbert in 1593, and Water Street bustled in 1600, making it the continent's oldest business district, but a permanent settlement was not established until early in the 17th century. Twice destroyed by the French and Indians, St. John's was permanently controlled by the British beginning in 1762. It served as a naval base during the American Revolution and the War of 1812. On Signal Hill in 1901, Marconi received the first trans-Atlantic wireless message. The first nonstop, trans-Atlantic flight was made from St. John's in 1919.

As a base for the province's fishing fleet, St. John's industries are mainly related to fishing, and include shipbuilding, manufacturing fishing equipment and marine engines, and the storing, preserving, and processing of fish. St. John's has Roman Catholic and Anglican cathedrals, and is the site of the Newfoundland Museum, Memorial University (founded in 1949), and Queen's College (founded in 1841).

St. John's has many fine parks throughout the city. One of the largest is C.A. Pippy Park. This park offers opportunities for recreation and relaxation that include hiking and cross-country skiing. It has picnic areas, a campground, golf course, and row-boat rentals. Bowring Park is located in the western part of the city. The park is noted for several very attractive and interesting pieces of statuary. It has been customary for various heads of state and members of the British Royal Family who have visited St. John's to follow the tradition of planting a tree in Bowring Park as a living reminder of their visit.

Victoria

Victoria, the capital of British Columbia, is located on the southeastern portion of Vancouver Island, at the east end of Juan de Fuca Strait. The 2000 population of the metropolitan area was estimated at 287,900.

Victoria is the largest city on the island, as well as its major port and business center. Industries in the city include sawmills, woodworking plants, grain elevators, and fish processing factories. Victoria is also the base for a deep-sea fishing fleet and the Pacific headquarters of the Canadian Navy.

The city was founded in 1843 as Fort Camosun, a Hudson's Bay Company post. It was later named Fort Victoria. When Vancouver Island became a crown colony in 1849, its new town (built in 1851–52) was called Victoria and named the capital of the colony. In the late 1850s, gold was discovered in British Columbia and Victoria became an important base for miners on their way to the Cariboo gold fields. The island was united with the mainland in 1866, and Victoria remained the capital. In 1871, it became the capital of the province.

Victoria, with its mild climate, beautiful gardens, and many parks is a popular center for American and Canadian tourists. The city's most famous garden is Butchard Gardens, which dates back to 1904. Other beautiful gardens worth visiting include those at Government House and Beacon Hill Park. Beacon Hill Park features ponds, gardens, forests, and one of the tallest totem poles in the world. The Dominion Astrophysical Observatory and the University of Victoria (founded in 1902 and elevated to university status in 1963) are located here. During the annual Victorian Days festival, inhabitants dress in Victorian clothing.

The downtown core of Victoria is small and packed with stores. Handmade chocolates, imported bone china, Irish linens, antiques, and English woolens are some of the items sold.

Nightlife includes the brilliantly lit parliament building, a small Chinatown, and an old section of town full of boutiques and restaurants. The city's provincial museum contains Indian, gold rush, early settler art and artifacts, and many superb old totem poles. A sawmill and logging museum is located in the nearby town of Duncan.

For the sports enthusiast, golf is available year-round at such courses as Royal Colwood, Olympic View, Glen Meadows, Cordova Bay, and Cedar Hill. To see harbor seals, porpoises, marine birds and killer whales, one cant take a three-hour, 50-mile boat trip into the Gulf Islands. For those interested in saltwater fishing, charters for both sail and power boats are available at Victoria's marinas.

Windsor

Windsor, Ontario, known as the "City of Roses," on the Detroit River, is a major border crossing between Canada and the United States. The Ambassador Bridge and the busy Detroit-Windsor river tunnel, which connect the two countries, carry countless commuters to their jobs in both cities, and serve the thousands of tourists who casually shop and dine and attend theaters and recreational activities in Detroit and Windsor.

A two-week-long International Freedom Festival is held jointly with Detroit in late June and early July, celebrating both the Canadian and the U.S. independence. The highlight of the festival is a huge fireworks display over the Detroit River. Windsor's riverfront is lined with parks. Jackson Park and Dieppe Gardens are the pride of the city.

With an estimated 2000 population of 262,000, Windsor has grown into a modern business and industrial center in the years since its incorporation as a village in 1854, then as a city in 1892.

Windsor was settled by the French at about the turn of the 18th century, just after the foundation of Detroit in 1701. It was headquarters for U.S. Gen. William Hull in the War of 1812.

Among the many products manufactured in Windsor are automobiles, pharmaceuticals, machine tools, and chemicals. Brewing and distilling facilities are major businesses here also. The city's educational institutions include the University of Windsor (founded in 1963), Assumption University (founded in 1857), and Holy Name (1934), and Canterbury Colleges (1957).

The town of Amherstburg, just a few miles south of Windsor, is one of the oldest settlements in the area, with an eventful history reflected in the numerous historic sites and buildings. When the British left Detroit, they established a fort and a navy yard here. Fort Malden National Historic Park contains part of the 1796 British earthworks. The Boblo Island amusement park can be reached by the Amherstburg ferry. Several intimate restaurants have recently given the town a reputation for fine cuisine. The population of Amherstburg is 5,700.

OTHER CITIES

ANTIGONISH is a city of 5,000 in northeast Nova Scotia, off St. George's Bay. The French first settled the region in 1762, followed by the British some 25 years later.

Antigonish exports lumber and fish and has nearby quarries. With its 117-year-old St. Ninian's Cathedral, the city is the seat of a Catholic diocese. The Antigonish Movement (a pioneering, self-help, cooperative program) was founded at local St. Francis Xavier University in 1930. Tourists visit the Highland Games which the city holds every summer; these have their origin in the Braemar Games of Scotland.

BRAMPTON, known as the "Flower City" because of its many nurseries, is located in southeastern Ontario, 20 miles west of Toronto. Founded in the 1820s, Brampton pleasantly blends old and new, and has preserved much of the architecture from its early days. Recently, the city has become industrialized, manufacturing metal products, automobiles, shoes, furniture, stationery, optical lenses, and communications equipment. Visitors to Brampton enjoy the Great War Flying Museum, which displays World War I aircraft, as well as the five-story-high White Star Slide, located in the Shopper's World mall. Brampton's population is approximately 268.000.

BRANTFORD is located in southeastern Ontario, about 22 miles southwest of Hamilton. It was founded in 1830 and named for the famous Indian chief, Joseph Brant, who led the Six Nations Indians from their homeland in upstate New York to this site on the Grand River. Today, Brantford retains many of its associations with the heritage and culture of the Six Nations Indians; there are exhibits in the Brant County Museum and the Woodland Indian Cultural Education Centre and Museum. Indian heritage is celebrated every August during the Six Nations Indian Pageant and at the Indian John Memorial Shoot, an archery contest held each June. Her Majesty's Chapel of the Mohawks, located in Brantford, is the world's only royal Indian chapel and the oldest Protestant church in Ontario. Brantford is also the place where Alexander Graham Bell invented the telephone and made the first long-distance call

from his home to Paris, Ontario, in 1876. Bell's home in Brantford is open to visitors; it is furnished just as it was when he lived here and many of his inventions are on display. Brantford has a population of approximately 76,070. Truck bodies refrigeration equipment, textiles, and agricultural implements are manufactured here. The city is also the birthplace of hockey's Wayne Gretzky.

CHARLOTTETOWN, capital and only city of Prince Edward Island, has a population of 15,300. It was named for Queen Charlotte, consort of George III. It is on the Gulf of St. Lawrence, near Prince Edward Island National Park.

Historic **DAWSON** (formerly called Dawson City) lies at the confluence of the Yukon and Klondike Rivers in western Yukon Territory. A town of only 1,790, Dawson in its heyday of the Klondike Gold Rush (late 1890s) boasted over 30,000 residents. The rapid exhaustion of accessible mines in the early 20th century dealt the community a serious blow. The town's status as administrative center of the territory was lost in 1953. Now a major tourist and distribution area, Dawson celebrates its past with annual Discovery Day celebrations in August. The cabins of writers Jack London and Robert W. Service have been restored. Other attractions include the restored turn of the century Palace Grande Theater, Post Office, gold dredge No. 4, the Steamer Kero, and the cabin of the famous Canadian author, Robert Service.

FREDERICTON is the capital of New Brunswick, located 60 miles northwest of St. John's in the south-central region. The city has military, political, and literary traditions dating to the post-Revolutionary War period. A stronghold of Empire Loyalists (Tories), Fredericton is named after Frederick, King George III's son. Canada's first university, the University of New Brunswick, is in this Georgian-style city. Riverside mansions recall earlier days of grace and charm. Loyalist traditions live on at Kings Landing

Historical Settlement. Fredericton is located alongside the Saint John River. The river is a focal point of city life. Each summer, the River Jubilee Festival pays tribute to the river. Tours and dinner cruises are available aboard the Pioneer Princess, a replica of the original paddlewheelers that once plied the river. Fredericton is also the home of the internationally renowned Beaverbrook Art Gallery. The gallery displays a permanent collection of 2,000 works of art. It is distinguished as being one of the most comprehensive British collections in Canada and the most complete representation of Canadian painting, historical and contemporary, east of Montreal. The population of Fredericton is approximately 44,000.

GANDER is a modern city of 10,000, 210 miles northwest of St. John's, Newfoundland. It is best known for its airport, one of North America's largest. Transatlantic flights have been handled in Gander since 1939. During World War II it was a critical connection for air ferries and Atlantic patrols. The area's many wild geese and the Gander River were the origin of the city's name. It was incorporated in 1954.

The manufacturing city of **GUELPH** is located in southeastern Ontario, about 15 miles northeast of Kitchener. Founded in 1827 on several hills, Guelph produces rubber goods; electrical apparatus; paint; carpets; clothing, cigarettes, woolen, cotton, and linen goods; and iron and steel products. Foundries and tobacco warehouses are located in the city. Guelph is characterized by maple trees, wide avenues, and fine old homes constructed of local limestone in early Canadian architecture. The city is the birthplace of Col. John McCrae (1872–1918), the poet and physician best known for his nostalgic poem, "In Flanders Fields," written in 1915; his birthplace is open to the public. The University of Guelph, founded in 1964, covers 1,110 acres and includes a 350-acre arboretum. Guelph boasts one of the largest mechanical floral clocks in the province; it contains six to seven thousand flowers. A

Spring Festival, featuring classical music, recitals, concerts, and song and dance programs, is held annually in late April and mid-May. Guelph's population is approximately 88,000.

KINGSTON, with a population of roughly 57,380, is strategically located in southeastern Ontario at the southern end of the Rideau Canal at the point where Lake Ontario flows into the St. Lawrence River. Fort Frontenac was built here by the French in 1673 and was destroyed by the Iroquois Indians shortly thereafter. Restored in 1695, the fort became a key point in reaching the Upper St. Lawrence River. The present city of Kingston, or "king's town," was settled by Loyalist refugees in 1793. In the early 1800s, the city seemed a likely target for an American invasion, so Fort Henry was built to guard the royal dockyards; it was used as a base for the British naval forces on Lake Ontario during the War of 1812. Fort Henry is currently a military museum. Kingston served as the capital of Canada from 1841 through 1844. Today, the city is an important transshipment point for the Welland Ship Canal and an outlet for traffic on the Rideau Canal. Aluminum sheeting, synthetic fibers, ceramics, mining equipment, ships, leather, and diesel engines are manufactured here. Kingston is the home of Queen's University (founded in 1841) and the Royal Military College of Canada (equivalent of West Point; founded in 1876). The city has an impressive concentration of 19th-century buildings that give it a unique appearance. Many of these buildings have been converted into pubs, restaurants, art galleries, and museums. The city is a departure point for boat tours along the Rideau Canal to Ottawa and around the scenic Thousand Islands. Kingston was the birthplace of organized hockey and the first league game was played here in 1885. The International Hockey Hall of Fame museum depicts the development of the sport through displays of equipment, photographs, and mementos.

KITCHENER, an industrial city in southeastern Ontario, is about 60 miles southwest of Toronto. Largely settled by the Pennsylvania Dutch in 1806, the area was then settled by Germans in 1825. The Germans named the city Berlin, but it was renamed in honor of Lord Horatio Kitchener, a British statesman. Kitchener honors its German heritage with an Oktoberfest, North America's largest. The city has a population of 178,000 (1996 est.); its metropolitan area, which includes the adjoining city of Waterloo, has a population of 346,000 (1990 est.). Manufactured items include furniture, textiles, shoes, appliances, and rubber products; industries include distilling, brewing, tanning, and meat packing. Kitchener is the site of St. Jerome's College, founded in 1864, and of Woodside National Historic Park, which commemorates the birthplace of William Lyon Mackenzie King, a Canadian statesman and former prime minister.

MEDICINE HAT, Alberta, lies on the South Saskatchewan River, 180 miles southeast of Calgary. This city of 40,000 is located in the heart of one of the biggest natural gas fields in the world. It is also on the Trans-Canada Highway and Canadian Pacific Railway. Medicine Hat is the home of several industries, among them pottery manufacturing, glassblowing, and flour milling. The mostly agricultural economy is dominated by ranching and vegetable growing. According to Indian legend, Medicine Hat acquired its name from a frightened Cree medicine man who lost his hat escaping from warriors. The city hosts an annual stampede and exhibition and has a highly regarded historical museum.

NIAGARA FALLS, with an estimated population of 70,500, is the site of one of the world's great natural wonders, drawing tourists from all over the world. The city itself is a manufacturing center located just below the falls in southeastern Ontario, opposite Niagara Falls, New York, to which it is connected by two bridges. Founded in 1853, the city was known as Clifton from 1856–1881, and was incorporated in 1904. The center of a large hydroelectric power complex, Niagara Falls also produces fertilizer, chemicals, abrasives, cereal, paper goods, silverware, and sporting goods. It is best known, however, as a bustling tourist town with several man-made attractions. A 25-mile park system stretches from above the falls downriver to Niagara-on-the-Lake. The falls are equally spectacular in the summer and in the winter when frozen; an illumination system also makes them a spectacular nighttime attraction.

Situated in a beautiful setting on Lake Ontario at the mouth of the Niagara River, **NIAGARA-ON-THE-LAKE** is one of the prettiest and best-preserved 19th-century towns in North America. Founded in 1780 and originally named Newark, Niagara-on-the-Lake was the first capital of Upper Canada from 1791–1796. Although the town was burned in 1813, parts of Fort Massassauga are still visible. Today, the city is best known for the Shaw Festival, a major annual theater event featuring the plays of George Bernard Shaw and his contemporaries. Performed in the Royal George Theatre, the Court House Theatre, and the modern Festival Theatre, the festival runs from early May through September. Located opposite Fort Niagara, New York, Niagara-on-the-Lake has a current population of 12,200.

Situated on the northeast shore of Lake Nipissing in northern Ontario, **NORTH BAY** is a busy year-round tourist city, well known to fishermen and hunters. It has a "golden mile" sandy beach with picnic facilities and shore-land parks, as well as numerous hiking trails. A transportation hub, North Bay produces lumber, dairy products, fur products, mining machinery and brass fittings; there are dairy farms in the area. The city is also home of the Quints Museum; the original Dionne family log farmhouse has been restored and now houses memorabilia from the world's first recorded surviving quintuplets. The annual Festival of the Arts, a series of cultural, musical, and social activities, is held in late September and early October. The local French community organizes sports and social events in early February for the Bon Homme Winter Carnival. North Bay's current population is 51,300.

OAKVILLE, located on Lake Ontario 22 miles southwest of Toronto, is a wealthy community of approximately 128,400 with an attractive harbor and an enduring, 19th-century charm. Automobiles, plastics, aluminum ware, and paper are produced in Oakville. The city is also a summer resort and has a golf course—Glen Abbey—designed by American pro golfer, Jack Nicklaus.

OSHAWA, situated on Lake Ontario 33 miles northeast of Toronto, is one of the main centers of Canada's automobile industry. Founded in 1795 as a lake port, Oshawa was incorporated as a town in 1879 and as a city in 1924. There are several old buildings near the lake-front that are preserved as part of the city's past. As an industrial city, Oshawa produces motor vehicles and parts, foundry products, electrical appliances, metal stampings, glass, plastics, textiles, pharmaceuticals, and furniture. The Canadian headquarters of General Motors is located here. The Canadian Automotive Museum, which displays collections from Canada's early car industry, is also located in Oshawa. The city's population is roughly 134,000.

PETERBOROUGH, a bustling city with many reminders of the past, is located in southeastern Ontario on the Otonabee River and Trent Canal, 13 miles north of the west end of Rice Lake and 70 miles northeast of Toronto. Sawmills were established on this site in 1821; the city was founded four years later and incorporated in 1905. Today, Peterborough is an industrial city whose products include electrical machinery, marine hardware, boats, plastics, lumber, carpets, and watches. Dairy farms are also

located in the area. In addition, Peterborough is the southeastern gateway to the Kawartha Lakes and is the major link in the Trent-Severn Waterway. The Hydraulic Lift Lock is the world's highest hydraulic lift and the symbol of the city. It literally lifts pleasure craft, along with the water in which they float, 65 feet straight up. There is constant traffic, especially on summer weekends; during winter, there is skating on the canal beneath the lift lock. Peterborough also boasts the highest jet fountain in Canada. The Centennial Fountain shoots water 250 feet up from Little Lake, just south of the city. Trent University was founded here in 1963. The population is roughly 62,500. Southeast of Peterborough is the industrial town of Belleville, located on the Bay of Quinte. With a population of 35,300, Belleville is the gateway to two great recreation regions—the Highlands of Hastings, with its clear lakes (Bancroft is a tourist center there), and the sandy beaches of Quinte's Isle to the south (Picton attracts tourists there). A popular vacation spot, Belleville has one of Ontario's finest yacht harbors, along with facilities for golf, fishing, and swimming. Southwest of Belleville, on the eastern terminus of the Trent Canal system, is Trenton, whose population is 15,100. A popular water-oriented city, Trenton offers sailing, swimming, and fishing in summer, and ice boating and ice fishing in winter.

Situated in south-central Saskatchewan, **PRINCE ALBERT** is an important distribution point for the northern reaches of the province. Its varied economic base includes oil refining, woodworking, paper milling, tanning, and food packaging. Tourism here centers on nearby Prince Albert National Park and the unique Lund Wildlife Exhibit. Visitors are often attracted to Prince Albert's numerous museums and art galleries. Outdoor enthusiasts also enjoy the area's excellent hiking and skiing trails, and beautiful lakes where fishing is abundant. The metropolitan area is the site of a federal penitentiary, a school for the retarded, and several

Indian reservations. Prince Albert has a population of about 34,000.

Situated in central British Columbia, 485 miles north of Vancouver, **PRINCE GEORGE** serves as an important provincial administrative and transportation hub. Explorer Simon Fraser founded the city in the early 1800s as a trading post on the river that now bears his name. The city grew with the opening of the Grand Trunk Pacific Railway in 1913. The community's approximately 66,000 residents rely heavily on the lumber industry, as well as on minerals, oil, and hydropower, for their livelihoods. Tourists and sportsmen know Prince George as a base for expeditions into the Cariboo district.

SAINT CATHERINES, "the Garden City," is an industrial city situated on the Welland Ship Canal, just south of Lake Ontario. Settled by the Loyalists in 1790, Saint Catherines was incorporated as a town in 1845 and as a city in 1876. It was once a depot of the Underground Railroad; was the site of the first Welland Canal, built in 1829; and had the first electric streetcar system in North America. Today, Saint Catherines produces automobile parts, machinery, electrical equipment, hardware, textiles, and hosiery. Fruit is packed and shipped from its harbor. Brock University, founded in 1962, was named for (Gen.) Sir Isaac Brock, who commanded the Canadian and British forces at the battle of Queenston Heights in 1812. The Niagara Grape and Wine Festival, marking the ripening of the grapes in the Saint Catherines area, is held annually in late September. The 10-day festival, begun in 1952 as a one-day observance, now includes more than 200 events. The population of Saint Catherines is approximately 124,000.

SAINT JOHN, New Brunswick's largest city, boasts an excellent harbor, large dry docks, and terminal facilities. It is a year-round port with shipping connections to Europe, North and South America, and the West Indies. The city is the commercial, manufacturing, and transportation center of the province. The city's major industries include brewing, tanning, fish processing, shipbuilding, and oil refining. Visited in 1604 by French explorer Samuel de Champlain, Saint John eventually became a French fort and trading post (1631), and in the ensuing years was captured and recaptured as England and France struggled for possession. Saint John is famed for its museums; its buildings dating to colonial times; and for the Reversing Falls, which are actually rapids caused by the famous high tides. Not far away is the former summer home of U.S. President Franklin D. Roosevelt at Campobello Island, now maintained jointly by Canada and the U.S. Historical attractions include the Carleton Martello Tower, a stone fortification surviving from the War of 1812; the Fort Howe Blockhouse, a replica of a 1777 blockhouse. Visitors are afforded a panoramic view of the city from the fort. Many of St. John's homes and buildings are worthy examples of historic architecture. The population of Saint John is about 102,000.

SARNIA is the center of Ontario's oil refining and petrochemical industries. Located on the Saint Clair River in southeastern Ontario, at the south end of Lake Huron, Sarnia is connected to Port Huron, Michigan, via the Bluewater Bridge, as well as by a railway tunnel. An important lake port, Sarnia produces lumber, plastics, sailboats, and automobile parts. Settled by the French in 1807 and by the English in 1813, Sarnia's waterfront offers a variety of recreational activities, including swimming, boating, and golfing. There are more than a dozen fully equipped marinas along 42 miles of white, sandy beaches. One of Sarnia's main attractions is fishing—trout, perch, whitefish, pickerel, walleye, chinook, and coho salmon may be caught from shore or boat. Water pollution problems have, occasionally, been serious. Those concerned about swimming in this region or eating locally caught fish are advised to contact

appropriate provincial agencies. Known as the "Salmon Capital of Ontario," the city is host to the annual Sarnia Salmon Derby in May. Thousands of sailors and spectators descend upon the city for the Port Huron-to-Mackinac Race each summer. The population is estimated at about 80,000.

SASKATOON, in Saskatchewan, is the potash capital of the world. Half of the world's potash reserve is located in this area. Industries located in Saskatoon include food and dairy processing, flour milling, brewing, tanning, oil refining, and meat-packing. The city also manufactures electronic equipment fertilizers, clothing, and chemicals. Saskatoon is the home of the Mendel Art Gallery, which houses a collection of works by Canadian artists. Other museums in Saskatoon include the Ukrainian Museum of Canada, which has contemporary and historical exhibits dealing with the early settlement of Saskatchewan and culture on the Ukrainian people, and the Western Development Museum, which features a "Boom Town" that recreates a 1910 village. Saskatoon also hosts several annual fairs, and festivals which attract tourists and natives alike. The city offers numerous opportunities for fine dining. The population is about 194,000; the city is the birthplace of hockey great Gordie Howe.

SAULT SAINTE MARIE was established on the site of a mission founded by Pere Jacques Marquette in 1668. It is situated at the falls on the St. Mary's River (the link between Lakes Huron and Superior), just opposite Sault Sainte Marie, Michigan. This is the site of one of the most active canals in the St. Lawrence Seaway system; lake freighters traveling to and from the upper Great Lakes use the locks to bypass the rapids. Tours of the locks are available. Two-hour cruises through both the American and Canadian locks, the world's busiest, are offered from late May until Thanksgiving. The Canadian lock, located at the edge of the St. Mary's River rapids, was completed in 1895

and is the oldest in the system. A pretty city with many old stone and brick buildings, Sault Sainte Marie's economy depends upon the Algoma steel plant, lumber, agriculture, and tourism. Although the city is considered part of the summer resort system, it also has many wintertime events. World class cross-country skiing trails are numerous and the downhill skiing is excellent. Groomed trails for snowmobiling are available. The Ontario Winter Carnival Bon Soo, featuring dog sled races, speed skating, polar bear swimming, and more is held here in late January/early February. To the east of Sault Sainte Marie, on the North Channel of Lake Huron, are several resort and vacation centers. Bruce Mines was named for Canada's first successful copper mines. Thessalon, a lumber town situated at the river mouth, has a large government wharf and marina. Iron Bridge, on the historic Mississagi River, is known for its sturgeon fishing. Blind River is a mining and lumbering center. A short distance inland is Elliot Lake, founded in 1954 when uranium deposits were discovered nearby. A modern town of 20,000 on the shore of one of the 170 lakes in the area, Elliot Lake offers winter and summer sports activities.

STRATFORD, Ontario, is located just north of London on the Avon River. Founded in 1832, the city produces furniture, brass, and leather and rubber goods. It is best known, however, for its deliberate resemblance to Stratford-upon-Avon, England, the home of William Shakespeare. The Stratford Shakespearean Festival in Ontario began modestly in 1953 and has since become a major world theatrical event, utilizing three theaters. While still based on a Shakespearean season, the festival now incorporates diverse forms of music and theater, from folk-singing to opera. The season runs from June through October. Stratford's population is over 27,000.

"The nickel capital of the world," **SUDBURY** is 40 miles north of

Georgian Bay in south-central Ontario. The city has a population of roughly over 90,000, and is in the middle of the country's most important mining region. Minerals were first discovered here in 1883; today, in addition to nickel, copper, gold, cobalt, sulfur, iron ore, silver, and platinum are mined. Industries include lumber milling, woodworking, brickworking, and machine shops. Sudbury is linked to other cities by the Trans-Canada Highway, as well as by two transcontinental railways. It acts as the area's main commercial and educational center.

THE FORD MINES is a mining community of 20,000, 50 miles south of Quebec City in southern Quebec province. It is known as one of the world's major asbestos-producing regions, but also mines chromium and feldspar (a crystalline mineral). Dairying, chromium and feldspar mining, saw milling, and fiberglass manufacturing are other commercial activities in Thetford Mines. It was founded in 1876 and became a city in 1912.

THOMPSON lies on the Burntwood River, 400 miles north of Winnipeg, in north-central Manitoba. This planned community was built in the late 1950s and has an estimated population of 14,700. The International Nickel Company is the principal employer. Its chairman, John Thompson, gave his name for the city when it was completed in 1961. The company's combination nickel mining-smelting-refining plant was the first of its kind in the Western Hemisphere. Thompson is linked to Winnipeg by air.

THUNDER BAY is Canada's third largest port, and the western terminus of the St. Lawrence Seaway. The twin cities of Port Arthur and Fort William joined to form Thunder Bay on January 1, 1970. The city is located in the midst of a rich mining and fishing region. Several industries in Thunder Bay are involved in brewing, flour milling, paper milling, truck and aircraft manufacturing, and shipbuilding.

The city is easily accessible by boat, highway, and rail. It has an estimated population of 114,000.

TROIS RIVIÈRES (Three Rivers), in Quebec, is the second oldest city in the province. Founded in 1634, it is predated only by Quebec City, which was established in 1608. The city has a strong manufacturing base. Factories in Trois Rivières produce clothing, electrical appliances, paper, textiles, shoes, and wood pulp. Abundant woodlands, combined with a large hydroelectric plant make the city one of the world's largest producers of newsprint. It has a beautiful 17th-century Anglican church, and a Gothic-style cathedral whose stained-glass windows are among the most exquisite on this continent. Approximately 51,800 people live in the city.

WHITEHORSE, the capital of the Yukon, is headquarters for the Royal Canadian Mounted Police. Its population is roughly 20,700. The Yukon was the site of the Klondike Gold Rush in 1898. The Gay Nineties days are relived every summer. Dramond Tooth Gerties in Dawson is a gambling casino, with blackjack and roulette tables. Other points of interest in Whitehorse include the McBride Museum, which features an in depth look at Yukon heritage and wildlife, a tour aboard the restored steamboat *S.S. Klondike* and a guided tour of the city.

YELLOWKNIFE, capital of the Northwest Territories, is one of Canada's youngest cities (1935). It is only 275 miles south of the Arctic Circle. From May through July, this is the land of the midnight sun. In late June, Yellowknife hosts the Pacific Western Midnight Sun Golf Tournament. The Northwest Territories covers one-third of Canada's land area, but the total population is only about 14,000. Coppermine, Cambridge Bay, Bathurst Inlet, and Bay Chimo are small communities north of Yellowknife.

COUNTRY PROFILE

Geography and Climate

The world's second largest country in land area (3,851,809 square miles), Canada is bordered on the north by the Arctic Ocean, on the northeast by the Atlantic Ocean, on the south by the United States, and on the west by the Pacific Ocean and Alaska.

Much of Canada's industry is concentrated in the southeast near the Great Lakes and the St. Lawrence River, in an environment similar to adjacent areas of the U.S. To the northeast are the rolling Appalachian country of southern Quebec, the Maritime Provinces, and the Island of Newfoundland. The most outstanding physical feature is the Shield, a rugged area of Precambrian rock which surrounds Hudson Bay and covers most of eastern and central Canada—almost half of the country. This semi-barren area, and the Arctic Archipelago to the north, are sparsely populated and as yet largely undeveloped.

Another major region is the Canadian prairies, an extension of the mid-continent Great Plains. This area lies between the western border of the Shield and the Canadian Rockies. It is the Canadian breadbasket, and an area that is also rich in petroleum, gas, and other mineral resources.

Far-western Canada, comprised mostly of British Columbia, is laced with towering mountain ranges. Most people here live on the temperate southwest coast and Vancouver Island.

The climate varies greatly in the many diversified regions—ranging from frigid to mild—but Canada generally may be described as lying in the cool temperate zone, with long, cold winters.

Population

More than two-thirds of Canada's 31.3 million people live within 100 miles of the U.S. border. Canadians and Americans are not "just alike," however, as many observers often assume. The Canadian character and outlook have been forged from a distinctive historical and social background which has produced a "Canadian way of life" that flourishes in a sovereign nation.

About 28% of the population is of British stock, about 23% of French, 15% is other European, and about 2% is indigenous Indian and Inuits (Eskimos). Canada's more than six million French-speaking citizens are mainly descendants of colonists who settled the country three centuries ago. They are concentrated in the Province of Quebec, although about 20% live in other parts of the country, mainly Ontario and New Brunswick. There is a sizeable French community in Manitoba as well.

The English-speaking population has been built up by immigration from the British Isles. The largest influx from the U.S. occurred during the American Revolution, when thousands of "Empire Loyalists" fled to Canada. Most settled in "Upper Canada," in southern and southeastern Ontario. Those Canadians who are of neither British nor French origin are mainly Germans, Ukrainians, Scandinavians, Italians, Dutch, Poles, Chinese, Indians, and Pakistanis.

Religion plays an important, though diminishing, role in the life of the Canadian. About 42% are Roman Catholics. The largest Protestant denomination, about 17% of the population, is the United Church of Canada—a union of Methodists, Congregationalists, and Presbyterians. Almost 10% are Anglicans, with Presbyterians, Lutherans, Baptists, and Jews next in number.

Government

Canada's parliamentary system of government reflects both its Old World heritage and its North American experience. The British North America Act of 1867 provided a written constitution, similar to that of the British. The lack of specific guarantees of rights, combined with profound regional disputes, led to serious consideration of a truly Canadian constitution in the late 1970s. After years of discussions, then-Prime Minister Pierre Trudeau "brought home the constitution" in 1982. Following British Parliament approval, Queen Elizabeth II and Trudeau signed the Constitution Act on Ottawa's Parliament Hill in April 1982. Included in the new constitution is a Charter of Rights and Freedoms.

Many of the country's legal and parliamentary practices are derived from ancient custom, as in Great Britain. On the other hand, the 10 provinces are united in a federal system resembling that in the U.S., though provinces have greater responsibilities and powers than have American states.

Queen Elizabeth II is the head of the Canadian state, and is a symbol of Canada's Commonwealth status. Her personal representative in Canada is the Governor-General.

Parliament consists of the Crown, the Senate, and the House of Commons, the latter clearly having the dominant voice in legislation. Its 282 members are elected for nominal five-year terms. The Senate's 104 members are appointed by the governor-general on the advice of the prime minister, and hold office until mandatory retirement at age 75.

Executive power is vested in the Cabinet, headed by the prime minister, who is the leader of the political party in power. The Cabinet remains in power as long as it retains majority support in the House on major issues.

Provincial government is patterned much along the lines of the central government. Each province is governed by a premier and a single, elected legislative chamber. A lieutenant governor, appointed by the governor-general, represents the Crown.

Criminal law, a parliamentary prerogative, is uniform throughout the nation, and is largely based on British law. Civil law is based on English common law, except in Quebec. Here, civil law is derived from the Napoleonic Code. Justice is administered by federal, provincial, and municipal courts.

During the past century, national politics has been dominated by two major parties, the Liberals and the Progressive Conservatives. While these parties have adopted many traditions from their British counterparts, there are substantial differences. The Liberals correspond, in very general terms, to the Democratic Party in the U.S., while the Progressive Conservatives would be the rough equivalent of the Republican Party. Distinctions between the two parties, however, are increasingly blurred since both take a pragmatic approach to Canada's problems.

Also represented in parliament and active in provincial politics is the New Democratic Party (NDP). The NDP corresponds roughly to the social democratic parties of Europe. The Communist Party is almost insignificant, and holds no seat in either the federal or provincial legislatures.

Canada is a member of the British Commonwealth, the United Nations, United Nations Educational, Scientific, and Cultural Organization (UNESCO), World Health Organization (WHO), North Atlantic Treaty Organization (NATO), and the following international associations: Inter-American Development Bank, International Energy Agency, International Sugar Organization, International Wool Study Group, and the International Wheat Council.

The Canadian flag consists of a red maple leaf on a white background, flanked by vertical bands of red.

Arts, Science, Education

The development of the arts in Canada reflects not only the country's culture and geography, but also bears the imprint of a rapidly growing nation. The existence of two dominant cultural traditions—French and English—has led to a diversity in the arts. Focal points of artistic activity have grown up in several metropolitan centers scattered about the country. Since World War II, economic growth has given Canadians greater means to practice and enjoy the arts, and the influx of immigrants has increased the pool of available talent.

All provincial governments, through various departments, agencies, or educational institutions, provide some assistance for professional and amateur artists within their borders. The federally funded, as well as privately funded, Canada Council administers a similar program on a national scale.

Well-known artistic groups include the Stratford Festival Company, the Montreal Symphony, Toronto's Canadian Opera Company, and the Winnipeg Ballet. All of these groups make extensive tours throughout North America, and occasionally tour abroad.

A technologically advanced nation, Canada needs and produces much scientific activity. Most major research projects reflect the increasingly interdependent industrial, university, and government laboratories. In addition, considerable scientific cooperation is undertaken with other nations—especially with the U.S. and the U.K.

All of Canada's activities in the field of atomic energy are the responsibility of the federal government. The most diversified program of scientific research is carried out by the National Research Council—a federal agency. On the other hand, most basic medical research is conducted by universities.

Education at the elementary and secondary level is the responsibility of provincial governments; curricula and teacher qualifications vary a great deal. In all provinces, public education is free. Ages of mandatory attendance vary from province to province, but are generally from seven to 15. In Halifax, Vancouver, and Winnipeg, free public education is controlled and funded by public school boards, as in the U.S. Private schools, primarily Roman Catholic, exist as well, and charge tuition. The literacy rate is estimated to be 99%.

In other Canadian cities, free public education is funded and controlled locally by two types of boards—either "public" or "separate." Except in Quebec, the public boards are nondenominational, reflecting a Protestant and English historical development; the separate boards are Roman Catholic. In Quebec, the public boards are Roman Catholic—further divided into boards for French- and English-speaking children; the separate boards are nondenominational, also with French and English subdivisions. Both types of boards fund public education from property taxes. Parents usually cannot elect to send children in the same family to schools controlled by different boards.

Education at the elementary level in Canada is considered to be on a par with schools in the U.S. At the secondary level, schools in Ontario and the western provinces are also considered to be at par, but in Montreal, Quebec City, and Halifax, schools at the secondary level do not always meet these standards.

In the non-French-speaking areas of Ottawa, Toronto, and Winnipeg, local school districts offer French-language instruction at all levels. In elementary schools, there are generally two tracks of instruction—a required French course, or an optional immersion program, which begins in kindergarten and offers instruction totally in French, with English being phased in gradually in the third or fourth grade. At the secondary level, French is usu-ally optional and is offered along with other languages, such as German and Spanish. At other places (outside Quebec), French is offered on an optional basis, primarily at the secondary level. In English-speaking schools in Quebec Province, French is also a required subject at all levels.

Canada's 60 universities range from small liberal arts colleges with as few as 1,000 students to multiversities (made up of colleges, faculties, and research institutes) with enrollments as high as 20,000. Most instruction is in English—although some institutions use French only—whereas both English and French are used at the University of Ottawa and two other institutions. There are numerous community colleges, usually called technical schools.

Commerce and Industry

The Canadian economy is highly developed, giving Canadians one of the highest standards of living in the world. Manufacturing is concentrated in transportation and communications equipment, engineering, and steel and consumer goods. Especially notable is the production of motor vehicles and parts, encouraged by the auto pact between the U.S. and Canada. Most manufacturing is concentrated in Ontario and Quebec.

Alberta is growing fast in industries related to oil and natural gas. Primary industries built on Canada's rich natural resources remain an important part of the economy and a major source of exports. Leading resource industries are: forest products; oil, natural gas, and hydroelectric power; grains and other agricultural products; mining of asbestos, potash, and nonferrous metals; and fishing. As in other developed countries, the service sector is growing rapidly.

The economy is closely linked by trade and investment with other countries, especially the U.S. Foreign trade, two-thirds of which is with the U.S., represents more than one-fifth of total output. There is considerable two-way direct investment between the U.S. and Canada, although the level of U.S. investment in Canada is higher, as is its relative importance in the economy.

Americans find that most products and services available in the U.S. are also available in Canada. Local prices are often higher, but this may be offset by a favorable exchange rate for the Canadian dollar.

The main office of the Canadian Chamber of Commerce is located at 55 Metcalf St., Ste. 1160, Ottawa, Ontario K1P 6N4. There are regional offices in all of the provinces.

Transportation

Except in the remote northern areas, Canada possesses an advanced transportation system in all modes comparable to that in the U.S. An extensive air network links all major and many minor traffic points with adequate connections to the rest of the world. Domestic air fares per mile are higher than in the U.S., and distances between population centers are considerably greater. A good highway system (with somewhat less emphasis on interstate-type roads) exists, and supports extensive truck, bus, and automobile traffic.

The Canadian railroad system, while vast, has many problems similar to those affecting the U.S. Although passenger service continues to exist, it is poor except in the Quebec-Windsor corridor.

Water transportation is important largely from the foreign trade viewpoint. Major ports exist at Vancouver, Montreal, other St. Lawrence River points, Halifax, and St. John (New Brunswick). The Great Lakes St. Lawrence Seaway and River System is an important domestic and binational transport route, which permits the movement of smaller-sized oceangoing vessels as far west as Duluth, Minnesota and Thunder Bay, Ontario.

All larger cities have public transit systems, generally buses. There are subways in Montreal and Toronto, and streetcars in Toronto and Calgary; plans are being formulated to develop rail systems in Edmonton and elsewhere. By and large, Canadian cities have public transportation arrangements at least as good as in American cities of similar size. They are better developed closer to the city's downtown center. Low population densities have inhibited the development of equivalent service in distant suburbs. The operation of public transport is frequently subsidized by provincial and local governments, making most fares reasonable.

In spite of extensive public transportation arrangements, Canada is as much an automobile society as the U.S. All American automobile manufacturers have plants in Canada, producing standard North American vehicles, and the greater portion of the automobile market in Canada is shared by these manufacturers. Most European and Japanese models found in the U.S. are also sold in Canada. Spare parts are available for all these vehicles. Repair facilities in the major cities compare to those in the U.S. There may be service problems with some European and Japanese cars outside the major cities, but most cars can be serviced readily except, perhaps, in remote areas.

U.S. grades of gasoline (leaded and unleaded) are widely available, and are sold in liters. Safety standards for cars are similar in the U.S. and Canada. Left-hand-drive vehicles are standard; traffic moves on the right. International highway symbols are used in Canada, and distances have been converted to the metric system. Seat belts and infant/child seat restraints are mandatory in the provinces of Ontario, Quebec, Saskatchewan, and British Columbia. Fines are imposed for non-use of seat belts and child restraints.

Communications

Telephone service, provided by the Bell Telephone Company of Canada in Ontario and Quebec, and by provincial companies in other provinces, is excellent. Canada (except for the Northwest Territories) is integrated with the U.S. direct distance dialing system. Telegraph services are operated by the two transcontinental railway companies, and by the federal government to outlying districts.

Mail service within and from Canada to other countries is satisfactory. All first-class mail is airmail within Canada at no extra cost, and letters to the U.S. require only a regular first- class stamp. There is no censorship, and customs formalities are minimal.

Broadcasting is well developed in Canada. Radio and TV stations operate in all major cities and carry extensive amounts of U.S. programming. There are two national TV networks (CBC and CTV), and independent TV stations also exist in many large cities. The Canadian Broadcasting Corporation (CBC) operates an extensive radio network, with domestic (AM and FM), northern, and international shortwave service. It operates dual networks for English and French programming; there are even French outlets in the western cities where the francophone population is limited. The Province of Quebec also has its own French-language broadcasting system. The Province of Ontario operates an impressive educational TV system which, at night, features nonacademic programs.

Direct reception of nearby U.S. radio and TV stations is possible in many parts of Canada. In most Canadian cities there is a well-developed cable TV system which relays most of the U.S. networks (including PBS), some distant Canadian stations for an additional charge, and distant FM radio as well.

About 109 daily newspapers are published in Canada—89% are in

English, the rest in French. Most major cities have at least two local papers, usually morning and evening. Ottawa has only one daily, *The Citizen*. About six Canadian newspapers publish a Sunday edition. Most cities receive major U.S. newspapers within a few days of publication. (*The New York Times* is available daily, including Sundays, in Ottawa, Toronto, Vancouver, and Montreal.)

Most American magazines and books are available, but usually at slightly higher prices. *Maclean's*, a biweekly, is the only national Canadian news magazine. *Reader's Digest* publishes a Canadian edition.

Health

Medical care in Canada is excellent. Competent doctors, dentists, and specialists in all fields are available, and most, except in some areas of Quebec, speak English. Canadian medical educational standards are equivalent to those in the U.S., particularly in dentistry and ophthalmology. There is a shortage of trained personnel and facilities in the physical rehabilitation field, although availability of these services has improved in recent years.

Laboratories and hospitals maintain high standards and are well equipped. Professional fees and hospital and prescription drug costs are comparable to those in the U.S. Pharmaceutical facilities are excellent.

There are no special health risks. Standards of community health and sanitation are very good, and no diseases are endemic to large cities; however, several possible health problems should be noted. Winnipeg's climate might affect visitors seriously afflicted with asthma, sinusitis, or Raynaud's disease, a circulatory vascular condition. Hay fever sufferers should remember that Toronto has the highest pollen count of any large North American city. While the hay fever season is short—about six weeks—persons with hay fever experience great dis-

comfort unless they take medication or remain in air-conditioned areas.

Clothing and Services

Americans find that tastes and standards in clothing are basically the same as in the U.S. The climate in winter makes warm clothes essential. For the most part, summers are somewhat cooler in Canada, but hot periods occur, and lightweight clothing is necessary. Wraps are usually needed for evenings, even in summer. Children dress casually, as in the U.S., but those who attend private schools ordinarily wear uniforms.

Ready-made clothes of all kinds are available at every price level. Items manufactured in the U.S. are expensive—often one-third higher than the American retail price.

Practically all services and supplies are available in the cities throughout Canada. The prices are often higher, but the current favorable exchange rate offsets the expense. Domestic help is difficult to find (as in the U.S.), and if the level of competence and experience is favorable, wages also are high. Professional catering and cleaning services are available.

NOTES FOR TRAVELERS

Passage, Customs & Duties
When entering from the United States, U.S. citizens must show either a U.S. passport or proof of U.S. citizenship and photo ID. U.S. citizens entering Canada from a third country must have a valid passport. A visa is not required for U.S. citizens for a stay up to 180 days. Anyone with a criminal record (including a DWI charge) should contact the Canadian Embassy or nearest Canadian consulate before travel. For further information on entry requirements, travelers may contact the Embassy of Canada at

501 Pennsylvania Avenue, N.W., Washington, D.C. 20001, telephone (202) 682-1740, Internet address: http://www.cdnemb-washdc.org; or the Canadian consulates in Atlanta, Boston, Buffalo, Chicago, Dallas, Detroit, Los Angeles, Miami, Minneapolis, New York, San Juan or Seattle.

U.S. citizens living in or visiting Canada may register at the Consular Section of the U.S. Embassy or at a U.S. Consulate General in Canada, and may obtain updated information on travel and security within Canada.

The U.S. Embassy is in Ottawa, Ontario, at 490 Sussex Drive, K1N 1G8, telephone (613) 238-5335, fax (613) 688-3082. The Embassy web site is http://www.usembassycanada.gov. The Embassy's consular district includes Baffin Island, the following counties in eastern Ontario: Lanark, Leeds, Prescott, Renfrew, Russell and Stormont; and the following counties in western Quebec: Gatineau, Hull, Labelle, Papineau, Pontiac and Tamiscamingue.

U.S. Consulates General are located at:

Calgary, Alberta, at Suite 1050, 615 Macleod Trail SE, telephone (403) 266-8962; emergency-after hours (403) 228-8900; fax (403) 264-6630. The consular district includes Alberta, Manitoba, Saskatchewan, and the Northwest Territories, excluding Nunavut.

Halifax, Nova Scotia, at Suite 904, Purdy's Tower II, 1969 Upper Water Street, Halifax, Nova Scotia B3J 3R7, telephone (902) 429-2480; emergency-after hours (902) 429-2485; fax (902) 423-6861. The consular district includes New Brunswick, Newfoundland, Nova Scotia, Prince Edward Island and the islands of Saint Pierre and Miquelon.

Montreal, Quebec, at 1155 St. Alexander Street, telephone (514) 398-9695; emergency-after hours (514) 981-5059; fax (514) 398-0702. The consular district includes south-western Quebec with the exception of the six counties served by the U.S. Embassy in Ottawa.

Quebec City, Quebec, at 2 Place Terrasse Dufferin, telephone (418) 692-2095; emergency-after hours (418) 692-2096; fax (418) 692-4640. The consular district includes the counties of Abitibi-West, Abitibi-East, St. Maurice, Trois-Rivieres, Nicolet, Wolfe, Frontenac and all other counties to the north or east within the province of Quebec. The new arctic territory of Nunavut is also in this district.

Toronto, Ontario, at 360 University Avenue, telephone (416) 595-1700; emergency-after hours (416) 201-4100; fax (416) 595-5466. The consular district includes the province of Ontario except the six counties served by the U.S. Embassy in Ottawa.

Vancouver, British Columbia, at 1095 West Pender Street, telephone (604) 685-4311; fax (604) 685-7175. The consular district includes British Columbia and the Yukon Territory.

Pets

Dogs and cats imported from the U.S. must be accompanied by a veterinarian's certificate showing that the dog or cat has been vaccinated against rabies during the three years preceding entry. From countries recognized by Canada to be free of rabies, a certificate issued by a veterinarian of the National Veterinary Service of the country of origin is required, certifying that the animal has been in that country for a continuous six-month period preceding shipment. From all other countries, a certificate issued by a veterinarian of the National Veterinary Service should certify that the animal was vaccinated against rabies not less than 30 days nor more than one year preceding shipment. Dogs and cats from countries other than the U.S. arriving without a certificate will be placed in quarantine for a 30-day period and vaccinated for rabies.

Firearms & Ammunition

Firearms are strictly controlled. As of January 1, 2001, visitors bringing firearms into Canada, or planning to borrow and use firearms while in Canada, are required to declare the firearms in writing using a Non-Resident Firearm Declaration form. Multiple firearms can be declared on the same form. At the border, three copies of the unsigned declaration must be presented to a Canadian Customs officer. The declaration will serve as a temporary license and registration certificate for up to 60 days. The Non-Resident Firearm Declaration costs $50 (Canadian). Visitors planning to borrow a firearm in Canada must obtain in advance a Temporary Firearms Borrowing License, which costs $30 (Canadian). The form must be signed before a Canadian Customs officer and the fee paid at the border. In order to save time at the border, Canadian authorities recommend that visitors complete the declaration form, but not sign it, and make two copies of the completed form before arriving at the port-of-entry. Requests made at the border for photocopies of the form may be denied. Full details on this new policy are available at the Canadian Firearms Centre web site, http://www.cfc-ccaf.gc.ca, under the heading "Visitors to Canada." The Non-Resident Firearm Declaration and the Temporary Firearms Borrowing License applications may also be obtained from this web site.

Canada has three classes of firearms: non-restricted, restricted, and prohibited. Non-restricted firearms include most ordinary hunting rifles and shotguns. These may be brought temporarily into Canada for sporting or hunting use during hunting season, for use in competitions, for in-transit movement through Canada, or for personal protection against wildlife in remote areas of Canada. Anyone wishing to bring hunting rifles into Canada must be at least 18 years old, and the firearm must be properly stored for transport. Restricted firearms are primarily handguns; however, pepper spray and mace are also included in this category. A restricted firearm may be brought into Canada, but an Authorization to Transport permit must be obtained in advance from a Provincial or Territorial Chief Firearms Officer. Prohibited firearms include fully automatic, converted automatics, and assault-type weapons. Prohibited firearms are not allowed into Canada.

In advance of any travel, please contact a Canadian embassy or consulate, or the Canadian Firearms Centre (http://www.cfc.ccaf.gc.ca) for detailed information and instructions on temporarily importing firearms. In all cases, travelers must declare to Canadian Customs authorities any firearms and weapons in their possession when entering Canada. If a traveler is denied permission to bring in the firearm, there are often facilities near border crossings where firearms may be stored, pending the traveler's return to the United States. Canadian law requires that officials confiscate firearms and weapons from those crossing the border who deny having them in their possession. Confiscated firearms and weapons are never returned.

Currency, Banking, and Weights and Measures

Canada covers seven time zones. The time in Newfoundland is Greenwich Mean Time (GMT) minus three-and-a-half. The time in Halifax is GMT minus four. The time in Ottawa, Toronto, Montreal, Quebec City, Hamilton, London, and Windsor is GMT minus five (Eastern Time in the U.S.). The time in Winnipeg and Regina is GMT minus six (Central Time in the U.S.). The time in Calgary and Edmonton is GMT minus seven (Mountain Time in the U.S.). The time in Vancouver is GMT minus eight (Pacific Time in the U.S.).

The unit of currency is the Canadian dollar, divided into half-dollar, quarter, dime, nickel, and penny coins, all similar in size and shape to U.S. currency. Canadian and U.S. dollars are fully convertible at banks. The conversion rate fluctuates.

Canada officially adopted the metric system in September 1977. Most road signs are now showing distances in kilometers and speed limits in kilometers/hour. Containers show contents and weights in both pounds and ounces, quarts and kilograms, and grams and liters.

LOCAL HOLIDAYS

Jan. 1	New Year's Day
Feb. 2	Groundhog Day
Feb. 14	St. Valentine's Day
Mar. 17	St. Patrick's Day
Mar/Apr.	Good Friday*
Mar/Apr.	Easter*
Mar/Apr.	Easter Monday*
Apr. 1	April Fool's Day
Apr. 22	Earth Day
Apr. 28	National Day of Mourning
May	Victoria Day*
May (2nd Sun)	Mother's Day*
June (3rd Sun)	Father's Day
July 1	Canada Day
Aug. (first Mon)	Civic Holiday (Calgary, Toronto, Ottawa, and Vancouver. Called Natal Day in Nova Scotia)*
Sept. 3	Labor Day
Oct.	Columbus Day*
Oct. (second Mon)	Thanksgiving* Day*
Oct. 31	Halloween
Nov. 11	Remembrance Day
Dec.25	Christmas Day
Dec. 26	Boxing Day
Dec. 31	New Year's Eve

*Variable

RECOMMENDED READING

The following titles are provided as a general indication of the material published on this country:

Berlitz Editors. *Canada 1992 Travellers Guide.* New York: Berlitz, 1992.

Bothwell, Robert. *Canada & The United States: The Politics of Partnership.* New York: Macmillan, 1992.

Canada 1991. New York: Bantam, 1991.

Eagles, et al. *The Almanac of Canadian Politics.* Concord, MA: Paul & Company Publishers, 1992.

Fodor's Canada 1991. New York: McKay, 1991.

Halsey, David. *Magnetic North: Take Across Canada.* San Francisco, CA: Sierra Club, 1990.

Harris, Bill. *Canada: Photo Journey.* Avenal, NJ: Outlet Book Co., 1991.

Harvey, David D. *Americans in Canada: Migration & Settlement Since 1840.* Lewiston, NY: Edward Mellen Press, 1991.

Hobbs, Pam. *The Adventure Guide to Canada.* Edison, NJ: Hunter Publishing, 1991.

LeVert, Suzanne. *Canada: Facts & Figures.* Let's Discover Canada Series. New York: Chelsea House, 1992.

LeVert, Suzanne. *Dominion of Canada.* Let's Discover Canada Series. New York: Chelsea House, 1992.

Lipset, Seymour M. *North American Culture: Values & Institutions in Canada and the United States.* Edited by Mary Williams. Orono, ME: Canadian-American Centre, 1990.

Malcolm, Andrew H. *The Canadians.* New York: St. Martin's Press, 1991.

Marchant, Garry. *Canada.* Edited by Kathleen Griffin and Martin Gamon. Oakland, CA: Compass America, 1991.

Marsh, James H., ed. *The Canadian Encyclopedia.* 4 vols. 2nd ed. Detroit: Gale Research, 1988.

Morris, Jan. O. *Canada: Travels in an Unknown Country.* New York: Harper Collins, 1992.

Pratson, Frederick. *Guide to Eastern Canada.* 4th ed. Old Saybrook, CT: Globe Peguot Press, 1992.

Pratson, Frederick. *Guide to Western Canada.* 2nd ed. Old Saybrook, CT: Globe Peguot Press, 1992.

The Penguin History of Canada. New York: Viking Penguin, 1988.

Watkins, Mel, and James Warren, eds. *Canada.* New York: Facts on File, 1992.

Weaver, P. Kent, ed. *The Collapse of Canada?* Washington, DC: Brookings Institution, 1992.

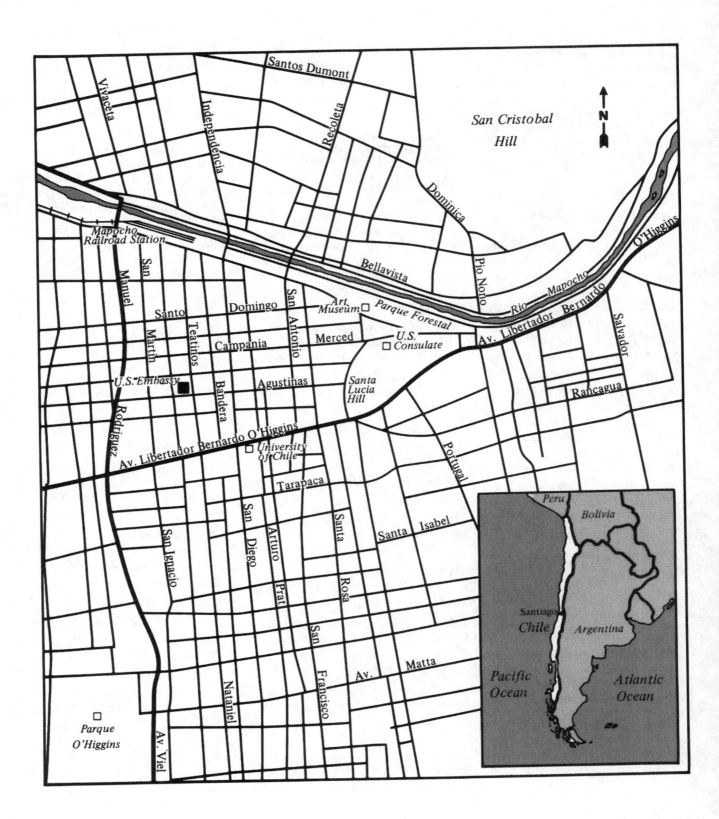

Santiago, Chile

CHILE

Republic of Chile

Major Cities:

Santiago, Viña del Mar, Valparaíso, Concepción, Antofagasta

Other Cities:

Arica, Chillán, Chuquicamata, Iquique, La Serena, Puerto Montt, Punta Arenas, Talca, Talcahuano, Temuco, Valdivia

EDITOR'S NOTE

This chapter was adapted from the Department of State Post Report dated July 1996. Supplemental material has been added to increase coverage of minor cities, facts have been updated, and some material has been condensed. Readers are encouraged to visit the Department of State's web site at http://travel.state.gov/ for the most recent information available on travel to this country.

INTRODUCTION

CHILE can accurately be described as a land of variety and geographic delight. The northern deserts; the rich fields in the central valley; the labyrinths of channels, inlets, fjords, and peninsulas in the south; and the Andes in the east all provide stark contrasts that give Chile a unique beauty. Its cultural, political, financial, and commercial activities have been influenced by these geographical features. Its history is as varied as its topography, and it is almost as much a "melting pot" as the United States. Although many nationalities have settled here, the population is homogeneous and nationalistic.

Ferdinand Magellan was the first European to behold the coasts of Chile when, in 1520, he made the crossing from the Atlantic to the Pacific through the strait that now bears his name. An expedition led by Diego de Almagro moved southward from Peru in 1536, but the conquest was halted due to unfavorable weather and hostile Indians. Six years later, the city of Santiago was founded. Historical sources reveal that the name Chile was derived from either the name of a native chieftain, from a river in the area, or from the sound of an indigenous bird.

MAJOR CITIES

Santiago

Founded in 1541 by Pedro de Valdivia, greater Santiago today is a modern city of 5,261,000 inhabitants. It is the cultural, political, financial, and commercial center of Chile. Santiago impresses foreigners as being more European than most Latin American cities—a reflection of its population characteristics and Chile's historical isolation from its neighbors. The city's high level of sophistication is apparent in the educated, neatly dressed populace, the posh shopping malls, and the efficient transportation system.

The city lies at the eastern edge of the fertile central valley, and some of its residential areas reach into the Andean foothills. The Andean peaks, which are snow-covered much of the year, are visible from the city's center on a clear day. Situated roughly 70 miles from the Pacific ocean, Santiago is at an altitude of about 1,700 feet.

Chile's standard of living, which ranks high in Latin America, is highest in Santiago, where most of the country's wealth and 40% of its population are concentrated. There is a small but active American community. Chile's other large population centers—Valparaiso, Concepcion, Temuco, and Antofagasta—have distinct personalities but are more provincial. Valparaiso has a long history as a vital and colorful seaport.

Food

Americans are usually delighted with Santiago's modern supermarkets which offer most of the variety of major US grocery chains. The colorful array of high quality fresh fruits and vegetables is one of the many attractions of Chile. However, they must be cleaned and soaked in a special disinfectant before being eaten. Winter produce is more limited but selection is still good. Fish and seafood from the vast Chilean coastline include many interesting, little-known varieties which Americans have come to enjoy.

Milk products manufactured in Santiago are good quality. The pasteurized milk in supermarkets comes in three varieties: natural whole milk, reconstituted, and low in butterfat. Condensed, evaporated, long life, and powdered milk are also sold. A variety of local cheeses are available, in addition to many kinds of imported cheeses. Other local dairy products include yogurt, margarine, butter, sour cream, cream cheese, cottage cheese, ricotta, and ice cream.

Local brands of cereal, cake mixes, snack foods, canned and frozen fruits and vegetables, and acceptable baby formula and strained foods are available, as well as the complete range of staples, such as flour, sugar, oils, vinegar, etc. Most locally produced food items in Chile are currently less expensive than in the U.S.

Chile is famous for its fine selection of excellent wines, which are inexpensive. Beer and soft drinks (including diet varieties) are also good quality.

Clothing

Located in the temperate zone, Santiago has four seasons. Clothing needs for this climate are the same as for the Bay area south of San Francisco. Winter is long but generally mild. June through September rainfall may be heavy but almost never freezes. During these months some poorly heated homes become damp and chilly, requiring warmer indoor clothing. Lightweight thermal underwear is useful. Bring raincoats, umbrellas, and boots.

Spring and autumn are sunny and mild with some rain. However, almost no rain falls during Santiago's warm, sunny and dry summer (December through March). Houses usually remain cool and pleasant.

The temperature drops at sundown, and cool summer evenings require a light wrap.

Chileans dress stylishly and shop windows display fashionable, well-made clothes. However, large sizes are difficult to find, and extra-long men's clothing is unavailable. Hand knit wool and cotton sweaters are a good buy here, as are leather goods. Chile manufactures lovely leather shoes, but, compared with US-manufactured footwear, the choice of lasts is smaller and most ready made shoes come only one width for each size. Long and narrow widths are available in only 2 or 3 stores. Locally made clothing is of good quality and reasonably priced, imported brands are more expensive.

Quality and workmanship among Santiago's seamstresses and tailors vary. Good men's suits can be made from the woolens, cottons, and synthetics locally available; a wider variety of material is available for women's wear. Dry-cleaning service is good.

Men: Men wear business suits for office and social functions. A dark suit is appropriate for almost all evening occasions. For year-round wear medium-weight wool blend suits are most practical, though some men prefer a heavier fabric for winter and wash-and-wear suits for summer. A raincoat is necessary, preferably washable with zip lining. A top coat may be useful; hats are a matter of personal preference.

Chile's four seasons require a variety of sportswear. Flannel or wool shirts are comfortable for winter. Attractive wool and synthetic knit shirts and sweaters are available usually for less than one would pay in the U.S. Slacks, shorts, and swim trunks are also available but styles and colors may be limited, and cuts may not fit everybody. Cotton knit underwear and socks are available.

Women: Chilean women tend to dress more formally than American women—even in the grocery store. They wear the latest European fashions in clothes, both in style and fabrics. A basic wardrobe of multipurpose clothing is more practical than many clothes of limited use.

Suits, wool dresses, knits, and two and three-piece combinations of wool and wool synthetic blends are popular for office, street or daytime functions from April through October. Some houses may be damp and chilly during this period, so warm clothing is needed. Skirts, blouses, and sweaters often are worn for office and informal meetings as well as at home. Slacks are acceptable at the office, jeans are worn on the weekends and for very casual occasions. (Here again, for Chileans, they are usually "designer" styles.) The widely varying temperatures during a 24-hour period often make the "layered look" the most practical.

In the summer (and occasionally in spring and autumn) women wear cotton, linen, and synthetic fabrics. Cool evenings usually require a light wrap. Stoles and blazers, as well as sweaters or sweater-coats, are useful.

Children: Generally children's clothes are attractive and inexpensive here Medium weight ski jackets are used a great deal. Boots are recommended. Sweaters that are easily washed, warm gloves, and light or medium-weight cotton thermal or knit long-sleeved pajamas are essential. Snowsuits are useful for winter trips to the ski resorts.

Satisfactory cotton knit and synthetic shorts and shirts are available for summer but may require special care compared with similar U.S. garments. This is also true of some of the highly styled children's clothes.

Most people buy their children's shoes locally. Leather shoes are generally well made and inexpensive. Sneakers such as Nike, Puma, and Diadora are sold in most stores and are expensive, but local brands are very reasonable.

School uniforms are required in Chile with the exception of nursery schools. However, the Nido de Aguilas School only requires uniforms through fifth grade. Some other schools where American students go do not require uniforms. No school

La Moneda, changing of the guard, Santiago, Chile

Susan Rock. Reproduced by permission.

uniforms should be purchased until you know in which school your children will be enrolled. Younger children sometimes wear coveralls or smocks over their uniforms—these may be purchased locally.

Boys' uniforms for those schools that require them usually consist of medium to dark gray trousers, white or light blue shirts, tie, and navy blue jackets with navy socks and black shoes. In winter boys may wear navy blue pea-jackets or ski jackets. Girls wear navy blue jumpers that must be purchased or made here in a specified style. Private schools for both girls and boys have different type of uniforms.

Teens in secondary grades at Nido de Aquiles wear the same clothing popular in a typical US high school, i.e., jeans, T-shirts, tennis shoes. Stylish teen apparel for boys and girls is sold in all the shopping areas.

Supplies and Services

Some well-known brands of American and international toiletries are available on the market but, if not made locally, may prove to be expensive. On the other hand, certain brands of face soaps and shampoos such as Camay and Silkience are manufactured here and are inexpensive.

Tailors and dressmakers charge less compared to the U.S. Laundry service, dry-cleaning, and shoe repair are good quality and also less expensive.

Service at beauty salons, which includes care of wigs, is good and comparable to U.S. The same is true of barber shops.

Simple car repairs and services are readily obtained for American (especially GMC) and foreign cars.

Auto rental rates locally are expensive, $60 and up per day.

Religious Activities

Chile is predominantly Roman Catholic, though Spanish-speaking Protestant congregations are also numerous. For the English-speaking community, the Santiago Community Church offers English language Protestant services, and the Holy Cross Order at St. George's School provides a Roman Catholic Mass in English during the Chilean school year. Other faiths represented in the city are Christian Science, Mormon, Baptist, Jewish, Greek Orthodox, and Seventh-Day Adventist.

The Santiago Community Church holds Sunday school for children. Through the International Preparatory School, Nido de Aguilas, and

other schools, Roman Catholic religious instruction is available. There is a Jewish day school. The Estadio Israelita (community center) offers religious instruction (in Spanish on Friday afternoons for children who do not attend the day school.

Education

Chile's established public school system is supplemented by numerous private schools for students in nursery through high school. The school year extends from March to mid-December with a vacation of two weeks in July and one week in September. All schools in Chile (public and private) schools require uniforms (see Clothing.)

Most American children attend Nido de Aguilas International School, (Casilla 16.211, Santiago 9), a coeducational, non-sectarian, N-12 school for students from Chile, the US, and numerous other countries. At Nido instruction is in English, and the curriculum, textbooks, and methods are US-based. The school is accredited by the U.S. Southern Association of Colleges and Schools. The student-teacher ratio is 20 to 1. Currently there are 750 students at Nido. The Headmaster is an American, as are approximately one-third of the teachers.

The elementary grades offer an individually guided program based on language arts, social studies, math, science, music, and art. The secondary school prepares students to meet the admission requirements of both US and Latin American universities.

Electives and special tutorial courses help to accommodate the varied educational backgrounds and needs of all international students. The International Baccalaureate (IB) program for grades 11 and 12 offers advanced level instruction in English, Math, Science, and Social Studies which can provide advanced placement in college.

College and career counseling for Chilean, American, and other international students is a regular part of the program. The standardized testing program to measure achievement annually includes the Iowa Test of Basic Skills for grades 2,4,6, and 8; the preliminary Scholastic Aptitude Test (PSAT) for grades 10 and 11; and the College Board Scholastic Aptitude Test; and National Merit Scholarship Test. The high school is a member of the National Honor Society. Junior and senior high school students can participate in Nido's active sports program and numerous extracurricular activities. The music program includes three bands, an orchestra, and a chorus. Nido's school calendar begins in early August and runs through the following June with a long break mid-December through February.

Several other schools offer an opportunity to study in English. Some of the schools that American children presently attend are: Santiago College (Pk-12), a bilingual school with courses taught in English at the elementary level and primarily in Spanish in grades 9-12; the International Preparatory School (Pk-12), a small British school; and the Santiago Christian Academy (K-12), a small Baptist missionary school with an American curriculum that follows the U.S. school calendar, but is not accredited by the Chilean Ministry of Education or the US Southern Association of Colleges and Schools.

Special Educational Opportunities

Spanish language training courses for adults are available through private tutors. The Chilean-North American Institute provides special study opportunities and many cultural activities, such as lectures on Chilean history and culture and exhibits on Chilean art, as well as Spanish and English language training. The Institute's library features facilities in both English and Spanish.

Courses in painting, judo, ceramics, ballet, guitar, folk singing and dancing, and other cultural subjects are offered at various institutes around Santiago. There are good professional schools in classical dance and a respected music conservatory with excellent instruction. Fees vary but compare favorably with stateside prices. French language courses are available at the Alliance Francaise and the French Bi-national Institute; German is taught at the Goethe Institute.

Admission to Santiago universities can usually be arranged for those fluent in Spanish and with adequate academic credentials. However, US colleges and universities do not always recognize credits from local universities. Several institutes offer computer training.

Sports

Chile has such a wide variety of tourist and sports activities throughout the year, that avid sports enthusiasts are hard-pressed to find the time to take advantage of all the opportunities. Even confirmed couch potatoes find themselves getting involved.

Tennis is played year round in private clubs or on the excellent public courts which provide ball boys and instruction for very modest fees. Most courts are clay, and players should bring balls from the States as they are expensive here. Both private and public squash courts are also available. Racquetball is a relatively new addition to the sports scene, but there are a few courts.

Homes with swimming pools are common in Santiago, but serious swimmers might prefer to join a private club with a larger pool. Also Sauna Mundt Spa located uptown offers an excellent indoor swimming pool. The city also has several public swimming facilities.

Golf is a favorite pastime in Chile, and the courses are lovely. Although all the golf clubs in Santiago are private, there are some public greens in the resort areas along the coast. Private country clubs range in price from prohibitively expensive (Club de Golf Los Leones) to fairly reasonable (Club de Golf Lomas de La Dehesa). Some of the more exclusive clubs have long waiting lists or are no longer accepting new member-

ships. For non-golfers, a sports club such as Stade Francais, which offers tennis, squash, swimming, and a restaurant may be more appealing and much less expensive. Gyms with weight machines and supervised exercise programs welcome memberships for a fraction of US prices.

Many water sports are popular throughout Chile. The lakes in the central valley and the south attract boaters and water skiers. In some of the coastal cities, motor and sailboats are available for rent.

White water rafting trips for beginners and experts can be arranged on certain rivers. Scuba diving requires a wet suit due to the cold ocean water.

Chile offers superb trout fishing from October through mid-April in the south-central part of the country and some mountain lakes.

However, the nearest fresh water fishing spots are over four hours away by car, and ideal trout and salmon fishing streams are a day away by car, bus, or train or about 3 hours by plane from Santiago. Deep sea fishing (broadbill, swordfish, and marlin) and surf casting are also available but less popular. Heavy tackle (20-25 pounds) is recommended; bring it with you. Hunting is popular, but Chile has no large game. Rifles may only be used in the extreme southern part of Chile. Most hunters use 12-gauge shotguns with No. 8 shot. Partridge, quail, doves, ducks, and rabbits are hunted throughout Chile, but very little game is found within a few hours drive of Santiago.

Horseback riding is a year-round activity in Santiago, where several academies and riding clubs rent horses and provide instruction. Riding trips of a few hours up to a week can be arranged, and during the summer there are children's camps that specialize in horseback-riding. There is also a polo club.

The mountains visible from Santiago offer a challenge to the day hiker as well as the experienced mountaineer. At 8700 feet, Provincia can be scaled in a day, while the Cajon de Maipo, southeast of Santiago, is a mountain climber's paradise, with peaks reaching over 20,000 feet. There are hiking and climbing clubs in Santiago, catering to the needs of beginners and experts alike. Experienced guides are available for the most challenging climbs.

Skiing ranks as the outstanding winter sports attraction in Chile, where some of the finest skiing centers in the hemisphere are located. The skiing season extends from June to October (and occasionally through November). The most popular ski areas—Portillo, 3 hours away from Santiago, (site of international championship competitions located on the international highway to Mendoza, Argentina); and Farellones, Colorado, Valle Nevado, La Parva, one hour away from Santiago (weather permitting)—offer slopes for every skill level. Hotel rooms are expensive and reservations for July and August must be made several months in advance. The slopes are never as crowded as are many in the United States.

Spectator sports include soccer, horse-racing, and rodeos. Team sports for youngsters are offered at Nido de Aguilas (which has good facilities) and some other schools, as well as some of the private clubs. There is a local softball league which welcomes players and fans alike.

Shoes, clothing, and equipment for nearly every sport areas available in Santiago. Prices and quality vary. For instance, European imported skis are expensive, but are comparable to U.S. prices, while good fishing gear is very expensive. Golf equipment is very high while a top quality tennis racket may be slightly less than in the States.

Touring and Outdoor Activities:

Pleasant day trips are possible outside the city. In the winter one can decide between an active day on the ski slopes or a leisurely lunch by the

sea as a Sunday excursion. Beautiful beaches are located within a 2-4 hour drive from Santiago. Some, however, are dangerous because of strong undertows and lack of lifeguards. The cold water makes swimming unattractive even in the summer. Hotel accommodations are adequate, but make reservations for the summer months well in advance.

Chile's largest summer resort, Viña del Mar, offers excellent hotels, a municipal gambling casino, nightclubs, golf and tennis facilities, a racetrack, and public beaches. Other fine beaches, located both south and north of Viña, often lack the accommodations and facilities of the more popular resorts, but are far less crowded. Most Chilean hotels are currently comparable to United States hotels cost wise.

Other attractive summer resorts are found in the lake region, about 500 miles south of Santiago. Known as the "Switzerland of South America," this area offers excellent trout fishing and some of the most magnificent scenery on the continent. Limited hotels require advance reservations during January and February.

The long list of summer touring activities includes: boat trips through the channels and fjords from Puerto Montt to Punta Arenas on the Straits of Magellan at the tip of the continent; the excursion to the Juan Fernandez Islands, 400 miles off the coast at Valparaíso; a visit to wilderness preserves such as the Torres del Paine Park near Punta Arenas; or a trip to Easter Island in the South Pacific.

In Chile's extreme north (1,300 miles from Santiago, two hours and 40 minutes by jet), Arica features year round spring weather, making it a popular spot in winter. It is also the base for excursions to the high Andean plateau and Lauca National Park, with vicuñas, flamingos and other Andean wildlife. All the major Northern seacoast cities—La Serena, Antofagasta, Iquique, and Arica—have a mild cli-

mate, sandy beaches, and sunshine most of the Year.

Opportunities for mountain climbing, hiking, and camping abound.

Camping facilities vary widely, but most provide baths and hot showers. Campsites are crowded during January and February, but usually are empty the rest of the summer. Camping equipment and supplies are readily available, but are usually less expensive if purchased in the U.S.

Note that tours to out of the way areas involving boats or air travel can be very expensive. In addition, the Pan-American Highway is mostly two lane and heavily traveled, making trips by car long and arduous.

Santiago is rather isolated from its neighbors. Lima is three and a quarter hours away by jet; however, Peru's prime attractions, the Incan cities of Cuzco and Machu Picchu, Buenos Aires (700 miles from Santiago), Montevideo, and Brazil are other favorite tourist destinations. Mendoza, Argentina is only 40 minutes away by jet or four to five hours by car; however, in winter the pass is often closed by snow.

Entertainment

In Santiago, the lovely Teatro Municipal is the center of an opera season, two ballet seasons, and two symphony orchestras that offer weekly concerts during the winter. Chamber music and choral groups perform frequently. Inexpensive businessmen's concerts are held weekly during the season at lunch time with sandwiches and beverages available in the theater lobby. Relatively economical season tickets are available.

Theater plays an active role in Santiago's cultural life. Several theaters present a variety of dramatic and satirical plays in Spanish throughout the year. The English-language amateur theater group, Santiago Stage, produces shows and is always delighted to have newcomers join.

The numerous movie theaters in the city and suburbs are good and inexpensive. All films are subject to censorship, with enforced minimum age limits set for each. Foreign films, which include many American films, are shown in their original language with Spanish subtitles.

Santiago has a few good nightclubs and discotheques. In general, Chileans prefer entertaining in their own homes, although young, unmarried adults frequently patronize clubs. Teenagers are generally pleased with the nightlife here. Several discos cater to their age group, and young people usually go with a group of friends. Unfortunately (for parents, at least) Chileans keep much later hours, and discos and private parties often begin between 11:00 pm and midnight, making typical US curfews difficult to enforce.

Plenty of average-to-very-good restaurants are available in Santiago. Service starts at about 2000 hours and is usually very good. Excellent inexpensive Chilean wines provide an elegant accompaniment to any meal.

Social Activities

Membership in the American Association of Chile is open to all Americans in Chile. Monthly meetings, usually a lunch or tea, provide a good opportunity to meet other Americans from the private sector. The Association sponsors a variety of activities, such as tennis, golf, bowling, bridge, library, quilting, and sewing groups, and several charitable activities.

The Rotary and the Lions Club have several local chapters. The US Chamber of Commerce has an affiliate in Santiago. Both the YWCA and the YMCA offer facilities for sports and cultural programs in the downtown area.

Special Information

Central Chile is one of the most seismically active places on earth, and destructive earthquakes have struck the country periodically throughout its history.

Residents of Santiago will frequently feel tremors which seldom result in damage.

Viña del Mar

Viña del Mar, a popular tourist spot near the Pacific Ocean, is Chile's second largest city. Located six miles east of Valparaíso, Viña del Mar has a population of close to 302,800. It is the country's largest summer resort, and also manufactures textiles, paint, glass, soaps, chemicals, and beverages. The area has first-class hotels, a municipal gambling casino and nightclub, golf and tennis facilities, a racetrack, beautiful parks and gardens, and public beaches. Other fine beaches may be found both south and north of Viña. These often lack the accommodations and facilities of the more popular resorts, but they are far less crowded.

Education

Mackay School, in Viña del Mar, is a boys' day school for kindergarten through grade 12. Founded in 1857 and governed by an elected board of governors, its admission requirements include tests and an interview.

The curriculum is Chilean-based, with English, French, and Spanish offered as foreign languages. Other elective classes are art, band, computer science, physical education, and vocational courses. Extracurricular activities include computer, drama, gymnastics/dance, guitar, literary magazine, newspaper, and rugby, soccer, and swimming. There are also special programs for children with learning disabilities.

The school year runs from March through December, with vacations in July and September. Enrollment is currently 651; there are 15 full-time and 50 part-time teachers. The staff also includes a math specialist, a counselor, and a nurse.

Mackay School is located in a coastal village about seven miles north of Viña del Mar. Facilities include language, computer, and science labs; a video studio; audiovisual room; library; cafeteria; and sports fields. The mailing address is Casilla 558, Viña del Mar, Chile.

Valparaíso

Valparaíso is the third largest city in Chile and the country's chief port. It is located 60 miles northeast of Santiago on the Pacific Ocean. Founded in 1536 by the Spanish conqueror Juan de Saavedra, the city was not permanently established until Pedro de Valdivia's arrival eight years later. The early history of Valparaíso was scattered with raids by English and Dutch pirates; it was bombarded by the Spanish fleet in 1866. Unimportant during colonial times, Valparaíso grew after the last severe earthquakes in 1907 and 1971.

Valparaíso is situated on a narrow waterfront terrace. Steep hills rise to give the city the effect of an amphitheater, with the wharves and business section below and the residential areas above. A cable railway is used to ascend some of the steeper areas. The city faces a wide bay and is partially protected by the breakwaters. The climate is generally mild, although severe winds do occur during the winter months.

As the principal port in Chile, Valparaíso has extensive modern dock facilities and handles the bulk of the country's imports. It manufactures chemicals, textiles, paint, leather goods, clothing, metal products, vegetable oils, and sugar.

Thousands of tourists annually visit Valparaíso, whose resident population is about 276,800. Visitors are attracted to the city's parks, theaters, cafes, colonial buildings, and museums.

Concepción

Concepción, 275 miles southwest of Santiago near the mouth of the Bío-Bío River, is one of Chile's commercial and industrial centers. It was founded in 1550 by Pedro de

Lower city along the bay, Valparaiso, Chile

Susan Rock. Reproduced by permission.

Valdivia about six miles from its present site. Throughout its history, Concepción has been completely destroyed by earthquakes five times. It was further damaged in 1960 by an earthquake, and it is the numerous restorations that have given the city its modern look.

Concepción produces glass, steel, textiles, sugar, and hides. Woodworking, food processing, glassmaking, and brewing are also important industries. Its port, Talcahuano, located just north of Concepción on the Pacific Ocean, ships products produced in the rich agricultural region to the east. Concepción has an estimated population of about 33,000 (2000).

Education

St. John's School, in Concepción, is a coeducational, proprietary school for pre-kindergarten through grade 12. Founded in 1942 and governed by an elected board, admission requirements include an application, past school records, tests, and an interview.

The curriculum is Chilean-based. French is offered as a foreign language, along with the following elective classes: art, chorus, computer science, and physical education. Extracurricular activities include ceramics, chess club, computers,

drama, yearbook, literary magazine, gymnastics/dance, guitar, and basketball, football, volleyball, hockey, and rugby.

The school year runs from the middle of March through December, with vacations in July and September. Enrollment in 1991-92 was 1,026; enrollment capacity is 1,260. There were 52 full-time and 20 part-time teachers. The staff also includes a counselor and a nurse.

St. John's School is located in a residential area of Concepción. Facilities include 45 classrooms, cafeteria, infirmary, a gymnasium, playing fields, and a 9,000-volume library; there are also science labs, computer labs, and a stadium nearby. The mailing address is Casilla 284, Concepción, Chile.

Antofagasta

Antofagasta, located 700 miles northwest of Santiago, is a port on the Pacific Ocean. It was founded in 1870 in Bolivian territory by Chileans wanting to exploit nitrates in the Desert of Atacama. This action, along with the city's occupation by Chilean troops, resulted in the War of the Pacific in 1879 with Bolivia. As a result of the Treaty of Valparaíso following the war, the area was ceded to Chile in 1884.

The economy of Antofagasta depends greatly on nitrates and copper exports, and the city is affected by fluctuations of these products in world markets. The city's industries include large foundries and oil refineries, food and beverage processing, and fish-meal production; it is also an international commercial center.

Antofagasta is surrounded by desert hills and has a pleasant, dry climate. Rainfall is scarce and necessitates the piping in of water from the San Pedro River, 280 miles away. The population was approximately 226,800 in 2000.

OTHER CITIES

ARICA, with a population that exceeds 180,000, is located in northern Chile, just south of the Peruvian border. Arica is situated on the Pacific Ocean at the northern limit of the Desert of Atacama. The city was originally part of Peru, but was occupied by Chile in 1880. Following the War of the Pacific, Arica was ceded to Chile, along with Tacna, through the Treaty of Ancon in 1883. After the Tacna-Arica Controversy was resolved in 1929, Chile retained jurisdiction over the city, but agreed to provide complete port facilities to Peru. Arica is currently a free zone, with both Chile and Peru maintaining customs facilities here. Access to the sea through Arica was also granted to Bolivia in 1920 via the Arica-La Paz Railroad. Today, Arica is a resort, and its port ships mineral exports—mostly copper, tin, and sulfur—for both Chile and Peru. Two major industries, automobile assembly and fish-meal processing, are located in Arica. The city is a major transportation center. It has an international airport, seaport, and railway links with neighboring Bolivia and Peru. With year-round spring weather, the city is popular during the winter months.

CHILLÁN, located in central Chile, is the birthplace of one of the nation's fathers of independence,

Bernardo O'Higgins. Chillán has had two severe earthquakes (1833 and 1939) since its founding in 1580. The city uses the raw materials (fruits, grains) from its rich farmland to produce wine and flour. Industries located in Chillán include shoe factories, flour mills, and lumberyards. Skiing is popular in the foothills of the nearby Andes. The resident population is approximately 163,000.

CHUQUICAMATA, about 125 miles northeast of Antofagasta, at an elevation of 10,435 feet, is located on the western slopes of the Andes. Chuquicamata is a mining town and has the world's largest copper-mining center. The open-pit copper mine, which dates to 1915, produces almost all of Chile's copper. Copper from this mine is transported south to Antofagasta for export. The population today is over 30,000.

IQUIQUE, a port on the Pacific, is located in northern Chile between Arica and Antofagasta, just 130 miles south of the Peruvian border. The city was founded in the 16th century and became part of Chile during the War of the Pacific in 1879. Rock and sand surround Iquique on the east; the city has fine beaches, a mild climate, and year-round sunshine. Water must be piped to Iquique from 60 miles away, as the area receives little rainfall. As a port, Iquique exports iodine and nitrates from the Atacama Desert. The city is an excellent place for deep-sea fishing. Tourism, based on sport fishing and beach facilities, also contributes to the economy. Fruits, sugarcane, and olives are grown near the city and exported through Iquique's port. The current population is about 160,000.

LA SERENA, 250 miles northwest of Santiago, is a popular beach resort noted for its cathedral and its gardens. With a population of close to 124,000, La Serena is situated on the Elqui River in a commercial and agricultural region known for vineyards and orchards. The city was founded in 1543 and was the site of

Chile's Declaration of Independence on February 12, 1818. La Serena has been damaged many times by earthquakes, but still retains its old world charm. La Serena is a popular tourist resort. The city has a mild climate and sunshine most of the year.

PUERTO MONTT is a port on the Gulf of Ancud, an inlet of the Pacific Ocean. With a population of just over 130,000, Puerto Montt is located 600 miles south of Santiago. Named for former Chilean president Manuel Montt, Puerto Montt was founded in 1853, and is an important area for fishing and sheep farming. The city's industries include fish canning, tanning, and sawmilling. Agricultural products, including potatoes and various grains, are grown near the city. The city is the southern terminus for the country's railroads and the starting point for navigation in the inland waterways and islands to the south. Puerto Montt is a popular resort with beautiful scenery—lakes, narrow fjords, forested hills, and peaks. During the summer, boat trips may be taken from Puerto Montt to Punta Arenas. There is an American School here; it is described in the Education section under Santiago.

PUNTA ARENAS, with a population of 120,000, is located in Tierra del Fuego. Sometimes called Magallanes, it is one of the world's two largest southernmost cities (Ushuaia, Argentina is further south), and the only one situated on the Strait of Magellan. Punta Arenas was founded in 1849 in order to secure Chile's claim to the strait, and was a busy coaling station until the Panama Canal was constructed. Today Punta Arenas is an important center for exporting Patagonian wool and mutton; naval and military facilities are also present in the area. Lumber and petroleum are exported through the city's port. Despite a long rainy season, Punta Arenas is a popular tourist resort and has one of South America's finest museums.

TALCA is about 150 miles south of Santiago near the Pacific Ocean. It is located in Chile's wine-producing region. Talca's industries include paper and flour mills, shoe factories, foundries, tanneries, and distilleries. The city was devastated by two earthquakes, in 1742 and 1928. Rebuilt in 1928, Talca now has a modern atmosphere with pleasant parks and avenues. The city is accessible by railroads and the Pan-American Highway. The population is estimated at 175,000.

TALCAHUANO is located on a small peninsula extending into the Pacific Ocean. It is in the State of Bío-Bío, approximately 50 miles north of Concepción. Talcahuano is an important manufacturing, and commercial center. Several industries are located here, among them flour milling, fish canning, and petroleum refining. Many products, such as hides, wool, fur, coal, and lumber are exported from Talcahuano's port. A large steel plant is located in nearby Huachipato. A Peruvian warship captured by Chile during the war of the Pacific is on display in Talcahuano's harbor. The city has a natural harbor that is considered the best in Chile. A leading commercial port, Talcahuano is also home of the country's naval base. The city suffered two earthquakes (1730 and 1960s). Its population today is about 270,000.

TEMUCO is 400 miles south of Santiago, on the Cautín River in central Chile. After its founding in 1881, other points to the south of Temuco began to be settled. The region was occupied by the Araucanian Indians, who are still an important part of life here. Temuco is a commercial city trading in livestock and agriculture produced in the region; grains, fruit, and timber are among the products traded and processed. Of interest in the city is an Araucanian museum. Temuco has a military air base, a cathedral, and several missionary schools. The city is accessible via railroads and the Pan-American Highway. The population was over 253,000 in 1997.

VALDIVIA is located in southern Chile, about 250 miles from Santiago. The city was founded as a fortress against the Araucanian Indians in 1552. When German immigrants arrived in the mid-19th century, the city began to grow with the introduction of its first two industries—beer and shoes. Other industries include lumber, metal goods, boats, and foodstuffs. Valdivia was mostly destroyed by an earthquake in 1960, but has been extensively reconstructed. Today, it has a population of about 122,000, and is a tourist center in the lake region.

COUNTRY PROFILE

Municipal market, Tenuco, Chile

Susan Rock. Reproduced by permission.

Geography and Climate

Chile is a narrow ribbon of land stretching almost 2,700 miles along the west coast of South America. Although it is one of the world's longest countries, its average width measures only 100 miles, and its maximum width, only 250 miles.

Santiago, Chile's capital and largest city, is almost directly south of Hartford, Connecticut. Valparaiso, the country's chief port, is farther east than New York City.

Wedged between the Andes on the east and the Pacific on the west, Chile is bordered by Peru to the north and Bolivia and Argentina to the east. Larger than any European country, except Russia, Chile covers an area of 292,257 square miles, about the size of California, Oregon, and half of Washington state combined. In the extreme south where the Atlantic and Pacific merge, the land becomes an archipelago with Cape Horn at its tip. Since Chile is south of the equator, the seasons are the reverse of those in the Northern Hemisphere. Santiago is about as far from the equator as are Atlanta and Los Angeles.

The Cordillera of the Andes which extends the length of the land is

Chile's dominant feature. Over 100 volcanoes dot the mountain system, and its relatively recent creation accounts for the country's often damaging earthquakes. This majestic chain has several peaks over 20,000 feet, including Mount Aconcagua (23,000 feet), the highest in the western hemisphere.

Chile has distinct geographic regions which can be roughly divided into four areas: the arid North; the fertile central valley midlands; the forested land and lakes in South-Central Chile; and the archipelagos, fjords, and channels of the far south.

The great northern desert or "Norte Grande" which constitutes one fourth of the country is one of the driest most barren areas on earth. Ironically this desolate, inhospitable land also produces rich mineral deposits such as copper and nitrates which are vital to the country's economy. Separating the northern desert from the central valley is a semiarid stretch of land known as the "Norte Chico" (Little North).

The central valley, where most of the population lives, begins with the Aconcagua River basin north of Santiago and continues on to the Bío-Bío River at Concepción. The nation's major industrial and agri-

cultural production is located in this section.

South-Central Chile below the Bío-Bío River is punctuated with an exquisite string of lakes running on a line from north to south and parallel to the Argentine border all the way from Temuco to Puerto Montt. This is the famous lake district, renowned for its beauty.

The archipelago south of Puerto Montt is usually rainy, with forested fjords and many glaciers and sea channels resembling southernmost Alaska. Still further to the south are the windy steppes and sheep country of Patagonia and Tierra del Fuego.

A number of Pacific islands are a part of Chilean territory. The Juan Fernandez Islands are 400 miles southwest of Valparaíso. The abandoned sailor, Alexander Selkirk, lived on one of these islands for 5 years; his adventures inspired Daniel Defoe's Robinson Crusoe. About 2,000 miles west of the continent is the famous Easter Island, or Rapa-Nui (Chilean since 1888), which is inhabited by Polynesians and is distinguished by gigantic stone monuments and carvings unique to the island. Chile also claims a wedge-shaped portion of Antarctica.

Chile's climate is as varied as its geography. In the far north, summers are warm and winters along the coast quite mild. Despite the fact that much of the north lies within the tropics, the cold Humboldt Current off the coast and the relatively short distance between the coast and the snow-covered Andean peaks to the east modify what might otherwise be a tropical climate. Precipitation is scant. In Santiago long, dry summers (December-March) feature warm days and cool evenings with temperatures reaching the low nineties. The June-September winter season is cold and rainy (14 inches of rain per year), with dampness and fog making the cold more penetrating, even though the temperature rarely drops to freezing. The weather in the capital is almost identical to that of Palo Alto and the southern bay region of California. The lake region is colder and wetter with annual rainfall reaching 100 inches. In the far south, the climate is colder still with gale force winds most of the year. Rainfall continues at the rate of 100 inches annually except in Patagonia where it drops to 20 inches a year.

Population

Chile's population is about 15.2 million (2000). Chile is mainly urban (83%), with almost 40% of its people living in the capital and environs. As in other developing countries, the population is youthful. About 30% of the population is under 15 years of age.

Chile is one of the more sparsely populated countries of Latin America (about 50 inhabitants per square mile). Its annual population growth rate is 1.5%. The family is usually a cohesive unit at all levels of society. A large middle class, with a nucleus of professional people, is important in business and government. But Chile also has a large poor class living in "poblaciones" (makeshift communities scattered in suburban areas of the larger cities). The rural population, including the indigenous Araucanian Indians, has a

standard of living generally well below that of the urban population.

The largest ethnic group is Spanish. Other principal groups include German, English, Italian, Yugoslav, and Arab. The population includes a small number of native Indians but almost no Asians or Blacks. The Indians live mainly south of the Bío-Bío River and in the Andean North. The most important group, the Araucanian Indians, has never been fully assimilated into Chilean society.

During the colonial period, European immigration originated almost entirely from Spain; early colonists were mainly Basques and Castilians. A small but influential number of Irish and English immigrants also came to Chile and played important roles in Chilean history. Bernardo O'Higgins, Chile's national hero, was of Irish descent.

After Chile won independence in 1810, many Irish, Scottish, and English immigrated to the new republic. In 1845 an official Chilean colonizing agency was set up in Europe to stimulate immigration, particularly from Germany. A small group of German colonists which arrived in 1850 was the first of a large-scale immigration that continued for 90 years. Most Germans settled in the Valdivia-Llanquihue-Chiloe area in the south, where towns have a decidedly Bavarian ambience. Spanish immigrants continued to arrive in large numbers throughout the 19th century and were joined by Italians, French, Swiss, British, Yugoslavs, and others. The twentieth century brought an influx of Middle-Easterners (principally Palestinians and Lebanese) as well as Europeans. Several thousand displaced persons resettled here after World War II.

Despite the diversity of their origins, few South American populations are more homogeneous than the Chileans. Their homogeneity and insularity are in large part the result of isolating geographic factors: mountains, deserts, a vast ocean, and long distances from outside cultural and political centers.

The Catholic religion predominates and is influential at all levels of society. However, religious freedom and separation of church and state are guaranteed by the Constitution. About 10% of the population is Protestant, and there is a small Jewish community.

Most Chilean holidays commemorate events important in the country's history or celebrate traditional feast days or holy days of the Catholic Church. The Fiestas Patrias, a 2-day celebration commemorating Chilean independence in mid-September, is the main patriotic holiday. The greatest religious festivals occur during Christmas and Holy Week. Some areas celebrate other religious holidays with centuries-old processions and dances.

Typical Chilean cuisine is simple, hearty, and rather blandly spiced. Beef, chicken, and seafood are the most popular main dishes. Cazuela, a stew of chicken, beef, pork, or fish, and the empanada (a pastry turnover filled with meat, fish, spiced onions, cheese, or even edible seaweed and served hot) are specialties.

Wine accompanies most meals. Other typical Chilean drinks include borgoña, red wine mixed with sparkling water and fruit; cola de mono, a Christmas drink similar to eggnog; chicha, grape or apple cider; and pisco sour, an indigenous liquor distilled from grapes, mixed with sugar syrup and lemon juice.

Public Institutions

Chile is a unitary republic with a highly centralized administrative structure and a strong executive. The President who serves a six-year term and cannot seek immediate reelection, appoints cabinet ministers and rector of state universities, as well as 13 regional administrators (intendentes), 51 provincial governors and numerous other officials. In December 1993, Eduardo Frei, the candidate for a coalition of center and moderate leftist political parties, was elected President with 58% of the vote. Frei, the son of a former president, took office in March 1994.

The bicameral Congress is made up of a Senate and a Chamber of Deputies. the Senate has 38 elected seats—two from each of 19 senatorial districts (circumscripciones)—and nine designated seats, which are variously filled by appointees of the Supreme Court, The National Security Council and the President. In addition, ex-presidents who have served six consecutive years also have the option of serving in the Senate for life. Senators are elected or appointed to eight-year terms. Half of the elected seats come up for reelection every four years.

The 120 members of the Chamber of Deputies are all elected, two from each of 60 electoral districts, and serve four year terms. Permanent commissions, roughly equivalent to committees in the U.S. Congress, work out the details of proposed legislation. Since reopening with the return to democracy in 1990, the Congress has been located in the port city of Valparaiso, 115 kilometers (about ½ hours by car northwest of Santiago.

Chile operates under a constitution promulgated during the military government of General Augusto Pinochet (1973–1990). That constitution provides for a democratic system, including an independent judiciary, while containing some limitations on popular sovereignty. It also grants considerable institutional autonomy to the armed services and national police.

Arts, Science, and Education

Santiago has traditionally been one of Latin America's most active centers of the fine and performing arts. Cultural events are generally held from March to November.

The Philharmonic Orchestra of Santiago and the Chilean National Symphony have subscription series, as do the Municipal Ballet and Opera. The National Ballet of the University of Chile also performs during the cultural season. The hub of ballet and opera activity is Santiago's superb Municipal Theater, which is a magnet for top foreign artists. The Beethoven Society of Santiago, the leading private cultural institution, offers a yearly subscription series featuring internationally recognized musicians during its May to September season.

Frequent concerts and recitals by local artists are held throughout the year. In January there is an international jazz festival in Santiago and in February there are two music festivals which attract international artists as well as local talent. One, held in Viña del Mar, features popular and rock and roll music; while the other, held in Frutillar on Lake Llanquihue, is devoted to classical music and provides a forum for Chile's young musicians. In addition, Santiago has a number of cultural FM radio stations.

Several professional theater companies in Santiago present exceptionally high quality productions by both Chilean and foreign playwrights. "Santiago Stage," the Anglo-American community's amateur theater group, produces plays in English each year. Many American and British films reach Santiago's cinemas only a few months after their release in the United States, and European and Latin American films are also frequently shown. Cinema films are usually shown in the original language with Spanish subtitles, though nearly all non-Spanish television films and other programs are dubbed in Spanish. Local "art" movie houses present re-runs of notable film classics.

Santiago has several good museums featuring pre-Columbian, folk, colonial, religious, and contemporary art; science; and Chilean history. Works by modern artists, sculptors, and photographers are exhibited and sold in the many private galleries. The National Library of Chile is one of the largest in Latin America. In addition, the Chilean-American Cultural Institute (BNC) has one of the most modern libraries in the capital.

Chile's folklore is rich. Examples of traditional music and dance are offered nearly every night of the year in several Santiago nightclubs and at festivals and special occasions outside the capital. Other night spots feature urban "folk" music, jazz, and tango. Santiago has several discotheques.

Chilean writers have won international fame for their achievements. Among the country's twentieth-century poets are the Nobel Prize winners Gabriela Mistral and Pablo Neruda, as well as Vicente Huidobro and Nicanor Parra. José Donoso, Maria Luisa Bombal, Isabel Allende, Manuel Rojas, and Jorge Edwards head the list of leading novelists. The country has also produced a number of fine short-story writers, essayists, historians, and playwrights.

Science

The Chilean government, universities, and other public and private entities actively encourage scientific activity.

Most universities have departments of science and technology and several of the country's finest centers of higher learning specialize in these fields. The Chilean Scientific Society publishes a scholarly journal.

Although Chile, unlike Peru to the north, was never the seat of a great Indian culture, archeological research centered in the northern desert has uncovered considerable evidence of pre-Columbian settlements showing southward extension of Incan and pre-Incan Andean civilizations.

Its location and clear desert air have made northern Chile the center of Southern Hemisphere astronomical research. Two of the world's largest observatories are located near La Serena, a day's drive north of Santiago; one is run by a consortium of U.S. universities.

Education

Chile has been a leader in public education in Latin America since the mid-nineteenth century. Of the country's universities, the oldest and most prestigious are the University of Chile, founded in 1842, and Catholic University, founded in 1888. The University of Santiago, dedicated mainly to science and technology is also important.

Valparaiso has three good-sized universities and Concepcion two. Most other provincial capitals have universities which serve their respective regions. Many private universities have been created over the past 15 years being the most prestigious Diego Portales University, Gabriela Mistral, Universidad Central, Andres Bello, etc.

Commerce And Industry

Chile's current government adheres to largely free market economic policies, including low and uniform tariffs (except on automobiles and a few other items regarded as luxury consumption) and an openness to foreign investment. As a result of these policies Chile has enjoyed several years of real economic growth, relatively low inflation, balance of payments equilibrium and, more recently, near full employment. In particular, the innovative use of debt-for-equity swaps has allowed Chile to make deep cuts in its debt to foreign bankers.

To lesson the country's dependence on mining activity, especially copper, the government has promoted development in areas such as forestry, fruits, and fishing in which Chile has a comparative advantage. As a result copper now accounts for less than 50% of Chile's export earnings compared to over 80% in the early 70s.

There are no quotas or embargoes on imports, and foreign goods are abundant, though generally somewhat higher priced than in the US. The US remains Chile's main trading partner with some 23% of the import market. Other important trading partners are Japan, Brazil, Argentina, Venezuela and Germany. Chile is ranked 34th among the U.S. trading partners.

Transportation

Automobiles

The axis of the generally adequate road network is a hard-surfaced highway running from Arica (in the North) to Puerto Montt which expands to four lanes near Santiago. Many other roads, however, are narrow and unpaved. Good paved roads link Santiago with Valparaíso and other cities on the central coast and connect central Chile with the Argentine border en route to Mendoza, Argentina, and the Argentine highway system. The road to the Argentine border is frequently closed by snow in winter.

Bus

Santiago offers a very comprehensive bus system. Although there are many new buses, the majority are run down, and they are all crowded during rush hour. However, the price is right—about a quarter. The subway system is always a pleasant surprise to newcomers. Clean and efficient, it costs even less than a bus.

The streets are teeming with taxis which are easily recognizable By their color—black with a yellow roof. The service is good and prices are reasonable. All taxis now have meters except tourist taxis at larger hotels, which charge a flat rate for certain trips. Taxis levy a legal surcharge on Sundays and daily after 9 p.m. which increases again after midnight. This surcharge is not shown on older meters, but newer meters indicate holiday and night rates. In addition there are "colectivos" or shared cabs that follow fixed routes. All black, with signs on the roof announcing their routes, "colectivos" can be flagged down like cabs.

Public transportation can meet most needs, but as in the US, at the price of some inconvenience and waiting.

Railway

Chile has a fairly extensive but old railway system, although at this time no rail passenger service operates north of Santiago. Sleeping cars and roll-on, roll-off cars for automobiles provide overnight rail service between Santiago and Puerto Montt. Most intercity buses are new and comfortable and follow fixed schedules. Some long-distance buses feature sleeping berths.

Air

Air service is well-developed and important to Chile's economy. Several domestic lines serve principal Chilean cities. Various carriers provide frequent flights between Chile and the US, including two American airlines. American and foreign passenger ships and freighters call at Valparaiso.

Communications

Telephone and Telegraph

Telephone service is very good. Privatization of long distance telephone service and local carrier completion has resulted in improved telephone service in all aspects. Calls can be made via the carrier of your choice (at last count there were six carriers operating in the Santiago area). International dialing rates are relatively inexpensive at this time, though the prices have been dynamic since the multi-carrier law went into effect in October of 1994. Local phone cards are available for placing long distance calls from any public phone in Chile or the United States. U.S. calling cards can also be used, though the rates tend to be slightly higher.

Radio And TV

Radio is Chile's most influential mass communications medium. There are a total of 300 AM and FM radio stations in Chile, with about 50 broadcasting from Santiago. Broadcasting is almost exclusively in the Spanish language, although a few English language programs can occasionally be heard. Several Santiago stations broadcast a broad range of American music in FM stereo. English language news can be heard on shortwave via the Voice of

America (VOA) and the British Broadcasting Company (BBC).

Santiago has six VHF TV channels, all of which broadcast in color, using the U.S. NTSC system. Programming includes a number of older U.S. television series and movie productions, local and imported soap operas, and a variety of news and local entertainment shows. There are no UHF stations. Some areas have access to one or two cable TV systems which carry the international versions of CNN, ESPN, TNT, HBO, AND MTV. There are also a number of stations from Europe and other Latin American countries as well as C-SPAN and Worldnet at certain times.

Newspapers, Magazines, And Books

English language books and magazines are scarce in Chile. Books in English can be obtained from a few local bookstores but they are expensive. The Chilean-American Cultural Institute (BNC) has 10,000 English language books and 115 U.S. periodicals. The American Association of Chile sponsors book groups which buy English language books for members' use, and the Santiago Lending Library is a volunteer organization which has a small but quality collection of fiction and nonfiction. (Both the latter charge a minimal monthly fee.) Students of Nido de Aguilas and their parents have access to the school library and some of the churches with English language services also have collections of books in English.

There is an English language weekly paper *The News Review,* also the international editions of *Time* and *Newsweek* are sold locally. American newspapers are available two to four days late through several newsstands. A subscription to the Miami Herald can be arranged with same day delivery, but it is expensive. The American Association of Chile publishes a monthly pamphlet, *The Spotlight,* which is full of information and practical advice for foreigners living in Chile. Likewise, The Journal of the American Chamber of Commerce is

geared to the needs and interests of the business community.

Chilean information media operate entirely in Spanish. *El Mercurio,* a conservative, Santiago morning publication, is Chile's most prestigious and influential paper. Several weekly news magazines representing various political points of view have a nationwide readership. In addition, there are magazines featuring women's fashions, science, economic-financial matters, and sports.

Health And Medicine

Medical Facilities

While in the US, individuals should obtain a yellow fever shot, which can be given only at approved vaccination centers. Though yellow fever is not found in Chile, the shot is required in some South American countries, and yellow fever immunization protects travelers in tropical and sub-tropical areas.

Most diseases or disorders can be treated in Santiago.

A number of local physicians have obtained medical training in the U.S. and Europe. Well-trained, English-speaking dentists and orthodontists also are available. The cost of doctor visits or dental care by these English-speaking or foreign-trained practitioners is comparable to US prices.

There are several hospitals in Santiago that provide the full range of medical services found in US hospitals, usually at a lower cost than in the US.

Many medical facilities provide round-the-clock emergency services, including ambulance transportation and duty medical personnel.

A number of pharmacies are open 24 hours on a rotating basis, and a few others are open 24 hours daily. The cost of some drugs is high, and many medications sold in the United States are not available in Chile.

Some commonly prescribed drugs in Chile are not approved by the U.S. Food and Drug Administration and may have serious side effects.

Eyeglasses, including bifocals and contact lenses, and lens prescriptions can be obtained in Chile.

To protect your skin from the dry climate, body lotions, moisturizer creams and bath oils should be used. Suntan preparations should be worn at the beaches and skiing areas. Exposure to the sun should be limited to prevent severe burning, which occurs rapidly in this climate.

Community Health

Community health standards are generally fair in Santiago and compare to those of other large Latin American cities. The sewage system and trash collection are efficient. Nevertheless, earthquake damage and sometimes deficient supervision of sewage systems during construction and repair, e.g., road pavement, metro construction, etc., causes the drinking water to be occasionally contaminated in certain areas of the city. Otherwise the water is purified and generally safe to drink. Just the same, many people go through an adjustment period to the water due, in part, to its high mineral content; and some prefer to boil their drinking water. (To be effective water should boil for five minutes; however, boiling will not affect the mineral level.) Outside the larger cities water may be contaminated, and bottled water is recommended. No unusual pests or vermin problems exist in Santiago.

Food and beverages are generally safe. However, care is required in choosing restaurants and preparing raw fruits and vegetables. Milk sold in paper or plastic containers, often reconstituted, is pasteurized and safe. "Long-life" sterilized milk which does not require refrigeration prior to opening is readily available. To avoid tuberculosis, boil fresh milk found on farms. Good quality powdered and liquid processed milk is sold on the local market.

Santiago has a serious smog problem. Although the pollution hangs all year long in the congested downtown area, it is particularly heavy in the winter months when the fumes of heating fuels are added to the dust and the exhaust of vehicles. Even the outlying suburbs generally have air pollution problems, and there are days when the smog reaches up the slopes of the Cordillera. As a result, respiratory and eye, ear, nose, and throat problems are common for employees and dependents. Minor eye irritations are endemic on bad days, and "smokers' hack" hangs on for many nonsmokers throughout the winter. Joggers often quit running for the duration of their tours here because of the air pollution.

Preventive Measures

Because Santiago appears to be a relatively clean, modern city, people are often surprised at the number of intestinal problems they experience here. Almost no one is immune to these upsets (indigestion and diarrhea), but new arrivals are particularly susceptible to attacks, and mild disorders occur regardless of precautions taken. While most people adjust rapidly, some experience recurring problems throughout their tours. More serious infections such as bacillary dysentery, amoebic dysentery and typhoid fever usually can be avoided, if care is taken.

Wash all salad ingredients, berries, and fruits in an appropriate solution. (First they should be washed in detergent, rinsed, soaked in a solution of one tablespoon of chlorine solution to one gallon water for 15 minutes, and then thoroughly rinsed again.) Antiseptic products such as Zonalin or iodine tablets are not as effective as a chlorine solution such as Chlorous or its local equivalent, Chlorous.

In restaurants, avoid fresh, unpeeled produce. Mayonnaise, custard, and creme fillings spoil quickly, especially in the summer months. Insist on the freshest seafood at markets and restaurants.

Typhoid and hepatitis do occur. All travellers are urged to renew typhoid and to be vaccinated against Hepatitis A.

Respiratory ailments are prevalent. Chile's climate, with its sharp temperature changes from day to night, coupled with the pollution and poorly heated houses, contributes to a high incidence of respiratory illnesses. Sore throats and sinusitis are common.

NOTES FOR TRAVELERS

Passage, Customs & Duties
A passport is required to enter Chile. U.S. citizens do not need a visa for a stay of up to three months. At the international port-of-entry, a fee, payable in U.S. dollars only, is levied on U.S. citizen visitors. The receipt is valid for multiple entries during the validity of the traveler's passport.

Dependent children under age 18 (including the children of divorced parents) arriving in Chile alone, with one parent, or in someone else's custody, are required to present a letter notarized before a Chilean consular officer in the United States certifying that both parents agree to their travel. To exit Chile, children traveling under one of these scenarios must present either the notarized letter used to enter the country or a letter of authorization signed before a Chilean notary if executed in Chile. In either case, the document presented must be executed not more than three months prior to entry or departure.

Travelers considering scientific, technical, or mountaineering activities in areas classified as frontier areas are required to obtain authorization from the Chilean government at least 90 days prior to the beginning of the expedition. The portions of Antarctica claimed by Chile are exempt from these pre-approval requirements. Officials at

the Torres del Paine National Park require mountain climbers to present an authorization granted by the Frontiers and Border Department, obtainable at the Chilean Embassy or Chilean consulates throughout the United States.

For further information concerning entry, exit, and customs requirements, travelers may contact the Chilean Embassy at 1732 Massachusetts Avenue, N.W., Washington, DC 20036, tel. (202) 785-1746, Internet - http://www.chile-usa.org. Travelers may also contact the Chilean consulates in Los Angeles, San Diego, San Francisco, Clara, Miami, Honolulu, Chicago, New Orleans, Boston, New York, Philadelphia, San Juan, Charleston, Dallas, Houston, and Salt Lake City.

Americans living in or visiting Chile are encouraged to register at the Consular Section of the U.S. Embassy in Santiago and obtain updated information on travel and security in Chile. The U.S. Embassy is located at Avenida Andres Bello 2800, Santiago; tel. (56-2) 335-6550 or 232-2600; after hours tel. (56-2) 330-3321. The Embassy's mailing address is Casilla 27-D, Santiago; the Consular Section's fax number is (56-2) 330-3005; and the e-mail address is "santiagoamcit@state.gov". The Embassy home page is: http://www.usembassy.cl, where Americans may also register on-line.

Pets

Importation of household pets is permitted. The animal must be vaccinated against rabies within 30 days before arrival.

Health certificate issued by the US Animal Health Dept. must be obtained prior shipping pet. Rabbis and Health certificate are to be presented to Chilean animal Health Dept. upon entering Chile. Shipping a pet as accompanied baggage is usually safer, cheaper and more convenient than sending the animal alone. Animals are not quarantined upon arrival.

Currency, Banking, and Weights and Measures

The Chilean peso (CLP, written $) is Chile's official currency. The official rate of exchange as of June 2002 is CLP$660.74 pesos = US$1.00. This rate changes slightly on a daily basis. Chile has 46 banking facilities, including several U.S. banks, many of which have numerous branches.

Chile uses the metric system of weights and measures.

Disaster Preparedness

Chile is an earthquake-prone country. Limited information on Chilean earthquake preparedness is available in Spanish from the Oficina Nacional de Emergencia de Chile (ONEMI) via the Internet at http://www.angelfire.com/nt/terremotos2. Other general information about natural disaster preparedness is available from the U.S. Federal Emergency Management Agency (FEMA) at http://www.fema.gov/.

LOCAL HOLIDAY

Jan. 1	New Year's Day
Mar/Apr	Good Friday*
Mar/Apr	Easter*
May 1	Labor Day
May 21	Battle of Iquique
June	Corpus Christi*
Aug. 15	Assumption Day
Sept. 11	Official Holiday
Sept. 18	Independence Day
Sept. 19	Day of the Army
Nov. 1	All Saints' Day
Dec. 25	Christmas Day

*variable

RECOMMENDED READING

These titles are provided as a general indication of the material published on this country. The Department of State does not endorse unofficial publications.

Alexander, Robert J. *The ABC Presidents: Conversations & Correspondence with the Presidents of Argentina, Brazil, & Chile*. Westport, CT: Greenwood Press, 1992.

Allende, Isabel. *The House of Spirits*. Alfred A Knopf, Inc.: New York, l986.

Aman, Kenneth, ed. *Popular Culture in Chile*. Boulder, CO: Westview Press, 1989.

American University. *Chile, A Country Study*. US Government Printing Office: Washington, DC, 1994.

Arriagada Herrera, Genaro. *Pinochet: the Politics of Power*. Boston, MA: Allen & Unwin, 1988.

Bizzarro, Salvatore. *Historical Dictionary of Chile*. 2nd ed., Iowa City, IA: University of Iowa Press, 1988.

Bradt, Hilary. *Backpacking in Chile & Argentina*. 2nd ed., Edison, NJ: Hunter Publishing, 1989.

Burr, Robert. *By Reason or Force, Chile and Balancing Power in South America, 1830-1905*. University of California Press: Berkeley, 1974

Committee on Foreign Affairs, US House of Representatives. *United States and Chile During the Allende Years, 1970-73*. US Government Printing Office: Washington, DC, 1975.

Constable, Pamela and Arturo Valenzuela, *A nation of Enemies: Chile Under Pinochet*. W.W. Norton & Co.: New York, 1991

Davis, Nathaniel. *The Last Two Years of Salvador Allende*. Cornell University Press: Ithaca, l985.

Drake, Paul W., and Ivan Jaksic, ed. *The Struggle for Democracy in Chile, 1982-1990*. Lincoln, NE: University of Nebraska Press, 1991.

Dwyer, Chris. *Chile*. New York: Chelsea House, 1989.

Falcoff, Mark. *Modern Chile, 1970-1989*. New Brunswick, NJ: Transaction Publishers, 1989.

Galvin, Irene Flum. *Chile, Land of Poets and Patriots*. Minneapolis, MN: Dillon Press, 1990.

Jacobsen, Karen. *Chile*. Chicago: Childrens Press, 1991.

Meehan, John. *With Darwin in Chile*. (Spanish translation, Con Darwin en Chile). Frederick Muller, Ltd.: London 1967.

Moran, Theodore H. *Multinational Corporations and the Politics of Dependence: Copper in Chile*. Princeton University Press: Princeton, 1974.

Nunn, Frederick. *The Military in Chilean History*. University of New Mexico Press: Albuquerque, 1976.

Rodriguez Monegal, Emir, ed. *The Borzoi Anthology of Latin American Literature* (Volumes I and II). Alfred K. Knopf: New York, 1977.

Samagalski, Alan. *Chile & Easter Island: A Travel Survival Kit*. Oakland, CA: Lonely Planet, 1990.

Sater, William F. *Chile & the United States*. Athens, GA: University of Georgia Press, 1991.

Sigmund, Paul. *The Overthrow of Allende and the Politics of Chile 1964-1976*. University of Pittsburgh Press: Pittsburgh, 1978.

———. *The United States and Democracy in Chile*. Johns Hopkins University Press, 1993.

Smith, Brian. *The Church and Politics in Chile, Challenges to Modern Catholicism*. Princeton University Press: Princeton, 1982.

Valenzuela, J.S. and A., eds. *Military Rule in Chile*, Johns Hopkins University Press, Baltimore, 1989.

Whalen, James Robert. *Out of the Ashes: Chile's Revolution Without Honor*. Washington, DC: Regnery Gateway, 1988.

Winter, Jane Kohen. *Chile*. New York: Marshall Cavendish, 1991.

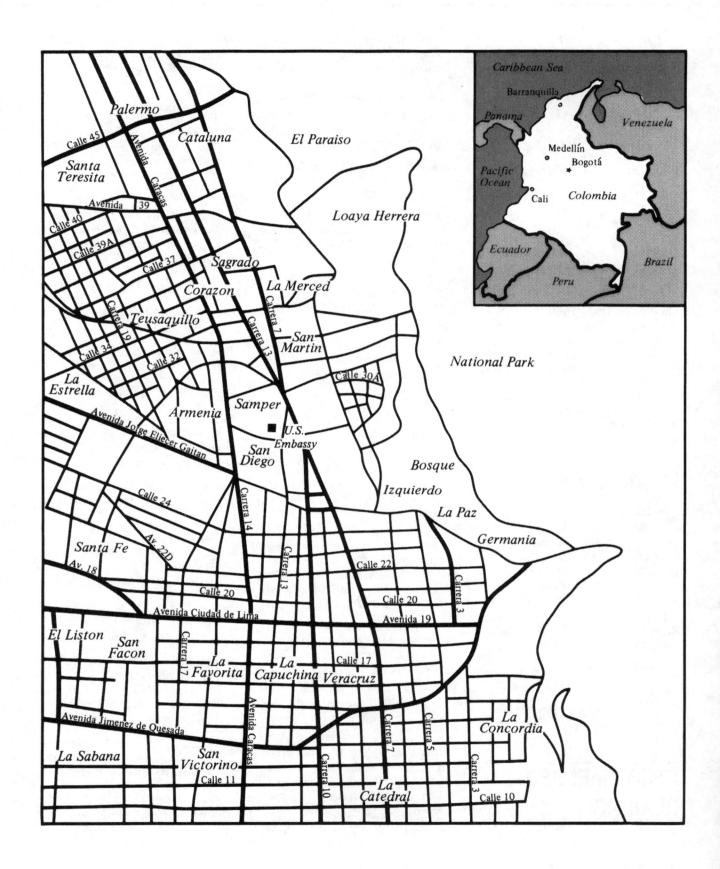

Bogota, Colombia

COLOMBIA

Republic of Colombia

Major Cities:
Santafe de Bogota, Medellín, Cali, Barranquilla, Cartagena, Bucaramanga

Other Cities:
Armenia, Bello, Buenaventura, Cúcutu, Girardot, Itagüi, Leticia, Manizales, Montería, Neiva, Palmira, Pasto, Popayán, Santa Marta, Tuluá, Tumaco, Tunja, Valledupar, Villavicencio

EDITOR'S NOTE

This chapter was adapted from the Department of State Post Report dated January 1997. Supplemental material has been added to increase coverage of minor cities, facts have been updated, and some material has been condensed. Readers are encouraged to visit the Department of State's web site at http://travel.state.gov/ for the most recent information available on travel to this country.

INTRODUCTION

COLOMBIA, washed by the waters of both the Pacific Ocean and the Caribbean Sea, is a land of geographical diversity and broad historical interest. It is a bridge between two great civilizations that flourished before the discovery of the New World—the Aztec to the north and the Inca to the south. It is a nation of cosmopolitan Andean cities and booming coastal ports, and yet it spreads across thousands of square miles of mountains, plains, and rain forests. Also, it is the most Spanish of the South American countries, although it has been independent since 1819.

Colombia is steeped in history. During its colonial era, it was one of the principal administrative centers of the Spanish possessions in the New World. Its present capital, Bogotá, was the seat of the viceroyalty of New Granada, which included what are now Venezuela, Ecuador, and Panama. After Colombia attained independence, Panama remained part of the republic for 90 years. Simón Bolívar, the great South American patriot, was the country's first president.

MAJOR CITIES

Santafe de Bogota

Bogota is considered a high-threat area for both terrorism/insurgency and crime. Individuals must exercise caution and follow effective security measures to minimize risks and vulnerabilities while in country. Although the security situation is closely monitored, caution must be exercised at all times.

The city of Bogota is nearly 8,700 feet above sea level, on a plateau of the Eastern Cordillera (range) of the Andes and is surrounded by peaks rising to 10,500 feet. The climate is cool and there are only two seasons, wet and dry; however, it is frequently wet in the dry season, and there can be lengthy dry periods in the wet season. The weather resembles early fall or spring in the north-central U.S. average temperature is 55 degrees F. The San Andres Fault line also runs through Colombia, and there are occasional earthquakes. The most recent, on June 6, 1994, was centered about 250 miles from Bogota, measured 6.2, and caused hundreds of deaths and did extensive damage.

Besides being the capital and largest city (population 6,834,000), Santafe de Bogota is also the cultural and economic center of the country. While a modern metropolis in some respects, the city's infrastructure has failed to keep pace with its growth. Combined with occasional power outages, traffic jams are frequent and monumental.

Well-kept residential areas, schools, shopping malls, grocery stores, and many restaurants and movie theaters assist in adjusting to living in this city.

The city has a mixed look from old world Spanish architecture which dominates in the southern part of the city, to modern high-rise apartments which dominate the north. Scattered throughout all areas of the city, however, are structures in severe conditions of decay. The lower windows of old and modern structures are heavily barred for security.

Bogotanos are proud of their cultural achievements. The city supports museums, universities, art galleries and many bookstores.

The English-speaking community is bolstered by a significant number of British and Canadian citizens, and many other people of European origin who live in the city. While Bogota is not considered a tourist center, about 1,000 Americans, mostly business representatives, visit the city annually.

Food

Bogota has an abundance of fresh foods and many varieties of fruits and vegetables; frozen seafood is carried by the better stores. Meat markets have large assortments of fresh meat. The quality is adequate, although meats are usually not aged and cuts often differ from those in the U.S.

Pasteurized milk is available in any supermarket and powdered milk is available, although expensive.

Local supermarkets are similar in style to those in the U.S. There is a variety of local and imported items, but fewer, smaller than in the U.S. There is usually a full stock of staple items. Some local supermarkets offer a variety of high-quality imported foods such as pate and smoked oysters, at very high prices.

Clothing

Clothing needed in Bogota is similar to that worn on the East Coast in the late fall season. The weather can be crisp and temperatures chilly. All-weather coats and umbrellas are a good idea. Styles for both men and women are fashionable and similar to that worn in the U.S.

Men: Colombian men tend to dress conservatively. Suits are worn more than sport coat-and-slacks combinations. Colors are also conservative-greys, dark blues and black predominate. Lightweight wool suits are recommended.

A wide variety of ready-made 100% wool and fine blended fabric suits and sport coats are available locally, but prices can be high. You will experience difficulty in obtaining ready-made suits in long sizes larger than 42.

Men's shirts must be tailor-made for sleeve length greater than 34.

Several tailors do excellent work and hand-tailored suits or of either imported or locally made material. Repair services are also available and reasonable. Socks and underwear are available, but do not equal U.S. quality.

Shoes are manufactured in Colombia, although it can be difficult to find a proper fit and the variety of styles is limited. Shoes and boots can be made to measure at reasonable cost.

Women: Shorts are rarely worn in Bogota, but are useful for tennis and trips to the "hot country." Skirts and sweaters or blouses are popular for daytime wear, as are lightweight suits and skirt-blouse-blazer combinations.

Jackets, short coats, and full-length fall coats are useful. Bring rain gear, including raincoat and umbrella.

Some name-brand lingerie is sold, but at higher prices than in the U.S.; therefore, bring a good supply of preferred items. Although nylons are sold, sizes are not U.S. standard. There are tailors and dressmakers who do good to excellent work at reasonable rates Beautiful fabrics are available locally, but are expensive.

Locally made shoes are not made to American specs, and sizes vary. Narrow sizes and larger sizes are especially hard to find. Shoes can be made to order at prices similar to good quality, ready-made American shoes.

Children: Children wear the same type of clothing worn in early spring or late fall in the U.S. Heavy cloth-

ing is not necessary, but a supply of wool sweaters or jackets is recommended. Wool sweaters are available locally, as are good-quality blue jeans of local manufacture (prices are higher than in the U.S., and quality is poorer.) Children's tennis shoes compare with U.S. makes and sell for similar prices.

Bring raincoats, umbrellas, and boots. Bring baby supplies in your luggage.

Small girls wear jeans for play and cotton dresses with sweaters or skirts and sweaters for school. Older girls can use wool suits, skirts and sweaters. Lightweight coats and jackets are useful.

Warm clothing such as sweaters, long-sleeved T-shirts, corduroy creepers, etc., are desirable for babies.

Slim and husky sizes are hard to find and children with narrow feet cannot be fitted locally.

Supplies and Services

Many popular American brand-name cosmetics and toiletries are sold in Bogota at high prices. If you prefer special brands, bring a supply. Toothpastes and shaving cream are reasonably priced and many U.S. name brands can be found. It is best to bring a supply of family medical and cosmetic needs.

Bogota has several good dry-cleaning establishments. Since quality of work varies even in the best establishments, it is often necessary to re-press clothing which has been cleaned. Most laundry is done in the home by maids.

Bogota has many good beauty shops, and barbershops. Major hotels give inexpensive, quality haircuts.

General Electric, Philco, Westinghouse, Phillips and Whirlpool are represented locally, but appliance repairs are generally of fair quality.

Aerial view of Bogota, Colombia

Religious Activities

There are a large number of Catholic churches in the city, and services are frequent during the week. There is one Catholic school which offers an English-speaking Mass on Sundays at 10:15 am. Masses are conducted by a group of American priests from the Mission of the Sacred Heart, and an order of Franciscan nuns offers instruction to the children. The chapel, located at Gymnasio Moderno, is located on Calle 74 between Carreras 9 and 11.

English-language Protestant, nonsectarian services are held in the Union Church on Sundays at 11:00 am. They also offer Sunday morning adult Bible study, Sunday School for children and a nursery service. The Union Church is located at Carrera 3a No. 69-06.

Additionally, there are three Jewish Synagogues, as well as a Baptist Chapel, Christian Science Church, and a Church of Jesus Christ of Latter-day Saints.

Education

Several English-language schools are available in Bogota. Parents are advised that all private schools in Colombia are Colombian-oriented and are administratively controlled by the Colombian Ministry of Education. Therefore, these schools are not, in the true sense, international in nature.

If you require special schooling for your child or desire some special type of education, curriculum, or extracurricular activities, contact either your agency or the school directly in Colombia for more information.

Colegio Nueva Granada is located at Carrera 2E No. 70-10. The mailing address is as follows:

Colegio Nueva Granada
Director
Apartado Aereo 51339
Bogota, Colombia

Instruction is in English, but Spanish is a required course for all students. The school is divided into elementary (kindergarten-5); middle school (grades 6-8); and high school (grades 9-12). Each of the three sections has its own principal and counselor. The director of the school is a US citizen and U.S.-trained, as are most of the administrative staff.

Nearly all the staff are trained teachers—about 70% hired locally (both American and Colombian) and 30% brought from the U.S. The school is accredited with the Southern Association of Colleges and Secondary Schools. The school year runs from late August to June.

A placement exam is required of all entering students before they are enrolled. It is given frequently during the summer months and at various times throughout the school year.

The school is coeducational with an enrollment of approximately 1,500 students. About 75% of the students are Colombian, 10% North American, and 10% dual citizenship (U.S./Colombian) 5% represent some 25 other countries.

The uniform of Colegio Nueva Granada as of the 1996–7 school year is as follows:

• White tennis shirts, plain while turtlenecks or mock turtlenecks, or white oxford shirts with the CNG monogram.

• Navy blue V-neck sweaters with two white stripes on the right sleeve.

• Navy blue gabardine trousers for boys and girls.

• Navy blue gabardine culotte-skirts for girls (optional).

• Navy blue CNG jacket - School tie for boys/girls on Fridays (middle and high school).

• Navy blue blazer with school emblem for boys and girls in middle and high school (optional).

• White, blue, or black tennis shoes or black, navy or brown leather shoes to be worn with white or blue socks

• A navy blue sweatsuit with CNG emblem required for elementary school.

The school sells uniforms on campus; plan to spend about $200 per child. Jewelry and hair accessories are to be conservative and blue and white color and size for use with a school uniform. Only stud earrings

for girls are allowed. No earrings will be permitted for boys, and length of hair must be appropriate for school. NOTE- "Appropriate" in Colombia means conservative.

Special Educational Opportunities

Locally, both the Universidad de los Andes and the Universidad Javeriana provide instruction in Spanish and other languages using the most modern teaching techniques.

Those interested in linguistics will find the Instituto Caro y Cuervo one of the best of its kind in the world.

Classes in painting, sculpture, and music can be arranged at the following institutions: Universidad de los Andes, Universidad Javeriana, Galeria de Arte Moderno, and Conservatorio de Música. Teachers of piano and guitar are available and fees are reasonable.

Bogota has several good universities in addition to Andes and Javeriana. Worthy of special mention are Colegio Mayor de Nuestra Señora del Rosario, Universidad Externado de Colombia, and Universidad de la Sabana. Special extension and night courses in many fields are offered at each. Instruction is in Spanish.

Recreation, Social Life, and Sports

Facilities for sports are limited and expensive. Although several country clubs have excellent golf and tennis courts, memberships are expensive.

Bogota has few public golf courses or public tennis courts. No swimming pools are open to the general public.

Arrangements can be made for horseback riding, and expert instruction is available at a reasonable cost. Many families make periodic weekend trips to the lower, hot country where swimming pools and tennis courts are available at the hotels and resorts. Spectator sports include soccer, boxing, wrestling,

horseracing, and bullfighting. Plaza de Santa Maria, the bull rink in the center of the city, has fights on Saturdays and Sundays between December and February. Soccer is very popular and fans avidly follow various local teams.

Lake Tota, northeast of Bogota, is a favorite fishing spot for foreigners and Colombians alike. The lake is high in a mountain basin in the Department of Boyaca. The lake can also be reached by flying to Sogamoso and taking a taxi about 18 miles to the lake. Its crystal clear waters are stocked and offer good trout fishing. Outboard motorboats can be rented. Two rustic hotels, plus the Tisquesusa, the Rocas Linda, and the Pozo Azul, offer comfortable accommodations. A small outboard motorboat (5-15 hp) is useful for trolling.

Trout fishing also can be found in Lake Neusa. Neusa is approximately a 1-1/2 hour drive north of Bogota. The drive is easy, and the roads are generally in good condition. Winding through the mountains, the roads take you through Pine and Eucalyptus forests. The entire trip is a steady climb into the mountains, probably 100 feet or more above Bogota. In Neusa, you can take a boat tour, or rent your own by the hour.

Deep-sea fishing is possible off the Atlantic and Pacific coasts, and the fishing enthusiasts will find trips to these areas rewarding. Fishing tackle is available in Bogota, but it is expensive.

Sailing is done on two of the man-made lakes near Bogota.

Scuba-diving and snorkeling can be done on the coast in Cartagena (1-hour flight from Bogota) or in the nearby island of San Andres or Santa Marta (both about a 2-hour flight from Bogota).

Hunting in Colombia requires a certain amount of planning and time. Dove hunting is popular, but the current security situation has resulted in the closing of many traditional hunting areas.

The hills surrounding Bogota offer ample opportunity for the mountaineer, and the snowpeaks of the Andes are a real challenge to the serious climber. The Laguna de Guatavita, origin of the legend of El Dorado, offers a delightful one-day adventure.

Additionally, there are a number of gyms and spas for weight-lifting and aerobics. Monthly or yearly membership fees are similar to those in the U.S. Many have saunas and/or steam rooms, and some offer massages, facials and other cosmetic features.

Touring and Outdoor Activities

By virtue of certain characteristics, such as dress, speech, mannerisms, cars and homes, Americans are susceptible to criminal attack. Consequently, common-sense security precautions should always be practiced when touring and sight-seeing in Bogota and elsewhere in Colombia. For example, women should not wear elaborate jewelry when visiting crowded shopping areas of the city. Carry as little money as possible and guard your wallet, purse, watch and valuables carefully.

Several museums display the historical, cultural and artistic heritage of the country. A fascinating collection, consisting of gold objects fashioned by the Indians who lived in Colombia before the arrival of the Conquistadores, is in the Museo de Oro at the Banco de la República.

On a mountaintop, 1,500 feet above the city, stands the Spanish-style church of Monserrate, considered the characteristic landmark of Bogota.

The original church, built in 1650, was destroyed by fire. About 25 years old, the present church commands a magnificent view of the city and surrounding plains. You can reach the church by the old, almost perpendicular "funicular" railway or the newer Swiss-built aerial cable car both of which take about three minutes.

A neighboring mountain peak, higher than Monserrate, is the site of the chapel of Guadalupe. This peak was the location of several earlier chapels dedicated to Our Lady of Guadalupe, patron saint of Latin America. The present chapel, with its huge dominating figure of the Virgin, is a 20th century work.

At the falls of Tequendama during the wet season, the Bogota River plunges 475 feet into a narrow gorge below. Only 15 miles southwest of Bogota, this waterfall can be reached by road.

Thirty miles north of Bogota by train or car lies the salt mine of Zipaquira—a solid mountain of rock salt. The mine has been worked since before the Spanish arrived, and while its tunnels penetrate deep into the mountain, the supply of salt has hardly been touched. On this site a massive Gothic-style cathedral has been carved out of the mountains. Illuminated by indirect lighting and severely simple in its decorations, the cathedral is impressive and unique. An interesting, colonial-style inn with a restaurant is on the grounds of the salt mine.

For a change of scenery and relief from the altitude and cool climate, the warm, tropical valleys that lead to the Magdalena River are ideal. Several resorts are within a few hours of Bogota. Girardot—l/2 hour by plane, three hours by car—is one of the most popular warm weather spots. Here, a large variety of tropical fruits and unusual pottery can be purchased in the town's center plaza.

Paipa, at about the same altitude as Bogota, can also be reached in about four hours by car. The Hotel Sochagota, in addition to its excellent conference facilities, is a popular first-class hotel fronting on a small lake. Activities center around the thermally-heated swimming pool but also include horseback riding, pool and billiards, and ping-pong. The hotel also has 12 detached cabañas, each with sleeping facilities for six, fireplace, efficiency-type kitchen, two bathrooms and private thermal bath facilities.

Barranquilla, with a population of over 1.2 million is the principal seaport on the mouth of the Magdalena River. One hour by jet from Bogota, the city is popular for its February carnival. Its famous Hotel del Prado is a large country club-like hotel with air-conditioned rooms, swimming pool, tennis courts and exercise facilities including a sauna. The hotel also maintains the Prado Mar Beach Club at Puerto Colombia for ocean bathing and fishing.

In March, Barranquilla is the site of the international tennis tournament called the "South American Wimbledon."

Cartagena, population 918,000, is about 70 miles southwest of Barranquilla on the Caribbean coast. The walled city dates back to the days of the Spanish Main. Its famous fortress of San Felipe de Barajas and ancient churches, including the Shrine of St. Peter Claver, make Cartagena one of the most interesting cities in Colombia. The city boasts a number of modern beachfront high-rise hotels as well as the older, colonial-style El Caribe Hotel. Most hotels have swimming pools; some have tennis courts. Nearby restaurants offer good seafood. In November, Cartagena commemorates its independence in a carnival atmosphere which includes the national beauty contest for the crown of "Miss Colombia."

Leticia is Colombia's principal town on the Amazon River, 670 miles southeast of Bogota. Accessible by air, Leticia provides tourists with such attractions as Amazon River excursions, visits to primitive Indian villages, and trips through dense rain forests. Leticia is located at the northern end of the Peru-Brazil border, and it is easy to cross over to one country for lunch and then to the other for dinner, and return to Leticia for the night.

Entertainment

The National Symphony has regularly scheduled concerts during most of the year, often with world-famous guest artists. Dance companies, chamber music groups, and concert artists perform seasonally. Theater is available from time to time, but its enjoyment is limited to those fluent in Spanish.

Movie theaters and video clubs are numerous; those in the downtown section and better residential areas are equal to theaters in the U.S. First-run American films are shown with Spanish subtitles, three-four months after their U.S. premiere. Movies at the best theaters cost about USD 8.00 per person. Bogota has few American-type nightclubs; however, several clubs have floor shows and dancing and offer a welcome change on a night out. Many restaurants serve continental and regional dishes.

The changing of the guard outside the Presidential Palace at 5:00 PM every afternoon is a colorful ceremony. Soldiers dress in 19th-century-style uniforms, including spiked helmets. Various festivals are held throughout the year in Colombia. Cartagena has a world-famous film festival, and annual fairs are held in Barranquilla.

Social Activities

Social life in Bogota depends greatly on your own initiative. Because of the large number of Americans and educated Colombians, it is possible to have a wide, varied circle of friends.

The American Women's Club admits all American women in Colombia and meets monthly. The American Society is open to all Americans living in Colombia. This club sponsors monthly social activities and a number of charitable programs.

Social contacts among Colombians who enjoy having foreign friends can be also be made through the Bi-National Center (BNC) and its various groups and activities and through a number of charitable, religious and social organizations.

Bogota has some resident business representatives from countries friendly to the US as well as about 40 other diplomatic missions. It is relatively easy to develop a circle of friends from among these groups.

Medellín

Medellín, with an estimated population of 3.8 million, is Colombia's second largest city. It is the capital of the Department of Antioquia, one of the country's most progressive areas. Although it was settled earlier, it was not officially established or named until 1675.

Medellín is an important industrial, commercial, and banking center and is located in a valley three to seven miles wide and about 25 miles long in the Central Cordillera of the Andes, about 150 air miles northwest of Bogotá.

Medellín, at an altitude of 5,000 feet, has a mild climate year round. Annual mean temperature is 70°F, with a temperature spread of 27°F. There are two rainy (winter) and two dry (summer) seasons of varying length each year. Rainfall averages about 55 inches annually.

The metropolitan area includes the city of Medellín and adjoining municipalities in the same valley. Total population of the valley is estimated at slightly above two million. The center of the city contains many large, modern office and apartment buildings. Despite a significant boom in recent years, however, a number of small businesses are still housed in converted residences.

Typical residential architecture is the one-story modern house, with red tile roof. There are two pleasant suburbs, 10 to 15 minutes from the city center, where the bulk of the foreign population resides. Comfortable, modern apartments are also available in the city.

Medellín, the original industrial heart of Colombia, remains a major center of indigenous capital, and supplies wealth and talent to all parts of the country. It is a banking and insurance center and headquarters for ANDI, the Colombian equivalent of the National Association of Manufacturers. Medellín's industries include food processing, woodworking, automobiles, chemicals, and metallurgy. The principal industry is the integrated manufacture of textiles, cotton, cotton-synthetics and, to a lesser degree, wool. Other important products are steel and steel products, tobacco, plastics, leather, cement, glass, beer, ceramics, electrical appliances, soft drinks, and packaging materials. Medellín is also an important marketing center for coffee, bananas, cement, and cattle. The Federation of Coffee Growers, which exports Colombia's foremost dollar-earning product, has a regional office in the city.

Americans, British, and Germans, with lesser numbers of Italians and French, comprise the small foreign community. The American element, about 600 persons, is almost indistinguishable, as many are married to Colombians, or are the product of Colombian-American marriages. There is a large number of English-speaking people in Medellín. Many Colombian professionals are U.S.-college educated, and still others are acquainted with the language through travel and study.

Although the city dates from the middle of the 17th century, only slight traces remain of the colonial era. Many social customs still reflect the Spanish past, but these too are being rapidly modified.

Antioquenos, as the people of the department are called, consider themselves apart from other Colombians. The colony of Antioquia began with the immigration of a small number of Spanish Basques and Andalusians. The early settlers, noted for their large families, occupied themselves primarily with gold mining. As the population grew and the gold supply diminished, the people turned to the land and cleared the high, healthful regions for food crops, and the middle levels for coffee production. Usually, the land was opened by the man who tilled it, and the small landholder pattern persists to this day. Larger families also meant forced migration, and the Antioqueno was the principal colonizer of the Departments of Caldas and Valle. Antioquia's population continues to grow rapidly, especially in Medellín proper (now over 1.6 million), which has attracted people from the rural areas in search of greater opportunities.

Antioquia is mountainous and, except for some fertile valleys and a banana-producing area in its northwest corner, is not well suited for agriculture. Cattle production is of growing importance. The Department of Chocó, which represents the other extreme within the Medellín district, is jungle-like, sparsely populated, and very undeveloped economically. Antioquia is Colombia's conservative stronghold and the Antioquenos, nearly all Roman Catholic, are devout supporters of the Church. A fairly rigid class structure persists and a large percentage of the wealth remains concentrated in the hands of a few families. Nonetheless, the region has traditionally provided opportunities for economic mobility to the industrious (or the fortunate), and an important and growing middle class exists.

Air travel is the most practical means of transportation in and out of Medellín. The airport, which operates during daylight hours only, is 10 minutes by car from the city center. Because of frequent fog and the lack of navigational aids, the airport is often closed and flight delays are common.

Driving in Medellín has certain risks, although the traffic is somewhat tamer than in Bogotá. Drivers in general, and bus and truck drivers in particular, are aggressive and undisciplined, and pay little heed to traffic lights or other controls. The size of the vehicle usually determines who gains the right-of-way, and under no circumstances should

pedestrians compete. Driving outside of the city calls for nerves of steel. The road network is limited, poorly maintained, and heavily used. Collisions are frequent and, although labor for bodywork is less expensive than in the U.S., import regulations result in much higher prices—and often delays—for repair parts.

Education

Two private schools in Medellín are considered adequate for the academic needs of American children. The Columbus School is a coeducational day school for kindergarten through grade 12. Founded in 1947 and sponsored by the U.S. Department of State, it is accredited in the U.S. by the Southern Association of Colleges and Schools.

The school follows both American and Colombian curricula. Most instruction is in English. French and Spanish are also offered. Extracurricular activities include computers, chorus, gymnastics, drama, newspaper, yearbook, and several participant sports. With a student body of about 900 (90% are Colombian), Columbus School employs 80 full-time and four part-time teachers; 43 are American. The staff also includes a counselor.

The school year runs from mid-August to mid-June, with a one-month vacation from mid-December to mid-January.

Columbus School is located on a mountainside, three miles northwest of Medellín. Facilities include seven buildings, 48 classrooms, science labs, computer lab, cafeteria, gymnasium, playing fields, and a 15,000-volume library. The mailing address is Apartado Aéreo 5225, Medellín, Colombia.

The Montessori School in Medellín is relatively new and plans to extend its grade structure by adding one grade each year. Currently, classes from kindergarten through grade eight are taught. The Colombian and American curricula are followed, with emphasis on English. Enrollment is divided between

Americans, Colombians, and several other nationalities. The school's directors are American. The mailing address is Apartado Aéreo 623, Medellín, Colombia.

Colegio Montelibano is a coeducational, day, company-sponsored school for pre-kindergarten through grade 12. It is located in the village of Montelibano, in the Córdoba Department, which is northwest of Medellín. Founded in 1980, the school is accredited by the Colombian Ministry of Education.

The school's curriculum is both U.S. and Colombian. Spanish is a required language; other courses offered include French, art, computer science, physical education, and vocational studies. Extracurricular activities are varied.

The school year, in English, runs from August to mid-June; in Spanish, the year runs from February to mid-December. Both calendars have a 10-day Easter vacation. The student body totals 387; enrollment capacity is 594. Of the 41 teachers, three are American.

Colegio Montelibano's facilities include science laboratories, an audiovisual room, and athletic fields. The school, on a 15-acre campus, is air-conditioned throughout. The mailing address is Apartado Aéreo 6823, Bogotá, Colombia.

Recreation

Because of the condition and extent of the roads, touring is not a popular pastime in the Medellín district. Nonetheless, a few nearby areas within a two-hour drive offer a change of scenery, and one of the prime pleasures of Colombians and Americans alike is the enjoyment of the surrounding countryside. Many Colombians own country homes, and these become the center of family life during weekends and the long Christmas season. Although Americans usually have no such refuge, nearby mountain areas provide many lovely spots for picnics.

Santa Fe de Antioquia is the original capital of the Department of

Antioquia. It has a population of about 18,000 and is a three-hour drive from Medellín. Situated on the bank of the Cauca River in what is locally termed the "hot country," the city contains many examples of Spanish colonial architecture.

Rionegro is about an hour's drive from Medellín. It is in an attractive valley at about 6,000 feet elevation. Rionegro was the site of the signing of the Constitution of 1863.

Quibdó, capital of the Department of Chocó, is on the banks of the Atrato River, which empties into the Caribbean Sea near the Colombian border with Panama. Chocó is sparsely populated by the descendants of escaped slaves who made their way to the hot, jungle-covered area bordering the Pacific coast of Colombia. The northern part of Chocó is said to have one of the most abundant rainfalls found anywhere in the world. Quibdó, with a population over 47,000, is about one hour by air, 15 hours by car.

La Pintada is a small town on the Cauca River two-and-a-half hours from Medellín and located in the "hot country." As another alternative for weekend outings, it offers an attractive landscape and a modest hotel with swimming pool. The model ranch of the Antioquian Cattle Fund is also located here.

Medellín's public athletic facilities are seldom used by Americans. There are private sports clubs, where membership is possible; Medellín also has two attractive private country clubs, each with a golf course, tennis courts, and swimming pool. Initial membership fees are expensive.

Spectator sports in Medellín consist chiefly of soccer matches, but baseball games are becoming popular among Colombians. Bullfights are held seasonally. Hunting and fishing are available, but facilities and accommodations within a reasonable distance from the city are almost completely lacking.

Church towers in Cali, Colombia

Horseback riding at country *fincas* (estates) is a popular pastime. Water-skiing and sailing are possible on a man-made lake about three hours from Medellín.

Entertainment

Among the many movie theaters in Medellín, 10 are considered first-class. Newly released American films with Spanish subtitles are shown.

Local civic organizations and private industries sponsor occasional concerts and musicals. Good amateur plays are presented several times during the year at the Pablo Tobon Theater. Several private clubs offer floor shows, and a few nightclubs are acceptable.

Medellín has active Rotary, Lions, and Kiwanis clubs, through which it is relatively easy to broaden one's contacts among other working professionals. Many women join the Pan-American Women's Association, a group composed mainly of members of the English-speaking colony, including Colombians. There are a number of opportunities in Medellín for international contacts.

Although Colombians are favorably disposed to the U.S., most Americans find that it requires a major effort to develop close personal relationships with them.

Special Note

In recent years, Medellín has been the center for a violent drug cartel. Because of this, the U.S. State Department advises against travel to this area. Visitors should check with the Embassy for further details.

As in many areas of the world, personal and physical security are increasing problems in Medellín. Nonviolent purse and jewelry snatchers abound on the streets, especially at night. Large amounts of money should not be carried, nor should jewelry be worn in public places.

Cali

Cali, Colombia's third largest city, rests in the southwest corner of the pear-shaped Cauca River valley, the principal center of cattle and sugar production. The city is also a manufacturing and distribution center between the Pacific coast port of Buenaventura and Bogotá. Cali is the capital of the Department of Valle del Cauca.

One of the oldest cities in the Americas, Cali was founded in 1536 by Sebastián de Belalcázar, who marched northward from Peru after aiding Francisco Pizarro in subjugating the Incas. Belalcázar's conquests afterwards were made a dependency of the Spanish viceroyalty of Lima. Parts of central Cali reflect the tastes of the colonial period, with palmed plazas lined by wood-roofed buildings. Charming bridges and walks along the river in the city's center date from the late 19th-century period. Newer sections of the city have incorporated varied contemporary influences.

Cali's elevation of 3,319 feet poses no physical challenge. Temperatures vary little throughout the year. Maximum daytime temperatures are in the low 80s; at night temperatures drop a little below 70°F, making it pleasantly cool in most residential sections of the city. Humidity remains at a comfortable low year round. Most of Cali's moderate rainfall occurs during the Northern Hemisphere's fall and spring months. Heaviest storms cause flooding in low sections of the city, but the rain usually comes in brief showers. Hurricanes, tornadoes, and cyclones are unknown. However, several minor earthquakes have struck the city in recent years.

Cali's metropolitan population is approximately 2.1 million, and its physical size is about that of Washington, DC. The city center is compressed into a small area. Growth of better suburbs has been along and into the foothills, while poorer sections have pushed out across the valley floor. The city's main activity, industry, is a product of favorable location and transportation. Moreover, more than half of Colombia's foreign trade passes through Cali en route to and from Buenaventura, on the Pacific coast. It is also headquarters for units of the departmental government, the Third Brigade of the National Army, and the Air Force Academy at Marco Fidel Suarez Base.

About 3,000 U.S. citizens reside in the district, more than two-thirds of whom live in Cali. Most are associated with some 100 partially- or wholly-owned U.S. firms doing business in the area. Some of the larger ones are Grace, International Paper, Goodyear, U.S. Rubber, Container Corporation, Corn Products, Home Products, Colgate-Palmolive, Gillette, Union Carbide, Squibb, and Quaker Oats. A substantial number of Americans are working with the Universidad del Valle at the International Center for Tropical Agriculture (CIAT).

Cali is becoming increasingly a center for tourism. The Pan American Games of August 1971 helped to bring the city to international attention, and its new Hotel Intercontinental and Palmaseca Airport have served as attractions to visitors. The Feria de Cali, with its week of bullfights, beauty contests, and parties, is perhaps the major social event in Colombia during the Christmas and New Year period.

Education

Most American children in Cali attend Colegio Bolívar. It is a coeducational day school for pre-kindergarten through grade 12. The school was organized in 1948 through the efforts of the American business community, and receives help from the U.S. Government Inter-American Schools Service. It is accredited by the Southern Association of Colleges and Schools and the Colombian Ministry of Education.

The curriculum is U.S.- and Colombian-based. Classes are in English, with additional mandatory instruction in Spanish beginning in the third grade. Elective classes include art, vocal music, computer science, and physical education. Among the extracurricular activities are yearbook, newspaper, literary magazine, field trips, scouting, and various sports. There is also a special program for children with learning disabilities.

The school year runs from the end of August to the middle of June, with vacations at Christmas and Easter. In 1991, the student body totaled 1,050; of the staff of 90 full-time and two part-time teachers, 45 were American. The staff also includes a counselor and a nurse.

Colegio Bolívar is located on 10 acres of land in a rural area about 10 miles from Cali. Facilities include 10 buildings, 42 classrooms, cafeteria, auditorium, an audiovisual room, science laboratories, computer lab, gymnasium, playing fields, swimming pool, and a 20,000-volume library. The mailing address is Apartado Aéreo 26300, Cali, Colombia.

Cali has three other English-language schools: Colegio Bennet, for kindergarten through grade 12; Jefferson School, offering courses through the 12th grade; and the British-American School, which accepts children from kindergarten through grade 12.

The Centro Colombo-Americano offers Spanish courses, and also maintains an English-language lending library. The city's main bookstore, Librería Nacional, has a limited selection of American paperbacks. Most principal American newspapers are available, as is *Time* magazine, but often these are a week old.

Recreation and Entertainment

The Cali area offers several points of interest for outings or weekend excursions. Twenty miles northeast of the city, near El Cerrito, is El Paraiso, a country house which was the scene of the 19th-century romantic novel, *La María*, written by Jorge Isaacs and describing life in his native valley. Operated by the Colombian Government, the house is preserved in minute detail complete with original furnishings, and is beautifully located at the foot of the Andes. A similar country house, Canasgordas, lies six miles south of Cali. It too was the setting for a novel—*Eustaquio Palacios El Alferez Real*. The house earlier served as the residence of Spanish colonial governors.

Within an hour's drive are various sugar refineries; Manuelita, in the city of Palmira, offers tours. Another site of interest is the Calima Dam and hydroelectric project, about a two-hour drive from Cali, in the western hills. En route to Calima lies the tranquil valley town of Buga, where lunch and an afternoon at Hotel Guadalajara's swimming pool provide a popular Sunday excursion. Buga's handsome 17th-century cathedral is being meticulously restored.

The nearest available beach with adequate hotel facilities is close to Tumaco (in Nariño Department), an hour away by plane. Hotel accommodations are adequate, but unpretentious. Other weekend trips can be made to the mountainous lake region near Pasto, where an attractive Swiss-run lodge is located, and to the interesting pre-Columbian archaeological site of San Agustín (in Huila).

Within certain limits, good recreational facilities are available in Cali year round. While no beaches are nearby and river swimming is discouraged, many Americans belong to one of several social clubs having excellent pools. Golf and tennis also are available.

Lake and ocean sport-fishing is possible within the district, but not near Cali. The Calima reservoir, one-and-a-half hours' drive from the city, is excellent for sailing, water-skiing, picnicking, or just for a change of scene. Dove hunting is available in the area, but big-game hunting requires a trans-Andean trip.

A number of good movie houses feature American films in English, with Spanish titles. Admission prices are low. Concerts and plays by local or visiting artists are given on occasion at the Teatro Municipal and at the conservatory. Visiting musical and dance troupes sometimes perform in Cali. Bullfights, featuring some of the world's best matadors, are given during the December *feria* week, and are also held at various times during the rest of the year. Boxing, baseball, soccer, and swimming meets are the available spectator sports.

Cali has many small nightclubs and discotheques, usually packed on Saturday nights. A handful of good restaurants in the city offer dinner at reasonable prices.

Cali has an American Women's Club and an American Men's Society.

Barranquilla

Barranquilla, capital of the Department of Atlántico, is the largest and most important northern coast city in the country. It is called the "Gateway to Colombia."

Although founded in 1629, it lacks the colonial atmosphere of many South American cities because there was little development here prior to the 20th century. Barranquilla emerged as an important seaport and industrial city with the

completion of the Bocas de Ceniza project, which created a deep-water river port at the mouth of the Magdalena River. This river serves as a major transportation link with the interior of the country.

Barranquilla spreads south from the river to a hilly area where most of the new housing and businesses are located. The city center and older suburbs show the effects of rapid growth and overcrowding found in most of the developing cities of the Third World. The population explosion (the estimated figure is over 1.2 million) has created a strain on city services, but new development programs are now underway, and municipal improvement has a high priority.

The biggest celebration in Barranquilla is Carnival, a four-day festival of parades, dancing, parties, and general festivities during which the city comes to almost a complete standstill. The popularity of Barranquilla for this mardi gras celebration—which in some cases rivals Rio in costumes and enthusiasm—is shown by the throngs of celebrants converging on the city. Pre-Carnival and post-Carnival celebrations abound as well and the outgoing Barranquillero is at its best during this joyous occasion.

Barranquilla is hot and humid year round, with cooling breezes during the windy season of December through February. The rainy seasons, April through June and September through November, bring torrential downpours which inundate certain streets and turn them into raging rivers. In parts of the city, curbs are 3-4 feet high in an effort to channel the water into the Magdalena River and out to sea. Knowledgeable Barranquilleros avoid these streets at all costs at the first sight of rain, since people, cars, and buses are frequently washed away.

Barranquilla's varied industrial base consists of chemical manufacturing, cement, metal fabrication, food processing, automobile assembly, textiles, shoes, publishing, sugar, beer, glass, perfume, and clothing manufacturing. The city is the major air terminus for northern Colombia and is served by several international airlines. A darker side to the recent growth of Barranquilla has been the massive drug-smuggling trade. Both the U.S. and Colombian governments have active control programs, and the U.S. Consulate is a focal point of this activity.

The American community in Barranquilla is small, but should expand with the development of the El Cerrejón coal mining project. This project will exploit vast coal reserves in the César and Guajira Departments and involve the construction of two airports, a seaport facility, and a railroad to transport coal to the coast.

The consular district includes the Departments of Atlántico, Córdoba, Sucre, Norte de Santander, Cesar, Bolívar, Guajira, Magdalena, and the Intendencia of San Andrés y Providencia.

Education

Barranquilla has three English-language schools. Colegio Karl C. Parrish is a coeducational institution for pre-kindergarten through grade 12. Accredited by the Southern Association of Colleges and Schools and the Colombian Ministry of Education, the school was founded in 1938. The Parrish School and other private schools in the area offer excellent bilingual education at the primary and secondary levels, and graduates are accepted at major universities throughout the world.

Colegio Karl C. Parrish follows the American-Colombian curriculum, with the study of Spanish required of all students. French is also offered, as well as computer science and physical education. Extracurricular activities include computer, newspaper, yearbook, and varied sports.

The school year extends from mid-August to the beginning of June, with vacations at Christmas and Easter. The student body totaled 727 in 1991; there were 66 teachers,

13 of them American. The staff also includes a reading specialist and a counselor.

Colegio Karl C. Parrish is situated on 20 acres just outside the city. Facilities include eight buildings, 35 classrooms, an audiovisual room, science laboratories, computer lab, playing fields, tennis courts, and an 8,000-volume library. Some of the classrooms are air-conditioned. The mailing address is Apartado Aéreo 52962, Barranquilla, Colombia.

The Marymount School is a coeducational day school for pre-kindergarten through grade 12. Founded in 1953, it is accredited by the Colombian Ministry of Education, and is operated by the nuns of the Order of the Sacred Heart.

The school uses both U.S. and Colombian curricula. The study of Spanish is required of all students. French is also offered, along with other electives and several extracurricular activities.

The school year runs from the beginning of September to the middle of June, with a three-week vacation at Christmas and a one-week vacation at Easter. The student body in 1991 numbered 1,325, under the tutelage of 110 full-time and 20 part-time teachers, of whom 35 are American. The staff also includes a counselor.

Marymount is located in a residential section in the northern part of the city. Facilities include ten buildings, 80 classrooms, a gymnasium, two playing fields, two science labs, swimming pool, auditorium, and a 17,000-volume library. The library and a typing room are air-conditioned. The mailing address is Apartado Aéreo 51766, Barranquilla, Colombia.

Colegio Albania is a coeducational, company-sponsored school for children in kindergarten through grade eight. The school is sponsored by Morrison Knudsen International and accredited by the Colombian Ministry of Education.

The curriculum is U.S.- and Colombian-based, offering the study of Spanish as well as other electives, and a variety of extracurricular activities, including a Boy Scout troop, drama, dance, yearbook, newspaper, and field trips.

The school year follows the usual calendar here. In 1991, the school had 746 students. There were 85 full-time teachers, 25 of whom were Americans.

Colegio Albania is located one hour by air from Barranquilla in an isolated camp. Its facilities include science and computer laboratories, tennis courts, two swimming pools, three playing fields, and two libraries. The school is completely air-conditioned. The mailing address is Apartado Aéreo 52499, Barranquilla, Colombia.

Another school attended by Americans is Fundación Colegio Bilingue, located in Valledupar, about 150 miles east of Barranquilla. The school is a coeducational day school covering pre-kindergarten through grade 12. It was founded in 1979 and is accredited by the Colombian Ministry of Education. The curriculum here is both U.S. and Colombian. French is offered in the secondary grade levels; other elective classes are art and vocational studies. There is also a program for students with learning disabilities.

The school year at Colegio Bilingue runs from the end of August to the first week in June, with vacations at Christmas, *Carnaval*, Easter, and national holidays. The student body currently totals 380. There are 32 full-time and three part-time teachers, of whom 11 are American. The staff includes a counselor. Fundación Colegio Bilingue is located just outside the central business district. The mailing address is Apartado Aéreo 129, Valledupar, Colombia.

Several other private elementary and secondary schools in Barranquilla follow the Colombian system, and classes are conducted in Spanish. Also, universities here offer

Street in Cartagena, Colombia

both graduate and undergraduate courses in a wide field of subjects, taught in Spanish. Anyone enrolling in these classes will need a working knowledge of that language.

Recreation and Entertainment

Several national parks located near Barranquilla have limited facilities, and their quality of maintenance is very low. They do, however, offer a chance to view local wildlife. No acceptable camping facilities are in the area, but interesting day trips can be made.

San Andrés Island, a one-hour flight from the city, offers excellent hotel accommodations, crystal clear waters abounding with fish and marine life, and white sand beaches. This island is also a free port, and its markets stock a wide variety of U.S. toiletries, appliances, clothing, and food.

In Barranquilla, tennis, golf, bowling, and water sports are available, but most facilities are in private clubs. The Barranquilla Country Club has swimming pools, tennis courts, and an 18-hole golf course. The Club Caujaral offers full recreational facilities. Guest membership cards can be obtained for temporary use of these clubs.

Each March, the city is the site of the international tennis tournament called the "South American Wimbledon."

Santa Marta, one-and-a-half hours by car from Barranquilla, has excellent beaches and good hotels. This Caribbean city is also noted for its Spanish architecture.

There are several beaches within a half hour of Barranquilla. Unfortunately, the sea here tends to be quite dirty because of silt from the Magdalena River, and swimming is not recommended. Many people spend the afternoon at local beaches sunbathing, people-watching, and eating fried fish and *patacones* (fried banana slices).

Barranquilla has several air-conditioned movie theaters showing recent releases of both U.S. and European films. These are reasonably priced and serve as a major form of entertainment. A film club shows revivals of classic films in one of the local theaters.

Another major form of entertainment here is the video cassette recorder. Rental centers with cassettes in English abound. Local television transmission is compatible with that in the U.S. and offers black-and-white and color programming in Spanish. Several current American series are dubbed in Spanish.

Radio programs range from *cumbia* (Colombian folk dance) to classical music. Stations broadcast in Spanish. A shortwave set is necessary for the reception of Voice of America (VOA), Radio Canada, and British Broadcasting Corporation (BBC).

Barranquilla has a wide range of excellent restaurants. French, Italian, Chinese, Arabic, and other specialties are available, as are restaurants featuring steak and ribs. Restaurants serving typical Colombian food, such as seafood or chicken with coconut rice, are also very popular. Fast-food restaurants are opening.

English-language editions of *Time* and *Newsweek*, the *Miami Herald* and, occasionally, the *New York Times*, are available. A small, cooperative lending library has books in English, and the Centro Colombo-Americano Library may be used by expatriates. The Centro Colombo-Americano often hosts art exhibits. Barranquilla public libraries do not shelve English-language books.

Cartagena

Cartagena, whose walled city dates back to the days of the Spanish Main, lies about 70 miles south of Barranquilla on the Caribbean coast. It was founded in 1533, and during the 17th century was a center of such importance in the Western Hemisphere that it was second only to Mexico City. During Spanish times, Cartagena (full name, Cartagena de Indias) was a strongly fortified town on an island, but one of its two entrances to the bay was barricaded by the Spanish after a heavy attack by English forces, and the city is now permanently linked to the mainland. The greatest of the Latin American heroes, Simón Bolívar, made Cartagena his headquarters in the Magdalena campaign of 1811.

The famous fortress of San Felipe Borajas, towering over the approaches to the city, and the ancient churches, including the Shrine of St. Peter Clavar, make Cartagena one of the most interesting cities in Colombia. The old town is a maze of narrow streets, houses with tiled roofs and balconies, and small shopping stalls—a contrast to the new, commercial city with its wide boulevards and the Plaza Bolívar, where a huge statue honors the memory of "The Liberator." Cartagena is a busy, modern city, handling the export of platinum, coffee, timber, and oil products. Cosmetics, textiles, sugar, tobacco products, leather goods, and fertilizer are produced here. Cartagena is one of Colombia's major ports. Aerovías Nacionales de Colombia (AVIANCA) flies in from New York and Miami, bringing businessmen to its industrial and commercial houses, and tourists to its fascinating historical sites and cosmopolitan attractions. The population of Cartagena was 918,000 in 2000.

Cartagena commemorates its independence each November in a carnival atmosphere, which includes the national beauty contest for the crown of "Miss Colombia." Candlemas Day, the religious feast of the Virgin de la Candelaria, is fervently observed every year on the second day of February at the monastery of La Popa, in the hills outside the city.

Cartagena is known throughout Colombia for its fine restaurants and its jazz and disco clubs. There are good hotels in the new city, attracting tourists throughout the year.

Education

George Washington School is a coeducational, day, proprietary school for children in pre-kindergarten through grade 12. Founded in 1952 and sponsored by the Office of Overseas Schools and the U.S. Department of State, it is accredited by the Southern Association of Colleges and Schools and the Colombian Ministry of Education.

Both U.S. and Colombian curricula are used. Spanish is offered, along with art, computer science, and physical education. Extracurricular activities include drama, gymnastics/dance, literary and news publications, field trips, and varied sports.

The school year extends from mid-August to the beginning of June, with vacations at Christmas, Easter, and U.S. and Colombian holidays. In 1991, the enrollment at George Washington School was 483. Of 27 full-time and seven part-time teachers, eight were Americans.

George Washington School is located on beach front property in Cartagena. Facilities include 20 classrooms, science and computer laboratories, athletic fields, cafeteria, and a 11,000-volume library. The mailing address is Apartado Aéreo 2899, Cartagena, Colombia.

Bucaramanga

Bucaramanga, the capital of Santander Department, is in north central Colombia, about 200 miles northeast of Bogotá. It is situated in the Cordillera Oriental of the Andes Mountains at an altitude of 3,340 feet. The city was founded in 1622, and many of its colonial monuments and buildings are still in evidence. Today, with a population of 1.5 million, Bucaramanga is a leading commercial city in the center of the country's coffee and tobacco area. Cacao and cotton are also produced. Several manufacturing ventures in the city produce cigars, cigarettes, textiles, straw hats, and iron products.

Known for its beautiful parks, Bucaramanga is often called Colombia's "garden city." It is also noted for the modern Universidad Industrial de Santander, which opened here in 1947.

Many American children in the area attend the Pan-American School, a coeducational, day, proprietary institution. Implementing a U.S. and Colombian curriculum (French is a required language), the school year extends from February to December, with vacations at Christmas, Easter, and from mid-June to mid-July. In 1991, the school had 318 students. Nine of the school's 24 full-time teachers were American. The school has a cafeteria, science lab, computer lab, and playing field. The school is located on five acres of land just outside the city; the mailing address is Apartado Aéreo 522, Bucaramanga, Colombia.

OTHER CITIES

ARMENIA, located in west-central Colombia, about 100 miles west of Bogotá, is a relatively new city. The city is situated in a rich agricultural region, best known for coffee and for the production of food and beverages. Other crops grown include corn, beans, silk, sugarcane, and plantains. Its population, counted with neighboring Calarcá, has already reached 306,000. As the capital of Quindío Department, it is the seat of a university, founded in 1962.

BELLO, at 4,905 feet above sea level, is located in northwestern Colombia. Situated on the Río Porce, in a fertile region, Bello was once a commercial center. Today, it is a part of the industrial complex of Medellín, located six miles south. The major industries are textile milling and brush manufacturing. Bello's estimated population is 370,000.

BUENAVENTURA is a Pacific port, about 50 miles west of Cali. Located on Cascajal Island in Buenaventura Bay, the city is the shipping point for the tobacco and sugar produced in the nearby Cauca Valley. Other items exported from here include coffee, hides, platinum, and gold. The city was founded in 1540, but was destroyed by Indian raids in the 16th century. Buenaventura's importance as a port increased with the building of the Panama Canal. It has steamer connections with Panama and is also the terminus of railroads in western Colombia. The current population is 271,400.

CÚCUTU (also known as San José de Cúcuta) is in northeast Colombia, 250 miles north of Bogotá. It is the capital of Norte de Santander Department, near the Venezuelan border on the Colombia-Venezuela highway. Cúcutu was founded in 1733 and captured from Spanish forces by Simón Bolívar in 1813. From here, Bolívar set out on his march to Caracas. Destroyed by an earthquake in 1875, Cúcutu was rebuilt, and today its population, including the environs, is 682,325. Cúcutu is an industrial city and the center of a rich coffee, oil, and mineral region. The city is linked by air, river, and railway connections with the cities of northeastern Colombia and Venezuela.

GIRARDOT is about 50 miles southeast of Bogotá, and one of the most popular warm-weather spots in the country. The city is noted for its numerous acacia trees. Also, large varieties of tropical fruits, as well as unusual pottery, can be purchased in the town's central plaza. Founded in 1853, Girardot is a commercial center whose principal products include coffee, livestock, and tobacco. The current population is close to 125,000.

Located in northern Colombia near the Río Porce, **ITAGÜI** was formerly a resort and local commercial center. Today, like other cities in the area, Itagüi is a part of the industrial complex of Medellín, located five miles northeast. The important industry in Itagüi is textile milling. Its population is close to 435,000 (2001).

LETICIA, capital of the Amazonas *comisaria* (lesser territory), is Colombia's principal town on the Amazon River, 670 miles southeast of Bogotá. Accessible by air, it provides tourists with such attractions as Amazon River excursions, visits to primitive Indian villages, and trips through dense rain forests. Leticia has practically no industry and relies on rubber gathering as a major economic activity. Leticia is located at the northern end of the Peru-Brazil border, and it is easy to make border crossings among the three countries in one day. The town, with a population of approximately 8,000, has been the site of several border disputes between Peru and Colombia. Peru ceded it by treaty in 1922, but seized it back 10 years later. The region was ultimately awarded to Colombia by the League of Nations in 1934.

MANIZALES, capital of Caldas Department, is 100 miles west of Bogotá and 125 miles north of Cali. Located at an altitude of 7,063 feet, it is a commercial and agricultural center in an area producing much of the country's coffee. The city was founded in 1847 by gold prospectors and there are gold and silver mines nearby. A cement plant is located in the city, as are factories producing agricultural machines, textiles, refrigerators, furniture, and leather goods. Manizales is the site of the University of Caldas. An earthquake destroyed Manizales in 1878, and it was leveled by fire in 1925. Situated in a higher and cooler setting than Cali, Manizales straddles a narrow ridge beneath snow-capped Mt. Ruiz, where adventurous souls have tried skiing on the 16,000-foot slope of year-round snow. The population today, including nearby Villamaria, is over 330,000.

MONTERÍA, with a population of over 230,000, is the capital of Córdoba Department. Situated in northwestern Colombia, it is an inland port on the Río Sinú. The city was originally a Zenúe Indian village used as a hunting post—Montería means "hunting" in Spanish. Industries here include lumbering, stock raising, and tagua nut production. The University of Córdoba is located here.

NEIVA, the capital city of Huila Department, is located in south-central Colombia, over 100 miles south of the nation's capital. Capt. Diego de Ospina claimed Neiva for the Spanish crown in 1612, after several others had tried unsuccessfully to establish the settlement. The city is basically agricultural, producing corn, rice, cotton, and sesame. It manufactures cement and cotton goods and processes marble. Neiva has excellent water, land, and air routes. The city's population in 2001 was approximately 349,000.

PALMIRA, with a population of well over 150,000, is located on the Pan-American Highway about 50 miles east of Cali and 175 miles southwest of Bogotá. At an altitude of 3,000 feet, Palmira is situated in the Cauca River valley, and is known as the agricultural capital of Colombia. Major crops in the area include coffee, tobacco, rice, corn, and sugarcane. Tours of the sugar refineries in Palmira are open to the public.

The city of **PASTO** is located in southwestern Colombia, just over 100 miles north of Quito, Ecuador. It is the capital of Nariño Department and is situated on a high plateau at the foot of the Galeras volcano. Pasto has flour and textile mills, sugar refineries, distilleries, and tanneries. Its principal product is wooden bowls finished with locally produced varnish. Founded in 1539, the city served as royalist headquarters during the revolutionary wars. The University of Nariño is located here. Pasto's population is almost 405,000 (2001 est.).

POPAYÁN, 75 miles south of Cali, is situated at an altitude of 5,500 feet on a volcanic terrace above the Cauca River. The city was founded in 1536 by Sebastián de Benalcázar and was the most important settlement in southwest Colombia during the colonial and immediate post-independence periods. During colonial times, Popayán prospered as a religious, cultural, and aristocratic trade center. Following Colombia's independence, Popayán lost much of its commercial importance, but retained its cultural prominence. There has been a university here since 1827. With a population of 230,137 (2001 est.), it is the capital of the Department of Cauca. Coffee is the chief commercial activity; mining is also done in the surrounding region. The city has several small manufacturing enterprises. These industries process food and beverages and manufacture building materials and clothing. Popayán is the repository of many priceless examples of Spanish colonial art and architecture. Numerous buildings destroyed in a recent devastating earthquake are now being restored. A visit to the city during Holy Week to view the internationally famous religious processions is worthwhile.

SANTA MARTA is situated in northern Colombia on the Caribbean Sea, 50 miles east of Barranquilla. Founded in 1525 by Rodrigo de Bastidas, Santa Marta is the oldest city in Colombia. It became an important banana shipping center in the late 19th century; today, the city's banana industry is operated by the United Fruit Company and is one of the most important in South America. The Atlantic Railway, which climbs through the beautiful mountains to connect Santa Marta with the interior, was completed in 1961. The city is also accessible by highway and air. With a population over 235,000, Santa Marta has fine beaches and is a tourist resort. Santa Marta is the home of the Technological University of Magdalena. Simón Bolívar died on an estate near here in 1830.

TULUÁ is situated in western Colombia, over 100 miles from Bogotá. It was originally settled by the Putimáes Indians and called Villa de Jerez by the explorers. The Indians resisted the Spanish attempts at conquest and, in 1636, Tuluá was established as a large cattle ranch and Indian village. It was not until 1814 that the city won municipal status. Primarily an agricultural center, Tuluá produces yeast, beef, and milk. An annual fair is held to display prize cattle and industrial goods. It is located near the Puerto Berío-Popayán railroad and the Pan-American Highway. The population here is almost 185,000.

TUMACO is located in southwestern Colombia, 375 miles from Bogotá. Situated on a small island just off the coast, it is Colombia's southernmost Pacific port. A commercial center, with about 160,000 residents, the city is the center of lumbering activity including plywood and molding factories. Gold mines are in operation near Tumaco. Tumaco exports ivory, nuts, cacao, tobacco, vegetables, coffee, and other items produced in the country's interior.

TUNJA, 85 miles northeast of Bogotá, on the Pan-American Highway, is the capital of Boyacá Department. The city was founded in 1529 and became independent from Spain in 1811. Many of its early structures are still standing. Situated in the Cordillera Oriental of the Andes, Tunja is a commercial center and distribution point for coal, emeralds, mineral water, and agricultural products produced in the area. Tunja is the home of the Pedagogical and Technological University of Colombia. The city is linked by rail and highway to Bogotá. Tunja's population is about 123,000 (2001 est.).

VALLEDUPAR, the capital city of César Department, has a population of approximately 354,000 (2001 est.). It is situated in northern Colombia, just west of the Venezuelan border. Founded in 1550, the city was prosperous during the colonial period but experienced setbacks during the 19th-century civil wars. Today, as a commercial hub, Valledupar produces bricks and ice. A large sawmill is also located here.

VILLAVICENCIO lies on the Meta River, about 50 miles southeast of Bogotá. Its position in the eastern foothills of the Andes makes it the gateway to the eastern plains of Colombia and the primary urban center of the llanos and forest region in this area of the country. Villavicencio is the capital of Meta Department. The climate here is warm, and the town is a cattle center with a frontier atmosphere. Industries include a distillery, a brewery, soap factories, coffee-roasting plants, and saddleries. Other products are coffee, bananas, rubber, and rice. The current population is about 340,300.

COUNTRY PROFILE

Geography and Climate

The Republic of Colombia (about 440,000 square miles), roughly the size of Texas, Arkansas, and New Mexico combined, is in northwest South America. Its location on the Caribbean Sea and Pacific Ocean, proximity to the Panama Canal, and economic potential give it a position of international importance.

As well as its frontier with Panama on the northwest, Colombia shares borders with Ecuador and Peru on the south, with Brazil on the southeast, and with Venezuela on the northeast.

The Andes dominate the western two-fifths of Colombia, giving it a very different character from the remaining three-fifths in the east. The Amazon region of southeastern Colombia lies below the Equator.

Well over 90% of the population is concentrated in the mountainous west and along the Caribbean and Pacific coasts. The remainder live is the Eastern Llanos, a large plains area, constituting 54% of the nation's area.

Most live on plateaus and mountain slopes, where elevation reduces the heat of the equatorial climate and contributes to the health and vigor of the people. By concentrating people in isolated pockets at high elevations, the mountain ranges determine not only settlement patterns, but also lines of communication and travel, which parallel the ranges in a north-south direction. Movement from rural to urban areas has been heavy, and nearly three-quarters of the population is now urban.

Colombia's climate varies with its different altitudes. Its three climatic zones are called "hot country," "temperate country," and "cold country."

Population

According to Colombian government statistics, the 2000 population was over 40 million. The population growth rate is 1,6%. Colombia is unique in Latin America in that 26 cities have populations over 100,000.

Due to recent improvements in health and sanitary conditions and a decrease in infant mortality, the population is relatively young: 31% are under 15 years of age, and only 5% are over 65.

In terms of total area, population density is a low 39 persons per square mile. This figure is misleading because the density per arable square mile is about 1,500 persons. Whether this ratio can be maintained or held down to a reasonable level through productive use of large jungle, forest, and plains areas is a major socioeconomic problem.

Settlement is divided into several broad regions. Each has been rather isolated by geologic obstacles to travel, so each has a high degree of economic independence of essential raw materials and fuel. Much of the prevalent regional sentiment can be traced to early settlement patterns.

When the Spanish Colonists entered what is now Colombia, they found a rather well-organized Indian population on the plateaus and high valleys of the Eastern Cordillera. A moderate climate, adequate natural resources, and Indian labor allowed the Cundinamarca-Boyaca area and parts of Tolima and Huila to develop into an economic entity which today has the heaviest concentration of people in the country. Here, Bogota became the economic, political, and cultural center of Colombia.

In the early 19th century, another population center developed along the northern end of the Eastern Cordillera when the export of cinchona bark became highly profitable. White settlers then appeared in significant numbers in what are now Santander and Norte de Santander.

A third population center developed in the area of the Departments of Antioquia and Caldas, usually called the Antioquia region. Other major population concentrations are in the Cauca River Valley (from Popayan to Cali and Cartagena), and the ocean ports: Buenaventura and the Pacific coast and the Cartagena-Barranquilla-Santa Marta region along the Atlantic shore.

Among the countries of Latin America, Colombia is commonly described as a mestizo nation, rather than a white or an Indian one, with a mixed and diverse society.

Colombians describe their society as tri-ethnic, due to mingling between Caucasians and peoples of African decent with the original Indians to form a new combination. This fusion has taken nearly four centuries and, consequently, most Colombians are of mixed origin. Ethnic boundaries have not been completely erased. Colombians still attach importance to ancestral characteristics, although these no longer demarcate distinct social groups.

Spanish is spoken throughout Colombia, except by small groups of

Indians who still speak aboriginal languages; however, these groups are becoming increasingly bilingual. San Andres, a small island Department in the Caribbean, is another exception; San Andreans speak English as a first language. Colombians are proud of their Spanish and consider it, especially that spoken by the upper classes in Bogota and other large cities, as the purest form of that language in Latin America today.

Colombia is overwhelmingly a Catholic country (approximately 90%.) Although freedom of worship is guaranteed by the Constitution, the Catholic Church receives some funds from the government and exercises considerable, although diminishing, influence over education. The church is the major social force in Colombia.

Public Institutions

The Republic of Colombia was established in 1823. In the same year, the United States became one of the first countries to recognize the new Republic and establish a resident diplomatic mission.

Colombia, unlike many Latin American countries, established an early tradition of civilian governments and regular free elections. Despite this background, Colombia's history has been marred by periods of violent political conflict. The period known as "La Violencia" in the 1940s and 1950s claimed between 100,000 and 200,000 lives. More recently, drug and guerrilla-related violence have plagued Colombian society. Since the early 1980s, the Colombian government has engaged in intermittent peace talks with guerrilla groups. In 1990, the guerrilla group M-19 (Movement of April 19) delivered its weapons to the government and scored surprising electoral gains as a legal political party. However, the two political parties, the Liberal and Conservative, soon shadowed the M-19 emergent preponderance. Two older and larger guerrilla armies, the Revolutionary Armed Forces of Colombia (FARC) and the National Liberation Army (ELN), remain in armed conflict with the government.

A military coup in 1953 brought General Gustavo Rojas Pinilla to power. Initially, Rojas enjoyed wide popular support, partly for his success in reducing La Violencia. When he did not promptly restore democratic government, however, he was overthrown by the military with the backing of the two major political parties (the Liberals and the Conservatives), and a provisional government took office in 1957.

In July 1957, the last Conservative president, Laureano Gomez (1950-53), and the last Liberal president, Alberto Lleras Camargo (1945-46), proposed the formation of a "National Front," under which the Liberal and Conservative parties would govern jointly. Through regular elections, the presidency would alternate between the two parties every four years; the parties would also share all other elective and appointive offices.

The first three National Front Presidents brought an end to La Violencia and the blind partisanship which had afflicted both parties. They committed Colombia to the far-reaching social and economic reforms proposed in the Charter of the Alliance for Progress, and, with assistance from the United States and international lending agencies, achieved major economic development.

The 1886 Constitution was substantially amended in 1991 by a 74-member Constituent Assembly. On July 4, 1991 a new Colombian Constitution was enacted. The new Constitution, one of the largest in the world, expanded citizens' basic rights. Among others, the most relevant is the "tutela" (immediate court action at the request of a citizen if he/she feels his/her constitutional rights have been violated and no other legal recourse is available). However, keystones to the constitutional reform in 1991 were the need to reform Congress and to strengthen justice administration by introducing the accusatorial system. Other relevant amendments were the approval of freedom of religion (in the past, Colombia's official religion was the Roman Catholic), civil divorce for all marriages, the election of a Vice-President, the election of governors, and dual nationality.

Colombia remains a democratic republic under a presidential system with Executive, Legislative and Judicial branches of government. Elected for a 4 year term, the President is the chief of the Executive Branch. He may not be reelected. The Vice-President runs for election on the same ticket as the presidential candidate, and both should be members of the same political party. The Vice-President fulfills the duties of the President in case of the President's resignation, serious illness, or death. However, the Vice-President may be assigned other special responsibilities, hold public positions, and even fulfill special presidential functions at the President's request. During the President's temporary absences, such as international trips, the Minister of the Interior or another minister in order of precedence performs his duties.

Colombia's bicameral Congress consists of a 102 member Senate elected on the basis of a nationwide ballot, and a House of Representatives whose number, currently 165, is elected proportionally by adult residents (age 18 and over) of the Departments and the Capital District. Congressional elections are held every four years, on a different date from the Presidential election. If a member of Congress is absent temporarily or permanently, his seat is taken by an alternate elected at the same time as the member.

Congress meets in two sessions annually, from March to June and from July to December. The president may convene special sessions at other times.

The country is divided into 32 departments, 1,025 municipalities—of which 30 cities have over 100,000 inhabitants—and the Capital District of Santa Fe de Bogota (herein referred to as Bogota). Governors and mayors are elected for a 3-year term.

Judicial power is exercised by subordinate courts and four high tribunals: The Constitutional Court (9 members elected by the Senate), the Supreme Court (20 members, highest criminal, civil and labor tribunal), the Council of State (26 members, highest tribunal for contentious administrative matters), and the Judiciary Superior Council (13 members, highest tribunal for justice administration and disciplinary issues of the judicial branch). The high court justices are elected for an 8-year term. Justices of the Constitutional Court, the Supreme Court and the Council of State may not be reelected.

The Office of the Prosecutor General (Fiscalía General de la Nación) was created under the 1991 Constitution and serves as the driving force in Colombia's accusatorial model of criminal investigation. The Prosecutor General is elected by the Supreme Court for a 4-year term and may not be reelected.

The Office of the Attorney General or Public Ministry (Procuraduría General de la Nación) oversees the performance of public servants. The Attorney General is elected by the Senate for a 4-year-term oversees the performance of public servants. The Attorney General is elected by the Senate for a 4-year term.

The Office of the Public Defender (Defensoría del Pueblo), under the Attorney General, is elected by the House of Representatives for a 4-year term to protect and defend human rights.

Arts, Science, and Education

Bogota is a cultural center with thriving theaters, orchestras, opera, museums and art galleries. Other major cities in Colombia also support the arts. The Centro Colombo-Americano in Bogota and its coun-

terpart Binational Centers around the country also provide venues for art presentations.

Visiting dancers, musicians and actors from all parts of the world perform in Bogota. Films from around the world are also screened in the many cinemas, including current U.S. movies in English with Spanish subtitles.

Bogota's bookstores, among the finest in Latin America, offer titles in English, French and German as well as Spanish. The American Library at the Centro Colombo-Americano has a solid and current collection of books and recent periodicals in English.

A small video library is also maintained there, and the annex where it is located offers service to visitors and students on weekend hours. Other libraries also hold small selections of English-language collections.

Colombia's literacy rate is over 91%. The basic structure of education in Colombia includes two years of preschool, five years of primary school, and six years of secondary school. Curricula for public and private elementary and high schools are developed by the Ministry of Education.

Under the 1991 Constitution, education is compulsory up to age 15. Previously, only the first five years were mandatory. The student population, including 500,000 at the university level, is estimated more than 4.5 million. The more than 230 institutions of higher education in Colombia offer programs in a wide variety of disciplines and at different types of institutions which grant degrees at the technical and/or professional levels. The biggest public university is Universidad Nacional de Colombia, with the main campus in Bogota and others in Medellin, Manizales and Palmira. Some of the oldest and most reputed private universities are Universidad de Santo Tomas, founded in 1580; Pontificia Universidad Javeriana, founded in 1622; and Colegio Mayor de Nuestra Señora del Rosario,

founded in 1653. Universidad de Los Andes in Bogota and Universidad del Valle in Cali are among the leading universities in the country and are known internationally for their academic excellence. Universidad Javeriana offers summer programs in Spanish language. Many Colombians do their graduate studies abroad.

Commerce and Industry

Colombia has a diversified economy which has enjoyed steady growth throughout the 1980s and 1990s. Contrary to popular opinion, cocaine trafficking does not play a major role in the overall Colombia economy nor does it provide significant foreign exchange earnings for the nation. Colombia is rich in natural resources and fertile agricultural land. It is the world's second largest producer and exporter of coffee. Other agricultural products include sugar, cotton, rice, bananas, corn, potatoes, yucca, cocoa, barley, flowers and sisal-like fiber ("fique"). Livestock also accounts for a large share of agricultural output, although in recent years the cattle industry has been in decline. Other products include petroleum, gold, platinum, silver, coal, iron, lead, limestone and salt. In addition, nickel exports are an important source of foreign exchange. Colombia's emeralds are world famous.

Coal and petroleum have become important exports in the last ten years. An affiliate of EXXON and the Colombian National Coal Company (Carbocol) together developed Colombia's giant north coast coal field. The project, named Cerrejon North, required an investment of US$3.2 billion and represents the largest U.S. investment in Colombia. Production began in 1985, and exports grew quickly to over US$600 million in 1990.

Occidental Petroleum Company and the Colombian national oil company Ecopetrol, jointly developed Caño-Limon, a major oil field in the Llanos near the Venezuelan border.

Development includes facilities for extraction and transport, and storage and export facilities in Coveñas on Colombia's north coast. The field's proven reserves are over one billion barrels. Production from the field has helped make Colombia self-sufficient in crude oil and a significant Latin American oil exporter (approximately 250,000 BPD). Colombia must still import a large percentage of its gasoline, due to insufficient refining capacity within the country.

Drummond Ltd. recently began operations in La Loma coal deposit. This bituminous coal has similar characteristics to that mined at the Cerrejon deposit and La Loma's project infrastructure is capable of producing up to 10 million tons a year to be exported via a private port venture. The government can create incentives for foreign investors in mineral development projects under the Mining Code.

Colombia enacted its 1991 Constitution under the principles of sustainable development and the protection of the country's rich biodiversity. The creation of the Ministry of the Environment and the National Environmental System sets a new framework for the government to plan strategies for the development of an environmental conscience in the public and private sectors; to develop policies for the efficient use of natural resources; to enforce environmental regulations; to control industrial pollution sources; and, to improve the institutional and legal framework of the environmental entities within the system.

In 1990, Colombia greatly accelerated an ambitious program of economic opening, called apertura, which is designed to make Colombia globally competitive. The country's industrial base, while growing slowly, is undergoing changes as Colombia frees its trade regime to allow more imports to enter at lower tariff rates. Less efficient industries are facing foreign competition, forcing them to modernize, improving technology and efficiency.

As part of the apertura program, legislation was passed at the end of 1990 to liberalize and modernize the foreign investment, foreign exchange, labor, tax and foreign trade regimes. Changes include legalization of 100% ownership of financial institutions by foreign investors, a reduction in currency controls, increased profit remittance ceilings, and more flexible hiring and firing practices. Prior licenses for imports have been virtually eliminated. Tariffs, although still high for luxury goods, have been reduced substantially. These laws will improve the already close financial and commercial ties between Colombia, the U.S. and Europe.

Foreign investment is permitted in all sectors of the Colombian economy with the exception of public security (defense and police) and nuclear energy. The government is interested in privatizing or bringing private investment into previously restricted sectors such as telecommunications and public works. Long distance telephone services are scheduled to be provided by competing private companies starting in 1997. Private oil and mineral extraction projects must still be approved by the Ministry of Mines and Energy, and financial sector investments must have the prior approval of the Banking Superintendency.

Until recently, the Colombian government maintained a policy of gradual devaluation (crawling peg) of the peso against the dollar to keep Colombian products competitive in world markets. Colombia's principal exports are coffee, oil, coal, textiles, leather products, bananas, cut flowers, fruits and citrus, cotton, sugar, tobacco, cement, lumber, shrimp, rice, cowhides, and precious metals.

Approximately 80% of Colombia's population lives outside Bogota. Much of the country's economic activity is spread among several modern and urbanized industrial centers. The cities of Medellin, Cali, Barranquilla, Cartagena, Bucara-

manga, Pereira, among others, play a significant role in the country's economy. The existence of four major ports and six international airports guarantees that goods may flow freely to and from Colombia without dependence upon Bogota.

The United States continues to be Colombia's largest trading partner, accounting for about 35% of its exports and 39% of its imports. The two nations formed the Joint Commission on Trade and Investment (TIC) in July 1990 to further economic ties and reduce barriers to trade between Colombia and the U.S. The TIC met most recently in May 1996.

Transportation
Local
Taxis are easily available and rates are reasonable. You may call via telephone, and one will be radio dispatched, or you can wave them down on the streets. As in most large cities, your wait may be long during rush hours and on rainy days. All taxis are metered and inexpensive by U.S. standards, except the green - and - white tourist taxis, which provide transportation to and from the first-class hotels.

Special arrangements can be made to hire taxis by the hour for local shopping trips, sight-seeing tours, etc. Bogota and most other cities in Colombia have bus service, but security and safety are poor.

Regional
Airline service within Colombia is good, ranging from Avianca's modern jet fleet to some "budget" airlines' DC-3s. Fares are expensive by U.S. standards for jet service. Connections between major cities are frequent and schedules are generally adhered to.

Bogota has a major international air terminal, with daily flights to the U.S., Europe, and other parts of Latin America. Barranquilla and other major cities also have adequate airport facilities with many international flights. Air fares for international routes are expensive; a round-trip excursion between Bogota and Miami between June through August and December through February, including taxes is approximately US$700. At other times, the fare is approximately US$500. Off-season special fares are currently offered twice annually. Both Continental and American Airlines service Colombia. The Colombian Government imposes a departure tax on international travelers of approximately US$23 which can be paid in local currency or U.S.dollars.

Colombian drivers are very aggressive and often do not obey local traffic regulations. Traffic is heavy, road conditions are often bad due to numerous potholes. Minor accidents are frequent. Maintenance and body work are normally good, but parts and labor are expensive.

Traffic moves on the right. All distances and speed limits are given in kilometers, and international symbols are used for stop signs, railway crossings, etc.

Communications

Telephone and Telegraph

Long distance telephone service is satisfactory. Calling the U.S. from Bogota is expensive, and you may wish to apply for a long-distance telephone credit card such as AT&T. A three minute call to Washington, D.C., costs about US$8.48 (plus US$1.49 per minute thereafter) during the week and US$4 (plus US$l per minute thereafter) on Sundays.

Colombia has complete domestic and international telegraph and FAX service.

Radio and TV

Colombia has many commercial radio stations and reception is good.

Programs are mostly Latin American music; however, some stations broadcast classical music and cul-tural programs and others give heavy play to American popular music, including rock and jazz. All broadcasts are in Spanish. English-language newscasts are heard on shortwave broadcasts by the VOA and American Forces Radio (AFRTS); reception is good. Numerous FM stereo stations operate in Bogota.

In 1992 the government began a program of restructuring Colombian television. Ownership has changed from completely government-controlled to shared public and private hands with the air-waves, transmission infrastructure and some of the production facilities owned by Inravision, the government's broadcasting regulatory authority. Sixty percent of airtime must be given to Colombian-produced programs. Foreign programs are shown to supplement local production.

Inravision operates three national channels. Programming includes local and world news, soap operas, sports, educational, entertainment and movies. There is also parabolica satellite antenna and Cable TV available for an additional fee, which offers several English-speaking movie channels as well as CNN and ESPN.

Newspapers, Magazines, and Technical Journals

All major cities have at least two daily newspapers; the two major dailies in Bogota, *El Tiempo* and *El Espectador*, are available in all cities and on the Internet. Most papers lack comprehensive coverage of international events, but *El Tiempo* and *El Espectador* offer adequate coverage. An English-language weekly newspaper is available. Internet access is relatively expensive.

A satellite edition of the *Miami Herald* is printed in Bogota on a same-day basis. The *International Herald Tribune* and the *New York Times* are sold in major tourist hotels one or two days after publication.

The Latin American editions of *Time* and *Newsweek* magazines are regularly available in all major cities Copies of most US magazines available locally are scarce and at least double Stateside prices.

Health and Medicine

Medical Facilities

Reputable and reliable doctors, dentists and optometrists practice in Colombia. Many have been trained in the U.S. and speak English.

The Santa Fe Clinic (Hospital) is generally recommended, although there are several other local facilities which offer good care. Equipment and technology at the Santa Fe Clinic are equal to those available in good hospitals in the U.S. Nursing care is acceptable and improving. Support services such as laboratories are also above average.

Barranquilla has a University Hospital and private facility, Clínica Bautista, where medical attention of good quality can also be obtained. Doctors and support services are also adequate.

Common medications are available in Colombia and cheaper than in the U.S. Bring any specific/prescription or other medicines (allergy, etc.) in airfreight or household effects, since many brand names are unavailable locally.

Community Health

The Colombian environment is generally healthy. Sanitation in Colombia varies, depending on the area, from adequate to lax. Diarrhea, amebiasis, infectious hepatitis and other diseases caused by contaminated food and water are more prevalent than in the U.S. Water is considered safe in some large cities, but not in villages or outside the cities. Pasteurized milk and milk products of high quality are available in the supermarkets in large cities, as is bottled water. As in the U.S., mumps, measles, chicken pox, and poliomyelitis as well as other viral infections are encountered here.

Rabies is prevalent is some areas of Colombia; however, at present, cases of rabies transmission to humans are very rare in the cities. Antirabies campaigns are nagging in Colombia.

Preventive Measures

Most foods can be freed of contamination by cooking or boiling, or, with fruits, by peeling. Lettuce and leafy vegetables are treated by washing well and rinsing. A soaking for 30 minutes in an iodine or chlorine solution provides added protection.

Recommended inoculations include typhoid, tetanus, polio, yellow fever, Hepatitis B and Hepatitis A. Have your shots checked before departing, and keep them current.

Bogota's high altitude causes short-term breathing difficulties, insomnia, and weight loss in some healthy individuals. Normally, these symptoms quickly subside.

Malaria suppressant pills (i.e., Aralen) are unnecessary in the major cities, but are suggested for individuals who plan to visit eastern Colombia, the Pacific Coast and the lower Magdalena River Valley.

NOTES FOR TRAVELERS

Passage, Customs & Duties

Air travel to Colombia is recommended; all major cities have airports American Airlines and Continental are currently the only U.S. flag carriers.

A valid U.S. passport is required to enter and depart Colombia. Tourists must also provide evidence of return or onward travel. U.S. citizens do not need a visa for a tourist stay of 60 days or less. Stiff fines are imposed if passports are not stamped on arrival and if stays exceeding 60 days are not authorized by the Colombian Immigration Agency (Departamento Administrativo de Seguridad, Jefatura de Extranjeria, "DAS

Extranjeria"). U.S. citizens whose passports are lost or stolen in Colombia must obtain a new passport and present it, together with a police report of the loss or theft, to the main immigration office in Bogota to obtain permission to depart. An exit tax must be paid at the airport when departing Colombia. For further information regarding entry and customs requirements, travelers should contact the Colombian Embassy at 2118 Leroy Place, N.W., Washington, DC 20008; telephone (202) 387-8338; Internet website - http://www.colombiaemb.org; or the Colombian consulate in Atlanta, Boston, Chicago, Houston, Los Angeles, Miami, New Orleans, New York, San Francisco or San Juan.

In an effort to prevent international child abduction, many governments, including Colombia's, have initiated procedures at entry/exit points. These often include requiring documentary evidence of relationship and permission for the child's travel from the parent(s) or legal guardian not present. Having such documentation on hand, even if not required, may facilitate entry/departure.

Colombia's specific procedures mandate that minors (under 18), regardless of nationality, who are traveling alone, with one parent or with a third party must present a copy of their birth certificate and written authorization from the absent parent(s) or legal guardian, specifically granting permission to travel alone, with one parent or with a third party. When a parent is deceased, a notarized copy of the death certificate is required in lieu of the written authorization. If documents are prepared in the United States, the authorization and the birth certificate must be translated into Spanish, notarized, and authenticated by the Colombian Embassy or a Colombian consulate within the United States. If documents are prepared in Colombia, only notarization by a Colombian notary is required. A permission letter prepared outside of Colombia is valid for 90 days. A

permission letter prepared in Colombia is valid for 60 days.

U.S. citizens living in or visiting Colombia are encouraged to register and obtain updated information on travel and security in Colombia either at the Consular Section of the U.S. Embassy in Bogota or via the Embassy's website (see website address below). The Consular Section is open for citizens services, including registration, from 8:30 a.m. to 12:00 noon, Monday through Thursday, excluding U.S. and Colombian holidays. The U.S. Embassy is located at Avenida El Dorado and Carrera 50; telephone (011-57-1) 315-0811 during business hours (8:30 a.m. to 5:00 p.m.), or 315-2109/2110 for emergencies during non-business hours; fax (011-57-1) 315-2196/2197; Internet website - http://usembassy.state.gov/bogota. The Consular Agency in Barranquilla, which provides some limited consular services, is located at Calle 77B, No. 57-141, Piso 5, Centro Empresarial Las Americas, Barranquilla, Atlantico, Colombia; telephone (011-57-5) 353-2001; fax (011-57-5) 353-5216; e-mail: conagent@metrotel.net.co.

Firearms & Ammunition

Colombian law prohibits tourists and business travelers from bringing firearms into Colombia. The penalty for illegal importation and/or possession of firearms is three to ten years in prison. It is advisable to contact the Embassy of Colombia in Washington or one of Colombia's consulates in the United States for specific information regarding customs requirements.

Pets

Pets must be accompanied by vaccination and health certificates certified by a Colombian consul. It is recommended that pets NOT be shipped as unaccompanied baggage.

Pets arriving at the airport as unaccompanied baggage after 2:00 PM cannot be cleared for entry until the next business day; unfortunately, the customs warehouse has no facilities for their proper care.

Currency, Banking and Weights and Measures

The basic monetary unit in Colombia is the Colombian peso (COP), a decimal currency. In writing, the same sign is used for both the peso ($) and the U.S. dollar ($) so they are often written either Col$, COP or Ps. Both paper currency and metal coins are used; the most common bills are in denominations of 1,000, 2,000, 5,000, 10,000, and 20,000 pesos. Coins are minted in values of 50, 100, 500, and 1000 pesos. The exchange rate in June 2002 was roughly COP$2,331.72 pesos per US$1.

Among U.S. banks with partially owned subsidiaries in Colombia are the First National City Bank and Bank of America.

Colombia is officially metric, with all distances measured in kilometers, heights in meters and temperature in Celsius. Many bulk commodities, however, such as coal and wood, are sold in "cargas," which vary according to the material weighed. Generally, it is the amount which can be loaded on a horse or burro. Bulk foodstuffs, such as fruits, vegetables, etc., are sold by the pound rather than by the kilo, and gas is sold in liters.

Disaster Preparedness

Colombia is an earthquake-prone country. U.S. citizens in Colombia may refer to information on dealing with natural disasters on the U.S. Embassy's web site at http://usembassy.state.gov/bogota/wwwhacsc.html. General information about natural disaster preparedness is available via the Internet from the U.S. Federal Emergency Management Agency (FEMA) at http://www.fema.gov/.

LOCAL HOLIDAYS

Jan.1	New Year's Day
Jan.6	Epiphany
Mar.	St. Joseph's Day*
Mar/Apr.	Holy Thursday*
Mar/Apr.	Good Friday*
May 1	Labor Day
May/June	Feast of the* Sacred Heart
May/June	Ascension Day*
June	Corpus Christi*
June	Saints Peter & Paul*
July 20	Independence Day
Aug.	Battle of Boyaca*
Aug.	Assumption Day*
Oct.	Columbus Day*
Nov.1	All Saints' Day
Nov.	Independence of Cartagena*
Dec. 8	Immaculate Conception
Dec. 25	Christmas Day

*variable

RECOMMENDED READING

These titles are provided as a general indication of the material published on this country. The Department of State does not endorse unofficial publications.

Bergquist, Charles, et al., eds. *Violence in Colombia: The Contemporary Crisis in Historical Perspective*. Wilmington, DE: Scholarly Resources, 1992.

Bogota: Cost of Living Survey. Rector, 1995.

Clancy, Tom. *Clear & Present Danger*. Putnam Publishing Group, 1989.

Colombia: A Country Study. USGPO, 1990, 4TH Ed. (Area handbook series)

Colombia: Financing Foreign Operations. Rector, 1995

Colombia in Focus: a Guide to the People, Politics & Culture. Monthly Review, 1996.

Colombia in Pictures. Minneapolis, MN: Lerner Publications, 1987.

Davis, Robert H., ed. *Colombia*. Santa Barbara, CA: ABC-Clio, 1990.

Decker, David R. & Duran, Ignacio. *The Political, Economic, & Labor Climate in Colombia*. University of Pennsylvania the Wharton School, Center for Human Resources, 1982.

Dix, Robert H. *The Politics of Colombia*. Greenwood Publishing Group, Inc., 1986.

DuBois, Jill. *Colombia*. New York: Marshall Cavendish, 1991.

Dydynski, Krzysztof. *Colombia: A Travel Survival Kit*. Oakland, CA: Lonely Planet, 1988.

Garcia Marquez, Gabriel. *One Hundred Years of Solitude*. Harper & Row: New York, 1970.

Giraldo, Javier. *Colombia the Genocidal Democracy*. Common Courage, 1995.

Gudeman, Stephen & Gutierrez, Alberto R. *Conversations in Colombia: The Domestic Economy in Life & Text*. Cambridge University Press, 1990.

Gugliotta, Guy & Leen, Jeff. *Kings of Cocaine: An Astonishing True Story of Murder, Money, & Corruption*. HarperCollins Publishers, Inc., 1990.

Hartlyn, Jonathan. *The Politics of Coalition Rule in Colombia*. New York: Cambridge University Press, 1988.

Haynes, Tricia. *Let's Visit Colombia*. Bridgeport, CT: Burke Publishing, 1988.

Henao J. *History of Colombia*. Gordon Press Publishers, 1976.

Henderson, James D. *When Colombia Bled: a History of the Violence in Tolima*. Univ. of Alabama, 1985.

Herman, Donald L., ed. *Democracy in Latin America: Colombia and Venezuela*. New York: Praeger, 1988.

Hutchinson, William R.; Poznanski, Cynthia A. & Todt-Stockman, Laura. *Living in Colombia: A Guide for Foreigners*. Intercultural Press, Inc., 1987.

Kline, Harvey F. *Portrait of Unit & Diversity*. Westview Press, 1983.

Lael, Richard L. *Arrogant Diplomacy: US Policy Toward Colombia, 1903-22.* Scholarly Resources, Inc., 1987.

Lang, James. *Inside Development in Latin America: A Report from the Dominican Republic, Colombia & Brazil.* University of North Carolina Press, 1988.

Morrison, Marion. *Colombia.* Chicago: Children's Press, 1990.

Oquist, Paul. *Violence, Conflict, & Politics in Colombia.* Academic Press, Inc., 1980.

Osterling, Jorge P. *Democracy in Colombia: Clientelistic Politics &*

Guerrilla Warfare. Transaction Publishers, 1989.

Parks, Taylor E. *Colombia & the United States.* Gordon Press Publishers, 1976.

Pearce, Jenny. *Colombia: Inside the Labyrinth.* New York: Monthly Review Press, 1990.

———. *Colombia: The Drug War.* New York: Watts, 1990.

Rosenberg, Tina. *Children of Cain: Violence & the Violent in Latin America.* New York: Morrow, 1991.

Stewart, Gail B. *Colombia.* New York: Macmillan Children's Book Group, 1991.

Washington Office on Latin America Staff. *Colombia Besieged: Political Violence & State Responsibility.* Washington Office on Latin America, 1989.

Wiarda, Howard J. *The Democratic Revolution in Latin America: History, Politics & US Policy.* Holmes & Meier, 1990.

Wickham-Crowley, Timothy P. *Guerrillas and Revolution in Latin America.* Princeton Univ. Pr., 1992.

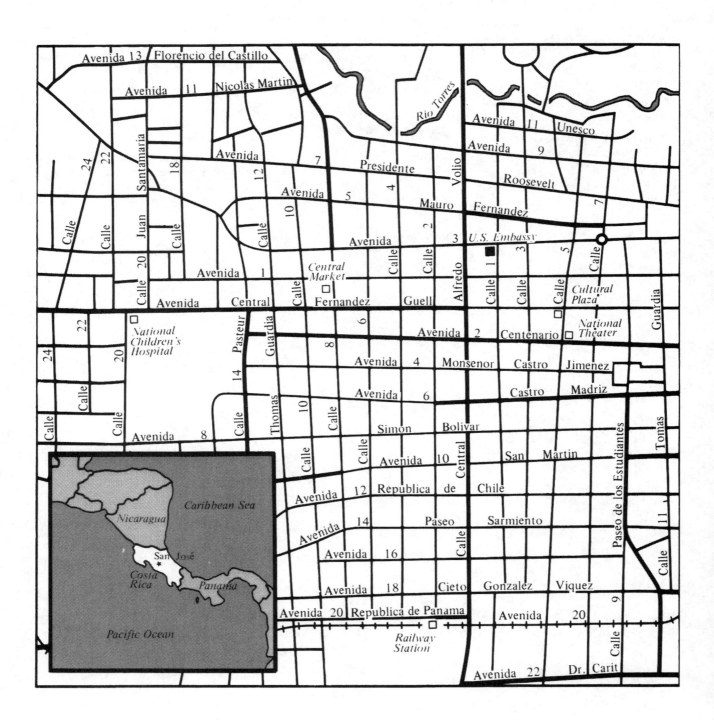

San José, Costa Rica

COSTA RICA

Republic of Costa Rica

Major City:

San José

Other Cities:

Alajuela, Cartago, Golfito, Heredia, Liberia, Limón, Puntarenas

EDITOR'S NOTE

This chapter was adapted from the Department of State Post Report 1999 for Costa Rica. Supplemental material has been added to increase coverage of minor cities, facts have been updated, and some material has been condensed. Readers are encouraged to visit the Department of State's web site at http://travel.state.gov/ for the most recent information available on travel to this country.

INTRODUCTION

Sometimes called the Switzerland of Middle America, Costa Rica straddles the mountain backbone that separates the Pacific from the Caribbean. Rugged ranges, topped by active volcanoes, climb sharply from lush jungles of the coastal regions and cradle a central plateau.

Legend holds that Columbus saw Indians wearing gold ornaments and named the region Costa Rica-Rich Coast. It enjoys a living standard considered the highest in Central America.

The explorers and "conquistadores" that were to come after Columbus did not find great native empires; instead, they found different tribes that were loosely connected or fragmented completely. While important Indian empires were falling-in 1532 the Incas and in the 1540s the Aztecs-Costa Rica was left alone, mostly because dreams of gold and jewels had proved to be illusions. It was not until 1559 that Spain decided to conquer Costa Rica.

Costa Rica is different from the rest of Central America because its people distribute their wealth, land, and power far more equitably. Its social welfare system and parliamentary democracy have no equal. To its everlasting good fortune, it was the most neglected of colonial Central America. It had neither of the two things the Spanish conquistadors wanted: mineral wealth (gold and silver), or an abundant Indian population to work their haciendas. The absence of minerals and indigenous workers meant that settlers worked their own land-and there was plenty of it to go around for centuries-to form a huge middle class of yeoman farmers. Money became so scarce at times that colonists had to substitute it with the Indian equivalent — cacao beans.

Wheat and tobacco were among the first products to be exported to Spain and other countries. Costa Rica was transformed by coffee in the 19th century. The brown bean attracted foreign capital and immigrant merchants and promoted road and railroad development. In one of the major engineering feats of the age, the San Jose-Puerto Limon railroad was completed in 1890, and from it a banana empire was built in the process. It connected the U.S. fruit centers of New Orleans and Boston with San Jose.

The country boasts a population close to 3.5 million people, which by standards of the region, is not large. Also, the growth rate is only 2.3% per year and is one of the most homogenous of the region. 98% of the people are classified as white or mestizo, and two percent as black or indigenous.

Costa Rica is also homogenous in regards to social classes. Most of the population is middle class, and even though poverty exists, it is not as large a problem as it is in other Latin countries. By the standards of a developed country, Costa Rican incomes are very low, but when compared to other neighbors, salaries and earnings prove to be much better. Besides the poor and middle classes, there is an upper class, which is very elitist. The preponderance of a middle-class produces an impression of class and social homogeneity.

Democracy is the source of tremendous pride in a country that can boast of having more teachers than policemen and of not having a standing army since 1948. Reform has always won over revolution and repression. Out of 53 leaders, only 3 have been military men and 6 can be considered dictators. Most Latin American countries can't affirm the same good fortune.

MAJOR CITY

San José

San José, with a metropolitan population of over one million, is almost completely surrounded by mountains, and just a few minutes' drive from the center of the city are foothills that offer a country atmosphere and lovely views.

The central part of the capital is divided into four quadrants by Avenida Central running east and west, and Calle Central running north and south. The arrangement of streets is logical, but initially confusing: Odd-numbered avenues (avenidas) are located north of Avenida Central and even-numbered avenues are to the south; odd-numbered streets (calles) are east of Calle Central, and even-numbered streets are to the west.

Street names or numbers are seldom used. Locations are given in relation to some landmark that may, or may not, be well known, such as a public building, a monument, a prominent intersection, or even a grocery store or gasoline station. Distances are expressed in meters ("metros" in Spanish), and 100 meters is roughly equivalent to a normal city block. At times the point of reference is a landmark that once existed but no longer is standing, a practice that works for longtime residents of San José but generally adds to the considerable confusion.

Most city streets in San José are paved, but many are narrow and rough, and congestion and noise are constant problems in the city. The pollution at times can be stifling. Potholes are a constant threat to the unwary, both in the city and in the countryside, and often are deep enough to damage vehicles. Open manholes are a danger as well, since theft of manhole covers seems to be a favorite activity in San José.

Downtown commercial buildings usually have two or three stories, but newer structures are much taller. Residential sections have many modern homes of brick, wood, or concrete construction, with either tile or galvanized metal roofs. Parks of all sizes are located throughout the city.

The temperature in San José is generally pleasant, with two seasons distinguished mainly by the rainfall. The dry season runs from December through April and the wet season extends from May through November. Even during the wet season the mornings generally are clear, with the afternoons and evenings dominated by heavy rains nearly every day. Relatively high winds often are present during the dry season.

The average temperature in San José is 70 to 75 degrees Fahrenheit. In December, the coolest month, the average temperature drops to around 65 degrees. Temperatures drop into the 50s at night throughout the year.

Humidity in San José averages 80 percent throughout the year, and during the rainy season mold and mildew are serious problems. Leave a light burning in closets, but for more serious measures, a dehumidifier must be used to prevent damage. Electronic equipment, books, records, tapes, and photographic equipment also suffer in the humidity, and should be protected if possible.

More than 20,000 private American citizens, most of them retirees, live in Costa Rica, and approximately one half million tourists from the U.S. visit the country every year. Smaller groups of foreign residents include Canadian, British, French, German, Italian, Chinese, Spanish, and other Latin Americans.

Precautions must be taken with regard to personal security. Pick-pocketing, muggings, and assaults are on the rise, especially in downtown San José.

Food

Many newcomers to San José are shocked at the prices for food and other purchases, which often approach or exceed U.S. prices and are not typical of Latin America.

Most fresh fruits and vegetables are available year round. They include bananas, papaya, melon, grapefruit, oranges, lemons, pineapples, strawberries, plantains, tomatoes, beets, eggplant, radishes, cucumbers, zucchini, potatoes (white and sweet), carrots, cauliflower, broccoli, spinach, squash, lettuce, cabbage, celery, green and wax beans, and several varieties of fresh and dried beans. Local fruits and vegetables are of good quality. Apricots, peaches, pears, apples, and grapes are not grown in commercial quantities in Costa Rica, but they are imported by the better grocers. Prices for all imported fruits are high.

Good quality fresh meats are available at all times, and beef, pork, chicken, and fish are plentiful. Mutton and lamb are seldom available on the open market, but can be ordered from some butchers. Beef prices and quality are slightly lower than in the U.S., while chicken, fish, and pork are sold at prices similar to those in the U.S. Fresh and frozen shrimp is available, but prices are quite high since most shrimp is destined for the export market.

Several dairies sell pasteurized milk similar in price and quality to American brands. Other dairy products such as chocolate milk, ice cream, skim milk, buttermilk, cottage cheese, sweet and sour cream, whipping cream, yogurt and eggnog, and a great variety of cheeses also are available. The overall quality of dairy products is high.

Local supermarkets are well stocked with snack foods, packaged foods, pasta, canned meats and fish, and soft drinks. Dry cereals are available at high prices. Flour, sugar, yeast, chocolate, and other baking items are available, but packaged cake mixes are of poor quality. A few frozen items are available, but choices are minimal. Supermarket chains stock many imported American foods, but the prices for all imported items are inflated.

Clothing

Since temperatures vary little, basically spring and fall weight clothing as well as summer attire are suitable for San Jose. Local tastes and standards are similar to those in the U.S. and are becoming increasingly casual. Some lightweight sweaters are handy during the rainy season, when evening temperatures are slightly cooler, and for trips to the mountains. Umbrellas and comfortable rain gear are necessary accessories for your San Jose wardrobe.

Shoes made in Costa Rica and other Central American countries are available at reasonable prices. Styles are similar to those found in the U.S. Finding shoes made with American lasts is difficult and consequently locally made shoes may not fit satisfactorily. Shoes, however, can be custom made for prices lower than in the U.S.

While shopping malls do exist, as indicated, the major differences are price, selection, and quality.

A wide selection of locally made material is available for home sewing, and some imported material is available as well. Care should be exercised in buying, as "seconds" sometimes appear on the local markets. Local department stores have adequate supplies of zippers, buttons, hooks, and facings, but some notions, especially fancy trimmings, are difficult to find. Some women have used local seamstresses, with varying success.

Children's casual clothing follows U.S. styles, with emphasis on slacks and jeans for both boys and girls, although girls are seen in dresses more often in Costa Rica than in the United States.

A recent change in regulations made school uniforms mandatory in all schools. Some uniforms can be purchased locally or from the U.S. Other uniforms are school specific and must be purchased locally. Prices for a complete uniform run between $40 and $50. Complete information about uniform requirements can be obtained from school representatives. Jackets, sweaters, and a water-repellent windbreaker with hood also should be included in a child's wardrobe. Locally made clothing is inexpensive, and of fair quality. Good quality, locally manufactured leather shoes are available in average widths, but extra shoelaces can be hard to find. Children's tennis shoes, made locally, are inexpensive and available in narrow to average widths, though no half sizes. Good quality boys underwear can be found, but underwear for girls is expensive if imported, and of inferior quality if made locally. Socks for both boys and girls are expensive. Infant clothing, as well as items such as receiving blankets, are available on the local market.

Supplies and Services

Some familiar American-brand and European-brand cosmetics, toiletries, and personal hygiene items are manufactured in Central America, and available at local drugstores and department stores. Common home medications found locally, and many medicines requiring a prescription in the United States, can be purchased over the counter. Generic medications are often sold.

A good supply of locally manufactured household products is available, such as soaps, detergents, floor wax, furniture polish, glass cleaner, insecticides (extreme care should be taken with some of the local products), and laundry supplies, although quality is below U.S. standards.

Locally made pots, pans, kitchen utensils, and dishes can be purchased at moderate prices. Imported varieties also are available for much higher prices.

Laundries and dry cleaners in San José have modern equipment, but only one chain of cleaners offers U.S.-style martinizing service. San José has few self-service laundromats.

Small repair shops in the city service appliances, stereos, and cameras, but the wait is long and the quality of the repairs is poor. Household repair services are unreliable as well. Basic household tools are useful. Prices for tools are higher in San José than in the United States.

Many hairdressers have adequate equipment and competent operators, some of whom speak English. Services tend to be inexpensive. Satisfactory shoe repair is available.

Domestic Help

Many Americans in San Jose prefer to hire a live-in maid, as a convenience and as a deterrent to burglary, which is a major problem. Reliable maids are difficult to find. Some families are employing part-time maids instead of full-time, live-in employees. It is common practice to employ one person to do the cleaning and cooking for a family. For those who do not want a live-in maid, or who cannot find one, a guard or housesitter is necessary whenever the entire family is away from the house.

Some people also employ a day laborer part time to do heavy work in the home, such as waxing floors and washing windows. Local gardeners also can be hired for reasonable prices, and most have their own equipment. Tools are available locally, but are more expensive than in the U.S.

The typical cash wage in 1997 for a live-in maid was around 40,000 colones a month, plus 19.5 percent of their monthly salary that must be paid into the Social Security system on a monthly basis.

Street in San Jose, Costa Rica

© Carl and Ann Purcell/Corbis. Reproduced by permission.

In addition to their salaries, both full-time and part-time domestics are entitled to two weeks paid vacation annually after 50 weeks of service, plus a Christmas bonus based on the number of months worked. Similar bonuses often are given to others, including garbage men, paper boys, and street sweepers. Maids are also entitled to severance pay when they are dismissed.

Full-time and part-time domestic employees are entitled to illness and maternity benefits of the Caja Costarricense de Seguro Social (the Social Security system). They are also covered under a Disability/ Old Age Retirement Plan. This is a compulsory program and in theory is funded through contributions by both the employer and employee. In fact, the employer generally pays the worker's share as well. Total contribution to the plan amounts to between 20 percent and 25 percent of the worker's salary. All domestic employees must be registered with the Caja.

Religious Activities
Catholicism is the state religion, and more than 90 percent of the population is affiliated with the Roman Catholic Church. Several local churches offer English services either Saturday or Sunday. Other denominations represented in San José include Episcopal, Baptist, Jehovah's Witnesses, Lutheran, Methodist, Mormon, and Seventh Day Adventist. San José also has a Jewish Synagogue.

Education
American children in Costa Rica have several educational alternatives, including some private schools that offer college-prep curriculums and operate on a U.S.-style August through June schedule.

During the past year, however, several newly arrived families have encountered problems with the school enrollment process. Missing required documents are the primary problem. These documents included: original school transcripts for the past two years, results of recent standardized achievements tests, passport or birth certificate, vaccination record, two passport size photos, letter of recommendation from the principal or counselor of the previous school. The schools require a personal interview and admission tests. Students will be tested on several academic subjects. The results of these tests often take up to three days to be released. Students will not be accepted until the results are known. Additionally, many arriving families fail to iden-

tify and contact the school they wish to use before arrival. These schools operate on a limited enrollment basis; failure to reserve a space early may preclude admission. Therefore, it is highly recommended that families with school-age children contact the selected school as soon as possible, ideally before May for the following August. This is especially important, if the family will arrive at after school begins.

Special Education
Parents should be aware that the schools have limited resources and/ or programs for students with special needs. In most instances, the buildings lack structures to facilitate the access of those in wheelchairs or with other physical disability requirements.

A few public schools in San Jose have devoted resources to establishing programs for children with educational requirements. These programs are below standards developed by schools in the U.S. and all such instruction is in Spanish. A few specially trained therapists are available, but physical, occupational, and speech therapists are in critically short supply. Parents should correspond directly with local schools for information about their child's special needs. Local school directors also can provide detailed information about curriculums, accreditation, student-to-teacher ratios, facilities, and extracurricular activities.

Private schools operating on a U.S. style schedule with classes in English, include: American International School (former Costa Rica Academy). Pre-kindergarten through 12th grade; 280 students; classes in English. Enrollment fee, $1000 one time payment per student, grades 1 - 12; school maintenance fee, $600 per family for 3 years; annual tuition: pre-kindergarten and kindergarten $2000; for 1/2 day program, $3500; for full day, 1st through 12th grade, $5150; bus fee, $900 annually.

For more information contact Director, Larry Lyons Apartado 4941-

1000 San Jose. Telephone: (506) 239-0376 E-mail: aiscr@cra.ed.cr

Country Day School: Pre-kindergarten through 12th grade; 800 students; classes in English. Enrollment fee, $375 per year; Annual tuition: pre-kindergarten half-day, $1832; kindergarten and prep half day, $2680; kindergarten and prep full day, $3995; grades 1 - 12, $5390; bus fee depends on the location of your residence.

For more information contact: Director, Timothy Carr Apartado 8-6170, San Jose Telephone: (506) 228-1187 or (506) 289-8406.

Marian Baker School: Kindergarten through 12th grade; 210 students; classes in English. Enrollment fee, $450; Annual tuition: kindergarten, $2500 1/2 day program; kindergarten, $3500 full day; prep. - 5th grade, $4500; 6th-12th grades, $5300. Bus fee, $540 per student.

For further information contact: Director, Linda Niehaus Apartado 4269, San Jose Telephone: (506) 273-3426 or (506) 273-3204 E-mail: mbschool@sol.racsa.co.cr

International Christian School: Pre-kindergarten through 12th grade; 530 students; classes in English. Enrollment fee, $190. PK $340 for 1st child enrolled, $220 for other siblings enrolled. Monthly tuition: pre-kindergarten half-day $160; kindergarten and prep half-day, $190; grades 1 - 6, $300; grades 7 - 12, $345.

For more information contact: Director, William Tabor Apartado 3512, San Jose Telephone: 236-7879 or 236-2970.

Each school may have additional fees not listed in the general pricing information provided, i.e., books, uniforms, school lunches, specialty or individual instruction classes, instrument rentals, maintenance and/or technology fees.

Private schools operating on the local February-November schedule,

with classes in English or in English and Spanish, include:

Lincoln School: Pre-kindergarten through grade 12; 750 students; classes in English. One-time family membership, $450; Enrollment fee, $180 per year; Registration fee, $50 per year; Monthly tuition: pre-kindergarten and kindergarten, $105; preparatory - grade 3, $150; grades 4 - 6. $170; grades 7 - 9, $175; grades 10 - 11. $185; grade 12, $245.

For more information contact: Director, John Dellman Apartado 1919-1000, San Jose Telephone: 235-7733.

Escuela Britanica: Kindergarten through grade 12; 800 students; classes half in English, half in Spanish. One time fee pet family, $310. Enrollment fee, $115 - $162 depending on grade level. Monthly tuition: $130 - $225, depending on grade level.

For more information contact: Director, David Lloyd Apartado 8184-1000, San Jose Telephone: 220-0719

Of the above schools, Costa Rica Academy (American International School (AIS) and Country Day School (CDS) are the most similar to American schools, and their familiarity may help ease the transition for some students.

There are several preschools available for children.

El Girasol: Ages 2-6, instruction in Spanish. Monthly fees: $90 with a matriculation fee of approximately $80.

For more information contact: Director, Nora Masis Apartado 6063, San Jose Telephone 232-8496

ABC Montessori: Ages 1-1/2 to 5 years; 60 students, instruction in English and Spanish. Enrollment fee, $95. Monthly tuition: $105; materials, $55; transportation, $28, School calendar: March through

November. Hours: 7:30 a.m. - 12:00 p.m.

For more information contact: Laura Patino, 759-1007 Centro Colon, San Jose Telephone, 232-1805.

Kiwi Kinder: Ages 2-1/2 to 5 years; 32 students; instruction in English. Enrollment fee, $80 per semester. Tuition per semester: 5 days per week, $775; 3 days per week, $525. School calendar: August through mid-June. Hours: pre-school, 8:00 a.m. - 12:00 p.m.; kindergarten, 8:00 a.m. - 3:00 p.m.

For more information contact: Director, Dianne Patterson Apartado 549-6150, Santa Ana Telephone: 282-6512

Special Educational Opportunities

The University of Costa Rica is situated on a modern campus in an eastern suburb of San Jose. The University has a faculty of some 2,500 and a student body of more than 30,000. Majors include history, art, law, education, science, economics, dentistry, medicine, microbiology, social work, agronomy, pharmacy, and engineering. Foreigners may take courses either for credit or on an audit basis. Admission requirements vary according to the courses desired and the individual's educational background. A good command of Spanish is necessary because all courses are taught in Spanish.

The Centro Cultural Costarricense-Norteamericano offers classes in Spanish at all levels, and private tutors of varying degrees of skill can be hired.

Courses in art are taught at the University of Costa Rica's School of Fine Arts, and in music at the National Conservatory. Many private teachers provide instruction in voice, music, painting, ballet, ceramics, swimming and diving, golf, tennis, and horseback riding.

Sports

The Costa Rica Country Club in Escazu is very expensive. It offers excellent facilities, including a heated swimming pool, tennis courts, a nine-hole golf course, saunas and exercise equipment, and a restaurant. The Costa Rica Tennis Club in La Sabana has a swimming pool, steam baths, tennis courts, and a restaurant. The Cariari Country Club, off the airport highway, offers an Olympic-size swimming pool, the country's only 18-hole golf course, tennis courts, exercise equipment, a nightclub, and a restaurant. The Indoor Club in Curridabat on the east side of San José, offers indoor and outdoor tennis courts, racquetball and squash courts, indoor and outdoor swimming pools, and a restaurant. And, the Los Reyes Country Club, located a half-hour drive from downtown San José, offers a nine-hole golf course, tennis courts, a swimming pool, and a restaurant. There are also several health clubs in the area that include: Spa Corobici, Hi-Line Gymnasio, San José Palacio, and Club Olimpico. For children, 6 months to 15 years, Kid's Gym offers classes in gymnastics and modern dance.

Joining the various clubs remains a costly proposition. Membership at the Cariari, for example, costs around $3000 initially, plus another $100 a month. Prices are increased frequently.

Horseback riding lessons are available at several stables, but most, including one of San José's best establishments, La Carana, cater to riders with their own horses. One stable in Guachipelin does offer lessons in dressage and jumping using horses they rent.

La Sabana park has a public swimming pool and many fields for soccer, baseball, softball, and basketball. A paved jogging track also circles the park. Other activities include swimming, golf, and tennis competitions, many of which are open to Americans.

Touring and Outdoor Activities

Costa Rica is a small country, and many interesting areas can be visited in a day trip from San José. They include the Braulio Carillo National Park; Poas, Irazú, Barva, and Arenal volcanoes; Lankester Gardens; beaches on both the Caribbean and Pacific coasts; the Sarchi ox cart factory; white water rafting trips, and a number of rustic restaurants reached after drives through the lush countryside. For those who prefer not to drive, there are scores of tour agencies that provide an abundance of packaged tours to all areas of the country.

After leaving San José the climate becomes either cooler or more tropical depending upon the destination, with altitude being the determining factor. Most day trips out of San José begin on divided highways, but the roads become less maintained outside the city. A few of these short trips include brief stretches on dirt roads.

Twenty-five percent of Costa Rica's land has been devoted to protected national parks and reserves, and visits to the parks can be the highlights of a stay in the country. The well-developed park system includes areas of dry forests, rain forests, and cloud forests, volcanoes, beaches on both coasts, caves, the highest mountain in Central America, nesting sites for several species of endangered sea turtles, and miles of hiking trails. Many of the parks are excellent sites for bird watching.

There are pristine beaches on both coasts, but most of the hotels are being developed along the Pacific. Several of the international hotel chains have accommodations at the more popular beaches. Small hotels, cabinas, and bed and breakfasts can be found at almost any beach. Camping is available at some of the parks and beaches, but campsites with facilities are limited.

Social Activities

Periodic business and social meetings, dinner parties, and many other informal social events provide opportunities for international contacts. Guest lists at such functions often include Americans, Costa Ricans, and nationals of other countries. The foreign segments may include people from the local or international business community, as well as people who have retired to Costa Rica.

The American Legion, Rotary Club, Lions, Masons, and several other fraternal organizations have branches in San José. Americans may join, although the memberships are mainly Costa Ricans.

Some of the many other international clubs that are available to join include: The Costa Rican Women's Club, Newcomers Club of Costa Rica, The Square Dance Club, National Bridge Association, and Women's Reading Group.

When invited to a formal dinner in a Costa Rican home, it is customary to send flowers.

OTHER CITIES

ALAJUELA, located in central Costa Rica 14 miles west of San José, was the capital of the country in the 1830s. With a metropolitan population of about 158,000, Alajuela is a commercial and agricultural center whose industries include sugar, coffee, and lumber. Four churches here are of outstanding architecture. The Juan Santamaria Museum is one of the city's principal tourist attractions. The museum features an exhibit of locally produced handicrafts. One wing of the museum exhibits the history of the Battle of Santa Rosa, where Costa Rican troops defeated filibusters led by William Walker in 1856.

CARTAGO is located on the Pan-American Highway, about 20 miles east of San José at the foot of Mt. Irazú. The city is situated at an elevation of 4,765 feet. Founded in 1563, Cartago was destroyed by the eruption of the Irazú volcano in 1723, and by earthquakes in 1841

Neighborhood in San Jose, Costa Rica

© Steve Kaufman/Corbis. Reproduced by permission.

and 1910. Because of these disasters, no authentic colonial buildings exist in Cartago. However, new buildings are built with colonial styling. Cartago was the political center of Costa Rica until 1821, when a more liberal government was seated in San José. It was in this rich coffee-growing region that the system of small plantations was begun, and many of the early colonial traditions survive. The population is estimated at close to 109,000. Cartago's principal church, the Cathedral of the Virgin of Los Angeles, is the scene of annual pilgrimages. Another attraction is the Church of Otosi, the oldest colonial church still in use in Costa Rica. In addition to regular services, the church houses a small museum of colonial and religious artifacts.

GOLFITO, surrounded by steep hills, is situated in southern Costa Rica off the Gulf of Dulce, about 100 miles south of San José. The heavy rainfall promotes the tropical rainforest vegetation found in this area. Golfito is a major banana port and belongs to the Banana Company of Costa Rica. The city handles about one-fifth of Costa Rica's seaborne trade. The city's population is estimated at 30,000.

HEREDIA, whose population is about 67,000, is located in central Costa Rica. It is the center of the nation's coffee and cattle industries. Founded in 1571, Heredia is a tourist attraction because of its colonial architecture. The lush vegetation of the area has earned Heredia the nickname "La Ciudad de las Flores" (city of the flowers).

LIBERIA, with a population of about 33,000, lies on the Liberia River in northwestern Costa Rica. Located near the Pan-American Highway, it is about 100 miles north of the capital. Liberia is a commercial center for grains, fruits, sugarcane, and livestock.

LIMÓN, on the Caribbean about 100 miles east of San José, is the leading port of the country, and a modern, busy city. It was founded in 1874 during the construction of the railroad to San José. Limón's major crops are coffee and bananas; cacao and timber also are exported from this city, whose population is about 68,000. Nearly 40 percent of the country's exports pass through Limón. Limón is a tourist resort. Several beautiful parks are located near the city. Cahuita National Park, with its lush flora and fauna, contains the only coral reef on Costa Rica's Caribbean coast. Tortuguero National Park is the most important nesting ground for the green sea turtle in the western Caribbean.

The park has an unique system of natural and man-made canals that serve as waterways for transportation and exploration. Columbus is said to have visited this area on his voyage in 1502.

PUNTARENAS is located about 60 miles west of San José on the Gulf of Nicoya. It was a major Pacific port before the building and expansion of Limón. With a population of approximately 92,000, Puntarenas is the center of the country's banana industry; coffee also is exported from here. Other industries include shark and tuna fishing and fish processing. Puntarenas is a picturesque resort.

COUNTRY PROFILE

Geography and Climate

At 19,730 square miles, about four-fifths the size of West Virginia, Costa Rica is, with the exception of El Salvador, the smallest country in Central America. It is bounded on the north and southeast by Nicaragua and Panama, respectively; on the east by the Caribbean Sea; and on the west and south by the Pacific Ocean. Limon, the major Caribbean port, is some 2,400 miles from New York; Puerto Caldera, the principal Pacific port, is located some 2,700 miles from San Francisco.

A rugged central massif runs the length of the country, north to south, separating the coastal plains. Even though Costa Rica lies totally within the tropics, the range of altitudes produces wide climatic variety. The country has four distinct geographic regions:

• The Caribbean Lowlands are hot and humid, and comprise about one-fourth of the total area of Costa Rica. It is the major banana exporting region. The lowlands contain less than 10 percent of the population.

• The Highlands are the economic, political, and cultural heart of the country, and include the Central and Talamanca mountain ranges and the Meseta Central where the capital, San José, is located. The Meseta, with elevations ranging from 3,000 to 4,500 feet, and adjacent areas contain nearly two-thirds of Costa Rica's population. The region has rolling, well-drained land, productive soil, and pleasant sub-tropical temperatures, with an annual rainfall of 60-75 inches. The central highlands have most of Costa Rica's improved roads, and there is direct access to both coasts by paved highway, rail, and air.

• The Guanacaste Plains comprise the rolling section of northwest Costa Rica, and include portions of the provinces of Guanacaste and Puntarenas, plus the Nicoya Peninsula. Despite having the lowest average annual rainfall and the longest dry season, the region is important for agriculture and livestock production as well as a popular area for tourism. The area contains 15 percent of Costa Rica's population.

Southern Costa Rica is the wettest part of Costa Rica with some 10 percent of the population.

Altitude determines the climate throughout Costa Rica. Areas below 3,000 feet have average annual temperatures of around 80 degrees, with little variation from month to month. The temperature drops from around 74 degrees at 3,000 feet to 59 degrees at 5,000 feet. Above 5,000 feet, the average annual temperatures can range as low as 40 degrees to the mid-50s, with occasional frost during the coolest months.

Palms abound in the freshwater and brackish swamps along the Caribbean coast, as do broad belts of mangroves along the Pacific shore and tidal streams and tropical hardwoods in the higher elevations. Logging operations, both legal and illegal, have stripped many previously wooded areas of Costa Rica,

and less than half the land now is forested. The broadleaf forests remaining contain mahogany, Spanish cedar, lignum vitae, balsa, rosewood, ceiba, nispero, zapote, Castilla rubber, brasilwood, and others. Oaks and grasslands once covered the Meseta Central, but the land there now is devoted largely to crops and pastures.

The country has approximately 12 active volcanoes; the last significant eruptions began in 1968. Seismic activity occurs on a regular basis in Costa Rica. The last major earthquake that caused considerable damage along the Atlantic coast was in April, 1991. Many buildings and homes in Costa Rica are built to withstand earth tremors.

Costa Rica long has been a haven for birdwatchers who track the 900-plus species. Animal life also is abundant. Deer, squirrel, opossum, tapir, monkey, porcupine, sloth, many species of reptiles, and several species of large cats can be found in some areas, although their ranges are constantly being reduced as their habitats are destroyed. Sport fishing on both coasts for tuna, swordfish, marlin, tarpon, and shark is popular, and opportunities for freshwater fishing also exist.

Costa Rica's economy traditionally has had an agricultural base, with the chief exports being bananas, coffee, sugar, and beef. Woodworking and leathercraft are the major handicrafts of the country. Tourism, along with the cattle industry, has grown rapidly in recent years, and non-traditional exports, both agricultural and manufactured, have become increasingly important as sources of revenue.

Population

In 1996, the population of Costa Rica was estimated to be 3.3 million. The San Jose metropolitan area, with a population of 1,230,848, accounted for over one-third of the country's people. Other provinces and their populations included Alajuela (607,486), Cart-

ago (381,420), Limon (258,369), Guanacaste (268,172), Heredia (272,711) and Puntarenas (379,002). Costa Ricans are called "Ticos" both by their Central American neighbors and among themselves.

According to the American Chamber of Commerce, more than 35,000 private American citizens, most of them retirees, live in Costa Rica, and approximately one half million tourists from the U.S. visit the country every year. Smaller groups of foreign residents include Canadian, British, French, German, Italian, Chinese, Spanish, and other Latin Americans.

Most Costa Ricans are Caucasians, and the country lacks the large indigenous Indian populations that characterize most other Central American countries. Small groups of Indians and Blacks live in Costa Rica, but together they account for less than 10 percent of the population. Descended from West Indian workers who began emigrating to Costa Rica in the late 19th Century, most Blacks live in the Limon Province on the Caribbean coast. Many speak English as their primary language.

Costa Rica's culture, like its racial composition, is relatively homogeneous. An old-line Spanish-Catholic tradition persists despite many changes brought about by an influx of people, goods, films, and books from other countries. Values of Latin American culture are evident in the great importance attached to family ties; a rather sedate, ritualized, conventional behavior; a yearly schedule of festivals; and an outwardly male-oriented and male-dominated society. Every town has its local patron saint whose day is celebrated with a "fiesta." Carnival in Limon in October, industrial and other fairs throughout the year are particularly interesting.

Public Institutions

Costa Rica is a vibrant democracy whose citizens have a strong sense of civic pride and considerable respect for human rights, peaceful resolution of conflicts and democratic institutions. The national government, which employs a comprehensive system of checks and balances, consists of the executive, legislative, and judicial branches, plus a highly respected Supreme Electoral Tribunal that oversees elections every four years. The 57-member Legislative Assembly has representatives from two major political parties as well as several minority parties. Overall, the president remains the single most influential political leader, but the Legislative Assembly wields considerable power. Since 1969, the Constitution has limited the president and legislative deputies to single terms, although deputies may gain reelection after sitting out one term.

Numerous political parties compete for elective office at the national and municipal levels every four years. The Social Christian Unity Party (PUSC) and the National Liberation Party (PLN) have dominated most recent elections. In February 1998, PUSC candidate Miguel Angel Rodriguez won the presidency by a narrow margin over PLN rival Jose Miguel Corrales. The PUSC also won a plurality in the Legislative Assembly.

Costa Ricans pride themselves on the country's abolition of its standing military in late 1948, a concept enshrined in the 1949 Constitution. Governments give priority to public spending on education and health care. A small civilian Public Force under the Public Security Ministry performs security and police functions. Costa Rica has exercised an international influence well beyond its relatively small size. The Figueres administration (1994 to 1998) hosted several regional conferences including the May 1997 San Jose Summit involving the U.S. President and his counterparts from Central America and the Dominican Republic.

Arts, Science, and Education

The arts are flourishing in Costa Rica. At the beautiful and historic National Theater, the Melico Salazar Theater, and other venues throughout San Jose, there is a steady stream of high-quality representations of the visual and plastic arts from Costa Rica and abroad. The National Symphony Orchestra offers an annual concert series, as does the Costa Rican Youth Symphony. The National Dance Company and university dance groups also perform during the year. Professional theater groups offer works in Spanish throughout the year, and an amateur theater group produces plays in English. Costa Rica hosts three major international festivals: the annual International Music Festival and, in alternate years, the International Festival of the Arts and the International Guitar Festival.

Several institutional and commercial art galleries are located in San Jose. The Museum of Costa Rican Art, located in the terminal of San Jose's original airport, now a large city park, features several exhibits every year by both Costa Rican and foreign artists. The Ministry of Culture, located in a restored liquor factory, houses the Museum of Modern Art and Design, exhibiting the more avant-garde works of local and foreign artists.

San Jose's movie theaters offer American films, with Spanish subtitles, shortly after original release, as well as films from Europe and the rest of Latin America. The San Jose metropolitan area has a variety of world-class museums. The National Museum, occupying a former fortress near the Legislative Assembly, has an excellent collection of pre-Columbian artifacts and a national history collection. The Central Bank's Gold Museum, located beneath the Plaza de la Cultura, near the National Theater, houses a stunning display of pre-Columbian gold artifacts. The Coin Museum is located in the same building. The Jade Museum, located in the National Insurance Institute, features one of the world's foremost collections of pre-Columbian jade pieces. The Children's Museum, established only in 1995, is located in a former penitentiary and offers a permanent display of history, science and technology with hands-on exploration for children. Other museums include the Serpentarium, the Museum of Natural Science, the Juan Santamaria Museum in Alajuela, and the Simon Bolivar Zoo.

Education is a national passion for Costa Rica, as reflected in the vast array of schools and universities throughout the country. The literacy rate, at 95 percent, is the highest in the region. Four state-supported universities and nearly forty private universities offer undergraduate and graduate courses in almost all major fields of study. The Centro Cultural Costarricense-Norteamericano, also known as the Binational Center (BNC), offers regular courses in English and Spanish as second languages, as do a host of commercial language schools. The BNC also houses an excellent lending library, which Mission families may join for a small annual fee, and offers art exhibits and performing arts events featuring American as well as Costa Rican artists.

Commerce and Industry

Costa Rica's economy emerged from recession in 1997 and is poised for relatively healthy growth for the near future. National account statistics from Costa Rica's Central Bank indicated a 1997 gross domestic product (GDP) of 2.2 trillion colones (USD 9.5 billion at the average exchange rate for the year), up 3.2 percent in real terms (measured in constant 1966 colones) from the year before, when GDP declined. Inflation, as measured by the Consumer Price Index, was 11.2 percent less than the 12.5 percent that was forecast The central government deficit decreased to 3.4 percent of GDP in 1998, down from 3.7 percent from the year before but still above the 3.0 percent target. Controlling the budget deficit remains the single biggest challenge for the country'; economic policy makers, as servicing the accumulated public sector debt consume approximately 30 percent of the government's budget and limits the amount of resources available for needed investments in public infrastructure.

Costa Rica's major economic re sources are its fertile land and frequent rainfall, its well educated population, and its location in the Central American isthmus, which provides easy accessibility to North and South American markets and direct ocean access to the European and Asian continents. With one fourth of it land dedicated to national forests, often adjoining picturesque beaches, the country has also become a popular destination for affluent retirees and ecotourists.

The country has not discovered sources of fossil fuels (apart from minuscule coal deposits), but its mountainous terrain and abundant rainfall have permit ted the construction of a dozen hydro-electric power plants, making it self-sufficient in all energy needs, except oil for transportation. Mild climate and trade wind make neither heating nor cooling necessary, particularly in the highland cities and towns where approximately 90% of the population lives.

Costa Rica has an extensive road system of more than 30,000 kilometers, al though much of it is in disrepair. All part; of the country are accessible by road. The main highland cities in the center of the country are connected by paved all-weather roads with the Atlantic and Pacific coast; and by the Pan American Highway with Nicaragua and Panama, the neighboring countries to the North and the South. Cost Rica needs to complete the Pacific coastal highway (and repair large sections of existing highway), build a new road along the Atlantic coast, and possibly construct coast-to-coast highway across the North ern plains of the country. These are probably the most pressing infra-structural need of the country.

Tourism, which has overtaken bananas as Costa Rica's leading foreign exchange earner, is once again growing after stagnating in the mid-1990s. Earning in 1997 from an estimated 812,000 visitors were reported at 750 million U.S. dollars, up from 684 million dollars the year before. The number of visitors in 1996 was 781,000. The numbers also show that tourists spend nearly 1,000 dollars per person per visit. In 1998 the Ministry of Tourism projected a 4-5 percent increase in the number of tourists visiting the country.

Costa Rica is also aggressively pursuing investment in the high technology sector. Largely due to the personal efforts of President Figueres to attract new investment in the sector, Intel Corporation began construction of a plant in 1997 to produce Pentium II microchips with an investment plant that reached 200 million dollars by the end of 1998. Intel's total planned investment was 400-500 million dollars by the end of 1999. A number of other high technology companies were already present in Costa Rica, and more are expected to follow.

Reflecting the evolution away from agriculture, 1997 growth was strong in the construction sector (16.4 percent), in industry (4.5 percent) and in commerce, restaurants and hotels (4.0 percent). Agriculture declined by 0.7 percent. Statistics for 1997 indicated a widening of the trade deficit and an increase of the current account deficit from roughly 1.1 percent of GDP in 1996 to 4.5 percent of GDP in 1997. During 1999, roughly 55 percent of total trade was with the U.S. As usual, bananas led the list of merchandise exports, but tourism earned more foreign exchange. However, despite the current account deficit, strong private capital inflows brought international reserves to over 1 billion dollars, a level approximating three months of imports.

Transportation

Automobiles

The majority of streets and roads in Costa Rica are rough and narrow. Many of the roads to the beaches and other out-of-the-way locations are not paved. A high clearance, rugged suspension vehicle, such as Ford Broncos, Chevrolet Blazers, Toyota Land Cruisers, Isuzu Troopers, Jeeps, Mitsubishi Monteros and Nissan Patrols, is recommended if significant travel away from San Jose is planned. Replacement parts, when available, are expensive.

It is strongly recommended to install anti-theft devices, such as an alarm or the Club as car burglary and theft are serious problems.

Both international and local rental car companies have offices in San Jose, but the cost is substantial and the quality of the rental cars is not always of a high standard. Costa Rica is a dangerous country in which to operate an automobile. Driving in San Jose, and throughout the country, is a challenge. Turns across one or two lanes of traffic are common; and pedestrians generally are not given the right of way. The narrow roads often are blocked by stalled, unmarked vehicles, pedestrians, or livestock. Yawning potholes, honking taxis, and smoke-belching buses with dangerous drivers, make Costa Rican traffic most unpleasant.

Liability insurance is a monopoly of the Costa Rican Government and must be purchased in the country. A comprehensive policy can be obtained in Costa Rica and several U.S. companies sell comprehensive policies for coverage in Costa Rica, although few have local offices or claims adjusters.

Since 1995, all imported vehicles must have catalytic converters.

Local

Within San Jose, taxis are efficient and inexpensive, by U.S. standards, although during rush hours and when it is raining, taxis seem to vanish. Taxis are mandated to have meters; passengers should insist that they be used, or at least determine the fare at the start of the trip.

Buses serve all parts of the city and surrounding suburbs. Service is inexpensive, but crowded, during rush hours, and some vehicles are in deplorable condition.

Regional

Costa Rica's principal cities are connected by air or highway with San Jose. The closest U.S. city is Miami, Florida, a two and a half hour non-stop flight. American carriers, American and United, as well as the national airline, LACSA, offer daily flights to Miami. Continental has a daily flight to Houston, Texas. American Airlines has a daily flight to Dallas, and Delta flies daily to Atlanta.

LACSA and other regional airlines include San Jose as a stop on their Central American schedules. Air travel within Costa Rica is very inexpensive, and many vacation spots can be reached easily by air. Travel to other Central American countries is quite expensive; a round-trip flight to Panama is $300, and Guatemala costs approximately the same. Few discounts are available.

Currently, most international flights land at Juan Santamaria Airport, a 25-minute drive from downtown San Jose. Another international airport, located near Liberia, opened recently.

Several steamship lines offer freight service to both the Pacific and Caribbean coasts of Costa Rica, and Cunard lines makes port calls at both Puerto Caldera and Limon. Both the Pacific and Caribbean ports are connected to San Jose by highway and air.

Communications

Telephone and Telegraph

An automatic telephone system covers all of Costa Rica. Long-distance calls may be placed from one's home, and direct-dial service to the United States and other Central American countries is available. Direct-dial rates to the continental United States range from $0.65 - $1.60 a minute, depending on the time of day, though the peak rate is expected to drop to $1.10 by the middle of 1998.

Radiografica Costarricense handles all international telegraphic messages.

Mail

International air mail service to San Jose is also available. The service is slow but generally reliable. Air mail and Special Delivery from almost any point in the U.S. to Costa Rica usually takes at least a week, and there can be a lengthy delay and considerable expense before a parcel can be collected from Customs.

TV and Radio

Short-wave reception is good in San Jose. The country has more than 80 commercial radio stations, almost half of them FM stations. Several broadcast in stereo, and a few offer regular classical music programming.

Twelve TV stations operate in San Jose, broadcasting in color and offering local news and entertainment programs, plus U.S. programs dubbed in Spanish. Cable television is available in most parts of San Jose, including the areas where most Americans live. Service is available on a monthly or bi-annual subscription basis and English-language programs from the U.S. include ABC, NBC, FOX and CBS networks, ESPN sports programming, several "superstations," two movie channels, and CNN news programs.

Newspapers, Magazines, and Technical Journals

Costa Rica has six daily newspapers in Spanish, plus two weekly commercial publications, the Tico Times and Costa Rica Today, in English. There are also four Spanish news magazines published weekly. Many American books and magazines are available at local book shops and newsstands, but prices are double those in the U.S. Consequently, magazine subscriptions and book club memberships are very popular.

The Centro Cultural Costarricense-Norteamericano, in the Los Yoses suburb of San Jose, maintains current periodicals and U.S. newspapers in its well-stocked library, the Biblioteca Mark Twain.

Health and Medicine

Medical Facilities

Costa Rica is known for the quality of its health care, and many competent surgeons, pediatricians, neurologists, dermatologists, gynecologists, cardiologists, general practitioners, dentists, and opticians work in San Jose. Many have trained in the U.S. or Europe, and some speak excellent English.

A number of local hospitals, clinics, and diagnostic laboratories are adequate for normal medical requirements, such as the Clinica Biblica or Clinica Catolica, both private medical facilities. Many Americans use the Clinica Santa Rita for maternity care.

Costa Rica also has an excellent social security (Seguro Social) hospital system with many hospitals in San Jose and other parts of the country. Costa Rica has the best children's hospital in Central America.

Essential medicines and medical supplies are available at local pharmacies, although prescriptions for some specific medications may be hard to fill.

Community Health

The general level of sanitation and health control in San Jose is below that found in the average U.S. city. Garbage is collected regularly, and San Jose has a central sewer system, but sanitary regulations sometimes are not rigidly enforced. The city's water supply is filtered and chlorinated, but the possibility of contamination is always present.

The altitude of San Jose (3,814 feet), the high humidity, the extremely high pollen concentrations at certain times of the year, and the general air pollution of the city can combine to affect persons with sinusitis, hay fever, or asthma. Colds and other respiratory problems occur with more frequency than in the U.S., because of the air quality, the pervading dampness during the rainy season, and the frequent and dramatic temperature changes from midday to evening.

Serious health hazards are found both in San Jose and in the provincial areas. These problems include common diarrhea, amebic dysentery, and bacillary dysentery. Common causes of intestinal diseases are contamination from flies, polluted water, and contaminated fruits and vegetables. Common sense precautions are necessary when dealing with food, particularly when traveling outside San Jose.

Cases of malaria have been reported in the coastal areas of Costa Rica that have altitudes of less than 2,000 feet at an increasing rate during the last few years. And in some regions of the country certain tropical diseases such as cholera and dengue still present a serious health hazard.

Use boiling as a means of water purification in areas where needed. Electronic water filtering systems are used in many restaurants and hotels. Commercially bottled water is available in San Jose.

Several dairies sell pasteurized milk and dairy products that are safe, but off-brand products should be viewed with suspicion. As in most countries, raw fruits and vegetables should not be eaten unless they have been properly washed, and this applies to produce purchased in local markets and grocery stores.

As of December, 1997, approximately 1,200 cases of AIDS had been diagnosed in Costa Rica, 60 percent of whom have died, and the number of undiagnosed HIV positives was estimated, as of December 1994, to be 15,000 to 20,000. AIDS testing is mandatory for certain groups, including blood donors, foreign applicants for temporary or permanent residence, patients consulting VD clinics or receiving treatment at Social Security hospitals, and prison inmates.

NOTES FOR TRAVELERS

Passage, Customs & Duties

A valid passport is required to enter Costa Rica. At the discretion of Costa Rican authorities, travelers are routinely admitted with a certified copy of their U.S. birth certificate and a valid photo identification. Foreign tourists are generally permitted to stay up to 90 days. Extension of legal stay beyond that time requires application to the Costa Rican Department of Migration. Tourists who have overstayed their 90-day limit without receiving a formal extension can expect to be fined at the airport as they depart the country. Those who have overstayed repeatedly, or have overstayed and wish to depart Costa Rica by land, must pay a fine to migration authorities in San Jose before departure. There is a departure tax for short-term visitors.

Additional information on entry and exit requirements may be obtained from the Consular Section of the Embassy of Costa Rica at 2114 S Street, N.W., Washington, D.C. 20008, telephone (202) 328-6628, or from a Costa Rican consulate in Atlanta, Chicago, Houston, Los Angeles, Miami, New Orleans, New York, Puerto Rico, San Antonio, or San Francisco. The Embassy of Costa Rica also maintains a web site at http://www.costarica-embassy.org/

Americans living in or visiting Costa Rica are encouraged to register at the Consular Section of the U.S. Embassy in San Jose and obtain updated information on travel and security within Costa Rica. The U.S. Embassy maintains a web site at http://usembassy.or.cr. Americans visiting Costa Rica are encouraged to inform the Embassy of their itinerary and contact information via the web site. This can also be accessed through the Department of State's web site at http://www.state.gov. The U.S. Embassy in Costa Rica is located in Pavas, San Jose, telephone (506) 220-3050. The Embassy is open Monday through Friday, and closed on Costa Rican and U.S. holidays. For emergencies arising outside normal business hours, U.S. citizens may call tel. (506) 220-3127 and ask for the duty officer.

Pets

The importation of pets into Costa Rica is controlled by the Ministry of Public Health. Entry permits from the Costa Rican Health Ministry must be obtained before the arrival of the pet in the country. Failure to obtain the necessary permit may result in the pet being refused entry or being detained by health authorities. The pet should arrive with the family and be declared as luggage instead of cargo.

The following documents should be certified by a Costa Rican Consul before the pet's departure for Costa Rica, and must accompany the pet: international health certificate from an accredited veterinarian (this document must be certified by the U.S. Dept. of Agriculture/ APHIS before presentation to the Costa Rican Consul, call 301-436-8590); certificate of vaccinations for rabies, distemper, parvovirus, and leptospirosis (if applicable to the species of pet); and certification that the pet is free from taenia equinococus. Plan ahead to have the vaccines given to your pets, as the rabies vaccine should be given at least 30 days prior to travel.

Costa Rican Government can require a quarantine period. Use proper cage or crate for shipment and bring a supply of pet food. If importing cats, bring a litter box, pooper scooper and cat litter. Cat litter is difficult to find; so, cat owners should bring a supply in their household effects.

American brands of cat and dog food are sold in local markets, at greatly inflated prices. Locally prepared pet food also is available, but the quality is not up to U.S. standards.

Firearms and Ammunition

Firearms are permitted in Costa Rica for persons over the age of 18. Firearm owners are authorized 1000 rounds of ammunition per weapon. Owners are advised to check with the U.S. Customs Service when shipping firearms from the continental U.S.

Currency, Banking, and Weights and Measures

The monetary unit in Costa Rica is the colon (C). Its exchange value with the U.S. dollar varies daily; in December 1999, the exchange rate was C296.00=US$1. Costa Rica has a small black market with the unofficial rates close to the rates obtained at banks. Counterfeit money has also been found on the black market.

Banking and exchange facilities exist in San Jose, but they are painfully slow-even a simple visit to a bank to cash a check can involve a wait of an hour or more. Travelers checks may be purchased at a some local banks.

The Banco Central de Costa Rica (the Central Bank) directs monetary policy and foreign exchange credit facilities, as well as supervising the banking system. Major commercial banks are government institutions; private banking institutions perform some banking functions, but their services are somewhat limited.

The dollar is freely convertible into colones. Major credit cards are widely accepted at hotels, restaurants, large department stores and supermarkets, but it is best to check before making your purchase.

Costa Rica uses the metric system, and officially, weights and measures are in kilograms, meters, and liters. Unofficially, and illegally, it is not uncommon to find American measures or Spanish colonial measures still in use.

Unleaded gasoline costs approximately $1.42 per gallon; leaded gasoline costs approximately $1.28 per gallon, and diesel fuel costs $1.06 per gallon in early 1995.

Disaster Preparedness

Costa Rica is an earthquake-prone country. General information about natural disaster preparedness is available via the Internet from the U.S. Federal Emergency Management Agency (FEMA) at http://www.fema.gov/.

LOCAL HOLIDAYS

Jan. 1	New Year's Day
Mar. 19	St. Joseph's Day
Apr. 11	Juan Santamaria
Mar/Apr.	Holy Thursday*
Mar/Apr.	Good Friday*
Mar/Apr.	Easter*
May 1	Labor Day
May/June	Corpus Christi*
June 29	Sts. Peter & Paul
July 25	Annexation of Guancaste
Aug. 2	Our Lady of the Angels
Aug. 15	Assumption Day (Mother's Day)
Sept.15	Independence Day
Oct. 12	Dia de la Raza/ Columbus Day
Dec. 25	Christmas Day

*variable

RECOMMENDED READING

The following titles are provided as a general indication of the material published on this country:

Barry, Tom. *Costa Rica: A Country Guide*. 3rd. ed., Albuquerque, NM: Inter-Hemisphere Education Resource Center, 1991.

Biesanz, Richard, et. al. *The Costa Ricans*. Prospect Heights, IL: Waveland Press, 1988.

Costa Rica, Guatemala & Belize on 25 Dollars-a-Day, 1991–92. Frommer's Budget Travel Guide Series. New York: Prentice Hall General Reference and Travel, 1991.

Creedman, Theodore S. *Historical Dictionary of Costa Rica*. 2nd ed. Metuchen, NJ: Scarecrow Press, 1991.

Cummins, Ronnie. *Costa Rica*. Milwaukee, WI: G. Stevens Children's Books, 1990.

Cummins, Ronnie, and Valerie Weber. *Children of the World: Costa Rica*. Milwaukee, WI: Gareth Stevens, 1989.

Edelman, Marc, and Joanne Kenen, eds. *The Costa Rica Reader*. New York: Grove Press, 1989.

Haynes, Tricia. *Let's Visit Costa Rica*. Bridgeport, CT: Burke Publishing, 1988.

National Democratic Institute for International Affairs Staff. *Democracies in Regions of Crisis: Botswana, Costa Rica, & Israel*. Washington, DC: Democratic Institute for International Affairs, 1990.

Peduzzi, Kelli. *Oscar Arias: Peacemaker and Leader Among Nations*. Milwaukee, WI: G. Stevens Children's Books, 1991.

Rolbein, Seth. *Nobel Costa Rica*. New York: St. Martin's Press, 1988.

Searby, Ellen. *The Costa Rica Traveler: Getting Around in Costa Rica*. 3rd ed., Occidental, CA: Windham Bay Press, 1991.

Sheck, Ree. *Costa Rica: A Natural Destination*. Sante Fe, NM: J. Muir Publications, 1990.

Wallace, David R. *The Quetzal & the Macaw: The Story of Costa Rica's National Parks*. San Francisco, CA: Sierra Club Books, 1992.

Winson, Anthony. *Coffee & Democracy in Modern Costa Rica*. New York: St. Martin's Press, 1989.

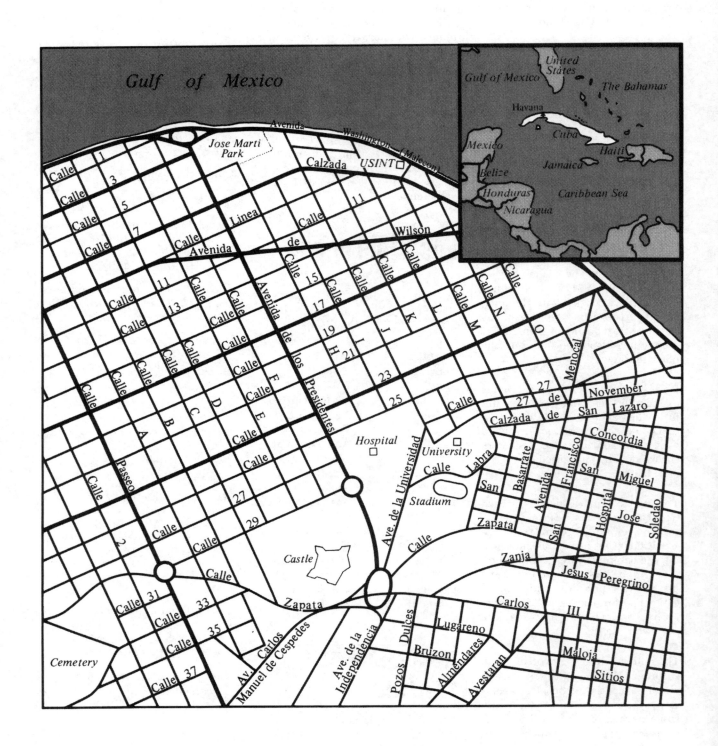

Havana, Cuba

CUBA

Republic of Cuba

Major Cities:

Havana, Santiago de Cuba

Other Cities:

Bayamo, Camagüey, Cárdenas, Ciego de Ávila, Cienfuegos, Guantánamo, Holguín, Matanzas, Santa Clara, Trinidad

INTRODUCTION

The island that is now the Republic of **CUBA** was discovered and claimed for Spain by Christopher Columbus on his first voyage to the New World in 1492. Except for a brief period of British occupation soon after the middle of the 18th century, it remained under Spanish control for nearly 400 years. The Cuban struggle for independence, born out of discontent with a failing economy, broke into open rebellion in 1868, and peaked 30 years later when the United States battleship *Maine* was blown up in Havana Harbor, thus igniting the Spanish-American War. Spain lost the war and relinquished its rights to Cuba in the Treaty of Paris.

Three years of U.S. administration followed before independence was proclaimed on May 20, 1902. Cuba's history since then has been one of dictatorships and revolutions, the most dramatic of which was in 1959 when Fidel Castro overthrew the Fulgencio Batista dictatorship with promises for a return to democratic rule. Lands and businesses were nationalized, and the economy came under the direction of the state. All political activity remains under the authority of Castro's ruling Communist Party.

Although the United States Embassy in Cuba was closed in 1961, there has been a U.S. Interests Section here since September 1977, subject to a bilateral agreement with the Cuban Government, and under the aegis of the Embassy of Switzerland.

MAJOR CITIES

Havana

Havana is a capital rich in history, architecture, and culture. Old Havana, characterized by narrow, cobbled streets, El Morro Castle dominating the harbor entrance, stately buildings, and beautiful wrought-ironwork, evokes its Spanish colonial origin. The United Nations has designated virtually all of that area as a World Heritage Site, in an effort to stave off its demise and destruction.

The Riviera Hotel, Hemingway haunts like La Bodeguita Restaurant (where everyone adds their name to the graffiti-filled walls), the once-dizzy but now more worn Tropicana Nightclub, crumbling yet still beautiful former private residences, the number of mid-century American cars... all combine to reflect Havana's heyday as a 1940s and 50s gambling and vacation hotspot.

In the years following the Revolution, much of the government's energy and revenue went into rural improvements in the country's infrastructure. Schools, roads, electricity, and health clinics helped widen Cuba's pro-revolutionary advances in terms of Latin American literacy and health indices. Since the demise of communism in Eastern Europe and the former Soviet Union, economic support and subsidies have collapsed, compelling far fewer expenditures in those areas in the 1990s, and laying clear the inefficiencies and poor management resulting from a generous subsidy.

Clothing

Standards of dress in Cuba for most occasions are informal. Summer weight clothing is appropriate year-round. Women find dresses or skirts a good choice. Men wear guayaberas or short-sleeved shirts. Light jackets or sweaters are useful during the winter months (November-February) and in the office building.

Clothing is available in some diplotiendas, but the variety is limited and generally quite expensive. You can have some clothing items made locally, and seamstress work is quite good.

Children's clothes are not available in any abundance or reasonable price range.

Supplies and Services

Dry-cleaning and shoe repair services are virtually nonexistent. The casual and tropical climate encourages more wash-and-wear clothing. Beauty parlors and barber shops offer acceptable services at an inexpensive price.

Religious Activities

From its Spanish legacy, Cuba developed an adherence to Roman Catholicism. From its African slave trade, Cuba absorbed tribal rituals and beliefs of ancestral gods. That vibrant mix, known today as Santeria, remains a widely-believed and practiced religion. Of course, more traditional services are conducted, virtually all in Spanish. More churches appear open to worship than in previous years, as the Cuban Government alternately tightens and loosens its control over the faithful. A few Protestant churches and Havana's diminishing Jewish community offer services, too.

Education

There are three international schools in Havana. L'école Francaise provides instruction in French for nursery school (age 2 and-a-half) through the fifth grade. Secondary courses (grades 6 through 8) are provided via correspondence courses graded in

© John Spaull/Corbis. Reproduced by permission.

Aerial view of Havana, Cuba

France. The Centro Educativo Espanol offers Spanish-language programs for children starting at age 2. Secondary courses are graded via testing reports from Spain. The International School of Havana (ISH) offers instruction in English from preschool through the high school level.

USINT children historically have attended ISH. The school is headed by an English-speaking principal (currently a citizen of the U.K.). All the teachers are Cubans and employees of Cubalse. Few have any formal training as educators. The Office of Overseas Schools (A/OS) rates the school as adequate through grade 6, yet parents of several children in the upper elementary grades (4-6) have been dissatisfied with the school's program. Still, with a new principal (1993) ISH is trying to move beyond past problems.

The few secondary educational courses offered operate under a University of Nebraska correspondence program or Mercer College (a British program. The International School currently follows a curriculum loosely based on the Fairfax County standard. All primary school textbooks are from the U.S.

Special Educational Opportunities

The International School of Havana is in the process of expanding its Adult Education Program (now limited to English as a Second Language), and has offered workshops on stress reduction and a Cuban Cinema Seminar. Casa de las Americas, an institute which studies the American continent, offers special seminars in literature. All instruction is in Spanish. There are no special facilities for those with physical, developmental, or learning handicaps.

Sports

Tennis, golf, horseback riding, swimming, snorkeling, scuba diving, wind surfing, water skiing, and fishing are year-round sports in Cuba Tennis courts can be rented or booked at several hotels.

Cuba has wonderful, unspoiled beaches, particularly at Varadero, two hours' east of Havana. That beautiful stretch of white sand beach ranks as one of the Caribbean's finest. Excellent beaches lie within 15 miles from Havana, while Herradura, the nearest coral reef for snorkeling or diving, is only an hour's drive west.

Cuba's coastal waters and coral reefs attract many fishermen and divers. You can charter deep-sea fishing boats at Marina Hemingway. Freshwater bass fishing is good at Hannabanilla, (called Treasure Lake on old maps of Cuba), a 5-hour drive into the mountains southeast of Havana. Scuba diving requires certification, which you preferably should have before arriving, along with your own equipment. Tanks can be recharged without problem.

The Havana Golf Club offers a nine-hole course, tennis courts, a squash court, bowling alley, pool and restaurant for a monthly fee. The Club Hipico Iberoamericano offers both Western and English-style horseback riding lessons and outings into Lenin Park. Some Americans enjoy bowling at the 24-lane alley built for the 1991 Pan-American Games, still in very good condition, and there is an outdoor roller-skating rink for rollerbladers of any age. Biking also remains a popular activity.

Touring and Outdoor Activities

Cuba's economic disintegration, reflected by its difficulty in sustaining consistent oil deliveries, has limited touring into the far reaches of the island. Gasoline may not always be available, and the quality of much of it is suspect. Still, one-day and one-tank drives afford an opportunity to enjoy a change of scenery from the city.

Beginning in 1994, however, the Foreign Ministry requires that all trips outside of Havana Province be reported to it in advance of the trip. There is no need to wait for authorization; only to inform MINREX of travel plans beyond the province borders.

Heading west from Havana into Pinar del Rio province, two areas attract interest. The waterfall and nearby orchid gardens at Soroa are just an hour's drive west of Havana. Running adjacent to the ridge of mountains known as Cordillera de los Organos, the highway to Soroa passes through large tracts of sugarcane and cattle-grazing pasture land.

Another hour brings you to Valle de Vinales, where the combination of soil and climate produce the best tobacco for Cuban cigars. These western mountains also offer rather dramatic contrasts to the agricultural lowlands, attractive vistas and cave exploration. Two hours east of Havana, in the province of Matanzas, visitors to Las Cuevas de Bellamar are guided through a small part of the extensive underground caverns.

Other more distant places of interest include Guama (a commercial crocodile farm), the cities of Trinidad and Cienfuegos (Spanish colonial architecture), and Santiago de Cuba (Cuba's second-largest and most important city, which sits close to Spanish-American War sites). Playa Giron, better known outside Cuba as the Bay of Pigs, is a three-hour drive southeast and worth an occasional weekend for snorkeling. Cayo Largo and Cayo Coco, island resorts being developed for Cuba's tourism industry, can be reached via small aircraft. All overnight travel outside of Havana should be arranged in advance in order to ensure accommodations, which can range from rustic to comfortable.

Entertainment

Frequent power outages may contribute to fewer performances of cultural events, but they have not diminished Cubans' interest in the arts. The National Ballet continues to stage various productions at the famous and still-lovely Garcia Lorca Theater. Jazz remains quite popular, and a yearly festival features local and international artists. Cuba has annually sponsored the Latin-American Film Festival—a Cuban film won Best Picture and critical acclaim in 1994—and a number of theaters show Spanish and American films.

Museums and art galleries provide occasional hours of enjoyable relief. The Museum of Colonial Art, Hemingway Museum, Museum of the Revolution, Museum of the City, and the Museum of Natural Science are worth visiting. Museo Historico in the nearby town of Guanabacoa displays extensive information on Santeria and other Afro-Cuban religions deriving from ancestral and spiritual worship.

Walking through parts of Old Havana is pleasurable. The beautiful and graceful Spanish Colonial architecture of the Havana Cathedral, its cobble-stoned plaza and adjacent buildings, evokes the grandeur of colonial Cuba. Stain glass windows, richly-detailed stucco and moldings, elegant doorways and window treatments, complement the historic if faded ambience of this U.N.-designated World Heritage site. Some caution is required, however, as purse snatchings have increased in recent years.

For nightlife, some hotels offer cabaret shows and discos, and of course, the famous Tropicana Nightclub continues its half-century plus reputation for dinner, drinks, and a dizzying floor show. Cuba's strong push

Street in Santiago de Cuba, Cuba

© Daniel Laine/Corbis. Reproduced by permission.

to promote its tourism facilities and industry likely will result in more nightclubs, restaurants, and evening entertainment opening in the future.

Santiago de Cuba

Santiago de Cuba, a port on the southern coast of the island, is the capital of Oriente Province. With a population of over 405,350 (2000 est.), it is the nation's second largest city. It was founded in 1514, and was the capital of Cuba until 1589. Santiago, its more commonly used name, was once a center for brisk smuggling trade with the British West Indies, but is probably better known as the scene of military activity during the Spanish-American War. U.S. ships established a blockade here in the harbor and, on July 3, 1898, in the final major battle of the war, destroyed the Spanish fleet led by Pascual Cervera y Topete. There also was heavy land fighting near the city when San Juan Hill was taken two days before the successful blockade.

The Spanish-American battles were not to be the final military struggles at Santiago—the city was once again the scene of heavy fighting in July 1953, when Fidel Castro (Ruz) led his first armed revolt against the government in power.

Santiago has many famous landmarks, among them the old cathedral in the city and the crumbling forts on towering cliffs above the harbor. Interesting old colonial buildings add to the charm of Santiago. Two major libraries, one central and one provincial, are maintained here, as is the 30-year-old Universidad de Oriente, which has facilities in several disciplines and a student body now numbering 12,000.

Wood, minerals, and agricultural products are Santiago's major exports. Iron, copper, and manganese are mined in the area. A new textile factory was opened here in 1984.

OTHER CITIES

Founded in 1513, **BAYAMO** is in eastern Cuba, 60 miles northwest of Santiago, on Cuba's longest river, Río Bayamo. The city is commercially active, manufacturing sugar, coffee, tobacco, and rice. There is a major condensed milk plant here. Copper and manganese are mixed in the area. The city is a patriotic favorite of Cubans. The Ten Years' War, 1868-1878, and the revolt of 1895 began in Bayamo. The population is about 141,000 (1995 est.).

CAMAGÜEY, with a population of almost 283,000 (2000 est.), is located in east-central Cuba. It is connected with Santiago and Havana by the Central Highway. Founded in 1515, the city prospered illegally by trading with the English and Dutch colonies in the Caribbean. Camagüey resisted Cuba's independence and several battles were fought nearby. The city maintains vestiges of its colonial architecture. Older parts of the city exhibit narrow, irregular streets and small plazas. Industries here include sawmilling, tanning, and dairying. The city is near major highways and railways, and has an international airport.

The port city of **CÁRDENAS,** on Cuba's north coast, is known as an important fishing port. The city's industries include rum distilleries, and sugar refineries. Cárdenas is 75 miles east of Havana and about 15 miles southwest of a fashionable spa, featuring white sulfur springs, in San Miguel de los Baños. A popular beach at Varadero is also nearby. Cárdenas has a population over 66,000.

CIEGO DE ÁVILA is in central Cuba, about 65 miles northwest of Camagüey. Situated in a fertile region, the city produces sugarcane, cattle, and tropical fruit. The population here is over 80,000.

The sugar port, **CIENFUEGOS,** is located about 140 miles southeast of Havana, on the south-central coast. Areas surrounding the city produce cattle, tobacco, coffee, rice, and sugarcane. Cienfuegos is home to several industries, among them are distilleries, coffee- and tobacco-processing plants. From May through November, the weather in Cienfuegos is hot and humid; winter temperatures are milder, with warm days and cool nights. The city is lovely—it boasts wide streets, numerous parks and promenades, a fine plaza, and interesting architecture. Visited by Columbus in 1494, Cienfuegos' port began operation in the early 1800s. Cienfuegos, site of Cuba's largest cement works, has a population of approximately 195,000.

GUANTÁNAMO, a city of 200,400 residents (2000 est.), is a major sugar-producing center in southeastern Cuba. Its history dates to the early 19th century when French colonists, fleeing the slave uprising in Haiti, established a settlement here. The area is probably best known to Americans because of the U.S. Navy base which has been in operation since 1903 at nearby Guantánamo Bay. The city's port is at Caimanera, on the west side of the bay. The city's chief industrial activities are sugar milling, coffee roasting, and the processing of chocolate, salt, and liqueurs. Guantánamo is accessible by railroad and highway.

HOLGUÍN, which lies in the fertile hill country of northeastern Cuba 70 miles north of Santiago, has twice been a rallying spot for insurgents—the first time during the Ten Years War (1868-78), and again in the period preceding the outbreak of the Spanish-American War (1898). Holguín was founded in 1720. It is one of the country's major commercial centers, and products grown in the region (sugar, coffee, tobacco) are shipped from its port, Gibara. The city, whose population was 243,000 in 2000, supports a university extension institute, with schools of engineering and economics.

MATANZAS, situated in western Cuba, on the road between Havana and beautiful Varadero, is known for its fine, deep-water harbor. The lush Yumurí valley in which it lies, and the fascinating caves in the area, have become tourist attractions. Known as the "Athens of Cuba," Matanzas has a public library, active cultural institutions, and numerous scholars and artists. The city offers beautiful monuments, plazas, and scenic drives. Among Matanzas' industries are sugar refineries, textile plants, fertilizer, and shoe factories. The city, founded in 1693, has a current population of about 123,000. A municipal museum is established here.

Calle Barcelona & Capitolio in Havana, Cuba

The 300-year-old city of **SANTA CLARA,** in the west-central part of the country, made its mark in recent history as the scene of a decisive battle in 1959, when Castro's guerilla forces overthrew the Batista government. This attractive city, nestled among the hills of Villa Clara Province, is the site of the Universidad de Las Villas, one of Cuba's three major institutes of higher learning; the school was founded in 1948, and currently has a student body of 8,500. Sugar and tobacco are the principal products of the area. The city is situated near the geographic center of the island and is a major junction for Cuba's railroads. Santa Clara has a population of 194,350.

Founded in 1514, and once Cuba's wealthiest city, **TRINIDAD** is situated in central Cuba, about 75 miles southwest of Havana. In order to maintain its colonial atmosphere and to celebrate famous former residents—including Spanish explorer Hernán Cortés—Trinidad has been declared a national monument. The city has numerous and varied industries, including sugar refineries, dairies, sawmills, and cigar and cigarette factories. Tourists enjoy its cool climate and mountainous landscape. Gold, amianthus, and copper deposits are found nearby. Trinidad has an airport railway that links with Cienfuegos, and good highways.

COUNTRY PROFILE

Geography and Climate

With more than 44,000 square miles (114,447 sq. km.) of land and 2,500 miles (4,000 km.) of coastline, Cuba rightfully lays claim to being the largest island in the West Indies, accounting for more than one-half of the total land area. The island stretches more than 745 miles (1200 km.) in latitude, yet only ranges from 20 to 125 miles (35-200 km) in longitude, lying about 90 miles (145 km.) south of Key West, Florida.

No larger than the state of Pennsylvania but contoured much differently, Cuba's coastline constantly breaks into literally hundreds of bays, inlets, and narrow, shallow rivers. The Isle of Youth (known as the Isle of Pines in pre-Revolution days), and some 1,600 keys and islets lie offshore. The deep-water harbors of Havana, Guantanamo, and Bahia Honda rank among the world's finest.

Topographically, three-fifths of Cuba displays flat or gently rolling fields and wide, fertile valleys - ideal for the sugarcane and tobacco crops which are the backbone and most recognizable symbols of the Cuban economy. The northern coast is low and marshy. Most of what remains, particularly at the southeastern end of the island, forms steep and at times formidable mountains. Three mountain ranges dominate the Cuban terrain, but by far the best-known and most rugged is the eastern Sierra Maestra, where peaks rise to almost 6,000 feet (1,829 m.) above sea level. Fidel Castro began his struggle there in the 1950s, and still today in speeches alludes to its historical significance in the Revolution.

Cuba is bordered on the north by the Gulf of Mexico and the Straits of Florida and on the south by the Caribbean Ocean. Prevailing trade winds combine with the warm waters of the Gulf Stream to produce a mild and semitropical climate. Cuba's mean temperature is about 77°F (25°C) in winter and only slightly more, perhaps 80°F to 85°F (26°C), in summer. Averages range only between 70°F (21°C) and 82°F (27°C) for the coldest and warmest months. Summer readings of as high as 100°F (37°C) have been recorded. Occasional near-freezing temperatures occur only in mountain areas.

Relative humidity varies from 60 to 70% in the daytime and from 80 to 90% during the night, regardless of the season, of which there are only two. The dry season lasts from November to April. During the May through October rainy season, Cuba receives up to 75% of its yearly rainfall, which averages 54 inches (137 cm.).

Population

Cuba's population is over 11 million, with an annual growth rate of 1.1% and a density of 200 persons per square mile. Most of the population is of Spanish and African origin. Spanish, the official language, has particularly Cuban traits in its spoken form.

About 70% of the population is urban. Havana, the capital, is Cuba's principal port and city, and has a population of 2.3 million. Other major cities include Santiago de Cuba, Camaguey, Santa Clara, Holguin, Matanzas, Cienfuegos, and Pinar del Rio.

Before 1959, Roman Catholicism was observed by about 85% of the population. The 1976 Cuban Constitution nominally protects freedom of religion. In practice, however, church attendance has only begun to grow in recent years, following years of official persecution of religious institutions. Various religions are sometimes permitted to publish literature for use within their churches. Religious public demonstrations or radio/television programming are not permitted.

Public Institutions

Under that same 1976 Constitution, Cuba is organized with a party-government-state structure. The Communist Party, described in the Constitution as "the highest force of the society and state," is headed by a Politburo. The Communist Party, Cuba's only legal political party, is the focus of power in the state.

Executive power within the government is vested in the Council of Ministers, which heads the government. Legislative power allegedly rests with the National Assembly of People's Power, which elects the Council of State, but in fact is a rubber-stamp body with no independent power. All courts, including the People's Supreme Court, are subordinated to the National Assembly of People's Power (and thus to the Council of State).

Administratively, Cuba is divided into 14 Provinces plus the Isle of Youth.

Arts, Science, and Education

Except for their enormous state of flux, few agree today on how to characterize the status of the arts and education in Cuba. One of the leitmotif's of the prize winning film, "Fresas y Chocolate", is derision of the low quality of popular education in Cuba. On the other hand, a long-time American admirer of the revolution, Carol Brightman, has written that:

> The so-called achievements of the revolution—lifelong health care, free and universal education, generous social security payments, free housing—have materially raised the standard of living of the vast majority of the population to levels undreamed of before 1959. (*The Nation*, v. 258,9: p. 299)

The strategy for long term economic recovery, emphasizing biotechnology, tourism development, and related fields such as medicine and

English teaching, and the stringencies of special period cutbacks, i.e., the reduction of Cuban book publishing from about 20 million volumes to 250,000, are forcing momentous changes, though few are discussed very openly. The enormous subsidies paid through the Ministry of Culture that kept tens of thousands of Cuban artists and intellectuals on the state's payroll have been reduced dramatically since members of the Union of Artists and Intellectuals (UNEAC) and the Union of Journalists (UPEC) were first allowed to work independently in 1992 and retain some or all of their hard currency earnings in 1993.

The Ministry remains the central authority for most museums and galleries, ballet and theater companies, musical groups, publishing houses, and the motion picture industry, but the ministry's personnel and activities have been cut back so far that it runs very little any more. Independent entities, such as the Pablo Milanes Foundation, have arisen as cultural impresarios and musical groups are increasingly arranging their own contracts with record companies and tourist hotels where they can be paid in dollars.

Museums now often depend on the revenue they can generate from tourists and international donors. Artisans sell their wares through co-ops and tourist stalls. The only Cuban films made in recent years have been foreign co-productions. The Ministry also retains responsibility for the "culturalization" of the people, but the legendary popular concerts and live performances of yesteryear are now generally restricted to TV appearances during rare home visits by big name performers.

The legendary cultural exports of the revolution, ranging from Alicia Alonso's ballet to a panorama of revolutionary films and Milanes' ballads, have decreased to a trickle. The 1993 Latin American Film Festival almost recouped some of the past glory by attracting a large number of films from other countries, but "Fresas y Chocolate" was the only Cuban film exhibited. The Cuban Institute of Cinematographic Art and Industry (INCAIC) and the film institute that Colombian novelist Gabriel Garcia Marquez helped found in 1986 continue to promote "Latin American film consciousness," just with much less Cuban content.

There are lots of cinemas, theaters and concert halls in Havana and spread around Cuba, but performances as advertised are much less reliable than in the past. Concertgoers are rarely surprised to hear a number not on the program, and having tickets for a performance of a particular opera or ballet does not insure that the performance will occur as scheduled. The Cuban National Ballet, founded by the "primissima" ballerina, Alicia Alonso, performs periodically, but performances are limited between foreign tours. Camaguey's dance company now rivals that of Havana, but it, too, is mostly on the road outside Cuba. Notable visiting artists from around the world occasionally visit Cuba, but in recent years they have come more to show solidarity than to perform.

Education is a pillar of the revolution, and teachers, after medical cadres and the military, have been among its most faithful. The independent employment allowed to artists and intellectuals remains unavailable to teachers. The regime maintains its claim of 96% literacy despite some evidence of functional illiteracy and criticisms of the educational system. Control of reading material has loosened greatly in recent years as the means to acquire it have diminished. In 1992-94 several Cuban universities and the National Library started accepting materials from the USIS book program. The pace of requests for more publications has now far outstripped the capacity to supply them. USIS also has distributed post-produced publications and donated newspapers and magazines, especially to support English teaching programs.

Cuban self criticisms of the waste, mismanagement, and inefficiency of their economy has rarely been applied to the educational system. The revolution succeeded in widespread school construction, especially in provincial areas, and in establishing a large-scale system of technical and normal education and the expansion of the country's public universities.

However, the well-endowed schools of the past are now all-but-forgotten when each new school year opens with a drive to raise funds to buy pencils and paper. During the prolonged blackouts of the special period, most schools lack electricity and all that goes with it, and water supplies and sanitary conditions are unreliable.

Despite all these problems, classes go on at all levels of the system amid the reductions, especially at the higher levels. Cuba's six universities and other centers of higher education appear to be losing enrollment, and concerns about the furloughing of faculty and other changes of status are mounting.

The big challenge for the universities in Pinar del Rio, Havana, Matanzas, Villa Clara, Camaguey and Santiago, as well as in the twenty or so other institutes of higher education is the lack of access to dollars. In 1993 these institutions were allowed to develop self-financing programs for the first time. Despite seemingly endless numbers of special courses, seminars and conferences for foreign students and academics, earnings appear limited.

Beside the lack of funds, many Cuban scholars trained in the former Soviet bloc now are without means of maintaining their scientific and professional development with respect to any international standard. In some faculties large-scale English programs have been started to retool the language capacities of the staff, and professional contact with visiting American scholars is eagerly sought out where it was once avoided. Professors are encouraged to participate in internationally-funded programs and to accept teaching opportunities in other countries that may generate some funds.

Academic and cultural contact with the United States is growing rapidly, largely at the initiative of U.S. institutions, but Cuban counterparts are quick to go along and often to take control of programs. From a low point during the mid-1980s when only a handful of academics traveled each year, today there are scores of U.S. visitors each month at the University of Havana, and several hundred Cubans visit the U.S. each year. The provincial educational centers are far less involved, especially in allowing faculty to travel, but U.S. institutions are beginning to focus their attention beyond Havana.

Commerce and Industry

Since the late 18th century, the Cuban economy has been dominated by sugar production and has prospered or suffered due to fluctuations in sugar prices. Sugar still accounts for about three-quarters of export earnings. Cuba has never diversified from its basic monocultural economy despite some development of tourism, nickel mining, pharmaceuticals, and biotechnology.

For almost 30 years, the defects in Cuba's economy and the effects of the economic embargo imposed by the U.S. in 1962 were partially offset by heavy subsidies from the former Soviet Union. But those supports ended with the collapse of COMECON in the late 1980s and with the demise of the Soviet Union in 1991. Cuba's break with its former patron and failure to undertake needed reforms combined to produce an unprecedented economic crisis. Its economy is estimated to have declined 40% from 1989 through 1992.

The economic prospects are not good, largely because of the Castro regime's decision to maintain the state's highly-centralized control over economic decision-making, the lack of energy supplies, and inputs for industry. The "Special Period in Peacetime" relies upon strict rationing of food, fuel, and electricity, and gives priority to domestic food production, development of tourism, and biotechnology production.

Basic public services are provided by the state, either free of charge or for minimal fees. Access to education through high school is still generally available, but urban housing and medical care have deteriorated, as have communications and transportation.

The state owns and operates most of Cuba's farms and all industrial enterprises. State farms occupy about 70% of farmland, while peasant cooperatives account for about 20%. Private farms account for about 10% of Cuba's agriculture. Cuba's manufacturing sector emphasizes import substitution and provision of basic industrial materials. In recent years, many Cuban firms have closed or reduced production because of shortages of foreign exchange and limited access to spare parts and imported components.

The U.S. has a comprehensive trade embargo on Cuba. The Cuban Democracy Act, signed into law in October 1992, revoked Treasury authority to issue licenses for most U.S. subsidiary trade with Cuba and bans for 180 days vessels which have entered a Cuban port from loading or unloading in U.S. ports. The legislation provides support for the Cuban people by permitting licensing for "efficient and adequate" telecommunications and for humanitarian donations to non-governmental organizations in Cuba.

With the loss of trade and aid from the former Soviet Union and Eastern Europe, Cuba has attempted to attract foreign investment and Western buyers for its nickel, petroleum, biotechnology, and other sectors. Except in tourism, minerals and mining, Cuba has had limited success in that effort because of the deterioration of the economy, its unpaid debt to Western countries, and the lack of clear title to expropriated property.

In 1993, the Cuban Government introduced measures to help revive the economy, including allowing more exiles from the U.S. to visit Cuba, expanding the permission for self-employment, and decriminalizing hard currency possession. In addition, Cuba also established the Basic Units of Collective Production (UBPCs), which allow greater control over the farms' administration and division of any profits with the farms' workers. However, concerned by the specter of a renascent capitalism and the possibility of corruption, the government already has limited the scope of such measures as self-employment.

Transportation
Local
Travel within and between Cuban cities is complicated by a dearth of reliable road maps, and signs or markers which are infrequently posted and poorly visible. Cuba's economic disintegration, after years of Soviet and Eastern Bloc support, has clearly manifested itself in gasoline shortages. Vehicle traffic in Havana is light, relative to past years when traffic jams and heavy pollution ringed the city. Yet if the volume of vehicular traffic is down, heavy bicycle traffic compensates, posing the latest and constant road hazard.

Driving is hazardous also due to potholes, obscure traffic signals, and parked or stalled cars in lanes of traffic. Dwindling revenue and central planning have contributed to the diversion of resources away from road repair and other infrastructural improvements. Power outages make signal intersections dangerous and leave many other streets in total darkness.

Rainy season flooding forces traffic off some streets, and it is not uncommon to encounter stalled cars and buses on the road even under good driving conditions. Vehicle inspection regulations are sporadically enforced at best. Spare parts, supplies, motor oil, etc. for privately-owned vehicles are seldom available, making maintenance and safety problematical. Indeed, the only thing keeping so many cars, including many vintage American models, running along Havana's boulevards is creativity and ingenuity.

Cuba's promotion of tourism has resulted in far more taxis plying the streets, although generally you can flag one only in front of tourist hotels and other hard currency locations. It is difficult to hail one on the street, but you can call for one. Bus transportation is erratic, unreliable, overcrowded, and not recommended.

Regional

Increasingly, even within Cuba's major cities, the road system reflects poor and infrequent maintenance. Secondary roads and more rural highways suffer from severe neglect, with little or no grass-cutting, no fencing to keep animals from wandering into traffic, few signs or other distance and safety markers, and crumbling pavement. Gasoline stations which are open, have fuel, and accept dollars are almost nonexistent in many outlying areas. The quality of refined petroleum in Cuba is questionable, and bad fuel has damaged or destroyed more than one fuel injector system. At $3.50 a gallon, the availability and price of gasoline confine most Americans to Havana or trips which can be achieved with one tankful.

Cubana de Aviacion serves Cuba's major cities but has limited international routes, which Americans are prohibited from using anyway. For domestic routes Cubana is the only airline from which to choose. There are a number of other international airlines and flights. Overnight train service, with a special car for dollar customers, transits Cuba from Havana to Santiago regularly.

Communications

Telephone and Telegraph

International telephone service is fair to acceptable, but frequently poor for local calls. Calls from Cuba to the States are subject to disconnection or dropped lines. It is virtually impossible to call Cuba from the States, and is getting more difficult.

Telephone rates vary based on the location called. Calls to the U.S. cost about $2.50 per minute, regardless of the time, distance or day of week. Calls to all other overseas destinations cost much more. Cellular telephone technology exists in Cuba, but rates are higher still. The quality of phone service discourages use of fax machines. Indeed, the quality of office and residential telephone service is questionable, as bills periodically reflect hundreds of dollars in calls never made. Radio and TV

For a large part of the population, radio and TV provide access to entertainment and information. Radio stations throughout the country offer programming varying from news and public affairs to sports, music, and soap operas. Western music is very popular in Cuba, and classical music programs are broadcast most of the day. Of course, some stations air programs with a more political orientation. Close proximity to the U.S. and favorable weather conditions permit some Florida radio signals to penetrate Cuban airwaves. Major shortwave radio signals from the VOA, BBC, and Armed Forces radio also can be picked up. USIA's Radio Marti' is easily received, but TV Marti' is actively jammed by Cuba.

The Cuban government maintains two TV stations which broadcast a variety of news, sports, political events and speeches, musical variety shows, soap operas, dramatic productions, cartoons and feature films from the U.S., Europe, Japan and the former Soviet Union, all but a few in Spanish. In recent years there has been a proliferation of privately-owned satellite dishes.

Health and Medicine

Medical Facilities

The quality of medical and dental care available in Havana has deteriorated. Hospitals designated to care for tourists and diplomats with relatively modern, imported equipment appear suitable for routine outpatient cases; but, pharmaceuticals are in short supply. A hospital's ability to provide a required medication on demand is open to question. A full range of medical specialists is available but secondary and follow-up care is not up to U.S. standards. Patients requiring evaluation or treatment of more complex cases are evacuated to Miami.

Community Health

Community public health and sanitation programs are collapsing. Mosquito bites and insect-borne diseases are common in Cuba. Garbage collection and disposal equipment is limited. Pick-up schedules are random and haphazard. Air pollution is common during sugarcane harvesting months (December through June). Trash burning in some residential neighborhoods adds to the problem.

Rain produces sewage backups jeopardizing public water supplies. While city water is adequately treated as it enters the municipal water system, tap water is not considered safe for internal consumption due to the deteriorated water distribution system. Sanitation during food preparation may be adequate, yet standards of cleanliness in food processing factories, markets and restaurants are marginal.

Upper respiratory and sinus problems are common in the Cuban climate. There are frequent flu outbreaks in the Fall and Winter (September through March) USINT personnel have experienced various minor ailments such as diarrhea, intestinal parasites, fungal infections, and conjunctivitis. With the breakdown of preventive public health programs and with periodic torrential rains and flooding, serious illnesses such as hepatitis, dengue fever, typhoid are a threat. The last major typhoid outbreak occurred in 1977. The last dengue fever epidemic was in 1981.

In 1993, an outbreak of optical neuritis affected about 50,000 Cubans, some seriously. Apparently in part the result of vitamin deficiencies, the outbreak subsided later in the year. No U.S. citizens were affected.

Preventive Measures

Boil all water. Raw fruits and vegetables should be scrubbed, soaked in a chlorine solution and rinsed in drinking water.

There is a shortage of medication in Cuba. U.S.-brand drugs are not available. You should bring a generous supply of mosquito repellent, sunscreen lotion, first-aid items, prescription drugs, and a full range of medicine cabinet drugs. If you wear eyeglasses or contact lens, bring a second pair.

There are no mandatory immunizations. Typhoid, influenza, hepatitis B, gamma globuli, and, for travel to Central America, yellow fever shots are recommended. Cuban authorities do not require any particular inoculations for persons coming from the U.S.

NOTES FOR TRAVELERS

Passage, Customs & Duties

The Cuban Assets Control Regulations of the U.S. Treasury Department require that persons subject to U.S. jurisdiction be licensed to engage in any transaction related to travel to, from and within Cuba. Transactions related to tourist travel are not licensable. This restriction includes tourist travel to Cuba from or through a third country such as Mexico or Canada.

The following categories of travelers are permitted to spend money for Cuban travel and to engage in other transactions directly incident to the purpose of their travel under a general license, without the need to obtain special permission from the U.S. Treasury Department:

• U.S. and foreign government officials traveling on official business, including representatives of international organizations of which the U.S. is a member.

• Journalists and supporting broadcasting or technical personnel regularly employed by a news reporting organization.

• Persons making a once-a-year visit to close family relatives in circumstances of humanitarian need.

• Full-time professionals whose travel transactions are directly related to professional research in their professional areas, provided that their research: (1) is of a noncommercial academic nature; (2) comprises a full work schedule in Cuba, and (3) has a substantial likelihood of public dissemination.

• Full-time professionals whose travel transactions are directly related to attendance at professional meetings or conferences in Cuba organized by an international professional organization, institution, or association that regularly sponsors such meetings or conferences in other countries.

• Amateur or semi-professional athletes or teams traveling to Cuba to participate in an athletic competition held under the auspices of the relevant international sports federation.

The Department of the Treasury may issue licenses on a case-by-case basis authorizing Cuba travel-related transactions directly incident to marketing, sales negotiation, accompanied delivery, and servicing of exports and reexports that appear consistent with the licensing policy of the Department of Commerce. The sectors in which U.S. citizens may sell and service products to Cuba include agricultural commodities, telecommunications activities, medicine, and medical devices. The Treasury Department will also consider requests for specific licenses for humanitarian travel not covered by the general license, educational exchanges, and religious activities by individuals or groups affiliated with a religious organization.

Unless otherwise exempted or authorized, any person subject to U.S. jurisdiction who engages in any travel-related transaction in Cuba violates the regulations. Persons not licensed to engage in travel-related transactions may travel to Cuba without violating the regulations only if all Cuba-related expenses are covered by a person not subject to U.S. jurisdiction and provided that the traveler does not provide any service to Cuba or a Cuban national. Such travel is called "fully-hosted" travel. Such travel may not by made on a Cuban carrier or aboard a direct flight between the United States and Cuba.

Failure to comply with Department of Treasury regulations may result in civil penalties and criminal prosecution upon return to the United States.

Additional information may be obtained by contacting the Licensing Division, Office of Foreign Assets Control, U.S. Department of the Treasury, 1500 Pennsylvania Avenue NW, Treasury Annex, Washington, DC 20220, telephone (202) 622-2480; fax (202) 622-1657. Internet users can log on to the web site through http://www.treas.gov/ofac/.

Should a traveler receive a license, a valid passport is required for entry into Cuba. The Cuban government requires that the traveler obtain a visa prior to arrival. Attempts to enter or exit Cuba illegally, or to aid the irregular exit of Cuban nationals or other persons, are contrary to Cuban law and are punishable by jail terms. Entering Cuban territory, territorial waters or airspace (within 12 miles of the Cuban coast) without prior authorization from the Cuban government may result in arrest or other enforcement action by Cuban authorities. Immigration violators are subject to prison terms ranging from four years for illegal entry or exit to as many as 30 years for aggravated cases of alien smuggling. For current information on Cuban entry and customs requirements, travelers may contact the Cuban Interests Section, an office of the Cuban government, located at 2630 16th Street NW, Washington, DC 20009, telephone (202) 797-8518.

U.S. citizens are encouraged to carry a copy of their U.S. passport with them at all times, so that, if questioned by local officials, proof of identity and U.S. citizenship are readily available.

The U.S. Interests Section (USINT) represents American citizens and the U.S. Government in Cuba, and operates under the legal protection of the Swiss government. The Interests Section staff provides the full range of American citizen and other consular services. U.S. citizens who travel to Cuba are encouraged to contact and register with the American Citizen Services section. USINT staff provide briefings on U.S.-Cuba policy to American individuals and groups visiting Cuba. These briefings or meetings can be arranged through USINT's Public Diplomacy office.

The Interests Section is located in Havana at Calzada between L and M Streets, Vedado; telephone (537) 33-3551 through 33-3559. Hours are Monday through Thursday, 8:30 a.m. to 5:00 p.m., and Friday, 8:30 a.m. to 4:00 p.m. After hours and on weekends, the number is 33-3026 or 66-2302. Should you encounter an emergency after normal duty hours, call these numbers and request to speak with the duty officer.

U.S. citizens who register at the U.S. Interests Section in Havana may obtain updated information on travel and security within the country. There is no access to the U.S. Naval Base at Guantanamo Bay from within Cuba. Consular issues for Guantanamo Bay are handled by the U.S. Embassy in Kingston, Jamaica. For further information on

Guantanamo Bay, please contact the U.S. Embassy in Kingston at telephone (876) 929-5374.

Pets

Cuba imposes no quarantine on arriving pets. However, all pets must have a certificate of good health signed by a veterinarian and dated within 10 days from the date of the animal's arrival in Cuba. Dogs and cats must have a veterinary certification showing the date of the last rabies vaccination. And all animals must be taken to a Cuban veterinarian shortly after arrival for a checkup.

Currency, Banking and Weights and Measures

Since the Cuban government legalized the use of dollars in July 1993, U.S. dollars are accepted for all transactions.

U.S. citizens and residents traveling under a general or specific license from the U.S. Treasury Department may spend money on travel in Cuba; such expenditures may only be for travel-related expenses at a rate not to exceed the U.S. Government's per diem rate. U.S. Treasury regulations authorize any U.S. resident to send up to $300 per calendar quarter to any Cuban family (except families of senior government and Communist party leaders) without a specific license from the Office of Foreign Assets Control. Treasury Department regulations also authorize the transfer of up to $1,000 (without specific license) to pay travel and other expenses for a Cuban national who has been granted a migration document by the U.S. Interests Section in Havana. For further information, travelers should contact the Office of Foreign Assets Control.

U.S. citizens and permanent resident aliens are prohibited from using credit cards in Cuba. U.S. credit card companies do not accept vouchers from Cuba, and Cuban shops, hotels and other places of business do not accept U.S. credit cards. Neither personal checks nor travelers checks drawn on U.S. banks are accepted in Cuba.

Both English and metric systems of weights and measures are used in Cuba, although the metric system predominates.

LOCAL HOLIDAYS

Jan.1 . . . . .New Year's Day
May 1 . . . . .Cuba Labor Day
July 25-27 . . . . . . .Cuban National Revolutionary Festival
Oct. 10 . . . . .Cuba Independence Day
Dec. 25. . . . . .Christmas Day

RECOMMENDED READING

These titles are provided as a general indication of the material published on this country. The Department of State does not endorse unofficial publications.

Azicri, Max. *Cuba: Politics, Economics, & Society*. New York: St. Martin, 1988.

Balfour, Sebastian. *Castro*. New York: Longman, 1990.

Bentley, Judith. *Fidel Castro of Cuba*. Englewood Cliffs, NJ: J. Messner, 1991.

Bernthal, Ron. *Saturday Night in Havana*. Thompsonville, NY: Mariposa Press, 1992.

Bonsal, Philip W. *Cuba, Castro and the United States*. University of Pittsburgh Press: Pittsburgh, 1971.

Crouch, Cifford W. *Cuba*. New York: Chelsea House, 1991.

Cuba: A Country Study. Washington: United States Government Printing Office, 1988.

Cummins, Ronald. *Cuba*. Milwaukee, WI: Gareth Stevens Children's Books, 1991.

Del Aguila, Juan M. *Cuba: Dilemmas of a Revolution*. Boulder, CO: Westview Press, 1988.

Draper, Theodore. *Castroism: Theory and Practice*. Praeger: New York, 1965.

Erisman, H. Michael, and John M. Kirk, eds. *Cuban Foreign Policy Confronts a New International Order*. Boulder, CO: Lynne Rienner, 1991.

Garcia, Cristina. *Dreaming in Cuban*. Alfred A. Knopf: New York, 1992.

Gebler, Carlos. *Driving Through Cuba: Rare Encounters in the Land of Sugarcane and Revolution*. New York: Simon & Schuster, 1988.

Geldof, Lynn. *The Cubans: Voices of Change*. New York: St. Martin, 1992.

Geyer, Georgie Anne. *Guerrilla Prince: The Untold Story of Fidel Castro*. Little, Brown & Company, Boston, 1991.

Graetz, Rick. *Cuba: The Land, the People*. Helena, MT: American World Geographic Publishing, 1990.

Graetz, Rick. *Havana: The City, the People*. Helena, MT: American World Geographic Publishing, 1991.

Habel, Janette. *Cuba: The Revolution in Peril*. Translated by Jon Barnes. New York: Verso, 1991.

Halebsky, Sandor, and John M. Kirk, eds. *Transformation and Struggle: Cuba Faces the 1990s*. New York: Praeger, 1990.

Horowitz, Irving Louis, ed. *Cuban Communism*. 7th ed., New Brunswick, NJ: Transaction Publishers, 1989.

Jacobsen, Karen. *Cuba*. Chicago: Childrens Press, 1990.

Kirk, John M. *Between God & the Party: Religion & Politics in Revolutionary Cuba*. Gainesville, FL: University Press of Florida, 1989.

Levine, Robert M. *Cuba in the 1850s: Through the Lens of Charles DeForest Fredericks*. Tampa, FL: University of South Florida Press, 1990.

Lockwood, Lee. *Castro's Cuba, Cuba's Fidel*. rev. ed., Boulder, CO: Westview Press, 1990.

McManus, Jane. *Getting to Know Cuba*. New York: St. Martin, 1989.

Martin, Lionel. *Early Fidel*. Lyle Stuart & Co.: Syracuse, N.Y., 1978.

Meduin, Tzvi. *Cuba, the Shaping of Revolutionary Consciousness*. Translated by Martha Grenzback. Boulder, CO: Lynne Rienner, 1990.

Mesa-Lago, Carmel, ed. *Revolutionary Change in Cuba*. University of Pittsburgh Press: Pittsburgh, 1971.

Miller, Tom. *Trading with the Enemy: A Yankee Travels Through Castro's Cuba*. New York: Macmillan, 1992.

Montaner, Carlos Alberto. *Fidel Castro and the Cuban Revolution: Age, Position, Character, Destiny, Personality, and Ambition*. New Brunswick, NJ: Transaction Publishers, 1989.

Morris, Emily. *Cuba*. Austin, TX: Steck-Vaughn, 1991.

Oppenheimer, Andres. *Castro's Final Hour*. Simon & Schuster: New York, 1992.

Perez, Jr., Louis A. *Cuba and the United States: Ties of Singular Intimacy*. The University of Georgia Press: Athens, Georgia, 1990.

Quirk, Robert E. *Fidel Castro*. W.W. Norton & Company: New York 1993.

Rabkin, Rhoda Pearl. *Cuban Politics: the Revolutionary Experiment*. New York: Praeger, 1991.

Smith, Wayne. *The Closest of Enemies*. W.W. Norton & Co.: New York, 1987.

Stewart, Gail. *Cuba*. New York: Crestwood House, 1991.

Suchlicki, Jaime. *Cuba: From Columbus to Castro*. 3rd ed., Tarrytown, NY: Pergamon Press, 1990.

Szulc, Tad. *Fidel: A Critical Portrait*. William Morrow & Co.: New York, 1986.

Thomas, Hugh. *Cuba: The Pursuit of Freedom*. Harper & Row: New York, 1971.

Timerman, Jacobo. *Cuba: A Journey*. Translated by Toby Talbot. New York: A.A. Knopf, 1990.

Tulchin, Joseph S., and Rafael Hernandez, eds. *Cuba & the United States: Will the Cold War in the Caribbean End?* Boulder, CO: Lynne Rienner, 1990.

Valladares, Armando. *Against All Hope*. Alfred A. Knopf: New York, 1985.

DOMINICA

Commonwealth of Dominica

Major City:
Roseau

Other City:
Portsmouth

INTRODUCTION

DOMINICA was the first island sighted by Christopher Columbus on his second voyage on Sunday *(dies dominica)*, November 3, 1493. At that time, the island was inhabited by Carib Indians, whose ancestors had originally come from the Orinoco Basin of South America. The Caribs had seized the island from the indigenous Arawaks in the 14th century. The Caribs fought against conquest, and the Spanish lost interest in the island because it apparently had no mineral wealth. Carib resistance also prevented the French and English from settling on the island in the early 1600s. In 1660, England and France agreed to let the native Caribs control the island without interference, but within 30 years Europeans began settling there. France took possession of Dominica in 1727 but forfeited it to Great Britain in 1763. Dominica was governed by Great Britain as part of the Leeward Islands from 1871 until 1939. Between 1940 and 1958, it was administered as part of the Windward Islands. From 1958 until 1962, it belonged to the short-lived Federation of the West Indies. After that federation broke apart, Dominica became an associated state of the Commonwealth of Nations in 1967 and an independent republic on November 3, 1978. Dominica fully supported the 1983 US-led military intervention in nearby Grenada.

MAJOR CITY

Roseau

Roseau, with a population of 21,000, is the capital of Dominica. Located on the southwest coast of the island on the south bank of the Roseau River, Roseau is the country's largest city. The town's name is taken from the French word for "reed" because the river's edge was once covered with reeds. Roseau has suffered from many catastrophes, including floods, fires, and ten hurricanes since 1781 (most recent in 1979, 1980, and 1989). Woodbridge Bay Deep Water Harbour, one mile north of Roseau, handles commercial and large cruise ships with a draft of 30 feet up to 500 feet in length. Agricultural plantations became the foundation of the economy. Coffee was the main crop during the French colonial era, and sugar production was later introduced by the British. The market near the mouth of the Roseau River is the city's center for commerce.

Recreation and Entertainment

Scuba diving and sailing are popular tourist activities. From Roseau, day trip hiking tours are available to explore the rugged natural beauty of Dominica's volcanic peaks, forests, lakes, waterfalls, and numerous rivers. Cricket is the national game of Dominica and is played all over the island.

The Botanical Gardens of Dominica lie just outside Roseau below the Morne Bruce hill. The gardens cover 40 acres and were first planted in 1890 from a converted sugarcane plantation. Since the gardens receive over 85 inches of rain per year, a wide variety of tropical ornamental plants can be grown. In the 1960s and 1970s, the gardens were a popular site for cricket matches. The aviary at the gardens is a breeding center for the endangered Jaco or Rednecked parrot *(Amazona arausiaca)* as well as Dominica's national bird, the Sisserou parrot *(Amazona imperialis)*. The Morne Trios Pitons National Park to the east covers 17,000 acres. The park is a natural undisturbed rainforest, and it contains Boeri Lake and Freshwater Lake, as well as the volcanic Boiling Lake and Middleham Falls. The Emerald Pool, a cave filled by a waterfall and surrounded by beautiful plants, is also located in the Morne Trois Piton National

Park. Trafalgar Falls north of the city is located in a lush gorge covered with ferns and orchids.

The Old Market Square area in downtown Roseau features several prominent early buildings. Dominica has several historic churches, including some in Roseau such as the Romanesque-style Cathedral of Our Lady of the Assumption. The architecture of older wooden buildings, complete with overhanging balconies, gingerbread fretwork, shutters, and jalousies, displays the historic influence of France. Many of the older buildings were restored to their original style after Hurricane David struck Roseau in 1979. In 1993, the Bay Front district opened as a waterfront promenade. The construction of a new seawall allowed land to be reclaimed for the project and now offers the city greater protection from rough seas. Fort Young, with its massive walls, was constructed during the 1700s for protection of the city; it became a hotel in the 1960s.

Roseau's art galleries feature the works of local artists who have received international recognition. There are three main annual arts festivals: Carnival, DOMFESTA, and Independence. Carnival has street parades, and beauty and costume pageants. Music is an important part of Carnival, which features calypso and a marching competition. DOMFESTA is a week-long festival held at the end of July which focuses on contemporary art. Independence celebrates Dominica's heritage with traditional food, costume, dance, and music.

OTHER CITY

PORTSMOUTH is Dominica's second-largest town, located on the northwestern coast. Nearby Prince Rupert's Bay is a natural harbor that was originally home to the Caribs. The sheltered bay was discovered by Columbus on his second voyage and later became a Spanish port for conquistadors going to South America. The town was originally planned as the capital, but the malaria-carrying mosquitoes in the nearby marshes led settlers to relocate to Roseau. Boat trips up the Indian River to see native flora and fauna are popular with visitors. Portsmouth has approximately 3,600 (1995) residents.

COUNTRY PROFILE

Geography and Climate

Dominica is part of the Windward Islands, and lies between Guadeloupe to the north and Martinique to the south. It lies in the middle of the Lesser Antilles chain of islands. Dominica has an area of 790 square miles and is 29 miles long (north to south) and 16 miles wide (east to west). Its terrain is the most rugged of all the islands in the Lesser Antilles, with many peaks, ridges, and ravines. There are several mountains with peaks that are over 4,000 feet above sea level. The Boiling Lake is the second-largest volcanic bubbling crater lake in world. Boeri Lake is a freshwater crater lake that lies 3,000 feet above sea level. Dominica's climate is fairly tropical. Temperatures average 77°F in the winter and 82°F in the summer. Annual rainfall ranges from 80 inches along the coast to 250 inches in mountainous inland areas. Almost one fourth of the land is planted with crops.

Population

Dominica's population is estimated at 64,000. The population density of 110 per square mile is one of the lowest in the West Indies. Over 90% of the population is descended from African slaves brought to the island in the 17th and 18th centuries. About 6% of the population is of mixed origins. The Carib Territory, some 3,700 acres on the northeast coast of the island set aside in 1903, belongs to the 3,400 descendants of the original inhabitants of the Caribbean islands. Due to the historic influence of the French, about 77% of all Dominicans are Roman Catholic. Smaller groups include Anglicans, Methodists, Pentecostals, Baptists, Seventh-Day Adventists, Baha'is, and Rastafarians. The Caribs' religious beliefs combine features of Christianity and nature worship. English is the official language of Dominica. Most of the population also speaks a French-based dialect called *kwéyòl*. Dominicans are increasingly using kwéyòl, which is unique but has elements in common with the dialects of St. Lucia and other islands with cultures influenced by France. Language in Dominica exhibits characteristics of Carib dialect and African phrases.

Government

Dominica became an independent republic on November 3, 1978.

Dominica has a Westminster-style parliamentary government, and there are three political parties: The Dominica Labor Party (the majority party), the Dominica United Workers Party, and the Dominica Freedom Party. A president and prime minister make up the executive branch. Nominated by the prime minister in consultation with the leader of the opposition party, the president is elected for a 5-year term by the parliament. The president appoints as prime minister the leader of the majority party in the parliament and also appoints, on the prime minister's recommendation, members of the parliament from the ruling party as cabinet ministers. The prime minister and cabinet are responsible to the parliament and can be removed on a no-confidence vote.

The unicameral parliament, called the House of Assembly, is composed of 21 regional representatives and nine senators. The regional representatives are elected by universal suffrage and, in turn, decide whether senators are to be elected or appointed. If appointed, five are

Street in downtown Roseau, Dominica

chosen by the president with the advice of the prime minister and four with the advice of the opposition leader. If elected, it is by vote of the regional representatives. Elections for representatives and senators must be held at least every 5 years, although the prime minister can call elections any time.

Dominica's legal system is based on English common law. There are three magistrate's courts, with appeals made to the Eastern Caribbean court of appeal and, ultimately, to the Privy Council in London.

Councils elected by universal suffrage govern most towns. Supported largely by property taxation, the councils are responsible for the regulation of markets and sanitation and the maintenance of secondary roads and other municipal amenities. The island also is divided into 10 parishes, whose governance is unrelated to the town governments.

The flag of the Commonwealth of Dominica consists of a green field with a cross composed of yellow, black, and white stripes. In the center is a red disk with 10 yellow-bordered green stars surrounding a parrot.

Arts, Science, Education

Education is compulsory between the ages of 5 and 15. Transportation to secondary schools is a problem for students in rural areas. Higher education facilities include a teacher training institute, a technical college, a nursing school, and a satellite center of the University of the West Indies. The Alliance Française of Dominica sponsors French-language classes for all ages and main- tains a library and cultural center in Roseau.

Commerce and Industry

Agriculture, with bananas as the principal crop, is still Dominica's economic mainstay. Banana production employs, directly or indirectly, upwards of one-third of the work force. This sector is highly vulnerable to weather conditions and to external events affecting commodity prices. The value of banana exports fell to less than 25% of merchandise trade earnings in 1998 compared to about 44% in 1994.

In view of the EU's announced phase-out of preferred access of bananas to its markets, agricultural diversification is a priority. Dominica has made some progress, with the export of small quantities of citrus fruits and vegetables and the introduction of coffee, patchouli, aloe vera, cut flowers, and exotic fruits such as mangoes, guavas, and papayas. Dominica has also had some success in increasing its manufactured exports, with soap as the primary product. Dominica also recently entered the offshore financial services market.

Because Dominica is mostly volcanic and has few beaches, development of tourism has been slow compared with that on neighboring islands. Nevertheless, Dominica's high, rugged mountains, rainforests, freshwater lakes, hot springs, waterfalls, and diving spots make it an attractive destination. Cruise ship stopovers have increased following the development of modern docking and waterfront facilities in the capital. Eco-tourism also is a growing industry on the island.

Dominica is a member of the Eastern Caribbean Currency Union (ECCU). The Eastern Caribbean Central Bank (ECCB) issues a common currency to all eight members of the ECCU. The ECCB also manages monetary policy, and regulates and supervises commercial banking activities in its member countries.

Dominica is a beneficiary of the U.S. Caribbean Basin Initiative (CBI). Its 1996 exports to the U.S. were $7.7 million, and its U.S. imports were $34 million. Dominica is also a member of the 14-member Caribbean Community and Common Market (CARICOM) and of the Organization of Eastern Caribbean States (OECS).

Transportation

A paved road circles the island. Both Roseau and Portsmouth receive ships. The Cabrits Cruise Ship Port, located in the northwest within the Cabrits National Park, handles only cruise ship traffic. There is a 2,500-foot airstrip north of Roseau.

Communications

In 1987 Dominica became the first country in the world to operate a telecommunications system that was entirely digital. There are five local radio stations and one cable television station. The island also receives broadcasts from neighboring islands. Two newspapers, the *New Chronicle* and the government's *Official Gazette*, are published in Roseau.

Health

Dominica's one general hospital, Princess Margaret Hospital, is in Roseau. There are also smaller hospital facilities in Portsmouth, Marigot, and Grand Bay, and 12 health centers scattered across the country. Tuberculosis and other respiratory problems are made worse by high humidity and rainy conditions.

Clothing and Services

Dominicans dress modestly. Tourists are advised that scanty clothes and swimwear are only to be worn on the beaches. Casual light cottons are worn during the day, with a light sweater for cooler evenings. Raingear and hiking shoes are recommended for the mountains and rainforests.

NOTES FOR TRAVELERS

U.S. citizens may enter Dominica without a passport for tourist stays of up to three months, but they must carry an original document proving U.S. citizenship, such as a U.S. passport, Certificate of Naturalization, Certificate of Citizenship or certified U.S. birth certificate; photo identification; and a return or onward ticket. For further information concerning entry requirements, travelers can contact the Embassy of the Commonwealth of Dominica, 3216 New Mexico Avenue, N.W., Washington, D.C. 20016, telephone:

(202) 364-6781, email: emb-domdc@aol.com, or the Consulate General of Dominica in New York at (212) 768-2480.

Dominica's customs authorities may enforce strict regulations concerning the temporary import or export of items such as business equipment, food and beverages, paints and varnishes, and chemicals. It is advisable to contact the Embassy of Dominica in Washington or the Consulate in New York for specific information regarding customs requirements.

Americans living in or visiting Dominica are encouraged to register at the Consular Section of the U.S. Embassy in Bridgetown, Barbados and obtain updated information on travel and security within Dominica. Consular Section hours are 9:00am-12 noon and 2:00pm-4:00pm, Monday-Friday except local and U.S. holidays. The U.S. Embassy is located in the American Life Insurance (ALICO) building, Cheapside, Bridgetown, Barbados, telephone 1-246-431-0225, fax 1-246-431-0179, e-mail: consular-bridge@state.gov or Internet: http://usembassy.state.gov/posts/bb1/wwwhcons.html

Disaster Preparedness
Dominica is a hurricane-prone country. General information about natural disaster preparedness is available via the Internet from the U.S. Federal Emergency Management Agency (FEMA) at http://www.fema.gov/.

LOCAL HOLIDAYS

January 1	New Year's Day
. . . .	*Carnival
. . . .	*Good Friday
. . . .	*Easter Monday
May 1	Labor Day
. . . .	*Whitmonday
July 2	Caricom Day
August (first Monday) . .	*Bank Holiday
November 3–4 . . .	National Holidays
December 25	Christmas

December 26 . . . . . Boxing Day
*Variable

RECOMMENDED READING

Philpott, Don. *Caribbean Sunseekers: Dominica*. Lincolnwood, Ill.: Passport Books, 1996.

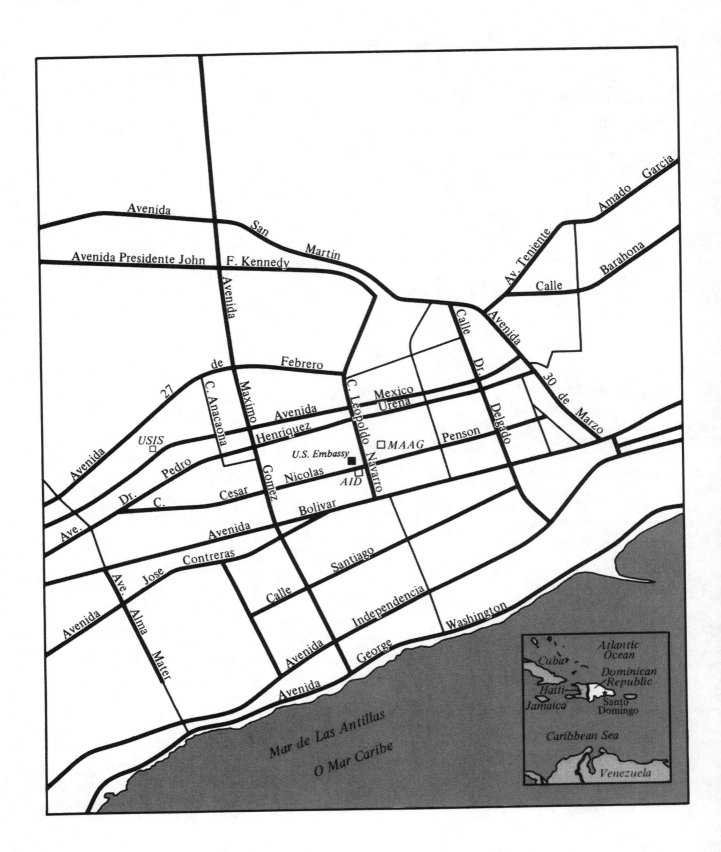

Santo Domingo, Dominican Republic

DOMINICAN REPUBLIC

Major Cities:

Santo Domingo, Santiago de los Caballeros, La Romana

Other Cities:

Azua, Baní, Barahona, Constanza, Higüey, Jarabacoa, La Vega, Puerto Plata, Samaná, San Cristóbal, San Francisco De Macorís, San Juan, San Pedro De Macorís

INTRODUCTION

The **DOMINICAN REPUBLIC** shares with the Republic of Haiti the tropical island of Hispaniola, one of the Greater Antilles situated between Cuba and Puerto Rico. Troubled by unstable political conditions throughout most of its history, it has had little chance until recent years to develop a sound economy capable of providing more than a subsistence level of living for most of its people. The period from the mid-1960s to the mid-1970s, however, was marked by rapid economic development and progress, and the 1982 peaceful transition of power indicates the nation's growing stability.

Since its discovery by Columbus in 1492 and its colonization by Spain, Hispaniola has been, for brief periods, under the nominal control of Great Britain, France, Haiti, and the United States (1916–24). A bloody revolution on the French-held western end of the island in 1791 led to the establishment of Haiti as an independent country. Haitian forces dominated the island for varying periods between 1801 and 1843. The Dominican Republic gained its independence in 1844 after a successful revolt against Haitian rule, but its political history remained stormy, with foreign intervention in the country's affairs from the late 1800s to the middle part of this century. Recent political events suggest a promise of permanent democratic tradition.

MAJOR CITIES

Santo Domingo

Santo Domingo, the oldest continuous European settlement in the Americas, is the capital and largest city of the Dominican Republic. It serves as the commercial, social, and political hub of the country, as well as the principal seaport. It is a fast-growing city which has more

than doubled its population in the last 10 years. The population is estimated at 3.6 million. Most inhabitants live in the older, poorer, *barrio* sections, bordering the Ozama River. Outside these areas and the commercial districts near the port, Santo Domingo is fairly modern, with new homes, apartments, and office buildings continually under construction. Here, streets and avenues are lined with palm and flame trees, and flowering shrubs.

La Plaza de la Cultura, on the western side of the city, is the most impressive cultural area in the Caribbean, boasting the Museum of Dominican Man (Museo del Hombre), with a collection of artifacts from the Indian migrations from South America through the Caribbean islands; the National Library (Biblioteca Nacional); and the National Theater (Teatro Nacional). Parks and playgrounds are numerous in the immediate outskirts of Santo Domingo, and nearby beaches lure Dominicans and tourists alike.

The present location of the nation's capital evolved through a series of incidents. Christopher Columbus made his first landing in the New World December 5, 1492, on the northwest coast of an island he named Hispaniola. On Christmas Day of that year, his flagship, the Santa María, was wrecked on the reefs of Cape Haitien, and from the salvaged timbers of this vessel the crew built the first European fort in the Western Hemisphere. Leaving a garrison of 40 men at the fort, Columbus set sail for further explorations and eventually went back to Spain. When he returned the following year on his second voyage, he found that the Indians had revolted against Spanish abuse, and had destroyed his small garrison. Columbus then ordered the construction of a new city, La Isabela, near the present city of Puerto Plata on the north coast of the Dominican Republic. His brother, Bartholomé (in English, Bartholomew), was made governor of Hispaniola.

In 1496, Bartholomé, enticed by rumors of gold, a good harbor, and fertile land, and disheartened by sickness and bickering among the colonists, transferred the seat of government to the south coast on the bank of the Ozama River. He named the new city Santo Domingo in honor of his favorite saint, Dominic. The spot served as Spain's stepping-stone to further explorations in the New World. Except for the period from 1936 to 1961, when the city was called Ciudad Trujillo, for (then) President Rafael Leonidas Trujillo Molina, this name has endured.

During the early 16th century, Santo Domingo was the staging area for the Spanish *conquistadors*. Among the famous explorers who contributed to the colorful history of the area were Ponce de León, Sir Francis Drake, Diego de Velázquez, and Hernán Cortés.

Clothing

Drip-dry materials, wash-and-wear cottons, and synthetic combinations will withstand repeated washings and the bright sun of the Dominican Republic. Because dry cleaning establishments are not up to U.S. standards, washable clothing is strongly recommended. For the most part, apparel that is suitable for a Washington, DC summer is appropriate all year in the Dominican climate. Jackets, sweaters, and shawls are needed for the rare cool

evening. Lightweight rainwear and umbrellas are useful during the rainy season; rubbers or boots are not. Hats and gloves are rarely worn. Sun hats, shades, and other protective clothing are recommended because the tropical sun can be hard on the skin.

Tropical-weight shirts and neckties are normal office attire but, for special functions, a white or dark business suit is appropriate. Black dinner jackets (never white) are worn on some occasions. Women dress simply in cool, sleeveless (or short-sleeved) dresses for office or other activities. Stockings are worn only for special occasions. Pantsuits may be worn to the office; slacks are acceptable for casual gatherings or for shopping. Shorts may be worn. Shoes are available locally, although they are expensive and often poorly made.

Children wear summer garments year round. Nightclothes suitable for U.S. summers are practical for older children, but infants and young children may need warmer wear in air-conditioned bedrooms. Children's shoes, both locally made and U.S. brands, are available. Teenagers in Santo Domingo are style and label conscious, and formal wear is worn much more in Santo Domingo than in the U.S.

Food

Several modern supermarkets in Santo Domingo offer a wide variety of U.S. canned and frozen foods including baby foods, but at high prices. Coffee, bread, rice, and a variety of other local products are found in most supermarkets. Supermarkets sell pasteurized milk, yogurt, butter, and cheese. They are usually safe to consume once checked for freshness.

Fresh foods on the local market are generally in good supply and of adequate quality. Farmers' outdoor markets and door-to-door vendors also sell fresh fruits and vegetables. Special outlets for meats, eggs, baked goods, and dairy products are available. Beef, veal, pork, poultry, fish, lobster, and shrimp are also

available locally. Due to the danger of ciguatera, a serious type of poisoning, do not eat fish at home or in restaurants. Both commonplace and tropical vegetables are found in season.

Local tropical fruits, including breadfruit, kumquat (nispero), gump (limoncillo), and guanabana, are plentiful and delicious. Lemons, as Americans know them, do not grow here; limes are used instead. Temperate zone fruits such as peaches, plums, and apples are imported occasionally, but are expensive.

Dairies sell pasteurized milk and will deliver. Milk in wax containers is preferable to bottled milk, as bottles may be contaminated. Local butter and cheese are usually safe, but should be checked for freshness.

The German-Jewish colony in Sosua, on the north coast, prepares excellent meats, cheeses, and good sandwich bread, all sold in Santo Domingo.

Fine local beers sell at prices approximately equal to those in the U.S. Most kinds of soft drinks are bottled here and sold at reasonable prices.

Supplies & Services

Beauty and barber shops are numerous in the cities and at the major resorts, with services varying from adequate to good. Tailoring is used mainly for alterations, but many American women find local dressmakers satisfactory. Shoe repair is satisfactory. All of these services are reasonable, but some radio, stereo, and television repairmen charge high rates. Cost estimates should be obtained beforehand. Laundries are available, but most expatriates prefer to have their laundry done at home. Washing and ironing should be supervised to prevent damage to fabrics, washers, and irons. At the few local dry cleaners, the quality of work is inconsistent.

Repair service is available on most cars, and prices for routine work are

City of Santo Domingo, Dominican Republic

reasonable. However, major repairs can mean delays while parts are ordered; this type of service is expensive and quality often only fair. Automatic transmission repair, electrical system adjustments, work on window and door fittings, and other jobs requiring a delicate touch are sometimes risky, depending upon the garage used.

Religious Activities

The Dominican Republic is officially Roman Catholic, but many other denominations maintain churches in the country. Members of the U.S. community in Santo Domingo usually attend English-language services at these churches: Epiphany Episcopal Church, Protestant Community Church, First Baptist Church, Parroquia Santiago Apóstal (mass in English), and Hebrew Synagogue Center (English prayer books, services in Hebrew each Friday). Other denominations, which have Spanish-language services, are Seventh-Day Adventist,

Plymouth Brethren, Latter-Day Saints, Assembly of God, Jehovah's Witnesses, and Roman Catholic.

Domestic Help

All types of servants are available. Generally, those who are experienced and well-trained pass from one expatriate family to another. Although efficiency and initiative are not outstanding characteristics, devotion to family and desire to please counterbalance these failings. Most servants speak only Spanish, but a few know some English. Many applicants for domestic work are illiterate and have no knowledge of American cooking or housekeeping, contrary to their claims. It is best to hire only on the recommendation of another employer, or to ask for advice at the U.S. Embassy personnel office, where a registry is kept on security-checked applicants.

The majority of Americans in the Dominican Republic (Santo Dom-

ingo, in particular) employ one or two full-time servants, and some have part-time yard boys and laundresses as well. Single people usually hire a maid for general housework, cooking, cleaning, and assistance with shopping at the local market. Some single people employ part-time maids. A family with children may need two servants, one acting as nursemaid in addition to helping with the housework. For security reasons, it is advisable to seek servants who will live in.

In addition to wages ($200-300 a month for live-ins), the employer furnishes all meals, uniforms, linens, and toiletries. Additional money is agreed upon to cover daily transportation for servants who live at home. It is customary to give a month's salary as a Christmas bonus to domestics who have been employed for a year. Some employers assist with medical expenses, and a certain amount of paternalism is involved in most employer-employee relationships. Servants customarily work a six-day week, with a paid two-week vacation after a year's service. Employers do not make obligatory payments for social or medical insurance.

Education

Most American children living in the capital attend the Carol Morgan School, a private, nonprofit institution providing coeducational instruction in English through grade 12. The curriculum parallels that of U.S. public schools, and the high school is accredited by the Southern Association of Colleges and Secondary Schools. The superintendent and teaching staff have U.S. certification. Of the total enrollment of 1,056, approximately 290 are Americans, 603 Dominicans (1994 est.), and the remainder other nationalities. School is in session from the last week in August to the first week in June, with a two-three week Christmas vacation, a week-long Easter break, and days off for the celebration of some U.S. and Dominican national holidays.

Carol Morgan School is just outside the city, in a complex of air-conditioned buildings. Spanish is taught as a foreign language in all grades, and four years of French are offered at the secondary level. The high-school curriculum is geared to college preparatory work. The physical plant has chemistry and physics laboratories, computer labs, 49 classrooms, infirmary, gymnasium, cafeteria, audiovisual facilities, and a 18,000-volume library. Physical education is offered in all grades, with intramural competition in volleyball, basketball, and softball. Extracurricular activities include a school newspaper, yearbook, literary magazine, dramatics and language clubs, and several special groups.

Santo Domingo has several other schools available to foreigners. Colegio Los Angelitos/St. George School has classes from nursery level to grade 12. The curriculum is bilingual. The school is large, well-organized, and follows a formal schedule combining British and American approaches to education. All teachers have certification. Resources and physical facilities are good. The school's name is Colegio Los Angelitos from nursery school through sixth grade, and St. George School in the upper-level classes.

ABC School offers a program based on U.S. and European educational systems. Enrollment is from kindergarten through grade six. Teachers either have college degrees or are university students.

American School of Santo Domingo provides coeducational instruction from pre-kindergarten through grade 12. The school is accredited by the Southern Association of Colleges and Secondary Schools in the U.S. The elementary classes receive instruction in English/language arts, mathematics, science, social studies, health, Spanish, art, music, and physical education. Special programs include remedial reading and comprehension, English as a second language, and mathematics. The high school follows a college preparatory program, covering all of the general areas of study, plus Dominican history and Spanish. Several electives are offered.

The George Washington School of English Education is also coeducational. An English curriculum is offered from nursery school to 12th grade.

Two nursery schools, Froebel School and Lucy's Lambs, are especially recommended. The Froebel School has excellent equipment and resources. The staff consists of a director and three assistants. The school has three classes: one for three-year-olds, a pre-kindergarten for four-year-olds, and a kindergarten for five-year-olds. Instruction focuses on the artistic, social, and academic aspects of the child's development.

Lucy's Lambs accepts children from ages two through five. There are two nursery classes for ages two through four, a pre-kindergarten for ages four through five, and a kindergarten for five-year-olds. Each class has about 20 children. The director and the kindergarten teacher are certified teachers. Instruction follows traditional approaches of learning colors, numbers, concepts, social adjustment, etc.

Recreation

Swimming, water-skiing, sailing, scuba diving, motor boating, baseball, softball, horseback riding, polo, volleyball, tennis, basketball, and cockfighting are among the more popular sports in the country. Americans in Santo Domingo enjoy these activities year round. Water sports are particularly popular, and several shallow, palm-lined beaches are within an hour's drive of the city. All major Santo Domingo hotels have swimming pools. Snorkeling and scuba diving are particularly interesting because of the clear water and the variety of marine life in the Caribbean. However, sharks and sea urchins are possible dangers.

Some of the finest fishing in the Caribbean may be found off the Dominican coast. Freshwater fishing and surf casting are popular, as well as fishing for marlin, sailfish, and other game fish. Some of the best spots include Cumayasa, La Romana, Cabeza de Toro, and Boca de Yuma, all east of Santo Domingo; Palmar de Ocoa and Barahona to the south; and Monte Cristi, Puerto Plata, and Samaná to the north.

Some Americans join the Club Náutico of Santo Domingo, about a 45-mile drive from the city. There is a clubhouse with dining room and bar, a small saltwater pool, a pier with a marina, and a fair beach. The club sponsors annual hunting and fishing tournaments.

Riding has become a popular sport, as have racquetball and running. For the latter, the city offers a few places for joggers, including the oceanfront or *malecon*, the six-mile perimeter of the Paseo de Los Indios Park, and the almost four-mile perimeter of the National Botanical

Gardens. Many informal walking groups exist in the country.

The Dominican Republic now has several golf courses, and others are being planned or built. One 18-hole course is at the Santo Domingo Country Club on the outskirts of the city; membership is open to non-Dominicans. Two other championship courses are 80 miles east of the capital in La Romana, beside the Caribbean. A fourth course, designed by Robert Trent Jones, is also of championship quality; it serves the tourist facilities around the seaport town of Puerto Plata.

Baseball is the national sport, and all games draw large crowds. There are two seasons. The professional winter season (which occasionally features players from the U.S. major leagues) lasts from late October to the end of January, and the summer season runs from April to September. Games during both seasons are played at Quisqueya Stadium in Santo Domingo, and at stadiums in Santiago de los Caballeros, San Pedro de Macorís, and La Romana.

Hunting is permitted in the Dominican Republic. Ducks, which migrate from North America in winter, and doves are the principal fowl hunted. Quail (in small numbers), *yaguaza* (a West Indian tree duck), and guinea hen are also hunted; no large game is found in the country.

The restored colonial section of the city is the location of Santo Domingo's principal tourist attractions. These include the Cathedral of Santa María la Menor, Torre del Homenaje, Alcazar de Colón, and the Museo de las Casas Reales (Royal Houses). The cathedral, built between 1523 and 1540, is one of the finest examples of Spanish Renaissance architecture in the Western Hemisphere. The onyx and marble monument inside the edifice was brought block by block from Barcelona, Spain. Santa María is the oldest cathedral in the New World, and is one of three places which claim to contain the remains of Christopher Columbus. The cathedral was completely rehabili-

tated in 1992 in time for festivities celebrating the 500th anniversary of Columbus' arrival in the New World.

Torre del Homenaje, part of Ozama Fortress, was erected in 1503, and reflects the power of colonial Spain. The Alcazar de Colón is the restored fortress palace built by Diego Columbus, son of Christopher, and first viceroy of the island; it contains some fine pieces of period furniture. Museo de las Casas Reales houses exhibits of historical interest, and is the former residence of the captain general of Hispaniola.

There are several other museums of interest in the city. The Museum of Dominican Man is best known for its collection of pre-Columbian artifacts; the National Museum displays works by well-known Dominican and regional artists; and the Museum of Natural History and Geography houses exhibits dealing with the topography, agriculture, and flora and fauna of the republic.

A number of parks are scattered throughout the city. The largest of these, beautiful Paseo de Los Indios, is three-and-a-half miles long and offers scenery, botanical specimens, and recreational facilities. A municipal amusement park in this area, Mirador del Sur, has a variety of attractions for small children. The Jardín Botánico Nacional Moscoso (botanical gardens named for Dr. Rafael M. Moscoso) covers an area of over 1,800,000 square meters, and contains special laboratories with hundreds of varieties of tropical plants. Other attractions are the Great Ravine, the Japanese Park, and the world's largest floral clock; small boating facilities are available in an artificial lake in the garden. The modern Parque Zoológico Nacional is spread over 1,250,000 square meters, and includes about five miles of roads and walks. Animals from different parts of the world are displayed in open areas which resemble their natural habitats. The zoo features the largest bird cage in the world, a unique African plain, and a children's zoo.

An Olympic park, with a complex of sports facilities, was built for the XII Central Caribbean Games in early 1974. The complex includes a stadium for soccer and track and field events, a covered sports palace with a seating capacity of 10,000, an Olympic-size pool, a cycling track, and court facilities.

The best beaches on the south coast are Boca Chica, 20 miles from the city; Guayacanes, Playa Caribe, Juan Dolio, and Villas del Mar, 30 miles; Barahona, 75 miles to the west; and Bayahibe, in La Romana, 80 miles to the east. Points of interest on the north coast are Puerto Plata and Sosua (about 150 miles from Santo Domingo) with their beautiful white-sand beaches.

Shopping in Santo Domingo is a real bargain because the Dominican *peso* trades favorably with most foreign currencies, and there is a wide variety of items from which to choose. Popular items include native handicrafts such as paintings, straw, macramé, and mahogany products. Amber, the country's national gem (more is mined in the Dominican Republic than anywhere else), is another good buy. Larimar, the sea-blue stone found in the western part of the country, is another recommended buy. There are duty-free zones in both Santo Domingo and Puerto Plata; Santo Domingo's is the largest duty-free area in the Caribbean.

Entertainment

Movies, shown in comfortable, air-conditioned theaters in Santo Domingo, are one of the principal means of entertainment outside the home. New and old U.S. films with original soundtracks and Spanish subtitles predominate, but British, Mexican, Italian, French, and German films are also shown. Santo Domingo has five popular gambling casinos at major hotels, and several nightclubs with floor shows. Also, various discotheques feature American music.

The National Theater is the center of a number of cultural presentations, including regular symphony concerts, occasional solo recitals, plays, ballets by visiting troupes, and operas or plays by local artists. The Binational Center (the Dominican-American Cultural Institute) and several private galleries offer exhibits by local artists.

Santiago

Santiago de los Caballeros is the "second city" of the Dominican Republic. Its name is commonly shortened to Santiago. Situated on the banks of the Río Yaque in the north-central part of the country, it is known for its Universidad Católica Madre y Maestra, a 23-year-old institution with a highly respected academic reputation. The university is considered the nation's best, and is supported by the Catholic Church and both public and private endowments.

Santiago was founded in 1504 by "30 Spanish gentlemen," and was rebuilt 60 years later after being demolished by an earthquake. It has endured not only several more earthquakes of varying intensity, but also a turbulent history of political insurrections. During the time that Rafael Trujillo was dictator in the middle years of this century, he tore down some of Santiago's finest old buildings, and erected what is widely considered to be an ugly "Peace Monument," and a $4 million suspension bridge that leads nowhere.

Santiago has grown considerably in the past quarter-century, and is home to 1.5 people. It is the commercial center of an agricultural region and the distribution point for several industries. These industries are centered on the production of rum, furniture, cigarettes, soap, pharmaceuticals, and leather articles. It is an especially clean city which keeps a crew of workers sweeping and washing the streets daily.

Santiago is noted for its excellent hotels and restaurants, and for the *paradores*, or *pensiones*, which attract the tourist trade. It is also famous for the fine Bermudez rum distilled here.

La Romana

La Romana is a seaport city of 133,000 in the republic's eastern province of the same name. Its popularity has increased in recent years with the completion of luxury tourist resorts, Casa de Campo and Club Dominicus, outside the city.

La Romana's name, meaning "The Scales," comes from earlier days when growers brought their crops to be weighed before shipment to Puerto Rican refineries. Its image has now changed to that of a spot popular with high society. It offers championship golf courses, superb tennis courts, good fishing facilities, swimming (off Catalina Island), a village inn, restaurants, a museum, and an exhibition hall.

The Casa de Campo complex near La Romana is fast becoming the Caribbean's most famous resort. Its 7,000 acres, spread out near the sea, include two championship courses designed by the golf architect Pete Dye.

About 10 miles from this luxurious resort is Altos de Chavón, an artist's replica of a 15th-century Spanish village. One of its famous attractions is a large, hillside amphitheater which serves as the site for cultural events. The tiny church in the village is popular for weddings.

La Romana itself is Gulf and Western Americas Corporation headquarters in the Dominican Republic, and also the site of the largest privately owned sugar refinery in the world. The city is home to several industries which manufactures soap, furniture, and shoes. The Abraham Lincoln School, a company-sponsored, English-language school, is open for students in pre-kindergarten through grade 12; admissions information is available from Fondación Gulf and Western, Central Romana, La Romana, Dominican Republic.

OTHER CITIES

AZUA (full name, Azua de Compostela) is located near the Caribbean Sea about 50 miles west of Santo Domingo. The original town, established in 1504, was destroyed by an earthquake, and Azua was rebuilt three miles inland at the foot of the Sierra de Ocoa. Trading includes rice, coffee, sugarcane, fruits, and timber. A paved highway connects the city with Santo Domingo. Azua's population is over 64,000.

BANÍ, capital city of Peravia Province, is located in southern Dominican Republic, 30 miles southwest of Santo Domingo. The city is a commercial center that produces rice, coffee, and bananas. Baní's population is close to 100,000.

BARAHONA (full name, Santa Cruz de Barahona) is situated on the Caribbean Sea in southwestern Dominican Republic, about 80 miles southwest of Santo Domingo. The city, site of a major port, has industries which include fishing, sugarcane, and fruits. It is also known for hunting. The city is accessible by air and roadway. Barahona's population is approximately 74,000.

CONSTANZA, 90 miles northwest of Santo Domingo over tortuous mountain roads, offers a scenery and climate change at 4,000 feet above sea level. The city's population is close to 15,200.

HIGÜEY, the capital city of La Altagracia Province, on the east coast, is known for its basilica, which houses the largest carillon in the Americas. The church represents the country's most outstanding example of modern architecture. The city is surrounded by fertile land where cacao, cattle, corn, rice, and dairy products are produced. A major highway links Higüey with Santo Domingo. The population of Higüey is about 83,700.

JARABACOA is a colonial city in the mountains, 60 miles northwest of Santo Domingo. It is now a small rural community with pleasant scenery, overlooking cloud formations in the lower mountain valleys. Potatoes, strawberries, apples, vegetables, and flowers are grown near the city. Jarabacoa has an estimated population of 13,400.

LA VEGA (full name, Concepción de la Vega) is the capital of La Vega Province in west-central Dominican Republic. Founded in 1494, La Vega is a commercial city in a fertile part of the country. Its crops include tobacco, coffee, cocoa, rice, and fruit. La Vega is located near the paved highway to the capital, and has an airfield. Its population is about 56,000.

PUERTO PLATA, situated on a crescent-shaped bay on the Atlantic Ocean, is an historic town where pirate ships docked in the 1500s. It became a free port during the 18th century, and later a coffee port, when plantation owners built their townhouses on the streets which now are part of a national preservation plan. In town, horses still pull carriages past gingerbread houses with latticed verandas. The city, originally named San Felipe de Puerto Plata, is the capital of Puerto Plata Province. About 130 miles north of Santo Domingo, Puerto Plata has a population of about 86,000. Tobacco, coffee, sugar, cacao, bananas, and hardwoods are exported here. Liquor, dairy products, pasta, and leather are manufactured in Puerto Plata. The city is among the country's ten greatest cattle producing areas. Recently, the area has become the site of a large, and still expanding, international tourist complex. Major resorts include Jack Tar Village, Playa Dorado Hotel, Dorado Naco, and Villas Dorados.

SAMANÁ (formerly called Santa Bárbara de Samaná), situated on the east coast, is about 170 miles from the capital. It was settled in 1864 by escaped slaves from the U.S., whose ship bringing them from the Underground Railroad was blown ashore. Their descendants, now numbering 7,000, speak English, and maintain several old Protestant churches built over the

years. Samaná, a seaside town, has excellent beaches and, as a spot for sport fishing, was once a favorite of Franklin D. Roosevelt. The city is a commercial and manufacturing center for coconuts, timber, rice, and marble. It has grown from a fishing village to a cruise port of note. Its population is about 38,800.

SAN CRISTÓBAL, 25 miles southwest of Santo Domingo, is the site of the Mahogany House, built and furnished by the late Rafael Trujillo. The city was the site of the signing of the Dominican Republic's first constitution in 1844. Founded in 1575, the city is situated in a region that produces rice, sugar, fruit, potatoes, livestock, and coffee. It is the capital of the province of the same name and has a population of approximately 124,000.

SAN FRANCISCO DE MACORÍS, the capital of Duarte Province, is located about 60 miles northwest of Santo Domingo. It is the busy center of an important sugar- and molasses-producing area. Timber, coffee, fruits, cacao, rice, hides, and wax are other major products of the district. The population of San Francisco de Macorís is about 130,000.

SAN JUAN (full name, San Juan de la Maguana), located in west-central Dominican Republic, was founded in 1508. The Battle of Santomé in 1844, which resulted in Dominican independence, was fought near San Juan. Markets include rice, fruit, corn, potatoes, and cattle. San Juan's population is roughly 50,000.

SAN PEDRO DE MACORÍS is located in the southeastern part of the country, about 40 miles east of Santo Domingo. The city's modern port handles most of the country's exports, which include molasses, timber, cattle, and sugar. Industries include corn milling, the manufacture of clothing, and soap and alcohol distilling. The Universidad Central del Este was founded here in 1970 and is located on the main road to Santo Domingo. The city's population is approximately

124,000. In recent years, San Pedro de Macorís has become a hotbed for baseball, producing more players per capita for U.S. major league teams than any other town ever.

Several other cities of interest are located within easy driving distance of Santo Domingo. On the north coast are La Isabela, Columbus' first settlement in the New World (1493); Sosua, settled by Jewish refugees from Germany in 1939; and Macao, 95 miles from Santo Domingo, noted for its beautiful, long beach.

COUNTRY PROFILE

Geography and Climate

The Dominican Republic occupies the eastern two-thirds of the island of Hispaniola, the second largest (after Cuba) of the Greater Antilles group, and shares a 224-mile border with Haiti to the west. The island is bordered on the north by the Atlantic Ocean, on the south by the Caribbean Sea, and on the east by the Mona Passage, which separates the Dominican Republic from the island of Puerto Rico, 71 miles away.

The country has a land area of 18,712 square miles, slightly larger than Vermont and New Hampshire combined. With its 1,000-mile coastline, it extends about 240 miles east to west, and has a maximum north-south width of about 170 miles.

Much of the terrain is rugged. Four nearly parallel mountain ranges traverse the country from northwest to southeast. The Cordillera Central is the largest range and divides the country into almost equal parts. Pico Duarte, at 10,128 feet the highest mountain in the West Indies, is within this range. The largest and most fertile valley, the Cibao, about 150 miles long and 10 to 30 miles wide, is in the upper central part of the country.

Dominican rivers vary in flow with the season, and are navigable only for short distances at their mouths, if at all. Their main use is for irrigation and hydroelectric power. The major rivers are the Ozama, Yaque del Norte, Yaque del Sur, Isabela, Higuamo, and Soco.

The climate varies little throughout the year. Although the country is in the tropics, temperatures seldom exceed 90°F, mainly because of constant trade winds. Temperatures in the coastal cities average about 78°F, with seasonal variations of five to eight degrees. Rainfall varies regionally, with about two-thirds of the annual 57 inches coming in the May-to-November rainy season. However, this period differs in various parts of the country; for example, the rainy season on the south coast occurs between May and November, and in the north from November to May.

Mildew, mold, rust, and insects are problems related to year-round high humidity. Furniture, leather goods, clothing, metal items, and books must be carefully aired and protected. The climate also contributes to prevalent upper respiratory infections, skin irritations, fungus, and stomach and intestinal complaints.

Hurricanes are a significant weather threat, particularly from mid-July through October, and have caused serious damage in recent years. The worst hurricane on record, which virtually destroyed Santo Domingo, occurred in 1930. Hurricanes David and Frederick, in August and September 1979, caused considerable damage to the city and countryside. In September, 1987, Hurricane Emily barely missed Santo Domingo. Earthquake tremors are felt occasionally, but have not had serious consequences since 1948.

Population

More than half of the Dominican Republic's 8.3 million inhabitants live in towns with populations over 10,000. The cities, however, are growing rapidly. The largest urban areas are Santo Domingo (3.6 million), and Santiago de los Caballeros (1.5 million).

The nation's population density of 171 persons per square mile makes it the seventh most densely populated country in Latin America, but it does not exceed that of most of the islands of the West Indies. Existing population pressure is accentuated by an annual growth rate of about 2%.

The nation's inhabitants are mostly descendants of both early European settlers and African slaves, but there are many relative newcomers of European and Middle Eastern origins. An estimated 16% of the population is Caucasian, another 11% are black, and the remaining 73% mixed Caucasian and Black. No traces of aboriginal Indians exist. No overt racial antagonism affects the relationship between the ethnic groups.

Spanish is the national language. It is spoken quite rapidly in the Dominican Republic, and many idioms and contractions are used in its colloquial form. English is spoken widely by the upper socioeconomic segment of society.

Under an accord with the Vatican in 1954, Roman Catholicism was formally established as the state religion, and the Dominican Government provides some financial support to the church. Freedom of worship is universal, however, and many Protestant denominations and missions of all faiths are found here.

Frequent colorful processions are held on various saints' day festivals. The nation's patron saint, Our Lady of Altagracia, is named after a vision of the Virgin Mary reported in the eastern part of the island in 1921. On holy days, mass is celebrated as a part of many public ceremonies.

The Dominican Republic does not have a large landholding class. A small but growing number of wealthy people dominate the country's social structure. For many years (1930–1961), this group held what little economic power was not monopolized by the ruling Trujillo family. The preponderance of the Trujillos in both the economic realm and in government ended with the dictator's assassination in 1961, but some of the established social patterns continue to linger. Upward mobility is geared largely to the acquisition of wealth, although increasing importance is being attached to education and professional achievement.

Two small groups top the social scale. One is composed of well-to-do persons whose extensive rural properties were not expropriated under the Trujillo dictatorship, and who have used their land to gain leadership in commerce and industry. Most of this group is centered around the northern cities of Santiago and Puerto Plata, but many maintain second homes in Santo Domingo. The second group is composed of former civil servants and military officials who attained prominence and wealth under previous governments. Their ranks include a few professionals and men of letters, but many of the latter fall into the small but growing middle class.

The middle class has suffered in recent years due to economic problems. It includes civil servants, private-sector managers, white-collar workers, teachers, and other professionals.

About three-fourths of the people are at the lower end of the socioeconomic scale. The majority earn a subsistence wage, have minimal education, live in substandard conditions, are largely rural, and are migrating to urban areas in the hope of improving their lot by serving as domestics or laborers.

Construction and public works projects employ substantial numbers of skilled and unskilled laborers in the urban areas, but not a sufficient number to offset the growing demand for jobs. It is estimated that more than 45% of the available labor force is unemployed or under-employed.

For many Dominicans, emigration is a viable alternative. Although the number seeking to enter the U.S., Venezuela, Canada, and Europe is increasing, the outflow is partially offset by significant illegal immigration of Haitians (estimated at 600,000) to the Dominican Republic.

Government

Originally a Spanish colony and later under Haitian rule, the Dominican Republic gained independence in 1844. Its subsequent history was characterized by alternating periods of authoritarian rule and instability. The collection of Dominican customs revenues was controlled by the U.S. from 1905 to 1940. A naval mission, chiefly composed of U.S. Marines, governed the country from 1916 to 1924.

Following Trujillo's assassination on May 30, 1961, the country again underwent a series of political crises, including the election and overthrow of the government of Juan Bosch, the first democratically elected president since 1930. This government lasted only seven months before it was toppled in a military coup in 1963. An attempt to restore constitutional government in April 1965 ended in civil war and the arrival of the Inter-American Peace Force (IAPF), of which U.S. forces were a part. Peace was restored, and the IAPF withdrew its last troops in September 1966.

In June 1966, Dr. Joaquín Balaguer was elected to a four-year term as president. During this period, his administration worked primarily to promote economic and social reforms. In June 1970, Balaguer was reelected to an additional four-year term. Although his second term was marred by both left- and right-wing terrorism and violence in 1970 and 1971, and by a minor short-lived guerrilla incursion in 1973, the country registered steady economic progress. Elections, in which an opposition alliance

abstained only days before (claiming unfair conditions), were held again in May 1974, and President Balaguer was returned to office for the third time. He was defeated for a fourth term in 1978 by the candidate of the Dominican Revolutionary Party, Antonio Guzmán (Fernández).

The 1982 elections brought Dr. Salvador Jorge Blanco to the presidency in an orderly succession, and a growing strength in the country's democratic institution has been demonstrated. The 1986 elections saw Joaquín Balaguer return to the presidency for a fourth term. Jacobo Majluta, the president of the Senate who opposed Balaguer in the balloting, conceded defeat after claiming irregularities in the closely fought race. Majluta lost by less than 44,000 votes. Balaguer was reelected to the presidency for a fifth term in August, 1990. The results of the May 1994 election were disputed, leading to scheduling of a new election in May 1996. Leonel Fernandez was elected president in a second round of voting and took office in August.

Under the constitution, executive power is vested in the president, who is assisted by a cabinet which includes secretaries of state for various areas of responsibilities, such as armed forces, foreign relations, finance, interior and police, education, fine arts and public worship, agriculture, industry and commerce, public health and social welfare, labor, public works and communications, and sports.

Legislative power is vested in a bicameral congress. There are 30 senators, one for each province and the National District (the city of Santo Domingo). As a result of the 1990 election, the Social Christian Reformist Party held 16 seats, the Dominican Liberation Party won 12 seats, and the Dominican Revolutionary Party gained two seats. The Chamber of Deputies has 120 members, one for each 50,000 inhabitants, based on the 1981 census.

The judiciary consists of local justices of the peace and civil courts of the first instance, special land courts in each province, district courts of appeal, and the Supreme Court of nine justices. Judges are nominated by the Senate. The judicial system does not include trial by jury.

Local authority emanates from the central government. The country is divided into 29 provinces, each administered by a governor appointed by the president. Santo Domingo and the municipalities are each governed by a mayor and a municipal council, elected by popular vote for four-year terms.

Besides the majority and opposing parties now in Congress (the Dominican Revolutionary Party (PRD) and the Reformists), several Communist parties and factions exist, as do others with Marxist leanings. These include the Dominican Communist Party (PCD), legalized in 1977; the Dominican Popular Movement (MPD); the Dominican Liberation Party (PLD); and the Anti-Imperialist Patriotic Union (UPA). These groups are active in intellectual circles, laboring classes, and student groups.

The Dominican Republic is a member of the United Nations and its various specialized agencies, the Organization of American States (OAS), the World Bank, the Inter-American Development Bank, and the International Monetary Fund (IMF), and is also a signatory to the General Agreement on Tariffs and Trade (GATT).

The flag of the Dominican Republic consists of two red and two blue sections divided by a white cross centered with the Dominican coat of arms.

Arts, Science, Education

The Dominican Republic has begun to achieve maturity in artistic, technical, and intellectual pursuits. In the past, opportunity to study abroad was limited and individual intellectual activity was discouraged. In recent years, an exciting ferment of new ideas, artistic expression, and an eagerness to discover and take part in the best intellectual and cultural developments has emerged. Santo Domingo's modern Cultural Plaza with its four museums, National Theater, and National Library is the scene of many artistic, musical, and theatrical productions. The opening of the National Theater in August 1973 signaled the beginning of a new cultural era for the country; the theater now draws artists and groups from around the world. The National Library, with a capacity for 200,000 volumes, and the Museum of Dominican Man were also inaugurated in 1973.

Individual artists who have achieved international renown include painters Gilberto Hernández Ortega, Guillo Perez, Ramón Oviedo, Candido Bido, Soucy de Pellerano, Ada Balcacer, Orlando Menicucci, Fernando Urena Rib, and Francisco Santos. Antonio Pratts Ventos, Domingo Liz, Ramiro Matos, and José Ramón Rotellini are leading sculptors who have done interesting work in metals and wood. Dominican architects show imagination and beauty in design.

Books of literary merit—novels, short stories, histories, and criticism—are published frequently. A five-volume anthology of Dominican literature has filled a need for gathering the best in the nation's writing. Popular music, *merengue*, *salsa*, and *nueva ola* performers are numerous. Several troupes of folkloric dancers and singers also perform.

Public education in the Dominican Republic has suffered greatly from a lack of funding, with the result that literacy may have slipped within recent years to less than 70%. Few families can afford to do without their children's labor, and only a limited number of free secondary schools exist. In general, schools are overcrowded, understaffed, and lack educational material and equipment.

Higher education is possible for only a fraction of the literate population. However, the oldest university in the Western Hemisphere, the 60,000-student Autonomous University of Santo Domingo (UASD), founded in the 16th century, has 10 times its enrollment of 20 years ago. Other excellent institutions are the Universidad Católica Madre y Maestra in Santiago, the Universidad Nacional Pedro Henríquez Urena and Instituto Tecnológico de Santo Domingo in the capital, and the Universidad Central del Este in San Pedro de Macorís. Although vocational and technical training cannot meet present needs, progress is being made in home economics, education, agriculture, commercial work, mechanics, electronics, metallurgy, and construction trades.

The principal institution for advanced technical training is the Instituto de Estudios Superiores. An English/Spanish branch of the World University of Puerto Rico is also active in Santo Domingo. Approximately 800 Dominican students attend universities in the U.S. annually, and several hundred also study in Europe (especially Spain) and in neighboring Latin American countries, particularly Mexico and Venezuela.

Commerce and Industry

Agriculture provides employment for roughly 17% of the Dominican labor force, and accounted for 15% of the total export earnings. Sugar, the mainstay of the economy, generates over $506 million annually. Other important agricultural products include coffee, tobacco, and cacao. The Dominican Republic also produces rice, potatoes, beans, plantains, yucca, and other crops for domestic consumption.

Industry has as its principal concerns sugar refining, textiles, pharmaceuticals, light manufacturing, and breweries that produce excellent local beer and rum. Mineral exports account for a substantial portion of total export value. In addition to recently discovered coal, the nation has important deposits of gold, silver, bauxite, and ferronickel.

The vigorous promotion of the Dominican Republic as a tourist haven has swelled the numbers of visitors to record levels placing the nation among the top Caribbean tourist destinations. Major resort complexes have been built on both coasts in an ambitious development program.

The U.S. is the principal trading partner of the Dominican Republic, and typically accounts for 70% of its exports and provided 46% of all imported goods. A relatively low inflation rate, import exonerations, low labor costs, and tax holidays help the investment climate. A long-needed revision of the basic foreign investment law is being considered to enhance the investment picture.

Transportation

Santo Domingo's international airport, Las Americas, is 19 miles from the city. It is served by the national airline, Dominicana (Compañía Dominicana de Aviación), American, Avianca, Viasa, ALM (subsidiary of KLM), Iberia, Lufthansa, Prinair, and Varig. Aeropuerto Internacional La Unión is the modern north-coast airport for the Puerto Plata/Playa Dorada/Sosua area.

Several private companies in the capital offer chartered, air-conditioned bus tours. A group of five persons can charter a car (*público*) at reasonable rates for trips to Santiago, San Cristóbal, or Barahona. Air charter service is available from Herrera Airport in Santo Domingo; also, daily service to Santiago, Puerto Plata, and other points on the island is provided by Alas del Caribe, the country's domestic airline.

Passenger and cargo ships call at Santo Domingo, Puerto Plata, Haina, and Port-au-Prince (Haiti) on an irregular basis. Freight lines of various registries call at Santo Domingo from all parts of the world.

The Dominican Republic has no passenger or freight railways. Private car lines and buses connect outlying cities to one another and to the capital. Air-conditioned express buses run daily on regular schedules from Santo Domingo to Bonao, La Vega, Moca, Santiago, Puerto Plata, San Pedro de Macorís, La Romana, and other towns in the interior.

Buses, minibuses, and *públicos* have regular routes throughout the capital. The latter, usually painted blue with red, white, or green roofs (depending on the zones they cover) cruise certain streets picking up as many passengers as the car will hold. Regular taxis are available at large hotels, as is private call-a-cab service; these taxis operate on a zone system, but drivers are occasionally willing to carry a passenger a short distance, called a *carrera*, for a minimum fare plus tip. It is advisable to settle on a fare before hiring a cab.

Traffic moves on the right. Laws are similar to those in the U.S., but local drivers are aggressive, making defensive driving necessary. It is against the law to smoke while driving. Traffic police control busy intersections, and their signals must be learned quickly and followed closely. Police cars are green and white; ambulances are white; fire trucks are red.

Santo Domingo is the hub of a fairly extensive road network. A hard-surfaced, four-lane highway leads from the capital to the international airport and beach areas east of the city, but the road narrows to two lanes about 30 miles out. A fairly good, two-lane, heavily traveled road connects Santo Domingo with Santiago de los Caballeros—the nation's second largest city—and with Puerto Plata on the north coast. There is a highway connecting Puerto Plata

eastward to the Samaná Bay area. Road networks throughout the republic are improving. Blacktop and gravel roads connect many outlying communities, although rural roads and bridges are often in poor condition. Vehicles with heavy-duty suspension and four-wheel-drive are generally required for these latter roads. Most Santo Domingo streets are blacktop, and their condition ranges from excellent to poor. The city has several divided boulevards. Most streets are narrow, particularly in the downtown shopping area, and permit only one-way traffic.

International driver's licenses are not valid in the Dominican Republic. Anyone without a license from his own country must take a written examination in Spanish and a road test to qualify for a Dominican license. Minimum third-party liability insurance is required; coverage should be obtained from a local firm, since few U.S. carriers are permitted to underwrite in the Dominican Republic.

Communications

Telephone service links all major points in the republic, and long-distance connections can be made to other countries without undue delay. There are some areas where growth has out-paced telephone expansion, but difficulties are minimal; local service is adequate. International mail is handled twice daily and normally takes three to five days for delivery to and from the eastern United States.

The Dominican Republic has over 200 radio stations, including shortwave and FM outlets. There are periodic newscasts all day, as well as interviews and all-round variety music programming.

Station HIJB (FM) has two classical music programs daily, "Gala Concert" at 1 p.m. and "Concert Hall" at 8 p.m. On Sundays, Texaco sponsors an opera at 1 p.m. Good shortwave radios can also pick up Voice of America (VOA), American Forces

Radio, and Puerto Rican, Jamaican, and Florida stations.

Santo Domingo has six television stations: Rahintel, Color-Visión, Teleantillas, Tele-Inde, and Tele-sistema, all privately owned; and Radio Televisión Dominicana, government-owned. All stations transmit in color. Programs include local and international news, weather, sports, variety shows, movies, and dramatic serials produced in Latin America and the U.S. The majority of programs are in Spanish. CNN and 18 other cable TV stations are available 24 hours a day. Many hotels have satellite dishes that allow them to receive foreign language broadcasts from countries around the world. U.S. TV sets can be used in Santo Domingo without modification. Usual broadcasting hours are 11 a.m. to midnight.

Nine major Spanish-language daily newspapers (Monday through Saturday) are published in the Dominican Republic. *El Caribe, Listín Diario, Hoy,* and *El Sol,* the morning papers, carry extensive news coverage and take independent political lines. *Última Hora, La Noticia,* and *El Nacional* are published in the afternoon. *El Día, Ya,* and *La Información* are published daily in Santiago, and serve the interests of the Cibao Valley. *El Nacional, La Noticia,* and *Listín Diario* have the only Sunday editions. Some of these papers subscribe to Associated Press, United Press International, and other news services. One major weekly news magazine, *Ahora,* is published locally. The *Miami Herald,* the *Wall Street Journal, Time, Newsweek,* and *The New York Times* arrive the same day or a day after publication. The English-language weekly, *The Santo Domingo News,* provides business and tourism news.

Health

Santo Domingo has many American-trained dentists and doctors, including specialists in obstetrics, pediatrics, neurosurgery, gynecology, cardiology, gastroenterology, dermatology, and diseases of the eye, ear, nose, and throat. Most doctors speak some English. Emergency aids, such as incubators, oxygen tents, and blood banks are available, and several laboratories are equipped to do routine tests. A number of hospitals and small clinics are adequate, but not up to U.S. standards, particularly in nursing care, cleanliness, and diet. Nonetheless, Americans use them for obstetrical care, pediatrics, some surgery, and other illnesses or injuries requiring relatively short periods of hospitalization.

Primarily because of poor storage methods, the inadequate disposal of garbage and other wastes, and the tropical climate, Santo Domingo is infested with flies, cockroaches, ants, mice, and rats. Other pests include termites, ticks, bedbugs, tarantulas, and mosquitoes. Non-poisonous snakes are also found here. Small lizards and frogs sometimes get into houses. Commercial exterminators are available.

Sanitation standards are loosely enforced, and unsanitary practices in the processing, storage, distribution, and sale of food are common. Several modern supermarkets in the capital, however, have improved their refrigeration and handling of fresh produce and meat. Most Americans prefer these stores over local markets, even though supermarket prices are much higher. City water, often filled with surface seepage and sediment after heavy rains, is not potable unless boiled for 10 minutes. Filtered bottled water is available.

Fruits and vegetables must be washed thoroughly with soapy water and soaked in an iodine or clorox solution. Fruits should be peeled. Locally bought meats should be served well done. Shellfish is safe if cooked thoroughly.

Domestic employees should receive periodic physical examinations and chest x-rays to rule out tuberculosis. They must be trained in good food-handling techniques and in personal hygiene.

Dominican health authorities, with the cooperation of the Pan-American Health Organization and other international agencies, are conducting active campaigns against disease. Although some progress has been made, observers agree that the task is formidable. Diseases which affect the local population include intestinal parasites, tuberculosis, dengue fever, AIDS, malnutrition, venereal disease and, in some rural areas, malaria. Periodic epidemics of influenza and gastro-intestinal infections exist. Diarrhea, accompanied by dehydration and fever, is common, and particularly debilitating to young children. Other complaints include upper respiratory, ear, and gynecological infections; skin irritations; and fungal infections. Animal rabies is a problem.

The following immunizations are recommended by U.S. authorities: yellow fever and tetanus-diphtheria for ages seven and up; DPT (diphtheria-pertussis-tetanus), measles, mumps, rubella, and polio for those under seven; anyone over age 12 should take gamma globulin every six months to prevent hepatitis. Inoculations against measles, tetanus, and rabies are available locally.

NOTES FOR TRAVELERS

Passage, Customs & Duties

A valid passport, or a U.S. birth certificate, Certificate of Naturalization or Certificate of Citizenship, along with photo identification, are required for both entry and exit. Because of the high incidence of fraud in the Dominican Republic and potential delays with Dominican Immigration, the U.S. Embassy strongly recommends that United States citizens travel with passports. Visitors who do not obtain a visa prior to entry must purchase a tourist card to enter the country.

Americans living in or traveling to the Dominican Republic are encouraged to register at the Consular Section of the United States Embassy

in Santo Domingo and obtain updated information on travel and security within the Dominican Republic. TheU.S. Embassy is located at the corner of Calle Cesar Nicolas Penson and Calle Leopoldo Navarro inSanto Domingo; telephone (809) 221-2171; after hours (809) 221-8100. The Consular Section is a half-mile away at the corner of Calle Cesar Nicolas Penson and Avenida Maximo Gomez. The American Citizens Services section can be reached by telephone at (809) 731-4294, or via the Internet at http://www.usemb.gov.do/nacsl.htm. Consular office hours are 7:30 a.m. to 12:00 p.m. and 1:00 p.m. to 2:00 p.m., Monday through Friday, except holidays. There is a Consular Agency in Puerto Plata at Calle Beller 51, 2nd floor, office 6, telephone (809) 586-4204; office hours are 9:00 a.m. to 12:00 p.m., and 2:30 p.m. to 5:00 p.m., Monday through Friday, except holidays. U.S. citizens may register at the Consular Section of the U.S. Embassy and obtain updated information on travel and security in the Dominican Republic.

Pets

A signed health and rabies vaccination certificate from a licensed veterinarian must be presented when importing a pet into the Dominican Republic, or the pet will be quarantined. Regulations change frequently; it is advisable to check beforehand with authorities.

Firearms & Ammunition

Dominican customs authorities strictly enforce regulations concerning the importation of firearms. Persons bringing firearms into the country, even temporarily, may face jail sentences and heavy fines. It is advisable to contact the Embassy of the Dominican Republic in Washington, D.C. or one of the Dominican Republic's consulates in the United States for specific information regarding customs requirements.

Currency, Banking, and Weights and Measures

The time in the Dominican Republic is Greenwich Mean Time (GMT) minus four (the same as observed during Daylight Saving Time on the U.S. east coast).

The sole monetary unit is the Dominican *peso*, written RD$. Currency is issued in the same denominations as U.S. currency, and the coins bear a close resemblance. The four American banks in the capital are Bank of America, Banco de Boston Dominicano (an affiliate of First National Bank of Boston), Chase Manhattan, and Citibank.

Officially, the Dominican Republic uses the metric system of weights and measures but, in practice, the U.S. system of ounces, pounds, inches, feet, gallons, and miles is commonly used.

Disaster Preparedness

The Dominican Republic is a hurricane-prone country. In the event of a hurricane alert, a notice will be posted in U.S. Embassy Santo Domingo's web page cited below. General information about natural disaster preparedness is available via the Internet from the U.S. Federal Emergency Management Agency (FEMA) at http://www.fema.gov.

LOCAL HOLIDAYS

Jan. 1	New Year's Day
Jan. 6	Epiphany
Jan. 21	Our Lady of Altagracia
Jan. 26	Duarte's Day
Feb. 27	Dominican Independence Day
Mar/Apr	Good Friday*
Mar/Apr	Easter*
May 1	Dominican Labor Day
May/June	Corpus Christi*
Aug. 16	Dominican Restoration Day
Sept. 24	Our Lady of las Mercedes
Oct. 14	Columbus Day
Dec. 25	Christmas Day

*Variable

RECOMMENDED READING

The following titles are provided as a general indication of the material published on this country:

Finlay, Barbara. *The Women of Azua: Work & Family in the Rural Dominican Republic.* Westport, CT: Greenwood Press, 1989.

Fodor's '89 Caribbean. New York: Fodor's, 1988.

Frommer's Dollarwise Guide to the Caribbean. New York: Prentice Hall, 1989.

Grasmuck, Sherry and Patricia R. Pressar. *Between Two Islands: Dominican International Migration.* Berkely, CA: University of California Press, 1991.

Haggerty, Richard A. *Dominican Republic & Haiti: A Country Study.* Washington, DC: Library of Congress, 1991.

Hillman, Richard S., and Thomas J. D'Agostino. *Distant Neighbors in the Caribbean: The Dominican Republic & Jamaica in Comparative Prospective.* Westport, CT: Greenwood Press, 1992.

Hinze, Peter. *Practical Travel A to Z: Dominican Republic.* Chatham, NY: Hayit Publishing USA, 1992.

Kryzanek, Michael J. *The Politics of External Influence in the Dominican Republic.* New York: Praeger, 1988.

Lowenthal, A.F. (ed.) *Exporting Democracy: The United States and Latin America.* Baltimore: John Hopkins University Press, 1991.

Lugo, Marta. *The Dominican Republic Guidebook.* Teaneck, NJ: Eurasia Press, 1989.

Nelson, William J. *Almost a Territory: America's Attempt to Annex the Dominican Republic.* Cranbury, NJ: University of Delaware Press, 1990.

Schoenhals, Kai, comp. *Dominican Republic.* Santa Barbara, CA: ABC-Clio, 1990.

Schoonmaker, Herbert Garrettson. *Military Crisis Management: U.S. Intervention in the Dominican Republic, 1965.* Westport, CT: Greenwood Press, 1990.

Vargas-Lundius, Rosemary. *Peasants in Distress: Poverty & Unemployment in the Dominican Republic.* Boulder, CO: Westview Press, 1991.

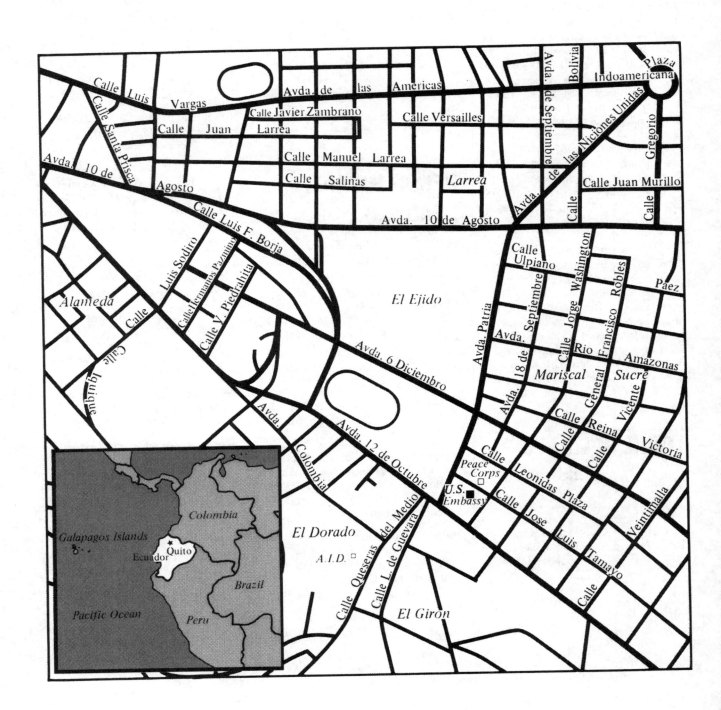

Quito, Ecuador

ECUADOR

Republic of Ecuador

Major Cities:
Quito, Guayaquil, Cuenca

Other Cities:
Ambato, Azogues, Babahoyo, Esmeraldas, Guaranda, Latacunga, Loja, Portoviejo, Riobamba, Tulcán

EDITOR'S NOTE

This chapter was adapted from the Department of State Post Report 1999 for Ecuador. Supplemental material has been added to increase coverage of minor cities, facts have been updated, and some material has been condensed. Readers are encouraged to visit the Department of State's web site at http://travel.state.gov/ for the most recent information available on travel to this country.

INTRODUCTION

Ecuador is not a large country, but it offers a striking variety of climates, customs, and cultures. The high, wide Andean plateau which dominates the country has been both a highway and a resting place for the Incan, Spanish, and mestizo civilizations which have shaped the nation's history. The lowland Amazonian jungle east of the mountains, home of several indigenous groups, is also the location of rough oil boom towns. The Pacific coastal plain to the west of the Andes is a land of tropical plantations, bustling port cities, and warm water beaches. Six hundred miles from the coast lie the Galapagos, a chain of volcanic islands which are home to unique species of wildlife and a small number of islanders.

Quito is a city of sun and sky, set in agricultural highlands and surrounded by high mountains and snow capped volcanoes. With a balance of equatorial sunshine and mountain chill, the climate varies little throughout the year. Some newcomers find it difficult to adjust to the thin air and burning sun at an altitude of 9,300 feet and even the most athletic need to wait a week before undertaking any strenuous activity.

Guayaquil is a complete contrast to the capital. It is a busy, noisy town where the natives are both more aggressive and more openhanded than the reserved inhabitants of the Sierra. Like most port towns, Guayaquil is a center of commerce, a place where the shrewd can make a fortune or can capture and direct enough of the city's rough energy to make a successful political career.

MAJOR CITIES

Quito

When Spanish expeditions overwhelmed the Inca Empire, the Inca leader Rumiñahui destroyed the city of Quito rather than surrender it to the conquerors. The Spanish built their own settlement, San Francisco de Quito, on the same site, at the southern end of the Pichincha Valley. It was an easily defensible location bordered by deep ravines and dominated by the smooth round hill now called the Panecillo.

Nestled in a high mountain valley surrounded by snow capped volcanoes, Quito will literally take your breath away with its natural beauty and altitude. The Andean setting, Spanish colonial architecture, Indian costumes, palm trees and bougainvillea, and steep hillsides with checkerboard patterns in vivid greens and yellows rising into the clouds a short distance from the sprawling city-all make Quito unique.

The colonial center of Quito has been declared a human heritage ("Patrimonio de la Humanidad") by UNESCO. This heritage is preserved today by zoning laws which forbid the demolition or exterior remodeling of the low, white-washed buildings in the center of the city. The old town, cut into squares by narrow streets with steep flights of steps, contains many colonial ecclesiastic monuments: La Compañia with its carved facade and gold-leafed interior; San Francisco, the

Aerial view of old Quito, Ecuador

Susan Rock. Reproduced by permission.

first spiritual center in South America, with a museum crowded with sculptures and paintings by Caspicara and Miguel de Santiago; San Augustin, a quiet convent with treasures in its ceilings and altars; the Cathedral, famous for art works of the Quiteño school; Santo Domingo monastery, with another museum of priceless paintings and sculptures, and many others.

The narrow streets of colonial Quito are a pleasure for an unhurried stroll on weekends when the city seems to shut down completely, though street crime compels caution. During the week the heavy traffic makes a walk through the center of town something of a struggle and it is unwise to venture through the colorful Ipiales street market with important documents or valuables. A respite from the bustling throngs of shoppers, vendors, and noisy traffic can be found in the broad plazas with well-kept parks bordered by churches and public buildings.

In the mid-20th century, Quito grew quickly. Industrial areas and crowded popular barrios developed to the south of the city. To the north, Quito spreads up a wide valley bordering the dormant Pichincha Volcano. Originally farmland dotted with villas built in fanciful Spanish, Moorish, or 1930s modern architecture, this area is rapidly becoming Quito's modern center. The Rio Amazonas shopping district runs from the park through a modern business center of high-rise office buildings that offer a variety of restaurants, shops, banks, and sidewalk cafes. Avenida Gonzales Suarez, Bella Vista, Quito Tenis and El Bosque are the areas where most of the diplomatic community lives.

Utilities

Most homes have reservoir tanks, pumps, and small electric water heaters. Houses and apartments have modern plumbing for the most part. Because of long waits for new phones, rent a house or apartment with a telephone already installed, a cordless phone may be convenient.

Electric current is the same as in the U.S.: 110v, 60 cycles, with 220v available for stoves and dryers. Do not rent a home without 220v triplephase current available for appliances.

Homes in Quito have no central heating, and evenings can be quite chilly. Some houses are colder than others; those with eastern and western exposure benefit from the strong equatorial sunshine and are warmer than those with north-south exposure.

At times in the past, Ecuador has experienced shortages due to lack of rainfall in the southern part of the country. Extended power rationing has often occurred during the winter months. The rationing has not occurred recently.

Food

Ecuador has a plentiful supply of tropical fruits and vegetables all year, with varieties not seen in North America. Avocados, artichokes, raspberries, strawberries, bananas, pineapples and papaya can be purchased all year, and peaches, apples, pears and other fruit can be found in season. Several markets in Quito have fresh produce, seafood, chicken and meat, cut flowers, and potted plants.

Beef, pork, lamb and veal can be bought in supermarkets and butcher shops. Filet mignon costs about half the U.S. price. Chicken is more expensive, and turkey costs about twice as much as in the U.S. Both American and European cuts of meat are available, though the beef here is usually unaged, and may be tough. Some families use meat tenderizers or marinade. A pressure cooker is very useful for cooking at high altitudes.

Although a wide variety of food items are available in Ecuador, including items imported from the U.S. and Europe, certain American food are difficult to find or very expensive.

Milk is pasteurized, though quality control is irregular, and comes in disposable paper cartons or plastic bags. Heavy cream is available in the supermarkets, and sour cream can be found in some stores. A variety of cheeses are available, though not of the same quality or variation as can be found in the states. Several brands of ice cream are considered safe, and several brands of good yogurt are available. Excellent pastry and a variety of breads can be purchased in Quito and the surrounding small towns.

Quito has two large supermarket chains; Supermaxi and Mi Comisariato, which are well stocked with groceries, dry goods, and fresh products at very reasonable prices. U.S. goods are available, but at somewhat higher prices than in the U.S. Comparable Ecuadorian and Latin American products are less expensive. Many small shops and delicatessens offer excellent quality food stuffs such as ham, sausages, cold cuts, pickles, olives, and pastas. In general, the cook who can use the local foods with imagination will find it economical to do without processed, packaged, imported goods.

Ecuadorian cuisine depends heavily on corn, potatoes, and pork. Wonderful soups are made with the great assortment of vegetables. One local specialty is locro, a potato soup with cheese and avocado; another is llapingachos, a potato and cheese pancake. Delicious "cebiche" (marinated seafood), "humitas" (baked corn cakes), and "empanadas" (pastries filled with meat or cheese) are standard fare.

Clothing
General: Light to medium weight clothing is used throughout the year in Quito. Due to varying temperatures during the course of the day, you will need sweaters, jackets, or raincoats, and an umbrella. In general, you can use almost anything in your wardrobe except heavy winter clothing. Bring summer clothing for trips to the beach and the jungle, and swimsuits for the heated pools in Quito. Warm up suits are a must for joggers and tennis players in Quito. Bathrobes and warm pajamas will be a comfort. Hats are useful for protection from the sun. A wide assortment of brimmed hats in beautiful colors and styles can be bought in Ecuador for much less than in the U.S. A lightweight coat will be welcomed on some of Quito's chilliest evenings. It is a good idea to bring a winter coat, in case a trip to Washington in January comes up. A down parka also comes in handy when visiting the volcanoes.

Many boutiques offer stylish clothing, dresses, and suits imported

from the U.S. and Europe, but prices are high. Locally made sweaters are inexpensive. Leather and suede coats for men and women may be made to order. Fashionable knitwear may be bought ready-made or made to order at reasonable prices. The quality of dry cleaning is good, and inexpensive.

Boots and shoes of good quality leather can be made to order. In women's shoes, U.S. sizes above 8½ are hard to find in ready-to-wear. In men's shoes, U.S. sizes above 9½ are also hard to find.

Men: Light to medium-weight suits are worn all year. Sport coats, sweaters, slacks, and long-sleeved sports shirts are useful for informal and casual gatherings. A raincoat with a zip-in lining is welcome on chilly evenings. Business and professional men do not wear hats except when watching sports events or other outdoor activities. Equestrians should bring riding helmets. Good tailoring is available at reasonable prices. Tuxedoes are occasionally needed; white dinner jackets are not worn.

Women: Blouses, skirts, sweaters, slacks, and jackets are standard daily wear in Quito. Because mornings and evenings are cool and temperatures at noon quite warm, a cardigan or blazer is usually worn or carried. Light-weight wool is the most practical material. Informal and casual clothes are worn at social gatherings outside the city on the weekends, but simple cocktail dresses are needed for dinner parties during the week in town. Long-sleeved dresses with jackets and dinner suits are good choices for chilly evenings. Shorts, short skirts and tank tops should not be worn in public. Bring a wraparound skirt or warm up suit to throw on after exercise classes or tennis.

Rainwear and a light or medium-weight coat, stole, or cape for evenings are necessary. Hats are not worn, except for protection from the sun. Embroidered capes and stoles, different kinds of sweaters, and ponchos are available locally. Dress-

makers are available and fabric can be purchased locally.

Children: Light to medium-weight clothes are the rule. Warm, inexpensive sweaters can be bought locally. Bring raincoats, boots, and shoes. You should bring with you any special sporting good attire or equipment. Warm pajamas or nightgowns, bathrobes, and slippers are recommended. Teenagers of both sexes seem to live in jeans or corduroy slacks and tennis shoes, but those who like discotheques and parties will need more formal clothing. Young men will probably want at least one sports coat and girls a nice dress, skirt or pantsuit.

Supplies and Services
The local pharmacies carry most medicines and drugs, but availability of item, varies from month to month. If you plan to sew or use a dressmaker's services, bring a supply of sewing accessories, especially thread and zippers. A wide range of fabrics is available at varying prices, but imported fabrics are expensive. Good quality woolens and synthetics are manufactured locally.

Bring basic tools, as well as any hobby and do-it-yourself equipment. Batteries of all sizes are available.

Stationery, quality envelopes, greeting cards, wrapping paper, and ribbon are scarce and expensive. Aluminum foil, plastic wrap, waxed paper, toilet paper and disposable diapers are available, but expensive. Plain paper napkins can be bought, but the quality is only fair, Candles are sold in different sizes and colors at U.S. prices, but the dripless variety are not available. Artists should bring all supplies.

Children's toys are very expensive. Bring toys for your children and for gifts. Bring lunch boxes for kindergarten and elementary school-age children.

Parts for common electrical appliances. electronic products, and cars are often available, but expensive. Parts ordered from the U.S. take a long time to arrive. and if sent airfreight they will spend one to two months awaiting customs clearance. Local mechanics are good. The cost of service on cars and appliances i, much lower than in the U.S. Painting is inexpensive.

Quito has many excellent hairdressers and barbershops and prices are lower than in the U.S. Hairdressers, masseuses. and manicurists will come to your home at reasonable cost. Several cosmetologists offer good service at low prices. Many reputable local artisans make and repair jewelry for much less than in the U.S. Good catering services are available in the city, and prices are reasonable. Good tailors and dressmakers are available at a range of prices.

Domestic Help

Domestic maids and gardeners are available for reasonable wages. Residents sometimes prefer live-in maids for babysitting duties and for security reasons, however, live-in maids are becoming harder to find. There are few trained nannies, although some maids handle childcare responsibilities well. Many maids can cook, but it is hard to find cooks who will handle other household duties or who are trained for representational duties. There are many good caterers who are available for parties. Many people in houses share the cost of a security guard with their neighbors.

A combination maid-cook is generally desirable for a single person or couple without children. Large families often hire more than one domestic employee. Domestic employees generally earn about $150 per month. Workers who come in by the day generally earn about $10 per day.

Under Ecuadorian law, domestic employees must be covered by Ecuadorian Social Security. Stringent laws cover employment and termination. These regulations are included in orientation material for new arrivals and should be read and followed carefully.

In addition to an annual salary, the domestic employee receives (per Ecuadorian law) a 13th, 14th, 15th, and 16th month salary plus a supplementary compensation, and a cost of living bonus. Live-out maids are also entitled to a transportation allowance. Although the employee and the employer are required to pay a portion of the employees income to the Social Security system, most employers in Ecuador pay the entire amount for their domestic employees. By law, domestic employees are entitled to one day off every two weeks, but in practice they receive one day off each week. Domestics are also entitled to 15 days paid vacation annually. Domestics are not entitled to any holidays. Employers are required by law to provide uniforms for their domestic help.

Religious Activities

Ecuador is primarily a Catholic country, and Quito is the seat of an Archbishop. About 70 Catholic churches in the city serve Spanish-speaking congregations. An English-language service is held in the Dominican Chapel each Sunday morning, and confessions may be heard.

Traditional Jewish services in Spanish and Hebrew are offered each Friday evening and Saturday morning at the Asociacion Israelita.

The community has a number of Protestant activities and services in English. The Advent-St. Nicholas Church (Lutheran and Anglican) offers a worship service and adult discussion group every Sunday morning at Isabel La Catolica 1431. The First Baptist Church has Sunday school classes and worship services. The Inter-denominational English Fellowship Church, sponsored by the World Radio Missionary Fellowship (which runs radio stations HCJB and Voz Andes Hospital), offers Bible school and services on Sunday and a teen group program.

The Seventh-day Adventists offer services on Saturday mornings and Sunday evenings and operate the Clinica Americana. Jehovah's Witnesses also have weekly services. The Church of the Latter-day Saints has Sunday services in Spanish.

Education

Quito has many public and private primary and secondary schools. Cotopaxi Academy, Alliance Academy, Colegio Menor and Colegio Americano are private schools usually preferred by Americans in Quito. Cotopaxi Academy and Colegio Americano receive limited grant support from the U.S. Government.

Cotopaxi Academy was founded in 1959 as a private, cooperative, American nonsectarian school offering classes from pre-kindergarten (for children from the age of 3) through grade 12. The school year runs from mid-August to mid-June. Some 750 students attend the school. About one-third are Americans, one-third are Ecuadorians, and one-third other nationalities. Instruction is in English, and both Spanish and English are taught as second languages. The teachers are certified in the U.S., and classes are limited to 20 students. An International Baccalaureate Diploma is offered for qualified students going on to universities around the world. It is located in a recently built campus in the northern part of the city.

Cotopaxi is affiliated with the Universities of Alabama, Kentucky, Massachusetts, and Pennsylvania for student teaching internship programs. It is accredited by the Southern Association of Colleges and Schools and the International Baccalaureate Office in Geneva.

In addition to the traditional academic subjects, classes are offered in art, band, physical education, computers, and French. Standard U.S. texts, teaching materials, and tests are used. Extracurricular activities include yearbook, newspaper, drama club, National Honor Society, Student Council, and several sports. Two guidance counselors are on the staff.

An integrated program for gifted students operates from prekindergarten to grade 12. Programs for physically handicapped children and those with learning disabilities are limited, but available from pre-kindergarten through grade 12 after the candidates undergo prerequisite screening. The staff includes a remedial reading teacher. For children in higher grades who have special problems, consult the school prior to arrival.

Alliance Academy, founded in 1929 for the children of missionaries is a privately supported college preparatory school. The school provides educational facilities to the children of Protestant missionaries from Quito, as well as those from other parts of Latin America. It has kindergarten through grade 12. The school year runs from early August to late May. Of some 500 students, 60% are children of missionaries from many different missions, and 40% are children of diplomatic and international business families.

Eighty percent are U.S and Canadian citizens. Children from other international families are accepted on a space-available basis. The Christian Philosophy of Education is the focus of the school. Daily Bible classes and weekly chapels are a required part of the curriculum. Students of all faiths are accepted.

Classes are taught in English, and Spanish classes are required for all students. The basic subjects resemble those in most U.S. schools. Electives include woodworking, art, typing, home economics, photography, shorthand, and yearbook publication. Advanced placement courses pre offered in math, English, and Spanish. Computer math and programming are also offered. The school is well supplied with learning materials, including three fully equipped science laboratories, elementary and secondary school libraries, and an audiovisual center. The library holds about 35,000 volumes, 800 films, 2,000 filmstrips, and videotaping facilities. Spanish and English are taught as second languages. Programs are available for the gifted as well as for the mentally handicapped. The school con-

Street scene in Guayquil, Ecuador

© Wolfgang Kaehler. Reproduced by permission.

ducts a full and varied sports and extracurricular program, including chorus, band, and orchestra.

Alliance Academy is accredited by the Southern Association of Colleges and Schools and belongs to the Southern Association of Independent Schools, the Association of Christian Schools International, and the Association of American Schools of South America.

Colegio Americano was founded in 1940 as a private coeducational school for students of all nationalities from pre-kindergarten through grade 12. A Junior College provides secretarial and business management training. The school year is

divided into trimesters extending from early October to mid-July, the traditional Ecuadorian school year. The current school population is 2,800. Most students are Ecuadorian. The 22-acre campus is 10 miles north of Quito.

The curriculum is divided into two sections: an international section offers courses similar to those at U.S. college preparatory, public schools; a national section offers subjects required of Ecuadorian schools. Instruction is in both English and Spanish. Courses in art and music are also taught. The school is accredited by the Southern Association of Colleges and Schools and by the Ecuadorian Ministry of

Education. A Comprehensive Learning Disabilities program from prekindergarten through grade 12 is offered, as well as guidance counseling and college counseling. Both English and Spanish are offered as second languages. Eighty-three percent of the graduating seniors go on to study in universities in the U.S. and Europe.

There is at least one English-speaking preschool. Some accept children from age 18 months.

Special Educational Opportunities

Universidad San Francisco, Catholic University and the National Polytechnic School offer academic instruction at the university level in Quito. San Francisco and Catholic Universities have faculties of Law, Economics, Engineering, and Philosophy. The Polytechnic School offers courses in electrical and chemical engineering and nuclear science. All classes are taught in Spanish. The admissions process is lengthy and difficult.

Catholic University offers a special 6 week intensive courses in Spanish for about $350. The course consists of 3 hours of class 5 days a week. Many Americans take this course. You can also find many schools in the city offering Spanish lessons at very reasonable rates. Tutors will also come to your house if requested.

Various well-known local artists accept students of all ages for private classes, and several resident Americans also give art lessons.

The National Conservatory of Music accepts students for voice training and instruction in musical instruments, especially piano and violin. Students attending the schools normally used by the American community may receive instruction in a variety of instruments. Students must have their own musical instruments, although the schools do rent smaller instruments.

The University of Alabama College of Education offers graduate studies

Susan Rock. Reproduced by permission.

View of Cuenca, Ecuador from Mirador Turi

in education in Quito. Visiting professors offer courses in secondary education, elementary and early childhood education, and administration and planning. Four-week courses are offered in the fall and spring and during the summer to fulfill credit requirements toward a Master's Degree or Ph.D.

Several museums in Quito have impressive collections of paintings, archeological objects, and historical manuscripts. The National Museum of History has a noteworthy manuscript collection. The Casa de la Cultura often sponsors exhibits and performances of local artists. The National Museum of Colonial Art has an outstanding collection of sculpture and paintings.

The premier museum in Quito is in the Central Bank located at the Casa de la Cultura. Divided into separate archeological and colonial exhibits, the museum shows carefully selected pieces in a well-designed arrangement. Tours are conducted in several languages, and the museum shows an English-language film describing the country's history and archeology. Another interesting ethnographic museum is located a few miles north of Quito at the Mitad del Mundc monument on

the Equator. Nearby are the partially excavated ruins of an Inca fortress with guides on weekends.

Sports

Soccer is Ecuador's most popular sport, and games are played in Quito year round at the Olympic Stadium. Bullfights are also popular. In December a series of bullfights are held to celebrate Quito Days and some of the world's leading bullfighters perform then.

Those interested in outdoor and indoor sports will not lack for opportunity in Ecuador. Local parks are well-kept and widely used on weekends, but you should be aware of the rising rate of pickpockets or robberies in the parks. Don't go with large amounts of money or important documents. There are tennis, racquetball, basketball and squash courts as well as bowling alleys. American instructors give classes in gymnastics, yoga, and aerobic exercises. Judo and karate are taught at the YMCA. Volleyball is very popular. Bicycling is possible in the parks, but dangerous on the road. Flying lessons are available. There is a small hang-gliding group. Several private clubs in and outside of the city have dining facilities, tennis courts, golf courses, and stables. You

Street in Cuenca, Ecuador

Susan Rock. Reproduced by permission.

can often join these clubs at costs ranging from $30 to $300 a month, plus initiation fees.

Opportunities for horseback riding abound. Buying and maintaining a horse is much less expensive than in the U.S. Lessons are available at different clubs, and riding competitions are held monthly. Polo players will find a small but enthusiastic group of colleagues in Quito.

Quito and its surrounding areas have several places for swimming. Swimming memberships are available at the Hotels Colon, Oro Verde and Quito. The Los Chillos Valley, south of Quito, has several pools and beautiful country clubs. Lago San Pablo, an hour's drive north of Quito, near Otavalo offers opportunities for windsurfing, water skiing and boating.

Health facilities are available in Quito, but range quite a bit in price and services offered. Several offer aerobics classes, weight machines and swimming pools. Memberships are available at the Hotel Hilton Colon, Oro Verde, Hotel Quito and the Elan gym (this list is not all inclusive). Prices range from $450 to $1,200 per year for a single membership.

Fishing enthusiasts can enjoy excellent freshwater and deep-sea fishing in Ecuador. Off the coast, deep-sea tackle is needed for the abundant marlin, tuna, dorado, and other species. Areas close to Quito have good stream and lake fishing for bass and trout. The best trout waters are located high in the mountains, in cold and rainy areas where parkas and waterproof pants are essential. A license to fish anywhere in Ecuador is required.

Good dove hunting can be found near Quito, partridge may be hunted in areas several hours away by car, and duck hunting is good on the coast. The Hunting and Fishing Club has a new clubhouse and excellent shooting range at Lago San Pablo. An overnight trip by car and horseback takes the hunter into good deer hunting country. Guns must be registered.

Mountain climbing, hiking, and camping are popular. Most of the mountains are not technically difficult, but the altitude-ranging from 14,000 to 20,000 feet-can cause problems. There are several climbing clubs. Mules and guides can be hired in villages near Chimborazo, Cotopaxi, Cayambe, and Tungurahua. Crude "refugios" on these

mountains offer shelter and cooking facilities. No one skis in Ecuador. The snow-covered peaks are steep and laced with crevasses. The Hash House Harriers has an active branch in Quito. This group sponsors runs twice a month and regularly organizes outings.

Ecuador is a paradise for the amateur photographer. Black-and-white, Kodachrome, and Ektachrome color film can be processed locally. Making pictures from slides is expensive. Film can be purchased locally but film speeds slower than 100 or higher than 400 are generally not available or difficult to find. It may be a good idea to bring extra film with you.

Touring and Outdoor Activities

Almost every corner of the country offers opportunities for interesting exploration. Anyone planning to take advantage of all possibilities will want to use a four-wheel-drive vehicle. Most sightseeing can be done on long weekends.

Less than an hour drive to the north of Quito is the equatorial monument at "Mitad del Mundo," marking the division between the Northern and Southern Hemispheres. Two hours from Quito is Otavalo, home of indigenous people known throughout the continent for their weaving. Their colorful Saturday morning market is a must for tourists, although you can now find a much smaller version of the market on any day of the week. The towns of Cotacachi and San Antonio de Ibarra, near Otavalo, are known for leatherwork and woodcarving respectively.

About three hours by car south of Quito on the Pan American Highway is Ambato, Ecuador's fourth largest city, which has an annual Festival of Fruits and Flowers held during Carnival. The region is known for its rug factories. Southeast of Ambato is the secluded and peaceful town of Baños, perched on the eastern edge of the Andean plateau at the foot of the Tungurahua volcano. Like many other resort towns in the mountains, Baños is known for its thermal springs. Metropolitan Touring offers an interesting trip by train from Quito to the colonial city of Riobamba, continuing through this area by bus, with stops at the local Indigenous markets.

In the southern part of the country, continuing on from Riobamba is Cuenca, Ecuador's third largest and perhaps most picturesque city, known for its artisan work and hand-woven rugs and woolens. There are many factories that do the finish work on the Panama hats which are made in small towns close to the coast. The ruins of an ancient Inca fortress are nearby. The province of Loja, in the southernmost part of Ecuador, is famous for the town of Vilcabamba, whose residents are known for their longevity.

Trips can be made by road or air into the Oriente and the jungle. The low-lying tropics are a pleasant contrast to Quito's cool climate. Metropolitan Touring operates a river boat trip down the Rio Napo, with excursions into the jungle, and dugout canoe rides. Visitors can reach the frontier oil towns by bus over rough roads if they prefer not to fly.

West of Quito, 3 hours by car down the Andean slope, is Santo Domingo de Los Colorados, home of Indigenous people who traditionally color their hair and skin with natural pigments. The area offers a wide variety of tropical fruits and other products. Farther down the road, 6-8 hours by car from Quito, is Guayaquil, the nation's largest city. Up and down the coast are beaches, some deserted, some dirty, some beautiful, and some highly urbanized, that offer a pleasant reprieve from Quito's altitude. The Galapagos Islands, 600 miles off the coast, are famous for their wildlife. In recent years Ecuador has taken great care to preserve the flora and fauna of the islands, strictly licensing and controlling the tourist industry that flourishes there. A proper tour of the islands takes at least a week. Ships operating in the tourist trade range from converted fishing sloops with room for no more than six passengers to luxurious cruise vessels offering all the comforts of a large hotel.

Entertainment

Quito has some comfortable cinemas that show films in English with Spanish subtitles. Most of the movies considered "children's" movies are dubbed in Spanish with no English subtitles. Well over half the films are American, and major releases usually arrive in Quito within a few months of their premiere in the U.S. The Casa de la Cultura also programs foreign film series in conjunction with various embassies.

The National Symphony Orchestra offers an annual series of concerts, often with guest artists and conductors. Live theater is active in Quito, with several amateur and semiprofessional groups presenting works in Spanish. An English-language amateur group, the Pichincha Players, presents one or two plays or musicals a year.

Many talented groups of Ecuadorian musicians offer concerts and perform in the late-night folk music houses. The music of the Andes is especially known for its use of pipes, guitars, percussion instruments, and the "charango," a mandolin-like instrument fashioned from the body of an armadillo. For those who prefer a different kind of popular music, there are several good discotheques in town.

Quito has a growing number of nightclubs, most of which are small. Elaborate floor shows and large orchestras are rare, although Ecuador is on the circuit for touring Latin American musical spectaculars. Casinos in the major hotels have slot machines, roulette, blackjack, and dice tables.

The city has an unusually large variety of good restaurants featuring Ecuadorian and international cuisines. Prices are reasonable except for imported items. A number of U.S.-style fast-food restaurants offer hamburgers, pizza, Mexican food and fried chicken for those suffering from culture shock.

Quito, Latacunga, Guayaquil, and Cuenca have annual "festival day" celebrations with fireworks and dancing in the streets. Many of the surrounding towns have their own smaller versions of these festivities.

Social Activities

No formal organizations exist exclusively for Americans. There are many opportunities for U.S. citizens to meet and work with Ecuadorians and other foreign nationals. Quito has 36 resident and 37 nonresident embassies, plus several international organizations. Membership in private clubs facilitates contact with influential Quito residents. The Damas Norteamericanas y Britanicas runs a small library, and supplies funds for many local charities through profits made at their Thrift Shop and annual Christmas bazaar. The Women's Christian Fellowship Group holds monthly meetings, weekly Bible study groups, and occasionally sponsors trips and seminars.

The Ecuadorian-American Chamber of Commerce has a large and growing membership, including many prominent Ecuadorian and U.S. resident business representatives. Each month the organization sponsors a luncheon with a well-known speaker.

The Rotary and Lions Clubs are active. The Ecuadorian Canine Association sponsors dog shows, registers purebreds, and is involved in other activities. Quito has both the Boy Scouts of America and the Cub Scouts pack. Both groups are active within the community. Also, there is a very active group of Girl Scouts.

Guayaquil

This sea level city, formally named Santiago de Guayaquil, was founded in 1538. Tropical, bustling and noisy, Guayaquil is located on the Guayas River and boasts a large deep-water seaport on the saltwater estuary 8 miles south of the center of town. The city is located 50 miles upriver from the Pacific Ocean. A few small hills rise abruptly in the northern residential section; the rest of the city is flat. With a population approaching 2,500,000, the city is growing rapidly, with extensive slums expanding on stilts over tidal estuaries. The city also has modern residential areas of attractive walled homes and gardens and many multistory apartment and condominium buildings. Temperatures are generally pleasant during the dry season from June to December, and no worse than Washington, DC in midsummer during the remainder of the year. Mosquitoes are common during the rainy season from January to May.

The business center is becoming increasingly modern, though unpainted cane buildings still exist side by side with modern high-rise structures on some streets. Many of the streets are in deplorable condition during most of the year despite patchwork repairs.

Guayaquil's vital commercial activity and frequently turbulent political life can help make for an interesting tour, though street crime and burglaries have become serious problems. The American community of several thousand new and long-time residents is well integrated with a much larger number of dual nationals, third-country citizens, and Ecuadorians who were educated or worked in the U.S.

Utilities

City water piped to houses is chlorinated and pure when it leaves the plant but is considered contaminated because of the old pipes and their proximity to sewer lines. Some areas of the city have frequent low pressure or water shortages because of distribution problems.

Standard two-wire, 110v, 60-cycle current is available for lights and appliances, including refrigerators and freezers. Water heaters, electric stoves, and some air-conditioners require U.S. standard three-wire, 220v-240v, 60-cycle current, which

is also available. Voltage regulators or surge protectors are highly recommended to protect specialized electronic equipment such as stereos, home minicomputers and microwave ovens against voltage fluctuations.

Food

Many tropical fruits and vegetables are available year round, and others in season. Some temperate zone fruits and vegetables are brought to Guayaquil from the cool mountain valleys. Prices are reasonable, but may rise during the rainy season.

Seafood, including fresh tuna, shrimp, crab, and oysters, is in good supply most of the time and is less expensive than in the U.S., but quality varies. Beef, chicken and pork are almost always available at prices similar to those in the U.S. Butter and cheese are of satisfactory quality. All imported foods are expensive. Soft drinks and beer are inexpensive, once the bottles are purchased. As a rule of thumb, bring in quantity anything nonperishable that you use often, such as Baker's chocolate, peanut butter, spices, cereal, or special cleaning aids.

Guayaquil has many good restaurants, fast food eateries and ice cream shops with prices similar to those in the U.S. Sanitation is almost never up to U.S. standards, therefore, salads, raw seafood and ice can cause stomach and intestinal problems.

Clothing

Men: Bring a dinner jacket (generally a dark jacket is used) only if you already have one. Men's clothing can be made here from local or imported material and tailors range from very reasonable to expensive. Lightweight suits, sport coats and slacks are worn in Guayaquil. A few dark conservative suits and some sporty outfits will fill most needs.

Women: You will need all your summer clothing here. Officers dealing constantly with the public, such as the principal officer and visa officers, wear dresses, suits, blouses and

skirts. For cocktail parties, dinners, and dances, the latest fashions are worn. Short-sleeved cocktail dresses for evening are comfortable most of the year.

Hats are not worn, except for brimmed sun hats. Sun-dresses and sandals are standard. Bring washable cottons, synthetics, and cotton blends. Tailors here make all types of clothing. Bring fabric and notions from the U.S. Cotton is more comfortable than synthetic material in this hot climate. Bring an ample supply of underwear and socks for everyone in the family.

Stoles, light sweaters, and scarves are used at night during the cooler season. Bring one or two autumn or winter outfits and party clothes for visits to Quito, Cuenca, and other mountain areas. Jackets and woolens are needed at that altitude, and warm slacks are useful. A great variety of stoles and ponchos are sold here at low prices.

Children: Bring a good supply of cotton clothing, shoes and sneakers. Blue jeans, warm jackets, rainwear and sweaters will also be needed.

The American School (Colegio Americano) and the Inter-American Academy both require school uniforms. At the Colegio Americano girls dress with skirts and boys wear blue jeans. Boys and girls are required to wear the same kind of shirt and physical education uniform. Black dress shoes are required except for the days students have gym class, when they bring white sneakers. The uniform for the Inter-American Academy may be purchased in the U.S. Girls wear dark blue jeans, slacks, or skirts with plain white shirts, and a blue jacket or sweater in cool weather. Shoes may be either leather or blue sneakers; sandals are not permitted. Boys wear blue jeans, white shirts. blue sneakers. and a blue jacket or sweater. The PE uniform for both boys and girls is plain blue shorts, white T-shirts, and blue or white sneakers. Reasonably priced blue jeans are available locally.

Supplies and Services

Most U.S. and European toiletries, cosmetics, cigarettes, and medicines are available, sometimes at less cost than in the U.S. Aluminum foil, plastic wrap, waxed paper and other paper products are more expensive than in the U.S., and are of inferior quality. Bring entertainment equipment. Video clubs abound in Guayaquil, with tape rentals from $1.00 to $2.00. An ice chest and beach supplies, particularly suntan lotion, are recommended.

The city has adequate shoe repair and dry-cleaning, radio, phonograph, and TV repair shops. Mechanics can repair most makes of automobiles, but service is from fair to unreliable, and generally slow. Automobile parts are readily available, but expensive.

A number of good tailors are available to make or alter clothing. Local hairdressers are good and reasonably priced. Single persons usually find they need at least a part-time maid, and many families have more than one domestic employee. Domestic employees' wages will run from $80 a month for a general maid to $120 a month for a cook, plus food and uniforms.

Religious Activities

The prevalent faith is Roman Catholic. One Catholic church offers an English Mass. Several Protestant denominations are represented in Guayaquil, but only the Guayaquil English Fellowship, and Interdenominational group, offers services in English. Several branches of the Mormon Church are here, with services in Spanish.

Education

Educational facilities through grade 8 are generally adequate. Colegio Americano, with kindergarten through grade 12, has a student enrollment of 1,656. It has a bilingual program, and operates from a spacious campus a few kilometers north of the urban areas. The school year is May through January. Spanish and English programs through grade six exist at present. The Colegio Americano is accredited by the Southern Association of Schools and by the Ecuadorian Ministry of Education.

Inter-American Academy was formed in 1978 when the former International Section split off from the Colegio Americano. It has kindergarten through grade 12, and is the only English-speaking school in Guayaquil at the high school level. It is accredited by the Southern Association of Schools, and offers an International Baccalaureate diploma. The Academy's diploma and credits are not recognized by the Ecuadorian Ministry of Education because it does not follow the Ministry's curriculum or calendar. The 1999 school year for the Academy starts in September. The 1998 student population is about 300. The school has limited athletic and laboratory facilities.

In addition to these schools, several Roman Catholic private schools have good reputations, but classes are taught entirely in Spanish. An excellent local German school is available for U.S students who speak German.

Several nursery schools are available. Several Spanish-language universities exist, but the largest (University of Guayaquil) is frequently disrupted by political demonstrations, including occasional gun battles between rival groups of students.

Sports

Swimming, tennis, basketball, soccer, baseball, volleyball, jogging, bowling, and golf are enjoyed in the Guayaquil area. Lessons are available. The Tennis Club and the Country Club have swimming pools, but membership is expensive. The pool at the Oro Verde Hotel offers club membership at $150 a year for families and $120 for singles. A municipal Olympic-size public pool with adjacent running track is located nearby. The clubs, Nacional and Garibaldi, are moderately priced alternatives with tennis and swimming facilities. A few families have small private pools. Hunting in Ecuador, particularly bird hunting, can be excellent. In the coastal region around Guayaquil, dove and duck hunting can be spectacular, since there are more than six species of dove and three major species of non-migrating ducks. The rice-growing regions are home to the large Muscovy duck and wintering grounds for blue teal. White-tailed deer and collared peccary are game animals hunted locally. Other game includes the jaguar, but hunting is difficult in the thick swamps and rugged hills. Ecuador has no specified hunting season or bag limit. Hunters should bring all their equipment, including ammunition.

The Mountain Climbing Association in Quito draws members from Guayaquil. See also Sports-Quito.

Touring and Outdoor Activities

Two beaches, Playas and Salinas, offer a cooler climate and swimming, fishing, and boating. Playas is 50 miles southwest of Guayaquil. A small, marginally adequate hotel is situated on a wide, sandy beach with a sheltered picnic ground. Furnished houses are sometimes available for rent on or near the beach. Beaches are generally uncrowded from May to December. The sun and the ocean currents should be treated with respect. The strong sunshine can cause severe sunburn even after short exposure. Ocean currents are very strong in the area and bathers must exercise caution.

Salinas, a resort town 85 miles west of Guayaquil, can be reached by asphalt road in 2 hours. There are more hotels, restaurants, and clubs than in Playas. Sailing and boating facilities are good. There are good beaches along the coast to the north, and a modern hotel nearby on the south coast. Salinas offers some of the best sport fishing (marlin and sailfish) in the world. Charters are expensive, but many fishing enthusiasts find it reasonable to go in groups. Good snorkeling is found among the coral formations in bays north of Salinas.

Over a long weekend, an excursion to the mountains becomes practical and offers a pleasant change in both climate and culture. The nearest city in the Sierra is Cuenca, about a 4 or 5 hour drive from Guayaquil. The road is subject to occasional landslides (especially during the rainy season) and fog banks, but the trip offers spectacular views. The train trip to Quito was a widely known tourist attraction, but service was suspended in early 1983 due to floods, and it is uncertain if service will ever be resumed.

Entertainment

Guayaquil has many movie theaters, some air-conditioned, that show fairly recent movies in English, with Spanish subtitles. Films considered to be for children however will be dubbed in Spanish without English subtitles. Concerts and plays are occasionally given by traveling American, Asian, or European groups. A Bi-National Center (Centeo Ecuatoriano-NorteAmericano), has an air-conditioned auditorium for public gatherings and cultural presentations, and a lending library with more than 4,000 volumes. Its small membership fee offers access to special programs, including movies, speakers, courses, and other activities. The Guayaquil Players, an English-language amateur theater group, stages productions two or three times a year.

Small but good collections of archeological antiquities are located in the Casa de la Cultura, the Municipal Museum, and the Museum of the Banco del Pacifico. Several small art galleries have weekly exhibits of artists from Ecuador and other Latin American countries.

Guayaquil's Independence Day, October 9th, is the most important local holiday. Indigenous festivals and markets can be seen all year by driving into the Andes. Horse races with pari-mutuel betting are held on Sundays throughout the year. Polo games and soccer games are held in season. Several hotels operate casinos. Bullfights are held twice a year.

Social Activities

About 2,500 U.S. citizens live in Guayaquil, providing a good opportunity for socializing with other Americans. The International Society has monthly dinners and several dances during the year. Numerous opportunities exist to meet and work with Ecuadorians and foreign nationals. The American-British Club is now the ABC International Women's Club. Many Ecuadorians have attended schools in the U.S. and welcome association with Americans. Guayaquileños are especially open and hospitable.

Cuenca

Cuenca, capital of Azuay Province in south-central Ecuador, is in one of the richest agricultural basins of the Ecuadorean Andes. A city with a population of 195,000 (1995 est.), it is approximately 68 miles southeast of Guayaquil and, because of its good rail and road connections, is the commercial center of southern Ecuador. One of its leading industries is the manufacture of Panama hats, made from the leaf of the *toquilla* palm which is brought to Cuenca from the coast. Other industries include tanning, sawmilling, flour milling, and paper milling. The city is also known for its artisan work and handwoven rugs and woolens.

Cuenca was founded by the Spanish in 1557 on the site of a native town called Tumibamba. It has been a Roman Catholic bishopric for more than 200 years. The churches and many other old buildings reflect the early Spanish influence in the area, and open-air flower and vegetable markets add to the charm of the older parts of the city. During its "festival days," there are beautiful fireworks displays, and dancing in the streets far into the night.

Cuenca has two universities, one public and one administered by the Catholic Church. The former, founded in 1867, has a student body of 20,000. About 3,000 students attend the latter.

Several good restaurants attract visitors, and a wide variety of entertainment is available. The city has two fine museums, the Provincial Archaeological and the Spanish Abstract Art Museum. The Ecuadoreans in Cuenca, as in other cities, are friendly and hospitable. Many speak English, but a knowledge of Spanish presents more opportunities to meet and socialize with the local population.

OTHER CITIES

AMBATO, capital of Tungurahua Province in central Ecuador, has a population of close to 111,500. It is about 50 miles south of the capital, on the Río Ambato, near Mt. Chimborazo. Due to its location, Ambato is susceptible to volcanic eruptions and earthquakes. Much of the city was destroyed during an earthquake in 1949. The city's historic landmarks include the mausoleum of Juan Montalvo, the noted 19th-century essayist, and a Renaissance cathedral. Along with sugarcane plantations, Ambato is known for its fresh fruits. Industries include tanning, leatherworks, food processing, and textile milling. Ambato is located on the Pan-American Highway and on the Guayaquil-Quito Railway. Miraflores, a suburb of Ambato, is a lush resort for the upper classes of Guayaquil.

The capital of Cañar Province, **AZOGUES** is located in south-central Ecuador, in a high Andean valley. Situated on the Pan-American Highway less than 20 miles north of Cuenca, Azogues has an estimated population of 13,840. The economy is based on agricultural products such as grains and fruit. Industries in the city include leather tanning and flour milling. The city's name comes from the Spanish word "azogue" which means "mercury." Mercury is a local resource, along with silver and copper.

BABAHOYO, capital of Los Ríos Province, is located in west-central Ecuador, less than 25 miles north of Guayaquil. On the southern shore of Río Babahoyo, the city is a trade center for the surrounding agricultural region. Sugarcane, rice, and fruits are grown. There is a government-owned distillery making alcohol, ether, and perfume. A technical university was opened here in 1971. The city has an estimated population of 43,000.

As the capital and major seaport of Esmeraldas Province, the city of **ESMERALDAS** is the chief trading center for the region. Located about 85 miles northwest of the nation's capital, Esmeraldas lies on the Pacific coast. The city is not strong industrially, but an oil refinery was completed in 1977 and new oil port facilities were opened in 1979. Its main exports are timber and bananas. Tourism has increased because of the addition of seaside resort accommodations, a pleasant climate, and a good highway to Quito. A technical university was opened here in 1970. The population in Esmeraldas is estimated at 131,000.

GUARANDA, capital of Bolívar Province, has an estimated population of 14,100. It is situated on a head-stream of the Río Chimbo in the Cordillera de Guaranda of the Andes. Less than 50 miles north of Guayaquil and about 75 miles south of Quito, Guaranda is an agricultural center trading corn, chincona, wheat, and timber. The city was an important transshipment point before the opening of Guayaquil-Quito Railway in 1908. Guaranda is linked by highway with the cities of Quito and Riobamba.

LATACUNGA, with a population close to 34,000, is the capital of Cotopaxi Province in north-central Ecuador. Located in an Andean basin on the upper Río Patate, the city is situated at an elevation of 9,055 feet. A pre-colonial city, Latacunga was favored by Incan royalty because of its hot springs. The city has been damaged by volcanic eruptions and subsequent earthquakes and, as a result, had to be rebuilt in 1797. Industrial activities include pottery, furniture manufacturing, and flour milling.

Located in south-central Ecuador, **LOJA,** capital of Loja Province, is situated on a small plain at the foot of the Cordillera de Zamora of the Andes. The city was founded in 1553 and has since been totally rebuilt as a result of an earthquake. Trade here is typical of the region (sugarcane, cereals, coffee, and cinchona). Industries include tanning and textile weaving, and the manufacture of light consumer goods. Loja has many beautiful marble buildings. Loja is on the Pan-American Highway and is an air link to principal Ecuadorean cities. The seat of a Roman Catholic diocese, the National University of Loja, and a technical university are all located in the city.

Founded in 1535 by Spanish colonists, **PORTOVIEJO** is situated in the Pacific lowlands of western Ecuador. The city is about 100 miles west of Quito, on the eastern bank of the Río Portoviejo. Formerly located on the coast, Portoviejo was moved inland because of Indian attacks. With an estimated population of 122,000, the city is an agricultural and lumbering center; products include cotton, coffee, cacao, and sugarcane. Light industries here include the manufacture of Panama baskets, hammocks, and hats. Portoviejo has been the seat of a bishopric since 1871; a technical university was opened in 1952. There are air and road routes connecting the city with Quito.

At an altitude of about 9,000 feet, **RIOBAMBA,** capital of Chimborazo Province, is situated in the central highlands of Ecuador. It is about 75 miles east of Guayaquil and the is the headquarters of the Guayaquil-Quito Railway. The city dates from pre-Inca and Inca times; it was settled by the Spanish in 1534, 12 miles south of its present location. Because of a landslide in 1797, Riobamba was moved to its present site near the Riobamba River. In 1830, the first Ecuadorian constitutional congress met at Riobamba and proclaimed the republic. Industries include carpets, textiles, cement, and cotton. Riobamba is known for its native artifacts. The city has a weekly fair that attracts Indians from the surrounding countryside. Many fine products can be purchased here. The population is about 81,000.

TULCÁN, with a population of nearly 34,000, is the capital of Carchi Province, in the northern tip of central Ecuador bordering Colombia. The city was severely damaged by an earthquake in 1923 and has since been rebuilt. Quito is about 75 miles to the southwest. Nearby sites include the natural bridge of Rumichaca over the Río Carchi and, in Colombia, only a few miles northeast, the shrine of Nuestra Señora de Las Lajas. Situated in a rich agricultural region, Tulcán processes sugarcane, coffee, cereals, and is known for its dairy products. The Pan-American Highway runs through the city.

COUNTRY PROFILE

Geography and Climate

Ecuador straddles the Equator, its namesake, on the west coast of South America, almost 3,000 miles due south of Washington, DC. It is roughly the size of Colorado. Two north-south ranges of the Andes Mountains divide the country into three distinct sections: the Costa, a belt of tropical lowlands 10-100 miles wide along the Pacific coast, where Guayaquil, the major city, is located; the Sierra, where Quito is located, is a highland plateau 3,000-10,000 feet high; and the Oriente, which are the jungle lowlands east of the Andes that make up about half of the country's area. In addition, the Galapagos Islands (Archipelago de Colon) lie 640 miles off the coast. The nine main islands are inhabited by some 15,000 people and an amazing variety of wildlife that has fascinated scientists ever since Charles Darwin visited there in 1836.

Ecuador claims an additional 100,000 square miles of territory in the Oriente, an area which includes navigable tributaries of the Amazon River. This territory was lost to Peru under the 1942 Rio Protocol of Peace, Friendship, and Boundaries, a fact which the Ecuadorian people and Government have never fully accepted. The national motto proclaims, "Ecuador was, is, and will be an Amazonian nation." Revising the treaty is one of the government's foremost foreign policy objectives. Efforts to settle the dispute have been unsuccessful because of strong nationalistic feelings in both countries. In 1995 an undeclared war took effect between Peru and Ecuador along the disputed southern border. Since 1995 the guarantors (U.S., Brazil, Chile and Argentina) have been very active in assisting Ecuador and Peru to resolve their differences.

Most of Ecuador is covered by equatorial forests. The rest consists of cultivated agricultural areas, some arid scrubland near the coast, and barren mountain ranges with 22 peaks over 14,000 feet high. These peaks include Chimborazo (20,561 ft.) and Cotopaxi, which is the second highest active volcano in the world (19,347 ft.). The spectacular array of snow capped volcanoes stretching north and south of Quito has been called the "Avenue of Volcanoes", and on a clear day the view from an airplane is breathtaking. On the Pacific slope the principal rivers are the Esmeraldas and the Guayas. Eastern Ecuador is part of the Amazon watershed. Its principal rivers are the Napo and Pastaza Rivers. None of the Amazon tributaries in Ecuador are navigable by oceangoing vessels.

Because of variations in altitude, Ecuador has a variety of climates. The lowland- are generally hot and humid Temperatures on the coast are moderated by the Humboldt Current to a range of 65° to 90°E Temperatures in the Sierra are generally cool, ranging from 35° to 75°E

Due to the altitude and thin air, temperature in direct sunlight can reach 85°F at midday. In the evenings it can range from pleasantly cool to very chilly. The tallest mountains are always syncopated, but it never snows in the inhabited altitudes, although it hails occasionally. During the Sierra dry season, from June through September, gusty winds are common.

In Quito the temperature pattern rarely changes from day to day or month to month. Mornings are cool and crisp, and midday is agreeably warm unless skies are overcast. Fog and mist may occur in the mornings or evenings as low-lying clouds spill over the sides of the valley. Since Quito is such a short distance from the Equator, sunrise and sunset vary only slightly from 6 am and 6 pm. Average annual rainfall in Quito is 50 inches, with 43 inches falling from October through May, and 7 inches from June through September. Relative humidity averages 75%. Occasional tremors are registered in the area, these may or may not be perceptible to residents. Earthquakes and volcanic eruptions are infrequent but do remain a possibility.

Population

Ecuador's population is 11,937,000; it is estimated that the population is 40% mestizo, 40% Indian, 10% white, 5% black, and 5% Asian and others. About half of the population lives on the Coast, where the principal group is mestizo. The average annual population growth rate is currently 2.3%. The term "mestizo" has a cultural significance in the Sierra; it is not simply a mixture of blood. An Indian who leaves his or her community, abandoning traditional dress, tribal ties, and native language, loses his or her Indian identity and is called a "mestizo."

Spanish is the official language, but Quichua, the language of the Incas, is still spoken by Indians constituting about one-third of the inhabitants. In the Oriente, several indigenous languages and dialects survive; some having no identifiable

link with any recognized language families.

Internal migrations are occurring from the highlands to the coastal area, and from the countryside to the cities. Today the population is divided about equally between the mountainous central highland region and the coastal lowlands. The urban segment of the population is about 55%.

Most of the population is Roman Catholic, though Protestant missionaries have been active in the country since the turn of the century. Religious freedom is observed.

Primary education is compulsory, and an estimated 85% of the population is literate. Both Catholic and Protestant missionaries have worked with indigenous peoples of the Oriente in conjunction with the Ministry of Education. Public university education is free, and there is an open admissions policy. Public and private university enrollment is large, although many students do not complete their degrees.

History

Perhaps 50 independent pre Columbian cultures flourished along the coast, in the Sierra, and in the Rio Napo Region before the Incas Conquered what is now Ecuador. Ceramics found in Valdivia date from 3200 B.C., are among the oldest found in South America. Archeologists have discovered rich gold works, ceramics, weavings, and mummies in several important sites. Around the year 1200, two important nations emerged: the Caras on the coast, and the Quitus in the Andes. These merged to form the Shyris nation, which was conquered by the Incas in the 15th century.

The Inca sovereign Huayna Capac consolidated his rule over the area in the early 1500s, just a few years before the first Spaniards landed on the shores of Ecuador. After seizing the treasures at Atacames on his first expedition along the coast from his base in Panama, Francisco Pizarro returned in 1532 to conquer the Inca kingdom, by then weakened by civil war. The last Inca king, Atahualpa, was held prisoner for ransom and then killed by Pizarro.

A long period of warfare against the native population followed and the Spanish conquest destroyed all but a few of the Inca fortresses and temples. Quito was not subdued until Sebastian de Benalcazar took possession of the area, establishing San Francisco de Quito on December 6, 1534, on the site of the ancient Quitu capital. Guayaquil was founded a year later. Gonzalo Pizarro was named governor of the colony in 1540 and organized an expedition in Quito which resulted in the discovery of the Amazon River by Francisco de Orellana. In 1563 Quito was made a Royal Audiencia, first as part of the Viceroyalty of Peru, and then the Viceroyalty of New Granada, after 1718. Exploration, colonization and religious conversion of the Indians continued for almost three centuries, until independence in 1822. The first schools were established by the religious orders of the Catholic Church. So many monasteries and sumptuous churches were built in Quito that it became known as "The Cloister of America." The combination of Spanish art and Indian handicraft led to a unique production of sculpture and painting in what is known as the Quiteño School of Colonial Art, with many extraordinary native artists, such as Caspicara, Goribar, and Miguel de Santiago.

Land which had been taken from the aborigines was granted to the religious communities and to the Spaniards who had served their king. During the 17th and 18th centuries African slave labor was brought from the Caribbean to work the new plantations and agriculture flourished. The colonial economy rested on three institutions: the encomienda (a system of serfdom), the mita (forced Indian labor in mines and public works), and the obraje (forced labor in textile factories). While the land belonged to the Spanish crown legally, the

encomienda was the cession of land and people to the privileged. The Indians were supposed to receive the care of the patron and be instructed in the Catholic faith, in exchange for personal services. The native population suffered greatly under this system.

A number of European scientists visited Ecuador in the 18th century: Charles de La Condamine of France headed a geodetic mission to confirm measurements of the equator, and Alexander Von Humboldt made significant discoveries in natural science. Intellectual societies flourished in the capital and became centers of liberal political thought.

Eugenio Espejo preached independence and influenced many wealthy merchants and nobles who resented Spanish oppression, taxation, and trade restrictions. In 1809 a group of citizens overthrew the Royal Audiencia, but Spanish rule was restored within 3 months. In 1820 Guayaquil again declared independence, and soon after Simon Bolivar sent Antonio Jose de Sucre into Ecuador to lead a decisive campaign against the Spaniards. Sucre won a great victory in a fierce battle on the slopes of Mount Pichincha overlooking Quito in 1822, liberating Ecuador and uniting it with the Federation of Greater Colombia.

The Republic of Ecuador began its separate existence in 1830, and Juan Jose Flores was elected the first President. The constitution established a presidential system of government, with a division of powers among the executive, the legislative, and the judicial branches. The new government was beset from the beginning by personal and sectional rivalries between the Coast and the Sierra. For many years political power alternated between the Liberal and Conservative Parties.

In the 19th century, political conditions were unstable, and during the first 95 years of its independence, Ecuador had a succession of 40 presidents, dictators, and juntas. In 1851 slavery was abolished, 60,000 Negroes were freed, and tribute

payments by the Indians were abolished. In 1860, 15 years of authoritarian rule by President Gabriel Garcia Moreno began. After his assassination in 1875 on the steps of the Presidential Palace, a period of liberal constitutional development followed. The greatest figure of this era was Eloy Alfaro, who completed the Guayaquil-Quito Railway and created the Public Health Service. Under his leadership new constitutions removed religious qualifications for citizenship, reestablished freedom of worship, confiscated Church estates, and secularized government education.

In the early 20th century, there was political unrest and economic distress following World War I. From 1925 until 1948, the country went through an even more troubled period, with 22 Chiefs of State. Twelve years of relative stability followed. Galo Plaza Lasso (former Secretary-General of the Organization of American States) was elected President in free elections in 1948 and was succeeded by Dr. Jose M. Velasco Ibarra who completed his presidential term, and in turn was succeeded by Dr. Camilo Ponce E., who also completed his presidential term. The next elected President was again Dr. Jose M. Velasco Ibarra, who did not complete his presidential term because he was overthrown by a military junta. Dr. Jose M. Velasco Ibarra was elected President on 5 occasions. After almost 2 decades under military governments, a constitutional government was elected, led by Dr. Jaime Roldos A., who died in an airplane accident in 1982 and was succeeded by his Vice-President Dr. Osvaldo Hurtado L. In 1984 there was an orderly transition from one democratically elected government to another when President Leon Febres Cordero took office. He, in turn, relinquished power to democratically elected Dr. Rodrigo Borja C. 1988-1992. Sixto Durán-Ballén was President for the period from 1992 to 1996. Abdalá Bucaram Ortiz was elected President in 1996 for a period of 4 years, however, his presidency was revoked in February 1997. Fabian Alarcón (February

1997 - August 1998) is the current interim president elected by Congress and further reconfirmed by popular consultation in May 1997. New elections will be held in 1998.

Public Institutions

Dr. Fabian Alarcón, Ecuador's sixth President since the return of democracy in 1979, was elected by Congress in 1997, after nation-wide popular protests forced President Abdala Bucaram to step down. Bucaram, who served 6 months in office, was widely viewed as Ecuador's most corrupt President in recent history. He fled to Panama to avoid prosecution. Alarcón was elected to serve as interim president until new elections are held in 1998.

President Alarcón was a compromise candidate from a small center-left party, the Radical Alfarista Front (FRA), who drew support from the larger center-left and center-right parties in Congress for his Presidency. He was elected by Congress to correct the corruption of the Bucaram government and to lay the ground work for a Constituent Assembly to overhaul the state. His party has grown from 3 to 12 deputies in Congress since he took office and he has managed to build a coalition with the larger parties from the right and the left supporting his reform agenda.

The Ecuadorian constitution provides for a separation of powers between executive, legislative, and judicial branches of government. With 14 formally registered political parties and a free press, Ecuador has a lively and open political environment. In the 1998 national elections, a new President, Vice President, and Provincial and Municipal Officials will be elected to serve 4-year terms. In addition, of the 82 members of the unicameral legislature, 12 will be elected at-large for 4-year terms ("National Deputies") and the remaining 70 will be elected by province for 2-year terms ("Provincial Deputies"). Following a 1997 constitutional reform, the 31 members of the Supreme Court are selected by the Congress from lists submitted by various social and professional organizations.

Ecuador's human rights record is generally good, although problems, principally involving abuse of authority and an ineffective judiciary, continue to exist.

Arts, Science, and Education

Quito's artistic tradition continued through the Republican era and flourishes today. Masters such as Oswaldo Guayasamin, Eduardo Kingman, and Oswaldo Viteri are joined by a younger generation that is gaining international fame. Marcelo Aguirre, one of these young painters, won the world's largest prize, the $250,000 Marco prize from Mexico, in 1995. Galleries such as La Galeria and Art Forum in Quito and Expresiones in Guayaquil spotlight the best in contemporary art.

The National Dance Company performs modern ballet and groups such as Humanizarte focus on indigenous dance forms. The National Symphony performs weekly concerts throughout Quito and elsewhere in the country. There are also a number of classical concerts offered by the Philharmonic Society and several chamber music groups. Private clubs and restaurants showcase traditional Andean music, Latin pop, and even jazz.

Traditional arts and crafts are very much alive. Indian wool weavings and rugs woven in Inca designs have been successfully commercialized and are sold in the world famous market city of Otavalo, which is located about 2 hours outside of Quito. The city of Cotacachi, near Otavalo, is known for its leather goods, and San Antonio de Ibarra, just a few miles north, is a center for wood carving. The city of Cuenca has a wide variety of art forms, including sophisticated ceramics and the famous "Panama Hats." Tigua, a small town near Latacunga, is famous for native paintings produced on stretched cowhides and furniture. A number of Indian communities combine colorful art forms with religious celebrations.

The government and a number of private organizations are working to preserve Ecuador's historic, archeological, and architectural heritage. Colonial Quito has been declared a "world cultural heritage site" city by UNESCO. Dozens of sites in Quito's historic center have been or are being restored. The Quito electric trolley system was built in an attempt to reduce the pollution and vibration that was harming many of the architectural treasures.

The Central Bank has long been a major player in the cultural world. The Central Bank's museums throughout the country showcase the artistic and archeological treasures of Ecuador. Perhaps the premier museum in Quito is the Central Bank museum at the Casa de la Cultura. The museum combines a large collection of pre-Columbian ceramics and gold with a historical review of Ecuadorian sculpture, painting, and furniture. The Guayasamin Foundation in the north part of the city pays homage to the work of Ecuador's best known painter. A major Quito city museum is due to be inaugurated, in the converted 16th century San Juan de Dios Hospital, sometime in 1998.

The Ecuadorian universities have lost much of their prestige over the past 25 years. Some 32 universities are recognized as "official" by the government. The two largest universities, the Central University in Quito and the University of Guayaquil, have launched reform projects, but it will take time for them to recoup the reputation for excellence they enjoyed 40 years ago. Most research takes place at the two technological universities, the ESPOL in Guayaquil and the National Polytechnic School in Quito. The Catholic University of Ecuador in Quito attracts some 200 U.S. students per year to study Spanish, while San Francisco University, founded just 7 years ago, has developed the nation's most impressive university campus in nearby Cumbaya while offering a 4-year liberal arts education similar to U.S. schools.

Ecuador's scientific community is small, however there is much work being done in biodiversity and other environmental areas. Researchers from around the world have come to Ecuador due to one of the richest environments on the globe. The Darwin Research Station in the Galapagos National Park is the center for studies of the islands. It receives funds from the Ecuadorian Government as well as international organizations for its activities. New research stations opened by Catholic University and San Francisco University in the Amazon basin are providing Ecuadorian and foreign scientists with the infrastructure to carry out projects there.

An increase in scientific activity is underway in Ecuador. The National Atomic Energy Commission is doing more extensive research with radio-isotopes, particularly in medicine and agriculture. Several experimental agricultural stations are active. The Central University and the National Polytechnic School have research labs. Other research is being conducted in cancer, pharmaceuticals, astronomy, and linguistics fields.

Commerce and Industry

Ecuador is largely an agricultural country and enjoys abundant, relatively unexploited, natural resources. Both the coastal and highland regions are rich agricultural areas. The Sierra (highland) Region largely produces traditional consumption crops, but has excellent potential fox export crops including flowers and vegetables. The coastal lowland produces mainly export crops, principally bananas, shrimp, coffee, and cocoa, as well as rice and sugarcane.

The main agricultural commodities accounted for approximately 43% of exports in 1995. Ecuador currently produces about 390,000 barrels per day of crude oil, about two-thirds of which are exported, accounting for 35% of total exports. Most of the oil is produced by state-owned Petroecuador, though foreign investors are conducting some exploration and development activities. Ecuador also appears to have extensive, underdeveloped mining potential, especially for gold. Ecuador's industrial sector produces largely for a domestic market which until recently has been heavily protected. Trade policy has been substantially liberalized in recent years, with current tariffs ranging from 5-20% and few nontariff barriers in place. Manufactured goods accounted for 20% of exports in 1995.

Economic growth in Ecuador has been uneven, influenced by international economic developments and natural disasters which have affected its petroleum and agricultural exports. Following a booming economy in the 1970s, which was driven by high petroleum prices, the 1980s was a decade of stagnation, as the debt crisis, inadequate domestic adjustment, and a volatile international oil market combined to thwart economic growth. Although economic growth has picked up in this decade, employment growth has been limited, and there is widespread agreement on the need for major structural reforms to revive economic growth. The economy grew by a rate of 2% in 1996, with inflation running at 31%. Open unemployment is around 7% and the informal sector employs over 40% of the urban workforce.

The Durán-Ballén government of 1992-1996 took a number of important steps to revitalize and restructure the economy. A major macroeconomics adjustment program was introduced, as were several important structural reform measures, including a budget reform law, liberalized investment regulations, a new capital markets law, hydrocarbons reform, customs

and tax reforms, new agrarian law, and a telecommunications privatization law. The government also reached an agreement with commercial banks on debt restructuring.

Economic reform stalled under the subsequent 6-month government of Abdalá Bucaram (August 1996 - February 1997) which was characterized by increased corruption and decreased investment. The current interim government of Fabian Alarcón (February 1997-August 1998) is faced with a number of challenges including implementing the Durán-Ballén era reforms, privatizing the state-owned telephone company, cutting the inflation rate to international levels and increasing social investment.

Transportation

Automobiles

City streets and principal intercity highways are reasonably well maintained. Many types of vehicles are used in Ecuador, from the smallest four-cylinder cars to the largest and most powerful luxury sedans. Automatic transmissions present no problems, except for replacement parts. Low-slung cars have problems when exploring remote areas. Heavy-duty shocks and suspensions are recommended. High road clearance and maneuverability are essential for this type of travel, and a good range of gears, heavy-duty tires, springs, shock absorbers, and a roll bar are recommended. An oversized radiator is a desirable safety feature. Four-wheel-drive vehicles, while expensive to rent, may be rented locally for recreational use or while waiting for your vehicle to arrive. Bring a new car or one in good condition. People who will not be traveling to remote areas will find a sedan or minivan to be an adequate means of transportation.

Unleaded gasoline is now readily available in Ecuador in two versions. The better quality is the "Super" gasoline which costs the equivalent of $1.35 per gallon. The lesser expensive "Eco" which costs the equivalent of $1.20, a low-octane regular leaded gasoline is also available for $1.10.

Most city streets are paved, although they are not always in good condition. Smaller towns usually have cobblestone or dirt streets. Travel by automobile can be slow, hard, and dangerous given the high number of unskilled drivers; some roads outside the cities are in poor condition and are very winding with steep drop-offs. The main roads are the north-south Pan American Highway that runs through Quito, the Quito-Guayaquil Road via Santo Domingo, and the Quito-Esmeraldas Road.

Local

Regular intercity bus service is available. Principal cities have numerous city buses. These are inexpensive, costing about $.05, but they are crowded and often in need of repair. The city of Quito is now served by an electric trolley system running from the southern to the northern areas of the city and vice versa, the cost is about $.25. Taxis are plentiful and the fares are reasonable. You can hail a taxi on the street or telephone to request one. If the taxi does not have a meter, negotiate the fare before beginning the trip. Taxis are difficult to find on the street, after 10:00 p.m. or when it is raining in Quito, but you can always request a taxi by phone.

Regional

American Airlines, SAETA and Ecuatoriana Airlines offer regular service to Quito and Guayaquil from Miami, with at least one flight daily. Continental provides daily service from Houston via Panama. There are several flights weekly to New York and also direct flights via Mexico or Miami to Los Angeles. Make your reservations well in advance of your trip, since all of these flights are crowded. Most are fully booked weeks in advance.

Mariscal Sucre is Quito's international airport. Ecuador has two international airlines (Ecuatoriana and Saeta) and three domestic airlines (SAETA, SAN, and TAME). Guayaquil is 30-45 minutes by air

from Quito, depending on the aircraft. Scheduled flights are also available to Esmeraldas, Cuenca, Lago Agrio, Coca, Loja, Manta, Machala, Tulcan, Portoviejo, Macas, and the Galapagos. The one-way fare from Quito to any continental Ecuadorian city is between $40 and $80.

Currently a round-trip flight from the capital to the Galapagos Islands costs about $390 for persons who are not permanent residents of Ecuador.

Communications
Telephone and Telegraph
The per minute rate for calls to the U.S. is currently approximately $1.10. You may want to research companies and rates for current programs and services before arrival in Ecuador. Companies such as AT&T, Sprint, and MCI all offer service in Ecuador. There is no time period with reduced rates. Most phones are touch tone and direct dial to the U.S. is readily available. Calls placed from the U.S. to Ecuador are considerably less expensive than those placed from Ecuador. Cellular phones have also become very popular within the country and sometimes are more reliable than the regular phone system. Phones purchased in the United States may not be able to be programmed for use within Ecuador, or it may cost up to U.S. $100.00 to program them. The price of cellular telephones and service is slightly higher than in the U.S.; you will need to check with the local companies for pricing and service information.

Mail
International airmail is expensive and not very dependable. Packages arriving by international parcel post and unaccompanied air-freight will be inspected and charged a duty.

Radio and TV
Quito has a wide range of AM radio stations presenting primarily Latin American and American popular music. Good FM radio stations oper-

ate here with most broadcasting in stereo. The FM service of HCJB, a missionary-run broadcasting organization, features light classical music and offers nightly news broadcasts in English. Short-wave reception is usually good. Both Voice of America and BBC can be received clearly. HAM radio operators should bring their own equipment, since the Ecuadorian Government issues licenses to those with a valid American license.

Quito and Guayaquil are served by a cable TV service that provides 50 channels, about one-fourth in English from the U.S. These vary as stations are added and dropped, but generally the three networks (ABC, NBC, CBS), Discovery, Fox, Warner Brothers, CNN, ESPN and a few rerun stations are available.

The cost for full service is about $35 monthly. Local stations broadcast in Spanish and include shows from all over Latin America, dubbed versions of many U.S. series and a variety of motion pictures.

Newspapers, Magazines, and Technical Journals
Quito has two independent morning newspapers, *El Comercio* and *Hoy*, and two afternoon papers, *Ultimas Noticias* and *La Hora*. Newspapers from Guayaquil, such as *El Universo* and *El Telegrafo*, are also sold in Quito. Newspapers are sold on the streets and in neighborhood stores and can be delivered to the home.

The Latin American edition of the *Miami Herald* is printed daily in Quito, using a direct satellite link and is currently available by subscription for around $400 per year.

The Latin American editions of *Time* and *Newsweek* magazines are available weekly at about $2.25 per copy and $75.00 per year by subscription. Other popular magazines from the U.S., France, Spain, and Germany are also available. The BiNational Centers in Guayaquil and Cuenca subscribe to numerous English-language periodicals and have libraries with fiction and nonfiction English-language books. The Damas Norteamericanas y Britanicas' Club operates a small rental library. AERA has a circulating library of bestsellers in fiction and non-fiction which is renewed regularly from the U.S., the cost of membership is $15 per year. Major hotels carry some paperback books. Several bookstores have limited stocks of books in English, but they are expensive.

Recordings of U.S. and European popular music are increasingly available. Those produced under license in Ecuador are relatively inexpensive (about $5), but imported recordings are costly. Selections of classical music are limited; recordings of Ecuadorian and Latin American popular and folk music are abundant, inexpensive, and of relatively good quality.

There are several video clubs, including the U.S. chain "Blockbusters," offering a wide variety of VHS tapes comparable to what would be found in the U.S. New movies take a significantly longer time to become available here than in the U.S.

Health and Medicine

Medical Facilities

There are several good hospitals for medical care and hospitalization. Many Ecuadorian physicians and dentists are trained in the U.S. or Europe and hospitals meet American standards. Though the local physicians and facilities are good, there are occasions that individuals are evacuated to Miami, Florida for medical treatment.

Quito has good dentists and orthodontists. Hygiene and quality of work is similar to the United States. Maj or dental problems such as root canal and crowns can be adequately accommodated here. Eye examinations and glasses are readily available in Quito. Contact lenses can also be fitted, though at a higher cost than in the U.S. German and American contact solutions are available on the local market, but

are also at a higher cost. It would be best to bring your own supplies if you prefer a specific brand. Contact lenses can be difficult to use due to the altitude and dryness of the climate. Bring a pair of prescription glasses as a backup. Most people find that the altitude and ultra-violet sun rays make sunglasses necessary. The sunlight is bright and sunglasses reduce the eye glare. Good dark sunglasses are difficult to find in Quito, bring a couple of pairs.

The local market does carry most of the medications available in the United States, but the availability at local pharmacies vary from month to month.

Local medical facilities are less adequate than Quito. Well trained physicians are available for consultation. The Clinica Kennedy is a small private hospital. Dental facilities are limited.

Due to the high humidity and temperature in Guayaquil, bring insect repellent and insecticides. Due to the risk of contracting malaria, insect repellent should be used when outside in the evenings. Insects are a problem in the homes, and U.S. brand insecticides (or bug sprays) are more effective in controlling their numbers. Antiseptic and antibiotic ointments are useful in prevention of bacterial skin infections.

Community Health

Quito and Guayaquil have central sewage systems, and garbage is collected regularly in most neighborhoods. However, sanitation facilities and public health controls are well below U.S. standards. Since the water system is subject to leaks and corrosion in the pipes, tap water is not safe.

Tap water should be boiled for 20 minutes.

The altitude can be a problem in Quito. During the first couple of days, most people experience some minor discomforts associated with the altitude. These symptoms

include shortness of breath, upset stomach, headaches, difficulty sleeping (including sleeping more than normal), dizziness, and loss of energy. After a period of adjustment, most individuals have no difficulty with the altitude. Colds and respiratory infections do require a longer convalescent period than at sea level.

Because of the thinness of the air and closer proximity to the sun, the equatorial sun is very intense. Skin irritation and sunburn can occur with short exposure to the sun. Use tanning products and sunscreens when outdoors. Bring a supply of sunblock with an SPF level of at least 8 but preferably higher. A wide assortment of brimmed hats can be bought locally, including the "Panama" hats (which are actually made in Ecuador).

Preventive Measures

Numerous diseases are endemic to Ecuador including cholera and rabies. Among the most common problems within the American community are intestinal parasites, hepatitis, viral infections and colds. Malaria is a problem below 5,000 feet (1,500 meters) in all areas of Ecuador, with the exception of the Galapagos Islands. Antimalarial medication should be taken by all persons living in or traveling to malaria areas including Guayaquil. Chloroquine-resistant malaria has been reported in parts of Ecuador, but neither Quito or Guayaquil are in these areas.

Vaccinations are a strong line of defense against diseases and illnesses while living in Ecuador. Yellow Fever injections are strongly recommended for Ecuador. Oral typhoid vaccine is another highly recommended vaccination for Ecuador. Hepatitis A vaccine is strongly recommended. Routine childhood immunization should be maintained including Hepatitis A and B, DPT, polio, MMR, and HIB. Tuberculosis is endemic in the country. It is advisable that immunization cards (the yellow shot cards) be reviewed in the United States before departing.

Soak fruits and vegetables in chlorine (Clorox) water for 20 minutes before being eaten raw. Wash fruits and vegetables with soap and water to remove dirt and pesticides before cooking.

Local milk is not considered to be pasteurized adequately for consumption without further boiling. Long-life milk and powdered milk can be purchased locally or in the commissary. Cheese and ice cream are processed adequately for consumption. All meat, including beef and pork, should be well done to prevent intestinal parasites. Do not eat mayonnaise based food because of risks of food poisoning. Food bought at the local supermarkets is safe and usually of good quality.

Have pre-employment medical examinations for domestic household staff members, especially if they will be cooking or caring for children. Establish strict standards for food handling and storage with your household staff.

NOTES FOR TRAVELERS

American Airlines has daily direct flights to Quito and Guayaquil from Miami. Some flights are non-stop and others may stop en route in Panama or Bogota. Continental Airlines has daily flights from Houston and New Jersey. SAETA and Ecuatoriana also arrive daily from Miami. Bookings on all airlines should be made well in advance of travel.

Immigration officials keep the international arrival card on file and return a carbon copy with the traveler's passport. Since you will have to surrender this copy upon leaving Ecuador, staple it to the last page of your passport. If you lose it, you may face a delay of 24 hours or more in obtaining a duplicate.

A valid U.S. passport is required to enter and depart Ecuador. Tourists must also provide evidence of return or onward travel. U.S. citizens do not need a visa for a stay of 90 days or less. Those planning a longer visit must obtain a visa in advance. U.S. citizens whose passports are lost or stolen in Ecuador must obtain a new passport at the U.S. Embassy in Quito or the U.S. Consulate General in Guayaquil and present it, together with a police report of the loss or theft, to the main immigration office in the capital city of Quito to obtain permission to depart. An exit tax must be paid at the airport when departing Ecuador. For further information regarding entry, exit, and customs requirements, travelers should contact the Ecuadorian Embassy at 2535 15th Street, NW, Washington, DC 20009; telephone (202) 234-7166; Internet - http://www.ecuador.org; or the Ecuadorian consulate in Chicago (312) 329-0266, Houston (713) 622-1787, Jersey City (201) 985-1700, Los Angeles (323) 658-6020, Miami (305) 539-8214, New Orleans (504) 523-3229, New York (212) 808-0170, or San Francisco (415) 957-5921.

U.S. citizens living in or visiting Ecuador are encouraged to register at the Consular Section of either the U.S. Embassy in Quito or the U.S. Consulate General in Guayaquil and obtain updated information on travel and security in Ecuador. The Consular Section in Quito is open for citizen services, including registration, from 8:00 a.m. to 12:30 p.m. and 1:30 to 4:00 p.m., Tuesday through Friday, excluding U.S. and Ecuadorian holidays. The Consular Section in Guayaquil is open for those services from 8:00 a.m. to 12:00 noon, Tuesday through Friday, excluding U.S. and Ecuadorian holidays. The U.S. Embassy in Quito is located at the corner of Avenida 12 de Octubre and Avenida Patria (across from the Casa de la Cultura); telephone (011-593-2) 256-2890, extension 4510, during business hours (8:00 a.m. to 5:00 p.m.) or 256-1749 for after-hours emergencies; fax (011-593-2) 256-1524; Internet web site - http://www.usembassy.org.ec. The Consulate General in Guayaquil is located at the corner of 9 de Octubre and Garcia Moreno (near the Hotel Oro Verde); telephone (011-593-4) 232-3570 during business hours (8:00 a.m. to 5:00 p.m.) or 232-1152 for after-hours emergencies; fax (011-593-4) 232-0904. Consular services for U.S. citizens in the Galapagos Islands are provided by the Consulate General in Guayaquil.

Pets

Pets are generally well accepted in Ecuador and relatively easy to bring into the country. Dogs and cats should have an up-to-date health certificate certified by your veterinarian. The certificate should include name of pet, age, sex, breed, color, and an up-to-date certification of rabies vaccination. You should carry these papers with you and make at least one copy to put in the animal's cage. Please note that pets greatly limit the choices for temporary quarters upon arrival, since many of the better hotels do not allow pets.

Firearms and Ammunition

The Government of Ecuador currently imposes the following size restrictions on the importation of personal firearms:

Handguns cannot exceed 9 mm; Rifles, limited to .22 to .30 caliber; Shotguns, 10, 12, 16, 20, 28, and 410 caliber.

Private weapons will only be used for recreational purposes, such as hunting and target shooting, and not for personal protection.

All are required by Ecuadorian law to register firearms. Upon registration, individuals will receive a weapons permit issued by the Ministry of Defense. This permit entitles them to possess and carry the weapon.

Carrying firearms about the city is dangerous, provocative and, generally, ineffective for protection. U.S. citizens abroad bearing or using weapons can lead to legal and diplomatic problems.

Possession and use of any firearm must be in compliance with Ecuadorian policy. Persons who maintain weapons in their homes are urged to be cautious in the use of such weapons. All weapons should be stored in a manner to preclude accidental discharge by children or domestic employees.

Currency, Banking, and Weights and Measures

The Ecuadorian unit of currency is the Sucre, designated "S/." and issued in bills of 5,000, 10,000, 20,000, and 50,000. Coins are minted in denominations of 50, 100, 500 and 1,000 Sucres. After several years of relative stability on the exchange market, the Sucre has deteriorated in value against the U.S. dollar from S/120$1 in 1981 to S/11,143-$1 in August 1999.

The metric system is used for both weights and measures, although food is often measured in "libras" (pounds). The ounce and the yard may be used in commerce. In hardware stores, gauges of pipes and fittings are often listed in U.S. measurements, as well as metric.

Taxes, Exchange, and Sale of Property

Ecuador has a direct sales tax (LVA.) of 10% which is collected on sales of goods and services, except for food items. A 10% service charge (tip) is included on most restaurant bills, along with the direct sales tax of 10%. It is not necessary to tip further, although an extra 5% is always appreciated when service has been excellent. An airport tax of U.S. $25.00 is charged to all persons leaving Ecuador. A tax of 10% is charged on the purchase of airline tickets when travel originates in Ecuador.

There are no currency controls in Ecuador and the Sucre is traded freely at any of a number of banks and exchange houses. Some find local Sucre accounts useful. Citibank maintains an exchange service in the Chancery, and you may cash personal checks, purchase Sucres or Sucre checks, and buy travelers' checks. Mastercard, Visa, American Express, and Diner's Club

credit cards are honored in most shops and restaurants.

Disaster Preparedness Volcanos

Beginning in September 1998, the Guagua Pichincha Volcano, located just west of Quito, has exhibited a significant increase in the number of tremors and an accompanying rise in magma level. Since October 1999, there has been an intermittent series of explosions. Volcanic ash has fallen on Quito during some of the explosions, causing temporary closings of area schools and the airport. In the event of a full-scale eruption, geological experts conclude that the city of Quito is protected from possible lava flows, avalanches, and lateral explosions by the bulk of Pichincha Mountain, which stands between the city and the volcano crater. Parts of Quito could be affected by secondary mudflows caused by heavy rains that usually accompany an eruption. The entire city could also be affected by slight to significant ash falls and resulting disruptions of water, power, communications, and transportation.

The town of Banos, a popular tourist destination located approximately 80 miles south of Quito, was evacuated in November 1999 because of the increased activity of the adjacent Tungurahua Volcano. The volcano has been ejecting significant amounts of ash and incandescent rocks. Geological experts advise that an explosive eruption could occur quickly and with little warning. The resulting pyroclastic flows would pose a significant and immediate threat to Banos and several small villages in the vicinity. Travelers are advised not to travel to Banos or the surrounding area.

The Quito City Government and the Ecuadorian Geophysical Institute continue to monitor these volcanoes and issue regular reports on their activity. Travelers are advised to pay close attention to the news media in Quito for updates on the situation. Besides Guagua Pichincha and Tungurahua, other volcanoes in Ecuador may, from time to

time, also exhibit increased activity. Further information about these and other volcanoes in the Western Hemisphere is available from the National Oceanic and Atmospheric Administration via the Internet at http://www.ssd.noaa.gov/VAAC/guag.html.

LOCAL HOLIDAYS

Jan.1	New Year
Feb.26, 27	Carnival
Mar/Apr.	Good Friday*
Mar/Apr.	Easter*
May 1	Labor Day
May 18	Battle of Pichincha
July 25	Founding of Guayaquil (Guayaquil only)
Aug. 10	Independence Day
Oct. 9	Independence of Guayaquil
Nov. 1	All Saints' Day
Nov. 2	All Souls' Day
Dec. 6	Founding of Quito (Quito only)
Dec.25	Christmas Day
*variable	

RECOMMENDED READING

These titles are provided as a general indication of the material published on this country.

Alban, Veronica, with photographs by Jean Claude Constant. *Los Andes Ecuatorianos*. Macalban Editores: Guayaquil, 1976. Parallel English text.

American University Foreign Area Studies. *Area Handbook for Ecuador*. U.S. Government Printing Office: Washington, DC. 1976. Gives general background and covers all areas.

Anhalzer, Jorge. *Through the Andes of Ecuador*. Ed. Campo Abierto: Quito, 1983. Mountaineering and snowcapped peaks with beautiful photographs;

Ayala, Enrique. *Resumen de la Historia del Ecuador.* Corporacion Editora Nacional, 1995. A good overview of Ecuador's history in Spanish.

Blanksten, George I. *Ecuador: Constitution and Caudillos.* New York: Russell and Russell, 1964. A detailed study of Ecuadorian Government and politics.

Bork, Albert William, and George Maier. *Historical Dictionary of Ecuador.* The Scarecrow Press, Inc., 1973. A panoramic view of the country from pre-Columbian days with the general political and social organization, the principal zones of archeological investigation, and similar matters of general interest presented in a dictionary format with concise informative paragraphs.

Brooks, John, ed. *The South American Handbook.* Trade and Travel Publications: England. Handy guide to all Latin American countries. Updated annually and fun to read.

Brooks, Rhoda and Earle. *The Barrios of Manta.* New American Library: New York, 1965. Written by and about Peace Corps Volunteers and conditions under which they worked in an Ecuadorian city.

Bustamante, Edgar, ed. Maravilloso Ecuador. *Circulo de Lectores: Quito, 1978.* Essays by contemporary Ecuadorian writers, covering the country region by region. Color photographs.

Corral, Pablo and Loup Langton. *Discovering Ecuador and the Galapagos Islands.* Imprenta Mariscal, 1994. An excellent photographic overview of the country produced by 38 international photographers.

Cueva, Juan. *Ecuador.* Ediciones Libri Mundi: Quito, 1980. Color photographs with captions in Spanish, French, English and German.

Eichler, Arthur. *Ecuador: A Land, a People, a Culture.* Ediciones Libri Mundi: Quito, 1982. A small general guidebook.

Elliot, Elizabeth. *The Savage, My Kinsman.* Harper and Brothers: New York, 1961. Deals with the primitive Auca tribe in the Oriente.

Fitch, John S. *The Military Coup d'Etat as a Political Process: Ecuador-1966.* Johns Hopkins University Press: Baltimore, 1977. General consideration of factors leading to coups, and specific details on post-war Ecuadorian politics.

Gartelmann, K.D. *Ecuador.* Imprenta Mariscal: Quito, 1975; rev. ed., 1979. Photographs. Text in Spanish, English and German.

Hassaurek, Fredrick. *Four Years Among the Ecuadorians.* Southern Illinois University Press: Carbondale, 1967. Edited from the 1867 edition written by an American Consul in Quito: an interesting commentary on Ecuador 100 years ago.

Hickman, John. *The Enchanted Islands: The Galapagos Discovered.* Anthony Nelson Ltd.: England 1985. History and Science with beautiful photographs.

Histografia Ecuatoriana. Banco Central del Ecuador, Corporacion Editora Nacional: Quito, 1985.

Hurtado, Osvaldo. *The Political Power in Ecuador.* 2nd English ed. Westview Press: Boulder, 1985. Analysis is made by Dr. Hurtado before his election to the vice presidency in 1979 and his ascension to the presidency of Ecuador in 1981. This edition contains updated information on the period since 1979.

Inter-American Development Bank. *Economic and Social Progress in Latin America.* Washington, DC, 1976.

Linke, Lilo. *Ecuador: Country of Contrasts.* Third edition. Royal Institute of International Affairs: London, 1960. A broad study of

Ecuador and an excellent basic reference.

Martz, John D. *Ecuador: Conflicting Political Culture and the Quest for Progress.* Allyn and Bacon: Boston, 1972. An overview of political developments in the contemporary period.

Meggers, Betty. *Ecuador,* Thomas and Hudson: London, 1966. An archeological study of the country and its people.

Mills, Nick. *Crisis, Conflicto y Consenso: Ecuador, 1979-84.* Corporacion Editora Nacional: Quito, 1984. An analysis of political relationship during the administrations of Jaime Roldos and Osvaldo Hurtado.

Oxandaberro, Roura. *Ecuador: Art/Folklore and Landscape.* Su Libreria: Quito, 1965.

Porras, Pedro. *Arqueologia del Ecuador.* 3d ed. Pontificia Universidad Catolica del Ecuador: Quito, 1984. The most up to date guide to archaeological finds in Ecuador.

Reyes, Oscar. *Breve Historia General del Ecuador.* 3 vols. 14th ed. Quito, 1981. A general but not brief, history of the country.

Salvat, Juan, and Eduardo Crespo, ed. *Arte Contemporaneo de Ecuador, and Arte Precolombino de Ecuador.* Salvat Editores Ecuatoriana S.A: Quito, 1977. Amply illustrated text treating painting, sculpture, and handicrafts.

Thomsen, Moritz. *Living Poor: A Peace Corps Chronicle.* University of Washington Press: Seattle, 1969. An excellent book written about the author's experiences as a Peace Corps volunteer in Rio Verde, Ecuador.

Zendegui, Guillermo de, ed. *Image of Ecuador.* Organization of American States: Washington, DC, September 1972. A well-written, 24-page summary of Ecuador and its people.

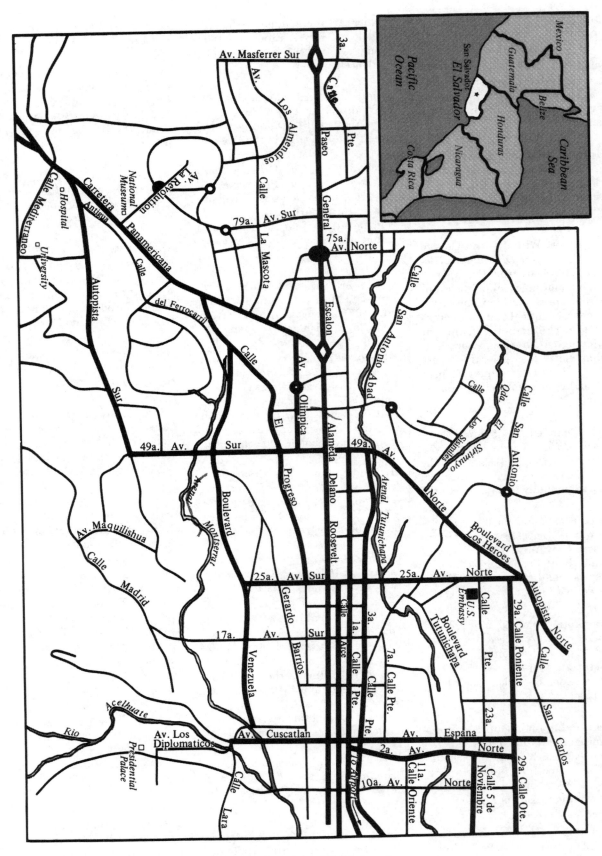

San Salvador, El Salvador

EL SALVADOR

Republic of El Salvador

Major City:
San Salvador

Other Cities:
Acajutla, Ahuachapán, Cojutepeque, La Libertad, La Unión, Nueva San Salvador, San Miguel, San Vicente, Santa Ana, Sonsonate, Zacatecoluca

INTRODUCTION

EL SALVADOR, the smallest of the Central American republics, shares with its neighbors a history marked by frequent uprisings and unremitting political discontent. Years of power struggles, and their resultant abuses of human rights, created such international concern and pressure in the late 1970s that a provisional government was accepted to initiate political and economic reforms. Under a new constitution, formulated in 1983, support of democratic premises and policies was established. In January 1992, a peace accord was signed between the Salvadoran government and the Farabundo Martí National Liberation Front (FMLN). The pact ended a 12-year civil war between the two parties.

What is now El Salvador was once two large Indian states and several principalities whose inhabitants were Pipils, a nomadic Nahua tribe similar to the Aztecs. The area was claimed for Spain in 1525 by Pedro de Alvarado, and remained a Spanish colony until 1821 under the captaincy general of Guatemala. In 1823, it became one of the five states of the Federal Republic of Central America and, when this federation was dissolved 15 years later, El Salvador began its existence as an independent republic.

MAJOR CITY

San Salvador

San Salvador, the capital and principal city of the Republic of El Salvador, is located in the "Valley of the Hammocks" at the foot of San Salvador volcano (6,398 feet high), about 19 miles from the Pacific Ocean. It is built on the volcanic belt which parallels the coast and, over the centuries, the city has suffered from such recurrent and severe earthquakes that it has had to be rebuilt frequently. Public buildings are constructed to resist shock, but an earthquake (measuring 7.5 on the Richter scale) rocked San Salvador October 10, 1986, killing 1400, injuring approximately 21,000, and heavily damaging the downtown area and the San Jacinto residential neighborhood. Two hundred aftershocks wrought additional destruction, and a state of emergency was declared. Among the buildings hit were all but one of the city's hospitals, and the U.S. Embassy on Avenida Norte.

The climate here is semitropical with distinct rainy and dry seasons, but no extreme seasonal temperature variations occur.

San Salvador is the economic, political, and cultural center of the country. It is an old city, established in 1524, and has been the country's capital since 1841, except for a three-year period in the mid-19th century. It is the site of a national university, founded almost 150 years ago.

The metropolitan population of San Salvador is 1.5 million, and includes the cities of Soyapongo, San Marcos, and Santa Tecla. While primarily Latin American in culture, many U.S. and Mexican influences are also apparent. Living standards of the Salvadorans belonging to the higher socioeconomic classes (and most foreigners) are comparable to those of the same strata in the U.S., although the standard is achieved at a greater cost. The city has modern, comfortable, fast-growing residential suburbs, several up-to-date shopping centers and supermarkets, and a less modern downtown area.

San Salvador hosts a large foreign colony, including about 3,000 U.S. citizens. Each year more North American tourists "discover" the country. Other principal groups in the city are Germans, Japanese, British, and other Latin Americans. The better educated Salvadoran frequently speaks English; however, local businessmen and officials often prefer to conduct business in Spanish. Almost no English is spoken in the open markets and other food markets in the city.

Education

The local educational system consists largely of private schools; the Spanish curriculum prepares students for entrance into Salvadoran universities. Few American children attend these schools.

School-aged dependents of Americans usually enroll at the American School (Escuela Americana). The institution is not U.S. Government-operated, but receives government support from grants and loans. It is a private, coeducational day school founded in 1946.

Located on a spacious 29-acre campus near San Salvador, Escuela Americana consists of 18 buildings, two cafeterias, three playing fields, four science labs, three computer labs, and two libraries with a total of 35,000 volumes.

Escuela Americana, in session from mid-August to late-June with a month-long recess over the Christmas holidays, maintains six subdivisions from preschool to high school levels. The preschool is for ages four to six; elementary school from grades one through five; junior high, grades six through eight; and the American high school, grades nine through 12.

Escuela Americana not only provides an American education at the elementary and secondary levels, but also serves to demonstrate American educational methods and practices. The schools are headed by an American principal and staffed by American and Salvadoran teachers.

The American high school is accredited by the Southern Association of Colleges and Schools, and follows a U.S. grading system. The high school curriculum is basically college preparatory. All students, grades one through 12, must study Spanish as a second language. Students also attend some classes that are taught in Spanish. Special efforts are made to help children who enroll without foreign-language capabilities.

The school has a small but active athletic program. Soccer—the national sport—is played instead of American football. The school has no swimming pool. Basketball and volleyball are also played at Escuela Americana.

Special educational facilities in El Salvador are limited. Americans rarely attend local universities. Some local teachers offer private lessons in painting, crafts, ballet, and music.

Recreation

Soccer is the most popular spectator sport among Salvadorans, and is played nearly every Wednesday and Sunday in the capital's stadium. Basketball, baseball, and softball also are major attractions, and the usual participant sports—swimming, golf, tennis, squash, fishing, hunting, and boating—are available.

Several interesting scenic and recreational areas are located within El Salvador, but few have attractive overnight accommodations. Public parks in various parts of the country have picnic and swimming facilities, but these are overcrowded on Sundays and holidays.

The most frequently visited places are Ilopango, a large crater lake about 10 miles east of San Salvador, which has both public and private recreational facilities; Coatepeque, a similar lake about 40 miles to the west; and Cerro Verde, a mountaintop park with a spectacular view of the volcano Izalco and surrounding countryside. All are accessible for a day's outing. A government-operated hotel at Cerro Verde opened in 1975.

The beaches near La Libertad, about 23 miles west of San Salvador on the Pacific, are popular, but also can be treacherous because of the strong undertow, unpredictable currents, and the possibilities of sharks close to the shore. Few public facilities are available on these beaches. Some of the beaches have black volcanic sand; some have white sand.

Excellent saltwater fishing is found in a large estuary about 30 miles from San Salvador. Since rented boats are unavailable, most fishing is done on invitation by friends who own boats. A fishing license is not required. Dove and duck are plentiful anytime, with no hunting season or legal limitations. Firearms permits and hunting licenses are required by law.

The National Archaeological Museum has a collection of artifacts recovered from pre-Columbian times. An Indian pyramid at El Tazumal is located not far from the city of Santa Ana, another is near San Andrés where digs have taken place. The most prestigious recent archeological find is Joya de Ceren, an entire city preserved in volcanic ash. The site is still under investigation.

Guatemala City, four to five hours away by car, is the largest capital in Central America. The volcanic highlands region is strikingly beautiful and offers several spots with good, moderately priced hotel accommodations. The country's unchanged Indian culture is fascinating. Ruins from the ancient Mayan civilizations can be seen in El Salvador,

Honduras (Copán), and Guatemala (Tikal). Many are accessible by car.

Entertainment

Entertainment facilities in San Salvador are limited to several comfortable cinemas that show American and European films (with Spanish subtitles), in addition to Latin American films and to an interesting and growing schedule of concerts. The Cine Presidente, a large national theater in the Colonia Benito area of the capital, is popular for both movies and concerts. The larger hotels, with dinner clubs and discotheques, are becoming popular. San Salvador has many good restaurants.

The American Society, open to all Americans in San Salvador, organizes luncheons, a Fourth of July picnic, and several other functions during the year. The American Women's Association has been active in various charitable activities; all English-speaking women in the city are eligible for membership.

OTHER CITIES

ACAJUTLA, with a population over 16,000, is situated near the Pacific coast, about 50 miles west of San Salvador. In 1524, the Spanish conquered the Indians and the city became a colonial port. As the country's major port, Acajutla exports coffee, balsam, and sugar. During summer, the city is a beach resort.

AHUACHAPÁN, in western El Salvador, is the capital of the department of the same name. It lies at the foot of La Lagunita volcano on the Río Molino. Its most important product is coffee. There are mineral baths here, drawn from hot springs located below the nearby Malacatiupan Falls. Ahuachapán has an estimated population of 20,000.

COJUTEPEQUE, a city of about 20,600 residents, is 22 miles east of the capital, near Lake Ilopango. It is a trading center; its market products include rice, sugarcane, cotton,

and coffee. Known in El Salvador for its cigars and smoked meats, Cojutepeque's landmarks include a Palladian-style church. A large festival is held here every August 29 in honor of St. John.

LA LIBERTAD, located on the Pacific Ocean, is 20 miles south of San Salvador. It is the chief seaport and port of entry for the capital city. La Libertad exports coffee and sugar, and is also a beach resort. Agriculture and fishing are primary economic activities. The population is about 16,000.

LA UNIÓN is approximately 100 miles east of San Salvador on the Gulf of Fonseca, an inlet of the Pacific Ocean. It is situated at the foot of the Conchagua volcano. With a population close to 57,000, La Unión is one of the country's major seaports, exporting cotton and livestock, as well as most of the foreign trade products. The city is situated at the southern terminus of a railroad system and is on the Inter-American Highway. La Unión was the scene of severe fighting during the civil war.

NUEVA SAN SALVADOR (formerly called Santa Telca) is located in west-central El Salvador, eight miles west of the capital. It was founded in 1854 after San Salvador was destroyed by an earthquake. When the capital was rebuilt, what is now Nueva San Salvador became a wealthy suburb. It is also in the midst of a coffee-growing region. The beach resort, Los Chorros, is nearby. The Salvadoran Institute for Coffee Research is in the city. The estimated population is 120,000.

SAN MIGUEL, a commercial center, is situated about 65 miles east of San Salvador, at the foot of San Miguel volcano (6,057 feet). Founded in 1530, and with a population of more than 182,000, San Miguel produces vegetable oil, leather goods, textiles, rope, tobacco products, pottery, and flour, and has textile and dairy industries. The town's industries suffered disruptions during the early 1980s

because of fighting between government troops and leftist guerrillas.

Located in a region of geysers and thermal springs, **SAN VICENTE** is at the foot of San Vicente volcano (7,155 feet). It is in central El Salvador, approximately 25 miles east of the capital. Originally the ancient Indian village of Tehuacán, the city was founded in 1635. It served as the capital (1834–39) and housed the national university (1854–59). Industries include textile manufacturing and sugar refining. San Vicente's population is over 20,000.

SANTA ANA is the second largest city in El Salvador and an important commercial and industrial center. Located in the northwestern part of the country, 50 miles from San Salvador, the city is also near the Santa Ana volcano which, at 7,828 feet, is the highest in the country. Santa Ana is the commercial and processing center for a region that raises sugarcane, coffee, and cattle. It also produces textiles, leather and wood products, cigars, and pottery. Industries include distilling and food processing. Historic landmarks include the Spanish Gothic cathedral and El Calvario colonial church. The population is approximately 213,000.

SONSONATE, about 40 miles west of San Salvador, is the commercial center of one of the richest agricultural regions in the country. Coffee, sugar, tobacco, and dairy products are produced here. Sonsonate, with a population of roughly 60,000, has two beautiful churches and is surrounded by parks and resorts located near the Izalco volcano. Colorful fiestas may be seen in the neighboring village of Asunción Izalco.

ZACATECOLUCA, in south-central El Salvador, is about 25 miles south of the capital. The city lies at the foot of the San Vicente volcano and has a population of around 26,000. Markets in Zacatecoluca include those for lumber, cement, salt, cotton goods, and baskets. The city was severely damaged by an earthquake in 1932. José Simeón

Cañas, who successfully fought to end slavery in Central America, was born here.

COUNTRY PROFILE

Geography and Climate

Most of El Salvador is situated on a plateau (about 2,000 feet above sea level) on the Pacific slope of the Central American Cordillera. With an area of 8,260 square miles, it is the smallest independent mainland state in the Western Hemisphere. Roughly rectangular in shape, it is bordered on the west by Guatemala, on the north and east by Honduras, on the southeast by the Gulf of Fonseca (which separates El Salvador from Nicaragua), and on the south by the Pacific Ocean.

Mountain ranges running from east to west divide El Salvador into three distinct regions: a hot, narrow Pacific coastal belt on the south; a subtropical central region of valleys and plateaus, where most of the population lives; and a mountainous northern region. Ninety percent of the land is of volcanic origin and many places still bear volcanic scars. Almost all of the arable land is cultivated.

El Salvador's climate is modified by its elevation and, except for the hot, narrow coastal region, is semitropical. The capital city of San Salvador, 19 miles from the Pacific, has a pleasant climate. Daily temperatures here average 73°F and range from 50°F to 90°F. Cool evenings moderate the sometimes uncomfortably hot afternoon peak hours. The country has distinct dry and wet seasons. The dry season (December to April) is dusty, particularly in the country. The hottest time of the year (March and April) precedes the rainy interval. During the wet season (May to November), the rain is not continuous, but usually falls in early evening, and is sometimes accompanied by thunder and strong winds. Rain patterns change during the season, and some June and September mornings are overcast. Occasional two- or three-day rainy spells occur. Mildew and insects can become problems during this season. Annual rainfall in San Salvador averages 66 inches.

Earthquakes and volcanic eruptions have been hazards in the past, and tremors occur periodically. Most tremors are felt during seasonal changes. A major earthquake in October 1986 caused damage to some sections of San Salvador and to other areas of the country. Hurricanes do not threaten El Salvador directly, but a strong Caribbean storm can generate heavy, damaging winds and rains as in 1974 with Hurricane Fifi.

Population

El Salvador is Central America's second most densely populated country, with an estimated 292 inhabitants per square mile. The population figure for 2000 was 5.9 million, of which roughly half was rural. The estimated annual growth rate is 1.85%. Because of unsettled conditions, many Salvadorans now live in neighboring countries and in the United States.

El Salvador's population is remarkably homogeneous with no significant minority. It comprises 90% *mestizo*, 9% Caucasian, and 1% Amerindian. The indigenous Indian population has been thoroughly assimilated, and only two or three Indian communities with native customs, dress, or dialects survive. Spanish is the national language and Roman Catholicism the predominant religion. Food varies from typically Latin to typically American. Clothing, houses, shopping facilities, and amusements in San Salvador resemble those in the U.S., but the atmosphere is distinctly Latin American.

Government

El Salvador is a democratic republic governed by a president and an 84-member unicameral Legislative Assembly. The president is elected by universal suffrage and serves for a 5-year term by absolute majority vote. A second round runoff is required in the event that no candidate receives more than 50% of the first round vote. Members of the assembly, also elected by universal suffrage, serve for 3-year terms. The country has an independent judiciary and Supreme Court.

The most recent presidential election, in March 1999, was free and fair, but voter turnout was low (39%). ARENA presidential candidate Francisco Guillermo Flores Perez faced Facundo Guardado of the FMLN party and won with 52% of the votes. Since Flores received just over 50% of the votes, a runoff was not required. Francisco Guillermo Flores Perez of the ARENA party began his 5-year term as president in June 1999, and cannot succeed himself. In the March 2000 legislative races, FMLN won 31 seats in the Legislative Assembly, the ARENA won 29, the National Conciliation Party (PCN) 14, the PDC five, and the Coalition Democratic United Center (CDU) and National Action Party (PAN) won 3 and 2 seats, respectively.

As of March 2002, defections and realignments in the Assembly left ARENA with 29 seats, the FMLN with 26, the PCN, 15, and the FMLN-splinter "Renewal Movement (MR)" 5. The governing ARENA party retains a working majority (43) with its PCN allies. The defection of five FMLN dissidents (MR) also stripped the FMLN of its ability to block qualified (two-thirds) majorities required for major legislation, including approval of international loans and confirmation of supreme court justices. The FMLN retains the capital city of San Salvador, where Hector Silva was re-elected overwhelmingly in 2000. Low voter turnout (35% in 2000) remains a concern.

In accordance with 1992 peace agreements, the constitution was amended to prohibit the military from playing an internal security role except under extraordinary circumstances. Demobilization of Salvadoran military forces generally proceeded on schedule throughout the process. The Treasury Police, National Guard, and National Police were abolished, and military intelligence functions were transferred to civilian control. By 1993--9 months ahead of schedule--the military had cut personnel from a wartime high of 63,000 to the level of 32,000 required by the peace accords. By 1999, ESAF strength stood at less than 15,000, including uniformed and non-uniformed personnel, consisting of personnel in the army, navy, and air force. A purge of military officers accused of human rights abuses and corruption was completed in 1993 in compliance with the Ad Hoc Commission's recommendations. The military's new doctrine, professionalism, and complete withdrawal from political and economic affairs leave it the most respected institution in El Salvador.

The Red Cross, Caritas, the Green Cross, and other privately supported refugee relief organizations are active. Additional organizations, such as professional and university student associations and chambers of commerce, also have active programs in the country.

El Salvador is a member of the United Nations, World Health Organization (WHO), and United Nations Educational, Scientific, and Cultural Organization (UNESCO), as well as the following international bodies: Inter-American Development Bank, International Wheat Council, Organization of American States (OAS), Central American Common Market, International Coffee Organization, and the Latin American Economic System.

The Salvadoran flag consists of three horizontal bands in light blue, white, and light blue, with a coat of arms on the white band.

Cory Langley. Reproduced by permission.

Small church on a hillside in San Salvador, El Salvador

Arts, Science, Education

In addition to overseeing the school system of El Salvador, the Ministry of Education maintains a Directorate General of Fine Arts, with schools of arts, music, and dance. It also sponsors the National Symphony Orchestra, the National Chorus, and National Theaters in San Salvador and Santa Ana.

The Ministry of Education maintains a national archaeological museum and sponsors several excavations of archaeological and anthropological interest. El Tazumal, located near the town of Chalchuapa in western El Salvador, is the major locale of pre-Columbian civilization in El Salvador. The site is open to visitors and includes a small museum. In San Salvador, the ministry sponsors a recently refurbished and expanded natural history museum and exhibit hall, with exhibits by local artists. Parks, recreational areas, and a zoo complete the city's leisure facilities.

The National Symphony Orchestra and the National Chorus give several concerts a year. The annual ballet season offers opportunities for students and professionals to perform. Several private art galleries exhibit the work of Salvadoran

artists, and semiprofessional theater groups offer several plays a year. The Salvadoran Institute of Tourism (ISTU) also sponsors cultural events which include folkloric productions and music and dance festivals, often held outside the capital, as well as annual crafts festivals in Panchimalco and Nahuizalco.

The Salvadoran Cultural Center in San Salvador has a modest library of Spanish and English books. Classes in English and elementary Spanish are offered, and frequent art exhibits and concerts are sponsored here.

Many classes have resumed at El Salvador's National University, which was closed in 1980 because of political unrest. Numerous private universities have arisen with the encouragement and support of the Ministry of Education. The second-largest and oldest of these private institutions is the Jesuit-administered Universidad Centroamericana José Simeón Cañas; it offers courses in engineering, economics, administration, and the humanities. The university library has over 40,000 volumes and has embarked on an expansion program financed by the Inter-American Development Bank. Albert Einstein University, founded in 1976, offers courses in engineering and architecture to some 8,500 students. Universidad José Matías Delgado, with over 9,000 students, has courses in law, economics, and communications, and a recently established School for Agricultural Investigation in Santa Ana. The American School in San Salvador offers a two-year program in English. In 1995, an estimated 70% of Salvadorans could read and write.

Commerce and Industry

The Salvadoran economy continues to benefit from a commitment to free markets and careful fiscal management. The impact of the civil war on El Salvador's economy was devastating; from 1979-90, losses from damage to infrastructure and means of production due to guerrilla sabotage as well as from reduced export earnings totaled about $2.2 billion. But since attacks on economic targets ended in 1992, improved investor confidence has led to increased private investment.

Rich soil, moderate climate, and a hard-working and enterprising labor pool comprise El Salvador's greatest assets. Much of the improvement in El Salvador's economy is due to free market policy initiatives carried out by the Cristiani and Calderon Sol governments, including the privatization of the banking system, telecommunications, public pensions, electrical distribution and some electrical generation, reduction of import duties, elimination of price controls on virtually all consumer products, and enhancing the investment climate through measures such as improved enforcement of intellectual property rights.

Natural disasters continue to plaque the Salvadoran economy. The damage caused by Hurricane Mitch to infrastructure and to agricultural production reduced 1998 growth by an estimated 5%. Because of the earthquakes that struck the country in January and February, the economy grew less than 2% in 2001.

Fiscal policy has been the biggest challenge for the Salvadoran Government. The 1992 peace accords committed the government to heavy expenditures for transition programs and social services. Although international aid was generous, the government has focused on improving the collection of its current revenues. A 10% value-added tax, implemented in September 1992, was raised to 13% in July 1995. The VAT is estimated to have contributed 51% of total tax revenues in 1999, due mainly to improved collection techniques.

Large inflows of dollars in the form of family remittances from Salvadorans working in the United States offset a substantial trade deficit and support the exchange rate. The monthly average of remittances reported by the Central Bank is around $150 million, with the total estimated at more than $1.9 billion for 2001. As of December 1999, net international reserves equaled $1.8 billion or roughly 5 months of imports. Having this hard currency buffer to work with, the Salvadoran Government undertook a "monetary integration plan" beginning January 1, 2001, by which the dollar became legal tender alongside the colón. No more colónes are to be printed, the economy is expected to be, in practice, fully dollarized, and the Central Reserve Bank dissolved, by late 2003. The FMLN is strongly opposed to the plan, regarding it as unconstitutional, and plans to make it an issue in the 2003 legislative elections.

Transportation

The usual mode of travel to El Salvador is by air. Ilopango International Airport is equipped for jet planes. Service is provided to the U.S. and Central American countries by TACA (Transportes Aéros Centro Americanos), LACSA (Líneas Aéreas Costarricenses), COPA (Compañía Panameña de Aviación), Belize Airways, and SAHSA (Servicio Aéreo de Honduras Sociedad Anonima).

Of the two main seaports in El Salvador, Acajutla is most important because of its all-weather dock facilities. Another port is Cutuco in La Unión. The Atlantic port generally used for surface freight shipments originating on the U.S. coast is Santo Tomás de Castilla, Guatemala, where cargo is loaded directly onto trucks bound for the Salvador customs warehouse.

Frequent bus service is available to all parts of the country, but is seldom used by Americans. In the cities, taxis are commonly used; they do not have meters, but operate on zone charges.

El Salvador's main roads are generally good, and most are paved. Back roads are often difficult and rough on both the passenger and the vehicle. Two principal branches of the Pan-American Highway pass through El Salvador—one crossing along the Pacific, the other at a more northerly point. Narrow roads, poor driving habits, livestock and pedestrians on the roads at night, and badly placed traffic signs constitute driving hazards.

The most practical mode of travel is by private car. Road transportation and a lack of recreational facilities within city areas make a car most desirable. An air-conditioned car, while not essential, makes traveling more enjoyable, especially because of the pollution from diesel vehicles. Driving is on the right.

Nearly all European and Japanese automobile manufacturers are represented in San Salvador. U.S. manufacturers are not well-represented and, for the most part, do not maintain spare parts in stock.

Communications

Telephone and telegraph service is available throughout El Salvador, with direct dialing to most of North America, South America, and Europe. International airmail is dependable; the rates are high for parcel post.

El Salvador's 75 commercial radio stations generally operate from 6 a.m. to 11 p.m. Several FM stations, including one which presents classical music, broadcast in stereo. A guerrilla group operates its own station. Over 90% of the homes have radios. Shortwave reception is good for Voice of America (VOA) and Armed Forces Radio broadcasts. VOA also broadcasts a daily program in Spanish (*Buenos Días America*) on medium-wave (Radio Centroamericana).

El Salvador has four commercial television channels that transmit in color. Standard U.S. color receivers are used. All channels transmit at least 16 hours per day. Government-owned channels 8 and 10 are used for educational and informational purposes. Salvadoran TV presents many U.S. programs with Spanish soundtracks. TV sets are costly here. Video recorders are widely used, and several cassette clubs offer a wide selection of movies.

San Salvador has four leading newspapers, *El Diario de Hoy, Diario Latino, El Mundo,* and *La Prensa Gráfica.* The Santa Ana newspaper is *Diario de Occidente.* The *Miami Herald, Chicago Tribune,* and the *New York Times* are home-delivered on an almost-daily basis, and international editions of *Time, Newsweek,* and European periodicals are sold at newsstands. The Union Church in San Salvador has an extensive lending library of paperbacks; these also can be purchased in the large hotels and from various bookshops.

Health

Many Americans use the Hospital de Diagnostico y Emergencias, a 155-bed general medical and surgical hospital with an emergency room. Standards are below those of U.S. hospitals. More complicated or serious illnesses are normally referred to Gorgas Hospital in the Canal Zone or to U.S. facilities. San

Salvador has a good obstetrical center and maternity hospital, a satisfactory pediatric clinic, and an adequate emergency facility and hospital with 25 beds. Medical laboratories here have most of the necessary equipment. Nearly every medical specialization is represented in San Salvador by physicians who have received training in the U.S. or Europe, and who speak English. Satisfactory dental and orthodontic care is available at costs considerably below those in the U.S.

No water purification plant exists in San Salvador. Most water comes from deep wells or springs and is chlorinated; however, contamination is common because of the many cross constructions in the water distribution system. Potable bottled water is available, and tap water, boiled rapidly for 10 minutes, is also safe.

A food sanitation program is conducted by Salvadoran authorities, with routine inspections similar to those recommended by the U.S. Public Health Service, and carried out by trained sanitarians. Qualified veterinarians and sanitarians perform ante mortem and post mortem meat inspections. While modern meat markets have refrigeration facilities, most meat is not refrigerated either at slaughter or in distribution. Some control of poultry processing has improved sanitation, slaughtering, and packaging. San Salvador experiences frequent power failures, and refrigerated items are not always kept at the proper temperature. Caution should be used in buying foods the day after a power failure.

The country has no planned rabies control program as practiced in the U.S. Dogs are not required by law to be vaccinated against rabies, nor must they be leashed. At intervals, attempts are made to eliminate stray dogs.

The most serious health problems in El Salvador are intestinal diseases, including typhoid fever, and amoebic and bacillary dysentery. These diseases are usually caused by care-

less handling of food and contamination of food and water. Other diseases present are influenza, malaria, dengue fever (in the coastal regions), frequent colds, and hepatitis.

Clothing and Services

Except for the slightly cooler mornings and evenings during November, December, and January, little temperature change occurs in El Salvador. However, a lightweight wardrobe should be augmented with clothing suitable for travel to cooler areas such as Guatemala. Certain Central American ready-made garments (shirts, underwear, and casual trousers) are available and satisfactory. An umbrella is needed for the rainy season. A warm robe and slippers are useful. Clothing, especially leather, can mildew during the rainy season. It is unwise to use light bulbs in closets to counteract mildew, as they are a fire hazard. Electric dehumidifier rods are fireproof, more effective, and are available locally. Portable dehumidifiers are useful for home storage areas.

Cockroaches, grasshoppers, crickets, and other insects can damage clothing and upholstery; regular spraying with insecticides can eliminate nearly all of these problems. San Salvador has a number of satisfactory fumigating companies.

Several local firms make shoes of acceptable quality, but sizes do not follow the U.S. scale. Local cobblers can make leather boots at well below U.S. prices. Imported shoes are sometimes available, but at higher-than-U.S. prices.

Men wear lightweight clothing, such as tropical worsted, throughout the year. During cooler months, heavier suits of lightweight worsted are suitable for evening outdoor parties. Men wear shorts only on the beach and while participating in sports.

Salvadoran society quickly reflects U.S. women's fashion trends. Simple cocktail dresses (long and short) are suitable for most evening functions. Conservative, washable cotton/polyester knits and synthetic-blend dresses should be made of durable material, as the strong sunlight and frequent laundering quickly make even good fabrics look drab. Boutique prices in San Salvador are higher than in the U.S. Slacks are worn extensively in the city and for casual parties. Shorts are worn only at beaches, clubs, and homes, or for private parties.

Washable fabrics are preferable for children's clothes. Boys and girls wear clothing similar to that worn in summer in the U.S. Satisfactory children's shoes are available locally, but the quality is below that of the U.S. and replacements are required more often.

A wide variety of food is available in El Salvador. Cuts of meat often differ from those in the U.S., and quality meat is often higher in price.

Fresh vegetables are available throughout the year. All vegetables should be thoroughly washed, soaked, and peeled, or cooked before they are eaten.

A wide choice of tropical and semi-tropical fruit is available; temperate-zone fruits are imported and expensive. All fruit needs careful washing.

Pasteurized milk and cream are available, but quality is poor. Powdered and canned milk are also sold locally.

Tap water is not potable unless it is boiled. Local firms deliver bottled drinking water weekly, as well as beer, carbonated soft drinks, soda water, and tonic by the case.

NOTES FOR TRAVELERS

Passage, Customs & Duties

El Salvador may be reached by commercial airlines which serve the capital from any part of the U.S., via Washington, DC, Miami, New Orleans, Houston, Los Angeles, and San Francisco. Travel by ship is seldom undertaken, and is not recommended.

A current U.S. passport and a one-entry tourist card are required to enter El Salvador. The tourist card may be obtained from immigration officials for a ten-dollar fee upon arrival in country. Travelers who plan to remain in El Salvador for more than thirty days can apply for a multiple-entry visa, issued free of charge, from the Embassy of El Salvador in Washington, D.C. or from a Salvadoran consulate in the United States. Travelers may be asked to present evidence of U.S. employment and adequate finances for their visit at the time of visa application or upon arrival in El Salvador. An exit tax must be paid, either in Salvadoran colones or U.S. dollars, when departing El Salvador from Comalapa International Airport in La Paz. Travelers should be aware that airlines operating out of Comalapa International Airport require U.S. citizens to present a valid U.S. passport when boarding flights bound for the United States. Airlines will not accept Certificates of Naturalization or birth certificates in lieu of a U.S. passport, and information to the contrary should be disregarded. U.S. citizens traveling to El Salvador for any reason without a valid passport should apply for a passport in person at the U.S. Embassy in San Salvador before attempting to return to the United States. Citizens applying for passports overseas are reminded that original proof of citizenship and identity is required before a passport can be issued. Photographic proof of identity is especially important for young children because of the high incidence of fraud involving children.

Americans living in or visiting El Salvador are encouraged to register at the Consular Section of the U.S. Embassy in the capital city, San Salvador, and obtain updated information on travel and security in El Salvador and neighboring countries. The U.S. Embassy is located at Final Boulevard Santa Elena, Urbanizacion Santa Elena, Antiguo Cuscatlan, San Salvador; telephone 011-503-278-4444. The Embassy's web site can be accessed at http://www.usinfo.org.sv. The Consular Section provides services for U.S. citizens from 8:15 a.m. to 11:30 a.m. on normal Embassy work days.

Pets

The following health requirements must be met for the importation of a pet: the animal must be vaccinated against rabies no less than 30 days before arrival in El Salvador, and a certificate from a qualified veterinarian is required, stating that the animal is free from contagious diseases. Shots against distemper, leptospirosis, and gastroenteritis parvo-viral are required. If a bird is imported, the veterinary certificate must show that the bird is free of pullorum and laryngotracheitis; this must be issued within 30 days before arrival of the bird and certified by the nearest Salvadoran consul.

Currency, Banking, and Weights and Measures

The time in El Salvador is Greenwich Mean Time minus six (the same as Central Time in the United States).

The monetary unit of El Salvador is the *colón*, but U.S. dollars are widely used.

El Salvador officially uses the metric system of weights and measures but, because of its proximity to the U.S. and the extensive trade between the two countries, U.S. standards are fairly well known and used. Gasoline, for example, is sold by the gallon rather than by the liter, and foods are sold by the pound.

Disaster Preparedness

El Salvador is an earthquake-prone country. There is also the risk of flooding and landslides. An earthquake measuring 7.6 on the Richter scale devastated much of El Salvador in January 2001. A second earthquake in February 2001 measured 6.6 on the Richter scale and caused significant additional damage and loss of life. The damage was most severe in the southern half of El Salvador between the cities of San Salvador and San Miguel. While reconstruction efforts are underway and the country is returning to normal, experts indicate that it is common for aftershocks to occur for months or longer following a major earthquake. There also is continuing danger from landslides, particularly during the rainy season that runs from May through October. The most recent data on flood and landslide risk can be found on the Government of El Salvador's web page at http://www.rree.gob.sv.

LOCAL HOLIDAYS

Jan. 1 . . . . New Year's Day
Mar/Apr. . . . . Holy Thursday*
Mar/Apr. . . . . Good Friday*
Mar/Apr. . . . . Holy Saturday*
Mar/Apr. . . . . Easter*
May 1 . . . . Salvadoran
                        Labor Day
Aug. . . . . Feasts of San
                        Salvador*
Sept.15 . . . . Salvadoran
                        Independence
Nov. 1 . . . . All Saints' Day
Nov. 2 . . . . All Souls' Day
Dec. 25 . . . . Christmas Day
*Variable

RECOMMENDED READING

The following titles are provided as a general indication of the material published on this country:

Americas Watch Staff. *El Salvador's Decade of Terror: Human Rights Since the Assassination of Archbishop Romero*. New Haven, CT: Yale University Press, 1991.

Bachelis, Faren Maree. *El Salvador*. Chicago: Childrens Press, 1990.

Barry, Tom. *El Salvador: A Country Guide*. 2nd ed., Albuquerque, NM: Inter-Hemisphere Education Resource Center, 1991.

Cheney, Glenn Alan. *El Salvador: Country in Crisis*. 2nd ed., New York: F. Watts, 1990.

Classen, Susan. *Vultures & Butterflies: Living the Contradictions*. Scottdale, PA: Herald Press, 1992.

Cummins, Ronnie. *El Salvador*. Milwaukee, WI: G. Stevens Children's Books, 1990.

Diskin, Martin. *Reform Without Change in El Salvador: The Political War in the Countryside*. Boulder, CO: Westview Press, 1993.

Golden, Renny, ed. *The Hour of the Poor—The Hour of Women: Salvadoran Women Tell Their Stories*. New York: Crossroad NY, 1991.

Haverstock, Nathan A. *El Salvador in Pictures*. Minneapolis, MN: Lerner Publications, 1987.

Krauss, Clifford. *Inside Central America: Its People, Politics, and History*. Summit Books: 1991.

Kufeld, Adam. *El Salvador*. New York: W.W. Norton, 1990.

Lido-Fuentes, Hector. *Weak Foundations: The Economy of El Salvador in the Nineteenth Century*. Berkeley, CA: University of California Press, 1990.

Prisk, Courtney E., ed. *The Comandante Speaks: Memoirs of an El Salvadoran Guerilla Leader*. Boulder, CO: Westview Press, 1991.

Ramos, Arnoldo. *El Salvador*. New York: W.W. Norton, 1990.

Smyth, Frank. *Wayward War: El Salvador & the American Global Vision*. Boulder, CO: Westview Press, 1993.

Wright, Scott, et al., eds. *El Salvador: A Spring Whose Waters Never Run Dry*. Washington, DC: PICA, 1990.

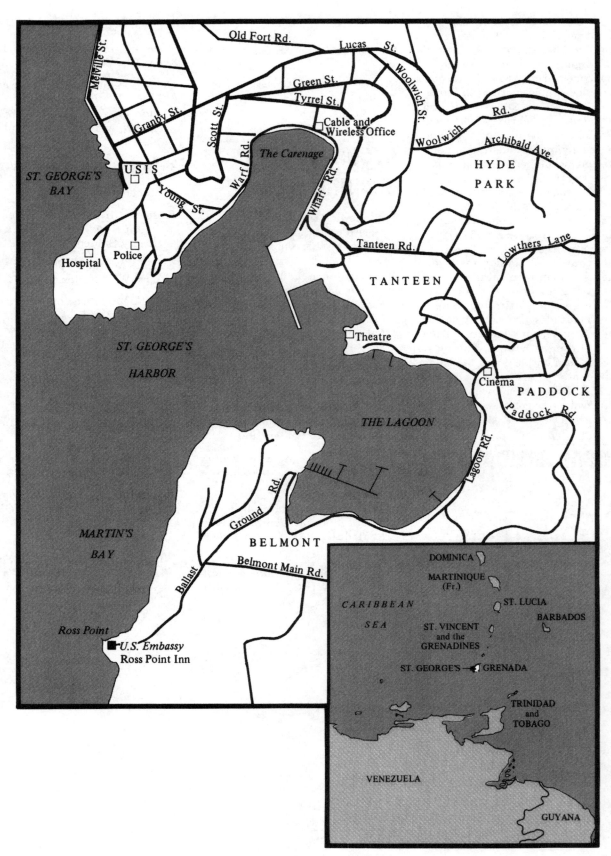

St. George's, Grenada

GRENADA

Major City:
St. George's

Other Cities:
Gouyave, Grenville, Hillsborough, Windward

INTRODUCTION

Volcanic in origin, the small island nation of **GRENADA** (pronounced "Gre-NAY-da") lies at the southernmost point of the Windward Islands in the eastern Caribbean. Its recent leap to instant recognition was prompted by a U.S.-led invasion against Marxist control in October 1983, and now, with a newly elected government in place, it is endeavoring to revitalize its economy and its reputation as a charming, picturesque tourist haven. Grenada is the only significant spice-producing area in the Western Hemisphere and, as such, is popularly referred to as the "Isle of Spice."

MAJOR CITY

St. George's

St. George's, the capital, lies at the southwestern end of the island. Its picture-postcard, almost landlocked harbor is considered one of the Caribbean's most beautiful. The town has a distinctly Mediterranean flavor, with its sun-washed buildings, some of them from the 18th century, and its steep, narrow streets. Towering behind the small city are lush green mountains, studded with fine residences and simple homes.

The hub of St. George's, where many important businesses are situated, is the waterfront, known as the Carenage. Brightly painted, wooden, inter-island trading vessels and larger freighters tie up alongside the harbor walls, and trucks can be seen loading or off-loading cargoes. Yachtsmen moor in the inner harbor and motor over in their tenders to shop at the waterfront stores. Fishing vessels unload their catches, which are sold in the nearby market square. One pier, 800 feet long, is capable of berthing cruise liners and other large ships.

Fort George, surrounded by steep walls, is in a prominent position at the entrance to the harbor. A curious feature is the Sendall Tunnel— in 1890, it was cut through St. George's Point to connect the Outer Harbor (also known as the Esplanade) with the Carenage. At the southern edge of town is a botanical garden.

Farther south is the residential area of L'Anse aux Épines, which has both large homes and simple, compact bungalows. Southeast of St. George's, the beautiful housing development of Westerhall Point overlooks the water.

The area population of St. George's is approximately 35,000.

Education

Education in Grenada follows the British system; children enter primary school at the age of five, and take the Eleven-Plus examination in sixth grade (age 11 or 12). Those who are successful then enroll in the government-run secondary schools, and take the "O" level exam at 16. Few students remain at school the extra two years to sit their "A" levels. The latter examination, required for entrance to British universities, is prepared and graded in England by Cambridge University.

Grenada's education, from an American point of view, is basic. The International School of Grenada

Carenage Harbour, St. George, Grenada

opened in 1984. It is a coeducational institution that covers pre-school through grade seven. A U.S. curriculum is followed using U.S. textbooks and assistance from the Broward County/Miami Department of Education. Enrollment is about 40 with six full-time and four part-time staff. There is no permanent facility; the school's four classrooms, small library, playing field, and administrative office are housed within St. George's University School of Medicine. Tuition is $1,300 annually. School is in session from the last week in August until the first week in June. Instruction is in English. Academic areas include language arts, math, social studies, science, French, art, music, computers, and physical education. There are no provisions for remedial programs or for students with severe physical, emotional, or learning disabilities.

Westmorland Primary is a good private primary school that is part of the Westmorland School, which is known to have the island's highest standard of education. However, the primary level has few vacancies and securing a place may be difficult. The school, covering nursery, kindergarten, and the early grades has an average class size of 24. It has a few trained Montessori teachers. The school year is divided into three terms and runs from early September to mid-July. There is another primary school, in the heart of St. George's, with a fairly solid reputation for teaching, but the physical plant is somewhat run-down, and has no telephone.

The vacancy situation at Westmorland Secondary is little better, with the lowest grade completely full and few places available in the more senior classes. Westmorland is a cooperative school owned by the parents of students and run by a board of management elected annually. First consideration is given to Grenadian children and, since the school has a capacity for only 320 students, it simply does not have enough latitude to accommodate many foreigners. Westmorland prepares students to the "O" level.

The school year at Westmorland is divided into three terms, extending from early September to mid-July. Vacations are held at Christmas and Easter, and on the long summer holiday.

Government-run secondary schools do not meet U.S. standards. American children enrolled in these schools might feel isolated and uncomfortable because of differences in culture, social background, or future expectations between themselves and the main student body. Parents of older children would, in most cases, have no option but to send them to the U.S. for secondary school.

No special facilities exist for children with learning disabilities or any other specific requirements.

Recreation

Pleasant drives amid breathtaking scenery of volcanic origin are among the most popular recreational attractions in Grenada. There are opportunities to see the beautiful Grand Étang (Great Pool) Lake in the rain forest; to drive through the resort developments at Fort Jeudy, Westerhall Point, L'Anse aux Épines, and Levera Beach; and to visit the spice-processing factories at Gouyave or Grenville.

The old French and British bastions, Fort Frederick and Fort George, are points of historical significance in town. Other attractions include Grencraft, (the Grenada handicraft center), the National Museum, Spice Island Perfume Factory, the botanical gardens, the Anglican church, the old Georgian buildings on Le Carénage (the Carenage), and the Yellow Poui art gallery.

Neighboring Trinidad and Barbados afford a change from the quiet, small-island atmosphere of Grenada, and offer good shopping facilities. Trinidad, 90 miles to the south (flying time, 35 minutes), is renowned for its colorful pre-Lenten carnival; the island has a Hilton Hotel and a Holiday Inn, as well as various smaller hotels. Port-of-Spain, its capital city, has several large shopping malls.

Barbados, 120 miles from Grenada, is an attractive, bustling island with good hotels and restaurants and a lively nightlife. In the off-season, shopping is particularly good. Duty-free shops stock a wider range of items than can be found on Grenada; the many fashionable boutiques sell colorful sundresses, sarongs, and beachwear suited to the Caribbean climate. Flying time from St. George's to Barbados is 45 minutes.

Farther north are Martinique and Guadeloupe, with their French ambience and delicious cuisine. An interesting spot in Martinique is the St. Pierre Museum, an eerie monument to the 30,000 who died when Mount Pelée erupted in 1902. In Guadeloupe, a day trip to a living volcano, La Soufrière, can be arranged.

Venezuela's sophisticated capital, Caracas, with its eternal spring climate, is another spot for enjoying the bright lights. It has all the usual big-city amenities, but is expensive. Confirmed hotel reservations are essential.

The two most popular spectator sports in Grenada are cricket and soccer; the former is played on Saturdays and Sundays from November to May, the latter from June to November.

Several participant sports are available. The Richmond Hill Tennis Club, although privately operated, welcomes visitors as temporary members; public courts are at Tanteen and Grand Anse. Many hotels also have their own courts.

Grenada Golf and Country Club at Woodlands, with a nine-hole course, is in a beautiful setting overlooking the sea. It is a 15-minute drive from St. George's. The club sponsors tournaments throughout the year, often involving teams from other islands. Social events include games evenings, dances, and film shows. Membership rates here are reasonable.

Sailing is popular in Grenada, and the island is headquarters for some of the finest yachts to be found in Caribbean waters. Berthing is either in the harbor or at a marina in suburban L'Anse aux Épines. The Grenada Yacht Club has more than 200 members, both Grenadian and foreign, and warmly welcomes newcomers. It sponsors various offshore races, including the annual Easter Regatta, and encourages visiting yachters from other Caribbean territories. The club, which has a sailing section, also serves as a social

center, holding dinners, cocktail hours, and barbecues all year. Mail and telephone facilities are maintained for offshore visitors.

The crystal-clear waters around Grenada make the island a yachting paradise, and cruising up the Grenadines, which extend from Grenada to St. Vincent, is especially rewarding. Sailing enthusiasts find a good selection of large, well-equipped yachts available with crew, and at reasonable rates, for daily or weekly charter. Carriacou Island sponsors an annual regatta the first week in August; races are held for work boats of all sizes, as well as for yachts. The many foreign vessels participating in this regatta make it one of the year's most important regional social events.

A combination of clear water, reefs, coral gardens, and tropical fish make scuba diving, spearfishing, and snorkeling excellent around Grenada.

From November to March, the waters offer good deep-sea fishing and boats for this purpose can be chartered by the day, week, or month. Small, open boats take parties out for a morning, or a day, to fish for snapper or grouper. It is advisable to ensure the availability of life jackets, especially for children, and to provide personal protection from the hot rays of the sun.

The Grenadian three-day fishing tournament, held the last weekend in January, attracts many large fishing cruisers, mainly from Trinidad. It is a popular sporting event and social get-together for the two neighboring islands.

Grenada has several attractive white sand beaches; the largest is Grand Anse, just south of St. George's, dotted with a number of hotels and guest cottages. There are no lifeguards, but the beach is relatively safe for bathing. Grand Anse Bay is popular for wind surfing. The many beautiful, quiet coves are good for picnicking and can be explored by car, although roads may be in poor condition.

Grenada has no public swimming pools or clubs with pool facilities. Some hotels will allow non-guests to use their pools, especially during the slow season.

Although few official sports clubs exist, some groups organize for informal activities such as bird-watching, hiking, or wind surfing. Small runs around the island are held every other Saturday, followed by an informal social gathering.

Entertainment

St. George's does not have a broad offering of formal entertainment. Apart from several popular discos, nightlife is non-existent. There is one poorly ventilated movie theater in St. George's which shows predominantly Kung Fu and "B" movies. Several video clubs exist which rent both current and classic movies.

Most of the restaurants feature local cuisine, and vary in quality. One of these, with a cheery, English-pub atmosphere, has become a favorite gathering spot for Grenadians, tourists, visiting yachters, and U.S. students from the American offshore medical school at the southern point of the island. Some of the hotels have weekly barbecue parties featuring steel-band music for dancing. One of the yacht marinas operates an outdoor snack bar which many find ideal for enjoying a late-evening rum punch and mingling with people from visiting yachts. The marina's Thursday night barbecue is often attended by Americans, mostly employees of the U.S. Embassy in St. George's.

In recent years, Grenada has celebrated its annual Carnival, the national festival, in mid-August. It is an exciting event, but considerably smaller than the huge pre-Lenten pageant held in neighboring Trinidad. Steel bands and calypso performers—both Grenadians and residents of other Caribbean territories—vie for prizes as they parade in colorful costumes on the streets of St. George's.

Amateur radio enthusiasts enjoy Grenada because of its friendly ham-radio community; the terrain provides excellent antenna setting. Permission to operate is granted upon presentation of a valid Federal Communications Commission (FCC) license; third-party traffic is allowed. An adequate transformer is needed for 110-volt equipment.

It should be noted that Grenada, because of its size, has limited entertainment facilities and few cultural or educational opportunities. Grenadians are friendly and hospitable, but the educated professional community is small in number. Social contact is, therefore, circumscribed, and loneliness can become a problem for single people or for young children. Those who have been assigned to the island on official or business tours of any length, advise newcomers to bring with them a good supply of games, books, records, and hobby equipment.

There is no U.S.-sponsored women's club, but American women are welcome to join the few local organizations. Volunteer workers are needed by the Red Cross, St. John's Ambulance Brigade, the Salvation Army, and the Society for the Prevention of Cruelty to Animals (SPCA). Children can join Boy Scouts, Girl Guides, and Cub and Brownie troops, but teenagers find that there are few organized activities for them.

OTHER CITIES

GOUYAVE (also known as Charlotte Town), with an estimated population of 2,900, and **GRENVILLE,** with a population of about 2,100, are on opposite sides of the main island of Grenada. Both of these small towns have spice factories.

The only other population center of any size in Grenada is too small to be called a city but, as the capital of the dependent island of Carriacou, **HILLSBOROUGH** draws yachtsmen and tourists to its modest accommodations. Market day, on Monday, brings the town to life. Many tourists also come here for leisurely walks through the hills or visits to the museum and the new Sea Life Centre. During Carriacou Regatta weekend, people come from all over the Grenadines to participate in the festivities. A highlight of the celebration is the big-drum dancing, an African tradition, in the market square.

WINDWARD, on Carriacou's east coast, is known for the building of wooden boats; many of its villagers are of mixed Scottish descent. Tyrell Bay, on the west coast, is also a boat-building center and a yacht anchorage.

COUNTRY PROFILE

Geography and Climate

Grenada, the southernmost of the Windward Islands, is situated in the eastern Caribbean, 90 miles north of Trinidad and 12 degrees north of the equator. The three-island nation includes Carriacou, the largest island in the Grenadine chain, and Petit Martinique. Grenada itself, roughly oval in shape, is 12 miles wide and 21 miles long. It comprises 133 square miles of rugged mountainous terrain, with lush tropical rain forests and little lowland. Its central mountains rise about 2,000 feet above sea level. The clear, clean air is fragrant with the aroma of the spices grown on the islands.

Carriacou has an area of 13 square miles, and its geographical characteristics are similar to Grenada's except for its lower elevations (approximately 1,000 feet above sea level). Petit Martinique, with a population of only 700, has no tourist facilities, but is famous for boat building.

Grenada's climate is sunny and tropical, averaging 80°F, with dry and rainy seasons. The dry interval,

Houses overlooking the harbor, St. George, Grenada

January through May, is more comfortable, with cooling trade winds, but also occasional showers. The rainy season, June through December, brings moderate to heavy rainfall which fluctuates considerably from year to year. Temperatures drop in the evening, making it pleasantly cool. Sunrise is at 6:30 a.m., and dusk varies between 6 and 6:30 p.m., according to the time of year.

Heavy rainstorms and high winds occur in the wet season, but violent hurricanes are rare.

Mildew can be a problem during the rainy months. Commercial desiccants are a help, but it is also advisable to avoid filling closets too full—this precaution keeps mildew to a minimum and discourages cockroaches, who like undisturbed, dark places. Other pests are mosquitoes, flies, moths, ants, termites, rats, and mice. Most of these can be controlled by taking particular care in household cleaning, and by proper disposal of garbage. Chinese coils, sold in supermarkets, repel mosquitoes; the scent of the coils is not unpleasant. Screens are strongly recommended. Because sand-flies are sometimes a nuisance on the beach, insect repellent should be kept available. Rust is another problem in the wet season, and furniture and appliances must be wiped dry often.

Population

Grenada was first sighted in 1498 by Christopher Columbus, on his third voyage to the New World. The island was inhabited by fierce aboriginal Carib Indians, who successfully discouraged attempts at settlement until French colonialists from Martinique purchased it from them in 1650 for "two bottles of brandy and a few trinkets." The Caribs eventually were eliminated, with the last remaining natives hurling themselves off the cliffs on the north part of the island rather than surrender. The spot where they died, Caribs Leap, is now a famous tourist attraction in the town of Sauteurs.

A series of bloody conflicts between Britain and France followed, with the British finally taking control of the island in 1783 under the Treaty of Versailles.

The French and British brought Africans to Grenada to work their plantations so the population is predominantly of African descent, over 90%, with mixed, East Indian, and Caucasian persons making up the rest of the population. The 1998 estimate put the population at over 96,000. In recent years, the rate of emigration has exceeded the birth rate, leading to a population decline. Most of the population is located in St. George's and four or five other coastal towns.

Christianity is the major religion; 53% of the people are Roman Catholic, 14%% are Anglican.

The Creole culture of Grenadians derives from their African, French, and English heritage. English is the spoken language, but often a French *patois* is heard. Some customs, such as the pre-Lenten carnival, date from the days of French rule. Racial tension is almost nonexistent. Grenadians are courteous and exhibit good-natured tolerance of foreign visitors and their ways; invariably, a smile begets a smile.

Government

Grenada became an independent nation within the British Commonwealth in February 1974. In a coup on March 13, 1979, the New Jewel Movement took control, setting up the People's Revolutionary Government under the leadership of Maurice Bishop. Disagreements within the party led to violence and the assassination of Mr. Bishop less than five years later (October 1983), prompting intervention by U.S. and Caribbean forces. This military action, which routed a Marxist government, has been called a welcome liberation by some, but an invasion by others. In December 1986, Benard Coard, Grenada's former prime minister, and 13 others were convicted of killing Maurice Bishop.

The constitution was restored after the events of October 1983, and the governor-general, Sir Paul Scoon, named an interim advisory council. In 1990, Nicholas Brathwaite was elected Prime Minister. Keith Claudius Mitchell followed as prime minister in 1995 and 1999.

Grenada is governed under a parliamentary system based on the British model; it has a governor general, a prime minister and a cabinet, and a bicameral Parliament with an elected House of Representatives and an appointed Senate.

Citizens enjoy a wide range of civil and political rights guaranteed by the constitution. Grenada's constitution provides citizens with the right to change their government peacefully. Citizens exercise this right through periodic, free, and fair elections held on the basis of universal suffrage.

Grenada's political parties range from the moderate TNP, NNP, and NDC to the left-of-center Maurice Bishop Patriotic Movement (MBPM -- organized by the pro-Bishop survivors of the October 1983 anti-Bishop coup) and the populist GULP of former Prime Minister Gairy.

Security in Grenada is maintained by the 650 members of the Royal Grenada Police Force (RGPF), which included an 80-member paramilitary special services unit (SSU) and a 30-member coast guard. The U.S. Army and the U.S. Coast Guard provide periodic training and material support for the SSU and the coast guard.

The United States, the United Kingdom, and Venezuela maintain resident diplomatic missions in the capital. In 2000, Grenada has an estimated population of 98,000. Grenada is a member of the United Nations, Organization of American States (OAS), Organization of Eastern Caribbean States (OECS), and Caribbean Common Market (CARICOM).

Grenada's flag consists of a red border with yellow and green triangles that form a central rectangle. There is a red circle in the center with a yellow star; there are three stars at the top and bottom of the red border, and a nutmeg to the left of center.

Arts, Science, Education

In 1972, the Commonwealth Caribbean member states formed the Caribbean Examinations Council (CXC) and, gradually, a new syllabus with more emphasis on regional matters has been developed. Some students still sit the British exam in certain subjects while Grenada converts to the new system. The University of the West Indies (UWI), which maintains campuses in several Commonwealth member islands, is responsible for the preparation and grading of the CXC tests.

The Grenada National College at Tanteen, St. George's, conducts courses in carpentry and joinery, refrigeration, electrical installation and maintenance, plumbing, auto mechanics, and machine shop engineering. Its commercial division teaches stenography and office skills.

A craft center, also at Tanteen, offers instruction in woodworking, shell and bamboo craft, tie-dying, ceramics, and pottery. It also sponsors a summer extension program for cottage-industry instructors who teach handicrafts in villages throughout the island.

Most Grenadians interested in higher education enroll in British or Canadian universities, but some first-year evening classes are being conducted by UWI's extension department at Marryshow House, St. George's. UWI is working to restore a full curriculum for its student body, which dramatically declined after the 1979 political coup, and more courses will be developed during the next few years. The university's reference library is open to its students and faculty, as well as to librarians and academics working in Grenada.

Grenada's lively folk culture, based on its African heritage, is superimposed with French and English elements. Modern dance troupes still perform the old slave dances—*bele*, *shamba*, and *piqué*. At festival time, such traditional characters as the "stickman," "horsehead," and "jab-jab" are recreated. At a newly built small theater adjacent to UWI, concerts, dance shows, and operettas are performed. Children from all over the country stage regular concerts and Christmas pageants.

Several Grenadian artists, notably Elinus Cato and Canute Caliste, have received overseas recognition for their primitive paintings. Grenadian sculptor and painter Fitzroy

Harack teaches ceramics at the Jamaica School of Art.

The country has produced a number of outstanding writers, including folk poet Paul Keens-Douglas and journalist T.A. Marryshow. An English-born priest, Rev. Raymond P. Devas, O.P., has written a comprehensive history of the island, as well as books on birds and wildlife. Wilfred and Eula Redhead have published plays and children's stories, rich in Grenadian folklore.

Island music also reflects the people's African ancestry. The calypso beat is strong here, as in Trinidad, and Grenadians have even made the claim that old-time calypso, or *kaiso*, originated on this island and was taken to Trinidad by a group of Grenadian slaves. The steel band is popular; on a typical evening, the "pan beat" can be heard echoing softly against the hills, as "pan men" practice their skills.

Commerce and Industry

Grenada's gross domestic product (GDP) in 2000 was estimated at about $394 million, with a per capita figure of about $4,400.

The economy of Grenada is based upon agricultural production (nutmeg, mace, cocoa, and bananas) and tourism. Agriculture accounts for over half of merchandise exports, and a large portion of the population is employed directly or indirectly in agriculture. Recently the performance of the agricultural sector has not been good. Grenada's banana exports declined markedly in volume and quality in 1996, and it is a question to what extent the country will remain a banana exporter. Tourism remains the key earner of foreign exchange.

Grenada is a member of the Eastern Caribbean Currency Union (ECCU). The Eastern Caribbean Central Bank (ECCB) issues a common currency for all members of the ECCU. The ECCB also manages monetary policy, and regulates and supervises commercial banking activities in its member countries.

Grenada also is a member of the Caribbean Community and Common Market (CARICOM). Most goods can be imported into Grenada under open general license but some goods require specific licenses. Goods that are produced in the Eastern Caribbean receive additional protection; in May 1991, the CARICOM common external tariff (CET) was implemented. The CET aims to facilitate economic growth through intra-regional trade by offering duty-free trade among CARICOM members and duties on goods imported from outside CARICOM.

Transportation

An international airport opened in October 1984 at Point Salines, on the southwest tip of the island. The old Pearls Airport was unable to accommodate commercial jets or night landings. Leeward Islands Air Transport (LIAT) runs daily round-trip flights to Carriacou and, from there, a boat can be taken to Petit Martinique. Carriacou has one or two clean, but somewhat rustic hotels; a third has recently been taken over by new management and is located out of town. Since they are all small and have limited occupancy, reservations should be made in advance. Boats leave for Carriacou twice a week from the Carenage in St. George's, or private accommodations are available from Grenada Yacht Services and Spice Island Charters.

Private cars and taxis are the principal means of transportation used by U.S. citizens on extended stays in Grenada. Some comfortable, newer minibuses travel certain routes around St. George's and to the airport but, for the most part, public transportation is inadequate. Taxis assemble for hire at designated places on the harbor front, at the airport, and at major hotels. Fares are higher than those in the U.S., but should be negotiated in advance, since cabs have no meters. Unmarked taxis can be identified by the letter "H" (for hire) in front of the license number.

Grenada's major roads have improved greatly since 1984, although some are still being rebuilt. Secondary roads are often in poor condition and badly maintained. Potholes are numerous; roads are narrow and often steep. A four-wheel-drive car is not essential, but useful if plans are to explore the island. The Japanese-made, Land Rover-type vehicles sold locally are well suited to the rugged driving conditions, but their small, under-padded rear seats make traveling in the back somewhat uncomfortable. Since they have no trunks, roof racks are necessary. Several lines of smaller Japanese jeeps, as well as some British models (all right-hand drive), are also sold in Grenada, but no American cars are available.

No import restrictions apply. If a new car is shipped to the island, it should be a right-hand-drive vehicle, preferably of a make and model sold in Grenada, as local mechanics work better with familiar cars, and parts are more readily available. Manual transmissions are more easily and cheaply serviced. As a rule, auto agencies satisfactorily service the cars they sell, as well as imported cars.

Before importing a used car, it is advisable to have it thoroughly overhauled, particularly the clutch and brakes, which wear out quickly in the mountainous terrain. Tires may have to be replaced sooner than expected. Spare parts for American-made cars, such as windshield wiper blades and arms, oil, air and oil filters, fan belts, contact points, and turn-signal flash units, should be kept on hand.

Air conditioning will make driving more comfortable, although repair delays are possible because of a lack of spare parts. Specially ordered air conditioners for cars bought in Grenada cost $1,000 or more.

Traffic moves on the left and no speed limits are posted. A Grenadian drivers license is required to drive in Grenada and can be obtained upon presentation of a valid U.S. drivers license and a completed application form.

Several rental firms offer mostly Japanese models, Volkswagens, or *minimokes* (modified dune buggies) at rates similar to those in the U.S. Some people rent minibuses by the day, week, or month at negotiable prices. As Grenada has no school bus system, parents sometimes jointly hire taxis or minibuses.

Communications

The government-owned Grenada Telephone Company operates a recently modernized, fully automatic dial system throughout the island. International telephone service is available 24 hours a day. Calls between Grenada and the U.S. are usually satisfactory.

Cable and Wireless, Ltd., provides international telex service Monday through Friday from 7 a.m. to 7 p.m., Saturdays to 1 p.m., and Sundays and public holidays from 10 a.m. to noon.

International airmail is received and dispatched Tuesday through Saturday by the Grenada General Post Office. Transit time for letters from the U.S. varies from six days to three weeks; letters from Grenada arrive in the U.S. in 7–14 days. Surface mail is erratic, and takes at least a month for delivery.

Radio Grenada operates an AM station providing music, local news, some Voice of America (VOA) programs, and a British Broadcasting Corporation (BBC) international roundup. AM broadcasts in English can usually be heard from Trinidad, Barbados, Montserrat, and The Netherlands Antilles. Spanish-language programs from Venezuela are also available. Although VOA and Armed Forces Radio can be received on shortwave, the quality of reception is often poor; equipment which

can be connected to outside antennas is advised. Radio Antilles in Montserrat broadcasts VOA news and other programs in the evenings on medium-wave.

Grenada-based Discovery TV transmits one channel in color, 7 days a week, from 9:00 a.m. to 11:30 p.m. Local Grenadian news and cultural programming is interspersed with American series reruns, cartoons, films and some NBA games. CNN midday news is broadcast in the evenings. Those who live on the south side of the island can usually pick up TV from Trinidad.

There are several weekly newspapers which largely confine themselves to events on Grenada and other Caribbean islands. International news takes a back seat to inter-island gossip. The weeklies are *The Grenadian Voice, The Informer, The Grenadian Guardian, The Grenadian Tribune,* and *The Indies Times.* The last three are affiliated with political parties. The current Latin American editions of *Time* and *Newsweek* are sold in book shops and supermarkets, and certain other popular U.S. magazines (*Good Housekeeping, Cosmopolitan, Harper's*) are also available, although at least a month old. Women's magazines, such as *Vogue,* are often stolen from the international mail.

Three small, but well-stocked, book shops sell a good range of paperback novels, as well as reference books and hardcover publications.

The Grenada Public Library on the Carenage in St. George's has a good selection of books and periodicals, many donated by the U.S., U.K., and Canadian governments. Reference materials are non-circulating and are restricted to Caribbean history, culture, and politics. Library lending cards are issued upon receipt of a refundable deposit and two recommendations from Grenadian residents. A small, but well-kept, reference library at the University of the West Indies, Marryshow House, is open to research scholars.

The collection contains many hard-to-find works by Caribbean writers.

Health

The General Hospital in St. George's is old and inadequately equipped, and the nursing care does not meet U.S. standards. Resident Americans in Grenada are advised to use the facility only for emergencies. However, the hospital does maintain an eye clinic which is currently updating its diagnostic services and equipment. Trained ophthalmologists from the International Eye Foundation run a clinic at the General Hospital which is open daily. For ordinary needs, St. George's has an up-to-date firm of opticians who perform eye examinations.

Two district hospitals are in operation—one in St. Andrew's Parish, the other on Carriacou. Health clinics, some of them with maternity facilities, are located throughout the island. The Simon Bolivar Clinic, a small, well-equipped dispensary is operated by the St. George's University School of Medicine on its Grand Anse campus.

Grenada has a few qualified specialists who were trained in England or the U.S.; their practices are in surgery, internal medicine, gynecology and obstetrics, and pediatrics. Preventive dental care should be arranged before moving to Grenada, however, several U.S. dentists are available locally by appointment a month in advance. Because there are no local orthodontists, those needing this particular type of care have to go to Trinidad or Barbados.

Local pharmacies carry adequate supplies.

Community sanitation includes sewage treatment and garbage collection (not up to U.S. standards). Water is treated at the source, but the distribution system and fluctuating pressure result in an unsafe yield. All drinking water must be boiled. Frozen foods are often suspect because of spoilage during

Grenada's frequent electrical outages.

Infectious hepatitis, dengue fever, gastroenteritis, and intestinal parasites are common. The tropical weather and high humidity are conducive to skin and fungal infections. Rabies is prevalent in animals.

Although none of the following inoculations are required for entry to Grenada, all are advised for anyone planning an extended stay: typhoid, polio, tetanus, gamma globulin for infectious hepatitis, and yellow fever. Children should be given measles, mumps, rubella, and diphtheria, pertussis, tetanus (DPT) shots, and everyone over the age of one should have pre-exposure rabies immunization. Children over 18 months should receive a Hemophilus influenza b (Hib) vaccination before going to Grenada, as outbreaks of meningitis occur on the island and the vaccine is not available locally.

Clothing and Services

Grenadians dress to suit the climate, but they are modest, and women rarely wear shorts or midriff garments in town. It is important that all clothing, including underwear and socks, be of extremely lightweight material; either cotton or a cotton blend is the most comfortable. With frequent laundering, necessitated by heat and high humidity, garments wear out quickly.

An umbrella is needed for the wet season's heavy, almost-daily rainstorms. Raincoats and heavy footwear are impractical in this heat. Beachwear and shorts are acceptable for adults and children in resort hotels and for recreation or relaxation; beach wraps are needed for lunches on hotel patios.

Office attire for men is either a shirt or *guayabera* and slacks, or a "jac suit," which is a short-sleeved, open-collared jacket worn with matching pants; no shirt or tie is needed for this practical outfit. Few Grenadians wear a regular jacket and tie in the office. The "jac suit" is also favored for social events, although a lightweight jacket and tie are equally appropriate. Jeans, although heavy for the climate, are popular in Grenada.

Working attire for women is usually a modest, short-sleeved dress, or a blouse with skirt or slacks, and sandals. Stockings are not normally worn. Sleeveless dresses are ideal for street wear in the humid months, but are not worn at work. Sundresses and straw hats are sold inexpensively by beach vendors. Stout canvas espadrilles are recommended for walking on beaches or along Grenada's rough roads.

Grenadian women are fashion conscious and like to dress up for parties. Home entertaining is popular in the foreign community and, since the same people travel in that circle, women find that they need substantial party wardrobes. Silk dresses, unless they are washable, are impractical, as St. George's one dry cleaner does only a rudimentary form of dry cleaning. A light stole is useful for cool nights.

Normal U.S. summer wear is suitable for children, with lightweight jackets or cardigans for cool evenings. Every child needs several pairs of sandals. Most Grenadian schools require uniforms (available locally).

Grenada has few high-quality clothing stores. There are a couple of attractive boutiques in St. George's, but stocks are limited and prices are not competitive with those in the U.S. Tourist shopping, however, is interesting, with a wide variety of straw items, spices, and coral handicrafts. Duty-free shopping is also available.

St. George's has several good tailors whose work is not expensive. There are also dressmakers, varying in skill. Shoe repair is fair. Beauty shops, although not elegant, have good reputations. Barbershops are adequate and reasonable in price. Repairs (electrical, auto, etc.) are available, but uneven in quality; progress is often slow and further hampered by periodic power outages and unavailability of materials.

The style of cooking in Grenada is Creole, similar to that of neighboring islands, with one or two specialties such as *lambie*, found in abundance in surrounding waters. On Saturday mornings, this variety of mollusk may be purchased directly from the conch boats at the Carenage. Local cooks have a touch with soups, and some notable ones are *callaloo*, made from a green bush with added seasonings, and *tannia*, from a root vegetable. Other island delicacies include crab-backs (seasoned crab meat served hot in the shell); souse, and black pudding.

In general, food prices are higher than in the U.S., but foreigners living here find that the supermarkets are well-stocked and carry a good supply of processed foods from the U.S., Europe, and other Caribbean territories. Small, family-run groceries abound. There is a wide variety of fresh fish, fruits and vegetables, bakery items, and imported candies and cookies. Most meats sold in the markets are local and of indifferent quality. Chicken is imported from the U.S. Powdered and evaporated milk and baby formula are readily available, as well as "flash" sterilized milk which does not need refrigeration. Although fresh milk is occasionally obtainable, it should be avoided, since some cattle are not tuberculin-tested.

French, American, and German wines are widely available, as is excellent rum from Trinidad and Barbados, marketed at reasonable prices. The local lager, Carib, is good; other beers are imported.

Domestic Help

Competent, trained maids and cooks work for moderate wages. An experienced domestic receives a monthly wage plus food, and many are prepared to live in or return in the evening to baby-sit. The employer's contribution to the compulsory national health insurance plan is 4% of the servant's salary. Under current codes, the employee serves a two- to three-month probationary period, is given two weeks' leave after one year of service, three weeks after two years, and a Christmas bonus of one month's pay. In addition, a maid/cook expects one-two days off each week; arrangements for weekends and holidays are fixed by the employer at the time of hiring.

NOTES FOR TRAVELERS

Passage, Customs & Duties

Direct service to Grenada from North America and other Caribbean islands is provided by British West Indies Airlines (BWIA). Leeward Islands Air Transport (LIAT) serves the country several times daily from Barbados and Trinidad. American, Pan Am, Eastern, and Air Canada provide connecting flights through Barbados.

U.S. citizens may enter Grenada with proof of U.S. citizenship, (a certified birth certificate, a Naturalization/Citizenship Certificate, or a valid or expired passport) and photo identification. U.S. citizen visitors who enter Grenada without one or more of these documents, even if admitted by local immigration officials, may encounter difficulties in boarding flights to return to the U.S. No visa is required for a stay of up to three months. There is an airport departure charge for adults and for children between the ages of five and thirteen years of age. For additional information concerning entry/exit requirements, travelers may contact the Embassy of Grenada, 1701 New Hampshire Avenue, N.W., Washington, D.C. 20009, telephone (202) 265-2561, e-mail grenada@oas.org, or the Con-

sulate of Grenada in New York at telephone (212) 599-0301.

Grenada customs authorities may enforce strict regulations concerning temporary importation into or export from Grenada of items such as firearms, antiquities, business equipment, fruits and vegetables, electronics, and archaeological items. It is advisable to contact the Embassy of Grenada in Washington, D.C. or the Consulate of Grenada in New York for specific information regarding customs regulations.

Americans living in or visiting Grenada are encouraged to register at the Consular Section of the U.S. Embassy in Grenada and obtain updated information on travel and security within Grenada. The U.S. Embassy is located on the right hand-side of the main road into Lance aux Epines in the "Green Building," and is approximately 15 minutes from the Point Salines International Airport. Telephone: 1-473-444-1173/4/5/6; fax: 1-473-444-4820; Internet: http://www.spiceisle.com; email: usemb_gd@caribsurf.com.

Pets

Grenada will permit entry of pets with proper documentation, including health certificates and proof of recent inoculation against rabies. The health certificate, stating that the pet is free from infectious diseases and rabies, must be issued by a licensed veterinarian and stamped with verification of that license. Both Trinidad and Barbados, still used by some as entry points to Grenada, have strict laws governing pet importation (other than from Great Britain or Ireland). A quarantine station and appropriate airport facilities are available in Trinidad.

Currency, Banking, and Weights and Measures

The time in Grenada is Greenwich Mean Time minus four hours.

Local currency is the East Caribbean dollar, which is pegged to the U.S. dollar at a rate of

US$1=EC$2.70. Bills, from $1 to $100, are printed in a series of colors, and coins are minted in six denominations. All currency carries the likeness of Queen Elizabeth II. Only a few hotels and stores accepts U.S. credit cards. Travellers checks are accepted everywhere.

Some effort is being made to introduce the metric system of weights and measures, but Grenadians continue to think in terms of pounds and miles, rather than kilograms and kilometers.

Disaster Preparedness

Grenada has experienced tropical storms during the hurricane season, from June through November. General information about natural disaster preparedness is available via the Internet from the U.S. Federal Emergency Management Agency (FEMA) at http://www.fema.gov/.

LOCAL HOLIDAYS

Jan. 1	New Year's Day
Feb. 7	Independence Day
Mar/Apr.	Good Friday*
Mar/Apr.	Easter*
Mar/Apr.	Easter Monday*
May 1	Labor Day
May/June	Whitsunday*
May/June	Whitmonday*
May/June	Corpus Christi*
Aug.	Emancipation Day*
Aug.13	Carnival Monday
Aug. 14	Carnival Tuesday
Oct. 25	Thanksgiving Day
Dec. 25	Christmas Day
Dec. 26	Boxing Day

*Variable

RECOMMENDED READING

The following titles are provided as a general indication of the material published on this country:

Brizan, George. *Grenada: Island of Conflict: From Amerindians to People's Revolution, 1498-1979.*

Atlantic Highlands, NJ: Humanities Press, 1984.

Burrowes, Reynold A. *Revolution and Rescue in Grenada: An Account of the U.S.-Caribbean Invasion.* Westport, CT: Greenwood Publishing Group, 1988.

Grenada. Edison, NJ: Hunter Publishing, 1990.

Heine, Jorge, ed. *A Revolution Aborted: The Lessons of Grenada.*

Pittsburgh, PA: University of Pittsburgh Press, 1990.

Lewis, Gordon K. *Grenada: The Jewel Despoiled.* Baltimore, MD: Johns Hopkins University Press, 1987.

Sanford, Gregory W., and Richard Vigilante. *Grenada: The Untold Story.* Lanham, MD: University Press of America, 1985.

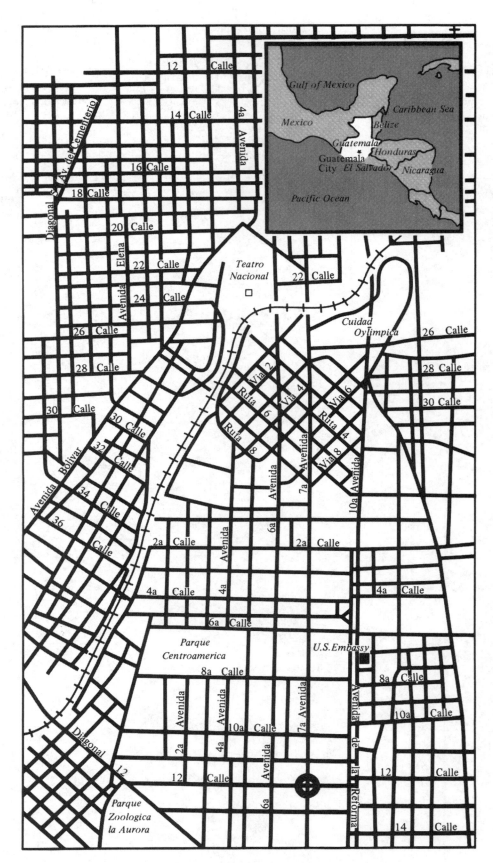

Guatemala City, Guatemala

GUATEMALA

Republic of Guatemala

Major Cities:
Guatemala City, Antigua

Other Cities:
Amatitlán, Chichicastenango, Chimaltenango, Chiquimula, Cobán, Esquipulas, Flores, Huehuetenango, Mazatenango, Puerto Barrios, Quezaltenango, San José, Zacapa

EDITOR'S NOTE

This chapter was adapted from the Department of State Post Report dated June 1996. Supplemental material has been added to increase coverage of minor cities, facts have been updated, and some material has been condensed. Readers are encouraged to visit the Department of State's web site at http://travel.state.gov/ for the most recent information available on travel to this country.

INTRODUCTION

GUATEMALA is one of the most diverse countries in the world. Its more than nine million inhabitants live in the highlands, the tropics, and the central plateau. Almost half of them are pure-blooded descendants of the Maya Indians, whose civilization flourished throughout much of Guatemala before the Spanish conquest in 1523.

Modern, comfortable Guatemala City, the capital, contrasts sharply with the rural interior. That area is characterized by Mayan ruins, mile-high Lake Atitlán, the ancient Indian cultures of Chichicastenango and Huehuetenango, and colonial Antigua, the proud capital of the country until it was leveled by two disastrous earthquakes in 1773. Guatemala has survived a turbulent history of dictatorships, political unrest, and economic instability, and is now pursuing a comprehensive plan for national development.

MAJOR CITIES

Guatemala City

Guatemala City, the capital, is a busy metropolis, and despite air pollution, dust in the dry season, and mud during the wet season, it is a fairly clean place. The colorful native dress of the large Indian population adds charm and uniqueness to this interesting city. Guatemala City (its full name is Santiago de los Caballeros de Guatemala la Nueva) is located slightly southwest of the country's geographical center at an altitude of about 5,000 feet, and is built on a long, narrow plain completely surrounded by hills and mountains. It is the largest city in Central America, with a population of 2.7 million (2000 est.).

The older buildings are Spanish-style, but starkly modern structures are rising rapidly. Residential districts are spreading beyond the town's outskirts, with newer homes either modern or Spanish colonial in design. Downtown Guatemala City's streets are narrow and, despite one-way traffic, congestion is bad and parking difficult. Several new shopping centers away from the city's center are gaining rapid popularity. Streets in the newer residential and business sections are relatively wide, attractive, and less congested.

The city has a number of interesting old churches. Large daily markets, the main source of fresh fruits and vegetables, are also centers for a variety of native textiles, blankets, and some pottery. The large block-size relief map of Guatemala, the National Palace, the Archeological Museum, and the Mayan ruins on the outskirts of the city are sightseeing attractions. Parks are always full, especially on Sundays and holidays. Aurora Zoo is small, but worth seeing.

In spite of the thousands of foreign tourists who stream through the city every month and the multinational, intercultural mix of residents, the city maintains a calm tolerant aura of well-being. Although some nightlife is available, Guatemala City is not a nighttime city, and quietly finishes most days well before midnight.

congregations, the Sephardic, Orthodox Ashkenazi, and a Reform group, hold regular services.

Education

The private educational system in Guatemala City is considered fairly good. Most schools require a birth certificate, a certification of good health, a vaccination certificate, and a transcript of education records. Although many private elementary and secondary schools operate in Guatemala, most American children attend the American or the Mayan School. Calvert System materials are not necessary, since these materials are provided by those schools using the system.

The American School (Colegio Americano) offers kindergarten through secondary school instruction. Despite its name, it is a private Guatemalan school with American administrators and some American teachers (the enrollment in 1991 was 1,600, of which 160 were American children). Accelerated courses are available in all grades for students planning to enter university or who will be transferred to other areas in the fall. Classes are conducted in both English and Spanish and students can elect to be taught in either language. Quality of instruction at all grade levels is considered adequate.

The secondary school is accredited by the U.S. Southern Association of Schools and Colleges. The number of American teachers usually averages 25% of the total faculty. Athletic activities consist of softball, water polo, track and field, basketball, baseball, soccer, volleyball, and swimming. Other extracurricular activities include drama, dance, choral and instrumental music, yearbook, newspaper, literary magazine, computers, and field trips. An intramural and playground recreational program is stressed. Bus transportation to and from school is provided at nominal cost.

The school year runs from mid-January through mid-October, with vacations during Holy Week and at midyear. The school is located on 52

David Johnson. Reproduced by permission.

Overview of city center, Guatemala City, Guatemala

The present city is the third permanent capital of Guatemala. It was founded in 1776 after Antigua was destroyed by earthquakes. An earthquake destroyed Guatemala City in 1917, but it was rebuilt on the same site. Guatemala City suffered less than did the countryside from the February 4, 1976 earthquake which killed 27,000, injured 76,000, and left more than one million homeless.

The level of living for Americans in Guatemala City is generally equal to that of a small U.S. city, but the cost of living is similar to that in Washington, DC. The American community, comprising some 6,500 persons in the capital and perhaps 1,000 elsewhere, is the largest single foreign group. The foreign community also includes much smaller German and British colonies.

Religious Activities

Roman Catholicism is the principal religion, and Catholic churches in the capital and throughout the country are staffed by native and foreign clergy in about equal numbers. Two of the churches, Villa Guadalupe and San Agustin are run by the American Maryknoll and Franciscan Fathers. Protestant services in English are offered by the interdenominational Union Church in Guatemala City and also by Episcopal, Lutheran, and Church of Christ congregations. Three Jewish

Central plaza, Guatemala City, Guatemala

David Johnson. Reproduced by permission.

acres of land in a residential area just outside the city. Facilities include an audiovisual room, auditorium, science labs, two computer labs, cafeteria, covered play area, gymnasium, swimming pool, and a 28,000-volume library. The mailing address is Apartado Postal 83, Guatemala City, Guatemala. U.S. mail may be sent in care of the U.S. Embassy, Guatemala, APO Miami, Florida 34024-5000.

The Mayan School (Colegio Maya) offers instruction for nursery through grade 12. It is a cooperative school sponsored by parents, administered by an elected board of directors, and fully accredited under the U.S. Southern Association of Schools and Colleges. The director and principal are American, as are at least 50% of the teachers and staff. The enrollment in 1991 was 340, almost equally divided among American, Guatemalan, and third-country nationals. General curriculum is taught in English with one class period daily in Spanish. Instruction provided in all grades is considered adequate. Art, physical education, and computer science may be elected. Extracurricular activities include drama, computers, yearbook, newspaper, field trips, and photography. Athletic activities comprise basketball, volleyball, baseball, and other orga-

nized sports. Playground equipment is also available for smaller children. Bus transportation is provided by the school.

The school year runs from the end of August to the beginning of June, with vacations at Christmas and Easter. The school is located on 12 acres of land about six miles from the city. Facilities include an audiovisual room, science and language labs, infirmary, cafeteria, a computer room, and a 10,200-volume library. The mailing address is Apartado Postal 2-C, Guatemala City, Guatemala. U.S. mail may be sent to APO 34024, Miami, Florida.

Recreation

Spectator events include frequent national and international soccer matches, bicycle and car races, and local wrestling. Baseball and softball are increasing in popularity and can be played year round. Joggers can be seen often here, and several organizations sponsor races throughout the year. Although Guatemala City has only two facilities, bowling is popular, with several regular city leagues and frequent national and Central American tournaments.

Golf courses and tennis courts are available for either membership or public use, as are several outdoor

and indoor pools. About two hours from Guatemala City, on the Pacific coast near the port of San José, is a large hotel with both fresh and salt-water pools. Ocean swimming on this coast, unfortunately, is not only dangerous because of strong undercurrents and occasional sharks, but also rather unpleasant because of the rough black sand, rocks, and narrow, limited "beach" areas. Caribbean beaches are lovely, almost virginal, territory, but not easily accessible.

Surf and deep-sea fishing are enjoyed on either coast where tarpon, barracuda, shark, sailfish, giant ray, red snapper, bonito, and jackfish are common. Lakes and rivers provide freshwater fishing.

Near Guatemala City, the volcanos Pacaya (8,345 feet), Fuego (12,851 feet), and Agua (12,307 feet) attract climbers and offer a rewarding view of both coasts on clear days. Pacaya, which is gently active much of the year, provides the unique opportunity for climbers to stand on one peak and view close at hand the lava activity on another. Climbing parties are organized during the dry season.

Wild game, such as deer, wild turkey, dove, geese, pheasant, duck, jaguar, and boar, is still plentiful in various parts of the country. Hunting is prohibited in most of Guatemala and hunters should obtain permission to hunt on private land.

Guatemala offers many opportunities for sight-seeing, as well as for sport. Lake Atitlán is two-and-a-half hours from Guatemala City by car over a good but winding road. Atitlán is generally considered the most beautiful lake in the country and is visited as part of the "must" excursion to Solola and Chichicastenango. Three large volcanos are nearby. Encircling the shores of the lake, 5,500 feet above sea level, are 12 Indian villages named after the Twelve Apostles. These villages can be reached by launch from the hotel area. Several good tourist hotels are located on the lakeshore in the town of Panajachel. Swimming and boating are pleasant pastimes.

Tikal, largest and one of the oldest of the ancient Mayan cities, is located in the midst of a dense tropical rain forest in the Department of Petén, in the northeast section of Guatemala. Due to daily flights and occasional special tourist or charter flights, these magnificent ruins, formerly almost inaccessible to the traveler, are now within a short flying time of Guatemala City. Overnight accommodations with meals are available at either of two adequate but non-luxury hotels.

The highland and northern jungle regions of Guatemala, difficult to reach because of poor or no roads, offer a complete change of scene and atmosphere. The towns of Flores and Sayaxche are the jumping-off points for jungle trips. Trips can be arranged by air and jeep to the sites of Mayan ruins, and bus service is usually available to many remote villages. Airline service is furnished to about 20 points within Guatemala. The road-building program is gradually opening up previously inaccessible regions, and tourist traffic is increasing.

Visiting Indian communities throughout the country during their various patron saint festivals offers unique opportunities to experience the flavor of the Guatemalan heartland and its hospitable people. These fiestas, which usually begin a few days before the actual patron saint's day, are usually characterized by special dances, processions, and a profusion of decorations, as well as firecrackers, native marimba or other instrumental music, and often a lively market. There are no limits, outside those of good taste, to taking photographs.

For those who want to become acquainted with Guatemala, the country, and its customs, the Trekkers Club offers frequent group trips at minimum cost. The club is international in membership. Meetings are held one evening a month at the Union Church with featured speakers, movies, and/or slide show-

David Johnson. Reproduced by permission.

Tree-lined street scene in Antigua, Guatemala

ings. Trips are usually planned for weekends. Members share the responsibilities for organizing and leading the excursions, as well as serving on the board of directors.

Guatemala is a friendly country, and most Americans establish fine and lasting friendships with Guatemalans. Many Guatemalans speak excellent English, having been educated in the U.S., and many others are studying English at the Instituto Guatemalteco-Americano de Cultura (IGA) and other institutions. Americans usually find ample opportunity for social contacts, both private and official, with Guatemalans. Social contacts between the American colony and other foreign colonies are frequent and interesting.

The American Society is an organization of U.S. citizens living in Guatemala. Membership includes official personnel, members of the business community, and others. The society endeavors to improve Guatemalan-American relations on the local level and performs an important welfare function. The group also sponsors several social functions each year, including an annual Fourth of July picnic and a children's Christmas Party, and holds bridge and craft classes for

members. Other clubs include a Rotary Club, Lion's Club, an English-speaking Masonic Lodge, an American Legion post, and a Toastmasters International Club.

While the primary aims of the American Chamber of Commerce of Guatemala are business and investment-oriented, the group has a large and active membership of firms and individuals who maintain a high community visibility. Their monthly luncheon meetings are frequently open to the public and their programs and service activities promote excellent, broad-based relationships. Membership fees are reasonable.

Entertainment

Entertainment is widely available in Guatemala City, and the scope is quite ambitious. Guatemala City boasts a 2,000-seat National Theater that hosts plays, dance performances, and concerts. The National Symphony Orchestra and the National Ballet each have a wide repertoire that is expanding each year. Several small city theater groups perform everything from musical comedy to serious drama. Guest artists and performers, often traveling under the sponsorship of the U.S. Government, are consistently well received, and add further dimension to the performing arts in Guatemala.

Recent U.S. films are shown at a number of theaters in Guatemala City, usually with Spanish subtitles. Mexican, Italian, French, and Argentine films are also featured, although less frequently. Guatemala City has several motion picture theaters, some of which are clean, modern, and as pleasant as any in the U.S.

Guatemala's art world is lively, especially the painting and sculpting. The binational center has at least one monthly exhibit, and frequent exhibits are held in the National Bank Building and smaller city galleries. Prices for art works, however, are comparable to those in the U.S. The National Palace displays examples of Spanish colonial art, and is decorated with vivid murals depicting the area's pre-colonial and Hispanic history. Several newer government buildings are decorated with facades of attractive modern sculpture.

One of the best sources of reading material is the IGA (the binational center) library, which has a collection of over 8,000 volumes in English and Spanish, and a bookstore offering current material. The American Club provides its members with a lending library of fiction and nonfiction best-sellers, and the Union Church maintains a library. Books are also available in commercial bookstores at import prices.

In addition to the first-class dining rooms of the major hotels, numerous good restaurants offer specialties ranging from typical dishes to French cuisine and Chinese food. Several popular restaurants specialize in "Argentine-style" beef. Many of the American fast food chains are represented in Guatemala.

Antigua

Antigua, previously named Ciudad de Santiago de los Caballeros de Guatemala, and sometimes called Antigua Guatemala, is located in the south-central part of the country, less than an hour by car from Guatemala City over a good road. Once a metropolis rich in beauty and culture, its mossy arches, well-preserved architectural ruins, and quiet parks and gardens are reminders of the magnificence of a bygone era.

Antigua was founded in 1542 by survivors of nearby Ciudad Vieja, which was destroyed by an earthquake and a flood. The city became the capital of Spanish Guatemala and, by the 17th century, was flourishing as one of the richest capitals of the New World, rivaling Lima and Mexico City. By the 18th century, Antigua's population was over 100,000; the university was the center of the arts and learning and the churches, convents, monasteries, public buildings, and houses were characterized by extreme luxury. Situated amongst three volcanoes (Agua, Acatenango, and Fuego), Antigua was destroyed by two earthquakes in 1773. The capital was moved to Guatemala City a few years later.

Today, Antigua is a picturesque city of ruins and old, restored homes. Buildings are characterized by Spanish facades, patios, and arcades. With a population over to 30,000, it is also a commercial center in a rich coffee-growing region. Now a major tourist center, Antigua has good, attractive hotels, one with a swimming pool, and all well-geared to tourist traffic. Shopping in Antigua is considered delightful. Spectacular festivities are held here during Holy Week. Those planning to visit during this period should make hotel reservations well in advance.

Visitors to Antigua will delight in its many interesting churches and landmarks. The Cathedral of San José, built between 1543 and 1680, was a magnificent structure, featuring 16 chapels, 60 cupolas, vaulted archways, high naves, and excellent paintings and sculptures. The facade and much of the wall structure stand today, along with the ruins of several domes. Excavation in 1935 revealed crypts beneath the cathedral. One is open to visitors and contains an altar, crucifix, and statues of saints. The conquistador of Guatemala, Don Pedro de Alvarado, is buried beneath the cathedral in an unidentified tomb. The present Church of San José was made from two of the original 16 chapels, which were restored in 1854. The cathedral was damaged in the 1976 earthquake, but has been reconstructed. Other interesting churches include La Merced Church, with lacy white stonework on its facade; and San Francisco, covering two square blocks, with its huge bell that tolls annually one stroke for each year of Guatemala's independence.

A few mansions, built during the colonial era, have been restored. Casa Popenoe, the House of Bells (converted into a shop), and the House of Lions all feature an austere outside wall encircling patios that contain fountains and gardens.

Ciudad Vieja (Old City) is about four miles from Antigua's central plaza, near the base of the volcano. The city was destroyed when it was engulfed by the eruptions of the volcano, Agua, in 1541. Parts of the city have been excavated. The church, built in 1534, was excavated intact; the third story of the governor's palace, built in 1527, has been exposed, but the first two floors remain buried.

There are several interesting Indian villages in the Antigua area that are accessible by car. Santa María de Jesús is less than seven miles from the foot of Agua volcano. Horseback and hiking expeditions to the volcano originate here. Just below Santa María de Jesús on the mountain slope is San Juan del Obispo. It is the site of the palace and former retreat of Antigua's colonial bishop; the palace is currently being rebuilt. Known for its hand-woven textiles, the village of San Antonio Aguas Calientes is five miles from Antigua.

Aerial view of the vegetable market in Guatemala

OTHER CITIES

Situated in the mountains of southeast Guatemala, the city of **AMATITLÁN** lies on the shores of Lake Amatitlán, 12 miles southwest of Guatemala City. The lake is badly polluted, however, and swimming is no longer safe. With a municipal population over 33,000, Amatitlán is the center of a popular weekend resort area for Guatemala City residents, and is particularly noted for its scenery. Beautiful vacation homes are built around the lakeshore and hot springs may be found throughout the region. Coffee and sugar plantations are also located in the area. Native skin divers find well-preserved relics of Mayan religious ceremonies that took place at the natural hot springs that empty into the lake. Fragments of pottery discovered on the bottom of the lake indicate that a cemetery of an ancient city could be buried in the silt.

CHICHICASTENANGO, about 90 miles west of Guatemala City, is the center of the Quiche Indian culture and a principal sight-seeing attraction. Located in the heart of the highlands at about 7,000 feet above sea level, Chichicastenango became the spiritual center of the Quiche following their defeat by Pedro de Alvarado in 1524. Often called Santo Tomás, the town is quaint and charming, with a main plaza connected by a maze of winding streets. It is the site of one of the most colorful markets in Central America. On market days, Thursday and Sunday, Chichicastenango is crowded with Indians in their colorful clothing. On Sundays especially, they practice their semi-pagan religious rites in the two ancient Roman Catholic churches on the main plaza. In the Dominican monastery, the famous Popul-Vuh manuscript of Maya-Quiche mythology was discovered. There are also several excellent collections of Indian relics, many of which are carved in jade.

CHIMALTENANGO is located 30 miles west of Guatemala City in the central highlands. This market center of over 30,000 was founded in 1526; today, its residents grow grains, sugarcane, and livestock. Brick-making is an important industry. Chimaltenango is noted for its church built on the Continental Divide, where water flows around the foundation—half to the Pacific and half to the Atlantic.

CHIQUIMULA lies 70 miles east of Guatemala City on the Río San José. The city has been ravaged by earthquakes, especially in the late 1700s during the colonial period. A colonial church remains, in ruins. Chiquimula's hinterland produces fruit, tobacco, sugarcane, and cattle. The city is linked to the capital by road and railroad and has a population of approximately 42,600.

COBÁN is situated in a rich coffee-growing area about 60 miles north of Guatemala City. Although an all-weather road connects the city to the capital, it is more easily accessible by plane. The hillside church, El Calvario, built in 1559, is located just outside of Cobán. Indian villages are also nearby and are known for their silverwork. Tourist attractions near the city include ancient Mayan pyramids and the Lanquin Caves, a series of underground grottoes stretching nearly 250 miles. The population of Cobán is approximately 23,000 (1989 estimate).

The town of **ESQUIPULAS,** located 75 miles east of Guatemala City, is known for its church that contains the figure of the Black Christ, revered by the Indians. Each year, more than one million pilgrims from Central America and Mexico visit the Black Christ. The six-foot image of Christ, completed in 1594, is made of balsa wood. The population of municipal Esquipulas is about 18,800.

Once a stronghold of the Itzá Indians, **FLORES** is located in a vast tropical jungle area in northern Guatemala. The town, with a population of about 14,000, is on an island in Lake Petén Itzá and is an export center for chicle, rubber, sugarcane, and lumber. It is accessible by road or plane but, during the rainy season, mud and flooding make driving hazardous.

HUEHUETENANGO is an old mining city on the slopes of the Altos Cuchumatanes Mountains, 75 miles northwest of Guatemala City. The name means Place of the Ancients, and ruins of an ancient Indian settlement called Zaculeu are located nearby. Lead, copper, and silver are mined in this city, which is also a major trading area for the local Maya Indians. Corns, beans, and potatoes are grown near the city. The estimated population of Huehuetenango is 37,200. The main Pan-American Highway is close by.

In the southwest, 60 miles southwest of Guatemala City, lies **MAZA-**

TENANGO. This commercial and manufacturing city provides a link between Pacific ports and the interior. Coffee, sugarcane, cacao, fruits and, especially cotton, are major crops. Mazatenango is connected to Guatemala City by road and railway.

PUERTO BARRIOS is located in eastern Guatemala, about 150 miles northeast of Guatemala City on the Bay of Amatique, an arm of the Caribbean's Gulf of Honduras. Named for Guatemalan politician Justo Rufina Barrios, Puerto Barrios is the capital of Izabel Department and the country's major port. Leading exports are coffee and bananas. Puerto Barrios had a population of 38,000 (1989 est.), is the terminus of the International Railways of Central America, and also is the eastern seaport for El Salvador. The city sustained heavy damage from the earthquake of 1976.

QUEZALTENANGO is Guatemala's second largest city, located in the western highlands about 75 miles west of Guatemala City. It can be reached in about three-and-a-half hours by highland route over the Pan-American Highway, which is paved all the way and generally in good condition. A mountain town at about 7,600 feet, it has a cool, invigorating climate and clean air. Its interesting old market offers excellent textiles and handicrafts. The city also has a multilevel shopping center. The development of hydroelectric power has helped Quezaltenango become one of the Central America's leading industrial cities. Principal industries in the city include mills, breweries, and textile factories. As the site of the ancient Quiche kingdom of Xelaju, Quezaltenango is also noteworthy for its hot sulfur baths and mineral springs. Many of Guatemala's best-known scholars, musicians, and writers have lived in the city. The population is approximately 90,000.

SAN JOSÉ, a commercial port on the Pacific Coast, is two hours from Guatemala City over a paved road. The nearby beaches of Chulamar, Likin, and Iztapa offer surf bath-

ing—limited, however, by a strong undertow at certain hours, and occasional sharks. The beaches are black volcanic ash, which is extremely hot in direct sun. Water-skiing, swimming, and fishing are possible on the canal and river that empty into the Pacific near Iztapa. Deep-sea fishing excursions can be arranged. Deer, wild pig, duck, and dove are also hunted in this area. The population is about 18,000.

ZACAPA is the capital of Zacapa Department in the eastern region, 25 miles from the Honduras border. This old community grew fast in the late 19th century with the completion of the Puerto Barrios-Guatemala City railroad. It now has approximately 34,000 residents. A principal railway junction, Zacapa is known for its cheese and cigars. Growers from the hinterland ship their products to the city; yields include corn, beans, sugarcane, and livestock. The 1976 earthquake caused extensive property damage.

COUNTRY PROFILE

Geography and Climate

Guatemala is the most northern and populous of the five Central American countries. Occupying 42,042 square miles, it is about the size of Tennessee. It is bordered on the north and west by Mexico, on the southeast by Honduras and El Salvador, on the east by Belize and the Caribbean Sea, and on the south by the Pacific Ocean. Guatemalan coastlines cover about 200 miles on the Pacific Ocean and 70 miles on the Caribbean.

The country is roughly divided into four geographic regions: the central-western highlands, the low northern plateau which is largely jungle, the southern volcanic regions of the Sierra Madre, and tropical coastal lowlands. The temperate mountain regions are the most densely populated.

Guatemala City's rainy season is May through October and its dry season, November through April. Temperatures are generally moderate during both seasons, ranging from an average low of 53°F in January to 60°F–85°F in April. Frost and snow are unknown, and flowers bloom year round.

Rainfall is heaviest from June through October; the annual average is approximately 52 inches. The wet months can cause mildew damage to clothing, shoes, luggage, and upholstered furniture. Frequent airing and the use of heating units in closets helps to prevent mildew. Long-stay travellers should consider bringing portable dehumidifiers. During the dry season, days are clear, and the sun is hot at midday with chilly to cold mornings and evenings. During these months it is dusty, foliage turns brown, grass and shrubs wither, and gardens must be watered.

Guatemala has 33 volcanoes, 4 within view of the city. Although most are inactive, Pacaya, about 27 miles south of Guatemala City, erupts occasionally with lava flows to nearby localities. Fuego, about 30 miles from the city, periodically produces impressive displays visible from Guatemala City.

Earth tremors are common. In 1976, a devastating earthquake struck Guatemala. Some 27,000 people were killed and over 1 million left homeless. Damage was greatest in areas with adobe housing. The modern sections of Guatemala City suffered light-to-moderate damage, but most of the city has been repaired. Before 1976, the last major earthquake to cause considerable damage occurred in 1917.

Population

The 2000 estimated population was 12.7 million—some 3 million of whom live in the capital and its suburbs. The annual population growth rate is about 3%. An estimated 43% of the nation's population is culturally Indian. The remainder, which includes Caucasians and people of mixed descent, speak Spanish and wear Western dress. Most of the small black population lives in the Caribbean coastal area.

Spanish is the principal urban language. It is necessary to have at least a basic knowledge of Spanish for day-to-day living. At least four major Indian languages and over 20 dialects are predominant in the villages where Spanish is not widely spoken. Many Indians, descendants of the Mayans, maintain ancient customs and wear colorful and distinctive regional dress. Many practice traditional Mayan forms of worship, often mixed with Christianity.

Public Institutions

Guatemala's 1985 Constitution and 1993 constitutional reforms provide for a popularly elected President and Vice President, a unicameral legislature representing the country's 22 departments, and an independent 13-member Supreme Court. All officials serve for 4 years.

Municipal officials are also elected. Political power has been concentrated in the executive branch, consistent with Hispano-Roman tradition. Department governors are appointed by the central government. Approximately 19 parties span a political spectrum from right to moderate left. The executive branch consists of 13 ministries: agriculture, livestock, and food; communications, transportation, and public works; culture and sports; economy; education; energy and mines; finance; foreign affairs; government; labor; national defense; public health and social welfare; and urban and rural development.

Autonomous or semiautonomous public institutions include the Guatemalan Telephone Company (GUATEL), Planning Council, Institute for Agricultural Transformation (INTA), the Electrical Development Institute (INDE), and the Bank of Guatemala.

As in much of Latin America, the national university, the University of San Carlos, is an institution of considerable importance and provides Guatemala with most of its technical experts and political leaders.

Arts, Science, and Education

Textiles and painting are Guatemala's primary art forms; many artists have gained international renown. "Artesania" thrives across the nation, producing colorful pottery, wood carving, and other objects. Exhibits by aspiring and established artists are held at the now autonomous Binational Center, Instituto Guatemalteco-Americano (IGA), and in other galleries. The Patronato de Bellas Artes promotes artistic expression and the preservation of Guatemala's rich heritage of both Indian and Spanish colonial art forms. To further bolster the arts, the government has recently boosted funding to the National Theater complex and a new corporate body modeled after the National Endowment for the Arts.

The National Symphony Orchestra and the National Ballet Company perform as funding permits. The Biannual Paiz Cultural Festival showcases every February in odd years, the performing and plastic arts.

Guatemala's national instrument, the marimba, known locally as "the voice of the trees," is played singularly or in groups of up to 20 musicians simultaneously playing five instruments. Though U.S. music, even "rap" with Spanish lyrics, is increasingly heard, marimba presentations still figure prominently in formal shows and at restaurants and theaters.

Perhaps the most interesting aspect of Guatemalan art and Indian culture is the profusion of native textiles. Guatemala's 23 ethnolinguistic groupings exhibit their different roots by distinctive costumes. The intricately hand-woven or embroidered women's "huipiles," or blouses, are famous among textile connoisseurs throughout the world. Many are trying to protect both family/community weaving enterprises and this dying art itself from machines churning out lesser quality tourist wares. The modern Ixchel Museum, built according to U.S. specifications, on the campus of Francisco Marroquin University, not only engages in this endeavor, it houses permanent and changing exhibits of indigenous textiles, and conducts educational programs.

Although many village men have adopted Western dress, interesting men's costumes can still be seen in the Lake Atitlan region, Chichicastenango, and in the Province of Huehuetenango.

Theater consists mainly of semiprofessional organizations whose performances follow no regular season. Productions are held in small theaters, the Binational Center, or the city's modern, attractive National Theater complex. The School of Theater at the Universidad Popular and the Teatro de Arte Universitario at San Carlos University also offer performances throughout the year.

The Guatemalan scientific community is based in the universities, the National Meteorological Service, and the Academia de Geografia e Historia. Several research centers formed under the auspices of the Central American Common Market, including the Central American Nutritional Research Center, are also headquartered in Guatemala City. Most scientific effort is directed toward economic development.

The San Carlos University, the national campus that enrolls upwards of 70,000 students for minimal fees, was founded in 1676. All lectures are in Spanish. The Faculty of Humanities corresponds to a school of liberal arts in the U.S., offering courses in philosophy, education, and literature. Courses in the sciences, engineering, medicine, and law are also available. Begin-

ning in the 1960s, four smaller private universities, Rafael Landivar, Mariano Galvez, Francisco Marroquin, and Del Valle, opened their doors to students and have continued to grow: the four universities sponsor 20-odd "extension" campuses across Guatemala's departments.

For decades, scholars, researchers, students, and culturally oriented tourists have been lured to Guatemala for its rich anthropological and archeological attractions. Epigraphers stand awed before the secrets of Tikal, now a national park; historians delightedly burrow through the treasures of the Archivo General de Centro America and the Centro de Investigaciones de Mesoamerica (CIRMA) in Antigua.

Commerce and Industry

Guatemala's GDP for 2001 was estimated at $20.0 billion, with real growth slowing to approximately 2.3%. After the signing of the final peace accord in December 1996, Guatemala was well-positioned for rapid economic growth over the next several years, though a financial crisis in 1998 limited its ability to achieve its potential growth rates.

Guatemala's economy is dominated by the private sector, which generates about 85% of GDP. Agriculture contributes 23% of GDP and accounts for 75% of exports. Most manufacturing is light assembly and food processing, geared to the domestic, U.S., and Central American markets. Over the past several years, tourism and exports of textiles, apparel, and nontraditional agricultural products such as winter vegetables, fruit, and cut flowers have boomed, while more traditional exports such as sugar, bananas, and coffee continue to represent a large share of the export market. Because of Guatemala's continued reliance on coffee exports, the recent downturn in world prices has contributed to Guatemala's rel-

atively slow growth over the past 2 years.

The United States is the country's largest trading partner, providing 35% of Guatemala's imports and receiving 27% of its exports. The government sector is small and shrinking, with its business activities limited to public utilities--some of which have been privatized--ports and airports and several development-oriented financial institutions.

Guatemala was certified to receive export trade benefits under the United States' Caribbean Basic Trade and Partnership Act (CBTPA) in October 2000, and enjoys access to U.S. Generalized System of Preferences (GSP) benefits. Due to concerns over serious worker rights protection issues Guatemala's benefits under both the CBTPA and GSP were reviewed in 2001. After passage of labor code reforms in May 2001, and the successful prosecution of labor rights violations against banana union workers dating to 1999, the review was lifted.

Current economic priorities include: Liberalizing the trade regime; Financial services sector reform; Overhauling Guatemala's public finances; Simplifying the tax structure, enhancing tax compliance, and broadening the tax base.

With 60% of all Guatemalans living in poverty, the country suffers from some of the worst mortality, illiteracy, malnutrition, and other social indicators in the hemisphere region. Providing $30–$50 million in annual assistance, USAID is working to address key constraints to Guatemalan development through the promotion of sustainable resource management, smaller and healthier families, improved basic education, enhanced trade and labor rights, and the sustained exercise of inalienable rights.

The headquarters for USAID's regional programs is also located in Guatemala. Through its regional programs, USAID promotes sustainable development throughout Central America, working with the

Central American Bank for Economic Integration, the Nutrition Institute for Central America, the Central American Commission for Environment and Development, the Permanent Secretariat of Central American Economic Integration, the Tropical Agricultural Center for Research and Education, the Inter-American Institute for Agricultural Cooperation, and a wide variety of nongovernmental organizations.

Transportation

Local

Buses, all private and independent, are the primary mode of public transportation within and between Guatemalan cities. In the capital, service is frequent, but most of the buses are old, smoke spewing, and noisy, and their drivers careless. Because of controversial increased prices and severe overcrowding on private buses, the city has recently inaugurated the use of converted semitrailers, with a capacity of 200 passengers, to offer express service along specified routes. Few buses are scheduled after 9 pm or 10 pm.; "ruleteros" (minibuses) pick up and discharge passengers along major streets until midnight. Taxis are available on a 24-hour basis, but are expensive and must be called by telephone or picked up at one of the several stations throughout the city. Use only recommended taxi companies such as those contracted by hotels. Since taxis are not metered, the cost should be settled before any trip. Tipping, though not expected, is always appreciated.

Regional

Interurban bus lines connect most towns and villages within the country. Although serviceable, these buses are often crowded and uncomfortable. Numerous tour agencies are available that offer comfortable transportation and guides at a reasonable cost; however, large-capacity rented vehicles and travel agency vans have been targeted by armed highway bandits.

Guatemala is a country brimming with natural beauty and color, and travel into the countryside is a welcome respite from city living. Much of the country cannot be visited safely by surface transportation. Roadblocks are occasionally set up by thieves posing as military or police officers, and travel after sunset anywhere in Guatemala is extremely dangerous.

All-weather paved highways traverse the country between Mexico, El Salvador, and both seacoasts. Other roads, which are gradually being improved, vary from two-lane, gravel topped hard bed to single-lane dirt. During the dry season, most unpaved roads are passable, though often dusty and rough. In the rainy season mountain roads are treacherous because of poor markings, frequent landslides, and washouts. Driving to Mexico City takes about 3 days via the coastal route entering Mexico at Tapachula. San Salvador is about 4 1/2 hours by car from Guatemala City.

Drivers in Guatemala take more risks than those in the U.S.; one must drive defensively whether within the city and faced with cars coming in the opposite direction on a one-way street or along the highways where large semitrailers will pass on a blind curve at high speed. Guatemalan law is strict with all parties in an accident, and cars are often impounded.

Infrastructure problems common to many Third World countries are present in Guatemala. Main roads to the larger towns and cities are paved and generally fair though plagued by deep potholes, washed-out bridges, and, during the long, rainy season, sometimes impassable because of mudslides and large fallen boulders. The major road to El Salvador, along which is located one of the schools attended by Mission children, suffers from erosion and is continually undergoing construction efforts.

Bus service is available twice daily between Guatemala and El Salvador. Bus companies offer service from Guatemala to Mexico and Honduras but may require a bus transfer at the borders. Travelers are urged to check with the Regional Security Office regarding guerrilla and criminal activity in the areas through which they plan to drive before planning any international travel. When traveling from El Salvador, the border crossing at Las Chinamas, El Salvador/Valle Nuevo, Guatemala, is preferred. When entering Guatemala from Honduras, the border crossings are at either El Florido or Agua Caliente. With all cross-border travel, travelers need plenty of time to complete border crossing formalities, which can be lengthy, in order to travel to a major town before dark. For group trips, chartered buses are available and border crossings are expedited.

Major car rental agencies, in convenient locations, offer car rental options, but rates are high, between $35–$50 a day for subcompact models. Insurance, both collision and liability, is required.

Tourism has recently increased between Guatemala and Costa Rica, with both the Costa Rican airline, LACSA, and Colombian airline, SAM, offering daily flights.

American Airlines provides three daily flights to and from Miami and one flight to and from Dallas each day. United offers daily service to and from Los Angeles, and Continental has one flight per day to and from Houston. The national airline, AVIATECA, has daily service between Guatemala City and Miami and Guatemala City and Los Angeles, and four flights per week to and from New Orleans, via El Salvador. AVIATECA also provides connections to Belize. TACA airlines offers a flight to Washington, D.C., and New York on a daily basis and provides connections to other Central American capitals. KLM, Iberia, and several other Latin American carriers also provide international connections.

Communications

Telephone and Telegraph

GUATEL, the government-owned and operated communications facility, provides internal and worldwide telephone service. Domestic rates are reasonable with the monthly usage rate averaging Q5. In 1995, a residential long-distance night call to Washington, D.C., cost $8 for 3 minutes and $2 for each additional minute. Direct-dialing is available 24 hours daily although service may be intermittent. An AT&T telephone calling card is useful in Guatemala. AT&T offers a more favorable rate on long-distance calling when the AT&T network is utilized. MCI and Sprint accounts also are operable in Guatemala City. The demand for new telephone lines and installations throughout the city has increased dramatically. GUATEL is currently in the process of modernizing their telephone network, which should facilitate the installation of new residential lines.

Telegraph service is also available through GUATEL to all worldwide locations. Internal usage is popular and fairly reliable. Western Union also provides a money transfer service to and from Guatemala.

Radio and TV

Guatemala City has over 65 Spanish radio stations. Thirty-four AM and 31 FM stations feature U.S.-style music, mostly of the pop hit parade variety. Some classical and jazz music programs are also available. News broadcasts can be heard three times daily on approximately 10 stations. Shortwave reception of VOA is good during the early morning or late evening hours. BBC programs (in English or Spanish) are also heard.

Five color TV channels, one government owned, broadcast a daily menu of mixed programs, including Spanish-dubbed U.S. series shows, feature films, Mexican soaps ("Telenovelas"), and music revues. Two channels provide regular news programs in Spanish three times daily, at 1 pm, 6:30 pm, and 9:45 pm, and one channel offers an early morning news broadcast from 7 am to 8 am. More than two dozen cable TV operators serve Guatemala City and offer a full range of U.S. programming in English. All major networks, with the exception of PBS, are available through cable, many transmitting 24 hours.

Newspapers, Magazines, and Technical Journals

Four morning and one afternoon papers are published daily in Spanish, including one official gazette. The two largest circulating dailies are *Prensa Libre* and *El Grafico*, both with ample international wire service news coverage. A weekly news magazine, *Cronica*, covers Guatemalan economic, political, and cultural news. English-language air express editions of the *Miami Herald*, the *New York Times*, the *Wall Street Journal*, and *USA Today* circulate at major hotels and newsstands. Latin American editions of *Newsweek* and *Time* appear promptly, and many popular English-language magazines and books are available throughout the city, although prices are double the U.S. price. Two locally published English-language news weeklies, *Central American Report* and *This Week*, contain regional political analyses. They are available only by subscription. Two, more widely distributed, weekly newspapers published locally, the *Guatemala News* and *Guatemala Weekly*, provide additional current event coverage for the English-speaking community.

Health and Medicine

Medical Facilities

Good, reliable medical services are available in Guatemala City. Competent and reputable doctors, dentists, ophthalmologists, and veterinarians are available. Most have studied or been trained in the U.S. or Europe and speak English. Specialization is common in most major fields and one or more physicians are available in each.

The major hospitals, clinics, and diagnostic laboratories are adequately equipped. The local supply of medicines, which can usually be bought without prescription, is adequate, but some may be difficult to obtain. If you take prescription drugs, bring a supply with you and arrange to have them sent to you as needed. If special medication is needed, bring a supply and a copy of the prescription.

Community Health

Guatemala City is about 5,000 feet above sea level. Healthy individuals rarely suffer ill effects from the altitude, though precautions must necessarily be taken to guard against overexposure to the sun's harmful rays. Guatemala's standards of sanitation are fair. Generally, health conditions in Guatemala City are good.

Diarrhea and amoebic and bacillary dysentery are not uncommon. These illnesses, as well as paratyphoid and typhoid fever, can be contracted from unpurified water and uncleaned vegetables. Hepatitis is endemic to the region. Safe drinking water remains a problem, but many Guatemalan communities are developing adequate supply and purification systems. Tuberculosis is the most serious contagious endemic disease and is prevalent in a large percentage of the Indian population. Although sanitariums exist, control of those infected with tuberculosis is inadequate, and the annual death rate from the disease is high. Smallpox has been eradicated.

In the coastal and other lowland areas of Guatemala, as well as nearby Lake Amatitlan, malaria is prevalent. Although a malaria eradication program is in operation, the incidence of the disease has increased significantly in the past few years. When traveling to these areas, appropriate prophylactic medication should be taken.

It is important to have window screens in residences to keep out disease-carrying mosquitoes and houseflies, and to eliminate or minimize breeding places in the immediate vicinity. The use of insect repellant is also recommended during times of the year when mosquitoes are more prevalent, and when traveling to lowlands and coastal areas.

Preventive Measures

Guatemala City's water supply is sporadic. During the dry season, water pressure occasionally drops so low that there is little or no water in many homes; in some instances, city water is turned off completely. Processed drinking water is delivered to the door and may be purchased in 5-gallon bottles for Q7.50. Most Americans use this or boil tap water to make it safe for drinking.

Although several dairies deliver pasteurized milk to homes, for consistency in quality and freshness, powdered or long-life shelf milk is recommended.

Locally purchased fresh fruits and vegetables should not be eaten raw, unless they can be peeled. Cooking is the only sure way to disinfect fresh fruits and vegetables. Another effective method is to immerse them in actively boiling water for one minute. Leafy vegetables treated in this manner will show only slight wilting on the outermost leaves, and the palatability of other sturdier vegetables and fruits will not be affected. An alternative method is to use a Clorox bleach solution for soaking fruit and vegetables.

NOTES FOR TRAVELERS

Passage, Customs & Duties

Flights to Guatemala can be arranged from the U.S. on the Guatemalan government-owned airline, AVIATECA, or on TACA. In February 1991, a new Guatemalan airline, Aeroquetzal, began U.S. service between Los Angeles and Guatemala City. Good connections also are provided by other carriers. Some expatriates drive to Guatemala from the U.S. if they have the time and stamina. Drivers are cautioned

that during the rainy months (May-October) the roads in Guatemala can be treacherous because of washouts, landslides, and earth tremors that create temporary impasses. No American passenger ships come to Guatemala, and travel by ship via Panama and air to Guatemala is not a commonly used route.

A valid U.S. passport is required to enter and depart Guatemala, even though many people, including some U.S.-based airline employees, mistakenly believe otherwise. U.S. citizens returning to the United States from Guatemala are not allowed to board their flights without a valid U.S. passport. Therefore, U.S. citizens are strongly advised to obtain a U.S. passport before departing the United States. Certificates of Naturalization, birth certificates, driver's licenses, and photocopies are not considered acceptable alternative travel documents. While in Guatemala, U.S. citizens should carry their passports, or photocopies of their passports, with them at all times. Minors (under 18) traveling with a valid U.S. passport need no special permission from their parents to enter or leave Guatemala. U.S. citizens do not need a visa for a stay of 90 days or less (that period can be extended upon application). An exit tax must be paid when departing Guatemala.

U.S. citizens living in or visiting Guatemala are encouraged to register at the Consular Section of the U.S. Embassy in Guatemala City and obtain updated information on travel and security in Guatemala. You may now informally register with the American Citizen Services Section via e-mail to amcitsguatemala@state.gov. Your registry information should include your complete name, date and place of birth, U.S. passport number, itinerary, contact information in both the United States and Guatemala. You may wish to attach a scanned copy of your U.S. passport and/or e-mail it to your own address or to someone in the United States. This will enable you to easily retrieve a copy

of your passport to facilitate a replacement.

The latest security information is available from the Embassy, including its website (see below). The Consular Section is open for citizens services, including registration, from 8:00 a.m. to 12:00 noon and 1:00 p.m. to 3:00 p.m. weekdays, excluding U.S. and Guatemalan holidays. The U.S. Embassy is located at Avenida La Reforma 7-01, Zone 10; telephone (502) 331-1541 during business hours (8:00 a.m. to 5:00 p.m.), or (502) 331-8904 for emergencies during non-business hours; fax (502) 331-0564; Internet web site - http://usembassy.state.gov/guatemala/.

Pets

All pets must be covered by certification of rabies inoculation. In addition, an import license issued by Guatemalan authorities is required for any pet arriving in Guatemala.

Currency, Banking, and Weights and Measures

The time in Guatemala is Greenwich Mean Time (GMT) minus six (or equivalent to Central Time in the U.S.).

The Guatemalan unit of currency is the *quetzalq*, which is on a par with the U.S. dollar. U.S. paper currency is widely accepted.

Various systems of weights and measures are used in Guatemala. Pounds and kilograms (2.2046 pounds) are the most common weight units, but more exotic units such as the *quintal* (100 pounds) are also used frequently. Gasoline is sold by the gallon (U.S.), but milk is sold by the liter. Common units of distance include centimeter, inch, foot, yard, *vara*, meter, kilometer, mile, and *legua*.

Disaster Preparedness

Guatemala is a geologically active country. Therefore, visitors should be aware of the possibility of earthquakes and volcanic eruptions, and the need for contingency measures. Occasional eruptions, such as those in January-February 2000 of Pacaya Volcano near Guatemala City, have forced evacuations of nearby villages and briefly closed Guatemala City's international airport. The major earthquakes in El Salvador in early 2001 caused damage, injuries, and deaths in Guatemala, albeit to a much lesser extent than her neighbor to the east. Both the Caribbean and Pacific coasts of Guatemala are vulnerable to hurricanes and tropical storms from June through November. Mudslides and flooding during the May to November rainy season often kill dozens of people and close roads. General information about natural disaster preparedness is available via the Internet from the U.S. Federal Emergency Management Agency (FEMA) at http://www.fema.gov/.

LOCAL HOLIDAYS

Jan. 1	New Year's Day
Mar/Apr.	Holy Thursday*
Mar/Apr.	Good Friday*
Mar/Apr.	Holy Saturday*
Mar/Apr.	Easter Sunday*
May 1	Labor Day
June 30	Army Day
Aug. 15	Feast of the Assumption
Sept. 15	Guatemala Independence Day
Oct. 20	Revolution Day
Nov. 1	All Saints' Day
Dec. 24 (from noon)	Christmas Eve
Dec. 25	Christmas Day
Dec. 31 (from noon)	New Year's Eve

*Variable

RECOMMENDED READING

The following titles are provided as a general indication of the material published on this country:

Barry, Tom. *Guatemala: A Country Guide*. Albuquerque, NM: Inter-Hemispheric Education Resource Center, 1990.

Brosnahan, Tom. *La Ruta Maya: A Travel Survival Kit*. Oakland, CA: Lonely Planet, 1991.

Canby, Peter. *The Heart of the Sky: Travel Among the Maya*. New York: HarperCollins Publications, 1992.

Cummins, Ronald. *Guatemala*. Milwaukee, WI: Gareth Stevens Children's Books, 1990.

Fauriol, Georges A., and Eva Loser. *Guatemala: A Political Puzzle*. New Brunswick, NJ: Transaction Publications, 1988.

Frommer's Budget Travel Guide Series. *Costa Rica, Guatemala, & Belize on 25 Dollars-a-Day, 1991-92*. New York: Prentice-Hall General Reference & Travel, 1991.

Greenberg, Arnold, and Diana Wells. *Guatemala Alive*. 2nd ed., New York: Alive Publications, 1990.

Harvard Student Agencies, Inc. Staff. *Let's Go, 1992: The Budget Guide to Mexico Including Belize & Guatemala*. Rev. ed., New York: St. Martin Press, 1991.

Jonas, Susanne. *The Battle for Guatemala: Rebels, Death Squads, and U.S. Power*. Boulder, CO: Westview Press, 1991.

Smith, Carol A., ed. *Guatemalan Indians & the State: 1540 to 1988*. Austin, TX: University of Texas Press, 1990.

Vlach, Norita. *The Quetzal in Flight: Guatemalan Immigrant Families in the United States*. Westport, CT: Greenwood, 1992.

Wright, Ronald. *Time Along the Maya: Travels in Belize, Guatemala, & Mexico*. New York: Grove Press, 1989.

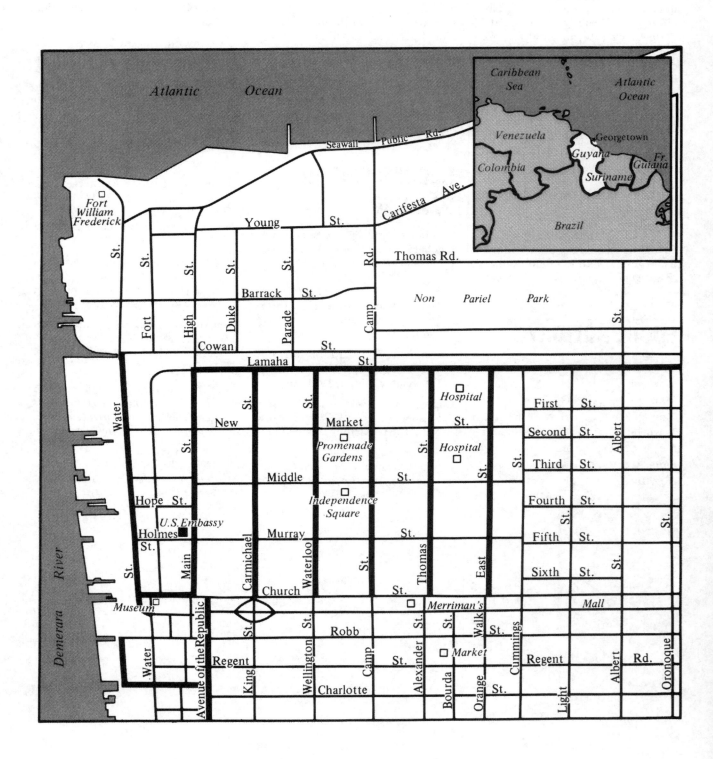

Georgetown, Guyana

GUYANA

Co-operative Republic of Guyana

Major City:

Georgetown

Other Cities:

Bartica, Corriverton, Linden, New Amsterdam

INTRODUCTION

GUYANA, the territory once known as British Guiana, has been a republic within the Commonwealth since February 1970. Its colonial history dates to the 17th century, when the Dutch West Indies Company developed sugar plantations in the settlements of Essequibo, Demerara, and Berbice. The British gained control early in the 19th century and eventually united the three settlements as a crown colony.

Guyana is a young country which has suffered from political unrest, and is still a land of ferment and change. Its unusual racial situation combines African, East Indian, Amerindian, and British cultures and institutions, struggling to build a sound economy. Guyana's topography includes a long, settled coastal area and a beautiful, isolated, and primitive frontier.

A tragic event in November 1978 brought worldwide attention to this small South American nation—900 members of a fanatic religious cult committed mass suicide in what came to be known as the Jonestown Massacre. Great numbers of the cult followers were American; U.S. Representative Leo J. Ryan and members of his party were ambushed and murdered when they arrived to investigate human abuses at cult headquarters.

MAJOR CITY

Georgetown

Guyana's capital city, Georgetown (pop. approximately 254,000), is located at the mouth of the Demerara River on the northeast coast of Guyana. Because it lies below sea level, it is protected by a seawall. Because there are no passable roads connecting it with any of the neighboring countries, and because its port is visited only by cargo vessels, Georgetown's only link to the outside world is by air. The only other communities of any size in Guyana are New Amsterdam (pop. 25,000), 70 miles east of Georgetown at the mouth of the Berbice River, and the bauxite mining town of Linden (pop. 35,000), 67 miles south on the Demerara River. Inhabitants of the three principal urban areas are predominantly African; those of the countryside are mainly East Indian.

Declining national income during the 1980s and deteriorating infrastructure has resulted in substandard living conditions for most Guyanese citizens. Beginning in 1991, however, because of privatization, foreign investment, and the government's economic recovery program, the gross domestic product (GDP) has grown at rates in excess of 6% a year, and wages and benefits, employment, and working conditions have improved. Most consumer goods, which virtually disappeared during the 1980s, are now widely available again but still unaffordable for many Guyanese. Many basic services such as electricity, transportation, and health care, remain limited and unreliable.

About 310 third country nationals and 1,135 U.S. citizens live in Guyana, most of them dual nationals born in Guyana or born abroad of Guyanese parents. There are 12 foreign missions in Georgetown: the High Commissions of the U.K., Canada, and India, and the embassies of

EDP Photos/Richard Lobban. Reproduced by permission.

Street in Georgetown, Guyana

Brazil, Colombia, Suriname, Venezuela, the People's Republic of China, Russia, Cuba, North Korea, and the U.S. The U.N. Development Program, the European Union, the World Health Organization, the Inter-American Institute for Cooperation in Agriculture (IICA), and the Inter-American Development Bank also have offices in Georgetown. The Caribbean Community (CARICOM) Secretariat is headquartered here. Most of the other major countries have nonresident ambassadors who visit Guyana from time to time and a dozen or so are also represented by Guyanese acting as honorary consuls.

Food

Grocery stores and public markets in Georgetown offer a variety of meat, poultry, fish, and seasonal fresh fruits and vegetables. Sanitary conditions in the markets are poor.

Common locally grown vegetables include cassava, plantains, yams, breadfruit, eddoes (a dry variety of sweet potato) and eggplant. These are high in carbohydrates and available in season only. Green and yellow vegetables—bora beans (a thin green bean), leaf lettuce, cabbage, pumpkin and various squash, cucumbers, onions, potatoes, spinach, callaloo, and tomatoes—are

available throughout the year. Local celery is adequate for seasoning, but unsuitable for relish trays. Green onions (scallions), small red and green peppers, and fresh thyme are usually available. Parsley is expensive and occasionally found. Locally grown rice that has been parboiled before packaging is cheap and a staple in the Guyanese diet.

Local oranges, grapefruits, tangerines, watermelons, bananas, pineapples, mangoes, papaya, yellow melons, and avocados are good and plentiful, although some are available only seasonally.

A wide variety of canned foods, including canned baby foods and pet food, are available but expensive.

Local meats are generally available and special orders can be placed at several meat stores. Fish, chicken and pork are usually good; prawns (shrimp) and red snapper are especially tasty. Cheese, butter, milk (UHT, evaporated, and powdered, but not fresh), and all other dairy products are available at most grocery stores.

Clothing

Dress for tropical weather. Summer clothing is worn year round. Cotton wash-and-wear and synthetic knit fabrics are suitable. Silks are

impractical because of the need for expert dry-cleaning. Nylon is an easy-care fabric, but uncomfortable in the heat. Woolens are generally not worn, except for men's tropical-weight wool suits.

Men: In the office most men wear slacks with a short-sleeved shirt and tie. Suits and slacks can be made to order locally.

Most social occasions are informal or casual. Casual events call for short-sleeved sport shirts or the guayabera. Reasonably priced short-sleeved guayaberas can be purchased locally. Long-sleeved guayaberas (difficult to purchase locally) may be worn in place of a suit on some occasions.

Women: Sport and straw hats are worn frequently for outdoor events because of the strong sun. Few women wear stockings. Slacks are popular, but shorts are worn only for sports or at home. Long dresses are occasionally worn but cocktail dresses are popular for receptions and dinners. In the office, most women wear cotton dresses or blouses and skirts. Short-sleeved cotton or cotton-blend sweaters are also worn. Light sweaters or stoles are sometimes needed. Bring a good supply of shoes, sandals, sneakers, old shoes, and rubber boots. A fold-up plastic raincoat is useful, as is an umbrella. Bring a supply of light-weight undergarments.

Children: Guyana is beginning to produce some good children's clothing, particularly inexpensive, attractive dresses Local clothing is limited in selection, size, and price, and even items of poor quality cost more than in the U.S. The American School does not require uniforms nor does the dress code prohibit jeans, shorts, sneakers, or jumpsuits.

Supplies and Services

Although toiletries and medicines can be purchased locally, the cost is usually high.

Laundry service is poor and slow. The only local dry-cleaning service in town is reasonably good. Georgetown has numerous seamstresses and tailors, whose work is inexpensive but varies in quality. Shoe repair is adequate. Most beauty shop operators have been trained in the U.S. or U.K. and offer good services. Most shops are unisex and offer acceptable haircuts.

Religious Activities

There are many religious denominations in Guyana, and Georgetown has churches, temples, and mosques of many faiths, although the order of service and the music may differ from U.S. churches. The East Indians are mainly Hindu or Muslim. The largest Christian church is Anglican (Episcopal), with about 110,000 members; Roman Catholics number about 60,000. Other denominations include Methodist, Seventh-day Adventist, Presbyterian, Christian Scientist, Lutheran, Jehovah's Witnesses, Baptist, Pentecostal, Church of Christ, Moravian, Assembly of God, Baha'i, and the Church of Jesus Christ of Latter-day Saints.

Education

Most Americans and international children attend the Georgetown American School, an institution sponsored by the U.S. State Department through its Office of Overseas Schools, from nursery through grade 12. Founded in 1971, the school's goal is to provide an education equal to that offered at better American public schools. American texts are used in all courses. The faculty is well qualified and includes several Americans, one of whom is the Director. In recent years enrollment has steadily increased and for 1996–97 stands at 115. Class size is quite small and individualized instruction is the norm. In 1993–94, grades 10–12 were offered for the first time.

The school year runs from September through mid-June. The school day begins at 7:45 and ends at 2:15. Classes in music, art, foreign languages, and physical education are an integral part of the curriculum. The school has a respectable library,

a science lab, and an adequate number of computers.

The Parent Teachers Association (PTA) is composed of the parents of students enrolled at the school. School policy is set by a seven-member Board of Directors, six of whom are elected annually by the parents, and one, usually the Embassy administrative officer, is appointed by the U.S. Ambassador.

Special Educational Opportunities

Few opportunities for advanced study or adult education exist in Georgetown, other than those offered by the University of Guyana. Foreign language instruction in Spanish and Portuguese is offered to the public by the Venezuelan and Brazilian embassies. Language instruction in German is also available. A few music teachers instruct beginning and intermediate students, but facilities for advanced musical education are nonexistent. Ballet and modern dance lessons are available to adults as well as children.

Sports

There is a nine-hole golf course about 10 miles from town which is rough but playable. There are several tennis courts and tennis and golf tournaments and competitions are common. The Pegasus and Tower Hotels and the Guyana Bank of Trade and Industry (GBTI) offer swimming, tennis, and weightlifting facilities for a membership fee. Annual dues for access to tennis and swimming at the Pegasus for a family with children are about US$600. GBTI is more reasonable. The Georgetown Club has a restaurant, bar and squash court, and annual dues are low.

Bicycles are widely used here for transportation among Guyanese, and bicycle racing is a popular sport. The National Park is an area where many people cycle, jog, or walk. It is not recommended that Americans walk/jog alone at the National Park or the seawall late in the evenings or early in the mornings.

Cricket and soccer are the two most popular sports for Guyanese. There are also rugby and basketball clubs and several karate groups. Another interesting sport, but not so common, is goat racing.

Touring and Outdoor Activities

Guyana's tourist attractions are not easy or cheap to get to. The east-west road offers endless views of rice and sugar plantations and the pavement on the north-south road ends at the bauxite mines. Few foreigners swim in either the ocean or the Demerara River. Ocean currents from Brazil carry silt from the Amazon to Guyana's coast and silt from Guyana's own rivers makes the ocean the color of thick coffee with mudflats to match. However, for those willing to travel by boat, truck, or small plane, Guyana offers a vast wilderness of undiscovered eco-tourism sites. Excursions can be arranged independently or through local travel agencies to sugar plantations (most of which have guest houses), jungle creeks, Amerindian villages, rustic tourist lodges (Timberhead, Shanklands, Madewini, and Kaow Island) and spectacular waterfalls. Guyana offers fabulous hunting (duck, deer, wild hog, and other exotic animals) and fishing. Birdwatchers find a large selection of species.

Kaieteur Falls, Guyana's best-known and most heavily visited tourist attraction, is five times higher than Niagara, but has no protective railings or tourist shops. Located in thick jungle 160 miles southwest of Georgetown, it is usually reached by chartered aircraft, but some choose to make the difficult 4-day overland trip by truck/boat/hiking.

Several ranches in the Rupununi Savanna offer comfortable overnight accommodations and various activities including riding, hunting, fishing, and swimming. Karanambo Ranch, which offers refuge to the endangered giant river otters, has been the subject of a *National Geographic* television special.

Adventurous types will want to consider investing in a sturdy four-wheel-drive vehicle. Although not essential, a winch, heavy-duty mud tires, and even a liftkit are all useful for driving trips deep into the interior. The adventurous will also want to consider investing in a boat of some type, as the best sporting and travel opportunities in the interior are on Guyana's numerous rivers and creeks. Individuals have found canoes, foldable kayaks, and aluminum boats with 25 horsepower outboard motors useful and enjoyable. The key to boating in Guyana is having a craft which your vehicle can transport from the road to the river. This generally means having both a four-wheel drive vehicle and a boat that can fit on or inside it. A boat that requires a trailer is restricted to those major rivers which can be reached by paved road.

The Swims Club, about 40 minutes south of Georgetown on the Demerara, offers not swimming but storage facilities and loading ramps for boats. Some people keep larger boats with inboard engines there for excursions on the river.

Points of interest in Georgetown include the Botanical Gardens which have an excellent zoo and an adjacent playground with slides, swings, etc. The National Museum in Georgetown is small, but its exhibits on the history of Guyana, Amerindian life and customs, gold and diamond prospecting methods, animals, and plants are well worth a visit.

For a change of scenery, vacation trips are possible to Antigua, Barbados, St. Lucia, Trinidad and Tobago, Grenada or other West Indian islands, and also to neighboring Venezuela, Suriname and French Guiana. The islands are popular for their excellent beaches and more cosmopolitan atmosphere. However, flight schedules usually require more than a 2-day weekend. Flying time is about 1 hour to Trinidad or 2 hours to Barbados or Antigua. Round-trip fares to those islands are about US$150. Hotel prices are high in season, mid-December to

mid-April, but considerably lower during the off-season. Some hotels give discounts to diplomats or residents of the Caribbean community.

Entertainment
The Guyana Theater Guild and other drama groups have several good productions throughout the year, but only one auditorium in Guyana, the National Cultural Centre, is air-conditioned. Many video clubs offer a wide selection of tapes. Movie theaters are not usually patronized by foreigners.

Occasional outdoor concerts by the Guyana Police Force and the Guyana Defense Force Bands usually are held in the Botanical Gardens or at the seawall bandstand. Visiting musical or dance groups occasionally perform in Guyana, usually under sponsorship of one of the embassies. The National School of Dance also offers occasional performances.

Social Activities
Four or five restaurants in town, including the Hotel Tower and Pegasus, allow private entertaining—the Cara Lodge Bottle Restaurant opened during 1996 and may be the best. However, most Americans entertain in their homes with informal cocktails or buffets. There are several floating bridge, poker, and games nights in Georgetown that many Americans participate in. Several charity balls are given throughout the year. Rotary, Lions, and Toastmasters Clubs all have active memberships in Georgetown.

OTHER CITIES

BARTICA, despite its small size, plays a big role in Guyana. Situated at the confluence of the Essequibo, Mazaruni, and Cuyuni Rivers, 40 miles southwest of Georgetown, it is a commercial center of a few thousand residents. Small oceangoing ships dock here, while critical roads to interior gold and diamond fields start in the town. Bartica has air service to Georgetown.

CORRIVERTON lies 70 miles southeast of Georgetown, in the far northeastern corner of Guyana. This city of about 11,000 is on an estuary of the Courantyne River, separating Guyana from Suriname. The villages of Springlands and Skeldon were united in 1970 to form Corentyne River Town, which later became known as Corriverton. It is a small port, as well as the terminus of a road from Georgetown. Area agricultural products include sugarcane and rice; cattle are also raised. Most residents of Corriverton are East Indian.

LINDEN is located 40 miles south of Georgetown on the Demerara River. It serves as a processing point for the bauxite mined extensively in the region. Linden's population of about 35,000 is linked to Georgetown by road and air.

NEW AMSTERDAM is a commercial and manufacturing center for Guyana's northeast lowlands. Situated on the Berbice River 50 miles southeast of Georgetown, New Amsterdam was built by the Dutch in 1740. By 1790, it had become the seat of colonial government, only to be seized by the British 13 years later. An Anglican cathedral bespeaks the British influence in an otherwise Dutch atmosphere. Agricultural activities include sugarcane and rice production, as well as cattle raising. The city is linked to Georgetown via highways and railroad. The population of New Amsterdam is approximately 25,000.

COUNTRY PROFILE

Geography and Climate

Guyana lies on the northern coast of South America, bounded on the north by the Atlantic Ocean, on the southwest and south by Brazil, on the northwest by Venezuela, and on the east by Suriname. Its 285-mile coastline extends from Punta Playa (near the mouth of the Orinoco River) in the northwest to the Corentyne River in the east. Guyana is 82,980 square miles in area, about the size of Kansas or Idaho.

The low-lying coastland, one of Guyana's three geographic regions, is a flat, often swampy strip of silt and clay about 5½ feet below sea level at high tide. Man-made concrete walls and earthen barriers keep the ocean back and prevent floods. Canals with sluice gates permit drainage to the rivers, and at low tide, to the sea. Most of the country's population and agricultural activity are concentrated in this narrow coastal strip between the Pomeroon and Corentyne Rivers.

The mountain region includes the Pakaraima Range, which lies along the western boundary between the Waini and Rupununi Rivers; a sandstone plateau 22 miles long and more than 9,000 feet above sea level; and the Kanaku Mountains, which lie on both sides of the Rupununi River near the Brazilian border.

The intermediate region, to the east and south of the coastal and mountain regions, is the largest of the three areas. It is mainly tropical forest and jungle, except for the Rupununi Savanna on the southwestern border with Brazil. Large rivers and their tributaries form a vast network of waterways. Rapids and falls hinder navigation and development along the larger rivers. The principal rivers are the Essequibo, Demerara, Berbice, and Corentyne. The Cuyuni, Mazaruni, and Rupununi are major tributaries of the Essequibo River.

Guyana's climate is typical of most tropical countries. Humidity ranges from an average low of 68% in October to 77% in May, and an average high of 79% in October to 86% in May through August. The average annual mean (AAM) is 73% in the afternoons and 83% in the mornings. The high humidity can cause mildew, but air-conditioning and sometimes dehumidifiers and light-bulbs in closets are used to prevent

its occurrence. Minimum temperatures in Georgetown, on the coast, range between 22–26°C (71–80°F) year around, with an AAM low of 75. Maximum temperatures range between 28–32°C (83–90°F), year round, with an AAM high of 86. The sea breezes (east-northeast trade winds) significantly mitigate the heat on the coast.

The coastal area typically has two wet seasons: May to mid-August, when about 40% of the total annual precipitation falls, and December to mid-January, which receive another 20%.

However, occasional rain may fall at any time of the year. Georgetown and the coast average 90 inches of rainfall annually; in the interior, 60–150 inches occur.

Population

Guyana's population of about 703,400 is divided between two major ethnic groups: Guyanese of East Indian origin, estimated at 49%, and those of African origin, 32%. Amerindians constitute about 6%, those of mixed heritage, 12%, and persons of Chinese and European origin comprise about 1%. About 60% live in rural areas; 30% of the labor force is in agriculture. About 50% of the population, including most Afro-Guyanese, is Christian, 9% Muslim, and 33% Hindu.

Guyana celebrates two Hindu and two Muslim holidays as well as Christmas and Easter. Dietary restrictions must be considered when entertaining Guyanese: pork should not be served to Muslims, nor beef to Hindus. Some Muslim Indians do not eat crustaceans, and some Guyanese are vegetarians.

Each ethnic group has made a unique contribution to the character of life in Guyana: the food and the music and dances of the Africans, East Indians, and Amerindians; and the language and legal, commercial, governmental, and educational structures of the British colonists.

Public Institutions

Guyana was a colony known as British Guiana until May 26, 1966. The Co-operative Republic of Guyana was created in 1970. Under the 1980 constitution, Guyana has a mixed parliamentary and presidential system of government. The President and members of Parliament serve for 5-year terms, unless earlier elections are called.

There is a 72-member unicameral parliament, elected by proportional representation, and an independent judiciary and an ombudsman. The Constitution provides for civil rights and the protection of minorities. The two main political parties are the largely Afro-Guyanese People's National Congress (PNC), which governed Guyana for 28 years, and the largely East Indian People's Progressive Party (PPP), which in October 1992 won Guyana's first free and fair elections after independence.

Principal social, philanthropic, and commercial organizations include the Georgetown Chamber of Commerce and Industry, Jaycees, Rotary, Lions, Kiwanis, and Toastmasters Clubs. The leading humanitarian organization is the Guyana Red Cross Society. The Boy Scouts, YMCA, and YWCA are active. Most denominations including the two largest, the Anglicans and Catholics—are represented on the Guyana Council of Churches.

Arts, Science, and Education

The University of Guyana is the mainspring of intellectual activity but is limited in scope. Located just outside of Georgetown, it offers degree programs in accounting, forestry, law, sociology. A university council under government authority administers the University's approximately 2,300 students, who are hampered by decaying facilities and a lack of books and qualified teachers.

Contemporary dance, steel bands, and drama are among Guyana's cultural attractions. Scientific work, mostly agricultural in nature, is carried on at state-sponsored stations throughout the country.

Commerce and Industry

Guyana's economy is dominated by agriculture and mining. Principal products are sugar, rice, bauxite, and gold. The most important gold mine, operated by Canadian firms, is the largest in Latin America. The state-owned bauxite and sugar companies are in World Bank-sponsored rehabilitation programs that may result in their eventual privatization. Timber, rice, and fishing assets have been divested, and an American company purchased 80% of the phone company in 1991. As a result, international telephone and fax service is excellent. Internet service is available from local service providers. Increased demand for machinery in the mining and agricultural sectors is attracting American exporters to Guyana. Major U.S. firms are also involved in offshore oil exploration and the food and beverage industry. The Guyana Electricity Corporation is to be divested shortly.

Guyana trades mainly with the U.S., the European Community, Venezuela, Canada, and with neighboring Caribbean countries that belong to CARICOM. Trade with Brazil, Japan, and Cuba is also of some importance. In 1992 the U.S. supplied 38% of Guyana's imports and purchased 38% of Guyana's exports.

Transportation
Local

Most of Georgetown's streets are paved, but in need of repair. Fast-moving, crowded minibuses are a traffic hazard for Georgetown drivers. Taxis are inexpensive and much safer.

Outside of Georgetown, about 450 miles of paved roads run mainly along the coast and the populated east bank of the Demerara River. A

paved two-lane road runs south to the airport (27 miles). From the airport, a highway (in better shape than most roads) continues south to Linden (67 miles from Georgetown). Another main road runs from Georgetown east to Rosignol (65 miles), where the Berbice River can be crossed on a car and passenger ferry. On the eastern side of the river, at New Amsterdam, the highway resumes to the Corentyne River and the border of Suriname. The Corentyne, like the Berbice, is wide and unbridged, and only passenger ferry service is available.

Most of the 1,500 miles of unpaved roads and trails in the interior are passable by truck or four-wheel-drive vehicles, but only during the dry season. Speedboats, launches, and steamers service many river communities. Many miles of roadless swamps and jungle separate coastal Guyana from Venezuela. A laterite road from Linden to the towns of Lethem and Bon Fim on the Guyana-Brazil border is under construction, but about 60 miles remains to be finished. A floating bridge across the Demerara River opened in 1978. The Essequibo, like the Berbice, must be crossed by car ferry. In many respects, Guyana is like an island.

Regional

The main gateway to Georgetown and Guyana is Timehri International Airport, 27 miles from the city, 45 minutes by car. The government-owned Guyana Airways Corporation (GAC) has direct, nonstop flights to and from New York and Toronto. BWIA, a carrier based in Trinidad and owned by the Government of Trinidad & Tobago, provides daily service to and from JFK New York via Barbados and to and from Miami via Trinidad. It also flies from Guyana to Antigua and Jamaica. American Airlines flies daily between the U.S. and Trinidad and the U.S. and Barbados, but passengers on all the flights except the New York-Barbados flight, must overnight before taking BWIA, LIAT or Suriname Airways to Georgetown. LIAT (Leeward Islands Air Transport) operates between Geor-

getown and Barbados with connections there to all the eastern Caribbean islands as well as Puerto Rico and the Dominican Republic. Suriname Airways flies 2 days a week from Paramaribo to Georgetown. A small Venezuelan airline, ASERCA, provides service to Venezuela; there is no direct service to Brazil.

Guyana Airways Corporation offers daily service to many domestic locations. Charter flights can easily be arranged to other areas. Other means of transportation are poor or nonexistent. Guyana has no deep harbors, so only small ocean freighters, mostly under 10,000 tons, and a number of bauxite carriers call at Guyana's ports.

Communications
Telephone and Telegraph

Telephone service is available in Georgetown and throughout the settled coastal area. International phone and fax service is excellent, and it costs less to call from Guyana to the U.S. than vice versa. Currently, a 3-minute call to Washington, D.C., costs about US$2.05, but rates may soon be increased. In Georgetown the annual phone rental is about US$18. Calls to nearby cities cost about US$0.04 for 3 minutes. Principal settlements in the interior have radio/telephone facilities. Extremely cheap telegraph service is available to and from the U.S. and the rest of the world. Telegrams to Washington, D.C., cost US$0.47 for 100 words; a 22-word night letter costs US$0.10, Internet varies from US$1 to US$54 a month.

Radio and TV

Guyana's two government-owned radio stations (Voice of Guyana and Radio Roraima) operate on two AM and two FM frequencies in Georgetown. Direct relays of the Voice of America (VOA) are used for special events, and VOA is available on medium wave, mornings and evenings. Georgetown has 15 TV stations, 1 of which is government owned. Many rebroadcast U.S. programs; including CBS and CNN newscasts and the "McNeil-Lehrer News Hour."

Newspapers, Magazines and Technical Journals

Two daily newspapers are published in Guyana: the state-owned *Chronicle* and the independent *Stabroek News*. The *Mirror* is the twice-weekly organ of the ruling Peoples Progressive Party (PPP) and the *New Nation* is the weekly organ of the People's National Congress (PNC). The Catholic Church publishes the *Catholic Standard* every Friday, often with important local news missed by the daily papers. The daily papers devote one or two pages each day to wire service reports of international news. The international editions of *Newsweek* and *Time* magazines are available each week, but many current foreign periodicals are not. Several small book- stores and the book departments of general stores offer a very limited selection.

Health and Medicine

Medical Facilities

Medical services in Guyana are extremely limited. Medical care is very marginal and serious medical or trauma cases will need evacuation to the U.S.

Guyana has several qualified, practicing dentists, but due to poor sanitary conditions in the offices visited, only one dentist has been identified for referrals for minor problems. There are no qualified orthodontists or periodontists, and few local dentists can maintain and adjust already-installed braces.

The few competent local physicians are extremely busy and sometimes hindered by shortages of medications and supplies. Specialists who are even fewer in number, work with the most basic equipment. Currently, there is no qualified cardiologist and only one urologist. The Georgetown Hospital recently commissioned a new ambulatory health-care facility which is being

plagued by shortages of medicines and qualified staff. CAT scan facilities are unavailable in the country and nursing skills are generally considered poor.

Local opticians and optometrists are qualified to fill prescriptions for glasses, but the quality of eye examinations is questionable. Choice of frames and lenses is limited. Two qualified ophthalmologists have private practices.

Local pharmacies stock common medicines, but supplies may be erratic. Purchasing medicines locally is done with caution and only products from approved manufacturers are chosen. Persons taking regular prescription medications are advised to bring an adequate supply to last until they can access local sources or arrange for regular supplies to be obtained from the U.S

Local laboratory facilities perform many routine tests but may be hampered by outdated supplies and shortages of reagents. Some tests which are considered routine in the U.S. may pose a problem here. Venipuncture techniques vary from technician to technician.

Community Health

The incidence of malaria in the interior of Guyana has increased over the years and cases number some 40,000 per year. Chloroquine-resistant falciparum malaria has been confirmed in the country along with infections from plasmodium vivax, plasmodium falciparum and mixed infections. There has been a slight increase in malaria cases reported in Region 4 (Demerara/Mahaica) which includes Georgetown, but malaria chemoprophylaxis is not advised for Georgetown at this time. All persons are advised to sleep under a mosquito net which has been sprayed with permethrin (permanone) and to use personal protective measures routinely. Persons traveling out of Georgetown to interior regions are advised to contact the Health Unit for advice on prophylaxis.

Microfilaria is prevalent in the Guyanese population, and the advanced state of infection of this parasite is seen in the form of noninfectious elephantiasis.

Tuberculosis is reportedly on the upsurge in certain regions of Guyana, especially in Region 4.

Cholera is also a threat with regular outbreaks in the neighboring countries.

Typhoid and intestinal parasites are now considered endemic in Guyana. Sporadic outbreaks of gastrointestinal diseases occur from time to time along with hepatitis.

Dengue fever has been reported in epidemic proportions in five countries in South America during the last 10 years. Cases of the more serious Dengue Hemorrhagic Fever (DHF) have been reported. The Vector Control Unit has reported confirmed cases of dengue fever in Guyana.

In Georgetown, city garbage collection is irregular, and garbage pileups and illegal dumping are widespread. Sewage disposal in the outskirts of the city is by septic tank. In the city itself, the underground sewer system is antiquated and inadequate, and presents many problems due to frequent blockages and overflows. The drainage system is not adequately maintained so there is often flooding and accumulation of stagnant water during the rainy season. Water supplies are usually adequate, but can be interrupted by low pressure or breaks in the water mains. Tap water is not safe to drink. It should be either filtered and boiled, or distilled.

Care is required when buying fresh food. Market standards are poor. Frequent and long lasting power outages may pose a threat to refrigerated stocks in commercial establishments or markets.

Preventive Measures

• Ensure that water for drinking is safe. Use milk treated by UHT or pasteurization. Powdered milk is also available locally. Wash fruits and vegetables well with detergent, then soak in a solution made up of one tablespoon of household bleach (5% chlorine) to one gallon of potable water for 15 minutes, then rinse well with potable water.

• Ensure that required immunizations are kept up-to-date. Immunizations required for Georgetown are yellow fever, typhoid, tetanus, polio, and hepatitis A and B.

• Check with the Health Unit before traveling out of town or into the interior to assess the need for malaria prophylaxis. Ensure that a high standard of sanitation is maintained in the home at all times. Keep surroundings clean, and grass and trees well trimmed.

• Use of sunscreen lotions to prevent burning by the strong tropical sun is a good idea. Use of insect repellant is also advised when going out in the evenings or when you expect to be in contact with grass.

• Have a full medical examination before coming to Guyana so that any existing problems can be treated.

NOTES FOR TRAVELERS

Passage, Customs & Duties

Travel to Guyana is by air, as no passenger ships call at Georgetown and it cannot be reached by road or rail from any other country. There are no U.S. carriers serving Guyana. American Airlines has daily flights from Miami to Trinidad and Barbados, but passengers must overnight in either country before taking a BWIA, Suriname Airways, or LIAT flight to Georgetown. American has flights twice a day from JFK New York to Barbados, both of which arrive in time to connect with a daily BWIA flight to Georgetown. BWIA, a Trinidadian airline, provides daily service to Georgetown

from JFK New York (via Barbados) and Miami (via Port-of-Spain). Guyana Airways Corporation (GAC) offers service from New York (via Curacao) three times a week and nonstop from Miami once a week. Leeward Islands Air Transport (LIAT) offers daily service from Barbados and via Barbados from other Caribbean Islands. LIAT has a strict excess baggage charge on all luggage over 20 kg. (44 pounds) and very limited cabin space for carry-on items. Suriname Airways provides air service from Paramaribo 2 days a week; which continues on to Trinidad and Venezuela.

A valid U.S. passport is required for U.S. citizens to enter and depart Guyana. On arrival in Guyana, visitors are granted a 30-day stay. Extensions of stay may be obtained from the Ministry of Home Affairs at 60 Brickdam Street, Georgetown. The Central Office of Immigration located on Camp Street, Georgetown, must then note the extension in the visitor's passport. Travelers for other than tourism purposes should check with the Ministry of Home Affairs for information about requirements for work permits and extended stays. U.S.-Guyanese dual nationals departing Guyana for the United States under a Guyanese passport must present to Guyanese authorities a U.S. Certificate of Naturalization or similar document establishing that they may freely enter the United States.

Americans living in or visiting Guyana are encouraged to register at the Consular Section of the U.S. 'in Georgetown and obtain updated information on travel and security within Guyana. The U.S. Embassy is located at 100 Young and Duke Streets, telephone 011-592-225-4900 through 54909, fax 011-592-225-8497. Hours of operation are Monday-Friday, 7:00 a.m. to 3:30 p.m., except local and U.S. holidays. For emergencies after hours, on weekends and on holidays, U.S. citizens are requested to call the U.S. Embassy duty officer at 011-592-226-2614 or 226-8298 or 227-7868

and to leave a message for pager number 6516.

Pets

It is difficult to import pets into Guyana. Pets brought into the country must have a valid health certificate showing rabies inoculations at least 30 days from the arrival and must have an entry permit from the Government of Guyana. Pets must arrive with or after the employee.

All pets must be quarantined for 90 days, unless they are coming from Britain or another country using the British quarantine system. However, the official Government of Guyana quarantine stations are usually full. Pet food must be supplied by the pet owner. The quarantine cost at the Government of Guyana, Ministry of Agriculture/police kennels is US$10 daily or US$900 for 90 days. Food, etc., is extra.

Many exotic birds found in Guyana are protected species. The Guyana Ministry of Agriculture will permit only those persons who have been legally residing in Guyana for more than one year to take an exotic bird out of the country when they leave. Those Americans who have legally resided in Guyana for more than a year and who would like to take back to the United States any birds or animals, including pets, listed in Appendices I, II and III of the Convention on International Trade in Endangered Species (CITES), must have a Wild Bird Conservation Act (WBCA) import permit from the U.S. Fish and Wildlife Service (USFWS). Please note that this is a U.S. regulation that applies regardless of distinctions among the three Appendices. U.S. residents and non-residents continue to arrive at U.S. ports of entry without WBCA permits, and they encounter difficulties. Individuals can obtain WBCA fact sheets and permit applications from the USFWS Office of Management Authority, Branch of Permits, 4401 North Fairfax Drive, Arlington, VA 22203, telephone (703) 358-2104, fax 703) 358-2281.

Currency, Banking, and Weights and Measures

Guyana's currency is the Guyana dollar (GYP). The current rate of exchange is US$1.00 = GYP$179.60. The rate is subject to change on a daily basis. Georgetown has five commercial banks; only the Bank of Baroda (India) and the Bank of Nova Scotia, a small private Canadian bank, are foreign-owned. A third foreign-owned, bank Citizens Bank of Jamaica has been licensed and opened in October 1994, as well as a new commercial bank—The Demerara Bank.

Commercial banks provide a full range of banking services, including sale and redemption of dollar or sterling travelers checks and cashing of personal checks.

American citizens are advised to exchange currency only with banks, hotels, and established money exchange houses ("cambios"). Many foreigners who opt to exchange money on the streets, lured by promises of higher exchange rates, are increasingly becoming victims of fraud and recipients of counterfeit currency. There is no legal recourse unless the police are successful in apprehending the perpetrator; even then there is no guarantee that the money will be recovered. Street vendors usually offer rates very near to bank or "cambio" rates, so there is little advantage to be gained by changing money outside the formal system.

Weights and measures are British, although the metric system was officially introduced in 1982. In many cases British units of measures are the same as American units. Liquid measurements differ; the imperial gallon is equal to 1.20094 U.S. gallons and the British cup is 10 ounces rather than 8.

LOCAL HOLIDAYS

Jan. 2	New Year's Day
Feb. 23	Republic Anniversary
Mar.	Phagwah*
Mar/Apr.	Good Friday*
Mar/Apr.	Easter*
Mar/Apr.	Easter Monday*
May 1	Labor Day
May	Eid-Ul-Azah*
July (first Monday)	Caribbean Day*
Aug.	Freedom Day*
Aug.	Youm-Un-Nabi*
October 23	Deepavali
Dec. 25	Christmas Day
Dec. 26	Boxing Day

*Variable

RECOMMENDED READING

These titles are provided as a general indication of the material published on this country. The Department of State does not endorse publications.

Asregadoo, Edward R. *Man from Guyana.* San Diego, CA: Libra Publications, 1990.

Burrowes, Reynold A. *The Wild Coast: An Account of Politics in Guyana.* Schenkman: Cambridge, Mass., 1984.

Carew, Nan. *Black Midas.* Seaker & Warburg: London, 1958.

Chambers, Frances, et al. *Guyana.* Santa Barbara, CA: ABC-Clio, 1989.

Daly, Vere T. *A Short History of the Guyanese People.* Macmillan Education: London, 1975.

Depres, Leo A. *Cultural Pluralism and Nationalist Politics in British Guiana.* Rand-McNally & Co.: Chicago 1967.

Gopal, Madam M. *Politics, Race, & Youth in Guyana.* Lewiston, NY: Edward Mellen Press, 1992.

Heath, Roy. *Orealla.* Allison and Busby: London, 1984.

Heath, Roy. *The Armstrong Trilogy: From the Heat of the Day, One Generation, Genetha.* Persea, 1994.

Hudson, W. H. *Green Mansions.* The World Publishing Co.: New York.

Jagan, Cheddi. *The West on Trial.* Seven Seas: Berlin, 1972.

Lerner Publications, Department of Geography Staff. *Guyana in Pictures.* Minneapolis, MN: Lerner Publications, 1988.

Mecklenburg, Kurt. K. *Guyana Gold.* Carlton Press: 1990.

Merill, Tim L., ed. *Guyana and Belize: Country Studies.* Federal Research Division, Library of Congress, U.S. Government Printing Office: Washington, D.C. 1993.

Mittleholzer, Edgar. *Children of Kwayana.* John Day Co., Inc.: New York, 1976. (Many novels by Edgar Mittleholzer, Guyana's most prolific writer, provide a good introduction to Guyanese life.)

Naipaul, V.S. *The Middle Passage.* Macmillan: New York, 1963.

Singh, Chaitram. *Guyana: Politics in a Plantation Society.* Praeger: New York, 1988.

Spinner, Thomas J., Jr. *A Political and Social History of Guyana, 1945-1983.* Westview Press: Boulder, Colo., 1984.

Williams, Brackette F. *Stains on My Name, War in My Veins.* Durham, NC: Duke University Press, 1991.

Port-au-Prince, Haiti

HAITI

Republic of Haiti

Major City:

Port-au-Prince

Other Cities:

Cap-Haïtien, Gonaïves, Jacmel, Kenscoff, Les Cayes, Pétionville, Port-de-Paix

EDITOR'S NOTE

This chapter was adapted from the Department of State Post Report dated August 1996. Supplemental material has been added to increase coverage of minor cities, facts have been updated, and some material has been condensed. Readers are encouraged to visit the Department of State's web site at http://travel.state.gov/ for the most recent information available on travel to this country.

INTRODUCTION

In October 1994, President Jean-Bertrand Aristide was restored to power in Haiti by a U.S.-led Multinational Force (MNF), ending 3 years of military dictatorship and extreme hardship for the Haitian people. Economic sanctions were lifted, and MNF troops were deployed throughout the country to ensure Haiti's peaceful transition to democratic rule. Shortly after Aristide's return, the international donor community met and pledged $1.2 billion to assist in the rebuilding of the Haitian economy and social institutions. Parliamentary elections were held in the summer and fall of 1995, and, in accordance with the constitution, elections for President were held in December 1995. President Rene Preval was inaugurated February 7, 1996, completing the first-ever peaceful transition from one elected President to another and giving Haitians a democratically elected government from the local level to the Presidency. A small U.N. or multinational peacekeeping mission is expected to remain in Haiti through 1996.

Haiti is a land with too many people and almost no natural resources. Its forests have been cut down and its topsoil washed into the sea. To the outside world, its name has become synonymous with "boat people" and voodoo. It is a land of hunger, poverty, pride, and beauty.

Americans living in Haiti find the climate delightful, the people handsome and approachable, the arts fascinating, the poverty appalling, and the overall experience unique to each person.

MAJOR CITY

Port-au-Prince

Port-au-Prince, the capital of Haiti, is located on the Gulf of La Gonave, formed by the two great peninsulas that define Haiti's coastline. These two peninsulas are often compared to the jaws of a crocodile that looks as if it is about to swallow Port-au-Prince.

To feel the pulse of Port-au-Prince, one can think of Haiti as "a fragment of black Africa which dislodged, drifted across the Atlantic and settled in the Caribbean." Following a successful slave revolt in 1804, this "bit of Africa" became the second independent country in the Western Hemisphere.

Port-au-Prince is a city with an uninspired waterfront and downtown area. The city has expanded onto adjoining hills with incredible vistas. At present, the city is a conglomeration of nondescript office buildings, slums, old Victorian houses with "gingerbread" trim, modern cement-block houses, and breathtaking million-dollar homes. The city's social system unofficially divides the populace into a majority of black African descent called "noirs" and a minority of mixed ancestry called "mulatres." This division continues to be the basis for the inequalities so glaringly visible in Port-au-Prince.

The city has few historic sites, but sight-seeing is ample for a short visit. Major attractions are the Episcopal cathedral with its Haitian Biblical murals, the Catholic cathedral, the Musee d'Art, and many private art galleries. Haitian handi-

Church in Port-au-Prince, Haiti

© Tony Arruza/Corbis. Reproduced by permission.

craft stores feature metal arts created from old oil drums, many with a delightful sense of humor. There are over 8,000 U.S. citizens living in Haiti, and about half of those registered are children under 18. The American business community in Port-au-Prince is not sizable.

Food

During normal times Port-au-Prince offers a surprising variety of food products, although many items are imported and retail at prices well above the U.S. level. These include packaged, canned, and frozen foods, occasional cottage cheese,

sour cream and French cheeses, but only dry or long-life (UHT) milk is available. Goods are often beyond their peak upon arrival and many past their expiration date as well.

Local beef, pork, and chicken are available, but the quality does not meet U.S. standards. Vegetables and fruit are available in season. Market women sell string beans, peas, avocados, beets, carrots, eggplant, tomatoes, squash, lettuce, cabbage, onions, garlic, parsley, special artichokes, cauliflower, potatoes, and radishes. Papayas, mangoes, oranges, grapefruit, tangerines, pineapples, bananas, and various melons are available in season but quality varies.

Uncooked vegetables or unpeeled fruit should be washed and treated with a chlorine solution as disinfectant.

Clothing

Lightweight clothing is worn year-round, with a sweater or jacket occasionally useful in the winter. The average temperature in Port-au-Prince is 80°F. Raincoats are not worn, as they are too warm, but umbrellas are useful. A lightweight sweater or jacket is needed for trips to the mountains.

Women: In public women wear dresses, skirts and blouses, or slacks and tops. Lightweight, washable cottons or synthetic cotton mixtures are most comfortable. A limited supply of Haitian-embroidered linen dresses are sold locally but at high prices.

Lingerie is available locally but is very expensive or of second quality. Nylon lingerie can be too hot for the Port-au-Prince climate. Hosiery is optional and rarely worn.

Locally made sandals are reasonably priced and available in the markets. It is wise to bring other footwear and tennis shoes from the U.S. Many beaches are stony, and sea urchins are numerous, so bathing shoes of some type are useful.

Children: Children in all grades at Union School wear uniforms. The uniforms, shirts and shorts are limited to the colors blue, white, and yellow and must be purchased locally. Play clothes are worn to children's parties. Most teenage entertaining is casual.

Supplies and Services

Most well-known brands of American toiletries and cosmetics are available but much more expensive. French and European toiletries and cosmetics often cost less.

Haitian fabric material is of poor quality, and imported fabrics are available but expensive.

Tailoring is inadequate for most types of men's clothing. Prices for low-quality tailor-made suits are reasonable.

Dressmakers are available. Seamstresses will come to the home at reasonable prices to make clothing for adults or children. Shoe repair often takes place on the street and is quite satisfactory. Good-quality dry-cleaning is hard to find.

In all of these service areas, language ability, or lack thereof, usually compounds any problem.

Religious Activities

Haiti is predominately a Roman Catholic country. Parish churches are located throughout the city, and the Port-au-Prince Cathedral is in the center city. Mass is traditionally said in French or Creole. An English mass is held on Sunday mornings at St. Louis de Gonzague Chapel in the downtown area.

Protestant services are held on Sunday mornings at the Episcopal Church of St. Jacques in Petionville and at the Quisqueya Chapel, a nondenominational church in Port-au-Prince. The Quisqueya Chapel also has Sunday School classes, Bible study groups, and a Sunday evening worship service. Services are held on Saturday mornings at the Church of the Adventist University of Haiti in Diquini.

Members of the Jewish and Muslim communities usually hold services in their homes to celebrate their holy days.

Vaudun (voodoo) plays a central part in the religious life of many Haitians. It is essentially a bringing together of beliefs and rituals of African origin, closely tied to Catholic practices. Some understanding of voodoo is essential to an understanding of Haiti.

Education

The Haitian school system includes primary through university levels and is based on the French system, with classes taught in French or Creole.

Most foreign children in Port-au-Prince attend the SACS-accredited Union School. Classes are taught in English, with French a required subject at all grade levels. The Union School is open to all nationalities and offers a program from preschool through grade 12. It has a capacity of 380 children and should be notified well in advance of enrollment plans for arriving children, particularly if they involve a midterm transfer.

When planning enrollment in the Union School, students should bring with them complete school records including report cards and test results. A one-time bonding fee of $150 per child is nonreimbursable. School hours are from 7:45 am to 1:30 pm. The school year normally begins toward the end of August and finishes in early June. Students at the Union School wear uniforms from kindergarten through grade 12, as do children in all Haitian schools. Children attending the Union School ordinarily have no difficulty transferring to U.S. schools.

The Union School has a Learning Center for children with mild learning difficulties, and it is generally recognized to have a very good elementary school program. Its high school curriculum has an advanced placement program, but there is no international baccalaureate available. The Quisqueya Christian School also provides English-language schooling from kindergarten through grade 12. The school is open to all nationalities and is attended by many American children. It currently has an enrollment of 200, and the staff are American educated.

Aerial view of Port-au-Prince, Haiti

Sports

Sports activities in Haiti are found primarily in private clubs. (There are no organized sports facilities such as the YMCA.) The Petion-Ville Club, about 3 miles from downtown Port-au-Prince, is on a hill overlooking the bay. Included in its 145 acres are a rugged nine-hole golf course, six tennis courts (four lighted), a 75-foot swimming pool (which can be enjoyed by children), and a clubhouse with dance floor, dining, bar, and locker accommodations. There are a number of tennis clubs in Port-au-Prince. These often have social facilities available in addition to the tennis courts. Most clubs require an initiation fee and/or monthly dues.

Touring and Outdoor Activities

A great deal of Haiti's outdoor life centers around its coastal waters and beaches. There are safe and pleasant beaches about a 60-minute

drive from Port-au-Prince, and a number have overnight and restaurant facilities. Swimming and snorkeling are ideal for all ages.

Scuba diving is popular in Haiti, but divers should bring their own tanks. There is one place in Port-au-Prince that will refill tanks, but only to 2,200 pounds unless you have your own compressor. There is no scuba-diving equipment available locally. The Cormier Plage Beach Resort, adjacent to Cap Haitien on the north coast, rents equipment. Scuba-diving instruction for certification is possible in Haiti at both beginning and advanced levels. The cost is 550 Haitian dollars.

Unstable political conditions have restricted the formerly good hunting for ducks, guinea hens, wild pigeons, and doves.

Kenscoff (45 minutes from Port-au-Prince) is a town at an altitude of 4,500 feet, set in mountains as high

as 6,500 feet. It is cool year-round and may even be cold in winter. Although the road has suffered wear and tear, people enjoy visiting Kenscoff on weekends. There are some wonderful places to hike. The scenery in the mountains is extraordinary, and travelers like to stop en route to visit the Baptist Fermathe Mission's arts-and-crafts shop and have lunch in its pleasant restaurant. For historic content, Forts Jacques and Alexandre can be added to the itinerary.

Cap Haitien (157 miles from Port-au-Prince; 6 hours by car), Haiti's second-largest city, is of primary interest because of its historic past. The famed Citadelle Laferriere, often referred to as the "eighth wonder of the world," was built on a 3,000-foot peak overlooking Cap Haitien. Below the Citadelle is Milot, where one can visit the ruins of Henri Christophe's Sans Souci Palace. Above Milot, horses can be rented for the uphill ride to the Citadelle. Cap Haitien has adequate hotel facilities, and nearby are two very pleasant seaside resorts.

Jacmel (73 miles from Port-au-Prince; 2 hours by car) is on the southern peninsula and well known for its beaches. It is a picturesque town with turn-of-the-century architecture, a small iron market, and a few small art galleries. Jacmel has beaches inside the town and nearby at Carrefour Raymond. The road to Jacmel is in fair condition, and the town has two good hotels with restaurants.

Les Cayes (125 miles from Port-au-Prince; 4 hours by car) is the principal city of the southern peninsula and the third-largest city in Haiti. The city itself has little to offer, but the road from the capital passes through beautiful and interesting country. One of the best beaches in Haiti, Port-Salut, is nearby and has a restaurant and hotel. Les Cayes has two satisfactory hotels, one on the outskirts and one in the city.

The Arts and Entertainment

The Haitian art scene has attracted world-wide attention since 1946, when English teacher DeWitt Peters brought Hector Hippolyte, Philomene Obin, and other greats of Haiti's primitive art scene to the attention of the world's art establishment. One of the unique experiences of living in Haiti is the chance to visit the studios and galleries of the artists carrying on this fascinating tradition.

Haiti has no concert or theater series, but the Philharmonic Orchestra of Saint Trinite Cathedral presents seasonal concerts of classical music, and the cathedral provides a locale for the all-too-rare performances by visiting soloists or chamber groups.

The Musee d'Art Haitien, on the Champs-de-Mars, houses both standing and rotating art exhibits.

Private art galleries abound in the Port-au-Prince area, but one that holds a special place in Haitian hearts is the Jean-Rene Jerome Museum, opened in the mid-1980s to honor the much-revered artist.

There are few archaeological sites in Haiti, but Dr. William Hodges of the Good Samaritan Hospital in Limbe has had as an avocation during his 30-year career in the country a search for the site where Columbus landed his first expedition on the north coast. If one is traveling to Cap Haitien by car, a stopover to visit Dr. Hodges' small museum in Limbe should be considered. For the real enthusiast, a journey to the east of Cap Haitien takes one to the site that Dr. Hodges' research leads him to conclude was the actual spot where Columbus established the first colony in the New World.

Port-au-Prince has several movie houses, of which the Imperial is the largest and most comfortable. Most films shown are French films, but even American films are dubbed in French.

There are a number of quite good restaurants in the area. Excellent French cuisine can be had at the pricier establishments. The larger hotels have dining rooms that feature special buffets, Sunday brunches, and an occasional floor show. A few nightclubs provide Haitian or disco music, and there are two hotel casinos.

Coverage of the entertainment scene in Haiti cannot neglect Carnival where dancing in the streets takes place every Sunday after Christmas and culminates in Mardi Gras, the two days before Ash Wednesday. Musical groups called rara bands dance across the countryside during the pre-Lenten season. Many Haitians join in these singing and dancing festivities, and drinking is excessive. Things tend to become rowdy, and foreigners usually prefer to watch these celebrations on television.

Social Activities

Most entertaining takes place informally in the home. Single people generally find sports clubs or outdoor activities the most satisfactory way to socialize. As most Haitians do not receive high salaries, it is often difficult for them to return hospitality. There is an American Women's Community Association (AWCA), which meets monthly. It provides a welcome to new American women, sponsors seasonal parties for the children, and is open to any activities or projects for which members indicate enthusiasm. The Women's International Gourmet Society (WIGS) meets monthly to sample different restaurant cuisine. The local churches have women's groups to which all are welcome. The Quisqueya Chapel sponsors periodic men's breakfasts at a local hotel. These are open to all men in the community.

OTHER CITIES

CAP-HAÏTIEN (also called Le Cap), about 85 miles north of Port-au-Prince on the northern coast, is Haiti's second largest city. It is of primary interest because of its historic past. There are ruins here of former colonial dwellings and buildings; nearby Milot is the site of the ruins of King Christophe's Sans Souci palace. From Milot, horses or burros can be rented for a two-hour ride to the Citadelle Laferrière, also built by Christophe, and surmounted on a 3,000-foot peak overlooking the nearby plain. The city has a modern harbor which handles one-ninth of Haiti's imports and exports. One of the world's largest sisal plantations is located in Cap-Haïtien. Pineapples, sugarcane, coffee, bananas, and cacao are grown near the city. From Port-au-Prince to Cap-Haïtien, the trip is four hours by car, or 35 minutes by air. Cap-Haïtien's 1995 population was about 100,600.

GONAÏVES is a port city on the Gulf of Gonave in western Haiti. The country's independence was proclaimed here in 1804, and today the city is a major commercial center. The region's agricultural products, including sugar, cotton, coffee, and bananas, are exported from the harbor. A main attraction in the city is the Musée du Centenaire. It was inaugurated in 1904 to commemorate the 100th anniversary of Haiti's independence. The Gulf of Gonave is situated in the pincers of two mountainous peninsulas and is considered one of the most beautiful in the world. The city's population is estimated over 40,000.

JACMEL, situated on the southern peninsula, is a picturesque town of about 216,600. It boasts a small iron market, a few small art galleries, and beaches at nearby Carrefour Raymond. The road to Jacmel recently was rerouted and paved.

KENSCOFF, 10 miles south of Port-au-Prince, and where visitors go on weekends to escape the heat of the capital city, is at an altitude of 4,500 feet. Its mountains rise as high as 6,500 feet. The area is cool all year, and sometimes even cold during the winter. In addition to the climate change, the road to Kenscoff and the town itself offer beautiful scenery and picturesque countryside. Along the road to Kenscoff, sightseers often stop to visit the Baptist Mission's arts and crafts shop or to explore the historic forts, Jacques and Alexandre. The town has about 3,000 people.

LES CAYES is the principal city of the southern peninsula and the third largest city in Haiti, with over 37,000 inhabitants. It is situated 90 miles from Port-au-Prince, but the trip takes several hours by jeep, and then only when roads are passable. The city itself has little to offer, but the road from the capital passes through beautiful and interesting country. One of the best beaches in Haiti, Port-Salut, is nearby. The city is Haiti's principal southern port. Coffee, bananas, cotton, timber, and hides are exported from Les Cayes. Historic landmarks include an arsenal and several forts dating from buccaneer times.

PÉTIONVILLE, a suburb of Port-au-Prince, is five miles southeast of the capital in the hills of the Massif de la Selle. The community is mostly a residential resort area, tied to Port-au-Prince by a twisting toll road. Pétionville's estimated

population is 69,5000 (1995). Its name derives from that of Alexandre Sab s Pétion, a hero of Haiti's war for independence in the early 1800s.

Historic **PORT-DE-PAIX** is a seaport town opposite Tortuga Island, 45 miles west of Cap-Haïtien. Its tumultuous history dates to 1665 and the founding of the city by French insurrectionists from Tortuga Island. They originally settled near Môle Saint-Nicolas, where Columbus landed on December 6, 1492. The first slave revolt took place in Port-de-Paix in 1679. The area flourished in the 19th century when, for a while, it was the colonial capital. A 1902 fire devastated the city, physically and spiritually. Today, Port-de-Paix relies on coffee, bananas, rice, sisal (a strong fiber used to make rope), and tobacco production, as well as fishing, for survival. Agricultural produce, logwood, and hides are exported. The municipal population is over 20,000.

COUNTRY PROFILE

Geography and Climate

Eighteenth-century Haiti, famed for its wealth and productivity, was known to the colonial world as the Pearl of the Antilles. Located in the Caribbean Sea on the western third of the island of Hispaniola, Haiti is a 10,700-square-mile area of primarily mountainous terrain, some of which rises above 8,000 feet, and 850 miles of spectacular coastline. Haïti shares the island of Hispaniola with the Dominican Republic, which occupies the eastern two-thirds.

Haiti's tropical climate produces seasonal rainfall, although large areas of the country are semiarid. Temperatures year-round range from 70°F to 90°F with humidity sometimes high along the coast. Average annual rainfall varies from nearly zero in some areas to 53

inches in Port-au-Prince. The two rainy seasons that Port-au-Prince experiences are from April to June and from August to mid-November. Rain and accompanying thunder/lightning storms usually occur at dusk and at night, but the days remain clear and sunny. There is a crisp dry season from December to April. Surrounding mountains protect Port-au-Prince from Caribbean hurricanes.

Population

With its current population estimated at approximately 7 million, Haiti ranks among the most densely populated countries in the world. Port-au-Prince, the capital, has more than 1.7 million inhabitants. Cap Haitien, on the north coast, is the second-largest city, with a population of 100,600. It is estimated that 95% of Haitians are of African descent. The remaining 5% include Haitians of mixed African-European descent plus immigrants from Europe and the Middle East. Haiti has both French and Creole as official languages even though only 20% of the population speaks French fluently. Creole is spoken and understood by all Haitians, but as a written means of communication it has to contend with Haiti's mere 45% literacy rate.

The culture and traditions of Haiti come from its African, Caribbean, and French roots. Following World War II, a significant number of Haitians began visiting or studying in the United States and Canada. Overseas Haitians now number around 1 million. This travel back and forth has made North American customs and habits increasingly familiar in Haiti. In an attempt to escape the country's grinding poverty (particularly during periods of political repression), tens of thousands of Haitians have attempted to enter the U.S. illegally, the vast majority in overcrowded, unseaworthy boats.

Public Institutions

The people of Haiti have fought with political instability since their independence in 1804. The country has had 21 different constitutions. But the most current Haitian constitution adheres to the principles of democracy and human rights as defined in the Universal Declaration of Human Rights of 1948.

The constitution provides for a system of representative government under which power is shared among branches.

The executive branch consists of a chief of state or president who is elected for a five-year term and is not eligible for immediate re-election or election for a total of more than two terms.

The head of government is the prime minister chosen by the chief of state from the membership of the majority party in Parliament; or, in the absence of a majority party, after consultations with the leadership of both parliamentary chambers.

The legislative branch consists of a senate made up of 27 members (three for each of the nine departments) elected by a direct popular vote at the departmental level for six-year terms and eligible for re-election for an indefinite number of terms. Terms are staggered on a two-year basis, one third of senators being elected every two years.

There is also a chamber of deputies consisting of 83 members elected by a direct popular vote at the municipal level for a four-year term, and eligible for re-election for an indefinite number of terms.

The Haitian judiciary is divided into four basic levels: justices of the peace; fifteen courts of first instance; five regional courts of appeal; and, The Haitian Supreme Court (Cour de Cassation).

The constitution also provides for an independent board of elections charged with the organization and supervision of electoral procedures and political decentralization through the election of mayors and administrative bodies responsible for local government.

The Prime Minister's government is composed of a cabinet that must be confirmed by parliament. This cabinet is called the Council of Ministers. The Council of Ministers is presided over by the President of the Republic.

Many political parties of different ideologies are active in the Haiti. Most parties are not well structured. They lack adequate financial resources, and their focus is on personalities and regional alliances rather than national policy priorities.

Despite the dictates of the constitution, politics remain volatile. Elections are often contested and military coups have called for intervention from the U.N. and other countries. After elections supervised by the United Nations in December 1990, Jean-Bertrand Aristide was inaugurated as President in February 1991.

But in September 1991, a military coup forced Aristide out of Haiti. The U.S.-led Multinational Force restored government three years later and Rene Preval, took office in 1996. Aristide returned to be elected to a second term in the 2000 elections, but these were boycotted by the majority of opposition leaders.

Legislative elections were held in both 1995 and 1997, with disappointing results. New legislative elections did not take place until May 2000. They were expected to reconstitute the legislative branch of government, which effectively ceased to function January 11, 1999. However, they were so flawed as to call into question the legitimacy of the Parliament, which was convened on August 28.

The international community has refused to offer the new Haitian government funding for their projects if they do not negotiate with the opposition in order to come up with an agreement that will satisfy both parties. Talks between the opposition and governing party aimed at resolving the political impasse have taken place under the mediation of the OAS (Organization of American States) and CARICOM (Community of Caribbean Nations), but have yet to result in an accord.

Arts, Science, and Education

Education is available in Haiti from preschool through university, although only 73% of 6- through 11-year-old Haitian children attend primary school. In driving through Port-au-Prince, one sees an extraordinary number of schools, including numerous preschools and kindergartens. Haitian parents prefer private schools over public ones and make great sacrifices to afford the tuition.

The University of Haiti, located in Port-au-Prince, is tuition free to those students who can pass the tough entrance exams. The university has schools of administration, agronomy, dentistry, economics, education, law, literature, medicine, and science. Most subjects are taught in French and in the French university tradition. Of late there has been some instruction in Creole, and the American educational system has influenced the curriculum at the Institute of Administration, Management, and Diplomacy (INAGHEI).

A significant number of art schools attempt to maintain the spirit of Haiti's 1940s explosion onto the world art scene. There are also institutes of science and technology and two private universities.

Commerce and Industry

Since the demise of the Duvalier dictatorship in 1986, international economists have urged Haiti to reform and modernize its economy. Under President Preval (1995-

2000), the country's economic agenda included trade/tariff liberalization, measures to control government expenditure and increase tax revenues, civil service downsizing, financial sector reform, and the modernization of two out of nine state-owned enterprises through their sale to private investors, the provision of private sector management contracts, or joint public-private investment. Structural adjustment agreements with the International Monetary Fund, World Bank, Inter-American Development Bank, and other international financial institutions intended to create necessary conditions for private sector growth, proved only partly successful.

In 1999, Haiti's economy began to falter after about 4 years of positive, though modest growth. Real GDP growth fell in 2001 by 1.2%. The Privatization program stalled. Macroeconomic stability was adversely affected by political uncertainty, low investment, a significant increase in the budget deficit, and reduced international capital flows. The lack of an agreement with the IMF has prevented the resumption of crucial international assistance. This recent weakening of the economy has serious implication for future economic development as well as efforts to improve the general standard of living.

External aid is essential to the future economic development of Haiti, the least-developed country in the Western Hemisphere and one of the poorest in the world. Comparative social and economic indicators show Haiti falling behind other low-income developing countries (particularly in the hemisphere) since the 1980s. Haiti's economic stagnation is the result of earlier inappropriate economic policies, political instability, a shortage of good arable land, environmental deterioration, continued use of traditional technologies, under-capitalization and lack of public investment in human resources, migration of large portions of the skilled population, a weak national savings rate, and the

lack of a functioning judicial system.

Haiti continues to suffer the consequences of the 1991 coup and the irresponsible economic and financial policies of the de facto authorities which greatly accelerated Haiti's economic decline. Following the coup, the United States adopted mandatory sanctions, and the OAS instituted voluntary sanctions aimed at restoring constitutional government. International sanctions culminated in the May 1994 UN embargo of all goods entering Haiti except humanitarian supplies, such as food and medicine. The assembly sector, heavily dependent on U.S. markets for its products, employed nearly 80,000 workers in the mid-1980s. During the embargo, employment fell below 17,000. Private domestic and foreign investment has been slow to return to Haiti. Since the return of constitutional rule, assembly sector employment has gradually recovered with about 25,000 now employed, but further growth has been stalled by investor concerns over safety and political instability.

If the political situation stabilizes, high-crime levels reduce, and new investment increases, tourism could take its place next to export-oriented manufacturing (the assembly sector) as a potential source of foreign exchange. Remittances from abroad now constitute a significant source of financial support for many Haitian households.

Workers in Haiti are guaranteed the right of association. Unionization is protected by the labor code. A legal minimum wage of 36 gourds a day (about U.S. $1.80) applies to most workers in the formal sector.

Transportation

Local

"Service" (sharing) taxis operate on defined routes. There is no safe, clean, or modern intercity or intracity public transport available. There are some private taxi services, but these are very expensive, particu-

larly for new foreigners and during any gasoline shortages.

Regional

During normal times, Port-au-Prince has daily nonstop flights to and from Miami and New York and regular flights to Santo Domingo, Montreal, Paris, Kingston, and Curacao. Reservations can be difficult to make during the peak travel seasons of summer and Christmas.

Communications

Telephone, Telegraph, and FAX

Port-au-Prince has a dial telephone system, which is subject to interruption during rainy seasons and electricity shortages. Intercity calls can be made within Haiti. Overseas calls can also be made at most local hotels with a USA-direct card.

Radio and TV

Under normal conditions there are about 46 independent AM/FM stereo radio stations in Haiti, 22 of which are located in Port-au-Prince. Most broadcast 16 to 18 hours a day, including the government-owned radio station Radio Nationale. Shortwave radios pick up all principal international networks, including VOA and BBC. The VOA Creole service program is rebroadcast daily in the capital.

There are three television stations in the capital. Television Nationale d'Haiti (TNH), the government-owned station, broadcasts all over the country, with an estimated audience of 500,000. It provides French- and Creole-language programs 18 hours a day, 7 days a week.

Tele-Haiti, a privately owned cable station, relays 14 separate channels of programs in English, French, and Spanish. These currently include CNN, HBO, the Learning Channel, the Disney Channel, and U.S. stations affiliated with CBS and NBC. Tele-Haiti (broadcasting 7 days a week, 24 hours daily) serves only Port-au-Prince and has approximately 100,000 viewers. Program quality is generally good, barring power failures. PVS-Antenne 16, a privately owned station broadcasting on UHF, beams French- and English-language programming 8 hours a day, 7 days a week to about 20,000 viewers in the capital.

Newspapers, Magazines, and Technical Journals

Local bookstores no longer supply major newspapers, but magazines such as *Time, Newsweek, L'Express,* and *Le Figaro* are available about a week after publication.

At present there are 15 newspapers in Haiti, including three French-language dailies in Port-au-Prince. One of these dailies has occasional articles in English. Radio, television, and newspapers draw on Agence France Presse, Reuters, and AP for international news.

The Haitian-American Institute library, open to Americans, has about 3,700 volumes and is probably the best lending library in the country; membership is 5 Haitian dollars per year. The Colony Club, a private lending library located at the Petion-Ville Club, is open Fridays from 4 to 6 pm and can be joined for a minimal fee.

A few commercial bookstores have American, British, French, and Haitian books, although the supply of novels in English is slim, and prices are higher than in the U.S. For small children there are few books available outside the school library. It is wise to subscribe to U.S. magazines and book clubs for both adults and children to make up for the dearth of current English-language reading material available in Port-au-Prince.

Health and Medicine

Medical Facilities

Port-au-Prince has a number of competent Haitian doctors, but lack of equipment limits medical facilities. Expert diagnostic service is not available. Locally, there are several competent dentists. A number of American- or Canadian-trained spe-

cialists in cardiology, pediatrics, and eye/ear/nose/throat are available.

Local oculists and optometrists can issue eyeglass prescriptions. Lens-grinding facilities are available, but special lenses must be ground outside the country. It is advisable to bring extra eyeglasses, contact lenses, and sunglasses with ultraviolet screening plus a copy of your current prescription. Selection of contact lens solutions is limited.

The Canape Vert Hospital in Port-au-Prince has a doctor covering the emergency room from 7 pm to 7 am. It has some air-conditioned private rooms, and most doctors are permitted to practice there. The rates are lower than in the U.S., but due to inadequate nursing care and lack of supplies, hospitalization is sometimes precarious.

It is advisable to bring any medications and over-the-counter drugs used regularly and to make arrangements with a U.S. pharmacy for refills. Pharmacies are available in Port-au-Prince but often stock only European pharmaceuticals.

Community Health

The level of community sanitation and public cleanliness throughout the country is far below American standards. Streets in Port-au-Prince are littered with refuse, and sewage often stagnates in open gutters. Port-au-Prince's sewerage system is totally inadequate for the city's needs. Local vegetables and fruit that cannot be peeled must be washed with soap and water and soaked in chlorine solution.

Preventive Measures

Malaria is a serious problem in rural Haiti. It is recommended that travelers take malaria-preventive medication.

Other diseases common to Haiti include hepatitis A and B, typhoid fever, tuberculosis, venereal disease (including AIDS), intestinal parasites, dengue fever, polio, and rabies. Due to the high incidence of some of these diseases, any hired household help should have a pre-

employment physical examination and periodic checkups.

Occasional cases of dysentery, diarrhea, or dengue fever occur among Americans living in Haiti. While no vaccinations are required for entry into the country (unless one is coming from a yellow-fever-infected area), the State Department recommends inoculations against typhoid fever, tetanus, diphtheria, polio, hepatitis B, measles, and rabies. Children should be up to date on all recommended immunizations. Immune globulin is recommended every 4 to 6 months for prevention of hepatitis A.

As the local water supply lacks fluoride, supplementation for children is important to prevent tooth decay. A supply of sunscreen is essential to prevent skin damage from the tropical rays.

NOTES FOR TRAVELERS

Passage, Customs & Duties

Haitian law requires travelers to have a passport to enter Haiti. In practice, officials frequently waive this requirement if travelers have a certified copy of their U.S. birth certificate. Due to fraud concerns, however, airlines do not board passengers for return to the United States unless they are in possession of a valid passport. The U.S. Embassy recommends that U.S. citizens obtain passports before travel to Haiti. The Haitian government requires foreigners to pay a fee prior to departure. For additional information regarding entry, departure and customs requirements for Haiti, travelers can contact the Haitian Embassy, 2311 Massachusetts Avenue, N.W., Washington, D.C. 20008, telephone (202) 332-4090, one of the Haitian consulates in Florida, Massachusetts, New York, Illinois or Puerto Rico, or via the Internet at http://www.haiti.org/embassy/.

U.S. citizens living in or visiting Haiti are encouraged to register at the Consular Section of the U.S. Embassy in Port-au-Prince and obtain updated information on travel and security in Haiti. The Consular Section is located on Rue Oswald Durand, Port-au-Prince; telephone 011 (509) 222-7011; fax 011 (509) 222-1641. Consular Section hours are 7:30 a.m. to 2:00 p.m. Monday through Friday, except U.S. and local holidays. The U.S. Embassy is located on Harry Truman Blvd., Port-au-Prince; telephone (509) 23-0200, 223-0354, 223-0955 or 223-0269; fax (509) 23-1641. Internet: http://usembassy.state.gov/haiti.

Pets

To be admitted into Haiti, a pet must have an Authorization to Import certificate, issued by the Haitian Department of Agriculture, which states the animal's breed and point of departure for Haiti. All pets are required to have a recent veterinarian's clearance stating that they have had a current rabies vaccination and are free from disease.

Currency, Banking, and Weights and Measures

The Haitian Government permits a free-market exchange of U.S. dollars for gourdes, the Haitian monetary unit. Most prices in Haiti are quoted in Haitian dollars, where a dollar equals 5 Haitian gourdes. The metric system of weights and measures is the official standard. U.S. weights and measures are also widely used.

Disaster Preparedness

Haiti, like all Caribbean countries, can be affected by hurricanes and other storms. Hurricane season runs from approximately June 1 to November 30 each year. Extensive flooding as a result of heavy rainfall has occurred in the past. General information about natural disaster preparedness is available via the Internet from the U.S. Federal Emergency Management Agency (FEMA) at http://www.fema.gov/.

LOCAL HOLIDAYS

Jan. 1	Independence Day
Jan. 2	Ancestor's Day
Feb/Mar.	Mardi Gras*
Mar/Apr.	Good Friday*
Mar/Apr.	Easter
May 1	Labor Day
May 16	Ascension Day
May 18	Flag and University Day
May 22	Sovereignty Day
May/June	Corpus Christi*
Aug. 15	Assumption Day
Oct. 17	Anniversary of the Death of Dessalines
Nov. 1	All Saints' Day
November 18	Anniversary of the Battle of Vertieres
Dec. 5	Discovery of Haiti by Columbus
Dec. 25	Christmas Day

* variable

RECOMMENDED READING

Much of the literature about Haiti is available only in French. The following is a suggested reading list of books in English. The more recent titles can be found in bookstores. Books published before 1989 may be available only in libraries. Novels and collections of short stories are indicated by an asterisk.

Abbott, Elizabeth. *Haiti: the Duvaliers and their Legacy.* Rev. ed. New York: Simon and Schuster, 1991.

Alternative Museum Staff. *Mon Reve: A Visual Record of Haiti Since the Departure of the Duvaliers.* New York: Alternative Museum, 1989.

Anthony, Suzanne. *Haiti.* New York: Chelsea House, 1988.

Bellegarde-Smith, Patrick. *Haiti: the Breached Citadel.* Boulder, CO: Westview Press, 1989.

Courlander, Harold. *The Drum and the Hoe.* University of California Press: Berkeley, 1981.

————. *The Bordeaux Narrative.* University of New Mexico Press: Albuquerque, 1990.

Danner, Mark. *Beyond the Mountains: The Legacy of Duvalier.* New York: Pantheon Books, 1991.

Dunham, Katherine. *Dances of Haiti.* Afro-American Studies Center: Los Angeles, 1983.

Dupuy, Alex. *Haiti in the World Economy: Class, Race & Underdevelopment Since 1700.* Boulder, CO: Westview Press, 1988.

Fass, Simon M. *Political Economy in Haiti: The Drama of Survival.* New Brunswick, NJ: Transaction Pubs., 1990.

Ferguson, James. *Papa Doc, Baby Doc, Haiti and the Duvaliers.* Basil Blackwell: London, 1987.

Fick, Carolyn E. *The Making of Haiti: the Saint Domingue Revolution from Below.* Knoxville, TN: University of Tennessee Press, 1990.

Greene, Graham. *The Comedians.* Viking: New York, 1966.

Griffiths, John. *Take a Trip to Haiti.* New York: F. Watts, 1989.

Haggerty, Richard A., ed. *The Dominican Republic and Haiti.* Area Studies Handbook Series. U.S. Government Printing Office: Washington, DC, 1991.

Haiti in Pictures. Minneapolis, MN: Lerner Publications, 1987.

Hanmer, Trudy J. *Haiti.* New York: F. Watts, 1988.

Hurston, Zora Neale. *Tell My Horse: Voodoo & Life in Haiti & Jamaica.* San Bernardino, CA: Borgo Press, 1990.

Lawyers Committee on Human Rights. *Paper Laws/Steel Bayonets: Breakdown of The Rule of Law in Haiti.* New York, 1991.

Leyburn, James. *The Haitian People.* New Haven, 1971.

Lyon, Danny. *Merci Gonaives: A Photographer's Account of Haiti and the February Revolution.*

Clintondale, NY: Bleak Beauty Books, 1988.

Pataki, Eva. *Haitian Painting: Art and Kitsch*. Adams Press, Chicago, 1986.

Rodman, Selden. *The Miracle of Haitian Art*. Doubleday: New York, 1971.

Thomson, Ian. *Bonjour Blanc: A Journey Through Haiti*. Hutchinson: London, 1992.

Trouillot, Michel-Rolph. *Haiti: State Against Nation: The Origins and Legacy of Duvalierism*. Monthly Review: New York, 1990.

University of Virginia. *Callaloo, Haiti: The Literature and Culture*. Johns Hopkins University Press: Baltimore, 1992.

Weinstein, Brian and Aaron Segal. *Haiti: The Failure of Politics*. Praeger: New York, 1992.

Wilentz, Amy. *The Rainy Season: Haiti Since Duvalier*. Simon and Schuster: New York, 1989.

Tegucigalpa, Honduras

HONDURAS

Republic of Honduras

Major City:
Tegucigalpa

Other Cities:
Amapala, Comayagua, Copán, La Ceiba, Puerto Cortés, San Pedro Sula, Santa Bárbara, Santa Rosa de Copán, Tela

EDITOR'S NOTE

This chapter was adapted from the Department of State Post Report dated June 1996. Supplemental material has been added to increase coverage of minor cities, facts have been updated, and some material has been condensed. Readers are encouraged to visit the Department of State's web site at http://travel.state.gov/ for the most recent information available on travel to this country.

INTRODUCTION

HONDURAS, whose name is derived from the depth, or *hondura*, of the waters which surround its northern shores, is an underdeveloped Central American nation, struggling to improve its economic and social circumstances. It has had a history of turbulence since the coming of the Spaniards early in the 16th century—political struggles, war with its neighbors, intervention by others in its internal affairs—all major deterrents to the encouragement of progress.

Honduras is a country of rugged and varied terrain, a predominantly rural aspect, and a strong Indo-Hispanic culture. Its ancient temple city of Copán was one of the great ceremonial centers of the vast Mayan empire.

MAJOR CITY

Tegucigalpa

Tegucigalpa, capital of the Republic of Honduras, is in a mountain-ringed valley about 3,200 feet above sea level. It is a provincial and picturesque city full of contrasts between the antique and the modern. At several points, streets of stairs connect one level of the city with another. At others, the city climbs the hillsides on terraces.

The predominant architectural style is Spanish colonial. Central Tegucigalpa is built around the traditional square. Narrow streets, remaining cobblestones, blank walls pierced by heavy doors and iron-grilled windows, and reddish tile roofs all add to an impression of architectural unity. But this unity is now being broken by the construction of new, modern buildings. Traces of former days contrast sharply with the new, modern residential sections surrounding the old town.

Spaniards founded Tegucigalpa in 1579 as a silvermining town with the imposing name of Real Minas de San Miguel de Tegus Galpa. In Indian language this means hill or mountain of silver. In 1880 the capital of the republic was transferred from Comayagua to Tegucigalpa. Until 1898, Tegucigalpa and Comayaguela, two settlements divided by the Choluteca River, were separate towns. The two were united in 1898 with the provision that each should retain its own municipal council. It was not until 1938 that they, together with other neighboring communities, were united to form the Central District.

Food

Pasteurized, fresh milk, as well as cheese, butter, eggs, cooking oil, and ice cream are available locally. Occasional shortages occur of items such as milk, eggs, flour, rice, beans, and chicken. Satisfactory locally bottled beer and soft drinks are also available.

Good quality frying chickens are available. Several outlets sell good quality beef (including fillet), veal, ham, and pork. Cuts and taste often differ from US meats. Good frozen and fresh lobster tails and shrimp are available at reasonable prices. Several supermarkets carry a fluctuating supply of local and imported food items and local meats. Items imported from the US are slightly

Courtesy of David Gibson

Overview of Tegucigalpa, Honduras

more expensive due to high transportation costs and import duties.

Fresh fruits and vegetables are available year round, but supplies vary with the season. Local vegetables include tomatoes, cabbage, broccoli, cauliflower, carrots, beets, corn, eggplant, and lettuce. Avocados, oranges, bananas, limes, melons, pineapples, and other tropical fruits are available year round.

Clothing

Summer clothing is suitable for most of the year in Tegucigalpa. Bring a complete wardrobe, as local selection is limited, expensive, and of lower quality. Local tailors and seamstresses are good, but quality materials are expensive. Tegucigalpa's weather is tropical by day and cool in the early morning and

evening. During the cool season (mid-November to February) it may be chilly during the day. At this time, lightweight wools and long sleeves are worn.

Men: Bring tropical-worsted, dacron, and other lightweight suits. One or two lightweight woolen suits or slacks with sport jackets are comfortable for cooler months.

Locally manufactured shirts (some well-known US brands) compare to those made in the US and cost about the same. Many men purchase locally made "guayaberas" (loose-fitting shirts), which are frequently worn at casual gatherings. Bring a supply of shoes, as those available locally are not the same quality as those made in the US.

Women: Bring a good supply of lightweight, synthetic, cotton, and cotton-blend clothes for the dry and rainy seasons. During the cool season, you may use long-sleeved synthetic knits, lightweight wools, sweaters, light jackets, and blazers. Include street-length dresses and skirts, separates, and sports clothes in your wardrobe. Shorts are inappropriate except for the beach. Rainy weather and unpaved streets are hard on shoes. Bring sandals, sport shoes, and boots for picnics and hiking. Bring plenty of lingerie and hose or panty hose, since sizes, styles, and colors are limited, and quality is only fair. Good quality imported items are expensive here.

Children: Local prices for imported children's wear are high and selection is limited. Children will need washable synthetic or cotton clothing most of the year with sweaters and/or jackets for cool months, and umbrellas. All schools in Tegucigalpa require uniforms for which materials can be purchased locally.

Supplies And Services

Local shops are open from 9 am to noon and 2 pm to 6 pm daily and 8 am to noon on Saturdays. Several large grocery stores are open on Sundays from 10 am to 6 pm.

Tailors and seamstresses are available in Tegucigalpa. Most make only simple, inexpensive clothes. A variety of material is available in all price ranges; however, quality material is expensive and selection is fair to poor.

Dry-cleaning is adequate for most fabrics, except leather. Laundry service is available. Shoe repair is satisfactory. Beauty shops and barbershops offer adequate service, but operators are not professionally trained, and sanitary precautions are not as strict as in the US. The barbershop in the Hotel Maya is cheap, excellent and hygienic.

Religious Activities

Most faiths are represented in Tegucigalpa. English-speaking Catholic and Protestant services are available. Tegucigalpa has several Catholic and Protestant Missions representing the Seventh Day Adventists, Assembly of God, Central American Mission, Baptist, Four-Squared Gospel, Jehovah's Witnesses, Mennonites, Lutheran, Mormon, Southern Baptist, and World Gospel Mission. The American community is also served by the nondenominational Union Church and an English-language Episcopal Church.

Most Hondurans are Roman Catholic. Highlights of the religious calendar in Tegucigalpa are Christmas and Semana Santa (Holy Week). Christmas week through New Year's Eve is celebrated with much gaiety and fireworks. Holy Week is rigorously observed. Most stores and all government offices remain closed from Wednesday through Sunday. Vehicular traffic on Good Friday is minimal. Honduran Catholics celebrate February 2 and 3 as feast days of the Patron Saint of Honduras, Our Lady of Suyapa.

Education

The largest school in Tegucigalpa offering a US curriculum is the American School. The school, a private institution organized under Honduran law, is not affiliated with the US Government. An elected school board, which includes US members, administers the school. About 10% of the student body are US citizens, 80% are Hondurans, and 10% are other nationalities. Enrollment is about 1,000, including pre-kindergarten through grade 12. Through guidance and financial support of the State Department's Office of Overseas Schools, it has improved significantly, upgrading teacher's professionalism and improving facilities. A new building for the high school was completed in 1991 and a new preschool complex will be completed in the Spring of 1995. The school has a large gym and modern exercise equipment.

Most classes are conducted in English with one period of Spanish-language instruction daily. The school follows the US curriculum through primary school (grade 6). Beginning in grade 7, students may choose from two curriculums: one prepares students to enter US colleges, the other prepares students for the National University of Honduras.

The American School is located in Colonia Las Lomas del Guijarro, a residential area. Overall, children of US parents do well at the American School, scoring above average on scholastic aptitude tests (SAT), many gaining acceptance to prestigious colleges of their choice in the US after graduation.

All students in grades K to 12 wear uniforms. Boys wear uniform pants, white, short-sleeved shirts, and dark socks. Girls wear jumpers with white, short-sleeved blouses and white socks. Girls may wear uniform pants with a white, short-sleeved blouse. All shirts/blouses must have the American School patch sewn on the sleeve. Material for the jumpers and uniform pants is available at the school as are the patches; shirts/blouses may be purchased from the school or local merchants and are readily available. A navy blue sweater or windbreaker is necessary for cooler days. Most students wear tennis shoes, or black or dark brown dress shoes on occasion. Kindergarten children wear the same uniform. The school, accredited by the Southern Association of Schools and Colleges, has a parent-teacher organization. Extracurricular activities include cheerleading, band, sports, drama, and chorus.

School begins in late August and ends in June. Advance registration is necessary; the address is:

American School
Tegucigalpa
APO AA 34022
Fax (504) 32-2380

Some American children attend Academia Los Pinares. A board of missionaries administers this school, located in a highland area 1/2 hour by bus from Tegucigalpa. A US curriculum is followed from kindergarten through grade 12. The Honduran curriculum is also offered in grades 7 to 12. Bible study is a required course, emphasizing moral values. The grading system is academically more rigorous than that of the American School. Classes are in English with one period of Spanish-language instruction daily. Pinares offers a full range of sports activities, plus band and chorus.

Enrollment at the beginning of the 1994-95 school year was 625 in pre-kindergarten through grade 12. The enrollment was 15% US citizens, 5% other nationalities, and 80% Hondurans. The school year runs from September to June. Academia Los Pinares students wear dark green uniforms with green-and-white checkered shirts. Many students wear tennis shoes. Socks are white.

Address all correspondence to:

Director, Academia Los Pinares
Apartado 143C
Tegucigalpa, Honduras, CA

American children also attend the Discovery School, a small private preschool and elementary school located in Colonia Payaqui, a residential area. A US curriculum and hands-on approach are followed from Kindergarten through sixth grade. Classes are capped at 15 students. Classes are in English with a daily Spanish class. Enrollment for is about 30 students, in three multi-grade classes, and about 20 in the preschool. Parents interested in sending a child to the Discovery School should write directly to the school.

Discovery School
TGU 00015
P.O. Box 025387
Miami, FL 33102-5387

The Mayan School and the Elvel School are two other English-language schools in Tegucigalpa. Several recently opened preschools offer varied curriculums. Parents wishing to enroll their children in a preschool should visit various facilities to determine which best suits their child's needs.

Special Educational Opportunities

The University of Honduras offers limited facilities for college age students and adults. All classes are taught in Spanish. Advanced study is usually undertaken abroad. French-language lessons are taught at the Alliance Francaise under the auspices of the French embassy. The Alliance offers an excellent curriculum from beginning to advanced studies. Guitar, piano, and marimba lessons are available.

Sports

Horseback riding is popular, and you can enjoy it year round. A stable near the outskirts of town offers English riding lessons. Horses are boarded for a monthly fee, which includes feed, utilities, rent, and membership. Lessons are available

on an hourly basis after the membership fee is paid.

There are two Country Clubs which offers tennis and golf memberships. The Hotel Honduras Maya and the Alameda Hotel offer pool memberships. The Country Club and Los Delfines del Maya have competitive swim teams for young people. Bosques de Zambrano, a 40 minute drive from Tegucigalpa has indoor and outdoor pools, skeet shooting, tennis courts, picnic grounds, and restaurant services.

Tegucigalpa has three ballet schools for children and adults. Karate and judo classes are available for all ages.

Little league baseball, basketball, and soccer are played at the American School. Adults can join in pickup basketball or volleyball games.

Scuba diving, snorkeling, and fishing in the Bay Islands are fantastic. An active scuba diving club (Honduras Underwater Group) makes regular trips to various diving areas. You can also charter sailing yachts in the Bay Islands or rent small cays for overnighting.

The rugged hills around Tegucigalpa and the La Tigre cloud forest offer excellent hiking opportunities. Tegucigalpa has limited museums, zoological parks, and playgrounds.

Amateur archeologists may be interested in the Mayan ruins scattered throughout the country. All archeological relics are the property of the state, and exportation is prohibited by Honduran law and a treaty with the US.

Bring all sporting equipment and special clothing with you since selection is limited and prices are high.

Touring and Outdoor Activities

The former Presidential Palace, which has been converted into a museum is a beautiful, old building

situated above the river. Near the palace is the more modern Congress building. A stroll through its columned patio area is interesting. A drive or walk up the cobblestone streets to the old La Leona section of the city leads to La Leona Park, with its lovely view of Tegucigalpa. In this area are a few colonial style homes. Concordia Park is a small popular park that has replicas of the Copan ruins.

The National Cathedral of San Miguel was begun in 1756 and consecrated in 1782. One of the oldest pieces in the church is the stone baptismal font. As you enter the valley of Tegucigalpa, you will see Suyapa Basilica, home of the Patron Saint of Honduras, the Virgin of Suyapa, etched against hills to the east.

The Pan American Agricultural School at Zamorano is about 25 miles from Tegucigalpa over a mountainous paved road. School grounds are beautiful and well kept, and the colonial style architecture of the buildings is attractive. Nearby is San Antonio de Oriente, a picturesque mining town, home of well-known Honduran primitive painter, Juan Antonio Velasquez. It is a morning's hike from the Pan American School grounds, or you can go by four-wheel-drive vehicle.

Valle de Angeles is about a 30minute drive over a paved road that winds through hills to the quaint village where you will find an arts and crafts center. Santa Lucia, near Valle de Angeles, is a small silver mining town perched on top of one of the many hills surrounding Tegucigalpa. The age of the principal church in Santa Lucia is unknown, but a wooden plaque dated 1598 was found in the old building.

Parque Aurora, a lovely park off the north road, has a lake for rowing, a picnic area, roller skating rink, miniature golf, playground equipment, and small zoo.

Comayagua, th colonial capital of Honduras, is situated in a broad

Street scene in Honduras

valley. It is a 90 minute drive on a paved road from Tegucigalpa. Comayagua's Cathedral, built over 400 years ago, is one of the most beautiful in Central America.

Lake Yojoa, the largest lake in Honduras, is about 2½ hours from Tegucigalpa. An hour's drive from Lake Yojoa is Pulhapanzak Falls. A jeep or four-wheel-drive vehicle is recommended.

Cedeno and Choluteca are reached by a paved road, the spur that connects Tegucigalpa with the Pan American Highway on the South Coast. A dirt road leads to the bathing beach of Cedeno on the Gulf of Fonseca, southwest of Choluteca. There is excellent fishing in the many shrimp farm canals near Choluteca.

The country's cultural heritage includes the remains of a great center of pre-Columbian civilization in America, the Mayan ruins of Copan. This Mayan center rose and mysteriously declined seven centuries before Columbus set foot on Honduran soil. Since their discovery in 1893, the ruins of Copan have been explored, excavated, and studied by some of the world's leading archeologists. Copan is one of the greatest ceremonial centers of temple cities of a vast empire evolved from ancient peoples who inhabited Mexico and Central America before the birth of Christ. Visit by car or tour bus. Ranging from 10 to 40 miles off the North Coast are several picturesque islands, the largest of which are Guanaja, Roatan, and Utila. Once the haven of buccaneers and pirates, the islands are now sparsely populated by friendly descendants of English settlers who welcome all visitors. The Bay Islands offer lovely scenery, excellent snorkeling and diving, sailing, relaxed atmosphere, and good food, especially seafood. Go by boat, scheduled airlines, or chartered aircraft.

Tela, on the North Coast, has fine, sandy beaches fringed by graceful palms. Telamar, a seaside resort, offers fair accommodations. La Ceiba also on the North Coast, is accessible daily by plane.

Entertainment

Movie theaters show current and old American films with English soundtrack and Spanish subtitles. They also feature some Mexican, Italian, French, and British films. Prices are low, even for first-run movies (L10 per person or $1.10). Several new, air-conditioned, multicinema movie theaters are in the suburbs, and several comfortable movie theaters are in town.

The National School of Fine Arts has showings of local art. Classes are conducted in ceramics, painting, woodcarving, and sculpturing. The average cost per class session is L25 (US $2.80). Photography is a popular hobby. You can find considerable human interest subject matter as well as panoramic scenes. Most popular types and sizes of film are available in the commissary as is developing service for black-and-white and color films. Mail-order firms in the US can also be used for processing.

Occasionally, cultural attractions are sponsored by the US Government and other embassies. Locally produced concerts, folk festivals, and plays are also offered. Plays in English and Spanish are presented by a local dramatic group, Teatro Reforma. Mixed Company, an amateur English-speaking theater group, also presents several plays a year. Both groups welcome Hondurans and members of the international community. The National University has a theater group that presents occasional plays in Spanish. Instituto Hondureno de Cultura Interamericana (Binational Center) presents concerts, lectures, and local art shows.

Social Activities

The English-speaking Women's Club of Tegucigalpa is open to any English-speaking woman, regardless of nationality, and offers an excellent opportunity to meet Hondurans, Americans, and women from other countries. The club offers a monthly entertainment program and a variety of classes such as oil painting, international cooking, discussion groups, bridge, book club, etc.

OTHER CITIES

AMAPALA is the chief Pacific port in Honduras. It is located in the southern part of the country, on Tigre Island in the Gulf of Fonseca. Lumber and coffee are shipped to Amapala by launch from the mainland for export. Amapala is about 70 miles southwest of Tegucigalpa and has a population over 4,000.

COMAYAGUA, located about 35 miles northwest of Tegucigalpa, was the most important city of colonial Honduras. Founded in 1537, Comayagua, the conservative stronghold, rivaled Tegucigalpa, dominated by liberals, in the political struggle following Honduras' independence from Spain in 1821. The two cities alternated as capital until 1880, when Tegucigalpa became the permanent site. Comayagua today is the center of an agricultural and mining region. It has colonial landmarks, including a magnificent cathedral. The population over 40,000.

COPÁN is a village of about 2,000 people on the Honduran-Guatemalan border, 125 miles northwest of Tegucigalpa. It is near the ruined city of Copán, considered to be the center of the ancient Mayan culture. Of note among the ruins is the Hieroglyphic Stairway, dating to the year 756 and bearing the lengthiest known Mayan inscription.

LA CEIBA, located in northern Honduras on the Caribbean Sea, is about 100 miles north of Tegucigalpa. Situated at the foot of Peak Bonito, La Ceiba has beautiful beaches and is a departure point for the Bay Islands. The city is a commercial and processing center for the surrounding agricultural region; coconuts and citrus fruits are shipped from its port. La Ceiba was Honduras' main banana port until disease destroyed the surrounding plantations in the 1930s. The population in 1995 was about 89,200.

PUERTO CORTÉS lies on the Gulf of Honduras near the Guatemalan border, about 100 miles west of La Ceiba. Founded in 1525, Puerto Cortés is the principal Atlantic port, exporting mainly bananas, but also coffee, coconuts, hardwood, abaca, and minerals. The population here is approximately 42,000 (1987 est.).

SAN PEDRO SULA is the second largest city in Honduras, located 100 miles northwest of Tegucigalpa. With a metropolitan population over 280,000, San Pedro Sula is a commercial center, producing foodstuffs, clothing, beverages, tobacco products, soap, and building materials. Industry here is small and consumer-oriented. The country's only railroad links northwestern banana and sugar plantations with the principal northern ports.

SANTA BÁRBARA is a commercial and administrative center in western Honduras, 80 miles northwest of Tegucigalpa. The community of over 26,000 residents, rests in the hot lowlands close to the Ulúa River and Lake Yojoa. In the city's outlying areas, livestock and sugarcane are economic mainstays; in the core, manufacturing of clothing and furniture is important. Nearby, ruins of the abandoned city of Tencoa have been found. Santa Bárbara can be reached by a spur from the Inter-Oceanic Highway; it has an airfield.

Situated 25 miles from the Guatemala border and 115 miles west of Tegucigalpa, **SANTA ROSA DE COPÁN** is the country's westernmost major city. It was founded in the 1700s and first called Los Llanos. Today it is the commercial hub of western Honduras, with 32,000 residents. The varied economy here includes tobacco blending and cigar making, and the production of lumber, furniture, leather products, clothing, and beverages. Good transportation is assured by access to several highways in Honduras and El Salvador; Santa Rosa de Copán also has an airfield. A nearby tourist stop is the ancient Mayan city of Copán, 25 miles outside of town. Several ruins can be seen, mostly buried under tropical vegetation. Courtyards, ball courts, and stone columns are among the sites.

TELA is situated in the northwestern region on the Caribbean Sea, between Puerto Cortés and La Ceiba. It is the headquarters for a large area of banana plantations, as well as a port and commercial center. Tela has an estimated population of 71,000.

COUNTRY PROFILE

Geography and Climate

The Republic of Honduras is situated in the middle of six republics comprising the Central American Isthmus between Mexico and Panama. Roughly triangular in shape, it has a 459-mile Caribbean coastline to the north and narrows in the south to 89 miles at the Gulf of Fonseca on the Pacific Ocean. It is bounded on the west by Guatemala, the southwest by El Salvador, and the east and southeast by Nicaragua.

Honduras has an estimated land area of 43,277 square miles, slightly larger than Tennessee. Second largest of the six Central American Republics, it ranks 14th in size among all Latin American nations. However, population distribution is unequal. The northeastern part (Mosquitia, consisting of eastern Department of Colon, most of Olancho, and all of Gracias a Dios) is thinly inhabited. It comprises 44.5% of the entire national territory and only 8.6% of the population.

Honduras also has insular possessions, including the picturesque Bay Islands formed by the summit of a submerged mountain range. The Bay Islands (Roatan, Utila, Guanaja, Barbereta, Santa Elena, and Morat) form one of the country's 18 departments. Farther northeast lie the Swan Islands, previously used by the US as a weather research station and now recognized as Honduran territory. Puerto Cortes (Honduras' first container-loading facility), Tela, La Ceiba, and Puerto Castilla are major Caribbean ports. Honduras has two secondary Pacific ports: Amapala, on Tiger Island in the Gulf of Fonseca, and San Lorenzo, on the mainland.

Honduran topography is exceptionally rugged. The Central American Cordillera crosses Honduras from east to west, making it the most mountainous of the six republics. The highest mountain peaks are in the southwest. Lowlands are the northern and eastern coastal plains, a narrow southern coastal plain, and river valleys. Principal rivers are in the north and flow into the Caribbean. Government estimates list 63.6% of the land surface as mountainous and 34.4% as plains and valleys.

Geographically and commercially, the country consists of two general regions: the highlands of the interior and southern Honduras and the tropical, banana-producing North Coast. Southern coastal lowlands are grouped with the highland region because of their economic linkage with Tegucigalpa, located in southwest central Honduras.

Tegucigalpa, located in a mountain basin at about 3,200 feet, is surrounded by jutting peaks, one of which reaches over 7,000 feet. The city proper lies at the foot of and on the slopes of Mount Picacho. It is 82 miles from the Gulf of Fonseca on the Pacific coast and 230 miles from the Caribbean to the north. The Choluteca River separates Tegucigalpa and its twin city, Comayaguela. Seven small bridges connect the twin cities.

Tegucigalpa's altitude renders a moderate climate, and most days are like spring. Moderate to cool nights relieve occasional hot days. Average monthly temperatures vary from 66°F in January to 74°F in May. Extreme temperatures as low as 44°F and as high as 90°F may occur. Seasonal differences vary more in rainfall than in temperature. The rainy season usually begins in mid-May and continues through mid-November, with heavy rains ending in late October. During the rainy season, rains occur in the late afternoons and early evenings, and days are mostly sunny and clear. From mid-November to February, cooler temperatures and strong winds prevail. The hot, dry season in Tegucigalpa can be uncomfortable and lasts for about 34 months, beginning as early as mid-January. It reaches its peak in April and continues until the first rains. During this time water shortages occur, the earth becomes brown and parched, and heavy dust and smoke from brush/grassland burnings hang in the air.

Population

Honduras' population is estimated at 6.1 million (2000), about 55 persons per square mile. Population distribution is concentrated in a rough crescent beginning at the South Coast, running through Tegucigalpa and Comayagua to San Pedro Sula, and then eastward along the North Coast through Tela to La Ceiba. Tegucigalpa, including Comayaguela (Central District), has a population of more than 800,000. Beginning in 1950, migration to the city from rural areas caused the population to rise sharply. Other population centers are San Pedro Sula, the country's industrial center; Puerto Cortes and La Ceiba on the North Coast; and Choluteca in the south.

The family is the basic social unit. Family ties extend to cousins, aunts, uncles, in-laws, and even godparents (known as "compadres"). Many families are large and often include representation from several social strata and different political affiliations. Although Roman Catholicism predominates, freedom of religion exists, and many other sects and denominations are represented.

Most Honduran Indians have been assimilated into the Hispano-American culture. Today, more than 90% of the population is comprised of mestizos, i.e., a mixture of white and Indian. A Caribbean black population is centered on the North Coast and the Bay Islands where most were born. Spanish is the official language, but North Coast blacks and most inhabitants of the Bay Islands speak an English dialect. A large colony of Catholic Palestinian emigrants is active in commerce and trade.

About 8,500 US citizens, many of whom are missionaries, reside in Honduras. Others are employed by

Mayan ruins in Copan, Honduras

Courtesy of Molly Flint

US-based firms and the US Government. A small international colony includes British, Chinese, German, Italian, French, Dutch, Finnish, Greek, and Spanish citizens. Although some Hondurans possess great wealth, a gap exists between upper class and middle-class groups and the poorer rural and urban populations. The middle class consists principally of professionals, merchants, entrepreneurs, and government employees.

Honduras is largely agricultural. More than 29% of the population depends on agriculture for its livelihood. Basic dietary staples are corn (usually prepared as tortillas), red beans, rice, fish, and eggs. Meat and fresh vegetables are added to the diet as one progresses up the economic scale.

Public Institutions

The 1982 constitution provides for a strong executive, a unicameral National Congress, and a judiciary appointed by the National Congress. The president is directly elected to a 4-year term by popular vote. The congress also serves a 4-year term; congressional seats are assigned the parties' candidates in proportion to the number of votes each party receives in the various departments. The judiciary includes

a Supreme Court of Justice, courts of appeal, and several courts of original jurisdiction--such as labor, tax, and criminal courts. For administrative purposes, Honduras is divided into 18 departments, with municipal officials selected for 4-year terms.

Reinforced by the media and several political watchdog organizations, human rights and civil liberties are reasonably well protected. There are no known political prisoners in Honduras, and the privately owned media frequently exercises its right to criticize without fear of reprisals.

Honduras held its sixth consecutive democratic elections in November 2001, to elect a new president, unicameral Congress, and mayors. For only the second time, voters were able to cast separate ballots for each office, and for the first time, denied the president-elect party's absolute majority in the Congress. The incidence of cross-voting between presidential and congressional candidates was marked.

The two major parties--the Liberal Party and the National Party--run active campaigns throughout the country. Their ideologies are mostly centrist, with diverse factions in each centered on personalities. The three smaller registered parties--

the Christian Democratic Party, the Innovation and National Unity Party, and the Democratic Unification Party--have increased their political muscle in the National Congress by doubling their representation. Despite significant progress in training and installing more skillful advisers at the top of each party ladder, electoral politics in Honduras remain traditionalist and paternalistic.

Under the 1982 Constitution, the Armed Forces are entrusted with ensuring both internal and external security. A branch, the Public Security Force (FUSEP), assumes police functions. The Armed Forces also play an important role in national political and economic affairs. They have supported the democratic process.

For administrative purposes, Honduras is divided into 18 departments. The chief official of each department is a governor appointed by the President.

Arts, Science, and Education

Tegucigalpa has six institutions of higher education. The National Autonomous University of Honduras (UNAH), founded in 1847, has its principal campus in Tegucigalpa with branches in San Pedro Sula and La Ceiba. UNAH and the local professional associations, such as the College of Engineers, share responsibility of issuing professional licenses. The public Universidad Pedagogica Nacional and the private Jose Cecilio del Valle University, a Catholic University, are also located in Tegucigalpa. Through extension programs, non-degree students can elect courses in painting, drama, archeology, and sculpture at any of these institutions. The newest private university in Tegucigalpa is the 1987 founded Central American Technical University (UNITEC). UNITEC offers 2-year programs, as well as BS and MS degrees in fields such as accounting, computer science, and human relations. The private

University of San Pedro Sula was founded in 1972 and offers degrees in business administration, economics, architecture, and anthropology.

In 1982 a scientific center of investigation was established at UNAH. The University has organized a marine biology center at La Ceiba. Despite these recent efforts, Hondurans pursue little scientific investigation and research.

The National School of Fine Arts and the National School of Music train qualified students. The Ministry of Culture and Tourism directs these institutions and sponsors the Cuadro Folklorico of Honduras and a Garifuna (a Caribbean coast ethnic group) song-and-dance group. The Institute of History and Anthropology, a part of the Ministry of Culture and Tourism, maintains a small museum in one of Tegucigalpa's historic houses and offers exhibits on topics of natural history, Honduran political history, and archeology. A study center at the museum conducts archeological studies and preserves Mayan artifacts. A second museum devoted to Honduran history can be found in downtown Tegucigalpa. A museum of North coast history and anthropology recently opened in San Pedro Sula. An excellent museum is located at the famous Copan ruins.

Aside from occasional visiting cultural presentations and the opportunity to attend courses at educational institutions, cultural opportunities are limited and do not compare with those available in larger regional cities in the US.

Commerce and Industry

Agriculture is the principal industry in Honduras. Although much farming is done at a low level of technology for basic staples such as corn and beans, commercial farming for export has become increasingly important in recent years. The tropical location combined with the mountainous terrain creates a variety of micro-climates suitable for a wide range of crops. Bananas, coffee, and sugar are the most important export crops; coffee alone accounts for some 30% of total exports. Nontraditional crops such as cantaloupes, watermelons, and vegetables such as cucumbers and squash are produced for the winter market in the US on an increasingly larger scale. Many other fruits, nuts, and vegetables are also grown but have not yet become significant exports.

Despite agriculture's importance, the Honduran countryside often seems empty when viewed from the roadside. This is due to both extensive forests and extensive cattle raising areas. Although cattle ranching remains important throughout Honduras, beef production has declined recently. The same may be said for the forestry industry. Although Honduras still has abundant forest reserves, primarily pine but with extensive tropical hardwood forests in some parts, poor government policies and inadequate reforestation have reduced commercial exploitation. Much of the population still uses wood as a primary fuel. This, along with clearing land for cattle and other food production, has resulted in deforestation in southern and central areas particularly.

The fishing industry is concentrated on the North Coast and in the Bay Islands. The large fishing fleet takes lobster, shrimp, and, increasingly, fin fish for both local and export markets. Farm-grown shrimp concentrated along the Gulf of Fonseca in the south form the base of a dynamic industry, which began in earnest in the early 1980s. As over-fishing in the north causes catches to decline, aquaculture in the south increases in importance. Recently disease has hurt production in the southern shrimp farms.

Honduras historically was a mining country, producing gold, silver, lead, and zinc. However, poor policies and low mineral prices have reduced mining's importance. El Mochito, the only large mine, still produces zinc and lead. Several smaller mines are active, and individuals do placer mining for gold on rivers in the east. No petroleum production exists, but onshore exploration activities were initiated in 1991.

Manufacturing consists primarily of consumer goods for local markets. The notable exception is, the booming apparel industry that generates considerable employment, primarily on the north coast. Many local apparel companies do assembly operations for well-known US brands and companies. In 1990, the first privately operated industrial park was inaugurated and others are expected soon. Occupants of these parks and free zones include US and Asian companies producing apparel for the US market.

Although not traditionally an important tourism destination, the industry shows signs of becoming more dynamic. Reef diving off the Bay Islands and well-preserved Mayan ruins are current attractions. Accommodations on the islands have improved and new development projects are in planning stages. Two American carriers (Continental and American), as well as several Central American airlines, serve Honduras.

Principal exports are bananas, coffee, sugar, shrimp, and apparel. Other exports include tobacco products, melons, winter vegetables, wood products, and minerals. Principal imports are petroleum products, fertilizers and pesticides, plastic resins, and paper products. A wide variety of machinery, vehicles, and consumer goods also reaches Honduran markets. The US buys about 55% of Honduran exports and provides 50% of its imports.

Transportation

Local

Individually operated buses and microbuses ("busitos") provide service within Tegucigalpa, San Pedro Sula, and nearby cities such as Choluteca and Danli. Bus fare is 75 centavos ($.08). No transfers are given, and often you must take several buses to a given destination. Taxi service is adequate in downtown areas of Tegucigalpa, but some drivers pick up as many passengers as possible along the way. Taxis can be hard to find in most residential areas and often you must walk to a main street. Major hotels and the airport in Tegucigalpa and San Perdo Sula have a fleet of cabs that charge two or three times normal rates. Taxis are not metered, so negotiate the fare first. Rental cars are available and taxis can be hired on a daily or hourly basis.

Regional

Rail service in Honduras is confined to the banana zone along the Caribbean coast and is not reliable.

Honduras has three international airports, located in Tegucigalpa, the capital city, San Pedro Sula, the commercial center and the coastal city of La Ceiba. Passenger and air freight services are reliable and efficient.

Air service from Tegucigalpa to Miami is provided by American Airlines and Taca Airlines. In addition, Taca provides service to New Orleans and Houston as well as to Guatemala City, San Salvador, Managua, San Jose, San Andres, and Panama. Continental Airlines provides air service from Tegucigalpa to Houston. Lacsa, a Costa Rican airline, provides air service via San Pedro Sula to Cancun, San Jose, Panama, Barranquilla, New Orleans, Los Angeles, and New York. Since delays can occur in receiving your baggage when coming from the US, include a change of clothing and toiletries in your carry on bags.

Islena, a domestic air carrier, connect Tegucigalpa with the North Coast and the Bay Islands. Charter service and aircraft rentals (small single and twin-engine equipment) are available from private flying services operating out of Tegucigalpa, San Pedro Sula, and La Ceiba. Small jets land in Teg-

ucigalpa, San Pedro Sula, and La Ceiba.

Of Honduras' 22,724 miles of roads, about 4,053 miles are paved. Potholes are constant hazards, particularly during the rainy season. Night driving is discouraged because of such hazards as poor road conditions, animals on the road, pedestrians, unlit vehicles, and heavy commercial traffic. It takes 4 hours to drive from Tegucigalpa to San Pedro Sula.

When political and security conditions permit, you can drive to neighboring Central American capitals.

Bus service is available from Honduras to principal cities of Central America. However, buses are often overcrowded and rarely meet US safety and comfort standards. There is, however, a comfortable and very reasonably priced express bus service between Tegucigalpa and San Pedro Sula.

Communications

Telephone and Telegraph

Telephone service is adequate, but obtaining a telephone in a new housing area is difficult.

Telecommunications of Honduras (HONDUTEL) provides domestic and international telephone service. The monthly rate for residential telephone service is L20 (US $2.25). Additional calls and/or increased calling time increase your phone bill. Direct-dial, long-distance calling within Honduras and to the US and many other countries is available. Costs are based on destination, and rates are available through operator assistance. Night rates are charged from 10 pm to 7 am daily. Direct-dial calls placed from the continental US to Honduras are considerably cheaper. AT&T credit card holders may use the less costly "USA Direct" service. Sprint 121 service is also available. Worldwide telephone service offers good connections.

Telegraph service, also through HONDUTEL, is available to all parts of the world at a rate of L7 ($0.8) per word, including name and address. An urgent telegram costs L1.40 ($.18) a word

Radio and TV

Radio reception is satisfactory. US-style music is featured on several stations, but news is exclusively in Spanish. A good shortwave radio is necessary to receive American stations and international broadcasts including the Voice of America (VOA).

Five local TV stations can be seen in Tegucigalpa, all with Spanish-language programming. Local viewing will improve your Spanish. Some local companies offer cable service with a wide range of stations, including major networks, CNN and entertainment-oriented stations (HBO Ole, CINEMAX, etc.).

Newspapers, Magazines, and Technical Journals

Six Spanish-language dailies are published in Tegucigalpa and San Pedro Sula. One weekly English-language newspaper is published in Honduras. Major sources of English-language news are the Latin American air express editions of the Miami Herald, the New York Times, the Wall Street Journal, the Washington Post, and USA Today. They normally arrive the day of, or day after, publication.

Overseas editions of *Time* and *Newsweek* are available at several newsstands at lesser cost. Several bookstores in Tegucigalpa carry limited selections of paperbacks, US magazines, and children's books. The Binational Center library carries a good selection of US newspapers, magazines, and some technical journals.

Health and Medicine

Medical Facilities

If you require medication for long-term conditions, bring an adequate supply and/or make arrangements with your physician and pharmacist to ensure a continued supply. Drugs may be obtained locally but are sporadically available. In addition, finding the exact item desired can be difficult.

Many local physicians have had part or all of their medical education in the US or Europe and enjoy the confidence of the community. Diagnostic facilities, such as radiology units and laboratories, provide most basic services. Three private hospitals are utilized frequently and two have emergency services. Hospitalization is usually limited to short stays, as comfort and nursing care are only fair and services limited.

Ophthalmology and optometry services are good. A new ophthalmology clinic has up-to-date outpatient care services and 24hour emergency services. Lenses, frames, glasses, and accessories are imported but are cheaper than in the US.

Routine dental care is quite good. Orthodontia is excellent and inexpensive. Many types of medical specialists are available and often are good.

Community Health

Honduras provides very little environmental sanitation or community health controls. Tap-water is considered contaminated and must be purified by the 3 minute boil-and-filter method before using for drinking, making ice cubes, brushing teeth, or washing fresh produce. All raw food products such as fruits, vegetables, and meats should be considered contaminated, and must be treated or properly cooked. Most endemic health hazards, including intestinal parasites and bacterial infections such as typhoid and infectious hepatitis, are directly related to water and food contamination. Pasteurized milk and other dairy products are available.

During the latter part of the dry season (February-April) water shortages occur. Many homes have water storage tanks (cisterns) with electric pumps in readiness for

shortages. During this same period, burning empty fields within the city results in an inordinate amount of smoke in the air. Upper respiratory infections and lung ailments, such as allergies and asthma, may be exacerbated during this period of dry, dusty, warm weather with smoke. If you are subject to any of these illnesses, bring a nebulizer, vaporizer and/or air purifier.

Rabies is present in Honduras but does not constitute a serious health problem. Mosquitoes and other flying insects are present in Tegucigalpa and can be somewhat controlled by repellents, sprays, and good screening. Malaria is exists outside Tegucigalpa, and malarial suppressants are recommended when overnighting in areas with elevation lower than Tegucigalpa. Crawling insects can be problems, and controlling them in homes requires constant care. To keep bugs out of food, use airtight containers.

NOTES FOR TRAVELERS

Passage, Customs & Duties

The best air travel to Tegucigalpa is via Miami on American Airlines (daily, nonstop flights are available). Luggage often does not arrive on the same flight as the traveler, therefore, use your carry on bag effectively (change of clothing, special medicines, etc.).

A valid U.S. passport is required to enter and depart Honduras. A visa is not required, but tourists must provide proof of return or onward travel. Visitors are given a permit to remain in Honduras for 30 days. Honduran immigration may grant up to two thirty-day extensions for a total of 90 days. Thereafter, tourists must leave the country prior to reentering. On departure, visitors are required to pay an exit fee, either in dollars or in local currency, at the airline counter.

Honduran customs authorities may enforce strict regulations concern-

ing temporary importation into or export from Honduras of items such as firearms, antiquities, medications, and business equipment. For example, Honduran law prohibits the export of antiques and artifacts from pre-colonial civilizations. To protect the country's biodiversity, it is illegal to export certain birds, feathers and other flora and fauna.

U.S. citizens who intend to stay in Honduras for an extended period of time and who bring vehicles or household goods into the country should consult Honduran customs officials prior to shipment.

For specific information regarding customs requirements, contact the Embassy of Honduras in Washington or one of Honduras's consulates in the United States.

Americans living in or visiting Honduras are encouraged to register at the consular section of the U.S. Embassy in Tegucigalpa and to obtain updated information on travel and security within Honduras. Travelers can register in person or fill out the form available on the Embassy website and fax it to the Embassy. Please include a copy of the data page of your passport and emergency contact information.

The U.S. Embassy and Consulate are located at: Avenida La Paz in Tegucigalpa, Honduras; Fax: 011-504-238-4357; Web site: http://www.usmission.hn; Telephone: 011-504-236-9320 or 011-504-238-5114. For information on services for U.S. citizens, ask for ext. 4400.

The Consular Agency in San Pedro Sula is located at: Banco Atlantida Building - 8th Floor, San Pedro Sula, Honduras, Telephone: 011-504-558-1580.

The Consular Agent at this office is available during limited hours to accept U.S. passport applications for adjudication at the Embassy in Tegucigalpa, perform notarial services and assist U.S. citizens with emergencies. Please call for office hours. The Consular Agent does not provide visa information or services.

Pets

The Government of Honduras' Ministry of Natural Resources has established import restrictions for pets. Before arrival, you must request an import permit and obtain a veterinarian certificate, which authorizes a 40 day in-house quarantine. Bring vaccination certificates for distemper, hepatitis, leptospirosis, and parvovirus. You must also bring, upon arrival in country, a health certificate not more than 14 days old and a rabies vaccination certificate that is at least 6 months, but not more than 1 year old. Local veterinarian services are fair to good.

Currency, Banking, and Weights and Measures

The official monetary unit is the lempira, named after a heroic Indian chief who fought against the Spanish conquistadors. It is usually written as L1 or 1 Lps.

Occasionally, the shopper will hear Hondurans use "peso". This monetary unit existed before the lempira was adopted and is currently equivalent to the lempira.

Lempiras are divided into 100 centavos. Bills the same size as US bills are issued in denominations of 1, 2, 5, 10, 20, 50, and 100 lempiras. Coins are issued in 1, 2, 5, 10, 20, and 50 centavos.

Currently, the official rate of exchange is L16.36=US$1. The Central Bank of Honduras regulates both imports and foreign exchange. The value of the lempira against the dollar (exchange rate) is subject to periodic adjustment according to supply of and demand for dollars and other political economic factors.

The official system of weights and measures is the metric system, but the US system is, used most in markets, shops, and gasoline stations. The old Spanish system (e.g., vara vs. meter) is used in legal affairs. Most mechanics and carpenters are also familiar with US weights and measures.

Disaster Preparedness

Honduras is prone to flooding and landslides from heavy rains, especially during the rainy season which generally occurs from June to December. Hurricane Mitch caused extensive damage and loss of life in October 1998. General information about natural disaster preparedness is available via the Internet from the U.S. Federal Emergency Management Agency (FEMA) at http://www.fema.gov/.

LOCAL HOLIDAYS

Jan.1 . . . . New Year's Day
Jan. 15 . . . . Martin Luther King's Day
Mar/Apr. . . . . Holy Thursday*
Mar/Apr. . . . . Good Friday*
Mar/Apr. . . . . Holy Saturday*
Mar/Apr. . . . . Easter*
Apr. 14 . . . . Day of the Americas
May 1 . . . . Honduran Labor Day
May 1 . . . . Labor Day
Sept. 15 . . . . Independence Day of Central America
Oct. 3 . . . . Birthday of General Francisco Morazan
Oct. 12 . . . . Discovery of America
Oct. 21 . . . . Honduran Armed Forces Day
Dec. 25 . . . . Christmas Day
*variable

RECOMMENDED READING

These titles are provided as a general indication of the material published on this country. The Department of State does not endorse unofficial publications.

Acker, Alison. *Honduras: The making of a Banana Republic.* South End Press: Boston, 1988.

American University. Foreign Area Studies. *Area Handbook for Honduras.* U.S. Government Printing Office: Washington, D.C., 1984.

Anderson, Thomas P. *Politics in Central America: Guatemala, El Salvador, Honduras and Nicaragua.* Praeger: New York, 1982.

————. *The War of the Dispossessed.* University of Nebraska: Lincoln, 1981.

Bair, Frank E., ed. *Countries of the World and Their Leaders Yearbook 1993.* Detroit, MI: Gale Research, 1993.

Bergsten, Horst, and Moran. *American Multinationals and Interests.* The Brookings Institution: 1978.

Chamberlain, R.S. *The Conquest and Colonization of Honduras.* Francisco Morazan: 1950.

Charnay, Desire. *The Ancient Cities of the New World.* AMS Press, Inc.: 1973

Coe, Michael. *The Maya.* Praeger Publishers: New York, 1973.

Durham, William H. *Scarcity and Survival in Central America: Ecological Origins of the Soccer War.* Stanford University Press: 1979.

Goetz and Morley. *The Sacred Book of the Ancient Quiche Maya.* University of Oklahoma Press: 1978.

Henderson, John S. *The World of the Ancient Maya.* Cornell University Press: Ithaca, 1981.

Houlson, Jane H. *Blue Blaze: Dangers & Delight in the Strange Islands of Honduras.* Birmingham, AL: Southern University Press, 1987.

Huston, R.G. *Journey in Honduras & Jottings by the Way.* Conway, NH: La Tienda, 1988.

Karnes, Thomas L. *The Failure of Union: Central America 1824-1975.* Arizona State University: Tempe, 1976.

Kepner and Soothill. *The Banana Empire.* Russell & Russell: 1963.

Lerner Publications, Department of Geography Staff. *Honduras in Pictures.* Minneapolis, MN: Lerner Publications, 1987.

MacCameron, Robert. *Bananas, Labor, and Politics in Honduras (1954-1963)*. Maxwell School: Syracuse University Press: 1983.

MacLeod, Murdo J. *Spanish Central America: A Socioeconomic History, 1520-1720*. University of California Press: 1973.

Meyer, Harvey. *Historical Dictionary of Honduras*. The Scarecrow Inc.: 1976.

McCann, Thomas. *An American Company: The Tragedy of United Fruit*. Crown: New York, 1976.

Morris, James A. *Honduras: Caudillo Politics and Military Rulers*. Boulder: Westview, 1984.

O'Henry. *Cabbages and Kings*. Doubleday & Co., Inc.: 1953.

Panet, J.P., and Leah Hart. *Honduras & the Bay Islands*. Champlain, NY: Passport Press, 1990.

Parker, Franklin D. *Travels in Central America 1821-1840*. University of Florida Press: 1970.

Peckenham, Nancy and Street, Annie. *Honduras: Portrait of a Captive Nation*. Praeger Publishers: New York, 1985.

Rosenberg, Mark B. and Shepherd, Philip L. *Honduras Confronts Its Future*. Lynne Rienner Publishers, Inc.: Boulder, 1986.

Soltera, Maria. *A Lady's Ride Across Spanish Honduras*. University of Florida Press: 1964.

Squier, E.G. *Honduras*. Trubner & Co.: 1970.

Stephens, John L. *Incidents of Travel in Central America*. Chiapas and Yucatan. In two volumes. Dover Publications, Inc.: 1969.

Stockes, William S. *Honduras*. Greenwood Press: 1973.

Stone, Doris. *Pre-Columbian Man Finds Central America*. Peabody Museum Press: 1976.

Thompson, J. Eric. *The Rise and Fall of Maya Civilization*. University of Oklahoma Press: 1977.

Williams, Mary. *Anglo-American Isthmian Diplomacy 1815-1915*. Russell & Russell, Inc.: 1965.

Wilson, Charles Morrow. *Empire in Green and Gold*. Greenwood Press: 1968. Fiction and Travelogs

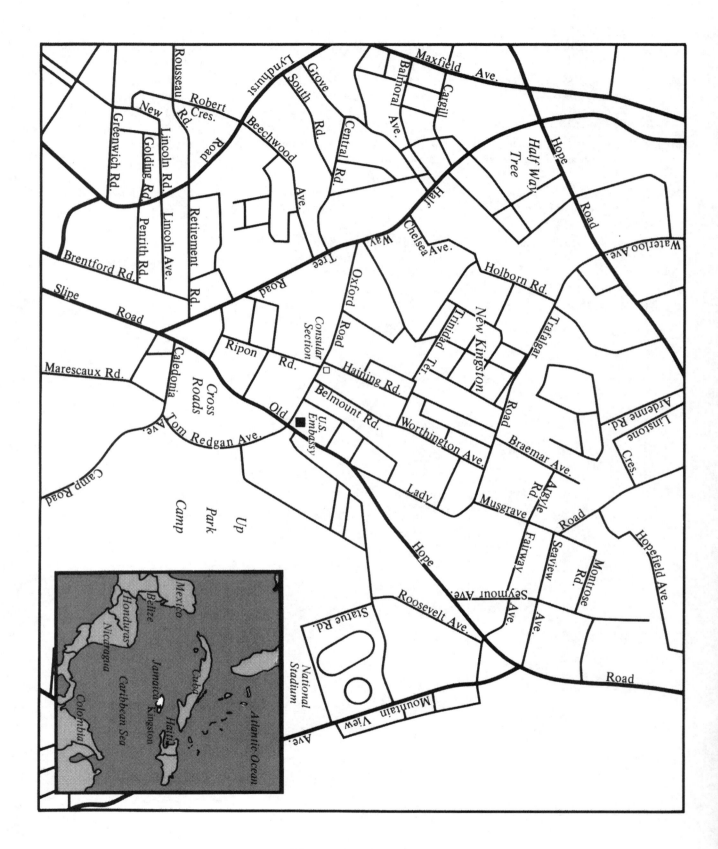

Kingston, Jamaica

JAMAICA

Major Cities:
Kingston, Mandeville, Montego Bay, Port Antonio

Other Cities:
Bath, Black River, Falmouth, Morant Bay, Negril, Ocho Rios, Savanna-La-Mar, Spanish Town

EDITOR'S NOTE

This chapter was adapted from the Department of State Post Report 2000 for Jamaica. Supplemental material has been added to increase coverage of minor cities, facts have been updated, and some material has been condensed. Readers are encouraged to visit the Department of State's web site at http://travel.state.gov/ for the most recent information available on travel to this country.

INTRODUCTION

Travelers have long regarded Jamaica as one of the most alluring of the Caribbean islands. Its beaches, mountains, and carnal red sunsets regularly appear in the world's tourist brochures, and, unlike other nearby islands, it democratically caters to all comers: You can choose a private villa with your own private beach; laugh your vacation away at a party-hearty resort; or throw yourself into the thick of the island's life.

Jamaica has a vivid and painful history, marred since European settlement by an undercurrent of violence and tyranny. Christopher Columbus first landed on the island in 1494, when there were perhaps 100,000 peaceful Arawak Amerindians who had settled Jamaica around 700 AD. Spanish settlers arrived from 1510, raising cattle and pigs, and introducing two things that would profoundly shape the island's future: sugar and slaves. By the end of the 16th century the Arawak population had been entirely wiped out.

In 1654 an ill-equipped and badly organized English contingent sailed to the Caribbean. After failing to take Hispaniola (present day Haiti and the Dominican Republic), the "wicked army of common cheats, thieves and lewd persons" turned to weakly defended Jamaica. Despite the ongoing efforts of Spanish loyalists and guerilla-style campaigns of freed Spanish slaves (cimarrones, "wild ones"-or Maroons), England took control of the island.

Investment and further settlement hastened as profits began to accrue from cocoa, coffee, and sugarcane production. Slave rebellions did not make life any easier for the English as escaped slaves joined with descendants of the Maroons, engaging in extended ambush-style campaigns, and eventually forcing the English to grant them autonomy in 1739. New slaves kept arriving, however, most of them put to work on sugar plantations. The Jamaican parliament finally abolished slavery on August 1, 1834.

Adult suffrage for all Jamaicans was introduced in 1944, and virtual autonomy from Britain was granted in 1947.

Post-independence politics have been dominated by the legacy of two cousins: Alexander Bustamante, who formed the first trade union in the Caribbean just before WWII and later formed the Jamaican Labor Party (JLP), and Norman Manley, whose People's National Party (PNP) was the first political party on the island when it was convened in 1938. Manley's son Michael led the PNP towards democratic socialism in the mid-1970s.

Jamaicans may have a quick wit and a ready smile, but this is not the happy-go-lucky island of Bacardi ads. Rastafarianism may mean easy skankin' to some, but its confused expression of love, hope, anger, and social discontent encapsulates modern Jamaica-a country that is struggling to escape dependency and debt.

MAJOR CITY

Kingston

The destruction of Port Royal by an earthquake in 1692 led to the settlement of Kingston to the north across the harbor. So rapid was growth that by 1703 it was declared by law the chief seat of trade and head port on the island. In 1872, it became the island's capital. After 1911, internal migration began to focus on Kingston, which led to the continuing trend toward movement from the countryside to principal urban areas. Kingston is now the largest English-speaking city in the Americas south of Miami.

Kingston is spread along the low coastal area surrounded by picturesque mountains. It is a bustling, sprawling city of striking contrasts. Typical of large cities, Kingston has areas of modern homes set in lovely gardens as well as sections of slums. The government is attempting to replace the "tin shanties" of the slums with low-cost housing developments.

The better suburban residential areas are close to several fairly modern shopping areas, which include supermarkets, drug stores, dry cleaners, small specialty shops, movie theaters, and boutiques.

The modern-day Port Royal, beyond the airport and across the harbor from Kingston, is considered one of the more valuable archeological sites in the Western Hemisphere. It was known as one of the richest and most wicked cities in the world before the 1692 earthquake, which plunged much of this buccaneer capital into the sea. Several old buildings are still standing, and there is an excellent museum. Restoration and an underwater archeological project are under way.

Kingston itself has several interesting old houses as well as galleries, museums, and other places to visit. The city features panoramic views of the mountains or the sea from nearly any point and offers many opportunities for an enjoyable tour.

Utilities

Electric service in Kingston is fair, with sporadic power outages. AC current is 110v, 50 cycles (the U.S. standard is 110v, 60 cycles). Many U.S.-made appliances function satisfactorily on 50-cycle current, but electric clocks, tape recorders, and some other equipment may not. Frequent voltage fluctuations sometimes damage electrical equipment.

Food

Supermarkets and small specialty shops in Kingston have a wide variety of meats, fruits, vegetables, and canned goods. The better quality shops and markets inspect their meat, but no government inspection is required. Prices are somewhat lower than those in the U.S. for all cuts of standard quality meats. Some American-type cuts of beef and pork are available. Fresh and frozen fish, lobster, and shrimp are available seasonally.

Vegetables range from tropical to standard fare and are available year round. Choices include white Irish potatoes (no baking), sweet potatoes, yams, beets, green beans, leaf lettuce, eggplant, green peppers, chilis, avocados, onions, scallions, celery, carrots, cucumbers, corn, tomatoes, varieties of pumpkin (squash), and several local varieties of vegetables. Quality is often below U.S. standards, and prices are moderately high, especially for potatoes and onions.

Fruits are also seasonal, with oranges, tangerines, grapefruit, limes, papaya, watermelon, mango, guava, pineapple, bananas, plantains, and other good local fruits available. Prices range from reasonable to high, although quality is good. All fruits and vegetables should be washed well before eating.

Clothing

Clothing suitable for men and women in southern Florida, southern California, and Hawaii is appropriate for Kingston. Some necessary items for men, women, and children are expensive but can be found here. A limited selection of lightweight fabrics is available. A few hard-to-find dressmakers can make dresses. Ready-made clothing is sold, and prices are often high. Careful shopping can produce good results.

Bring a good supply of shoes, especially for women and children. These are hard to find in the right size, and quality is below U.S. standards. Imported shoes are available but are expensive. For possible trips to cooler climates or the U.S., include some warm clothing. Also bring blue jeans, sports clothes, slacks, and a pullover if you like mountain holidays.

American-style sportswear is worn here. Long patio dresses are worn, but short sundresses are popular for informal evening wear.

Drip-dry fabrics are ideal but are expensive here. Due to the climate and need for frequent laundering, elastic deteriorates rapidly.

For the infrequent cool evenings, sweaters or light evening wraps, depending on the function attended, will suffice. Men need only a lightweight tropical suit, even for the coolest Kingston weather.

Children wear typical play clothing, particularly shorts and T-shirts, tennis shoes, and sandals.

Supplies and Services

Bring your favorite cosmetics and toiletries, as well as prescription medications.

The quality of dry cleaning is fair. Barber shops are generally adequate and less expensive than those in the U.S. Beauty shops are nearly up to U.S. standards and charge U.S. prices.

Domestic Help

"Helper," not "maid," is the term used by Jamaicans and foreigners alike for domestic help on the island. Most Jamaican helpers are female. Most types of household help are available, but reliable,

Business district of Kingston, Jamaica

well-trained workers, especially cooks and gardeners, may be difficult to find.

The Jamaican legal minimum wage is low, and most U.S. travelers pay more generous salaries. The standard pay for a dayworker, for instance, ranges from J$200 to J$300 a day, with average weekly salaries (40-hour maximum workweek) of J$1,000 to J$1,500.

Various arrangements are made for helpers food, bus fare, and lodging. Helpers daily hours are not rigidly set, and various schedules can be arranged to suit your family needs. Gardeners are generally competent, but are hard on American lawnmowers and tools.

If uniforms are desired, employers must furnish them. Once a year each helper receives 2 weeks' vacation with pay. In some cases, a helper is given quarters and lives in.

Helpers and employers must make modest weekly payments to the National Insurance Scheme, the Jamaican social security system. Payments for hospitalization or unemployment are not required, though often made by the employer. If a helper who has been employed at least 4 weeks is discharged without cause, 2 weeks severance pay is required.

Although local custom is not strongly established on this point, the employer should pay the costs of some medical services for a helper in case of sickness or injury. Public hospitals provide a wide range of free services, although receiving them can be time-consuming.

Religious Activities

Most major faiths are found in Jamaica. A partial list of denominations in Kingston includes Anglican, Baptist, Friends (Quaker), Jewish, Methodist, Mormon (Latter-day Saints), Presbyterian/Congrega-

tional, Roman Catholic, and Seventh-day Adventist. All services are in English.

Education

In the Jamaican school system, students take two important examinations, the Common Entrance and the Caribbean Examination Council (CXC). In 6th grade, at the end of January, every Jamaican student takes the Common Entrance Exam to enter high school. Doing well means acceptance in one of the nation's better high schools; doing poorly means the child cannot attend high school except as a private placement. In 1996, more than 55,000 Jamaican students sat the exam to earn one of fewer than 20,000 places. During the latter terms of 5th grade and the first term of 6th grade, students attend extra classes at the schools to prepare for the Common Entrance Exam. In its favor, the exam tests student abilities in math mechanics, adding, multiplication, etc., math reasoning and problem solving, spelling, English grammar, parts of speech, and reading comprehension. Students learn using rote memorization methods; yet they leave the Jamaican schools with a thorough grounding in the basics of math and English.

At senior level, grades 7-11, the Jamaican curriculum prepares students for the Caribbean Examination Council Exam. If students pass this exam, they go on to "A" level courses in 12th and 13th grades, and after that, to university. No Jamaican school will admit a student to the 12th grade unless the student passes the CXC.

The Jamaican high school curriculum treats science and math courses differently from the U.S. A Jamaican student studies a science course such as chemistry, biology, physics, etc., throughout 3 years and earns course credits only at the end of the third year. The Jamaican math curriculum incorporates general math, algebra, geometry, etc., into one mathematics course, whereas, under a U.S. curriculum, these are individual courses taught in separate years. In both math and science, it is difficult for a student to carry a useful transcript crediting the student with having completed algebra, geometry, the sciences, etc., to the U.S. or another school. Finally, as the high school begins at 7th grade, foreign language instruction also starts at that grade level.

Under the Jamaican education system, a person may teach in a classroom with 3 years' university certification. The student to teacher ratio is higher in Jamaican schools than in U.S. schools. Values and morals, such as integrity, responsibility, self-control, and self-reliance, are part of the Jamaican school philosophy. The students address their teachers as "Sir" or "Miss." Schools in Jamaica may not have the modern and well-equipped facilities of American schools, for example, full-scale libraries, computer and scientific laboratories, physical education gymnasiums, and sports field; nevertheless, facilities are more than adequate and children receive an education equal to U.S. standards.

In Jamaica, children enter kindergarten at age 4; thus for Americans attending Jamaican schools, the age and grade do not correspond with the U.S. system and American children may frequently be a year older than classmates. The Jamaican schools tend to place incoming children based on age, so parents should work with the school in placing their child. Some students do very well, in effect, "skipping a grade," but parents must consider whether the U.S. school system will readmit the child at the advanced grade or return the child back to a grade more suitable for the child's age, maturity, and intellectual and social development.

American International School of Kingston: AISK was founded in 1994 to meet the growing demands for a school that would offer quality education that more closely follows the U.S. curriculum and style of education. It is applying for accreditation from the Southern States Association. Class size is small (no more than 15 students per class), allowing for more individualized attention.

The school year runs from early September through to late June or very early July and is divided into three terms, the Christmas, Easter, and summer terms. The Jamaican education system separates into preparatory schools, pre-kindergarten to grade 6, and high schools, grades 7 to 13. AISK follows a traditional American grade division: an elementary program for grades pre-kindergarten through 6, a middle school for grades 7 and 8, and a high school from grades 9 to 12.

Since it does not offer a program to prepare students for the two major Jamaican exams, Common Entrance and Caribbean Examination Council, AISK is a real alternative for children from the U.S. and other diplomatic missions, American and international business families, and Jamaican families who do not need their children to sit the Common Entrance Exam because their children will attend high school abroad.

For grades 9-12, the school is fully accredited with the University of Nebraska and uses the university's directed home study program under the supervision of two high school teachers. Facilities include a library configuration that includes separate libraries for the lower grades (pre-kindergarten through 6) and upper grades (7-12), totaling over 5,000 volumes. Two computer labs with CD-ROM and access to the Internet are available to the students at AISK.

Because of the small class size, there is an emphasis on hands-on learning, and students may learn according to their own needs. The curriculum for the early grades includes Spanish, French, and art. The school emphasizes the development of the individual student. The goal of the school, at all levels, is to help students achieve their highest potential.

The high school at present does not provide facilities found in many U.S. schools. The home study system is quite different from a normal high school program, and while students lose out on a "normal high school social scene," they gain in their ability to work independently. Two students graduated in 1995 from 12th grade, and they were both accepted into Canadian universities. Students attending AISK's high school program will have no problem entering a U.S. high school when they leave Jamaica.

Hillel Academy: Hillel Academy, founded in 1969 as the Jewish community's contribution to education in Kingston, is nondenominational and religious instruction is optional. The curriculum is designed to prepare students for the CEE, CXC, and SAT examinations, as many Jamaican students attend university in the U.S. Hillel is in the process of applying for accreditation from the Southern States Association. Class size is large (28-30) per class, and this can be a problem for

Jamaican novelty market

some children who require more individualized attention.

The highly regarded preparatory school is nursery, called reception, to grade 6, and the senior school is grades 7-13. The 1995-96 enrollment was 662 students.

The prep school offers a curriculum that is closely linked to that of U.S. schools. Many of the textbooks used are from the U.S., particularly in math and science. Language arts is based on a Caribbean curriculum and uses Caribbean textbooks; for example, within the Caribbean curriculum the word "harbor" is spelled with a "u," harbour. Students in the 5th grade begin to prepare for the Common Entrance Exam, given in January of 6th grade. The prep school offers a library, computer lab, art and music programs, French and Spanish languages, and after-school activities such as soccer, netball, tennis, martial arts, and ballet.

Hillel, which is building a swimming pool in time for the 1996 summer term, will offer swimming instruction as part of the physical education classes and swimming as an intramural sports program.

Although the senior school has experienced some problems in the past with curriculum and discipline, the school has installed a new principal in the high school, and the reports are that firm discipline and school structure are making changes in the school. All students are required to take French and Spanish the first 3 years of senior school.

Hillel is on an 8-1/2-acre campus at the foot of the mountains. Blue uniforms are required but may be bought from a local manufacturer. Black shoes are required for both boys and girls. Boys wear dark socks and girls wear navy socks. Bring both shoes and socks to post

as well as crew socks and white tennis shoes, which are needed for physical education. White shorts for phys. ed. can be bought locally, and the phys. ed. T-shirt will be sold by the school in the appropriate "house color" for your child.

Hillel Academy
Dr. Hyacinth Hall (Director)
51 Upper Markway
Kingston 8, Jamaica
Tel: (809) 925-1980

Special Educational Opportunities

The University of the West Indies has its largest campus in Kingston. It is a modern institution offering liberal arts, natural sciences, and medical training. Entrance requirements are at the level of 1 year of college in the U.S. It is possible to enroll in selected classes but difficult to enroll for a degree program.

The Edna Manley College of the Visual and Performing Arts includes the Schools of Dance, Drama, Art, and Music. Each offers programs for both adults and children.

Opportunities for learning languages such as French, German, and Spanish are available at the Alliance Française, the Jamaica-German Society, and the Institute of Bolivar y Bello. Private tutors are also readily available.

A number of facilities exist in Kingston for educating the handicapped, although equipment and staff are limited. These schools have limited space, and each should be explored for specific needs. Day programs are offered by the Jamaica Association for the Deaf, the Salvation Army School for the Blind, and the Mona Rehabilitation Center for the physically handicapped. Carberry Court Special School has day and boarding programs for the severely mentally handicapped. None of these programs meets U.S. standards.

Mico Care Center offers a 9-week remedial program for those with multiple handicaps. The Jamaica Association for Children with Learning Disabilities is a resource facility for assisting children while in their regular school program.

Sports

Jamaicans are sports conscious. Chief sports are soccer, cricket, golf, tennis, swimming, sailing, and horseback riding. Smaller groups are active in squash, rugby, scuba diving, snorkeling, basketball, and softball. Local sports groups and clubs accept foreign nationals.

There is a Saturday baseball league for students that begins in the fall. It is held on the campuses of local schools. Coaches and assistants are always welcome.

Although scuba gear is available for rental, it can be purchased here at higher-than-U.S. prices.

The Jamaica Sub-Aqua Club, a branch of the British Sub Aqua Club (BSAC), gives scuba diving lessons for a minimal fee. BSAC certification with the club is required to participate in club-sponsored dives, arranged every weekend. PADI certification can be obtained at the Buccaneer Scuba Club in Port Royal and through some of the north coast hotels.

Jamaica has virtually no continental shelf, and the drop-off starts 200 yards from shore. Scuba diving and snorkeling enthusiasts enjoy exploring the many networks of caves, canyons, and crevices. The Ocho Rios area has traditionally had one of the Caribbean's finest reef communities. Over 50 species of coral include giant pillar, lettuce, antler, star and rose cup, and staghorn, as well as a wide variety of beautiful sponges and seaweed. Hurricane damage to the reefs in 1988 was extensive, particularly on the south side of the island.

Sergeant majors, tangs, and peacock flounders are among the many fish species to be seen. The island has over 800 species of shells.

There is saltwater sport fishing for jack, blue marlin (record 600 lbs.), sailfish, kingfish, dolphin, tuna, barracuda, tarpon, and snapper. Freshwater catches are snook, mullet, and others. Windsurfing is enjoyed at several north coast resorts. Water-skiing can be found in several places, especially at Blue Hole (Port Antonio) and Doctor's Cave (Montego Bay).

For joggers and walkers, the favorite spot to do laps is the Mona Reservoir. Daily running is also possible at the Police Officers' Club in Kingston. Running on the streets is not recommended because of dogs, traffic, and crime.

Constant Spring Golf Club offers a challenging 18-hole course marked by hills and narrow fairways. Entrance fees are moderate as are annual dues. Greens fees are low. Social membership entitles you to squash, badminton, tennis, and swimming. The initiation fee for social membership is moderate when compared with U.S. private club fees. The clubhouse has a newly renovated bar and lounge room and snack bar. The pool area has also been renovated. There are no playground facilities at the club.

Caymanas Golf and Country Club is 12 miles from Kingston. Its facilities include a good 18-hole golf course and some tennis courts. Membership fees approximate those of the Constant Spring Club.

The Jamaica Golf Association (JGA) has a special arrangement for members of a Jamaican golf club. For a small annual fee, you may join JGA and play any course in Jamaica for about half price. There are 11 good golf courses on the island.

Kingston's Liguanea Club has a swimming pool; lighted tennis, badminton, and squash courts; a restaurant and bar; and an exercise room. The club has several dances a year and is used for other events. A special golf membership is available at Liguanea for play at the Caymanas golf course.

The Royal Jamaica Yacht Club has facilities available for those interested in sailing, boating, and fishing. Social events are also held. The club is located near the international airport, and its large veranda affords a panoramic view of the harbor, Kingston, and the mountains. Entrance fees and annual dues are moderate. Anyone with a desire to "crew" on sailboats should join the club and meet the boat owners.

Physical fitness clubs and health spas are available. The Spartan Health Club, for instance, offers universal weight lifting equipment, aerobic exercise classes, steam room, and shower facilities. Future Fitness is a state-of-the-art facility housed in the Wyndham Hotel. The air-conditioned facility offers aerobics as well as weight training, Stairmasters, bikes, and treadmills.

Kingston does not have extensive outdoor recreational opportunities for children. The city has a small zoo and botanical gardens where children can ride bikes or rollerblade. Schools have limited playgrounds. Most families do not have sufficient space for bikes, except for tricycles. Children usually get their outdoor exercise in their own yards.

Many Jamaicans enroll their children in full-time nursery schools at the age of 2 or 3. Because of this, Americans find their own young children frequently lack playmates. Therefore, most families enroll young children in a nursery 5 days a week, at a reasonable cost.

There is little informal play between children of neighboring families in most neighborhoods in Kingston. Parents often schedule lessons or activities for the afternoons, especially for school-age children, since schools finish between 1:30 and 2:30 p.m. Tennis and golf lessons as well as piano, dance, and ballet lessons are popular. The Tae Kwon Do Club is enjoyed by all ages interested in self-defense.

Because summers are hot and humid, swimming is popular. Some families have homes with swimming pools, but beaches are some distance from Kingston.

Children will want to play indoors in the heat of the day when they first arrive, especially in summer.

Touring and Outdoor Activities

The most popular form of outdoor activity on the island is beach-going. The north coast of Jamaica has luxury resorts, hotels, and private villas every few miles. The off-season from mid-April to mid-December offers lower rates.

Bicycle riding is not recommended in Kingston because of erratic driving habits, potholes, and overzealous dogs. There also have been incidents of bikers being attacked and bikes stolen. The University of the West Indies campus offers several miles of quiet, scenic roads for riders of all abilities and ages. There are several tour companies that offer bike excursions into the

Blue Mountains. Bring a car rack, helmet, and rear-view mirror.

Another popular outdoor activity is a weekend or day trip to Newcastle, a Jamaican Defense Force training center about an hour's drive from Kingston. At 4,000 feet, the weather can be quite cool so warmer clothes are advised. Hiking is a popular outdoor activity.

Bird watching is popular, and over 250 species can be seen, including 25 found only in Jamaica. Resident species shared with neighboring countries are of special interest, since some have developed differences in behavior and appearance peculiar to Jamaica. Bring binoculars.

Garden clubs have regular outdoor shows. The Orchid Show is an annual event enjoyed by many.

Touring is popular. Kingston-area locales include historic sites at Port Royal, Castleton and Hope Botanical Gardens, the National Gallery, and the nearby Blue Mountains. Touring elsewhere is an easy day's drive from Kingston.

Negril, on the western end of the island, has 7 miles of white-sand beach and uninhibited simplicity.

To the east of Negril along the north coast is Montego Bay, tourist capital of the island with its beaches, hotels, and attractions. The area includes several excellent golf courses and Rose Hall, Jamaica's most famous great house, which echoes with the mystery of Annie Palmer (the "White Witch"), its former mistress with a murky past. Nearby is Greenwood, once owned by the Barrett family whose best-known members were poet Elizabeth Barrett Browning and Sarah Barrett, "Pinkie" in Sir Thomas Lawrence's portrait.

Falmouth, despite its neglect, is a charming north coast port. It is still the best-preserved late 18th- and early 19th-century town on the island. The old Georgian buildings are worth a sight-seeing tour.

The St. Ann's Bay/Discovery Bay/Runaway Bay area, where Columbus landed in 1494, is another interesting locale. Columbus Park, Columbus Statue, and the ruins of the first Spanish settlement, Seville Nueva, are here. Visitors to the area can tour the caves near Runaway Bay, which the last Spanish governor of Jamaica used as a safe haven while fleeing the British. Discovery Bay is the home of the University of the West Indies Marine Lab.

Ocho Rios is the resort area for the central north coast. The offshore reefs are among the finest in the Caribbean. Just south of Ocho Rios is Fern Gully, a rain forest where the road twists through a ravine. Also in the area is Jamaica's leading tourist site, Dunn's River Falls. Brimmer Hall Plantation (coconut and bananas) and Prospect Estate (pimento, citrus, and cattle) offer tours.

On the northeast coast near Port Maria is "Firefly," former home of Noel Coward. "Golden Eye," once home of James Bond's creator, Ian Fleming, is in Oracabessa.

Port Antonio, once vacation home of actor Errol Flynn, is considered Jamaica's most beautiful port and is the sport fishing capital of the island. The beauty of the area, the beaches, rafting on the Rio Grande River, Blue Hole (the world's largest natural swimming pool), Folly (ruins) built by an American millionaire for his love, Nunsuch Caves, Somerset Falls, and Maroon "jerk" pork and chicken still attract many visitors to its hotels and villas.

The trip back to Kingston along the coastal road to the east of Port Antonio is rewarding. Beautiful coastal scenes, extensive coconut and banana plantations, the John Crow Mountains, and interesting villages provide a pleasant break from tourist areas.

A 424-mile primary highway circles the island and several highways cross the mountainous interior from north to south. The two main north-

Jamaica

Cities of the World

south roads used to cross the center of the island from Kingston are also interesting. A third, mostly paved road runs between Kingston and Buff Bay via Newcastle (41 miles). It is a narrow road through small villages and over Hardware Gap, the highest point on the primary road net, offering beautiful scenery. From Kingston to Annotto Bay (28 miles), a good but narrow road winds through the mountains. Along the way is Castleton Botanical Gardens, founded in 1862. These lovely gardens were severely damaged by the 1988 hurricane but have been restored. They provide a good setting for weekend picnic outings.

The other road crossing the island from Kingston begins by going west. It passes the Arawak Museum at White Marl, Caymanas race track, and Spanish Town, the old capital. Spanish Town is unique among Jamaican cities and has the longest history of settlement (1534) plus the finest collection of historic buildings and monuments on the island. It is also home of the National Archives.

From Spanish Town, the road winds its way north through the canyon of the Cobre River, across the narrow Flat Bridge, past Bog Walk, Linstead, and Ewarton (Alcan alumina plant), and over Mount Diablo (2,250 feet). At Moneague, where three small lakes periodically appear, the road branches to the left to St. Ann's Bay or to the right through Fern Gully to Ocho Rios.

Because of reasonable air fares and the proximity to Miami, Cayman Islands, and Haiti, it is easy to take trips out of Jamaica.

Entertainment

Two drive-in theaters and three walk-in theaters are frequented by Americans. Several theaters offer a selection of stage presentations: drama, reviews, variety, musicals, and pantomime. Kingston also has several active dance theater movements, the Jamaica Philharmonic, and several choral groups.

The island has several fine museums. The Institute of Jamaica has general displays. The Arawak Museum near Spanish Town and the Port Royal Museum with buildings and collections of relics of the Buccaneer heyday are all within the Kingston area.

The National Gallery of Art (downtown) and several smaller art galleries have excellent collections of Jamaican art. Regular exhibits of paintings, sculpture, ceramics, and native crafts are held in Kingston.

There are many colorful activities that are interesting to newcomers, including Jonkanoo dancing, a curious type of costumed, masked folk dancing of African origin that is seen during the Christmas season. Carnival is a popular event, celebrated the week after Easter with both adult and children's carnivals.

"Eating Jamaican" is not to be missed. Two popular dishes are ackee with saltfish and rice with peas (beans). Other specialties include curried goat, fricasseed chicken, escovitched fish, Port Royal's fried fish and bammy, jerk pork, jerk chicken, soups such as pepperpot and pumpkin, and gungo peas. Desserts such as sweet potato puddings, plantain tart, bulla, gizada, cut cakes, and grater cakes are popular.

Kingston has good restaurants offering Jamaican, British, Chinese, American, Indian, French, and Italian cuisine. Most restaurants are moderately priced compared to the U.S.

Social Activities

The American Women's Group is a social club for all American women. It has monthly programs and activity groups.

The American community, through various sponsors, celebrates our holidays-Christmas, Fourth of July, and Halloween-in traditional fashion.

Americans have opportunities to meet members of the foreign community. There are several active international groups such as the Diplomatic Association of Jamaica, the Consular Corps, International Proxy Parents and the Rotary Club.

Mandeville

Mandeville is a busy mountain city noted for beautiful gardens and a climate where both tropical and subtropical plants flourish. As a market center for the surrounding agricultural areas and a dormitory town for the two major bauxite and alumina installations, it is Jamaica's most flourishing parish capital. A U.S. Agency for International Development (USAID) contract post is in operation here. The city has a population of about 34,000.

Mandeville, at an elevation of 2,000 feet above sea level, maintains a year-round comfortable climate where neither air conditioners nor heaters are needed. The rainy seasons are basically in May and October.

Five shopping centers, reasonably good medical facilities, pharmacies, banks, restaurants, and a good library are available. Both radio and television reception are good. There are churches of many denominations, with varied activities sponsored within each church. Service clubs include Rotary, Jaycees, Lions, and Kiwanis.

Schools for Foreigners

Belair School, an independent coeducational, boarding institution, offers classes from kindergarten through grade 12 for children of all nationalities. Founded in 1967, it is sponsored by two bauxite companies. It is accredited by the Southern Association of Colleges and Schools.

Belair's curriculum is a combination of programs typically found in U.S. academic and college-preparatory schools, and has subjects leading to the Cambridge GCE ordinary-level examinations. The current enrollment (mostly Jamaican) is over 650,

348

and the staff numbers 45. Uniforms are required.

The elementary school is situated on a two-acre campus near the center of town; the preparatory and high school are located on a separate 11-acre campus. There is a 10,600-volume library. Further information can be obtained from the school at 43 DeCarteret Road, Mandeville.

Montego Bay

Montego Bay, on Jamaica's northwest coast, is the tourist capital of the island, with its good harbor and fine beaches. The city's permanent population of close to 75,000, is swelled each year by the thousands of visitors who are drawn to the yacht races, the excellent golf courses, beach parties, garden tours, and nightlife. The world's largest reggae festival, Sunsplash, is celebrated here each August.

Montego Bay was, for many years, one of several small ports on the north coast from which sugar was shipped. Many of the old buildings in town have been restored and now house restaurants and shops. Shopping centers are found downtown and close to the resort areas.

The Cage, a jail built in 1807 for runaway slaves, is now a museum. Historic mansions have also been restored as museums, and are a glimpse into life of the colonial era. Among Montego Bay's plantation houses are Rose Hall, which echoes with the mystery of Annie Palmer, the "white witch" who is said to have dabbled with the occult; and Greenwood, once owned by the family of Elizabeth Barrett Browning.

There are several trips that visitors may take to see the mountains and countryside around Montego Bay. The Governor's Coach is an all-day drive which winds through the mountains, stopping to visit the villages of Ipswich Caves and Appleton, and to tour a rum factory.

Port Antonio

Port Antonio, which lies on a divided bay in the northeast corner of the island, is a lovely port city called the "greenhouse of the gods" for its lush vegetation. It is almost the length of the island (134 miles) away from Montego Bay and 65 miles from Kingston, separated by the Blue Mountains. It is the fishing capital of Jamaica; dolphin, kingfish, wahoo, and bonito, with blue marlin are at their seasonal height in September and October.

Cruise ships dock here only infrequently, but the beauty of the area attracts numerous visitors to the town's hotels and villas. Attractions include the beaches; rafting on the Rio Grande River; Blue Hole, the world's largest natural swimming pool; Mitchell's Folly, the ruins of a palatial vacation villa built just after the turn of the century; nearby Somerset Falls; and Nonsuch Cave. Old Fort George, now part of the high school's grounds, is one of the town's few historic monuments, located at the tip of the peninsula.

Long a popular jet-set haunt, Port Antonio is still the site of many private villas nestled in the lush hillsides and along shoreline coves. The late Errol Flynn once had a home on the bay, and his former wife operates two boutiques in town and runs a 2,000-acre cattle ranch nearby. Port Antonio has a current population of approximately 13,000.

OTHER CITIES

BATH is located in southeastern Jamaica, 30 miles east of Kingston. The town of approximately 2,000 is famous for its hot springs and botanical gardens, the second oldest in the hemisphere. A runaway slave discovered the springs in the late 17th century; soon after, the area became a mecca for travelers from all over the island. The waters are supposedly helpful in the treatment of skin conditions, as well as rheumatic problems. The Bath Hotel has hot springs tanks for rent, in addition to outdoor bathing supplied by a bamboo pipe.

BLACK RIVER is a community of about 2,700 situated at the mouth of the Black River in the southwest, 30 miles south of Montego Bay. This quiet fishing town, once a main logging point, comes to life at the covered market on Fridays and Saturdays. The Waterloo Guest House here was the first house in the country to have electricity. Tourists enjoy visiting the Holland Estate and sugar factory. The acclaimed "Bamboo Avenue" is on the way to the town of Lacovia, less than 10 miles upriver.

FALMOUTH, despite years of destruction and neglect, is a charming north coast port. It is still the best-preserved late 18th- and early 19th-century town on the island. All the old Georgian buildings are worth a visit. Built as the capital of Trelawny Parish at the height of the area's sugar-growing prosperity, the town has been declared a national trust and plans for its restoration are being considered. Falmouth's population is about 4,000.

MORANT BAY, capital of St. Thomas Parish 30 miles southeast of Kingston, is a small town that played a big role in Jamaican history. This was the scene of the Morant Bay Rebellion of 1865, led by Deacon Paul Bogle. A protest march on the courthouse led to street battles and, eventually, mass executions. The governor was recalled in the ensuing controversy and Jamaica gained new status as a Crown Colony. The nearly 3,000 residents of Morant Bay now have rebuilt the courthouse, with a statue of Paul Bogle set prominently in the front. Near the town are the highly saline Yallahs Ponds and the remnants of a signal tower, now a national monument.

NEGRIL, on the western end of the island, has seven miles of white sand beach and uninhibited simplicity. The country's newest resort town, Negril is two hours from Montego Bay. Hotels and tourist facilities have been constructed since the area was discovered by the "flower children" of the 1960s, but Negril's natural beauty remains because no building can be taller than the highest tree. Restaurants abound, and there is a wide range of accommodations, although the town is small, with a population of less than 2,800. During Jamaica Race Week, many yachts drop anchor in Negril harbor.

OCHO RIOS, once a small fishing village, is now the resort area for the central north coast, a scenic two-and-one-half-hour drive from Montego Bay. Its offshore reefs, although severely damaged by Hurricane Allen in 1980, are among the finest in the Caribbean. Ocho Rios, which has a population of 11,000, is the site of the University of the West Indies Marine Laboratory. Just south of town is Fern Gully, a rain forest where the road twists through an old riverbed. Also in the area are the 168-year-old Brimmer Hall Plantation (coconut and bananas) and Prospect Estate (pimento, citrus, and cattle), which conduct tours. Near Ocho Rios is Dunn's River Falls, a 600-foot cascade, and perhaps Jamaica's most famous beauty spot. Surrounded by lush vegetation, the water cascades over rocks to the waiting sea. Guided tours are available for climbing the falls. Daily tours to the falls are available from all of Jamaica's main towns. Also nearby is the Shaw Park Botanical Garden and Bird Sanctuary. In the vicinity, on the north coast near Port Maria, are Firefly, the former home of Noel Coward; and Golden Eye, once the residence of Ian Fleming, creator of the fictitious James Bond.

SAVANNA-LA-MAR, 25 miles southwest of Montego Bay on the west coast, has a most unfortunate past. The city of 12,000 has been ravaged by hurricanes that at one time demolished it. A fort—today used as a large swimming hole— was likewise considered a disaster. An admiral derisively noted in 1755 that it was the very worst in Jamaica. Savanna-La-Mar, whose name means "plain by the sea," is an active sugar port.

SPANISH TOWN, 20 miles west of Kingston in the island's foothills, is unique among Jamaican cities. It has the longest history of continuous settlement (1534), plus the finest collection of historic buildings and monuments on the island, among them the Anglican cathedral, built on the foundation of a Spanish chapel erected in 1524. The town also houses the National Archives. Formerly called Villa de la Vega and St. Iago de la Villa, Spanish Town became Jamaica's most important city after the destruction of Port Royal by an earthquake in 1692. It served as the capital until 1872, when the seat of government was moved to Kingston. The city, with a current population estimated at 107,000, is the commercial and processing center for the surrounding rich agricultural region.

COUNTRY PROFILE

Geography and Climate

The island of Jamaica is perhaps best noted for its lush and scenic tropical beauty: the rugged spine of blue-green mountains rising to 7,400 feet; warm, clear Caribbean waters with exciting underwater reefs; and the picture-postcard north coast with its white-sand beaches.

Jamaica is the third-largest Caribbean island and lies nearly 600 miles south of Miami, Florida. The island is 146 miles long and 51 miles across at its widest point. Except for narrow coastal plains mainly on the island's south side, the landscape is one of sharp, crested ridges, unique "cockpit" formations, and deep, twisting valleys. Almost half the island is more than 1,000 feet above sea level. Some 50 percent of the island is used for agriculture, 40 percent is woodland, and the remaining 10 percent is divided between mining and urban areas.

Jamaica has about 120 rivers. Most flow to the coast from the central mountain ranges. Those on the north side tend to be shorter and swifter than those on the south side. Only one is navigable for more than a short distance.

Kingston, the capital, is on the southeast coast and has the world's seventh-largest natural harbor. From sea level at city center, the terrain rises to 1,800 feet. The suburban residential areas of St. Andrew in the foothills of the mountains are slightly cooler than the rest of the city.

Jamaica enjoys a favorable, though warm and humid, climate. Average temperatures are about 80°–95°F, May through September, and 70°–85°F during the cooler months. The higher mountainous regions reach a low of 50°F in the cooler months. Northeast trade winds help maintain a feeling of relative comfort.

Temperature and rainfall are markedly affected by the changes in elevation and geography of the island. Rainfall varies from an annual average of 25 inches at the Kingston airport to an average of 250 inches at Blue Mountain Peak. Suburban residential areas of Kingston receive about 50 inches on the average. Rainfall is generally heaviest during April–May and October–November, though these are not rainy seasons in the tropical sense. Mildew is a problem during these months. Relative humidity in Kingston ranges from 63 percent in February to 86 percent in October.

Jamaica is in the earthquake and hurricane belts but has not had a disastrous earthquake since 1907, even though every year has a few tremors. In September 1988, the island was struck head-on by Hurricane Gilbert, the first since 1980. The main force of the storm affected the entire island, especially the eastern coastal areas, and caused widespread damage, mainly to crops and vegetation, coastal properties, utilities, and roofs.

The island suffers from periodic droughts. The water situation in Kingston was improved dramatically by the completion of the Blue Mountain Water Scheme. Occasional water shortages do occur.

Jamaica has no dangerous wild animals. Black widow spiders and scorpions are present but rare. Many varieties of soft-bodied lizards and nuisance insects-particularly cockroaches, ants, and termites-present some problems. Mosquitoes and houseflies are troublesome in the Kingston area. Grass ticks and fleas are also annoying to outside pets.

Jamaica has over 600 insect species as well as 250 bird species-25 of which belong only to Jamaica. About 120 species of butterflies, including the world's largest (6" wingspan), are also found here. The island is especially noted for its fireflies, otherwise known as blinkies or peeny-waullies.

A profusion of flowering shrubs, trees, and cacti reflects Jamaica's great variation of climate and topography. Hundreds of imported plants are well established. Pimento or allspice is from an indigenous plant, and Jamaica is the world's largest producer. The ortanique, developed in Jamaica, is a cross between an orange and a tangerine. Jamaica also has over 220 species of native orchids, over 500 different ferns, more than 300 mosses, and many fungi.

Population

Jamaica's population of 2.5 million, according to 1993 estimates, is distributed unevenly, with large, sparsely populated areas in the mountainous interior of the island. Kingston is the island's largest city, with an estimated population of 700,000 for the Kingston-St. Andrew metropolitan area. Nearby Spanish Town, with 112,000 inhabitants, and Greater Portmore, with nearly 500,000, although in the adjacent parish of St. Catherine, are in effect extensions of the Kingston metropolitan area. Montego Bay,

with a population of 85,500, is the largest urban concentration outside of the greater Kingston area.

A colorful, complex cultural heritage makes Jamaicans a unique people. Their society is multiracially integrated, and the term "Jamaican" does not carry a particular color connotation. Jamaica's population is about 90 percent African or mixed descent. The remaining 10 percent are chiefly European, Chinese, East Indian, and Lebanese.

Over 70 percent of the population is under 35-the mean age is 18. The economic and emotional focus of the home is frequently the mother, as reflected by the title of Jamaican sociologist Edith Clarke's book, *My Mother Who Fathered Me.*

The language in Jamaica is English, but it varies from precise Oxford English to Jamaican patois. Because of differences in phraseology, inflection, and word usage, new arrivals may experience some difficulty in understanding Jamaican English, particularly on the telephone. Given time, most difficulties disappear. The exception is with patois, sometimes called Jamaican Creole. Understanding it takes time and attention.

While most Jamaicans speak standard English, a combination of patois and English is commonly encountered in dealings with street vendors, domestic helpers, and artisans. Most Jamaicans are familiar with the dialect, although few speak only patois. However, modern Jamaican theater includes much dialogue in rapid patois, which may be difficult to follow, even after extended exposure to it.

Religion is an important facet of the Jamaican character and a major stabilizing influence. Most Jamaicans are Christians, with Baptists now representing the largest single denomination. The Church of Jamaica, successor to the Church of England (Anglican) since the 1880s; Church of God; and Roman Catholic Church have substantial followings.

Many other denominations are also represented, including Moravians, Seventh-day Adventists, Methodists, Presbyterians, and Latter-day Saints (Mormons). There are also small Jewish, Muslim, and Hindu communities.

Also found are religious groups unique to Jamaica: the Revivalists, whose Afro-Christian blend of religion has a high trance-invoking emotional content, and the bearded, "dreadlocked" Rastafarians, who worship "Jah," whose earthly representative was the late Emperor Haile Selassie of Ethiopia.

Jamaican culture and traditions are largely African and British, but ties with North America are increasing. This is due primarily to the large number of Jamaicans who have lived in or visited the U.S. and Canada, the importance of North American tourists and the bauxite industry to the island's economy, and the influence of U.S. television shows and media.

Public Institutions

Jamaica is an independent member of the British Commonwealth. The British Monarch is the Head of State and is represented by a Jamaican Governor General nominated by the Prime Minister. The government is based on the Westminster parliamentary system and has an elected 60-member House of Representatives and an appointed 21-member Senate. Since the early 1940s, the Jamaican political scene has been dominated by two closely matched political parties: the Jamaica Labor Party (JLP) and the People's National Party (PNP). A third party, the National Democratic Movement (NDM), was formed in 1995 by former JLP chairman, Bruce Golding.

The government is elected for a 5-year term, but elections can be held earlier under certain circumstances. The ministries of government are directed by ministers selected from majority party members of the House and Senate and appointed by the Governor General, acting on the advice of the Prime Minister. An experienced though somewhat understaffed civil service carries out governmental functions.

In the March 1993 general election, the PNP won a 52 to 8 majority in the House of Representatives. Jamaica's Prime Minister is P.J. Patterson, leader of the PNP, who succeeded Michael Manley when he retired for health reasons in 1992. Edward Seaga, leader of the opposition JLP, was Prime Minister from 1980 to 1989.

Legal institutions generally follow British practice. Cases are tried before an independent judiciary ranked in an ascending hierarchy of Petty Sessions Courts, Resident Magistrate Courts, Supreme Court, and Court of Appeal. Certain cases may be sent on appeal to the U.K. Privy Council for final determination.

The island is divided into three counties, which have no present-day functions. Within these counties are 14 parishes. Kingston and the suburban parish of St. Andrew are combined for administrative purposes into the Kingston and St. Andrew Corporation. Local government functions are handled by Parish Councils, which are to be elected every 3 years. They depend on support from the central government and can be dissolved if the national government believes parish affairs are being mismanaged.

Arts and Science

Culture. Jamaica has long been noted for the richness and diversity of its culture and the quality of its artists. In the area of theater, the island has produced such notable actors as Madge Sinclair, the Honorable Louise Bennett-Coverley, and Charles Hyatt. A variety of plays can be seen daily in the capital city of Kingston. Jamaica has an international reputation in dance, especially through the National Dance Theater Company, which fosters the development of traditional dance forms. The country also has a high reputation for its many fine paint-

ers, sculptors, and writers. Music is another field in which Jamaica is well known, particularly for reggae, which has been made famous by singers such as the late Bob Marley.

Music. Jamaica's music is perhaps its most revealing form of folk expression. Frank, natural, and spontaneous, it springs from the soul of the people and often reflects historical circumstances. The songs record joys and sorrows, wit, philosophy of life, and religion.

Traditional Jamaican music is percussive, polyrhythmic, and repetitive. Vocals rely heavily on the call-and-response form, while drums control the accompanying dances. The major influences are evident in the structure and behavior of Jamaican melody and harmony: the older heritage of African music and rhythm and the more recent legacy of European religious and popular music, introduced over the centuries of British rule.

Popular music has steadily evolved over the last 20 years from mento to ska to reggae. Reggae has been internationally promoted through the late Rasta folk hero and international pop star, Bob Marley. Other prominent reggae artists include Dennis Brown, Jimmy Cliff, and the late Peter Tosh. Several Jamaicans also have gained international recognition in the fields of classical music and jazz; Curtis Watson and Monty Alexander are notable examples. The philosophy, doctrine, and music of the Rastafarians heavily influence reggae in instrumentation, lyrics, movement, and delivery. The latest musical movement is called "DJ music." Similar to American rap music, it relies heavily on rhythmic chanting and emphasizes experiences of inner-city youth. Other forms of popular music include "dance hall," "dub," and "soca," a form of merengue music heard primarily during Carnival celebrations.

Art. Jamaican art is varied and reveals no predominant cultural or ethnic influences except, perhaps, very stylized African motifs. Many

of the established Jamaican painters and sculptors have achieved acclaim outside this country, particularly in the U.S. and Britain, where many of them were trained. Sophisticated works can be obtained in various media: oils, acrylics, watercolors, silk-screen prints, woodcuts, sculpture, ceramics, pottery, and textile arts. There is a fairly large group of expatriate artists-mostly from the U.S. and the Commonwealth-resident in Jamaica.

Kingston is the art center of the island, with many artists, the art school, and several well-respected high-quality galleries. Three broad categories of art are discernible: intuitive, abstract, and representational. Representational is the dominant mode. The National Gallery of Art maintains a large collection of Jamaican and Caribbean art from the 18th century to the present.

Crafts. Local craftwork is strongly influenced by cultural heritage and finds expression in straw, semiprecious stones and jewelry, wood, clay, fabric, shell, and bamboo. A substantial amount of the alabaster, embroidered cutwork, and appliqué craftwork is exported to the U.S. An attractive cluster of craft shops is located on the grounds of Devon House, a historic site.

Dance. The National Dance Theater Company (NDTC) was formed in 1962. Many of the troupe's more recognized members studied in England and the United States. The NDTC emphasizes indigenous dance and experimentation. NDTC choreographers have produced an extremely varied and culturally rich repertoire. The revived folk dances are actively performed on the island. They are presented at cultural festivals, on TV, and in resort areas.

Drama. Drama has expanded considerably in the past decade. During the 1980s, Jamaican playwrights typically produced works based on social currents and issues of the day. Today, the theater offers a broad base, ranging from comedy and reviews to serious drama.

Festivals. Jamaica places much emphasis on the cultural heritage of its people. The artistic and cultural awakening has been accompanied by a keen search for roots in folk forms based chiefly in colorful and intensely rhythmic dances and songs. This is best reflected in the annual festival celebrated from the last two weeks in July until Independence Day, the first Monday in August. Winners of "all island" parish dance, song, poetry, and drama competitions perform during the festival. Other high-profile festivals include the Ocho Rios Jazz Festival, the Reggae Sunsplash Festival, and Carnival. Festivals provide an avenue of expression for Jamaicans at every level of society.

Science. Organized scientific investigation in Jamaica dates back to 1774 when the Botanical Department and the gardens at Bath were established. The Institute of Jamaica-which includes the West Indies Reference Library, the National Gallery of Jamaica, and several museums-is the most significant cultural organization in the country. Its Natural History Division is the chief source of information on Jamaican flora and fauna. The Institute also produces publications on Jamaican history and culture. Perhaps one of the most active units of the Institute is the Edna Manley College of the Visual and Performing Arts where students are instructed in dance, drama, music, and the fine arts.

Systematic geological surveys began over 100 years ago. In 1942, with the realization of the potential of bauxite, extensive research began, which led to the creation of a separate Geological Department in 1951.

Important areas of scientific research include geology, mineralogy, biochemistry, food technology, nutrition, agro-industry, crop and soil agronomy, epidemiology, ecology, and marine biology.

The Meteorological Office of the Jamaican Government and the Seismic Research Unit of the University of the West Indies compile and disseminate information to the public.

Commerce and Industry

Jamaica's pattern of trade and production has historically been based on the export of its principal agricultural products (sugar, bananas, coffee, cocoa, spices, etc.), as well as other foreign exchange earners (bauxite/alumina, rum) in exchange for imports of oil, machinery, manufactured goods, and food products (principally wheat, corn, rice, soybeans, butter). However, the fast growth of tourism, textile production, and the proliferation of service industries have changed the island's trading habits.

Tourism has been Jamaica's primary foreign exchange-earning industry since 1983. Total visitor arrivals have remained well over one million annually. Stopover visitors (visitors staying one night or more) average 65 percent of total arrivals, two-thirds of which come from the U.S. Hotel room capacity on the island is 19,760 and is expanding. In 1994, total foreign exchange earnings from tourism accounted for an estimated US$977 million. The second largest source of foreign exchange in 1994 was remittances (approximately US$600 million).

Jamaica has large commercial deposits of mineral resources such as limestone (two-thirds of the island), bauxite, gypsum, marble, silica sand, and clays. The mining and processing of bauxite continues to be the major economic activity. Net export earnings from bauxite/alumina (levies, royalties, local cash inflows) amounted to US$231 million in 1994. Development of this industry is greatly influenced by worldwide aluminum consumption and price fluctuation in the international market. The agricultural sector generates about 8 per-

cent of GDP and employs over one-quarter of Jamaica's work force. Jamaica has a favorable climate and varied soil types. Major traditional export crops are sugar, spices, bananas, coffee, citrus, allspice, and pimento. Other crops of growing importance include yams, tropical fruits and vegetables, legumes, and horticulture.

Other nontraditional products have also strengthened Jamaica's export performance during the last few years. These include garments, cut flowers, ornamental plants, gourmet food items and spices, handicrafts, and furniture. World-renowned Jamaican products such as Blue Mountain coffee, cigars, and Red Stripe beer have experienced growth in demand. The U.S. continues to be Jamaica's leading trading partner, exporting an average of US$1.06 billion annually to Jamaica and importing approximately US$415 million worth of Jamaican goods during the 1992-94 period. Jamaica's other leading trading partners are the U.K., Canada, Venezuela, and Japan.

The Jamaican economy grew by 0.8 percent in 1994 following a modest growth of 1.2 percent in 1993. This resulted from growth in the agricultural sector, mining, tourism, financing, insurance, and other service sectors. The pace of economic growth in 1994 slowed somewhat due to tight monetary and fiscal policies, high inflation, and declining real incomes for the majority of the population. In addition, the servicing of a heavy debt burden, the deterioration in earnings from the bauxite/alumina industry, and high interest rates have further constrained economic growth.

Jamaica faces several ongoing economic problems. Although the external debt has been modestly reduced over the last 3 years, debt servicing still constitutes about 40 percent of the government fiscal budget, constraining both growth and the government's policy options. The stock of debt is approximately US$3.6 billion, or US$1,440 on a per-capita basis. Privatization, tariff reform, liberalization of foreign exchange controls, and tight fiscal and monetary policies are some of the major policies implemented over the past few years to enhance economic growth and development.

Transportation
Automobiles
Driving is on the left, but either left-hand or right-hand drive cars may be imported. Left-hand-drive cars must usually have headlights re-aimed. Because of the narrow roads and in the interest of safety, serious consideration should be given to bringing a right-hand-drive vehicle.

Current Jamaican Government policy forbids the importation of vehicles over 3 years old (date of manufacture to date of entry into Jamaica).

Compact cars rather than larger American model cars are better suited to the narrow, winding Jamaican roads. A car with a high road clearance is an advantage because of the many potholes. Lighter colors are preferable, as they are cooler. An air-conditioner is desirable. Garages can service most American, Japanese, or European makes, but service is below U.S. standards.

Spare parts are expensive and sometimes hard to find, especially for older and less common models. Bring a basic supply of oil filters, radiator hoses, fan belts, and spark plugs, as well as points and condensers if your car uses them. Spare parts can also be obtained from Miami with delivery in only a few days, in most cases. Also, bring a basic tool supply and repair manuals for your make and model of car. Durable tires in good condition are necessary because of often poorly kept roads.

You must have a Jamaican license to drive. Automobile registration is accomplished by obtaining (1) an import license for your car at the time of importation, (2) compulsory local liability insurance, and (3) a certificate of vehicle fitness.

Certificates of car fitness must be renewed annually. Besides being in good condition, all cars must have turn indicators. Those on U.S. cars are acceptable.

Communications
Telephone and Telegraph
Telephone service is available to most of the island, but service is below U.S. standards. Calls from one exchange to another are treated as long-distance calls despite relatively short distances, with rates determined by the mileage between exchanges. A direct-dialing system serves the whole island. Service to the U.S. by satellite is generally adequate.

A 3-minute, station-to-station call from Kingston to Washington, D.C., costs about US$5.27 at full rate and US$4 at the reduced rate (night and all day Sunday and on Jamaican holidays). AT&T calling cards can be used, and many U.S. long-distance companies offer collect-call services from Jamaica. Direct-dialing from the U.S. is possible using area code 809 and the Jamaican seven-digit number.

International telegraph service is good, and rates are moderate. Cables are sent via JAMINTEL Limited through the Jamaican postal service. Local service and delivery are erratic.

Mail
Local airmail service is available to and from the U.S. Transit time to Washington or New York is about 10 days, with some fluctuations in service. The airmail letter rate to the U.S. is J$1.10 per ounce. Surface mail and international parcel post depend on sailing schedules to Jamaica and are unreliable. Delivery time from the U.S. varies from 2 to 6 months. International letter mail service ranges from -excellent to disastrous, while local mail can disappear or take weeks to travel a few miles.

Radio and TV
AM and FM radio reception in the Kingston area is excellent. There are several major national radio networks, including RJR Limited and the Jamaica Broadcasting Corporation (JBC). Radio stations offer a wide variety of programming, including music, talk shows, local and international news, and religious programs.

Shortwave reception from the U.S. and U.K. is fair to good, with occasional interference; some people find a shortwave set desirable. Voice of America (VOA) shortwave broadcasts get good reception in early morning and evening and have excellent news and sports coverage.

JBC has also operated a TV station since 1963. JBC-TV transmits Jamaican, U.S., U.K., and Canadian programs. A privately owned station, CVM-TV, broadcasts many popular American sitcoms and movies. Both stations offer regular local and overseas news programs. As a result of recent legislation governing cable TV service, a wide variety of cable programming is now, available through several local cable providers. Rates are comparable to those in the U.S. TVs made in the U.S. can be used in Jamaica.

Video rental stores can be found in Kingston. The vast majority of available tapes are VHS, not Betamax. Ordering of VCRs and color TVs can be done through the commissary at U.S. retail prices, plus transportation. There are now almost 20,000 satellite dishes in Jamaica that receive the whole range of U.S. TV offerings.

Newspapers, Magazines, and Technical Journals
The *Miami Herald* and the *New York Times* are usually available at local newsstands late on the day of publication. Limited international coverage is provided by the *Daily Gleaner,* the *Herald,* and the *Observer,* Jamaica's three main newspapers. Copies of these papers are usually available for perusal at

the Jamaica Desk (ARA/CAR) in the Department of State.

English and American magazines are available locally. American magazines are marked up at least 12%. Subscriptions to U.S. magazines will save money. Send them by pouch, if you don't mind them arriving at least 2 weeks late and occasionally in batches of two or three. Subscriptions to the international editions of *Time* or *Newsweek* will ensure that the magazine arrives during the week of publication. Books printed in England are available from several booksellers. U.S. bestsellers are months late arriving at local shops and difficult to find. Books cost more than in the U.S.

The Public Affairs Library has about 2,200 volumes, ranging from art to technology and the social sciences, as well as general reference works. The library also subscribes to 69 U.S. periodicals. The Kingston and St. Andrew Parish Library is part of the islandwide free public library service. It has about 75,000 volumes.

Health and Medicine

Medical Facilities

General practitioners and specialists are available. Many have received specialty training in the U.S., Canada, or U.K. These doctors are highly qualified and good diagnosticians even without the benefit of sophisticated equipment. Fees are generally lower than those in the U.S., particularly in the specialty areas. There are many good dentists whose fees are also lower than those in the U.S. Many professionals have migrated to the U.S., and in several specialty areas it is sometimes difficult to get appointments quickly.

Several small and generally adequate private hospitals are found in and around Kingston. People go to the U.S. for special treatment or surgery. Local doctors recommend trips to the U.S. if they believe their

own facilities are inadequate. The regional medical officer, who visits Kingston every 4 to 6 months, has stated that no elective surgery should be done in Jamaica. Miami is the designated medical evacuation point.

Community Health

Community sanitation in Kingston has improved in the past few years. Drains and plumbing are inspected sporadically. Insects are a constant nuisance, and there is not a regular spraying program to control the breeding grounds. Trash and garbage disposal in the urban areas has also improved. In rural areas, it is an individual matter. Sewage facilities and treatment are adequate in Kingston.

Preventive Measures

Some infectious diseases are influenza, whooping cough, scarlet fever, and German measles. It is now mandatory for students entering school for the first time to have documents verifying that they have been immunized against whooping cough, tetanus, diphtheria, measles, polio, and tuberculosis before admission is approved.

Rabies, yellow fever, and malaria are not present in Jamaica, but mosquitoes do transmit the unpleasant dengue fever. Cases of dengue fever rose dramatically in late 1995, but the problem is being addressed through aerial spraying and reduction of mosquitoes' breeding areas.

Quality pasteurized milk is available in Kingston. The commissary also stocks U.S.-origin milk and dairy products, but they are expensive.

Avoid excessive exercise during the heat of the day. Because of the large areas of dense foliage and high pollen levels, the climate can be unpleasant to asthma and sinus sufferers.

LOCAL HOLIDAYS

Jan. 1	New Year's Day
Feb/Mar.	Ash Wednesday*
Mar/Apr.	Good Friday*
Mar/Apr.	Easter*
Mar/Apr.	Easter Monday*
May 23	National Labor Day
Aug.1	Emancipation Day
Aug. (first Monday)	Independence Day*
Oct. (third Monday)	National Heroes' Day*
Dec. 25	Christmas Day
Dec. 26	Boxing Day

*variable

NOTES FOR TRAVELERS

Passage, Customs & Duties

Those arriving from areas where yellow fever is known to exist must be immunized.

U.S. citizens traveling as tourists can enter Jamaica with a U.S. passport or a certified copy of a U.S. birth certificate and current state photo identification. They must also have a return ticket and sufficient funds for their visit. U.S. citizens traveling to Jamaica for work or for extended stays are required to have a current passport and must obtain a visa before arriving. A departure tax is collected when leaving the country. For further information, travelers can contact the Embassy of Jamaica at 1520 New Hampshire Avenue NW, Washington, DC 20036, telephone (202)452-0660, the Jamaican Consulate in Miami or New York, or one of Jamaica's honorary consuls in Atlanta, Boston, Chicago, Houston, Seattle or Los Angeles. Travelers may also contact Jamaican representative in the

United States through the Internet at http://www.emjam@sysnet.net or at http://www.emjam@emjam-usa.org.

U.S. citizens are encouraged to register with the Consular Section of the U.S. Embassy in Kingston. The Consular Section is located on the first floor of the Life of Jamaica Building, 16 Oxford Road, Kingston 5, telephone 1-876-935-6044. Office hours are 7:15 a.m. to 4:00 p.m. with window services available Monday through Friday, 8:30 a.m. to 11:30 a.m. For after-hours emergencies involving American citizens, a duty officer can be contacted at 1-876-926-6440. The Chancery is located three blocks away at the Mutual Life Building, 3rd floor, 2 Oxford Road, Kingston 5, telephone 1-876-929-4850 through -4859.

There is a Consular Agency in Montego Bay at St. James Place, 2nd floor, Gloucester Avenue, telephone 1-876-952-0160, fax 1-876-952-5050. Office hours are 9 a.m. to 12:00 noon, Monday through Friday.

The U.S. Embassy also has consular responsibility for the Cayman Islands, a British dependent territory. Please refer to the British West Indies Consular Information Sheet for information about the Cayman Islands. There is a Consular Agency located in the office of Adventure Travel, Seven-Mile Beach, George Town, Grand Cayman, telephone 1-345-946-1611, fax 1-345-945-1811. Office hours are 8 a.m. to 12:00 noon, Monday through Friday.

Pets

With the single exception of animals born and bred in the U.K., which have never had rabies shots, importation of pets is not allowed.

To bring animals from the U.K., the following procedure must be taken. You must have a certificate from the Ministry of Agriculture, Fisheries, and Food at Hookrise, Surrey, England, proving that the animal was born and bred in the U.K. This certificate must then be presented to the Veterinary Department at Hope Gardens in Kingston to receive an import permit. These steps must be taken before the animal arrives.

Several excellent veterinarians practice in Kingston.

Currency, Banking and Weights and Measures

The currency is the Jamaican dollar. Bills are printed on different-colored paper in denominations of $2, $5, $10, $20, $50, $100, and $500 while coins are minted in denominations of 5¢, 10¢, 25¢, 50¢, $1, and $5. The official exchange rate fluctuates within a 30¢ "band" or margin, and is adjusted at regular intervals. As of January 1996, it was US$1 = J$40. The exact exchange rate at any given time may be obtained from the Jamaica desk in ARA.

With the exception of gasoline, which is sold by liter, all other units of measure (inches, feet, yards, miles, etc.) and weight (pounds and ounces) are the same as in the U.S. However, there is an ongoing national project under way to convert the country to the metric system. Some road signs and consumer product labels already reflect these changes.

U.S. dollars or travelers checks may be converted readily into Jamaican currency at airports, banks, and hotels. While some north coast resorts will accept U.S. dollars, all official transactions must be made in Jamaican currency.

You may buy U.S. dollar instruments, including travelers checks, from local banks by presenting an airline ticket showing travel off the island.

Disaster Preparedness

Jamaica, like all Caribbean countries, can be affected by hurricanes. Hurricane season runs from approximately June 1 - November 30 each year. The Office of Disaster Preparedness and Emergency Management (ODPEM) has put measures in place in the event of an emergency or disaster. General information about natural disaster preparedness is available from the U.S. Federal Emergency Management Agency (FEMA) at http://www.fema.gov/.

RECOMMENDED READING

These titles are provided as a general indication of the material published on this country. The Department of State does not endorse unofficial publications.

Apa Productions. *Insight Guide to Jamaica.*

Black, Clinton V. *The Story of Jamaica.* Rev. 1965.

Black, Evon. *Beautiful Jamaica.* 1975.

Cargill, Morris. *Jamaica Farewell.* Secaucus, NJ: Lyle Stuart, 1978.

Clark, Edith. *My Mother Who Fathered Me: A Study of the Family in the Selected Communities in Jamaica.* Winchester, MA: Allen Unwin, 1976.

Craton, Michael M. *Searching for the Invisible Man: Slaves and Plantation Life in Jamaica.* Cambridge, MA: Harvard University Press, 1978.

Henriques, Fernando. *Family & Color in Jamaica.* 1953.

Henzel, Perry. *The Power Game.* 1983.

Ingram, K.E., ed. *Jamaica.* Santa Barbara, CA: ABC-Clio, 1984.

Insight Guides. *Jamaica.* Englewood Cliffs, NJ: Prentice-Hall, 1983.

Kaplan, Irving. *Area Handbook for Jamaica.* 1976.

Kaplan, John. *Marijuana-The New Prohibition.* 1970.

Knight, Franklin W. *The Caribbean: The Genesis of a Fragmented Nationalism.* Oxford University Press, 1978.

Looney, Robert. *The Jamaican Economy in the 1980's: Economic Decline and Structural Readjust-*

ment. Boulder, CO: Westview Press, 1986.

Lowenthal & Comitas. *Consequences of Class & Color.* 1973.

———. *Work and Family.* 1967.

Mikes, George. *Not by Sun Alone.* 1967.

Morrish, Ivor. *Obeah, Christ, and Rastaman: Jamaica and Its Religions.* Greenwood, SC: Attic Press, 1982.

Nettleford, Rex. *Mirror, Mirror- Identity, Race and Protest in Jamaica.* 1970.

———. *Caribbean Cultural Identity: The Case of Jamaica.* 1979.

Senior, Olive. *A-Z of Jamaica Heritage.* Portsmouth, NH: Heinemann Educational Books, 1983.

Sherlock, P.M. *This Is Jamaica: An Informal Guide.* 1968.

Slater, Mary. *The Caribbean Islands.* 1968.

Thelwell. *The Harder They Come.*

White, Timothy. *Catch a Fire: The Life of Bob Marley.* New York: Henry Holt, 1983.

Waters, Anita M. *Race, Class and Political Symbols: Rastafari and Reggae in Jamaican Politics.* New Brunswick, NJ: Transaction Books, 1985.

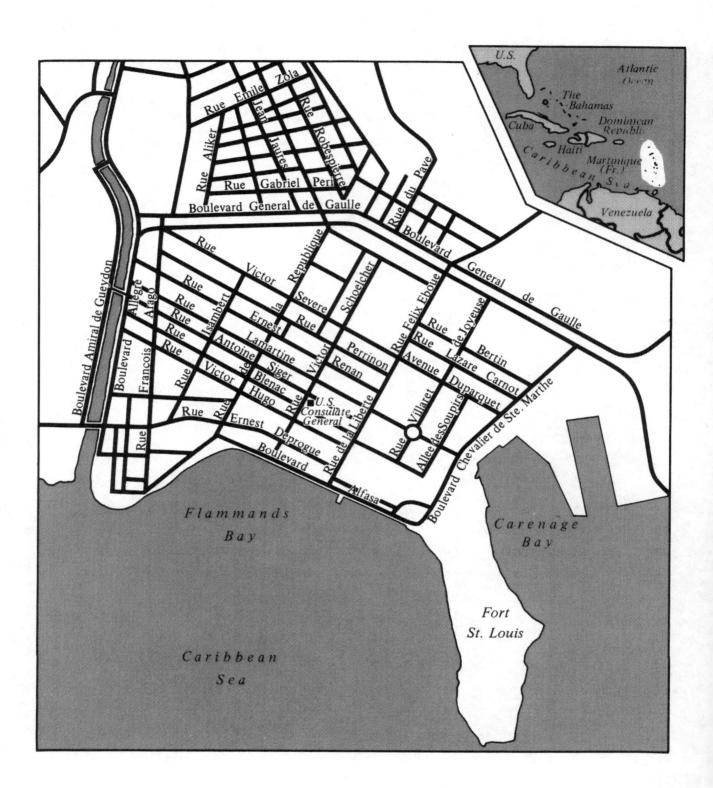

Fort-de-France, Martinique

MARTINIQUE

(including Guadeloupe and French Guiana)
Departments of Martinique, Guadeloupe, and French Guiana

Major City:
Fort-de-France

Other Cities:
Basse-Terre, Cayenne, Grand Bourg, Kourou, Le Vauclin, Les Trois-Ilets, Maripasoula, Pointe-à-Pitre, Saint-Laurent-du-Maroni, Saint-Pierre

INTRODUCTION

In the 16th and 17th centuries, France amassed a vast empire in North America and the Caribbean. Today, the three Overseas Departments of France in the Western Hemisphere—Martinique, Guadeloupe, and French Guiana—encompass virtually all that remains of that imperial sovereignty.

MARTINIQUE is one of the most beautiful islands in the Caribbean, and its beauty is matched by the richness of its history. Although discovered by Columbus, the island was taken for France in 1635 and has since been a possession of that country, except for three short periods when it was under British occupation. A singular feature of its history is that it has bred a race of queens. Joséphine, who was to become Empress of France; her daughter Hortense, who became Queen of Holland; Madame de Maintenon, morganatic wife of Louis XIV; and Aimée Debuc, the *sultan validah*, or queen mother, of Turkey— all were born on Martinique.

Named for Santa María de Guadelupe de Estremadura by Christopher Columbus when he landed here in 1493, **GUADELOUPE** offers a blend of cultures, manifested in colorful dress and a variety of culinary delights. **FRENCH GUIANA** was probably discovered by Columbus on his third voyage in 1498. It has good beaches, but its principal charm lies in the unspoiled inner regions, reachable only by air or motorized canoe. The infamous penal colony, Devil's Island, was located off French Guiana.

MAJOR CITY

Fort-de-France

Fort-de-France, with more than 100,000 residents, is the only significant metropolitan center on the island. The city is picturesque in that the architecture is colorful, and the effects of the tropics tend to explain, and even soften, the rather shabby aspect of much of the town. Open drainage ditches alongside some streets are an eyesore and a nuisance, but they no longer carry sewage and are gradually being covered up.

Martinique was first settled by Europeans in 1635, and many parts of the island are associated with the history of the past three centuries. However, the climate, earthquakes, and the total destruction in 1902 of Saint-Pierre, then the island's principal city, have erased many vestiges of the past. It was only after Saint-Pierre was destroyed by the volcanic eruption of Mount (Mont) Pelée that Fort-de-France gained prominence. Interesting archaeological sites exist on the island, once the scene of important developments of Arawak and Carib cultures dating back to the beginning of the Christian era.

Martinique and Guadeloupe are densely populated, tropical, and agricultural. Sugar, bananas, pineapples to a lesser extent, and assistance from metropolitan France are the economic underpinnings of the islands, providing them with a standard of living higher than that of most of the rest of the Caribbean. French culture is pervasive. The tourist industry has been slow to develop, although tourists are much in evidence during winter. They arrive aboard cruise ships, but generally leave after spending less than a day on Martinique.

Martinique lies about halfway down the arc of the Lesser Antilles that extends from Puerto Rico to Trinidad. It is some 900 miles north of the equator, about 280 miles from the South American mainland, and 4,400 miles from metropolitan France. Guadeloupe is 100 miles north of Martinique. Its island dependencies of French Saint-Martin and

View of Martinique

Saint-Barthélemy are 150 miles north of Guadeloupe proper and about 100 miles from the U.S. Virgin Islands. French Guiana, wedged between Brazil and Suriname on the north coast of South America, extends from the second to the sixth degree of north latitude.

Clothing

Lightweight clothing is worn throughout the year; washable, wrinkle-free fabrics are preferable. Cotton underwear and children's clothes can be purchased locally. Good quality yard goods are available, but expensive.

Men wear clothing similar to that worn in Washington, DC in the summer. Dark suits are appropriate for evenings. Women rarely need hats (except sunhats) or gloves; these are worn almost exclusively at church ceremonies. Dressy cottons are comfortable and suitable. During winter, some women wear cocktail dresses of silk and brocade. Also necessary is an ample supply of low-heeled shoes for walking over the rough sidewalks and streets in town. Shoes may be found locally, but none narrower than a B width. A coat is never needed but, on occasion, a fabric stole is useful.

Food

A number of supermarkets are found in Fort-de-France, including large ones in residential districts. Most stock is imported, and prices are high. Variety of produce is usually good, although delay in transport can result in occasional shortages. A few American brands are carried locally, usually manufactured under license in Europe.

Locally produced meat and fish have their own sizable markets in downtown Fort-de-France, and several similar markets sell local fruits and vegetables.

Supplies & Services

A few tailors and dressmakers do good work relatively inexpensively. Shoe repair is adequate. Dry cleaning and laundry services range from fair to good, but are expensive by U.S. standards. Beauty shops have reasonable prices, offer adequately skilled service, and are beginning to install up-to-date equipment. Radio and other household repair service is apt to be casual, with disregard for deadlines or commitments.

Pharmacies are well-stocked with French drugs, but precise equivalents of American products are not always available.

Education

All local education is in French. The public and parochial elementary and secondary schools have lower academic standards than in metropolitan France, although they operate according to the same system. Kindergartens are both available and good. During the past few years, Americans have enrolled children in elementary schools or kindergartens in Fort-de-France, but it is hard to gain admission to some of these institutions.

American children who speak French have no difficulty making friends among the children in the various communities on Martinique, either local or from metropolitan France.

High school students are normally sent to boarding schools in the U.S. or elsewhere. For teenagers who want to stay with their parents and are willing or able to follow French courses, education is possible here.

Fort-de-France has a school of music and a number of private music and dance teachers. Tutoring is available in diverse subjects to those whose French is adequate. A branch of the University of the Antilles and Guiana, a government-owned institution whose headquarters are on Guadeloupe, offers a four-year program in some subjects and a two-year program in others.

Recreation

The Martiniquais are sports-minded. Everyone, it seems, plays or closely follows one or more sports. Football (soccer), cycling, and basketball are among the more popular games. In recent years, Americans have enjoyed sports such as tennis (four courts are available through membership in two tennis clubs), riding (two riding stables are in the residential environs of Fort-de-France), golf (one nine-hole course 45 minutes from Fort-de-France), gymnastics, and judo classes for both men and women. Boating is popular and may be attractive to those willing to assume the expense involved. Sailing lessons under French governmental auspices are inexpensive and popular. Martinique is a fairly good spot for scuba diving, spearfishing, and snorkeling.

Being a beautiful mountainous island, Martinique would seem to offer much in the way of outdoor activities. However, much of the island's potential is undeveloped, and the hot, humid climate is not conducive to sustained physical effort. Few parks or public recreation areas exist on the island, and the only beaches near Fort-de-France are artificially made beaches adjoining the principal hotels, mostly across the bay in Trois Islets area. Black volcanic beaches are in the north, and beautiful white-sand stretches in the south are accessible within an hour's drive.

Hiking in and around Fort-de-France is difficult because of the climate and the total lack of serviceable sidewalks or footpaths. The higher mountains have trails for hardy hikers. Only in French Guiana is there any worthwhile hunting. For those who enjoy the out-of-doors, nature studies are attractive.

The area around Victor Hugo, Schoelcher, and Antoine Siger Streets in Fort-de-France is replete with boutiques and duty-free shops. There are also a department store, a designer fashion shop, and an arts and crafts center in this area.

There are a few small museums on Martinique. The sugar-plantation birthplace of Empress Josephine has been turned into an historical repository and included here is a display of Napoleon's love letters. Other archives include the Volcanological Museum in Saint-Pierre, a new gallery dedicated to Paul Gauguin, and a small museum that displays pre-Columbian and colonial artifacts.

There are 30 hotels on Martinique. Discotheques, nightclubs, and gambling casinos light up the night, but dining seems to be the favorite evening activity; an endless choice of restaurants feature French and creole cuisine.

Twice a year, a small company of actors comes from France, once to

produce classical French plays and once to sing operettas. Occasionally a musician, a traveling lecturer, or a local artist offers his talent for public enjoyment. There is considerable interest in music here, and amateur musicians can find ample scope to develop their talents in a congenial atmosphere.

The American community on Martinique is small, and is confined to a few business people, missionaries, several American spouses of French citizens, and some Martiniquais who have acquired American citizenship after living in the U.S., but have chosen to retire in the Antilles. Social organizations, such as the local bridge club, attract many of these Americans.

The most socially active times of year are the Christmas/New Year holiday season and pre-Lent carnival, and early summer. Most social life is centered around the family and, for this reason some single Americans assigned here have found it difficult to establish contacts. Reasonable fluency in French is the principal requirement for establishment of professional and personal relationships.

OTHER CITIES

BASSE-TERRE, the capital of Guadeloupe, located at the southern tip on the island which bears the same name, is a banana port and commercial center. It was founded by the French in 1643 and, with a population of roughly 14,000, it retains its French colonial atmosphere. The city is in the mountainous section of the island. The volcanic peak, Soufrière, emits sulphurous fumes, but has not erupted in several years, and can be climbed. Basse-Terre's beaches are volcanic sand and, therefore, black. Snorkeling is good on the reefs off the west and south shores. Fort St. Charles, built to protect the port between 1650 and 1780, now houses the local historical museum. Fishermen from the island of Les Saintes come to Basse-Terre daily to sell their catch; Saturday is the best day to visit the native market. Other sites on this island include Carbet Falls Gorge, the archaeological park at Trois Rivières, and the rain forest.

CAYENNE, the capital of French Guiana, is located at the mouth of the Cayenne River which empties into the Atlantic Ocean. The city was founded in 1643 by the French. An Indian massacre destroyed the town, and it was not resettled until 1664. Great Britain, France, and the Netherlands fought for control of Cayenne and the surrounding region during the 17th century, and it later was occupied (from 1808 to 1816) by both the British and the Portuguese. The development of the city has been slow because of internal strife, the tropical climate, and the prevalence of disease. The harbor is shallow, making it necessary for deep-water ships to anchor some distance out. Exports include rum, timber, essence of rosewood, and gold. The Pasteur Institute here specializes in the study of tropical diseases. Several buildings from Cayenne's colonial days still stand, and there are many lovely parks. The city gave its name to the pungent pepper which is derived from plants that grow in profusion in this area. The 2000 population of Cayenne was approximately 52,000.

GRAND BOURG is the capital of Marie-Galante Island, Guadeloupe. Situated in the far southwest corner of the island, it has a protected beach and is known for its Creole-sauce seafood. Two hotels are available: Le Salut and Solédad. El Rancho, a new entertainment complex, offers a movie theater, restaurant, discothèque, and overnight accommodations.

KOUROU is located about 30 miles west of Cayenne and has a population of about 6,500. From 1851 to 1946, it was the center of the penal settlements in Guiana. The most famous of these was Devil's Island, built in 1852 on îles du Salut, an island in the Caribbean off the coast of French Guiana. Used largely for political prisoners, its most famous was Alfred Dreyfus. Excursions may be taken to these offshore islands, where the crumbling remains of the prisons can be seen. Today, Kourou is the site of an extensive space center from which the European Space Agency launches commercial satellites.

LE VAUCLIN is one of Martinique's most scenic areas, situated in the southeast, 16 miles from Fort-de-France. This fishing town of 3,000 has a palm-lined beach that suddenly comes to life with the arrival of the fishing boats. Salt marshes and the other worldly Savane des Pétrifications are nearby. The latter is an arid region where veins of lava flows appear to be petrified wood.

LES TROIS-ILETS, on Martinique, is six miles south of Fort-de-France Bay. It is best known as the birthplace of Joséphine Beauharnais (1763-1814), the Creole beauty who became the first wife of Napoleon. Her house, La Pagerie, has been partially restored. The church where she was baptized can be visited, as well as a museum of the Napoleonic era. The estimated population of Les Trois-Ilets is 1,500.

MARIPASOULA lies on the Lawa River, 140 miles southwest of Cayenne, on French Guiana's western border. This village of about 550 is the threshold to Wayana Indian territory. The Wayanas are warm, friendly people; they are hunters who follow colorful rituals. Maripasoula has a small airstrip and an inn near the water to accommodate visitors.

POINTE-À-PITRE is the largest city on Guadeloupe, with a population estimated at 27,000 in 1995. It is located on the island of Grande-Terre, at the southern entrance of the Rivière Salée, the narrow, shallow ocean channel that separates Basse-Terre and Grande-Terre. Pointe-à-Pitre is its island's main port. More than 900 ships call each year; chief exports are rum, coffee, sugar, and bananas. Yachting is a major business, with close to 1,500 pleasure boats based here. Pointe-à-Pitre is also the finishing point (in November and December) for the Route de Rhum Rade, a 3,700-mile solo transatlantic event that begins at Saint-Malo, France. The marketplace at Pointe-à-Pitre is one of the most colorful in the area. Fort Fleur d'Epée, at Bas du Fort near Pointe-à-Pitre, was used to repel the British invasions of the 1700s. The new Edgar Clerc Archaeological Museum houses a collection of Arawak and Carib Indian artifacts from the Lesser Antilles. The stores in Pointe-à-Pitre have a fine selection of perfume, crystal, gold jewelry, and rum. There is also fine dining, especially at the little Creole restaurants, as well as dancing, and shows.

SAINT-LAURENT-DU-MARONI is a city of approximately 14,000 people on the Maroni River, 120 miles northwest of Cayenne, French Guiana. Shipping and the making of parquet flooring are the main economic activities here. This seaport was once a receiving station for prisoners during the prison era. All but the incorrigibles were housed here; ruins of the prison remain. Saint-Laurent-du-Maroni is the starting point for river excursions. The Atyp and Peslier hotels are said to provide basic, reasonable accommodations. The area nightspots bring this quiet community to life during the evening.

SAINT-PIERRE, 12 miles northwest of Fort-de-France, Martinique, was the first city the French founded in the area, in 1635. It was the scene of one of the most horrendous volcanic calamities of all time in 1902. Mont Pelée's last eruption wiped out all but one of the city's 30,000 people. The survivor was a prisoner in solitary confinement—in an underground cell. Saint-Pierre, in its heyday, was renowned as the "little Paris of the West Indies." The steps and some columns from its beautiful opera house are all that remain of that

Street scene in Martinique

Courtesy of Carolyn Fischer

era. The city is now a tourist stop, and caters to that trade with the Musée Vulcanologique. On a hill is La Factorerie, a large restaurant run by a student-restaurateur staff. A black-sand beach in the southern district is popular. Saint-Pierre's estimated population is 5,000.

ISLAND PROFILE

Geography and Climate

Martinique, part of a group of islands known as the Lesser Antilles, stretches across the entrance to the Caribbean Sea. This archipelago, in the shape of an arc bowed out toward the Atlantic Ocean, extends for 450 miles from the Virgin Islands southward, almost to the coast of

South America. The northern part of the group is called the Leeward Islands; the southern half, the Windward Islands. Many of the islands are the result of volcanic eruptions forcing the ocean bed up 10,000 or more feet. From prehistoric times, this string of islands has stretched across the throat of the Caribbean like a chain of smoldering furnaces about to burst into flame.

It is customary to speak locally of the period from December to May as the dry season when, in fact, some lowering of precipitation and temperature occurs. Throughout the year, however, the mean temperature in the capital, Fort-de-France, varies only slightly, from a low of 76°F to a high of 81°F, while humidity ranges from 65 to 95%. The weather fluctuates from hour to hour; rain showers are quickly followed by bright and sunny weather, and the heat is almost invariably

lifted by the trade winds. The relief brought by these prevailing easterlies makes an otherwise difficult climate more comfortable, particularly in the evenings.

Because of the consistently high temperature and humidity, insects are numerous; lack of screening makes them particularly noticeable. Rust and mildew must be continually combatted.

Guadeloupe is actually two islands, the mountainous Basse-Terre and the flat Grande-Terre, which together resemble the shape of a butterfly. Separated by the Rivière Salée, the islands are connected by a drawbridge. The highest point is the volcano Soufrière, which rises 4,850 feet. November through April are usually the coolest and driest months. Temperatures vary from 74°F in January to 87°F in August;

humidity varies from 77% in April to 85% in August.

French Guiana, the largest of France's overseas departments, with an area of 32,252 square miles, is situated in the northeast corner of South America. Suriname is on the west, and Brazil on the east and south. The land consists of low-lying coastal plains, with tropical forest to low hills. The climate is sub-equatorial, and the temperature averages 80°F throughout the year. Annual rainfall amounts to more than 100 inches, with the wet season extending from December through June.

Population

The population of Martinique is estimated at 412,000 (June 1999). One-third of the population lives in or near Fort-de-France, the island's only major city. Migration of young people to metropolitan France in search of career opportunities limits the annual population growth rate to about 1%. Guadeloupe, Martinique's sister island 100 miles north, has about 421,000 residents. French Guiana's population is approximately 168,000 (1999 est.), half of whom live in Cayenne area.

French is spoken by virtually everyone in all three places, although a Creole *patois* is often heard. A good knowledge of French is essential for daily living, as well as for official and social requirements. The American community is quite small, and the few Frenchmen who know English usually prefer to speak their own language.

The people of Guadeloupe and Martinique are generally friendly toward Americans and other foreigners. The islands are 90% African and African-Caucasian-Indian mixture; 5% Caucasian; and less than 5% East Indian, Lebanese, and Chinese. French Guiana is 66% black or mulatto; 12% Caucasian; 12% East Indian, Chinese, and American Indian; and 10% other. A large proportion of the administrative and military cadre is metropolitan French.

Government

Since 1946, French Guiana, Guadeloupe, and Martinique have borne the formal designation, Départements d' Outre Mer (overseas departments) of France. The senior French official is the prefect/commissioner of the republic, a title which replaced that of "prefect" in 1982 in all French departments under a decentralization policy. The prefect/commissioner reports to the secretary of state for Overseas Departments and Territories who, in turn, reports to the minister of the interior.

Each of the overseas departments/regions has a general council, whose members are elected from each canton, and a regional council whose members are elected by proportional representation. The policy of decentralization provides that many of the powers formerly held by the prefect will be transferred to the elected assemblies. The French military commandant for the French Antilles and French Guiana, normally a general of brigade, has headquarters in Fort-de-France, as does the French Regional Navy commandant.

The French flag, consisting of three vertical bands in blue, white, and red, is flown in Martinique, Guadeloupe, and French Guiana. Martinique and Guadeloupe also have their own territorial flags. Guadaloupe's flag consists of a broad horizontal red band, separated from green stripes at the top and bottom by narrower white stripes. In the red band there is a gold star offset toward the hoist. Martinique's flag has a light blue field with a centered white cross; a white serpent is in each of the four blue quarters.

Arts, Science, Education

Education is compulsory through age 16; literacy is about 80–90% in all three areas.

Two cultural centers in Fort-de-France present musical groups, including some American musicians or ensembles from metropolitan France. (Many Martiniquais are well versed in the history of American jazz.) Occasionally, local groups perform plays, sometimes in Creole. An international guitar festival has been a cultural highlight in recent years. Some opportunities are available for amateur musicians to participate in local chamber music groups. The Ballet Folklorique de la Martinique performs three or more nights weekly at various tourist hotels.

Fort-de-France has a small museum that displays pre-Columbian and colonial artifacts. A small museum across the bay, La Pagerie, is devoted to Empress Josephine of France, who was born on Martinique in 1763.

Commerce and Industry

While the resources of French Guiana remain virtually unexploited, the economies of Martinique and Guadeloupe are based on sugar, bananas, rum, pineapples, tourism, and spending by the French government. Manufacturing is peripheral and in support of the agricultural base. Local markets are dominated by metropolitan France, and the prevalence of imported over locally made products contributes to the high cost of living.

Martinique's gross domestic product (GDP) is nearly $4 billion, or about $$10,000 per capita (1995 rates). Ten percent of the labor force is engaged in agriculture, which includes bananas, pineapples, vegetables, flowers, and sugarcane for rum. Industry in Martinique includes construction, rum, cement, oil refining, and tourism. Exports include refined petroleum products, bananas, rum, and pineapples; imports are petroleum products, foodstuffs, construction materials, vehicles, clothing, and other consumer goods. France is Martinique's major trading partner.

Guadeloupe's GDP is approximately $3.7 billion, or $9,200 per capita. Over half of the labor force is engaged in services, commerce, and government. Guadeloupe's industry includes construction, cement, rum, and tourism. Bananas, sugar, and rum are the main exports; imports include vehicles, foodstuffs, clothing and other consumer goods, construction materials, and petroleum. Franc-zone countries are Guadeloupe's major trade partners.

French Guiana's GDP is about $1 billion, or $6,000 per capita. Sixty percent of the French Guianese labor force work in services, government, and commerce. Agricultural products include limited vegetables for local consumption, as well as rice, corn, manioc, cocoa, bananas, and sugar. Industries include construction, shrimp processing, forestry products, rum, and gold mining. French Guiana exports include shrimp, timber, rum, and rosewood essence. Among the imports are foodstuffs, consumer goods, producer goods, and petroleum.

Transportation

Travel among the three departments is mostly by air. American Airlines flies between New York and Fort-de-France on weekends. Air France has flights between Miami and Fort-de-France, usually with stops at Port-au-Prince, Haiti, and San Juan, Puerto Rico. Three or four ships (freighters) sail monthly between the U.S. and Martinique.

Leeward Islands Air Transport (LIAT), whose headquarters are in Barbados, and Air Guadeloupe provide scheduled service between Martinique and several neighboring islands. Air France also operates between Martinique and Guadeloupe and between each of these and French Guiana. One or two commuter airlines offer service to nearby islands, geared to the tourist trade. Except for Air France, schedules and reservations can be erratic.

The scheduled bus service in Fort-de-France is rarely patronized by Americans. Taxis are expensive. For any extended stay, a personal or rented car is the most convenient method of transportation. Since the town streets are narrow, with few available parking spaces, and roads elsewhere are equally narrow and winding, compact cars are advisable. A U.S. license may be used on the island for a visit of up to 90 days.

Communications

Local telephone service is adequate. Calls to the U.S. can be dialed directly from Martinique, but operator assistance is required for some calls in the reverse direction. Telegraph and airmail service vary in adequacy.

The local radio station, Radio-Télévision Française d'Outre-Mer (RFO) broadcasts daily from early morning until late evening. Programs are produced locally, with occasional dramatic and discussion programs produced in metropolitan France. Medium-wave receivers pick up Radio Caraïbe from the nearby island of St. Lucia, and Radio Antilles from Montserrat—both stations broadcast in English and French and, occasionally, in Creole. About a dozen small, private FM radio stations broadcast in Martinique. Some medium-wave English-language stations in St. Lucia and Barbados, and the Voice of America (VOA) station from Antigua, can often be received. A shortwave is useful and recommended for American Armed Forces Radio, VOA, and British Broadcasting Corporation (BBC) broadcasts. Shortwave reception varies from fair to good.

Television is aired on the same time schedule as is radio. Except for the locally produced daily news, most programs originate in metropolitan France.

Newspapers are barely adequate in reporting local news, and coverage of international developments is superficial. All popular French periodicals and most Paris newspapers appear on local newsstands, usually several days to two weeks after publication. Scarcely any English-language books, either hardback or paperback, are on sale in Martinique, although some bookstores do stock standard French works, fiction and nonfiction. The public library in Fort-de-France has a few English-language books.

Health

Local doctors, dentists, oculists, and opticians are competent for normal needs. Serious or complicated medical problems may require recourse to medical services in San Juan, Puerto Rico, or in the continental U.S. Physical facilities are improving, but remain below American standards; emergency treatment and laboratory work are particularly poor. Maternity facilities are adequate for routine deliveries only; these are normally accomplished without anesthesia and without the presence of a physician.

The water supply in Fort-de-France is safe. Reconstituted, canned, and pasteurized milk is available. Raw fruits and vegetables should be thoroughly cleaned, although this precaution has limited value since it is often ignored by those who prepare food eaten outside American homes.

A yellow fever vaccination is required for travel to French Guiana. Inoculations against typhoid, tetanus, poliomyelitis, and the common infantile diseases are advisable. Common serums and vaccines are available locally.

The invariability of the tropical climate must be included among debilitating factors for those not accustomed to prolonged periods in this type of climate.

The government public health machinery is adequate, but tropical conditions and human indolence encourage diseases and unhealthy conditions. Unsanitary conditions in most eating places, the questionable standard of food preparation, and prevalence of insects encourage disease. A person of generally good health can expect to build up an immunity to most health hazards. Although filariasis, leprosy, bilharzia, and venereal diseases are present among the local population, only dysentery, skin infections, kidney and liver ailments, flu, mononucleosis, and dengue fever have affected Americans.

NOTES FOR TRAVELERS

Passage, Customs & Duties

Fort-de-France can be reached on flights scheduled by American carriers out of New York, Miami, and San Juan.

Passports are required of U.S. citizens entering the French West Indies. Visitors who arrive on a commercial air carrier with a round-trip ticket may enter for up to 90 days without a visa. For further information, travelers can contact the Embassy of France at 4101 Reservoir Road, N.W., Washington, DC 20007; telephone 1 202 944-6000; or the nearest French consulate in Atlanta, Boston, Chicago, Houston, Los Angeles, Miami, New York, New Orleans or San Francisco; Internet: http://www.info-france-usa.org.

There is no U.S. Embassy or Consulate in the French West Indies. For assistance in the French West Indies, U.S. citizens may contact the U.S. Consular Agency at 9 Rue Des Alpinias, Dedier, Fort de France, Martinique, Monday-Friday from 9:00 a.m. to 12:30 p.m., except local and U.S. holidays; telephone (011) (596) 71-96-90 or fax (596) 71-96-89. The mailing address is P.O. Box 975, CEDEX 97246, Fort de France, Martinique. For after-hours service, American citizens may contact the U.S. Embassy in Bridgetown, Barbados, telephone 1-246-436-4950. U.S. citizens living in or visiting the French West Indies are encouraged to register at the Consular Section

of the U.S. Embassy in Bridgetown, and obtain updated information on travel and security within the French West Indies. The Consular Section is located in the American Life Insurance Company (ALICO) Building, Cheapside; telephone 1-246-431-0225; fax 1-246-431-0179; Internet: http://usembassy.state.gov/posts/bb1/wwwhemb1.html. The Consular Section is open for American Citizens Services from 7:30 a.m. to 4:30 p.m., Monday-Friday, except local and U.S. holidays.

Passports are required of U.S. citizens entering French Guiana. Visitors who arrive on a commercial air carrier with a return ticket may enter for up to 90 days without a visa. For further information on entry requirements, travelers can contact the Embassy of France at 4101 Reservoir Road, N.W., Washington, DC 20007; telephone 1-202-944-6000; or the nearest French Consulate in Atlanta, Boston, Chicago, Houston, Los Angeles, Miami, New York, New Orleans or San Francisco. Internet: http://www.info-france-usa.org.

There is no U.S. Embassy or Consulate in French Guiana. Americans living in or visiting French Guiana are encouraged to register at the Consular Section of the U.S. Embassy in Paramaribo, Suriname, and obtain updated information on travel and security within French Guiana. The U.S. Embassy is located at Dr. Sophie Redmondstraat 129, Paramaribo; telephone (011) (597) 472-900. The Consular Section is open for American Citizens Services from 8:00 a.m. to 10:00 a.m., Mondays and Wednesdays, except local and U.S. holidays, or by appointment. In an emergency after normal business hours, American citizens may contact the duty officer by pager at (011)(597) 088-0338.

Pets

Pets may be imported provided they have health certificates and documentation of recent vaccination against rabies. No quarantine

restrictions are imposed on dogs and cats.

Currency, Banking & Weights and Measures

The local currency is the French franc. Chase Manhattan Bank has offices in Martinique.

The metric system of weights and measures is used.

The time in Martinique and Guadeloupe is Greenwich Mean Time (GMT) minus four hours (or equivalent to U.S. Eastern Daylight Saving Time, year round). The time in French Guiana is Greenwich Mean Time minus five hours (the same as U.S. Eastern Standard Time).

Disaster Preparedness

The French West Indies can be affected by hurricanes. The hurricane season normally runs from June to the end of November, but there have been hurricanes in December in recent years. General information about natural disaster preparedness is available via the Internet from the U.S. Federal Emergency Management Agency (FEMA) at http://www.fema.gov/.

LOCAL HOLIDAYS

Jan. 1	New Year's Day
Feb/Mar	Carnival*
Mar/Apr.	Good Friday*
Mar/Apr.	Easter Monday*
May 1	Labor Day
May 8	Veterans Day
May 22	Emancipation Day
May/June	Ascension Day*
May/June	Pentecost
May/June	Pentecost Monday*
Aug. 15	Assumption Day
Nov. 1	All Saints' Day
Dec. 25	Christmas Day

*variable

RECOMMENDED READING

The following titles are provided as a general indication of material published on this country:

Horowitz, Michael M. *Morne-Paysan: A Peasant Village in Martinique*. New York: Irvington Publishers, 1983.

Laguerre, Michel S. *Urban Poverty in the Caribbean: The Martinican Experience*. New York: St. Martin, 1990.

Miles, William F. *Elections & Ethnicity in French Martinique: A Paradox in Paradise*. Westport, CT: Greenwood Publishing, 1985.

Smith, A.L., and M.J. Roobol. *Mt. Pelee, Martinique: A Study of an Active Island-Arc Volcano*. Boulder, CO: Geological Society of America, 1991.

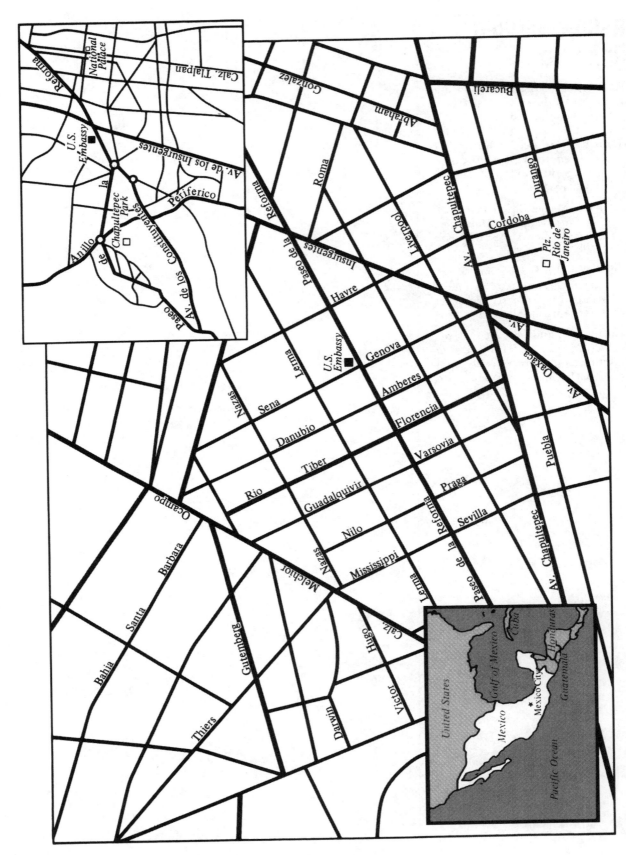

Mexico City, Mexico

MEXICO

United Mexican States

Major Cities:

Mexico City, Guadalajara, Monterrey, Ciudad Juárez, Tijuana, Hermosillo, Matamoros, Mazatlán, Mérida, Nuevo Laredo, Puebla

Other Cities:

Acapulco, Aguascalientes, Campeche, Chihuahua, Ciudad Obregón, Coyoacán, Cuernavaca, Culiacán, Durango, Guanajuato, Guaymas, Irapuato, Ixtapalapa, Jalapa, La Paz, León, Manzanillo, Mexicali, Morelia, Nezahualcóyotl, Oaxaca, Orizaba, Pachuca, Poza Rica, Puerto Vallarta, Querétaro, Saltillo, San Luis Potosí, Tampico, Taxco, Tepic, Toluca, Veracruz, Xochimilco, Zacatecas

INTRODUCTION

Mexico's rich past offers a visitor's backdrop of enchantment. Pyramids where Aztec priests performed human sacrifices still stand, approaching in bulk Egypt's largest. Monuments recall the exploits of a handful of Spaniards who toppled a mighty empire in a conquest unparalleled in history. Towns retain the flavor of a Spanish colony that flourished-even boasted a university-half a century before Jamestown began.

Mexico City, a metropolis of delightful climate and modern buildings amid historic charm, lies ringed by snow-capped volcanoes that slope down to pine forests, deserts, and balmy tropical beaches.

The first people to inhabit this land may have arrived 20,000 years before Columbus. Their descendants, including the Mayan and Aztecs, built a succession of highly developed civilizations that flourished from 1200 B.C.E. to C.E. 1521.

Hernán Cortex landed near modern day Vera Cruz in 1519. King Montezuma II invited the Spaniards into his palace and they promptly took him hostage. After the Spanish conquistadors destroyed the Aztec Empire, the position of the conquered peoples deteriorated rapidly. The Indian population fell from an estimated 25 million at the time of conquest to 1 million by 1605.

From the 16th to 19th centuries, a new colonial society emerged, stratified by race and wealth. The upper echelon was European, in the middle were people of mixed European-indigenous heritage, and at the bottom were the descendants of the native peoples.

Mexico began agitating for independence in the late 1700s and early 1800s. The struggle for independence was long and fitful, however, and freedom from Spain was not finally realized until 1821.

Culturally, politically, and economically, Mexico is experiencing rapid change. For a country composed mostly of peasants before the Revolution (1910-20), Mexico has undergone broad and rapid urbanization. Mexico City emerged as one of the world's largest cities at the end of the 20th century. The economy has dramatically about-faced, embracing open-market policies and free-trade links with the U.S. and countries throughout the Americas.

MAJOR CITIES

Mexico City

Mexico City, formally known as Mexico, Distrito Federal (D.F.), is a cosmopolitan capital. The glass-walled sky-scrapers lining the Paseo de la Reforma, the stunning architecture of the Museum of Anthropology, the variety of international restaurants, deluxe hotels, the Lomas residential area with its stylish homes, and modern department stores and supermarkets are all signs of a world metropolitan center. But surrounding this glittering center are mass housing developments and barrios typical of the rapidly growing capital of a developing country. Heavy industry and millions of motor vehicles make the city one of most polluted in the world.

Cityscape of Mexico City, Mexico

Mexico City lies in a long, flat valley on the high plateau of central Mexico. Many of the peaks encircling the city are volcanic-including glacier topped Popocateped, "The Warrior," and Iztacchihautl, "The Sleeping Lady." "Pogo" and "Izta" provide a spectacular setting for the city on the days when a drop in air pollution makes them visible.

Although Mexico City is only 19 degrees N. of the Equator, the high altitude (7,350 feet) creates a fall-like climate all year. Thus, despite its tropical latitude, the city has a pleasant average temperature range of 53 to 79°F in the warmest month (May), and 42 to 70°F in the coolest month (January). The two seasons are dry and rainy. The latter lasts from June through September when several hours of rain fall daily, usually in the afternoon and evening; but mornings are sunny. Nights and evenings after the storms are cool and damp. The weather is coolest November through February when night and early morning temperatures can drop to freezing. March through May are the warm and dusty. These months are at the end of the dry season. Average humidity range is 44%-73% and annual rainfall averages 30 inches, 90%% of which falls between May and October.

Utilities

Electricity is the same as in the U.S.: 110 volt, 60 hertz, alternating current. Buildings use liquid propane gas for hot water and cooking.

Water pressure varies and is often low; so many residences have reserve storage tanks to occasionally supply water when the city water is off for several hours or days.

Mexico uses the same two-prong outlets as in the U.S., but many residences have been upgraded with standard three-prong, polarized, and grounded outlets that are more common in the U.S. Electrical blackouts of several hours are not unusual during the rainy season. Voltage fluctuations are common; so surge suppressors, voltage regulators, and uninterruptible power supplies for electronic equipment are useful. Kitchen and bathroom outlets are rarely found with ground fault circuit interrupters, which are required by most U.S. electrical codes.

Food

A variety of groceries, including fresh fruits and vegetables, packaged foods (both domestic and imported), dairy products, and meats are available. Supermarkets stock fresh or frozen meat and fish, dairy products, fresh produce, and canned or packaged goods. Major U.S. food packagers produce such goods in Mexico as cereals, bakery products, and beverages-but sometimes with a slightly different taste than what you may be accustomed to. Widely available fresh fruits include pineapple, papaya, watermelon, and cantaloupe year round; as well as seasonal mango. Several large markets have unusual and common Mexican and tropical fruits and vegetables. Many specialty shops sell ethnic foods-including Middle-Eastern locally produced fresh kosher meats, and imported frozen foods. Most food items are available at reasonable prices, but imported items are only available at prices higher than in the United States. Most of the larger supermarkets feature sections devoted to imported goods. Smaller shops specializing in U.S. products are located in Lomas, Polanco, and a few other areas. All necessities and many other items are available.

Locally produced mixes and canned foods are of varying quality and very limited variety. Prepared frozen and packaged meals are imported and expensive. A large variety of Mexican cheeses are available. Many of the available cheeses are similar to common European and American types. Strained baby foods are expensive and of lower quality.

Mexican beer is good and very reasonably priced. Bottled soft drinks (including diet sodas or "lite" as they are known locally) are available at modest prices.

Clothing

Clothing needs in Mexico City do not vary a great deal throughout the year. Warm clothing is useful for cold spells in the winter (November to February) and rainy season (June to September). Temperatures can vary anywhere from 70°F to 40°F It is suggested that you take a few sweaters, a raincoat, and an umbrella.

Lightweight summer clothes are essential for travel to low-altitude areas where the climate is hot and humid, but are only needed in Mexico City from March through June when temperatures may reach up to 90°F. Remember that Mexico is approximately 7,300 feet above sea level; so mornings and evenings can be cool and even though it may

reach into the 90s in the sun, it can still be on the cool side in the shade.

Clothing of all kinds is available at prices comparable to the U.S., but the quality varies. Mexico City has large shopping malls, several different department store chains, and a large variety of small boutiques. Sears, Liverpool, and Palacio de Hierro are among the larger department stores. A wide variety of locally made and imported clothing is available.

Take U.S. swimsuits and underwear for children and adults. Some Mexican-made clothing, particularly stockings and pantyhose, often do not fit tall women (approx. 5'6" and taller). Mexican shoes are stylish and well made, however shoes do not go beyond American size eight for women. Narrow shoe sizes are very scarce.

Men: In Mexico City, men wear light- to medium weight business suits. The darker colors (black, brown, charcoal gray) are the most popular. Lightweight suits are comfortable in the spring and for traveling to low altitudes. Mexican shoes are stylish and well made, but do not go beyond American 10 for men. Narrow shoe sizes are very scarce. Take or order from the U.S. any sportswear, shirts, shoes, pajamas, underwear, and socks that you will need. These items are sold locally; but the quality and variety may not appeal to American tastes. It is suggested that you take along a supply of buttons (for suits) and thread. Buttons very frequently 'pop-off' at the most inconvenient time and thread sold locally may not be of very good quality.

Good tailors are available varying with prices. Hats or shorts are rarely worn in Mexico City, except for sports activities. A dark suit is appropriate.

Women: Take wool or cotton suits and dresses with jackets. Mexico City temperatures can change rapidly during the day, particularly during the rainy season. Long-sleeved blouses, sweaters, jackets,

and layered clothing are very useful; homes and offices are rarely heated. Pantsuits are very popular.

The dress for receptions, cocktail parties, dinners, and similar events varies according to rank and representational activity. Most Mexican women wear current U.S. fashions for both afternoon and evening social events. Shorts are not worn except for recreation, or at resorts. Locally made dresses are available in a variety of styles, including both current fashions and Mexican ethnic. Imported clothing from the U.S. and Europe is available. Good Mexican textiles are available; but some are not pre-shrunk, colorfast, or drip-dry.

Patterns sold locally cost twice as much as those in the U.S. The selection of such sewing accessories as thread is limited and the quality is often poor. Well-crafted silver, brass, and copper jewelry is less expensive than in the U.S. Native semi-precious stones such as turquoise, opals, and topaz in silver or gold mountings-are also available.

Children: Children's clothes are available in great variety. Price and quality vary, depending upon the store. Some parents take children's clothes from the U.S. or order from catalogs. Dress for all ages is similar to that in the U.S., although teenagers in Mexico seem very fashion conscious. Some schools require uniforms. European-style baby clothing is readily available, but American style clothing is not. Disposable diapers are available in the commissary and on the local economy; however some locally made disposable diapers have been known to cause severe diaper rash on some children. Children's shoes and sneakers are available at both a satisfactory price and quality.

Supplies and Services

A variety of both domestic and imported supplies and services are available on the local economy. Many U.S. brands of health or beauty aids are manufactured and sold locally. Most medications can be bought at local drugstores and may cost less than in the U.S.

Film and developing are readily available, including 45-minute processing. Prices, quality, and service compare favorably with the U.S. Quality engraving and printing can be done locally.

Dry-cleaners and commercial laundries are slower, but competitive in price to those in the U.S. Pick-up and delivery from your residence is also available. Beauty shops and barbershops are numerous and compare favorably with those in the U.S. in price and service. Reasonably priced shoe repair is available. Audio, video, and personal computer equipment repair services are satisfactory; however, some parts are scarce and the work can be expensive. Service and repair on U.S. cars are fair. Dealer service is available for Chrysler, Ford, GM, Nissan, and VW models that are assembled in Mexico. It is suggested that you contact your local dealer in the U.S. to verify all warranty information.

Most stores and markets are located close to such tourist centers as the Zona Rosa (Pink Zone), Polanco (very popular neighborhood), and the Zocalo (Historic Center). The real bargains are in handcrafted silver, gold, copper, tin, onyx, leather, textiles, pottery, blown-glass, and paintings. Stores usually open at 10 am or 11 am, but the time may vary according to the owner's whim. They usually remain open until 7 pm or 8 pm. Many specialized stores open only half- days on Saturday and most stores close on Sunday, except for those stores located in the malls.

Domestic Help

Many U.S. expatriates have such domestic help as maids, gardeners or chauffeurs; however, few speak English. Truly skilled cooks are hard to find. Almost all domestic employees hired locally are Mexican. The Government of Mexico is strict about visas and work permits for foreign domestics because of the large number of Mexicans available.

Although many domestics live in, they can also be hired on a part-time "live-out" basis for laundry and cleaning purposes. Families with small children may find it helpful to have a live-in domestic to look after children, since good babysitters are very scarce. Most homes and many apartments have separate servants quarters. The cost of a domestic employee's salary, Christmas bonus, meals, uniform, severance pay, and Social Security has increased in recent years; but it is still significantly less expensive than in the U.S. An employer is liable for three months of severance pay upon departure once an employee has completed 30 days of employment. It increases at the rate of 20 days a year. One-third of the wage is retained to cover costs of room and board for live-in domestics. Domestic employees are entitled to one day off a week, Mexican holidays, and six to twelve days, paid vacation days a year. Employers have the option of enrolling servants in the IMSS health program or paying their medical expenses directly.

Religious Activities

Mexico City's large English-speaking community is served by several English language religious institutions, including but not limited to Catholic, Baptist, Christian Science, Church of Christ, Greek Orthodox, Jewish (Conservative), Latter-day Saints, Lutheran, Methodist, Quaker, Seventh-day Adventist, Union Evangelical, Interdenominational, and Unitarian religions/beliefs. Announcements for the times of services appear regularly in the English-language daily newspaper, The Mexico City News.

Education

The following schools offer programs from pre-school through sixth grade: Lomas Altas, Sierra Nevada, and Eaton. These schools are located in the Lomas de Chapultepec neighborhood.

The American School Foundation (ASF) (Address: Bondojito 215, Colonia Las Americas, Delegacion Alvaro Obregon, 01120 Mexico, Distrito Federal, Mexico)

As a bicultural and bilingual school, its program is different than the U.S. schools. It offers accredited co-educational programs in pre-primary, primary (first to fifth), middle school (sixth to eighth), and high school (ninth to twelfth) levels. The SACS in the U.S. accredits the ASR The school also has Mexican accreditation, by the Secretariat of Public Education (SEP) for all grade levels and the National Autonomous University of Mexico (UNAM), Mexico City, for the high school program.

ASF receives some grant aid from the Office of Overseas Schools (A/OS); but, it is not affiliated with the U.S. Embassy. Under the terms of the Government's grant to the school, AFS must accept all children who meet admission standards. AFS has about 2,200 students-approximately 50% of whom are Mexican, 25% American, and 25% other nationalities. Classes in primary school are conducted half-day in Spanish and half-day in English. However, children with little-to no Spanish attend "Special Spanish" classes. In middle school, Spanish is taught as a second language. The ASF campus includes indoor and outdoor play areas, tennis courts, and an indoor swimming pool. An intramural sports program includes American football, soccer, and basketball.

The school year starts in mid-August and ends in late June. Two-week vacations occur both at Christmas and Easter. Uniforms are not required.

Children coming from schools with other than an American curriculum and children with poor academic records may be required to take an admission exam.

Summer activities include remedial and enrichment programs, in addition to a half-day Summer Camp Program. Extracurricular activities include drama, Model United Nations, a variety of sports,

National Honor Society (NHS), and various clubs.

Greengates: (Address: Avenida Circunvalacion Poniente 102, Balcones de San Mateo, 53200 Naucalpan, Estado de Mexico, Mexico). A private, coeducational school based on the British system that offers kindergarten through high school. Applicants are tested for acceptance and placement. The school year is from mid-August through late June. Classes are taught in English. Spanish is required as a second language and French is offered beginning in grade six.

The school requires elementary and junior high students to wear uniforms. An after-school activity program includes art, drama, music, chess, and photography. About 30 nationalities are represented. Summer programs include remedial education, arts, crafts, and sports. Expenses are within the education allowance.

Lomas Altas: (Address: Montanas Calizas 305, Lomas de Chapultepec, Mexico 11000 D.F. Tels 520-5375, 2027986, fax: 520-2276.) Lomas Alias is growing in popularity for younger children (up to the sixth grade). The school is a private, coeducational school for children from pre-school through sixth grade. There are regularly long waiting lists for spaces. Early registration is recommended No uniform is required. The school year is from mid-August through to the end of June. The majority of children attending the school are Mexican. Beginning in the first grade, half the day's curriculum is conducted in Spanish and half in English. For younger children, the classes are all in English.

Westhill Institute: (Address: Monies Carpatos, No. 940, 11000 Mexico D.F) Westhill is a private, coeducational school, founded in 1992. The school has two campuses. Kindergarten through grade 6 is located in Lomas de Chapultepec. Older children go to the campus in Santa Fe. Uniforms are required.

The standard curriculum includes some class work in Spanish and French.

In addition, numerous other schools-such as Montessori, French, German, and religious-are available. Many nursery schools and kindergartens are available and one or two have summer programs. Most schools have bus service.

Except for Greengates School, most schools must conform to the Government of Mexico requirements to teach Spanish at least half of every school day in elementary grades and follow the approved curriculum.

Special Educational Opportunities

UNAM has a school for foreign students, that offers programs in Latin American Studies and intensive Spanish. Most courses are in English, including those in Mexican history and culture. The university offers many degrees-including economics, dentistry, engineering, and the humanities.

A wide range of courses and programs is offered at The Ibero-American University (Universidad Ibero Americana) and the University of the Americas, Mexico City (Universidad de Las Americas).

Universidad Internacional de Mexico, located in Mexico City, is part of the U.S. International University of San Diego, California. The U.S. campus is accredited by the Western Association of Schools and Colleges. It offers undergraduate degrees in business administration, general studies, and psychology as well as graduate programs in management and organizational development, psychology, international business administration, and business administration. All course work is in English.

Sports

The athletic facilities at numerous private clubs are open. The ASF campus includes lighted tennis courts and an indoor swimming pool, available for community use for a nominal fee. A swimming pool

at the YMCA is available for a small charge. Gold's Gym, located in Mexico City, offers various types of equipment and personal trainers for variable membership dues.

The Maria Isabel Sheraton Hotel has some athletic club facilities, including exercise classes. The Camino Real Hotel rents tennis courts by the hour.

Runners must take time to adapt to Mexico City's higher altitude. Heavy traffic and air pollution dampen some runners' enthusiasm, but Chapultepec Park and other locations provide pleasant surroundings for running. Runners must remember that crime is relatively high in Mexico City; so you must be cautious of where and when you choose to run.

As in most Latin countries, soccer is a favorite spectator sport. Other sports include horse racing, jaialai, American football, baseball, softball, basketball, and polo. Bullfights are held almost every Sunday. Horseback riding is popular among Mexicans. Few riding clubs are available in Mexico City and its environs. You may rent horses to ride "Mexican saddle" in the countryside around Mexico City.

The Government of Mexico requires special permits to possess firearms or to use them for hunting.

Freshwater fishing for trout and bass is good.

Some of the world's best deep-sea fishing and beaches are at such Pacific coast resorts, as Acapulco and Ixtapa Zihuatanejo (Guerrero), Puerto Vallarta (Jalisco), Puerto Escondido and Huatulco (Oaxaca) near the Gulf of Tehuantepec, Mazatlan (Sinaloa), and Los Cabos (at the southern tip of the 1,000-mile-long Baja California Peninsula). The Gulf of California (also known as the Sea of Cortes) resorts include Guaymas (Sonora). The Gulf of Mexico resorts include Veracruz and Tampico (Veracruz). Caribbean resorts include Cancun and Cozumel (Quintana Roo). Mountain climbing is popular at the nearby volcanoes of Popocateped ("Pogo" is the second-highest mountain in Mexico) and Iztacchihautl; and at the Pico de Orizaba (the highest mountain in Mexico and the third highest in North America, on the Puebla/Veracruz border) it is popular with the hardy who are also accustomed to high altitudes (17,000 feet above sea level). The lower slopes provide extraordinary beauty and offer an attractive alternative of hiking and scenery. The city of Puebla (altitude 7,030 feet), located on the eastern side of "Pogo" and "Izta," was one of the first Hispanic cities in Mexico. It has museums and buildings reflecting the Spanish colonial period. The Battle of Puebla, which marked Mexican victory over

French forces on May 5, 1862, is celebrated in today's Cinco de Mayo festivities.

Touring and Outdoor Activities

Touring and sightseeing possibilities are excellent. Mexico abounds in archeological sites from the indigenous, meso-American civilizations of the pre-Hispanic era.

The Great Temple, the seat of the Aztec civilization, is in the Zocalo (or central plaza), in downtown Mexico City. Founded in 1325 as Tenochtitlan, it was conquered by Hernando Cortes in 1521. An adjacent museum displays artifacts found at the site. The pyramids of the Sun and the Moon, dating from C.E. 500, are found at Teotihuacan (also known as the City of the Gods), about a 45 minute ride northeast of Mexico City. Tula (Hidalgo), the capital of the Toltec civilization, is a one-hour drive northwest of Mexico City, off the toll road to Queretaro. Mayan sites are everywhere when you visit the Yucatan Peninsula.

The downtown Mexico City area includes excellent museums, the Cathedral, the National Palace with murals by Diego Rivera, glass factories, old churches, convents, and colorful markets. Chapultepec Park is a popular, lake-centered woodland.

It is several miles square and located near the Polanco and Lomas areas of Mexico City. It has a zoo, bridle paths, picnic areas, playgrounds, miniature trains, botanical gardens, bicycle paths, row boats, a colorful amusement park, fine restaurants, and Atlantis-an aquatic animal park.

Mexico City's central location makes weekend trips easy to low altitudes, scenic resorts, and towns by car, train, bus, or plane. Many old haciendas have been converted into beautiful hotels and resorts. Located within a day's excursion, south of Mexico City is Cuernavaca, Morelos (altitude 5,060 feet), known as the City of Perpetual Springtime; and Taxco, Guerrero (altitude 5,760 feet), a colonial town noted for silver manufacturing.

The Spanish colonial town of San Miguel de Allende, Guanajuato (altitude 6,140 feet) is two hours to the north. Toll roads fan out from Mexico City to these and other areas of interest.

Summer activities for children are somewhat limited. Summer jobs are not always available for high school and college-age students; so many families spend a few weeks traveling during summer.

Entertainment

Mexico City's performing and visual arts programs are international in scope. The National Institute of Fine Arts (INBA) offers a broad range of cultural activities at its numerous concert halls, theaters, museums, and other facilities. The Palacio de Bellas Artes and the National Auditorium are the traditional venues for performing arts programs. In recent years, newer facilities have suffered in various parts of the city. World class symphony orchestras, chamber orchestras, chamber ensembles, opera companies, jazz groups, modern dance companies and ballet companies perform periodically at Bellas Artes. Superb art exhibits, are held frequently.

The National Museum of Anthropology hosts programs of dance and music from Mexico's indigenous cultures.

Mexico's famed Ballet Folklorico performs each Wednesday and Sunday a Bellas Artes. UNAM administers an extensive cultural program, which often includes American activities held at their Centro Cultural, in the southern part of the city. Tickets for INBA and UNAM programs are moderately priced.

There are several amateur theater groups in addition to commercial theater groups. Movie theaters show first-run American movies about three months after their release in the U.S. at inexpensive prices.

Video clubs feature a selection of movies, most of which are in VHS format. DVD is sometimes available.

Dining out is reasonably priced and varied. The cosmopolitan nature of the city is nowhere more evident than in the variety of restaurants, with specialties ranging from the various regions of Mexico (Yucatan, Veracruz, etc.) to countries and cultures around the world. Mexican food in Mexico is very different from the Mexican-style food that has become so popular in the U.S. International restaurant offerings include anything from the Argentine-style "parrilla" to Middle Eastern cuisine. Good caterers are available throughout Mexico.

Mexicans normally eat their main meal as early as 2:00 pm and then have light dinner after about 9:00 pm. It is always better to make a restaurant reservation for parties larger than six. Nightclubs are everywhere you look in Mexico City.

Chapultepec Park boasts the National Museum of Anthropology, a handsome building housing one of the world's most extensive collection of pre-Hispanic artifacts from cultures indigenous to Mexico.

Church in Guadalajara, Mexico

Lecture tours in English are available. The Museum of Modern Art provides an overview of 80 years of Mexican art, as well as numerous excellent foreign and Mexican exhibits. The Rufino Tamayo Museum, includes collections of paintings and sculptures by 20th-century artists from Mexico, the U.S., and Europe. Chapultepec Castle and museum, the residence of the Austrian Archduke Maximilian (1864-67), overlooks the eastern end of the park and Paseo de la Reforma.

Other fine museums include the San Carlos, the Pinacoteca Virreinal, the Frida Kalo, the National Museum of the Viceroyalty (the Spanish Colonial Period), and the Anahuacali Museum which features Diego Rivera's pre-Hispancic collection.

For those interested in Mexico City's active art scene, the city offers more than a dozen fine commercial art galleries, which periodically show the best of Mexican and-to a lesser extent-foreign artists. Artists also regularly exhibit in several out-door parks.

Social Activities

Well-known organizations with branches in Mexico City include: the American Benevolence Society, the American Legion, Boy Scouts, Girl Guides, Daughters of the American Revolution, Junior League, Lions, Navy League, Kiwanis, Knights of Columbus, Shriners, Hash House Harriers, St. Andrews, and various U.S. college alumni clubs. The American Society offers a wide variety of social activities.

A good knowledge of Spanish and a real effort to make friends helps to develop friendships. Many clubs within Mexico, such as Damas Diplomaticas and The Newcomers' Club, offer monthly meetings, speakers, tours to various sites in Mexico, dinners, and dances.

Guadalajara

Metropolitan Guadalajara, with a population of more than five million inhabitants, including approximately 50,000 resident U.S citizens, sits 5,092 feet above sea level on a broad plateau. A dramatic canyon, "La Barranca," forms the city's natural northern boundary; picturesque mountains rise to the east and west and Lake Chapala lies to the south.

Guadalajara enjoys a temperate climate year round. Dry, sunny days are interrupted by brief thundershowers during the summer rainy season (June through October). Ninety percent of the average annual rainfall of 35 inches falls during these five months. Because of its altitude, Guadalajara escapes coastal heat and humidity. The average temperature range varies from 45 to 75°F in January and 55 to 90°F in May. The climate which is comparable to that of San Diego except for the greater rainfall, has been instrumental in attracting thousands of tourists as well as American retirees.

A city of brightly colored tropical flowers, Guadalajara proudly blends its historic past with modern development. The Cathedral, government buildings, and expansive plazas of the city center stand as impressive remnants of Mexico's colonial heritage. Plaza Tapatia, a downtown pedestrian mall, offers hours of pleasant strolling amidst greenery, fountains, shops, and restaurants in the city's historic center. It is also the location of the Cultural Cabanas Institute, which houses the world-famous Orozco ceiling murals.

Utilities

Electric service is the same as in the U.S.: 110 volt, 60 hertz, AC. Voltage regulators or surge suppressors can protect televisions, stereos, and computers from electrical surges. Both are available locally. It is advisable to unplug the equipment when not in use and to not use the equipment in the middle of thunder and lightning storms.

Food

Guadalajara is home to such American chains as Wal-Mart Super-Center, Sam's Club, and Costco in addition to Mexican chain super-center-type stores. Many American products manufactured in either the U.S. or in Mexico can be found in these stores. However, those products made in the U.S. may not be routinely stocked by the store. It is best to stock up on desired goods when you find them in local stores. Additionally, there are innumerable specialty food stores, bakeries, and outdoor markets that offer a wide variety of products.

Frozen foods are readily available, and low-calorie, low-fat products are becoming more widely available. Pasteurized milk (whole and skim), cheeses, and heavy cream may be safely purchased in supermarkets.

City tap water is safe for bathing and cleaning, but not for drinking.

Bottled drinking water is sold in virtually all stores and delivery service may be established such that the water is delivered to your home on a set schedule.

It is necessary to disinfect fruits and vegetables before eating them. Disinfectant drops and powder are readily available in all local grocery stores.

Clothing

Guadalajara boasts an enviable spring and summer climate year round. Light and medium weight clothing is comfortable in all seasons. Heavy winter clothing is not needed. Take a raincoat and umbrella for the mid-June to October rainy season. Summer clothes are perfect for travel to low-altitude, warmer areas. Take your bathing suit for use at local pools and for the enjoyment of nearby beaches. Formal social occasions are rare; most functions are informal. A plain, dark suit for men or cocktail dresses for women is appropriate attire.

Guadalajara has several large, American-style shopping malls, and a variety of clothing styles is available in the many boutiques and department stores. Leather jackets, shoes and boots are available at reasonable prices as there are many manufacturers of leather goods in the area. Large sized shoes and clothing are scarce.

Supplies and Services

Housekeepers are available on apart-time or live-in basis. Wages are very reasonable in comparison to U.S. rates.

Gardeners are also available at a reasonable fee. Their services are generally needed every two weeks during the rainy season and less frequently for the remainder of the year. Medical care, furniture design, and construction, automobile and appliance repair, and other services can be found at a lower cost than in the U.S.

Religious Activities

Several churches, including Catholic, Lutheran, Episcopal, and Pres-

byterian churches offer English services. A Jewish community offers services in Spanish and Hebrew.

Education

Guadalajara is home to five private and two public universities as well as several smaller institutions of higher learning. Also, a good number of excellent high schools and grammar schools exist where the language of instruction is Spanish.

The American School offers a coeducational, bilingual program from pre-kindergarten through high school. The student body consists of nearly 1,300 students, more than 80% of whom are Mexican. Children with special educational needs may not be well served there or by any other school in Guadalajara. The teaching staff is multinational, but predominantly Mexican. Most of the remainder is from the U.S. or Canada. It is accredited by the Southern Association of Colleges of Schools. The school year runs from late August to late June with two-week vacations at Easter and Christmas.

Pre-kindergarten, elementary, and high school level courses have summer sessions. Uniforms are not required.

The John F. Kennedy School offers instruction from kindergarten through grade six. Kindergarten is taught completely in English; pre-first grade for six year-olds offers two subjects in Spanish and the rest in English; and primary school beginning at age seven is taught in Spanish and English on alternating days. Bus service is not available.

The Lincoln School, which offers prekindergarten through grade 12, has two different teaching programs: the bilingual program is taught half in Spanish and half in English; the traditional, bicultural program offers 90% of material in English, with the remaining 10% in Spanish. The school is built on Christian principles, with mandatory 20-minute devotions each morning. Bus service is not offered.

Sports

Guadalajara's climate encourages a wide variety of outdoor sports. Swimming, tennis, hiking, and horseback riding are popular. Five 18-hole golf courses, a nine-hole course and one practice range are available in Guadalajara. Both private clubs and city recreation facilities offer swimming, tennis, racquetball, basketball, and other sports.

Touring and Outdoor Activities

Guadalajara is situated in close proximity to many areas worth visiting. The neighboring towns of Tonala and Tlaquepaque offer an enormous selection of artisan crafts at very affordable prices. Tonala hosts exciting market days every Thursday and Sunday for additional shopping pleasure.

Lake Chapala and the lakeside village of Ajijic are only an hour away. Beyond the lake are the picturesque towns of Mazamitla and Tapalpa.

For beach lovers, there are many options within about four hours' driving from Guadalajara. Puerto Vallarta, the principal beach resort in the consular district, is 25 minutes away by plane or approximately four hours by car. Manzanillo, another important beach town, is three hours away by car and home to great fishing as well as the largest seaport on Mexico's Pacific coast. Additional beaches include Barra de Navidad, Nueva Vallarta, and Tenacatita.

The neighboring states of Michoacan, Guanajuato, and Zacatecas are also, easy-to-reach destinations for vacations or long weekends.

Entertainment

Touring musical and dance companies from Mexico and other countries are often featured in the stately Degollad Theater or Cultural Cabanas Institute. Additionally, the University of Guadalajara presents an exceptional Ballet Folklorico every Sunday morning at the Degollado Theater.

Busy downtown street, Tijuana

Susan Rock. Reproduced by permission.

There is a large and active American Society to welcome new American residents. The Mexican American Cultural Institute also sponsors program, of interest.

Depending on the neighborhood in which they live, families either have cable television or a satellite television service on which various American television shows are shown, and such Popular cable channels, as ESPN, and CNN are widely available.

Monterrey

Monterrey stretches from the arid plains near the U.S. border south to the northern tier of traditional, colo-nial Mexico. The most distant major city in the district, Durango, is a six-hour drive from Monterrey. The total population of the district is estimated at nearly 12 million, of which an estimated 3.8 million live in the Monterrey metropolitan area. About 57,000 U.S. citizens live within the district, with 28,000 residing in greater Monterrey.

Monterrey is Mexico's third largest city and second most important industrial and financial metropolis. The capital of the state of Nuevo Leó It is located in the northeastern part of Mexico, about 150 miles from the Texas border. Monterrey is the hub of the most prosperous urban area in all of Mexico.

The area's geography and history have given the people of Monterrey, otherwise known as "Regiomontanos," an individualistic-reserved character. The trend setting business community is conservative in its politics, religion, and social structure. Monterrey is advanced in its approach to technical innovation and economic opportunities; closer to American than traditional Latin concepts in business practices; and devoted to the family, hard work and the expansion of the family enterprise. The "Group of Ten," are 10 large industrial conglomerates that play a crucial role in Mexico's economy.

Monterrey is situated in a semi-arid valley at an altitude of 1,766 feet and is bounded on three sides by rugged mountains. About two hours to the southeast of the city is one of Mexico's most important citrus-producing areas. Most of the surrounding countryside, however, is semi-arid and covered with brush.

While only minimal rainfall occurs during the November to April dry season, the average rainfall is 20 inches a year. Half the rain falls during August, September, and October. Summer temperatures usually begin in mid-March and last though October. Spring-like weather with warm days and cool nights occurs from November to March, but the cooler weather worsens the seemingly omnipresent smog. The average monthly temperatures vary from 50-74°F in January to 74-98°F in June and July. Summer highs regularly top 100°F for several weeks at a time; from mid-November through January, the mercury can sporadically plunge into the 30s overnight.

Dust can be an irritant year round, especially during the dry season, and chronic respiratory problems are aggravated by frequent thermal inversions. The phenomenal growth Monterrey experienced during the last decade has threatened the fragile ecology of the semi-arid region. Government efforts to reduce pollution have thus far had little effect.

Utilities

Piped natural gas is commonly used for stoves and water heaters. Electric current is the same as in the U.S.: 110 volt, 60 hertz, AC. Power outages are rare but fluctuations are common, making voltage regulators or surge protectors for PC's essential. Due to scarce rainfall, many houses are equipped with water tanks and some with cistern systems, which ensure water 24 hours daily.

Transportation

Public transportation within the suburbs and in Monterrey is adequate; nevertheless, you may want to bring a personnally owned vehicle for a longer stay.

Driving in this area is not for the faint-hearted. Regulations concerning driver's licenses are loosely enforced and locals are known for their aggressive driving habits.

Food

Fish, seafood, and poultry are also regularly available. Most fresh fruits and vegetables familiar to Americans, plus a wide variety of tropical fruits, are sold here. The arrival of the South Texas grocery chain H.E.B. in Monterrey in 1997 elevated the food shopping experience to U.S. standards. Baby food, low fat, sugarfree and numerous ethnic foods are available year round. Most Americans make occasional trips to the Texas border towns to purchase hard-to-find specialty items or to take advantage of the lower prices. All cuts of good quality meat are available, but at prices higher than those in the U.S.

Clothing

Although clothes are often more expensive in Monterrey than in the U.S., tailors are a bargain.

Hats are seldom worn by men, except with sport clothes or for protection from the sun and rain. In summer, men often wear cotton suits; men's fashions are conservative, with business suits universal among government and private sector contacts. A variety of women's clothing is worn. Slacks are often seen, but shorts are appropriate only for sporting activities. Women should bring what they would wear for the office, parties, or at home in the U.S. Although Mexican shoes are stylish and reasonably priced, many Americans have difficulty finding their shoe sizes. Attractive sandals for summer are available.

Religious Activities

English-speaking services are held at the Fatima (Roman Catholic), All Souls (Anglican) and Union Churches, the latter serving a broad based Protestant congregation. The independent Castillo del Rey offers English language Bible study. There are also services for Jewish (Orthodox), LDS, Baptist, Presbyterian, Methodist, Pentecostal, and independent congregations, some of whose services may be translated into English upon request.

Education

The American School Foundation of Monterrey, a private, coeducational school offering classes from nursery through grade 12. Instruction is in English with Spanish courses for American children. The school is accredited by SACS.

The school year runs from mid August to mid June. Current enrollment exceeds 2,000 students-of whom more than 10% are American. The preschool and elementary school operate at the Rio Missouri Campus and serve more than 1,000 children. A beautiful state-of-the art middle school and high school opened on a separate campus in August 1996. Students in high school have the opportunity to earn both a U.S. high school diploma and its Mexican equivalent. The school offers a rigorous college preparatory program and includes support services for children with mild learning difficulties.

Several children also attend the American Institute of Monterrey, a smaller bilingual school that is not accredited in the U.S.

Medical Facilities

Monterrey is known as the Houston of Mexico, boasting the best medical care facilities in all of Mexico. A full range of U.S. trained, English - speaking specialists is readily available to assist with virtually any medical problem. Nevertheless, some patients, in consultation with MED, would be advised to seek treatment in the U.S.-particularly expectant mothers. For dental and orthodontic needs, local professionals offer competent service at only a fraction of the stateside cost.

Sports

Public soccer fields and a jogging course are located in a long section of a dry riverbed. Few public tennis courts are in the city. Residents can join a number of reasonably priced gyms with weight rooms, aerobics, tennis courts, and small pools. The better equipped sports clubs in Monterrey are more costly. Two expensive equestrian clubs in the area offer riding and jumping. The city has a few bowling alleys, roller skating rinks, and small ice skating rinks. There are three private golf courses, but only one club offers membership-which is costly. Unfortunately, the heat and pollution limit the number of outdoor activities that can be enjoyed safely and comfortably.

Hiking and rock climbing are popular diversions in the nearby Chipinque and La Huasteca Parks, and in other nearby mountainous areas as well. The State of Nuevo Leon is actively encouraging adventure and ecotourism. Fishing is possible in several lakes in the region, although a boat is essential in most and rentals are unavailable. Lake Guerrero, a five-hour drive away in the neighboring state of Tamaulipas, allows bass fishing, although guides and lodging are expensive. Tamaulipas and Nuevo Leon allow dove, quail, duck, and/or goose hunting. Finally, the northern border region allows whitetail deer hunting, although most of this takes place on private ranches and can cost hundreds of dollars per day. Hunting weapons are subject to strict control and to cumbersome, expensive licensing requirements.

Touring and Outdoor Activities

Nearby attractions and their facilities include: Chipinque (picnic area, a restaurant, beautiful hiking trails, and a scenic view); Horsetail Falls (picnic area, waterfall, and burro riding); Presa de la Boca (picnic area, boating, and water skiing); the Grutas de Garcia (caverns); Huasteca Canyon (picnics and hiking); and Plaza Sésamo an amusement and water park for children.

The city of Saltillo, Coahuila, is about an hour's drive from Monterrey. Situated at a higher elevation than

Monterrey, Saltillo offers a slightly cooler climate, a smattering of Spanish colonial architecture, and shopping for serapes. Most other handicrafts come from central or southern Mexico. Dog and horse shows (including "charreadas"), are announced in advance in the newspaper. Bullfighting is a popular spectator sport in Monterrey. During the October - May season, bullfights are held on Sunday afternoons and holidays. Monterrey boasts two professional soccer teams and two Mexican baseball teams similar to the AAA class in the U.S. The baseball season lasts from March through August.

Entertainment

Monterrey has many good, moderately priced to expensive restaurants offering Mexican, German, French, Italian, Arab, and Asian cuisine. A full range of fast food shops is available, including many U.S. chain restaurants. Several modern movie theaters show current U.S. films at reasonable prices. Younger adults frequent a few nightclubs. Although known more as an industrial center than a cultural center, Monterrey offers a growing and varied bill of fare for the performing and plastic arts-including sporadic performances by the symphony, ballet, and opera. The city boasts such art galleries and museums as El Museo de Monterrey, the Glass Museum, and the Museum of Contemporary Art. The Museum of Mexican History is also worth a visit.

Social Activities

Many Americans participate in the American Society of Monterrey [ASOMO], which sponsors a Fourth of July party, Christmas dance, Halloween party, Easter egg hunt for children, and other social events.

Opportunities for socializing with the local people are limited, particularly for single adults, since social events usually are for families and often take place at expensive private clubs.

Ciudad Juárez

Ciudad Juarez (commonly called Juarez) is Mexico's fourth largest city with a population of more than 1.5 million. It is the largest of all cities along the U.S.-Mexico border. Juarez is a blend of old and new. Because of its proximity to El Paso, it has strong cultural and economic ties to the U.S. Many families in Juarez have U.S. citizen relatives on the other side of the border. Still, Juarez is proud of its heritage and its history as the chief city of the state of Chihuahua, "Cradle of the Mexican Revolution." Although Juarez Mexicans are very friendly in a social or business setting, they rarely welcome new friends into the close family circle. Invitations to dine at someone's home are rare.

Many industrial plants have been established in Ciudad Juarez to take advantage of low labor costs. The "twin plant" or "maquiladora" concept, with labor-intensive plants in Juarez and El Paso, creates an appearance of one city separated only by long lines at the immigration checkpoints over the Rio Grande. It is responsible for the extremely low unemployment rate and the rapid growth of the city. El Paso, on the other hand, has not coped well with the changes brought by NAFTA. Unemployment is high. Good jobs are scarce.

Ciudad Juarez is located 3,700 feet above sea level in an arid desert region surrounded by treeless mountains. The region enjoys cloudless days, low humidity, and an average rainfall of less than 10 inches a year. Rainfall is less than an inch per month, except for July through September, when Juarez receives one to two inches a month. The average temperature range varies from 30 to 67°F in January to 67 to 100 °F in July. Both temperatures and humidity have been rising in the last several years. Juarez enjoys a change of seasons similar to that of Washington, D.C. Dust storms, Juarez's most unpleasant climatic feature, can occur at any time of the year and can cause difficulties for persons suffering from allergies.

Food

Modern supermarkets abound in both Ciudad Juarez and El Paso. Shopping for food and other daily necessities presents no problem. Food costs are lower than in Washington, D.C., especially for plentiful fresh fruits and vegetables. Locally produced alcoholic beverages are inexpensive and of good quality. Anything that cannot be obtained in Juarez is available in El Paso.

Clothing

A seasonal wardrobe is necessary in Juarez, with emphasis on lightweight clothing in view of the long summer. In winter, medium-weight suits for men and women are appropriate. Although subfreezing temperatures are rare, penetrating winds make hats, gloves, and lined coats useful. Rain is infrequent, so little rainwear is needed; but take umbrellas.

Fashion trends in Juarez follow those in the southwestern U.S., except that shorts are seldom worn in public. Suits and dresses are appropriate for work but after hours dress is casual. Formal dress is rarely required. Several representational functions require informal dress (suit and tie).

Women in Juarez dress more formally than American women for luncheons and the like. El Paso is one of the best places in the U.S. to buy boots. Many manufacturers are head-quartered in El Paso and factory outlets are numerous. Western wear is popular on both sides of the border.

Supplies and Services

Domestic servants speak only Spanish. Full time, live-in maids have proven impossible to find. Part-time maids are available and charge $25 to $30 per day. If you need a full-time maid or nanny, the wisest course would be to take one with you.

Religious Activities

Protestant and Roman Catholic churches are located in Ciudad Juarez and in El Paso. All services in Juarez are held in Spanish. El Paso offers a Synagogue and temple. Evangelical groups are well represented on both sides of the border.

Education

Americans with school-age children may use any of El Paso's public or private schools. The public schools are overcrowded.

Juarez has at least four Montessori preschools. The University of Texas at El Paso (UTEP), with an enrollment of 13,000, grants bachelor and masters degrees. Night and summer courses are available.

Voice and music lessons are available at El Paso Community College. The Universidad Autonoma de Chihuahua maintains a branch in Juarez, where evening courses are offered.

Sports

Such sports as golf, tennis, and horseback riding represent popular forms of entertainment. Other enjoyable activities available on the border are hiking and camping. Many excellent campsites are within driving distance. Whitewater rafting is also available. Snow skiing is available in the Ruidoso-Cloudcroft highlands. Spectator sports events include UTEP basketball and football. UTEP hosts the NCAA John Hancock Sun Bowl in winter. El Paso has a good minor league baseball team, the Diablos.

Touring and Outdoor Activities

Touring attractions include day trips to White Sands National Monument, the Carlsbad Caverns, Hueco Tanks State Park, and Elephant Butte Lake. Manageable in a day is Silver City, New Mexico, with its nearby ghost town and the Gila Cliff Dwellings. Some of the more interesting weekend trips include the city of Chihuahua, capital of the state of Chihuahua, about four hours south by train or car. The Mennonite Community in Cuauhtemoc, Chihuahua, about 220 miles south of Juarez, is fascinating.

Big Bend National Park; Santa Fe, Taos, and Albuquerque, New Mexico; Houston, Dallas, Phoenix, and Las Vegas are frequent U.S. destinations made more appealing by fares to Los Angeles and San Diego that can be found as low as $99 on Southwest.

Entertainment

Juarez boasts many good restaurants in all price ranges, including Chinese, Mexican and seafood. Tacos, burritos, and hamburgers are local favorites. Brown bag lunches are also popular. El Paso and nearby Las Cruces, New Mexico, also have good restaurants. Gourmet restaurants are rare. The best discotheques and nightclubs that are open until dawn in the area are in Juarez.

Mariachi clubs abound and bands can be hired for private functions. The downtown area has many bars and clubs with live entertainment. El Paso has country/western clubs in abundance, as well as top forties nightclubs. A comedy club occasionally attracts nationally known comedians. Movie theaters on both sides of the border show the most recent U.S. releases. Video clubs are numerous and inexpensive. The El Paso YMCA, YWCA, El Paso Community College, and UTEP offer various art classes for both adults and children. The unusual scenery inspires painters and photographers. Other cultural activities include the El Paso Symphony Orchestra, touring dance groups, plays, lectures, and rock concerts.

Tijuana

Tijuana lies just south of San Diego, California. Its vegetation and terrain are identical to that of southern California. The city is 75 feet above sea level and about 5 miles from the ocean. It is built on and around a group of large hills, which are part of the Pacific coast range of mountains.

The climate is similar to that of San Diego. The temperature range in Tijuana varies from 42 to 68°F in January and 63 to 82 °F in August. Sunny days and low humidity help maintain comfortable conditions year round.

More than 80% of the rainfall occurs from November to March and averages only eight inches a year. Thus, vegetation on the hills surrounding the city is sparse, leading to dusty conditions year round. During periods of heavy rains, mud slides and clogged gutters often occur. Several minor earthquakes have shaken but have caused no damage to Tijuana.

Food
Foods available in California are also sold in Tijuana, but Americans normally shop in California supermarkets.

Clothing
Take warm sweaters, woolen clothing, and raincoats for winter-which is the rainy season. Formal wear is seldom needed. The women of Tijuana are fashion conscious and are always well dressed.

Religious Activities
Although Roman Catholicism is predominant among the general population, Tijuana has several Protestant churches and a Jewish Synagogue. However, no English-language services are available. Those wishing to attend services in the U.S. usually must cross the border before 9:00 am to avoid long lines on weekends.

Education
Most American children are enrolled in U.S. schools in the San Diego area. Parents often spend considerable time shuttling their children to and from afterschool activities.

Recreation & Entertainment
Because of Tijuana's proximity to the U.S., take advantage of the many recreational activities offered on both sides of the border. Although downtown San Diego is only a 25-minute drive from Tijuana, unpredictable waits at the border, varying from five minutes to one hour, make planning activities in the U.S. more complicated. Camping, fishing, hunting, swimming, and sailing take place on both sides of the border. The Tijuana Country Club has an 18- hole golf course that nonmembers may use for a nominal fee. Tijuana offers horse racing, dog racing, jai alai, and bullfights. San Diego has professional football, baseball, and indoor soccer teams.

The Tijuana Cultural Center offers the full range of theater arts, art galleries, exhibits, and musical events. A wide variety of theater and concerts are also available in San Diego. Located near the Cultural Center is the Rio de Tijuana Plaza-a large complex of department stores, boutiques, and specialty shops. Most Americans shop in San Diego. Tijuana has many excellent restaurants. Tijuana's nightlife consists of bars and hotels with live entertainment, several discotheques, and downtown bars designed for young U.S. tourists.

Other recreational activities include the San Diego Zoo, Wild Animal Park, and Sea World. Disneyland is an approximately three-hour drive from Tijuana.

Hermosillo

Hermosillo, though named for one of the early explorers of the region, is in fact the "pretty little place" its name implies in Spanish. It is a city of modern houses, broad, tree-lined streets, pleasant parks, and several universities, with a population of nearly 700,000. The town is located near a river in the middle of the Sonoran desert, 800 feet above sea level, 180 miles south of Nogales, Arizona, and 60 miles inland from the Gulf of California.

Hermosillo is the hub of a small transportation network that provides the city with adequate bus, and air transportation north to the U.S. and south to central Mexico. Both Aeromexico and Mexicana offer daily flights to Mexico City, Guadalajara, Tijuana, Mexicali, and other destinations in Mexico. Tucson, Phoenix, Los Angeles, Las Vegas, and Houston are also served by non-stop flights from Hermosillo's international airport 7 miles west of town.

Thousands of Americans pass through the city en route to the seaside resorts of Bahia Kino and Guaymas/San Carlos on the shore of the Sea of Cortez, as well as to points farther south. Traditionally, the American colony was so small and well integrated into the local community that it was not recognizable as a group. However, the opening of a major Ford Motor Company plant, several maquilladora factories, and mining operations over the last two decades have expanded the size of the American community. This has had considerable influence on housing, schools, and social life in the community.

Hermosillo is the capital city of Sonora, the second-largest state of Mexico, which is part of the great southwest desert of the North American Continent. Geographically, the state has the same soil and climate as southern Arizona, New Mexico, western Texas, and the desert regions of California.

The relative prosperity of Sonora acts as a magnet to draw people here from other parts of Mexico (two of the state's largest cities-San Luis and Nogales-are situated on the border and in the new Nogales consular district). The railroad passes through Hermosillo, providing freight service from Mexico City and Guadalajara to the U.S.

Sonora's relative prosperity has, as noted, been attracting new residents from other parts of Mexico, fostering a substantial middle class. Visitors are often astonished by the number of new cars and pickups on the roads, by the well-dressed matrons and teenagers thronging the sidewalks in town, and by the often elegant houses in the better residential neighborhoods.

The climate is hot and dry, yet healthful.

Summer, from May to October, brings daily temperatures of more than 100°F; rainfall averages less than 8 inches a year concentrated in two rainy seasons, one in July and August, the other in December and January. Winter months, from November to April, are cool and spring-like. Sinaloa, which includes the world famous beach resort of Mazatlan, has a more moderate climate, with considerably more rainfall.

The consular district, which covers the southern two-thirds of Sonora and all of the State of Sinaloa, has increased rapidly with respect to both population and output. The economy is farm based in the large, irrigated lowlands of western and southern Sonora, and rain-fed agriculture in Sinaloa. Cotton and wheat are the most important crops. The region is also a major producer of cattle, shrimp, poultry, oranges, grapes, and winter vegetables. Industrial output is increasing, and copper mining has always been important. The district has traditionally had close economic ties with Arizona.

Utilities

Electric service is the same as in the U.S.: 110 volt, 60 hertz, AC. Voltage regulators or surge suppressors to protect televisions, stereos, and computers from electrical surges are available locally. However,

houses are not grounded for electrical purposes like they are in the U.S., so surge suppressors may not offer adequate protection. In order to better protect expensive electrical equipment, especially during the rainy season, it is advisable to unplug the equipment when not in use and to not use the equipment in the middle of thunder and lightning storms.

Food

Hermosillo is home to American chains like Wal-Mart SuperCenter, Sam's Club, and Costco, as well as Mexican chain super center-type stores. Many American products and brand names can be found in these stores, whether they are manufactured in the U.S. or in Mexico. However, those products made in the U.S. may not be routinely stocked by the store, so it is best to stock up on desired goods when you find them in local stores.

Frozen foods are readily available, and low-calorie, low-fat products are becoming more widely available. Pasteurized milk (whole and skim), cheeses, and heavy cream may be safely purchased in supermarkets.

City tap water is safe for bathing and cleaning, but not recommended for drinking.

It is advisable to disinfect fruits and vegetables before eating them. Disinfectant drops and powder are readily available in all local grocery stores.

Clothing

During the summer months, daytime temperatures can reach 115°F, and summer weight clothing is a must. Light-to medium-weight clothing is comfortable the rest of the year, with a sweater sometimes necessary on winter evenings. Heavy winter clothing is not needed. Formal social occasions are rare; most functions are informal.

Hermosillo currently has no large, American-style shopping malls. Although the city center has many shops with all varieties of shoes and clothing, many residents (Mexican

and American alike) go to Tucson for major shopping.

Supplies and Services

Housekeepers are available on apart-time or live-in basis. Wages are very reasonable in comparison to U.S. rates.

Gardeners are also available at a reasonable fee. Their services are generally needed every two weeks during the rainy season and less frequently for the remainder of the year.

Generally all services, including competent medical care, furniture design and construction, automobile and appliance repair, etc., can be found at lower than U.S. prices.

Education

Hermosillo is home to three large universities (one private and two public) as well as several smaller institutions of higher learning. The language of instruction in the public schools is Spanish, with English instruction introduced at the secondary level.

The Instituto Irlandes offers a bilingual program from prekindergarten through high school, with boys and girls in separate classes in the upper grades. The Instituto Mexicano Americano de Relaciones Culturales (IMARC) offers bilingual instruction, on the American model, from pre-kindergarten through grade 6. However, since the overwhelming majority of the students are native speakers of Spanish, the bilingual schools are not geared to students who enter with no knowledge of that language. While this does not seem to present too much difficulty at the preschool and kindergarten level, it could be problematic for children entering at a higher grade.

At the secondary level, the Instituto Technologico y des Estudios Superiores de Monterrey (perhaps Mexico's best private university, with campuses across the country) has a college preparatory school (grades 10 and up) and offers the international baccalaureate program.

Sports

Although summer can be too hot, Hermosillo's climate during the rest of the year encourages a wide variety of outdoor sports. Swimming, tennis, hiking, and horseback riding are popular. There is a country club with an 18-hole golf course, various hunting clubs, a shooting and archery range, horse and auto racing facilities, and a Mexican winter-league baseball team.

Touring and Outdoor Activities

The immediate vicinity of Hermosillo offers ample opportunity to explore the Arizona-Sonora Desert, with many petroglyph sites. To the east are the mountains of the Sierra Madre Occidental, which can offer some respite from the heat of the lower elevations. In the south of Sonora is the colonial town of Alamos.

For beach lovers, there are two options within about an hour and a half drive from Hermosillo. San Carlos (about 80 miles to the south), with a growing American community, has several resort hotels, two marinas, fine beaches, and a Club Med, as well as shops that carry articles from all over Mexico. Bahia Kino (about 70 miles to the west) is more of a traditional beach town, with a large fishing fleet and fewer tourist services. Mazatlan, in Sinaloa, is about eight hours away by car, but can also be reached by direct flights from Hermosillo, as can the resort areas of lower Baja California.

Los Mochis, in northern Sinaloa, is the western terminus of the Copper Canyon Railroad, which goes into the neighboring state of Chihuahua.

Entertainment

The entertainment scene, apart from the many movie theaters showing both English and Spanish language films, consists of small clubs with a variety of musical formats. Touring theater and

dance companies from around the country are often featured in the

Casa de Cultura, the Municipal Auditorium, or at the University of Sonora.

Matamoros

Matamoros is located on the south bank of the Rio Grande, about 20 miles inland from the Gulf of Mexico. With Brownsville, its sister city in Texas, Matamoros forms a metropolitan area of around 600,000 inhabitants. Matamoros, the larger of the two cities, has more than 400,000 residents.

The Rio Grande Valley, or the Valle, as it is called locally, comprises a population of about 1.5 million and includes the city of Reynosa in Mexico (approximately 65 miles upriver from Matamoros), and the cities of Harlingen and McAllen in Texas. Gulf sea breezes temper the tropical climate. The temperature range in Matamoros varies from 78 to 98°F in July and 50 to 60°F in January. The rainfall varies from one half inch in March to five inches in September. Temperatures at mid-day in summer can range well above 90°F with high humidity. Spring and autumn days are mild and brilliant. Winter is sunny and warm, except for an occasional "norther" when temperatures can drop suddenly to near freezing.

The Matamoros and Reynosa areas are home to more than 250 border industries, or "maquiladoras" These factories import parts duty free into Mexico, assemble them, and send them back to the U.S. or other countries, again duty free. A wide range of U.S. and foreign companies have plants, including Zenith, General Motors, AT&T, and Converse, among others. The area also has a large "agribusiness" center.

Matamoros has a thriving tourist industry, providing facilities to American winter visitors and retirees. Thousands of college students spending spring break at nearby South Padre Island visit Matamoros during March of each year. Shopping and restaurants are among Matamoros' chief attractions.

Domestic Help

Maids, both live-in and daily, are available but the cost has risen due to competition in the labor market surrounded by the rapidly expanding maquiladora sector. Day maids earn $15 to $20 per day. Live-in maids are available but tend to be younger, less experienced, and requiring of more supervision.

Food

All food needs can be met at modern supermarkets in Brownsville and Matamoros. Local produce is of excellent quality. U.S. produce is abundant in Brownsville, and most vegetables are available fresh, year round. Seafood, especially gulf shrimp, is also of high quality. Matamoros city water is not potable but inexpensive, sterilized drinking water is readily available.

Clothing

Business dress is informal and sports wear is acceptable year round. During the summer, an open-necked shirt and jacket are popular. Light spring and fall weight clothing is worn during the short winter season, although occasional cold spells make heavier clothing practical for a few weeks each year. Few social events will require black tie or formal attire; black tie dress can be rented in Brownsville.

Religious Activities

Most faiths are represented in Brownsville, which has many Catholic or Protestant churches and a Synagogue. Although Roman Catholic churches predominate in Matamoros, congregations of evangelical and Protestant denominations also exist.

Education

There are no English schools in Matamoros. Public schools are available in Brownsville free of charge to dependents, but most dependents attend private schools in Brownsville. The cost per pupil of private education is $2,000 to $3,000 per year. A full range of classes and subjects is available to more

© Kelly-Mooney Photography/Corbis. Reproduced by permission.

Street in Mazatlan, Mexico

advanced students at The University of Texas Southwest College in Brownsville, which has a modern library with an excellent selection of periodicals and journals.

Recreation and Social Life

Most social activities revolve around civic organizations, business luncheons, Rotary, Lions, etc. The State of Tamaulipas organizes a cultural festival in the fall and the University of Texas at Brownsville offers cultural programs throughout the academic year.

The Texas Rio Grande Valley is becoming famous as a recreational area for winter and summer tourists. South Padre Island, about 25 miles from Brownsville, offers excellent swimming, surfing, sailing, and deep-sea fishing. Golf is popular and can be played year round at the numerous public and private courses. The Rio Grande Valley also offers restaurants and first run movies.

Mazatlán

Mazatlán is an old, Mediterranean-style port city on Mexico's west coast. Located 780 miles south of Nogales, Arizona, it is situated on a picturesque peninsula. At the harbor's entrance, the highest recorded

lighthouse in the Western Hemisphere, El Faro, rests atop one of Mazatlán's few hills. The city's history goes back to the early part of the 19th century, but its growth is relatively recent. The population numbers approximately 400,000 full-time residents, increased by large numbers of Americans and other tourists who visit throughout the year.

The weather in Mazatlán is excellent, particularly during the winter season, November through March. In these months, temperatures range from 85°F in the daytime to 65°F at night. The tropical summer, lasting from April to October, is hot and humid with frequent thunderstorms.

Mazatlán's economy is influenced most directly by the commercial fishing dock, which makes it a shrimp capital of the world, and by the Pacífico Brewery. Agriculture is also an important industry; the northern part of the State of Sinaloa has become the chief supplier of winter vegetables for the United States. Since Mazatlán is the biggest and busiest seaport between San Diego and Panama, U.S. Navy ships make it a port of call.

Mazatlán itself actually is more than 300 years old, but it was not

incorporated until 1837. A few remnants of the colonial section remain, and they can be seen on a walking tour of the town's streets and alleys.

Most foods are available, and prices are less than or compare favorably with U.S. prices. Fish and seafood abound. Drug store items are, generally, not expensive, but some items cost more than U.S. equivalents, and some cost less. Special medications should be brought from the U.S.

Schools for Foreigners

Mazatlán has no American schools, but the Instituto Anglo-American (grade one through high school) teaches in both English and Spanish. Enrollment is small, and American students are often the children of U.S. citizens who are part-time residents during the winter. Other schools attended by American children are ICO (Instituto Cultural de Occidente), a private, coeducational school run by Italian priests (grades one through 12); Colegio Remington (girls only, run by nuns for grades one through nine); and Colegio El Pacífico (nonsectarian, grades one through 12). Most American children in Mazatlán attend boarding schools in the U.S.

Recreation

Mazatlán's beaches are beautiful, and ocean temperatures seldom dip below 65°F; the surf is well-suited for swimming and surfing. North Beach and Las Gaviotas (the sea gulls) are considered the best spots. Fishing for marlin, sailfish, and other large fighters is popular. Hunters may move through the nearby foothills in search of duck, dove, goose, and quail. Mazatlán means "place of the deer" in the Nahuatl language, and deer still abound in the area.

The Club Campestre and El Cid both have fine golf courses, with memberships available. El Cid also has tennis courts and a swimming pool.

There are several air-conditioned theaters, a large baseball stadium, and a bullring in the city. Three television channels and seven radio stations provide news and entertainment in Spanish. Social events are informal, but both the American and Mexican communities are active.

Mazatlán's pre-Lenten *carnaval* is famous throughout Mexico.

Mérida

The Yucatan is noted for the friendliness of its inhabitants and its impressive archeological remains. Home of the Maya, it is strewn with ruins and relics of their culture. Merida itself is built on the site of the old Mayan ceremonial center of T'Ho. The area has a long history of separatism from the rest of Mexico. The Yucatecan habits, culture, and outlook differ from those of the rest of the country. It is home to three million people, the majority of whom live in the state of Yucatan, with smaller populations in the States of Campeche and Quintana Roo. Merida's population exceeds 600,000 and is mostly of mixed Maya or Spanish descent. English is widely understood in the metropolitan areas. Thousands of American tourists visit the district annually. New resorts on the Caribbean coast have become increasingly popular with U.S. tourists.

Merida is about 19 miles from the sea and 25 feet above sea level. The climate is tropical, with average humidity of 72% year round. There are three seasons: rainy season, May through October with more than 80% of the 38 inches of annual rainfall; cool or winter season, November through February; and dry season, March and April. The average temperature in Merida ranges from 73 to 93°F in June and 64 to 83°F in January.

Supplies and Services

Electricity is the same as in the U.S. It is subject to spikes, so surge protectors are strongly recommended. Satellite and cable TV are available.

Domestic help is reasonably priced. Live-in as well as daytime or hourly help is available.

Local authorities are concerned with growing water and automobile pollution and are beginning to monitor growth and contamination.

Food

Food is readily available in the several large supermarket chains that operate in Merida. The central market downtown is also available for those who love chaos and olfactory challenges. Most U.S. goods are available, but sometimes irregularly. Locally all kinds of meats, fresh fruit, and vegetables can be found at reasonable prices.

Clothing

U.S. type clothing is available in Merida. There are a variety of local department store chains and small shops. These all carry some U.S. brands.

There are also a few upscale department stores that have recently been constructed. American made products can be more expensive than in the U.S. Locally made clothing can be of poorer quality than in the U.S., as well. Extra care should be taken with leather goods and clothing in storage to avoid the ravages of humidity and mildew.

Coat and tie or formal dress is rarely worn at work. Men wear slacks and a shirt. Women wear cotton or lightweight dresses.

Religious Activities

Both Catholic and Protestant services are found within the consular district. One Catholic parish offers English-language services on Sunday.

Education

There are two bilingual schools operating in Merida. One is a Catholic institution, which is open to all; the other is secular. Both are considered suitable up to junior high level. All other schools are conducted in Spanish. Most other private schools are run by Catholic religious orders.

Limited special education is available.

Recreation and Social Life

Tennis, fishing, boating and golf are common in the area. The Club Campestre has tennis courts and a swimming pool. Cancun and Merida both have 18-hole golf courses. The beach at Progreso, where cottages may be rented, is about a 20-minute drive by car. Scuba diving and snorkeling are popular at Isla Mujeres, Cancun and Cozumel. All sports equipment, including tennis balls, is expensive. Many people take their own.

Merida has a few air-conditioned movie theaters, a large baseball stadium, a bullring and a few small museums. Social life is informal. Membership to the Club Campestre, the Golf Club, the Rotary Club and the Lions Club is open. Members of the international community sponsor events from time to time. The International Women's Club is actively involved with charitable events.

Nearby attractions include the archeological sites at Uxmal, Chichen Itza, and Palenque, among others.

All kinds of sports, summer schools, and summer camps are available for children or youngsters of any age. These activities are, for the most part, organized by their schools or church communities. Merida has several parks, a zoo, and programs for children (in Spanish).

Nogales

Nogales has been a border pass through the mountains since the middle 1800s, with a U.S. Consulate first established in 1886. The Consulate was closed in 1970 but reopened in 1998. Visitors are often surprised after expecting sand hills and finding a mountainous and pleasant countryside instead. The name refers to a now disappeared stand of black walnut trees, although the hills are still covered with a native scrub oak. The river valleys glisten with the leaves of huge cottonwoods, green in the summer and golden in the fall. The riverbeds are usually dry; but torrential summer rains often fill them to overflowing, closing roads and washing out bridges. The weather in the western deserts can be dramatic. Nogales is located 60 miles south of Tucson, Arizona and 140 miles to the north of Hermosillo, Sonora, on the U.S./Arizona-Sonora, Mexico border.

Long a vital entry point into the U.S. from western and northern Mexico, Nogales has grown in the past 20 years from a pleasant, small town to a booming factory town with growth fueled by NAFTA maquiladora factories that assemble primarily U.S. made parts into goods exported around the world. There are approximately 90 factories in Nogales and another 50 to 100 in other border communities along the Arizona/Sonora border. These factories have caused tremendous growth, with many residents of central and southern Mexico moving north to seek employment. These factories account for 35,000 jobs in Nogales and another 35,000 jobs elsewhere in the consular district. The produce industry has also grown tremendously with 60% of all winter produce consumed in the U.S. and Canada passing through Nogales, Sonora, and processed in Nogales, Arizona. Most of the produce comes from areas in Sonora and Sinaloa. Cattle ranching, mining, and small farms still comprise an important part of the economy of the region. Nogales is also a major border crossing for Americans going south for the winter into Mexico and to the Pacific beaches year round.

Sonora has traditionally been a relatively prosperous state with a well-developed middle class. The capital of Sonora, Hermosillo, is a bustling and growing commercial and industrial center of almost a million. Unofficial estimates put the population of Nogales at 250,000. Agua Prieta and San Luis Rio Colorado, two other important border cities in this consular district, are also large and growing. Puerto Penasco, a shrimp fishing port and vacation destination for Arizonans located at the top of the Gulf of California, has become a major resort and residence for Americans. The history of northern Sonora is inextricably linked to that of Southern Arizona. It begins with Father Eusebio Kino, a Jesuit priest-who first brought European farming ideas and Christianity to the region. The churches he established are still functioning and form a tour route for those interested in Spanish colonial churches. The pleasant towns that have grown up around these churches (two of which are in Southern Arizona) form the heart of the region. Commercial and family ties between Northern Sonora and Southern Arizona are very strong and make this a unique region united culturally and historically.

The climate has dramatic temperature changes but can usually be described in two phrases: warm and sunny in the day, cool at night. The summers are hot but the nights cool off. Winter nighttime temperatures dip into the 20s and 30s but the days usually warm up to the 60s and 70s. It is very dry except in the summer rainy season in July and August. Shorts and tee shirts are the summer dress. Sweaters and jackets are appropriate for the winter. It snows on occasion, although old timers say less and less due to the increase in cars and concrete.

Utilities

Electricity is the same as in the U.S. (110v, 60 hertz, AC). Voltage regulators or surge protectors are recommended for sensitive, electronic equipment. Satellite and cable are both options for television.

Food

All food needs can be met at modern supermarkets on either side of the border. Nogales, Sonora, water is not potable; but drinking water can be purchased at reasonable cost and is plentiful.

Domestic Help

Domestic help is available at a reasonable cost. Live-in maids, as well as daytime or hourly help are available.

Religious Activities

Roman Catholic churches predominate in Nogales, Sonora. However, there are small Protestant congregations and both Catholic and Protestant denominations may be found in Nogales, Arizona. Jewish and other religious communities are very limited in "ambos nogales." However, Tucson has a large and active Jewish community, as well as other religious groups.

Education

Although there are a few, self-described bilingual schools in Nogales, Sonora, instruction in these and all schools is predominantly in Spanish.

Recreation & Social Life

Tennis courts and bowling alleys are available in Nogales, Sonora. Golf is popular and can be played throughout the year at several public and private courses in Nogales, Arizona.

Entertainment in Nogales, Sonora and Arizona is limited mainly to dining; although there is also a modern movie theater in Nogales, Sonora. Southern Arizona, especially Tucson, offers a limitless variety of city and country cultural and shopping opportunities. Tucson has an opera, active theatre, a ballet, and a variety of sports events. Northern and central Sonora offer beaches, beautiful countryside, and Kino mission churches.)

Nuevo Laredo

Nuevo Laredo combines the convenience of shopping in the U.S. with the attractions of living abroad. Nuevo Laredo is the most important port of entry on the U.S.-Mexican border for shipping and for travelers to the interior of Mexico. Of its estimated 300,000 inhabitants, only about 10% speak English.

Nuevo Laredo is located on a gently rolling plain, with mountains skirting the southwestern boundary of the consular district. Brush, cactus and scrub vegetation abounds, as do more tropical plants. The city itself is 542 feet above sea level; and the climate is sunny and hotter than Washington, D.C., but much less humid. The daily temperature range averages 78 to 96°F in August and occasional high temperatures in winter are not uncommon. The average daily temperature range in January is 44 to 64°E Annual rainfall is 18 inches. May, June, and September usually have the greatest rainfall.

Food

Adequate food supplies are available locally and at supermarkets in Laredo, Texas. Gourmet food items are not readily available.

Clothing

During the hot season, lightweight clothing is a must. Office attire for men is usually the traditional Mexican guayabera or sport shirts with slacks. Suits are worn occasionally. The guayabera is also appropriate for informal evening wear. Women wear cotton or linen dresses, blouses, skirts, and slacks. Men often wear sport shirts and slacks at social gatherings while women favor airy cottons. For more formal occasions, men wear black or white dinner jackets; women may wear either long or short cocktail dress in a wide array of fabrics and styles. During winter, custom occasionally requires formal attire (dinner jackets for men, gowns for women). Fall and spring weight suits, dresses, overcoats, and rain boots are used during winter when temperatures can drop into the 30s. All wearing apparel needed for this climate is available in Laredo, Texas.

Supplies and Services

Necessary supplies and services are available in both Laredos. In Laredo, Texas, there are two large shopping centers featuring nationally known department stores and boutiques.

Religious Activities

Roman Catholicism is the predominant religion in both Laredos. Most Christian denominations are represented in Laredo, Texas and services in English are available.

Education

Schools in Nuevo Laredo are overcrowded and instruction is in Spanish. Children are usually enrolled in public or private schools in Laredo, Texas. Full curriculums for undergraduate and some graduate level degrees are offered at Texas A&M International University and Laredo City College.

Puebla

Puebla, capital of the state whose name it bears, is a city of over one million about 75 miles southeast of Mexico City. Its official name is Heróica Puebla de Zaragoza, in honor of Gen. Ignacio Zaragoza, who defeated the French here in 1862 in their attempt to establish Maximilian's empire.

Aside from the renown for its cotton mills and onyx quarries, and as a major commercial center, Puebla is known for the colorful Talavera tiles which adorn its buildings and churches. The cathedral on the main plaza, built during the 16th and 17th centuries, is one of the finest in Mexico. The city also claims to have the oldest theater in North America.

Puebla has several other notable buildings, among them the 340-year-old Biblioteca Polafoxiana, with 50,000 priceless volumes; the regional museum, dating from the 17th century; and the university founded in 1578 by Jesuit priests.

Founded by the Spanish in 1532 as Puebla de los Ángeles, the city early served as a link between the coast and the capital. It was taken by Winfield Scott in the Mexican War in 1847.

OTHER CITIES

ACAPULCO, in Guerrero State, southwest Mexico, is a fashionable international resort on the Pacific Ocean. Its fine natural harbors, surrounded by cliffs and promontories, once served as a base for Spanish explorers. Acapulco played an important role in the development of the Philippines between the years 1565 and 1815, when Spanish galleons made commercial voyages across the Pacific to Manila. After Mexican independence was achieved, the city lost its status as a major port. In the 1920s, a road was constructed to Mexico City, and Acapulco became a tourist center and, again, an important port during World War II. This city of 462,000, whose full name is Acapulco de Juárez, stretches out along bays and cliffs, and its many fine beaches attract thousands of swimmers and sunbathers. In the evenings, high divers can be seen at La Quebrada, performing for enthusiastic crowds. Acapulco's economy is heavily dependent on tourism, with the copra (coconut oil) industry second in importance. In its amphitheater, overlooking the sea, the city plays host to art exhibits and to musical and theatrical productions. A historic spot in Acapulco is San Diego Fortress (Fuerte de San Diego), where Mexico's last battle for independence was fought. The star-shaped fortress, which once defended the town and harbor against pirate raids, is now a museum. A summer school for foreigners, founded in 1955, provides tourists with courses on Mexican arts and archaeology.

AGUASCALIENTES is the capital of Aguascalientes State, 100 miles northwest of León in central Mexico. The city (whose name means "hot waters" in Spanish) is also known as "the perforated city," because of its extensive network of tunnels. These were dug in pre-Columbian times and have never been fully explored. City records date to 1522, when Cortés sent Pedro de Alvarado to conquer western territories; native tribal

Pyramid in Chichen Itza, Mexico

Courtesy of Andrea Henderson

attacks forced Alvarado to retreat. The city was founded in 1575 by a royal decree of Philip II, surviving in the early years as a wilderness outpost besieged by Indians. Modern Aguascalientes is a railroad center, known also for its orchards and vineyards, and for the ranches which breed bulls for *corridas*. An important native industry is drawn linen work. The broad-based economy includes railroad repair shops, textile factories, potteries, tobacco factories, and distilleries. Aguascalientes boasts lovely churches, especially San Juan de Dios, San Francisco, and La Parroquia; they contain excellent examples of colonial art. The annual San Marcos Fair features fireworks, parades, and an art exposition. Rail, highway, and air connections from Aguascalientes to other areas are good. The city has an estimated 643,360 residents.

CAMPECHE, the capital of Campeche State, is situated on the west coast of the Yucatán peninsula, 550 miles east of Mexico City. The largest city between Villahermosa and Mérida, Campeche is the first landing place (1517) in Mexico of Cortés and his *conquistadors*. Founded as a settlement by Don Francisco de Montejo in 1540, the old city wall and remains of 11 fortifications built in the 17th and 18th

centuries for protection from pirate raids attract tourists. Today, the city produces alligator leather and Panama hats (*campeche* is the Spanish word); logwood, mahogany, cigars, rice, sugarcane, tobacco, and cotton are exported. A university was founded here in 1756. Campeche's population is currently 217,000.

CHIHUAHUA, 100 miles south of the Rio Grande River in the northern region, is a state capital with a population of about 670,000. It was first settled in the 1500s, prospering late in the colonial period as a mining center. Chihuahua was twice captured by American forces during the short but fierce Mexican-American War of 1846–48. The city enjoys good transportation links to other areas, allowing easy access to its university, as well as to adjacent cattle ranches. Notable public buildings here number among Mexico's architectural treasures. The church of San Francisco is arguably the best example of 18th-century Mexican architecture. Chihuahua's plaza contains a monument to the religious leader, Miguel Hidalgo y Costilla, and his companions in the war for independence (1821), who were executed here. Center of a rich silver-mining, timber, and ranching district, the city is famous for the *chihuahuitas* (miniature dogs) bred in the area. From Chihuahua, inter-

esting side trips may be taken to the old mining town of Aquiles Sérdan, and to Aldama in the center of an important fruit-producing area.

CIUDAD OBREGÓN is located in northwest Mexico, 65 miles southeast of Guaymas. Situated in the fertile Yaqui Valley, the city is known for its contemporary buildings and complexes of storage elevators, grain mills, cotton gins, and numerous other industries. Agricultural products grown in the valley are irrigated by the Alvaro Obregón Dam, 35 miles northeast of the city. Cotton, wheat, rice, sesame, and corn are grown here. Boating and fishing are possible in the area. Sportsmen come here to hunt duck, dove, and quail; turkey, wild boar, deer, and bear may be found in the mountains to the east. Ciudad Obregón's population is 181,700.

COYOACÁN, a southern suburb of Mexico City, was settled by Cortés in 1521 and was the initial seat of Spanish government in New Spain. Cortés' palace stands in the city's main square and is now the Palacio Municipal. Russian communist leader Leon Trotsky was assassinated here in 1940. Landmarks include the Dominican Monastery (built in 1530) and the Church of San Juan Bautista (built in 1583). The Frida Kahlo Museum, the house occupied for more than a quarter-century by the artist and her husband, muralist Diego Rivera, is located here. Coyoacán's current population is approximately 360,000.

Located 120 miles south of Mexico City is **CUERNAVACA,** an internationally famous resort, with facilities for golf, horseback riding, tennis, and water sports. Spanish conquistador Hernán Cortés seized the Indian settlement here in 1521; it later became a seat of a marquessate and finally, a state capital. Cortés' palace was decorated with murals by Diego Rivera (1886–1957) in 1929. Along with the Franciscan cathedral and nearby ruins (at Alpuyeca, 23 miles southwest), the city is a fascinating tourist stop today. Cuernavaca's Borda Gardens—Emperor Maximilian's retreat—has attracted many wealthy Mexicans and foreigners; the mansion was built by José de la Borda, who made his fortune in silver mining in the Taxco area. Besides tourism, agriculture and industry are important. Crops include fruit, corn, beans, and wheat. Various plants, mills, and factories constitute the industrial base. Furniture, fine silver, and leather goods may be purchased here; on market days, Indians sell their wares in the streets and plazas. There is a university here, and a modern expressway links the area with Mexico City. Cuernavaca's approximate population is 338,000.

Situated at the base of the Sierra Madre Occidental Mountains, 30 miles from the Gulf of California, **CULIACÁN** (Culiacán Rosales) served as a base for Spanish expeditions in the early colonial era. The center of an important agricultural area, the city's surrounding farms raise corn, sugarcane, tobacco, and many varieties of fruit, which are irrigated by a sophisticated water system. Culiacán's location on the west-coast artery of the Pan-American Highway provides outstanding transportation for its approximately 307,000 residents.

DURANGO (officially called Victoria de Durango), an important political and religious center in early history, is located in northwest-central Mexico, 250 miles north of Guadalajara. Situated at an altitude of 6,314 feet on a level plain formed by foothills of the Sierra Madre Occidental, Durango is in a region known for its rich iron, gold, and silver deposits. Irrigated by surrounding mountain streams and by the water of the Río Tunal, the area produces cotton, corn, barley, and wheat; it is also a lumbering center. Several industries are located in the city, including cotton and wool mills, glassworks, iron foundries, sugar refineries, flour mills, and tobacco factories. Durango is the capital of Durango State, and was founded by Don Francisco de Ibarra in 1563. The main plaza, with an attractive garden, is the site of thrice-weekly

band concerts. Durango has also been the scene of location filming for some Hollywood studios; a number of the movie sets are permanent fixtures here. Durango's population is about 258,000.

GUANAJUATO, the capital of Guanajuato State in central Mexico, was founded in 1554 in the Cañada de Marfil ("ivory ravine"). It is a city of narrow, steep, winding, cobblestone streets (some with rough stone steps), veined underneath with silver-mine shafts. For a while, the mine at La Valenciana, high above the town, filled the silver vaults of Spain. Silver, gold, and lead deposits are still being mined nearby. Guanajuato has so many important colonial churches and buildings—many showing a Moorish influence brought by the Andalusians who were among Guanajuato's early settlers—that the city has been declared a colonial monument. The city, now home to the International Cervantes Festival each spring, figured prominently in the wars and revolutions of the 19th and early 20th centuries because of its geographical location. The royalist garrison of Alhóndiga de Granaditas, originally a granary in Guanajuato, was besieged and captured by Hidalgo y Costilla at the outbreak of the war against Spain. Guanajuato is a resort center today. The painter Diego Rivera was born here in 1886, and his house (with sketches for murals) is now a museum. Running nearly the entire length of the main street of Guanajuato is the Calle Subterráneo, an underground road which was constructed after a devastating flash flood in 1905. The University of Guanajuato was established there in 1945. Guanajuato's estimated population is 141,215.

GUAYMAS, located in northwest Mexico 90 miles southwest of Hermosillo, is one of the country's best seaports. Situated on the Gulf of California, Guaymas was originally settled by Indians in 1760. The settlement was a Spanish-Mexican free port and opened to common trade in 1841. Guaymas is actually two communities; the city, with its

shrimp docks, freighters, and tankers in the harbor, is separated from the resort area along Bocochibampo Bay by a hilly peninsula. Swimming, skin diving, water-skiing, tennis, hunting, and horseback riding are popular resort activities. The city is also popular among fishermen. Big runs of marlin and sailfish usually occur in late June, July, and August. The Fiesta de la Pesca (Fishing Festival) is held in May; an international fishing tournament is held in July. San Carlos, about 13 miles northeast, is another popular vacation center. In 2000, Guaymas had an estimated population of 130,000.

Situated in a central Mexican farming district known for strawberries, **IRAPUATO** is 140 miles east of Guadalajara. A rapidly expanding industrial center, Irapuato was founded in 1547 and was the scene of many battles during the colonial era. The city's central mall, a renovated shopping area surrounding the plaza and cathedral, prohibits motor vehicles. The current population of Irapuato is 440,000.

IXTAPALAPA, a southeastern suburb of Mexico City, was once a flourishing Aztec town. The Aztecs lighted new fires at the beginning of each 52-year cycle atop nearby Cerro de Estrella (Star Hill). The fertile land surrounding Ixtapalapa produces corn, alfalfa, wheat, beans, and vegetables. A number of industries are becoming an important economic asset. Ixtapalapa has a population exceeding 1.2 million.

JALAPA (Enríquez), capital of Veracruz State, is situated 150 miles east of Mexico City, just a few miles inland from the Bay of Campeche. Built on the fifth tier of a hill called Macuiltepec at an altitude of 4,500 feet, the city was once a Spanish stronghold and a stagecoach stop. Today, Jalapa is a mountain resort and an important commercial center for coffee and tobacco. Much of the city's colonial atmosphere is evident in the red tile roofs, balconies, carved doors, and window grills along the narrow, cobblestone streets. In contrast, modern build-

View of Aculpulco, Mexico

Courtesy of Paul Droste

ings line wide streets in the newer section of town. Often called the "Flower Garden of Mexico," Jalapa is known for its mild climate. The University of Veracruz, founded here in 1944, has a well-known dance company and symphony. The estimated population is about 212,000.

LA PAZ is situated on La Paz Bay about 90 miles north of the southern tip of the Baja Peninsula, and 720 miles south of San Diego, California. With fine port facilities, La Paz is the capital of Baja California Sur State as well as the commercial center of the area. Isolation prevented permanent settlement of La Paz for three centuries; the area's only regular inhabitants were privateers who dropped anchor in the bay. The Spanish finally settled La Paz in 1811. Mining and pearl diving provided growth and the city soon replaced Loreto as the territorial capital. Both industries declined about 1930, and La Paz faded until it was rediscovered by tourists and sportsmen. Now, La Paz boasts a growing number of fine resorts and fleets of pleasure craft. The city is linked to the Mexican mainland by air-conditioned, automobile-passenger ferries. Luxury crafts make the overnight run from Mazatlán six times weekly; sailings are twice weekly from Topolobampo near Los Mochis. Flights regularly depart from the jet-capacity airport. La Paz's population is about 196,000.

LEÓN, also in Guanajuato State, was once the second largest city in Mexico. Founded in 1576, it was almost washed away by floods (most notably in 1888), diminishing its prominence. A dam was later built as protection from such disasters. León lies in a river valley on the main rail line between Mexico City and El Paso, Texas, and is a commercial, agricultural, and mining center with a population of over one million. It is known especially for its production of gold and silver embroidery and silver-trimmed leather goods. Steel products, textiles, and soap are manufactured in the city, which contains tanneries and flour mills. The area also produces serapes, spurs, and knives. Most of León's buildings are of colonial architecture. Adding to the charm of the city are flowering plazas, fine old portals around the central square, and the colorful market. Cathedrals and churches are of additional interest, and sulphur baths are nearby.

MANZANILLO, with a population of 124,000, is Mexico's leading Pacific port. Situated in the south-western part of the country, the city is 350 miles west of Mexico City and 130 miles southwest of Guadalajara. A bronze bell is rung from a high point west of the city to announce approaching vessels. Manzanillo has a spacious waterfront, and narrow streets ascend the hillside of the city. The tropical climate allows the banana and coconut plantations that line the shoreline to flourish. Manzanillo is a haven for fishermen (especially from November through March) who flock here to catch sailfish, marlin, red snapper, yellow-tail, shark, and other tropical varieties. Skin diving and water-skiing are among the popular water sports. The best still-water beaches are near Bahía de Santiago, eight miles north. Beaches near Coco and Las Ventanas have heavy surf and strong currents. The beach close to Cuyutlan, about 26 miles southeast, is known for the "green wave," a mountainous swell that crests during April or May.

The city of **MEXICALI,** at the northern extremity of Baja California State, is adjacent to Calexico, California. It is a duty-free port, with customs offices open 24 hours. Irrigation programs have helped this desert region to flourish. Mexicali is now a focus for commerce, and also has gained wealth and note as a gaudy border resort. The city market, in an arcaded building, sells everything from handicrafts to food. A university is located here. The city is accessible by highway, railroad, and air from the southwestern United States and from many points in Mexico. The population is currently about 765,000.

MORELIA, 150 miles west of Mexico City, is a major intellectual and art center of about 620,000 residents. The country's oldest institution of higher learning, Colegio San Nicolás, is located here, as are a classic baroque cathedral and colonial governor's palace. Since the late 1500s, Morelia has also been Michoacán State's capital and agricultural hub, processing the vegetables and cattle grown nearby. An unusual three-mile-long aqueduct was built near Morelia in 1785 for famine assistance. Transportation here is good.

NEZAHUALCÓYOTL is Mexico's second largest municipality after Mexico City, located directly east of the Federal District (Distrito Federal). This suburb of approximately 2.5 million is tied to Mexico City by a highway and shared bus lines; its residents are greatly dependent on the capital for their jobs. A new city in Mexican terms, Nezahualcóyotl was marshland, considered uninhabitable, at the beginning of the 20th century. However, the tremendous growth of the Federal District's population made the area attractive by the late 1940s. The agglomeration of numerous area cities formalized municipal administration in 1963.

OAXACA, the capital of Oaxaca State, is situated at an altitude of 5,000 feet in a semi-tropical valley, surrounded by the summits of the Sierra Madre del Sur, 230 miles south of Mexico City. Once the center of the Mixtec and Zapotec civilizations, Oaxaca was founded as an Aztec garrison post in 1486 and was conquered by the Spanish in 1521. Oaxaca is the center of a noted handicrafts market; the area produces leather goods, hand-loomed cottons, tempered machetes and daggers, and carved idols. The nearby village of San Bártolo Coyotepec is known for its black pottery; the towns of Teotitlán and Ocotlán are weaving and pottery centers. Oaxaca is a mixture of colonial and modern periods and has a great many 16th-century buildings. The city's market is colorful on Saturdays when the Indians visit town to sell their merchandise. Original costumes of the state are worn here during July and December fiestas. Guides in the city are available for tours to nearby Monte Albán (a major religious city, with ruins of the Zapotec Indians), Mitla, and Zaachila. Oaxaca's population is about 170,000.

A major manufacturing city, **ORIZABA** is situated at an altitude of 4,211 feet in eastern Mexico, 150 miles east of Mexico City. The 18,000-foot volcano, Citlaltépetl, looms over the far reaches of the landscape here. Once an Aztec garrison post, Orizaba was chartered as a city in 1774. Today, it has some of the country's largest cotton mills. Other industries include breweries, cement plants, marble quarries, and coffee and fruit plantations. There are also important textile centers in the nearby towns of Río Blanco, Ciudad Mendoza, and Nogales. The city was nearly leveled by a strong earthquake in August 1973, but has since been rebuilt. Orizaba has a pleasant climate and an estimated population of 125,000.

Founded by the Spanish in 1534, the city of **PACHUCA** is the center of an area that produces about 15 percent of the world's silver. The capital of Hidalgo State in central Mexico, Pachuca is 50 miles north of Mexico City at an altitude of 8,150 feet. The surrounding hills are extensively tunneled and heaped with slag piles; smelters and ore-reduction plants are also located in the area. Landmarks of interest in Pachuca are the Church of San Francisco (built in 1596) and the Monument to Independence. There is also a university, founded in 1869. The mining town of Mineral del Monte overlooks Pachuca, at a distance of about seven miles. It has narrow, almost vertical cobblestone streets and houses. Pachuca's population is about 110,000.

POZA RICA is Mexico's chief petroleum-producing center. Located 150 miles northeast of Mexico City, the city pipes crude oil and gas to refineries in distant cities. Oil derricks, refineries, storage tanks, and oil wells dot the landscape around Poza Rica. The city itself features wide boulevards, modern buildings, and a population of about 196,000. Eleven miles south of Poza Rica is the ceremonial city of El Tajin, which reached its peak about A.D. 800. The city is accessible by highway and is served by Mexico's domestic airlines.

PUERTO VALLARTA, a coastal town in west-central Mexico, 100 miles west of Guadalajara, is a thriving resort combining a scenic locale with extensive recreational facilities. Situated on the Bahía de Banderas, Puerto Vallarta's older buildings with red tile roofs on narrow, stony streets are in counterpoint with more modern structures on the upper slopes of the mountains that surround the bay. Popular daytime activities include swimming and surfing at nearby beaches, deep-sea fishing, tennis, golf, and horseback riding. Hunting for deer, quail, iguana, and jaguar is excellent in the mountains to the east. Aquatic sports fishing is also extremely popular in Puerto Vallarta. Sight-seeing craft are available along the shoreline, and boats for sport fishing may be chartered. Puerto Vallarta's nightlife is lively, and includes nightclubs, hotel bars, and discotheques. Cruise ships stop here regularly; a ferryboat service operates twice weekly between Puerto Vallarta and Cabo San Lucas, at the southern tip of the Baja Peninsula. The city is a major port through which bananas, coconut oil, hides, and fine woods are exported. The current population is about 183,700.

QUERÉTARO lies in a valley 160 miles northwest of Mexico City at an altitude of 5,900 feet. The capital of Querétaro State, the city was already an Otomí Indian settlement before the Spaniards discovered the New World, and was absorbed as part of the Aztec Empire in the 15th century. Captured by the Spanish in 1531, Querétaro was the headquarters for Franciscan monks who established missions in Central America and California. Emperor Maximilian was executed here on June 19, 1867. Querétaro today is known for its exquisite parks, squares, and gardens. An aqueduct, built by the Spanish more than 200 years ago, is still in use. Opals are mined in the area and sold by sidewalk vendors. There are several churches of interest in Querétaro. A university, founded here in 1775, was elevated to its present status in 1951. Querétaro is the site of one of Mexico's oldest and largest cotton factories. The factory also produces textiles, pottery, and processes food crops grown near the city. Querétaro's population is about 640,000.

SALTILLO is the capital and leading industrial city in Coahuila State. It lies at an altitude of 5,244 feet in a broad valley surrounded by imposing mountains, about 660 miles north of Mexico City. Founded in 1575, Saltillo is a modern city of 577,000 residents, but retains much of its Spanish colonial heritage. In the early part of the 17th century, Saltillo was headquarters for explorations to the northern part of the country. Between 1824 and 1836, it was the capital of a territory that included present-day Texas northward to the region of Colorado. Saltillo's altitude and dry climate make it a popular summer resort. Golf, tennis, swimming, polo, and hunting are available. Saltillo produces textiles in its numerous mills, and is especially known for the serapes woven here in brilliant hues and striking patterns. Gold, silver, lead, and coal mines are in the area. Educational institutions include the 15,000-student University of Coahuila, an institute of technology, an agricultural college, and the Institute for Iberoamerican Studies. Saltillo's market sells local products and handicrafts.

SAN LUIS POTOSÍ, a major industrial center, is located 250 miles northwest of Mexico City in an agricultural region. Founded as a Franciscan mission in 1583, the city was twice the seat of the national government under Juárez, in 1863 and 1867. The economy of San Luis Potosí depends mainly on the production of gold, silver, and industrial metals. A number of other industries are located here. Livestock raising is important, and hides, tallow, and wool are exported. Some of Mexico's richest silver mines are located in the city. The city is also a railroad hub and distribution center. Landmarks in San Luis Potosí include several notable churches and a cathedral. Its university, established in 1859, was elevated to university status in 1923. A pedestrian mall, with some of the city's finest shops, is located on Hidalgo Street. The population of San Luis Potosí is 670,000.

A seaport and petroleum center, **TAMPICO** is located in east-central Mexico on the north bank of the Río Pánuco, six miles inland from the Gulf of Mexico and about 200 miles northeast of Mexico City. The city developed around a monastery founded in 1532. It was abandoned in 1683 following its destruction by pirates, and resettled again in 1823. Tampico today is a transportation center and one of Mexico's principal seaports. Exports include oil, copper ore, sugar, coffee, hides, livestock, and agricultural products. Oil tanks and refineries extend for miles along the south bank of the river. The city is also a tourist center and seaside resort known for its hunting, golfing, and fishing. The popular Miramar Beach is nearby. Tampico's current population is about 295,000.

TAXCO (formerly called Taxco de Alarcón), situated 50 miles southwest of Mexico City, is a world-famous silver capital. Perhaps the oldest mining center on the continent, it was originally an Indian town called Tlacho in the 1400s. Spanish conquest a century later brought silver-mine development, which has been constant to this day. Taxco, with some 60,000 residents, treasures its colonial past and atmosphere to the extent that the entire city has been declared a national monument. New construction must conform to old architectural styles; even the cobblestone streets may not be altered. The charm of this community has brought tourists from all over the world to sight-see and to buy unique handmade silver items from countless shops and vendors. Sundays in Taxco are market days. Indians sell their wares in the plaza, where licensed guides are available. The city's many spectacular fiestas draw visitors from across the country. Eighteenth-century landmarks include the magnificent Church of Santa Prisca and Sebastián—a richly decorated edifice built by José de la Borda, one of Taxco's most cel-ebrated and prosperous citizens; Figuera House, finished in 1767 and restored in 1943 as an artist's studio; and Humbolt House (Casa de Villanueva), a restored Moorish-inspired masterpiece. Built on a hill in the middle of the Sierra Madre Mountains, Taxco is considered a difficult city for drivers. Its narrow, twisting streets—often without street signs—encourage use of the plentiful taxis, as well as leisurely walking.

TEPIC is located near Mexico's west coast, about 110 miles northwest of Guadalajara at the foot of an extinct volcano, Sángangüey. Dating back to the 16th century, Tepic's isolated position contributed to its slow development. Today, it is a fascinating combination of old and new, with busy streets and broad plazas. Tobacco is grown on plantations in the area and processed in local factories. Processing plants, refineries, and rice mills are located in Tepic. Several shops in the city offer Indian handicrafts. The cathedral in Tepic, built about 1750, has two Gothic towers. Ingenio de Jala Falls, which flow only in the rainy season, are in this area; El Salto, a beautiful waterfall, is west of the city. Tepic, with an estimated population of 305,000, is the capital of Nayarit State.

The commercial city of **TOLUCA** is 35 miles west of Mexico City at an altitude of 8,500 feet. Founded in 1530, it is, today, a community with many beautiful gardens, cooler in climate than Mexico City because of its higher elevation. Toluca produces dried meats, sausage, wine, dairy products, and native handicraft. The city's industries include brewing and distilling, textile manufacturing, and food processing. The extinct volcano, Nevada de Toluca, towers above the city 27 miles to the southwest. At 15,000 feet, its peak is snow-capped most of the year; the beautiful Lake of the Moon and Sun in the crater are formed by melting snow. With a guide, it is possible to drive to the top of the volcano and then down into the crater. Also near Toluca are several interesting Indian villages. Toluca, whose formal designation is Toluca de Lerdo, has a population of 666,000. The city is the capital of México State.

One of Mexico's chief ports, **VERACRUZ** (full name is Veracruz Llave) is situated on the Gulf of Mexico, 260 miles east of Mexico City. The original settlement, Mexico's oldest, was founded in 1519 by Cortés and named La Villa Rica de la Vera Cruz (Rich Town of the True Cross). The present city and port date from 1599. Veracruz was the principal Mexican port for Spanish trade fleets from the 16th through 18th centuries, even though it was frequently sacked by pirates. The city was captured twice by the French, in 1838 and 1861, and by U.S. troops under Winfield Scott in 1847. Veracruz is the main port of entry from eastern and gulf ports; its port facilities were expanded and modernized after 1946. The city is also the terminus of two railroads and produces most of the country's cigars. In town, Veracruz's old buildings on cobbled streets contrast with modern structures. The area of old lighthouses is particularly interesting. Swimming, fishing, and boating are popular here. Band concerts are regularly held at the Plaza de la Constitución. The Mexican Naval Academy is located in the nearby coastal village of Antón Lizardo. Villa del Mar and Mocambo beaches are just south of Veracruz; they are often muddy and, sometimes, sharks lurk offshore. Veracruz's population is 460,000.

XOCHIMILCO, situated on the western shore of the lake whose name it bears, is 10 miles south of Mexico City. The city is intertwined with numerous waterways which are all that remain of what once was an extensive lake. The famous *chinampas*, or "floating gardens," were originally rafts woven of twigs, covered with earth, and planted with flowers; the rafts usually contained small huts and moved through the lake with oars. Through time, the roots of the vegetation on the rafts attached themselves to the lake bottom, and each "garden" became an "island." The number of these artificial islands increased until they formed a vast meadow interspersed with waterways. Flat-bottomed boats filled with flowers are today's floating gardens. Xochimilco is a prime tourist attraction, as well as a Sunday-outing spot for the natives. The Convent and Church of San Bernardino predate 1535. A campus of the Autonomous Metropolitan University of Mexico City is located in the city. The estimated population of Xochimilco is 170,000.

The mining town of **ZACATECAS** in central Mexico, 160 miles northeast of Guadalajara, is the capital of Zacatecas State. The town was built on the slopes of Cerro de la Bufa at an altitude of 8,075 feet. Zacatecas was taken by the Spanish in 1548 and vast quantities of silver found here were shipped to Spain. Until the 19th century, the mines around Zacatecas yielded one-fifth of the world's silver. Although surrounded by agricultural and cattle-raising regions, Zacatecas is principally a center for silver mining. Zacatecas is characterized by closely built houses, an aqueduct, stone steps, and steeply inclined streets, all of which give the city a medieval look. In contrast are the modern facilities housing the University of Zacatecas and its museums of anthropology and mining. Colonial buildings include the Municipal Palace, Theater of Calderón, and Church of Santo Domingo; an 18th-century convent is located in the suburb of Guadelupe. Zacatecas' population is 123,700.

COUNTRY PROFILE

Geography and Climate

Mexico is located in North America. It borders the Caribbean Sea and the Gulf of Mexico between Belize and the U.S. and borders the North Pacific Ocean between Guatemala and the U.S. Its land mass covers approximately 1.9 million sq. kms, or slightly less than three times the size of Texas, and has approximately 9,330 sq. kms of beachfront property. In July 1999, the population was estimated at 100.3 million.

Within Mexico, there are 31 states and one Federal District-Districo Federal, the country's capital. Independence Day for Mexico was September 16, 1810. It is celebrated widely throughout the country. The flag has three equal vertical bands of green, white, and red with a coat of arms-in the form of an eagle perched on a cactus with a snake in its beak-centered on a white band.

With a climate that varies from tropical to desert, the terrain ranges from high rugged mountains to low coastal plains and high plateaus to desert. Its lowest elevation point is at Laguna Salada at -10 meters. The highest point is the Volcano, Pico de Orizaba, at 5,700 meters.

Mexico has such natural hazards as tsunamis on the Pacific coast, volcanoes and destructive earthquakes at the center and south, and hurricanes on the Gulf of Mexico and Caribbean coasts.

The main agricultural products are corn, wheat, soybeans, rice, beans, cotton, coffee, fruit, tomatoes, beef, poultry, diary and wood products. The Mexican currency is in pesos. The June 2000 exchange rate is 9.84 pesos=US$1; but periodic fluctuations occur.

Population

Mexico has an estimated population of 100 million. It is the world's most populous Spanish-speaking country and the second most populous Latin American country.

Contemporary Mexico is an urban society, with close to 70% of the total population living in cities and 23% (18 million) in the Mexico City metropolitan area. Mexico is also a young nation. Almost 40% of Mexicans are less than 15 years old. Nearly 50% of the population lives in the high plateau central region (14% of the country).

About two-thirds are "mestizo" (mixed indigenous and Spanish blood). Mexican customs and traditions are an intricate mixture of the Spanish and the indigenous. Mexico has largely avoided racial divisions by proudly considering its population a distinct Mexican race, celebrated as Dia de la Raza on the October 12 annual holiday. Economic conditions determine social class.

Roman Catholicism is the predominant religion. Small groups of Protestant Christians are often related to and supported by U.S. churches.

Mexico began an aggressive and far reaching national family planning effort in 1973 to reduce the population growth rate from its all-time high of 3.5% then to 1% for the year 2000.

Spanish is the national language, spoken by 97% of the population. In some remote areas, only Indian dialects are spoken. The literacy rate is about 75%.

Public Institutions

The country's official name is the United Mexican States (Estudos Unidos Mexicanos). The 1917 constitution provided for a federal republic, which is now composed of 31 states and the Federal District where the capital is located. The government is made up of executive, legislative, and judicial branches.

The military forces are small and have stayed out of politics since 1946. The Cabinet is politically important; from the 1930s through the 1990s, all Mexican presidents had come directly from the Cabinet. The President, elected for a single six-year-term ("sexenio"), proposes and executes laws that are passed by Mexico's congress; and has the power to govern by decree in many economic and financial areas. No Vice President is elected; if an incumbent dies or leaves office before a term has been completed, the Congress elects a provisional President.

Until the National Action Party's victory in Mexico's 2000 presidential election, the Institutional Revolutionary Party (PRI) had been in power since its founding in 1929. It had won every presidential election and controlled the Congress by overwhelming majorities.

The Congress is composed of two houses: a 128 seat Senate, and a 500 seat Chamber of Deputies. Through a complex formula of proportional representation, the opposition parties are guaranteed at least 150 seats in the Chamber.

The judicial system, which is based on Roman civil law, consists of a Supreme Court and Federal and local courts. The President appoints Supreme Court justices with Senate approval.

The unicameral legislatures of the state governments are headed by elected governors, who serve for six years. In the absence of a county government system, there are only local governments at the municipal level. Mayors and city council members are popularly elected for three year terms.

Arts, Science and Education

Mexico City is the cultural hub of the country. The arts play an important role in national life and are heavily subsidized by the government. Influences of indigenous cultures, the Spanish colonial period, as well as North American contemporary culture are evident in architecture, literature, and art.

The richness and diversity of Mexico's cultural heritage and reflected by murals of Diego Rivera, Jose Clemente Orozco, and David Alfaro Siqueiros; paintings by Rufino Tamayo; and writings by Octavio Paz, Juan Rulfo, Carlos Fuentes, and Carlos Monsiváis.

Major arts festivals include the Cervantino International Festival in Guanajuato and Mexico City; the Festival of Mexico City's Historical Center; the International Music Festival in Morelia, Michoacán; the International Festival of Contemporary Art in León, Guanajuato; the Jose Limón International Dance Festival in Mazatlán; and the Festival of the Borders in Mexicali and Tijuana.

Nine U.S.-Mexico binational centers from Hermosillo to Merida promote understanding between "Estadounidenses" and Mexicans through the teaching of English to more than 30,000 Mexicans annually; teaching Spanish to foreigners; and sponsoring cultural and educational activities. Benjamin Franklin libraries, which receive support from the Public Affairs Section of the U.S. Embassy, are located in Mexico City, Guadalajara, and Monterrey.

Education is highly centralized under the Federal Secretariat of Public Education (SEP). Mexicans who can afford to send their children to private schools almost always choose to do so. More than 90% are educated under public SEP auspices. Teachers comprise half of the Federal workforce. Some 70% of Mexicans complete only primary school; about 10% finish some higher education, including university, teaching training colleges, or two-year technical institutes. The main teacher training institutions are the Universidad Pedagógica Nacional and the Escuela Normal Superior.

Traditionally, Mexican students have attended public universities-the most prestigious of which was the National Autonomous University of Mexico (UNAM), one of the oldest institutions of higher education in the Americas. Two-thirds of the older Mexican political leaders are UNAM alumni. Government-subsidized tuition fees of approximately two cents per year have limited UNAM's resources. An attempt by the rector to raise tuition to approximately US$200 provoked a student strike that began in April 1999 and ended in February 2000 when police retook control of the UNAM installations.

Other options for public education include: the Instituto Politecnico Nacional, the alma mater of President Zedillo (the first President not to have graduated from UNAM); the Universidad Autónoma Metropolitana with its three campuses in the Mexico City metropolitan area, and 31 autonomous universities, many of which have multiple campuses located in the various states.

Today, about 25% of university students are enrolled in private universities. The Instituto Tecnologico y de Estudios Superiores de Monterrey has 27 campuses linked by satellite across the country. Other recognized institutions of higher learning are the four campuses of Iberoamericana University; Instituto Tecnologico Autónomo de Mexico (ITAM), where most of the technocrats from the Salinas and Zedillo administrations studied; and the University of the Americas in Puebla. El Colegio de Mexico also has an excellent research reputation.

Given the interest among Mexicans in continuing their studies in the U.S., the U.S. Department of State has facilitated 12 U.S. educational advising centers across the country. A 13th center was inaugurated in Chiapas in January 2000. There are currently more than 9,600 Mexicans studying in the U.S., making Mexico the 10th largest source country for foreign students in the U.S.

Commerce and Industry

During the last 20 years, the Mexican economy has undergone a dramatic reorientation away from protectionist policies. After decades of import-substitution practices and extensive state intervention, Mexico is now cited as a model for countries intent on pursuing outward-looking and market-oriented economic policies. In 1994, Mexico entered into a comprehensive free trade agreement with the United States and Canada-the North American Free Trade Agreement, or NAFTA; and in 1999, Mexico concluded a similar agreement with the European Union. Tariff levels, as high as 100% before Mexico's 1986 accession to GATT (now WTO), currently average about 4% on a trade-weighted basis. The Mexican Government's divestiture then of airlines, banks, the telephone company, mines, and steel plants were major elements of a successful privatization program that has continued. Reduction and elimination of subsidies made a major contribution toward transforming a fiscal deficit that had reached a height of 16.0% of Gross Domestic Product (GDP) in 1987. It resulted in a very manageable 1.2% deficit in 1998. By turning increasingly to private capital for such basic infrastructure investment as toll roads and ports, the government has been able to expand budget outlays on education, health, and agricultural development.

GDP growth for 2000 was at the start of the year set to be around 3.6%. Inflation closed 1999 at less than 13%, and the central bank targeted an inflation rate of 10% for 2000. At more than $30 billion, in late 1999, foreign exchange reserves stand near their all-time high.

NAFTA significantly expanded U.S.Mexican economic ties. In 1999, Mexico overtook Japan as the second largest trading partner of the United States. NAFTA also raised Mexico's attractiveness as a recipient of foreign direct investment (FDI). During the first five years of NAFTA, the country cumulatively received $36 billion in FDI, twice the amount received during the five years prior to the signing of the accord. FDI reached $10 billion in 1998 alone, and is on target to exceed that level by 2000. About 54% of that investment comes from the U.S., which is further evidence of the two countries, increasing commercial integration. Awards of major projects to American firms are common and American companies comment frequently on the greatly improved business climate.

Mexico has a number of strengths empowering it to embark on a period of sustained economic growth. It is the world's seventh largest oil producer; is ranked ninth globally in proven petroleum reserves; and is well endowed with such minerals as silver-of which Mexico is the world's number one producer-copper, and zinc. Its manufacturing sector continues to grow. Automotive parts and textiles are its most significant products. Mexico is also an important producer of steel, glass, cement, and petrochemicals. Manufactured products account for about 90% of its exports compared to 80% in 1993 and only 14% in 1982. In-bond assembly and manufacturing is the fastest growing sector in Mexico contributing to export growth. It employs more than one million workers.

To achieve its ultimate economic aspirations, Mexico must overcome a 24-year history of economic collapses brought about mostly by fiscal mismanagement. Mexico exhibits extreme regional differences in development. The richer, more vibrant and dynamic North contains the country's most modern industrial plants and is tightly integrated with the U.S. economy. The poorer, lagging South contains outdated plants and an inadequate infrastructure. Central Mexico shows signs of both regions. There also are extreme differences within some sectors, particularly agriculture. Modern and efficient export-oriented industrial estates coexist with poor and inefficient subsistence farms. The banking sector, which collapsed with devaluation of the peso, is undercapitalized and leaves businesses with little access to credit. As a result, the formal economy cannot generate sufficient jobs to absorb all of the new entrants into the labor market, pushing many of them into the informal sector. Other problems plague income distribution, nutrition, health care, education, and public services. Forty million people live under the poverty line; 26 million live in abject poverty. Of Mexico's 7.5 million unionized workers, 3.5 million belong to the Confederation of Mexican Workers and 1.5 million to the Confederation of Independent Unions.

Transportation

Automobiles

Traffic and parking make power steering and automatic transmissions desirable. In Mexico City, drive with closed windows to keep out pollution. In the more temperate climates, such as Guadalajara, air-conditioning is optional but desirable.

General Motors, Ford, Chrysler, Nissan, Honda, and Volkswagen cars are made in Mexico. Adequate repair services are available for those makes and for the American Motors Jeep and Renault, which were made in Mexico until 1986. Basic model cars are the easiest to service. The cost of parts is slightly higher than in the U.S., and parts for late model American cars-even though a vehicle with the same model name is manufactured in Mexico-may not be available in Mexico and must be ordered from the U.S.

Some cars, especially large ones with optional equipment, can lose up to 25% of their power in Mexico City's high altitude. Tune vehicles for high altitude driving to ensure efficient operation.

Petroleos Mexicanos (PEMEX), the national petroleum company, sells vehicle fuel. Two grades (both unleaded): Premium (93 octane) in a red pump and Magna (87 octane) in a green pump. Therefore, retain catalytic converters on your vehicle. A few stations in cities and along major highways sell diesel. Keep fuel tanks at least half full, as stations are fewer and farther between than in the U.S. and may occasionally run out. Fuel is sold by the liter (3.785 liters equal 1 gallon). Use a locking gas cap.

Gasoline prices in Mexico are established by authorities in Mexico City and not by individual franchises.

Since 1991, all cars manufactured in Mexico are equipped with catalytic converters to reduce vehicle emissions that contribute to an acute air pollution problem in the Valley of Mexico-which includes Mexico City and adjacent areas in the State of Mexico.

Driving is on the right. Traffic congestion is common in cities. Mexico honors a valid drivers license, regardless of origin. Dependents who are more than 16 years of age can obtain a drivers permit for a small fee. The Mexican Department of Tourism provides a reliable highway emergency assistance patrol called "Angeles Verdes" (Green Angels), easily identifiable in a green truck. Toll roads ("cuota") are designated by the letter "D" after the highway number and are faster and safer than free ("libre") routes. The toll roads en route to the border are more expensive than comparable roads (interstates and highways) in the U.S. But it is worth the extra cost for the excellent roadbeds and uncrowded conditions.

Wandering livestock, unlighted vehicles, and unmarked road hazards make nighttime driving dangerous on all highways.

Road courtesies in Mexico, particularly on the long stretches of two-lane highway between Mexico City and the border, are different than in the U.S. 2-way traffic will often move over to the shoulders to allow vehicles to pass in the center of the road. Unwary U.S. drivers risk head on collisions if they do not pick up on this quickly. Also, drivers wanting to pass will turn on their left turn signal and leave it on until the pass is completed. Large trucks, as well as cars, often use the same signal to inform a vehicle behind them that it is safe to pass.

Mexican law requires drivers entering Mexico to have liability insurance issued by a Mexican company. Several U.S. and Mexican insurance companies offer plans that cover a driver for 30 days after crossing the border. Comprehensive and collision insurance are available from both U.S. and Mexican companies.

Cars purchased in Mexico come with temporary registration, but no temporary registration is available for imported cars. Therefore, all imported cars should have foreign registration and plates, preferably valid for at least four months from date of arrival to avoid being stopped by the police until Mexican plates are obtained.

Mexican vehicles may be sold locally, and Mexico has no restrictions on types of cars that may be imported.

Local

Licensed taxi service is readily available and inexpensive; a small tip is customary. The taxis are painted in various distinctive colors, include the word "taxi," have distinctive license plates, and either have meters or display rates. Airports often have buses or special taxi service ("transporte terrestre"), which is preferred. When using city buses and the metro subway system, observe security precautions that are appropriate for a large city.

"Combis" (or "peseros") are vans, smaller than buses, that carry passengers over assigned routes, to provide a convenient service. Licensed, chauffeured rental cars are also available, at prices comparable to taxi service in the U.S.

Mexico has extensive, inexpensive bus service throughout the country. Quality of service ranges from air-conditioned, luxury buses with reserved seats, that serve tourist destinations to often overcrowded buses providing the basics.

Regional

Railroad passenger service within Mexico is inexpensive, but covers only a few routes-including a few connections with the U.S.-and is being improved with new equipment.

Air service is good between major Mexican and U.S. cities. Within Mexico, air routes fan out from Mexico City. Domestic air travel however is expensive. Air travel between Mexican cities along the border is accomplished more easily by using U.S. airports.

Communications

Telephone and Telegraph

Local and international services are adequate, and both domestic and international calls may be dialed directly. TelMex, the former Mexican national phone company and currently the leading private phone company in Mexico, provides the connection for a reasonable fee. Calls to the U.S. from Mexico are comparable in cost to calls from the U.S. to Mexico. International calls outside of North America are expensive. Telephone service within Mexico is inexpensive. Telegrams are accepted in English and may be billed to home telephone numbers. Domestic and international FAX service is available.

Long distance is feasible by several carriers other than TelMex; Alestra (AT&T-Bancomer), Avantel (MCI-Banamex), and Miditel. Local service is still provided by TelMex.

Along with standard landlines, Mexico has two major providers of cellular phone services - TelCel and USACell. Both are affiliated with major telecommunications companies: TelCel with TelMex (Telefonos de Mexico) and USACell with Avantel, a division of MCI. Prices are very competitive between the two providers and only slightly higher than that which is available in the U.S. Both suppliers offer contracts that provide the phone, "free minutes," and access to the cellular network. At the end of the contract, the purchaser owns the cell phone. Typical contracts run for 18 months. TelCel also offers an alternative to a contract called the Amigo phone, where one buys the phone and pays for the minutes separately to be used as needed. The cell phone units offered for both contract and the Amigo plan are the same phones available in the U.S. They include, but are not limited to: Motorola, Nokia, Ericsson, and Philips with both digital and analog features. GSM technology is not supported in Mexico.

Telephone calls made with a credit card offer a wide variety of applications. Unfortunately, security is not up to the same standards as the U.S., and caution is recommended when using credit cards to place calls.

Mail

The most direct means for mail service is via post office boxes in U.S. border cities or international mail.

Radio and TV

Mexican television (TV) broadcasts on the same standard (NTSC) as in the U.S. and Mexican TV companies generally operate with state-of-the-art equipment. Two networks dominate Mexican television. Televisa is the older and highest rated one, but TV Azteca-privatized in 1994-has proven itself to be a worthy adversary. Each network broadcasts on three or four channels, featuring soap operas ("telenovelas"), series, variety shows, children's programs, sports (including major U.S. broadcasts), movies, and news coverage. Although most programs are produced or dubbed in Spanish, some movies are shown in the original language with subtitles. The UHF spectrum is not as occupied as in the U.S. That is mostly due to the fact that pay television became available in most major market neighborhoods and in hundreds of small towns at reasonable prices before smaller companies resorted to UHF frequencies. Though "pay TV" companies initially simply passed through U.S. network signals, they now relay the "Latin" services that many U.S. companies have set up. There are also cable-only programs (including an all news service in Spanish) produced nationally. C-Band dishes enjoyed an early heyday, but direct-to home broadcasts on the Ku-Band are taking a greater market share.

The radio spectrum in Mexico City is saturated by radio stations operating mostly with state-of-the-art equipment. All companies, some of which own as many as 12 stations, have at least one morning news magazine program that runs 3 to 4 hours. The leading stations include live reports from the U.S. and other world capitals, though they empha-size local and national events. Many Spanish-language AM and FM broadcasts feature music in English. Along the border, U.S. broadcasts are also available.

Newspapers, Magazines, and Technical Journals

Although sold at prices substantially higher than in the U.S. -a wide selection of U.S. magazines and newspapers and a limited selection of books can be found in most Mexican cities. The international editions of Time and Newsweek are sold locally, as are the editions of such major magazines as U.S. News & World Report, Popular Science, People, The Economist. The News, an English-language paper published in Mexico City, covers local events in eastern and central Mexico including Monterrey, with stateside and international coverage taken from major U.S. newspapers. The Guadalajara Colony Reporter has similar coverage for the Guadalajara area. Delivery of local Mexican papers, as well as a selection of U.S. papers (The New York Times, The Miami Herald, The Los Angeles Times and The Wall Street Journal), is available in Mexico City and at the nine U.S. Consulates throughout the country. USA Today, the Miami edition of the International Herald Tribune, and papers from neighboring U.S. states are also available. El Financiero also publishes a weekly international edition in English, that focuses on economic and financial issues. It is sent to U.S. subscribers.

Mexico has specialized magazines in English on such subjects as computers, cars, scientific innovations, medical journals, and women that are sold in major cities at bookstores and popular restaurants.

Health and Medicine

Medical Facilities

Pharmacies in the cities carry most drugs at reasonable prices, but occasional shortages occur. Although many prescription and over-the-counter medications that are manufactured in Mexico are manufactured by Mexican affiliates of U.S. firms, there may be some minor differences in formulation; thus, consult with a health practitioner before purchasing locally manufactured medications. Take prescriptions and an adequate supply of prescription medications. If you plan to have refills sent from the U.S., make arrangements beforehand. A supply of basic medicine chest items should also be taken.

The American-British Cowdray (ABC) Hospital in Mexico City, staffed partially by English speaking, U.S. trained physicians, is recommended for emergencies and routine hospitalizations. There are other well-equipped private hospitals available with similar staff. Mexico City has many English speaking U.S. trained physicians, including medical and dental specialists. For major medical and surgical problems, patients may be evacuated to the U.S. The designated evacuation point is Miami, Florida.

Ciudad Juarez: The full range of medical services is available in El Paso, Texas.

Guadalajara: English-speaking, U.S.-trained physicians and several well equipped hospitals and clinics are available and provide adequate medical care.

Hermosillo: Hospitals and clinics in Hermosillo are adequate for routine and emergency care. Many doctors are U.S. trained and certified. A full range of medical services is available in Tucson, Arizona, a four-hour drive or a one-hour flight away.

Matamoros: The full range of medical services is available across the river in Brownsville, Texas, and other nearby cities in the Rio Grande Valley.

Merida: The incidence of diarrheal diseases and hepatitis is high. Malaria is rare; but there are incidents of other diseases transmitted by mosquitoes. Medical facilities are inadequate despite the presence of

competent doctors and dentists. In the event of serious illness, the patient will be evacuated to Mexico City or Miami, Florida.

Monterrey: Medical facilities in Monterrey are modern and adequate. Two large, well-equipped private hospitals have been approved for routine and emergency care. U.S. trained and highly specialized physicians and dentists are available. Difficult or unusual cases may be evacuated to Texas.

Nuevo Laredo: Use the medical and dental facilities in Laredo, Texas, or the medical center in San Antonio, Texas.

Tijuana: Complete health care is available across the border in the San Diego or Chula Vista area.

Tuxtla Gutierrez: A USDA installation is in this southern Mexico region. Private clinics and hospitals are minimally adequate, despite many well trained physicians. In the event of serious medical problems, evacuation to Mexico City or to Miami, Florida, will be authorized.

Community Health

Air pollution is widely recognized as a problem in Mexico City. In a study published in the spring of 1999, the World Resources Institute rated Mexico City as the number one city in the world for health risks to children age 5 and under due to air pollution. This pollution is due in part to rapid urbanization and industrialization, but mostly to the huge and ever growing number of vehicles. The air quality has improved in some categories since the early 1990s. According to the Mexican Government, the lead and sulfur dioxide levels are consistently within the acceptable levels, as defined by the World Health Organization; and the nitrogen dioxide and carbon monoxide levels are rarely above them. The levels for declaring environmental emergencies were recently tightened in response to evidence of negative health effects from ozone and particulate matter. Although there

were fewer ozone peaks above 330 parts per million annually in the past few years, it is still above acceptable levels over 85% of the year. Suspended particulate matter (PM 10) exceeds the standards 20% to 30% annually. Because of the continuing concerns about pollution, the standard length of tour remains at two years.

Tap water is not safe to drink. Boiling, iodine, or chlorine treatment is necessary.

Tuberculosis is still present in the general population; thus domestic employees should be screened for it. Malaria and other serious tropical diseases are present only in southern rural areas of Mexico. Persons who will reside or travel in southern Mexico should be vaccinated for yellow fever before departing the U.S. because of a yellow fever is endemic in parts of southern Mexico and Central America.

Intestinal infections are prevalent in Mexico. Most infections are due solely to the fact that Mexican bacteria are different from U.S. bacteria. Nevertheless, parasitic infections (including ameba and giardia) are common. Therefore, select food sources and restaurants carefully. Clean and treat raw vegetables and fruits with iodine. Unpasteurized dairy products may carry brucellosis and tuberculosis. Therefore, purchase only reliably pasteurized and refrigerated products.

Marijuana and cocaine and other addictive drugs are readily available, despite Mexican efforts to control drug trafficking. Drug offenders, including teenagers, are often jailed for lengthy periods.

Preventive Measures

Cigarette smokers should be particularly aware that they risk increased cardiopulmonary problems due to the altitude and pollution. The combination of altitude in Mexico's high plateau and pollution in the Valley of Mexico with smoking may be dangerous for pregnant women and the fetus. Numerous health clubs are available throughout the city. Those who wish to exercise outdoors should do so in the morning, when the pollution levels are lowest.

Rabies is endemic in Mexico, thus keep pet immunizations current. Rabies vaccine is available in the Health Unit for all who wish to be vaccinated. It may be especially advisable for children, joggers, and rural workers to be vaccinated.

Recommended immunizations for Mexico include diphtheria, tetanus, polio, MMR, and yellow fever. Infectious (viral) hepatitis is endemic in Mexico; therefore gamma globulin injections every four to six months are recommended for those over 12 years old.

Newcomers to high altitude should allow time for acclimatization. In the first several weeks, you should avoid overeating, alcoholic beverages, and excessive physical exertion. Light-headedness, insomnia, slight headaches, and shortness of breath are common initial reactions to the altitude. Adequate rest and fluids help alleviate the discomfort.

NOTES FOR TRAVELERS

Passage, Customs & Duties

The Government of Mexico requires that all U.S. citizens present proof of citizenship and photo identification for entry into Mexico. A U.S. passport is recommended, but other U.S. citizenship documents such as a certified copy of a U.S. birth certificate, a Naturalization Certificate, a Consular Report of Birth Abroad, or a Certificate of Citizenship are acceptable. U.S. citizens boarding flights to Mexico should be prepared to present one of these documents as proof of U.S. citizenship, along with photo identification. Driver's permits, voter registration cards, affidavits and similar documents are not sufficient to prove citizenship for readmission into the United States.

Travelers should be aware that Mexican entry regulations require Spanish translations of all legal documents, including notarized consent decrees and court agreements. Enforcement of this provision is not always consistent, and English-language documents are almost always sufficient.

A visa is not required for a tourist/transit stay up to 180 days. A tourist card, also known as a FM-T, available from Mexican consulates and most airlines serving Mexico, is issued instead. Travelers entering Mexico for purposes other than tourism require a visa and must carry a valid U.S. passport. The Government of Mexico charges an entry fee to U.S. citizens traveling to Mexico's interior.

Upon arrival in Mexico, business travelers must complete a form (Form FM-N 30 days) authorizing the conduct of business, but not employment, for a 30-day period. U.S. citizens planning to work or live in Mexico should apply for the appropriate Mexican visa (Form FM-2 or 3) at the Mexican Embassy in Washington, DC or nearest Mexican consulate in the United States. U.S. citizens planning to participate in humanitarian aid missions, human rights advocacy groups or international observer delegations also should contact the Mexican Embassy or nearest Mexican consulate for guidance on how to obtain the appropriate visa before traveling to Mexico. Such activities, undertaken while on a tourist visa, may draw unfavorable attention from Mexican authorities because Mexican immigration law prohibits foreigners from engaging in political activity. U.S. citizens have been detained or deported for violating their tourist visa status. Therefore, tourists should avoid demonstrations and other activities that may be deemed political by Mexican authorities. This is particularly relevant in light of the tension and polarization in the state of Chiapas. U.S. citizens and other foreigners have been detained in Chiapas and expelled from Mexico for allegedly violating their visa status or for

interfering in Mexican internal politics.

Mexican regulations limit the value of goods brought into Mexico by U.S. citizens arriving by air or sea to $300 per person and by land to $50 per person. Amounts exceeding the duty-free limit are subject to a 32.8 percent tax. For further information concerning entry and visa requirements, travelers may contact the Embassy of Mexico at 1911 Pennsylvania Avenue N.W., Washington, D.C. 20006, telephone (202) 736-1000, or its web site at http://embassyofmexico.org, or any Mexican consulate in the United States.

Americans living in or visiting Mexico are encouraged to register at the U.S. Embassy or at one of the U.S. Consulates, in order to obtain updated information on travel and security within Mexico. The U.S. Embassy is located in Mexico City at Paseo de la Reforma 305, Colonia Cuauhtemoc, telephone from the United States: 011-525-080-2000; telephone within Mexico City: 5-080-2000; telephone long distance within Mexico 01-5-080-2000. You may also contact the Embassy by e-mail at: ccs@usembassy.net.mx.

U.S. Consulates General are located in:

Ciudad Juarez: Avenida Lopez Mateos 924-N, telephone (52)(1) 611-3000.

Guadalajara: Progreso 175, telephone (52)(3) 825-2998.

Monterrey: Avenida Constitucion 411 Poniente 64000, telephone (52)(8) 345-2120.

Tijuana: Tapachula 96, telephone (52)(6) 681-7400.

U.S. Consulates are located in:

Hermosillo: Avenida Monterrey 141, telephone (52)(6) 217-2375.

Matamoros: Avenida Primera 2002, telephone (52)(8) 812-4402.

Merida: Paseo Montejo 453, telephone (52)(9) 925-5011.

Nogales: Calle San Jose, Nogales, Sonora, telephone (52)(6) 313-4820.

Nuevo Laredo: Calle Allende 3330, Col. Jardin, telephone (52)(8) 714-0512.

U.S. Consular Agencies are located in:

Acapulco: Hotel Continental Plaza, Costera Miguel Aleman 121 - Local 14, telephone (52)(7) 484-03-00 or (52)(7) 469-0556.

Cabo San Lucas: Blvd. Marina y Pedregal #1, Local No. 3, Zona Centro, telephone (52)(1) 143-3566.

Cancun: Plaza Caracol Two, Third Level, No. 320-323, Boulevard Kukulcan, km. 8.5, Zona Hotelera, telephone (52)(9) 883-0272.

Cozumel: Plaza Villa Mar in the Main Square - El Centro, 2nd floor right rear, Locale #8, Avenida Juarez and 5th Ave. Norte, telephone (52)(9) 872-4574.

Ixtapa/Zihuatanejo: Local 9, Plaza Ambiente, telephone (52)(7) 553-2100.

Mazatlan: Hotel Playa Mazatlan, Rodolfo T. Loaiza #202, Zona Dorada, telephone (52)(6) 916-5889.

Oaxaca: Macedonio Alcala No. 407, Interior 20, telephone (52)(9) 514-3054 (52)(9) 516-2853.

Puerto Vallarta: Edif. Vallarta, Plaza Zaragoza 160-Piso 2 Int-18, telephone (52)(3) 222-0069.

San Luis Potosi: Edificio "Las Terrazas", Avenida Venustiano Carranza 2076-41, (52)(4) 811-7802.

San Miguel de Allende: Dr. Hernandez Macias #72, telephone (52)(4)152-2357 or (52)(4)152-0068.

Pets

There are no quarantine requirements for pets, but they require specific documents issued by an officially recognized veterinarian, and authenticated ("visado") by the Mexican consul with jurisdiction over the place of issue.

All Pets entering Mexico require a certificate that they were examined and found free of evidence of infectious or parasitic disease; this should be done within 10 days of arrival in Mexico. Dogs require proof of vaccination against rabies, viral hepatitis, leptospirosis, and distemper not less than 15 days or more than one year before arrival, and of parvo-virus vaccination not less than 15 days or more than 150 days before arrival.

Cats require proof of vaccination against rabies and feline panleucopenia not less than 15 days or more than 1 year before arrival.

Prior to travel, the Mexican consul in the U.S. requires certification from the U.S. Department of Agriculture (USDA), Animal and Plant Health Inspection Service-Veterinary Services (APHISVS), that the veterinarian issuing the documents is officially recognized.

Pets traveling with their owners are cleared into Mexico with only these documents. Those pets who are shipped to Mexico require a free entry permit, which takes a month or more to obtain after the owner has arrived in Mexico. Pets shipped to Mexico must arrive in the morning to allow time for same-day customs clearance, as there are no pet storage facilities at airports.

Firearms and Ammunition

The Mexican Government has significant restrictions on the types of firearms and ammunition that may be imported into the country. Generally, the Mexican government prohibits the importation of .357 and .45 caliber handguns, rifles with a caliber of .30 and larger, and shotguns with barrels shorter than 25 inches.

Currency, Banking, and Weights and Measures

The monetary unit in Mexico is the peso. The symbol used to designate pesos is the same as the dollar symbol, except that it has only one vertical line. The peso-dollar exchange rate is subject to change. Current currency notes include the following denominations: 500, 200, 100, 50, and 20. Coins in circulation include: 10, 5, 2, 1 peso, and .50, .20, .10, and .05 centavos.

The current exchange rate is approximately 9.4 Pesos=US $1.

Mexican banking facilities are similar to those in the U.S.

Carry U.S. dollar travelers checks. Travelers already in Mexico may obtain travelers checks from the travel agency at the U.S Embassy. U.S. dollars in cash or travelers checks are accepted widely, and can be exchanged at most banks or cambios (foreign exchange dealer), including those at border crossing points and international airports. Dollars and travelers checks are accepted at most hotels and many stores and restaurants, but at a less favorable rate of exchange. Major U.S. credit cards, e.g., American Express, Master Card, and Visa, are widely accepted in Mexico. Sears stores in Mexico accept Sears cards from the U.S. Credit cards can also be obtained locally with a peso account. The majority of gasoline stations in Mexico do not accept credit cards.

Taxes, Exchange, and Sale of Property

A 15% value-added sales tax is applied to most goods and services. Hotels charge an additional 2% lodging tax that is not required to be itemized separately on your bill. Rather, it is usually included in the retail price of goods. It is always smart to ask if the price includes IVA (taxes); It is customary to leave a tip for baggage handlers, porters, chambermaids, tour guides, and drivers. Avoid leaving U.S. coins. Taxi drivers expect a tip only when an extra service is provided.

Hunting licenses are required. There is a value-added tax (IVA-impuesto al valor agregado) averaging 15% on most goods and services except on food, medicines, newspapers, residential rents, and physicians' fees.

Security Precautions

The Department of State rates Mexico City's crime situation as CRITICAL (its highest designator). Walking in an isolated area anywhere in the city, especially after dark, raises a real risk of armed robbery. The use of roving taxis, those with green and white license plates, is discouraged because of the threat of robbery by the drivers or their criminal accomplices.

Disaster Preparedness - Earthquakes & Volcanos

Since December 1994, the Popocatepetl Volcano, situated 38 miles southeast of Mexico City, has registered varying levels of seismic activity, including the release of vapor, gas, ash, and incendiary material. Depending on the levels of activity, the Mexican National Center for Disaster Prevention restricts access or closes parks and hiking trails on the mountain's slopes. U.S. citizens planning to hike in the area should be alert to any warnings or signs posted, and should contact the U.S. Embassy for the latest information about seismic activity.

Civil defense officials in the states of Jalisco and Colima are closely monitoring activity at the Volcan de Colima, (also known as Volcan de Fuego), located in south-central Jalisco. The volcano produced a number of gas exhalations, explosions and ash falls in February 1999. There is also active lava flow on the south side of the mountain. A major eruption is possible. U.S. citizens should exercise caution if planning to travel to the area surrounding the volcano. They should contact the U.S. Consulate General in Guadalajara, Mexico, at telephone 011-523-825-3429 for the latest information. Updated information may also be obtained in Spanish and in English at web site http://www.ucol.mx/volcan.

LOCAL HOLIDAYS

Jan. 1	New Year's Day
Jan. 6	Day of the Kings
Feb. 2	Candlemas
Feb. 5	Constitution Day
Feb. 24	Flag Day
Feb/Mar.	Carnival*
Mar. 21	Juarez's Birthday
Mar/Apr.	Holy Thursday*
Mar/Apr	Good Friday*
Mar/Apr	Easter Sunday*
May 1	Labor Day
May 5	Anniversary of the Battle of the Puebla/Cinco de Mayo)
May 10	Mother's Day
Aug. 15	Assumption
Sept. 1	El Diadel Informe
Sept. 16	Independence Day
Oct. 12	El Dia de la Raza/Columbus Day
Nov. 1	All Saints' Day
Nov. 2	Day of the Dead
Nov. 20	Revolution Day
Dec. 12	Our Lady of Guadelupe
Dec. 23	Feast of the Radishes (Oaxaca only)
Dec. 25	Christmas Day
Dec. 28	Holy Innocents' Day
Dec. 31	New Year's Eve

*variable

RECOMMENDED READING

The following titles are provided as a general indication of the material published on this country:

Art

Goldman, Shifra M. *Contemporary Mexican Painting in a Time of Change.* Austin: University of Texas Press, 1981.

Harvey, Marian. *Mexican Crafts and Craftspeople.* Philadelphia,

PA: The Art Alliance Press; London: Cornwall Books, 1987.

Los Angeles County Museum of Art. *Sculpture of Ancient West Mexico: Nayarit, Jalisco, Colima:* a catalogue of the proctor Stafford collection at the Los Angeles County Museum of Art/Michael Kan, Clement Meighan, H.B. Nicholson. Albuquerque, NM: Los Angeles County Museum of Art in association with University of New Mexico Press, 1989.

Mexico: Splendors of Thirty Centuries / Introduction by Octavio Paz. Boston: Little, Brown & Co.; New York: Metropolitan Museum of Art, 1990.

Oettinger, Marion. *Folk Treasures of Mexico: the Nelson A. Rockefeller Collection.* New York: Harry N. Abrams, 1990.

Oles, James. *Frida Kalo, Diego Rivera, and Mexican Modernism: from the Jacques and Natasha Gelman Collection.* San Francisco, CA: San Francisco Museum of Modern Art, 1996.

Olmec Art of Ancient Mexico. Edited by Elizabeth E Benson & Beatriz de la Fuente; with contributions by Marcia Castro-Leal. Washington, D.C.: National Gallery of Art, 1996.

Paz, Octavio. *Essays on Mexican Art.* New York: Harcourt Brace Jovanovich, 1993.

Portillo, Jose Lopez. *Quetzalcoatl, in Myth, Archeology, and Art.* New York: Continuum Pub. Co., 1982.

Rivera, Diego. *Diego Rivera, a Retrospective.* New York: Founders Society Detroit Institute, 1986.

Rochfort, Desmond. *Mexican Muralists: Orozco, Rivera, Siqueiros.* San Francisco: Chronicle, 1993.

Sayer, Chloe. *Costumes of Mexico.* Austin: University of Texas Press, 1985.

Schele, Linda. *The Blood of Kings: Dynasty and Ritual in Maya Art.* Fort Worth, TX: Kimball Art Museum, 1986.

Smith, Bradley. *Mexico: A History in Art*. New York: Doubleday & Co., 1968.

Stierlin, Henri. *Art of the Aztecs and Its Origins*. New York: Rizzoli, 1982.

Yampolsky, Mariana. *The Edge of Time: Photographs of Mexico*. Austin: University of Texas Press, 1998.

Economic

Armstrong, George M. *Law and Market Society in Mexico*. New York: Praeger Publishers, 1989.

Mexico Faces the 21st Century. Edited by Donald E. Schulz and Edward J. Williams. Westport, CT: Praeger, 1995.

Mexico's External Relations in the 1990s. Edited by Riordan Roett. Boulder, CO: Lynne Rienner Publishers, 1991.

Orme, William A. *Understanding NAFTA: Mexico, Free, Trade and The New North America*. Austin: University of Texas Press, 1996.

Riner, D.L. *Mexico: Meeting the Challenge*. London; Mexico: Euromoney Publications in association with Auritec Asesores, Banco Internacional, 1991.

Society and Economy in Mexico. Edited by James W Wilkie. Los Angeles: University of California, 1990.

The Mexican Peso Crisis: International Perspectives. Edited by Riordan Roett. Boulder, CO: Lynne Rienner Publishers, 1996.

History

Aguilar Camin, Hector. *In the Shadow of the Mexican Revolution: Contemporary Mexican History, 1910-1989*. by Hector Aguilar Camin and Lorenzo Meyer; translated by Luis Alberto Fierro. Austin: University of Texas Press, 1993. viii, 287 p. 972.08 CAM

At the Crossroads: Mexico and U.S. Immigration Policy. Edited by Frank D. Bean... [et al.] Lanham, MD: Rowman & Littlefield, 1999. 322 p. 325.273 CRO

Between Two Worlds: Mexican Immigrants in the United States. David G. Guti'rrez, editor. Wilmington, DE: Scholarly Resources, 1996. xxvii, 271 p. 973.04 BET

Camp, Roderic Ai. *Crossing Swords: Politics and Religion in Mexico*. New York: Oxford University Press, 1997. 341 p. 261.7 CAM

Camp, Roderic Ai. *Politics in Mexico: The Decline of Authoritarianism*. New York: Oxford University Press, 1999. Edition: 3rd ed. 279 p. 320.972 CAM

Centeno, Miguel Angel. *Democracy Within Reason: Technocratic Revolution in Mexico*. University Park: Pennsylvania State University Press, 1994. 272 p. 320.972 CEN

Cornelius, Wayne A. *Mexican Politics in Transition: The Breakdown of a One-Party-Dominant Regime*. San Diego: Center for U.S.-Mexican Studies, University of California, San Diego, 1996. 122 p.: ill. 320.972 COR

Dunn, Timothy J., 1961-. *The Militarization of the U.S.-Mexico Border, 1978-1992: Low-Intensity Conflict Doctrine Comes Home*. Austin: Center for Mexican American Studies, University of Texas at Austin, 1996. xii, 307 p.: map 972 DUN

Electoral Patterns and Perspectives in Mexico. Edited by Arturo Alvarado Mendoza. San Diego: Center for U.S.-Mexican Studies, University of California, 1987. 287 p. 324.972 ELE

Encyclopedia of Mexico: History, Society & Culture. Eitor, Michael S. Werner; cartographer, Tom Willcockson; indexer, AEIOU, Inc.; commissioning editor, Robert M. Salkin. Chicago: Fitzroy Dearborn Publishers, 1997. 2 v.: ill., maps REF 972.003 ENC

Erfani, Julie A. *The Paradox of the Mexican State: Rereading Sovereignty From Independence to NAFTA*. Boulder, CO: Lynne Rienner Publishers, 1995. 238 p.: ill. 320.972 ERF

Farriss, Nancy M. (Nancy Marguerite). *Maya Society Under Colonial Rule: The Collective Enterprise of Survival*. Princeton: Princeton University Press, 1984.

Fodor's Mexico, 1998-. New York: Fodor's Travel Publications, 1998- v. ill., maps REF 917.2 FOD

Griswold del Castillo, Richard. *The Treaty of Guadalupe Hidalgo: A Legacy of Conflict*. Norman: University of Oklahoma Press, 1990

Guti'rrez, David (David Gregory). *Walls and Mirrors: Mexican Americans, Mexican Immigrants, and the Politics of Ethnicity*. Berkeley: University of California Press, c1995. 320 p. 323.116 GUT

Herrera, Celia. Uniform Title: [Francisco Villa ante la historia.] *Pancho Villa Facing History*. New York: Vantage Press, 1993.

Johns, Michael; 1958. *The City of Mexico in the Age of Diaz*. Austin: University of Texas Press, 1997.

Katz, Friedrich. *The Life and Times of Pancho Villa*. Stanford: Stanford University Press, 1998. 985 p.: ill. 972.08 KAT

La Problernatica de las Etnica en Mexico. Victor Campa Mendoza. Mexico: Scientyc Ediciones, 1998. Edition: 3a ed., corr. y aumentada 400 p. S 972.004 PRO

Mazarr, Michael J. Mexico 2005: The Challenges of the New Millennium. Michael J. Mazarr: foreword by Federico Reyes-Heroles. Washington, DC: CSIS Press, 1999. 175 p. 972.08 MAZ

McGregor, Peter. *Essential Mexico*. United Kingdom: AA Publishing, 1996. 128 p.: ill. REF 917.2 MCG

Mexican Literature: A History. Edited by David William Foster. Austin: University of Texas Press, 1994. x, 458 p. 860.997 MEX

Mexico Under Zedillo. Edited by Susan Kaufman Purcell and Luis Rubio. Boulder, CO: Lynne Rienner Publishers, 1998. 151 p. 972.08 MEX

Mexico, From Independence to Revolution, 1810-1910. Edited, with commentary, by W Dirk Raat.

Lincoln: University of Nebraska Press, 1982.

Morales-Gomez, Daniel A. *The State, Corporatist Politics, and Educational Policy Making in Mexico*. Westport, CT: Praeger Publishers, 1990. 197 p. 379.72 MOR

Morris, Stephen D., 1957-. *Political Reformism in Mexico: An Overview of Contemporary Mexican Politics*. Boulder, CO: Lynne Rienner Pub., 1995. 261 p. 320.972 MOR

New Writings From Mexico. Edited by Reginal Gibbons. Evanston, IL: TriQuarterly, Northwestern University, 1992. 420 p.: ill. 860 NEW

Opposition Government in Mexico. Edited by Victoria E. Rodriguez and Peter M. Ward. Albuquerque: University of New Mexico Press, 1995. 255 p. 320.972 OPP

Polling for Democracy: Public Opinion and Political Liberalization in Mexico. Edited by Roderic Ai Camp. Wilmington, DE: SR Books, 1996. 186 p. 303.38 POL

Rebellion in Chiapas: An Historical Reader. [compilation, translations, and introductory material by] John Womack, Jr. New York:

New Press, 1999. xvii, 372 p. 972.75 REB

Reed, Glenn and Rober Gray. *How To Do Business in Mexico: Your Essential and Up-to-Date Guide for Success*. Austin: University of Texas Press, 1997. xvi, 181 p. REF 658.848 REE

Reed, John, 1887-1920. *Mexico Insurgente*. Mexico: Editores Mexicanos Unidos, 1989.

Revolution in Mexico: Years of Upheaval, 1910-1940. Edited by James W Wilkie. Tucson: University of Arizona Press, 1984.

Rural Revolt in Mexico: U.S. Intervention and the Domain of Subaltern Politics. Edited by Daniel Nugent; foreword by William C. Roseberry. Durham, NC: Duke University Press, 1998. Edition: 2nd ed., expanded ed. 384 p. 327.720 RUR

Sayer, Chloe. *Costumes of Mexico*. Austin: University of Texas Press, 1985.

Smith, Michael Ernest; 1953. *The Aztecs*. Cambridge, MA: Blackwell Publishers, 1997.

Subnational Politics and Democratization in Mexico. Edited by Wayne A. Cornelius, Todd A. Eisenstadt & Jane Hind-

ley. San Diego, CA: Center for U.S.-Mexican studies, University of California, 1999. viii, 369 p. 320.972 SUB

Taylor, Lawrence J. *The Road to Mexico*. Text by Lawrence J. Taylor; photographs by Maeve Hickey. Tucson: University of Arizona Press, c1997. 179 p. 917.2 TAY

The Evolution of the Mexican Political System. Edited by Jaime E. Rodriguez O. Wilmington, DE: SR Books, 1993. 322 p.: ill. 972 EVO *Prospects for Mexico*. Edited by George W Grayson. [Washington, D.C.]: Foreign Service Institute, U.S. Dept. of State, 1988. 286 p.: ill. 972.083 PRO

U.S. Commission for the Study of International Migration and Cooperative Economic Development. *Unauthorized Migration: Addressing the Root Causes: Research Addendum*. Washington, D.C.: The Commission, 1990. 2 v. REF 325.73 USC

Van Delden, Maarten, 1958. *Carlos Fuentes, Mexico, and Modernity*. Nashville, TN: Vanderbilt University Press, 1998. ix, 262 p. 863 VAN

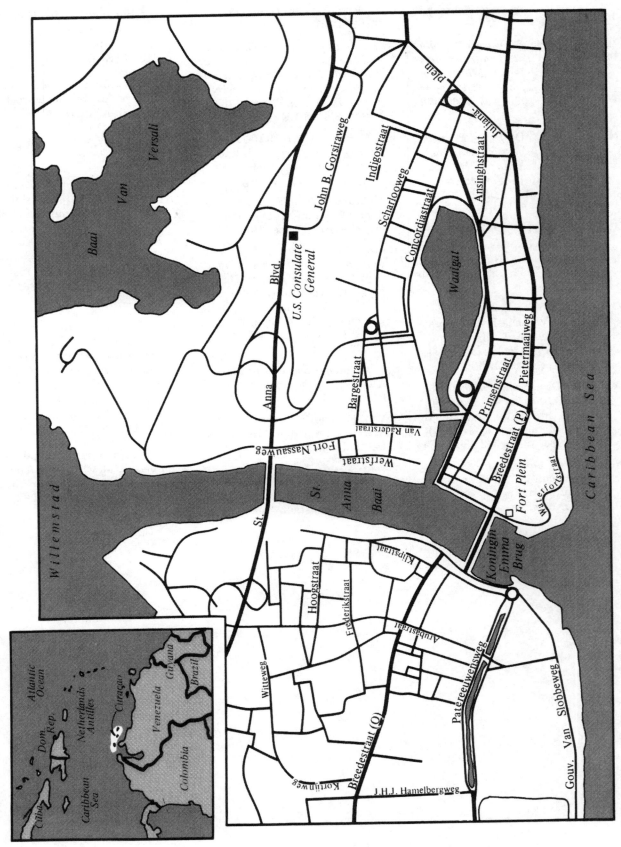

Willemstad (Curaçao), Netherlands Antilles

NETHERLANDS ANTILLES

(including Aruba)

Major City:
Curaçao (Willemstad)

Other Cities:
The Bottom, Kralendijk, Oranjestad, Philipsburg, Sint Nicolaas

This chapter was adapted from the Department of State Post Report 2000 for Netherlands Antilles. Supplemental material has been added to increase coverage of minor cities, facts have been updated, and some material has been condensed. Readers are encouraged to visit the Department of State's web site at http://travel.state.gov/ for the most recent information available on travel to this country.

INTRODUCTION

THE NETHERLANDS ANTILLES, a Dutch colonial possession for the greater part of three centuries, and once a center for slave trade in the Caribbean, has been an autonomous territory of the Kingdom of the Netherlands since 1954. Aruba, one of the three largest islands (the others are Curaçao and Bonaire) withdrew from the federation in January 1986 to form its own domestic government. In 1990, however, Aruba requested and received from the Netherlands a cancellation of the agreement that would have granted independence in 1996. It remains under Dutch protection and, unofficially at least, is still referred to as an integral part of the Antilles group.

The islands are a fascinating blend of Afro-Spanish-Dutch culture—a tapestry of sites, peoples, and languages. The countryside is rich in history, and in natural marvels which draw increasing numbers of tourists each year to these jewels in the sun.

MAJOR CITY

Curaçao

During the colonial period Curaçao was a center of slave trade in the Caribbean. After emancipation of the slaves in 1863, Curaçao lost much of its economic importance until 1916 when Royal Dutch Shell built an oil refinery on the shores of Schottegat Harbor. Shell pulled out in 1985, and the Venezuelan petroleum company took over operation of the refinery. Curaçao also has the largest repair dry-dock in the Caribbean, a container port, an important offshore financial sector and several resort hotels.

The total number of American citizens residing on the island fluctuates but is in the neighborhood of 1,000. The overall "foreign colony", including Dutch nationals, makes up about 10% of the total population. Curaçao has as many as 40 nationalities represented, including a large percentage of Indians, Chinese and Indonesians.

Although Curaçao has been associated with the Netherlands for about 300 years, visitors to Curaçao find that a knowledge of Spanish is as helpful as Dutch. English is spoken and understood to one degree or another by a large percentage of the local population; Papiamentu is the language of daily life.

The town of Willemstad contains most of Curaçao's 150,000 population. Dutch architecture predominates in the older sections of the city. Homes in the suburbs are more modern and spacious.

Utilities

The city water supply consists exclusively of distilled, potable seawater. Electric current in Curaçao is 110v-130v, 50-cycle, single-phase AC.

Any American appliance, which relies on 60-cycle current for its timing (such as clocks, record players and tape recorders) must be converted for 50-cycle current in order to operate properly. If possible, have this done in the U.S. before shipment (transformers can only convert voltage, not cycles). Transformers and all types of electrical equipment and appliances are

Wathey Square in Philipsburg, Netherlands Antilles

available locally but at high prices. Most major brands can be serviced locally. The local power supply sometimes experiences surges, spikes and/or brownouts.

UPS's and/or surge protectors are recommended for computers, TV's, VCR's, stereos and other sensitive electronic equipment. They can be purchased locally but are less expensive in the States.

Food

Almost all food is imported. A good variety of canned and frozen foods, including baby foods, of U.S. and Dutch origin are available in modern supermarkets. Fresh produce is flown in regularly, mostly from the U.S. and Venezuela, but are not necessarily in stock at all times. Boats from Venezuela sell produce and fish at a central area in Willemstad called the "floating market."

Curaçao imports all its meat, mostly from Argentina, the Netherlands,

New Zealand, Denmark and the U.S. Quality is satisfactory although sometimes tougher than we are accustomed to in the U.S. and special cuts, particularly beef and veal, are often unavailable. Most frozen poultry is of U.S. origin. Eggs of good size and quality come from local sources. Butter and cheese are imported from the U.S. and the Netherlands. Frozen fish and seafood products come from as far away as Norway and Iceland. Fresh fish from South American and Caribbean sources is available and safe.

Since transportation costs are included, food prices are comparatively high.

Clothing

Men: At work, clothing suitable for summer in Washington is appropriate. Casual dress is typical at other times. Both European and American men's clothing is available but relatively expensive. A dark suit is

necessary and suitable for most representational purposes.

Women: Curaçao really has only one season-summer. Bring summer wear. Light cotton is preferable to polyester blends. Women wear short dresses at most evening social affairs not identified as "casual" or "sport." All kinds of women's clothes are available in Curaçao at prices higher than those in the U.S. A fair selection of women's shoes is usually, but not always, available; some American women have found excellent buys in European brand shoes.

Children: Infant and children's clothes are available at prices much higher than those in the U.S. but the selection is limited in size and style and the quality is sometimes inferior. Children's shoes are available in American sizes. Baby items (such as diapers) are much more expensive than in the U.S.

Supplies and Services

Nearly all well known brands of American and European toiletries, cosmetics, personal hygiene supplies, home medicines and drugs are available on Curaçao. Prices range from less than those in the U.S. to up to 50% higher on some items. A good range of liquor and tobacco items is available through duty-free suppliers.

Most basic services found in a small community can be found on Curaçao but the quality varies widely. Tailors and dressmakers charge reasonable prices and their work can range from fair to excellent. A wide assortment of cottons and dress fabrics are available but sewing notions offer a limited selection.

Dry-cleaning facilities are available and the services provided are acceptable. Beauty shops compare with those in the U.S. and those in major tourist hotels have good operators and service. Costs are comparable with those in the U.S. Barbershops also have reasonable prices.

Radio and TV repair is adequate and reasonable but parts are not always available locally. Simple plumbing and electrical maintenance repair is available at reasonable prices. Automobile repair is satisfactory but, once again, parts are not always available locally.

Curaçao has a public library with a modest collection of books and publications in English. Several hotels and restaurants maintain a "swap" shelf of English language paperbacks.

Domestic Help

Domestics from English-speaking Caribbean islands are available but require permission from the Curaçao government to live and work here. Local law entitles maids to a three-week paid vacation annually, with supplementary pay for meals is not taken in the employer's home. Employers are obliged to provide health insurance for maids; the premium is about $360 a year. Wages for part-time help are about $2 per hour, plus transportation, or about $150 a month for house servants. The rate for gardeners is from $2 to $3 per hour.

Religious Activities

Curaçao prides itself on having the oldest continuously operating synagogue in the Western Hemisphere. Services are in English and Hebrew. Several Roman Catholic Churches offer services in Dutch and Papiamentu and at least one offers Mass in English. A Dutch Reformed Church holds services in Dutch; a Methodist Church and an Anglican Church hold services in English; and a Seventh-day Adventist Chapel and a few evangelical churches hold services in Papiamentu and English. The Protestant Church of Curaçao, with several locations in the city, holds services in Dutch and English.

Education

The International School was started in Curaçao in September 1968. The school is open to children of Curaçao residents. Grade levels include K-12. All subjects are taught in English, the curriculum is American and the school is accredited in the U.S. There are extensive extracurricular activities available for all ages, even some for adults. School enrollment for the last few years has averaged over 200 students. Parents are responsible for transportation. Tuition varies depending on grade and ranges from approximately $4,500 to $8,000 per year.

The local government supports a complete system of elementary and high schools equivalent to 12 grades or more in the U.S. Local schools are parochial (Catholic or Protestant) or public, with classes conducted in Dutch and Papiamentu. All schools have the same basic curriculum. Academic standards are good. The school year runs from August 15 to July 15, with 60 holidays during the year, including a one-month summer vacation. American children attending a local school above first grade will have difficulty adjusting to schooling in a foreign language. Intensive language training of several months is often necessary. Children are usually put back one or two grades and then promoted grade-by-grade to their regular level as they learn Dutch. Reasonable tuition fees are charged.

Special Educational Opportunities

Papiamentu lessons are available locally but are expensive. Individual language training in Dutch, Spanish and Papiamentu is available through tutors at reasonable rates. Textbooks are available at the local bookstores.

The Curaçao Music School offers classes and individualized instruction in piano, rhythm instruments, orchestral instruments, guitar, accordion and choral group singing. Individual tutoring in both music and art is also available through independent tutors.

Sports

Water sports of all kinds are popular. Curaçao has numerous small beaches, some public and others that can be used for a small fee. Swimming, snorkeling, scuba diving, water skiing, sailing and windsurfing are possible year round. Curaçao has an extensive number of dive sites, as well as an underwater park, for scuba divers; equipment rental and instruction are available from several Dive Shops. Other sports are available through clubs.

Membership in local clubs, or private membership at local resorts, provides for the use of swimming pools, bar and restaurants, as well as tennis, basketball, Ping Pong, soccer, yachting, sailing, water sports and horseback riding.

The Curaçao Golf and Squash Club has the island's only golf course. It has nine holes with oiled sand greens. The club sponsors weekend tournaments and has a small clubhouse where refreshments are served. A squash court is located near clubhouse.

The Curaçao Yacht Club and other private marinas offer facilities for sail and powerboats.

Harbor and Haystack Mts., Netherlands Antilles

For those interested in flying, a small flying club offers small plane rentals and flight instruction but the rates are high.

Baseball and soccer games are played enthusiastically with local and inter-island competition. A large sports stadium with facilities for various spectator sports is located at Brievengat.

Both U.S. and European sports clothing and equipment can be purchased locally but usually at prices higher than those in the U.S.

Touring and Outdoor Activities

The Curaçao Museum has a permanent exhibition of antiques, paintings and artifacts.

Periodic art exhibits are held there and at the Centro Pro Arte and Centro Cultural de Curaçao. A museum of Jewish history is associated with the synagogue. A commercial Seaquarium displays local marine life and there is a small botanical garden and zoo located in one of Willemstad's suburbs.

A national park surrounds Mt. Christoffel, which provides a panoramic view of the west end of the island to climbers. On a high ridge near the airport are the Hato Caverns, the grottos of Curaçao. Near the west end of the island is Boca Tabla, an unusual sea cave.

Entertainment

In addition to a local cinema that shows current U.S. and European movies, several video rental stores offer recent video releases. The Centro Pro Arte has facilities for ballet, symphony orchestras, operas and plays but offerings are limited and infrequent. Most of the theatrical events are in Dutch or Papiamentu. Several tourist hotels in Curaçao offer entertainment with orches-tras, dancing and floorshows. Many have casinos and one has a discotheque. Several private discotheques are open as well.

The period between Christmas and Carnival is full of special events. A fireworks display and late night partying celebrate the New Year. Carnival time in February brings out street processions with flamboyant costumes, floats, and street dancing. Several bridge clubs are available for the enthusiast.

Social Activities

Private entertaining and official contacts provide the main source of contact with the American community. An American Women's Club holds regular meetings and sponsors social activities several times a year. A local chapter of the U.S. Navy League sponsors receptions for U.S. Navy and Coast Guard ships during port calls.

Daily opportunities exist to meet host country nationals through work and socially. Local branches of Rotary, Kiwanis and Lions Clubs provide social contact with the Antillean and international communities.

OTHER CITIES

Saba's main town, **THE BOTTOM,** is home to about half of the island's total population of 1,000. Saba is just five square miles in area, and is an extinct volcano that rises 3,000 feet above sea level. Vegetation here is lush and there are many gardens and fruit trees. The island's four villages are connected by a single crossroad.

KRALENDIJK, the capital and chief town of Bonaire, lies on the west coast of the island, and has a population of close to 3,000. It is directly opposite the tiny island called Klein (small) Bonaire, noted for its choice snorkeling and scuba diving. Bonaire proper is casual and unspoiled, and is known as one of the best diving areas in the world. There are more than 50 choice diving spots; the average water temperature is 80°F. The beaches are secluded and several of them have sea-carved grottoes. Bonaire has six hotels and resorts, including two casinos. The island is nicknamed Flamingo Island and is home for a flamingo sanctuary, a breeding ground for 10,000 birds of that species. Washington National Park, on the northwestern shore, is a game preserve. Other interesting sites are the salt pans (solar salt works) and slave huts in the south; Rincon, the island's oldest village; and Willemstoren, Bonaire's 150-year-old lighthouse.

ORANJESTAD is the capital of Aruba and has about one-third of that island's 68,000 inhabitants. It is situated on the western side of the island. Aruba has an unusually flat landscape and interesting rock formations. Vegetation includes a wide variety of cacti and *divi-divi* trees, which are shaped by the cooling trade winds. Its beautiful beaches, most notably seven-mile-long Palm Beach, are where most of the hotels are located. Aruba has more than 1,500 hotel rooms, 15 nightclubs, 60 restaurants, five casinos, and 51 low-duty stores on its main street. The Aruba Historical Museum opened in 1984 and displays Arawak Indian implements as well as furniture made by the island's early settlers. A betting facility located in the Aruba Holiday Inn and Casino, allows tourists to bet on football and other sports events. Aruba also has an annual carnival, which runs from mid-January through mid-March.

The principal town of St. Eustatius is **ORANJESTAD** (the same name as Aruba's capital), with a population of about 1,600. The island is undeveloped and has several small plantations.

PHILIPSBURG, with a population of about 11,000, is the capital of the Dutch portion of St. Maarten. As with all of the Netherlands Antilles, tourists can enjoy the beaches and water sports, as well as shopping along Front Street in Philipsburg.

SINT NICOLAAS is the former capital of Aruba, located 12 miles southeast of Oranjestad. A refinery closed here recently, seriously depressing the economy. The area has not developed a reputation as a tourist stop, but the adjacent beaches are considered attractive. No resort hotels are in the vicinity. The Aruba Golf Club, however, has accommodations just north of Sint Nicolaas. The community is also known by its Spanish designation, San Nicolás.

COUNTRY PROFILE

Geography and Climate

Curaçao is the largest of the "ABC" islands (Aruba, Bonaire and Curaçao) which lie just off the coast of Venezuela. Curaçao is 38 miles long, 7 miles wide at its widest point, and 2-1/2 miles wide at its narrowest point. Sint Christoffelberg, at 1,260 feet on the western end of the island and Tafelberg, at about 600 feet near the eastern end are the most prominent geographical features. Tafelberg has provided limestone for the construction industry for several years and now resembles a stepped mesa. Numerous small and large bays indent the island's southern coast. The largest of these, which comprises the inner harbor known as the Schottegat, is surrounded by the city of Willemstad.

Curaçao and the other ABC islands are hot year round. Temperatures seldom exceed 90°F during the day or fall below 80°F at night. Relative humidity averages 70% annually and seldom varies far from that average. The effect of the heat and the humidity, however, is lessened by the almost constant northeast trade winds. The ocean temperature averages 80°F and only varies a few degrees between summer and winter. Rainfall averages only 22 inches annually, most of which falls during the months of November and December, and the islands are below the hurricane belt so that particular danger is absent. Drought resistant plants, such as cactus, thorn tree; and succulents predominate. August, September and October are the warmest months; December, January and February are the coolest.

Mildew can occur when dehumidifying air-conditioning is not used, especially during the "rainy" season (October to January). Outdoors, items rust and fade quickly in the salt air and harsh sun. Lizards roaches, flies, ants, rodents and mosquitoes are common.

In addition to the ABC Islands, the consular district includes the Windward Islands of Saba, St. Eustatius (or Statia and Sint Maarten. They are located south east of Puerto Rico and about five hundred miles northeast from Curaçao. Also of volcanic origin, they differ from the ABC

Islands primarily in that they have more annual rainfall and lusher vegetation. The most populous and economically developed of the Windward group, Sint Maarten, shares its island with the French Department of Saint Martin.

Population

The population of the Netherlands Antilles is approximately 185,000. Curaçao has about 150,000; Sint Maarten, 23,000; Bonaire, 10,000; St. Eustatius, 1,500; Saba, 1,000. Aruba's population is around 90,000. About 85% of Curaçao's population is of African derivation. The remaining 15% is made up of various races and nationalities, including Dutch, Portuguese, North Americans, natives from other Caribbean islands, Latin Americans, Sephardic Jews, Lebanese and Asians.

Four languages are in common use. Papiamentu is the native vernacular in Curaçao, Bonaire and Aruba. Dutch is the official language, though both English and Spanish are widely used on the ABC Islands. English is the predominant language in the Windward Islands.

Roman Catholicism predominates but several other churches are represented, these include Anglican, Jewish, Muslim, Protestant, Mormon and Baptist. The Jewish community is the oldest in the Western Hemisphere, dating from 1634.

Public Institutions

Willemstad, Curaçao, is the capital of the Netherlands Antilles, which is a separate entity in the Kingdom of the Netherlands. The Antilles are governed by a popularly elected unicameral "Staten" (parliament) of 22 members. It chooses the Prime Minister (called Minister President) and a Council of Ministers, consisting of six to eight other ministers. The Governor, who serves a 6-year term, represents the Queen of the Netherlands. Defense and foreign affairs are the responsibility of the Neth-

erlands but, otherwise, the islands are largely self-governing.

Local government is in the hands of each island. Under the direction of a Kingdom-appointed Island Governor, these local governments have a "Bestuurscollege" (administrative body) made up of Commissioners who head the separate government departments.

Aruba separated from the Netherlands Antilles on January 1, 1986, and now enjoys equal status (status aparte) with the Antilles within the Kingdom of the Netherlands. Its government structure is similar to that of the Netherlands Antilles.

Aruba, Bonaire, Curaçao and Sint Maarten have quasi-governmental chambers of commerce, which are, among other things, the official registries of business firms on those islands. They also have trade and industry functions, which are comparable to an American Chamber of Commerce.

Arts, Science, and Education

The educational system is based on the Dutch model, with upper grades split into academic and vocational tracks. The University of the Netherlands Antilles, with law, business and technical faculties, is located on Curaçao. Many students also pursue higher education in the Netherlands or the United States.

Commerce and Industry

Oil refining, tourism, and offshore financial activities are the mainstays of the Curaçao economy. The Netherlands and the European Economic Community provide financial and development aid annually. Local agriculture and manufacturing is very limited. Most consumer goods are imported, often from the U.S. but also from the Netherlands and other European countries.

Transportation

Automobiles

Curaçao has well over 50,000 vehicles. Driving is on the right. Gasoline prices are currently approximately US$3.80 per gallon. Routine service station maintenance is adequate and reasonable but spare parts and body repair work are expensive. The high humidity, salt air and intense sunlight cause automobile tires and bodies to deteriorate rapidly. Undercoating is recommended and may be done locally at reasonable prices. Overall, roads are fair to good but some parts of Curaçao can only be reached by rough dirt tracks.

Curaçao has no restrictions on automobiles other than normal traffic regulations and compulsory automobile insurance. Third-party liability insurance as well as property damage, collision, and fire and theft insurance can be obtained locally from several Dutch firms. If you present a statement from a previous insurance company stating that you have made no claims in the last five years, a discount of up to 50% is offered; or for each consecutive accident-free year a 10% discount will apply. Full coverage collision insurance is recommended for more expensive vehicles. Several car rental agencies operate on the island at tourist prices.

Local

Three types of public transportation are available: buses, privately owned vans operating as buses and taxicabs. Buses are crowded and run irregularly. The private vehicles operating as buses pick up passengers at specific locations for a flat fee. Taxi fares are fixed (no meters) but are geared to tourists and are relatively expensive.

Regional

American and United (through an ALM code-share) Airlines offer daily service between Curaçao and the U.S. Aruba and Sint Maarten also have daily U.S. connections via U.S. carriers. The Netherlands, Venezuela, Colombia, Trinidad and the Dominican Republic have direct connections with Curaçao. Regional airlines provide service between the islands within the consular district. Several local travel agencies are equipped to arrange personal travel anywhere in the world.

Communications

Telephone and Telegraph

Local telephone service is usually reliable although not always of the best quality and outages are not unexpected. The monthly charge is $10 plus 10 cents for each four minutes of use for local calls. Long distance calls may be dialed direct to anywhere in the world at any hour but are very expensive.

Internet

Several local companies provide internet access on Curaçao; however, service is very expensive compared to the U.S. Access currently ranges from $60 per month for unlimited access to three times that. The less expensive service provider has oversubscribed and it is very hard to connect during peak hours. In addition to the Internet access fees, you still have to pay the local per-minute phone charges that can effectively double your costs if you are a heavy user.

Mail

UPS-International, Federal Express and DHL also serve Curaçao.

Radio and TV

Curaçao has one TV station (Tele-Curaçao), which broadcasts in color. Most shows are in Papiamentu. Venezuelan TV can also be received on Curaçao. Cable TV is available, and presently CNN, ESPN, BBC World, HBO Ole, Cinemax, A&E, TBS, ABC, CBS, NBC and others are featured. Major American and European sporting events are generally carried via cable. Television sets are available locally at prices higher than in the U.S. Local television broadcasts on NTSC format and an U.S. television set works with no conversion necessary.

Local radio stations provide a wide range of music choices. Most radio

stations broadcast news in Papiamentu and Dutch; however, periodic English news broadcasts are transmitted by some of the stations.

Newspapers, Magazines, and Technical Journals

U.S. newspapers from New York and Miami are available the day after publication. Daily newspapers are printed in Curaçao in Dutch and in Papiamentu. Magazines in English, Dutch and Spanish are available at newsstands but are more expensive than in the U.S. It is less expensive to subscribe to magazines than to pay local newsstand prices, even for airmail editions. Magazines can be pouched but take from three weeks to one month to arrive. Many popular books are available in English at local bookstores but, once again, are more expensive than in the U.S.

Health and Medicine

Medical Facilities

There are two private hospitals and one public hospital available on-island which provide adequate services for most any medical problem. The doctors are trained in Europe and in the U.S. and overall their quality is good to excellent. Many dentists practice in Curaçao; some have been trained in the U.S. and many in Europe. Specialists, both medical and dental, are either available locally or visit the island periodically from the U.S. or Europe.

Community Health

Community health standards are good. Tap water is distilled from seawater and is of good quality, although turbidity (suspended particles) is frequently high. Fresh foods are safe to eat.

Preventive Measures

Normal health precautions are in order, but some potential dangers warrant special mention. Precautions should be taken against the strong sun and heat, which can cause dehydration. Swimmers should be cautious of sea urchins and other stinging creatures on the

sea floor. Some common trees at Curaçao beaches have a poisonous sap (irritating) which rain can wash onto the unwary. Dengue fever has been reported in Curaçao.

Most medicines are available, but local pharmacy prices tend to be higher than in the U.S. Some over-the-counter medicines available in the U.S. are not available in Curaçao or are available by prescription only. You may wish to bring a supply for special needs.

NOTES FOR TRAVELERS

Passage, Customs & Duties

Travel to Curaçao is by air.

A valid U.S. passport or a U.S. birth certificate accompanied by a valid photo identification must be presented. While a U.S. passport is not mandatory, it is recommended since it is more readily recognized as positive proof of citizenship. Tourists may be asked to show onward/return tickets or proof of sufficient funds for their stay. Visitors may enter for two weeks, extendable for 90 days by the Head Office of Immigration. For further information, travelers may contact The Royal Netherlands Embassy, 4200 Linnean Avenue, N.W., Washington, D.C. 20008, telephone (202) 244-5300, Internet: http://www.netherlands-embassy.org, or the Dutch consulates in Los Angeles, Chicago, New York, and Houston.

The Netherlands Antilles, like most Caribbean territories, are subject to the threat of hurricanes. General information about natural disaster preparedness is available via the Internet from the U.S. Federal Emergency Management Agency (FEMA) at http://www.fema.gov/.

U.S. citizens living in or visiting the Netherlands Antilles are encouraged to register with the U.S. Consulate General in Curaçao located at J.B. Gorsiraweg #1, Willemstad, Curaçao, telephone (599-9)461-

3066; fax (599-9)461-6489; e-mail address: cgCuraçao@interneeds.net.

Pets

Pets are admitted duty free and are not placed in quarantine. Dogs and cats must have rabies inoculations and certificates of good health issued within ten days of their arrival. Pet foods, medications and veterinary services are available locally. Fleas, ticks, heartworms and other infestations are a constant problem on the island.

Firearms and Ammunition

The Netherlands Antilles Government maintains strict control over the number of firearms and amount of ammunition on the islands and requires that a permit be issued prior to importation. As a further means of control, local authorities limit the number of authorized dealers in firearms. Sales to individuals can be made only to those licensed to own weapons, and the dealers must register all sales with the government.

Currency, Banking, and Weights and Measures

The medium of exchange in the Netherlands Antilles is the Netherlands Antilles florin, also called the "guilder." The exchange rate is currently fixed at US$1 =NAF 1.78. Local banks cash U.S. Treasury checks and exchange U.S. currency; however, a service fee is frequently charged. You do not need to buy Netherlands Antilles florins before arrival in Curaçao; US dollars are widely used and accepted. Have a supply of small bills with you for tips and taxi fares.

Local banking facilities are comparable to those in the U.S. and arrangements can be made to cash U.S. checks. U.S. ATM/Debit Cards can be used in some local automatic tellers and will allow you to withdraw either US$ or NAF. Many local stores accept VISA and/or MasterCard.

No limit is placed on the amount of money (dollars or other currency) brought into the Netherlands Antilles. Nor are limits placed on amounts taken out. Reporting procedures are in effect for large or unusual monetary transactions. Local bank accounts may be useful but are not necessary.

The metric system is the official standard for weights and measures.

LOCAL HOLIDAYS

Jan. 1	New Year's Day
Feb/Mar	Carnival Monday*
Mar/Apr.	Good Friday*
Mar/Apr.	Easter*
Mar/Apr.	Easter Monday*
Apr. 30	Queen's Birthday
May 1	Labor Day
May/June	Ascension Day*
May/June.	Pentecost*
May/June.	Whitmonday*
July 2	Curacao Flag Day
Dec. 25	Christmas
Dec. 26	Boxing Day

*variable

RECOMMENDED READING

The following titles are provided as a general indication of the material published on this country:

Tourist and travel information is available from the Curaçao Tourist Offices at the following addresses:

The Curaçao Tourist Board 330 Biscayne Boulevard Miami, FL 33132. Tel: (305) 374-5811 Fax: (305) 374-6741 Toll Free: (800) 445-826.

The Curaçao Tourist Board 475 Park Avenue Suite 2000, New York, NY 10016 Tel: (212) 683-7660 Fax: (212) 683-9337 Toll Free: (800) 270-3350 E-mail: CuraVao@ix.net-com.com

Several Internet sites can provide additional current information. Use the search words "Curaçao," "Netherlands Antilles," and "Willemstad."

The following bibliography contains a sample of available English language material.

Coomans, Henry E. *Building Up The Future From The Past*. DeWalburg Press: Netherlands, 1990.

De Groot, G. *The Netherlands Antilles*. Bosch & Keuning: Netherlands, 1978.

De Roo, Jos. *Curaçao, Scenes and Behind the Scenes*. Van Dorp-Eddine: Curaçao, 1979.

Dyde, Brian. *Islands to the Windward*. Macmillan: London, 1987.

Emmanuel, Isaac S. and Suzanne A. *History of the Jews of the Netherlands Antilles, Vol. I and II.*

Glasscock, Jean. *The Making of an Island: Sint Maarten, St Martin, 1985*. Goilo, E. R. Papiamentu Textbook. De Wit: Aruba, 1972.

Hannau, Hans. *Aruba Pictorial*. De Wit: Aruba, 1981.

—*The Netherlands Antilles*. De Wit, Aruba, 1975.

—*Curaçao in Full Color*. De Wit, Aruba.

Hannau, Hans and Bernard Mock. *Beneath the Seas of the West Indies*. Hastings House: New York, 1979.

Hartog, Dr. Johan. *Aruba: Short History*. Van Dorp: Aruba, 1980.

—*Curaçao, A Short History*. De Wit: Aruba, 1979.

—*History of St. Eustatius*. De Wit: Aruba, 1976.

—*St. Maarten, Saba, St. Eustatius*. De Wit: Aruba, 1978.

—*A Short History of Bonaire*. De Wit: Aruba, 1978.

—*U.S. Consul in 19th Century Curaçao*. Van Dorp & Co., N.V: Aruba and Curaçao, 1971.

Heinen, G. *The Image of Curaçao.* Witgeverij ICS: Netherlands, 1997.

Howes, Barbara, ed. *From the Green Antilles: Writings of the Caribbean.* Granada: London, 1971.

Johnson, Will. *Saban Lore: Tales from My Grandmother's Pipe.* Saba, 1983.

Karner, Frances, P. *The Sephardics of Curaçao.* Van Gorcum: Netherlands, 1969.

Maslin, Simeon J. *Synagogue Guidebook.* Mikve Israel-Emanuel: Curaçao, 1975.

Reimar, Dietmar. *Caribbean Underwater World, Curaçao & Klein Curaçao.* Nautiphot: Germany, 1991.

Romer, Dr. Rene. *Curaçao.* UNICA, 1981.

Sekou, Lasana M. *National Symbols of St. Martin.* House of Nehesi: St Martin, 1996.

Smit, Sypkens. *Beyond The Tourist Trap, A Study of St Martin Culture.* Koninklijke Bibliotheek: Netherlands, 1995.

Tuchman, Barbara W. *The First Salute.* Alfred A. Knopf. New York 1988.

Van Dalen, Henk H. *The Netherlands Antilles.* Bosch & Keuning: Netherlands 1994

van den Bor, W. *Island Adrift: The Social Organization of a Small Caribbean Community: The Case of St. Eustatius.* Smits Publishers: Netherlands, 1981.

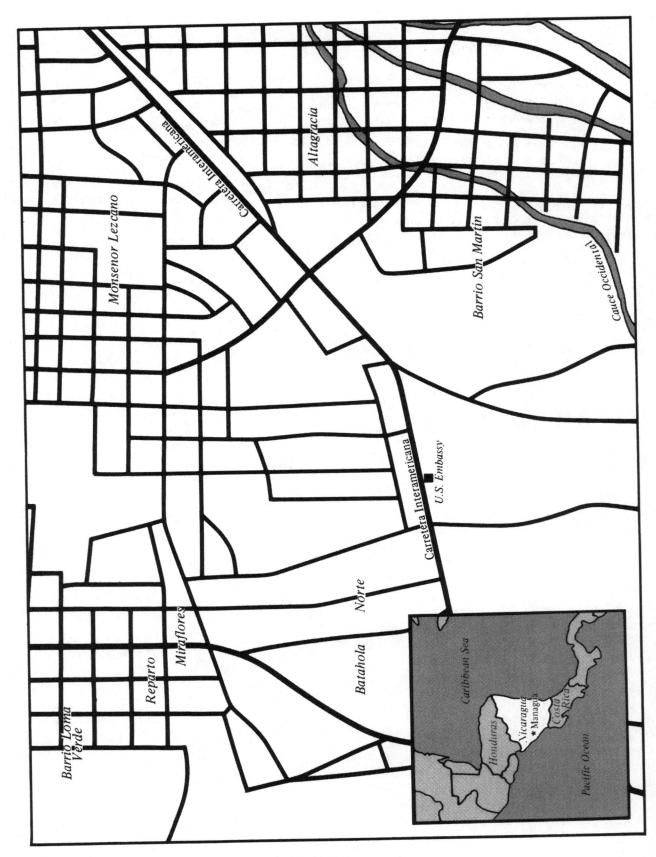

Managua, Nicaragua

NICARAGUA

Republic of Nicaragua

Major Cities:
Managua, León

Minor Cities:
Bluefields, Chinandega, Corinto, Diriamba, Estelí, Granada, Jinotega, Jinotepe, Masaya, Matagalpa

EDITOR'S NOTE

This chapter was adapted from the Department of State Post Report 1999 for Nicaragua. Supplemental material has been added to increase coverage of minor cities, facts have been updated, and some material has been condensed. Readers are encouraged to visit the Department of State's web site at http://travel.state.gov/ for the most recent information available on travel to this country.

INTRODUCTION

NICARAGUA, which has suffered relentless exploitation by dictators and foreign interests since its discovery in 1502, emerged from a decade-long civil war in the early 1990s. In 1996 the nation achieved its first peaceful transition of power in 100 years. However, it must still overcome a turbulent history of political strife and natural disasters as it struggles to achieve and maintain political and economic stability.

MAJOR CITIES

Managua

The capital, Managua, with a rapidly growing population of about 1 million, is the largest city and the commercial and political center of Nicaragua. It is located on the southern shore of severely polluted Lake Managua in western Nicaragua at latitude 121, longitude 861, and 110 feet above sea level.

Earthquakes destroyed Managua twice, once in 1931 and again in 1972. The earthquake on December 23, 1972, reduced the city's downtown to rubble. Businesses and residents relocated to the outskirts of the city, and there has been no reconstruction in the once bustling center. Therefore, Managua has no real business or commercial district. Offices and shops are often housed in residences and scattered throughout the city. Hostilities in 1978 and 1979 caused additional destruction, especially in the industrial section, along the north highway to the airport.

Construction during the Sandinista regime came almost to a standstill except for the burgeoning shanty towns. As the rural poor have poured into the city looking for work, this substandard housing, with no sanitary facilities of any type, has literally sprouted in every neighborhood and has replaced earthquake ruins as the dominant scene in Managua.

Food

Shopping for food in Nicaragua requires patience and flexibility; but, with perseverance, you can maintain a balanced, varied diet. A variety of goods is now readily available in local supermarkets.

Open markets, such as the Huembes Market off the Masaya Highway, offer the best selection of fresh fruits and vegetables. Seasonal fruits and vegetables common to the tropics are usually good quality and cost less than in the U.S. Mangoes, bananas, papaya, cantaloupe, watermelon, pineapple, nispero, citrus, and jocote are typical fruit selections, while vegetables are limited to potatoes, yucca, beets, lettuce, cabbage, onions, cilantro, garlic, parsley, tomatoes, celery, peppers, cucumbers, carrots, squash, broccoli, avocado, green beans, and occasionally asparagus, mushrooms, cauliflower, and eggplant. Imported apples, grapes, pears, and strawberries are sometimes available in supermarkets. Open markets also sell dried beans, rice, and some spices. You may also find staples such as flour, sugar, and oil as well as some packaged and canned goods, toiletries, and sundries. However, the commissary sells such items in better quality, if higher prices.

meat and seafood well, and avoid raw seafood.

Those with babies should bring in their hand luggage, or mail ahead, a large initial supply of formula (powdered keeps better in the heat) or baby food they may need. Baby food produced in Central America is not always up to U.S. standards.

Clothing

Informal attire is acceptable on most occasions, including in the office. Open-collar dress shirts or locally made guayaberas and slacks are worn by men for work and social events. Ties, suits, and sport jackets are occasionally worn. An event requiring a suit will usually indicate as much on the invitation. At the office, women wear short dresses, skirts, or slacks. Nylons are often seen but are a matter of choice. At dinners and receptions attended by Nicaraguans or the diplomatic community, women dress somewhat more formally than the men; however, at the same function you may see sequins and cotton dresses. Being improperly attired is almost impossible.

Warm-weather clothes are necessary, especially washable cottons. Avoid "dry clean only" apparel, because local dry cleaners are not always reliable. In addition, long sleeves are often useful at outdoor receptions during the first three months of the dry season, especially on the South Highway, which is cooler than the rest of the city. Lightweight sweaters and jackets are also useful for trips to cooler countries in the region. Local shoes, sandals, and cowboy boots are available. Some shoes are imported from the U.S. or Europe, but selection is limited, and prices are high.

Men: Men's clothing can be made at are reasonable cost. Tailors can copy styles, but quality material is scarce. If you are interested, bring all fabric and notions.

Women: Dressmakers are available at low prices, though they may not be reliable. Some can skillfully copy designs from fashion magazines or

Courtesy of United Nations

Market in Managua, Nicaragua

Good selections of meat and fish can be found at supermarkets, butcher shops, and delicatessens. Processed pork products such as luncheon meat, ham, and smoked chops are subject to questionable handling, and therefore, not recommended for purchase except at Delikatessen Bavaria. Local chickens are small and, currently, more expensive than those the commissary sells. Various distributors sell lobster, shrimp, and other seafood, frozen for export.

Shoppers in the open markets provide their own bags. Young boys will besiege you to guard your car or to help carry your groceries for a small tip.

Milk products are readily available. The commissary sells long-shelf-life whole milk; canned, condensed, and evaporated milk; and assorted cheeses, cream, cottage cheese, and sour cream. One reliable source for local cheese, the La Perfecta Company, produces about six varieties of fresh and aged cheeses, but not

every type is available at one time. The factory, where the best selection can be found, is on the North Highway. The Eskimo Factory produces good-quality ice cream in several flavors.

There are bakeries where whole wheat bread, French bread, rolls, etc., can be found. An Italian-style pasta shop will prepare carry-out meals if you provide the casserole dish. Local beer and soft drinks are good and inexpensive if you buy refill bottles.

Generally, Nicaraguan production and handling methods fall short of U.S. sanitary standards; therefore, wash all raw vegetables and fruits properly. Washing in detergent, soaking in a bleach solution, and then rinsing thoroughly is recommended. However, this will not kill amebic dysentery spores or other types of contamination. The surest ways to avoid food contamination and food-borne illness are peel or cook fruits and vegetables, cook from an existing model. They rarely use patterns. You must furnish fabric and notions, which, if available here, are very expensive. Many Nicaraguans do beautiful hand or machine embroidery as well.

Children: Children's clothes can be made at a reasonable cost from bright cotton bought locally or in the U.S. A limited ready-made supply is available here, but quality is mixed.

Supplies and Services

Bring all contact lenses supplies from the U.S. Few medicines are available in Nicaragua.

Household items bought here can cost two or three times the U.S. price. La Galeria sells electric appliances, radios, cameras, TV's, video machines, perfumes, clothing, liquor, and toys-all at high prices.

Good-quality wicker and wooden porch furniture can be ordered to specification. Several well-known Nicaraguan artists' works may be purchased. Lovely machine embroidered linens are made in Masaya and Granada. Finely woven, decorative hammocks are a Nicaraguan trademark; and woodcrafters, basketweavers, and potters make gift items in various parts of the country. Although these items are not the bargain they once were, they are usually reasonably priced when compared to buying them in the U.S.

Managua has several good restaurants, including two pizza and two sandwich shops. Restaurant prices are high, especially, if you order imported liquor or wine.

A maid will do almost all laundry. Drycleaning establishments exist, but they get mixed reviews. Some have been known to lose or ruin clothing. Some people save dry cleaning for trips to Costa Rica or the U.S.-thus, the need for washable clothing. Garment bags are useful during the dry season, when dust permeates the air. Bring extra hangers. Plastic ones are best as metal ones may rust in the rainy season.

Managua has several beauty and barber shops. Some have relatively modern equipment, but few have sufficient supplies or trained personnel. Some people take advantage of trips outside Nicaragua to have their hair cut and styled, though this industry in Managua is improving.

Dealers in radio and electric appliances, including General Electric, Westinghouse, Philco, and Sony, provide repair service, but replacement parts are scarce. Parts catalogs, which usually come with appliances when purchased, are valuable for ordering parts from the U.S. Bring parts that you feel you may have to replace.

Simple picture framing is available at a reasonable cost. Some people take items to Costa Rica to be framed. At numerous hardware stores, stock is limited and prices for quality, imported goods are high.

Domestic Help

Domestic help is loosely defined as employees engaged in household, gardening, guard, and similar services. They may, or may not, live in. Live-in help is entitled to room, board, and three uniforms as well as salary. Live-out help receives only salary and, perhaps, uniforms. The first month of employment is a trial period for both employer and employee. Either party can then terminate employment for any reason without incurring additional legal obligations. A work contract with employees is not required, but recommended.

Domestics specialize in cooking ("cocinera"), caring for children ("china"), laundry ("lavandera"), gardening ("jardinero"), guards ("celador"), and cleaning ("limpieza"), etc. Most employees combine various specialties required by the family. Because of the high crime rate, all homes should have at least one employee, or family member, home at all times. Potential loss from break-ins outweighs the cost of a competent, honest employee.

After each six-month period, domestic employees get 15 days of paid vacation, but most employees prefer double pay (for the 15 days) in lieu of time off. In December, local law requires the payment of a Christmas bonus equal to a month's salary. Keep a written record, signed by the employee, of wage payments to prevent complications over the amount of Christmas bonus or severance payments due when employment is terminated. Additional provisions regulate days off, sick leave, severance pay, and other matters.

Religious Activities

Most Nicaraguans are Roman Catholic. Catholic Churches in Managua celebrate Masses on Saturdays, Sundays, and Holy Days at various hours from 5 am or 6 am through noon and in the evenings. Mass is celebrated in English at the Lincoln School every Sunday at 9:30 am.

Nondenominational English services are held on Sundays at 8 am at the Nicaragua Christian Academy. Baptist, Mormon, Seventh-Day Adventist, Jehovah's Witnesses, and other missionary congregations conduct services in Spanish at various times during the week. Managua has no synagogues.

Education

For primary and secondary students, the American-Nicaraguan School (ANS), established in 1944, offers English instruction from the nursery and kindergarten levels through grade 12 by American, Nicaraguan, and some third-country national teachers. The school is accredited by the Southern Association of Schools and Colleges. Graduates have successfully attended many U.S. colleges and universities. The school has about 1,250 students and 104 teachers. The school year for all students roughly follows the U.S. system: first semester, early August to mid-December; second semester, early January to early June.

Bus service is available for a monthly fee. Preschool students attend from 7:30 am to 11:30 am; all other students from 7:40 am to 2:10 pm. Uniforms, consisting of dark blue pants or skirts with white shirts or blouses, are required for all grades here, as they are for all schools in Managua. You may bring shirts or blouses and sew the school patch (available in the business office) on to them. Books are provided. The school offers a standard U.S. college preparatory course, a business course, and a "bachillerato" program in Spanish. One honors course is offered. Spanish-as-a-second language is required at all levels, beginning at grade 2. Advanced placement classes are also available to students, beginning in their sophomore year. These classes are first-year college courses that students can take for college credit. ANS has five science labs, a full computer laboratory, a 5,000-volume library, new gym, outdoor sports facilities, a covered outdoor stage, and counseling quarters. Afterschool sports, drama, and community service activities are offered.

The Nicaraguan Christian Academy (NCA), established in 1991, has grown rapidly. Its current enrollment is 106 with 13 teachers (ten Americans, two Nicaraguans, and one third-country national). NCA has a 40% native English-speaking student body. Its out of the city location, just off the South Highway, makes it all the more appealing to those who live on that side of town. What it lacks in facilities, it makes up for in personal attention in its small classes. Pre-kindergarten hours are 8:30 am to noon; kindergarten, 7:30 am to noon; and grades 1 to 12, 7:30 am to 2:15 pm. NCA's classes begin early September and continue until mid-June.

The Lincoln International School, a Catholic school established in 1991, is located across the highway from NCA and currently has 500 students taught by 40 teachers. The percentage of native-English speakers is unknown. Hours are 7:45 am to 3 pm, and classes start in mid August.

Notre Dame School, a Catholic school established in 1992, currently has 290 students enrolled (10% of whom are native English speakers) with 24 teachers. The hours are 7:45 am to 2:15 pin and the school year begins mid-August. It offers three diplomas: Nicaraguan, U.S., and International Baccalaureate. Although the last three newly established schools have limited facilities, they offer quality education.

Special Educational Opportunities

Nicaragua has numerous institutions of higher education including the National Autonomous University of Nicaragua (UNAN), the Jesuit-run Central American University (UCA), the Harvard-affiliated Central American Institute of Business Administration (INCAE), the University of Mobile, the American Autonomous University (UAM), the National Agrarian University (UNA), the Polytechnical University (UPOLI), the National Engineering University (UNI), and the Catholic University (UNICA). (See Arts, Science, and Education.)

Some private or small group classes are offered in tennis, swimming, dancing, art, music, and bridge. Instruction in Spanish and other foreign languages is available. Anyone with a skill to teach will find that the community is receptive to new activities. Very limited special educational opportunities are available.

Managua does not have adequate teaching facilities for children with physical or emotional handicaps or learning disabilities.

Sports

The Intercontinental Hotel, the Camino Real Hotel, the Casa de Espana, and the Casa Grande have swimming pools. "Cabana Club" memberships are available at the Intercontinental. Swimming can be enjoyed at various Pacific Ocean beaches, at Lake Xiloa, and Laguna de Apoyo. Montelimar, a private beach on the Pacific, has the only first-class overnight accom-

modations in Nicaragua outside Managua.

The Camino Real and Casa de Espana each have two night-lit tennis courts. Casa Grande has one court with night-lighting; the Ticomo Apartments has two day courts. For a minimum fee, Casa de Espana accepts temporary members and offers swimming, tennis, bar, and restaurant facilities.

A modern eight-lane bowling alley, with a sandwich shop, outdoor roller skating rink, and a video gameroom is located off the Masaya Highway.

Nicaragua has many areas for boating, but boats are expensive. For those with access, small-boat sailing is available and popular. Lake Managua, however, is not used for water sports because it is both shallow and contaminated. Rental boats are not generally available, except for fishing areas like San Juan del Sur, where rates are expensive and safe boating measures (such as providing life preservers) are not always practiced. Lake Nicaragua has tarpon, shark, and sawfish. (Lake Nicaragua is the only freshwater lake in the world where sharks have been found.) Guapote, a fish similar to bass, is found in many lakes and streams.

Baseball is the national sport; soccer is number two. Basketball is played in schools, colleges, and is sponsored commercially. Professional and amateur boxing is popular and a source of national pride.

Riding stables featuring Western-style riding lessons are available. Horses can be purchased, but few houses have sufficient grounds to stable a horse. Bring special riding equipment or clothing. Saddles are available locally.

Several regularly scheduled sports events take place at the Casa Grande, such as volleyball, basketball, softball, and exercise classes. Everyone is invited to join. Many people are involved in the local chapter of the Hash House Harriers, a running and walking club.

Touring and Outdoor Activities

Nicaragua has panoramic natural beauty; and its mountains, volcanoes, and lakes offer many new experiences to visitors. Fine hunting, fishing, hiking, bird watching, and boating are available, if you are the rugged outdoor type. However, few package trips exist. You have to make your own arrangements and provide all your own equipment. Hotels, lodges, sanitary facilities, and potable water are nonexistent; and a four-wheel-drive vehicle is essential. Managua has little tourist activity, but local travel agencies offer trips throughout Nicaragua. Cities outside the capital have retained their colonial flavor with low one-story houses, built around an inner patio, lining the sidewalks. The church always faces the main square park and together they usually form the geographic and social center of the town.

Located about an hour's drive from Managua, past the town of Masachapa, southwest of Managua, Montelimar, was once the private hideaway of the Somoza family. Converted to a tourist complex by the Sandinista government and now owned by a Spanish firm, it boasts the best accommodations outside of Managua. You can go for the day and take a picnic or eat at one of the restaurants. Comfortable rooms and cabins are available for overnight guests.

On the Pacific, Pochimil Beach is ½ miles from the town of Masachapa (37 miles southwest of Managua). It has a wide, gently sloping beach. The Nicaraguan Government opened a tourist center with picnic facilities at Pochomil in 1982. The beach is usually quiet on Saturdays and crowded on Sundays or during the Easter season. The undertow and cross currents can be hazardous.

Poneloya beach is 12 miles beyond Leon on a paved road. A hotel is available where you can change clothes and buy food and drinks; however, the accommodations do not appeal to most for an overnight

Aerial view of Managua, Nicaragua

© Nik Wheeler/Corbis. Reproduced by permission.

stay. The undertow and cross currents are also hazardous.

San Juan del Sur, located about 95 miles southwest of Managua on the Pacific, can be reached via a poorly paved side road from the Pan-American Highway. It has excellent deep-sea fishing, and you can rent fishing boats by making arrangements in advance.

Lake Xiloa is a crater lake 10 miles from Managua offers swimming, boating, and water skiing. An extensive tourist complex has been built, and the spot is popular as a nearby recreation area. Snacks and drinks are available.

The semiactive Masaya Volcano is 13 miles from Managua on the Masaya Highway. The park has paved roads, observation areas, picnic locations, a museum with a restaurant, and excellent views of the smoking volcano with molten lava in the crater. On the Atlantic coast, the Caribbean seaport of Bluefields can be reached by Nica or Costena Airlines or by poor roads and boat. English is the predominant language in this deeply tropical region. Its West Indies atmosphere differentiates it from the rest of the country.

There are two Corn Islands, both typical tropical isles with waving palms and broad beaches. The larger one is about three miles long and located 40 miles off the coast of Bluefields. Overnight facilities can be obtained in private homes on the islands, but they are primitive. There are no hotels.

Travel to neighboring countries by car is possible, and many people take advantage of the opportunity to escape Managua's heat, shop, and become acquainted with other Central American cultures. San Jose, Costa Rica (about a 7-hour drive), at an altitude of over 3,000 feet, is a modern city with a cool climate. Tegucigalpa, Honduras (about a 5-hour drive), is also over 3,000 feet. The drive to San Salvador takes some 10 hours and to Guatemala City, almost 14 hours. Major roads within Nicaragua are generally in fair condition, depending on the season and money available to patch them; however, the Pan-American Highway is usually passable year round.

All Central American capitals, and Mexico City, can be reached quickly by air on the many regional and U.S. airlines that serve Managua. (See Transportation Regional.) For current information, contact the airlines. Approximate round-trip fares from Managua as of April 1997 were: San Jose, $196; Tegucigalpa, $200; Guatemala City, $350; San Salvador, $240; Mexico City, $490; Miami, $574; Houston $788.

Entertainment

Managua has limited entertainment. Most There is one modern movie theater with two screens. First-run movies arrive within a few months of their U.S. release date. The four cable companies receive 40-65 channels. Rates range from $20-$30 a month.

A few foreign cultural groups perform in Managua each year, usually in the Ruben Dario Theater, which is one of the finest in the region. Local folk-dance groups perform there as well. There are usually a couple of major popular music festivals, with artists from other Latin American countries. The Ministry of Culture sponsors some events in the Ruins of the Grand Hotel where a theater has been built.

There are local disco-type nightclubs, as well as clubs that feature Nicaraguan and Latin American musical groups. Some restaurants, including Los Ranchos and the Lobster's Inn, are available for large parties. The Intercontinental and Camino Real Hotels have party, banquet, and conference rooms. However, entertaining is usually done at home. Caterers are available, as well as small musical groups, although prices are high.

Social Activities

The American-Nicaraguan Society, open to all members of the U.S. community, sponsors several events during the year. There is also the relatively new Christian Ladies Tea Group, which meets monthly at the Casa Grande.

The International Women's Club consists of women who are native Nicaraguans, some who married Nicaraguans and settled here, those who came to Nicaragua with their husbands to live, and women living here for only a short time. Their meetings are conducted in English. The Nicaraguan English Speaking Theater (NEST) is composed of members from throughout the community and offers two productions a year which are highly attended.

Nicaraguans are usually open and hospitable. As the country has attained normalcy, so have relations between our two governments. Even though foreign investment is starting to return after having plummeted during the Sandinista years, there is still only a small foreign business community.

The Alliance Francaise offers language classes and a variety of entertainment, including movies, lectures, plays, and social dances year round.

León

Nicaragua's former capital, and second largest city, can be reached by paved highway, 42 miles from Managua, and has a population of 147,000. It is the seat of part of the University of Nicaragua (UNAN), and several of its faculties are located there. Leon's large 18th-century cathedral contains the tomb of Ruben Dario, Nicaragua's world-renowned poet.

OTHER CITIES

BLUEFIELDS is located in southeast Nicaragua on Bluefields Bay, about 170 miles east of Managua. Situated at the mouth of the Escondido River, it is Nicaragua's chief port on the Caribbean Sea. From here, bananas, coconuts, shrimp, lobsters, and hardwoods are exported. In the 16th and 17th centuries, Bluefields was a meeting point for English and Dutch pirates. In 1678, it became the capital of the British protectorate over the Mosquito Coast. Today, Bluefields is the capital of Zelaya Department and has a population of about 25,000.

Situated in the Pacific coastlands about 70 miles northwest of Managua, **CHINANDEGA** is a thriving industrial city. It is the capital of Chinandega Department as well as a processing point for the hinterland. Revolutionary battles took place here in 1927, and again in 1978–1979. Crops grown near the city include bananas, sugarcane, and cotton. Chinandega's industries produce furniture, perfume, and toilet water. Several sawmills, metalworks, and tanneries are located in Chinandega. Its 1995 population was about 67,800. A line of the Pacific Railway passes through Chinandega; the city is connected to Managua by highway.

CORINTO, located on the Pacific Ocean about 75 miles northwest of Managua, is Nicaragua's chief port. Sugar, hides, coffee, cotton, and wood are exported from here. With a population of approximately 20,000, Corinto is also a railroad terminus.

DIRIAMBA is a 26 miles southwest of Managua, on the Pan-American Highway, and lies in the heart of a coffee-growing region. Limestone quarries and saltworks are also located near the city. It is situated at an altitude of 2,000 feet and has a pleasant climate. Diriamba was heavily damaged during the 1978-79 civil war. Casares and La Boquita are two undeveloped black sand beaches on the Pacific out of Diriamba.

ESTELÍ is an agricultural hub on the Estelí River, 70 miles north of Managua. The downtown area was virtually ruined in the heavy fighting of the revolution in 1978–1979. The Spanish settled Estelí near prehistoric stone figures; today, it is a commercial center on the Pan-American Highway. Industries in Estelí include hat manufacturing, sawmilling, and tanning. Several crops are grown near the city, among them tobacco, cotton, fruit, vegetables, and sesame. The estimated population of this departmental capital is 30,600.

GRANADA, Nicaragua's oldest city, formerly the country's commercial center, was founded by Hernandez de Cordoba, Nicaragua's colonizer in 1523. Its population is about 75,000. The epitaphs on the marble tombs of Granada's cemetery provide a fascinating history of the city's turbulent past. The city is on the northwestern shore of the country's large freshwater Lake Nicaragua, 28 miles over paved highway from Managua. Here tourists are attracted to a group of beautiful lake islands, "Las Isletas." Ometepe and Zapatera, volcanic-formed islands in the lakes, are well-known sites for pre-Colombian artifacts.

JINOTEGA is a departmental capital in northern Nicaragua, 70 miles north-northwest of Managua. Coffee, tobacco, corn, beans, potatoes, wheat, and fruits are grown here. Several industries, including coffee processing, tanning, hat manufacturing, and flour milling are located in the city. A highway connects the city to Matagalpa. Jinotega's estimated population is 17,000.

JINOTEPE lies in the Diriamba Highlands, about 25 miles south of Managua. It is the capital of Carazo Department in addition to being an important commercial and manufacturing point. Quarries are located nearby and coffee, rice, sugarcane, and sesame are grown in surrounding farmland. The city's church contains a rare reliquary of precious gems. The area honors St. James the Great, its patron, with an annual festival. The city was heavily damaged during the 1978–79 civil war. An estimated 18,000 people live in Jinotepe, which is situated on the Pan-American Highway.

MASAYA, the "City of Flowers," 16 miles from Managua, has a population of 95,000. The town is well known to natives, and tourists as well, as Nicaragua's handicrafts center. Embroidered dresses and shirts, shoes, handbags, fiber floormats, hand fans, hammocks, black coral jewelry, wicker furniture, small gifts crafted of wood, and filigree-gold- and - silver work are available. One of the country's better-known restaurants, the Tip Top, which specializes in chicken dishes, is nearby.

MATAGALPA. This town is 81 miles north of Managua on a paved branch of the Pan American Highway and has a population of about 63,000. The city, at an altitude of 2,100 feet and consequently a cooler climate, is set in hilly country and surrounded by beautiful coffee plantations. The Selva Negra (Schwarzwald) Mountain Hotel has a restaurant. Near Matagalpa on the Dariense Cordillera.

COUNTRY PROFILE

Geography and Climate

The largest of the Central American Republics, Nicaragua borders Costa Rica to the south and Honduras to the north. It covers 57,143 square miles (about the size of Wisconsin) including the region's largest fresh water lakes-Lake Nicaragua and Lake Managua which total 3,500 square miles. The country is divided into three geographic sections: the drier Pacific coastal plain to the west with its low mountain ranges near the sea; the wetter and cooler mountainous extension of the Central American Highlands which runs from northwest to southeast across the middle of the country; and the hot and humid flat Atlantic lowlands along the east coast.

Most of the population is located in western Nicaragua on the fertile lowland Pacific Plains which surround the lakes and extend north to the Gulf of Fonseca. This region is the political and commercial heart of the country. Lake Managua and Lake Nicaragua dominate the map of this area, and a series of young volcanoes, many still active, dot the coastal plain paralleling the Central American Highlands. The tallest volcanoes reach 5,700 feet, and two are visible from Managua.

The mountain highland provinces of Matagalpa and Jinotega, northeast of the volcanoes and lakes, are more sparsely populated and Nicaragua's

major coffee producing areas. The easternmost section of the highlands receives the warm, wet Caribbean winds and is mainly sparsely settled rain forest, with a few operating gold mines near the town of Bonanza.

Eastern Nicaragua, with one-third of the total national territory which is an area about the size of El Salvador, has about 10% of the population and is tropical rain forests and pine-flats. The region, largely ignored by the Spanish, was a British protectorate until 1860. Even today, many of the people along the Atlantic coast prefer to speak English.

Nicaragua's climate varies with altitude and season. The summer, or dry season, from mid-November to mid-May, is hot and dry, with cooler nights. Winter, better described as the rainy season, from mid-May to mid-November, is hot and humid, with short, heavy tropical showers that may occur daily, often accompanied by violent electrical storms. Streams flood in the rainy season and dry up the rest of the year. The average daily high temperature in Managua ranges from 79°F to 93°F. Nights are usually temperate. Temperatures in the mountains can dip as low as 61°F, while the east coast high may be a humid 84°F.

Nicaragua offers appealing landscapes from the primitive Caribbean island beauty of Corn Island, to the lovely lake views near the colonial city of Granada, to the stark beauty of the semiactive volcano located between Managua and Masaya. Volcanic Lakes Xiloa and Apoyo, near Managua, are excellent for swimming and day sailing, and provide relief from the heat. Pacific Ocean beaches are nearby, and the cooler rainforest mountains of Esteli and Matagalpa are just a few hours drive away. (Note: Accommodations outside Managua are limited. See Recreation and Social Life.)

Managua never fully recovered from the 1972 earthquake, in which the entire city center was destroyed, and suffered further neglect through the 1980s. Today, it remains mostly deserted, with visible earthquake ruins. Managua is now a widely scattered collection of neighborhoods that rim an empty hub, with no centrally located business or shopping district. However, the area near the recently inaugurated Cathedral appears to be becoming the city's new focal point.

Population

In 1995, the Government of Nicaragua conducted a census of the country's population, but the final results of this census have not been published. In 1996, however, voter registration predictions, based on preliminary results of the 1995 census, were found to be underestimated across the board. Observers, therefore, suspect that the 1995 census was flawed, particularly in remote rural areas of north and central Nicaragua, where conditions make it extremely difficult to conduct an accurate census. The national estimate is 4.4 million, with almost 1 million in Managua alone.

Nicaragua's history of political centralism, and geographic and ethnic diversity, has led to the development of three distinct societies. In the western one-third, known as the Pacific and where the bulk of the population, wealth, and political power is concentrated, the people are Spanish-speaking, predominantly Catholic mestizos.

Despite its minute population, the east coast has more ethnic diversity-primarily Caribbean black and Miskito, Sumo, and Rama Indians. These groups differ culturally and linguistically from each other, and, from their Spanish-speaking countrymen in the west and center. The foreign influence in this region, primarily from England but also from the U.S., shares dominance with the Hispanic culture. Caribbean English and Spanish are spoken by many communities of the Caribbean coast, but in the indigenous communities Miskut, Rama, and Sumo predominate.

The central corridor of Nicaragua, where most fighting occurred in the 1980s, has registered tremendous growth, both in terms of population and economic activity, since 1990. This growth is due in part to Nicaraguans returning to their country since the end of the war in 1990. In this region, a largely mestizo, Spanish-speaking population is pushing into areas populated almost exclusively by the indigenous peoples who predominate in the east coast.

Public Institutions

The election held October 20, 1996, culminated Nicaragua's transition to demos racy that began with the 1990 election of President Violeta Chamorro. President Chamorro's tenure followed over 10 year; of Sandinista rule and armed conflict between the Sandinista Popular Army (EPS and the Nicaragua Resistance (RN). During President Chamorro's nearly sever years in office, the government achieved major progress toward consolidating democratic institutions, advancing national reconciliation, stabilizing the economy privatizing state-owned enterprises, and reducing human rights violations.

In all, Nicaragua's 35 political parties participated in the 1996 elections, independently or as part of one of five electoral coalitions. With nearly 52% of the vote the center-right Liberal Alliance, a coalition of five political parties and sectors of another two, won the presidency for it leader, Armoldo Aleman, a plurality in the national legislature, and a large majority of the mayoral races. The Sandinista National Liberation Front (FSLN) ended in second place with 38%. Only two out of 14.` mayors belong to third parties. The firs transfer of power in recent Nicaraguan his tory from one democratically elected president to another occurred January 10, 1997 with the Aleman administration'; inauguration.

Nicaragua is a constitutional demos racy with executive, legislative, judicial and electoral branches of government. It 1995, the executive

and legislative branches negotiated a reform of the 198' Sandinista constitution, giving the National Assembly impressive new powers and in dependence, including over taxation (formerly, an exclusive executive branch power) and the power to elect Supreme Court judges and other important public officials.

Both the President and the Member; of the unicameral National Assembly (legislature) are elected to concurrent five-yea terms. The President is head of state, as well as the head of government.

The National Assembly consists of 90 deputies elected from party lists, draws at the department and national level, plus, those defeated presidential candidates who obtained a minimal quotient of votes. In the 1996 elections, the Liberal Alliance won a plurality of 42 seats, the FSLN won 36 seats, and nine other parties won the remaining 15 seats.

The Supreme Court supervises functioning of a still largely ineffective, and overburdened, judicial system. As part of 1995 constitutional reforms, the Supreme Court's independence was strengthened by increasing the number of magistrates from organizing and conducting elections, plebiscites, and referendums. Magistrates and their alternates are elected to five-year terms by the National Assembly.

Freedom of speech is a right, guaranteed by the Nicaraguan constitution, and vigorously exercised by its people. Diverse viewpoints are freely and openly discussed in the media and in academia. Nicaragua does not use state censorship. Other constitutional freedoms include peaceful assembly and association, freedom of religion, and freedom of movement within the country, as well as foreign travel, emigration, and repatriation. Domestic and international human rights monitors operate freely within the country.

Both the military and police are increasingly professional and apolitical. In February 1995, General Joaquin Cuadra replaced then-Sandinista army commander General Humberto Ortega, in accordance with a new military code, enacted in 1994. He has espoused greater professionalism in the renamed Army of Nicaragua.

President Aleman has established a civilian-led Ministry of Defense to ensure that civilians assume their appropriate role in setting national defense and security policies. A new police organization law, passed by the National Assembly and signed into law in August 1996, further codified civilian control and professionalizing of that law enforcement agency.

Arts, Science, and Education

The Sandinista regime encouraged the arts, and the current government continues to support them, within budget constraints. There are a National School of Dance, National School of Fine Arts, and a National Conservatory of Music, along with several private schools dedicated to the arts.

Although the works of Nicaraguan plastic artists and artisans are internationally known, the nation's true pride is its poets. Indeed, it has been said that every Nicaraguan is a poet. Ruben Dario, a late 19th-century Nicaraguan poet, is credited with introducing modernism to Spanish poetry. He is internationally known and highly honored in his native land. A museum dedicated to his memory is located in Leon, and the impressive National Theater is named after him.

The national university scene continues to develop, as private universities continue to grow and prosper alongside Nicaragua's traditional, state-funded universities.

The Central American University, UCA, has a law school, social sciences/humanities faculties, and the only journalism program in the country. The National Autonomous University of Nicaragua in Leon (UNAN-Leon, enrollment: 7,000 students), was founded in 1812. This state-run university has the most prestigious law and medical schools in Nicaragua. The state-run National Autonomous University of Nicaragua in Managua, UNAN Managua, was founded in 1941 as the Central University of Managua. It was officially part of UNAN-Leon until 1982. Its enrollment is 15,000 students and its degree programs include strong business and economics programs. It is the only university that trains the nation's primary and secondary schoolteachers, including teachers of English.

The Central American Business Administration Institute, INCAS (enrollment: 200 students), offers a solid, U.S.-style graduate business program. In 1996, the MBA program was reinstated after a 13-year absence. The Business School of Harvard University financially supports and exchanges faculty with INCAS.

The private Catholic University, UNICA (enrollment: 1,500 students), opened in 1993 on land donated by the Managua mayor's office. It is openly aligned with the Catholic Church and has right-of-center political interests, but it accepts students (with good grades) of all faiths and political leanings. It is now retrenching after an initial, ambitious growth spurt and has trimmed its course offerings and cut engineering as a major.

The American University, UAM (enrollment: 1,500 students), opened in 1993 in four small buildings, but has expanded dramatically since then. It runs one of only two international relations/diplomacy programs in Nicaragua, has a medical school, and recently established a dentistry program. UAM has recently been concentrating on its business course offerings and developing its computer science program. The University of Mobile Latin American campus (enrollment: 300 students), was founded in San Marcos in 1993. It is a private, U.S.-accredited, English-language branch of the Alabama university of the same name. This campus boasts the most modern facilities in Nicaragua. Each professor reportedly has a Ph.D. or Master's degree. It offers computer science, English literature, marine biology, biology, environmental technology, finance, accounting, business administration, economics, marketing, and tourism degrees. It owns and operates the University Hotel in Jinotepe as part of its hotel and restaurant management program.

The Polytechnical University, UPOLI (enrollment: 2,500 students), is a technical and scientific institution founded in 1967. It is administered by the Baptist Convention, with some government funding. The National Engineering University, UNI (enrollment: 8,000 students), was founded in 1982. Curriculums cover all engineering fields, except agriculture and forestry. UNI does a good job of selling services to the private sector and also receives assistance from European governments. The quality of instruction and equipment is fair but improving. Until SPRINT recently appeared on the scene, UNI served as Nicaragua's hub for Internet users.

The National Agrarian University, UNA (enrollment: 1,500 students), founded in 1990, was previously the Agricultural College of UNAN-Managua. UNA works closely with the Ministry of Agriculture and the Ministry of Natural Resources.

The Centro Cultural Nicaraguense-Norteamericano (CCNN), a nonprofit binational center, offers English- and Spanish-language instruction, a 6,000-volume library of American books, and a wide assortment of U.S. periodicals.

Commerce and Industry

Nicaragua began to institute free market reforms in 1991 after 12 years of economic free fall under the Sandinista regime. Despite some setbacks, the country has made dramatic progress: privatizing almost 350 state enterprises, reducing inflation from 13,490% to 12%, and cutting the foreign debt by 50%. The economy began expanding in 1994 and grew a very strong 5.5% in 1996 (its best performance since 1977). As a result, total GDP reached $2.029 billion.

Despite this growing economy, Nicaragua remains the second poorest nation in the hemisphere with a per capita GDP of $476 (below where it stood before the Sandinista takeover in 1979). Unemployment, although falling, is 16%, and another 36% are underemployed. Nicaragua suffers from persistent trade deficits. That, along with a high-debt service burden and government fiscal deficit, leaves the nation highly dependent on foreign assistance (which equaled 22% of GDP in 1996).

One of the key engines of economic growth has been production for export. Exports rose to $70 million in 1996, up 28% from 1995. Although traditional products such as coffee, meat, and sugar continued to lead the list of Nicaraguan exports, during 1996 the total value of nontraditional exports surpassed that of traditional goods for the first time. The fastest growing of these new products were "maquila" goods (apparel), bananas, gold, seafood, and new agricultural products such as sesame, melons, and onions. Rapid expansion of the tourist industry in 1996 made it the nation's third largest source of foreign exchange. The U.S. is the largest trading partner by far; the source of 26% of Nicaragua's imports, and the destination of 45% of its exports.

Nicaragua is primarily an agricultural country, but construction, mining, fisheries, and general commerce have also been expanding strongly during the last few years. The economy in 1996 saw increasing net inflows of foreign private capital, which totaled about $190 million. The private banking sector continued to expand and strengthen. Private banks, which did not exist six years ago, currently hold 70% of the nation's deposit base.

Nicaragua now appears poised for rapid economic growth. However, long-term success at attracting investment, creating jobs, and reducing poverty depend on the Nicaraguan Government's ability to stay on track with an International Monetary Fund Program, resolve the thousands of Sandinista-era property confiscation cases, and continue to open its economy to foreign trade.

Transportation

Automobiles

Because of unreliable public transportation, a car is essential in Managua. The most popular cars are small-sized, four- or six-cylinder, U.S., or Japanese models. Many people, especially those who like to explore off-the-beaten track, have found four-wheel-drive vehicles very useful on Nicaragua's poor road system. High ground clearance for speed bumps and potholes is also an asset, and the high cost of gasoline (some $2.50 a gallon) makes fuel economy a priority. Several Japanese and American (GM and Ford) distributorships have vehicles that sell above U.S. prices, but they do not meet U.S. specifications. Several car rental agencies, including Budget and Avis, have vehicles available at higher U.S. prices.

At Managua's several garages, repair quality varies. Labor is cheaper than in the U.S., but parts and tires cost much more than U.S. prices; and, most parts are not available locally at any price.

Cars shipped to the U.S. Despatch Agent in Miami are surface shipped to Puerto Cortes, Honduras, and transported overland to Managua. Send your car in good mechanical condition with good tires and undercoating. The tropical climate, humidity, rain, dust, and rough road conditions all contribute to heavy wear-and-tear on tires and vehicles. Don't bring a convertible-they offer less protection from the elements and are more susceptible to vandalism.

Unleaded gasoline, including super and diesel, is readily available, but expensive.

All vehicles must have local third party-liability insurance coverage (cost $107) before you receive license plates. Driving, especially at night, is often hazardous due to poor local driving habits, a lack of streetlights, and the rundown condition of vehicles and roads. In addition, pedestrians, vendors, beggars, and animals often wander in the driving lanes with no idea of the dangers they cause to themselves and to others.

Local

Local transportation is crowded with unsafe conditions. Most taxis are mid 70s Japanese models or Soviet-made Ladas in poor condition. Cabdrivers can, and do, pick up additional passengers; therefore, routes are usually indirect. The local bus system connects all parts of the city for a low fare but buses are scarce, uncomfortable, overcrowded (as much as triple the capacity), and in need of repair. Numerous pickup trucks, "camionetas," carry passengers as well. At rush hour, the crowded camionetas resemble cattle trucks.

Drivers who frequently fail to observe traffic rules are at fault in a large percentage of the traffic accidents. The disorderly driving of buses and taxis aggravates the already difficult driving conditions.

Regional

Augusto Cesar Sandino Airport, 11 kilometers from Managua, handles international traffic, including jet service.

Managua is currently served by several airlines, including Continental, American, Nica, Aviateca, TACA, COPA, Iberia, and LACSA. American carriers offer daily direct flights to Miami and three times a week to Houston. The national airline, Nica, is the only major airline that provides both domestic and international service. Tickets for all airlines are purchased in U.S. currency, and credit cards are accepted.

Nicaragua has a primary highway system connecting principal cities by paved but poorly maintained roads. The highway network is mostly confined to the populous western part of the country. One paved road extends east to Rama, and an unpaved road goes to Puerto Cabezas; the latter is often impassable in the rainy season. The Pan American Highway (all paved but poorly maintained) is the country's major travel artery. It enters Nicaragua in the north at El Espino and exits in the south at Penas Blancas on the Costa Rican border.

Various privately owned bus companies have lines connecting Managua with all of western Nicaragua. Many are vans. Buses also run on a limited schedule to Costa Rica and Honduras.

Communications

Telephone and Telegraph

Local- and long-distance telephone service is available in Managua. International telephone and telegraph are handled by the Nicaraguan Telecommunications and Post Office Company (TELCOR). Direct dialing to the U.S. costs about $1.15 a minute. If you have AT&T, SPRINT, and MCI cards you can make direct calls. The number of telephone lines is severely limited, new phones are hard to obtain, malfunctions occur frequently, and repairs are slow. Local and in-country calls are often difficult to make; overseas calls are more easily made.

Radio and TV

Managua has 120 radio stations broadcasting on both AM and FM. With the return to democracy, censorship has been lifted, and news programs have proliferated. Other offerings are usually limited to music and some religious programming. For best FM reception, bring an external antenna (indoor or outdoor).

Shortwave radio reception is fairly good using built-in antennas. Broadcasts in English by VOA, BBC, and others are common and offer a variety of programs. To operate a ham radio, you must request and receive a license from the Radio Club of Nicaragua. If you are approved, TELCOR issues you permission to go on the air.

The eight TV stations currently on the air include privately run channel 2; Sandinista-affiliated Channel 4; private, conservative, channel 8; privately owned business-oriented channel 10 and channel 12, privately owned channel 19; channel 21, a religious broadcaster, and private music and youth-oriented channel 23. Almost all offer a mix of Latin soap operas, sports, and movies, some of which are dubbed, and some, subtitled. Several cable TV operators are active in the areas in and offer a full range of U.S. programming for about $20-$30 a month.

Newspapers, Magazines, and Technical Journals

Nicaragua's print media are no longer subject to censorship. Managua has four daily newspapers: La Prensa is an independent newspaper owned by former President Chamorro's family; Barricada, no longer the official organ of the FSLN, still favorably reports the Sandinista's programs and views; El Nuevo Diario, which has the largest circulation, is supportive of the Sandinistas but highly critical of the U.S.; La Tribuna, privately owned, conservative, and independent, began publishing in 1993.

Several weekly magazines are published; best known among them are: El Semanario-political news and commentary, generally pro-Sandinista and Confidencial-left-of-center news and commentary.

Several U.S. news and business magazines such as Time, Newsweek, and Fortune, as well as the Miami Herald and the New York Times are available, but slightly delayed, at local newsstands.

Health and Medicine

Medical Facilities

Local hospitals are far below U.S. standards; however, considerable improvements have been noted in the Baptist and military hospitals since 1990. Most medicines are available. X-ray, ultrasound, and endoscopy equipment is new. No elective surgery is done incountry. Some emergencies, however, can be, and have been, properly handled. Serious cases can be stabilized and evacuated either by Air Ambulance or commercial airline. Medical evacuations are authorized to Miami. Expectant mothers return to the U.S. for delivery. Many local laboratories are now equipped to perform almost all tests.

Community Health

Reports on local dental care are mixed. Some have had good experiences, but others have not. Some local dentists are well trained, but even those find it difficult to acquire high-quality equipment, which is expensive in a practice setting that will not financially support such purchases. In general, basic dental care (i.e., cleaning, polishing, and fillings) can be done locally. Have more complicated procedures, such as root canals, done elsewhere. Orthodontic care is available and at a lower cost than in the U.S.

Opticians and optometrists are available, and lens-grinding facilities exist and can be used if needed. Prices are higher than the level of quality warrants and, if you need glasses, bring them. Bring sunglasses also.

Public sanitation measures are rudimentary at best with resulting health and hygiene hazards. Garbage collection is erratic and collection areas are usually strewn with refuse, which is scattered by impoverished individuals "dumpster diving" in search of usable items and feral dogs and rodents foraging for something edible.

Shanty towns, without water or sewage systems, have sprung up in every neighborhood. These areas are a reservoir of contagious illnesses such as typhoid, cholera, infectious hepatitis, and mosquito-borne illnesses.

Despite local government efforts to maintain the water system, and even chlorinate the water supply, the water system is aging and has been a victim of earthquakes, illegal tapping into the water mains by shanty town residents that increases the risk of contamination, and frequent water shortages in the dry season that leave stagnant water in the system that appears at faucets when the flow is restored. For these reasons, regard suspiciously any water that has not been boiled, or otherwise treated. Carry bottled water when you travel outside Managua.

Mosquito-borne illnesses are endemic. Malaria, in the form of vivax malaria, is present in most parts of the country, and dengue-fever infection rates are the hemisphere's highest. Budget restrictions severely hinder mosquito spraying to limited times and areas, which is only minimally effective.

Most food sold in public markets is handled and stored in unsanitary conditions. Perishable items in these markets are not well refrigerated, and erratic power supplies make proper storage impossible even in those shops that have refrigeration.

Suitable facilities are not available for the handicapped.

Preventive Measures

Typhoid, polio, tetanus, and diphtheria vaccinations are recommended before leaving the U.S. Incidents of infectious hepatitis are increasing in Nicaragua, and Hepatitis A and Hepatitis B vaccine are recommended as a preventive measure.

Intestinal diseases affect everyone at one time or another, but you can experience fewer episodes if you take suitable precautions with food, your personal hygiene, and your household help. Boil or filter drinking water and water for ice. Fruits and vegetables should be washed thoroughly, peeled, or soaked in chlorine (chlorox) or iodine solution. Cook meats and seafood well before eating. If intestinal diseases occur, you can find medications to deal with them at local pharmacies.

During the dry season, dust and wind make life uncomfortable for those who suffer from sinusitis, allergies, and other respiratory ailments. Asthmatics must also contend with mold that forms during the rainy season; however, using a room dehumidifier can help relieve the problem.

The most hazardous insects in Managua are houseflies, mosquitoes, spiders, and scorpions. Roaches, ants, and other common household insects can be controlled with aerosol bombs. Regular fumigation is necessary. Poisonous snakes are seen occasionally.

Malaria is a hazard. It is recommended that chloroquine, a malaria suppressant, is taken weekly. Several U.S. travelers have been affected by dengue fever which, at times, reaches epidemic proportions. Keeping bedroom windows screened, or closed with air-conditioning, cuts down on possibility of mosquito bites. Mosquito netting is a good idea, especially for small children, and you can purchase it locally.

NOTES FOR TRAVELERS

Passage, Customs & Duties

A U.S. passport, valid for six months beyond the duration of the visit, is required to enter Nicaragua. Tourists must also have an onward or return ticket and evidence of sufficient funds to support themselves during their stay. U.S. citizens do not require a visa, but a tourist card valid for 90 days must be purchased upon arrival. Tourist card fees and airport departure taxes must be paid in U.S. dollars. Visitors remaining more than 90 days must obtain an extension from Nicaraguan immigration. Failure to do so prevents departure until a fine is paid. For further information regarding entry, departure, and customs requirements, travelers should contact the Embassy of Nicaragua at 1627 New Hampshire Avenue, N.W., Washington D.C. 20009; telephone (202) 939-6570 or (202) 939-6531; e-mail at embanic_prensa@andyne.net; or a Nicaraguan consulate in Atlanta, Houston, Los Angeles, Milwaukee, Miami, New Orleans, New York, Pittsburgh, San Francisco, or San Juan, Puerto Rico.

Although many restaurants and hotels now accept credit cards, especially in Managua, acceptance is not as widespread as in the U.S. Travelers checks are accepted at a few major hotels and may be exchanged for local currency at authorized exchange facilities ("casas de cambio"). There are few automatic teller machines, particularly outside Managua. English is not widely spoken.

Nicaragua is prone to a wide variety of natural disasters, including earthquakes, hurricanes and volcanic eruptions. General information about natural disaster preparedness is available via the Internet from the U.S. Federal Emergency Management Agency (FEMA) at http://www.fema.gov.

U.S. citizens living in or visiting Nicaragua are encouraged to register at the Consular Section of the U.S. Embassy in Managua and obtain updated information on travel and security in Nicaragua. The U.S. Embassy is located at Kilometer 4½ (4.5) Carretera Sur, Managua; telephone (505) 266-6010 or 268-0123; after hours telephone (505) 266-6038; Consular Section fax (505)266-9943; e-mail: consularmanagu@state.gov; web page http://usembassy.state.gov/managua

Pets

Pets must have a certificate of rabies vaccine, health certificate, and certificate of origin (pet shop receipt, veterinarian's proof of origin, etc.) The health certificate must be certified by the Nicaraguan Embassy or Consulate before departing for Managua.Send the following information in advance of arrival: a) pet's species, b) breed, c) name, d) color, e) weight, f) sex, and g) height (in inches).

Firearms and Ammunition

Government of Nicaragua regulations require clear proof of ownership during customs inspection. A Government of Nicaragua firearms permit application must be filled out (with accompanying photos of the applicant).

Currency, Banking, and Weights and Measures

All currency transactions are regulated by the Government of Nicaragua. The official unit of money is the cordoba, exchanged (September 1999) at a rate of 012.04 (cordobas) to US$1. Local currency can be obtained at licensed money exchangers (Casas de Cambio) or local banks. All other currency transactions are illegal and should be avoided. U.S. currency can be obtained and personal checks may be cashed at Bancentro.

Nicaragua is partially on the metric system; weight is normally measured in pounds rather than kilograms, but distance is measured in kilometers.

No limitation is placed on amount of dollars or traveler's checks you can bring into the country. Traveler's checks are accepted by local banks, but the rate is likely to be below that available at a Casa de Cambio.

LOCAL HOLIDAYS

Jan. 1	New Year's Day
Mar/Apr.	Holy Thursday*
Mar/Apr.	Good Friday*
Mar/Apr.	Holy Saturday*
Mar/Apr.	Easter Sunday*
May 1	Labor Day
July 19	Anniversary of the Revolution
Sept. 14.	Battle of San Jacinto
Sept. 15.	Independence Day
Dec. 8	Immaculate Conception
Dec. 25	Christmas Day

*variable

RECOMMENDED READING

The following titles are provided as a general indication of the material published on this country:

Most current literature on Nicaragua was written in 1980s. Many of these books are biased toward one side or the other of the civil war that ravaged Nicaragua during that decade. A few books of a general nature on Nicaragua and its people are listed here. Most information on Nicaragua is included in larger studies on Central America.

Federal Research Division Library of Congress. *Nicaragua: A Country Study.* (Area Handbook Series.) 1994.

Barrios de Chamorro, Violeta. *Dreams of the Heart.* (1996). The autobiography of President Violeta Barrios de Chamorro.

Christian, Shirley. *Nicaragua: Revolution in the Family.*

Cuadra, Pablo Antonio. *El Nicaraguense.*

Deidrich, Bernard. Somoza. Gallegois, Paco. *Nicaragua Tierra de Maravillas.*

Garner, J.D. *Historia de Nicaragua.*

Garvin, Glenn. *Everybody Had His Own Gringo!*

Harrison, Lawrence. *Underdevelopment is a State of Mind.* (Contains a section comparing Nicaragua and Costa Rica).

Herrera Zuniga, Rene. *Nicaragua, El derrumbe Negociado, Los avatares dc un Cambio de Regimen.* (1994).

Kaplan, Robert. *A Twilight Struggle.* A voluminous analysis of U.S. Policy on Nicaragua.

Kinzer, Stephen. *Blood of Brothers.*

Nunez, Orlando, ed. Nunez, Orlando et al. *La Guerra y el Campesinado en Nicaragua.* (A Sandinista analysis of the causes for the emergency of the Nicaraguan Resistance.)

Randall, Margaret. *Sandnno' Daughters. Sandnno' Daughters Revisited: Feminism in Nicaragua. Las Relaciones internacionaels y la formacion del poderpolitico en Nicaragua.* (1991).

Schwartz, Stephen. *A Strange Silence: The Emergence of Democracy in Nicaragua.* (1992)

Spalding, Rose J. *Capitalists and Revolution in Nicaragua: Opposition and Accommodation 1979-1993.*

Vilas, Carlos M. *Between Earthquakes anc Volcanoes: Market, State, and the Revolutions in Central America.*

Waiter, Knut. *The Regime of Anastasio Somoza, 1936-1956.*

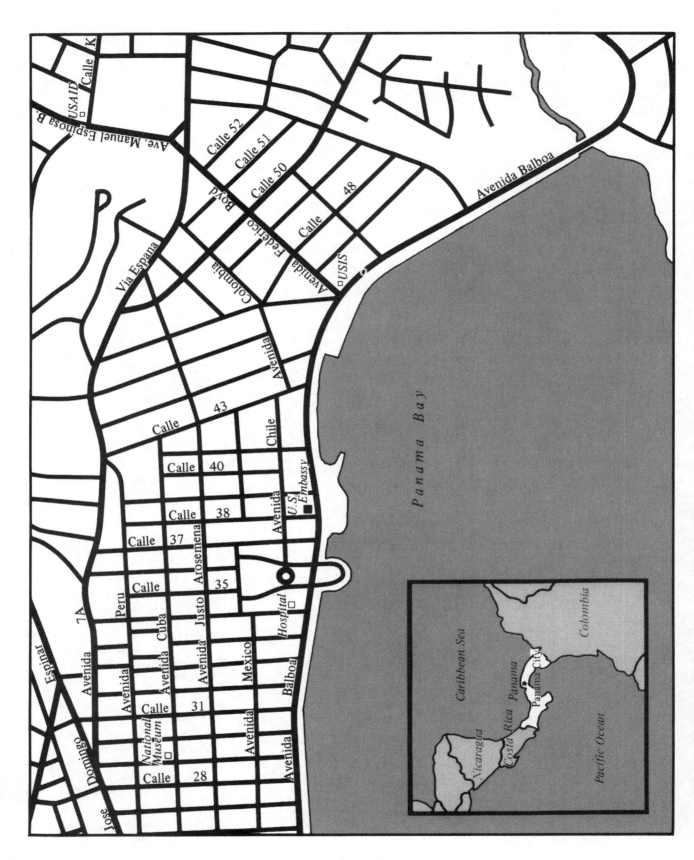

Panama City, Panama

PANAMA

Republic of Panama

Major City:

Panama City

Other Cities:

Balboa, Chitré, Colón, Cristóbal, David, Portobelo, Santiago

EDITOR'S NOTE

This chapter was adapted from the Department of State Post Report dated August 1996. Supplemental material has been added to increase coverage of minor cities, facts have been updated, and some material has been condensed. Readers are encouraged to visit the Department of State's web site at http://travel.state.gov/ for the most recent information available on travel to this country.

INTRODUCTION

PANAMA, because of its strategic position on the isthmus connecting the North and South American continents, was a major center for exploration and expansion during the 16th and 17th centuries. In 1821, some years after the decline of Spanish colonial power in the Western Hemisphere, the territory became part of Greater Colombia.

The question of a waterway across the isthmus, linking the Atlantic and Pacific oceans, and Colombia's refusal to ratify a treaty allowing construction, led to Panama's revolt and secession. The United States supported Panama with military forces, and recognized the new state on November 6, 1903. A treaty was signed, giving the U.S. perpetual control over what came to be known as the Canal Zone, a designation that no longer applies. The covenant was amended in 1977, and implemented in 1979, with provision for ending U.S. military presence in Panama on the last day of this century, and for turning over responsibility and operation of the canal to the Panamanians.

MAJOR CITY

Panama City

Panama City, the capital and principal city of the Republic of Panama, is situated on the Pacific side of the country. In 2000, it had an approximate population of 1,088,00. Often called the "Crossroads of the World," it offers a uniquely international ambience and an active life with modern shopping centers, art expositions and many excellent NSrestaurants.

Food

A wide variety of American and ethnic foods are available at modern supermarkets in Panama City. Seafood, meat, fruits, vegetables, and canned and packaged goods are readily available in Panamanian shops, although prepared foods which are imported from the U.S. or elsewhere can be expensive. Restaurants vary widely in both cost and cuisine. A full lunch can be had for seven dollars. There are also numerous top quality restaurants specializing in seafood, or any type of ethnic food, around the city. Pizza Hut, Dominos Pizza and other vendors offer home and office delivery.

Clothing

Summer clothes are worn year round in Panama. Cottons are the most comfortable, but cotton blends are satisfactory. Fabrics that are 100% synthetic neither absorb moisture nor "breathe" and are uncomfortable in Panama's humid climate. Many office buildings are overly air-conditioned so a light jacket or sweater can come in handy.

All types of clothing suitable for the Panamanian climate are available in retail shops in the Canal area, although selection may be limited at any given time. Prices in the local retail stores can be higher than U.S. prices, and size ranges are limited.

Men: Normal attire for male staff during working hours is a suit and tie. It is also preferred by many Panamanians. Some men use either the "guayabera" or a short-sleeved shirt. Casual sports attire is the rule outside the office. The guayabera, a long, untucked embroidered shirt, is frequently worn for daytime or evening social functions and can be purchased locally.

Women: Female officers and staff members are most comfortable in lightweight suits or tailored or otherwise professional-looking one or two-piece dresses. A blazer, whether in a traditional color or something more tropical, is a useful addition to a working wardrobe. Casual outfits should be brought for general use, and beachwear, shorts, and slacks for recreational purposes. Shorts are not generally worn on the streets, but pants are acceptable. Sun hats are useful when outdoors. In recent years, the trend in female formal wear in Panama has been towards street-length rather than long gowns.

Children: Department of Defense schools do not enforce a dress code. Girls wear mostly shirts or blouses with slacks, jeans or skirts. Boys wear long pants (mostly jeans) or shorts with T-shirts or sport shirts. Private schools require school uniforms, which vary from school to school.

Supplies and Services

American brands of toilet articles, cosmetics, home medicines, drugs, tobacco products, cleaning materials, and household and entertainment accessories are readily available in retail stores in Panama City, but at prices higher than in the United States. Local brands are available at retail stores for very reasonable prices.

Panama City has good facilities for shoe repair, laundry and dry-cleaning, and radio and automobile repair. Beauty and barbershops are also available. You can take advantage of competent tailoring and dressmaking services here.

Religious Activities

Although Panama is a predominately Catholic country (approximately 85%), places of worship of all denominations—with services in both English and Spanish—are

City view in Panama

Cory Langley. Reproduced by permission.

located in Panama City and the Canal area. Sunday schools and church-related activities are numerous.

Education

Department of Defense Dependent Schools (DODDS) operates a school system in the canal area including grades K-l2, as well as a two-year college curriculum. The schools are modeled on the U.S. public school system and are accredited by the Middle States Association of Colleges and Secondary Schools. Instruction is in English. The schools are modern and well-equipped. Special education is available for children ages three and older. DODDS also has a talented and gifted program. Bus transportation is available for students in grades Kindergarten through twelfth grade. The school year runs from late August until mid June.

La Escuela Internacional de Panama (the International School of Panama) is the alternative school most often attended by American students, and is increasingly used due to the gradual closure of the DODDS system in Panama. Classes presently include grades K-12. The school's academic program meets the requirements of the Panama-

nian Ministry of Education and it has been accredited by the Southern Association of Colleges and Schools of the United Schools. Instruction is in English except for a 40-minute class in Spanish each day.

Applications for admission to the International School are accepted at any time during the year. Classes are limited to a maximum of 24 students. All students are tested by the school counselor or other qualified staff member at the time of registration. If you would like to initiate the admission process before arriving in Panama, you may send your child's Iowa Test (ITBS) results or the equivalent. Following testing, the school's Admissions Committee will review the completed application to evaluate the student's potential and to determine whether acceptance will contribute to a balance of nationalities, transient vs. local population, language capability, personal interests, and personalities. The school year runs from early August to late June, with approximately seven weeks of vacation from just before Christmas until the end of January.

There are two other private schools: St. Mary's Parochial School and the Episcopal School of Panama both schools are well regarded in Panama. St. Mary's Parochial School, located in the canal area, offers classes for pre-school through the twelfth grade. Instruction is in English and Spanish. Registration is held one day during the first week of March. Preregistration is not possible.

The Episcopal School of Panama (Colegio Episcopal de Panama) is a small college preparatory school. Both English and Spanish are taught as first languages. This school has a waiting list. Both of these schools are in session from April through December.

There are several good nursery schools on the military bases, in the canal area, and in Panama City. Those located on the military bases conduct classes in English from September through June. All others, as a general rule, are bilingual with a preference toward Spanish, and are in session from April through December. It is best to postpone any decision until parents can visit the schools to determine which will best suit the needs and personality of their child.

For most schools you will need proof of age (for pre-kindergarten and kindergarten), a copy of the student's last report card, and an up-to-date immunization record. All schools that comply with the regulations set forth by the Panamanian Ministry of Education (all but DODDS) require that the birth certificate or a photocopy of the passport, and the previous year's school record be translated into Spanish and notarized.

Special Educational Opportunities

The Panama Canal College, part of the Department of Defense School system, offers a two-year college course with Associate degrees available in Business Administration, Accounting, Business Data Processing, and others, including Secretarial skills. Current full-time tuition is $716 per semester for sponsored dependents under the age of 21. Dependent spouses may attend on a part-time basis (up to

eleven credits), at a charge of $65.00 per credit hour.

The Panama Canal branch of Florida State University is located at Albrook Air Force Base. The university offers Bachelor of Arts degrees in Interamerican Studies, International Affairs and Social Science. In addition, students may complete up to 90 semester credit hours towards the 120 required for a degree in Business Administration. The last thirty credit hours must be taken in Florida. Tuition at Florida State is $90.00 per semester credit hour.

Florida-based Nova University offers several degrees at the Panama Learning Center, which was founded in 1977. These include a Bachelor of Science degree in Professional Management, a Master of Arts degree in Applied Linguistics and Teaching English as a Second Language, and a Master's degree in Business Administration, and Computer Programs. The cost per credit hour ranges from $125.00 for undergraduates to $200.00 for graduate courses.

The University of Oklahoma has an extension campus at Albrook, offering a Master of Educational Psychology and a Master of Public Administration. Current tuition is $203.75 per credit hour.

The above institutions are fully accredited. For additional information, they may be contacted at the following addresses:

Panama Canal College
DODDS, Panama Area
Unit 0925
APO, AA 34002

Florida State University
Panama Canal Branch
Unit 0922
APO, AA 34002

The University of Oklahoma
Education Service Center
Unit 0924
APO, AA 34002

Nova University
Panama Center
Unit 0924
APO, AA 34002

The University of Panama is located in Panama City. In general, you must successfully complete a five-year course to obtain a degree. The University will accept certificates from recognized secondary schools. Many classes are held in the evening and all instruction is in Spanish. For further information contact the University of Panama at Urbanizacion El Cangrejo, Republic of Panama.

The YMCA in the Canal area holds classes in Spanish, cooking, art, oil painting, ceramics, design, jewelry making, bridge, swimming, scuba diving and a variety of other subjects.

Sports

Organized athletic programs for adults are limited, but you can participate on an individual basis in almost any warm-weather sport. A number of swimming pools, tennis courts, golf courses, and stables are found throughout the city and the canal area. You can purchase athletic equipment of all types locally or at the sport shops on the bases.

Several hotels offer memberships to use their pools and other recreational facilities. There are also several quality health clubs in the city, as well as the gymnasiums on the bases, that offer aerobics and weightlifting. A variety of private social athletic clubs in Panama include the Club de Golf de Panama, the Club de Montana Altos del Lago, the Club de Yates y Pesca, and the Club Union.

Canal area facilities for children (organized by the Youth Recreation Program) include swimming, bowling leagues, league baseball and softball (December through April), soccer (in the Spring), Little League football (August through October), and lessons in judo, scuba diving, karate, and gymnastics.

Deep-sea and fresh-water fishing in the waters in and around Panama are among the best in the world. You can use most types of freshwater and saltwater tackle. Fishing in Gatun Lake for Peacock Bass is a popular pastime. Private boat skiing, fishing, and cruising is facilitated by the availability of various water crafts from several different locations for modest fees.

For the hunter, a variety of wild fowl, small game animals, and some larger animals such as deer abound. Most hunters in Panama use a shotgun, but air rifles are also used occasionally. Panama has a trapshoot club, as well as several rifle ranges in the canal area. Neither a hunting nor a fishing license is required in the Republic of Panama. The Panamanian Government does requires a gun permit. The canal area has some easily-met licensing requirements, although there are some restrictions.

Horse racing, boxing and baseball are the favorite spectator sports in Panama. A local track holds races each week.

Baseball, basketball, softball and soccer are played extensively on the amateur level, and facilities are available for squash, racquetball, volleyball, and weight training.

Touring and Outdoor Activities

One small zoo is located in the Canal area. The Panama Canal Experimental Gardens are a popular spot for visits or picnics. Barro Colorado Island is a biological research center and forest preserve that is located in Gatun Lake within the canal system; day trips are made to explore this site where the Smithsonian Institute researches local flora and fauna.

Museums include the Canal Area Museum, Museum of Contemporary Art, the National Museum of Panama, and the Museum of the Panamanian Man, with its interesting collection of pre-Columbian pottery and gold artifacts.

Another point of interest is the ruins of "Panama La Vieja," the first Panamanian city on the Pacific side of the isthmus, which was founded by the Spaniards in 1519. It was destroyed by the pirate Henry Morgan in 1671. The Church of San Jose, with its famous Golden Altar, is another well-known site located in the colonial sector of Panama City. According to legend, the altar was saved from the assaults of Morgan the Pirate in the year 1671 when it was painted with whitewash to look like wood.

You can find a moderate change of climate in El Valle (2,000 feet) in the Cordillera de Veraguas, 80 miles from Panama, where a fair hotel is available. Boquete and Volcan are 350 miles away. At elevations of 4,000 and 7,000 feet, they offer spectacular mountain scenery, a cool climate, and good hotels. Contadora Island in the Las Perlas Archipelago is seventeen minutes by air from Panama City. The resort-like island offers a hotel, private homes that may be rented, and beautiful beaches.

San Jose, Costa Rica, is accessible by air at a reasonable price. The Colombian island of San Andres, as well as Bogota, Medellin, Cali, Barranquilla, and Cartagena in Colombia are also within easy reach by air. Country clearance must be obtained from the U.S. Embassy in Bogota prior to any travel to Colombia. By car, San Jose, Costa Rica is about thirteen hours from Panama City.

Beaches are available on the Pacific side (Panama Bay) approximately 60-90 minutes from Panama City. Beaches on the Atlantic side (Caribbean Sea) can be reached in a two- to three-hour drive. Both areas provide a number of good beaches and varied facilities.

Entertainment

Panama City has a number of fine indoor theaters, as well as those in the canal area, where first-run American films are shown. Those shown in the city are in English with Spanish subtitles. Video stores also abound. No professional theater exists, but a few small theater groups produce plays periodically in Spanish and English. The Ancon Theater Guild has an active production schedule and there has been high interest and involvement from the mission community. The Balboa High School drama department presents two productions per year.

Concerts are presented by visiting musical artists and dance groups, either under the sponsorship of the National Concert Association, The National Institute of Culture or various Embassies. The national symphony and the ballet company also perform periodically.

A few cocktail lounges feature small combos and the major hotels have Happy Hours with local variety artists.

During the dry season, folk dancing in native costumes can be seen at the picturesque ruins of Old Panama and in some interior towns. A number of small fairs and festivals are held in the provinces at various times during the year. The ATLAPA Convention Center attracts a few big name musical and dance groups; most of the productions charge big-city prices for tickets.

Social Activities

Ample opportunities exist for social contact with both Panamanians and American residents of Panama and the American civilian and military population in the canal area. Many resident Americans play important roles in business and professional circles.

There are a number of social, vocational and fraternal organizations in the canal area. The Panama Audubon Society offers unique bird and nature study opportunities, and a Junior Audubon Society was established in 1986 to sponsor monthly outings and activities for children ages nine and over. The "Who's New" is another active and well-organized club where Americans may meet and mix with people of other nationalities. This club offers a book study group, children's play groups, bridge, tennis and a variety of other activities in addition to monthly coffees.

Extracurricular activities for school age children include Boy and Girl Scouts and Little League sports as well as the activities organized by the Youth Recreation Centers on the military bases.

Apply the same techniques here to get to know people that you would to develop social contacts in any overseas community. While knowledge of Spanish helps considerably, many Panamanians speak English. Memberships in local international fraternal organizations such as the Lions Club and Rotary Club are available.

OTHER CITIES

BALBOA, at the Panama Canal's Pacific entrance, is the largest town in the area formerly designated as the Canal Zone. It has a population of only 3,000, but is the administrative headquarters of the new joint Panama Canal Commission, which replaced the U.S. governing body in October 1979. An American naval base remains here, with military forces of more than 10,000. Balboa is the port for Panama City.

Situated 90 miles southwest of Panama City, **CHITRÉ** is the capital of Herrara Province. The Río de la Villa flows by, nourishing locally grown livestock and agricultural products. Chitré is a marketing center that produces ice and beverages. Transportation facilities for this city of approximately 34,700 include a road link to the Pan-American Highway and an airfield.

COLÓN is the second largest city in Panama, with a population of 141,000 (2000 est.) Located at the Caribbean entrance to the Panama Canal, Colón is situated at the northern terminus of the trans-Panama railroad. The city was founded in 1850 by Americans constructing the railroad, and was originally named Aspinwall after William H. Aspinwall, one of the builders. The name was changed to Colón ("Columbus" in Spanish), in honor of Christopher Columbus, in 1890. An important port and commercial center, Colón was made a free trade zone in 1953.

CRISTÓBAL, a suburb of Colón, is also an important port in this area. It has a population of about 12,000. Rainbow City, formerly called Silver City, with a population of 3,000, adjoins Cristóbal.

DAVID, 200 miles west of Panama City, is the fourth largest city in the country and the capital of mountainous Chiriquí Province. It dates to 1738, when gold prospectors set up camp here. David, though modern, maintains old traditions. San José Church has two bell towers—one to call to worship, another to warn against Indian attack. This major commercial area's economy depends on industries such as meatpacking, food processing, and tanning. David may be best known for the saddles and harnesses made here. The city is located near Enrique Malek Airport and had a population of roughly 103,000 in 2000.

PORTOBELO (also called Porto Bello and Puerto Bello) is located on the Caribbean side of Panama, about 20 miles northeast of Colón. Founded in 1597 just west of Christopher Columbus' earlier colony of Nombre de Dios, Portobelo lies in a banana-growing region and has an excellent harbor. Once a thriving colonial city, Portobelo was linked to Panama City by a stone highway. As a port, it sent out and received the royal Spanish fleets and was a transshipment point for Spanish Pacific riches. Portobelo declined with the building of the trans-Panama railroad and the Panama Canal, and has a population of just under 3,000 (1992 est.) Sir Francis Drake died aboard ship near here in 1596, and was buried at sea.

SANTIAGO is one of Panama's oldest cities, situated about 110 miles southwest of Panama City. The capital of Veraguas Province, it thrived in colonial times, as many historic buildings indicate. Santiago is an agricultural marketing center with local gold deposits. The municipality has an airfield and is on the Pan-American Highway. Approximately 61,000 people live in Santiago.

COUNTRY PROFILE

Geography and Climate

The Republic of Panama, occupying the isthmus connecting the North and South American continents, is situated between 77° and 83° west longitude and 7° and °30' north latitude. Covering an area of some 29,208 square miles, the Republic of Panama is slightly smaller than South Carolina. It is bounded on the north by the Caribbean Sea, on the south by the Pacific Ocean, on the east by Colombia, and on the west by Costa Rica. Due to the configuration of the isthmus, in Panama City the sun rises over the Pacific.

The Panama Canal Commission, in conjunction with a binational board of directors, operates the 43-mile canal which passes through the isthmus between the Atlantic (Caribbean) and Pacific oceans. Under the Panama Canal Treaty of 1977, the Commission will remain a U.S. Government agency until December 31, 1999, at which time the canal comes under total Panamanian control.

Panama has two well-defined regions: the Atlantic Watershed, which is covered by tropical rain forest, and the Pacific Watershed, whose narrow valleys and coastal plains receive less rainfall. Mountain ranges form the backbone of the Isthmus. Although some peaks reach 11,000 feet, the "cordillera" descends in the canal area to a height of only 290 feet.

Panama has a year-round tropical climate. During the dry season, which runs from January through April, there is only sporadic rainfall. The rainy season extends from May through December, with heaviest precipitation between September and November. The average annual rainfall in Panama City, on the Pacific side, is 69 inches; in Colon, on the Atlantic side, 128 inches. Temperatures and humidity vary only slightly between the two seasons. During the rainy months, average relative humidity is 85%; in the dry season, only 55 to 75%. The average annual temperature in Panama City is 26°C (80°F), with an average maximum of 30°C (87°F) and an average minimum of 22°C 3°F). Colon's temperature and humidity are about the same. Nearly constant year-round breezes provide some relief from the heat, especially at night.

Population

In 2000 Panama's estimated population was 2,821,085. Nearly half of the country's population is located in the province of Panama, with the next largest concentrations located in the provinces of Chiriqui and Colon. Approximately two-thirds of the population is located in these three of the country's nine provinces.

Rodrigo de Bastidas, one of the captains accompanying Columbus on his second voyage to America, discovered the Isthmus of Panama in 1502. Columbus visited Portobelo, a small bay on the Atlantic, on his fourth voyage in 1502. Panama City was founded in 1519, about 5 miles east of its present site. Because of its strategic position, Panama City became the crossroads of Spanish exploration and expansion in America.

At the time of Columbus, more than sixty Indian tribes were living on the isthmus. Today, however, Indians comprise only 6% of the population. While the majority of these are Kuna and Guaymi, a small group of Chocoe Indians remain in the southeastern part of the Darien Province.

Direct descendants of the Spaniards who colonized the country remain influential, but no longer dominate Panama's social, economic, and political life. Mixed-blooded Panamanians share prominent political and professional status with the Spanish-descendant group, and participate fully in Panama's diverse and influential social circles. Much of Panama's population is a mix of Spanish-Indian and black Hispanic ancestry. Immigrants from China, India, Europe, the Middle East, and South and Central America can be found in the growing middle class. Blacks of West Indian descent, whose ancestors provided most of the labor in digging the canal, tend to be concentrated in the provinces of Panama and Colon. While North American influence on Panama's basically Hispanic culture is evident in Panama City and Colon, the history and heritage of these distinct ethnic groups have combined to form the modern Panamanian way of life.

In the interior provinces, the ethnic makeup is more homogenous. The Spanish-Indian mixture is preponderant, and North American influence on customs and mores is relatively minor.

Spanish is the official language of the country. Although many Panamanians speak English, a working knowledge of Spanish is useful for shopping, communicating with servants, taking taxis, speaking with neighbors, and, especially, traveling in the interior.

Public Institutions

On November 28, 1821, the country declared its secession from Spain and associated itself with Colombia. This alliance existed in one form or another until November 3, 1903, when Panama was established as an independent republic.

Panama's constitution, which was adopted in 1972, provides for a representative democracy with direct popular election of the president and legislators, an independent judiciary, and a broad range of individual and civil rights. The constitution delineates the respective powers of the three branches of government, and contains extensive sections establishing broad economic, social and cultural rights and objectives for all its citizens. There have been several notable amendments. The last two, passed in 1994, abolished the Panamanian military and created an agency of the Panamanian government to deal with the reverted areas of the Panama Canal zone.

Operation Just Cause, which began on December 19th, 1989, ended years of political instability in Panama with the reinstatement of President Guillermo Endara's administration and the removal of Manuel Noriega as national leader. 1994 saw a return to free, fair, and violence-free elections for Panama, in which Ernesto Perez Balladares won the Presidency as the head of a multi-party coalition. Balladares won with only 33% of the popular vote, but his party, the Revolutionary Democratic Party (PRD), regained a near-majority in the Legislature. One of the first moves of this administration was to amend the Constitution to abolish the military, breaking with the tainted past of the Noriega era.

Legislators are chosen in a complicated process. Certain seats are granted to the party winning the plurality of the popular vote in the electoral circuits, while others are awarded by proportional representation in the more populous areas, and still others are reserved for Indian minorities. Legislators are nominated by a party and are subject to its discipline.

The 1983 constitutional reforms significantly increased the powers of the Legislative Assembly relative to the other branches of government. In contrast to the situation that prevailed between 1968 and 1984, the legislature now has a significant hand in budget matters and in establishing public institutions. Legislators are able to interpellate and censor Ministers and to impeach and try Presidents and Supreme Court justices. They may override a presidential veto of approved legislation with a two-thirds majority vote. The Assembly also has the power to declare war and to grant amnesty for political crimes. In addition, it must approve the appointment of Supreme Court justices, the Attorney General, the Solicitor General or Prosecutor, and other high administrative officials.

The Executive Branch is comprised of the President of the Republic, two Vice-Presidents, and the Ministers of State, or Cabinet Secretaries. The President and Vice Presidents and other elected authorities serve five-year terms. Voting is by direct and secret ballot, and a plurality is needed for election.

The President is responsible for appointing the Cabinet, coordinating the government, and maintaining public order. Along with the Cabinet, the President approves and promulgates laws passed by the Legislature and ensures their enforcement; appoints police, provincial governors and heads of various public agencies; prepares the national budget for submission to the legislature and conducts the country's foreign affairs.

The President, Vice Presidents, and Ministers of State together form the Cabinet Council, which appoints the Magistrates of the Supreme Court of Justice, the Attorney General, and the Solicitor General, or Prosecutor, subject to legislative approval.

The President and Vice Presidents may be removed from office for abusing their constitutional duties, for violent actions or coercion during an electoral process, or for preventing the meeting of the Legislative Assembly. The President and Vice Presidents need not belong to the same political party.

The Judicial Branch is comprised of the Supreme Court of Justice, the Electoral- and other Tribunals. The latter are created by the Legislature, while the first two are constitutionally decreed.

Under the 1983 constitutional amendments, Supreme Court Magistrates are appointed by the Cabinet Council and confirmed by the Legislature for staggered ten-year terms, with two magistrates appointed every other year, or as present magistrates resign or retire. The nine-member court is divided into three-judge panels for civil, criminal and administrative cases.

Its decisions are final and binding. The Judicial Branch is the ultimate interpreter of the Panamanian constitution and of the constitutionality of the laws and decrees of the Executive and Legislative Branches.

A separate three-judge Electoral Tribunal oversees elections, with one member chosen by the Supreme Court, the Legislature, and the Executive, respectively. Supreme Court justices choose the magistrates who sit on other tribunals, and the magistrates in turn choose the judges who sit on the lower courts. All sitting judges are prohibited from engaging in any other employment except as law professors, and from participating in political activities, except as voters. Although the Constitution provides for the right to trial by jury, the Legislative Assembly is empowered to determine whether this right will apply in cases against the President, Supreme Court Justices or members of the Legislative Assembly.

The Public Ministry, or Attorney General's office, is separate from the Ministry of Government and Justice and is constitutionally a part of the Judicial Branch. The Attorney General is appointed for a 10-year term. The Constitution mandates setting aside at least 2% of the annual government income for the Judicial Branch, thereby establishing its financial independence from the Legislature and the Executive. The Attorney General also oversees Panama's criminal police investigative agency, the Judicial Technical Police (PTJ).

Panama is a civil law country, with most law created by legislative codes rather than judicial decision. In 1983, the Legislature enacted new criminal and administrative codes. Implementation of some of these reforms has been delayed, however, for budgetary reasons.

Panamanian Public Forces. On December 20, 1989, the former Panamanian Defense Forces (PDF) were neutralized by U.S. armed

forces during Operation Just Cause and, over the next several days, were diminished as an effective military force. As a result, the PDF was disbanded.

Panama no longer desires a military, and in 1994 the Constitution was amended, abolishing the standing army. The Panamanian Public Forces (PPF), a civilian law enforcement organization comprised of police, air, and sea services was created in the wake of Operation Just Cause. It drew heavily on the ranks of the former PDF because of the urgent requirement to reestablish law and order throughout Panama.

The PPF, the Panamanian civil police force, remains Panama's national security force. Challenged by rising international crime and narco-trafficking activity, the PPF continues to adapt to Panama's security concerns. Its efforts in this direction are aided by the U.S. Department of Justice, as well as other agencies. Resource limits are placing financial constraints on the PPF's ability to face up to dynamic crime challenges.

The Panamanian National Police (PNP) is charged with maintaining law and order nationwide. Directed by a civilian attorney, the PNP falls under the control of the Minister of Government and Justice. The police draw heavy criticism from opposition groups and the media for a variety of reasons related to its own transitional problems. The PNP still has no organic law upon which to establish itself firmly. In the meantime, and with U.S. assistance, it strives to build confidence, establish institutional roots, and—most importantly—serve the Panamanian public.

The Panama Canal Treaty. The Panama Canal Treaty was negotiated by four different U.S. Administrations over a period of thirteen years. This treaty, along with a separate treaty pertaining to the neutrality of the Canal, and a host of ancillary agreements, was signed on September 7, 1977. The U.S. Senate gave its consent to ratification of the Canal Treaty on April 18, 1978.

As a result of the treaties, control of the Canal is presently in the process of being turned over to the Government of Panama. On December 31, 1999 Panama assumed ownership of and full operational responsibility for the Canal. The Panama Canal Commission, which operates the Canal, is a U.S. Government agency; however, its administrator is Panamanian.

The Department of Defense, under the terms of the Carter-Torrijos Treaty of 1977, is in the process of withdrawing U.S. forces from Panama. This process is scheduled to be completed by the year 2000. The U.S. military drawdown will include the closure of U.S. Military PX and Commissary facilities, Gorgas Hospital, DODDS schools and other social facilities and services to which embassy personnel now have access.

In 1994 the newly elected government amended the Constitution to create the Interoceanic Regional Authority (ARI) to plan for and implement the reversion of all lands formerly belonging to the U.S.

The U.S. Embassy in Panama has the responsibility of ensuring that the treaties and their related agreements are carried out smoothly and effectively and to ensure that the rights of the U.S. Government and of American citizens in Panama are respected.

Arts, Science, and Education

Panama's intellectual and cultural life largely revolves around activities sponsored by the Instituto Nacional de Cultura (INAC), the National Concert Association, and, from time to time, the University of Panama. INAC sponsors the National Theater, School of Dance, School of Plastic Arts, Symphony Orchestra, and Ballet.

Architecture is rich and varied, ranging from colonial to modern in private homes, public buildings, commercial office buildings, and high rise condominiums.

A fairly active art colony is to be found here, and several Panamanian artists have achieved international recognition. Accomplishments in music, drama, dance, and literature have been less notable in the last few years.

In the Canal area, research projects conducted at Gorgas Hospital (renowned for its work in tropical medicine), by the Middle America Research Unit of the National Institutes of Health, the Smithsonian Institution's Tropical Research Institute on Barro Colorado Island, and the Gorgas Memorial Institute are of international import. And, of course, the Panama Canal represents one of the greatest engineering feats of modern times.

Panamanians have historically attached great importance to education. This is reflected in its literacy rate of 83%—one of the highest in Latin America. There are a number of very good private schools in the country. Many graduates of the Instituto Nacional, a public school known throughout the country, have subsequently entered Panamanian political life. The Ministry of Education is working hard to improve instructional facilities and teacher preparation throughout the country.

The University of Panama consists of a main campus in Panama City and branches in three provincial capitals. Total enrollment is approximately 45,000. The Technological University of Panama, also based in Panama City, has branches in seven provinces and an enrollment of 8,000. A private Catholic university, Santa Maria la Antigua, has an enrollment of 4,500. American officers receive a cordial welcome at these universities, and many opportunities exist for exchanges and cooperative programs. Instruction is in Spanish.

The Panama Canal College, a two-year institution linked to the U.S. Department of Defense, is open to all qualified individuals. Several other U.S. institutions, including Nova, Florida State and Oklahoma universities, also offer courses in Panama. Instruction in these universities and at the Panama Canal College is in English, and course credits can be transferred to institutions in the United States.

Commerce and Industry

Panama's economy is based primarily on a well-developed services sector that accounts for 76.5% of GDP. Services include the Panama Canal, banking, insurance, government, the Colon Free Zone, and the transisthmian oil pipeline. Manufacturing, mining, utilities, and construction together account for 16.5% of GDP. Manufacturing is principally geared to production of items such as processed foods, clothing, chemical products, and construction materials for the domestic market. Agriculture, forestry, and fisheries account for the remaining 7% of GDP. Principal primary products include bananas, shrimp, sugar, coffee, meat, dairy products, tropical fruits, rice, corn, and beans. The sectors of the Panamanian economy with the greatest potential for substantial growth are mining, tourism, and maritime services.

From 1968 until 1989, Panama was governed by a military regime which implemented a statist plan of economic development. The government nationalized various private enterprises and instituted price controls on many goods, some of which still exist today. In 1990 the newly reinstated democratic government embarked on a reform program to liberalize trade and modernize government operations. These reforms were diluted, however, by entrenched special interest groups.

In 1994 a new government was elected and took office with an even more ambitious program of reforms, including GATT/WTO accession and labor code reforms. The Government of Panama has recently taken initial steps toward privatization of the state-owned telecommunications company and has revoked the government-owned electricity utility's monopoly on electricity generation. Reform of the national labor code, although one of this administration's top priorities, is being met with strong opposition by the various labor organizations.

The use of the U.S. dollar as Panama's currency means that fiscal policy is the government's principal macroeconomic policy instrument. Because Panama does not issue its own currency, government spending and investment are strictly bound by tax and non-tax revenues and the government's ability to borrow.

Panama Canal business rose in 1994 over the previous year. Ocean-going transits increased 2.6% to 12,671 or 34.7 vessels daily, and net tonnage, on which tolls are assessed, jumped 7.9%. Toll revenues rose 3.1% to US$425 million. The near-term outlook is for continued moderate to strong growth in both tonnage and toll revenue projected for 1995 and 1996. Work on expanding the canal's capacity by widening the Gaillard Cut through the continental divide continues and numerous other maintenance and upgrade projects are constantly in progress.

The development of areas reverting to Panama under the Panama Canal Treaties will present many opportunities for the Government of Panama, as well as investors. Projects in tourism, industry, and environmental areas will be possible. The exact nature of these projects will be determined by a development plan which is being prepared by Panama's Interoceanic Regional Authority (ARI).

The Colon Free Zone is the largest of its kind in Latin America and rivals Hong Kong in overall activity. Total imports to the Free Zone reached US$5.0 billion in 1994, an increase of 11.5% per 1993. Free Zone trade is expected to show solid

Ships in Moraflores Locks, Panama

growth during 1995 as it has already made many of the adjustments necessary to deal with market liberalization in Latin America. U.S. exports to the free zone totaled approximately US$370 million in 1994. The free zone's contribution to real GDP increased to 9.2% in 1994.

Transportation
Local
Taxi service is readily available and generally adequate. City buses are often very poorly maintained however, and riding them is not recommended for safety and security reasons.

Regional
Panama has two major highways. The Transisthmian Highway links Panama City to Colon. A Branch of the Inter-American Highway extends from the Costa Rican border to the town of Chepo, about 35 miles beyond Panama City. Both roads are two-lane and paved. There is also a recently finished road between Chepo and Colombia. Streets within Panama City and Colon are adequate. Many are subject to flooding during the rainy season.

American Airlines and Continental Airlines, COPA, and other major foreign carriers operate daily flights to the United States and other parts of the world from Panama's Tocumen International Airport. All flights to or from Panama enter and exit the U.S. from either Houston or Miami. AERO-PERLAS and ALAS-CHIRICANAS are local carriers that provide service to Panama's provinces, Contadora and the San Blas Islands. These flights operate from Paitilla Airport, a ten-minute drive from the city center.

Communications
Telephone and Telegraph
Telephone service in Panama City is good, although in some sections of the city residents must wait long periods for initial installation of a telephone.

Long-distance service is available to all parts of the country. Facilities are excellent for overseas calls to the United States (with direct dialing from Panama City) and to other parts of the world via radio or satellite. Rates vary depending on country and time zone.

Telegram facilities are excellent and provide worldwide service.

Radio and TV
There are both English and Spanish-language AM and FM radio programs and commercial TV stations

(including one educational channel), some of which broadcast sporting events and reruns of American feature programs and movies (all dubbed).

The Southern Command Network (SCN), an affiliate of the Armed Forces Radio and Television Service, broadcasts on AM and FM radio in English on a 24-hour basis. SCN-TV presents news programs, sports events, old movies, reruns of U.S. feature programs and Saturday-morning children's programs in English. SCN-TV broadcasts daily: the weekly schedule is published in the base newspaper, The Tropic Times. American variety and series programs are broadcast in English. Live TV coverage via satellite of some news programs or sporting and special events is also provided. The station broadcasts Monday through Sunday from 6:00 a.m. until midnight, plus additional late night movies on weekends.

Cable TV is available in Panama City and provides a variety of satellite programming, including the Disney Channel, HBO/Showtime, CNN, and ESPN. There is usually an installation fee; monthly fees are upwards of $40.

Local cinemas are comparable in quality to those in the U.S., yet prices are much lower. First run movies are shown in English with Spanish subtitles. Local video stores rent both VHS and Beta tapes at reasonable prices comparable to stateside, usually with Spanish subtitles.

Newspapers, Magazines, and Technical Journals

Six Spanish-language newspapers (including three tabloids) are published on a daily basis. The English-language international edition of The *Miami Herald* is published locally.

Airmail editions of *USA Today* are available on the bases. Copies of the *New York Times* and the *Wall Street Journal* are occasionally available at the major hotels. Along with the *Washington Post,* they are also

available through subscription, but rates are higher than in the U.S. Home delivery of U.S. newspapers is available, but delivery is one day late.

The Latin American issues of *Time* and *Newsweek* are sold at most newsstands, drug stores, and in major hotels, usually within days of their domestic editions in the United States. Other U.S. magazines (on topics such as cars, sports, and outdoor hobbies) are available on the bases. Prices are comparable to those in the United States, although tax must be paid when purchased off the bases.

Health and Medicine

Medical Facilities

Health care services for U.S. citizens residing in Panama are generally excellent. Nearly all medical and surgical specialties are represented. Many of the local dentists and orthodontists are considered to be on a par with those in the United States, and prices are slightly lower than U.S. prices.

In conjunction with the U.S. military drawdown in Panama Gorgas Hospital is scheduled to close in 1998; however Paitilla Hospital is up to U.S. standards. Many Americans have been very pleased with the quality of care received there.

Many standard medications are available from Gorgas Hospital or from local pharmacies in Panama.

Community Health

For a tropical region, Panama's community health standards are good. With normal precautions one can avoid most health hazards. The cities of Panama and Colon have potable and fluoridated water supplies, although water should be boiled before drinking for 24 hours following water cutoffs. Travelers to more remote parts of the country should boil their water or use a water purifier. Milk is pasteurized and bottled under sanitary conditions, as are locally produced beers and other

beverages. Domestically produced meats are packaged and sold under generally sanitary conditions in the larger grocery stores. Local fruits and vegetables should be thoroughly washed before eating. Fresh fish and seafood are plentiful and inexpensive. Between the local markets and bakeries there is little one cannot find in Panama.

Trash is collected daily in most areas of Panama City. Roaches, ants, and other insects as well as mice and rats are ever present in this tropical climate, but, with vigilance, they can be kept under control. Until recently, Panama City had an active mosquito control program.

Common medical complaints include colds and other upper respiratory infections. Sinus and asthmatic conditions may be aggravated by the humidity, molds, and pollens. Swimmer's ear is a common complaint among both children and adults.

More serious illnesses such as malaria and yellow fever are virtually nonexistent in Panama City, but persons travelling to the interior of the country may be at risk. Hepatitis is considered a significant health threat, and individuals are encouraged to keep their gamma globulin inoculations current. Tuberculosis is endemic and common among residents of the poorer areas. Dengue fever cases are on the increase.

Preventive Measures

Persons being assigned to Panama should ensure that their Yellow Fever, Typhoid, and Tetanus/ Diphtheria immunizations, as well as a TB skin test are current. Hepatitis-A vaccine or gamma globulin is also recommended.

Immunization requirements for Panamanian schools vary. The Department of Defense schools require the following immunizations:

Oral Polio Vaccine—3 doses of Trivalent, at least one of which was administered after the fourth birthday.

Diphtheria/Tetanus/Pertussis*—3 doses, given singly or in combination, at least one dose of which was administered after fourth birthday and the last dose was given within ten years.

Measles (Rubeola)
Mumps
Rubella—1 dose of live attenuated vaccine given singly or in combination on or after 15 months of age. Individuals immunized after one year of age but before 15 months need not be reimmunized.

*Pertussis immunization is not required for individuals after their seventh birthday.

NOTES FOR TRAVELERS

Passage, Customs & Duties
U.S. citizens are encouraged to obtain a U.S. passport before traveling to Panama. Although entry into Panama is permitted with any proof of U.S. citizenship (such as a certified birth certificate or a Naturalization Certificate) and official photo identification (such as a driver's license), travelers may experience difficulties entering and/or exiting Panama when not in possession of a valid U.S. passport. Panamanian law requires that travelers must either purchase a tourist card from the airline serving Panama or obtain a visa from a Panamanian embassy or consulate before traveling to Panama. Further information may be obtained from the Embassy of Panama, 2862 McGill Terrace, N.W., Washington, D.C. 20009, tel. (202) 483-1407, or the Panamanian consulates in Atlanta, Chicago, Houston, Los Angeles, Miami, New Orleans, New York, Philadelphia or Tampa.

U.S. citizens transiting the Panama Canal as passengers do not need to obtain visas, report to customs, or pay any fees. U.S. citizens piloting private craft through the canal should contact the U.S. Embassy in Panama City for details on required procedures.

Panamanian customs authorities may enforce strict regulations concerning temporary importation into or export from Panama of items such as firearms and ammunition, cultural property, endangered wildlife species, narcotics, biological material, and food products. It is advisable to contact the Embassy of Panama in Washington or one of Panama's consulates in the United States for specific information regarding customs requirements.

U.S. citizens living in or visiting Panama are encouraged to register at the Consular Section of the U.S. Embassy in Panama and obtain updated information on travel and security within Panama. The Consular Section of the U.S. Embassy is located on Panama Bay, Panama City, at Balboa Avenue and 39th Street. The international mailing address is Apartado 6959, Panama 5, Republic of Panama. The U.S. mailing address is U.S. Embassy Panama, Department of State, Washington, D.C. 20521-9100. The telephone number of the Consular Section is 011-507-207-7000/7030 (after hours, 011-507-207-7000); fax 011-507-207-7278; web site http://www.orbi.net/usispan/ and e-mail is usispan@pty.com.

Pets
Panama requires a veterinary certificate of health and certification of vaccination against rabies, distemper, hepatitis, leptospirosis, parvovirus (dogs) and feline panleucopenia (cats) for each arriving pet. Each certificate must be authenticated by a Panamanian consul to be acceptable. This can be done by sending your pet's health certification to the following address for a consular stamp. There is a fee for this service.

Consulate General of Panama
2862 McGill Terrace NW
Washington, D.C. 20008
202-483-8413/8416(fax)

All incoming pets are placed in quarantine. If your pet arrives on a commercial flight to Tocumen Airport it must be examined by a Panamanian vet at the airport prior to being moved to quarantine. If your pet arrives on Friday it may not be examined and released until Monday. There is a transportation fee of $13.50, as well as admission and importation permit fees.

The following documents are required for your pet to enter Panama: a health certificate for the animal (good for only ten days), a rabies vaccination certificate, a stamp from a Panamanian Consulate as outlined above, and a copy of your travel orders. These documents are to be attached, in an envelope, to the outside of the animal's cage.

Currency, Banking, and Weights and Measures
The official currency of Panama is the Balboa (B/) which is on par value to the U.S. dollar. The Balboa exists only in coin form and, in Panama, is interchangeable with U.S. coins. The official paper currency of Panama are U.S. dollar bills.

Both the U.S. system of weights and measures and the metric system are used in Panama. Speed limits are posted in miles per hour in some places, kilometers per hour in other places, some signs give both miles and kilometers per hour, and in many areas the limits are not posted.

Complete banking facilities are available at many banks in Panama City, including branches of Chase Manhattan, Citibank, Bank of Boston and American Express. Many local retail outlets accept personal checks drawn on U.S, banks.

You can purchase or cash travelers checks locally without difficulty. To deposit or cash U.S. checks in Panamanian banks, a service charge is assessed. Major U.S. credit cards are widely accepted in shops, hotels and restaurants.

LOCAL HOLIDAYS

Jan. 1 . . . . New Year's Day
Jan. 9 . . . . Day of
            Mourning
Feb/Mar . . . . Carnival*
Mar/Apr. . . . . Good Friday*
Mar/Apr. . . . . Easter*
May 1 . . . . Panama Labor
            Day
Nov. 3 . . . . Independence
            Day from
            Colombia
Nov. 4 . . . . Flag Day
Nov.10. . . . . Uprising of Los
            Santos
Nov. 28 . . . . Independence
            Day from Spain
Dec. 8 . . . . Mother's Day
Dec. 25 . . . . Christmas Day
*variable

RECOMMENDED READING

The following titles are provided as a general indication of the material published on this country. The Department of State does not endorse unofficial publications.

Abbot, W. *Panama and The Canal* (1976). Gordon Press Publications.

Anderson, Charles L.G. *Old Panama and Castilla del Oro. Sudwarth: 1911 0.*Narrative history of the discovery, conquest, and settlement by the Spaniards of Panama, Darien, Veraguas, and other parts of the New World.

Anguizola, Gustavo *Phillipe Bueneau-Varilla: The Man Behind The Panama Canal* (1980). 480p. Nelson-Hall, Inc.

Avery, R. *America's Triumph at Panama (1976).* Gordon Press Publications.

Bair, Frank E., ed. *Countries of the World and Their Leaders Yearbook 1993.* Detroit, MI: Gale Research, 1993.

Barry, Tom. *Panama: A Country Guide.* Albuquerque, NM: Inter-

Hemispheric Education Resource Center, 1990.

Behar, D., and G. Harris. *Invasion: The American Destruction of the Noriega Regime in Panama.* Los Angeles, CA: Americas Group, 1990.

Bennett, Wendell C. *Ancient Arts of the Andes* (1954). Museum of Modern Art, New York. This book discusses the Indian art of Panama which is related to the pre-Columbian art of the Andes.

Biesanz, John and Mavis. *The People of Panama (1955).* Columbia University Press: New York. A readable introduction to the people and an analysis of the social conditions in Panama and the canal area.

Billard, Jules B. "Panama, Link Between Oceans and Continents." (March 1970) *National Geographic Magazine.* Vol. 137, pp. 402-440.

Chidsey, Donald Barr. *The Panama Canal, an Informal History.* (1970) Crowan: New York.

Cobb, Charles A. Jr. "Panama, Ever at the Crossroad." (April 1986). *National Geographic Magazine.*

Coniff, Michael L. *Black Labor on a White Canal: Panama. 1904-1981.*

———. *Panama and the United States: The Forced Alliance.* Athens, GA: University of Georgia Press, 1992.

Crane, Philip M. *Surrender in Panama: the case against the treaty* (1978). 180p. Green Hill Publications.

Dinges, John. *Our Man in Panama: The Shrewd Rise & Brutal Fall of Manuel Noriega.* New York: Random House, 1991.

Donnelly, Thomas, et al. *Operation Just Cause: The Invasion of Panama.* New York: Free Press, 1991.

Du Val, Miles P. *And the Mountains Will Move.* (1947) Stanford University Press: Stanford, California. Scholarly account of the digging of the Panama Canal from the start of the French effort

through the successful American achievement.

Flanagan, Edward M., Jr. *Battle for Panama: Inside Operation Just Cause.* McLean, VA: Brasseys, 1993.

Gordon, Burton *A Panama Forest and Shore* (1983). Boxwood Press.

Hogan, J. Michael. *The Panama Canal in Americas Politics: Domestic Advocacy and the Evolution of Policy* (1986). 304p. Southern Illinois University Press.

Howarth, David A. *Panama: 400 Years of Dreams and Cruelty* (Also called The Golden Isthmus.) McGraw: New York, 1966. Readable history of the isthmus from Balboa's exploration in 1513 to 1964.

Jorden, William J. *Panama Odyssey*

Keeler, Cylde E. *Land of the Moon Children: The Primitive San Blas Culture in Flux* (1956). University of Georgia: Athens, Georgia. An account of the findings of Dr. Keeler after four summers spent with the Cuna Indians in the San Blas Islands.

Keeler, Cylde E. *Secrets of the Cuna Earth Mother: A Contemporary Study of Ancient Religions* (1960). Exposition: New York. 1st ed. Notes on the religion and lives of the Cuna Indians and a comparison of the religion with some in the Far East.

Keller, Ulrich, ed. *The Building of the Panama Canal in Historic Photography* (1983). 176p. Dove Macmillan Publishing Co. Inc.

Kempe, Frederick. *Divorcing the Dictator: America's Bungled Affair with Noriega* (1990). 352p. Putnam Publishing Group.

Koster, R.M., and Guillermo Sanchez. *In the Time of the Tyrants: Panama: 1968-1990.* New York: Norton, 1990.

LaFeber, Walter. *The Panama Canal: The Crisis in Historical Perspective.* New York: Oxford University Press, 1990.

Langstaff, Eleanor D. *Panama* (1982). 184p. ABC-Clio, Inc.

Liss, Sheldon B. *The Canal: Aspects of The United States-Panamanian Relations* (1967). University of Notre Dame Press: Notre Dame, Indiana. A history of the relations of the two nations from 1903 to 1966, with emphasis on the post-World War II years.

Mack, Gerstle. *The Land Divided* (1944). Knopf: New York Documented history of the Panama Canal and other isthmian canal projects, embracing the entire concept of the interoceanic communication of Panama.

Marsh, Richard O. *White Indians of Darien* (1934). Putnam: New York. Account of an exploratory trip in the Darien.

McCullough, David. *Path Between the Seas* (1977). Simon & Schuster: New York,. Perhaps the best book written on the construction of the canal.

Melditz, Sandra W. and Dennis M. Hanratty, eds. *Panama: A Country Study* (1989). 4th ed. 1989. USGPO.

Mellander, Gustavo Adolfo. The United States in Panamanian Politics: *The Intriguing Formative Years.* The Interstate Printers & Publishers, Inc.: Danville, Ill., 1971.

Minter, John E. *The Chagres, River of Westward Passage* (1948). Rinehart: New York. The Chagres River as it influenced the history of the Isthmus of Panama.

Moore, Evelyn. *Sancocho* (1947). Star & Herald Co.: Panama, 2d ed. Stories and sketches of Panama. Drawings by Jan Koerber.

Navarrete Talavera, Ela. *Panama: Invasion o Revolucion* (1990) 356p. Group Editorial Planeta.

Nyrop, Richard F., ed. *Panama: a Country Study* (1990). 3rd. ed. 300p. USGPO.

Oliver, Carl R. *Panama's Canal.* New York: Franklin Watts, 1990.

Panama Canal Company. *The Panama Canal Fiftieth Anniversary* (1964). Panama Canal Information Office: La Boca, Canal Zone. The story of a great conquest. This book celebrates the 50th anniversary of the operation of the Panama Canal.

Pirer, Rene. *The Fifteen Wonders of the World* (1961). Random: New York. A history of the Panama Canal. Translated by Margaret Crossland.

Priesley, George. *Military Government and Popular Participation in Panama* (1985). 200p. WestView Publishing Co.

Ropp, Steve C. *Panamanian Politics: From guarded nation to National Guard* (1982). 174p. Greenwood Press Inc.

St. George, Judith. *The Panama Canal: Gateway to the World.* New York: Putnam Publishing Group, 1989.

Sanchez Borbon, Guillermo and Richard Kosyer. *In the Time of the Tyrants* (1990). Norton.

Scranton, Margaret E. *The Noriega Years: U.S.-Panamanian Relations, 1981-1990.* Boulder, CO: Lynne Rienner, 1991.

Simon, Maron. The Panama Affair (1971). Scribner: New York An account of the French Isthmian Canal venture.

Summ, G. Harvey and Tom Kelly, eds. The Good Neighbors: America, Panama, and 1977 Canal Treaties (1988). 135p. Ohio University Press.

The Americas Group Invasion: The American Destruction of the Noriega Regime in Panama (1990). The Americas Group.

The South American Handbook. Rand McNally, Chicago, Illinois. Issued annually, this handbook provides detailed current information on central and South American and Caribbean countries.

Vazquez, Ana M. *Panama.* Chicago, IL: Childrens Press, 1991.

Wali, Alaka. *Kilowats and Crisis: A Study of Development and Social Change in Panama* (1988). 250p. WestView Publishing Co.

Weeks, John. *Panama: Made in the U.S.A.* New York: Monthly Review Press, 1990.

World Bank. *Panama: Structural Change and Growth Prospects* (1985). 384p. World Bank.

Zimbalist, Andrew, and John Weeks. *Panama at the Crossroads: Economic Development & Political Change in the Twentieth Century.* Berkeley, CA: University of California Press, 1991.

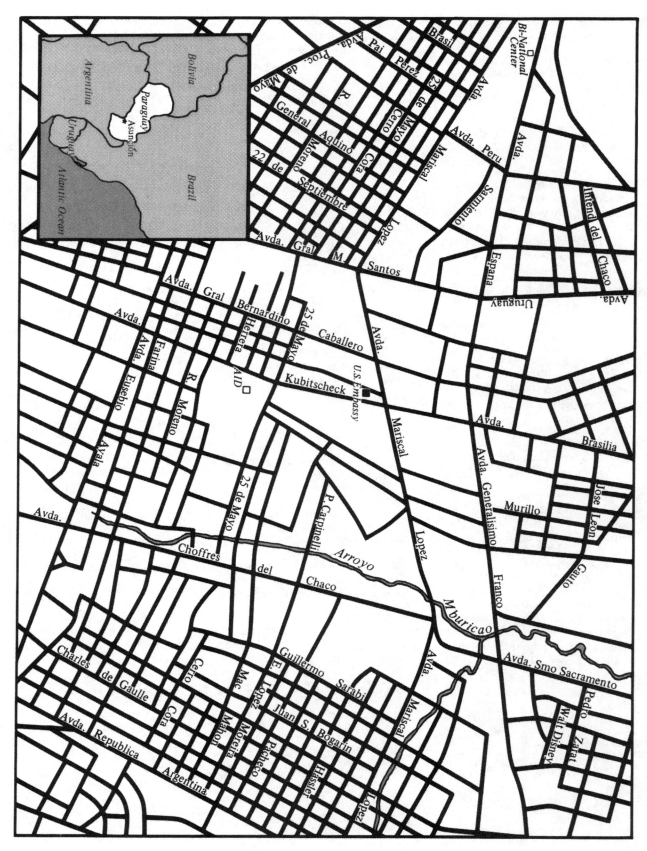

Asunción, Paraguay

PARAGUAY

Republic of Paraguay

Major Cities:
Asunción, Encarnación

Minor Cities:
Caacupé, Caazapá, Ciudad Del Este, Concepción, Coronel Oviedo, Luque, Pedro Juan Caballero, Pilar, Villarrica

INTRODUCTION

Located in the heart of South America, Paraguay is a landlocked, agricultural country about the size of California. The Parana-Paraguay River system is Paraguay's commercial access to the outside world. The eastern section of Paraguay, where most of the population lives, consists of rolling, fertile, farming areas and grasslands. The western section, called the Chaco, is a low lying plateau covered with grassy meadows, bogs, spiny bushes, palms, and small trees. Lack of roads and navigable rivers makes much of this region inaccessible. Paraguay's climate is variable and unpredictable. It is subtropical, with summer and winter seasons opposite those in the U.S.

Older than Buenos Aires, Asuncion, the capital, has not yet lost its aura of provincialism and isolation. With profuse, colorful year-round blossoms in residential gardens and along tree-lined avenues, Asuncion retains a quiet charm. Entertainment is diverse, with ready access to the nearby countries of Brazil, Argentina, and Uruguay. Paraguayans are generally well-disposed toward Americans, and informal acquaintances can easily be made with coworkers, neighbors, and at school events. Social life, however, centers on the family and contact with outsiders is somewhat limited. The people do appreciate it when someone takes the trouble to learn their native language, Guarani.

MAJOR CITIES

Asunción

Older than Buenos Aires, Asuncion has not yet lost its aura of provincialism and isolation. Founded on August 15, 1537, and once the capital of the colonial River Plata Viceroyalty, it remains the center of Paraguayan activity. Increasing numbers of visitors (mostly from Argentina and Brazil) are attracted to Paraguay during the Southern Hemisphere winter. Modern hotels and office buildings are springing up beside weathered structures of an earlier vintage in Asuncion's bustling downtown shopping and business area. With profuse, colorful year-round blossoms in residential gardens and along tree-lined avenues, Asuncion retains a quiet charm.

Utilities

Short water outages occur occasionally in Asuncion. Laundry areas and kitchens do not always have hot water. Showers are much more common than bathtubs.

Short power outages occur occasionally. Electrical current is 220v, 50-cycle, AC. Appliances using 110v current in the U.S. need transformers. A 1,500w transformer is necessary for high wattage appliances. Do not bring electric clocks as they require an impractical conversion.

Food

As an agricultural country, Paraguay offers ample locally produced fruits and vegetables as well as beef, pork, and poultry. Staple items and processed foods are not offered in the variety found in the U.S. Foods that are imported or not produced in large quantities can be expensive.

Several large markets in the city sell a variety of seasonal fresh fruits and vegetables, beef, pork, chicken, freshwater fish, flowers, plants, herbs, and a jumble of household items.

Meat is also sold in small butcher shops and supermarkets. It is inspected but not always refrigerated and is sold freshly butchered. Beef is plentiful, but the variety of cuts is limited. Poultry, pork, hot dogs, cold cuts, and some good freshwater fish are available. Veal is uncommon, and lamb is rare. Supermarkets sell some precut, packaged meat and poultry.

Good-sized supermarkets, scattered throughout the city, compare on a smaller scale to U.S. supermarkets. They also carry wines and liquors, and depending on size, some kitchenware, hardware, toys, stationery supplies, and clothing.

Most processed food is imported. Since Paraguayans depend primarily on fresh foods, the selection of canned fruits, vegetables, soups, or meals-in-a-can is small. Similarly, their tastes do not demand great variety in snack foods, convenience foods, sauces, and salad dressings. Paraguayan cheeses and those most commonly imported are bland types. More robust and highly flavored cheeses are imported in small amounts. Either skim or whole milk is available with a long shelf life and does not need refrigeration until ready to use. Yogurt is available in limited flavors and cottage cheese and cream cheese are available at times.

No canned pet food is sold, although dry pet food is available. You can buy liver and kidneys from local neighborhood pickup trucks or butcher shops. Mix it with kitchen scraps, for an inexpensive, yet nourishing, pet food.

The selection of vegetables has expanded over the years due to the influxes of agricultural technologies brought in by Japanese and Taiwanese immigrants. You can find a good selection of fresh green vegetables in local oriental markets or the Tuesday agro shopping fair in the Mariscal Lopez Shopping Center.

No home is more than a couple of blocks from a neighborhood grocery store ("dispensa"), which stocks a little of everything. Bakeries offer a good assortment of white and brown bread and rolls. Specialty shops sell cakes and pastries, cold cuts and sausages, and ice cream. Yard area permitting, a home garden can add diversity to seasonal menus. Insects can be a minor problem, but most plants grow quickly and well.

Frozen foods are not normally available in Asuncion.

Clothing

Styles are much the same as in the U.S., but are influenced by the long, hot summers and short, cold winters. Although almost any article of clothing can be found in Asuncion, the choice is somewhat limited by U.S. standards. The search can be time-consuming for those unfamiliar with Asuncion's local shops. Children's clothing is also available here. Bring underwear, socks and hosiery, diapers and baby clothes, and bathing suits. Jeans are popular for school and casual wear.

Dressmakers and tailors can make formal gowns, dresses, skirts, and blouses for women; shorts, sunsuits, and other clothing for children; suits, slacks, and jackets for men. A good selection of fine wool, cotton, and dressy fabrics can be found locally, whereas greater diversity in synthetic and wash-and-wear fabrics is available in the U.S. Asuncion's cobblestone streets are hard on all footwear; women's shoes with low or thick heels are practical. Sandals are popular in summer, when stockings are not usually worn.

Woolen or other warm clothing is needed during the June to September winter for the many cold, damp days and nights. Sweaters or jackets that can be layered or removed are particularly useful. Bring cotton flannel sleepwear and warm slippers. Umbrellas and raincoats are necessary.

Locally made embroidered shirts, blouses, and dresses of fine cotton

fabric called "aho-poi" are a good and useful buy in Asuncion.

Men: Bring a good supply of lightweight suits, sport coats, slacks, and shirts. Casual clothes may be worn to all restaurants and to some cultural events. In Paraguay's short cold season, some winter weight wool suits, sport coats, and slacks will be useful.

Women: Loose fitting cotton daytime dresses are more comfortable in summer heat than nylon and certain other synthetics such as polyester knit. Dressy cottons or other washable fabrics are suitable for casual evening wear. For more formal events, simple to elaborate cocktail dresses are appropriate. Heavier weight dresses are needed for winter wear; jackets or stoles are useful. Hats or gloves are seldom worn, but occasionally a hat to shield the sun's rays or leather gloves to ward off the morning cold are practical.

Supplies and Services

Imported medicines, drugs, toiletries, and cosmetics are available locally, but can be expensive. Certain U.S. brand toiletries, such as Johnson's Baby Powder, are made under license in Argentina and Brazil and are less expensive than those produced in the U.S. If generic brands satisfy you, you will find most everything here.

U.S.-type hardware items and tools, including garden tools, are available locally but are higher in price and limited in variety. Lovely nanduti lace or "aho-poi" embroidered placemats and tablecloths, guest towels, and doilies are handmade in Paraguay and sold at reasonable prices. Items difficult to find or expensive locally are: books, stationery, greeting cards in English, cocktail napkins, party supplies, special sewing or craft materials, games, toys, sports equipment, fishing gear, pool supplies, flashlights, anti-mildew products, and airtight storage containers.

Tailors and dressmakers, cobblers, and barbershops offer satisfactory services at reasonable prices. Most hairdressers are small-scale neighborhood establishments unlike U.S.-style salons. Several higher quality salons offer many services at better prices than those in the U.S. Prices and quality vary. Drycleaning is acceptable. Laundry is generally done at home; hotel laundry facilities are expensive. Inexpensive, good quality work is done on picture framing, furniture upholstering, and drapery making. Attractive wicker and rattan furniture is made locally. Appliance and auto repair shops are reasonable but often do not meet U.S. standards and may not have parts. When thinking of items to bring with you for your car, remember filters, belts, spark plugs, and extra tires. Caterers supply food and equipment for large parties.

Domestic Help

Well-trained domestic help is rare, and good cooks are hard to find. Any help will probably speak Spanish and Guarani, rarely English.

Large families may have a maid and a nursemaid. Laundresses, cleaning ladies, or gardeners usually come once or twice a week. Wages do not represent the total expense to the employer. Food is provided to day workers, and live-in servants may receive food or allowances. Most houses have quarters for one live-in servant; the employer supplies furniture, bed, and bath linens. Work dresses, uniforms, and routine medical aid may also be provided. After completing 1 continuous year of service, servants receive a 13th-month bonus (Christmas bonus). For employees who work less than 1 year, a bonus will be established taking 1/12 of the total amount of all salaries paid during the calendar year. Under Paraguayan Law 1085, domestics-including regularly employed cooks, maids, laundresses, gardeners, chauffeurs, and nursemaids-must be covered by social security. It is not elective with either the employer or the domestic. All servants must have a medical examination at the employer's expense.

Religious Activities

Since most Paraguayans are Roman Catholic, Spanish-language Catholic churches abound. Mass is regularly held in English on Sundays and holidays for English-speaking Catholics by American priests of the Redemptorist Order. The Anglican (Episcopal) Church and Baptist Fellowship hold services and Sunday school in English every Sunday. Anglican and Baptist churches also have services in Spanish, as do the Free Will Methodists, Assemblies of God, and Seventh-day Adventist. The Lutheran and Mennonite churches offer German-language services. Services in Spanish can also be found at the Church of Jesus Christ of the Latter-day Saints (Mormon), Jewish Synagogue (which also has a social club), and the Russian Orthodox Church.

Education

Many primary age school children attend the American School of Asuncion, accredited by the Southern Association of Colleges and Schools. The American School offers kindergarten through grade 12. Separate kindergartens for 4- and 5-year olds are available, but the education allowance only pays for the latter. First graders must have turned 6 before the opening of school in August.

Instruction is in English, but Spanish is taught as a native language, beginning with K-5. Both the U.S. standard and the Paraguayan curriculums are offered. Almost all teachers, except Spanish instructors, are U.S. citizens and U.S. certified. The school has no speech therapist. Some remedial tutoring is provided.

The school teaches standard U.S. curriculum subjects-language arts, math, science, and social science. General electives include French, Italian, special Spanish, Latin, German, economics, computer, creative writing, photography, government, sociology, biology, music appreciation, art, typing, and PE. Home economics and shop courses are not offered. The school has occupied its building since 1963 and has been

expanding and improving the facilities since then. The school has a library, a science lab, a dark room, a tennis court, an art room, locker/shower facilities, a canteen, and a computer room.

Hours are 8 am to 3 pm for all grades. Hot lunches are available in the canteen for children who do not bring their lunches. Lunch boxes and vacuum bottles are sometimes available locally.

The two-semester school year ends in July and begins in August, with a 2-week break between school years. A 2 1/2-month midterm vacation lasts from December through mid-February. The school observes all Paraguayan and some U.S. holidays.

The Asuncion Christian Academy is an interdenominational school sponsored by the evangelical missions in Paraguay. It provides Christian academic education to English-speaking children from pre-kindergarten through grade 12. Instruction is in English, but Spanish is also taught. The school calendar is similar to that of the American School. Classes are from 7:15 am to 12:30 pm. Teachers must have U.S. certification; materials and methods are U.S. based.

Another option is the Pan American International School, also accredited by the Southern Association of Colleges and Schools. The PAIS offers education to students in grades K through 12. Instruction is in English. In addition to the required curriculum at PAIS, classes in drivers education and industrial arts are also available. Classes are from 8:00 am to 3:30 pm for grades 5 to 12 and 8 am to noon for kindergarten through grade 4.

Neither the American School nor the Christian Academy has a dress code.

Attendance at any other local school requires Spanish-language fluency. In some subjects, standards of the Paraguayan institutions are high, and Paraguayan students may be ahead of their American contemporaries. Curriculums naturally are geared to the local education system, with emphasis on Paraguayan history and geography. Teaching stresses rote memorization. English is sometimes taught as a foreign language.

The best private Spanish-language institution is the well-regarded Colegio Internacional. Established by the American Disciples of Christ Church, the school offers kindergarten, primary, and secondary classes. Instruction is by local teachers. English is taught as a foreign language. The extracurricular program, which includes music and sports, is excellent. The most prestigious Catholic boys school, San Jose, and the leading Catholic girls school, Santa Clara de Jesus, offer 12-year academic programs. The Santa Clara School, run by Catholic nuns, has coeducational kindergarten and primary classes, and a 4-year secondary school for girls only. The Goethe Institute, subsidized by the German Government, offers instruction in German and Spanish.

The University of Alabama at Tuscaloosa offers a Masters of Education program in the American School of Asuncion campus..

Special Educational Opportunities

Private instruction in Paraguayan harps and guitars is available. The instruments themselves are inexpensive and available locally. Piano lessons, and group ballet and Spanish dancing classes are available for children and adults.

With permission from local authorities, foreigners may attend lectures at the National University, gratis. All instruction is in Spanish. No academic credits are awarded.

Several nursery schools are available for preschool children. Only two are conducted in English, however, and the number of places in these are limited. Parents who wish to enroll their children should make a reservation well in advance. The names of some of the nursery schools are: Maria's Pre-School

(English-speaking), English Playgroup (English-speaking), and Casita de Sandy (Spanish speaking).

No special educational facilities for handicapped and learning-disabled English-speaking children exist.

Sports

Participant and spectator sports are available year-round in Asuncion. Some clubs, such as the Yacht and Golf Club and Asuncion Golf offer special rates for diplomats or waive initiation fees. The Yacht and Golf Club includes swimming, tennis, weight lifting, and squash. The American School has outdoor facilities for soccer, basketball, volleyball, and baseball, which are available to the community.

Asuncion has one bowling center with 12 automatic lanes. Rates are reasonable. Shoes may be rented for a small additional fee.

The main spectator sport in Paraguay is, of course, soccer. Rugby, basketball, volleyball, tennis, and boxing are also popular. Motorcycle and cross-country automobile races are held from time to time.

Fishing on the Paraguay River is principally for dorado, a large, fighting game fish, and several large varieties of catfish. Paraguay sponsors international fishing competitions in spring.

Popular fishing areas are Guraty, a 20-25-minute drive from Asuncion, where you can rent boats; Santa Rosa, 85 kilometers down river by boat; and Ayolas (300 kilometers south), which has a modern hotel and boat rentals. Villa Florida, a small town on the Tebicuary, a tributary of the Paraguay River, has hotel or camping facilities and boat rentals. Swift currents and an abundance of small piranas make swimming unsafe in these rivers. Fishing equipment brought with you and should include a heavy-duty rod, combination of trolling and bait-casting reel capable of holding 200 yards of 40-pound test line, large spoons, and plugs and wire leaders,

as both surubi (catfish) and dorado sometimes exceed 30-40 pounds. Motors are not usually available for rental and are expensive locally. Small boats (3-8-passenger motor launches) may be purchased locally. Garages service them. Dock-and-storage facilities are available near Asuncion, as well as at the Sajonia Club.

Most hunting is for game birds such as duck, perdiz (South American tinamdu), and doves. Crocodiles, wild boar, deer, jaguar, and puma are found in remote regions of the Chaco, but their status as endangered species means they are generally illegal to hunt. Although hunting on public land has been banned for several years to allow stocks to increase, hunting continues on many private lands. Paraguay does not require either hunting season or fishing licenses. To hunt, you must have access to private land.

For all practical purposes, big game hunting is impossible, since access to the Chaco is difficult. Bird shooting, especially perdiz, is very popular and easily accomplished, providing one gains access to a nearby "Estancia." Usually, any of the cattle ranches within 1 hour of Asuncion will have a large population of perdiz. A bird dog is a must for perdiz. The perdiz, a quail-like bird, prefers to run whenever possible. Without a dog, chasing perdiz could be futile in some areas. If you are a bird shooter, bring all your equipment, including reloading components. Although U.S.-made ammunition is very expensive, it is possible to buy Brazilian ammunition at lower cost, about like U.S. prices. Bird dogs, although available, are expensive and difficult to find. Bring your own. A 12-gauge shotgun will probably be most versatile; however, keep it light and chokes open. If you are a die-hard bird shooter, then the traditional lightweight 20 would be ideal.

Touring and Outdoor Activities

Museums and buildings of interest in Asuncion include the Ethnological and Archeological Museum, the Military History Museum, the National Pantheon, and the Casa de la Independencia. Near the Cathedral is the first seminary in Asuncion, which has several exhibits of religious artifacts, memorabilia from both wars, and some personal effects of Monsignor Bogarin, former Archbishop of Asuncion. The Bank of Asuncion has restored the former home of one of Mariscal Lopez's brothers, Benigno, and it contains an interesting historical exhibit of currency used in Paraguay. The Botanical Garden contains the Museum of Natural History and a small Indian museum as well as picnic areas, sports fields, and the zoo.

Not far from Asuncion, the town of San Lorenzo has an Indian artifacts museum and shop near the only Gothic style church in Paraguay. Capiata boasts a private mythological museum, which also has a display from the Triple Alliance and Chaco wars, and a collection of religious wooden statues carved by Indians, who had been instructed by the Franciscans. San Bernardino is Lake Ypacarai's most developed resort town with hotels, a casino, and concerts. On the other side of the lake is Aregua, which has picnic facilities and rowboat rentals. The town of Itaugua is the home of nanduti, a lace product found only in Paraguay. Every year in December pilgrims trek the 50+ km walk from Asuncion to Caacupe to see the Shrine of the Blue Virgin. Capiata also has a private mythological museum, which has a display from the Triple Alliance and Chaco wars.

Full day or weekend camping trips can be made to Pirareta Falls, Chololo Falls, and Cristal Falls, all less than 100 kilometers from Asuncion. All three have camping areas, and Chololo has a restaurant.

You will need 2 or 3 days to visit the ruins of several Jesuit mission towns in southern Paraguay. Some of the travel is on secondary, unpaved roads. Hotel accommodations are available at Encarnacion or Tirol del Paraguay, a hillside

Ann Kalosh. Reproduced by permission.

Man standing in a truck in Concepcion, Paraguay

resort. A comfortable, round-trip, 2-day ship excursion can be taken upriver to Concepcion.

The sprawling Chaco begins almost immediately northwest of Asuncion. For longer trips beyond all-weather roads, you need a four-wheel-drive vehicle, as well as camping gear, mosquito netting, and insect repellent. This area is reminiscent of the early American West with its vast open spaces, herds of cattle, and colorful cowboys. It is also a bird-watcher's paradise, and game animals abound here.

The world-famous Iguazu Falls are spectacular. The falls are located at

the juncture of the Parana and Iguazu Rivers where the Paraguayan border meets with those of Brazil and Argentina. The falls can be reached in 5 hours by car. An overnight bus can also be taken for those who wish to see the falls and return the same day. It is here that the International Friendship Bridge crosses the Parana to Brazil. At the falls, accommodations in all three countries range from camping areas to luxury hotels.

In planning road travel, you must consider high gas prices as well as the type and conditions of roads to be traveled. Hotels and restaurants are found in larger towns and on both sides of the borders with Argentina and Brazil, but make reservations in advance. Prices are comparable to those in Asuncion.

To have a real change of scene, you must travel to one of the more developed neighboring countries. Visits to cosmopolitan centers such as Buenos Aires, Montevideo, Cordoba, Sao Paulo, Rio de Janeiro, or Santiago offer shopping, cultural, and entertainment diversions not found in Asuncion. Ocean beach resorts in Brazil and Uruguay provide a refreshingly different ambiance.

Entertainment
Commercial entertainment in Asuncion consists of films, plays, concerts, discos, a hotel gambling casino, karaoke bars, and hotels and restaurants with dancing and/or floor shows. Asuncion has several movie theaters that offer a fair selection of American and foreign films (mostly double features), including older action films and juvenile favorites. Shopping del Sol, Villa Mora Shopping Center, Excelsior Shopping Center, the Hiperseis Shopping Center and Multiplaza Shopping Center all have modern movie theaters showing relatively new movies.

Modern and classical plays are presented (in Spanish or Guarani) at the Arlequin Teatro. The Centro Cultural Paraguayo-Americano (which boasts the best theater in town) and the cultural centers of other foreign missions also present plays and host film presentations, gallery shows, and concerts by musicians from their respective countries. Argentine, Uruguayan, and American professional groups bring occasional theater or music to Asuncion.

Entertainment at clubs and restaurants is principally local talent, with folkloric presentations such as the guarani, the polka, and the bottle dance performed regularly. Asuncion has a variety of good restaurants, many of which offer ethnic menus such as Brazilian, Chinese, French, German, Japanese, Korean, and Lebanese.

Local festivals, all comparatively low-key and subdued, include a pre-Lenten carnival and the Festival of St. John's Eve featuring demonstrations of faith or bravado by people walking barefoot on hot coals. Most towns have processions on their patron saint's name day, and festivals in artisan towns near Asuncion are held during the winter tourist season. Photography is unrestricted at these events. Paraguayans are generally quite willing to have their pictures taken, although Indians expect to receive a tip or may set a price themselves.

Social Activities
American women, some years ago, organized a club known as Las Amigas Norteamericanas del Paraguay. Among its social activities are monthly meetings, visits to nearby places of interest, handicraft work, coffees, and luncheons. Its charitable activities include welfare work, participation in fund raising projects of other organizations, and an annual fair.

Paraguayans are generally well-disposed toward Americans, and informal acquaintances can easily be made with coworkers, neighbors, and at school events. As with many Latin societies, however, social life centers on the family and contact with outsiders is somewhat limited.

Church or cultural center activities, where shared interests form a common bond, provide some opportunities for meeting Paraguayans and other foreigners. Several business clubs, including Lions and Rotary, exist throughout the country. Charitable groups in which Americans participate besides Las Amigas and missionary organizations include: Damas Diplomaticas, a group of women from the diplomatic community who meet socially to raise money for charity; the International Women's group organizes different activities including visits to cultural centers and talks on diverse subjects; and the Red Cross, whose activities include sewing and conducting charity sales. The American School PTA sponsors various activities and events. The Damas Britan-

icas annual Caledonian Ball is popular with many Americans.

Encarnación
Encarnación, in the deep, southeastern part of Paraguay, is the country's second largest city (in terms of stable population figures) and an important port on the Alto Paraná, across from the Argentine city of Posadas. It serves as a major rail terminus for passengers, goods, and livestock; trains are ferried from there into Argentina and on to Buenos Aires.

Encarnación, with a population of about 31,000, is a busy commercial and manufacturing center, whose products from the surrounding rich agricultural area include lumber, tobacco, tea, rice, and maize. Several Japanese farm colonies nearby contribute heavily to agricultural production.

Founded in 1614, Encarnación was originally named Itapúa. It is now the capital of Itapúa Province. In 1926, the city was severely damaged by a tornado, but over the past half-century has rebuilt and expanded into an active community. Its people speak either Spanish or *Guaraní*; there are few hotels or shops where English is heard. British or other European newspapers occasionally are available at the airport outside the city. The library in Encarnación has some titles in English. No English-language schools are in operation.

Encarnación has a television station (Channel 7, Itapúa), which serves the southeastern part of the country. It is a subsidiary of one of the major channels in Asunción.

OTHER CITIES

CAACUPÉ serves as the capital of La Cordilerra Department, 30 miles east of Asunción. Surrounded by the Cordillera de los Altos Mountains, Caacupé is the destination of pilgrims from all over the continent. Its central plaza contains the

Shrine of the Blue Virgin of the Miracles, whose feast day is December 8th. The city is an important agricultural processing center; tile manufacturing is another economic activity. The National Agronomic Institute is located here and does crop research. Caacupé is an important resort center. This community of approximately 10,000 people is linked to Asunción by a paved highway.

Founded in the early 1600s, **CAAZAPÁ** is a departmental capital on the edge of the Brazilian Highlands in the south. The economy depends on lumbering, agriculture, and tanneries. A regional hospital, several educational institutions, and an agricultural college are situated here. A monument to the city's founder, Friar Bolaños, stands in the city of about 3,000. A railway and highway provide transportation to Asunción, 50 miles northwest.

The city of **CIUDAD DEL ESTE**, formerly Puerto Presidente Stroessner, is a river port on the Brazilian border which grew from a small village to a population of 90,000 during its boom years, when the Itaipú Dam was being constructed across the Paraná River. The city was carved out of the jungle in 1957, and when work began on the dam in the mid-1970s, the population exploded. Now, with the completion of the dam, which was formally opened in November 1982, Ciudad del Este's fortunes have begun to regress. Thousands of families whose livelihood depended on the dam construction and attendant businesses, have left the area seeking other means of support. During the city's flourishing years, it was a black-market haven, and people from neighboring Brazil flocked across the border to buy cheap contraband. Some of this illegal activity continues, but not in the same bold proportions as during the boom years. The city is linked to Brazil by the 1,600-foot Puente de la Armistad Bridge. One of the principal tourist attractions is the Iguaçu Falls, which are located outside of the city. Its population is approximately 111,000.

CONCEPCIÓN is an eastern trading port on the Paraguay River about 125 miles north of the capital. The city, founded in 1773, is also called Villa Concepción. Several banks and commercial establishments are located here. Several industries are located here, including sawmills, flour mills, tanneries, cotton gins, and sugar refineries. The 1995 population was approximately 25,600.

CORONEL OVIEDO, also in eastern Paraguay, is a town of 22,700 residents. It serves as the administrative center of Caaguacú Department. Oranges, sugarcane, and tobacco are grown near the town. The town has a hospital and a Catholic cathedral.

LUQUE, 10 miles outside of Asunción, made history in the late 1860s when war erupted with Argentina, Brazil, and Uruguay. For six years it was the national capital. Luque's produce and industry supply Asunción. Its population is estimated at 25,000.

PEDRO JUAN CABALLERO is on the Brazilian border in eastern Paraguay. It is the capital of the Amambay Department and one of the largest towns in the region. Cattle ranching and coffee growing are primary economic pursuits.

PILAR, capital of Ñeembucú Department, lies 60 miles south of Asunción. This port on the Paraguay River handles most of the agricultural products of the adjacent districts. It is also important in manufacturing. Manufacturing industries in Pilar include sawmills, textile mills, and distilleries. The city is linked with the rest of the country via the Asunción-Encarnación highway. Approximately 13,000 live in Pilar, which has an airport.

VILLARRICA, in south-central Paraguay, is a long-established commercial center about 70 miles southeast of the capital. Founded in 1570, it is the capital of Guairá Department, and the shipping point for a region producing cattle, tobacco,

sugarcane, wine, fruit, and *yerba maté* (Paraguayan tea). It is also known for its sugar refineries, textile mills, shoe factories, flour mills, distilleries, and sawmills. The population, which has a large percentage of people of German descent, is about 21,200. Villarrica's cathedral is a pilgrimage center.

COUNTRY PROFILE

Geography and Climate

Located in the heart of South America, Paraguay is a landlocked, agricultural country about the size of California. It shares its borders with Brazil, Argentina, and Bolivia.

The Parana-Paraguay River system is Paraguay's commercial access to the outside world. Rivers and their tributaries largely define Paraguay's boundaries, and the Paraguay River divides the country into two dissimilar sections, east and west.

The eastern section consists of rolling, fertile farming areas and grasslands, together with large, wooded areas and jungle patches near the Brazilian border. Most of the country's population live in the east and engage in small-scale agriculture. Asuncion and other commercially important towns-Encarnacion, Ciudad del Este, Pedro Juan Caballero, Concepcion, Coronel Oviedo, and Villarrica-are in this area, and most are accessible by paved roads. The western section, nearly two-thirds of Paraguay's total area, is called the Chaco. It is a low lying plateau covered with grassy meadows, bogs, spiny bushes, palms, and small trees. Lacking roads and navigable rivers, much of the region is inaccessible. Only 3% of the population live in this area.

The riverfront elevation of Asuncion is 177 feet above sea level. Residential areas are situated on low hills that rise another 200 feet. Eleva-

Government palace in Asuncion, Paraguay

© AFP/Corbis. Reproduced by permission.

tions throughout Paraguay are moderate, the highest range of hills, located in the eastern region, rises to about 2,000 feet.

Paraguay's climate is seasonal and subject to abrupt changes. It is subtropical, with summer and winter seasons opposite those in the U.S. Winds are generally moderate, but high winds accompanied by thunder and electrical storms are common, especially in summer. The long, hot summer lasts from October through March, with January average maximum temperature 917 and mean temperature 81°F Severe hot spells with very high humidity are common. Temperatures often exceed 100°F during the day from December to February (the official record high temperature is 109°F), with little relief at night.

Winter extends from June through August. Cold snaps of 4 or 5 days with temperatures in the low 40s and high 30s are interspersed with several days in the upper 70s and low 80s. Frosts occur rarely. The official record low in Asuncion is 32°F, although the damp air and improper ventilation make it seem much colder. With frequent and abrupt changes, from winter to summer-like weather and back again (temperature changes of 20°F-50°F are common), a high incidence of respiratory and bronchial illness occurs in winter.

Relative humidity ranges between 67% and 78% (monthly averages) year round and is particularly high in summer. This causes problems in keeping certain foods crisp, and clothes and shoes may mildew.

Asuncion's average 59-inch annual rainfall is well distributed seasonally. Slightly greater amounts fall in hotter months. Torrential rains cause annual floods in riverside communities. The Chaco, which receives little rainfall, becomes semiarid in its western most reaches. During rainy periods, however, water covers large areas due to the impermeable clay subsoil.

Mosquitoes and a tiny gnat-like insect called "Mbarigui" are the most troublesome insects. Cockroaches appear at times in even the cleanest kitchens; but fast, good exterminators are available. Flies, ants, spiders, crickets, silverfish, and moths also prevail. Store woolen clothing in naphthalene during summer. Less common are rats, mice, bats, scorpions, and tarantulas. Depending on how developed a neighborhood is, animals in residential areas can include numerous stray dogs, cows, grazing mules and horses, and a few snakes. Children should avoid any unfamiliar animal.

Population

Much of Paraguay is sparsely populated. Most of its 5.2 million people are concentrated in the smaller eastern half of the country. About 600,000 people live in Asuncion, the political, economic, and cultural center of the country. Asuncion's population triples during the day with the influx of workers from surrounding cities. Nearly 35% of the country's population reside in the greater Asuncion metropolitan area.

Almost complete assimilation of the early Spanish settlers by the native Guarani Indians has developed a distinctive racially homogeneous Paraguayan strain, which makes up most of the population. The important minority groups include some 100,000 unassimilated Indians, representing 17 different ethnic groups.

As a result of the expansion of the Brazilian economy up to and across its border with Paraguay, about 300,000 Brazilians live in the border area where many engage in mechanized farming. This phenomenon continues on and has begun to cause some border tensions. Most of these immigrants are from southern Brazil, which is predominantly European. About 20,000 Argentines live along the Argentine border. Other minority groups include 40,000 Germans, 10,000 Koreans, 8,000 Japanese, 2,000 Chinese, 1,000 Poles, 300 French, and 300 English. Some 20,000 Russian, Canadian, Mexican, and U.S. Mennonites live in agricultural communities scattered throughout the country. Paraguay has traditionally welcomed immigrants.

The official U.S. community (including dependents and Peace Corps volunteers) numbers 290. Of the 2,836 nonofficial Americans registered at the Embassy, many are missionaries and business representatives and their dependents, along with some students and retired persons.

The Paraguayan population is predominantly Roman Catholic. The 1992 constitution recognizes religious freedom and states that no confession will have official character. The constitution also states that relations between the state and the Catholic Church are based on independence, cooperation, and autonomy. Although all religious groups had been tolerated, in 1979 the Paraguayan Government took legal action against groups such as the Jehovah's Witnesses, the Children of God, and the Hare Krishna movement, whose teachings on patriotic and family allegiances conflicted with Paraguayan law and custom. In a related attempt to restrict the growth of religious cults, recent legislation has prohibited the conferring of legal status on any new religious groups. Spanish is the language of government, business, and education and is used among the educated. Paraguayans are proud of their native heritage and of the Guarani language, also recognized as an official language.

Guarani is used almost exclusively in rural areas and is widely spoken in urban areas. Anyone learning even a few words of Guarani will find it greatly appreciated by Paraguayans.

Paraguayans are not as class conscious as some Latin Americans. All share a pride in their ethnic heritage and a fierce patriotism born of devastating, protracted wars with neighboring countries. Although extremes of wealth and want exist, display of great wealth is still uncommon; and conversely, abject poverty is less visible here than in many Latin American countries. Life, particularly in rural areas, can be hard, but social differences that divide groups are neither deeply felt nor well defined. This is due, in part, to the availability of land for those willing to homestead, to the almost total elimination of the landed Spanish aristocracy under the dictatorship of Jose Gaspar Rod-

riguez de Francia in the early 1800s, and to the leveling effect of the War of the Triple Alliance (1864-70), in which up to 70% of the male population was killed.

Public Institutions

Paraguay has had a turbulent political history. The area, first colonized in the early 16th century, achieved independence from Spain in 1811. Left with a legacy of authoritarian rule by its early leaders and nearly destroyed by the War of the Triple Alliance (1864-70), it has been plagued by a major conflict with Bolivia (Chaco War, 1932-35), periods of near anarchy, and civil wars interspersed with several prolonged periods of relative tranquility. The last major conflict was the 6-month civil war of 1947.

On February 3, 1989, a coup d'etat overthrew 34 years of authoritarian rule. In May 1989, under the new President of the Republic, Paraguay began the long process of transition from authoritarianism to democracy. A new constitution took effect in June 1992, providing for a stronger Parliament, an independent judiciary, municipal autonomy, and limited decentralization of administrative authority.

Paraguay's two major, traditional political organizations, the Colorado and Liberal Parties, have each ruled the country for prolonged periods. Few ideological differences separate them. In 1991, a third party, the Encuentro Nacional, was formed. The Colorado Party, the dominant political force during the authoritarian years and the democratic transition, is likely to remain so for some time.

The traditional Liberal Party is split into several fragments. The largest of these, the Authentic Radical Liberal Party (PLRA), was the principal opposition party in the later years of authoritarian rule. The Liberals and "Encuentristas" hold a sizable minority of congressional seats. A small Christian Democratic Party (PDC) also participated in nationwide municipal

elections in the early 1990s, but has had little active role since then.

In March 1999, the Vice President of Paraguay was assassinated in a plot widely attributed to a disaffected former Army commander who enjoyed the protection of Paraguay's President. After mass public protests several days later, in which several protesters were killed, both the President and the former Army commander fled the country. The then-Senate President became President of the Republic, in accordance with the Constitution, and formed a "national unity" government with members of the Liberal and Encuentro Nacional parties.

Although the military was highly politicized during the first years of the democratic transition, it remains an influential institution in Paraguay and ha; been supportive of the attempt to trans. form Paraguay into a modern democracy The army (10,000 troops), navy, and air force (1,000 each) lack modern equipment and training in many areas, but remain receptive to civilian control. It many isolated areas, the armed forces arc the sole representative of government.

Arts, Science, and Education

The Centro Cultural Paraguayo Americano (BNC) sponsors numerous cultural activities and has a 12,000-volume library with both Spanish and English titles, including one of the country's most complete collections of Paraguayan works. As well as teaching at average of 6,000 students English, the center offers concerts, theater, gallery shows, and lectures and seminars on various topics. The Center opened a second branch in 1998.

Of the fine arts, painting and graphics are the most developed in Paraguay The Contemporary Arts Museum, the Ceramics Museum, the Museo del Barro Manzana de la Rivera, and the U.S.

Cultural Center gallery, as well as other binational institutions, exhibit Paraguayan and foreign artwork throughout the year. Asuncion has a part-time symphony that performs during winter in various auditoriums. Paraguayan folk musicians perform at various sites throughout the year. Paraguay's most popular theater groups present Spanish and Guarani comedies at the city's several theaters. Ballet troupes perform occasionally at the Municipal Theater or other locales. Cultural missions of France, the E.R.G., Argentina, Brazil, Japan, and the U.K. present music, theater, and films at their institutions.

Paraguay's two institutions of higher education are the National University of Asuncion and the Catholic University of Asuncion. Both have adjunct faculties in the larger cities of the interior.

Little scientific activity exists beyond instruction at the National University. Scientific museums include the Ethnographic Museum and the Museum of Natural Science.

Commerce and Industry

Paraguay is predominantly an agricultural country with vast hydroelectric potential but no known significant mineral or petroleum resources. The Paraguayan economy is extremely vulnerable to the vagaries of weather. It exports cotton, soybeans, cattle, and electricity. It also has a fairly lucrative business of reexporting products made elsewhere. Paraguay imports foodstuffs, machinery, transportation equipment, fuels and lubricants, and textiles. Its principal trade partners are Brazil, Argentina, Chile, U.S., and Western European countries. The U.S. maintains a healthy trade surplus with Paraguay. From a base of $375 million in 1991, U.S. exports to Paraguay rose to $913 million at the end of 1997. This represents a 24% annual increase. In 1998, Paraguay's total

registered exports amounted to $1,002 million and total registered imports were $2,377 million.

Since the 1980s, the economy has experienced a series of peaks and valleys. The decade of the 80s began with the final 2 years of rapid construction of the Itaipu Dam (with the largest hydroelectric-generating capacity in the world) fueling annual growth of 10%. From this peak, the economy alternated periods of recession with modest growth. The 1988-89 period saw solid economic growth averaging 5% a year. During 1990 and 1991, the pace of expansion sustained by the Paraguayan economy in the preceding 2 years began to slow. From 1992-98 the economy has grown at an anemic 2.5% per year. The year 1999 was the second consecutive year of negative economic growth.

The February 1989 coup d'etat marked the end of 34 years of repressive regime and the beginning of a transition process to democracy in Paraguay. Since then, successive administrations have implemented modest economic reform packages and have flirted with privatization of state-run telephone, electrical, and water companies. Some reforms include the unification of the exchange rate, the elimination of preferential foreign exchange rates and foreign exchange controls, expenditure reductions, and implementation of a new tax code. In the financial sector, interest rates were freed, and new savings instruments were authorized. Price controls on some basic products were also eliminated, and tax incentives to encourage investment and attract foreign investors were provided. The Government is now studying privatization of state-run enterprises and modernization of the state. Paraguay continues to have one of the lowest foreign debts in Latin America.

Since ending the 34-year Stroessner dictatorship in 1989, the Government of Paraguay has made significant progress in reinserting the country into the world community. On March 26, 1991, Paraguay

joined Argentina, Brazil, and Uruguay in signing the Treaty of Asuncion, to create Mercosur, a common market and customs union that went into effect in January 1995. Mercosur signed free trade agreements with Chile and Bolivia in 1996, and similar arrangements are under negotiation with Mexico, Peru, and the European Union. Paraguay became a member of the World Trade Organization (WTO) in January 1995.

Transportation

Automobiles

Driving is on the right. Although distances traveled within Asuncion are not great and travel into the countryside is not extensive or frequent, most find a car necessary here. Unleaded gasoline is available countrywide. Fuel prices vary considerably due to fluctuating exchange rates. Unleaded (97 octane) costs about $2.73 a gallon; regular gasoline (95 octane, unleaded with alcohol) $2.53 a gallon; regular gasoline (85 octane, unleaded with alcohol) $2.15 a gallon; and diesel fuel $0.92 a gallon (April 2000). Currently, unleaded gasoline is sold without alcohol additives; regular gasoline does contain some alcohol. Various U.S., Japanese, Brazilian, and European-origin cars are driven here. Many vehicles are available locally; costs are higher than vehicles from the U.S. Brazilian and Japanese vehicles are the most common, but none sold locally meet U.S. safety requirements and smog control specifications.

Sport cars with low-road clearance are unsuitable for local cobblestone streets and unpaved roads. A diesel-powered car or low-consumption compact would be most economical and would probably have fewer maintenance problems. U.S. cars hold up well, although obtaining spare parts can involve long delays when repairs are needed as many are not available locally. Most parts purchased here are expensive. Service is fair-to-good.

Local

Of Paraguay's 28,000-kilometer road network, 2,700 kilometers are paved. Some roads are graded earth or gravel and are susceptible to closure from rains and flooding for considerable periods of time. The southeast portion of the country, east of the Paraguay River, where the major economic activity of the country is concentrated, has the best roads. Most of the main towns in this area, and from Asuncion to Rio de Janeiro, Sao Paulo, Montevideo, and Buenos Aires, are linked by paved or all-weather roads. Considerable highway expansion and improvement is planned or in the construction stage. Emphasis is on making the Chaco more accessible year round, routing truck transport of agricultural products to the Brazilian Port of Paranagua, and integrating the hydroelectric projects at Itaipu and Yacyreta into the national economy.

Road travel is the most common transportation for domestic freight and passenger travel. More than 50% of road traffic consists of trucks and buses. Excellent bus service is available to Rio de Janeiro and Buenos Aires, but distances and travel times are long.

Public transportation in Asuncion consists of taxis and buses. Radio taxis are available and reliable either by phone or at stands throughout the city; they are more scarce at night. City bus routes are extensive, with fullest and most frequent service downtown. Unfortunately, bus stops and routes are not well marked. Buses are noisy, uncomfortable, and in ill-repair. During rush hours they are dangerously over-crowded. To add to the adventure, buses often slow down rather than stop to discharge and pick up passengers. Bus travel is not recommended.

Regional

Paraguay's external ties are mainly through air, road, and river transport. Great distances and poor and sometimes impassable roads limit overland travel. Most travel in the interior is for business, not pleasure.

Paraguay's most important transportation system is the inland waterway that connects Paraguay's inland ports with the Atlantic Ocean. It begins with the Paraguay River that runs north-south across the country and the Parana River that serves as a border with Brazil and Argentina, and continues past the Argentine Port of Rosario to Buenos Aires. Together with the Rio de la Plata, it constitutes a 3,170-kilometer system of transport, handling over 60% of the international traffic in the area.

Asuncion, the largest port, serves Paraguay's most important productive areas and is the only port with modern berthing facilities and cargo-handling equipment. Facilities are limited, however, and transit areas are very congested. With completion of the Itaipu, Yacyreta, and Corpus hydroelectric projects, water levels on the Parana River should increase from Encarnacion to Saltos del Guaira. This will open the Parana River to oceangoing vessels and increase the importance of both Encarnacion and Ciudad del Este as inland ports.

For other than leisure sightseeing, air transportation is the only practical means of international travel to and from Asuncion. Asuncion is served by Silvio Pettirossi International Airport, a Category 3 airport. As such, there are no direct flights via U.S. carriers to the U.S. TAM offers daily flights between the U.S. and Asuncion. American Airlines offers daily flights to Miami, New York, and Dallas through Sao Paulo, Brazil. Varig also offers daily flights to Miami or New York through Sao Paulo. Airlines connecting Asuncion with other capitals and major cities include: American Airlines, Aerolineas Argentinas, Varig, PLUNA, LAN Chile, Lloyd Aereo Boliviano, Iberia, and TAM. The internal airline, ARPA, operates with a Cessna Caravan from Monday to Friday. Domestic air traffic is small but important, as it is often the only means into other sections of the country, especially during bad weather. Airfields range from an all-weather airport under construction at Mariscal Estigarribia (halfway between Asuncion and Santa Cruz, Bolivia), where only military flights operate; to a restricted all-weather airport under the control of the Itaipu Binational Authority, north of Ciudad del Estate; to an International Airport named Guarani located in Minga Guazu, and to a few concrete strips in the more remote interior.

There is also daily bus service between Asuncion and Buenos Aires, Sao Paulo and Foz de Iguazu. There are very comfortable, air-conditioned executive buses, in addition to the regular buses.

Communications

Telephone and Telegraph

Asuncion's telephone system is good but suffers from maintenance and repair problems. Long-distance service is available almost worldwide, with good connections. Calls to the U.S. are normally of excellent quality. Costs for a long distance call to anywhere in the continental U.S. are: weekdays (Monday through Saturday) $2.23 a minute; Sunday, $2 a minute.

Access to AT&T's USA Direct is now available. Also, you can join MCI and U.S. Sprint calling systems.

An ordinary telegram to the U.S. costs about 31 cents a word (with a 7-word minimum). Night letter (telegram): 7-word minimum and 21-word maximum costs 16 cents a word.

All costs listed above and throughout this report change considerably, depending on the prevailing exchange rate.

Mail

The Paraguayan mail system is becoming more reliable, but do not send money or valuables through the mail.

Radio and TV

Asuncion has four TV stations and two cable TV stations: Channel 2, Channel 4, Channel 9, and Channel 13. Channel 9 and Channel 13 have their national networks on subsidiary channels. Cable TV is growing. The main cable companies, CVC/TVD and CMM, carry channels from Argentina, Brazil, Chile, Germany, Italy, Mexico, Spain, Venezuela, and the U.S. (ESPN, CMM carries HBO Ole, CVC carries CNN in English and Spanish).

The main news programs are transmitted by Channels 4, 9, and 13 at noon and at 8 pin and cover news from around the world. Most of the series shown come from the U.S. and are dubbed into Spanish.

The color system used in Paraguay is PAL-N (similar to Uruguay and Argentina). A bistandard set NTSC/PAL-N will allow you to watch TV and view American video movies. A good 20-inch bistandard (or "binorma") TV set currently costs about $350 if purchased here. U.S. color TV sets are not compatible with the PAL-N system. A bistandard video recorder would allow you to tape from local TV

Several video-cassette clubs operate in Asuncion. These clubs do not operate with the same standards found in the U.S., and selection of tapes is not as varied.

Paraguayan TV stations may be received on indoor antennas.

In Asuncion, some 10 AM stations and 12 FM stations are available. There are some 30 other stations outside of Asuncion. All broadcast popular and traditional Latin music, local news, and sports. Most of the FM stations transmit music in stereo, including the latest U.S. and British popular music.

For English-language broadcasts, bring a shortwave radio, or you can buy one locally. A simple longwire outdoor antenna can help to bring in shortwave stations.

Bring stereo equipment. The 50 cycle current means that in addition to the 110v-220v transformer, however, phonographs and tape recorders without DC motors require modification. Phonographs may require a different pulley; tape recorders may need a different capstan. Both can usually be bought from the manufacturer. If possible, have these adjustments made before arrival. Newer equipment, however, is multivoltage and multicycle (as is computer equipment). Please check before departure.

Newspapers, Magazines, and Technical Journals

Six independent daily newspapers are printed in Asuncion; one of them, *Ultima Hora,* has morning and afternoon editions. *Ultima Hora* and *ABC Color* have the largest circulations. Papers can be purchased from newsboys at street corners or at kiosks. Home delivery can also be arranged.

The following newspapers are located on the worldwide web as indicated: *Ultima Hora* at http://www.ultimahora.com.py; *ABC Color* at http://www.abc.com.py; *Noticias El Diario* at http://www.diaiionoticias.com.py. *Time, Newsweek,* and *People* are sold at newsstands. The only English-language newspaper available is the *Buenos Aires Herald,* which usually arrives in Asuncion on the day of publication. Subscriptions from the U.S. arrive from 1 day to 2 weeks after being sent.

Many English-language periodicals may be read at the Roosevelt Library of the Centro Cultural Paraguayo-Americano, Asuncion's BNC.

Health and Medicine

Medical Facilities

Although several well-trained physicians and surgeons practice in the city and several hospitals are adequately staffed and equipped to handle most emergency medical and surgical problems, persons

requiring complicated diagnostic work and all but minor surgery cases are normally evacuated to Miami. Many doctors are U.S. trained, including dentists, orthodontists, ophthalmologists, obstetricians, pediatricians, and surgeons. There are four hospitals used often by U.S. citizens and military personnel in the country. They are the Baptist Hospital with 44 beds, the Hospital Privado Frances with 55 beds, the Migone Hospital with 34 beds, and the Sanatorio San Roque with 66 beds. The four hospitals provide emergency rooms, intensive care units, lab and x-ray facilities, and doctors on 24-hour call.

Community Health

Most of Asuncion (73%) has a modern municipal water supply, and unfluoridated tap water connected to the system (CORPOSANA) is considered safe to drink. As a health precaution, however, all drinking water should be boiled and/or treated. Most hotels and larger homes are connected to the system. When contracting for a house, determine whether the CORPOSANA system has been installed. If not, note that well water, in and outside the city, must be boiled at least 10 minutes to ensure potability. Asuncion's sewers empty untreated waste into the Paraguay River. Many restaurants observe acceptable standards of health. Routine inspections are not considered to be reliable, however.

Milk is available in several forms. It is very safe to use long life milk which is available in all stores. The quality is good and it is sold at a good price. Powdered milk is also available.

Preventive Measures

Regional endemic diseases include measles, rabies, hepatitis, typhoid fever, tetanus, diphtheria, polio, parasitic diseases, and tuberculosis. Immunized healthy Americans taking normal sanitary precautions, however, are relatively safe from most diseases. Malaria suppressants are unnecessary. Be sure to have your Hepatitis A vaccine and other routine immunizations up to date before departing.

Certain precautions are important. Wash all vegetables and fruits thoroughly, and have yearly physical exams for all household help. Since hookworm is prevalent, wear shoes or sandals outdoors. Fungi infections are common during the hot summers, and allergies aggravated by the many lovely flowering trees are common. Frequent climatic changes, particularly in winter, cause colds and other upper respiratory infections.

NOTES FOR TRAVELERS

Passage, Customs & Duties
Travel time by air from the east coast to Asuncion is about 12 hours. American Airlines flies from New York, Washington, D.C Dulles, and Miami to Asuncion through Sao Paulo. Since delays are common, allow for adequate transit time where travel involves changes from one flight to another.

Ship travel from U.S. ports to Buenos Aires does not have regular service. From Buenos Aires, passengers for Asuncion can continue by plane or bus; however, air travel is more practical.

For entry into Paraguay by road, you will need all essential vehicle documents such as ownership and registration, certified in the form of a vehicle transit pass (Libreta de Paso) obtained from the automobile club of the country from which entry into Paraguay is made.

Travelers without Brazilian or Peruvian visas are not allowed out of the airport even if they have missed their connection. Peru requires visas in diplomatic and official passports, not in tourist passports.

Unaccompanied air baggage may take 6-8 weeks to arrive and be cleared in Asuncion. Include all essential items in your accompanied luggage.

A passport is required. U.S. citizens traveling as tourists or for business do not need a visa for stays up to three months. Persons planning on working, formally or informally, or staying longer than three months, may require a visa and should seek information from the Paraguayan Embassy or consulate on the corresponding visas prior to travel. Although Paraguayan law allows changes in visa status, the procedure is lengthy and can be cumbersome. In addition, individuals wishing to reside in Paraguay for any length of time should have their civil documents (birth and marriage certificates, etc.) certified and authenticated by the Paraguayan Embassy or Consulate in the U.S. as well as translated into Spanish. For current information concerning entry and customs requirements for Paraguay, travelers may contact the Paraguayan Embassy at 2400 Massachusetts Avenue N.W., Washington, D.C. 20008, telephone (202) 483-6960. Internet: http://www.embassy.org/embassies/py.html; or the Paraguayan consulate in Los Angeles, Miami, or New York.

Americans living in or visiting Paraguay are encouraged to register at the Consular Section of the U.S. Embassy in Asuncion and obtain updated information on travel and security in Paraguay. The U.S. Embassy is located at 1776 Mariscal Lopez Avenue; telephone (011-595-21) 213-715. The Consular Section is open for U.S. citizens services, including registration, Monday through Thursday from 1-5 pm and Friday from 7:30 am to 11:30 am, except for U.S. and Paraguayan holidays. The Consular Section's Internet e-mail address is: usaconsulasuncion@hotmail.com. (This e-mail address is not checked on a regular basis.)

Pets
All types of pets may be imported. A USDA veterinary certificate of good health and certificate of inoculation against rabies (at least 15 days prior to travel) are the only required documents. If you are staying overnight or transiting along the way before reaching Asuncion, permission to have your pet enter that country will be needed. All pets may be exported as well, except birds and wild animals indigenous to Paraguay. Pets purchased locally should be inoculated against distemper and rabies every 6 months.

Firearms and Ammunition
All firearms must be registered in country with the local government.

Currency, Banking, and Weights and Measures
The monetary unit of Paraguay is the Guarani and can be purchased with dollar instruments in the fluctuating free market through licensed banks and exchange houses. The rate of exchange (ROE) is about US$1=G3,503 (June 2000). Currently, only one U.S. bank remains active in Paraguay and that is Citibank N.A. Paraguay officially uses the metric system of weights and measures.

LOCAL HOLIDAYS

Jan. 1	New Year's Day
Mar. 1	Heroes Day
Mar/Apr.	Holy Thursday*
Mar/Apr.	Good Friday*
Mar/Apr.	Easter*
May 1	Paraguay Labor Day
May 15	Paraguay Independence Day
June 12	Chaco Armistice
Aug. 15	Founding of the City of Asuncion
Sept. 29	Victory at Boqueron
Dec. 8	Virgin of Caacupe Day
Dec. 25	Christmas Day

*variable

RECOMMENDED READING

The following titles are provided as a general indication of the material published on this country:

Abou, Selim. *Jesuit Republic of the Guaranis (1609-1768) and Its Heritage.* Crossroad Pub. Co.: New York, 1997.

American University. *Area Handbook for Paraguay.* U.S. Government Printing Office: Washington, D.C., 1990.

Arnold, Adlai E. *Foundations of an Agricultural Policy in Paraguay.* Praeger: 1971.

Attenborough, David. *The Zoo Quest Expeditions.* Penguin Books: New York, 1982. This paperback reedition of three of Attenborough's books includes his Zoo Quest in Paraguay. Anecdotes about filming and collecting animals.

Barrett, William E. *Women on Horseback: The Story of Francisco S. Lopez and Elisa Lynch.* Doubleday: Garden City, 1969. A novel about Francisco Solano Lopez and the famous Madame Lynch.

Brodsky, Ayln. *Madame Lynch and Friend.* Harper & Row: New York, 1975. A biographical account of the lives of Irish adventurer Elisa Lynch and Francisco Lopez.

Durrell, Gerald. *The Drunken Forest.* Rupert Hart-Davis: London, 1956. Amusing account of animal collecting in Argentina and the Paraguayan Chaco Region.

Fretz, Joseph Winfield. *Immigrant Group Settlements in Paraguay.* Bethel College Press: North Newton, Kansas, 1962.

Fretz, Joseph Winfield. *Pilgrims in Paraguay.* Bethel College Press: North Newton, Kansas, 1953. Both are studies of colonization by Mennonite and other immigrant groups, mainly European and Asiatic in Paraguay by an American Mennonite scholar.

Frings, Paul. *Paracuaria: Art Treasures of the Jesuit Republic of Paraguay.* Matthias-Gronewald-Verlag: Mainz, Germany, 1982. This book, with texts in English, Spanish, and German, contains information about the Jesuit ruins in Paraguay and efforts to restore the ruins. Includes background information on the Jesuit republic and photographs of the art works.

Garner, William. *The Chaco Dispute: A Study of Prestige Diplomacy.* Public Affairs Press: Washington, D.C., 1966. The only English-language diplomatic history of the Chaco War. (1928-1938).

Greene, Graham. *The Honorary Consul.* Simon & Schuster: New York, 1973. (Also available in paperback from Pocket Books, a subsidiary of Simon & Schuster.) A popular novel about a British Honorary Consul who is mistaken for an American Ambassador and is abducted and held by Paraguayan revolutionaries.

Greene, Graham. *Travels With My Aunt.* Bantam Books: New York, 1971. In this comic novel, Henry and his aunt Augusta travel to Paraguay.

Hay, James Eston. *Tobati: Tradicion y cambio en un pueblo paraguayo.* CERI/Universidad Catolica, Pilar: Asuncion, 1999. An analysis of the change and development of a small Paraguayan town, Tobati. [This book should be available in English by 2002. English language copies may be obtained at research libraries, through University Microfilms or through Inter-Library Loan: Hay, James Eston, Tobati: Tradition and Change in a Paraguayan Town. Ph.D. Dissertation, University of Florida, 1993.]

Kolinski, Charles J. *Independence or Death.* University of Florida Press: Gainesville, Florida, 1965. A history of the War of the Triple Alliance, 1865-70.

Lambert, Peter and Nickson, Andrew, Eds. *The Transition to Democracy in Paraguay.* St. Mar-

tin's Press, Inc.: New York, NY, 1997. The most up-to-date assessment of Paraguay after the transition from the Stroessner dictatorship.

Land of Lace and Legend, An Informal Guide to Paraguay. Compiled by Las Amigas Norteamericanas del Paraguay, 1977. It describes many features of life in Paraguay.

Lewis, Paul. *Socialism, Liberalism, and Dictatorship in Paraguay.* Praeger: New York, 1982. This book places General Stroessner and his regime into the context of Paraguay's political culture. It deals with the struggles between Liberals and those who represented an indigenous socialism, shows how Stroessner rose to power, and describes his regime's structure and organizational support. Stroessner's policies with respect to economic development and foreign affairs are described and the state of the opposition under Stroessner is discussed.

Lewis, Paul H. *Paraguay Under Stroessner.* The University of North Carolina Press: Chapel Hill, 1980. A political biography of the President of Paraguay that is rich in historical background and anecdotal detail. An excellent and educational book on contemporary politics of Paraguay.

McNaspy, C. J. *Lost Cities of Paraguay: Art and Architecture of the Jesuit Reductions, 1607-1767.* Loyola University Press: Chicago, 1982. Gives an account of the Jesuit Reductions (missions) and describes sites in Paraguay, Argentina, and Brazil. The best book in English to date on this subject.

Miranda, Carlos R. *The Stroessner Era: Authoritarian Rule in Paraguay.* Westview: Boulder, 1990. The author describes the political culture of, and the history of authoritarianism, in Paraguay before embarking on an in-depth study of the ideological bases of the Stroessner era, the politics of control of the Stroessner regime, and economic development and the pattern of co-optation during his dictatorship. He also examines the reasons for the demise of the Stroessner regime.

Pendle, George. *Paraguay, A Riverside Nation*. Third Edition, Royal Institute of International Affairs: 1967. This short volume reads like an extended encyclopedia article. Recommended as the best single book dealing with the historical, economic, and sociological aspects of Paraguayan life. Includes a comprehensive annotated bibliography.

Raine, Philip. *Paraguay*. Scarecrow Press: New Brunswick, New Jersey, 1956. An informative, comprehensive treatment by a U.S. Foreign Service officer.

Sergice, Elman R. and Helen S. Tobati. *A Paraguayan Town*. University of Chicago Press: Chicago, 1954. A detailed study of life in a representative rural town.

Warren, Harris G. *Paraguay, An Informal History*. University of Oklahoma Press: 1949. Probably the best book in English for a historical overall view of the country.

Stover, Richard. *Six Silver Moonbeams: The Life and times of Augustin Barrios Mangore*. Querico Pubs.: Clovis, CA, 1992. This book is a comprehensive and authoritative biography of the world's greatest guitarist/composer, Agustin Pio Barrios (1885-1944), also known as Nitsuga Mangore. This extensive treatment of Barrios' life and music brings to light many facts about the amazing "Paganini of the guitar from the jungles of Paraguay."

Paraguay and the Triple Alliance: The Post-war Decade, 1869-1878. University of Texas Press: Austin, Texas, 1978. A well-written, well-researched study of the years after Paraguay's disastrous war with Brazil, Argentina, and Uruguay.

Warren, Harris Gaylord. *Rebirth of the Paraguayan Republic: The First Colorado Era, 1878-1904*. University of Pittsburgh Press: Pittsburgh, 1985. Warren writes a comprehensive history of Paraguay, based primarily on archival sources, from the watershed years of 1869-1870 to the Colorado defeat in 1904.

Washburn, Charles A. *The History of Paraguay*. Two volumes, 1871. An interesting autobiographical and historical account by an American diplomat in Paraguay at the time of the War of the Triple Alliance.

Whigham, Thomas. *The Politics of River Trade, Tradition and Development in The Upper Plata, 1780-1870*. University of New Mexico Press: 1991.

White, Edward Lucas. *El Supremo*. Durron: New York, 1934. A good historical novel of Paraguay under Dr. de Francia.

White, Richard Alan. *Paraguay's Autonomous Revolution: 1810-1840*. University of New Mexico Press: Albuquerque, 1978. A new look at the revolution carried out by Dr. de Francia following independence.

Williams, John Hoyt. *The Rise and Fall of the Paraguayan Republic, 1800-1870*. University of Texas Press: Austin, Texas, 1979. Examines this critical period of Paraguayan history as a period rather than a study of personalities.

Zook, David H., Jr. *The Conduct of the Chaco War*. Bookman Associates: New Haven, Connecticut, 1960. An interesting, in-depth treatment of this little-understood war from a politico-military viewpoint.

The following Internet sites are a few of many with information on Paraguay: http://travel. state.gov/ paraguay.html http://www.odci.gov/ cia/publications/factbook/pa.html http://lcweb2.loc.gov/frd/cs/ pytoc.html http://www.wtgon-line.com/data/pry/ pry.asp http:// www.latinworld.com/sur/Paraguay/ http://travel.lycos.com/Destinations/ South America/Paraguay/.

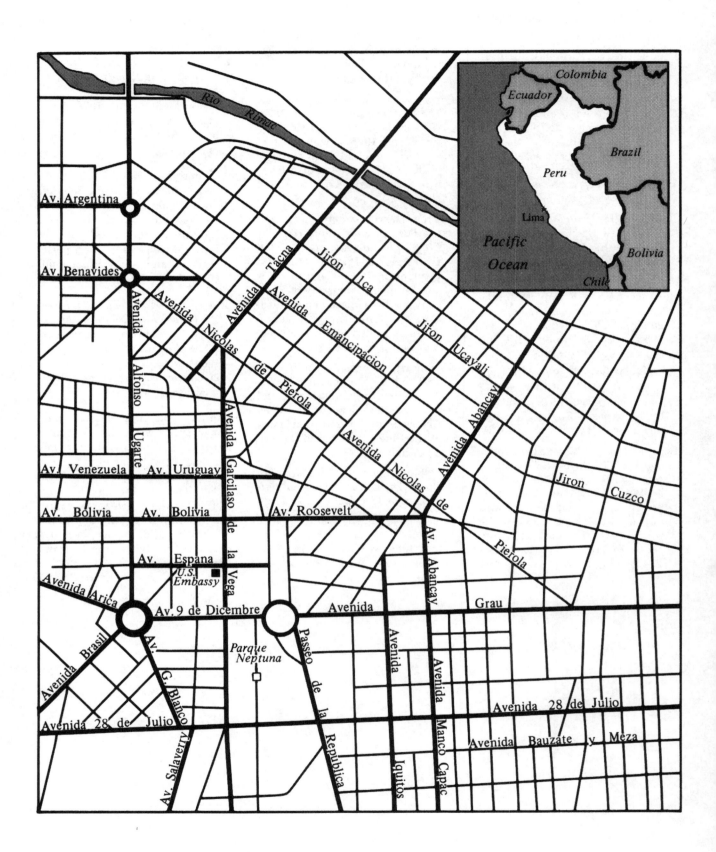

Lima, Peru

PERU
Republic of Peru

Major Cities:
Lima, Arequipa

Other Cities:
Cajamarca, Callao, Cerro de Pasco, Chiclayo, Chimbote, Cuzco, Huancayo, Ica, Iquitos, Pisco, Piura, Pucallpa, Trujillo

EDITOR'S NOTE

This chapter was adapted from the Department of State Post Report 1999 for Peru. Supplemental material has been added to increase coverage of minor cities, facts have been updated, and some material has been condensed. Readers are encouraged to visit the Department of State's web site at http://travel.state.gov/ for the most recent information available on travel to this country.

INTRODUCTION

PERU is a nation of diversity and contrast. Historically, it was the nucleus of the great Inca civilization and, subsequently, the administrative center of the Spanish colonial empire in South America. Geographically, Peru includes the desert coastal region with its populous cities of Lima, Arequipa, Trujillo, Chiclayo, and Piura; the mountainous central area of the Andean chain; and the jungle region forming the headwaters of the Amazon Basin.

Situated on the Pacific coast of the continent, Peru shares frontiers with five South American republics—Ecuador and Colombia to the north, Chile to the south, and Brazil and Bolivia to the east.

MAJOR CITIES

Lima

Lima lies in the center of Peru's coastal desert area on the Rimac River, 8 miles from the Pacific Port of Callao and about 475 feet above sea level. Its coordinates are 12 degrees south latitude and 77 degrees west longitude, the same longitude as New York City, 3,500 miles north. The Pan American Highway links Lima with Ecuador (600 miles north) and with Chile (720 miles south).

Although only 12 degrees south of the Equator, Lima is not tropical. The Pacific Ocean's cool Humboldt Current moderates the Peruvian coastal climate. Two distinct seasons occur: summer and winter. Winter is cool and damp with overcast skies; summer is moderate and generally pleasant. Rain is practically nonexistent in the area though light mist and drizzle persist throughout the winter.

Lima was founded by Francisco Pizarro on January 18, 1535, and named the "City of Kings," probably because the site was discovered on Epiphany. The seat of the viceroy was established here in 1542 with jurisdiction over all Spanish territory in South America except Venezuela.

The City of Kings has changed in the past 25 years from a quiet city of Spanish colonial charm into a modern-day metropolis. Although many colonial landmarks still stand, new office buildings and hotels tower over the dignified mansions and churches of the 17th and 18th centuries. Greater Lima with its suburbs covers roughly 400 square miles and has a population of over 7 million, making it the fourth-largest city in South America. By day the city teems with business and traffic; at night it assumes a typical Latin American cosmopolitan appearance, offering excellent restaurants, nightclubs, discotheques, concert halls, and movie theaters.

The area is rich in centuries-old plazas and churches. Inca and pre-Inca ruins are nearby, and artisan objects of silver, leather, and alpaca wool are available. Many modern entertainment and sports facilities are also available.

Utilities

Electricity in Lima is 220v, 60 cycles, but the voltage varies. Some houses and apartments are wired

459

Courthouse and plaza in Lima, Peru

Susan Rock. Reproduced by permission.

for both 110 and 220. Keep in mind that 110v appliances require a transformer. Most areas have enough water, but severe shortages can occur, particularly in summer. Telephone, electricity and water service are reliable in Lima.

Food

American-style supermarkets are abundant in most residential areas. Markets offer a variety of locally produced and processed goods. Many small specialty shops can be found throughout greater Lima, but imported foodstuffs are expensive.

Delicious fresh domestic and imported fruits and vegetables, both tropical and temperate, are sold in Lima year-round. Bananas, melons, oranges, and such tropical fruits as papayas, mangoes, and maracuya (passion fruit) are of good quality and reasonably priced. Apples, plums, peaches, strawberries, watermelon, pears, etc., are also available in season. Small limes are used for drinks and in cooking. Fresh fruit juices including strawberry and melon are popular. Many fresh herbs and spices are sold in the supermarkets.

Fish, fresh meat, and chicken are generally available. Beef, pork, and some cuts of lamb are good, but quality varies. Cook pork thoroughly.

Fresh, pasteurized milk is available at some local supermarkets (La Molina brand is preferred but sometimes hard to find). Many Americans buy boxed, long-life milk. Powdered or canned milk is available. Local and imported cheeses are plentiful and varied. There is no lack of good cheeses in Lima. Ice cream is not very expensive and may also easily be made at home.

Seven brands of beer are brewed in Peru and good Chilean wines are available locally. World-famous "pisco" brandy (distilled from grapes) is widely served and "pisco sours" are traditionally offered as a gesture of hospitality. Locally bottled soft drinks include Coca-Cola, Pepsi Cola, Canada Dry Ginger Ale, Seven-Up, and tonic. The bright yellow Inka Cola is a favorite Peruvian soft drink.

Peruvian cuisine excites the palate and is imaginative and varied, with many dishes based on fresh fish and seafood. Corn, potatoes, and chicken are combined with such fresh herbs as basil and coriander (Chinese parsley) to make delicious soups. Rich desserts are popular. Restaurants are exceptionally good, though expensive.

Clothing

All items of apparel are sold locally but imported items are expensive. The style and fit of locally produced apparel are different. Local tailoring and dressmaking services are good. Excellent fabrics may be purchased here. Peru is famous for export of a high-quality cotton.

Attractive, good-quality shoes are available, but expensive, and large, half-size, and narrow sizes are hard to find.

Men: Most Peruvian men dress conservatively, wearing shirts and ties to both office and social gatherings. In summer, sport shirts and slacks are acceptable for day and evening wear.

Women: Women will find woolen and other medium-weight warm dresses or suits practical for office or social wear during winter. Evening jackets and wraps are necessary in winter and frequently lightweight shawls are needed in summer. Shorts are rarely seen in public in the city, but are common at clubs, picnics, and at home.

Dress slacks are generally acceptable, depending upon style and fabric, and are suitable for coffees, luncheons, teas, meetings, and cocktail parties. Street-length dresses or separates are worn more frequently.

Children: Uniforms required for various schools should be purchased locally. Black athletic shoes are acceptable to uniform standards and could be purchased in the U.S. Although kindergarten-age children do not wear uniforms, they will need them when they enter first grade. During March, school children are not required to wear uniforms because of the heat.

Supplies and Services

American and European brands of toilet articles and cosmetics are expensive here; domestic brands are more reasonably priced and some are satisfactory.

Pharmacies are well stocked with antibiotics, vitamins, and U.S.-patented medicines at controlled prices comparable to those in the U.S.

Photography enthusiasts could bring a supply of film, but remember that it deteriorates if stored in a humid climate for long. Most film types are sold locally.

Tailoring, dressmaking, shoe repair, hairdressing, barbering, laundry, dry-cleaning, and other services are available at reasonable prices.

Domestic Help

A maid's salary is currently about $150 to $200 per month. For full-time help, the employer also must pay a social security tax of about 18% of monthly salary. Both live-in maid and day maids are easy to find. Besides monthly pay, the employer must provide uniforms, food, and for daily domestics, transportation money. Live-in servants need a simple bed and chest of drawers, available locally at modest prices. Some find that to have domestic help is essential because their presence helps improve home security and because air pollution and dust create constant cleaning problems.

Gardeners, and ironing persons, are available as day workers, who can be hired to wash and wax floors, clean windows, and polish furniture (jobs maids generally do not do). Gardeners generally have their own lawn mowers. Good caterers are available for special entertaining at reasonable prices.

Peruvian law requires employers to give servants 15 days vacation when they complete a year of continuous service. Also, 15 days indemnity will be due domestic workers for each full year of service.

Religious Activities

The Lima Cathedral, originally built in the 16th century, has been almost entirely reconstructed and is currently used primarily as a museum. Lima has many other Catholic churches, some of considerable historic and artistic interest. Masses in English are conducted at the Santa Maria Reina Chapel, Avenida Sta. Cruz, Ovalo Gutierrez, in Miraflores.

Three Protestant churches have Sunday services in English: the Anglican Church of the Good Shepherd at Av. Santa Cruz 491, Miraflores. Sunday services include Holy Communion at 8:00 a.m. with Morning Service at 10:00 (Creche and Sunday school available). The International Union Church at Av. Angamos 1155, Miraflores offers interdenominational Worship Services in English on Sundays at 10:30 and Sunday school at 9:30 (adults) and at 10:15 (children). The Union Church also offers Bible Studies on Friday, March to November. The New Life Bible Fellowship at Av. La Molina Este, 142 Rinconada del Lago, offers an interdenominational English Worship Service on Sunday at 11:00 a.m. in Iglesia Vida Nueva en Cristo. Nursery is available. Several Jewish congregations offer services in Hebrew and Spanish, with many English-speaking members of the congregation. Asociacion Judia de Beneficeacia Eculto de 1870 is located at Jose Galvez 282, Miraflores (4451089), Central Social y Cultura Sharon at Dos de Mayo (440-0290) and Union Israelita del Peru can be contacted at 4400290. Mormon services in English are also offered. Lima has missionaries from many Protestant denominations, but their church services are usually in Spanish. The YMCA and YWCA are active in the Lima community.

Education

School-age children usually attend the Colegio Franklin D. Roosevelt, an international school in Lima. Instruction is in English and programs are offered for preschool age children (3 and 4-year old), as well as kindergarten through grade 12. Colegio Roosevelt is accredited by the U.S. Southern Association of Colleges and Secondary Schools. This private, coeducational, nondenominational school, was established in 1946 to provide schooling for dependents of major U.S. companies in Peru. Its curriculum is primarily designed to prepare students for future enrollment in universities. The school has about 1,300 students (kindergarten through grade 12). The student population is currently 1,337 with U.S. citizens making up 26%, 52% Peruvian, and the remaining 22% of the students are third country nationals.

The large campus is quite impressive. Separate buildings are used for the high school, middle school, elementary school, multipurpose media facility, and the gymnasium. Many faculty and administrative personnel are U.S. citizens. School begins the first week in August and continues until early July, with a 2-1/2 month holiday from mid December through February. The school does not have a cafeteria. Children either carry their lunches or purchase snack food.

Guidance counselor interviews of secondary students assist in class scheduling. To assist administrators, the school recommends that copies of official transcripts, standardized tests, report cards, letters of recommendation and any additional information that would be helpful, be forwarded to FDR prior to your arrival. English, history, social studies, Spanish, science, math, and physical education are standard offerings in the high school as well as elective courses. International Baccalaureate (IB) courses and diploma as well as Advanced Placement (AP) are available. Additionally, Roosevelt offers a strong computer education program. Extracurricular activities include sports (baseball, basketball, soccer, field hockey, tennis, softball and volleyball). Photography Club, Drama Club, National Honor Society, student government and Varsity Club. Gifted and talented children programs are offered. Students with diagnosed mild learning disabilities are included in regular classes with support from a specialist. However, it should be noted that Coleglo Roosevelt has limited

Town square in Arequipa, Peru

resources for special needs students. Programs for students with learning difficulties or those in advanced curriculums do not compare with those offered in U.S. public school systems. It is important to contact the school before enrollment to discuss how best your child can be accommodated. All relevant information should be forwarded, along with academic and health records, before arrival to enable the school to better evaluate individual students. More detailed information regarding resources for special needs students at FDR can be obtained from the Overseas Briefing Center.

The school offers a short summer activities program. Colegio Franklin Delano Roosevelt can be contacted at: (phone) 51-1-435-0890, (fax) 51-1-4360927 or (e-mail) fdr@amersol.edu.pe.

Their web site address to be contacted is: www amersol. edu.pe.

Peru has many national and private universities, including 14 in Lima. One semester courses like those given in U.S. colleges and universities are generally not offered here. Agriculture and engineering are taught at national universities in Lima. All courses are in Spanish and enrollment is restricted.

The University of San Marcos in Lima is the oldest in the Americas (founded May 13, 155 1) and the largest in Peru. Its faculties include humanities, law, medicine, sciences, economics, education, and veterinary medicine. But this university has been plagued with student disturbances and is suffering an economic crisis.

The Catholic University is the largest private university in Lima. During July and August it sponsors a special program for U.S. students, as does the University of Lima, which has an excellent School of Communications. The University of the Pacific specializes in business education and other related programs.

Special Educational Opportunities

The Binational Centers offer a language program to teach Spanish to foreigners in Peru. In addition, English language classes are available. You can also arrange inexpensive private language tutoring.

Sports

Sports facilities, aside from various spectator sports, are primarily limited to private clubs, gymnasiums, or health studios. Lima has many popular, but expensive, sporting clubs and several tennis, golf, swimming, and riding facilities. Some clubs have almost impossible admission requirements, but others have memberships available that range from expensive to moderate. Clubs usually require initiation fees or shares (some of which can be sold on departure) plus monthly or quarterly dues. Several modern, well-equipped health studios and gymnasiums in the area provide exercise facilities, boxing, wrestling, weight lifting, etc. An active softball league operates on weekends at Roosevelt School.

The American Association is a social/charitable membership organization for U.S. citizens and Canadians living in Lima. Among its activities are group trips to outlying areas, a monthly restaurant night, and other social events. It sponsors a community picnic each year on Labor Day and a joint Canadian/U.S. Independence Day celebration in July.

Touring and Outdoor Activities

Almost every area and town in Peru has its own unique festivals and celebrations. These are mostly colorful religious events. Comfortable, clean tourist hotels operate in the most frequently visited towns. Reservations for all in-country travel can be made through several local travel agencies. The South American Explorers' Club has an office in Lima with extensive files on trips within Peru. Membership costs $30 per year.

Nearby Pacific Ocean beaches offer swimming and surfing, but the undertow and currents are sometimes dangerous, and many nearby beaches are contaminated by raw sewage. About 20 to 30 miles south of Lima are clean, pleasant beaches that are also safe for children. These include the Punta Hermosa and Santa Maria beaches. Surfing in Peru deserves special mention. The many coastal beaches provide a variety of waves rarely seen in other localities. However, the water is usually quite cold, so surfers require wetsuits as well as surfboards. Both are expensive in Peru. A group of sailing enthusiasts in

Lima holds regattas during the summer for Lightning class craft.

Both expensive surf and small boat fishing are available at Pucusana (30 miles south) and Ancon, though it is hard to get small boats in summer. Trout fishing is available at Lake Titicaca, on the Altiplano in southeast Peru about 810 miles from Lima, and in neighboring mountain streams, but not in the vicinity of the city.

Three aviation clubs are located about 12 miles from the city center. These include a flying club, a gliding club, and a parachute club. Fees vary and at times have been high by U.S. standards. A good working knowledge of Spanish is needed to participate in the activities of these clubs.

Lima has facilities for target, skeet, and trap shooting. You may rent or board horses at several stables and riding clubs. Inter-Club riding competition is well organized and competition keen. Spectator sports include horse races (held on Tuesday, Thursday, Saturday, and Sunday), polo, colorful bullfights (October–November), soccer, basketball, cockfights, and professional boxing and wrestling.

Bring any sports equipment you plan to use here, particularly tennis and squash racquets, scuba equipment, surfboards, golf clubs, badminton sets, ping-pong, volleyball, hunting and fishing equipment, bicycles, yard equipment for children, baseball gloves, balls and bats. Local equipment ins expensive. A game known as "fronton" is also popular and is similar to outdoor paddle ball.

Lima offers a wide choice of good restaurants for business lunches and social dining. Sidewalk cafes and drive-in restaurants abound in the city. Some snack bars feature American-type services and food. Certain tourist areas offer more elegant dining. Many popular restaurants specialize in Chinese food, pizza, fried chicken, or Peruvian Creole food. Many U.S. fast-food

franchises such as Burger King, Kentucky Fried Chicken, and Domino's Pizza operate in Lima.

Entertainment

Several theaters in Lima show first-run movies. American films are popular and are widely shown with original soundtracks and Spanish subtitles. Lima also has live theaters with most performances in Spanish. An active amateur theater group, sponsored by the British community, regularly presents plays in English.

The National Symphony Orchestra offers concerts during winter, at times featuring vocal or instrumental artists from Europe, the U.S., or other Latin American countries. The city has a local ballet company, and international ballet companies occasionally perform. International soloists participate in the elegant Municipal Theater's annual opera season.

Lima has several nightclubs with dance orchestras and floorshows, discos, and good jazz bars. These clubs are expensive and prices vary according to the entertainment offered.

Peruvians celebrate their country's independence on July 28 and 29 with military parades, official receptions, and religious ceremonies.

Social Activities

Most entertaining in Lima is done in private homes, clubs, or hotels.

Peruvians are conservative and reserved about admitting outsiders to their social and family circles, but they are friendly to Americans. With a little time and effort you can make valuable and pleasant friendships. It is a good idea to reconfirm appointments, particularly social engagements, the same day or the day before.

Social organizations open to membership by Americans (some by invitation only, others by application) include the American Society of Peru, the Toastmasters, the American Women's Literary Club, the Lima Women's Chorale, Good Companions (British theater group), Lions, Rotary, and several sport clubs. For children, Lima has active affiliates of Cub Scouts, Boy Scouts, and Girl Guides. Bring transfer cards if you wish to enroll your children in one of these groups.

Arequipa

Arequipa is 475 miles southeast of Lima, at the foot of the dormant volcano, *El Misti*, one of Peru's highest points (19,031 feet). The city proper, at an altitude of 7,550 feet, is the capital of Arequipa Department and had a metropolitan population of about 635,000 in 1990.

Arequipa was founded in 1540 by Francisco Pizarro on the site of an Inca town. It is situated on an oasis, in an arid region that grows crops for local consumption. The city is an important commercial center for southern Peru and northern Bolivia, producing leather, nylon, textiles, and foodstuffs. A steel mill and textile plants also are in operation.

Tourism is an important industry here. Incan ruins, hot springs, and bathing resorts are among Arequipa's tourist attractions. Examples of Spanish colonial architecture, almost completely destroyed in an 1868 earthquake, have been restored. Santa Catalina, a cloistered convent, is said to be an architectural marvel. Arequipa has been called the "white city" because of the light-colored *sillar* (building stone) which dominates the area.

There has been a university in Arequipa since 1821. The city is the seat of a Catholic diocese, the publishing center for two newspapers, and the site of several provincial banks and a Chamber of Commerce. One of Peru's three seismological stations is located here; the others are in Lima and Huancayo. The city is prone to severe earthquakes. The latest earthquake in the 1960s devastated the city.

Prescott Anglo-American School in Arequipa is a coeducational day school for pre-kindergarten through grade 12. It was founded in 1965 and is accredited by the country's Ministry of Education. Its curriculum is Peruvian, with Spanish a required language. Six members of its staff of 70 are U.S. citizens. Enrollment is about 1,140. Prescott is located a few miles from the center of the city; the mailing address is Apartado 1036, Arequipa, Peru.

OTHER CITIES

The ancient Inca city of **CAJAMARCA** is situated 350 miles north of Lima in Cajamarca Province. Conquistador Francisco Pizarro captured and executed Inca chief Atahualpa here in 1532. The colonial presence is evident in the cathedral and San Francisco Belén Church. Cajamarca relies on mining, agriculture, and manufacturing for its economic well-being; tourism is increasing in importance. The thermal springs known as "Baths of the Incas" are near this provincial capital of approximately 93,000. A main trading hub of the northern Andes, Cajamarca has adequate transportation via road and air.

CALLAO, on the doorstep of the capital city, is the chief seaport of Peru. It is situated on Callao Bay, only eight miles west of Lima. The city is the capital of Lima Department, and had a metropolitan population of approximately 575,000 in 1989. Founded in 1537, at the same time that Francisco Pizarro established Lima, Callao was incorporated as a town in 1671. As the gateway to Lima, it was frequently attacked. Sir Francis Drake captured the town in 1578. It later was held by Spanish loyalists until 1825, even though Peru had gained its independence in 1821; the Spanish also bombarded the city in 1866. Callao was occupied by Chile from 1881 to 1883 during the War of the Pacific. Major expansion of its harbor was undertaken in 1958. The harbor, which is sheltered by a small peninsula and an island, handles more than half of the nation's imports and exports. Metallurgical industries, shipbuilding factories, breweries, and sugar refineries are found in Callao. Exports include minerals, wool, refined metals, fish oil, and fish meal. Callao was totally destroyed in 1746 by an earthquake and a tidal wave, and again severely damaged in 1940; however, many colonial landmarks survive.

CERRO DE PASCO rests in Peru's central highlands 112 miles northeast of Lima. One of the highest cities in the world at an altitude of 14,436 feet, it gained renown for its mining in the mid-1630s. Silver dominated the industry for 200 years. Today the original silver deposits are long depleted, replaced by gold, copper, lead, zinc, and other minerals. Cerro de Pasco is the capital of Pasco Province and has an estimated population of 70,000.

CHICLAYO, with a 2000 population of about 517,000, is a maritime city in northwestern Peru, 400 miles north of Lima. The capital of Lambayeque Department, it is situated on the coastal desert between the Pacific Ocean and the Andes Mountains. Chiclayo gets little rainfall and may go years at a time without receiving any, but Andean streams are used for irrigation. The artificial watering enables the area to raise sugarcane and the greatest part of the country's rice. Chiclayo has a university, founded in 1962, and an agricultural college, established in 1963. The city has many parks and gardens and a large marketplace.

CHIMBOTE, one of Peru's fastest-growing urban areas, was reconstructed as a model city less than 20 years ago. The city, 225 miles northwest of Lima on the Pacific coast, made international headlines in 1970 when a massive earthquake struck. The unique natural harbor accounts for the important import/export business here. This involves agriculture, manufactured goods, and bulk materials. Excellent transportation for this community of 253,000 is provided by an airport and by the city's location on the Pan-American Highway. Chimbote is also the terminus of a local railroad.

CUZCO (also spelled Cusco) is 300 miles southeast of Lima at the junction of the Huatanay and Tullamayo rivers. Situated at an altitude of 11,200 feet, Cuzco's population, close to 300,000, is predominantly Indian. Cuzco once was the capital of a vast Inca empire, known as the "City of the Sun." It is thought to have been founded in the 11th century by Manco Capac, the first ruler of the Incas. At that time, the city had massive temples, fortresses, walls, and beautiful palaces. Today, the Temple of the Sun is the site of a Dominican convent. Ruins of some of the Inca buildings survive, notably the fortress of Sacsahuaman. Francisco Pizarro took Cuzco for the Spanish in 1522, destroyed much of the ancient city, and constructed a colonial city, using many of the old walls as foundations for new buildings. The Renaissance cathedral of La Merced is the most noteworthy of the many churches in Cuzco. An earthquake destroyed a broad area of the city in 1950, but most of the historical buildings have been restored, and Cuzco still is considered the "archaeological capital of South America." The National University of Cuzco was built in 1597. The Feast of Into Raymi is the important festival here. Close to Cuzco is the ancient, terraced, "lost city" of Machu Picchu. Cuzco is a commercial and industrial center. Among the industries are textile, beer, and rug production. The city is linked by air, highway, and railroad with Lima.

HUANCAYO, a city whose metropolitan-area population was estimated at 327,000 in 2000, is situated in central Peru, on the Montaro River. A university, founded in 1962, and a national seismological station are located here. Huancayo is the hub of a large Indian district. Many Indians come to Huancayo to trade at the city's central market. The city has many beautiful examples of modern and religious architecture. Huancayo is a major commercial and tourist center for Peru's Central Andes region. In 1966, the Museo Cabrera was opened. It contains pottery and engraved stones from the ancient Nazca culture.

ICA, on the river whose name it bears, is 170 miles southeast of Lima. The capital of Ica Department, this city of 161,400 (1993 est.) is located next to the Pan-American Highway. The Spanish settled here in 1563. Ica, twice destroyed by earthquakes, is today a commercial center for the cotton, wool, and wine produced in the region, and is also a summer resort. A university was founded in Ica in 1961. The shrine of Our Lord of Luren, site of many pilgrimages, is located here.

IQUITOS is in northeastern Peru, 1,270 miles northeast of Lima. The capital of Loreto Department, it lies on the Amazon, approximately 2,300 miles from the river's mouth. Founded in 1863, Iquitos, with a 2000 population of 367,000, is the farthest inland port of appreciable size in the world. The city became important early in the 20th century with the boom in rubber, but declined soon afterward when the market collapsed. Today, rubber, coffee, cotton, and timber are exported from Iquitos. The Andes Mountains are a barrier to the transport of commercial goods to the Pacific, so Iquitos' products are exported via the Atlantic Ocean. A university was founded here in 1961. Iquitos is the cultural, religious, and tourist center of eastern Peru.

PISCO is a port on the Pacific Ocean, about 130 miles south of Lima, with a population of about 56,000. Large vineyards surround the city, and one of its major industries is the production of Pisco brandy. Cotton is also cultivated and processed in the area. Other industries in Pisco include textile manufacturing and cotton seed milling. Subsistence farming and fishing are also pursued. Adjacent to Pisco, on the Paracus Peninsula, are ruins from a pre-Incan civilization.

PIURA, 425 miles northeast of Lima, is situated in the Piura valley of the Peruvian coastal desert. San Miguel de Piura, originally situated on the coast, was the first Spanish settlement in Peru, founded by Francisco Pizarro in 1532. Because of unhealthy conditions, the city was moved to the present inland site of Piura, about 35 miles southeast of its port, Paita. Sebastián de Benalcázar set out from here to conquer Ecuador. Severely damaged by an earthquake in 1912, this city of 325,000 (2000 est.) residents has developed into a commercial center for corn, rice, cotton, and sugarcane produced in the region. The cotton market in Piura is extensive; several cotton gins and cottonseed oil mills are located in the immediate area. A technical university opened here in 1961.

In east-central Peru about 80 miles from the Brazil border sits **PUCALLPA,** half civilized, half rain forest frontier town. This city of approximately 172,300 (1993 est.) residents was opened to the outside world in 1945 upon the completion of the Lima-Pucallpa highway. First settled in the early 1530s, Pucallpa is the largest city in Ucayali Department, as well as a market center and industrial district. Primary industries in Pucallpa include sawmills and plants for extracting rosewood oil. It is accessible by air or river traffic; there are no paved roads. This area has become headquarters for several missionaries and colonizers.

TRUJILLO is a coastal city in northwestern Peru, about 300 miles north of Lima. Its port, Salaverry, is nine miles to the west. The capital of La Libertad Department, Trujillo has a metropolitan population of about 652,500. The city was founded in 1534 and played an important role in the fight against Spanish rule. Independence was declared in 1820 and, in 1825, Trujillo served as Peru's provisional capital, as well as main headquarters for Simón Bolívar. In 1617, a wall was built to protect the city from English pirates; today, the wall is one of the principal points of interest. Situated in a fertile oasis of the coastal desert, Trujillo is a thriving commercial and industrial center. Rice and sugar are processed here, and the city also produces textiles, leather goods, and food products. The University of La Libertad was founded in Trujillo in 1824. Four miles west are the ruins of the pre-Incan city of Chan-Chan, believed to have been established between 800 and 1000. Chan-Chan is recognized as the capital of the pre-Incan civilization of Chium, and once had 200,000 inhabitants. Walls, decorated in relief designs, are part of the ruins today. In 1990, Trujillo had an estimated population of 532,000.

COUNTRY PROFILE

Geography and Climate

Peru is on the west coast of South America, south of the Equator, between 0 and 18 degrees south latitude and 70 degrees and 81 degrees west longitude. It is the fifth most populated country in Latin America, and it is three times the geographic size of California.

The country has four distinct geographic areas: the narrow coastal desert region (about 25 to 40 miles wide), barren except for irrigated valleys; the Andean highlands or sierra, containing some of the world's highest mountains; the "ceja de montana" (eyebrow of the mountain), a long narrow strip of mountainous jungle on the eastern slope of the Andes; and the selva or rain forest area, which covers over half the country, including the vast Amazon River Basin and the Madre de Dios River Basin.

The sierra, which makes up over one-fourth of Peru, is an area of uneven population distribution, rich in mineral wealth. Many of its inhabitants live at elevations above 10,000 feet. The selva region is sparsely populated and only partially explored. The climate in the ceja de montana varies with the elevation from temperate to tropical.

Because Lima lies on an axis of instability in the Earth's crust, seismic activity is common. Light earthquakes called "temblores" occur but seldom cause damage. For example, between May 1998 and May 1999, 85 light earthquakes occurred. A strong earthquake occurred in Lima, Callao, and environs on May 24, 1940, causing major damage and claiming over 2,000 lives. Also, serious earthquakes occurred in Cuzco (1950), Arequipa (1958 and 1960), the Lima-Callao area (1966–74), and Chimbote and the Callejon de Huaylas (1970).

Peru lies below the Equator; therefore its seasons along the Pacific Coast are the reverse of those in the Northern Hemisphere. Summer lasts from about mid-December through April in that region and is generally pleasant, with warm, sunny days and cool, comfortable nights. February is usually the warmest, with an average temperature of about 79°F, but humidity averages 83 percent. Temperatures rarely range above the mid-80s. Only two distinct seasons occur in the highlands: the rainy season from December to April and a dry period the rest of the year. Temperatures in the sierra fluctuate considerably with the weather and altitude.

Winter along the coast lasts from May or June to November. The weather is chilly and damp. Sunny days in Lima's winter are rare, particularly in July, August, and September. Rain is virtually unknown; however, a fine mist often falls and fog is common. The coolest, dampest months are July and August, with average temperatures about 60°F and rarely falling below the low 50s. Humidity is high all year, especially in winter, requiring constant vigilance against mildew and mold.

Population

Peru's 1999 population was estimated at 25.23 million, with a population growth rate of about 1.7 percent per year. The nation's population consists of many ethnic groups, of which about one-third

live in the Lima metropolitan area. Indigenous peoples constitute about 35 percent of the population, while Peruvian of mixed indigenous and European descent ("mestizo") comprise almost 50 percent. Whites comprise almost 10 percent of the population, while Asians and Blacks make up less than 5 percent of the total population. In the Lima metropolitan area, the population is overwhelmingly mestizo and white, with relatively large Japanese and Chinese communities.

Peru has two official languages - Spanish and the foremost indigenous language, Quechua. Spanish is used by the government and the media, and in most forms of education and commerce. English is spoken by many educated Peruvians, and is understood in most major hotels and in many restaurants and shops catering to tourists. Amerindians who live in the Andean highlands speak Quechua or Aymara and are ethnically distinct from the diverse indigenous groups, who live on the eastern side of the Andes and in the tropical lowlands adjacent to the Amazon basin. All of the indigenous languages are losing ground with increases in indigenous people moving to the largest cities, where Spanish is the most commonly used language.

Public Institutions

When the Spanish arrived in the early 16th century, the territory now known as Peru was part of the Inca Empire that extended from southwestern Colombia to central Chile. Its conquest by a handful of adventurers led by Francisco Pizarro (who founded Lima, which he called the "City of Kings") was facilitated by the aftereffects of the succession struggle in the Inca Empire between two half-brothers, Atahualpa and Huascar.

Peru was part of Spain's American empire for almost 300 years. Several prominent leaders of South American wars of independence played a role in Peru's liberation: San Martin proclaimed Peru's independence on July 28, 1821; and Bolivar was President of Peru from 1824 to 1826. Sucre won the battle of Ayacucho in 1824 (generally considered the last major engagement of the wars of independence).

Since becoming independent, Peru and its neighbors have been engaged in intermittent territorial disputes. Chile's victory over Peru and Bolivia in the War of the Pacific (1879–83) resulted in a territorial settlement in which Peru lost Arica and Tarapaca Provinces to Chile. Following a serious clash between Peru and Ecuador in 1941, the Rio Protocol (of which the U.S. is guarantor) established the current boundary between the two countries. Occasional brief skirmishes have occurred over the years along a part of the border area still undemarcated. Major fighting broke out on the Peru-Ecuador border (limited to a sparsely populated jungle area) in January 1995 until a cease-fire was brokered by the four Rio Protocol guarantors in March. The U.S. participated in observing the cease-fire, and along with Brazil, Argentinia and Chile, helped facilitate the signing of a global and definitive peace agreement on October 26, 1998.

Throughout Peruvian history, the military has played a prominent role. Coups have repeatedly interrupted civilian, constitutional government. The last period of military rule lasted from 1968 to 1980.

For centuries, the Peruvian Indian population has cultivated the coca plant (*Erythroxylum coca vas coca*), whose leaf is chewed as a mild stimulant and specific against altitude sickness, used as an herbal tea, or used for some traditional or religious ceremonies. In the 1870s, the pharmaceutical industry isolated the cocaine alkaloid, a powerful local anesthetic, but also a highly addictive stimulant with significant potential for abuse.

An initial burst of cocaine abuse in Europe and the U. S. subsided at the time of World War I, but in the 1970s, escalating demand for cocaine in the U.S. again led to vast expansion in the limited traditional coca crops by much greater cultivation destined for illicit drug production. Since that time, cocaine has become the most significant illicit substance of abuse in the U.S., and is a growing problem for the rest of the world.

Peru is overwhelmingly the world's largest producer of raw material for cocaine, and the illegal drug trafficking industry has since the 1980s become recognized by the Peruvian people as one of their greatest domestic problems, a source of financing for terrorist groups, corruption of democratic political and judicial institutions, economic and social distortion, and devastation of the Amazon environment.

Peru returned to democratic rule in 1980 when Accion Popular led by American-educated Fernando Belaunde Terry came to power. In the 1985 elections, Alan Garcia of the center-left American Popular Revolutionary Party (APRA) won the presidency and a controlled majority of the two Houses of Congress. American- educated Alberto Fujimori, an independent candidate, was elected President in 1990. On April 5, 1992, with the support of the armed forces, President Fujimori suspended the constitution and closed down the country's congress and courts in what became known as "the auto-coup." Following pressure by the international community, Fujimori called national elections to choose a new unicameral congress in November 1992 to draft a new constitution. Fujimori's political movement, Cambio 90/Nueva Mayoria, won a majority of seats; several traditional political parties boycotted the election.

The new constitution, which the congress drafted, was narrowly approved in a nationwide referendum in October 1993. Unlike the previous constitution, the new one allowed a sitting president to run for reelection, which Fujimori did and won by a landslide in April 1995. In 1996, the Congress passed legislation interpreting the consti-

tutional term limits for president, that made it possible for Fujimori to seek reelection in the 2000 national elections. The new legislative body is a unicameral congress with 120 members elected at large. President Fujimori's party holds 71 seats, and a variety of other groups, the largest of which is Union Por El Peru, hold the rest.

Under President Fujimori, many of the problems that haunted his predecessors—including terrorism, significant human rights violations, and hyperinflation—have been eliminated or greatly reduced. Some 30,000 persons, including thousands of noncombatants, died between 1980 and 1995 as two insurgencies challenged the government. A turning point was the September 1992 capture by police of Abimael Guzman, the founder and leader of Peru's largest terrorist group, Sendero Luminoso (Shining Path). However, other serious problems remain, including poverty, high unemployment, the illicit drug industry, and a controversial judicial branch.

Peru is divided into 24 departments and the Constitutional Province of Callao (the country's chief port, adjacent to Lima). The departments are subdivided into provinces that in turn are composed of districts. Municipal government is a distant second in power to the central government, with regional government a mere appendage of the latter.

Arts, Science, and Education

As Spain's most important viceroyalty in South America, Peru was an art-producing center. Art continues to be appreciated in Lima, where numerous commercial art galleries and museums exist. During the last three decades, painters such as Gerardo Chavez, Alberto Quintanilla, and Jose Carlos Ramos have gained international stature along with Peru's renowned painter Fernando de Syszlo and sculptor Victor Delfin. A younger generation of promising artists has also sprung up at a time when Peru's economy provides more opportunity to promote the arts.

Peru is well known for its writers and poets. Mario Vargas Llosa is one of the world's most renowned contemporary novelists. His novels and essays are read abroad and have been widely translated. His bestselling titles include *Green House*, *Conversation in the Cathedral*, *Aunt Julia and the Scriptwriter*, and *The War of the End of the World*. His most recent is *A Fish in the Water*. Other poets and writers are Julio Ramon Ribeyro, Alfredo Bryce Echenique, Antonio Cisneros, and Blanca Varela.

With the recovering economy and the strengthened internal security situation in Peru, the country is resuming its cultural life. Musical offerings, including opera, are also available in Lima. Internationally known soloists, ensembles, and conductors perform with either the National Symphony Orchestra or under the sponsorship of the Philharmonic of Lima. The three famous tenors Luciano Pavarotti, Placido Domingo, and Jose Carreras, for example, all visited Peru during 1995. Top foreign singers, folk dancers, and ballet groups perform in Lima every year, and quality chamber groups present concerts during the May–December season. U.S. artists perform under the auspices of USIS and Peru's Binational Centers (BNC's) in Lima or in provincial cities.

The Peruvian theater has had a long and colorful history. Today, it is a popular national institution, with many active professional and amateur university groups. An increasing number of professional companies continue performing regularly, with several specializing in modern theater. USIS and the Lima BNC recently staged the Tennessee Williams play *The Night of the Iguana* with great success.

The Good Companions, a nonprofessional theater group sponsored by the British community, performs in English several times yearly at the British Theater under the auspices of the British Council.

Spanish and English classes, a varied program of cultural presentations, and a modest bilingual library are available to Americans and Peruvians at the Lima Binational Center and its branch in Miraflores (Instituto Cultural Peruano Norteamericano-ICPNA), where more than 10,000 Peruvians study English. Other Binational Centers, also supported by English teaching, are located in Arequipa, Cuzco, Trujillo, Chiclayo, Piura, and Huancayo. Americans are encouraged to request the monthly activities bulletin of the Lima ICPNA's and to visit the provincial centers, where they are assured of a cordial welcome.

Commerce and Industry

Peru is a developing country blessed with extensive natural resources that enhance its potential for development. Rich mineral deposits in the Andes, abundant timber resources in the Amazon region, and an unusually bountiful supply of fish along the country's long coastline form a solid base of natural wealth. The arable lands along the coast offer the potential for considerable growth in agriculture, with sufficient investment in irrigation and other agricultural technologies.

In 1997, Peru's Economy grew by 7.2 percent, while inflation, at only 6.5 percent, fell to its lowest level in a quarter century. Peru's economy faltered in 1998, however, as the combined adverse effects of the Asian crisis (which depressed metal prices), the El Niño weather phenomenon (which hurt the important fishing industry) and the Russian crisis (which caused foreign investors to withdraw portfolio investments and foreign banks to suspend lines of credit to Peruvian banks) took their toll. The 1998 Gross Domestic Product grew by 0.7 percent while the inflation rate fell to 6.5 percent. The following year saw

an estimated growth of about 3 percent.

Confidence in the Peruvian economy stems from the program of fiscal discipline undertaken by President Alberto Fujimori since his first term in office (1990). His policies halted the hyperinflation of the 1980s and put Peru on an unprecedented growth path. He succeeded in reinserting Peru into the global financial community by committing to repay official debt to foreign creditors, and by his efforts to stem terrorist activity.

The Peruvian Government actively seeks to attract both foreign and domestic investment in all sectors of the economy. In 1991, the Peruvian government began an extensive privatization program, encouraging foreign investors to participate. From 1991 through 1998, privatization sales totaled about $7 billion, of which foreign investors purchased the vast majority. Foreign investors have the same rights as national investors to benefit from any investment incentives, such as tax exemptions. Foreign direct investment has been spurred by the significant progress Peru has made over the last eight years toward economic, social, and political stability.

The Peruvian economy was not as hard hit during 1998 and early 1999 as some other Latin American economies (such as Brazil's which was forced to devalue its currency at the beginning of 1999). Most observers attribute the relative calm in Peruvian financial markets to its fiscal and monetary discipline, the size of its international reserves, and its floating exchange rate. Nevertheless, at the start of 1999 business leaders in Peru and others were calling for the government to spur domestic demand by increasing government spending.

The U.S. government advises the American Business Community that the best prospects for investment include mining, oil, and gas, construction, telecommunications, food processing, food packaging, and personal security equipment. Tour-

Marketplace in Peru

Cory Langley. Reproduced by permission.

ism-related products (such as hotel and restaurant supplies) are also promising. In the services sector, consulting services (especially in the areas of finance and tourism) and licensing of franchises are also good prospects.

Transportation

Automobiles

General traffic and driving practices differ greatly from those in the U.S. Traffic signs are widely disregarded. Improper signaling, failure to signal, and excessive speeding are frequent. Traffic signals frequently fail, compounding congestion and confusion. Lima's traffic can be nerve racking at first, but most people soon adjust to the improvised driving patterns. Traffic in Peru moves on the right as in the U.S.

Leaded gasoline is available in 84 and 95 octane and unleaded at 90 and 97 octane. The latter grades are most commonly used by those with American cars but do not give the same performance as U.S. high test. The cost of a gallon of gasoline in 1995 was almost double U.S. rates. Nowadays the cost of a gallon is between 6 and 7.87 new soles. Your catalytic converter may be removed here to accommodate the local leaded gasoline at more reasonable prices.

Local

Taxis, buses and smaller microbuses abound. Buses are crowded but inexpensive. Regular taxi service is available at reasonable prices but the condition of most taxis is poor. Passengers should agree upon a price before entering the vehicle. Telephone dispatched taxi service is also available at higher rates.

Regional

Lima, an important air hub of South America, has a large, fairly modern airport, served by American Airlines, Delta Airlines, United Airlines and Continental Airlines. Other international airlines serving Lima include Air France, Lan-Chile, Viasa (Venezuela), Avianca (Colombia), Varig (Brazil), Aero Peru, Iberia (Spain), LAB (Bolivia), Lufthansa (Germany), Alitalia (Italy), and others.

The ships that regularly service Callao Port and offer passenger transportation are from the Crowley American Transport and Maersk Lines. Their ships depart every 15 days or so from Miami, New Orleans, Houston, and New York.

Communications

Telephone and Telegraph

Long-distance telephone and telegraph services to and from the U.S. and other countries are good and getting better.

All services are routed via satellite. AT&T, MCI and Sprint direct dialing to the U.S. is available through the Peruvian telephone company (Telefonica, a member of the ITU). It is possible to dial direct to almost any country in the world.

Radio and TV

Lima has 32 AM and 36 FM radio stations that provide news and popular Latin American, classical, contemporary, European, American, and Peruvian music. World news coverage in Spanish is adequate, and reception is good. Peru's leading news radio station is Radio Programas del Peru (RPP): BO 730 AM and 89.7 FM. VOA shortwave reception is good, and VOA Spanish programs are regularly rebroadcast on Radio Miraflores (1250 AM), RPP, and others.

Seven TV stations operate in Lima. One of them, Channel 5, transmits 24 hours daily, while the others start in the morning or at midday and broadcast until late at night. All broadcasts are in color and use the standard American television (NTSC) system. Most programs are the same as in the U.S. - soap operas, Westerns, audience participation, domestic comedies, old movies, and dubbed U.S. shows. All are commercial with 8 to 22 minutes of advertising an hour. Two Peruvian companies provide cable TV service to metropolitan Lima. The monthly fee is approximately $40 for about 50 channels including some from Europe, Chile, Mexico, Brazil, Argentina, and the U.S. (CNN, ABC, NBC and CBS, but ESPN, TNT, FOX, and HBO are not the U.S. premium channels).

Recent enacted Peruvian telecommunications laws aim to make the content of Peruvian TV more educational and cultural. American TVs with a transformer to convert 220v current to 110v will receive local programs. However, cables, rabbit ears or access to an external antenna is required. Bring radio, TV equipment, VCRs, and TV cassettes from the U.S. as they are expensive here.

Ham radio operators, who hold a valid U.S. license, are entitled to operate in Lima.

Licenses also can be obtained locally. Prior notice and payment of a small fee must be given to the Ministerio de Transportes y Comunicaciones, Direccion General de Telecomunicaciones.

In the past few years, VCRs have become very popular. Many places rent English-language films, both current and classic, as well as U.S. TV shows. Tapes, the majority of these available for VHS systems at moderate prices, are often pirated so the quality is poor. However, a U.S. video chain (Blockbuster Video) has opened several stores.

Several local Internet Service Providers (ISPs) offer standard dial up services for those bringing personal computers. Surge protectors are advisable. 28.8 kbps to 54 kbps modem speeds are available depending on the telephone lines servicing the area where the user resides. ISPs provide communications and browser software for most standard operating systems. ISP subscription fees vary but closely parallel those in the U.S. ranging from $10.50 to $19 per month. Red Cientifica Peruana (RCP) is the longest established and perhaps the best known ISP with full, 24-hour dial-up service. America On Line (AOL) and other U.S. Internet services are available, but users must pay a per-minute charge for connect time via long distance telephone lines.

Newspapers, Magazines, and Technical Journals

Lima has a competitive press with 16 daily newspapers. The most influential is the 159 year-old paper of record, conservative *El Comercio.* Well-informed readers often also consult center-right *Expreso* and center-left *La Republica.*

Gestion tries to be Peru's version of *The Wall Street Journal. El Peruano,* the government gazette, is the only medium that publishes the text of official communications. Other

dailies are more or less sensationalistic and colorful.

Three political magazines are published in Lima. The most influential is centrist *Caretas;* followed by independent, center-left *Si;* and the more popularly oriented *Gente.* Two respected intellectual bimonthlies, *Debate* and moderate leftist *Quehacer,* are published along with a wide range of specialized periodicals on economics and other fields.

Newspapers are relatively expensive. Newsstands sell copies at 58 cents to 88 cents daily and 66 cents to $1.11 on Sundays with home delivery costing more. The official daily *El Peruano* costs a hefty 88 cents. Magazines have become quite expensive (at about $3).

Lima has distributors of most major U.S. dailies. At one of them, Durlar, at Tiziano 205, San Borja, phone 475-8025, you can buy or arrange for delivery of the *Wall Street Journal,* the *New York Times,* the *Washington Post,* and the *International Herald Tribune,* all 1 or 2 days old. They may also be ordered by mail. The international edition of the *Miami Herald,* which has been printed in Lima and available for same-day sale, including home delivery, is being renegotiated at the time of this writing. Newsstands sell *Time, Newsweek,* and a few other popular American magazines. Prices are higher than those in the U.S. Some bookstores, mostly in Miraflores and San Isidro, sell English-language books.

Health and Medicine

Medical Facilities

Lima has several good private hospitals called "clinicas." These clinics lack some of the high-tech equipment found in the U.S. but are more than adequate for emergency situations and stabilizing patients. The physicians are trained in Peru, Europe, and in the U.S. Many are U.S.-board certified.

Individuals should have planned elective surgery done in the U.S. In general U.S. health insurance is not accepted and payment is expected at the time of the visit (expenses generally are reimbursable as allowed through your specific insurance plan). Dental care including orthodontia is available by both U.S.- and Peruvian-trained dentists. Individuals should have a general dental examination prior to arrival.

Community Health

Lima has a high incidence of hepatitis A, measles, typhoid, diarrheal disease, and tuberculosis. Poverty, overcrowding, and malnutrition are common. Malaria, yellow fever, dengue, and rabies are common in the jungle.

Expatriate families are generally healthy. They experience the same illnesses as in the U.S. in addition to gastro-intestinal infections, usually from contaminated food or water. Winter (May through November) is cool and humid. The cool, sunless weather increases the number of colds, bronchitis, asthma, and allergy-related complaints. Due to many factors, e.g., terrorism, high crime, need for increased residential security, and periodic water shortages, and the long, sunless, gray winter, many individuals experience stress-related symptoms and occasional depression.

Preventive Measures

The following are suggestions for staying healthy in Peru:

• Use bottled water, as tap-water is not potable. Commercially prepared soft drinks and beer are considered safe.

• Vegetables and fruit require disinfection with a chlorine solution before eating. Avoid salads and raw vegetables and fruits in restaurants. Do not buy from "ambulantes" (street vendors).

• It is recommended that you start the hepatitis A and the hepatitis B series before coming. Yellow fever immunization is required for jungle travel and for travel into some other countries (such as Brazil) from Peru. Have this vaccine before you come to Peru. The following immunizations should be kept current: typhoid; diphtheria; tetanus; polio; measles, mumps, and rubella; and HIB.

• Individuals who will be working in the jungles and/or traveling or living in outlying areas should take the pre-exposure rabies and hepatitis B vaccines prior to arrival.

• Hand-carry your immunization record as you would your passport.

• Bottled drinking water is not adequately fluoridated.

• Automobile accidents commonly occur. Seat belts and child-restraint systems are strongly recommended.

• Before traveling outside Lima, check for malaria precautions, as the malaria prophylaxis medication recommended depends on the area of jungle travel within Peru. Generally, Mefloquine or Doxycycline are recommended. Notes for Travelers

NOTES FOR TRAVELERS

Passage, Customs & Duties

A valid U.S. passport is required to enter and depart Peru. Tourists must also provide evidence of return or onward travel. U.S. citizens do not need a visa for a tourist stay of 90 days or less. U.S. citizens remaining in Peru more than 90 days must pay a monthly fee to extend their visa for up to three additional months, for a total of six months. U.S. citizens, including children, who remain in Peru over six months without obtaining a residence visa will have to pay a fine in order to depart Peru.

Visitors for other than tourist or family visit purposes must obtain a Peruvian visa in advance. Business visitors should ascertain the tax and exit regulations that apply to the specific visa that they are granted. U.S. citizens whose passports are lost or stolen in Peru must obtain a new passport and present it, together with a police report of the loss or theft, to the main immigration office in the capital city of Lima to obtain permission to depart. An airport tax of $25 per person must be paid in U.S. currency when departing Peru. There is also a small airport fee for domestic flights. For further information regarding entry requirements, travelers should contact the Peruvian Embassy at 1625 Massachusetts Avenue, NW, Suite 605, Washington, DC 20036; telephone (202) 462-1084 or 462-1085; Internet http://www.peruemb.org; or the Peruvian Consulate in Chicago, Houston, Los Angeles, Miami, New York, Patterson (NJ), San Francisco, or San Juan.

You can fly to Peru from most sections of the U.S. in less than 16 hours (6 hours nonstop from Miami).

Remember that the seasons are the reverse of those in the U.S., so pack your luggage accordingly.

The Government of Peru prohibits the exportation of ancient Indian artifacts and colonial art. The U.S. Government supports this policy and, in accordance with the GOP Law No. 12958 of February 22, 1958, and Decree of Law 18780 of February 4, 1971 (available in General Services Office). The packing companies in Lima are prohibited from packing and shipping items that appear to be antiques. Due to the large number of facsimiles, the packing companies cannot differentiate between the real item and a copy. In order to avoid delays, acquire in advance a certification from the Instituto Nacional de Cultura verifying that the item is a copy and may be exported.

U.S. citizens living in or visiting Peru are encouraged to register at the Consular Section of the U.S. Embassy in Lima and obtain updated information on travel and security in Peru. The Consular Section is open for American Citizen Services, including registration, from 8:00 a.m. to 12:00 noon weekdays, excluding U.S. and Peruvian holidays. The U.S. Embassy is located in Monterrico, a suburb of Lima, at Avenida Encalada, Block Seventeen; telephone (51-1) 434-3000 during business hours (8:00 a.m. To 5:00 p.m.), Or (51-1) 434-3032 for after-hours emergencies; fax (51-1) 434-3065 or 434-3037; Internet web site - http://usembassy.state.gov/lima. This web site provides information but does not yet have interactive capability to respond to specific inquiries. The U.S. Consular Agency in Cusco is located in the Binational Center (Instituto Cultural Peruana Norte Americano, ICPNA) at Avenida Tullumayo 125; telephone (51-8) 24-51-02; fax (51-8) 23-35-41; Internet address consagent-cuzco@terra.com.pe. The Consular Agency can provide information and assistance to U.S. citizen travelers who are victims of crime or need other assistance, but it cannot replace U.S. passports. U.S. passports are issued at the U.S. Embassy in Lima

Pets

Pets must have a certificate of good health issued by a registered U.S. or foreign veterinarian. A Peruvian consul must then notarize this document. A certificate of rabies inoculation is also necessary for dogs and cats. Dog owners are especially cautioned that Lima has high infestations of fleas and mites that are difficult to control. Owners should bring appropriate pesticides and shampoos to aid in treatment.

Firearms & Ammunition

Local law provides that law enforcement and military personnel are authorized to import handguns in calibers up to .45 (pistol) and .357 (revolver). All others are limited to 9mm and .38 calibers respectively. Shotguns up to 16 gauge and rifles up to .44 caliber are permitted. Personal full automatic weapons are not allowed. All firearms brought

into Peru must be taken out of the country when you leave.

Currency, Banking & Weights and Measures

Peru's currency changed on January 1, 1986, from the sol to the inti. On January 1, 1991, the currency changed from the inti to the new sol. In December 1999, the exchange rate is new soles 3.49 = $1.

A legacy from the years of hyperinflation is that many businesses price items in U.S. dollars. Payment is usually made in the sol equivalent value but many stores readily accept U.S. dollars as well. Counterfeiting, both of U.S. dollars and soles, is a problem and caution should be exercised when conducting transactions.

Peru uses the metric system of weights and measures, except for gasoline, which is sold by the gallon.

Specific Health Risks

Visitors to high-altitude Andean destinations such as Cusco (11,000 feet), Machu Picchu (8,000 feet), or Lake Titicaca (13,000 feet) should discuss the trip with their personal physician prior to departing the United States. Travel to high altitudes could pose a serious risk of illness, hospitalization, and even death, particularly if the traveler has a medical condition that affects blood circulation or breathing. Several U.S. citizens have died in Peru from medical conditions exacerbated by the high altitude. All people, even healthy and fit persons, will feel symptoms of hypoxia (lack of oxygen) upon arrival at high-altitude. Most people will have increased respiration and increased heart rate. Many people will have headaches, difficulty sleeping, lack of appetite, minor gastric and intestinal upsets, and mood changes. Most people may need time to adjust to the altitude. To help prevent these complications, consider taking acetazolamide (Diamox) after consulting your personal physician, avoid alcohol and smoking for at least one week after arrival at high altitudes, and limit physical

activity for the first 36 to 48 hours after arrival at high altitudes.

LOCAL HOLIDAYS

Jan. 1	New Year's Day
Mar/Apr	Holy Thursday*
Mar/Apr.	Holy Friday*
Mar/Apr.	Easter*
May 1	Labor Day
June 29	St. Peter and St. Paul
July 28-29	Independence Days
Aug. 31	St. Rose of Lima
Sept. 5	Labor Day
Oct. 12.	Combat of Angamos
Nov. 1	All Saints' Day
Dec. 14	Immaculate Conception
Dec 25.	Christmas

*variable

RECOMMENDED READING

These titles are provided as a general indication of the material published on this country.

Area Handbook for Peru. American University. Foreign Area Studies. U.S. Government Printing Office, 1993.

Barndt, Deborah. *Education and Social Change: A Photographic Study of Peru*. Kendall/Hunt Publishing Co., 1980.

Bingham, Hiram. *Lost City of the Incas*. Yale University Press, 1930. (Paperback edition).

Caraway, Caren. *Peruvian Textile Designs;* International Design Library, Stemmer House, 1983.

Carey, James C. *Peru and the United States, 1900-1962*, Notre Dame Press, 1964.

De Soto, Hernando. *The Other Path: The Invisible Revolution in the Third World*. Harper and Row, 1990.

Frost, Peter. *Exploring Cusco*. Nuevas Imagenes S.A., 1989.

Gilbert, Dennis L. *The Oligarchy and the Old Regimes in Peru*. Latin American Dissertation Series, Ithaca. Cornell Univ. Press, 1977.

Gorman, Stephen M. *Post-Revolutionary Peru: The Politics of Transformation*. Westview Press, 1982.

Hemming, John and Edward Ranney. *Monument of the Incas*. Little, Brown, 1982.

Insight Guides-Peru. Houghton Mifflin Co., 1994.

McClintock, Cynthia and Abraham Lowenthal. *The Peruvian Experiment Reconsidered*. Princeton University Press, 1983.

Minta, Stephan. *Aguirre: The Re-Creation of a 16th Century Journey Across South America*. Henry Holt and Company, 1993.

Morales, Edmundo. *Cocaine: White Gold Rush in Peru*. University of Arizona Press, 1989.

Morris, Robert. *Contemporary Peruvian Theater*. Texas Tech Press, 1977.

Moseley, Michael E. T*he Incas and their Ancestors*. Thomas and Hudson, Ltd. 1992.

Palmer, David Scott. *Peru: The Authoritarian Tradition*. Praeger Publishers. 1980.

Palmer, David Scott, ed. *Shining Path of Peru*. St. Martin's Press, 1992.

Peru in Pictures. Lerner Publications, Department of Geography Staff, Lerner, 1987.

Pike, Frederick B. The Modern History of Peru. Praeger Histories of Latin America. Praeger, 1967.

Poole, Deborah & Gerardo Renique. *Peru: Time of Fear*. Latin America Bureau. 1992.

Poole, Richard. *The Inca Smiled: The Growing Pains of an Aidworker in Ecuador*. One World Publications, 1993.

Prescott, William H. History of the Conquest of Peru. Modem Library, 1936. (Paperback edition). Basis for information on many subsequent publications.

Rachowiecki, Rob. *Peru: A Travel Survival Kit,* Lonely Planet, 1986.

Simpson, John. *In the Forests of the Night. Encounters in Peru with Terrorism, Drug-Running and Military Oppression*. Random House, 1993.

Stap, Don. *A Parrot Without a Name: The Search for the Last Unknown Birds on Earth*. University of Texas, 1990.

Stein, Steven. *Populism in Peru: The Emergence of the Masses and the Politics of Social Control*. University of Wisconsin Press, 1980.

Vargas Llosa, Alvaro. *The Madness of Things Peruvian: Democracy Under Siege*. Transaction Publishers, 1994.

Vargas Llosa, Mario. *A Fish in the Water: A Memoir.* Farrar Straus Giroux, 1994. *Aunt Julia and the Scriptwriter.* Farrar, 1982. (Paperback, AVON, 1985.) *The War of the End of the World.* Farrar, 1984.

Washington Office on Latin American Staff. *Peru in Crisis: Challenges to a New Government.* WOLA, 1990.

Werlick, David P *Peru: A Short History,* Southern Illinois University, 1978.

Wethey, Harold H. *Colonial Architecture and Sculpture in Peru*. Harvard University Press, 1949.

Wright, Ronald. *Cut Stones and Crossroads: A Journey in Peru.* Viking Penguin, 1988.

ST. KITTS AND NEVIS

Federation of St. Kitts and Nevis

Major City:
Basseterre

Other City:
Charlestown

INTRODUCTION

Christopher Columbus landed on St. Christopher in 1493, naming the island after his patron saint. French and English colonists settled in the region in the 1600s, and the colonists shortened the name to "**ST**. **KITTS** island." The settlers fought and eliminated the native Carib people. Sugar was the mainstay of the economy until well into the 20th century. St. Kitts-Nevis-Anguilla became part of the Leeward Islands Federation in 1871. In 1967, the three islands became an associated state. In 1969, Anguilla islanders rebelled and that island was permitted to secede in 1971. St. Kitts and Nevis became an independent federated state within the Commonwealth on September 19, 1983. In 1996, the premier of Nevis announced plans for the island to eventually secede from the federation and return to British control.

MAJOR CITY

Basseterre

Basseterre is the capital of St. Kitts and Nevis, with a population of 12,000. The city lies along the southern coast of St. Kitts's central region. The economy of St. Kitts was traditionally based on growing and processing sugarcane, but tourism and export-oriented manufacturing have assumed larger roles. The government-owned St. Kitts Sugar Manufacturing Corp. is still the largest industrial enterprise in the country.

Port Zante is Basseterre's new cruise ship port. Thirty acres of land have recently been reclaimed from the sea and added to Basseterre, which has building codes that encourage an 18th-century architectural style. The cruiseship terminal can handle vessels of up to 75,000 tons with a draft of 30 feet, and a marina takes yachts up to 70 feet long with a draft of 12 feet. Bradshaw International Airport (scheduled for completion in mid-1998) has one of the largest runways in the Caribbean and can handle jumbo jet traffic.

Recreation and Entertainment

Popular local team sports include basketball, cricket, soccer, netball, and volleyball. Mountain biking, horseback riding, and scuba diving and snorkeling over the coral reefs are popular tourist activities. The most popular dive sights on St. Kitts are Monkey Shoals, Coconut Tree Reef, Nags Head, Sandy Point, and the shipwrecked freighter of the River Taw. Local dive operators can provide instruction and equipment. There is a championship 18-hole golf on Nevis where PGA professionals offer private lessons.

The St. Kitts Sugar Manufacturing Corporation's sugar conducts factory tours, as does the St. Kitts Breweries Ltd.

Basseterre's Georgian architectural style attracts tourists. St. George's Anglican Church was originally built in 1670 as a French Catholic church, and it has been destroyed both intentionally and accidentally several times over the centuries. The present building dates from 1869. Independence Square, in the center of Basseterre, was once a slave market. Brimstone Hill has a massive old fortress that took 100 years to build. The fortress covers 38 acres and rises almost 800 feet above the Caribbean.

The St. Christopher Heritage Society has a display of photos that shows the history, culture, and marine life of the island.

OTHER CITY

CHARLESTOWN is the main town on Nevis. The Museum of Nevis History is located at the birthplace of

US statesman Alexander Hamilton. The museum features displays of rare pre-Colombian artifacts and colonial-era objects. Several resorts offer golden beaches, hiking trails, water sports, golf, tennis with accommodations ranging from modest plantation inns to luxury hotels.

COUNTRY PROFILE

Geography and Climate

St. Kitts lies about 5 miles southeast of the Netherlands Antilles and 45 miles northwest of Antigua in the Leeward Islands chain of the Caribbean Sea. Nevis lies two miles off the southeast coast of St. Kitts. The total area of St. Kitts is 104 square miles, and Nevis covers 36 square miles. Both islands are of volcanic origin. In the northwest of St. Kitts is the country's highest peak, Mt. Liamuiga (3,793 feet), and on the southern peninsula lies the Great Salt Pond. The highest point on Nevis is Mt. Nevis, at 3,232 feet. Temperatures stay between 68°F and 84°F throughout the year. The average annual rainfall is 43 inches, with the wet season lasting between May and November.

History

At the time of European discovery, the islands of St. Kitts and Nevis were inhabited by Carib Indians. Christopher Columbus landed on the larger island in 1493 on his second voyage and named it after St. Christopher, his patron saint. Columbus also discovered Nevis on his second voyage, reportedly calling it Nevis because of its resemblance to a snowcapped mountain (in Spanish, nuestra senora de las nieves or our lady of the snows). European colonization did not begin until 1623-24, when first English, then French colonists arrived on St. Christopher's island, whose name the English shortened to St. Kitt's island. As the first English colony in

© Wolfgang Kaehler/Corbis. Reproduced by permission.

Clock Tower and town square in Basseterre, St. Kitts

the Caribbean, St. Kitts served as a base for further colonization in the region.

St. Kitts was held jointly by the English and French from 1628-1713. During the 17th century, intermittent warfare between French and English settlers ravaged its economy. Meanwhile Nevis, settled by English settlers in 1628, grew prosperous under English rule. St. Kitts was ceded to Great Britain by the treaty of Utrecht in 1713. Both St. Kitts and Nevis were seized by the French in 1782.

The Treaty of Paris in 1783 definitively awarded both islands to Britain. They were part of the colony of the Leeward Islands from 1871-1956, and of the West Indies Federation from 1958-62. In 1967, together with Anguilla, they became a self-governing state in association with Great Britain; Anguilla seceded late that year and remains a British dependency. The federation of St. Kitts and Nevis attained full independence on September 19,1983.

Population

St. Kitts and Nevis has a population of 43,400. There are about 298 per-

sons per square mile, but the density on St. Kitts is twice that of Nevis. Over 90% of the population is of black African descent. There are minorities of mixed race persons, Indo-Pakistanis, and Europeans. The largest religious groups are the Anglican Church, the Church of God, the Methodist Church, the Moravians, the Baptists, Seventh-Day Adventists, the Pilgrim Holiness Church, and the Roman Catholic Church. English, spoken with local expressions, is the country's language.

Government

As head of state, Queen Elizabeth II is represented in St. Kitts and Nevis by a governor general, who acts on the advice of the prime minister and the cabinet. The prime minister is the leader of the majority party of the house, and the cabinet conducts affairs of state. St. Kitts and Nevis has a bicameral legislature: An 11-member senate appointed by the governor general (mainly on the advice of the prime minister and the leader of the opposition) and an 11-member popularly elected house of representatives which has eight St. Kitts seats and three Nevis seats. The prime minister and the cabinet are responsible to the Parliament.

St. Kitts and Nevis has enjoyed a long history of free and fair elections, although the outcome of elections in 1993 was strongly protested by the opposition, and the RSS was briefly deployed to restore order. The elections in 1995 were contested by the two major parties, the ruling People's Action Movement (PAM) and the St. Kitts and Nevis Labor Party. Labor won seven of the 11 seats, with Dr. Denzil Douglas becoming prime minister. In March 2000 elections, Denzil Douglas and the Labour Party were returned to power, winning eight of the 11 seats in Parliament. The Nevis-based Concerned Citizens Movement (CCM) won two seats and the Nevis Reformation Party (NRP) won one seat. The PAM party was unable to obtain a seat.

Under the constitution, Nevis has considerable autonomy and has an island assembly, a premier, and a deputy governor general. Under certain specified conditions, it may secede from the federation. In June 1996, the Nevis Island Administration under the concerned citizens movement of Premier Vance Amory announced its intention to do so. Secession requires approval by two-thirds of the assembly's five elected members and also by two-thirds of voters in a referendum. After the Nevis Reformation Party blocked the bill of secession, the premier called for elections for February 24, 1997. Although the elections produced no change in the composition of the assembly, Premier Amory pledged to continue his efforts toward Nevis' independence. In August 1998, a referendum on the question of independence for Nevis failed and Nevis presently remains in the Federation. The March 2000 election results placed Vance Armory, as head of the CCM, the leader of the country's opposition party.

Constitutional safeguards include freedom of speech, press, worship, movement, and association. Like its neighbors in the English-speaking Caribbean, St. Kitts and Nevis has an excellent human rights record.

Its judicial system is modeled on British practice and procedure and its jurisprudence on English common law. The Royal St. Kitts and Nevis police force has about 340 members.

Two thin diagonal yellow bands flanking a wide black diagonal band separate a green triangle at the hoist from a red triangle at the fly. On the black band are two white five-pointed stars.

Arts, Science, Education

Education is provided by the government and compulsory for 12 years. The Clarence Fitzroy Bryant College in Basseterre, completed in 1996, offers courses in vocational fields, the arts, sciences, and general studies, with plans to offer associate degrees as well as classes in conjunction with the University of the West Indies. The College of Further Education also provides higher education.

Commerce and Industry

St. Kitts and Nevis was the last sugar monoculture in the Eastern Caribbean. Faced with a sugar industry, which was finding it increasingly difficult to earn a profit, the Government of St. Kitts and Nevis embarked on a program to diversify the agricultural sector and stimulate the development of other sectors of the economy.

The government instituted a program of investment incentives for businesses considering locating in St. Kitts or Nevis, encouraging both domestic and foreign private investment. Government policies provide liberal tax holidays, duty-free import of equipment and materials, and subsidies for training provided to local personnel. Tourism has shown the greatest growth. By 1987, tourism had surpassed sugar as the major foreign exchange earner for St. Kitts and Nevis.

The economy of St. Kitts and Nevis experienced strong growth for most of the 1990s, but hurricanes in 1998 and 1999 contributed to a sharp slowdown in growth. Growth was only 1% in 1998 and 2.8% in 1999, compared to 7.3% in 1997. Tourism in particular suffered in 1998 and 1999 as a result of the hurricanes which forced the closure of one of the major hotels and heavily damaged the cruiseship pier. Significant new investment in tourism as well as continued government efforts to diversify the economy are expected to improve economic performance. Consumer prices have risen marginally over the past few years. The inflation rate was 3%-4% for most of the 1990s.

St. Kitts and Nevis is a member of the Eastern Caribbean Currency Union (ECCU). All members of the ECCU, The Eastern Caribbean Central Bank (ECCB) issues a common currency for all members of the ECCU. The ECCB also manages monetary policy, and regulates and supervises commercial banking activities in its member countries.

Transportation

The only railway on St. Kitts is a small line used by the government to transport sugarcane and processed sugar. Main roads circle each island. A state-run motorboat service shuttles passengers between the two islands. There is regular freight service to St. Kitts and Nevis from the US and Europe. Most ocean freight is now fully containerized. The deepwater harbor handles ships which service the islands. Smaller carriers sail between St. Kitts and Nevis and Puerto Rico, the US Virgin Islands, and St. Maarten.

Driving on St. Kitts and Nevis is on the left-hand side of the road. Seventy-five percent of the main road is in reasonably good condition, having been recently resurfaced, and secondary roads are also fairly good. The islands have good police enforcement of traffic regulations. More detailed information on roads and traffic safety can be obtained from the Ministry of Tourism, Culture and the Environment, Bay Road, Pelican Mall, P.O. Box 132, Basse Terre, St. Kitts, tel. (869) 465-8970.

Communications

The telephone system is operated by the government and international telecommunications services are privately operated. St. Kitts has one AM/FM radio station, and Nevis has two other AM stations. There is also one television broadcast station and two cable television systems. St. Kitts and Nevis has three newspapers: *The Democrat* (published by the opposition Peoples Action Movement), *The Observer* (independent), and *The Labour Spokesman* (affiliated with the governing Labour Party).

Health

There are over 40 physicians and 190 nurses in the country.

Medical care is limited. Doctors and hospitals often expect immediate cash payment for health services. U.S. medical insurance is not always valid outside the U.S. In some cases, supplementary medical insurance with specific overseas coverage, including provision for medical evacuation, has proved useful. For additional health information, travelers may contact the Centers for Disease Control and Prevention's international travelers hotline at (404) 332-4559; Internet http://www.cdc.gov.

LOCAL HOLIDAYS

Jan.1	New Year's Day
Feb	Carnival*
Feb. 22	Independence Day
Mar/Apr.	Good Friday *
Mar/Apr.	Easter*
Mar/Apr.	Easter Monday*
May 1	Labor Day
May/June	Whit Sunday (Pentecost)*
May/June	Whit Monday*
May/June	Corpus Christi*
June 8	Queen's Official Birthday
Aug. 2	Emancipation Day
Aug. 30	Feast of St Rose of Lima (Rose Festival)
Oct. 4	Thanksgiving
Oct. 17	Feast of St Margaret Alacoque
Nov. 1	All Saints' Day
Nov. 2	All Souls' Day (Fet le Mo)
Nov. 11	Remembrance Day
Nov. 22	Feast of St Cecilia
Dec. 13	National Discovery Day
Dec. 25	Christmas
Dec. 26	Boxing Day

*Variable

NOTES FOR TRAVELERS

A valid U.S. passport or certified U.S. birth certificate and a picture identification that contains both name and date of birth are required of U.S. citizens entering St. Kitts and Nevis. Visitors should also have a valid return ticket. St. Kitts and Nevis immigration recommends that visitors put their full home address in the U.S. on their arrival cards in order to facilitate the entry process. Stays of up to one month are granted at immigration. Anyone requiring an extension must apply to the Ministry of National Security. There is an airport departure tax. For further information, travelers can contact the Embassy of St. Kitts and Nevis, 3216 New Mexico Avenue, N.W., OECS Building, Washington, D.C. 20016, telephone (202) 686-2636, the Permanent Mission to the UN in New York at (212) 535-1934, or the Internet at http://www.stkittsnevis.org.

U.S. citizens living in or visiting St. Kitts and Nevis are encouraged to register at the Consular Section of the U.S. Embassy in Bridgetown, Barbados and obtain updated information on travel and security within St. Kitts and Nevis. Consular Section hours are 9:00 am-12 noon and 2:00 pm-4:00 pm, Monday-Friday except local and U.S. holidays. The U.S. Embassy is located in the American Life Insurance (ALICO) building, Cheapside, Bridgetown, Barbados, telephone 1-246-431-0225, fax 1-246-431-0179, e-mail address: Consular-Bridge@state.gov or Internet home page: http://usembassy.state.gov/posts/bb1/wwwhcons.html.

Disaster Preparedness

St. Kitts and Nevis is a hurricane-prone country. General information about natural disaster preparedness is available via the Internet from the U.S. Federal Emergency Management Agency (FEMA) at http://www.fema.gov.

ST. LUCIA

Saint Lucia

Major City:
Castries

INTRODUCTION

The second largest of the four Windward Islands, the Arawaks migrated to **ST. LUCIA** from South America during AD 200–400. The Caribs gradually replaced the Arawaks during AD 800–1000. Tradition has it that Columbus sighted the island on St. Lucy's Day (December 13) in 1498. The Dutch, English, and French all tried to establish trading posts on St. Lucia during the 17th century but the Caribs successfully defended their island for many years. Possession of the island changed between the British and French several times until 1814, when Britain took permanent possession. Unlike other islands in the area, sugarcane monoculture did not dominate the island's economy. Sugar was grown, along with tobacco, ginger, and cotton. Bananas became the main cash crop in the 20th century. Slavery was abolished in 1834 and indentured East Indian workers were brought to the island during the late 1800s. St. Lucia became an associated state with full internal self-government in 1967 and on February 22, 1979 it became an independent member of the Commonwealth of Nations.

MAJOR CITY

Castries

Castries, located along the harbor of Port Castries on the northwestern coast, is the capital of St. Lucia. Port Castries has been the hub of St. Lucia's economic activity for over a century. During the early 20th century, the port was an important coaling station in the Caribbean for ships crossing the Atlantic to and from South America. The town has a population of approximately 53,000, or about one-third of St. Lucia's population. Vigie Airport on the outskirts of Castries provides service to neighboring Caribbean islands. The port of Castries is a deepwater harbor with six berths and a cargo handling capacity of 365,000 tons per year. The main commodities shipped from the port include bananas, sugarcane, rum, molasses, cocoa, coconuts, limes, and various tropical fruits and vegetables. The Castries Market has operated for over 100 years and features hundreds of vendors selling tropical fruit and vegetables, spices, and local crafts.

Recreation

A fortress on Mt. Fortune (852 feet) overlooks Castries, and Vigie Beach is nearby. Coral reefs with colorful marine life attract divers. Since the island is volcanic, there are also some spectacular steep drop-off dive sites. The most popular dive sites include Anse Chastanet reef, the Key Hole Pinnacles, Superman's Flight, the Coral Gardens, Fairy Land, and Anse La Raye. There are also two wreck dives to explore. There are dive operators that provide equipment and training. Sulphur Springs in nearby Soufrière is a drive-through volcano and features a 7-acre crater lake and pools of bubbling sulfur-laden steam. The National Forest covers 19,000 acres and is a favorite of birdwatchers and hikers.

The Diamond Botanical Gardens dates back to the 1700s, when France's King Louis XIV wanted a place for his troops to enjoy the natural hot springs. The gardens feature a variety of tropical fruit trees, shrubs, vines, and flowers. Pigeon Island National Park contains the old barracks, magazines, and ramparts of Fort Rodney, which dates from the era when the British and French battled over control of the island. The museum at the fort used to be the British officers' dining area and was restored to show how it looked in 1808.

St. Lucia has several smaller hotels that allow visitors the chance to experience the authentic culture and cuisine of the island.

Entertainment

Jump Up is a weekly street fair and dance held Friday nights in Gros Islet, a small village north of Castries. St. Lucians and tourists alike pack the town's single street to enjoy Caribbean soca and reggae music, food, and drink. The Carnival celebration occurs every February and features a traditional Caribbean parade of colorful costumes and calypso music. The finals of the calypso competition and the naming of the Carnival King and Queen are held over the weekend, followed by a party in the streets that begins at 4:00 AM on Monday morning. The international Atlantic Rally for Cruises is a yacht race held in December that finishes in Rodney Bay. The St. Lucia Jazz Festival occurs in May and includes Caribbean and Cajun music shows, rhythm and blues, and contemporary and traditional jazz.

COUNTRY PROFILE

Geography and Climate

St. Lucia is a part of the Windward Islands group of the Lesser Antilles in the Caribbean sea. The island's total area is 239 square miles, or 3.5 times the size of Washington, D.C. The island is situated between Martinique to the north and St. Vincent to the southwest. The island is volcanic; the southern part is younger and more mountainous than the hilly and more level northern half. The highest mountain is Mt. Gimie, at 3,145 feet above sea level. Better known are the two peaks on the southern coast, Grand Piton (2,619 feet) and Petit Piton (2,461 feet), which together form one of the scenic highlights of the West Indies. The average yearly temperature is 79°f, with the warmest temperatures in September and the coolest in January. The average annual rainfall along the coast is 91 inches,

© Wolfgang Kaehler. Reproduced by permission.

View of Soufriere, St. Lucia

but more than 150 inches on the mountains.

History

St. Lucia's first known inhabitants were Arawaks, believed to have come from northern South America 200-400 A.D. Numerous archaeological sites on the island have produced specimens of the Arawaks' well-developed pottery. Caribs gradually replaced Arawaks during the period 800-1000 A.D.

Europeans first landed on the island in either 1492 or 1502 during Spain's early exploration of the Caribbean. The Dutch, English, and French all tried to establish trading

outposts on St. Lucia in the 17th century but faced opposition from hostile Caribs.

The English, with their headquarters in Barbados, and the French, centered on Martinique, found St. Lucia attractive after the sugar industry developed in 1765. Britain eventually triumphed, with France permanently ceding St. Lucia in 1815. In 1838, St. Lucia was incorporated into the British windward islands administration, headquartered in Barbados. This lasted until 1885, when the capital was moved to Grenada.

St. Lucia's 20th-century history has been marked by increasing self-government. A 1924 constitution gave the island its first form of representative government, with a minority of elected members in the previously all-nominated legislative council. Universal adult suffrage was introduced in 1951, and elected members became a majority of the council. Ministerial government was introduced in 1956, and in 1958 St. Lucia joined the short-lived West Indies Federation, a semi-autonomous dependency of the United Kingdom. When the federation collapsed in 1962, following Jamaica's withdrawal, a smaller federation was briefly attempted. After the second failure, the United Kingdom and the six windward and leeward islands--Grenada, St. Vincent, Dominica, Antigua, St. Kitts-Nevis-Anguilla, and St. Lucia--developed a novel form of cooperation called associated statehood.

As an associated state of the United Kingdom from 1967 to 1979, St. Lucia had full responsibility for internal self-government but left its external affairs and defense responsibilities to the United Kingdom. This interim arrangement ended on February 22, 1979, when St. Lucia achieved full independence. St. Lucia continues to recognize Queen Elizabeth II as titular head of state and is an active member of the Commonwealth. The island continues to cooperate with its neighbors through the Caribbean community and common market (CARICOM), the East Caribbean Common Market (ECCM), and the Organization of Eastern Caribbean States (OECS).

Population

St. Lucia has a population of about 156,000, about one-third of which lives in Castries. The population density is about 669 persons per square mile. About 90% of the population consists of descendants of slaves brought from Africa in the 17th and 18th centuries. There are small numbers of mixed race persons, East Indians, and descendants of Europeans. About 80% of the population is Roman Catholic; there are also Anglican, Methodist, Baptist,

and Seventh-Day Adventist churches. English is the official language, spoken by 80% of the population. Almost all the islanders speak a French patois based on a mixture of African and French grammar and a vocabulary of mostly French with some English and Spanish words.

Government

In 1814, Britain took permanent possession of St. Lucia, after having changed hands several times between Britain and France. St. Lucia's democratic tradition began in 1924, when a few elected positions were added to the appointed legislative council. St. Lucia became an associated state with full internal self government in 1967 and an independent member of the Commonwealth in 1979.

St. Lucia is a parliamentary democracy modeled on the Westminster system. The head of state is Queen Elizabeth II, represented by a Governor General, appointed by the Queen as her representative. The Governor General exercises basically ceremonial functions, but residual powers, under the constitution, can be used at the governor general's discretion. The actual power in St. Lucia lies with the prime minister and the cabinet, usually representing the majority party in parliament.

The bicameral parliament consists of a 17-member House of Assembly whose members are elected by universal adult suffrage for 5-year terms and an 11-member senate appointed by the governor general. The parliament may be dissolved by the governor general at any point during its 5-year term, either at the request of the prime minister--in order to take the nation into early elections--or at the governor general's own discretion, if the house passes a vote of no confidence in the government.

St. Lucia has an independent judiciary composed of district courts and a high court. Cases may be appealed to the Eastern Caribbean Court of Appeals and, ultimately, to

the Judicial Committee of the Privy Council in London. The island is divided into 10 administrative divisions, including the capital, Castries. Popularly elected local governments in most towns and villages perform such tasks as regulation of sanitation and markets and maintenance of cemeteries and secondary roads.

St. Lucia has no army but maintains a paramilitary Special Service Unit within its police force and a coast guard.

Politics in St. Lucia has been dominated by the United Workers Party (UWP), which has governed the country for all but 3 years since independence.

The flag has a blue background. In the middle is a yellow triangle surmounted by a black arrowhead whose outer edges are bordered in white.

Arts, Science, Education

Education is compulsory and provided by the government for ten years. An education complex in Castries has a teacher-training center, a technical school, a secretarial school, and a branch of the University of the West Indies. There is a research laboratory on the island serving the needs of banana growers in the region.

Commerce and Industry

St. Lucia's economy depends primarily on revenue from banana production and tourism with some input from smallscale manufacturing. There are numerous small and medium-sized agricultural enterprises. Revenue from agriculture has supported the noticeable socioeconomic changes that have taken place in St. Lucia since the 1960s. Eighty percent of merchandise trade earnings came from banana exports to the United Kingdom in the 1960s.

In view of the European Union's announced phase-out of preferred access to its markets by Windward Island bananas by 2006, agricultural diversification is a priority. An attempt is being made to diversify production by encouraging the establishment of tree crops such as mangos and avocados. A variety of vegetables are produced for local consumption. Recently, St. Lucia added small computer-driven information technology and financial services as development objectives.

St. Lucia's leading revenue producers--agriculture, tourism and small-scale manufacturing -- benefited from a focus on infrastructure improvements in roads, communications, water supply, sewerage, and port facilities. Foreign investors also have been attracted by the infrastructure improvements as well as by the educated and skilled work force and relatively stable political conditions. The largest investment is in a petroleum storage and trans-shipment terminal built by Hess Oil. The Caribbean Development Bank (CDB) funded and airport expansion project.

The tourism sector has made significant gains, experiencing a boom during the last few years despite some untimely and destructive hurricanes. In 1999, 50% more tourists visited the island than in 1996, including 261,000 stayover tourists and 423,000 cruise- ship visitors. The development of the tourism sector has been helped by the government's commitment to providing a favorable investment environment. Incentives are available for building and upgrading tourism facilities. There has been liberal use of public funds to improve the physical infrastructure of the island, and the government has made efforts to attract cultural and sporting events and develop historical sites.

St. Lucia is a member of the Eastern Caribbean Currency Union (ECCU). The Eastern Caribbean Central Bank (ECCB) issues a common currency for all members of the ECCU. The ECCB also manages monetary policy, and regulates and supervises commercial banking activities in its member countries.

St. Lucia is a beneficiary of the U.S. Caribbean Basin Initiative and is a member of the Caribbean Community and Common Market (CARICOM) and the Organization of Eastern Caribbean States (OECS)

Transportation

The Hewanorra International Airport on the southern tip of the island has direct flights to New York, Toronto, London, and Frankfurt. Ferries from Port Vieux on the southern coast link St. Lucia with St. Vincent and the Grenadines. All of the island's towns and villages are linked by all-purpose roads.

Vehicles travel on the left, traffic approaches from the right. Roads are narrow with steep inclines/declines throughout the island. Road conditions vary from fair to poor with few guard rails in areas that have precipitous drop-offs from the road.

Communications

There is a fully automatic telephone system. St. Lucia has 4 AM and an FM radio stations and a television station. Television programs are usually local programming, videotapes, and broadcasts from Barbados and Martinique. *The Voice of St. Lucia* is published twice a week, while *Crusader* and *Star* are weeklies.

Health

St. Lucia has five hospitals with over 500 beds. The Victoria Hospital provides a range of medical treatment, while the Golden Hope Hospital specializes in psychiatric cases. There are also over two dozen health centers scattered throughout the island. Malnutrition and intestinal difficulties are the main health problems.

Doctors and hospitals often expect immediate cash payment for health services. U.S. medical insurance is not always valid outside the U.S. In some cases, supplementary medical insurance with specific overseas coverage, including medical evacuation, has proved useful. For additional health information, travelers can contact the Centers for Disease Control and Prevention's international travelers hotline at 1888-232-3228, via CDC's toll-free autofax service, 1-888-232-3299, or via the Internet http://www.cdc.gov.

LOCAL HOLIDAYS

Jan. 1	New Year's Day
Feb	Carnival*
Feb. 22	Independence Day
Mar/Apr.	Good Friday*
Mar/Apr.	Easter*
Mar/Apr.	Easter Monday*
May 1	Labor Day
May/June	Whit Sunday (Pentecost)*
May/June	Whit Monday*
May/June	Corpus Christi*
June 8	Queen's Official Birthday
Aug. 2	Emancipation Day
Aug. 30	Feast of St. Rose of Lima (Rose Festival)
Oct. 4	Thanksgiving
Oct. 17	Feast of St. Margaret Alacoque
Nov. 1	All Saints' Day
Nov. 2	All Souls' Day (Fet le Mo)
Nov. 11	Remembrance Day
Nov. 22	Feast of St. Cecilia
Dec. 13	National Discovery Day
Dec. 25	Christmas
Dec. 26	Boxing Day

*Variable

NOTES FOR TRAVELERS

For stays up to six months, U.S. citizens may enter St. Lucia without a passport, but must carry an original document proving U.S. citizenship (U.S. passport, Certificate of Naturalization, Certificate of Citizenship or certified copy of a U.S. birth certificate), photo identification, and a return or onward ticket. For further information concerning entry requirements, travelers can contact the Embassy of St. Lucia, 3216 New Mexico Avenue, N.W., Washington, D.C. 20015; telephone (202) 364-6792; or St. Lucia's Permanent Mission to the UN in New York. Internet: sluonestop.com.

The U.S. does not maintain an embassy in St. Lucia. U.S. citizens requiring assistance can contact the U.S. Embassy in Bridgetown, Barbados; telephone 1 (246) 436-4950. The Consular Section of the Embassy is located in the American Life Insurance Company (ALICO) building, Cheapside, Bridgetown; telephone 1 (246) 431-0225. Hours of operation are Monday-Friday, 8:00 a.m. to 4:00 p.m. except local and U.S. holidays. U.S. citizens may register in the Consular Section of the Embassy at Bridgetown and obtain updated information on travel and security in St. Lucia and within the region.

Disaster Preparedness

St. Lucia is a hurricane-prone area. General information about natural disaster preparedness is available via the Internet from the U.S. Federal Emergency Management Agency (FEMA) at http://www.fema.gov/.

ST. VINCENT AND THE GRENADINES

St. Vincent and the Grenadines

Major City:
Kingstown

INTRODUCTION

ST. VINCENT may have been inhabited as early as 5000 BC. Agrarian Arawaks immigrated from South America. The Caribs eventually conquered the Arawaks, killing all the men and incorporating the women into their group. Christopher Columbus allegedly sighted the island on January 22, 1498, the feast day of the island's namesake. European settlers later arrived with African slaves. In 1675, slaves from a Dutch shipwreck made it to the island of Bequia and were given shelter by the native, or Yellow Caribs. Slaves from Barbados and St. Lucia later managed to escape to the island. The mixture of slaves and Yellow Caribs created a new group known as the Black Caribs. The Caribs ardently fought off European settlement on St. Vincent until the 18th century. Tensions between the Yellow Caribs and the Black Caribs led to conflict and territorial division. The perpetual hostilities delayed colonial development of the island, while several nearby islands already had an advanced sugar industry. In 1700 the French divided St. Vincent, with the west going to the Yellow Caribs and the east going to the Black Caribs. French settlers began cultivating coffee, tobacco, indigo, cotton, and sugar on plantations worked by African slaves starting in 1719. Great Britain controlled St. Vincent from 1763 until French rule was restored in 1779. The British got control back in 1783. Under the British, sugar production fell throughout the 1800s, and arrowroot became the leading cash crop by 1900. St. Vincent is still the world's leading producer of arrowroot, which is used to make starch. St. Vincent became a crown colony in 1877, and a legislative council was created in 1925. The island was granted associate statehood status in 1969 and became the last of the Windward Islands to gain independence on October 27, 1979.

MAJOR CITY

Kingstown

Kingstown, the capital, is located on the southwestern coast of the island of St. Vincent and has a population of about 27,000. The town overlooks Kingstown Harbour and is protected by Berkshire Hill to the north and Cane Garden Point to the south. Cruise ships put into Kingstown Harbour. The E.T. Joshua Airport is located on the southern tip of St. Vincent near Kingstown. Local transportation is provided by open-air buses and small minibus taxis sporting colorful hand-painted names and designs. Campden Industrial Park, about three miles west of the city, is a 30-acre enclave that serves as the principal industrial area of the country. The East Caribbean Group of Companies has operations there that handle animal feed processing, bag production, and flour and rice milling. In 1989 a fire destroyed much of Kingstown's center, but reconstruction in 1990 emphasized increasing tourism.

Recreation and Entertainment

St. Vincent has numerous beaches for swimming and surfing. The waters along the black sand beaches of the Atlantic coast are choppy and conducive to surfing and windsurfing, while the waters along the golden sand beaches of the Caribbean coast are calm and more pleasant for swimming. Cricket is played throughout the islands, and several local players have gone on to represent the West Indies at the international level. International sports are played at the Arnos Vale Playing Field. Soccer, netball, volleyball, and basketball are also popular. Soccer is the most widely played sport, and there are 14 local leagues that organize team play. Indoor sports such as squash and table tennis are played in the suburbs of Kingstown. Weight training, karate, and taekwondo are also becoming

Harbor view, St. Vincent

popular. Swimming, sailing, and windsurfing are popular aquatic activities. Dominoes is a popular game among groups of men.

Bay Street is Kingstown's waterfront district, with shops and a few hotels. The Cobblestone Inn was built in 1814 as a sugar warehouse and was restored to its original Georgian style. St. George's Anglican Cathedral also is an example of Georgian architecture, and contains several Kempe and Munich stained glass windows. St. Mary's Roman Catholic Cathedral originally was built in 1823, and was most recently renovated in the 1940s. The cathedral is a mixture of Romanesque, Gothic, and Moorish designs.

The General Post Office in Kingstown features stamps produced by the government that are prized by international collectors. St. Vincent Philatelic Services, Ltd. in Kingstown works with an agency in New York to produce nine collectible issues per year. Kingstown's vegetable market is one of the island's main commercial centers.

The St. Vincent Botanic Gardens and Museum on the outskirts of Kingstown features tropical foliage and brightly colored songbirds. It is the most ornate garden in the Caribbean and the oldest of its kind in the Western Hemisphere. The gardens occupy 20 acres and were founded in 1765 as a nursery for plants useful to medicine and commerce. The French introduced exotic Asian spices (such as cinnamon) to the gardens. Cloves were brought from Martinique and nutmeg and black pepper plants from French Guiana. Breadfruit trees brought from the South Pacific by Captain Bligh were introduced in 1793. The St. Vincent National Museum at the gardens contains stone, ceramic, and shell artifacts dating from 500 BC to AD 1200 left behind by the pre-Columbian inhabitants of St. Vincent and some of the other islands in the Grenadines. The Parrot Breeding Center at the Botanic Gardens is trying to increase the population of the islands' national bird, the St. Vincent parrot (*Amazona guildingi*). Fort Charlotte, west of Kingstown, sits atop a ridge 600 feet above sea level and was completed in 1806. A museum at the fort depicts the history of the Black Caribs on the island.

Cultural activities on St. Vincent include several festivals, arts and crafts exhibitions, dancing, and folksinging. The national carnival festival, known as Vincy Mas, is celebrated in early July. Costumed, steel, and calypso bands give performances, and there are beauty shows. The Music Festival has been held every other year since 1956 and features vocal, choral, and instrumental performances. There is also an annual school drama festival. There are plans to build a performing arts center in Kingstown. The Kingstown Free Library has a display of Carib artifacts.

COUNTRY PROFILE

Geography and Climate

St. Vincent and the Grenadines is located 21 miles southwest of St. Lucia and about 100 miles west of Barbados in the Caribbean Sea. Scattered between St. Vincent and Grenada are more than 100 small islands called the Grenadines, half of which belong to St. Vincent and the other half to Grenada. The Grenadines belonging to St. Vincent include Union Island, Mayreau, Canouan, Mustique, Bequia, and many other uninhabited cays, rocks, and reefs. St. Vincent has an area of 134 square miles, with a coastline of 52 miles. Bequia, the largest of the Grenadines, has an area of 7 square miles. St. Vincent is a rugged island with dark volcanic sand beaches. Its highest point is Soufrière, an active volcano that rises 4,048 feet above sea level. Only 5% of St. Vincent's surface has slopes of less than 5°. The low-lying Grenadines have wide beaches and shallow bays and harbors. The islands have a pleasant tropical climate throughout the year, with the average temperature ranging from 77°F in January to 81°F in September. The rainfall on St. Vincent averages about 91 inches per year, but more than 150 inches may fall in the mountains. The islands lie in the Caribbean hurricane belt and were devastated in 1780, 1898, and 1980.

Population

St. Vincent and the Grenadines has a population of about 122,000, with over 90% living on the main island. Only about a dozen of the country's 120 islands are populated. About 66% of the islanders are descen-

dants of slaves brought from Africa. About 20% is of mixed origins and about 3.5% is of European descent. Some 5.5% of the islanders are descendants of 19th-century East Indian indentured laborers. About 2% of the people are indigenous Caribs. The mixture of Africans and the native Caribs (Yellow Caribs) created an ethnicity known as the Black Caribs. Some scholars believe that the African origin of the Black Caribs came from escaped slaves, while others believe they descended from a stranded group of 13th century West African explorers. Today, the few remaining descendants of the Yellow Caribs live at Sandy Bay. The majority of the population is Anglican or Methodist. There is also a significant Roman Catholic minority. English is the official language of the country. Some islanders speak a French patois, which uses a mixture of African and French grammar, with a vocabulary using mostly French words, with some English and a few Spanish words. A minority of the islanders speak French as a first language.

Government

St. Vincent was one of the last of the West Indies to be settled by Europeans. The British and French agreed to leave the island to the native Caribs in 1660, and the island had a sizable Carib population until the 1720s. The island was formally taken by the British in 1763, who ruled thereafter except during 1779–83, when its was under French control. St. Vincent was administered as a crown colony from 1833 until 1960. Upon independence in 1979, St. Vincent and the Grenadines kept the British monarch as the nominal head of state, represented by a governor-general.

St. Vincent and the Grenadines is a parliamentary democracy within the Commonwealth of Nations. Queen Elizabeth II is head of state and is represented on the island by a governor general, an office with mostly ceremonial functions. Con-

trol of the government rests with the prime minister and the cabinet.

The parliament is a unicameral body with a 15-member elected house of assembly and a six-member appointed senate. The governor general appoints senators, four on the advice of the prime minister and two on the advice of the leader of the opposition. The parliamentary term of office is 5 years, although the prime minister may call elections at any time.

As in other English-speaking Caribbean countries, the judiciary in St. Vincent is rooted in British common law. There are 11 courts in three magisterial districts. The Eastern Caribbean Supreme Court, comprising a high court and a court of appeals, is known in St. Vincent as the St. Vincent and the Grenadines supreme court. The court of last resort is the judicial committee of Her Majesty's Privy Council in London.

There is no local government in St. Vincent, and all six parishes are administered by the central government.

The flag consists of three vertical bands of blue, yellow and green; centered on the yellow band are three green diamonds arranged in a V-pattern.

Arts, Science, Education

Primary education lasts for seven years and is provided by the government but not compulsory. There are about 65 primary schools. The government-assisted School for Children with Special Needs serves handicapped students. At the secondary level, there are a teachers' training college and a technical college. Government agencies sponsor adult education, vocational training, and agricultural training.

Commerce and Industry

The St. Vincent economy has traditionally been dependent on agriculture, but the government has attempted to diversify the economy in recent years. Agriculture now accounts for about 9% of GDP compared to 11% in 1996 and 13% in 1993. Bananas account for more than 80% of agricultural output. and account for upwards of 60% of the work force and about 35% of merchandise exports. Such reliance on a single crop makes the economy vulnerable to external factors. St. Vincent's banana growers benefit from preferential access to the European market. In view of the European Union's announced phase-out of this preferred access, economic diversification is a priority.

Tourism has become a very important part of the economy. In 1993, tourism supplanted banana exports as the chief source of foreign exchange. The Grenadines have become a favorite of the up-market yachting crowd. The trend toward increasing tourism revenues will likely continue. In 1996, new cruise-ship and ferry berths came on-line, sharply increasing the number of passenger arrivals. In 2000, total visitor arrivals were about 280,700. A relatively small number of Americans--under 1,000--reside on the islands.

St. Vincent is a member of the Eastern Caribbean Currency Union (ECCU). Eastern Caribbean Central Bank (ECCB) issues a common currency for all members of the ECCU. The ECCB also manages monetary policy and regulates and supervises commercial banking activities in its member countries.

St. Vincent and the Grenadines is a beneficiary of the U.S. Caribbean Basin Initiative. The country belongs to the Caribbean Community and Common Market (CARICOM), which has signed a framework agreement with the United States to promote trade and investment in the region. St. Vincent also is a member of the Organization of Eastern Caribbean States (OECS).

Transportation

St. Vincent is on the main air routes of the Caribbean, with direct flights to Trinidad and Barbados as well as other islands to the north. The international airport is located on St. Vincent near Kingstown and there is another on the east coast, near Georgetown. There are also small airports on Bequia, Canouan, Mustique, and Union Island. All of the Grenadines have excellent harbors served by a ferry service out of Kingstown.

Harbors in the Grenadines are being expanded to increase potential tourism. There is a road on St. Vincent that connects all of the main towns with the capital.

Vehicles travel on the left, and traffic approaches from the right. Roads are narrow, with steep inclines/declines throughout the island. Taxis and buses tend to be relatively safe, but the buses are often overcrowded. Vans are generally overcrowded and frequently travel at high rates of speed. Rural mountainous roads are the more dangerous areas for road travel. Night driving should be done with great caution and is discouraged in mountainous areas because the roads are not well marked, there are few, if any, guardrails, and the roads are often steep and winding.

Communications

Cable and Wireless (West Indies) operates the islands' telecommunications services. There are two AM radio stations, one television station, and four weekly newspapers.

Health

The general hospital in Kingstown has over 200 beds and is equipped with x-ray, dental, and eye clinics. There are three rural hospitals, two on St. Vincent and another on Bequia.

Clothing and Services

Sandals are an important beach accessory, as the sand can become very hot. Comfortable, casual clothing is the norm, but it is considered improper to wear swimwear when in town. A raincoat and light sweater may be needed for the higher altitudes of St. Vincent, where it can get wet, windy, and cool.

LOCAL HOLIDAYS

*Variable

NOTES FOR TRAVELLERS

For stays up to six months, U.S. citizens may enter St. Vincent and The Grenadines without a passport. U.S. citizens must carry an original document proving U.S. citizenship (a U.S. passport, certificate of naturalization, certificate of citizenship or a certified copy of a U.S. birth certificate).

Photo identification, a return/onward ticket and/or proof of sufficient funds are also required.

For further information concerning entry requirements, travelers can contact the Embassy of St. Vincent and The Grenadines, 3216 New Mexico Ave., N.W., Washington, D.C. 20016, telephone (202) 364-6730, or the consulates in Los Angeles, New Orleans, and New York.

The United States does not maintain an Embassy in St. Vincent and The Grenadines. U.S. citizens requiring assistance may contact the U.S. Embassy in Bridgetown, Barbados; telephone 1 (246) 436-4950. The Consular Section is located in the American Life Insurance Company (ALICO) building, Cheapside, Bridgetown; telephone 1 (246) 431-0225. Americans are encouraged to register at the Consular Section of the Embassy in Bridgetown and obtain updated information on travel and security in St. Vincent and The Grenadines and within the area.

RECOMMENDED READING

Bobrow, Jill and Dana Jinkins. *St. Vincent and the Grenadines: Gems of the Caribbean.* Waitsfield, Vt.: Concepts Publishing Inc., 1993.

Philpott, Don. *Caribbean Sunseekers: St. Vincent & Grenadines.* Lincolnwood, Ill.: Passport Books, 1996.

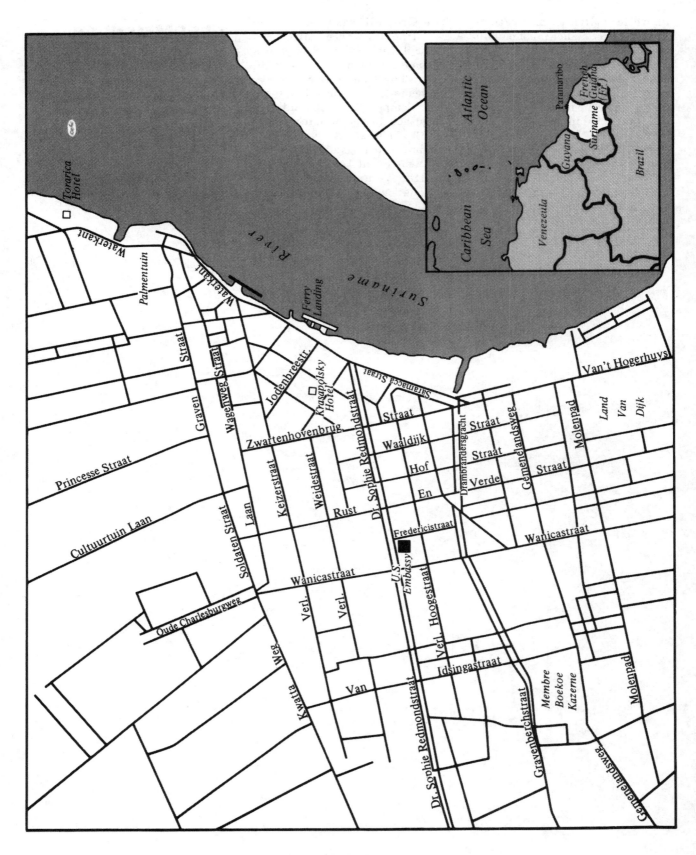

Paramaribo, Suriname

SURINAME

Republic of Suriname

Major City:
Paramaribo

Other Cities:
Albina, Moengo, Nieuw-nickerie, Totness, Wageningen

EDITOR'S NOTE

This chapter was adapted from the Department of State Post Report dated July 1993. Supplemental material has been added to increase coverage of minor cities, facts have been updated, and some material has been condensed. Readers are encouraged to visit the Department of State's web site at http://travel.state.gov/ for the most recent information available on travel to this country.

INTRODUCTION

SURINAME, which, as Dutch Guiana, was an autonomous territory within the Kingdom of the Netherlands until 1975, is an independent, racially and ethnically mixed country on the northeast coast of South America. It retains much of its Dutch heritage in language and culture, while striving to develop an identity within the context of its geographical environment.

Suriname is currently pursuing institutional changes in a concerted effort to recover from a 1980 military coup and an escalating austerity alien to this once prosperous colony. From the beginning, it has been faced with a small population and an economic development largely restricted to a narrow coastal band, and the suspension of Dutch aid in the wake of the military takeover has created additional hardships. Growing inflation and foreign exchange restrictions continue to strain immediate plans for development.

MAJOR CITY

Paramaribo

Suriname's capital city, Paramaribo, is located 12 miles inland, on the west bank of the Suriname River. Founded in 1613 as a trading post with the Indians it was, at various times, subject to alternating British and Dutch administration. The city expanded and developed greatly during the 18th century, but declined somewhat during the next century after two damaging fires. At present, many of Paramaribo's structures date from the early and mid-20th century, and exhibit a characteristic Dutch-colonial, tropical style of architecture. The canals are reminiscent of the Netherlands.

Some 180,000 people live in Paramaribo and its immediate suburbs. The city is the heart of Suriname's political, cultural, and intellectual life, serving not only its own population, but also that of the entire country. Older cultural traditions prevail in isolated jungle villages.

Paramaribo is not generally afflicted by floods, although heavy rains can, at times, exceed the city's drainage capabilities and create isolated flooding on some streets and in low-lying areas.

About 350 American citizens live in Suriname. Most are connected with the U.S. Embassy, or are in Protestant missionary work.

Resident foreign embassies include those of the U.S., the Netherlands, India, Brazil, Venezuela, the former U.S.S.R., the People's Republic of China, Indonesia, South Korea, Japan, Libya, France, and Guyana. A number of other countries are represented by honorary consular officers. Cuba established a trade mission in 1981, but its advisers were expelled after the U.S. invasion of Grenada in October 1983.

Schools for Foreigners

The American Cooperative School, operated by American Protestant missionaries, provides classes in grades kindergarten through 8. Instruction is in English and meets U.S. standards. The school year runs from late August until May.

Street in Paramaribo, Suriname

Suriname has a dual religious and secular educational system, conducted in Dutch. Schools are run by Catholic and Moravian Churches as well as by the state. While some foreign children enroll in the Suriname schools at Paramaribo, the necessity of learning Dutch and the problems of transferring credits make this difficult (if not impossible) for Americans. Standards vary from school to school, with the best schools having an excellent record in placing students in universities here and abroad.

Suriname's Anton de Kom University (in the capital) has faculties of medicine, law, technical and social sciences, and natural resources. Other institutions of higher education also operate in Suriname.

Recreation

The most popular national sport is soccer. Basketball and cricket are also available, and adult teams play regularly. Weight lifting, badminton, horseback riding, and aerobic exercise classes are also pursued by Americans. A nine-hole golf course is four miles from Paramaribo. Formerly a rice paddy, it is flat and low, and drainage, though extensive and well planned, is a problem during the rainy season. Americans have found Paramaribo an excellent place to learn to play golf under uncrowded but rustic conditions.

Hunting and fishing also evoke a great deal of interest, as neither requires any unusual equipment. Both, however, can involve hard trekking in deep forests. Stringent laws govern ownership of firearms and ammunition. Rifles and pistols are prohibited, and an individual may own only one shotgun. Guides and transportation to the best hunting areas are expensive; hunting without a guide is definitely not recommended. It may be necessary to hire a power boat and/or plane to get to the desired area. Dogs are needed for some kinds of hunting.

A gun club uses pistols (owned by the club) at a range near Paramaribo three times a week, traps at Paranam once a month, and rifles (owned by the club) at a range near Zanderij Airport, also monthly.

Fishing in the Suriname and Saramacca Rivers, Afobakka Lake, and the surrounding streams is not unduly inconvenient, but trips to the interior or saltwater fishing are as difficult to organize as hunting trips. Tarpon is the principal sport fish, with catfish and other species also popular. Many excellent streams and rivers in Suriname are suitable for small boats. It is possible to do some fishing from the river banks.

Camping and hiking are difficult because of heat, insects, and lack of organized campsites and marked trails, but adventurous types might enjoy these sports at several of the national parks here. Bicycling is popular, although heavy traffic makes it risky.

There are neither ocean beaches nor lakes suitable for swimming. Several tannic acid-colored rivers and creeks offer interesting and safe swimming and water-skiing. The city has one public swimming pool, and four private clubs maintain their own pools.

The Suriname Aero Club has a Cessna plane and operates both a ground school and a flying school. For beginners, at least a basic knowledge of Dutch is necessary, since the ground course and examination are conducted in that language. Costs are somewhat higher than those in the U.S., but not prohibitively so.

Some opportunities exist for sight-seeing. The visitor can drive to Kola Creek, Brokopondo Dam, Groningen, Joden Savanna, or Nieuw-Amsterdam for outings; some facilities for picnicking are available. It also is possible to drive to Cayenne, French Guiana, and to the border of Guyana. The scenery and climate in these places are similar to that of Suriname. French Guiana, however, offers the added attraction of French wines, cheeses, and meals, making it a popular place to visit. Trips to the interior by plane or boat are interesting, but can be expensive.

Entertainment

Paramaribo has one small museum (Fort Zeelandia), a natural history collection, a small zoo, and numerous public parks. There are 10 movie theaters, but not all of them are patronized by Americans. Films in English are popular at most of the theaters, and five establishments specialize in Indian movies. Movies are censored and may be restricted to certain age groups. A film league offers art films about every two weeks, and one drive-in theater shows an occasional movie in English.

Suriname's government-owned TV channel (STVS) broadcasts every evening and offers American variety programs and occasional feature films. A private TV station (ATV), inaugurated in 1987, offers American, Brazilian, and European programs, mostly in English.

Videotapes in VHS or Betamax can be rented from commercial sources at low cost. The Beta format, popular here, offers the most variety.

Although the country has no legitimate theater, the Suriname Cultural Center (CCS) and Ons Erf sponsor occasional plays, concerts, and other cultural presentations. Plays are almost always in Dutch or Sranan Tongo. Modest parades and trade fairs are sometimes held on holidays.

Average-to-good Chinese, Javanese, and Korean food is served in at least five restaurants in Paramaribo. Prices are higher than those at good U.S. restaurants. A few continental-style restaurants are here.

No special or unusual etiquette is required when participating in any form of entertainment. Bush Negroes often object to being photographed in their villages.

The Torarica Hotel stages floor shows on weekends—usually a solo performance by a singer, dancer, or musician. It also has a dance band and a casino and restaurant. A few local discos and nightclubs cater to young people. Good Chinese and Javanese food is served in at least five restaurants, with prices comparable to those at good U.S. dining establishments. There is a good continental-style restaurant at the Ambassador Hotel, and a disco next to the Krasnapolsky Hotel.

Paramaribo is a friendly city. It is easy to meet people through personal introductions. Among men's and women's service clubs, Rotary, Lions, Kiwanis, Jaycees, Optimists, Soroptimists, and Toastmasters are represented in Paramaribo. Anyone interested in social work may volunteer with the Salvation Army, Red Cross, YWCA, the family planning organization (LOBI), or one of many other secular and religious groups.

The American community is too small to support exclusive social activity, even in Paramaribo. Most of the non-Surinamese middle-class expatriate community is composed of Dutch Europeans and some Belgians, with few other foreigners. Social calls and social affairs among both Surinamese and Dutch are more structured than U.S. custom requires. Close friends usually do not call on one another without prior notice.

OTHER CITIES

ALBINA is a seaport town on the west bank of the Maroni (Morowijne) River. Besides being a district capital, it is the largest city on the French Guiana border.

MOENGO lies on the Cottica River in the northeast part of the country. The local economy depends on extensive bauxite deposits.

NIEUW-NICKERIE is Suriname's major coastal town in the northwest, across from Corriverton, Guyana. It is the capital of the Nickerie District. The city is an important port through which rice, cocoa, and lumber is exported.

TOTNESS is the capital and largest village of Coronie District. Situated on the Atlantic Ocean, halfway between Nieuw-Nickerie and Paramaribo, Totness has a government guest house and bus connections to Paramaribo. The village's main road traverses a great forest of coconut palms.

The small town of **WAGENINGEN** has great status in the field of agriculture. It lies on the Nickerie River, 30 miles southeast of Nieuw-Nickerie, in the northwest. Located in the heart of the country's rice-producing area, Wageningen is the home of one of the world's largest fully mechanized rice farms. The road from Nieuw-Nickerie is newly rebuilt.

COUNTRY PROFILE

Geography and Climate

Roughly square, Suriname lies on South America's northeast coast, bounded on the east by French Guiana, on the south by Brazil, and on the west by Guyana. Most of the 220-mile shoreline on the Atlantic ocean consists of mud flats and swamps. Suriname's inland boundaries with French Guiana and Guyana are in dispute.

Suriname (this is the Dutch spelling, but the English spelling, Surinam, is often seen) has a land area of about 63,000 square miles, and is about the same size as Georgia. However, most Surinamers live in the 1,900-square mile, narrow coastal plain in and around Paramaribo, Moengo, and Nieuw-Nickerie.

Suriname's coastal area is flat. Hills and low mountains, reaching a maximum height of about 4,000 feet (1,230 meters), rise in the heavily forested interior. Between these two zones lie the savanna lands, 30 to 40 miles in width. Large rivers and streams bisect the country from the south to the north and provide major transportation routes between the coast and the interior. However, they hinder east-west land transportation.

Suriname has a tropical rainforest climate—hot and humid all year. Daytime temperatures average about 90°F (27°C), although evening and night readings are considerably lower (about 70°F, or 21°C). Interior temperatures, not moderated by coastal breezes, are slightly more extreme.

Most Americans find the climate notably more agreeable than they had anticipated. On a normal day, outdoor activities such as golfing, fishing, and jogging are pleasant except between 10 a.m. and 4 p.m. when the sun is high.

Seasons are distinguished only by more or less rain, with annual rainfall averaging 87 inches. December to February and April to August are generally the periods of heaviest rainfall. The hottest months are September and October, with temperatures averaging 89°F (35°C). Suriname lies outside the hurricane and earthquake area.

Population

Suriname's estimated population is 434,000 (2000 est.). Because of emigration to the Netherlands between 1972 and 1980, there was a significant decline in total numbers. The people are a mixture of several ethnic and racial classifications, with Hindustanis (37%) and Creoles (32%) the two largest groups. Others represented in the population include Javanese (15.3%), Bush Negroes (10.3%), Amerindians (2.7%), Chinese (1.7%), and Europeans, one percent.

The Hindustanis (East Indians) are predominately Hindu, but include a substantial Muslim minority. They are descended from contract farm laborers brought to Suriname in the latter part of the 19th century. Hindustanis are still heavily engaged in agriculture, but have become increasingly urbanized and are often active in business and commerce.

Creoles, of mixed African, European, and other ancestry, are descendants of African slave laborers emancipated in 1863. In this century, they have filled the ranks of civil service and office jobs.

The Javanese, who are descended from farm laborers brought to Suriname on contract from Java, in Indonesia, are chiefly active in agricultural life in the rural areas of Suriname. They have retained their own language. The Bush Negroes, or Maroons, are descended from escaped African slaves. Many escaped before losing their African culture, which has been maintained in some primitive villages along streams and rivers in the interior. Although such communities still exist far removed from the developed coastal region, many Bush Negroes are now abandoning their traditional life-style to move to population centers in search of better education and job opportunities.

Amerindians, descendants of original pre-Columbian inhabitants, also live in tribal villages along interior streams and rivers. They are less hospitable and desire more privacy than Bush Negroes. Certain small Amerindian tribes in Suriname have been discovered only recently.

The Chinese, many born in China, are mostly shopkeepers, business people, and restaurateurs. They speak Chinese (Hakka and Cantonese) among themselves, and support a Chinese newspaper.

Caucasians are mainly descended from Dutch farmers who came here in the 18th and 19th centuries, though some are descended from early Jewish, French, and German immigrants. A small community of expatriate Europeans, mostly from the Netherlands, work in some local businesses.

Approximately 350 Americans reside in Suriname, mostly in Paramaribo. Mostly Protestant missionaries, they spend some of their time in the interior.

Each ethnic group maintains its identity and customs. Some wear distinctive clothing. Almost all celebrate their own holidays, observe their own religions and, except for sophisticated city dwellers, associate with members of their particular groups in exclusive or semi-exclusive social clubs and societies. Political parties are racially or ethnically oriented. The government seeks to break down such barriers and forge a national identity.

The official language of Suriname is Dutch, but *Sranan Tongo* (literally, Suriname tongue), also called Surinamese, a non-tonal English-based Creole tongue, is the lingua franca. Dutch is taught in school and used exclusively by the government; government publications and newspapers are in that language, as are radio and television.

English is widely understood and almost all educated people speak it fluently. A great many Surinamers speak three or even four languages—Sranan Tongo, Dutch, and English, plus Hindi, Chinese, or Javanese. The latter three are used extensively in Paramaribo.

Freedom of religion is legally protected in Suriname. Hindus and Muslims comprise the two largest religious groups, but there are also many Roman Catholics and other Christians (primarily Moravians) and a small number of Jews and Baha'is. A significant number of Amerindians and Bush Negroes follow animistic religions, although the majority of both groups profess Christianity in either its Catholic or Moravian form.

Government

The popularly elected government that ruled Suriname after the end of Dutch colonial rule was overthrown in a military coup in February 1980. The sergeants who took power in 1980 were at first welcomed as reformers. Their gradual leftward drift, however, increasingly alienated the generally conservative middle-class Surinamese majority, and the repressive methods they employed to maintain control eventually cost them most of their popular support.

The executions of 15 opposition leaders in 1982 led to the suspension of Dutch and American development aid. Combined with a decline in world market prices for bauxite and alumina (Suriname's chief export commodities), the aid suspension led to a general economic downturn that had reached a critical stage. When an insurgent group began a series of attacks on military and economic targets in the interior, the government gave in to international and domestic pressures and announced that a new constitution would be adopted by the end of March 1987, and that

national elections would be held in November of that year.

Eighty-eight percent of Suriname's eligible voters took part in the elections, in which a coalition of traditional, ethnic-based, pre-coup parties called the Front for Development and Democracy won with an 85 percent majority.

Under the new constitution, the 51-member directly elected National Assembly is the highest authority in Suriname. The President, chosen by the Assembly, is both head of government and head of state. The Vice President, also elected by the Assembly, is chairman of the Council of Ministers that, together with the President and Vice President, makes up the government. Like the Assembly members, the President and Vice President are elected for five-year terms.

Despite the democratic elections of 1987, Suriname's political situation remained extremely unstable. Although the army had relinquished control of the government, it remained powerful and influential. The army often sharply criticized the new government's economic policies. A series of confrontations between the government and army caused relations to worsen. By 1990, the tensions between the two parties had come to a head. On December 24, 1990, the army launched a successful military coup against the government. President Ramswewak Shankar was overthrown and replaced by Johannes Samuel Kraag. A military council established shortly after the coup announced that Kraag would govern on an interim basis until new elections could be held.

The military fulfilled this promise by holding democratic elections in May 1991. Election results showed that the New Front Coalition, consisting of three ethnically-based parties and the Surinamese Labor Party, captured 30 of 51 seats. The pro-military National Democratic Party obtained only 10 seats. The rest of the seats were divided among several small opposition parties. On

September 6, 1991, the National Assembly and other elected representatives of districts and subdistricts met to select a new President. The New Front Coalition candidate, Ronald Venetiaan, became Suriname's new president after gaining 80 percent of the vote.

Economic difficulties caused Venetiaan's popularity to decline over the succeeding years, and he was replaced by NDP candidate Jules Wijdenbosch in elections held in May 1996. These elections marked the first peaceful transfer of power between democratically elected governments since Suriname gained independence.

In May 1999, after mass demonstrations protesting poor economic conditions, the government was forced to call early elections. The elections in May 2000 returned Ronald Venetiaan and his coalition to the presidency. The New Front ran its campaign on a platform to fix the faltering Surinamese economy. But while the Venetiaan administration has made progress in stabilizing the economy, tensions within the coalition and the impatience of the populace have impeded progress.

Suriname is a member of the United Nations, World Health Organization (WHO), and United Nations Educational, Scientific, and Cultural Organization (UNESCO), as well as European Communities, International Bauxite Association, Inter-American Development Bank, Nonaligned Movement, Organization of American States and Latin American Economic System.

The flag of Suriname consists of green, white, red, white, and green horizontal bands, with a yellow star in the middle of the red band.

Arts, Science, Education

Some local cultural activities are available. Occasional plays and concerts are offered at the Suriname Cultural Center, Ons Erf Cultural Center, and elsewhere. Two or three times a year, foreign groups (Chinese acrobats, American jazz ensembles) arrive for performances. Live theater is confined to two companies which produce plays in Dutch and Sranan Tongo. A music school offers instruction in a wide range of instruments. There are several small ballet schools in Paramaribo.

Each government cultural center maintains a public library with a limited collection of English editions. English-language paperbacks and hardcover books are available from several retail outlets in Paramaribo, but are expensive. Ons Erf, a Roman Catholic Church organization, maintains an arts and crafts center and sponsors activities for younger children.

Suriname's main ethnic groups—Creoles, Hindustanis, and Javanese—maintain associations which occasionally sponsor cultural activities.

Suriname has an extensive educational system, with compulsory free schooling until age 14. Its Anton de Kom University has faculties of medicine, law, natural resources, and social and technical sciences. However, transfer of individual course credit to or from the U.S. is unlikely, even when a non-Dutch-speaking person is allowed to enroll. Teacher-training institutes, secondary schools, and technical schools also provide degrees. Nurses and dental technicians are trained in conjunction with the medical faculty. The adult literacy rate was approximately 93 percent in 1995.

The government and the Roman Catholic and Moravian Churches provide education from kindergarten through secondary school. All instruction is in Dutch, except at the American Cooperative Elementary School, administered by the Suriname Aluminum Company (SURALCO), and in two private schools administered by American missionaries. Lectures in English are sometimes given at the university. Many students still attend high

schools and universities in the Netherlands; a growing number study in U.S. universities.

The Government Language Center offers courses in Dutch, English, Spanish, and Sranan Tongo. French is offered by the Alliance Française, Spanish by the Andrés Bello Center, and Portuguese by the Brazilian Cultural Center. The Indonesian and Indian centers give instruction in their native folk art and dance.

Commerce and Industry

Approximately 70 percent of Suriname's exports by value are bauxite and its aluminum derivatives. The attractiveness of Suriname's bauxite reserves has diminished in recent years as more economical sources have been developed elsewhere in the world and the worldwide marketing of bauxite and aluminum has become more complex. SURALCO, a subsidiary of ALCOA and the biggest private firm in Suriname, has reduced its labor force as its bauxite and aluminum shipments have fallen and internal costs have risen.

Agriculture is important as a major source of employment. Rice, citrus, other tropical fruits, vegetables, seafood, and a few other commodities are available. The principal food crop is rice. Suriname also produces half of the sugar it consumes. Commercial fishing is undertaken by Japanese, Korean, and Surinamese companies using imported labor. Shrimp is a major export; the catch has diminished since 1982 as the shrimp have at least temporarily moved to grounds closer to Guyana. However, production of other foodstuffs is inadequate to meet the needs of the country. Importation of a wide variety of foods is, therefore, necessary.

Forestry is an important sector of the economy, dominated by the state-owned company, Bruynzeel, which exports products derived from tropical hardwoods.

Wheat, potatoes, some poultry, milk powder, cheese, and many other commodities must be imported. Protective tariff and nontariff barriers and import substitution plans have been put into effect, sometimes limiting the variety of foods available on the local market. Local manufacturing consists of saw mills, shrimp-packing plants, a cigarette factory, a rum distillery, a brewery, soft drink bottlers, and a few other small industries.

A rapid deterioration in the Surinamese balance of trade began in 1983. It was brought about both by reduced bauxite revenues and by termination—due to Dutch displeasure with Suriname Government actions regarding human rights—of Dutch development aid. The virtual disappearance by late 1984 of freely available foreign exchange finally induced the government to impose stringent restrictions on import of consumer and industrial goods.

High wages, low foreign exchange levels, a small domestic economy, and little experience in exporting limit Suriname's competitiveness in international markets. Nonetheless, the country's GDP was an estimated $1.48 billion in 1999. Per capita income is ten times that of the poorest Caribbean islands.

Suriname is a member of the Lome Convention and has observer status in the Caribbean Common Market (CARICOM). The U.S. has traditionally been the country's largest trading partner, accounting for approximately one-third of export-import trade. The remainder has been carried on with European nations, Japan and, to an increasing extent, neighboring countries in the Caribbean and South America. This pattern may change, however, as the Surinamese Government does more centralized procurement in bulk from lower cost sources.

The Suriname Chamber of Commerce and Industry can be reached at P.O. Box 149, Mirandastraat 10, Paramaribo.

Transportation

Suriname's extensive rivers and streams are important avenues of transportation. Some rivers are navigable by ocean freighters for 100 miles inland. Hundreds of miles of smaller rivers are navigable by smaller boats and barges, which are used widely for moving people and freight. The boats of the Amerindians and Bush Negroes are vital to them.

Surinamese Luchtvaart Maatschappij NV (SLM) offers flights between major populated areas. The only practical means of reaching some interior areas is by small plane, using the recently built "grasshopper" airstrips. Chartered flights to these small fields are very expensive. Zanderij International Airport, 25 miles south of Paramaribo, can accommodate large jets. Zanderij is served by KLM, ALM, SLM, Guyana Airways, and Brazil's Cruzeiro do Sul, which connect the country with the U.S., Europe, and major South American cities. A small airfield on the edge of the city is limited to twin-engine propeller craft.

Suriname has no passenger rail transportation. River transport is one way to visit the interior and some coastal areas.

Buses serve Paramaribo, but service is erratic and the buses are hot and usually crowded during rush hours. Motorbikes, motorcycles, scooters, and bicycles are important local means of transportation. Traffic is hazardous, especially for riders of two-wheeled vehicles. Paramaribo has several taxi companies. Cabs are hard to find, but it is possible to phone for service.

Private cars are the best means of transportation in Paramaribo, particularly small vehicles, as some streets are narrow, and good maneuverability is necessary in traffic. Cars are not used very often for trips outside the city. Traffic moves on the left (although cars for right-hand traffic are numerous), and visitors are cautioned to be careful when crossing streets, as it is easy to forget which way traffic is coming. The bicycle and motorbike paths can be hazardous, too, as the latter have the right-of-way.

Prices of small foreign cars are comparable to U.S. prices, and spare parts for these vehicles are more readily available than for large American cars. Insurance can be purchased at reduced rates (10 percent per year up to five years) with a statement from previous insurers that no claim has been made within five years. For other than liability, it is wise to purchase additional insurance through a U.S. company, as rates are more reasonable. A driver's license can be obtained for a small fee by presenting a valid U.S. license and two photos.

Communications

Postal, telegraph, and telephone systems connect Suriname's cities with one another and with the outside world. These services are quite reliable, and the rates reasonable. Suriname has a dial telephone system; direct dialing from the U.S. is possible using country code 597. International airmail letters arrive almost daily from the U.S., with transit time averaging 15 days. Surface mail takes two months or longer. Local mail service is slow, although reasonably reliable.

Government-owned, commercial stations provide news and entertainment in local languages, Dutch and English. Shortwave radio can pick up Voice of America (VOA), Armed Forces Radio, British Broadcasting Corporation (BBC), a few U.S. stations, and numerous Spanish and Portuguese broadcasts. The television broadcasts provide many recorded programs from the U.S., with some in color. The news is reported in Dutch.

Government publications and newspapers are in Dutch. The government cultural center maintains a public library with a limited collection of English editions. A few very expensive English-language paperbacks and hardcover books are available from one or two outlets in Paramaribo.

Health

Paramaribo has medical facilities which are satisfactory for all but the most serious health problems. Local doctors have received their training in the Netherlands, Suriname, and the U.S. Several good dentists with modern equipment practice in the city. Eyeglasses can be fitted satisfactorily, as there are several eye specialists and opticians. Some common prescription and patent medicines are available, but most prescription medications are unavailable.

The general level of sanitation and health in Paramaribo, although not up to U.S. standards, is good. Garbage is collected weekly. Government efforts have eliminated yellow fever, malaria, and rabies from the capital area. Locally produced food, milk, bottled drinks, and meat are safe.

Tap water is potable in Paramaribo, Nieuw-Nickerie, and Moengo. In small villages and in the interior, waterborne diseases are always a possibility because of various unsanitary health practices. Skin infections are fairly common. It is inadvisable to walk barefoot, since schistosomiasis and other parasites can be contracted through exposed skin. The coastal area has been free of yellow fever and malaria for many years, but these diseases are still found in the interior. The visitor should take anti-malarial drugs when traveling in those regions.

Suriname's high humidity aggravates arthritis, sinusitis, rheumatism, and bronchial asthma. The damp, warm air encourages fungus growth which can affect the skin or cause allergic reactions. Numerous plants and flowers are also sources of allergies. The climate is debilitating to many Americans, particularly those arriving from cooler climates. New arrivals may feel weak and tired and may require extra sleep during their first few weeks in Paramaribo. The tropical sun is surprisingly strong, and direct exposure at midday can cause uncomfortable burns in 15 to 20 minutes.

Mosquitoes are prevalent in some lower lying parts of Paramaribo. Some people use mosquito nets when sleeping in rooms that are not air-conditioned, especially in some areas outside the capital, where mosquitoes may carry malaria. Mosquito and insect repellents are widely used. The many insects found in this tropical region result in frequent, but mild, bites, which sometimes become infected despite precautions. Outside heavier-populated sections, there are poisonous reptiles and wild animals. Caution should be exercised by wearing proper clothing and keeping alert when in forested areas.

Clothing and Services

The warm, humid climate of Suriname normally necessitates only lightweight summer clothing, except in some air-conditioned offices and buildings. Evenings in the rainy season are cooler than in the dry season. It rains almost daily, so an umbrella is necessary for each family member. Because of the high humidity, raincoats are seldom worn.

Men normally wear light cotton shirts and lightweight suits. At many social occasions, casual attire is acceptable.

Women generally wear skirts or slacks while shopping in the city. Shorts should not be worn in public. Pants and pantsuits are often seen in casual social situations. Clothing accessories can be purchased in Paramaribo, but selection is limited, and prices are higher than in the U.S.

Basic services are adequate. The city has two laundries and two dry cleaners. Work is fair, and prices are higher than to those in the U.S. A few dressmakers, tailors, hairdressers, and barbers do good work at reasonable rates. Repairs of any

kind are adequate, but slow. Qualified technicians for some repairs do not exist in Paramaribo. However, many auto garages, especially those of dealers, have modern facilities, skilled mechanics, and do adequate work, although parts are often in short supply.

Virtually all miscellaneous household items, supplies, medicines, and tobacco are difficult to find locally. Since nearly everything must be imported, prices are high. It is advisable to have on hand a supply of special or unusual medicines or toiletries.

Domestic Help

English-speaking domestics are not only hard to find, but are rarely willing to live in. A full-time maid works six hours a day, six days a week, is paid at least $300 a month, plus food and transportation, and is paid overtime for evening work.

Part-time gardeners often will do heavy tasks when required. For entertaining, ample extra help is available.

Expatriates should be careful not to hire persons with illegal residential status in Suriname, as is often the case with Guyanese and Haitians.

NOTES FOR TRAVELERS

There are several routes from the U.S. to Paramaribo, the easiest being the SLM flight from Miami, which departs twice a week. Transit can also be through Curaçao, Netherlands Antilles, from Miami; or through Port-of-Spain, Trinidad, from either New York or Miami.

A passport, visa and, if traveling by air, return ticket are required for travel to Suriname. There is a processing fee for business and tourist visas. A business visa requires a letter from the sponsoring company detailing the reason for the visit.

There is an airport departure charge and a terminal fee. Travelers arriving from Guyana, French Guiana and Brazil are required to show proof of a yellow fever vaccination. For further information, travelers can contact the Embassy of the Republic of Suriname, 4301 Connecticut Avenue, N.W., Suite 460, Washington, D.C. 20008, telephone (202) 244-7488, email: embsur@erols.com, or the Consulate of Suriname in Miami, 7235 NW 19th Street, Suite A, Miami, Fl 33126, telephone (305) 593-2697.

While the situation in the countryside is stable at present, there is insufficient police authority over much of the interior of Suriname to offer assistance in an emergency. Unaccompanied travel to the interior, particularly the East-West highway between Paramaribo and Albina, is considered risky due to the high incidence of robberies and assaults along this route. Isolated acts of violence, particularly in but not limited to the interior, may occur. Travelers to remote areas of the interior of Suriname should be aware that they may encounter difficulties because of the lack of government authority throughout the interior and inadequate medical facilities in some areas. The ability of the U.S. Embassy to assist in an emergency situation may be hampered by limited transportation and communications in some areas.

The rate of violent crime has increased. Burglary and armed robbery are increasingly common in the capital city of Paramaribo, as well as in the outlying areas. Banditry occurs along routes in the interior of the country where police protection is inadequate. An increasing number of tourists report being attacked and robbed. Visitors may wish to exercise caution when traveling to the interior without an organized tour group, and secure their belongings carefully while staying in Paramaribo. Visitors may find it useful to carry photocopies of their passport, drivers license, credit cards and other important papers and leave the originals in a safe place.

Travelers to Suriname may experience disruptions in travel plans because of the unreliability of scheduled airline service to and from that country. Suriname Airways (SLM), operating in conjunction with Antillean Airways, serves as the only direct air link between the U.S. and Suriname. Limited flight schedules and ongoing technical problems commonly result in delays. Additionally, transportation to the interior is unreliable. Interior flights are often delayed, sometimes for days, because of mechanical difficulties, fuel shortages, and runway conditions. Dutch is the official language of Suriname; however, English is widely used, and most tourist arrangements can be made in English.

Household pets must have veterinary certificates stating that they are free from disease and have had rabies shots. Quarantine is waived if the documentation is in order. No kennels are available.

Stringent laws govern ownership of firearms and ammunition. Hunting licenses are obtained only after acquiring a permit to own a shotgun, and importing and registering a shotgun is a long, slow process. An individual may own one shotgun. Twelve and 16-gauge shotguns are used almost exclusively. Rifles or pistols are forbidden.

Travelers should note that natives object to being photographed.

Paramaribo has Roman Catholic, Southern Baptist, Dutch Reformed, Lutheran, Moravian, Baptist, Assembly of God, Jehovah's Witnesses, Pilgrim Holiness, AME, and Seventh-Day Adventist churches, an Anglican mission, two synagogues, a Baha'i center and several Muslim mosques and Hindu temples. English services are held regularly each Sunday at the Anglican mission and the AME church. A Catholic mass in English is offered once a month. Many Americans attend an interdenominational Protestant service held each Sunday.

The time in Suriname is Greenwich Mean Time (GMT) minus three-and-a-half.

The Suriname *guilder* (Sf) is the monetary unit. Currency controls are stringent.

The metric system is used. An additional unit of weight measurement is the Dutch *pond*, which equals 500 grams, 46 more than in an American pound.

Americans living in or visiting Suriname are encouraged to register at the Consular Section of the U.S. Embassy in Paramaribo to obtain updated information on travel and security within Suriname. The Embassy is located at Dr. Sophie Redmondstraat 129, telephone (011)(597) 472-900. The Consular Section hours of operation for routine American citizen services are Mondays and Wednesdays from 8:00 a.m. - 10:00 a.m., or by appointment, except on American and Surinamese holidays. U.S. citizens requiring emergency assistance evenings, weekends, and holidays may contact an Embassy duty officer by pager at (011)(597) 088-08302. The U.S. Embassy in Paramaribo also provides consular services for French Guiana. For further information on French Guiana, please refer to the separate Consular Information Sheet on French Guiana.

LOCAL HOLIDAYS

Jan. 1	New Year's Day
Feb/Mar	Holi Phagwa*
	Id al-Fitr*
Mar/Apr.	Good Friday*
Mar/Apr.	Easter Monday*
Mar/Apr.	Easter*
May 1	Labor Day
July 1	Emancipation Day
Nov. 25	Independence Day
Dec. 25	Christmas Day
Dec. 26	Boxing Day

*variable

RECOMMENDED READING

The following titles are provided as a general indication of the material published on this country:

Beatty, Noelle B. *Suriname*. New York: Chelsea House, 1988.

Hoogbergen, Wim. *The Boni Maroon Wars in Suriname*. Kinderhook, NY: EJ Brill, 1990.

Price, Richard. *Alabi's World*. The Johns Hopkins University Press, 1990.

Stedman, John G. *Stedman's Surinam: Life in an Eighteenth-Century Slave Society*. Edited by Richard Price and Sally Price. Baltimore, MD: Johns Hopkins University Press, 1992.

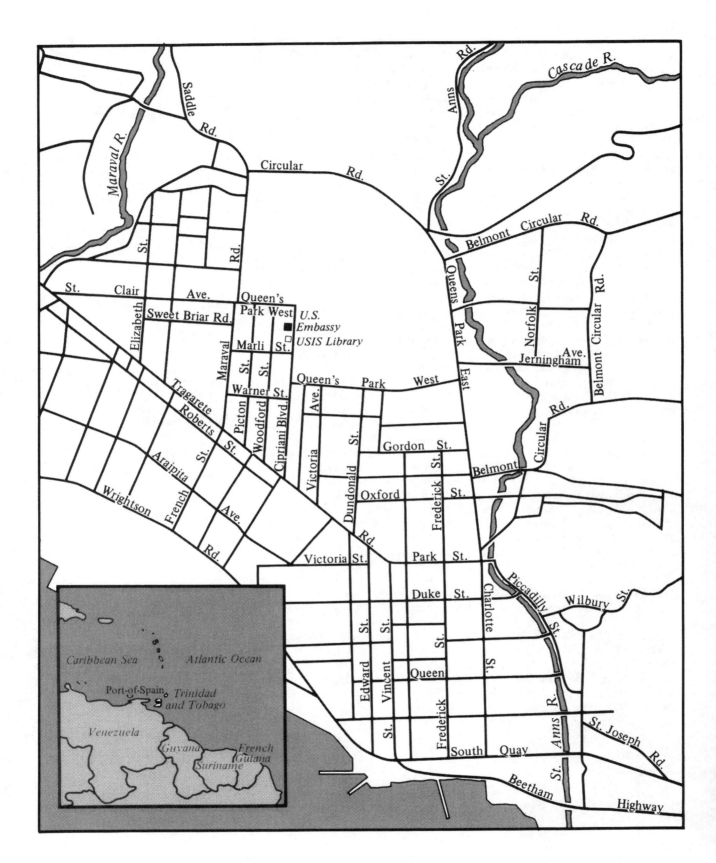

Port-of-Spain, Trinidad and Tobago

TRINIDAD AND TOBAGO

Republic of Trinidad and Tobago

Major City:
Port-of-Spain

Other Cities:
Arima, Chaguanas, La Brea, Lopinot, Saint Joseph, San Fernando, Sangre Grande, Scarborough, Tunapuna

EDITOR'S NOTE

This chapter was adapted from the Department of State Post Report 1999 for Trinidad & Tobago. Supplemental material has been added to increase coverage of minor cities, facts have been updated, and some material has been condensed. Readers are encouraged to visit the Department of State's web site at http://travel.state.gov/ for the most recent information available on travel to this country.

INTRODUCTION

Trinidad does not conform to the stereotypes of a Caribbean resort island. In fact, while it is blessed with great natural beauty and some good beaches, it is not a premier tourist destination. Tourism is growing rapidly on the sister island of Tobago, which is only a 20-minute flight away. What Trinidad lacks in tourist infrastructure, however, it more than makes up for in its unique ethnic and cultural flavor. Its abundant natural resources (oil and gas) have provided it the means to chart its own course, politically and economically, and make it a leader in the region. First-time visitors are often surprised at the level of industrialization in the country. It is a relatively prosperous nation as

measured by per capita GDP. Its population and landmass are larger than all of the Windward Islands combined. Even its geologic origins set it apart; it was originally a part of the South American mainland before it broke off thousands of years ago. This means that its flora and fauna are as varied as those of South America, but concentrated in a much smaller area. It is one of the world's premier destinations for bird watchers, boasting several hundred species, especially hummingbirds. Trinidad includes mountain ranges with peaks as high as 3,000 ft, as well as flat lands used for agriculture, and wetlands.

The Venezuelan coastline, less than 10 miles away, is visible from Port of Spain, yet cultural and language differences mean there is relatively little contact with Venezuela. Trinidadian society is a vibrant and unique mixture of races and national origins, with the two largest groups being of African and of Indian descent. In addition, there are smaller, but significant numbers of people of Chinese, Syrian, Lebanese, English, Portuguese, Spanish, and French origin.

Life for the community is good in Port of Spain, particularly for families and those who like outdoor activities. Port of Spain is as safe as many large U.S. cities, the weather

is good, and medical care and other facilities are adequate. The people are open and friendly toward Americans, the business infrastructure is reasonably modern and efficient, and housing and schools are good. While some of the conveniences Americans take for granted are not always available, one can dial direct to family in the U.S., easily access the internet and watch many stateside channels on cable TV, or find the latest video releases as well as decent bagels. At the same time, opportunities abound to be enriched by an interesting and unique culture.

MAJOR CITY

Port-of-Spain

Port-of-Spain is located between the sheltered Gulf of Paria and the mountains of the Northern Range that rise sharply from the sea to an altitude of 3,000 feet. With a metropolitan population of over 200,000 this bustling port city is on many important air and sea routes of the eastern Caribbean.

The city itself is situated on flat land, with hills rising on three sides and the sea on the fourth. Downtown streets are narrow and congested. The downtown businesses are immediately inland from the dock and waterfront. On nearby Woodford Square stands the Red House, which is the center of government and houses parliamentary offices as well as the House of Representatives, and the Senate. Many political and social functions take place at Woodford Square or on the recently refurbished Brian Lara Promenade.

Further inland is the Savannah, cultural and recreational hub of the city, with its surrounding road often called the "world's largest roundabout." This huge, grassy, oval park is the site of numerous cricket and soccer games, food vendors, and spectators on park benches. A 2-1/2 mile long paved walk around the Savannah is used by roller skaters, joggers, baby strollers, and pedestrians. Many Carnival activities take place on the Savannah.

Many of Port of Spain's cultural attractions are located around the Savannah, including Queen's Hall (used for concerts and other performances), the Botanical Gardens, a zoo, the Hilton Hotel, and historical houses, many in Victorian style architecture.

With U.S.-style shopping malls and supermarkets in many locations, Port of Spain is a growing city with many of the conveniences of the United States.

Utilities

Since electric current is the same as in the U.S. (I 10v, 60-cycle AC), transformers are unnecessary. Plugs and outlets are American or a locally available three-prong type.

The electrical system experiences occasional surges and outages. Line conditioners are recommended for sensitive electronic items such as computers.

During the dry season (January-June) water supplies are low, and restrictions may be placed on watering lawns and washing cars. Water pressure and supply problems can be a serious problem in hilly suburbs.

Food

Supermarkets similar to those in the U.S. are located conveniently throughout the city. Smaller family-run groceries, vegetable-fruit stores (called greengrocers here), and roadside stands sell vegetables, fruits and fish. Well-stocked store shelves hold many familiar brands.

Food prices, except for government controlled items, are comparable or higher than in the U.S., since prices for imported food reflect freight costs and some import duties. Products come from the U.S., Canada, UK, Venezuela, Jamaica, and elsewhere. Government-controlled items are sold at below market prices and are supported by government subsidies. These include rice, sugar, flour, and some imported foods such as butter and cheese.

Some items, which are solely imports, include baby food, cake mixes, pickles, olives, and canned and dehydrated soups. Locally produced coffee is available, but stronger than U.S. coffee. American ground coffee is available. Good quality juices produced locally can be had both sweetened and unsweetened. Both local and imported candy and snacks are widely available at reasonable prices. Local and imported nuts (peanuts, cashews, walnuts, and almonds) are available, but expensive.

Staples such as eggs, bread, butter, yogurt, cream and milk (fresh, UHT and powdered) of good quality are widely available at reasonable prices. U.S.-style breakfast cereals, both local and imported, as well as rice and pasta products are also widely available.

A wide variety of fresh, canned and frozen fruits and vegetables are found in local supermarkets, neighborhood shops and roadside stands. While there are many fruits and vegetables not commonly found in the U.S., the availability of fresh herbs and the variety of vegetables overall is less than that found in Washington, D.C. area supermarkets.

Fresh fish and shrimp can be purchased at the downtown central market, roadside stands, or from fishermen returning with their catch. Frozen fish is available at supermarkets. Local pork is good, as are New Zealand mutton and lamb. Beef cuts differ from those in the U.S. both in texture and taste and are often tougher and drier. Sausages, ham and luncheon meats are available.

Miller and Miller Genuine Draft are the only U.S. beers available locally.

Trinidadian cuisine reflects the nation's cultural diversity. "Creole" cooking includes dishes based on rice mixed with chicken, pork and various local vegetables. On their way to work, many Trinidadians enjoy a quick breakfast of fresh coconut water and jelly sold by vendors along the Savannah and Independence Square. Callaloo, a popular soup, is made from taro leaves, okra, pumpkin, coconut, and crabs. Other favorites are cow heel soup, crab backs, souse (pickled pig's feet), and pastels (ground beef wrapped in crepe-like pancakes and banana leaves). East Indian dishes include roti (usually beef, chicken, or pork with potatoes and curry spices wrapped in a large, thin bread), spicy hot curries, and chutney. Most Chinese food is Cantonese, but is prepared to suit Trinidadian taste and is somewhat different from what one finds in U.S. Chinese restaurants. Wild meats, such as manicou (possum), armadillo, iguana, deer, and wild boar are delicacies here. Trinidadians especially enjoy fish including shark, king fish, red snapper, Spanish mackerel, flying fish, shrimp, carite, and cascadura (a fresh water fish).

Clothing

Lightweight summer clothing is worn year round by both men and women in Port of Spain. Due to Trinidad and Tobago's tropical climate, clothing made from natural fibers (cotton, linen, etc.) or a blend

Carnival in Port of Spain, Trinidad

© Wolfgang Kaehler. Reproduced by permission.

of natural and synthetic fibers is more comfortable than all synthetic materials. Clothing wears out quickly under the frequent laundering made essential by the high heat and humidity.

Men: Dress is casual and informal, although evening functions often require "lounge suits," the local term for dark business suits. At more casual functions, sport shirts and slacks are commonly worn, as are "shirt jacks," which are similar to the Latin American guayabera or African safari suit and are very popular among Trinidadian men. During the rainy season, showers can be expected nearly every day. Umbrellas are therefore essential. Raincoats and galoshes are not worn here due to the hot climate. Loose-fitting clothing made of natural fibers is the most comfortable.

Women: Women wear dresses, suits, or skirts to the office. Stockings are rarely worn due to the high

humidity. Plan to bring a good supply of dresses for social occasions, as parties and other social events are numerous throughout the year. Trinidadian women are generally smartly dressed no matter what dress is specified by the invitation. Casual and dressy short dresses or skirts are favored at most social functions.

More formal evening functions require long dresses or fancy short dresses.

Informal social functions require only skirts and blouses/tops.

Local boutiques sell the latest fashions, including interesting local designs, at relatively high prices. Fabric shops offer a wide variety of materials at reasonable prices. Seamstresses are numerous and many can sew without patterns; their prices vary.

Children: Clothing worn during summer in the U.S. is suitable here. Washable, lightweight materials with natural fibers are best. One sweater or feather-light jacket should be all the outer wear needed. Most children wear sandals or comfortable canvas shoes. They are available here at reasonable prices. Most schools require school uniforms, which can be purchased locally. The International School requires black or white shoes or sneakers, of which more styles are available in the U.S.

Supplies and Services

Locally made laundry soaps and cleansers are available at reasonable prices. Imported soaps, cleaners, disinfectants, fabric softeners, grease cutters, and waxes are more expensive.

Numerous name brand cosmetics and personal hygiene items are sold locally, including hair care products, lotions, nail polish, deodorants, foot powders, and shampoos. Except for a few locally made products, they are more expensive than in the U.S. Several brands of locally made diapers are sold at reasonable prices.

Photographic equipment is expensive and limited in variety. Film and black-and white and color processing services are available at higher than U.S. cost.

Attractive shops sell most of the kitchen items found in the U.S., but at higher prices.

There are several reasonably-priced but unreliable dry cleaners. Beauty and barber shops resemble those in the U.S.

Domestic Help

Domestic help can be found and hired at rates considerably below those in the United States. Few families hire more than a full-time maid and part-time gardener. Live-in maids are hard to find, because most employees prefer day work. Some families employ maids and waiters for representational functions, at hourly or evening wages. Baby-sitters are inexpensive but sometimes hard to find. In addition to wages, employers should provide meals or cash equivalent, uniforms, and a contribution to the compulsory National Insurance plan. If the employer requires the employee to have a pre-employment medical check-up, this should be done at the employer's expense.

Religious Activities

Freedom of worship exists in Trinidad and Tobago. Most religions have places of worship. The Roman Catholic, Anglican (Episcopalian), Presbyterian, Methodist, Hindu, and Muslim faiths predominate. There are no synagogues, but a small Jewish community (mainly foreign residents) organizes activities and observances.

Education

The school year begins in early September and ends in mid-July, with Christmas and Easter vacations dividing it into three terms. The school week is Monday-Friday except for holidays. All Trinidadian schools above nursery level require uniforms that are inexpensive and well suited for the tropics.

Good preschools for 2-5-year-olds are available and are held in the teacher's home. Teacher-pupil ratio, physical setup of the classroom, and the teacher's training and method vary widely. Drilling on numbers and alphabet is a primary activity, and children have less freedom of movement than in U.S. nursery schools. However, some Montessori-type schools exist, and other schools have teachers who include some Montessori methods in games and activities.

Primary schooling (PreK through 12) is available at The International School of Port of Spain (ISPS). In April 1999, ISPS moved into a US$4.5 million dollar, purpose-built educational facility on the banks of the Diego Martin River. ISPS is growing rapidly and is modeled on the American educational system and reflects a college preparatory curriculum. As an accredited, private independent school, it continues to expand course offerings and extra-curricular activities.

Special Educational Opportunities

The Venezuelan Embassy and the National Institute for Higher Education (Research Science and Technology) (NIHERST) in Port of Spain conduct free courses in Spanish conversation for adults. A similar service is provided in French by the Alliance Francaise for a nominal fee. Private teachers offer special courses in crafts, music, modern dance, and arts.

The University of the West Indies is located at St. Augustine, about 12 miles east of Port of Spain. Degree courses are offered by the faculties of agriculture, engineering, social sciences, the natural sciences, and the arts. The University also offers some non-degree courses in Port of Spain and at St. Augustine. The cost for non-degree study at UWI is high, but many of the more popular departments (engineering, sciences, and premedical) are difficult to enroll in due to enrollment limits.

Sports

Trinidad and Tobago's primary national sports are cricket and soccer. Swimming, tennis, golf, boating, and fishing are also popular and are available in and around Port of Spain. Port of Spain has several parks, including a botanical garden and a small zoo.

Beaches in Trinidad are not resorts, but they are convenient to Port of Spain and are well used all year. The most popular beach is located at Maracas Bay on the north coast, about 35 minutes from Port of Spain. The smaller, less crowded, Las Cuevas Beach is 5 miles farther. There are beach houses for rent on the East Coast (about two hours' drive from Port of Spain) and on the small islands off the northwest coast (reachable through a short water taxi ride) which are popular weekend getaway spot. Swimming can be dangerous at any beach in Trinidad because of frequent heavy surf, rip-tides, and undertows. However, Maracas and several of the other more popular beaches have lifeguards. Several sports facilities provide swimming pools in Port of Spain at lower rates than the U.S. Tobago offers resort-type facilities, including hotels on or near the beach and a golf course. Many people find weekends on "Robinson Crusoe's Island" a welcome change from Port of Spain's routine. Tennis facilities in the city are frequently crowded, but adequate; equipment and clothing are expensive. The Tranquillity Square Lawn Tennis Club has five clay courts and one all-weather court. This private club accepts member referral and tennis is quite competitive. The Trinidad Hilton has two all-weather courts, but expect a short wait for half-hour of playing time. The Trinidad Country Club in Port of Spain has a large swimming pool (and a children's pool), six tennis courts, playground (swings, slide), bar, and eating facilities. As of June 1997, the cost was approximately US$110 initiation fee per adult and US$150 annual

View of Speyside, Tobago

fees for families. Although these three private clubs are the most popular, smaller clubs exist. It is also possible to reserve an hour's play at a good all-weather public court.

Opportunities for scuba diving and spearfishing are fair in Trinidad and excellent in Tobago. The waters around Trinidad are generally murky and devoid of coral reefs, with dangerous currents. These conditions coupled with the lack of diving instruction and rental equipment, means divers should be experienced and outfitted before attempting dives in Trinidad. By contrast, Tobago diving is well organized with equipment and instruction available; the reefs, clear water, and tropical fish provide for excellent diving opportunities. Deep sea fishing is quite good, and there are some charter boats available.

Port of Spain has several boating clubs and marinas: the Trinidad and Tobago Yacht Club, Trinidad and Tobago Yachting Association, Island Properties, Power Boats, Crews Inn and Peake's, among others. The Yacht Club has boating facilities for members and guests. Power Boats and Island Properties, as well as Peake's, have haul-out and full service facilities for boats. The recently established Crews Inn is a world class marina for power and sail boats and includes a supermarket, hotel, bank, bookstore, and other features such as boat slips with full electrical, cable TV and telephone hookups. The Trinidad and Tobago Yachting Association, which is only for sailboats and dinghies, offers competitive sailing in a number of large and small boat categories. It also sponsors children's boating classes. Sailboats and powerboats can be purchased locally, but prices are high and selection limited.

St. Andrews Golf Club, situated in a valley 5 miles north of Port of Spain, offers an 18-hole golf course, restaurant, swimming pool, driving range, and putting green. Similar facilities and less expensive 18-hole course are located at Point-a-Pierre, 45 minutes south. A nine-hole public golf course, in an attractive valley northwest of town, is also available.

Small game hunting in the forests and duck hunting in the swamps is possible, but only with shotguns. Rifles are not legal hunting weapons here. Game is scarce and all but the most dedicated hunters find that the results are not worth the effort. The Trinidad Rifle Association and Trap and Skeet Association offer firing range facilities for shooting pistols, as well as skeet, small bore, and high-power rifles.

Good hiking opportunities are enhanced by an active Field Naturalists Club, which sponsors monthly hikes to out-of-the-way spots. Informal group hiking is a common event. Opportunities are outstanding for bird watchers and butterfly collectors. The internationally known Asa Wright Nature Center near Arima provides overnight facilities for amateur and professional naturalists.

Other recreational opportunities include several karate schools, dancing schools, fitness centers, amateur theater, model building club, stamp club and various women's clubs.

Sports equipment and attire compare to those used in the U.S. and can be purchased locally, but prices are higher.

Port of Spain has an active Hash House Harriers Club that organizes trail runs every other week in different parts of the country. Unlike Hash groups in many other countries, the group is not dominated by ex-pats. There is a good mix of locals and foreigners. The hash is a good way for newcomers to meet people and see the country.

Touring and Outdoor Activities

Many staff members enjoy visits to nearby islands and to the Venezuelan mainland. Visitors traveling by British West Indian Airways (BWIA) to Trinidad should include Tobago on their ticket, at no extra charge and get a free trip to Tobago within a year. A quiet, peaceful island, Tobago boasts lagoons, beaches, and undersea coral gardens with tropical fish, and an 18-hole golf course.

Barbados, 200 miles away, offers more tourist infrastructure than Tobago, excellent beaches and a wide selection of good restaurants and hotels. Moderate excursion rates are available during the off season. Caracas, Venezuela is another popular destination for long weekends, offering restaurants and shopping as well as a change from the typical Caribbean atmosphere. Georgetown, Guyana is an exotic break for the adventurous, where

Amerindian villages and huge rivers and waterfalls can be visited. Grenada, 90 miles north of Trinidad, is known as the "Isle of Spice". The most southerly of the Windward Islands, it offers beautiful beaches and several good hotels. St. George's, the capital city, has excellent yacht facilities. Moderate excursion rates are available during the off-season. Grenada is the southern gateway to the Grenadines, an increasingly popular cruising and sailing ground.

Entertainment

Port of Spain has a number of reasonably priced restaurants featuring continental, Indian, Italian, Thai, American, Chinese, and local Creole cuisine.

Several hotels and three or four nightclubs offer entertainment featuring steel bands, calypso, and other local music and dance bands. For the younger crowd, several discotheques play current U.S. disco and pop music favorites, local and Jamaican dance music.

Three large-screen movie theaters and a drive-in present mostly U.S. films. Other venues sometimes offer cultural events, plays or shows. An active semi-professional theater workshop group welcomes foreigners. In addition, interested visitors might participate in other smaller theater and dance groups. Video rental stores are used by many Americans.

The entertainment highlight is the annual Carnival. Many feel that Trinidad's pre-Lenten Carnival is second only to Rio's in grandeur and twice as enjoyable, since it is safer and more informal. Many Americans each year join one of the colorful "Mas" bands (masquerade groups). There are also numerous other special cultural events, festivals and competitions. The period between Christmas and Carnival is filled with "fetes" (parties) and is characterized by local calypso and steelband competitions leading to the national finals which take place the weekend preceding Carnival. During this time, one can visit

numerous local "pan yards" in the evenings to hear the world's premier steelband rehearsing intricate arrangements of specially commissioned competition tunes.

On a year-round basis, however, entertainment possibilities are less varied in Port of Spain than in a comparable U.S. city. Bring books, records, games, and hobby materials.

Trinidad is a destination which most young families find enjoyable because of the outdoor living, the friendliness and hospitality of the Trinidadians, and the relative safety and lack of serious health and political hazards.

Social Activities

Port of Spain has many opportunities for social activity. Trinidadians are friendly and very hospitable. Americans are welcomed at the many fetes that occur throughout the year. During the Christmas and Carnival season nonstop fetes are held. Most parties are informal. Other types of home entertainment include cocktail parties, dinners, bridge parties, and buffet suppers. Club activities include films, barbecues, and dances for members.

Some other clubs include the Horticultural Society, Trinidad and Tobago German Club, the Orchid Society, the Field Naturalists Society, Living Waters Christian Community, an informal Jewish community, and other groups.

Families with small children find opportunities for social contact in such groups as Cub Scouts, Boy Scouts, Sea Scouts, Girl Guides, and Brownies. Older children and teenagers find few organized groups to join. Most American service clubs such as Rotary International and Lions, have branches in Trinidad and Tobago.

OTHER CITIES

ARIMA, the nation's other population center is on Trinidad. It is about 15 miles east of Port-of-Spain, and many of its residents work in the capital. The population of Arima is about 24,600.

CHAGUANAS is a market center in western Trinidad, 12 miles southeast of Port-of-Spain. This town of roughly 6,100 residents is noted for its busy Saturday open-air market. Everything from produce to glassware and gadgets is offered for sale, spread out on blankets and displayed in small wooden stands.

LA BREA lies on the Gulf of Paria in the southwest, in one of Trinidad's most unusual regions. The adjoining Pitch Lake has become a major tourist attraction and the city itself has benefitted. The area is covered with pitch, so houses and buildings in La Brea tilt in all directions. Roads are full of potholes, and huge cracks. The pitch erupts and subsides quickly, even in the heart of town. Pitch Lake, referred to as "magnified elephant skin," is actually a massive field of resin, almost 300 feet deep. The lake supplies tons of asphalt from its more than 100 acres. La Brea's population is an estimated 1,500.

LOPINOT is a picturesque village tucked into a valley in north-central Trinidad, about 12 miles east of Port-of-Spain. The village dates to the 1800s, when it was founded by the Count de Lopinot. The Frenchman and his settlers were awarded the region by the British, and proceeded to carve out a thriving plantation from the dense forest. The count's estate is now a principal tourist spot, the house a museum with memorabilia and photos. The gardens are meticulously tended and are highly popular for picnickers. Residents of Lopinot are a mixture of French, Spanish, Amerindian, and African, and are known for their distinctive songs and instrumentation. Other features here include a church that was moved from a nearby town, linked caves with curious stalactites, and a dubiously interesting colony of white cockroaches—the only such species in the world—found in the caves.

SAINT JOSEPH is the former capital of Trinidad, situated seven miles east of Port-of-Spain on the main highway. Its population is approximately 4,100.

SAN FERNANDO, on the island of Trinidad, was founded in 1786. With a population of approximately 33,600 (1995 est.), it is a business and industrial center of growing importance. It is a seaport city, and several industrial plants have made their headquarters here.

One of Trinidad's most important market centers is **SANGRE GRANDE,** 25 miles southeast of Port-of-Spain. It has a population of about 9,000, and is the hub of St. Andrew County.

SCARBOROUGH is the chief town of Tobago, although it has only about 6,000 residents. It is situated near the island's Rockley Bay. Because Scarborough is in a resort area, it has hotels, several banks, and a car rental agency.

TUNAPUNA, 10 miles east of Port-of-Spain on Trinidad's main highway, is near the home of the St. Augustine campus of the University of the West Indies. The city's population is an estimated 10,000.

COUNTRY PROFILE

Population

Christopher Columbus discovered, named and claimed Trinidad for Spain in 1498. Sir Walter Raleigh made brief bids for possession of the island in 1595. The indigenous inhabitants of the islands - the warlike Caribs, who flourished in Tobago, and the more peaceful Arawaks, who outnumbered the Caribs in Trinidad - were ultimately subdued and enslaved by the Spanish. By the end of the 18th century, they were almost extinct.

Africans were brought to Trinidad as slaves in 1702 to boost cacao production. When the Spanish crown opened the island to immigration in the last quarter of the century, French planters and their slaves came by the thousands from other Caribbean islands and France, bringing their knowledge of sugarcane cultivation.

The Spanish ceded Trinidad to the English in 1797. Tobago, after changing hands among the Dutch, French, and British several times during the 16th and 17th centuries, was finally captured by the British in 1793.

When slavery was abolished throughout the British West Indies in 1834, plantation owners turned to indentured laborers from India, and some 150,000 arrived in Trinidad between 1854 and 1917. By 1921 East Indians accounted for almost one-third of Trinidad's population; today they comprise a slim plurality.

Trinidad was the site of a large U.S. military presence during World War II, serving as a huge naval base and training site for many of the troops headed for North Africa. It also protected supply routes for oil for the allied forces. German U-boats stalked allied supply and troop ships headed for the war in Europe, sinking many in the waters surrounding Trinidad and Tobago. A small, privately run military history museum outside of Port of Spain details this and other fascinating military chapters in the history of the islands. U.S. military bases and other facilities on the island were returned by the U.S. to Trinidad and Tobago in the 1960s.

A plurality of the population is Christian (Roman Catholic 30%, Anglican 11%, also Presbyterian, Baptist and other faiths). 24% are Hindu and 6% Muslim. There are also smaller groups following African derived religions.

Trinidad and Tobago's population is just under 1.3 million, of which over 50,000 live in Tobago. Greater Port of Spain, with about 200,000 inhabitants, is by far the largest city, followed by San Fernando, Arima and

Chaguanas. The largest town in Tobago is Scarborough. Over 2,000 Americans live in Trinidad and Tobago, many of local origin. Family and cultural ties with North America are strong, with sizable Trinidadian communities resident in New York, Florida and Toronto, Canada.

Most of the rural population in Trinidad lives in small roadside agricultural villages. The larger villages usually contain a church or temple, a police station, a primary school, recreational club/bar and small grocery stores.

The two major folk traditions are Creole and East Indian. Creole is a mixture of African elements as influenced by Spanish, French, and English colonial culture. Many East Indians have retained their own way of life and Hindu traditions and religious rites such as cremation and Divali (Festival of Lights). A smaller proportion of the East Indian population is Muslim. The entire population speaks English, often flavored with expressions derived from Trinidad's cultural heritage.

The people of Trinidad and Tobago enjoy social events called `fetes' all year. One of the world's biggest fetes - Carnival - takes place each year on the Monday and Tuesday before Lent. This festival features parades with huge groups of masqueraders dancing in spectacular costumes through the streets of Port of Spain, accompanied by large sound trucks or steel bands, and calypso singers accompanied by brass bands performing at calypso "tents." The French introduced Carnival as an urban festival and it was celebrated initially among the upper class Creoles. In time it also became a means for the Afro-Trinidadian masses to break out of their normal routine, sometimes to express ridicule or to indirectly attack their social superiors and the government. It has now become a truly national event, with most segments of the population actively participating.

Public Institutions

Trinidad and Tobago is a democratic country with a parliamentary form of government. On August 31, 1962, the United Kingdom granted independence to Trinidad and Tobago as a member of the British Commonwealth with a Governor General as the Queen's personal representative. On September 24, 1976, Trinidad and Tobago adopted a new constitution, which established the country as a republic within the British Commonwealth. The Queen was replaced as head of state by a President elected by Parliament, and the position of Governor General was abolished.

The major governmental institutions, based on the British model, remained the same as those established by the 1962 constitution. They are: A Cabinet (currently 17 Ministers appointed and led by a Prime Minister).

A bicameral Parliament consisting of a 36-member House of Representatives and a 31-member Senate. Members of the House of Representatives are elected in parliamentary elections held at least every five years. Members of the Senate are appointed by the President: 16 on the advice of the governing party, six on the advice of the opposition party, and nine at the President's discretion.

A judicial system which has a Court of Appeals as its highest level in the country. Final appeals may be taken to the Judicial Committee of the Privy Council in London.

In November 1995, the United National Congress (UNC), in coalition with the small National Alliance for Reconstruction (NAR) party, formed a government, with Basdeo Panday of the UNC as Prime Minister. The coalition took over from the People's National Movement (PNM) Government headed by Patrick Manning. The PNM was founded in 1958 under the leadership of Dr. Eric Williams. Dr. Williams in 1962 became the first Prime Minister of the newly

independent country, continuing in office until his death in 1981. In 1986 the PNM was swept out of office by the National Alliance for Reconstruction (NAR), led by A.N.R. Robinson. In 1991, the PNM returned to power only to be defeated in 1995 by the UNC/NAR coalition.

Trinidad and Tobago belongs to a number of international organizations through which it exerts some influence on world affairs. On gaining independence in 1962, Trinidad and Tobago joined the United Nations and became a member of the Commonwealth of Nations. In 1967, it was the first Commonwealth Caribbean country to seek membership in the Organization of American States (OAS) and the Inter-American Development Bank (IDB). Trinidad and Tobago was a founding member of the Caribbean Free Trade Association (CARIFTA), and its successor organization, the Caribbean Community (CARICOM). It is a member of the Non-Aligned Movement (NAM) and identifies with developing countries on many North-South economic issues.

Familiar organizations, such as the Red Cross, YMCA, YWCA, Boy Scouts, PTA, Jaycees, Lions Club, Kiwanis Club, Rotary Club, American Legion, etc., play significant roles in the community and welcome participation by foreign residents.

Arts, Science, and Education

The educational program inherited from the colonial administration was patterned on the British model, with structure and content resembling those of other Commonwealth Caribbean members. Students completing secondary school now take the Caribbean Examinations Council (CXC) examinations instead of the General Certificate of Education (GCE) exams prepared and graded in the U.K.

While Trinidad has one of the hemisphere's highest literacy rates and has produced scholars of international renown, some educational problems persist. School facilities tend to be outdated, in poor condition and overcrowded. Teacher salaries and training are also well below the private sector. Not all teachers have university degrees; some have received pedagogical training, others have specialist diplomas, and some have general secondary education. Higher education is available in Trinidad and Tobago at the St. Augustine Campus of the University of the West Indies, located on the outskirts of Port of Spain.

In the literary field notable writers include Alfred Mendes, C.L.R. James, Samuel Selvon, Earl Lovelace and Sir Vidiandhar Surajprasad Naipaul. Selvon's work most often deals with the poor people of Trinidad at home and abroad, and his style is both humorous and sympathetic. Naipaul's novels show a deep sensitivity toward the racial and cultural complexity of Trinidadian society and an understanding of its tensions and prejudices. Trinidad's leading poet and playwright is Pulitzer Prize-winner Derek Walcott, a St. Lucian by birth, who is now teaching in the United States.

The music and dance of Trinidad and Tobago and the festivals that inspire and preserve them reflect the country's kaleidoscopic colonial heritage and its multicultural population. Each element of the social mosaic-the Spanish and English colonizers, the French immigrants, the African slaves, and the East Indian indentured laborers, as well as smaller communities of Chinese, Syrians and Lebanese-has contributed to a national folkloric tradition which is among the world's richest.

The calypso, the musical genre that has drawn international attention to Trinidad, evolved from folk culture but is considered a popular political music form. Today's calypso has been described as "witty, smutty, topical, and full of double entendre." Stimulated by the commercialization of the music and the hotly contested annual competition for Carnival calypso monarch,

composers turn out some 40 or 50 "hit" songs each year. Soca, a high energy dance music, Indo-Trinidadian "chutney" music, Indian style "tassa" drum bands, and the limbo dance are also all of Trinidadian origin.

Trinidad's most notable contribution to world culture, however, may be the steel drum ("pan"). Several decades ago urban Afro-Trinidadians found that empty steel drums and similar objects were ideal for music making. The thousands of 55 gallon oil drums, discarded by the U.S. Naval Base at Chaguaramas during World War II, furnished an ample supply. From primitive beginnings they were slowly developed to be able to reproduce the entire chromatic scale. The bands, which can number over 100 musicians, typically have bass, guitar, and cello pans in the rhythm section, while tenor and "double second" pans play the melody. Pan music has become very refined and, aside from calypso tunes, now includes popular, jazz and classical pieces.

In the field of the visual arts, Boscoe Holder, who excels in figurative paintings, Noel Vaucrosson, a watercolorist, and Pat Chu Foon, a painter and sculptor, are well known. Peter Minshall, who designed the opening ceremonies at both the Barcelona and Atlanta Olympic Games, has become one of the stand-outs among the many talented "mas" (Carnival band) producers.

Clothing designers, producing a typical Caribbean style, have also come into their own in recent years.

Port of Spain has several small theaters and two larger auditoriums, which feature original and foreign plays and musical performances. While Trinidad and Tobago's cultural "market" is not large enough to draw many foreign acts (aside from Caribbean music shows), occasionally visits by lesser known foreign musical and dance groups liven up the local cultural scene.

Commerce and Industry

Endowed like neighboring Venezuela with rich deposits of oil and natural gas, Trinidad and Tobago became one of the most prosperous countries in the Western Hemisphere during the oil boom of the 1970s, ranking third in per-capita income behind the United States and Canada by 1981.Oil revenues enabled the nation to embark on a rapid industrial and infrastructural development program, within the framework of a "mixed economy," in which government investment in state corporations played a major role. Oil wealth also fueled a dramatic increase in domestic consumption.

With the collapse of oil prices in the early 1980s, Trinidad and Tobago entered into a difficult period of economic recession. In mid-1988, worsening economic conditions forced the government to begin a stringent adjustment program guided by the International Monetary Fund. This included devaluing the currency, adopting strict austerity budgets, rescheduling foreign debt, and in 1990 imposing a 15% value-added tax (VAT) on most goods and services.

By 1997, the country successfully recovered from its decade of economic decline, posting three straight years of real GDP growth (3.5% in 1994,23% in 1995 and 3.1% in 1996). Trinidad and Tobago's international debt rating and per capita income are now among the highest in the hemisphere, and the country is viewed as an economic and political leader in the Caribbean. New U.S. business investment has been running at about US$1 billion a year since 1995.

As part of its economic restructuring, the government adopted a more welcoming attitude toward foreign investment. Since 1992 almost all investment barriers have been eliminated, and the government has aggressively and successfully courted foreign investors. U.S. firms, mostly in the hydrocarbon sector and related downstream petrochemical industries, invested over US$2.5 billion from 1996 - 1998, placing Trinidad second only to Canada in the hemisphere in per capita U.S. direct foreign investment. There are no currency or capital controls, and the TT dollar has been in a lightly-managed, stable float since early 1993. The government has concluded a Bilateral Investment Treaty and an Intellectual Property Rights agreement with the United States.

In moving toward a more liberalized economy based on open competition, the government has privatized many state-owned industries and reduced subsidies to those that remain in the public portfolio. Companies all or partially divested since 1994 include the National Fisheries Company, British West Indian Airways (BWIA), National Flour Mills (NFM), the Trinidad and Tobago Electricity Commission (T&TEC), and the Water and Sewerage Authority (WASA).

Inflation averaged over 12% annually during the economic downturn of the early 1980s, and over 8% a year during the restructuring period in the first half of the 1990s. Through a combination of prudent monetary policies and fiscal restraint in public-sector budgets, the government has been successful in bringing inflation under control. Consumer prices rose 5.3% in 1995, and just 3.6% in 1996.

Despite serious efforts to diversify its economy, Trinidad and Tobago remains heavily dependent on the energy sector, which accounts for one-fourth of total GDP and 20% of government revenue and a maj or share of foreign exchange earnings. Production of crude oil has been steadily declining over the past decade, but the discovery of large reserves of natural gas, primarily in off shore fields, has fueled the development of petrochemical and metals industries. There are now over 20 large industrial plants in Trinidad, with most dependent on natural gas as a feedstock or running on inexpensive natural gas-generated electricity. At current trends Trinidad and Tobago will become the world's largest exporter of ammonia and methanol by the year 2000.

Since 1989, Trinidad and Tobago, in partnership with many major international oil companies, has pursued an aggressive oil and gas exploration campaign. BP Amoco, the biggest player in Trinidad's energy sector, produces half of the country's crude oil and the largest share of natural gas. BP Amoco, in partnership with Cabot (Boston), Repsol (Spain), British Gas and the National Gas Company (TT) has constructed a US$1 billion liquefied natural gas plant in southern Trinidad, the largest industrial project in the Caribbean, which began operating in early 1999.

Trinidad and Tobago is highly trade dependent, using the foreign exchange earned by its commodity and energy exports to buy consumer goods. The U.S. is by far Trinidad's most important trading partner, supplying about half of all imports and buying half of all exports.

Trinidad's exports are concentrated in a few sectors: oil, gas and downstream petrochemical products (chiefly fertilizers), and iron and steel. Thanks to its energy and commodity exports Trinidad has run a trade surplus in all but two of the last 20 years. Since the floating of the TT dollar in 1993, exports of manufactured products such as diapers, beer, soft drinks, processed foods, air conditioning equipment and plastic products have increased significantly, particularly to the country's CARICOM neighbors with whom T&T runs a ten to one trade surplus.

Trinidad and Tobago's agricultural sector is still dominated by sugar, which was introduced in colonial times. But despite preferential market access arrangements with the U.S. and the European Union, sugar production has generally been unprofitable, due to high costs and low volume. The state owned sugar company Caroni (1975) Ltd. has made attempts to diversify into areas such as citrus production, livestock and aquaculture with limited success. Other export crops include cocoa, coffee and cut flowers, but none is currently a significant foreign exchange earner. Agriculture still only accounts for about 2% of GDP The fishing sector is receiving increased attention both for the local market and for exports, but over fishing by commercial shrimp trawlers and coastal pollution are threatening once abundant fishing grounds.

In the oil-boom years, neither the government nor the people showed much interest in tourism. After the economic decline of the 1980s, however, Trinidad and Tobago has witnessed a positive change in attitudes toward tourism, and government has targeted the tourism industry for greater development. Currently largely confined to Tobago, tourism in Trinidad and Tobago is low-key and only accounts for 1% of GDP Fewer than 200,000 tourists visit the islands each year, many of these during Carnival. Lack of sufficient hotel rooms and limited air transportation links are challenges in marketing T&T as a tourist destination. The marine pleasure yacht subsector has been a bright spot in the country's tourism picture in recent years. Since 1990 annual sailing yacht arrivals have increased from several hundred to well over 3,000. The government is focusing efforts on the development of ecotourism destinations, taking advantage of acclaimed diving sites off the coast of Tobago and the impressive biological diversity of both islands.

The country's labor force numbers around 521,000, according to the latest figures. In 1998, official unemployment reached its lowest level in a decade at 14%, falling from 21.1% in 1993. The largest employment sector is services, accounting for 30% of total employment. Other significant sectors are trade, restaurant and hotels (18%), construction (13.6%), and manufacturing (10.3%). The vital, but capital intensive, hydrocarbon sectors employ only a small percentage of the labor force.

Trinidad and Tobago has an active labor movement. Although only about a quarter of the national labor force is unionized, the unions enjoy a relatively high public profile. Unionization in the industrial and public sectors is higher than in most other sectors. The Labor Ministry serves as conciliator in labor disputes, and the Industrial Court, to which disputes are referred when collective bargaining fails, has a record of fair, but slow, adjudication.

Transportation

Automobiles

Poor public transportation makes a personal car necessary in Port of Spain. Traffic moves on the left, so right-hand-drive vehicles predominate. Only right-hand-drive (RHD) cars are sold locally. There are dealers for nearly all Japanese and Korean brands and an increasing number of European models. U.S.-made right-hand drive Fords and Jeeps recently entered the market. Shipping a car to Trinidad, preferably of a make that is sold locally, is less expensive than purchasing one on the island.

A local driver's license (good for three years) is required and a valid U.S. license will facilitate its issuance.

Third-party liability insurance, required by law, is available locally at reasonable rates. A five-year claim-free statement from a previous insurer entitles you to a discount. Local auto insurance rates other than third party liability are high and vary according to the driver's age and safety record. Collision and comprehensive insurance is also available locally, but the rates are higher than U.S. firms.

Although some improvements are under way, many roads and streets (with the exception of a few major highways) are narrow, full of potholes, and poorly maintained. Wear and tear on cars is rapid and narrow

roads are often congested; small cars are recommended. Four-wheel-drive sport utility vehicles are also very popular, especially for those who enjoy exploring the dirt roads and secluded beaches of the island.

The typical Trinidadian driving style may surprise newcomers. Some drivers are aggressive and have little reluctance about straddling the center of the road. Driving with high beams on at night is fairly common. Taxis stop suddenly to pick up or discharge passengers. Newcomers quickly learn to drive defensively at all times but find that driving on the left is not as hard as it appears.

Local

Private cars and taxis are the primary means of local transport, but buses cover limited routes which concentrate on connecting Port-of-Spain with nearby towns and villages. The country no longer has a railway system.

Taxi stands are located in several areas of Port-of-Spain, including hotels and the airport. Taxis can also be summoned by telephone or hailed on the street. Travel by taxi on a daily basis is expensive; ask the fare beforehand, as taxis are not metered. Taxis are not identified by signs, or by uniform painting, but by the first letter "H" on the license plate. Route taxis or maxi-taxis (minibuses) are restricted to special routes. They display a sign in the windshield, but the color coding designates their area. Passengers are picked up and let off along the route. Fares are reasonable and many local residents rely on maxi-taxis for transportation.

Car rentals are higher than in the U.S. and usually require a large cash deposit or credit card. A typical compact car averages US$45 a day when available, but long term rates are lower.

Trinidad has no school bus system. The lack of organized school transportation further congests the morning rush hour.

Regional

Popular regional destinations include Caracas, San Juan, Miami, Barbados, Grenada, and other islands. Air connections are reasonably good to all of these places. Regional airlines, British West Indian Airways (BWIA), Liat and American Airlines offer regular service from Port of Spain.

There are hourly 20-minute flights daily between Trinidad (Piarco Airport) and Tobago (Crown Point Airport). The fare is currently US$48 round trip. Airport taxi fares on both islands are standard and are displayed at each terminal. Establish the fare before hiring a taxi.

A ferry also operates between Trinidad and Tobago. The round trip fare is US$8 and US$10 for economy and tourist class tickets and US$20 for an average sized car (cost is based on car's weight). A cabin costs an additional US$26 and must be booked early. The trip takes 5 1/2 hours from Port of Spain to Tobago, but only 5 hours return because of the favorable current. Car rentals in Tobago cost about US$45 a day; reserve in advance in Port of Spain.

Communications

Telephone and Telegraph

A modern telephone system has been installed throughout the island. Trinidad and Tobago follows the North American Dialing Plan and uses the international area code 1-868.

You can dial international calls to the United States direct from home or office by simply dialing 1, the area code, and number. Worldwide connections are good, but costs are well above U.S. discount rates. Credit card billing to the U.S. saves money on longer calls, but costs more for short calls due to operator assistance. As of June 1997, calls to Washington, D.C., is approximately US$1.00 per minute, if charged to a TT number.

TSTT International Cable Service offers worldwide telegram delivery, but incoming service has not always been reliable.

Internet services are available in Trinidad through private vendors or TSTT.

Mail

International airmail from the U.S. is received about five times a week and takes from 3 to 10 days, depending on the point of origin. Airmail from Trinidad to the U.S. costs approximately US400 for a standard letter. There are reports, however, of lost or stolen mail, especially items such as magazines, catalogs and packages.

Radio and TV

Trinidad has fourteen local radio stations, three on AM and the balance FM, which offer almost exclusively international pop and local music. There is almost no classical, jazz, rock or world music programming. World news is broadcast regularly, but U.S. news coverage is limited.

Cable TV service is available through several companies providing about 40 or more channels, mostly from the U.S., including some network stations. The one government-owned TV station operates separate programs on two channels. Both transmit in color. Programs are mainly imported series, most of them from the U.S. Some locally produced shows as well as news programs are shown. A video cassette recorder (VCR) is useful for additional entertainment, with video stores located throughout Trinidad. Tapes, often of only fair quality, rent for approximately US $2 each per week.

Trinidad and Tobago is on the U.S. scanning and frequency system, so TV sets manufactured for use in the U.S. will work in Trinidad without adaptation. Ship TVs, stereos, VCRs, radios, etc., from the U.S. as they are more expensive in Trinidad. Service and parts for the better known models can be obtained locally and repair work is relatively inexpensive.

Newspapers, Magazines, and Technical Journals

Three morning newspapers and several weeklies are published locally. The papers subscribe to the Caribbean News Agency (CANA), AP, etc. All give coverage to overseas news highlights, but in-depth international reporting is inadequate. The quality of the journalism varies widely.

U.S. daily newspapers are not currently available in Trinidad, except on the Internet on a limited and delayed basis at some hotels. The current Latin American editions of Time and Newsweek are available, at close to U.S. prices, at newsstands and bookstores. Popular American magazines, such as Good Housekeeping, Vogue, Glamour and House Beautiful are also available, but are often at least a month old and more expensive. Subscribe to magazines in the U.S. and have them mailed via pouch.

Port of Spain has various bookstores, stocked with books and paperbacks published locally, and in the U.K. and the U.S. However, they are not comparable in selection to U.S. bookstores and prices are considerable higher. The Port of Spain City Library has a large selection of British and American classics and popular novels.

Health and Medicine

Medical Facilities

Trinidad and Tobago has a relatively large number of competent general practitioners and specialists who have trained in the U.K., U.S., and Canada. Some doctors practice in private clinics, but most maintain private offices located throughout the country.

Government-operated clinics are open to those who cannot afford private care. The Mount Hope Medical Sciences Complex is fitted with state-of-the-art equipment but, like other government hospitals which have well-trained staff, conditions often do not meet U.S. standards.

Private clinics also offer good-quality care; such as the St. Clair Medical Centre.

In a major medical emergency, when medical evacuation is not feasible, the St. Clair Medical Clinic has been designated the facility for use. Doctors are in attendance around the clock, and life-support equipment is available. Medical care in Trinidad and Tobago is adequate for routine procedures, but the U.S. is generally preferable for specialized treatment.

Most Americans and other foreigners use local dentists trained in the U.K., U.S. or Canada. Orthodontic care is available, as are eye specialists. Eyeglass frames are imported and expensive, but locally ground lenses are relatively cheaper. Overall, the cost of medical, hospital, and dental care is much lower than in the U.S.

Prescription drugs, medicines and remedies available locally are mostly British and U.S. products. A full range of items is available from well-stocked pharmacies, but some brands may be unfamiliar. Prices are also generally higher than in the U.S. Bring a supply of any medical items you use regularly, including contact lens supplies, prescription drugs, over-the-counter remedies, first aid supplies, and cosmetics. Many items can be ordered later by pouch.

Community Health

Community sanitation in residential areas is good. Garbage is collected three times a week in most neighborhoods and garden clippings are collected weekly. Port of Spain and its suburbs are connected to a central sewage disposal system; outlying areas rely on septic tanks.

Water, for the most part, is potable. Certain residential areas (particularly elevated ones) are subjected to water shortages, however, most of these residences have water storage tanks.

Food purchased from street vendors and small restaurants can be of mixed quality. Qualified food handlers display a "food handler's badge." Fruits and vegetables are generally safe after being washed.

Preventive Measures

Epidemics are rare in Trinidad and Tobago. However, gastroenteritis in children continues to be a problem, particularly in the rural areas. South American cholera generally does not reach Trinidad and Tobago, but precautions such as vigilant hand-washing and avoidance of food and drink from street vendors are advisable. Mosquito-borne dengue fever has increased in frequency in recent years. Yellow fever outbreaks occur roughly every ten years.

Newcomers may suffer from heat rash due to the high temperature and humidity. The weather may also affect those who suffer from hay fever, bronchial asthma, and fungal infections, and prolong other infections. Mosquitoes, sand flies and chiggers can cause discomfort outdoors.

Typhoid, gamma globulin, and yellow fever inoculations are not required for travelers coming from the U.S. to enter Trinidad and Tobago, but they are recommended for those who plan to travel to South America. Immunization can be obtained locally.

NOTES FOR TRAVELERS

Passage, Customs & Duties

Two daily flights from Miami to Port of Spain are available on American Airlines. In addition, non-American carriers provide regular service to Port of Spain from the U.S., Canada, Venezuela, and the U.K. as well as interisland service. Reservations may be difficult to obtain during certain seasons, especially Christmas and Carnival.

A passport is required of U.S. citizens for entry to Trinidad and Tobago. U.S. citizens do not need a visa for stays of 90 days or less. Work permits are required for certain types of compensated and non-compensated employment, including missionary work. For further information concerning entry, employment and customs requirements, travelers may contact the Embassy of Trinidad and Tobago, 1708 Massachusetts Avenue, N.W., Washington, D.C. 20036, telephone (202) 467-6490 or the consulates of Trinidad and Tobago in Miami at (305) 374-2199 or New York City at (212) 682-7272, or by email at embassyttgo@erols.com

Americans living in or visiting Trinidad and Tobago are encouraged to register at the Consular Section of the U.S. Embassy in Port-of-Spain, Trinidad and obtain updated information on travel and security. The U.S. Embassy is located at 15 Queen's Park West in Port-of-Spain, telephone 1-868-622-6371, Consular Section fax 1-868-628-5462. Hours of operation are 7:30 a.m.-12:00 noon, Monday-Friday, except U.S. and Trinidad and Tobago holidays.

Pets

All pets imported into Trinidad and Tobago except birds, are subject without exception to a six-month quarantine.

The animal must have a health certificate from a U.S. Government veterinarian, stating vaccinations received, disease history, etc. The animal must be confined in an escape-proof cage. (Dogs must have a collar and leash).

The owner must also provide all the food, two feeding bowls and a padlock with two keys for the bin in which the food will be kept and locked- the owner keeps one key.

Birds are not quarantined, but must have a similar permit and Health Certificate, along with a Species Certificate showing that the species may be imported.

Currency, Banking, and Weights and Measures

The local currency is referred to as the Trinidad and Tobago dollar, TT dollar or just "TT". Effective April 13, 1993, the Government of Trinidad & Tobago announced the floating of the TT dollar. As of September 1999, the exchange rate was approximately TT$6.30 to US$1. Coins and bills have the same denomination as U.S. money, but the bills are issued in different colors.

All weights and measures were converted to the metric system in early 1982. However, you will find that both systems are used.

LOCAL HOLIDAYS

Jan.1	New Year's Day
Mar. 30	Spiritual Baptist Liberation Shouter Day
Mar/Apr.	Good Friday*
Mar/Apr.	Easter*
Mar/Apr.	Easter Monday*
May 30	Indian Arrival Day
May/June	Corpus Christi*
June 19	Labor Day
Aug. 1	Emancipation Day
Aug. 31	Independence Day
Dec. 25	Christmas Day
Dec. 26	Boxing Day

*variable

RECOMMENDED READING

These titles are provided as a general indication of the material published on this country.

History and General

Ahye, Molly. *Golden Heritage: The Dance in Trinidad and Tobago*. Port- of-Spain, Trinidad: Moonan Printers Ltd.

Anthony, Michael. *The Making of Port of Spain*. Port of Spain, Trinidad: Key Caribbean Pub., 1978.

Black, Jan K. and others. *The Area Handbook for Trinidad and*

Tobago. American University Press: Washington, DC, 1976.

Brathwaite, Lloyd. *Social Stratification in Trinidad: A Preliminary Analysis.* Mona, Kingston: USER, U.W L., 1975. Carmichael, Gertrude. *History of the West Indian Islands of Trinidad and Tobago.* Fernhill: New York, 1961.

Christopher, C.A. *Nationhood 18: A Progress Review of Trinidad and Tobago in 18 years of Nationhood.* Trinidad and Tobago: Enform Publications, 1980.

De Verteuil, Fr. Anthony. *The Years Before.* Trinidad: Inprint Caribbean Ltd., 1975.

Deosaran, Ramesh. *Eric Williams, the Man, His Ideas, and His Politics (A Study of Political Power).* Signum Publishing Co. Ltd., 1981.

Edwards, S. Hylton. *Lengthening Shadows: Birth and Revolt of the Trinidad Army.* Trinidad and Tobago: Inprint Caribbean Ltd., 1975.

Fraser, Lionel Mordaunt. *History of Trinidad.* London: Cass 1971.

Naipaul, V. S. *Loss of El Dorado.* Knopf. 1970.

Naipaul, V.S. *The Middle Passage.* Penguin Books, Ltd.: 1962.

O'Connor, P.E.T. *Some Trinidad Yesterdays.* Port of Spain, Trinidad: Inprint Caribbean Ltd., 1975.

Ryan, Selwyn D. *Race and Nationalism in Trinidad and Tobago.* University of Toronto: 1972.

Sudama, Trevor. *Of Society and Politics. Miscellaneous Commentaries on Trinidad and Tobago.* Siparia, Trinidad: Sookhai's Printery, 1979.

Williams, Eric. *From Columbus to Castor.* Deutsch: London, 1970.

Williams, Eric. *History of the People of Trinidad and Tobago.* Transatlantic: New York, 1970.

Geography and Description

First Geography of Trinidad and Tobago. Cambridge University Press: 1968.

The Caribbean Handbook 1984-1985. Edited by Clayton Goodwin. St. John's, Antigua, W l.: Ft. International, Head Office: P.O. Box 1032.

Herklots, G.A/C. *Birds of Trinidad and Tobago.* William Collins and sons, Ltd.: London, 1965.

Zubert, Christian. *Trinidad and Tobago.* Editions Delroisse: Boulogne, France.

Fiction

Lovelace, Earl. *The Dragon Can't Dance.* Logman Group Ltd.: 1979.

Lovelace, Earl. *Salt.*

Michener, James. *The Caribbean.*

Naipaul, V. S. *A House for Mr. Biswas.* McGraw-Hill: 1962.

Naipaul, V. S. *Miguel Street.* Vanguard: 1980.

Stewart, John. *Last Schooldays.* Deutsch: London 1971.

Walcott, Derek. *Fortunate Traveller.* Farrar, Straus, Giroux Inc.: 1982.

Walcott, Derek. *Another Life.* Cape: London, 1972

TURKS AND CAICOS ISLANDS

Turks and Caicos Islands

Major City:
Grand Turk

INTRODUCTION

Archeological expeditions have uncovered artifacts indicating Arawak habitation of the **TURKS AND CAICOS ISLANDS** at one time. Today, only eight of the 30 islands are inhabited. The Turks and Caicos Islands may have been the site of Columbus' landfall on his first voyage in 1492. Traditionally, however, Juan Ponce de Leon gets the credit for the European discovery of the islands in 1512. The islands then served as a hideout for pirates and as a port of call for explorers and merchants. The first European residents were Bermudians who, starting in the 1670s, came regularly to collect salt. The Caicos Islands were settled by Loyalist farmers who fled the southern states after the United States won independence from Britain. After slavery was abolished in 1838, the planters left and their former slaves remained. The islands were placed under the government of the Bahamas until 1848, and the islands were largely self-governing under the supervision of Jamaica until 1873. From 1874 until 1959, the islands were a dependency of Jamaica. The islands were under Bahamian control until the Bahamas became independent in 1973. In 1976, the Turks and Caicos Islands became a crown colony.

Independence was originally planned for 1982, but a change in government brought a reversal of that policy. The islands are still a crown colony.

MAJOR CITY

Grand Turk

Grand Turk (also known as Cockburn Town) is the main town among the islands, located on Grand Turk Island. The population of Grand Turk is about 4,000. The traditional economic activity was salt collection, but that industry ceased in 1964. Tourism and lobster fishing are the main economic activities. Offshore financial services have also become increasingly important. The main port for the Turks and Caicos Islands is at Grand Turk, and there are other ports at Salt Cay, Providenciales, and Cockburn Harbour on South Caicos. Grand Turk, South Caicos, Providenciales, and North Caicos have international airports. Cable and Wireless (West Indies) Ltd. provides national and international public telecommunications services. An Intelsat station on Grand Turk links the island to the USA, Bermuda, and the United Kingdom.

Recreation and Entertainment

The Provo Golf Club on the island of Providenciales has an 18-hole championship course. Scuba diving, snorkeling, yachting, fishing, horseback riding, tennis, and cycling are popular activities for visitors. The Turks and Caicos National Park covers 325 square miles and has 33 protected dive areas. There are organized whale-watching excursions for visitors. Grand Turk is known for its 19th-century architecture and horse carriages. There are historic windmills and salt-raking operations on nearby Salt Cay. The library in Grand Turk doubles as a museum. Its principal attraction is a display of Lucayan Indian artifacts. Churches and benevolent societies are important centers of social life throughout the Turks and Caicos Islands.

COUNTRY PROFILE

Geography and Climate

The Turks and Caicos Islands consist of two island groups separated by the Turks Island Passage, which is 22 miles across and about 7,000 feet deep. The island group consists

Ann Kalosh. Reproduced by permission.

Resort in Providenciales, Turks and Caicos Islands

of 40 mostly uninhabited islands and cays. The Turks group has two inhabited islands (Grand Turk and Salt Cay), six uninhabited cays, and numerous rocks surrounded by a triangular reef. The Caicos group has six main islands (North Caicos, Middle Caicos, East Caicos, South Caicos, West Caicos, and Providenciales). The total land area of the islands is 166 square miles, or 2.5 times the size of Washington, D.C. Providenciales is the main island and has 200 miles of beaches, 200 miles of wildlife preserves, and 65 miles of coral reefs. The Turks group islands are low and flat, and surrounded by reefs and sunken coral heads. The land mass is limestone, with shallow creeks and mangrove swamps. The highest elevation is only 163 feet above sea level on Providenciales. There are limestone caves on Middle Caicos. Temperatures range from a low of 61°F to a high of 90°F, with April–November the hottest months. There are almost constant trade winds from the east. Rainfall averages 21 inches per year, and hurricanes are a frequent occurrence.

Population

The islands have a population of about 17,000, or approximately 33 persons per square mile. About half

the population lives on Grand Turk, and the other half resides primarily on South Caicos and North Caicos. Only six of the 40 islands are inhabited. Over 90% of the population is of black African descent. The remainder are of mixed, European, or North American heritage. Most islanders are Christian; the main sects are Baptist, Methodist, Anglican, and Roman Catholic. English is the official and common language spoken in the islands, interspersed with many local words and phrases.

Government

The islands experienced a great deal of autonomy under the supervision of Jamaica until 1873, and were made a dependency of Jamaica from 1874 until 1959. The Turks and Caicos were then placed under Bahamian control until the Bahamas became independent in 1973. In 1976, the islands became a crown colony. The Turks and Caicos Islands were supposed to become independent in 1982, but a change in government brought a reversal of that decision. The islands are still a crown colony. The 1976 constitution, revised in 1988, established a ministerial system in which a governor, representing the British monarch, has responsibility over external affairs, defense, and internal secu-

rity. An Executive Council consists of eight members of the Legislative Council, three nominated and five appointed by the governor. Derek H. Taylor was appointed as chief minister in January 1995 by the governor. The Legislative Council has 19 seats, of which 13 are elected. The legal system is composed of Legislative Council acts, certain laws of Britain's parliament, and a few Jamaican and Bahamian statutes. A magistrate conducts weekly hearings to administer justice.

The flag is the Blue Ensign of Great Britain with a shield of the colony in the fly; the shield is yellow with a conch, lobster, and Turk's head cactus represented in natural colors.

Arts, Science, Education

Education is provided free of charge and is compulsory for children aged 7–14. Six years of primary education are followed by five years of secondary school. There are no higher educational institutions on the islands.

Commerce and Industry

The economy is based on tourism, fishing, and offshore financial services. The US was the leading source of tourists in 1996, accounting for more than half of the 87,000 visitors; tourist arrivals had risen to 93,000 by 1998. Offshore financial services have become an increasingly important part of the islands' economy. With no direct taxation, the US dollar as the local currency, confidentiality, and a growing financial sector, there are over 10,000 offshore companies registered with the government. The Offshore Financial Center Unit was established in 1989 to promote the islands as a financial center. The government also actively tries to attract captive insurance companies from the US. An offshore registry program with the United Kingdom enables British merchant ships to register with the Turks and Caicos Islands. The program cuts crew costs while enabling vessels to sail under the protection of the Red Ensign flag of the United Kingdom.

Transportation

The islands have about 75 miles of roads; the roads on Grand Turk and South Caicos are paved. The main seaports are Grand Turk, Cockburn Harbour on South Caicos, Providenciales, and Salt Cay. The islands have seven airports and four paved runways long enough to handle commercial jets. There are also three small unpaved landing strips on the uninhabited islands.

Communications

International telecommunications service is available through Cable and Wireless (West Indies) Ltd. There are three AM radio stations and several cable television stations. Broadcasts are also received from the Bahamas. The *Turks and Caicos News* is a weekly newspaper published in Grand Turk.

Health

Grand Turk has a 30-bed hospital and an outpatient and dental clinic. There are 11 more outpatient and dental clinics on South, Middle, and North Caicos, Providenciales, and Salt Cay.

LOCAL HOLIDAYS

January 1	New Year's Day
. . . .	*Good Friday
. . . .	*Easter Monday
May	*Commonwealth Day
June	*Queen's Official Birthday
August (first Monday) . . .	Emancipation Day
August 30	Constitution Day
October (second Monday) .	Columbus Day
October	*Human Rights Day
December 25	Christmas
December 26	Boxing Day

*Variable

RECOMMENDED READING

Boultbee, Paul G. *Turks and Caicos Islands.* Santa Barbara, CA: Clio Press, 1991.

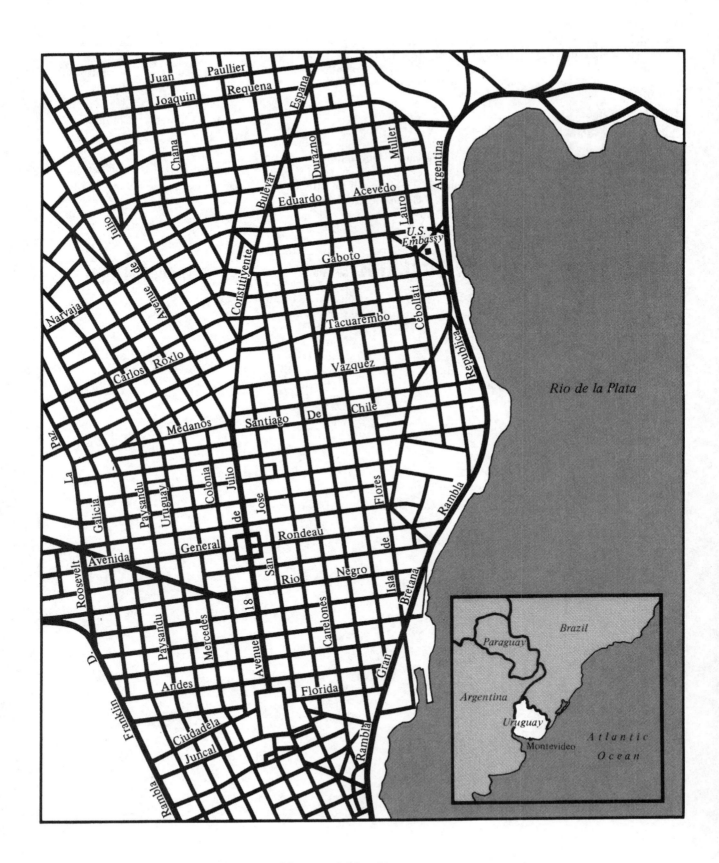

Montevideo, Uruguay

URUGUAY

Oriental Republic of Uruguay

Major City:
Montevideo

Other Cities:
Colonia del Sacramento, Fray Bentos, Minas, Paysandú, Punta del Este, Rivera, Salto, Treinta y Tres

EDITOR'S NOTE

This chapter was adapted from the Department of State Post Report 1999 for Uruguay. Supplemental material has been added to increase coverage of minor cities, facts have been updated, and some material has been condensed. Readers are encouraged to visit the Department of State's web site at http://travel.state.gov/ for the most recent information available on travel to this country.

INTRODUCTION

A wedge of a nation tucked between Brazil and Argentina, Uruguay is the smallest and, after Ecuador, the most densely populated republic in South America.

Rolling grasslands of black, potash rich soil make raising cattle and sheep the lifeblood of the nation's economy. Also important are tourism and financial services. Montevideo, home of 45% of Uruguay's population, gears much of its industry to processing wool, meat, and hides. White-sand beaches and luxurious resorts stretch along the Atlantic shoreline, bringing Uruguay renown as a vacation playland. It has one of the highest living standards in South America and a broad program of social welfare.

A constitution provides for a republic with three autonomous branches of government. Under it, there prospers a progressive land where beef is the national dish and soccer the national game.

On the east coast of South America, south of Brazil and east of Argentina, Uruguay is comparable in size to Oklahoma. The country consists of a low, rolling plain in the south and a low plateau in the north. It has a 120-mile Atlantic shoreline, a 235-mile frontage on the Rio de la Plata, and 270 miles on the Uruguay River, its western boundary.

Prior to European settlement, Uruguay was inhabited by groups of indigenous peoples collectively known as the Charruas. The Spanish visited Uruguay in 1516, but the Portuguese were first to settle it. After a long struggle, Spain wrested the country from Portugal in 1778, by which time almost all of the indigenous people had been exterminated. Uruguay revolted against Spain in 1811, only to be conquered in 1817 by the Portuguese from Brazil. Independence was reasserted with Argentine help in 1825, and the republic was set up in 1828.

A military coup ousted the civilian government in 1973. The military dictatorship that followed used fear and terror to demoralize the population. After ruling for 12 years, the military regime permitted election of a civilian government in November 1984 and relinquished rule in March 1985; full political and civil rights were then restored.

Subsequent leaders have contended with high inflation and a mammoth national debt. Uruguay has pushed for constitutional and economic reforms aimed at reducing inflation, partially through tax increases and privatization.

MAJOR CITY

Montevideo

The southernmost capital in the hemisphere, Montevideo is the industrial, commercial, educational, and cultural center of Uruguay. It is situated on the northern shore of the estuary formed by the Uruguay and Paran Rivers, known as Rio de la Plata, 120 miles east-southeast of Buenos Aires.

Like most Latin American cities, Montevideo has the "Ciudad Vieja," (Old Quarter) characterized by nar-

Downtown plaza in Montevideo, Uruguay

took pride in its architecture, boulevards, and boardwalk. The architectural tradition has been diluted with multistoried buildings, however, and is tarnished by poor maintenance and rubbish collection.

Utilities

Electrical current is 220v, 50 cycles, single phase throughout Uruguay. U.S-made 110v, 60 cycle appliances, except for clock radios or timers, can be used with stepdown transformers.

Voltage fluctuations often occur during peak periods with occasional power failures. Battery operated radios and clocks, several flashlights, candles and a camping lantern are useful.

The telephone system functions well.

Food

Beef, the staple of the Uruguayan diet, is abundant, of good quality, and inexpensive. Pork and poultry are more expensive than in the U.S. Veal is difficult to find, and lamb (mutton) is only available at certain times of the year (August–January). Local cold-cuts are tasty and of good quality. Purchase freshly-baked bread daily. A wide variety of pastries and cookies is also available. A good selection of fish from the Rio de la Plata is often sold at reasonable prices along the river front and in local outdoor markets. Shellfish is expensive and available occasionally.

Fresh milk, cream, and milk products such as yogurt, ice cream, and cheese are one of the advantages of living here. Ice cream is good but about twice the U.S. cost. Long-life milk in cartons is also available.

Fruit and vegetables abound in season and become more available each year. Wash green leafy vegetables and fruits that are not peeled thoroughly before eating.

Many Americans enjoy buying produce and variety foods at outdoor markets (ferias) that are set up daily in different parts of the city

row streets and colonial buildings. There stands the city's oldest church (Basilica Metropolitana), the first city hall (Cabildo), and remnants of the original walled settlement (Ciudadela). Across the harbor rises a 435-foot hill, El Cerro, with an old fortress at its peak commanding a view of the greater part of Montevideo. It is believed the city was named after the hill—Monte Video—from "I see a hill" - uttered by a Portuguese sailor aboard a ship of one of the earliest explorers.

The old city contains much of Montevideo's commerce and banking. In the newer section are "galerias," housing many small shops under one roof, often connecting two streets in midblock. Many wide, tree-lined avenues, along with numerous plazas and monuments, give the city a parklike atmosphere, although poor maintenance of streets and buildings detract from the city's overall beauty. Among the more attractive areas to the east are the residential suburbs of Pocitos, Punta Gorda, and Carrasco. The architectural diversity, terra cotta roofs, and ironwork balconies, and beaches make Montevideo's suburbs pleasant.

In its time, Montevideo was the pearl of Latin American cities, well planned and designed to take advantage of the riverside. The city and dismantled in early afternoon. Most neighborhoods are served by a feria at least twice a week. Also, many permanent vegetable and fruit stands are available, some of which sell select produce and hard-to-find items. Also, some companies deliver milk, cheese, fresh bread, and pastry to your house daily.

Uruguayan supermarkets are smaller and have fewer items than in the U.S. Some supermarkets and many smaller stores stock imported foods.

Montevideo's typical restaurant is the "parillada." (A parillada has a huge grill where meat is slowly barbecued over coals of a wood fire.) The food is very good and prices are reasonable. A few restaurants offer Italian, German, Chinese, French, and Swiss cuisines. A few seafood restaurants are in Punta del Este and other coastal towns.

Rarely do restaurants open before 8 p.m. Because of the late dinner hour, tea is fashionable in Uruguay. Several tea shops offer a variety of sandwiches and pastries. Also many snack shops and sidewalk cafes are open throughout the day and into the night. These serve pizza, "chivitos" (the delicious Uruguayan variation of a steak sandwich), and other foods from snacks to full meals. The atmosphere is informal. A McDonald's has recently opened restaurants in Montevideo, Atlantida, and Punta del Este. Pizza Hut, Burger King, and Subway are also present in Montevideo.

Clothing

Clothing needed in Uruguay is similar to clothing worn during equivalent U.S. seasons.

Men: Local tastes in menswear are like those in the U.S. and Western Europe. Office and commercial workers wear suits and ties year round. For informal occasions, Uruguayans follow the latest fashions in sportswear. Shirts are available in common neck and sleeve lengths. Topcoats, heavy sweaters, scarves, and hats are worn in winter. Most foreign residents limit their pur-chases of local menswear to wool sweaters, leather jackets, and high quality fabrics that they have made into custom-tailored suits (at reasonable prices).

Although quality varies considerably, shoes are available in most sizes at higher-than-U.S. prices. Those with narrow feet will have difficulty finding shoes. Uruguay's export lines are not available on the local market.

Women: Clothing for women in Montevideo is surprisingly fashionable and similar to that worn in the U.S. and Western Europe. Currently, short or cocktail length dresses are being worn for dinners, parties, and receptions Suits, jackets with skirts and blouses, or dresses are appropriate office wear as well as for luncheons or teas. Casual outfits are needed for asados. No restrictions on the use of pants or shorts exist. Hats are rarely worn.

Warm clothes are needed in winter. Include some wool garments against the penetrating damp cold of Montevideo (indoors and out). As Montevideo's social life is much more active in fall, winter, and spring (March–November) than in summer, you will need a number of dressy, but warm outfits. Summer days can be humid and air-conditioning is rare so cotton, cotton blends, and rayon fabrics are suitable.

A variety of ready-made women's clothing is available locally; prices are higher than in the U.S. Some export-quality wool clothing is available locally. Quality knitwear is available; prices on wool and orlon products are reasonable. Quality hosiery and undergarments are expensive; selection is limited. Leather, suede, otter, fox, and nutria coats are available in many styles at popular prices.

A limited selection of apparel fabrics is available but very expensive. Good jewelry, especially amethyst and topaz, is available at reasonable prices.

Children: Ready-made clothing is attractive, but with the exception of knitwear, expensive, wears out quickly, and is difficult to clean.

All Uruguayan school children wear uniforms that must be purchased locally. The Uruguayan-American School does not require uniforms. The British, Scottish, and Italian schools, which are open to Americans, do require uniforms.

Jackets and coats for children are available at higher-than-U.S. prices. Children's shoes, including tennis shoes, are attractive and expensive, but not durable. Corrective shoes may be satisfactorily custom made here.

Infant wear in local stores is almost entirely wool or orlon knit; few terrycloth suits are available. Undershirts, polo shirts, and overalls are found, but prices are high and styles are not practical. Infant shoes are readily available.

Teenage clothing is limited and expensive.

Supplies and Services

Prescription drugs are generally available. Bring a supply of nonprescription medicines with you, including, but not limited to, acetaminophen, aspirin, antacids, and cold medicines.

Bring cosmetics, home perms, nail polish, and hair coloring from the U.S. Paper products such as toilet paper, tissues, sanitary products, and paper towels are sold locally, but are of poor quality and expensive.

Cameras cost two to three times U.S. prices. Most types of film can be purchased and developed locally at high prices. Families find film ordered and developed through U.S. film mail-order companies satisfactory.

Children's toys are very expensive. Those not imported from the U.S. seldom meet American safety standards. Bring toys for your children and for gifts. Also bring lunch boxes, book bags, and school supplies for schoolchildren.

Most household appliances can be repaired locally but not always quickly or cheaply, especially if new parts are needed. TV service is good. Watch repair is of good quality. Shoe repairs are done quickly. Auto maintenance is adequate and reasonable, but spare parts are expensive and sometimes difficult to obtain. Bodywork is done well at reasonable prices.

Both beauty shops and barbershops are good. Adequate dry cleaning is available, but expensive; dry cleaning service is available through the commissary.

Diaper services are nonexistent. Laundry is normally done at home. Laundry service is Laundromat style: clothing is washed and pressed. Iron-on mending tape is useful to repair clothes and is available here.

Domestic Help

It is easier to find daily or part-time, rather than live-in, domestic help. Domestic help is relatively expensive. A few families with small children have a live-in servant. Other families and single people hire a daily housekeeper, part-time cleaning woman, or housekeeper/cook. It is easy to find someone to prepare party food, and good waiters are reasonable.

Employer obligations regarding time off, vacation, year-end bonus, severance pay, social benefits, etc., tied to regularly rising salaries, have sharply increased costs for domestic help.

Religious Activities

Montevideo has four churches that have English-language services: Christian Brothers (Roman Catholic), Christ Church (interdenominational Protestant), the Cathedral of the Most Holy Trinity (Episcopal), and the Church of Christ Science. Many other Christian sects are represented, holding services in Spanish.

© Bettmann/Corbis. Reproduced by permission.

Skyline of Montevideo, Uruguay

With a fairly large Jewish population, Montevideo also has two synagogues, one conservative congregation and the other, orthodox.

The Church of Jesus Christ of the Latter Day Saints also holds weekly sacrament meetings in Spanish. There are approximately 55,000 church members and 365 missionaries throughout the country.

Education

Uruguay has free public education from kindergarten through university. Many private and parochial schools also exist. Instruction is in Spanish, and private schools that do not provide instruction in Spanish must offer it as a second language. The local school year runs from March to mid December, with a midterm vacation in June/July and a spring vacation in September. Montevideo's public schools, some of which offer good education and excellent facilities, are generally overcrowded and work on two or three shifts, 5-6 days a week. The private British and St. Andrew's Schools and a Christian school also offer instruction in English.

The Uruguayan-American School (UAS), founded in 1958, moved to its Carrasco location in 1978. It ful-

fills the requirements of an American school abroad. Sufficient classroom space is available in three separate buildings located on a spacious campus. The school offers food service (optional), and bus transportation can be arranged.

UAS provides classes in English from nursery school through grade 12. The school uses an American curriculum, methodology, textbooks, and American or bilingual teachers. All classes are coeducational. The school is accredited by the Southern Association of Colleges and Schools. The school capitalizes on its overseas location to provide instruction in Spanish as well as other regional studies for U.S. and international students.

The student body numbers about 160, of which 60% is American; 20% Uruguayan; and the remainder come from various countries. The small high-school student population (50-65 students) does not enable the school to provide many extracurricular activities. Classes in art, music, computer science, and physical education are included in the curriculum. However, because of its size, the school offers limited electives/materials and sports facilities. The school has an 8,000-volume library and offers complete counseling services.

The school's first semester runs from early August through December, followed by a 10-week summer vacation. The second semester starts in late February and ends late June. UAS is the official testing center in Uruguay for the Scholastic Aptitude Test and the American College Test.

The British School is coeducational for kindergarten through grade 12. Located in a large attractive complex in Carrasco, the student population is primarily Uruguayan, with some British and a few Americans. It uses a British curriculum, but American history and government are also taught. American children accustomed to the American system may have difficulty adjusting to the British system, particularly in adjusting to the different way of teaching mathematics. However, the school offers excellent sports.

Coeducational St. Andrew's (Scottish) School has students from kindergarten through grade 8. Located in Pocitos, with adequate play facilities, it uses a U.K. curriculum.

The British School and St. Andrew's School have first semester from March to June and second semester from late July to early December.

Special Educational Opportunities

The University of the Republic and the Catholic University of the Republic Damaso Antonio Larranaga, both located in Montevideo, are the country's only universities. Instruction at the University of the Republic is free and facilities are open to all foreign residents. However, courses seldom are transferable for credit at U.S. colleges and universities. Uruguay does have the University of Maryland, European Division. All courses are taught in English, and the professors are local, American, and British.

Sports

Uruguay's national pastime is soccer, locally called football (futbol). Teams enjoy fanatical support, especially the rivalry between the two best clubs, Nacional and Pe

arol. Montevideo's Centenario Stadium holds about 70,000 people and games are frequent. Tickets are reasonably priced.

Five-a-side soccer is currently the most popular sport among Uruguayans. Uruguyans and Americans alike can participate in informal league play.

Swimming is popular and enjoyed 4 to 5 months every year. Uruguay's beaches extend from Montevideo to the Brazilian border. The river and beach front in Montevideo are polluted and unsafe for swimming. Bathing and surfing is possible beyond Atlantida (28 miles east of Montevideo). Several private clubs with swimming pools are available in Montevideo.

Tennis is popular and some municipal courts are available. Several private clubs offer membership with reasonable entrance fees and monthly dues.

Golfers will find two challenging 18-hole courses in Montevideo. The Golf Club of Uruguay has a beautiful course in Punta Carretas, a residential area bordering the Rio de la Plata. Facilities include a large dining room, snack bar, swimming pool, and tennis and paddleball courts.

The Cerro Golf Club is across the bay from the downtown area, about 40 minutes by car. Less crowded than Punta Carretas, neither is crowded in the U.S. sense. The Cerro Golf Club offers light luncheons and its bar/gameroom is open Wednesday afternoons, weekends, and national holidays.

Riding is also popular. The Hipico and the Polo Club (which also has two tennis courts and a large swimming pool) offer all facilities needed for the care and maintenance of horses. Fees for horse rentals, including jumpers, are reasonable.

Horse racing is a popular diversion, and Montevideo has a good track in the northern part of the city. Bullfighting and cockfighting, popular

in many Latin American countries, were outlawed here many years ago.

Montevideo has three sailing clubs: Montevideo Yacht Club, Nautilus Yacht Club, and Montevideo Rowing Club. The Montevideo Yacht Club has several Marconi-rigged fin keelboats for members. Water sports other than swimming are just beginning to develop in Montevideo. Water skiing, surfing, and sailboarding are popular in Punta del Este.

Uruguay offers good freshwater fishing in the interior and surfcasting along the coast. The Rio Negro is famous for its large dorado, an excellent game fish. The best fishing is in Punta del Este where weakfish, blackdrum, and bluefish are most often caught. Boat rentals are expensive, particularly during summer. Bring your own tackle for shoreline and freshwater angling.

Good hunting is available within a relatively short drive of the city. Partridge, plover, dove, pigeon, and duck are among the game birds available. A permit and permission from the property owner to hunt on private property are required. Guns and ammunition are available in Montevideo, but at very high prices.

Almost all sporting equipment available in Montevideo is imported and expensive. Tennis balls are especially expensive. Bicycles are popular with both children and adults. Bicycles sold here are expensive.

Paddleball is the new rage. Squash courts are available through several inexpensive clubs. Racquetball is relatively new to Montevideo, though two clubs have opened with several courts.

Touring and Outdoor Activities

Montevideo has a number of historic sites that are worth visiting, including the Cabildo (city hall) and El Cerro fortress. A planetarium offers scheduled shows.

The city has several parks and plazas, many with play facilities, and a botanical garden. The Legislative Palace boasts 47 kinds of native marble and is interesting to visit when either house is in session. A short drive into the country will take you into cattle and sheep country, land of the Uruguayan gaucho. Traffic in the interior is usually light and a Sunday drive can be relaxing.

Uruguay is unique in South America in that practically any point of the country is within a day's drive of the capital. Popular tourist attractions are the resort towns of Atlantida, Piriapolis, and Punta del Este. Beyond Punta del Este are many worthwhile sights on the way to the Brazilian border. Punta del Este's popularity with wealthy Argentines and Brazilians has pushed prices well past an official American's normal budget.

The town of Colonia, founded by the Portuguese in 1680, lies 100 miles west of Montevideo along the coast, and has several museums and restored 17th-century colonial buildings. Colonia is 1 hour from Buenos Aires by hydrofoil.

The city of Minas is 78 miles north of Montevideo in the interior. Known for its quarries of high-grade marble and mineral water springs, its lakes and hills present a change from the seaside. The pleasant interior towns of Salto and Paysandu, located along the Uruguay River, can also be reached in less than a day's drive. The Termas (hot springs) del Arapey, especially nice in winter, are less than 30 miles from Salto.

To the north, on the Brazilian border, are the towns of Rivera and Artigas. Located in the area between these cities are geological fields where amethyst and topaz are found. The Brazilian border town of Chuy, just 140 miles northeast of Punta del Este, offers a popular duty-free shopping area. Brazilian coffee and other consumer goods are available at advantageous prices. Also near the border are two restored old forts, Santa Teresa and San Miguel, and the lovely small beach resort of La Coronilla. Near both forts are charming government-run inns (paradores), which are worth an overnight stay or even an extended vacation. Comfortable, reasonably priced hotels and several good restaurants are also in the area.

Brazil, Argentina, and Chile offer a multitude of tourist attractions. One of the most popular is Iguazu Falls, which most travelers consider a must. You can reach this series of unharnessed falls on the Brazilian-Paraguayan-Argentine border by automobile, bus, or air.

Entertainment

Montevideo has many movie theaters showing recent American and European films. Movies in English have Spanish subtitles. Admission prices are comparable to the U.S.

Montevideo has two casinos, the Parque Casino and the Carrasco Casino. Another is in Atlantida, a half-hour drive from Carrasco. No nightclubs exist; however, some restaurants with floor shows and a few lively late hour discotheques are available for teenagers and the twenties crowd.

Social Activities

The American Association holds monthly luncheon meetings. Membership enables you to meet Americans and Uruguayans representing business interests and other organizations in Uruguay. The association sponsors an annual golf tournament.

The American Women's Club is an active community service and social group composed principally of the spouses of Americans in Montevideo. The club holds monthly meetings at its Carrasco clubhouse, except during summer. Among its activities are a thrift shop, which sells used articles to raise funds for charity, and a number of social events.

Both the Lions and the Rotarians welcome Americans as guests or members of their numerous Montevideo chapters.

Membership in a tennis, golf, or yacht club can be another excellent way of meeting people.

An English-language Cub Scout pack operates at the Uruguyan-American School, and scouting is also widespread among Uruguyans. Spanish-speaking Boy Scout troops meet at the British School.

Private entertaining usually takes the form of luncheons, cocktail parties, coffees, teas, buffet suppers, and small dinner parties. Uruguayans are open to social contacts, and representational activities are frequent.

OTHER CITIES

COLONIA DEL SACRAMENTO (also called Colonia), about 80 miles west of Montevideo in the far southwest, is Uruguay's most colonial-flavored city. Situated on the Río Plata across from Buenos Aires, Argentina, it was settled by the Portuguese in the late 17th century, and later by the Spanish. Tourism plays a big role in the local economy, and sites such as the parochial church, museum, viceroy's mansion, and lighthouse, are favorites. The ruins of the city's bullring, visited by throngs of Argentines until bullfighting was outlawed in the 1930s, can be viewed. Colonia del Sacramento serves as a commercial and manufacturing center for adjacent hinterlands. Its location makes it an important border crossing and trade zone. Connections to Buenos Aires are available via hydrofoil, ferry, and airplane. Travel to Montevideo is possible via highway and railway. Uruguay's main agricultural research center and a dairy industry school are located here. Colonia del Sacramento has roughly 17,000 residents.

FRAY BENTOS houses the largest meat packing plant in a country that once outstripped Argentina in beef exports. Situated in the southwest about 160 miles northwest of Montevideo, the city is the capital of Río Negro Department. In 1969, the Puerto Unzué bridge was constructed in Fray Bentos. This bridge has greatly facilitated trade between Uruguay and Argentina. Fray Bentos was founded in 1859 as Independencia, but later was renamed for a religious hermit who lived nearby. It has a population of about 20,000.

MINAS is a mining city of about 35,000, situated in thickly forested hills 75 miles north of Montevideo. Its name, meaning "mines" in Spanish, was given in recognition of the nearby marble and granite deposits which support this picturesque spot. Juan Antonio Lavalleja (1786-1853), a leader of Uruguayan independence, was born here. He directed the *Treinta y Tres*, or "Thirty-Three Immortals," who declared the country's independence from Brazil in 1825 under the motto "liberty or death." After three years of war, a British-mediated treaty confirmed Uruguay's status as a sovereign state. The thirty-three revolutionaries, meanwhile, became politicians. Lavalleja's equestrian statue has a prominent place. Considered interesting for the visitor are the church, nearby caves, and the local park—Parque Salus. The Cascada de Agua del Penitente waterfall also is a local attraction. The city is noted for its bottled mineral waters.

PAYSANDÚ, an often-used crossing point to Argentina on the Río Uruguay, gives the visitor a sense of history with its major attractions. The cathedral has cannonballs still embedded in its walls from the 1865 War of the Triple Alliance, when Paraguayans briefly held the town. In the next building is a museum in the Silesian college. Paysandú features several budget hotels, and a local tourist information office. Many industries are located in Paysandú, among them tanneries, breweries, distilleries, flour mills, meat processing plants, and textile factories. The city is a busy port through which goods are shipped to northwestern Uruguay. This

departmental capital has a population of about 75,000.

PUNTA DEL ESTE has emerged as one of South America's most popular resort and conference centers. Located about 70 miles due east of Montevideo on the Atlantic coast, the city hosted several important political conferences in the 1960s, including the 1961 meeting which proclaimed the Alliance for Progress and a 1967 meeting of the presidents of the American republics. Foreigners, principally Argentines, Brazilians, and Chileans, vacation here regularly, visiting the many restaurants, casinos, and recreational facilities. Fishing is a popular pastime. Punta del Este, linked to Montevideo by a major road, has a population of over 10,000.

RIVERA is a city of 57,000 people on the Brazilian frontier, about 270 miles north of Montevideo. A street separates it from the Brazilian city of Santa Ana do Livramento. Rivera serves as capital of Rivera Department, as well as being the largest Uruguayan city on the border. Nearby are the Cuchilla de Santa Ana Mountains and livestock-growing regions. The city is home to several industries which manufacture mosaics, brooms, cigars and cigarettes, and textiles. Rivera is a trading center for the fruits, grains, and vegetables grown in the region. There is a local airport and good road connections.

SALTO is the last of the major population centers to be found when traveling up the Río Uruguay. The capital of Salto Department in the northwestern part of the country, it is a city of about 77,000, known as a rail and shipping center for agricultural products and livestock.

It is situated in the midst of a large area of vineyards and citrus orchards. The vineyards near Salto are considered the best in Uruguay. Many of these vineyards produce tomatoes, corn, wheat, and strawberries. For many years, a boat-building industry has operated here. Meat processing and wine production are also important indus-

tries. Salto lies opposite Concordia, Argentina. Salto is linked by rail, river, highway, and air services with Montevideo.

TREINTA Y TRES lies 150 miles northeast of Montevideo, near the Olivar River. This departmental capital takes its name from the *Treinta y Tres*, or "Thirty-Three Immortals," who led the successful revolt for independence from Brazil in 1825. The city's approximately 26,000 residents enjoy the Quebrada de los Cuervos National Park about 25 miles outside of town.

COUNTRY PROFILE

Geography and Climate

La Republica Oriental del Uruguay (the Oriental Republic of Uruguay, or literally translated, the Republic East of the River Uruguay) covers an area of 72,200 square miles, slightly larger than North Dakota.

Topographically, the country is divided into three parts. The southern area is a belt of gently undulating alluvial plains; the western part, an extension of Argentina's flat pampas; and the northern area, an extension of southern Brazil's low regions and broad valleys. Maximum elevation above sea level is about 2,000 feet; the average being about 490 feet. Few natural forests exist, but extensive forestation has been undertaken.

Except for a small subtropical area in the northwest, the climate is even throughout Uruguay. Temperatures are generally mild but seasons are distinct: summer daytime temperatures average 70°F and rarely exceed the mid-90s; autumn (March–May) is mild; and spring (September–November) is often damp, cold, and windy. In winter, monthly temperatures range from 44°F to 60°F with occasional frost, although humidity, averaging 75 percent year round, intensifies the cold. Average annual rainfall is 39.5 inches.

Population

Uruguay's population (2.97 million) is composed primarily of Spanish and Italian ancestry. The native Indians were killed or forced to migrate during colonization in the last century. Some 4 percent of the population is of African descent, mostly Brazilian immigrants. Small colonies of German, East European, Armenian, and British citizens also live here. Most of the elderly "anglos," who speak English as their primary language, are second and third generation dual-nationals whose ancestors came in the last century to work in the many British-founded companies. A small colony of Swiss lives in an area called Colonia Suiza located about 100 miles west of Montevideo. The various languages of their former country are still spoken and they retain the customs of their forebears as well.

About 45 percent of Uruguay's total population lives in Montevideo. Salto and Paysandu, with about 100,000 inhabitants each, vie for the honor of being the second largest city. Several other cities are in the 25,000–40,000 population range. Uruguay does not share Latin America's concern with the population explosion; a low birth rate and emigration result in an annual growth rate of less than 1 percent. Families are small and close.

Life expectancy in Uruguay is 70 years and the literacy rate is about 94 percent, the highest in Latin America. Spanish is the official language. Religion does not play a dominant role in the lives of Uruguayans, many of whom classify themselves as agnostics. Roman Catholicism is the predominant faith but many are Protestants. Montevideo has a relatively large Jewish and Mormon communities as well.

Public Institutions

Traditionally one of the strongest democracies in Latin America, Uruguay, in the early 1970s, experienced a gradual transfer of power to the Uruguayan military because of the government's inability to cope with a violent leftist urban guerrilla group, known as the Tupamaros. The process culminated in the dissolution of parliament in 1973 and the ouster of the elected President in 1976. Civilian, democratic rule returned to Uruguay on March 1, 1985, after the military agreed to hold parliamentary and presidential elections in November 1984. The military banned several leading politicians from participating in the 1984 elections, a proscription that was removed by the new civilian government before the 1989 elections. National elections were held without incident in 1989, 1994 and 1999.

Uruguay's constitution, adopted in 1967 and partially suspended during military rule, provides for a republic with three autonomous branches of government. The President and vice-president, elected by popular vote, serve a single 5-year term but can be reelected after an interval of 5 years. They are assisted by a cabinet, made up of 12 ministers and the heads of various state entities, appointed by the President.

The legislative branch consists of two houses, a Senate (30 members) elected at large, and a Chamber of Deputies (99 members) elected proportionally from the 19 provinces (departamentos). Although each province has at least two deputies, most come from Montevideo, where about 45 percent of the country's population resides. It takes a two-thirds vote of Parliament to overturn vetoes or remove executive branch officials. In special cases, such as national crises, Parliament can also be called into session as a unicameral General Assembly.

The judicial branch consists of a five-person Supreme Court, whose primary duties are interpreting the

Constitution and dealing with claims against the government. Appeals courts, criminal courts, and justices of the peace deal with other matters of law. Supreme Court justices are appointed by the President and must retire at age 70. Special courts oversee the election process, audit government departments, and arbitrate appeals against administrative acts.

Uruguay's 19 departments (provinces) are organized similarly to the national government. An "intendente," or departmental governor, is elected by popular vote and is assisted by a departmental council or "junta departamental," chosen on a proportional basis. Montevideo, the capital city, is treated as a one of the 19 departments and has a similar governmental structure.

The major political parties, the National ("Blanco") and Colorado parties, in the past embraced about 90 percent of the electorate. The two parties have seen their share of the vote decline to approximately 65 percent of the electorate. The "Broad Front" a coalition of the Communist Party, Socialist Party, and various leftist factions, is now a major force in Uruguayan politics. A fourth political force, the New Space Coalition, is a social democratic grouping that consists primarily of two social democratic parties that split from the Broad Front in 1989.

Uruguayan politics value consensus and compromise over confrontation. The Colorado and Blanco parties share the administration of the independent state enterprises, and political agreements to split Cabinet posts are not uncommon. Almost all politicians pride themselves on their refusal to let ideological differences result in personal animosity.

Arts, Science, and Education

Montevideo is the cultural center of the country and activities are varied and continuous. Most, however, occur during the school year,

March–November. Cultural mainstays are the S.O.D.R.E. (Servicio Oficial de Difusion Radiotelevision y Espectaculos), the official government radio and television network; the Intendencia Municipal; and the Centro Cultural de Musica, a local nonprofit organization that organizes international events.

S.O.D.R.E. offers a 15–18 week symphony season featuring Uruguayan and internationally famous conductors and performers. Concerts are broadcast on the government TV channel. Short opera and ballet seasons usually follow the symphony season. Since the S.O.D.R.E. theater was destroyed by fire in 1971, most of its programs are held at the Sala Brunet, a smaller hall, which has recently been refurbished. S.O.D.R.E. also sponsors events at the Teatro Solis (1,300 seats). SODRE is building a new cultural center that should be completed soon.

The Centro Cultural de Musica offers 8 to 10 cultural events during the year. Tickets for season and individual performances are less expensive than in the U.S. Expect to wait in line overnight when the season subscriptions go on sale. Except for extraordinary occasions, all events take place at the Teatro Solis.

The Intendencia Municipal sponsors the Comedia Nacional, the national repertory company, which plays at the Teatro Solis and Sala Verdi. In addition, the municipal government has a popular and varied program of cultural activities. For instance, the municipal symphony (Orquesta Filarmonica de Montevideo) repeats its weekly Teatro Solis concerts in different neighborhoods and all programs are free.

Other theaters presenting professional productions are the Teatro Circular, El Galpon, Teatro del Centro, and the Teatro del Notariado. The Montevideo Players, an amateur acting society with English and American participants, produces two or three plays a year in English.

The U.S. established binational center, known as the Alianza Cultural Uruguay-Estados Unidos de America is a large complex in downtown Montevideo. It houses an English teaching center (over 4,000 students), one of the city's most prestigious galleries, and one of its most sought after theater spaces. The Biblioteca Artigas-Washington, a USIS library, is located in the same complex and is considered to be the most up-to-date library in the country. The Alianza encourages Americans to participate in all of its programs and invites licensed English teachers to join the teaching staff.

Public education in Uruguay is free through the university level, and many people receive advanced degrees in numerous disciplines. Since 1985, a number of private, fee-charging universities have also begun operating. In 1993, the University of Maryland began offering courses at Alianza.

Commerce and Industry

Uruguay's economy is based on services (mostly tourism and financial services), along with exploitation of renewable natural resources and related industries. Natural-resources exploitation and related activities benefit from Uruguay's level terrain, temperate climate, abundant rainfall, and natural pastures. Although Uruguay exported mainly cattle hides during colonial times, the principal export products have been beef and wool for more than a century, and Uruguay has developed such additional exports as textiles, garments, shoes, and rice.

In the last decade, the most dynamic sectors of the economy have been transport and communications, construction, commerce, and tourism; industry and financial services have the lowest growth rates. Although Uruguay has no-known hydrocarbon deposits, it is generously endowed with hydroelectric resources, now mostly devel-

oped. Electric production from the world's fourth largest hydroelectric complex, at Salto Grande (a joint venture with Argentina), began in late 1979. Social indicators place Uruguay among Latin America's most advanced countries. Uruguay has long had one of the highest literacy rates in Latin America, and the income distribution is much more equitable than in most Latin American countries. Between 1990 and 1994, urban poverty was reduced by 50% to only 6%, the lowest in Latin America (Latin American average is 40%). Moreover, Uruguay's income distribution resembles that of industrialized countries; a per capita income of US$6,000 places it among the upper middle income bracket in the World Bank classification. However, despite good social indicators, unemployment has been slightly lower - 10% in recent years. During the 1950s, with good export performance from farm and cattle products fueled by World War II and the Korean war, Uruguay provided incomes that were among the highest in Latin America, gaining the nickname "The South American Switzerland." However, as in many Latin American countries, Uruguay shifted its economic interests inward in the early 1960s, following an import-substitution model. For the next decade, Uruguay shut its doors to the world, protecting its industries with high import tariffs. Results were disastrous; export growth was low, inflation was high and volatile, and productivity performance and GDP growth were substandard. At the same time, with the creation of the European Economic Community which cut off traditional agricultural markets in Europe, Uruguay's agricultural sector suffered a serious setback. General stagflation ensued. These factors contributed to political instability during the 1960s and early 1970s.

In the early 1970s, the government adopted a program of gradual economic liberalization, loosened control over the economy, reduced public sector employment, and opened the economy to international trade. Exports of processed items, including leather goods, foods, textiles, fish, marble, and granite, surged. By 1981, the dollar value of Uruguay's exports had more than doubled from their worth a few years earlier.

Even before the advent of global recession in the early 1980s, the Uruguayan economy suffered from an artificially high fiscal exchange rate and chronic public sector deficits. To finance its deficit and to maintain the exchange rate, and because of readily available international funds, the government borrowed heavily from abroad. By 1982, the total external debt was more than three times the amount at the end of 1978. Global recession compounded Uruguay's woes as exports and investment inflows declined and capital flight accelerated.

In November 1982, with the country well into a serious recession, the fixed-exchange rate was abandoned, and the peso was devalued almost 100% from 14 to 28 pesos per US$. The GDP declined by 9.4% in 1982, 5% in 1983, and a further 1.8% in 1984. Unemployment peaked at more than 16% in 1983.

However, since 1985, Uruguay's growth trend has recovered. It has maintained an open-capital account in that interest rates are market determined, and there are neither price controls nor restraints on currency exchange. Between 1985 and 1990, the average annual growth was 3.4%; it reached 4% between 1991 and 1996. The GDP in 1999 was about $21 billion, and most estimates indicate that Uruguay will continue to have annual growth unless external shocks arise.

The LaCalle and Sanguinetti administrations affirmed Uruguay's commitment to the economic liberalization process, which had begun in the 1970s. Furthermore, they have implemented some important structural reforms. First, the social security system was modified to convert the highly deficit-ridden public system into a mixed system of both public and private providers;

combined with laws passed on capital market and investment funds, this change should stimulate capital market operations and national savings. Second, educational reforms in progress are expected to have a positive impact on future human capital. Despite the setback of privatization by a 1992 referendum, private-sector access to previously state owned activities continues. Controlled by moderate and left-of-center parties, respectively, both the national and the Montevideo state governments encourage the private sector's growing economic role.

Managed by the government, the Uruguayan exchange system is based on a band inside, within which the exchange rate can float. As of December 1990, the estimated rate was 11.7 pesos to the dollar. The annual inflation rate has steadily declined for the past 6 years, decreasing from 130% in 1990 to about 4% in 1999.

Uruguay is a member of Mercosur, a regional common market, with Argentina, Brazil, and Paraguay. Argentina is Uruguay's largest trading partner, followed by Brazil, the U.S., and Germany. With Mercosur integration into the economies, duties among Mercosur's members were exchanged for a common external tariff applying to most products. Chile and Bolivia are associate members of Mercosur in that they do not belong to the Common Market, but rather, to the free trade area; negotiations with other countries are being held.

Transportation

Automobiles

Roads in and around the capital are fair-to-poor with many potholes. Many streets are poorly identified and illuminated. Intercity highways are well maintained and generally excellent, but the all weather aspect of some of these roads requires caution. More traveled routes, such as the highway between Punta del Este and Montevideo, have service

stations, tow trucks, and other facilities.

Gasoline is sold by a government company, ANCAP, as well as by ESSO, Texaco, Shell, and other international oil companies. The better grade of gas is of lower octane than that used in the U.S., but American cars operate adequately with it. Moderate detergent oil is used.

Local

Bus service is cheap and extensive within Montevideo. Taxis are readily available at reasonable fares.

Intercity bus service, the most popular transportation method, is frequent to most parts of the interior. Modern buses, including sleepers, connect Montevideo with Brazil and Argentina. Bus tickets are cheaper than in the U.S.

Regional

Several international airlines fly from Uruguay to other parts of Latin America, North America, and Europe. Many international flights board in Buenos Aires, only 25 minutes by air from Montevideo, but some flights require a wait of several hours and an expensive and time-consuming change of airports. Pluna, the government-operated airline, and others offer flights to Argentina, Chile, Paraguay, and Brazil.

Communications

Telephone and Telegraph

The telephone network works reasonably well. Cellular phones are available in Montevideo and Punta del Este. Telephone connections outside Uruguay, especially to the U.S., are good but very expensive. English-speaking, long distance operators are usually on duty.

USA Direct service through MCI, AT&T, and Sprint is available and much less expensive than regular international operator-assisted calls to the U.S. Telegraph and fax facilities connecting Montevideo with

North America and Europe are good but expensive.

Radio and TV

Montevideo has some 35 radio stations including 12 FM. Radio programming consists of music, news programs, and soap operas. The tango, the music of the Rio de la Plata area, is heard on many stations, but modern rock from the U.S., Brazil, and Europe is more popular.

Shortwave reception is quite good in Montevideo, outside the downtown area. Listeners can pick up VOA, BBC, and the Armed Forces Radio Service. The best reception is from 8 p.m. to midnight. Uruguay has four TV stations that offer color TV transmission, and five cable channels provide additional programming. American TV's can be used here but will receive only black-and-white images unless they are converted to the PAL-N color system.

Newspapers, Magazines, and Technical Journals

Newspapers, as well as several weekly papers, are published in Montevideo. The Buenos Aires Herald, an English-language daily, is expensive.

Time and Newsweek are regularly available. Some technical journals from the U.S. and Europe are sold in two or three bookshops specializing in foreign literature. Many bookstores sell paperbacks in English.

The Artigas-Washington Library at the Uruguayan-American Alianza is colorful, attractive, and modern. In addition to a selection of about 12,000 books in both English and Spanish, it provides members with an extensive audiovisual section, which includes audio cassettes, tapes, records, video tapes, and films, plus a broad selection of U.S. magazines and journals.

Health and Medicine

Community Health

Montevideo experiences few health problems. In rural Uruguay where livestock is raised, hydatid disease (echinococcosis) can be contracted by humans via food contaminated with dog feces. Avoid contact with strange dogs anywhere in South America. Other intestinal parasites and worms are uncommon in Uruguay.

Hepatitis A occurs occasionally in Montevideo. Have gamma globulin injections every 4-6 months or get the Hepatitis A vaccine.

Montevideo has four seasons. Spring and summer are very pleasant. Winter is cold, wet, and windy; hence, frequent colds and sore throats occur. Upper respiratory tract allergies and lower tract allergies may be aggravated.

Tap water is safe to drink in Montevideo and in most urban areas; it does not have to be filtered or boiled. Occasional breaks in the city water lines do occur. Since the water is low in fluoride, children under age 12 should take fluoride supplements.

Montevideo is located on the River Plate, and there are beaches along the river from the city to the Atlantic Ocean, about 45 miles up the coast. Beaches within the city limits are polluted. Most sports clubs have swimming pools that are usually well cared for and safe.

Except for seasonal mosquitoes, few insects are of concern in Montevideo. Parents should caution children against touching the "bicho peludo" (green or black hairy caterpillar) which inhabits gardens, trees, and plants. This caterpillar may be poisonous, causing an allergic skin reaction when touched.

Good dental care is available in the city of Montevideo and currently costs about one-third less than in the U.S.

Most Uruguayan doctors are graduates of the local medical school, although many have received further training in the U.S. and in countries in Europe. Many speak English.

Well-trained, qualified nurses usually have attended at least 3 years of nursing school. Nurses aides, who have on-the-job training, handle most of the floor duty. Hospitals. The British Hospital is adequate for routine medical care. Advanced procedures may involve medical evacuation to the U.S. Pharmacies. Most drugs, except tranquilizers and stimulants, certain antibiotics, hormones, and cardiac drugs are available without a prescription. One can usually find American drugs or good-quality equivalents. Bring special prescriptions from the U.S.

Thousands of babies are born each year in Montevideo without incident. Because of adequate hospital care and facilities, Uruguay has one of the lowest infant mortality rates in the Hemisphere. State Department policy, however, now recommends medical evacuation to Miami, Florida, for labor and delivery.

In an emergency, call the Servicio de Emergencia Medico Movil (SEMM). This service dispatches an ambulance and physician to anywhere within the limits of Montevideo. Their care extends to accident victims as well as to people with chronic illnesses.

The British Hospital has an emergency room.

For children: Vaccines standard in the U.S. are recommended for Uruguay.

Adults: The only recommended immunization is tetanus-diphtheria (every 10 years). Yellow fever, typhoid, and cholera vaccines are neither required nor recommended. Adults born after 1956 may need a measles vaccination. Although not absolutely necessary, Hepatitis A and B vaccinations should be considered.

NOTES FOR TRAVELERS

Passage. Customs & Duties

Carrasco Airport is about 13 miles from downtown Montevideo. The airport building has a currency exchange booth that is open during business hours only. The port where oceangoing vessels dock is near downtown Montevideo, just a few minutes from the better hotels.

A passport is required. U.S. citizens do not need a visa for a visit of less than three months. For further information on entry requirements, contact the Embassy of Uruguay at 2715 M Street, N.W. Third Floor, Washington, D.C. 20007, tel. (202) 331-1313; E-mail: uruwashi@iamdigex.net; Embassy home page: http://www.embassy.org/uruguay/. Travelers may also contact the Consulate of Uruguay or the Honorary Consul in: Boston, Chicago, Honolulu, Los Angeles, Miami, New Orleans, New York, Reno, Salt Lake City, San Francisco, San Juan, Puerto Rico or Seattle.

Americans living in or visiting Uruguay are encouraged to register at the Consular Section of the U.S. Embassy in Montevideo and obtain updated information on travel and security within Uruguay. The U.S. Embassy is located at Lauro Muller 1776; telephone (598)(2) 408-7777; fax (598)(2)408-4110 or -8611. Internet: http://www.embeeuu.gub.uy/. Consular Section hours are Monday, Wednesday, and Friday, 9:00 a.m. to 11:00 p.m. and 2:00 p.m. to 4:00 p.m.

Pets

Pets with a certificate of good health may be imported into Uruguay. Dogs and cats require also a certificate of rabies vaccinations. These certificates should be endorsed and authenticated by an Uruguayan consul in the U.S. or other point of departure before shipment.

Travelers with pets may find it more convenient to fly to Montevideo via Brazil rather than Argentina, since a delay in Buenos Aires may be experienced if they must change airports to take a connecting flight. Pets leaving the area of the Buenos Aires international airport (Ezeiza) are considered as having entered Argentina and must be examined by an Argentine veterinarian. If a veterinarian is not immediately available, long delays may result. Since U.S. health and rabies certificates are valid in Argentina, travelers with pets should continue on to Montevideo on the same plane or change to a connecting flight that departs only from Ezeiza Airport.

Another consideration is the requirement that no pets are allowed in the cabin of any plane departing from Argentina. All pets are placed in the freight compartment. Since some planes do not have pressurized freight compartments, you may have to spend a number of hours in Ezeiza Airport waiting for a suitable plane.

Firearms and Ammunition

Only the following nonautomatic firearms and ammunitions may be brought to Uruguay:

Semiautomatic Pistol or Revolver, 1; Rifle, 1; Shotguns, 2. Ammunition for above firearms, 1,000 rounds. Uruguayan Government approval of a revolver may be more easily obtained than for semiautomatic pistols, as the latter are generally reserved for police and military use.

Currency, Banking, and Weights and Measures

Since March 1, 1993, the basic currency unit in Uruguay is the Uruguayan peso. The current rate of exchange is $11.84 as of March 31, 2000.

Uruguay has many banks, some with numerous branches throughout the country. Some foreign banks, including Citibank, First National City Bank of New York, American Express Bank, and Bank of Boston, have branches in Montevideo. Travelers checks may be purchased through banking facilities at the Chancery. Please note that they are not readily accepted at local retail facilities, which prefer cash.

Adequate banking facilities exist in Montevideo, but long lines and short banking hours make it impractical to have peso checking accounts. The metric system of weights and measures is used.

LOCAL HOLIDAYS

Jan 1	New Year's Day
Feb/Mar.	Carnaval*
Mar/Apr.	Holy Week
Apr. 19	Desembarco De Los 33 Orientales
May 1	Uruguayan Labor Day
June 18	Natalicio De Artigas
July 18	Jura De La Constitucion
Nov. 5	Dia De Los Difuntos
Oct 12	Discovery of America
Nov 1.	All Saints' Day
Nov 2.	All Soul's Day
Dec. 8	Blessing of the Waters
Dec. 25	Christmas

*variable

RECOMMENDED READING

These titles are provided as a general indication of the material published on this country.

Alinsky, Marvin. *Uruguay: A Contemporary Survey*. Frederick A. Praeger: New York, 1969.

American University. *Area Handbook for Uruguay*. Government Printing Office: Washington, D.C., 1971.

De Skerkinin, Betty. *The River Plate Republics: Argentina, Uruguay, Paraguay*. Corvard-McCann: New York, 1947.

Dobler, Lavinia G. *The Land and People of Uruguay*. Lippincott Philadelphia, 1965.

Ferguson, J. Halcro. *The River Plate Republics-Argentina, Paraguay and Uruguay*. Time-Life Books, New York,: 1965.

Greenbie, Syndey. *Republics of the Pampas, Argentina, Uruguay, Paraguay*. Tow Peterson and Company: Evanston, IL, 1943.

J. D. Holzhauer. *West From Montevideo, Uruguay by Bike*. Cassell Publishers: London, 1989. Available from Sterling Publishing Co., 2 Park Avenue, New York, New York 10016.

Jackson, Sir Geoffrey. *People's Prison*. Faber and Faber: London, 1973.

Pan American Union. *Uruguay*. Washington, D.C. 1966.

Pender, George. *Uruguay*. Oxford University Press: London, 1965.

Street, John. *Artigas and the Emancipation of Uruguay*. Cambridge: Cambridge University Press, 1959.

Vangor, Milton Isadore. *Jose Batalle y Ordonez of Uruguay: The Creator of His Time, 1902-1907*. Harvard University Press: Cambridge, MA, 1963.

Weinstein, Martin. *Uruguay: The Politics of Failure*. Greenwood Press: Westport, CT, 1975.

Caracas, Venezuela

VENEZUELA

Major Cities:
Caracas, Maracaibo

Other Cities:
Barquisimeto, Ciudad Bolívar, Colonia Tovar, Cumaná, Maracay, Mérida, San Cristóbal, Valencia

EDITOR'S NOTE

This chapter was adapted from the Department of State Post Report dated September 1994. Supplemental material has been added to increase coverage of minor cities, facts have been updated, and some material has been condensed. Readers are encouraged to visit the Department of State's web site at http://travel.state.gov/ for the most recent information available on travel to this country.

INTRODUCTION

Venezuela is important to the U.S. Venezuelans have practiced democracy successfully since 1958, and their success is an example for others in Latin America. Moreover, Venezuela is a principal trading partner for the U.S., ranking among the top 20 markets for U.S. exports. It traditionally has been a reliable supplier of petroleum products to the U.S. and currently is the second largest exporter to the U.S. of oil and its derivatives.

Caracas is at times a challenging place to live. It is crowded, noisy, and jostling, and it is often difficult to get services performed that are routine at home. But it can be exciting, and close at hand are oases of beauty and tranquility that make the city livable: the rugged wilderness of the Avila mountain range ranging up to 6,000 feet over the city, the jewellike Los Chorros park, and the Parque del Este where early risers jog among hundreds of tropical birds. And, when long weekends or vacations permit, there is a varied universe of natural beauty ranging from the desert of Falcon State, to the spectacular high Andes; from the mesa country of the east with the world's highest waterfall, to the still largely unexplored Amazon jungle. Venezuela has over 1,300 varieties of birds and extraordinary flora, including magnificent orchids and frailejons.

Venezuela's varied beauty, strategic location, and natural resources, as well as its varied social structure, combine to make a tour here challenging and interesting.

MAJOR CITIES

Caracas

Caracas occupies a garden-like valley rimmed by the majestic Avila Mountain that forms a rugged barrier between the valley and the Caribbean. It is the political, cultural, and economic center of the nation.

Its architecture is a mixture of colonial and mainly modern styles. In the older western part of the city, some of the old world Spanish colonial charm has been retained. To the east are the newer areas, characterized by skyscrapers and freeways with modern, comfortable residential areas dotting the valley floor and spreading up the mountain sides.

In contrast with the modernity of much of Caracas and the genteel charm of the historical sections are the "ranchitos" or shack settlements built by the poor immigrants from the interior regions and immigrants from neighboring countries.

Justifiably, the Caraquenos refer to Caracas as "The City of Eternal Spring." Caracas has a mean average temperature of 71 degrees F. Daytime temperatures range from 60 degrees to 80 degrees during the dry season to a maximum of 80 degrees to 90 degrees during the hot parts of the summer rainy season. Nights are cool and pleasant year round. Winter temperatures have even dropped to the low 50s. A consistent east-west wind blows almost every day, keeping the atmosphere of the valley clear. There is no daylight savings time in Caracas, therefore it becomes dark every night at about 7 pm.

The eastern part of the city has many familiar American features: major arteries ablaze with neon signs advertising U.S. products, supermarkets, some department stores, air-conditioned theaters showing American films, and even soda fountains and drive-in restaurants. Late-model American cars literally congest the streets and nearly every home displays a TV antenna to receive one of the Spanish-language TV stations.

The American appearance, however, is superficial. Caracas is a distinctively Latin city. The dominant culture is Spanish with the vitality and zest of a Caribbean orientation to the world. The combination is not Venezuelan, but Caraqueno. Caracas has the amenities of a large, cosmopolitan city. It boasts a number of excellent restaurants, a good selection of movies, and a variety of theatrical and musical productions. The city has many nightclubs and discotheques, a concert and symphony series, several museums, a thriving art market, a zoo, and an ultramodern racetrack.

Food

Generally, Caracas offers a broad range of quality food products though you may have to search for certain imported items. Recent government-imposed restrictions will probably lessen the availability of many imported items. Shopping is done at the large, American-style supermarkets that abound, at convenient corner stores (abastos), and at the farmers' markets (mercado libre).

Supermarkets are generally well stocked, but some items are unavailable for months at a time. Cleanliness in supermarkets is not up to U.S. standards. Due to uncertainty about the effects of import prohibitions, it is not clear whether speciality shops will continue to carry unusual imported items.

Many Americans find the "mercado libre" both fun and economical. Arrive early to get the best quality fresh fruits and vegetables.

There is a wide variety of locally grown vegetables that are quite good, though not consistently up to U.S. standards. Some Americans take advantage of the excellent quality of fresh fruits and vegetables sold by vendors from trucks. Some deliver. Bananas, papaya (locally called lechosa), coconuts, pineapples, mangoes, melons, and citrus fruits are abundant. Local peaches and apricots are disappointing. Fresh-squeezed fruit juices, sold everywhere, are excellent and cheap.

Bread, meat, and fish are available in supermarkets. Bakery goods are generally excellent. Many Americans prefer to buy these items at the bakeries, at the butcher, and at the fish shops that dot the residential areas. Some deliver. Good quality beef is available. Venezuelan beef is range-fed and not normally aged. It is less tasty and less fatty than the U.S. corn-fed animal. Pork is excellent and reasonably priced. Local lamb is sometimes available. Veal is almost never available. Seafood is always obtainable and of good quality, with prices less than those in the Washington area. Shrimp, which is relatively inexpensive, and red snapper (pargo) are especially popular. Cold-cuts and sausage are varied and plentiful.

Fresh pasteurized and homogenized milk is available throughout the year.

Canned foods are expensive compared to fresh foods available on the local market. Most stores carry a variety of canned food imported from the U.S. or made locally under license. Neither the selection nor the quality of baby foods is comparable to what is available in the U.S. Infant formula is available, although all brands are not in stock at the same time.

Local cheeses are acceptable, but sometimes lack flavor and may be more salty than in the U.S. A few imported European cheeses are available, in particular Gouda and Edam from Holland. Good quality eggs are plentiful.

Venezuelan ice cream is excellent. It is available in the usual flavors plus some tropical fruit flavors not found in the U.S.

Paper products are available but some are of inferior quality. Imported paper towels, toilet tissue, Kleenex, etc. are available in the commissary.

Frozen vegetables, fruits and fruit juices are sometimes available, but variety is limited and in some cases products may have been thawed and refrozen.

Some American fast food chains, such as McDonald's, Burger King, Pizza Hut, Domino's Pizza and Baskin & Robbins, have locations in Caracas.

There is a MAKRO Superstore in Caracas that is similar to the PACE Warehouse stores in the U.S. Membership is required. There are American products as well as Venezuelan products and many items are sold in bulk.

Clothing

General: Caracas' climate can be quite warm from April through September, and pleasant and cooler in December and January. Therefore, you will need a summer-weight wardrobe the year round although spring-weight clothes can be worn December through February. Bring a good umbrella for the rainy season. Raincoats are seldom seen here as they are usually too hot to wear. Sunglasses are necessary. Sportswear and beachwear suitable for the U.S. are fine for the clubs and beaches.

There is a wide selection of formal clothing for women in Caracas. Larger men's and women's sizes are not normally available. Good casual clothing is expensive and hard to find. Shoes are of good quality and reasonably priced.

Men: Summer-weight suits are more comfortable in Caracas' warm climate, therefore highly recommended. The quality of dry-cleaning is good and reasonably priced.

Sport shirts, guayaberas, and slacks are worn for informal occasions everywhere in Venezuela. Shorts are seldom seen on the streets except for joggers, cyclists, and other sports enthusiasts.

Dark suits will suffice for almost all occasions in the evening. Business and professional men rarely wear hats in Caracas.

Women: Women should bring what they would wear in late spring or summer in Washington or New York. Normal daytime wear is cotton, linen and other light fabrics. Blue jeans are popular for casual wear. You will need dressier cotton dresses and skirts and blouses for luncheons and coffees. Women dress up for evening occasions and follow the latest European and U.S. fashions. Cocktail dresses or nice evening dresses are normally worn to cocktail parties and dinners. Evening pants are permissible. Silk, satin, sheer knits and jerseys are popular fabrics. Fur stoles are seldom seen but a light sweater, shawl, or dressy jacket is useful for the cooler evenings. Hats are not currently being worn.

Beautiful and expensive fabrics are available. Women's shoes are stylish and of good quality with prices comparable to similar quality shoes in the U.S. Large size women's shoes (over size 9) or extra wide women's shoes are virtually impossible to find in Caracas.

Children: Durable summer wear is the best clothing for children in Caracas. Blue jeans are very popular among all ages. Bring light sweaters for cool evenings and mornings. Heavy pajamas or sleepers with feet are needed for infants in winter (December-February).

Venezuelan law requires that all school children wear uniforms.

Some American-style shoes are made and sold in Caracas. They are somewhat wider than standard American shoes. The quality of children's shoes varies.

For teenagers, one dressy outfit for occasional parties or school functions may be required. Jeans are universal wear for day-to-day activities. T-shirts are very popular.

Supplies and Services

Supplies: Popular American brand name, but locally produced toiletries, cosmetics, and household supplies can be found in Caracas. Drugs and medicines are price controlled and can often be bought at prices below those in the U.S., many without prescriptions.

Basic Services: Tailoring, drycleaning, laundry, shoe repair, radio and TV repair, electrical work, plumbing, fumigation, and auto repair are available and generally adequate. Standards of workmanship and cost vary considerably. Good hairdressers and barbers are available at prices substantially lower than in major cities in the U.S.

Keep in mind that it is the custom here for stores to be closed anywhere between 12:30 pm and 3:00 pm in the afternoon, and to close in the evening at about 7:00 pm, even in the malls. Note: many establishments in Caracas close during the Christmas holidays from about December 15 to January 15.

Religious Activities

There are several major English-speaking church communities in Caracas: St. Thomas More, a Roman Catholic parish, is served by an Italian priest. The United Christian Church, an interdenominational Protestant Church; the Bethel Baptist Church; and the El Salvador Lutheran Church all have American ministers. St. Mary's Anglican Cathedral (Anglican-Episcopal) has a British bishop. There is also the First Church of Christ Scientist and the Centro Evangelico Pentecostal. They all have services in addition to religious instructions and Sunday school or Bible studies for the children on Sunday mornings. The Mormon community has several wards throughout the city. The Jewish (orthodox and conserva-

tive) congregations have several synagogues: Jabad-Lubavitch Yeshiva Gedola of Venezuela, or Shalom Synagogue and Union Israelita de Caracas. Services are conducted in Spanish and Hebrew. There is also an outstanding and beautiful mosque that has been completed recently that is the tallest in South America.

These congregations offer a variety of social activities that provide good opportunities to meet others from the international community. Church announcements are printed in the English-language newspaper.

Education

Dependent Education. Good schools are available in Venezuela. Most American children attend one of two schools: Campo Alegre (Campo) which ranges from pre-kindergarten through grade 12 and Colegio Internacional de Caracas (CIC) which also ranges from kindergarten through grade 12. Documentation required for enrollment is a school transcript, transfers, grade cards, or school records. Entrance placement examinations are always given to assure correct placement. A certificate of medical examination and immunization record is also required. It is best obtained before arrival, but can be obtained in Venezuela.

Both schools are private. They require a registration fee, tuition payments, and transportation fees.

By Venezuelan decree, uniforms are required at all schools in all grades.

The school year extends from late August through early June. The program of instruction closely parallels the American system. Both schools use a contained classroom system at the elementary level and departmentalized classes in middle and secondary school. Students or graduates from these schools are qualified to enroll in public or private schools and colleges and universities in the U.S. since they both are accredited by the U.S. Southern Association of Schools and Colleges. Instruction is in English. A majority

City of Caracas, Venezuela

David Johnson. Reproduced by permission.

of teachers are recruited from the U.S. and are U.S. certified. The Venezuelan Ministry of Education requires that all students receive some instruction in Spanish and certain civics and history courses. Library, science labs, and computer facilities are all considered more than adequate when compared with U.S. averages.

Each of these schools has a full-time administrative staff that operates under the direction of an annually elected Board of Directors. The schools also sponsor Parent-Teacher-Student Associations (PTA) and provide ample opportunities for formal consultation and informal exchanges between parents and

teachers. A full-time nurse is on duty at both schools.

Both schools offer honors, advanced placement and International Baccalaureate courses for talented students, as well as physical education programs, although varsity sports are not emphasized as they are in most U.S. schools. Varsity teams offer basketball, soccer, volleyball and softball. They have limited schedules, but an advantage is that a higher percentage of students have an opportunity to participate in sports than in large U.S. schools. CIC has athletic facilities that include a full-sized football field, a tennis court and swimming activities. Campo has a gymnasium, out-

door courts and a playing field used for softball and soccer.

There are some extracurricular activities and periodic evening social activities for the older children. Bus transportation is available to both schools from most neighborhoods where Americans live. The consensus here is that both schools offer a solid education. Most children tend to have to work harder than in U.S. schools, unless they were in a specialized, accelerated program in the U.S. Special resources for children with learning disabilities are available at the schools, but are limited.

Campo Alegre is situated in a residential area of Las Mercedes and has an excellent but crowded physical plant including a gymnasium, many science labs, Macintosh computer labs and a cafeteria. It is centrally located and access is easy. Enrollment is currently just over 1000 with 52 nationalities represented. Class sizes range from 13-22. The well-qualified and dedicated staff has written Essential Agreements in all curricular areas to enhance and reinforce the basic educational beliefs on which the school's philosophy is written.

Campo's programs are driven by 23 student outcomes and based on a belief that an international school setting is an enriching and positive factor in the education of children who will live and work in a global society. The school's curriculum includes Advanced Placement and International Baccalaureate at the secondary level. Computer studies begin in kindergarten and continue through high school. There is an excellent physical education program that engages students in gymnastics, dance, ball skills and track and field.

Campo's physical education department recently hosted the first Caribbean Volleyball Tournament with participants from Costa Rica, Bolivia, Dominican Republic and other schools in the Caribbean area. A school psychologist directs a program of intervention for students needing special help, both educationally and socially. Counselors at all levels are available for students and parents. Parents are kept well informed through regular reporting, conferences, a weekly newsletter (Campo News), and a program of parent forums on key instructional progress and issues (Parents Ask and Family Nights).

A comprehensive "English as a Second Language" program is well articulated with the other curriculum within the school. All elementary students have one period each day of Spanish. Spanish and French are offered at the secondary levels. A new middle school offers a program specifically designed to meet the needs of students from 12-14 years of age. Over 95 percent of the graduating classes enroll in college and the school offers a full range of placement and achievement tests (PSAT, SAT, ACT, AP). The school has a 650-seat auditorium with stage and orchestra pit that is well used by the Drama Program provided for Campo students and staff alike.

Campo is also a center for many English-speaking community functions. Art, music and cultural events are available for all students. Campo also has a chapter of the Junior and Senior Honor Society. Escuela Campo Alegre participates in the Merit Scholar program and the annual International Schools Model United Nations Assembly in The Hague, Holland. Cub and Boy Scouts, Brownies and Girl Scouts are popular as after school activities. A school-sponsored Activities Program offers a wide range of activities from a weekend adventure program at the secondary school to an elementary cooking class. The school is a member of the National Association of Independent Schools, the Association of South American Schools and the European Council of International Schools.

Colegio Internacional de Caracas has a large campus on a hilltop commanding a sweeping view of the valley with ample space for sports

activities, as well as special events for students and their parents. On campus a canteen serves full lunches or snacks, and supplies food and drink for special get-togethers. Present enrollment of CIC is about 550, in grades nursery through 12, the largest single group being North American. The balance of the students are from around 40 other countries. Students enjoy relatively small classes and a high degree of individual instruction.

Clubs and after school activities are available for all students varying with student interest and adult supervisor availability. Art, music, drama, cultural development and global awareness are stressed in the elementary school and supported with classroom instruction at almost every level. CIC has a chapter of the Junior and Senior National Honor Society and presently offers a program for gifted and talented students at the elementary level. This program will be extended in 1994-95 or earlier, although the Advanced Placement and International Baccalaureate programs already present challenging opportunities for the able students in the secondary school. The school also provides Resource Center services for children with mild learning disabilities, mild emotional handicaps, and attention deficit disorders. Tutoring services are also available at the Center through the Boost Program. The school participates in the National Merit Scholar program, the Close Up educational visit to Washington, and sponsors the yearly South American Model United Nations Conference attended by more than 200 students. CIC students also participate in the Model United Nations Assembly in The Hague, Holland. Over 95 percent of the graduating classes enroll in college, and the school offers a comprehensive guidance and counseling program, including the services of a psychologist. Achievement, college entrance and placements tests such as Metropolitan Achievement Tests, PSAT, SAT, and ACT are offered on campus, as are Advanced Placement

courses and the full International Baccalaureate Program.

Advanced programs are offered in English, French, Spanish, Italian, History, Math, and Science. Two modern media centers support the learning needs of the faculty and students. A laboratory and classroom-based comprehensive computer literacy program in the elementary school, and two computer laboratories in the secondary school, provide students access to these skills. CIC also offers summer school and summer day camp programs for students. A school-to-school program with a sister district in Bremerton, Washington, provides CIC faculty with opportunities to receive in-service and other professional development experiences.

Several other good, private schools in the Caracas area have been used by some North American families. However, none are accredited. The Washington Academy, located in Valle Arriba, offers bilingual education for kindergarten through eighth grade. The Jefferson Academy, also located in Valle Arriba, offers bilingual education for pre-kindergarten through sixth grade.

Caracas has many good, private nursery schools, some English speaking, some bilingual. A list can be obtained from the CLO coordinator. Neighborhood Spanish-speaking nurseries are numerous.

Other international community schools

Escuela Britanica offers kindergarten through grade six. The curriculum closely follows the British system. Uniforms are required. The education is excellent, but application must be made early.

Colegio Francia has a complete elementary school with instruction in French and Spanish. At the Colegio Humbolt, instruction is in German and Spanish for both elementary and high school grades.

Venezuelan Schools
There are numerous private elementary and secondary schools in

Caracas, many of which are Catholic.

Special Educational Opportunities

For Spanish-speaking students, college classes are available at several universities. Universidad Simon Bolivar is free but entrance is very difficult for foreigners. Universidad Andres Bello and Universidad Metropolitana are private and charge tuition. Another private university, IESA, the Institute of Higher Studies in Administration, offers postgraduate studies in business administration and management. Due to the general difficulty of transferring foreign credits to the U.S., many have chosen to audit classes. International House offers graduate degree work in English for M.E. degrees through Marymount College and is initiating a Masters degree program in Business.

The Audubon Society (La Sociedad Conservacionista Audubon de Venezuela), maintains an environmental reference library, holds meetings and has various excursions. The office is located in the Paseo las Mercedes shopping center. The Caracas Circulating Library maintains a collection of current best sellers in English, both fiction and nonfiction, as well as a children's library. It is open 3 days a week, 1 day being Saturday mornings. The cost is about $5 to join and $5 per month.

The Caracas Playhouse, an English-language theater group, produces plays and musicals with the purpose of developing amateur theater in Caracas. Previous experience is not required for participation.

Spanish and English instructions are available through the Centro Venezolano Americano. The CVA also has a lending library and sponsors a wide variety of cultural programs. Other languages may be studied through various institutions such as the Centro Venezolano Italiano and Alianza Francesa. English and Spanish language lessons are also offered through Instituto Cultural Venezolano Britanico.

The Venezuelan-American Association of University Women offers a biannual study group program that is open to nonmembers as well as members. Courses are offered in drawing, painting, sculpture, photography, calligraphy, interior design, batik, education (including Venezuelan Field Study), bridge, mini-lectures on countries of the world, world religions, shorthand and typing, Indians of Venezuela, music, languages, cooking, and physical fitness.

Classes in music, dance, physical fitness, arts and crafts, languages, and many other subjects are available at commercial institutions and from individuals.

Sports

Sports activities in the immediate Caracas area are limited, principally because of the lack of public facilities. There are few public swimming pools in Caracas. One of them, Parque Miranda, has swimming instructions in an olympic-size pool and offers swim team competition.

Clubs in Caracas are excellent, fully equipped and provide a wide range of facilities. Many are also very expensive. There are no public golf courses in Venezuela. There are also no public tennis courts, but at least one semi-public court exists and there is a tennis club that some Americans have joined.

Jogging is a popular sport here, particularly since the climate allows this activity year round; however, jogging is usually done in daylight hours at Parque del Este. The Hash House Harriers has a run twice monthly on Sunday afternoons in different neighborhoods of Caracas. Everyone does not run, and many people walk the route. Hiking is another popular activity. Excellent but steep trails lead up the sides of the Avila Range, and the varieties of flora are unbelievable. The plateaus offer opportunities for sports such as softball, volleyball, soccer, etc., and picnicking is also popular. The physically fit can hike to the top and view the Caribbean Sea and port

city of La Guaria on one side and on the other side have an airplane's view of Caracas. There is no charge for climbing the Avila and overnight camping is easily accommodated, however there are no facilities except for running water in some places.

Venezuela offers a range of challenges for every kind of fisherman. One can troll for monster marlin, tuna, wahoo, sailfish and other saltwater prizes along Venezuela's Caribbean coast, angle for trout in pristine Andean lakes or land peacock bass, catfish, and other freshwater game fish in the country's many rivers. The second major draw for any angler is the abundance and large size of fish in Venezuela's waters that have not been "fished out" as have many areas of the world that have long been popular for this sport. Side by side with offers for beach, jungle and Andean tours, one now finds that nearly all major travel and tourism agencies offer fishing packages for both salt- and freshwater. A license is not required.

Hunting is not popular here and the rules and regulations are vague and unenforced. There is a hunting season, however, and all endangered species are off limits to hunters at all times. A hunting license is not required, however guns must be registered.

Spectator sports are as popular among Caraquenos of all ages as they are among Americans. Professional baseball leagues, often featuring major league American and Venezuelan players, have a full schedule of games after the U.S. season ends. The general level is that of a triple A league in the U.S. Soccer is followed by many Venezuelans. Some of the finest teams in the world tour here occasionally and are worth seeing. A major bullfight season is held annually in Caracas' Nuevo Circo with well-known bullfighters from Spain, Mexico, Venezuela, etc. Tickets are reasonably priced, but seldom advertised. Horseraces are held every Saturday and Sunday year round at a superbly designed and equipped track. The spacious stands are nearly always filled. A large percentage of the city's residents bet the weekly "5 and 6" (Cinco y Seis) ticket (picking five or six winners out of the last six races). Bi-weekly night races are held.

Touring and Outdoor Activities

Caracas has several historical churches and museums, including the birthplace of Simon Bolivar, a museum of fine arts, a museum of natural history, a science museum, and a museum of contemporary art. There is also a lovely colonial museum, the Quinta Anauco, which features evening concerts during certain times of the year, and a unique and interesting Children's Museum. There are also some fine parks within the city. Strollers may enjoy Parque del Este or Parque Los Chorros, which is located at the base of the Avila, and offers a pleasant escape from the traffic and the noise. Parque del Este also has a small zoo and is a popular spot for early morning joggers. The suburb of El Hatillo on the outskirts of Caracas offers quaint colonial style shops, houses and restaurants. There are many shops in El Hatillo but one, Hannsi's, sells handicrafts from all over South America.

Beaches within a short drive from Caracas are crowded on weekends and unfortunately the water is polluted. For longer trips, the beach at Cata to the west of Caracas or Rio Chico to the east are popular on weekends. The islands in the Morrocoy National Park, 3–5 hours from Caracas by car, and then reachable only by boat, offer beautiful beaches and great snorkeling. Camping is allowed on these islands although there are no facilities. The islands of Los Roques, reachable only by air (30 minutes from Caracas), are beautiful and offer excellent snorkeling, too. Camping is allowed there also, but again, no facilities. Beaches in Venezuela are not like the beaches of Florida and California. They are generally very short in length and width and are not the

© Yann Arthus-Bertrand/Corbis. Reproduced by permission.
Church and museum in Maracaibo, Venezuela

type of beaches where one can take a nice long walk. However, some are beautiful and some have very crystal clear water.

There are several offshore islands that offer wonderful opportunities for snorkeling. Bonaire, one of the islands in the Netherland Antilles, is perhaps the best example. Scuba diving is also quite popular and there are certified diving instructors in Caracas who offer classes in English on a regular basis.

An interesting 1-day excursion from Caracas over winding but paved roads is to Colonia Tovar, a settlement of German immigrants about 40 miles from Caracas. The picturesque houses and cuisine remind one of the Bavarian Alps. Another pleasant day trip out of Caracas is to Los Teques where one can ride a narrow gauge train to El Encanto Park. When the train is operating, the trip affords lovely scenery and a chance to enjoy a picnic lunch at the end of the line. It is also near the Arte Murano glass factory, a favorite spot for buying Venetian style glass.

In the Andean region of Venezuela one can enjoy spectacular and beautiful scenery. The teleferico in Merida, when working, gives one a sweeping view of the mountains,

while the Hotel Los Frailes, once a monastery, offers charm and beauty. Popular activities in this area are mountain climbing, trout fishing, and horseback riding. On the opposite side of Venezuela is the tropical jungle in the State of Bolivar. Canaima is a small settlement in the jungle at the base of the spectacular falls of the Carrao River. This place of imposing beauty is a perfect trip for those who admire adventure and is accessible only by air. An added attraction is an aerial view of Angel Falls, highest in the world (3,312 feet). It was named for an American aviator, Jimmy Angel, who landed above them in 1937. It rivals the Grand Canyon in the U.S.

For birdwatchers and anyone interested in exploring the countryside, the local Audubon Society organizes outings regularly. The most interesting require a four-wheel drive vehicle and overnight camping.

Trips to nearby Caribbean islands are also popular. The Venezuelan island of Margarita combines the charm of old Spanish colonial forts and churches with some nice beaches. Curacao, Aruba, Bonaire, Barbados, Trinidad and Tobago are other interesting islands to visit. Trinidad is especially exciting during Carnival when the entire island closes down and "jumps up" for 4 days to the music of hundreds of steel bands.

For the really adventurous traveler, there are canoe trips to the base of Angel Falls that require a few days, trips into the interior to visit missionaries working among primitive Indians (which require special permission), flights over the Grand Sabana area near the Brazilian frontier, boat trips down the Orinoco from Puerto Ayacucho to Ciudad Bolivar, and camping on the llanos (plains).

Traveling in Venezuela is often disorganized. Planes often get overbooked and sometimes trips don't go as planned. The best approach to this is to arrive very early at the airport and to have lots of patience.

Many apartments have nice window boxes for plants, herbs or flowers. There are numerous nurseries in Caracas and the climate is excellent for gardening. Most plants flourish here. Orchids are especially popular and are the national flower.

Entertainment

Caracas enjoys a diversity of international cuisine with Argentine-style steak houses, Italian, Spanish, Chinese and French restaurants being the most popular. Some restaurants provide music and dinner dancing. Caracas is truly a city of spectacular restaurants. Caraquenos love to dine out and it shows in the atmosphere, ambiance and diversity of their restaurants. The city also has many night clubs, and private discotheques and jazz clubs are becoming increasingly popular. A woman should have a male escort to enter clubs in Caracas at night.

Modern movie theaters, including several drive-ins, are located throughout the city. The majority of films shown are American with Spanish subtitles, but French, Italian and Mexican movies are also presented. Venezuela does not yet have a highly developed feature length film industry but sophisticated "soap operas", aired during prime-time by local TV stations are avidly followed by many.

Sports fans can expect to see regular season major league baseball games weekly in addition to the playoffs and the World Series. Professional basketball and the Super Bowl have also aired here in the past.

Social Activities

Caracas is a cosmopolitan city, offering opportunities to get involved. The extent and direction of social activities depends largely on your initiative. There are a number of organizations to help newcomers get introduced.

Groups and activities within the American community include the Venezuelan-American Chamber of Commerce, Rotary Club International, Lions Club International, the Audubon Society, a hiking club, "Circulo Excursionistas" and scouting. The Centro Venezolano-Americano sponsors social and cultural events.

The Venezuelan-American Association of University Women (VAAUW) offers membership to university graduates only. Those who attended college for two years may join as associate members. However, their excellent and varied courses and many of their programs and activities are open to nonmembers.

The Children's Service League is a volunteer organization that works with children and young adults, raises money for hospitalized and handicapped children, and annually helps 20 institutions and hospitals. CSL activities include sewing workshops, a mini-bookstore, a bridge competition and a bowling league, as well as the design, preparation and sale of its annual collection of Christmas and note cards. The CSL holds a Christmas Bazaar at which these cards and handicrafts are sold.

The Newcomer's Club emphasizes welcoming you to Caracas with tips on how to adapt to its culture and social life. It is a good place to meet other newcomers who live in your own area.

Maracaibo

Maracaibo, the capital of Zulia State and Venezuela's second largest city (population was estimated at 1.9 million in 2000), is situated in the coastal lowlands, on the western shore of Lake Maracaibo. The lake, South America's largest, bounds the city on the east and south. The six-mile-long Rafael Urdaneta Bridge, which is the longest prestressed concrete span in the world, spans the narrow, northern neck of the lake and connects Maracaibo with the eastern shore. To the north, the lake opens into the Gulf of Venezuela and in the south, beyond the lake, rise the Andes.

Although 170 miles away, Pico Bolívar, the country's highest point, is visible from the city on a clear day. Called both the Bolívar Coast and Costa Oriental del Lago, this area is the center of Venezuela's petroleum industry. Scattered all along this coast and on the waters offshore are thousands of wells tapping the extensive deposits of the Maracaibo Basin, which provides 80 percent of the nation's oil.

Maracaibo was founded in 1571 and soon became an inland trading center. The city and the surrounding area underwent tremendous expansion following the discovery of oil in 1917. Production of Venezuela's three largest national oil companies is headquartered in the Maracaibo area. Directly across the lake from the city is El Tablazo, a huge petrochemical complex, and up the gulf coast on the Paraguaná Peninsula at Amuay is the world's largest oil refinery. Numerous petroleum-related companies, many of them U.S. firms, operate in and around Maracaibo.

Clustered around the port are the colonial-style buildings and narrow streets of the old city. This is the site of the Cathedral of Maracaibo and the Palacio de las Aguilas, which serves as the seat of state government. Farther from the port, the architecture is more modern, with many multistory apartment and office buildings. Nearer the outskirts of the city, prosperity is less obvious, and modern buildings give way to brick and corrugated tin shacks.

The U.S. consular district of Maracaibo serves the coastal states of Zulia and Falcon and the Andean states of Táchira, Mérida, and Trujillo. An estimated 4,000 Americans live in this district—mostly in Maracaibo and across the lake on the Bolívar Coast in the oil towns of Cabimas, Las Morochas, Tia Juana, and Lagunillas. Because of the long history of American business participation in the area, Americans are generally well regarded, and many mixed-nationality families live here.

Maracaibo is hot and humid throughout the year, although winter months are slightly cooler. Daytime temperatures are usually 90°F or above, with 75 percent humidity. Annual rainfall is about 20 inches. The moderate rainy season begins in May, with rain becoming more frequent toward November.

Schools for Foreigners

Schooling in English is available from pre-kindergarten to 12th grade at Escuela Bella Vista, which is accredited by the Southern Association of Colleges and Schools. Some 30 nationalities are represented among the approximately 300 students; most are American and Venezuelan. There are approximately 40 full-time teachers, half of which are American. Although academic classes are conducted in English, Spanish-language courses are required at all grade levels. The quality of teaching is good, and students in the upper grades can choose from a variety of electives.

Bella Vista has good facilities, including an air-conditioned 14,500-volume library, cafeteria, two gymnasiums, science lab, computer lab, covered play area, a ball field, and tennis courts. Extracurricular activities include instrumental music, drama, school newspaper, yearbook, computers, gymnastics, soccer, volleyball, basketball, softball, track and field, tennis, and field trips. The school has neither special facilities

for teaching children with learning disabilities, nor any programs for gifted students.

The school year runs from late August to mid-June. Venezuelan holidays are observed. Bella Vista is located at Calle 67, entre Avenue 3D y 3E, La Lago, Maracaibo. Mail can be addressed to Apartado 290, Maracaibo, Venezuela.

Special educational opportunities are offered at the University of Zulia, where those competent in Spanish can audit courses. Medicine, dentistry, law, engineering, and the humanities are taught at the university.

El Centro de Bellas Artes, established by Venezuelans and foreigners interested in fine arts, sponsors moderately priced classes and individual instruction in painting, sculpture, ceramics, leather work, and metalwork. The Spanish-speaking instructors are competent. Fees are moderate. Academia de Música, run by the State of Zulia, offers instruction in voice and various musical instruments. Private music and ballet instruction are also available.

Recreation

Boating and other water sports on Lake Maracaibo are available, but limited by the lake's pollution. The majority of beaches in the immediate area are neither attractive nor well maintained. Good beaches are several hours away. Several professional sports stadiums host soccer and baseball, which are very popular. During the annual Feria de La Chinita, bullfights are presented in the Plaza de Toros.

Recreational facilities for children and teenagers are virtually nonexistent outside of private clubs, causing some problems for families. Most sports activities take place during evening hours when it is slightly cooler. A public park, Paseo del Lago, has been constructed on the lake shore, and facilities there include a jogging course, baseball diamonds, soccer fields, and children's play equipment. The popular

Paseo often draws Maracuchos for evening recreation, but upkeep of the facilities is inadequate.

Maracaibo has only limited hunting opportunities; most hunting is for fowl and takes place on privately owned haciendas. Opportunities for fishing are more plentiful. This sport is possible in some parts of the lake, as well as in the Gulf of Venezuela. In the Andes, trout fishing is available.

An informal group of English-speaking men meet at Escuela Bella Vista for mixed sports once a week, alternating among basketball, soccer, and other games. Most other sports activities require membership in clubs, which are expensive. Among these private clubs are Los Andes Yacht Club, Maracaibo Country Club, Club Náutico, and the German Club; many English-speaking expatriates belong to the latter.

The nearest place of interest outside of town is the Río Limón area, about 30 miles north of the city. From there, the visitor may take a boat trip up-river to see the Paraguaná Indian villages built on stilts over the water. A bridge crosses the river for car trips to the Indian villages of Sinamaica and Paraguaipoa farther up the coast from Río Limón. A modest beach resort, Caimara Chico (Balneario) on the Gulf of Venezuela, is near Sinamaica.

A pleasant change of scenery and climate is possible by visiting the Andean villages of La Puerta and Timotes, about 160 miles (three to four hours by car) from Maracaibo. Many Maracuchos have vacation cabins there, and some small inns cater to tourists. Valera and Mérida, farther down the Andean chain, are the nearest Andean cities accessible by air (about 45 minutes flying time). Alternatively, Mérida, a charming university town, is about a nine-hour drive, and from there one can travel into the Andes.

Aruba, a popular resort island, is less than an hour's flight from Maracaibo, and Caracas is about one hour by air or nine hours by car.

Entertainment

Maracaibo has many movie theaters, but few of them show first-run films. American movies are popular and are usually screened with Spanish subtitles. British, French, and Latin American films are also shown. Prices are reasonable.

Occasionally, it is possible to attend live performances presented by touring Venezuelan and international groups. Additionally, the binational center presents a full cultural program during the year. The Maracaibo Players, an amateur English-speaking dramatic group, stages two annual plays. The Maracaibo Symphony Orchestra, with several American members, gives reasonably priced Thursday evening concerts at Teatro Bellas Artes. Ticket prices are reasonable.

Maracaibo has several good restaurants. Steak is popular with Venezuelan diners, and this popularity is reflected in the number of good steak houses in town. Traditional Venezuelan cuisine—or criollo—is featured in several restaurants. The city also has a variety of Chinese, Italian, Spanish, and French dining spots. Numerous soda fountains and tea shops serve American-style sandwiches and ice cream. There also are a few American-style fast food restaurants.

For those interested in history, Maracaibo offers the Urdaneta Museum. This museum chronicles the history of Spanish settlement in the Maracaibo area.

The ability to communicate in Spanish is essential to a full social life. American men sometimes join the local Rotary, Lions, Jaycees, Toastmasters, or Masonic organizations; women join various church-connected groups or the Maracaibo Women's Tennis Club or Ladies Club. Maracaibo has an active North American Association.

Special Information

Maracaibo is located only about 50 miles from the Colombian border. The Guajira Peninsula, shared by the two countries, is north of Maracaibo, and this area (particularly the Colombian side) is known as a drug-trafficking center where law enforcement resources are extremely limited. Border areas south and southwest of Maracaibo are lightly populated, largely wilderness regions from which come sporadic reports of Colombian guerrilla activity and kidnappings. Travel to any border area should be carefully considered.

OTHER CITIES

BARQUISIMETO, established in 1552, a few years before the founding of Valencia, is the capital of Lara State in northwestern Venezuela. It is situated at an altitude of 1,856 feet at the northern end of the Cordillera Mérida, 170 miles southwest of Caracas. Barquisimeto is situated in a productive agricultural area. Cacao, sugarcane, sisal, and coffee are grown near the city. Several industries in the city produce cement, twine, and food products. A 230-foot tower built in 1952 to commemorate the city's 400th anniversary is a well-known landmark. Barquisimeto is the home of Central-Western University. In 2000, the city had an estimated population of 914,000.

CIUDAD BOLÍVAR is the commercial hub of the plains (*llanos*) region of the east. It lies on the south bank of the Orinoco River, 280 miles southeast of Caracas. The city dates to 1764, when it was called San Tomás de la Nueva Guayana de la Angostura. Simón Bolívar, the South American liberator, declared Gran Colombia's independence from Spain here in 1819; the city was renamed in 1846 in his honor. Ciudad Bolívar is a river port and the principal docking area on the Orinoco. Exports include gold, diamonds, cattle, horses, skins, hides, timber, and agricultural products. Fishing and tourism also are important in Ciudad Bolívar; the late June catches of the sapoara fish are popular, and gold trinkets made here—especially charms—are considered the best in Venezuela. The

city is home to the Jesus Soto Museum, which features works by Venezuelan and European artists. This state capital has an estimated population of 308,000. The planned city of Ciudad Guayana (or Santo Tomé de Guayana) is situated 60 miles to the east at the juncture of the Orinoco and Caroní rivers. It has a population of about 692,000.

The small "Black Forest" village of **COLONIA TOVAR** lies in the mountains 40 miles west of Caracas. Known for its German sausage, flowers, and jams, the town becomes congested with visitors from Caracas on Sundays. German immigrants founded Colonia Tovar in 1843; it remained virtually isolated until modern roads were built in the vicinity in the 1940s.

CUMANÁ is South America's oldest Hispanic community, located 200 miles east of Caracas on the main highway. Dating to 1521, the city of approximately 208,115 people (2000 est.) is known for Fort Antonio and other colonial-era churches and houses. Beset by earthquakes, especially the massive devastations of 1766 and 1929, Cumaná lies near large salt beds and sandy beaches. Sardine canning supports many here. Cumaná is nestled in a rich agricultural area. Sugarcane, beans, tobacco, coffee, cacao, and fruits are grown here. The city is the home of Eastern University.

MARACAY, with a population of 460,000 in 2000, is the capital of Aragua State in the north, 50 miles southwest of Caracas. The center of Venezuela's cattle industry, it was, during the early years of this century, headquarters for the military government which ruled the country. The city is home to many industries which produce textiles, rayon, sugar, rubber, paper, cement, and food stuffs. Maracay is linked to Caracas via the Pan-American Highway.

MÉRIDA is the capital of Mérida State, 325 miles southwest of Caracas. Situated deep in the Cordillera Mérida Mountains at an altitude of

5,400 feet, this is an agricultural hub for neighboring hinterlands producing coffee, tobacco, and vegetable oils. Mérida is the highest city in Venezuela. The "Five White Eagles," a local name for looming mountain peaks, provide a stunning backdrop for Mérida's 21 parks, most notably the Park of the Five Republics. This park has the world's first Simón Bolívar monument (erected in 1842) and contains soil from each of the countries he freed. Recreational activities in the area include mountaineering and fishing. Andean tourists enjoy Mérida's cathedral, zoo, colonial museum, university campus, and unusual cable car. The cable car is the highest and longest in the world, climbing to above 15,000 feet. There are several hotels here. Mérida is known for its candied fruits and *ruanas* (Andean poncho-like woolen cloaks). Mérida's current population is approximately 230,000 (2000 est.).

SAN CRISTÓBAL, founded in 1561, is the capital of Tachira State in western Venezuela. A mountain city situated at the end of the Cordillera Mérida, it suffered great human loss and property damage in an earthquake which shook that part of the country in 1875. The 2000 population was estimated at 329,000. San Cristóbal is a commercial center for the cassava, corn, sugarcane, coffee, and pineapples grown near the city. The city's industries include factories which produce textiles, leather goods, shoes, cement, and cigarettes.

VALENCIA, the capital of Carabobo State in northern Venezuela, is one of the principal industrial and transportation centers in the country. It is situated at the western end of Lake Valencia, approximately 80 miles west of the capital. The city dates to the mid-16th century. It is an important producer of automobiles and parts, pharmaceuticals, food and dairy products, garments, cement, furniture, rubber goods, fertilizers, paper, textiles, soap, and vegetable oils. Colegio Internacional de Carabobo, offering a U.S. curriculum for pre-kindergarten through grade 12, is located five miles from the center of Valencia. The school has two computer labs, a science lab, an auditorium, cafeteria, recreational area, athletic field, and a library with nearly 13,500 volumes. Extracurricular activities include drama, dance, yearbook, literary magazine, field trips, and various trips. The school has approximately 25 full-time and 10 part-time teachers. Half of those teachers were American. Of the school's approximately 260 students, about 80 are American. Further information may be obtained by writing to the school at Apartado 103, Valencia. Valencia's population was estimated at 832,000 in 2000.

COUNTRY PROFILE

Geography and Climate

Venezuela is located on the north coast of South America, and covers 352,150 square miles—about the size of Texas and Oklahoma combined. Caracas' altitude is about 2,700 feet above sea level, giving the city a permanent springtime climate.

The Orinoco River and the various mountain ranges, all branches of the Andes chain, divide the country into four distinct regions:

South of the Orinoco River are the wild and largely unexplored Guyana Highlands, rich in mineral resources and in developed and potential hydroelectric power. They are characterized by rugged relief and mesa-like formations. The climate ranges from temperate in the Gran Sabana to tropical on the fringes of the plateau.

North of the Orinoco are the "llanos" or plains. During the dry season (December-April) the entire area is almost desert-like. But during the rainy season, flooding rivers make the area muddy and practically impassable.

Spurs of the Andes Mountains run along each side of the Maracaibo basin and part of the seacoast. The bulk of Venezuela's population traditionally has lived in these highlands attracted by the temperate weather and fertile soil.

A tropical coastal plain stretches along most of Venezuela's 1,750-mile coastline. This narrow strip of land between mountains and sea widens in the west to form the Maracaibo basin. The climate is uniformly hot and humid.

Population

Venezuela's population in 2000 was 18,105,000. Over 38 percent of the population was under 15 years of age, and 66 percent was under 30. Rapid population growth and migration from rural areas have produced densely populated cities containing over 84 percent of the population, while vast areas of the interior are sparsely populated.

Venezuela proudly regards itself as being a melting pot. About 20 percent of the population are Caucasian, 9 percent are black, 2 percent are Indian, and the remaining 69 percent are mixed race (mestizo).

Caracas is especially cosmopolitan. Around a quarter of its residents are immigrants and their descendents from Spain, Portugal, and Italy, most of whom came after the World War II. Smaller numbers of immigrants from other European countries also play an important role in the city's commercial and professional life. In the 1970s, the booming Venezuelan economy attracted large numbers of people from the other Caribbean and Andean countries. There are about 24,000 Americans in Venezuela, many of whom live in Caracas.

Public Institutions

Discovered by Columbus in 1498 on his third voyage to the New World, Venezuela was first explored by Alonso de Ojeda in 1499. According to legend, Ojeda named the country

Venezuela (Little Venice) after seeing the Indian houses on stilts in Lake Maracaibo. It was one of the first New World colonies to revolt against Spain (1810), but it was not until 1821 that independence was achieved. Francisco de Miranda began the task. It was completed by the great hero and statesman of Latin America, Simon Bolivar, Venezuela's national hero and native son.

Venezuela, together with what are now Colombia, Panama, and Ecuador, was part of the Union Gran Colombiana until 1830, when it withdrew and began its own existence as a sovereign state.

Until as recently as 1958, Venezuela's political history as an independent nation could be characterized as rule by a series of military dictators.

During General Juan Vicente Gomez' rule (1908-35), oil was discovered in the Maracaibo Basin, and Venezuela changed from a poor, largely agrarian country to one of the richest nations in Latin America.

The modern political forces set in motion by the new oil economy produced a brief experiment in democracy 1945-48, a military coup followed by a 10-year period of dictatorship under General Marcos Perez Jimenez, and finally the restoration of democracy in 1958. Former Presidents are Romulo Betancourt from the Accion Democratica (AD) Social Democratic party 1959-64; Raul Leoni (AD) 1964-69; Rafael Caldera from the Social Christian COPEI party 1969-74; Carlos Andres Perez (AD) 1974-79; Luis Herrera Campins (COPEI) 1979-84; Jaime Lusinchi (AD) 1984-89; Carlos Andres Perez (AD) 1989-93. Perez was removed peacefully after he was indicted by the Supreme Court. Ramon Velasquez became interim president until February 1994, when Rafael Caldera was once again inaugurated. President Hugo Chavez Frias came into office in February 1999.

Venezuela is a representative democracy. The constitution of 1999 provides for the direct election of the President every 6 years. The President is chief of state and head of the national executive branch, and he or she appoints the Vice-President. The President is assisted by Cabinet Members with the rank of Minister. State governors, legislators and municipal councilmen are elected locally.

The legislative branch consists of a unicameral National Assembly. The 165 representatives are elected by popular vote to serve 5-year terms.

The judicial branch consists of a Supreme Court and other courts on all different levels of government. The Republic of Venezuela is composed of 23 states and the Federal District that includes much of the Caracas metropolitan area.

Arts, Science, and Education

Venezuelan cultural life is centered in Caracas, a reflection of the capital's overwhelming political and financial influence. A quarter of the country's population lives in Caracas, a dramatic shift from the situation at the end of World War II when the city's population was about 250,000. In response to the petroleum boom and this population shift, numerous cultural and artistic institutions have been established. The luxurious Teresa Carreno performing arts complex opened in 1983 and is one of the most architecturally dramatic in the world. The Venezuelan Government has made a strong commitment to fostering culture, education, and the arts, backing these efforts with considerable state funding.

The National Cultural Council (CONAC), the major government funding source, actively promotes the arts and culture outside of Caracas as do individual state arts councils. Regional development councils, large state industries and private foundations also contribute

to the arts. Foreign embassies sponsor performing artists on tour and the U.S.-Venezuelan binational centers also promote cultural and artistic activities.

Music is perhaps the best developed of Venezuela's cultural attractions. There are four major orchestras in Caracas alone. The National Symphony gives regular concerts at the Teresa Carreno Theater and often has visiting conductors and soloists. World-renowned musicians have performed with the National Symphony. The newer Municipal Orchestra was established to accompany the Municipal Opera and a variety of ballet and dance groups.

The Philharmonic Orchestra also has a regular concert season. Additionally, there is an active and excellent youth orchestra with several other youth orchestras around the country that nurture provincial talent and send their best students to Caracas for membership in the national youth orchestra. Also, choral music is pervasive with many groups each devoted to a particular choral speciality (baroque, modern, etc.). Popular music—jazz and rock—is popular in Venezuela, and occasionally well-known entertainers come to Caracas. Most recently, Kenny G., Guns N' Roses, Robert Plant, and the B-52's have performed here. However, salsa and merengue remain the most popular among Venezuelans.

The Caracas Metropolitan Opera has a regular season in June and July, performing the standard repertoire with a mixture of artists from their own opera school as well as from Europe and the U.S. The opera school also gives workshop productions throughout the year, and independent entrepreneurs sponsor ad hoc performances.

Ballet has received enormous stature and impetus with the great success of the now world-renowned New World Ballet of Caracas which has two regular seasons, spring and fall. Many experimental groups are being spawned, founded by Venezuelans trained abroad. There are well-established ballet schools in Caracas as well as major cities of the interior, which give recitals. Many accept non-Venezuelan students. Baryshnikov has performed in Caracas as recently as 1993. Caracas is an active theater city with several plays being performed at any given time. Additionally, there are experimental groups, University players, children's theater, a black theater group near Caracas (Teatro Negro de Barlovento), the well-established Caracas Players who perform in English, and a venerable tradition of puppetry. Caracas has an annual theater festival, and is also the host of a biennial international theater festival. The International Theater Institute (ITI) has an office in Caracas.

The Venezuelan Institute of Folklore sponsors traditional festivals, regional fairs and dance groups in an effort to foster and preserve traditional Venezuelan culture. Such festival and other activities are often associated with local saints' days. For example, a popular dance known as Los Diablos Danzantes de Yare (the Dancing Devils of Yare) is performed on the feast of Corpus Christi. The village is approximately 50 miles from Caracas and the event draws a considerable crowd from the capital. Although this festival represents African influence on Venezuela, other festivals reflect the dominant Spanish influence on the country's folklore.

Private sector scientific activity is generally limited to instruction and some research, primarily in the social sciences. However, the Government's National Council for Scientific and Technological Investigations (CONICIT) plays a major role in developing science and technology in Venezuela. A bilateral agreement in science and technology between the U.S. and Venezuela provides the framework for mutually advantageous cooperative endeavors by our two countries in this field.

The arts flourish in Venezuela. The capital alone has three major museums: one devoted to Venezuelan painters, another to contemporary art beginning in the late 19th century and the third to fine arts with representations of all periods and all countries. Art galleries dot the city and are numerous, some with international connections. Provincial capitals also support local art museums. Venezuela's internationally known artists include Jesus Soto, Carlos Cruz, Hector Poleo, Alejandro Otero and his wife, Mercedes Pardo, and Cornelis Zitman. Art shows and auctions sponsored by such public service organizations as the Venezuelan American Association of University Women, the North American Association and Hadassah as fund-raising events, are very well attended.

The Venezuelan education system currently finds itself in a state of crisis. Educational planning was based on the premise of ever-increasing oil wealth, although petroleum revenues have, in fact, decreased in recent years. The oil boom's legacy, therefore, is an educational system that is overextended and underfunded. Yet the government remains committed to the notion that every citizen is entitled to a free education. The result is a student population that has increased more than seven times since 1958, including a university population that has risen more than 30 times in this period, and a Ministry of Education budget that has increased more than two-fold, yet is still considered inadequate.

There have been significant gains since the 1950s as a result of the government's policy of "Massification" of education. The adult literacy rate, for example, was 91% in 1995. In 1950, there were only four universities in Venezuela; today there are over 90 institutions of higher education. In 1958, there were 853,683 students in the entire system; today there are over 6 million.

The issue today in Venezuela is not quantity, but quality. The Ministry of Education has one of the largest budgets of any government department and its efforts now lie in adapting the curriculum to the demands of an increasingly technological society, in expanding compulsory education, and in upgrading teacher qualifications. However, the current financial difficulties and a demographic bulge (75 percent of the population is under 35 years of age) are likely to cause some dissatisfaction in the future.

Commerce and Industry

Venezuela is one of the wealthier nations in the hemisphere. In 1992, its GDP, measured at the official exchange rate, was $146.2 billion (2000 est.), or $6,200 per capita. The Government dominates the economy; State companies control the petroleum, minerals and basic industries. However, in 1989, an economic adjustment program was started in order to provide Venezuela with a market-oriented, diversified, and export-competitive economy.

Petroleum is and has been the cornerstone of the Venezuelan economy for over 50 years. The petroleum sector dominates the economy, accounting for roughly a third of GDP, around 80% of export earnings, and more than half of government operating revenues in 2000. A strong rebound in international oil prices fueled the recovery from the steep recession in 1999. Nevertheless, a weak nonoil sector and capital flight undercut the recovery. Venezuela is the fourth-leading supplier of imported crude and refined petroleum products to the U.S. This takes into account crude oil and refined products, as well as indirect imports via Caribbean refineries. Venezuela is one of the founding members of the Organization of Petroleum Exporting Countries (OPEC). Venezuela's huge oil reserves will keep it a major oil producer for at least the next hundred years.

Venezuela's total exports in 2000 were $32.8 billion. Its most important nonpetroleum exports include aluminum, steel, iron ore, petro-chemicals, seafood, cement, coffee, cacao, and fruit. More than half of Venezuela's exports are to the U.S. It imported $14.7 billion worth of merchandise in 2000. Principal imports include machinery, transportation equipment, semi-manufactured goods and agricultural commodities. The U.S. supplies 53 percent of all imports.

In contrast to the highly concentrated pattern of Venezuela's exports, the internal economy is quite diversified. Hundreds of small- and medium-sized industries provide many of the products needed by a growing local market for consumer goods. In the late 1950s and early 1960s, Venezuela encouraged foreign and domestic investment in the automobile, tire, and food production industries to reduce imports of consumer goods. During the boom years of the 1970s, Venezuela allowed more imports to satisfy growing domestic demand, while restricting foreign investment in line with general Andean Pact policy. Recently, however, Venezuela has liberalized foreign investment rules, and the Government has embarked on an ambitious privatization program.

Transportation

Local

Many consider a car to be essential in Caracas, although taxis and por puestos are plentiful. Traffic is usually heavy both during the week and on weekends leaving the city. Parking can be very difficult, particularly in older sections, but parking garages exist in many areas of the city. Bicycles and motorbikes are not safe due to the steep hills and heavy traffic. Most apartment buildings provide lockable parking for their tenants. Traffic moves on the right side of the road.

Public transportation in Caracas consists of buses, taxis, collective taxis (por puestos) and the clean and modern Metro system. All are overcrowded during morning, noon and evening rush hours. Buses are

sometimes used by Americans, but they are slow and not always clean, comfortable or safe. Por puestos, which are cheap and travel fixed routes, are quite dependable.

The Metro system is clean and efficient though the network has not yet been fully completed. It runs through most major parts of town but service is not available to a few of the better parts of Caracas.

Taxis can be found on most main streets although they are scarce during rush hours and late at night. Several taxi companies have dispatcher service. Fares are currently inexpensive compared to the rates in major U.S. cities. There is a minimum charge and tips are not generally expected, although tipping is becoming more expected than previously. Prices increase with the lateness of the hour, the holiday seasons and out-of-town destinations. Take a map along, since many drivers are unfamiliar with the city.

International and Regional

The primary highway system is good, but often poorly marked, particularly in residential areas of cities. All major routes and connecting roads are paved. Mountain roads and some main roads suffer from landslides and washouts during the rainy season. Gas stations and garages can be found throughout the country.

All commercial flights, both domestic and international, use Maiquetia airport, about 15 miles from Caracas. American Airlines has daily flights to the U.S.—through Miami, San Juan and JFK in New York. United has daily flights—through Miami and New York. Two Venezuelan airlines, Avensa and Viasa, also have daily flights to the U.S.

Two national airlines, Avensa and Linea Aeropostal Venezolana (LAV), serve the principal cities of the country and many outlying areas not accessible by road. Both airlines have jet service between Caracas and the main cities of Venezuela.

Many carriers from Central and South American countries fly into Caracas, making travel to these countries relatively easy. There are also airlines from the United Kingdom, Spain, Germany and Holland that fly into Caracas regularly.

Travel to some of the Caribbean islands may be complicated because of limited flight schedules.

Reservations to and from the U.S., particularly during the summer, Christmas and Easter seasons, are difficult to obtain on short notice. Personnel planning on arriving during these periods should request reservations well in advance.

Communications
Telecommunications
Local telephone service is relatively reliable when the phone lines are working; however, some people have problems with the phone lines going totally dead for weeks and sometimes even months. Long-distance calls within Venezuela may be dialed directly. Some sections of Caracas also have direct dialing to the U.S. and such calls take little time. If it is necessary to go through the long-distance operator, delays may be expected during peak periods. AT&T and MCI calling cards can be used in Caracas to call the U.S. direct, and collect calls can be made as well. The American company, GTE, acquired a controlling interest in the Venezuelan phone company in 1992. Service has improved dramatically and is expected to continue to do so.

Radio-telegraph service between the U.S. and Venezuela is very good. Local telegrams within Venezuela, however, are unreliable and sometimes slower than regular mail.

Radio and TV
Caracas has a variety of TV programs in Spanish and English. There are satellite dishes on many of the buildings that capture HBO, Showtime, USA, Disney and news channels such as CNN. Cable is also available from two cable TV compa-

nies in Caracas at a cost comparable to the same service in the U.S. The Super Bowl, World Series, U.S. Open, and other major American sporting events are telecast here. Spanish soap operas are popular here along with game shows and sitcoms. Some American series are dubbed in Spanish.

Radio stations in Caracas are similar to those in the U.S. There are stations broadcasting Latin American music, U.S. rock, jazz and classical, in the same broadcast bands (FM and AM) as in the U.S.

Newspapers, Magazines, and Technical Journals

Caracas has a lively and competitive press with seven daily newspapers. There are three major papers: conservative, business-orientated El Universal; center-left El Nacional, and centrist El Diario de Caracas, which feature in-depth coverage of Caracas and foreign news. Caracas also has an English-language newspaper, The Daily Journal, which publishes opinions of well-known U.S. columnists and uses wire services as its principal source of news. There are also two good daily financial newspapers. In addition, The Miami Herald and the The Wall Street Journal can be purchased at Caracas newsstands a day or two late, or received via mail subscriptions. Some 20 magazines are published in Venezuela. Among the more prominent news magazines are Bohemia, Zeta, Autentico, Momento, and Elite, Numero, Veneconomia and Venezuelan Economic Review are good sources of local economic news.

Health and Medicine

Medical Facilities

Caracas has many highly respected general practitioners and specialists of all types, many of whom have had U.S. training and speak English fluently. There are several clinics organized by groups of doctors that include facilities similar to well-equipped hospitals in the U.S. The quality of nursing care is generally below U.S. standards.

Caracas also has many U.S.-trained dentists, and many dental offices measure up to a great degree to the standards in the U.S., although some Americans have encountered problems. The cost of dental work in Caracas is generally lower than in the U.S.

Eye examinations by U.S.-trained specialists are available at reasonable prices, as are lenses and frames for glasses.

Selected pharmacies are open 24 hours daily on a rotational basis for use in case of emergencies. The schedule is printed in newspapers.

Community Health

Since 1936, a national health program has made Venezuela the largest relatively malaria-free tropical area in the world, although some resistant strains have shown up in the southern and eastern parts of the country. Many other diseases, including rabies, once endemic to the country, have been controlled.

Although health standards among the upper- and middle-classes are good, overall health conditions suffer from poor sanitation in the shack communities that surround the cities. Infectious hepatitis, amebiasis, and other intestinal problems, such as diarrhea caused by virus, bacteria or parasites, are health problems that may affect Americans. Gastroenteritis is one of the principal public health problems in Venezuela. Dengue fever, spread by mosquitos, is a rapidly expanding disease in most tropical areas. Individuals are advised to wear protective clothing and use insect repellent.

The climate in Caracas favors some allergy sufferers. However, the altitude, climate, and prevalence of tropical pollens during all seasons aggravate asthma and hay fever conditions. Sinus problems may also be aggravated. The frequency of respiratory infections such as colds is similar to that in the U.S.

Preventive Measures

The yellow immunization card is normally not checked when entering the country, but yellow fever vaccination is required for entry into many of the surrounding countries and islands. Because the vaccine is inconvenient to obtain locally, it is essential that visitors be vaccinated before arriving. Typhoid and tetanus immunizations are recommended. Immunizations against cholera are considered unnecessary. Gamma globulin has reduced the incidence of hepatitis A and personnel should take this injection every 3-6 months. Malaria is a problem in only a few areas. Mefloquine (lariam) or doxycycline is the recommended prophylaxis against malaria. The incidence of polio is similar to that of the U.S.

Sunburns are a common problem due to the close proximity of the equator, and you should use a good sunscreen to protect your skin. Sunscreens and suntan products are available in local pharmacies.

The city's faulty water pumping system has resulted in intermittent interruptions of the water supply in parts of the city. Tap water is not safe to drink and should be boiled before consumption. Nonfluoridated bottled water is available, and most apartments have bottled water delivered.

Caution should be used in eating tossed salads, slaws, raw or rare meat, and other possible sources of parasites. Cooking, boiling, or peeling is recommended. It is recommended not to eat raw seafood in the smaller towns outside Caracas.

NOTES FOR TRAVELERS

Caracas has many flights from the U.S. arriving daily. United Airlines has daily flights from New York and Miami. American Airlines has daily flights from New York, Miami and San Juan. Viasa, a Venezuelan airline has daily flights from New

York, Miami, Houston and San Juan. Avensa, another Venezuelan airline has daily flights from New York and Miami, and Aeropostal has a daily flight from Orlando.

A valid passport and a visa or tourist card are required. Tourist cards are issued on flights from the U.S. to Venezuela for persons staying less than ninety days. For current information concerning entry, tax, and customs requirements for Venezuela, travelers may contact the Venezuelan Embassy at 1099 30th St. N.W., Washington D.C. 20007, tel: (202) 342-2214, Internet: http://www.embavenez-us.org. Travelers may also contact the Venezuelan consulates in New York, Miami, Chicago, New Orleans, Boston, Houston, San Francisco or San Juan.

U.S. citizens living in or visiting Venezuela are strongly encouraged to register at the consular section of the U.S. Embassy in Caracas or the Consular Agency in Maracaibo and obtain updated information on travel and security within Venezuela. The U.S. Embassy is located at Calle Suapure and Calle F, Colinas de Valle Arriba, Caracas. The Embassy is open from 8:00 a.m. to 5:00 p.m., Monday-Friday, telephone (011)(58)(212) 975-6411. In case of an after-hours emergency, callers should dial (011)(58)(212) 975-9821.

Cross-border violence occurs frequently in remote areas along the Colombian border in Zulia, Tachira, Apure and Amazonas states. U.S. citizens should consult the U.S. Embassy if they plan to visit these areas. Kidnapping, smuggling, and drug trafficking are common along the border between Venezuela and Colombia.

Most crime is economically motivated. Pickpockets concentrate in and around crowded bus and subway stations, along with the area around "Parque Simon Bolivar" near the "Capitolio" area in downtown Caracas. There have been cases of theft from hotel rooms and safe deposit boxes. The "barrios"

(the poor neighborhoods that cover the hills around Caracas) and isolated urban parks, such as "El Calvario" in the "El Silencio" area of Caracas, can be very dangerous. Most criminals are armed with guns or knives, and will use force. Theft of unattended valuables on the beach and from rental cars parked in isolated areas or on city streets is common. A guarded garage is not always a guarantee against theft. Travelers are advised not to leave valuables or belongings in open view even in locked vehicles. There have been incidents on Margarita Island where tourists have been targeted for robbery and theft.

Armed robberies are common in urban and tourist areas and travelers should exercise caution in displaying money and valuables. Also, four-wheel drive vehicles have been targeted in several recent carjackings.

Sporadic political demonstrations occur in urban centers. These tend to focus primarily on or near university campuses or secondary schools, and sometimes turn violent. Most tourist destinations, however, remain unaffected. The number and intensity of demonstrations have fluctuated widely. Merida, a major tourist destination in the Andes, is the scene of frequent student demonstrations.

Travelers may keep informed of local developments by following the local press (including "The Daily Journal," an English-language newspaper), radio and TV, and by consulting their local hosts, including U.S. and Venezuelan business contacts, hotels, tour guides, and travel organizers for current information on demonstrations, the purpose and location of which are often announced in advance.

U.S. citizens visiting certain areas along the border with Colombia may be subject to search and seizure. For further information regarding travel to these areas, contact the U.S. Embassy in Caracas.

A number of U.S. citizens have reported that Venezuelan officials at airports, immigration offices, and police stations have demanded bribes. U.S. citizens should report immediately to the U.S. Embassy any such demand.

U.S. citizens who do not have Venezuelan cedulas (national identity cards) must carry their passports with them at all times. Photocopies of passports prove valuable in facilitating their replacement if lost or stolen.

All pets entering Venezuela require a health certificate and a rabies certificate, issued by a veterinarian within the last 12 months, certifying that the animal is free from infections or contagious diseases, including rabies. For pets entering from the U.S., these certificates must be accompanied by a letter from the U.S. Department of Agriculture, certifying that the person signing the health certificate is a veterinarian. A Venezuelan consul must stamp and sign the health certificate and rabies certificate (and letter, if applicable). These documents must accompany the pet when shipped. Inquiries should be directed to the Venezuelan Embassy in Washington, D.C. Pets must not arrive as cargo; they must accompany the owner.

An exit permit is necessary to take a pet out of Venezuela. It is obtained from the Venezuelan Ministry of Agriculture. A rabies vaccine certificate and health certificate must be obtained from a veterinarian and these certificates must then be taken to the Ministry of Agriculture to obtain the exit permit. This must be done 15 days before actual departure. Pets must leave accompanied.

The basic Venezuelan currency unit is the Bolivar (abbreviated "Bs.") and is divided into 100 centimos. The bolivar is widely believed to be overvalued by as much as 50%.

Foreign exchange transactions must take place through commercial banks or exchange houses at the official rate. Hotels and banks often restrict transactions to their clients only. Money exchange by tourists is most easily arranged at "casas de cambio" (exchange houses). Credit cards are accepted at most upscale tourist establishments. Visa, MasterCard and American Express have representatives in Venezuela.

Bills are printed in denominations of Bs. 5, 10, 20, 50, 100, 500, and 1000. Venezuelan coins, followed by their local names, are: Bs. .25 (medio); or Bs. .50 (real); Bs. 1.00 (bolivar, bolo, or "B" as pronounced in English); Bs. 2.00 (dos bolivares); and Bs. 5.00 (cinco bolivares).

The metric system is used in all local weights and measures.

LOCAL HOLIDAYS

Jan. 1	New Year's Day
Jan. 6	La Paradura del Niño (Parade of Baby Jesus)
Feb/Mar.	Carnival*
Mar/Apr.	Palm Sunday*
Mar/Apr.	Holy Thursday*
Mar/Apr.	Good Friday*
Mar/Apr.	Holy Saturday*
Mar/Apr.	Easter*
Mar. 19	St. joseph's Day
Apr. 19	Declaration of Independence
May 1	Labor Day
May 3	La Cruz de Mayo
May/June	Ascension Day*
May/June	Corpus Christi*
June 24	Battle of Carabobo
July 5	Independence Day
July 24	Bolivar's Birthday
Aug. 15	Assumption Day
Oct. 12	Dia de la Raza/ Columbus Day
Nov. 1	All Saints' Day
Dec. 8	Immaculate Conception
Dec. 25	Christmas Day

*variable

RECOMMENDED READING

These titles are provided as a general indication of the material published on this country. The Department of State does not endorse unofficial publications.

General Information and Background

Alexander, Robert Jackson. *Venezuela's Voice for Democracy: Conversations and Correspondence with Romulo Betancourt.* New York: Praeger Publishers, 1990.

Bauman, Janice and Young, Leni. *Guide to Venezuela.* Ernesto Armitano ed.: Caracas, 1989.

Dalton, L. *Venezuela.* Gordon Press: 1976.

Ellner, Steve. *Venezuela's Movimiento al Socialismo: From Guerrilla Defeat to Innovative Politics.* Duke University Press: Durham, N.C., 1988.

Fox, Geoffrey. *The Land and People of Venezuela.* Harper Collins Publishers: U.S.A., 1991.

Good, Kenneth. *Into the Heart: One Man's Pursuit of Love and Knowledge among the Yanomama.* New York: Simon & Schuster, 1991.

Haggerty Richard. *Venezuela: A Country Study.* U.S.G.P.O: Washington, 1984.

Hellinger, Daniel. *Venezuela: Tarnished Democracy.* Boulder, CO: Westview Press, 1991.

Herman, Donald L., ed. *Democracy in Latin America: Colombia & Venezuela.* Westport, CT: Greenwood Publishing, 1988.

Hofer, Hans. *Inside Guides, Venezuela.* Hofer Press Pte. Ltd: Singapore, 1993.

Kaye, Dorothy Karmen. *Venezuelan Folkways.* Blaine-Etheridge: 1976.

Living in Venezuela. Venezuelan-American Chamber of Commerce and Industry: VenAmCham, 1993.

Lombardi, John V. *Venezuela: The Search for Order, The Dream of Progress.* Oxford University Press: New York, 1982.

Lye, Keith. *Take a Trip to Venezuela.* New York: F. Watts, 1988.

Masur, Gerhard. *Simon Bolivar.* University of New Mexico Press: Albuquerque, 1969.

Moron, Guillermo. *A History of Venezuela* (translated from Spanish). International Publications Service: New York, 1971.

Morrison, Marion. *Venezuela.* Chicago: Childrens Press, 1989.

Naim, Moses. *Paper Tigers & Minotaurs, The Politics of Venezuela's Economic Reforms.* Carnegie Endowment: 1993.

Rheinheimer Key, Hans. *Topo: the Story of a Scottish Colony Near Caracas, 1825-1827.* Brookfield, VT: Gower Publishing, 1989.

Waddell, D.A.G., et al. *Venezuela.* Santa Barbara, CA: ABC-Clio, 1990.

Winter, Jane Kohen. *Venezuela.* New York: Marshall Cavendish, 1991.

Specialized Studies

Betancourt, Romulo. *Venezuela's Oil.* George Allen & Unwin: London 1978.

Bond, Robert D. ed. *Contemporary Venezuela and Its Role in International Affairs.* University Press: New York, New York, 1977.

Carillo, Jorge Salazar. *Oil in the Economic Development of Venezuela.* Praeger Publishers: New York, 1976.

Martz, John D. and Myers, David J. eds. *Venezuela: The Democratic Experience.* Praeger: New York, 1977.

Powell, John Duncan. *Political Mobilization of the Venezuelan Peasant.* Harvard: 1971.

Ray, Talton. *The Politics of the Barrios of Venezuela.* Berkeley: 1969.

Tugwell, Franklin. *The Politics of Oil in Venezuela.* Stanford University Press: Stanford, 1975.

Wright, Winthrop R. *Cafe Con Leche: Race, Class, and National Image in Venezuela.* Austin, TX: University of Texas Press, 1990.

INDEX

U

V